The Palgrave Handbook on the Philosophy of Friedrich Schiller

Antonino Falduto • Tim Mehigan
Editors

The Palgrave Handbook on the Philosophy of Friedrich Schiller

palgrave
macmillan

Editors
Antonino Falduto
Department of Humanities
University of Ferrara
Ferrara, Italy

Tim Mehigan
School of Languages and Cultures
University of Queensland
St. Lucia, QLD, Australia

ISBN 978-3-031-16797-3   ISBN 978-3-031-16798-0 (eBook)
https://doi.org/10.1007/978-3-031-16798-0

© The Editor(s) (if applicable) and The Author(s), under exclusive licence to Springer Nature Switzerland AG 2023

This work is subject to copyright. All rights are solely and exclusively licensed by the Publisher, whether the whole or part of the material is concerned, specifically the rights of translation, reprinting, reuse of illustrations, recitation, broadcasting, reproduction on microfilms or in any other physical way, and transmission or information storage and retrieval, electronic adaptation, computer software, or by similar or dissimilar methodology now known or hereafter developed.

The use of general descriptive names, registered names, trademarks, service marks, etc. in this publication does not imply, even in the absence of a specific statement, that such names are exempt from the relevant protective laws and regulations and therefore free for general use.

The publisher, the authors, and the editors are safe to assume that the advice and information in this book are believed to be true and accurate at the date of publication. Neither the publisher nor the authors or the editors give a warranty, expressed or implied, with respect to the material contained herein or for any errors or omissions that may have been made. The publisher remains neutral with regard to jurisdictional claims in published maps and institutional affiliations.

Cover illustration: © Grafissimo / Getty Images

This Palgrave Macmillan imprint is published by the registered company Springer Nature Switzerland AG.
The registered company address is: Gewerbestrasse 11, 6330 Cham, Switzerland

Preface

I.

Long considered a marginal figure in the history of philosophy, Friedrich Schiller has returned to the forefront of philosophical debates. There are many reasons for such a return. For one thing, the progress of philosophy itself in recent decades has opened the door to a variety of new approaches and perspectives. With the waning of the division between "analytic" and "continental" approaches in philosophy of late has come a readiness to reconsider the value to philosophy of all such oppositions. In the deeper, ancestral split between philosophy and its "other" imaginative literature, glossed since time immemorial as the "ancient quarrel", attempts to maintain the ground of philosophy solely with reference to the primacy of reason, or, which is nearly the same thing, the analytical path of logic in "the space of reasons" (Sellars), increasingly seem unconvincing. Issues of greater moment such as a looming climate disaster and biodiversity catastrophe have crowded into the space of reasons in an era of the post-modern, even if only as a backdrop, to upset once settled accommodations of thought. Philosophy, like all other branches of knowledge in the last few decades, has been obliged to reconsider its origins, its nature, and its purpose at a time of unprecedented global change.

But if philosophy itself has responded to great change at its margins, there has also been change in the internal discussion relating to one of the signature philosophers of the modern period, Immanuel Kant—a figure of supreme importance for Schiller. The need to appraise Kant's legacy properly, a task once limited to the Kantian "revival" in the German-speaking world in the last few decades of the nineteenth century and the early part of the twentieth century, was registered as a new concern in Anglo-American philosophy in the second half of the twentieth century. As this interest in Kant grew in the wake of inquiries undertaken by Strawson, Sellars, Allison, Ameriks, and Guyer, among others, so did the interest in those coevals considered important for both the transmission of Kant's critical philosophy and its revision. In stages, then, light was dispersed retrospectively over a cast of gifted interpreters and expositors of

Kant's legacy, some of whom engaged with Kant directly in the last few years of his life. Among these "gifted interpreters" who engaged directly with Kant and—a rare thing—who also drew a response from Kant himself (in the second edition of Kant's treatise *Religion within the Bounds of Pure Reason*) was Friedrich Schiller, outwardly a poet rather than a philosopher, but a thinker, nevertheless, who had received philosophical training in his youth. The appearance in 1790 of Kant's third Critique, *The Critique of the Power of Judgment*, precipitated a profound engagement on the part of Schiller with Kant's moral and aesthetic thought. Though the philosophical results of this engagement are confined to an intense five-year period from the early 1790s of fevered reading and prolific production of insights, a large proportion of which was to find its way into print during Schiller's lifetime, it is also the case that Schiller, much like the philosopher K. L. Reinhold, Schiller's colleague at the University of Jena, undertook a protracted reckoning with Kant, but also drew on inspiration derived before this period from a variety of philosophical sources and traditions. It is to this process of evolution of Schiller as a thinker that the present undertaking aims to draw attention. The claim of this volume is that Schiller's thought in his Kantian period was to bring into view an independent project—one whose outlines are consistent with positions he adopts in his earlier thought and creative writings. The essays gathered in this volume seek to bring forward for discussion and assessment the status of this independent project.

A further reason for the present undertaking may be found in the fact alluded to above that Schiller's contribution to philosophical debates has not always received the attention it clearly merits. When Schiller's role in the history of philosophy is recorded, his theoretical suggestions are apt to be confined to the field of aesthetics and to his relation to Kant. Notwithstanding two extant handbooks published in German devoted to Schiller's life and work in general (Koopmann 1998; Luserke-Jaqui 2005), a handbook on the *philosophy* of Friedrich Schiller outright, whether composed in English or any other language, is still lacking. With *The Palgrave Handbook on the Philosophy of Friedrich Schiller*, we aim to make good this desideratum as well as to draw scholarly attention to Schiller's philosophy in new ways. Part of this latter ambition flows from a comprehensive discussion of a range of topics and topic areas that Schiller's writings enriched ranging from education and philosophical anthropology through to aesthetic and moral theory. It also consists in refreshing acquaintance with Schiller's biography and intellectual background insofar as it advanced what we wish to call in this volume his "philosophy".

II.

Friedrich Schiller's rise to become one of the leading writers and thinkers of his age could not have been foretold from his beginnings. Though an intellectually precocious child, Schiller was no scion of a wealthy aristocratic family. Nevertheless, perhaps on the strength of his father's service in the Seven Years' War, the young Schiller came to the attention of Karl Eugen, Archduke of the

Duchy of Württemberg, who had established a military academy in his own name, the "Karlsschule". Despite the school's conservative credentials, Schiller received a liberal education there and looked destined early on to enter the law. That he changed tack and moved into the medical sciences is only partly explained by the ministrations of the Archduke, who took a close interest in the pupils under his dominion. The shift in orientation Schiller underwent during his schooling can also be put down to wide-ranging, sometimes opposed, interests that were to become characteristic of the attitude he would strike in the world. These interests were revealed in the first decade of his career as a dramatist, for example, in the tension between the counterposed attractions of idealism and materialism, or, during his middle years as a professor at the University of Jena when most of his important aesthetic writings were composed, between the drive to rational intellectualism and an equally powerful pull towards physical sensation, or, finally, during his last years in Jena and Weimar, in the distinction he noted between the "naïve" poetic genius of his friend Goethe and his own attachment to philosophical "sentimentality". These apparent opposites, though consistent with the reach of an expansive intellect, were also to lead Schiller into intellectual isolation, and for a time, until a sympathetic benefactor stepped forward, relative penury. In his maturity Schiller's divergent interests meant that he was neither wholly a political opponent of a waning feudal aristocracy, nor unreservedly a denizen of an emerging artistic community, nor even thoroughly an elder statesman in the manner of Goethe presiding over a new literature at a moment of its greatest early flourishing as a world language. Schiller's interests leant towards all these things, and yet he was also none of them singly. Schiller's contributions to his society, since they spoke to contrasting features of his character and intellectual bearing all at once, are unique in European letters. His importance can be understood as Beethoven understood it in his own day—as inspiration for a new type of sensibility and a new conception of living. A progressive spirit in the same vein as Schiller, Beethoven memorialised this importance in the final movement of his Ninth Symphony by making Schiller's "Ode to Joy" into an anthem for the new age to come.

Given the significance of Schiller the man—a significance fully appreciated by Schiller's coevals Goethe and Beethoven no less than the great Scottish critic Thomas Carlyle, who released a life of Schiller soon after his death (Carlyle 1899)—it seems surprising that Schiller's reputation as a thinker was to face major obstacles. In the German setting, these obstacles can be put down to the difficulty his aesthetic theory faced in gaining a proper hearing next to Immanuel Kant's critical philosophy, in the light of whose brilliance it could seem a pale shadow. In the Anglophone setting, where Kant's philosophy was obliged to face its own hurdles, the situation presents somewhat differently. This is due to problems attaching to the reception of aesthetic theory in this setting as much as it had to do with the style and quality of Schiller's thinking. Nevertheless, it must also be said that Schiller's reputation was understood in English-speaking countries from the outset to be due to poetic more than philosophical considerations, indeed that Schiller's philosophy, such as it was taken to be, could appear secondary in view of the monumental achievement of his dramatic writing and his poetry. That Schiller's aesthetic writings largely (though by no means exclusively) emerged during an intense period of focus in his Jena years on Kant's third *Critique* in particular was disposed to excite little attention when measured against turbulent dramas such as *The Robbers*, *Fiesco*, *Intrigue and Love* and *Don Carlos*—works in which Schiller's reputation as a progressive thinker in the vein of the Enlightenment was secured. And yet it is also the case that the later dramatic work from *Wallenstein* and *Maria Stuart* through to *William Tell* would not have been possible without the "silent" half-decade in which Schiller clarified his intentions within the domain of aesthetics in areas relating to tragedy and the function of the sublime as well as in foundational areas of meta-theory dedicated to the justification and defence of aesthetic "truth". It is to insights arising from a period of focus on Kantian philosophy that the towering achievement of the late dramas owe their resonance and profundity.

Be that as it may, it is also the case that the reception of Schiller's aesthetic theory in the Anglophone domain was delayed for reasons pertaining to the understanding of aestheticism itself. For one thing, as the philosopher Dewey pointed out in *Art as Experience* as early as 1934, there is "no word in the English language that unambiguously includes what is signified by the two words 'artistic' and 'esthetic' [*sic*.]" (Dewey 2005: 48). As Dewey observes, "there is a certain verbal awkwardness in that we are compelled sometimes to use the term 'esthetic' to cover the entire field and sometimes to limit it to the receiving perceptual aspect of the whole operation" (*ibid.*). The halfway house that has long been obtained in English is that the term "artistic" tends to stand for the productive dimensions of aesthetic activity, whereas "aesthetic" is more frequently taken to denote its receptive dimensions. The modification to these linguistic circumstances observable today is that the word "creative" has stepped forward to augment the meaning of "artistic" just adumbrated. The consequence of the use of both terms, however, is that the productive dimensions of the aesthetic in the Anglophone setting are freighted towards art and discourses of art, thereby undercutting the ambition of aesthetics to issue any kind of knowledge claim. In today's intellectual debates, where views about the existence of "two cultures" of art and science have enjoyed a certain prestige, particularly in the wake of C. P. Snow (Snow 1959), aesthetics can look like an internal preoccupation of the "culture" of art and not, as Schiller intended, long before such a proposal about the organisation of fields of endeavour was vented, a concern for knowledge (*Wissenschaft*) as such. Thus, if Schiller's intentions are to be followed, one must strip away the glasses of today which are not naturally suited to appraising many of the claims he advances. Only then can one appreciate the consciously allusive use of the term *ästhetisch* in his Kantian writings, which depends on reciprocal relations running between aesthetic productivity and receptivity. That Schiller's aesthetics necessarily encompasses both productive and receptive aspects bulks large, for example, in the *Kallias Letters*, where an objective claim arising from beauty as "freedom in appearance" is made, or in the essay *On Grace and Dignity*, where an aesthetic attitude bound up with a productive bearing (grace) is argued alongside an attitude consistent with a receptive or suffering bearing (dignity).

A direct result of these circumstances in the Anglophone context is that Kant's aesthetic theory has fared rather better than Schiller's, and not just because of the philosophical eminence of the former. For, if aesthetics is held not to be independently productive of moral thinking, but only illustrative of it, as Kant suggests in the *Critique of the Power of Judgment*, and if "perception and enjoyment" represents a default reading of the term "aesthetic" in English, as Dewey maintains (Dewey 2005: 48), it is surely the case that Schiller's argument in the *Aesthetic Letters* that the "aesthetic condition" is capable of carrying out moral work in its own right will not be immediately evident and, rather more seriously, could even be regarded as philosophically incoherent. So long, then, as a productively determined or enabled aesthetics makes no decisive inroads into ethical theory, as is the case with Kant's moral theory, claims that art has the capacity to make an independent contribution to morals are likely to fall on deaf ears.

And yet it is precisely these kinds of claims with which Schiller's "philosophy" is associated and, equally, by which it stands and falls. In the tradition that claims such as these inaugurated, the aesthetic and the ethical have often been considered of a piece. This proximity of the ethical and the aesthetical animated the Romantic thought of poetic thinkers after Schiller from Hölderlin, Schelling, Hegel, and Nietzsche in the nineteenth century through to Thomas Mann, Rilke, Robert Musil, and Paul Celan in the twentieth century. For many of these poets and thinkers, Schiller was a talisman. Schiller's thought was also of interest to the neo-Kantians in the second half of the nineteenth century and has had an impact along various lines of development since then through to the critical theory and post-structural thought of our own day. For many reasons, then, a volume dedicated to bringing together the most current and valuable research on Schiller's philosophy in the interests of assessing the currency of this philosophy and the rich intellectual heritage it brought about is a worthy ambition. Such is the purpose of *The Palgrave Handbook on the Philosophy of Friedrich Schiller*.

III.

The volume is organised into six parts and seeks to provide a comprehensive overview of the dominant contours of Schiller's theoretical work, with essays dealing, respectively, with Schiller's biography and intellectual development (*PART I. Biographical and Historical Background*); with overviews of Schiller's philosophically relevant writings, in which each single text by Schiller is treated per se (*PART II. Schiller's Theoretical Writings*); with overviews of Schiller's contribution to the topics of philosophical anthropology, aesthetics, morals, political theory, philosophy of history, and pedagogy (*PART III. Schiller's Philosophical Topics*); with the relevance of his theorising activity in the context of his literary work (*PART IV. The Relevance of Schiller's Philosophical Thought in the Context of His Entire Work*); with his relation to Kant and the Kantian tradition (*PART V. Kant, the Kantian Tradition, and Schiller*); and, finally, with his legacy in the history of thought, in particular in relation to German idealism, the Romantics, the neo-Kantians, Alexander von Humboldt, Georg Wilhelm Friedrich Hegel, Karl Marx, and Critical Theory (*PART VI. Schiller's Philosophical Legacy*).

A special feature of this volume is the interpenetration of literary and philosophical perspectives and approaches, which represents a novelty in Schiller's scholarship and, more generally, in the wider field of scholarly philosophy dedicated to men and women of letters who are, at the same time, thinkers and poets. Up till now, as discussed above, Schiller has mainly been valued as a literary figure, which is to say, whose principal contributions have been understood to be to the field of imaginative literature. In resistance to this tendency, *The Palgrave Handbook on the Philosophy of Friedrich Schiller* treats the literary approach alongside the philosophical approach so that a comprehensive picture of Schiller's significance for modern thought can come into view.

In assembling this volume—a project which was conceived by the editors after a chance meeting at a conference several years ago—we would like to acknowledge and thank the 32 leading scholars whose coming together made this project possible. Working with and within this team of distinguished scholars, who responded cheerfully to every demand and deadline, was a pleasure from the beginning. An immediate measure of the visibility of Schiller's philosophy today, indeed, can be witnessed in the impressively broad range of expertise represented in the work of these scholars, in the far-reaching discussions linking specialists from Germany and other European countries with their counterparts in the Anglophone domain, and finally, in the partnership of two editors—communicating almost daily over a period measured in years rather than months—based respectively in the University of Ferrara in Italy and the University of Queensland in Australia.

Ferrara, Italy	Antonino Falduto
St. Lucia, QLD, Australia	Tim Mehigan
July 2022	

References

Carlyle, Thomas: *The Life of Schiller: Comprehending an Examination of His Works* (1825), New York 1899.
Dewey, John: *Art as Experience*. New York: Penguin 2005.
Koopmann, Helmut (ed.): *Schiller-Handbuch*. Stuttgart: Kröner 1998.
Luserke-Jaqui, Matthias (with Grit Dommes, eds.): *Schiller-Handbuch. Leben—Werk—Wirkung*. Stuttgart: Metzler 2005.
Snow, C. P.: *The Two Cultures*. Cambridge: Cambridge 1959 (first edition: 1993).

Contents

Part I	**Biographical and Historical Background**	1
1	J. Chr. Fr. Schiller: A Life as Mensch of Letters Jeffrey L. High	3
2	Schiller and His Philosophical Context: Pleasure, Form, and Freedom Jennifer A. McMahon	55
3	The Development of Schiller's Philosophical Attitude: Schiller's Philosophical Education Laura Anna Macor	73
Part II	**Schiller's Theoretical Writings**	89
4	Writings from Schiller's Time at the Karlsschule in Stuttgart (1773–1780) Jeffrey L. High	91
5	What Effect Can a Good Permanent Theatre Actually Achieve? (1785) Sandra Vlasta	129
6	Philosophical Letters (1786) Antonino Falduto	137
7	On the Cause of the Pleasure We Derive from Tragic Objects (1792) Carsten Zelle	147

xii CONTENTS

8 On the Art of Tragedy (1792) 163
   Jens Ole Schneider

9 Kallias, or Concerning Beauty (1793) 171
   María del Rosario Acosta López

10 On Grace and Dignity (1793) 189
   Heiner F. Klemme

11 Concerning the Sublime (1793) / On the Pathetic (1801) 201
   Carsten Zelle

12 Detached Reflections on Different Questions of Aesthetics
   (1793) 217
   Mirjam Schaub

13 Letters on the Aesthetic Education (1795) 231
   Tim Mehigan

14 Concerning the Necessary Limits in the Use of Beautiful
   Forms (1795) 247
   Anne Pollok

15 On Naïve and Sentimental Poetry (1795/96) 261
   Gideon Stiening

16 On the Sublime (1801) 273
   Carsten Zelle

Part III Schiller's Philosophical Topics 291

17 Schiller and Philosophical Anthropology 293
   Wolfgang Riedel

18 Schiller's Aesthetics: Beauty Is Freedom 319
   Violetta L. Waibel

19 Schiller on Morals 341
   Jörg Noller

20 Schiller on Politics and Political Theory 353
   Daniel Stader

21	Schiller's Philosophy of History Andree Hahmann	371
22	"Upward to Freedom": Schiller on the Nature and Goals of Aesthetic Education Robert B. Louden	389

Part IV	The Relevance of Schiller's Philosophical Thought in the Context of His Entire Work	403
23	The Role of Philosophy in Schiller's Plays Giovanna Pinna	405
24	The Role of Philosophy in Schiller's Poetry Matthew Feminella	423
25	The Role of Philosophy in Schiller's Prose Matthew Cipa	441

Part V	Kant, the Kantian Tradition, and Schiller	457
26	Schiller and Kant on Grace and Beauty Paul Guyer	459
27	Karl Leonhard Reinhold's Influence on Schiller's Reception of Kant Martin Bondeli	477
28	The Controversy Between Schiller and Johann Gottlieb Fichte Emiliano Acosta	497
29	Schiller on the Aesthetics of Morals and Twentieth-Century Kant Scholarship and Philosophy Katerina Deligiorgi	511

Part VI	Schiller's Philosophical Legacy	525
30	Schiller and the Birth of German Idealism Hans Feger	527

31 Schiller and Early German Romantics (Kleist, Hölderlin, Goethe) 541
Tim Mehigan

32 The Neo-Kantians and Schiller's Transcendental Idealism 559
Frederick C. Beiser

33 Schiller's Horen, Humboldt's Rhodian Genius, and the Development of Physiological Ideas in Mythical Form 573
Elizabeth Millán Brusslan

34 Friedrich Schiller and Georg Wilhelm Friedrich Hegel 591
Valerio Rocco Lozano

35 Schiller and Marx on Alienation 607
Gabriel Rivero

36 Schiller and Critical Theory 625
Claudia Brodsky

Author Index 655

Subject Index 659

Notes on Contributors

María del Rosario Acosta López is Professor at the Department of Hispanic Studies and Cooperating Faculty in the Department of Philosophy in UC Riverside. She teaches and conducts research on Romanticism and German idealism, aesthetics and philosophy of art, contemporary political European philosophy, and more recently, on the areas of decolonial and Latin American studies. She is the author of a book on silence and art in German Romanticism (2006) and a monograph on Friedrich Schiller and the political sublime (2008) and has edited and co-edited volumes and special issues on Hegel (2008), Schiller (2008, 2018), *Critique in German Philosophy* (2020), *Contemporary Political Philosophy* (2010, 2013, 2014), and *Philosophy and Memory in Colombia* (2016, 2019, 2022).

Emiliano Acosta is Associate Professor at the Vrije Universiteit Brussel, invited professor at the Universities of Ghent and Catania, and Alumnus of the Young Academy of the Royal Flemish Academy of Sciences and Arts of Belgium. He is the author of *Schiller versus Fichte* (2011) and *Plato lezen* (2020).

Frederick C. Beiser has taught in many universities in the USA, including Yale, Harvard, Penn, Wisconsin, Colorado, and Indiana, and is currently Professor Emeritus of Philosophy at Syracuse University, New York. He has been a major contributor to work on the history of modern philosophy, especially the history of German philosophy (Kant and German idealism) and the English Enlightenment. His book *The Fate of Reason: German Philosophy from Kant to Fichte* won the Thomas J. Wilson Prize for the Best First Book. He has won Thyssen and Humboldt research fellowships to study at the Free University of Berlin and was a Guggenheim fellow. He received an NEH Faculty Fellowship (at Indiana University), and he has won awards for his outstanding teaching.

Martin Bondeli was "Privatdozent" for Philosophy at the Universities of Berne and Fribourg (Switzerland). He is the editor of *Karl Leonhard Reinhold: Gesammelte Schriften* (Schwabe, Basel 2007ff.) and the author of books on

Kant and German Idealism, inter alia *Der Kantianismus des jungen Hegel* (1997), *Apperzeption und Erfahrung (2006), Reinhold und Schopenhauer (2014), Kant über Selbstaffektion (2018)*, and *Im Gravitationsfeld nachkantischen Denkens: Reinhold und Hölderlin* (2020).

Claudia Brodsky is Professor of Comparative Literature at Princeton University and Ancien Directeur de Programme at the Collège International de Philosophie, Paris. Her books include *The Imposition of Form: Studies in Narrative Representation and Knowledge* (1987); *Lines of Thought: Discourse, Architectonics, and the Origin of Modern Philosophy* (1996); *Birth of a Nation'hood*, co-Ed. with Toni Morrison (1997); *In the Place of Language: Literature and the Architecture of the Referent* (2009); *Inventing Agency: Essays in the Literary and Philosophical Production of the Subject* (2017); *Words' Worth: What the Poet Does* (2020); *The Linguistic Condition. Kant's Critique of Judgment and the Poetics of Action* (2021); and *Kant and Literary Studies*, Ed. (Cambridge UP, forthcoming).

Matthew Cipa is an academic in the School of Communication and Arts and the School of Languages and Cultures at the University of Queensland, Australia. He is the author of *Is Harpo Free? and Other Questions of the Metaphysical Screen* (forthcoming, SUNY Press).

Katerina Deligiorgi is Reader in Philosophy at the University of Sussex. She is the author of *The Scope of Autonomy: Kant and The Morality of Freedom* (OUP 2012) and *Kant and The Culture of Enlightenment* (SUNY 2005) and editor of *Hegel: New Directions* (Acumen and McGill-Queens 2006).

Antonino Falduto is a Lecturer (tenured Associate Professor) in Philosophy at the University of Ferrara, Italy. He was Assistant Professor (*wissenschaftlicher Mitarbeiter*) at the Johannes Gutenberg-Universität Mainz and at the Martin-Luther-Universität Halle-Wittenberg (Germany) and Postdoctoral Research Fellow at the University of St Andrews (UK). He is the author and editor of numerous works on the philosophy of Enlightenment (including *The Faculties of the Human Mind and the Case of Moral Feeling in Kant's Philosophy*, Berlin/Boston 2014).

Hans Feger is Adjunct Professor for Philosophy at Free University Berlin. He specialised on German idealism, existentialism, moral philosophy, and aesthetics in an intercultural context. His main books are *Die Macht der Einbildungskraft in der Ästhetik Kants und Schillers* (1995, Japanese translation 1996); *Poetische Vernunft. Moral und Ästhetik im Deutschen Idealismus* (2007); and *Handbuch für Literatur und Philosophie* (2012). He has published numerous books as editor and many articles on practical philosophy, German literature, moral theory, and aesthetics. He coordinates the *German-Asian Graduate Group of Humanities* at Free University Berlin, is the international editor of the *Yearbook for Eastern and Western Philosophy*, and is principal investigator of the German-Chinese Alumni Network (DCHAN) of the Humanities in Germany.

Matthew Feminella is Assistant Professor of German at the University of Alabama, Tuscaloosa. He has published widely on topics in seventeenth- and eighteenth-century German literature, ranging from the contemporary conceptions of sleepwalking in the works of Grimmelshausen to the intellectual tradition of the theatrical mask in the German-speaking world around 1800, as well as the German reception of Voltaire's *Candide* and emergence of German theatre historiography.

Paul Guyer is the Jonathan Nelson Professor of Humanities and Philosophy at Brown University. He is the author, editor, and translator of numerous works on Kant, as well as of *A History of Modern Aesthetics* in three volumes (2014). Among his most recent books are *Kant on the Rationality of Morality* (2019), *Reason and Experience in Mendelssohn and Kant* (2020), and *A Philosopher Looks at Architecture* (2021). He is currently completing *The Impact of Kant's Moral Philosophy*.

Andree Hahmann is Associate Professor of Philosophy at Tsinghua University, Beijing. He is working on topics from ancient and modern philosophy. He is the author of *Aristoteles gegen Epikur* (2017), *Aristoteles' »Über die Seele«: Ein systematischer Kommentar* (2016), and *Kritische Metaphysik der Substanz. Kant im Widerspruch zu Leibniz* (2009).

Jeffrey L. High is Professor and Section Chair of German Studies at California State University, Long Beach, as well as Guest Professor at the German Summer School of the Pacific in Portland, Oregon. He is the author of *Schillers Rebellionskonzept und die Französische Revolution* (2004), the editor of *Schiller's Literary Prose Works* (2008), and the co-editor of *Who Is This Schiller Now?* (2011), *Heinrich von Kleist: Artistic and Political Legacies* (2013), *Inspiration Bonaparte?* (2021), and *Heinrich von Kleist: Artistic and Philosophical Paradigms* (2022).

Heiner F. Klemme is Full Professor for the History of Philosophy at the University of Halle-Wittenberg. He has widely published on Kant and modern philosophy. His books include *Kants Philosophie des Subjects* (1996) and *Sich selbst erhalten. Kants Apologie der Vernunft heute* (2023). He is also (co-)editor of the journal *Kant-Studien*, the series *Kantstudien-Ergänzungshefte*, and of the volumes *Reception of the Scottish Enlightenment in Germany: Six Significant Translations, 1755–1782* (2000), *The Reception of British Aesthetics in Germany: Seven Significant Translations, 1745–1776* (2001), *The Bloomsbury Dictionary of Eighteenth Century German Philosophy* (2016), and many other books and collections.

Robert B. Louden is Distinguished Professor of Philosophy at the University of Southern Maine, USA. Recent publications include *Johann Bernard Basedow and the Transformation of Modern Education* (Bloomsbury, 2021) and *Anthropology from a Kantian Point of View* (Cambridge University Press, 2021). A past President of the North American Kant Society, Louden is also the co-editor and translator of two volumes in the *Cambridge Edition of the Works of Immanuel Kant*.

Laura Anna Macor is Associate Professor of History of Philosophy at the University of Verona, Italy, and a member of the Beirat of the Hölderlin-Gesellschaft (Tübingen). She is interested in German philosophy, with a special focus on the Enlightenment and early idealism, which she deals with from an interdisciplinary perspective open particularly to literature. She is the author of *Der morastige Zirkel der menschlichen Bestimmung. Friedrich Schillers Weg von der Aufklärung zu Kant* (2010), *Die Bestimmung des Menschen (1748–1800), and Eine Begriffsgeschichte* (2013), and a co-editor of *Hegel y Hölderlin, una amistad estelar* (2021).

Jennifer A. McMahon is Emeritus Professor in Philosophy at the University of Adelaide. She is the author of *Art and Ethics in a Material World: Kant's Pragmatist Legacy* (Routledge 2014) and *Aesthetics and Material Beauty: Aesthetics Naturalized* (Routledge 2007). McMahon edited *Social Aesthetics and Moral Judgment* (Routledge 2018) and special journal issues, including a Focus Issue for the highly regarded *Curator: The Museum Journal* (62/1, 2019) on "The Ancient Quarrel Between Art and Philosophy in Contemporary Visual Art Exhibitions", and for the inaugural issue of the *Australasian Philosophical Review* (March 2017) on "The Pleasure of Art". Her most recent reference article is a substantial contribution to the literature on pleasure and imagination, titled "Beauty" in the *Oxford Research Encyclopedia of Literature* (online 2020), also in hard copy within the *Oxford Encyclopedia of Literary Theory* (2022). She has contributed chapters to various research books including *Palgrave Kant Handbook* (2017) and the *Routledge Handbook of Liberal Naturalism* (2022).

Tim Mehigan is Professorial Chair of German at the University of Queensland, Australia, and Fellow of the Australian Academy of Humanities. He is the author of *Robert Musil and the Question of Science* (2020) and *Heinrich von Kleist: Writing after Kant* (2011). With Barry Empson he provided the first English translation of K.L. Reinhold's *Essay on a New Theory of the Human Capacity of Representation* (2011).

Elizabeth Millán Brusslan is a professor and chair of philosophy at DePaul University in Chicago. She has published in the areas of aesthetics, German idealism/Romanticism, and Latin American philosophy. Recent publications include *The Palgrave Handbook of German Romantic Philosophy* (2020) and "The Political Implications of Friedrich Schlegel's Poetic, Republican Discourse," in *Practical Philosophy from Kant to Hegel*, edited by James Clarke and Gabriel Gottlieb (Cambridge: Cambridge University Press, 2021). She is currently finishing a book-length study on Alexander von Humboldt as a romantic critic of nature.

Jörg Noller is currently Deputy Professor at the University of Konstanz and "Privatdozent" at the University of Munich. He has authored and co-authored numerous books and articles on Kant and classical German philosophy, among others *Kant's Early Critics on Freedom of the Will* (ed. and transl. with John Walsh, Cambridge University Press 2022).

Giovanna Pinna is Professor of Asthetics at the University of Molise, Italy. Her main research area is the philosophy and culture of the Goethezeit. She is the author of *Introduzione a Schiller* (2012, on Schiller's philosophical work) and provided Italian commented translations of Schiller's *Letters on aesthetic education* (2020²), of his early theoretical writings (2012), as well as of his philosophical poems (2005). She also published the first modern edition, with commentary, of K. W. F. Solger's *Vorlesungen über Ästhetik* (Meiner 2017).

Anne Pollok is *wissenschaftliche Mitarbeiterin* at Johannes Gutenberg Universität Mainz, after receiving tenure as Associate Professor at UofSC in 2019. She is the author of *Facetten des Menschen: Zur Anthropologie Moses Mendelssohns* (2010) and numerous essays on anthropology, history, aesthetics, and practical philosophy in the Enlightenment era, as well as on the philosophy of culture.

Wolfgang Riedel is Senior Professor of German Literature and History of Ideas at the University of Würzburg, Germany, and Fellow of the Bavarian Academy of Sciences in Munich. Books on Schiller: *Die Anthropologie des jungen Schiller* (1985); *"Der Spaziergang"* (1989); *Jacob Friedrich Abel. Eine Quellenedition* (1996—as editor); Volume 5 of Schillers Werke (SW 5, 2004, ²2008—as editor); and *Um Schiller. Studien zur Literatur- und Ideengeschichte der Sattelzeit* (2017).

Gabriel Rivero is Assistant Professor at the Martin Luther University Halle-Wittenberg. He is the author of *Zum Begriff der Ontologie bei Kant. Eine entwicklungsgeschichtliche Untersuchung* (2014) and the editor of volume 30 of the journal *Aufklärung. Interdisziplinäres Jahrbuch zur Erforschung des 18. Jahrhunderts und seiner Wirkungsgeschichte* (2018) dedicated to the topic: "Pflicht und Verbindlichkeit bei Kant. Quellengeschichtliche, systematische und wirkungsgeschichtliche Beiträge". He has also written several articles related to Kant's conception of metaphysics, the concept of obligation, and the theory of property and state

Valerio Rocco Lozano is Associate Professor of History of Modern Philosophy at the Universidad Autónoma de Madrid and Director of the Círculo de Bellas Artes. He is currently Tasks Leader of the European research project entitled "FAILURE. Reversing the Genealogies of Unsuccess, 16th–19th Centuries". He is the author of *La vieja Roma en el joven Hegel* (2011), and has edited eleven collective volumes on German Idealism, philosophy of history, and philosophy of Europe.

Mirjam Schaub is Professor of Aesthetics and Philosophy of Culture at the Department of Design at the University of Applied Sciences in Hamburg (HAW), Germany. She is the author and editor of numerous works on, among others, Kant, Bergson, and Deleuze, and on the sense and non-sense of examples in philosophy and aesthetics. Among her most recent books are *The Walk Book* (with Janet Cardiff, 2005), *Beauty of Theory* (as co-editor, 2013), and *Performing Radicalness. An Untold History of Popular Culture* (forthcoming, 2023).

Jens Ole Schneider is Postdoc and Research Fellow at the Friedrich Schiller Universität Jena. He is the author of *Aporetische Moderne. Monistische Anthropologie und poetische Skepsis. 1890–1910* (2020). Besides that, he published various papers on Friedrich Schiller, Christoph Martin Wieland, Thomas Mann, and Hugo von Hofmannsthal. Currently, he is working on a book about visuality and power in German dramatic literature of the seventeenth and eighteenth century.

Daniel Stader is Assistant Professor (*wissenschaftlicher Mitarbeiter*) at the Department of Philosophy of Martin-Luther Universität-Halle-Wittenberg (Germany). He earned his PhD with the dissertation *Unmündigkeit. Kant und die Dynamik der Herrschaft* (2021). He works on Kant, critical theory, anthropology, hermeneutics, as well as political and social philosophy in general.

Gideon Stiening is Professor of German Literature at the University of Munich and Scientific Coordinator at the SFB 1385 "Law and Literatur" at the University of Münster. He is the author of *Literatur und Wissen im Werk Georg Büchners. Studien zu seinen wissenschaftlichen, politischen und literarischen Texten* (Berlin/Boston 2019). He is the editor of *Friedrich Schiller: Briefe über die ästhetische Erziehung des Menschen* (Berlin/Boston 2019—in the series *Klassiker Auslegen*), as well as the co-editor, with Matthias Löwe, of *Ästhetische Staaten. Recht, Ethik und Politik in Schillers Werk* (Baden-Baden 2021).

Sandra Vlasta is Lecturer (tenured Associate Professor) in English at the University of Genoa, Italy. She was a Marie Skłodowska-Curie Fellow at the Johannes Gutenberg Universität Mainz (Germany) and the Nottingham Trent University (UK), where she undertook research on European travel writing around 1800 (https://travelwriting.uni-mainz.de), and Lecturer at the Department of Comparative Literature at the University of Vienna (Austria). She is the author of *Contemporary Migration Literature in German and English: A Comparative Study* (2016).

Violetta L. Waibel is Professor of European Philosophy at the University of Vienna. Important publications include *Hölderlin und Fichte. 1794–1800*, Paderborn 2000; *Spinozas Affektenlehre und ihre Rezeption im Deutschen Idealismus, der Romantik und der Moderne*, as editor—Hamburg 2012; *Natur und Freiheit. Akten des 12. Internationalen Kant-Kongresses / Nature and*

Freedom. Proceedings of the 12th International Kant-Congress (5 volumes), ed. by Violetta L. Waibel, Margit Ruffing and David Wagner, assisted by Sophie Gerber, Berlin 2018; and *Ein Zeichen sind wir, deutungslos'. Hölderlin lesen, Ikkyū Sōjun hören, Musik denken*, as editor—Göttingen 2020.

Carsten Zelle is a professor emeritus of modern German literature, in particular literary theory and rhetoric, at the German Department of the Ruhr University in Bochum. He is the author of *Die Doppelte Ästhetik der Moderne. Revisionen des Schönen von Boileau bis Nietzsche* (1995) and *"Angenehmes Grauen". Literaturhistorische Beiträge zur Ästhetik des Schrecklichen im 18. Jahrhundert* (1987). With Rudolf Behrens, he edited most recently *Die Causes célèbres des 19. Jahrhunderts in Frankreich und Deutschland* (2020). He was the long-time editor (until 2019) of the journal *Das achtzehnte Jahrhunder* and is now an honorary member of the *Deutsche Gesellschaft für die Erforschung des achtzehnten Jahrhunderts*.

Key to Abbreviations

Works by Kant and Schiller are referenced primarily using the abbreviations listed below. Further works cited in endnotes are given with their full publication information. When citing an English translation, the German source is also indicated. Where there is no mention of an English version, the translation is the author's own.

Works by Friedrich Schiller

Works by Schiller are referenced in the text parenthetically, primarily using the abbreviations listed below. Works cited only in endnotes are given with their full publication information.

There are at least three German editions of Schiller's works that are currently widely used by scholars.

The edition primarily relied upon in this volume is the one edited by Fricke and Göpfert, which exhibits an identical paging as the new one edited by Alt, Meier, and Riedel. These editions are the following ones and will be referred to as

SW   Schiller, Friedrich. 1959. *Sämtliche Werke*, ed. Gerhard Fricke and Herbert G. Göpfert. München: Hanser. Identical paging as:
Schiller, Friedrich. 2004. *Sämtliche Werke*, ed. Peter-André Alt, Albert Meier and Wolfgang Riedel. München: dtv.
References to these editions are given in the form SW 5: 30, indicating volume and page number.

The other two editions are:

NA   Schiller, Friedrich. 1943ff. *Werke* [known as *Nationalausgabe*], ed. on behalf of the Goethe- und Schiller Archiv, of the Schiller-Nationalmuseum and of the Deutsche Akademie, originally by Julius Petersen and Hermann Schneider; after 1961: ed. on behalf of the Nationale Forschungs- und Gedenkstätte der klassischen deutschen Literatur in Weimar (Goethe- und

	Schiller-Archiv) and of the Schiller-Nationalmuseum in Marbach by Lieselotte Blumenthal and Benno von Wiese; after 1979: ed. Norbert Oellers and Siegfried Seidel; after 1992: ed. on behalf of the Stiftung Weimarer Klassik and the Schiller-Nationalmuseum Marbach by Norbert Oellers. Weimar: Böhlau.

References to this edition are given in the form NA 8: 5, indicating volume and page number.

FA   Schiller, Friedrich. 1988ff. *Werke und Briefe in zwölf Bänden* [known as *Frankfurter Ausgabe*], ed. Otto Dann, Heinz Gerd Ingenkamp, Rolf-Peter Janz, Gerhard Kluge, Herbert Kraft, Georg Kurscheidt, Matthias Luserke, Norbert Oellers, Mirjam Springer, and Frithjof Stock. Frankfurt a. M.: Suhrkamp.

References to this edition are given in the form FA 8: 5, indicating volume and page number.

Furthermore, the abbreviations of the translations listed below will be used:

AE   Schiller, Friedrich. 1967. *On the Aesthetic Education of Man in a Series of Letters*. Transl. E. M. Wilkinson and L. A. Willoughby. Oxford: Oxford University Press.

ESS   Schiller, Friedrich. 1993. *Essays*, ed. Daniel Dahlstrom and Walter Hinderer. New York: Continuum.

GD   Schiller, Friedrich. 2005. *On Grace and Dignity*. Transl. J. V. Curran. In *Schiller's 'On Grace and Dignity' in its Cultural Context: Essays and a New Translation*, ed. Jane V. Curran and Christophe Fricker, 123–170. Rochester: Camden House 2005.

KAL   Schiller, Friedrich. 2003. *Kallias or Concerning Beauty: Letters to Gottfried Körner*. Transl. S. Bird-Pollan. In *Classical and Romantic German Aesthetics*, ed. J. M. Bernstein, 145–184. Cambridge: Cambridge University Press.

MPL   Schiller, Friedrich. 1978. *Medicine, Psychology and Literature*, ed. Kenneth Dewhurst and Nigel Reeves. Berkeley: University of California Press.

Works by Immanuel Kant

Works by Kant are referenced in the text parenthetically, using the abbreviations listed below. When available, authors have used the standard English translations. Works cited only in endnotes are given with their full publication information. Where there is no mention of an English version, the translation is the author's own. As is standard in Kant scholarship, each parenthetical reference to Kant's writings gives the volume and page number(s) of the Royal Prussian Academy edition (*Kants gesammelte Schriften*) (Ak), which are included in the margins of the translations.

Ak   Kant, Immanuel. 1900ff. *Kants gesammelte Schriften*. 29 vols. Ed. Preussische Akademie der Wissenschaften and successors. Berlin: Reimer, later de Gruyter. References to this edition are given in the form Ak 8: 5,

	indicating volume and page number. Where applicable, the number of the *Reflexion* (R) is given in addition to the volume and page number.
A/B	Kant, Immanuel. 1998. *Critique of Pure Reason* (1781, 1787). Trans. and ed. Paul Guyer and Allen W. Wood. Cambridge: Cambridge University Press [Ak 3, 4]. The volume number is not included in references to the *Critique of Pure Reason*.
Anth	Kant, Immanuel. 2007. *Anthropology from a Pragmatic Point of View* (1798). Trans. Robert B. Louden. In *Anthropology, History, and Education*, ed. Günter Zöller and Robert B. Louden, 231–429. Cambridge: Cambridge University Press [Ak 7].
CF	Kant, Immanuel. 1996. *The Conflict of the Faculties* (1798). Trans. Mary J. Gregor and Robert Anchor. In *Religion and Rational Theology*, ed. Allen W. Wood and George di Giovanni, 233–327. Cambridge: Cambridge University Press [Ak 7].
CJ	Kant, Immanuel. 2000. *Critique of the Power of Judgment* (1790). Trans. Paul Guyer and Eric Matthews. Ed. Paul Guyer. Cambridge: Cambridge University Press [Ak 5].
CPrR	Kant, Immanuel. 1996. *Critique of Practical Reason* (1788). In *Practical Philosophy*, trans. and ed. Mary J. Gregor, 137–271. Cambridge: Cambridge University Press [Ak 5].
FI	Kant, Immanuel. 2000. *First Introduction to the Critique of the Power of Judgment*. Trans. Paul Guyer and Eric Matthews. In *Critique of the Power of Judgment*, ed. Paul Guyer, 1–51. Cambridge: Cambridge University Press [Ak 20].
G	Kant, Immanuel. 1996. *Groundwork of the Metaphysics of Morals* (1785). In *Practical Philosophy*, trans. and ed. Mary J. Gregor, 41–108. Cambridge: Cambridge University Press [Ak 4].
IUH	Kant, Immanuel. 2007. *Idea for a Universal History with a Cosmopolitan Aim* (1784). Trans. Allen W. Wood. In *Anthropology, History, and Education*, ed. Günter Zöller and Robert B. Louden, 108–20. Cambridge: Cambridge University Press, 2007 [Ak 8].
MM	Kant, Immanuel. 1996. *The Metaphysics of Morals* (1797). In *Practical Philosophy*, trans. and ed. Mary J. Gregor, 363–602. Cambridge: Cambridge University Press [Ak 6].
OBS	Kant, Immanuel. 2007. *Observations on the Feeling of the Beautiful and Sublime* (1764). Trans. Paul Guyer. In *Anthropology, History, and Education*, ed. Günter Zöller and Robert B. Louden, 23–62. Cambridge: Cambridge University Press [Ak 2].
OT	Kant, Immanuel. 1996. *What Does It Mean to Orient Oneself in Thinking?* (1786). Trans. Allen W. Wood. In *Religion and Rational Theology*, ed. Allen W. Wood and George di Giovanni, 7–18. Cambridge: Cambridge University Press [Ak 8].
PP	Kant, Immanuel. 1996. *Toward Perpetual Peace* (1795). In *Practical Philosophy*, trans. and ed. Mary J. Gregor, 315–51. Cambridge: Cambridge University Press [Ak 8].
Pro	Kant, Immanuel. 2002. *Prolegomena to Any Future Metaphysics That Will Be Able to Come Forward as a Science* (1783). Trans. Gary Hatfield. In *Theoretical Philosophy after 1781*, ed. Henry Allison and Peter Heath, 49–169. Cambridge: Cambridge University Press [Ak 4].

Rel	Kant, Immanuel. 1996. *Religion within the Boundaries of Mere Reason* (1793). Trans. George di Giovanni. In *Religion and Rational Theology*, ed. Allen W. Wood and George di Giovanni, 55–215. Cambridge: Cambridge University Press [Ak 6].
RL	Kant, Immanuel. 1996. *On a Supposed Right to Lie from Philanthropy* (1797). In *Practical Philosophy*, trans. and ed. Mary J. Gregor, 605–15. Cambridge: Cambridge University Press [Ak 8].
RPT	Kant, Immanuel. 2002. *On a Recently Prominent Tone of Superiority in Philosophy* (1796). Trans. Peter Heath. In *Theoretical Philosophy after 1781*, ed. Henry Allison and Peter Heath, 429–45. Cambridge: Cambridge University Press [Ak 8].
TP	Kant, Immanuel. 1996. *On the Common Saying: That May Be Correct in Theory, but It Is of No Use in Practice* (1793). In *Practical Philosophy*, trans. and ed. Mary J. Gregor, 277–309. Cambridge: Cambridge University Press [Ak 8].
WE	Kant, Immanuel. 1996. *An Answer to the Question: What Is Enlightenment?* (1784). In *Practical Philosophy*, trans. and ed. Mary J. Gregor, 15–22. Cambridge: Cambridge University Press [Ak 8].

PART I

Biographical and Historical Background

CHAPTER 1

J. Chr. Fr. Schiller: A Life as Mensch of Letters

Jeffrey L. High

Es reden und träumen die Menschen viel
Von bessern künftigen Tagen,
Nach einem glüklichen goldenen Ziel
Sieht man sie rennen und jagen,
Die Welt wird alt und wird wieder jung,
Doch der Mensch hoft immer Verbesserung!
Schiller, "Hofnung" (1797; *NA* 1: 401)

Schiller was born in Marbach am Neckar, not in the country that is known as Germany today, but in the Duchy of Württemberg, one of the some three-hundred states of the Holy Roman Empire of the German Nation (926–1806). The seat of the empire was in the capital city of the most powerful of the German-speaking states, Vienna, Austria, ruled at the time of Schiller's birth by Empress Maria Theresa (1717–1780) and Emperor Franz I (1708–1765) of the Habsburg/Habsburg-Lorraine line, which governed the empire from 1440 until its dissolution in the face of aggression led by Napoleon Bonaparte (1769–1821) in 1806. Although Schiller is frequently and somewhat misleadingly referred to by the title of nobility "von Schiller," he was born and raised in relative poverty and received his patent of nobility for his service to the empire as an artist, philosopher, and historian on November 16, 1802, just over two years before his death in 1805 at the age of forty-five. Schiller was in fact a subject of Duke Carl Eugen of Württemberg (1728–1793) and was born and raised a "Sklave" (slave) by rank, if not in spirit, as one of his early literary

J. L. High (✉)
California State University, Long Beach, CA, USA
e-mail: Jeffrey.High@csulb.edu

© The Author(s), under exclusive license to Springer Nature Switzerland AG 2023
A. Falduto, T. Mehigan (eds.), *The Palgrave Handbook on the Philosophy of Friedrich Schiller*, https://doi.org/10.1007/978-3-031-16798-0_1

role models—the poet, journalist, and musician Christian Friedrich Daniel Schubart (1739–1791)—described the subjects of Europe's petty feudal tyrants, and of Carl Eugen in particular. "Leibeigenschaft" (bondage) was the law for all inhabitants but the nobility in Württemberg until 1817.

Schiller's parents provide a paradigmatic case of the emerging tensions between feudal tradition, increasing freedom of thought, and upward mobility, producing in a son who attended law school before becoming a Doctor of Medicine in 1780, one of seventeen international political activists declared citizens of the French Republic in 1792, and the recipient of a patent of nobility. His paternal grandfather was village sheriff (Schultheiß) in Bittenfeld, and all four of his grandparents were professional bakers; his mother, Elisabetha Dorothea Kodweiß (1732–1802), continued the tradition, barely making ends meet during her husband's military service for the first three years of Schiller's life in a small apartment in Marbach. His father, Johann Caspar Schiller (1723–1796), served in the Seven Years' War and rose from ensign in 1745, to army medic in 1753, to lieutenant in 1758, to captain in 1767, finally retiring from the Württembergian army in 1785, at which time he was appointed by the duke to supervise the botanical gardens at the residence in Ludwigsburg, where he was promoted to sergeant-major in 1794. He directed the forestry academy in Ludwigsburg and became a pioneer in cultivating fruit trees, and Schiller helped him publish his book, *Die Baumzucht im Großen* (Aboriculture on a Large Scale, 1795), which was considered a standard work for over a century. None of these accomplishments resulted in anything but a meager existence. In even more difficult financial times, Schiller's parents also had five daughters, two of whom died very young, and one who died at the age of eighteen: Elisabetha Christophina Friederika "Fina" (1757–1847, later Reinwald), Luise Dorothea Katharina (1766–1836, later Franckh), Maria Charlotte (1768–1774), Beata Friederike (May 1773–December 1773), and Caroline Christiane "Nanette" (1777–1796).

In 1762, the Schiller family moved into a modest apartment in Ludwigsburg, and in 1764 into more affordable rooms in the shop of a blacksmith in nearby Lorch, where Schiller received instruction in Latin and Ancient Greek from Pastor Philipp Ulrich Moser (1720–1792), who provided the inspiration for the eponymous, sympathetic, and serious character in Schiller's first drama, *Die Räuber* (The Robbers, 1782). From 1766 to 1772, Schiller attended the Latin School in Ludwigsburg. Without exception, Schiller—or "Fritz," as he was known—is described as an unusually bright child, whose most striking characteristic was his willingness to give his few possessions to less fortunate children, a habit his father forbade him. In almost every available description of his youth—most of which merely restate bourgeois fabrications of the nineteenth century—one reads how the six/seven-year-old Schiller delivered play sermons, an anecdote that generally leads to the disingenuous conclusion that Schiller was, at some point after his childhood, genuinely religious. The only evidence for such a conclusion is a few letters with pious greetings either written to relatives under the watchful eyes of his parents, composed under strict supervision while a teenager in college, or delivered in his sister Christophina Schiller's one reminiscence of how their father had decided early that Schiller would become a clergyman (*NA* 42: 3). Theology, however, was not only a common subject of study for future state servants, whether or not they were particularly pious, but also launched many a pedagogical, literary, and philosophical career for a growing class of first-generation college students, all of whom were male. There are only two recorded remarks from Schiller on the topic, one firsthand to the duke in the paper, "Bericht an den Herzog Karl Eugen über die Mitschüler und sich selbst" (Report to Duke Karl Eugen on the Classmates and on Myself; Fall 1774), written just before his fifteenth birthday, in which he wrote that he would like to become not a minister, but a "Gottesgelehrter" (theologian; *NA* 22: 15), a subject not offered at the Karlsschule, an institution that he very much hoped to leave. Schiller, however, did not study theology, and the second remark on the topic appears in a reminiscence of Schiller's classmate Karl Philipp Conz (1762–1827) regarding an encounter in 1781 that establishes the irrelevance of the first, during which Schiller stated that he was happy to have studied medicine: "Was wäre ich denn? Ein Tübingisches Magisterchen" (What would I be? A little magistrate in Tübingen; *NA* 42: 19). There is no evidence that Schiller ever gave the matter any further thought, and there is a great deal of evidence that religious studies was not a spiritual interest for Schiller, but a sub-field of anthropology, history, and psychology, and possibly even a disingenuous argument for leaving the Karlsschule. His only acquaintances who ever implied that Schiller had religious tendencies as an adult were his servant Georg Gottfried Rudolph (1777–1840) and his sister-in-law Caroline von Wolzogen (1763–1847). In line with her own increasingly religious worldview, Wolzogen appears to imagine a religious Schiller on a number of occasions: upon Schiller's death in 1805 (*NA* 42: 431–432)—in testimony that was rebutted by Schiller's close friend Wilhelm von Humboldt (1767–1835)—in her biography *Schillers Leben* (Schiller's Life) of 1830, and in a letter of 1840 to Schiller-biographer Gustav Schwab (1792–1850; *NA* 42: 279).

At the age of thirteen, Schiller was ordered by the duke to attend the strictly regimented military academy the duke himself had founded and personally supervised, the Hohe Karlsschule, which had begun as a military orphanage at Castle Solitude in 1770, became a military academy in 1773, moved to Stuttgart in 1775, received university status from Emperor Joseph II (1741–1790) in 1781, and was disbanded in 1794 by Carl Eugen's brother, Duke Ludwig Eugen (1731–1795)—one of the very few (dubious) accomplishments in his short reign after the death of his brother. Schiller spent eight years studying at the Karlsschule, at first studying law from 1773 to 1775 without any particular passion or success, before being granted permission to change majors and study medicine in 1775 upon the creation of a medical program. Schiller thrived as a medical student, regularly receiving awards for his work—three of which he received during Johann Wolfgang von Goethe's (1749–1832) visit to the Karlsschule in December 1779—and demonstrating a defiant tendency for unconventional, dialectical, and interdisciplinary approaches, as well as a critical edge that his professors found disrespectful toward established scholars, and a literary style and ironic sense of humor they likewise found inappropriate (*NA* 21: 24).

Schiller's earliest poems, influenced foremost by those of Friedrich Gottlieb Klopstock (1724–1803), demonstrate what he described as his "brennender Hass" (burning hatred) of despotism in all its forms, but, in particular, in its most virulent and destructive form, that of the military conqueror and occupier. Sixteen years after his birth in the geographical and chronological midst of the Seven Years' War (1756–1763), Schiller's first published poems are concerned with two forms of enslavement that he lived with from birth to death: native serfdom and foreign occupation, as evident in barely veiled expressions of support for the US-American War of Independence in his first two published poems, "Der Abend" (At Dusk, 1776/1777) and "Der Eroberer" (The Conqueror, 1776/1777). Already these first poems demonstrate the Deist concept of gods as poetic projections and a concept of judgment and immortality as secular matters strictly limited to human morality and human history, ideas he likely adapted from his reading of Moses Mendelssohn's (1729–1786) *Phädon, oder über die Unsterblichkeit der Seele* (Phaedo, or On the Immortality of the Soul), an adaptation of Plato's seventh dialogue on the death of Socrates, a resonant work that had appeared in four editions (1767, 1768, 1769, and 1776) by the time Schiller was sixteen years old. Here, too, the seeds of his strategic, kaleidoscopic blur of metaphors become evident, an approach necessary for free expression at the Karlsschule that served him well in outmaneuvering censors throughout his career. Between the ages of twelve and sixteen, Schiller also drafted at least four dramas prior to *Die Räuber*, including *Die Christen* (The Christians, 1772)—about which we know nothing—*Absolon* (1772), the content of which is hinted at in Schiller's description of Absolon's pursuit of power through deception in the first Karlsschule speech; and the plan for *Der Student von Nassau* (The Student of Nassau, 1775). *Cosmus von Medicis* (1776), which Schiller destroyed, dealt with the hatred between two brothers and their competition for the same woman, and likely left traces in *Die Räuber*, from which he read excerpts of a draft to classmates at the Karlsschule and which he completed in late 1781. Aside from *Die Räuber*, the only other theater work from Schiller's university years to survive is the two-scene "lyrical operetta" *Semele* (1779/1782; *NA* 5: 195–245), a singspiel inspired by Ovid's *Metamorphoses* about a fatal affair between the Theban princess Semele and Zeus that begot Dionysis and led to her death, a work that Schiller disavowed in an early meeting with his future wife Charlotte von Lengefeld (1766–1826) and later chose to leave out of his collected works edition.

After changing his major from law to medicine in 1775, Schiller wrote two philosophical speeches—"Rede über die Frage: Gehört allzuviel Güte, Leutseeligkeit und grosse Freygebigkeit im engsten Verstande zur Tugend?" (Speech on the Question: Does all too much Kindness, Sociability, and great Generosity necessarily Constitute Virtue?, 1779) and "Die Tugend in ihren

Folgen betrachtet" (The Consequences of Virtue Considered, 1779–1780; *NA* 20: 30–36). Both speeches were assigned by the duke to be written in praise of Baroness Franziska von Hohenheim (1748–1811)—the duke's mistress from 1772 until 1785, when she became his second wife—on consecutive birthdays. Although both speeches have been widely overlooked by scholars, they lay the philosophical foundation for a lifelong program of promoting a reasoned, secular alternative to faith-based role models, embarking from and concluding with the Scottish Enlightenment/*Common Sense* thesis that the destiny of humankind is happiness, and the path to happiness is virtue, both of which rely on what became the familiar Schillerian connection between moral rationalism and sensual foundation. A striking feature of the First Virtue Speech of 1779 is Schiller's relative silence toward Christ and his focus on pagan characters as moral exemplars and perversions, demonstrating with all clarity that virtue is a universally human potential that cannot be brought about through coercion. Thus, Socrates, without any possible knowledge of more recent divine revelation, serves as Schiller's most sublime figure in all of antiquity (*NA* 20: 3). In addition to the two speeches, Schiller wrote one assigned report on the religious conviction, moral constitution, dislikes, inclinations, hygienic habits, and relationships to faculty of classmates, the aforementioned "Bericht an Herzog Karl Eugen über die Mitschüler und sich selbst." This was followed by a minor case study on the depression of a classmate, "Über die Krankheit des Eleven Grammont" (On the Illness of Cadet Grammont, 1780; *NA* 22: 19–30), and three medical dissertations. Schiller's first dissertation, *Philosophie der Physiologie* (Philosophy of Physiology, late 1779), was criticized by committee members Johann Friedrich Consbruch (1736–1810), Christian Klein (1741–1815), and Christian Gottlieb Reuß (1742–1815) for its literary style and academic inconsistency, unwittingly describing the text's primary virtue in their review, namely, Schiller's interdisciplinary virtuosity, which combines the science of physiology with philosophical treatises and literary examples (*NA* 21: 114–115)—including the reckless prank of citing his own drama *Die Räuber* as a medical case study. Schiller's second unsatisfactory submission, *De discrimine febrium inflammatoriarum et putridarum* (On the Difference between Inflammatory and Putrid Fever, November 1780; *NA* 22: 31–62), a more traditional scientific treatise written in Latin, though rich in literary language and citations, focuses almost exclusively on the physical processes that accompany fevers, and was rejected for its general sloppiness. Schiller's third successful submission, *Versuch über den Zusammenhang der thierischen Natur des Menschen mit seiner geistigen* (Essay on the Connection between the Animal Nature and the Intellectual Nature of the Human Being, November 1780; *NA* 20: 37–75), though likewise criticized for poetic expression and excessive imagination, was approved; the thesis, written in German, was subsequently published by Cotta in Stuttgart. After completing his comprehensive examinations, Schiller received his doctorate on December 15, 1780, having just turned twenty-one years old.

Upon receiving his medical degree, Schiller was assigned to serve as Assistant Medical Officer in Stuttgart. From February 1, 1781 until September 23, 1782, Schiller sublet a very modest and—according to his classmate Georg Friedrich Scharffenstein (1760–1817)—spectacularly messy room in an apartment, in a building that belonged to the father of another of Schiller's classmates, the author and publisher Balthasar Haug (1731–1792), who had printed Schiller's first two published poems in 1777. His landlady was a captain's widow, Luise Dorothea Vischer (1751–1816), with whom Schiller had an affair, immortalized as "Laura" in a series of popular love poems, one of which was later set to music by Franz Schubert (1797–1828), and for which Schubart admonished Schiller in the poem "An Schiller" that revolution, not love poetry, was his calling. During this period, Schiller embarked on his first attempts at publishing journals, serving as co-editor for *Wirttembergisches Repertorium der Litteratur* (Württembergian Repertorium of Literature), a quarterly journal co-edited with former classmate Johann Wilhelm Petersen (1758–1815), which appeared three times from 1782 to 1783, and *Anthologie auf das Jahr 1782* (Anthology for the Year 1782), which, as its title implies, only appeared once. Here, too, on June 7, 1784, Schiller made the acquaintance of Henriette von Wolzogen (1745–1788), the widowed mother of four Karlsschule students, including his classmate Wilhelm von Wolzogen (1762–1809), who was to become Schiller's brother-in-law after Wolzogen married Schiller's recently divorced sister-in-law Caroline von (Lengefeld) Beulwitz in 1794 (*NA* 23: 146–147).

Seldom in the history of rises from utter obscurity to stardom has there been a story like that of Schiller and *Die Räuber*, which saw Schiller recognized as among the most resonant authors from the stages of continental Europe in 1782 to those of New York City by 1795. The play shocked the audience at its January 13, 1782 premiere at the Nationaltheater Mannheim with its violent and emotional rant against any form of coercion, featuring dueling sublime criminal brothers who embody the antagonism of drives that informs Schiller's Karlsschule writings. The timeliness, rebellious energy, and originality of Schiller's "dramatischer Roman" (dramatic novel; *NA* 3: 244) marked the play early—morally and politically—as a future canonical subversive work, and, according to one account, left audiences in a state ranging from insensible to ecstatic to outraged. In addition to the reality of highway robbers in the 1770s, including a substantial number of displaced Seven Years' War veterans, the play was inspired by three of Schiller's favorite works, Schubart's essay *Zur Geschichte des menschlichen Herzens* (Toward a History of the Human Heart, 1767), Johann Anton Leisewitz' (1752–1806) *Julius von Tarent* (1774), and Friedrich Maximilian Klinger's *Die Zwillinge* (The Twins, 1776), all of which feature extreme cases of sibling rivalry. After the tumultuous premiere and successful performances in Hamburg, Leipzig, and Erfurt in 1782, *Die Räuber* was alternately condemned by the literary authorities—Goethe and Christoph Martin Wieland (1733–1813)—repeatedly banned from the stage for "endangering the youth" until the early 1800s, embraced by the very young—Friedrich

Hölderlin (1770–1843) and Ludwig Tieck (1773–1853)—and met with awe by Samuel Taylor Coleridge (1772–1834): "Who is this Schiller, this convulser of the heart?" (Coleridge 1: 96–97).

Written almost completely while Schiller was still in medical school, the play features a number of the theories that inform his early philosophical and scientific writings. At the most basic level, the conflict is driven by the binary opposition of Karl Moor's one-sided revolution of feeling and self-individuation versus Franz Moor's one-sided domination of reason and self-indulgence that precludes the possibility of *positive* societal order (as opposed to mere coerced obedience to tradition), due to a failure to achieve the inner harmony of humanity's rational and sensual natures. Both the Enlightenment materialist villain, Franz Moor, and the ideologically dangerous *Sturm und Drang* idealist, Karl Moor, declare war on distinct aspects of social tradition in response to injustices. In 1782, in *Württembergisches Repertorium der Litteratur*, Schiller describes the conflict: devoid of compassion due to childhood trauma, the second-born and unattractive Franz exploits the most recent developments in enlightened and progressive thought—moral, religious, and civil law; reason, equal rights, modern medical theory, and the dismissal of Christian beliefs—to create a system of vice designed to usurp his father's throne, which is by birthright his brother's. Franz exposes the romantic concept of love as a mask for the fulfillment of animal sexual drive, deconstructs fatherly love to reveal the narcissistic pride of a failed artist for his deeply flawed creation, and orchestrates a complicated plan for the psychosomatic murder of his father. Conversely, Karl, to whom nature and tradition have given everything, has every reason to be invested in the philosophy of love, wisdom, virtue, and happiness that has privileged him over his brother, and which is too easily shattered when he is deceived into believing that his father has disowned him, leading him to direct a war on society most notable for its recklessness, rape, arson, and murder. Thus, ironically, Franz and Karl, both of whose primary virtue is resistance, arrive at similar conclusions and become what Schiller calls "Ungeheuer mit Mäjestät" (monsters with majesty; *NA* 3: 244) via two very different paths, both in pursuit of, among other goals, the allegorical representation of virtue, Amalia, whose character and selfless sacrifice demonstrate the balance of feeling and reason that constitutes inner freedom.

According to Scharffenstein, Schiller achieved his goal to write a book the oppressors would have to burn (NA 42: 16): *Die Räuber* was censored in Bavaria and Austria, and never performed in its original form in Schiller's lifetime. In short, in his own words, Schiller—who had played the gadfly at the Karlsschule for most of his stay—also demonstrated many of the qualifications to become a proper outlaw. After the newspapers had reported on the positive reception of *Die Räuber*, the duke learned that Schiller had broken the law by leaving the state twice in four months to attend both the play's premiere in January—in a carriage with Dorothea Vischer and Henriette von Wolzogen—and a further performance in Mannheim on May 25. The duke had Schiller arrested, imprisoned him for fourteen days, and forbade him in a public announcement to write any further dramas. Ironically, while in jail from June 28 to July 12, Schiller worked on his drama, *Die Verschwörung des Fiesko zu Genua. Ein republikanisches Trauerspiel* (The Fiesco Conspiracy at Genoa; A Republican Play of Mourning), a study in anti-republican tyranny (Abel 1: 304). Soon thereafter, in the night from September 22 to 23, 1782, Schiller fled with his classmate, musician Johann Andreas Streicher (1761–1833), in a cloak-and-dagger action planned to take place during royal wedding fireworks, featuring false names and passports, stolen horses, a calculated misdirection maneuver, two broken pistols for show, and—as scheduled—a unit guarding the Stuttgart South Gate in which only classmate and friend Scharffenstein would recognize the defectors (Alt 2009, 306). In order to avoid detection in Mannheim, Schiller (Dr. Schmidt), a military deserter and fugitive, and Streicher stayed at the inn "Zum Viehhof" (The Cattle Pen) in Oggersheim from October 13 to November 30, 1782, where he continued work on *Fiesko* and *Kabale und Liebe*, originally titled *Luise Millerin*. On December 7, 1782, Schiller arrived at the inn "Zum Hirsch" (The Stag) in Meiningen, where he was received by a stranger, court librarian, and author Wilhelm Reinwald (1737–1815) and found asylum at the home of Henriette von Wolzogen in Bauerbach under the pseudonym "Dr. Ritter"—all elements of the Gothic tradition Schiller's works would soon inform. Reinwald went on to publish frequently in Schiller's journals and married Schiller's sister Christophina, a private art instructor twenty years his junior, in 1786. Despite the many testimonials regarding the despotic conditions at the Karlsschule and the tyranny of Carl Eugen, the duke's mild response to Schiller's defection and the fact that Schiller's family suffered no consequences for the actions of a renegade son demonstrate the duke's fondness for the defiant subject Schiller as much as the arbitrariness of a despot who had also sent local publisher and poet Schubart to a decade (1777–1787) in the dungeon Hohenasberg, overlooking Asberg near Stuttgart, for little worse. Schiller's rise from obscurity to international prominence was, as Thomas Mann (1875–1955) wrote, "ein blutendes Trotzdem" (a bleeding act of defiance; Mann VIII: 372), and, for all the dialectical contrariness that marked his works from the medical theses to his final dramas, Schiller owed much to his simultaneous education and experience of coercion at the Karlsschule (Thomas, 24).

As was the case with Schiller's early and late philosophical treatises, in which happiness leads to happiness, and freedom yields freedom, the cause and effect of Schiller's exile in Mannheim were the same, namely, his relationship with the theater director Freiherr Wolfgang Heribert von Dalberg (1750–1806) and his prospects for a position as house dramatist at the Nationaltheater Mannheim. On July 27, 1783, Schiller was appointed house playwright by Dalberg. The first fruit of this collaboration was Schiller's second drama, *Fiesko*, the prophetic play of mourning by no means focused on the downfall of the reckless and opportunist titular character, but rather on his entirely resistible rise, which threatens the future of the flawed and vulnerable, if humane, republic, a focus seemingly self-evident in its subtitle. As the follow-up to the wild success of *Die*

Räuber, Fiesko was a box-office failure, leading Schiller to rework the drama to feature an optimistic ending, in which Fiesko surprises all by revealing that what appeared to be selfish ambition was in fact a test of the republican resolve of his supporters. Schiller was disgusted with the Mannheim theater audience's discomfort with the historical tragedy of the stolen dream of a republic, and summarized the *Fiesko* experience in a letter of May 5, 1784 to Reinwald: "Den Fiesko verstand das Publikum nicht. Republikanische Freiheit ist hier zu Lande ein Schall ohne Bedeutung, ein leerer Name—in den Adern der Pfälzer fließt kein römisches Blut" (The audience did not understand *Fiesko*. In this state, republican freedom is a sound without a meaning, an empty signifier—no Roman blood flows in the veins of the Palatines; *NA* 23: 137). Not only Schiller and his audience in Mannheim were disappointed in their taste agendas, but, for entirely different reasons, the censors in Vienna responded to the frank portrayal of the selfish motivations of those who usurp the freedom of the people by substantially rewriting *Fiesko*, deleting the word "Freiheit" (*freedom*) as well as the author's name (Glossy, 35).

Writing in Bauerbach near Meiningen, Schiller completed his third drama, *Luise Millerin*, in July 1783. At the urging of prominent actor and playwright August Wilhelm Iffland (1759–1814), Schiller published the play with the revised title *Kabale und Liebe. Ein bürgerliches Trauerspiel* (Intrigue and Love: A Bourgeois Play of Mourning) in March 1784, and the play premiered to mostly positive reviews in Frankfurt on April 9—starring the poet and actress Sophie Albrecht (1756–1840) as Luise Miller. Not all of the reviews were positive: the prominent author and critic Karl Philipp Moritz (1756–1793) denounced the language and the story of courtly corruption, inter-class romance, blackmail, and murder-suicide as "Schillerschen Schmutz" (Schillerian filth) and "Unsinn" (nonsense; *Staats- und gelehrte Zeitung*, 831–833). Like Gotthold Ephraim Lessing's (1729–1781) title character in *Emilia Galotti* (1772), the middle-class protagonist Luise Miller, whose mother harbors dangerous social ambitions, becomes the focus of both noble and bourgeois suitors in a labyrinthine conspiracy to preempt her involvement with Ferdinand von Walter—the son of the president of a corrupt minor feudal state run by a prince whose court and behavior closely resemble those of Schiller's Duke Carl Eugen—by marrying her off and sealing her fate as an unhappy wife and mistress. With her path to happiness effectively rendered hopeless by class tradition and the extraordinary efforts of the court, Luise consumes a drink poisoned by Ferdinand, who has been misled into a jealous rage. Ironically, it was Ferdinand's liberal view of love that first led Luise to dream that they could be happy together, a view diametrically opposed to that of his opportunist father, who had murdered his predecessor in order to rise to power. In Act I, Scene 7, father and son engage in a heated debate pitting the base hunger for power against the ideal of true love, featuring the terms "Glück" and "Glückseligkeit" (happiness) five times in less than half a page (*NA* 5: 37–38, footnote). In Act II, Scene 2, the moral failure of the state is revealed in all clarity in a detailed adaptation of a scene from the historical Ochsenfurt Mutiny of mercenaries of

May 10, 1777, which took place less than 90 miles from Ludwigsburg, ending with the troops' ironic declaration of defeat, "*Juchhe nach Amerika!*" (Hurrah! To America!; *NA* 5: 50). Schiller himself indicated in 1784 that he was indeed aware that the numerous references to happiness—or the lack thereof—and political freedom in *Kabale und Liebe* were understood as criticism of pro-British German rulers in the conscious context of the sale of German mercenaries to fight for England in the US-American War of Independence. This is evident in his specific reference to the United States in his May 1, 1784, letter to his theater director Dalberg: "Iffland wird den *Kammerdiener* spielen, den ich, mit Wegwerfung aller amerikanischen Beziehungen, wieder ins Stük hineingeschoben habe" (Iffland will play the Courtier, whom I have reinserted into the play, while throwing out all American references; *NA* 23: 134).

During his tenure as house poet in Mannheim, Schiller led the complicated personal life of a young celebrity, including a Gothic pursuit of a grifter known only as Julia, an infatuation with Charlotte von Wolzogen—who was the daughter of his landlady Henriette von Wolzogen, and who served as one of the models for his character Luise Miller—and with the daughter of his publisher Christian Friedrich Schwan (1733–1815), Anna Margaretha Schwan (1766–1796), to whom Schiller proposed in April 1785 after he left Mannheim; her father rejected the proposal without consulting his daughter. In May 1784, Schiller began a years-long affair with the married noblewoman Charlotte Sophia Juliane von Kalb (1761–1843), whose husband was an often-absent French military advisor during the US War of Independence, and who was also an acquaintance of Goethe, Johann Gottfried von Herder (1744–1803), and Jean Paul Richter (1763–1825). At the urging of Kalb and Dalberg, Schiller presented himself to Duke Carl August of Sachsen-Weimar-Eisenach (1757–1828) on December 26, 1784 in Darmstadt, and read to him from a draft of *Don Karlos* (1787). The following day, the duke conferred on Schiller the honorary title "Rath" (councillor), bringing Schiller one step closer to Weimar, and Goethe. In October of 1785, in the company of Henriette and Wilhelm von Wolzogen, Schiller briefly met his future mother-in-law Louise Juliane Eleonore Friederike von Lengefeld (1743–1823) and her two daughters, the recently married Caroline von Beulwitz (1763–1847) and the unmarried Louise Antoinette Charlotte von Lengefeld (1766–1826).

Expecting his dismissal as house dramatist in Mannheim, Schiller hoped to find employment as the secretary of the "Kurpfälzische Deutsche Gesellschaft" (German Society of the Electorate of the Palatinate), to whose members he delivered the lecture "Vom Wirken der Schaubühne auf das Volk" (On the Effect of the Stage on the People) on June 26, 1784. A revision of the speech appeared in 1785 in the first issue of Schiller's second journal *Rheinische Thalia* (Rhenish Thalia) published in Mannheim by Schwan - as "Was kann eine gute stehende Schaubühne eigentlich wirken?" (What Effect Can a Good Permanent Theater Actually Achieve?), and then again in 1802 as "Die Schaubühne als moralische Anstalt betrachtet" (The Stage considered as a Moral Institution) in Schiller's *Kleinere prosaische Schriften* (Schiller's Shorter Prose Works). Schiller's promotion of the educational benefits of a national theater, first attempted by Lessing in Hamburg, contrasts the superior benefits of the "autonomous process of self-fashioning" (Moggach, 534) through aesthetic education with the merely heteronomous functions of the law and religion, which only enforce negative laws, which Schiller states become superfluous for morally educated individuals: "Wenn keine Moral mehr gelehrt wird, keine Religion mehr Glauben findet, wenn kein Gesez mehr vorhanden ist" (When morality is no longer taught, religion no longer believed, when laws no longer exist; *NA* 20: 92), audiences will still experience "heilsame Schauer" (healing sense of horror) and a "lebendige Glut zur Tugend, brennender Haß des Lasters" (lively glow for virtue, burning hatred of vice; *NA* 20: 92) at the sight of the misdeeds of Medea, Lady Macbeth, and Franz Moor. Thus, the process entails self-enlightenment and liberation from the legion of "Schlachtopfer vernachläßigter Erziehung" (victims of neglected education; *NA* 20: 98) by learning from the failures of one's predecessors. In keeping with Schiller's thesis that the aesthetic experience revives and promotes wholeness through reconciliation of e.g. amusement and instruction, rest and exertion, the state of aesthetic reception appears here as "einen mittleren Zustand" (an intermediary state; *NA* 20: 90) between animal physical sensation and human intellect that was already present in his first and third dissertations, in which it appeared as a "Mittelkraft" (transmutative force; *NA* 20: 13) between the material world and the intellect. The advantage of the stage is threefold: first, the medium of the stage is pleasurable (even more so than literature) rather than punitive; second, the experience of the medium is liberating rather than coercive; thus, "So gewiß sichtbare Darstellung mächtiger wirkt, als toder Buchstabe und kalte Erzählung, so gewiß wirkt die Schaubühne tiefer und daurender als Moral und Geseze" (Just as certainly as visual portrayal has a more powerful impact than the dead letter and cold narration, it is also certain that the stage has a deeper and more lasting impact than morality and law; *NA* 20: 93); and third, relatively speaking, the stage offers a level of freedom of speech only possible in the public sphere in the realms of art and—as Immanuel Kant (1724–1804) would explain in his December 1784 essay, "Was ist Aufklärung?" (What is Enlightenment?)—academia, in particular regarding criticism of rulers and state and religious institutions.

Not surprisingly, one of dozens of plays Schiller cites in the *Schaubühne* essay is Lessing's *Nathan der Weise* (Nathan the Wise, 1779), which was subjected to severe censorship and had premiered only a year earlier when Schiller was twenty-four years old. Lessing's play provides the model of presenting a meaningful exposé of the holy trinity of tyranny and majority bullying—political tyranny, church tyranny, and church-state-approved mob tyranny against minority interests—in an entertainment medium featuring the portrayal of the aesthetic education of a prince (Sultan Saladin) and an intolerant crusader knight toward not only tolerance but compassion. Schiller's interest in characters who autonomously turn the historical condition of the human being, or fate in the most modern sense, into an object of free will serve as models, including Pierre Corneille's (1606–1684) portrayal of Augustus' forgiveness of and offer of friendship to Cinna in *Cinna ou la Clémence d'Auguste* (Cinna: or The Clemency of Augustus, 1641; *NA* 20: 93) and the sublime dedication of the title figure in Julius von Soden's (1754–1831) *Franz von Sickingen* (*NA* 20: 93; *NA* 23: 313), allowing Schiller to conclude that just as the stage is superior to the law and religion, "wie groß wird mir da der Mensch, wie klein und verächtlich das gefürchtete unüberwindliche Schicksal!" (how great the human being appears to me, how small and contemptuous dreaded insurmountable fate!; *NA* 20: 93). The theater radiates reconciliation and happiness beyond the individual to "Menschen aus allen Kraisen und Zonen und Ständen" (individuals of all spheres and realms and classes), transcending historical situation and unfettered by convention in the awareness of belonging to "*Ein* Geschlecht" (*One* race) driven by reason to freedom and happiness through an "allwebende Sympathie" (all-interweaving compassion) and of what it means "Mensch zu seyn" (to be a human being; *NA* 20: 100).

In late 1784, Schiller had announced his second journal, *Thalia*, named after the Greek muse of joyous art, only the first issue of which was entitled *Rheinische Thalia*, which appeared in March 1785, with a conspicuously ingratiating dedication to Duke Carl August, his future patron. In his announcement of the journal of November 11, 1784, Schiller delivers by now characteristically defiant political and aesthetic rhetorical gestures that continue to inform his legacy as a social critic with serious street credibility, among them the statement: "Ich schreibe als Weltbürger, der keinem Fürsten dient" (I write as a citizen of the world, who serves no prince; *NA* 22: 93), proceeding to state that he lost his family and his fatherland, Württemberg, due to the political response to his first drama, *Die Räuber*. The first issue of *Rheinische Thalia*, which sets the tone for the next seven years of the journal, displays Schiller's remarkable rate of production and versatility, featuring seven items—all written by Schiller—including the *Schaubühne* essay, the novella adapted from Denis Diderot (1713–1784), "Merkwürdiges Beispiel einer weiblichen Rache" (A Remarkable Example of Female Revenge), and the first acts of *Don Karlos*, two further essays on theater and the Mannheim Museum, and the results of an essay contest on theater for which Dalberg had provided the prompts. *Rheinische Thalia* was not a sales success, but subsequent issues as *Thalia* beginning in 1786 sold well under the supervision of the first of Schiller's two most important publishers, Georg Joachim Göschen (1752–1828) in Leipzig, a friend of Schiller's future confidante Johann Gottfried Körner (1756–1831), who helped Göschen establish his publishing house, and the second being Johann Friedrich Cotta (1764–1832) in Stuttgart. *Thalia* continued in seven issues through 1791, when Schiller's serious illness postponed work until the first issue of *Neue Thalia* in 1792.

In April 1785, Schiller took leave from his friends and romantic entanglements in Mannheim, meeting last with his former classmate and fellow outlaw Streicher, with whom he had fled Württemberg, both vowing to succeed—Streicher as orchestra conductor, and Schiller planning to pursue a law degree in Leipzig and a career as a politician. Streicher went on to become a renowned piano maker, composer, and a close friend of Ludwig van Beethoven (1770–1827). At the beginning of June 1784, the rather desperate Schiller had received a package including the gifts of a wallet and individual miniature portraits of two young couples in Dresden who were great admirers of his work: the portrait artist Dora Stock (1760–1832), the diplomat, author, and future revolutionary exile Ludwig Ferdinand Huber (1764–1804), and the salon host Minna Stock (1762–1843)—a scene from whose childhood appears in the eighth book of Goethe's *Dichtung und Wahrheit*, in which he describes visiting the Stock family in Leipzig during his student years—and one of Schiller's most influential friends and collaborators, author and Saxon and Prussian state administrator Körner. Having no place to go after the termination of his position as house dramatist in Mannheim, Schiller took their open invitation quite literally; he stayed in Körner's residence in Leipzig-Gohlis in the summer of 1785 and arrived in Dresden in early September, at first vacationing with them in Loschwitz, and then living with the newly married Minna and Gottfried Körner in Dresden until 1787, having created a studio and apartment in their garden house in Loschwitz on September 12, 1785. During this period, Dora Stock assisted the portrait artist Anton Graff (1736–1813) with his well-known portrait of Schiller, as well as producing three of her own, one of which was a pastel copy of Graff's portrait. The Körners, who were extraordinarily well-connected in the theatre scene, constructed a small but impressive theater in their home, where scenes from *Don Karlos* were first performed; Dora Stock later became the first to perform as Johanna in an in-house reading of Schiller's *Die Jungfrau von Orleans* (The Maid of Orleans, 1801), and her nephew Carl Theodor Körner (1791–1813), who became a prominent dramatist at the Burgtheater in Vienna and an anti-Napoleonic soldier-poet, became the first to portray Schiller's Wilhelm Tell as a child.

In the summer and fall of 1785, while in Gohlis—today part of Leipzig—at the invitation of Körner's friend, the manor lord and patron of the arts Johann Hieronymus Hetzer (1723–1788), Schiller worked on the first three acts of his fourth completed drama *Don Karlos* and what was to become his best-known lyric work, the philosophical poem "An die Freude" (Ode to Joy). In late 1785, Schiller wrote as the defiant voice of the Age of Happiness, and his use of "Freude" (joy) here—the sensual counterpart to the political-philosophical term "Glückseligkeit" (happiness)—is an expression of the feeling of enthusiasm that both drives and accompanies the crowning achievement of reason and virtue—political freedom—and the overthrow of tyranny, violent if necessary—both of which are prerequisites of happiness. Although Schiller concluded in 1803 that it was "ein schlechtes Gedicht" (a bad poem) that "einem fehlerhaften Geschmack der Zeit entgegen kam" (catered to a flawed taste of the time; *NA* 30: 206), even by then, twenty-one years before the premiere of Beethoven's setting, Schiller and Körner recognized the widespread popularity of the "Volkslied" (people's song) in several letters in September and October of 1800 (*NA* 38/1: 347; *NA* 30: 206). Indeed, Beethoven's setting of Schiller's poem was preceded by approximately forty other melodies between 1785 and

1824, among them settings by Körner and Schubart, and fourteen of which appeared in the published collection, *Vierzehn Compositionen zu Schillers ODE AN DIE FREUDE* (Fourteen Compositions for Schiller's ODE TO JOY), in 1800 (Hildebrandt, 123). In a series of packages sent to his publisher Göschen from November 29 to December 23, 1785, were the poem Schiller had referred to as "das Gedicht an die Freude" (the poem To Joy; *NA* 24: 28–29) from its very first mention—not "An die Freiheit" (Ode to Freedom), as has been speculated without compelling evidence—followed by Act II of *Don Karlos*, the poems "Freigeisterei der Leidenschaft" (Libertinism of Passion) and "Resignation," both of which he suspected would be censored, and the latter of which contains the leitmotivistic secularist line: "Die Weltgeschichte ist das Weltgericht" (world history is the final judgment; *NA* 1: 168). In the same weeks, Schiller submitted the anonymous "Verbrecher aus Infamie" (Criminal of Infamy), and the final version of "Philosophische Briefe" (Philosophical Letters, 1786). In this work, a fictional dialogue adapted from discussions between Schiller and Körner, the enlightened Raphael seeks to debunk the theosophy of the younger Julius, causing the latter to experience an existential crisis. However, according to Schiller, it is natural and positive that the promotion of "Sceptizismus und Freidenkerei" (skepticism and libertinism; *NA* 20: 108) necessarily causes feverish convulsions of the human mind that accompany the progression from the "Irrthum" (error) of half-enlightened and mystical conviction to the triumph of "Wahrheit" (truth; *NA* 20: 108).

Four years in the writing, *Don Karlos. Infant von Spanien*, Schiller's royal family portrait, revolutionary philosophical-political debate, and drama of forbidden love between former fiancé-turned-stepson Don Karlos and former fiancée-turned-stepmother and Queen of Spain Elisabeth of Valois, is among Schiller's best-known works and was his fourth completed drama in the six years between 1781 and 1787. Work on *Don Karlos* began in May 1782 at the villa of Henriette von Wolzogen in Bauerbach when Dalberg, the director of the Nationaltheater Mannheim, sent his newest theater author, Schiller, Abbé Saint-Réal's (1639–1692) historical novella *Dom Carlos, nouvelle historique* (1672) as a suggestion for a drama. Significantly, along with *Kabale und Liebe*, the drama becomes Schiller's second to demonstrate his interest in the US War of Independence, and the second of what will be six dramas to address the war of liberation as a prerequisite for the pursuit of happiness of a population facing the horrors of occupation and oppression. Schiller's awareness of the parallels between the liberation of the Netherlands and that of the British colonies and their significance for his biography as well as his art are reflected in his letter to Henriette von Wolzogen of January 8, 1783, written during the early phase of his work on *Don Karlos*: "Wenn Nordamerika frei wird, so ist es ausgemacht, daß ich hingehe" (If North America becomes free, then it is settled that I will go there; *NA* 23: 60). In Act III, Scene 10 of *Don Karlos*, arguably among the most significant scenes in the history of the dramatic portrayal of the struggle between absolutism and the rights of the human individual, Schiller's advocate of humanity, Marquis Posa, and Philipp II—the ruthless ruler of Spain and of an empire on which the sun never sets—face off in a debate over heteronomy and autonomy. Schiller's Posa both opens and closes his argument with a play on Schiller's concept of the "Weltbürger, der keinem Fürsten dient"—"Ich kann nicht Fürstendiener sein" (I cannot be the servant of a prince; NA 6: 180)—in the process delivering the play's signature line—"Geben Sie / Gedankenfreiheit" (Give freedom of thought; NA 6: 191)—and invoking the late eighteenth-century political concept of happiness literally twelve times in nine pages (High 2010, 102; NA 6: 181–189). Despite the success of his first four dramas, few authors of canonical status have been as critical of their own works as was Schiller, and his dissatisfaction with the early dramas resonates in his letters on his completion of his fifth drama, the *Wallenstein Trilogy*, some twelve years after the completion of *Don Karlos*.

Beginning in 1787, Schiller's circle of influential acquaintances expands, and his tale of upward mobility takes further steps toward Weimar. In early 1787, Minna Körner reports that Schiller is "ganz toll und blind verliebt" (quite mad and blindly infatuated; NA 42: 106) in Henriette von Arnim (1768–1847), a relationship that the Körners opposed and which ended badly. In July 1787, Schiller accepted Charlotte von Kalb's invitation to visit Weimar, where he met Herder and Wieland, but missed Goethe, who was on his famous Italian Journey. On August 9, 1787, Schiller writes to Körner that he thinks of Henriette von Arnim "fast zu oft" (almost too often; NA 24: 128). He writes to Körner on November 19, perhaps ironically, that he had recently visited the home of Wieland in Oßmannstedt and would ask for the hand of Wieland's second daughter, Maria Carolina Friederica Wieland (1770–1851), whom he had seen only once, if he thought he were worthy (NA 24: 178–179). At the end of November 1787, Schiller again visited Henriette von Wolzogen in Bauerbach, where Wilhelm von Wolzogen suggested that Schiller should join him in visiting his aunt Luise von Lengefeld and his two self-described "super-klugen Cousinen" (super-clever cousins; CvW *Nachlass*, 156) Charlotte von Lengefeld—whose hand in marriage represented the financial hopes of her family—and her unhappily married sister Caroline von Beulwitz, in Rudolstadt, which they did on December 6. In 1788, after a summer of pursuing relationships with both sisters, Schiller hoped to become engaged to marry Charlotte von Lengefeld, the daughter of the widowed Luise von Lengefeld and the Superintendant of Forests (*Oberforstmeister*) at the court of Schwarzburg-Rudolstadt, Carl Christoph von Lengefeld (1715–1775), as well as the godchild of Goethe's confidante and inspiration, the author Charlotte von Stein (1742–1827), who was herself lady in waiting to Duchess Anna Amalia of Sachsen-Weimar-Eisenach (1739–1807). Charlotte von Lengefeld was also a close friend of the poet, essayist, and translator Karl Ludwig von Knebel (1744–1834), who was, along with Wieland—one of Germany's leading writers and the editor of the best-selling journal *Teutscher Merkur*—the tutor of the two princes of Saxe-Weimar, and a close friend of Goethe. Indeed, it was Knebel who introduced Goethe to Duke Carl August in Frankfurt in 1774, who in turn had invited Goethe to move to Weimar, which Goethe did in

1775. After the death of her husband in 1775, Luise von Lengefeld served as "Hofmeisterin" (house tutor) to the princes of Schwarzburg-Rudolstadt at the residential palace Heidecksburg, which stands above Rudolstadt.

According to repeated testimony by all involved, Schiller's potential mother-in-law, a devout Christian in search of a like-minded and financially secure husband for her daughter, would not readily have consented to the engagement, had Schiller—an unemployed celebrity commoner and renowned secularist—not found a permanent and respected position. Only in the spring of his courtship, Schiller had published the highly controversial poem "Die Götter Griechenlandes" (The Gods of Ancient Greece) in Wieland's *Teutscher Merkur* (German Mercury) of March 1788, at which point readers who had somehow failed to recognize his hostility toward organized religion could not but admit the obvious. With no job, no patent of nobility, no religion, and a scandal brewing, Schiller, who otherwise mentions the Bible explicitly only very few times, goes on a charm offensive, mentioning the Bible three times in letters from July and August of 1788 and March 1789, all addressed to the Lengefelds and intended for the ears of the "*Cher Mere*," for whom he orders an ornate English Bible just as the reactions to his poem begin to pour in (*NA* 25: 73; *NA* 25: 89). In March 1788 in the *Teutscher Merkur*, an anonymous and critical essay on polytheism appeared, as Schiller put it, "von *Herrn* v. Knebeln und Herdern zusammengestoppelt" (thrown together by Herr v. Knebel and Herder; NA 25: 56); in the August 1788 issue of *Deutsches Museum*, very recent Catholic convert and poet Friedrich Leopold Graf zu Stolberg (1750–1819) published an outraged accusation of blasphemy lamenting the sad relationship of the naturalist to the deity; in *Thalia*, Körner published a defense of Schiller and his poem; Catholic-leaning poet Novalis (Friedrich von Hardenberg, 1772–1801) expressed support for the "vortrefliches Gedicht" (outstanding poem; Novalis, 18–20); in April 1789, Schiller cites a letter in which popular poet Gottfried August Bürger (1747–1794) defends Stolberg's good heart and simultaneously ridicules his "Schwachsinnigkeit" (feeblemindedness; *NA* 25: 251), stating that he expects more defenses of Schiller's poem. The responses culminate in a spirited defense of the poet's freedom of expression by world explorer and revolutionary thinker Georg Forster (1754–1794) entitled "Fragment eines Briefes an einen deutschen Schriftsteller über Schillers 'Götter Griechenlandes'" (Fragment of a Letter to a German Author on Schiller's "Gods of Ancient Greece") in the May 1789 issue of *Neue Litteratur und Voelkerkunde* (New Literature and Ethnology; High 2013, Secularism, 319). Thus, by early 1789, the potential son-in-law had become an infamous atheist, yet, at the height of the scandal, Schiller achieved the requisite profile of a prospective husband when, at the urging of a family acquaintance and distant admirer, Goethe, he was named to a position as unsalaried Professor of History (technically Philosophy) at the University of Jena on May 11, 1789. At the age of twenty-nine, Schiller's engagement on December 22, 1789 to the highly educated, enlightened, and popular daughter of a poor, but connected, noble family had not only brought about the personal happiness he had sought, but expanded his relatively small circle of acquaintances to include those who led him ever closer to Weimar—then the seat of German culture—first cultivated by Duchess Anna Amalia, who had served as regent since her husband's death in 1758, and now ruled since 1775 by her son, the Duke Carl August.

The prose works that Schiller published in his journals from 1782 to 1789 and, to a somewhat lesser extent, his first four dramas, had an impact on transnational Gothic literature in the 1790s that was possibly unmatched. Of the many characteristics that comprised the Gothic mood in the eighteenth century, or what Edgar Allen Poe (1809–1849) later tellingly called "Germanism" and "gloom"—political, legal, and social failure; corruption, the inquisition, persecution, rebellion, and superstition; executions, frame-ups, murders, seances, special effects, pacts with the devil, and ventriloquism; confidence men, conspiracy, and disguises; evil monks, ghosts, prisoners, robbers, and spies; dungeons, forests, lairs, and castle ruins; and redundant and disingenuous claims of truth—Schiller delivered all in the eight years (1782–1789) that immediately precede the resonant German-English Gothic explosion of the 1790s. As a result, most of the leading British authors of the 1790s demonstrate an intimate familiarity with Schiller's works, and the most strident critics of British Gothic literature cite Schiller as an important, if often unwelcome, presence behind the phenomenon (High 2011, 49). Schiller's production as an author of novellas achieved watershed status on the merits of his final two completed works of seven attempts at literary prose, "Der Verbrecher aus verlorener Ehre" (The Criminal of Lost Honor, 1786; originally "Der Verbrecher aus Infamie") and *Der Geisterseher* (The Spiritualist, 1787–1789).

"Der Verbrecher aus verlorener Ehre"—a psychological character study that Schiller refers to as a "Leichenöffnung" (autopsy) of the human animal (Christian Wolf)—reveals how individuals, societies, churches, and justice systems create rather than reform criminals, and provides a model for a new single-narrative frame novella, along with the frame novellas that constitute *Der Geisterseher*—each told by a new narrator and featuring the now-familiar genre-critical phrases "die Begebenheit, die sich [...] ereignet hat" (the occurrence that took place; *NA* 16: 70), "merkwürdige Begebenheit" (unusual occurrence; *NA* 16: 77), "daß die erzählte Begebenheit sich wirklich ereignet habe" (that the occurrence narrated actually took place; *NA* 16: 92), "seltsame Wendung" (curious turn; *NA* 16: 71), "das Unerwartete dieser Wendung" (the unexpectedness of this turn; *NA* 16: 86), and the "Todesfall [...] der sich [...] ereignet" (death that had occurred; *NA* 16: 102). Ironically, although Schiller had conceived of *Der Geisterseher* in order to reap the per-page commission from his publisher, it quickly became an international Gothic pop-cultural phenomenon and one of Schiller's best-selling works; the enthusiastic reception of the serial work left him once again profoundly annoyed with the public's taste. By the time Schiller's struggle with the broad popularity of and his personal distaste for *Der Geisterseher* had begun, literary prose had become a necessary financial evil, and Schiller produced a series of unhappy outbursts, referring to his hit as "der verfluchte Geisterseher" (the cursed *Geisterseher*), and describing his work as "schlecht" and "Schmiererei" (bad and scribbling), while bemoaning the project as a "sündlichen Zeitaufwand" (sinful waste of time; *NA* 25: 30; High 2011, 60), and wondering in a letter to Körner of March 17, 1788, if a demon had inspired it. As he reported to Körner on January 29, 1789, once it became a popular success, the project would not hold any further attraction for Schiller until he found a way to accessorize the Gothic tale with the insertion of a predictably less popular philosophical dialogue—"Philosophisches Gespräch aus dem *Geisterseher*," in many ways a continuation of the *Philosophische Briefe*: "Stelle Dir vor, daß mir der Geisterseher anfängt, lieb zu werden" (just imagine, the Spiritualist is beginning to grow on me; *NA* 25: 188). Upon completion of the philosophical dialogue, which did not appear in subsequent book publications, Schiller promptly abandoned the project as a fragment.

Despite working on *Wallenstein* and the never-realized *Don Karlos* prequel *Die Maltheser* (The Maltese Knights) in the early 1790s, after the publication of *Don Karlos* in 1787, Schiller did not complete another dramatic work until *Wallensteins Lager* (*Wallenstein's Camp*) in 1798, a fact that has led to a great deal of speculation regarding possible explanations for his sudden lack of dramatic production. It has long been a commonplace and facile approach to explain both Schiller's lack of dramatic production in the early 1790s and his intensive study of Kant's works—in particular *Critik der Urteilskraft* (*Critique of the Power of Judgement*, 1790)—as a result of his ostensible political disappointment with the course of the French Revolution. This flight-from-politics theory finds apparent support and a starting point in Schiller's letter to Körner of February 8, 1793, in which he laments the unconstitutional execution of Louis XVI, and in the letter to Prince Augustenburg of the next day, which eventually evolved into the *Ästhetische Briefe* (*Aesthetic Letters*, 1795). In the former, Schiller expresses his disgust at the January 21, 1793 execution of Louis XVI: "Was sprichst Du zu den französischen Sachen? […] Ich kann seit 14 Tagen keine *französischen* Zeitungen mehr lesen, so ekeln diese elenden Schindersknechte mich an" (What do you say to the events in France? […] I have not been able to read any French newspaper for the past fourteen days; that is how much these wretched henchmen disgust me; *NA* 26: 183). Although there can be little doubt that Schiller would have embraced the revolutionary rule of law in France, if he had ever believed in its success, all the sources extant indicate that, rather than expressing unreflected enthusiasm at the outset, Schiller, the universal historian, expressed only a prescient concern for the consequences of its failure. Reflecting back on February 9, 1790, Caroline von Wolzogen writes: "Die Greuelsczenen hatten dort begonnen. […] Schiller hatte diese Begebenheiten schon bei ihrem ersten Entstehen ernst und ahnungsvoll aufgenommen; er hielt die Franzosen für kein Volk, dem echt republikanische Gesinnung eigen werden könnte" (The scenes of horror there had begun […] already from the outset, Schiller had viewed these events seriously and with a sense of foreboding; he did not consider the French to be a people capable of adopting a truly republican character; *NA* 42: 127). Since demonstrating Schiller's ostensible disappointment in the French Revolution would require some expression of his early enthusiasm, the fact that there is no such expression to be found renders the notion rather empty. Often overlooked in this discussion is the inescapable fact that, in the period between 1784 and 1789, Schiller had completed one drama, which he had begun in 1783 and which was largely complete by the end of 1785. Thus, one will have to look beyond the revolution and Kant for the reasons. According to the evidence, beginning in 1788, a number of personal and professional preoccupations interrupted Schiller's dedication to drama and led to a shift in focus. Among his preoccupations were his marriage, his health, and his new position as professor—ironically, one that he had embraced foremost in order to secure an income that would qualify him to become a husband in the first place, and one whose duties his fragile health made increasingly difficult to fulfill.

On May 11, 1789, Schiller moved into his first apartment in Jena, where he immediately began writing lectures on a number of demanding topics, having never taught before and with no formal education as historian or philosopher. By the time he arrived in Jena, Schiller was already preparing for his wedding to Charlotte von Lengefeld, which took place on February 22, 1790, in what is now called the *Schillerkirche* in the suburb Wenigenjena. In addition to the historical and aesthetic studies required of an author, editor, critic, and professor, financial concerns dominated Schiller's letters during the first four years of the French Revolution. As was the case with *Der Geisterseher*, Schiller sought to write a great deal of the material for *Thalia*, so that he could take advantage of the per-page commission. In a letter to Körner of November 26, 1790, Schiller stated that even if he were ready to write drama again, he could not afford to stop publishing on history, if only "um meine Existenz bestmöglichst zu verbessern" (in order to improve my financial situation as best as possible; *NA* 26: 58). This income from writing was of the utmost importance, since his professorship was actually an honorary position, and originally provided him with an honorarium plus student tuition totaling some 400 *Reichsthaler*, which, as Schiller explained in a letter to Körner of December 12, 1789, constituted approximately half of a minimal annual income (NA 25: 354–355).

Schiller's first mention of Kant appears in a letter to Körner of July 23, 1787 (*NA* 24: 111), and the first evidence of Schiller's interest in Kant's works appears in a letter to Körner of August 29, 1787, regarding University of Jena Professor of Philosophy Karl Leonhard Reinhold's (1757–1823) promotion of Kant's essays that had appeared in the *Berliner Monatsschrift*, and in particular regarding Kant's *Idee zu einer allgemeinen Geschichte in weltbürgerlichen Absicht* (Idea for a Universal History with a Cosmopolitan Purpose, 1784). On May 26, 1789, Schiller delivered his inaugural lecture to a packed auditorium at the University of Jena, "Was ist und wozu studiert man Universalgeschichte?" (What is and to what end does one study universal history?), addressing a scholarly approach recently popularized foremost by Adam Ferguson (1723–1816), Christian Garve (1742–1798), Herder, and Kant. True to his mission to publish as much as possible based on his university research, Schiller's publications closely follow the topics of his university lectures. Thus, the beginning of the final decade of the eighteenth century finds Schiller at the height of his work as a historian, which had first sparked his interest in Kant, had already produced a best-selling historical work and the drama *Don Karlos*, and would lead directly to his next history book and next drama project *Wallenstein*, which he worked on intermittently in 1791 and 1794. The research for *Don Karlos* had also laid the groundwork for Schiller's best-selling historical work, *Geschichte des Abfalls der vereinigten Niederlande von der Spanischen Regierung* (History of the Revolt of the United Netherlands against Spain, 1788), which had first secured him the professorship in Jena. In the events and documents of the Dutch War of Liberation, where the North American colonists had found a legal precedence to support an actual rebellion in the Dutch *Plakaat von Verlatinghe* (Act of Abjuration, 1581), Schiller discovered a moral-legal argument with which to threaten feudal rulers with a modern historical-political inevitability, which he clearly formulates as a warning to all occupiers and oppressors: "Die Kraft also, womit es handelte, ist unter uns nicht verschwunden; der glückliche Erfolg, der sein Wagestück krönte, ist auch uns nicht versagt, wenn die Zeitläufte wiederkehren und ähnliche Anlässe uns zu ähnlichen Thaten rufen" (Thus the power that they wielded has not left us; the happy result that crowned their act of courage will not fail us, when the cycle of history repeats and similar contexts call us to similar deeds; *NA* 17: 11). As ever, Schiller is foremost interested in the past to the extent that it educates by reflecting the present and modeling the future; consequently, Schiller argues in a letter to Caroline von Beulwitz of October 12, 1788, that even as a historian, it is not "historische Warheit" (historical truth) that is of importance to his historiography, but human interest and the potential to excite readers by revealing "innere Wahrheit" (inner truth) and "philosophische und künstlerische Wahrheit" (philosophical and artistic truth). In *Ueber das Pathetische*, Schiller returns to the topic, stressing how relatively insignificant "historische[…] Realität" (historical reality) is for the aesthetic experience of fiction or history, which is in the end a form of fiction (*NA* 20: 218).

In the summer of 1790, Schiller lectured on the history of the Thirty Years' War and the theory of tragedy, while he continued work on his second and final historical monograph, the popular *Geschichte des Dreyßigjährigen Kriegs* (History of the Thirty Years' War), which he published in five serial installments in Göschen's *Historischer Kalender für Damen* (Historical Calendar for Ladies) in 1791–1793. During the same period, Schiller published several shorter historical works, including further essays on the liberation of the Netherlands, and essays on the history of politics, including the essays "Die Gesetzgebung des Lykurgus und Solon" (The Legislation of Lykurgus and Solon, 1790) and "Die Sendung Moses" (The Mission of Moses, 1790), a secular analysis of Moses as politician and his contributions to an initially positive transition from polytheism to constitutional monotheism that had long since become both a guarantee of pseudo-virtue and a hindrance to true virtue and freedom. Schiller criticizes precisely this problem in a March 1793 letter to

Körner regarding Kant's *Religion innerhalb der Grenzen der bloßen Vernunft* (*Religion within the Limits of Reason Alone*, 1793–1794), of which Schiller concludes that Kant had unwittingly lent support to the history of surrogate virtue and pseudo-civilization by reconciling philosophy with "Kindervernunft" (reason of children) and thus had merely "das morsche Gebäude der Dummheit geflickt" (patched up the rotting house of stupidity; *NA* 26: 219).

In a letter to Körner of November 26, 1790, Schiller indicated his intention to conduct rigorous aesthetic studies before returning to drama or poetry: "Das Arbeiten im dramatischen Fache dürfte überhaupt noch auf eine ziemlich lange Zeit hinausgerückt werden. Ehe ich der griechischen Tragödie durchaus mächtig bin und meine dunklen Ahnungen von Regel und Kunst in klare Begriffe verwandelt habe, lasse ich mich auf keine dramatische Ausarbeitung ein" (Work in the field of drama is likely to be postponed for quite a long time. Before I have thoroughly mastered Greek tragedy and have transformed my obscure notions of rule and art into clear concepts, I will not embark on any drama project; *NA* 26: 58). On January 11, 1793—ten days before the execution of Louis XVI and before news of his death sentence could reach Jena—Schiller reports to Körner that in his preparations for *Kallias* he has recently read "Burke, Sulzer, Wepp, Mengs, Winkelmann, Home, Batteux, Wood, Mendelsohn," in addition to five or six compilations, and hopes to read yet more works on aesthetics (*NA* 26: 174). Thus, Schiller's study of aesthetics prior to his encounter with Kant had been broad, beginning with his college years and including a great number of the Scottish Enlightenment works Kant himself had read prior to writing *Grundlegung einer Metaphysik der Sitten* (*Groundwork for the Metaphysics of Morals*, 1785) and *Critik der Urteilskraft*, corroborating the conclusion of Franz Mehring (1846–1919)—"In gewissem Sinne war Schiller schon Kantianer gewesen, ehe er Kants Philosophie kennenlernte" (In a certain sense, Schiller was already a Kantian before he became familiar with Kant's philosophy; Mehring, 316)—and of Laura Anna Macor that Schiller was a "Kantianer ante litteram" (a Kantian prior to reading Kant; Macor 2011).

Schiller himself was clearly convinced that the nature of his publishing opportunities and commitments and his professorial duties were a major hindrance to his literary production which had all but stopped in 1787, not that he was happy with the arrangement. As the work on *Geschichte des dreyßigjährigen Kriegs* neared completion, Schiller wrote to Körner on September 21, 1792: "Sage mir nun woran ich mich jetzt zuerst machen soll? Mir ist ordentlich bange bey meiner wiedererlangten Geistesfreiheit. […] Ich hätte Lust mir durch ein Gedicht die Musen wieder zu versöhnen, die ich durch den Calender gröblich beleidigt habe" (Now tell me what should I now do first? I am truly frightened by my regained intellectual freedom. […] I would like to use a poem to reconcile myself with the muses, whom I have grossly offended through my work on the Calendar; *NA* 26: 152). In a letter to Körner of October 15, 1792, Schiller explained why it was practical for him as an author and editor to forego poetry and continue his comprehensive study of aesthetics:

Ich wollte Poesie treiben, aber die nahe Ankunft der CollegienZeit zwingt mich Aesthetik vorzunehmen. Jetzt stecke ich biss an die Ohren in Kants Urtheilskraft. Ich werde nicht ruhen, biss ich diese Materie durchdrungen habe und sie unter meinen Händen etwas geworden ist. Auch ist es nöthig, dass ich, auf alle Fälle, ein Collegium ganz durchdenke und erschöpfe, [...] um mit Leichtigkeit, ohne Kraft- und Zeit-Aufwand etwas lesbares für die Thalia zu jeder Zeit schreiben zu können. (NA 26: 161).

[I wanted to practice poetry, but the imminent arrival of the semester compels me to pursue aesthetics. Now I am up to my ears in Kant's Urteilskraft. I will not rest until I have thoroughly worked through this material, and it has become something concrete in my own hands. By all means, it is also necessary that I thoroughly think through and exhaust a subject [...] in order to be able to write something presentable for Thalia on short notice, with ease and without expenditure of energy and time.]

Thus, although Schiller's work beginning in 1787 shows a change of focus from drama and poetry to literary prose, history, and philosophy, this change clearly occurred several years before the outbreak of the French Revolution and before he studied Kant. Nowhere did Schiller or any acquaintance express the belief that a preoccupation with the revolution, or with Kant, caused this shift.

In 1792, gothic-revolutionary dramatist and Schiller-translator Jean Henri Ferdinand La Martelière's (1761–1830) adaptation of Schiller's *Die Räuber*, entitled *Robert, Chef du brigands* (Robert, Leader of the Robbers, 1792) was performed weekly at the Theatre du Marais in Paris. To some extent as a result, on August 26, 1792, the National Assembly in Paris awarded French citizenship to Schiller and other internationally prominent progressives and revolutionaries—among them Joseph Priestley, Thomas Paine, Jeremy Bentham, William Wilberforce, Joachim Heinrich Campe, Johann Heinrich Pestalozzi, George Washington, Alexander Hamilton, James Madison, Klopstock, and Tadeusz Kościuszko, who, "par leurs écrits & par leur courage, ont servi la cause de la liberté, & préparé l'affranchissement des peuples" (by their writings and courage served the cause of freedom and the liberation of humanity; Schmid 10). The honor was announced in the August 28 issue of *Le Moniteur Universel*, and the aristocratic annoyance with Schiller's involvement became evident as soon as the news arrived in Weimar. In a letter from Charlotte von Stein to Charlotte Schiller of September 14, 1792, Stein asks: "[...] was hat denn Schiller zur Vertheidigung oder zum Lobe der Revolution geschrieben?" (what has Schiller ever written in defense or in praise of the revolution? C.v.S. 2: 288), and quietly relays a position expressed by Duchess Louise von Sachsen-Weimar (1757–1830) in a letter to Stein of September 10, 1792, in which the Duchess expressed her hope that Schiller would decline the citizenship offer (Wilson, Document 216). This epistolary evidence dispels one of the most stubborn myths regarding Schiller and the French Revolution, namely that his six-year silence on the subject of his French citizenship from August 1792 to March 1798 was due to his being unaware of the honor until actually receiving the documents in 1798. On the contrary, the list of honorees was anything but a secret and had been reprinted in *Minerva, Schleswiges Journal*, and *Wiener Zeitschrift* (Saine, 308n). A number of documents show that Schiller was widely criticized in Weimar for even this passive involvement with the French Revolution and for the equally passive transgression registered, when student demonstrators in Jena sang "Ein freies Leben führen wir" (A Free Life We Lead; Wilson 1999, 225) from Schiller's *Die Räuber*, about which the privy councilors in Weimar expressed their dissatisfaction with Schiller's inferred complicity (Wilson 1999, 225). Poet, scientist, long-time Goethe colleague, and Privy Counselor Christian Gottlob Voigt (1743–1819) wrote to the duke that Schiller's French citizenship had resulted in a number of playful criticisms (Wilson 1999, 226), including Professor Heinrich Paulus' complaint to the duke of the students' "Raeuber- und Sauflieder" (robber and drinking songs), Privy Councilor Christian Friedrich Schnauß (1722–1797) complaining that "Schiller hätte auch etwas Besseres machen können" (Schiller could have come up with something better; Wilson, 226), and Duke Carl August writing on his birthday on October 12, 1792, to his mother that, at the moment, *Die Räuber* is his measure for annoying works of art (Carl August, 115).

In spite of the aristocratic discomfort in Weimar with Schiller's revolutionary reputation and recognition, his letter to Körner of November 26, 1792, is the closest he came to expressing expectations for the French revolutionaries:

> Seitdem ich den Moniteur lese habe ich mehr Erwartungen von diesen. […] Man hat darinn alle Verhandlungen in der Nat.Convention im Detail vor sich und lernt die
> Franzosen in ihrer Stärke und Schwäche kennen. Die Maynzischen Aspecten werden sehr zweifelhaft für mich, aber in Gottes Nahmen. Wenn die Franzosen mich um meine Hofnungen bringen, so kann es mir einfallen, mir bey den Franzosen selbst beßere zu schaffen. (*NA* 26: 169–170)
> [Since reading the Moniteur I have more expectations from them. […] You have all the negotiations in the National Convention in front of you in detail and you get to know the French in their strengths and weaknesses. The prospects in Mainz are becoming very doubtful for me, but in God's name. If the French rob me of my hopes, it may occur to me to create better ones for myself among the French.]

In his first reference to hopes here, Schiller notes that his prospects for a position at the university in Mainz were growing dimmer with every day of the French occupation there since the creation of the Mainz Republic, led by Schiller's erstwhile literary ally Forster. Citing dissatisfaction with Jena, financial concerns, and the need for a less demanding work schedule due to his health, Schiller produces a series of letters to Körner, Caroline von Beulwitz, Charlotte Schiller, and Huber dating back to November 1789 that reveals his serious desire to leave Jena for Mainz, where he hoped that his supporter Karl Theodor Anton Maria Reichsfreiherr von Dalberg (1744–1817)—Coadjutur in Erfurt, and future Prince-Archbishop of Konstanz (1800)—could provide him a more comfortable position upon becoming Elector of Mainz, which did not occur until 1802 (High 1995, 181–182). In a letter to Körner of December 21, 1792, Schiller strongly criticizes Forster's rise to President of the French Rhine Republic in Mainz, predicting that the experiment would end in "Schande und Reue" (disgrace and regret) for Forster, and closing with a condemnation of the Mainz revolutionaries: "Für die Mainzer kann ich mich gar nicht interessiren; denn alle ihre Schritte zeugen mehr von einer lächerlichen Sucht sich zu signalisieren, als von gesunden Grundsätzen, mit denen sich ihr Betragen gegen die Andersdenkenden gar nicht reimt" (I cannot conjure up any interest in the Mainzer; for their every step bears witness more to a ridiculous addiction to drawing attention to themselves than to sound principles, which in no way rhyme with their behavior towards dissidents; *NA* 26: 171). Schiller's objection to the dictatorial nature of the puppet republic and its virtue signaling as well as his concern for the freedom of thought of "Andersdenkende" provide a paradigmatic example in the microcosm of Mainz for his wariness of dogmatism.

Schiller's second reference to his hopes "bey den Franzosen" refers to his plan to travel to Paris to deliver a constitutional defense of Louis XVI, whose trial on charges of treason had been debated for the better part of November and began on December 3, 1792, and here Schiller's French citizenship appears to have played its intended role to some unintended extent. Based on his letters, Schiller paid less attention to the revolution from 1789 through August of 1792 than he did after being named a French citizen. His regular reading of the *Moniteur* and his plan to defend the French Constitution in Paris of November–December 1792 all took place in the four months after the announcement of his French citizenship. The nature of the weakness and strength in the National Convention becomes clear to Schiller in the November 13 speeches by two representatives, which were printed in the *Moniteur* of November 14: St. Just, who proposed the unconstitutional execution of the king without trial, and Morisson, who argued the king's immunity based on the constitution. On November 23, three days before Schiller's letter to Körner, the Stuttgart (somewhat irregular) daily, the *Fortgesetzte Schubart'sche Chronik* (Schubart's New Chronicle), published a translation of Morrison's speech. In the November 20 issue, *Chronik* publisher Gotthold Friedrich Stäudlin (1758–1796) had published a personal plea on behalf of Louis XVI. In the November 23 issue, Stäudlin referred back to this plea and then quoted the *Moniteur* of November 14 in a footnote to his report "*Ludwig XVI.*," citing Morisson's argument that although he personally sees the king's guilt and would rather see the king punished for his crimes, there is nonetheless no provision in the constitution for punishing a king for pre-constitutional crimes, and that doing so would be a very bad step for a young state seeking to institute the rule of law: "Es ist wahr, Ludwig hat Unzählige der Unsrigen gemordet: aber wenn wir ihn durch neuere Geseze strafen wollen, so werden wir an ihm eben so sehr zu Mördern" (It is true that Louis murdered too many of our people to count: but if we want to punish him with newer laws, then we become just as much his murderers; Schubart, 769–770).

Just a few days later, Schiller links his vague reference to better hopes with travel plans. Inspired by the reports described above, Schiller intends to travel to Paris to deliver a defense of the king and the constitution. In the first week of December, Caroline von Beulwitz and Wilhelm von Humboldt offered to accompany Schiller to France (*NA* 34/1: 202; *NA* 34/1: 204), and in a letter of December 21, Schiller asks Körner to find him a translator for his defense:

> Kaum kann ich der Versuchung widerstehen, mich in die Streitsache wegen des Königs einzumischen, und ein Memoire darüber zu schreiben. […] Hätte jeder freisinnige Kopf geschwiegen, so wäre nie ein Schritt zu unserer Verbesserung geschehen. Es gibt Zeiten, wo man öffentlich sprechen muß, weil Empfänglichkeit dafür da ist, und eine solche Zeit scheint mir die jetztige zu sein (*NA* 26: 171–172).
>
> [I can hardly resist the temptation to get involved in the dispute about the king and write a position paper about it. […] If every liberal mind had always been silent, no step toward our improvement would ever have happened. There are times when one has to speak publicly because there is a receptive audience, and the present appears to me to be such a time.]

That Schiller believed there was an audience for such a plea (*Empfänglichkeit*) resulted from his awareness of the legal argument of representatives such as Morisson and from Schiller's knowledge of his French citizenship, an indication that the National Convention knew and respected him. Fellow citizenship-honorands Cloots, Paine, and Priestley (who did not serve) were all elected to the National Convention in September. In a letter of December 27, 1792, Körner lambastes the French revolutionaries for their "politische Sophisterei" (political sophism; *NA* 34/1: 214) before agreeing to arrange for a translator for Schiller's speech (*NA* 34/1: 213). At this point, Körner's skepticism toward the project apparently prompted Schiller to proceed without him (*NA* 34/1: 213). On December 30, both Beulwitz and Schiller wrote in strictest secrecy to family friend Rudolph Zacharias Becker (1752–1822) to recruit him as translator of Schiller's plea (*NA* 26: 657). The fate of Louis XVI was decided less than three weeks later on January 17, and he was executed on January 21, 1793. Some three weeks after the execution of Louis XVI, on February 8, 1793, Schiller informs Körner: "Ich habe wirklich eine Schrift für den König schon angefangen gehabt, aber es wurde mir nicht wohl darüber, und da ligt sie mir nun noch da" (I really had already started writing a text for the king, but I had second thoughts, and there it still lies; *NA* 26: 183).

During his three years as professor in Jena, Schiller had often lamented the combination of his poor health and the financial necessity of work as professional historian and philosopher—not only a barrier to his aspirations as a dramatist, but to some important extent the work of a bread-fed scholar that he had decried in the *Universalgeschichte* lecture. Indeed, before he even began in his new position, Schiller jests in a letter to Körner of March 9, 1789, that if he could find a wealthy wife, he could make a living as a writer and that then the University of Jena "möchte mich dann im Asch lecken" (could then kiss my ass; *NA* 25: 222). In February 1791, Schiller suffered the first serious bout of the lung affliction that effectively ended his academic career and would eventually end his life. As a Doctor of Medicine and not yet thirty-two years old, by May of 1791 Schiller was keenly aware that his time was growing short. That summer, Schiller received notification that reports of his near fatal condition and indeed news of his death had spread in Denmark, where Schiller's admirers, radical Danish poet and freemason Jens Immanuel Baggesen (1764–1826), Duke Friedrich Christian von Schleswig-Holstein-Augustenburg (1765–1814), and court minister Ernst Heinrich Count von Schimmelmann (1747–1831) held a private memorial service. Upon hearing of the service, Jena philosopher Reinhold informed Baggesen that, although Schiller was indeed dangerously ill, he was in fact still alive. In a letter to Schiller of November 27, 1791, the duke and the count employ the cosmopolitan rhetoric of Schiller's Don Karlos and Marquis Posa in their offer of a stipend to promote his writing and alleviate his workload: "Zwey Freunde, durch Weltbürgersinn mit einander verbunden, erlassen dieses Schreiben an Sie [...] Nehmen Sie dieses Anerbieten an edler Mann! Der Anblick unsrer Titel bewege Sie nicht es abzulehnen [...] Wir kennen keinen Stolz als nur *den* Menschen zu seyn [...] Ihre Brüder" (Two friends bound together by a sense of cosmopolitanism issue this letter to you [...] Accept this offer, noble man! Let not the sight of our titles persuade you to reject it [...] We know no pride other than to be human beings [...] your brothers; *NA* 34/1: 114). In his letter to Körner of December 13, 1791, Schiller writes, somewhat optimistically: "Ich habe einmal Muße zu lernen und zu sammeln, und für die Ewigkeit zu arbeiten" (For once I have the leisure time to learn and collect, and to work for eternity; *NA* 26: 117). A day later, Schiller writes the first of his letters to Duke Augustenburg, which later appeared revised in serial form as the first of the *Ästhetische Briefe* in *Die Horen* (The Horae). Despite the stipend, which would be extended for three years, the task of writing to maintain a steady income remained a matter of pressing concern until 1795, by which time, as he wrote to Abel on April 3, 1795, Schiller had received a guarantee from Duke Carl August of a doubled stipend in the very likely event of permanent disability (*NA* 27: 169). Schiller would remain weakened for the rest of his life, yet, in accord with the ideas presented in his third dissertation, he faced his final fourteen years with the defiant conviction that his physical state, dictated by nature, could not be considered part of his self, but rather "etwas Auswärtiges und Fremdes" (something external and foreign), a resistance of fate Goethe later attributed to Schiller's "Evangelium der Freiheit" (gospel of freedom; Safranski, 8).

From 1790 to 1793, intermittently interrupted by his illness, Schiller wrote the majority of his moral-philosophical essays, all of which stem in part from his experience as a creative artist and his continued study of the most recent works of philosophy, preeminently those of Kant. They comprise to a significant degree the results of his Summer 1789 and 1790 university lectures on the theory of tragedy and his Winter 1792–1793 lectures on aesthetics, and almost all of the essays appeared in the third iteration of his second journal, which appeared as *Neue Thalia* beginning in 1792. In the first issue of January 1792, Schiller published the essay *Über den Grund des Vergnügens an tragischen Gegenständen* (On the Cause of the Pleasure We Derive from Tragic Objects), which hearkens back to the *Schaubühne* essay of 1784 in Schiller's description of the mechanisms of entertainment and morality, in which the audience benefits by cursing history's great criminals while enjoying on the stage the very horror of their crimes, and while experiencing both the pain and the joy of watching tragic heroes face coercion with moral resistance. In the second issue of *Neue Thalia* of March 1792, Schiller published *Über die tragische Kunst* (On the Art of Tragedy), in which he responds to Lessing, Mendelssohn, and Kant's theories of the sublime in a practical consideration of the means and ends of tragic art, namely the experience of the moral enjoyment of one's own compassion.

From January 25 to February 23, 1793, Schiller and Körner composed the series of letters that were to constitute the unrealized book project, *Kallias*, the artistic ends of which, beyond the quest for an objective definition of beauty, are stated clearly in the first paragraph of the first letter: "Die Untersuchung über das Schöne, wovon beynahe kein Theil der aesthetik zu trennen ist, führen mich in ein sehr weites Feld, wo für mich noch ganz fremde Länder liegen. Und doch muss ich mich schlechterdings des Ganzen bemächtigt haben, wenn ich etwas befriedigendes leisten soll" (The investigation of the beautiful, which can hardly be separated from any part of aesthetics, has led me into a wide field [...] And yet I must become master of the whole realm if I am to produce any satisfying work; *NA* 26: 175; Concerning Beauty, 145). To that end, Schiller engages Kant's distinction between *pulchritude vaga* (free beauty) and *pulchritude fixa* (adherent beauty), which appears in Section 16 of *Die Kritik der Urteilskraft*, seeking to demonstrate that the beautiful includes works of art created according to rules, and that if both nature and art can bring about the same reaction to beauty in the subject by overcoming the logical nature of their object, then there is no reason to distinguish between them as "Freiheit in der Erscheinung" (freedom in its appearance). *Über Anmut und Würde* (On Grace and Dignity) appeared in *Neue Thalia* in mid-July 1793, presenting in part results of Schiller's work on *Kallias* and the *Augustenburgerbriefe*. In his thesis statement that grace is "die durch Freiheit bewegten Gestalt" (the form moved by freedom), Schiller addresses a long-term interest in the natural gestures of actors, which had appeared in essays from "Über das Teutsche Theater" (On German Theater, 1782) to *Kallias*. *Vom Erhabenen* (Concerning the Sublime) appeared in the third and fourth issues of *Neue Thalia* in September 1793 and August 1794, again embarking from Kant's theory of the sublime in an explication of how the imaginative faculties of mathematical recognition or desire facilitate the disinterested experience of pleasure at viewing tragic or awe-inspiring events in the realms of both nature and art; again, Schiller is more driven by the concerns of the creative artist than those of the aesthetic philosopher. *Ueber das Erhabene* (On the Sublime), composed between 1794 and 1796, and first published in Volume 3 of the 1801 edition of Schiller's *Kleinere prosaische Schriften*, analyzes the concept of the sublime as the portrayal and experience of moral resistance against coercion: "Alle andere Dinge müssen; *der Mensch* ist das Wesen, welches will. Eben deswegen ist *des Menschen nichts so unwürdig*, als *Gewalt* zu erleiden, denn *Gewalt* hebt ihn auf" (All other things must; the human is the being that wills. Precisely for this reason, nothing is so unworthy of the human being as to suffer violence, for violence negates them as human beings; *NA* 21: 38). In "Über das Pathetische" (On the Pathetic) composed in 1793 and first published in 1801, Schiller posits that "das übersinnliche Prinzip" (the supersensual principle)—the triumph of active freedom of the will over instinct—distinguishes the human from the animal; thus the portrayal of suffering without resistance is one of mere animal determinism, and not the stuff of tragedy. *Zerstreute Betrachtungen über verschiedene ästhetische Gegenstände* (Reflections on Different Aesthetical Objects) appeared in the fifth issue of *Neue Thalia* in October 1794. Here, Schiller attempts to demonstrate how Kant's concept of beauty as the subjective basis of taste can be expanded by the objective experience not of *beauty* but of the *beautiful* and the sublime. In art, specifically in drama, and in particular in the tragedy, a mediation process occurs in the dynamic subjective experience of objective beauty on the stage.

In the winter of 1792–1793, Schiller wrote to his former foil Duke Carl Eugen of Württemberg to ask whether he, as fugitive and persona non grata, could be allowed to visit his family in Ludwigsburg for what would be his first and only visit to his home state in the eleven years since his exile in 1782. Although the duke did not respond directly, he let it be known that Schiller was free to visit, and would be ignored, and in September 1793, after visiting Heilbronn in August, the Schillers rented the second floor of the house at Wilhelmsstraße 17, where, on September 14, they welcomed the first of four children, Karl Ludwig Friedrich (1793–1857), who was followed by Ernst Friedrich Wilhelm (1796–1841), born in Jena; Karoline Luise Friederike (1799–1850), born in Weimar; and Emilie Henriette Luise (1804–1872), born in Jena. In addition to parenting and running the household, like her sister, who published the serial novel *Agnes von Lilien* (1796–1797) in Schiller's journal *Die Horen*, Charlotte Schiller was a lifelong writer and the author of the unpublished novel *Die heimliche Heirat* (The Secret Marriage). While Schiller was in Ludwigsburg, he visited with a number of old friends, his childhood friend, politician and poet Anselm Karl Elwert (1761–1825); his college friend Hoven, and his Karlsschule professor Abel, now at the University of Tübingen. On 24 October, Duke Carl Eugen died. According to Hoven, he and Schiller visited the grave of the recently deceased duke in November 1793, eliciting a surprising gesture of reconciliation from Schiller: "Da ruht er also […] dieser rastlos tätig gewesene Mann! Er hatte große Fehler als Regent, größere als Mensch; aber die erstern wurden von seinen großen Eigenschaften weit überwogen, und das Andenken an die letztern muß mit dem Toten begraben werden" (So there he rests [...] this tirelessly active man! He had great faults as a regent, greater as a man; but the former were far outweighed by his great qualities, and the memory of the latter must be buried with the dead; *NA* 42: 176–177). While in Ludwigsburg, at the end of September, Schiller met the aspiring poet Hölderlin, then twenty-three years old. Although Schiller never embraced Hölderlin's poetry, he did play a role in aiding Hölderlin's eerily familiar escape from his mother's wish that he become a minister in order to pursue a career as a poet. In a letter of May 28, 1793, Charlotte von Kalb had asked Schiller to help her find a *Hofmeister* for her son Fritz, and Schiller ultimately recommended two fellow Württembergians whose acquaintances he had made in Ludwigsburg and Tübingen, Hölderlin and philosopher Georg Wilhelm Friedrich Hegel (1770–1831), who—along with a third, philosopher and a future husband of Caroline Schlegel, Friedrich Wilhelm Joseph Schelling (1775–1854)—had until recently been roommates while studying theology at the University of Tübingen's Tübinger Stift seminary. In March 1794, Schiller met the publisher Cotta in Tübingen, who had published his dissertation, in a meeting arranged by Abel, and the two quickly agreed to work together. In May, Schiller returned to Jena. At the University of Jena, Schiller met the student and future linguist, political theorist, diplomat, and educational reformer Wilhelm von Humboldt. The two became collaborative spirits and met regularly, even twice daily, from 1794 to 1797, remaining friends until Schiller's death. Humboldt's affinity with Schiller's educational and political ideas is evident in his contributions to secularism in Prussian educational reform against the wishes of his colleague, the seminal figure in the history of hermeneutics, Friedrich Daniel Ernst Schleiermacher (1768–1834), in the founding of the Friedrich Wilhelm University at Berlin (later Humboldt University), and in his work toward convincing Austria to join the anti-Napoleonic coalition in 1813. Humboldt quickly became active publishing in Schiller's journals, as would Goethe just shortly thereafter.

Before Schiller's relationship with Goethe began in earnest in 1794, a collision between the two appeared inevitable. In December 1779, just after Schiller's twentieth birthday, Duke Carl August of Weimar and Goethe made an appearance at the Karlsschule to bestow the annual student awards, three of which were silver medals awarded to Schiller as a medical student. On September 7, 1788, soon after Goethe's return from his Italian Journey, he and Schiller spoke cordially for the first time at the home of the Lengefelds in Rudolstadt, but, while Schiller was impressed with what he saw, he did not get the impression that the feeling was mutual, as he expresses in a letter to Körner of September 11: "[...] ich zweifle, ob wir einander je sehr nahe rücken werden. [...] er ist mir, (an Jahren weniger als an Lebenserfahrungen und Selbstentwicklung) so weit voraus, daß wir unterwegs nie mehr zusammen kommen werden" (I doubt whether we can ever become very close [...] he is so far ahead of me (less in years than in self-development) that we shall never come together on our paths; *NA* 25: 107). As late as March 9, 1789, Schiller could conclude in a letter to Körner: "Dieser Mensch, dieser Göthe ist mir einmal im Wege, und er erinnert mich so oft, daß das Schicksal mich hart behandelt hat. Wie leicht ward *sein* Genie von seinem Schicksal getragen, und wie muß *ich* biss auf diese Minute noch kämpfen!" (This person, this Goethe, is in my way for better or worse, and he reminds me so often that fate has treated me harshly. How easily his genius was borne by his fate, and how I must still struggle to this minute!; *NA* 25: 222). By the time Goethe first truly engaged Schiller in 1794, their remarkable collaboration during the final decade of Schiller's life appeared highly unlikely, as Goethe reports: "Als ich ihn kennen lernte, glaubte ich, er lebte keine vier Wochen mehr" (When I first met him, I was convinced that he would not live another four weeks; Safranski, 7). Schiller's letters show that he was preoccupied with his health until 1794, when he makes clear his decision not to linger on his illness and to use his remaining time as productively as possible, as he explained in his letter to Goethe of August 31, 1794: "Eine große und allgemeine Geistesrevolution werde ich schwerlich Zeit haben, in mir zu vollenden aber ich werde thun was ich kann, und wenn endlich das Gebäude zusammenfällt, so habe ich doch vielleicht das Erhaltenswerthe aus dem Brande geflüchtet" (I will scarcely have time to complete a great and comprehensive intellectual revolution within myself, but I will do what I can, and when the building finally collapses, I may have saved that most worth preserving from the fire; *NA* 27: 32). To this end, as was the case with coffee, alcohol, and tobacco, according to Humboldt, Schiller sought to make of his illness a creative advantage, which he confirms in a letter to Garve of November 6, 1797: "Auch die Kränklichkeit ist zu was gut, ich habe ihr viel zu danken" (Even illness is good for something, I owe it a great deal; *NA* 29: 156).

After their meeting in Ludwigsburg, the first collaboration between Schiller and Cotta was to be a political quarterly, edited by Schiller, *Die Allgemeine Europäische Staatenzeitung* (The General European Political Journal), which would be entirely dedicated to the analysis of European politics, a contract for which Schiller signed on May 28, 1794 (*NA* 27: 206–207)—a serious indication that Schiller was perceived as an important political thinker at a point in history when legend would have it he had turned his back on politics. By July 10, 1794, however, Schiller's preference for the literary journal Die Horen over the Staatenzeitung, which he pleaded repeatedly in letters to Cotta, finally won out (NA 27: 7–8, 21). *Die Horen* was to feature an impressive list of contributors, including the new collaborators Goethe, August Wilhelm Schlegel (1767–1845), Humboldt and his younger brother Alexander von Humboldt (1769–1859), as well as, among others, Louise Brachmann (1777–1822), Friederike Brun (1765–1835), Fichte, Herder, Amalie von (Imhoff) Helvig (1776–1831), Sophie (Schubart) Mereau (later Brentano; 1770–1806), Elisa von der Recke (1754–1833), and Caroline von Wolzogen.

The announcement of Schiller's third journal, which appeared on December 10, 1794, has proven significantly more controversial than its actual contents, providing many scholars with a model of Weimar Classicism that is relatively rare beyond a very small set of texts. Already long weary of the divisive debates over the triumphs and failures of a French Revolution that had become best known for its spectacular, unconstitutional violence toward French citizens and subjects of the German states, in particular regarding its propagandistic promotion in Johann Friedrich Reichardt's (1752–1814) journals *Deutschland* and *Frankreich*, Schiller's announcement seeks to fill a market niche with a healing national forum promoting an aesthetic education of the individual that would reconcile division:

> Zu einer Zeit, wo das nahe Geräusch des Kriegs das Vaterland ängstiget, wo der Kampf politischer Meinungen und Interessen diesen Krieg beinahe in jedem Zirkel erneuert und nur allzuoft Musen und Grazien daraus verscheucht, wo weder in den Gesprächen noch in den Schriften des Tages vor diesem allverfolgenden Dämon der Staatskritik Rettung ist, möchte es ebenso gewagt als verdienstlich sein, den so sehr zerstreuten Leser zu einer Unterhaltung von ganz entgegengesetzter Art einzuladen. (*NA* 22: 106)
>
> At a time when the near roar of war frightens the fatherland, where the struggle of political opinions and interests renew this war in almost every circle and all too often scare off the muses and graces, where neither in discussion nor the writings of the day offer salvation from this all-pursuing demon of state criticism, it may be as daring as it is meritorious to invite the so very distracted reader to a form of entertainment of an entirely opposite kind.

The announcement responds to the partisan writing that had divided German intellectuals since the French Revolution began in 1789, bringing with it attacks on both pro- and anti-revolution authors, and a crackdown in many states in which the degree of censorship intensified just when late Enlightenment thinkers had reason to hope that progressive evolution might preclude revolution. As a result, the concept of German constitutional unity through a national literature and theater, as proposed by Lessing, one Schiller had all but propagandistically pursued since the publication of "Ueber das gegenwärtige teutsche Theater" in 1782, had suffered a setback. Just as Schiller's *Schaubühne* essay had suggested the long-term preparation of the people for self-government through aesthetic education, his announcement of *Die Horen* delivers the decidedly patient and by this point leitmotivistic motto—at a point when patience was in short supply—of a national forum dedicated to "[…] dem stillen Bau besserer Begriffe, reinerer Grundsätze und edlerer Sitten, von dem zuletzt alle wahre Verbesserung des gesellschaftlichen Zustands abhängt" (the steady creation of better concepts, purer principles, and nobler manners, upon which all true improvement of the state of society ultimately depends; *NA* 22: 107). In stark contrast to its programmatic foreword, *Die Horen*, and likewise Schiller's *Musen-Almanach* were critical enough of the French Revolution and its German supporters, and so alternatively pro-evolution through aesthetic education, that Schiller and Goethe's foils soon seized on the disharmony between the announcement and the actual product in reviews of *Die Horen*. Even a glance at the contents of *Die Horen* suffices to demonstrate that the desire to lead discussions of the political future away from discussions of the French Revolution proved impossible. Neither Schiller nor Goethe delivered much that did not in some regard address the most recent developments in France, and three of the four contributions that comprised the first issue featured allusions to France that were at best ill-concealed: Goethe's poem "Epistel," the first installment of his novella *Unterhaltungen deutscher Ausgewanderten* (Discussions of German Emigres), and Schiller's *Ästhetische Briefe*. There were, however, a large number of contributions that adhered to the program of *Die Horen* as announced. One of the breakout hits of the journal was Caroline von Wolzogen's serial novel *Agnes von Lilien*, which some believed had been written by Goethe or Schiller and which attracted the attention of Anne Louise Germaine (Madame) de Staël (1766–1817).

In 1795 and 1796, Schiller completed work on his most important treatises on the philosophy of art, which comprise to a significant degree the results of his continuing lectures on the theory of tragedy and his Winter 1792–1793, Winter 1794–95, and Summer 1795 lectures on aesthetics, and all of which were first published in *Die Horen*. *Über die notwendigen Grenzen beim Gebrauch schöner Formen* (On the Necessary Limits in the Use of Beautiful Forms, 1795) appeared in the ninth issue of *Die Horen* in September following Schiller's rejection of Fichte's essay "Über Geist und Buchstabe in der Philosophie" (On Spirit and Letter in Philosophy), Fichte's criticism of the obscurity of Schiller's philosophical essays, and Schiller's statement in the 26th of the *Ästhetische Briefe* that he would return to the topic of "Grenzen des schönen Scheins" (limits of the appearance of beauty; *NA* 20: 401). Schiller proposes that there is a danger in the proliferation of portrayals of morality as an appeal to aesthetic feeling without interruption by focused rational cognition. Schiller's essay *Über das Naive* (On the Naïve) appeared in the eleventh issue of *Die Horen*, and Humboldt responds in an effusive letter of November 1, 1795, praising Schiller's unique ability to fuse "Geist" (intellect) and "Natur" (nature): "Diesen Charakter, sagen Sie, theilen Sie mit allen Modernen, und hierin bin ich ganz und gar Ihrer Meynung, nur ist diese Eigenthümlichkeit in Ihnen [...] stärker als sonst irgendwo, darum sind Sie, wenn ich so sagen darf, der *modernste*" (You say that you share this character with all moderns, and in this I agree with you entirely, only this peculiarity is stronger in you [...] than anywhere else, which is why you are, if I may say so, the most modern"; *NA* 36/1: 6). *Über naive und sentimentalische Dichtung* (On Naïve and Sentimental Poetry) appeared in the 11th, 12th, and 13th issues of *Die Horen* of November, December, and January 1795/1796. Schiller proposes categorizing poets and poetry as naïve (direct narrative description) or sentimental (self-reflective portrayal) in approach—in contrast to Friedrich Schlegel, without consideration of literary-historical era or content—citing most of the ancient Greeks, Shakespeare, and Goethe as examples of the former and himself, Euripides, and the majority of modern authors as examples of the latter.

There can be little doubt that the most enduring contribution to *Die Horen* was the serial publication of Schiller's own *Über die ästhetische Erziehung des Menschen in einer Reihe von Briefen* (*Letters on the Aesthetic Education of the Human Individual in a Series of Letters*, 1795), which, far from representing a flight from politics, Schiller called his "politische[s] Glaubensbekenntniß" (political confession) in a letter to Garve of January 25, 1795 (*NA* 27: 125), a confession that embarks from the insight in the *Augustenburgerbriefe* that "man wird damit anfangen müssen für die Verfassung Bürger zu erschaffen, ehe man den Bürgern eine Verfassung geben kann" (one will have to begin creating citizens for the constitution before one can give the citizens a constitution; *NA* 26: 265). Despite the stated significance of the French Revolution for the *Augustenburgerbriefe* and its self-evident presence in their universalist revision, the *Ästhetische Briefe* are not Schiller's newly conceived view of the prerequisites of enduring political progress in response to the horrors of the French Revolution, but a restatement of ideas regarding the individual pursuit of happiness that he had articulated prior to 1789, perhaps nowhere more clearly than in the *Schaubühne* essay, in which the goal is to convince wise rulers that the path to widespread autonomy and happiness can best be achieved by art, which has the unique ability to reconcile by inspiring the people themselves to become "Quellen der Glückseligkeit" (sources of happiness; *NA* 20: 90). In the sixth of the *Ästhetische Briefe* (*NA* 20: 319), Schiller's diagnosis of the ills of modernity borrows from the concept of "Leichenöffnung" (autopsy) that he first learned as a medical student and expanded to psychological analysis in "Der Verbrecher aus verlorener Ehre" (*NA* 16: 9). The forensic analysis of the state of humankind reveals a division of individuals into classes of half-enlightened "Barbaren" (barbarians) and unenlightened "Wilde" (savages), driven at best to achieve a state of pseudo-virtue through the enforcement of negative duties—resulting in a "Surrogat der wahren Tugend" (substitute for true virtue; *NA* 26: 331), and at worst by the unchecked rage of "rohe gesetzlose Triebe" (base, lawless drives; *NA* 26: 319), both sharing the same inhumane end: "Der *Nutzen* ist das große Idol der Zeit, dem alle Kräfte frohnen und alle Talente huldigen sollen" (*Utility* is the great idol of our age, for which all powers are supposed to toil and to which all talents are supposed to pay homage; *NA* 20: 311). Unlike the ancient Greeks, who ostensibly led whole lives, Schiller presents a picture of the fragmented existence of the modern subject: "Ewig nur an ein einzelnes kleines Bruchstück des Ganzen gefesselt, bildet sich der Mensch selbst nur als Bruchstück aus, ewig nur das eintönige Geräusch des Rades, das er umtreibt, im Ohre, entwickelt er nie die Harmonie seines Wesens, und anstatt die Menschheit in seiner Natur auszuprägen, wird er bloß zu einem Abdruck seines Geschäfts, seiner Wissenschaft" (Forever chained to a single small fragment of the whole, the human being develops into nothing but a fragment; whose ear is forever subjected to the monotonous sound of the wheel that they turn, they never develop the harmony of their being, and instead of putting the stamp of humanity upon their own nature, they become nothing more than the imprint of their occupation; *NA* 20: 323).

As in the dissertations and in the *Schaubühne* essay, so in *Ästhetische Briefe*, the fragmented individual, divided between animal physical sensation and human intellect, is reconciled through the "Mittelkraft" (medial force) into "einen mittleren Zustand" (a medial state) between physical and mental activity, ideas rearticulated as the "dritten Character" (third character state) in the 18th, 20th, and 23rd of the *Ästhetische Briefe*. In the 15th letter, this reconciliation of drives results in the state of freedom from internal and external coercion that constitutes the state of play: "Denn [...] der Mensch spielt nur, wo er in voller Bedeutung des Worts Mensch ist, und er ist nur da ganz Mensch, wo er spielt" (The human being plays only there, where they are human beings in the fullest sense of the term, and they are only fully human beings there where they play; *NA* 20: 359). Only in this aesthetic state, in which the violence of passions and the rigidity of principles are reconciled, is the human being free to practice compassion by making "fremde Gefühle zu den unsrigen" (other people's feelings our own; *NA* 20: 350). After a long century of widespread critical skepticism toward Schiller's political ideas, twenty-first century observers of wobbling republics are finding it increasingly difficult to ignore the fact that these are not post-revolution reactions but post-progressive radical ideas that directly address the concrete political dangers of an orthodoxy of ignorance and the foundational political thesis of the 9th letter that "Alle Verbesserung im Politischen soll von Veredlung des Charakters ausgehen" (All improvement in the political realm should begin with the ennoblement of individual character; *NA* 20: 332), resulting in the regulative idea of movement toward "*Totalität* des Charakters" (wholeness of character; *NA* 20: 318). After a run of only two years, Schiller and Cotta ended the journal due to workload considerations and falling subscription rates. Nonetheless, *Die Horen* is considered to be among the most significant journalistic contributions to philosophy and literature in European history.

Schiller's parallel project to *Die Horen*, *Der Musen-Almanach* (1795–1799), which followed a format popularized in France, constitutes perhaps the best-known such publication internationally due to the renown of the editor and contributors as well as the quality and subsequent resonance of the content, particularly regarding poetry. In addition to Schiller and his many enduring *Musen-Almanach* contributions—"Der Ring des Polykrates," "Der Taucher," "Die Kraniche des Ibycus," "Die Bürgschaft," and "Das Lied von der Glocke"—featured authors included Goethe, Karoline von Günderrode (1780–1806), Herder, Hölderlin, A.W. Schlegel, Tieck, and two Schiller proteges, the actress and poet Sophie Albrecht and Sophie Mereau. In contrast to his constant grumbling about many of his other contributors, Schiller predicts a brilliant career for Mereau after reading her novel *Eduard und Amanda*:

"Für die Horen hat mir unsere Dichterin Mereau jetzt ein sehr angenehmes Geschenk gemacht, und das mich wirklich überraschte. [...] und wenn sie auf diesem guten Wege weiter fortgeht, so erleben wir noch was an ihr" (Our poet Mereau has now given me a very pleasant gift for *Die Horen*, and it really surprised me [...] and if she continues on this good path, we can look forward to big things from her; *NA* 29: 93). Mereau continued to be productive, but died after childbirth in 1806, as did Günderrode, who committed suicide after the traumatic end to a relationship. If, as Schiller wrote, the muses had been run out of the German states by the roar of French canons and internal partisan political debate, the appearance of Schiller and Goethe's many partisan and political *Xenien* in *Der Musen-Almanach* of 1797 did nothing to encourage the muses to return. The *Xenien* comprised 414 critical distiches by Schiller and Goethe aimed at the mediocrity of their rivals—a very large number of which were specifically intended to expose the artistic haplessness and political insightlessness of their growing number of adversaries.

In a letter to Goethe of November 23, 1795, Schiller laments his growing legion of literary enemies (*NA* 28: 110)—a number of them members of the extended *Göttinger Hain* group—who now, after Schiller's legendarily harsh review of his poetry, included Bürger, Friedrich Schlegel, to whom Schiller took an instant disliking, and August Wilhelm Schlegel. Bürger's tenuous alliance with Schiller, which had begun with his defense of "Die Götter Griechenlandes" in 1788, proved short-lived. According to Schiller-critic Caroline (Michaelis, widowed Boehmer) Schlegel (later Schelling; 1763–1809), Schiller's legendarily harsh review of Bürger's poetry in 1791 had robbed her friend of "alle menschliche Ehre" (all human honor; Caroline Schlegel, 1: 225). To some extent as a response to Schiller's review of Bürger's poetry, August Wilhelm Schlegel criticized Schiller's moralizing tone in a poem entitled "An einen Kunstrichter" (To a Critic, 1792) in the *Göttinger Musenalmenach*, and published a decidedly frosty review of *Thalia* (*AWS* 10, 30–36). By late 1792, Schiller had already lost his patience with a number of the friends of the Schlegel circle—Stolberg, who had accused Schiller of blasphemy in 1788; Forster, whose participation in the Rhine Republic had annoyed Schiller; and Schiller's erstwhile friend, the diplomat and author Huber. Huber had been all but disowned by the Schiller circle after he abandoned Körner's sister-in-law Dora Stock while sharing a house in Mainz with his future wife Therese (Heyne) Forster (1764–1829), Forster himself, and Therese's childhood friend, Caroline Böhmer.

Somewhat surprisingly, after the death of his former University of Göttingen professor and ally Bürger in 1794, and after his first unfriendly review of *Die Horen*, August Wilhelm Schlegel joined the teams of *Die Horen* and *Der Musen-Almanach* in 1795, arriving in May 1796 in precisely the kind of position he had aspired to, precisely where he had aspired to be—in Jena, working with Schiller and Goethe (as well as his friend Humboldt), and soon finding himself in the middle of a tribal turf war involving friends and family. Shortly after marrying in July 1796, Caroline Schlegel joined August Wilhelm Schlegel in Jena, as did Friedrich Schlegel. Based on all evidence prior to 1796, despite their reservations the Schlegel brothers were genuine Schiller admirers, and both aggressively sought his approval and patronage. The constellation of characters in their circle, however, made fruitful collaboration increasingly difficult, notably Friedrich Schlegel himself—"who could be a menace," was "an unruly presence," and who "effectively destroyed August Wilhelm's good working relationship with Schiller" (Paulin, 67)—and Caroline Schlegel, who, like her brother-in-law, was found annoying by many, including her friends, Therese (Heyne-Forster) Huber (Hoock-Demarle, 137) and her short-term sister-in-law Dorothea Mendelsohn (Veit) Schlegel (Roetzel, 378).

Despite the best efforts of Körner to convince Schiller of Friedrich Schlegel's respect for him, Schiller's reluctance to work with Schlegel led the latter to seek work with yet another Schiller-adversary, Reichardt, and the two collaborated on a series of hostile reviews of *Die Horen* that appeared in Reichardt's rival journal, *Deutschland*, attacking everything from the hypocrisy of the announcement of *Die Horen*, to Goethe and Schiller's dishonesty, to their "diktatorische[n] Übermuth" (dictatorial arrogance; *NA* 2/2: 485) in a review rumored by Woltmann to have been written by Caroline Schlegel (*NA* 37: 31–32). To this, both Charlotte Schiller—in whose circle Caroline Schlegel was referred to as "Madame Luzifer" (Oellers 1990)—and later, in May 1797, Körner took an instant dislike to her, likely due in some part to her proximity to the estranged Huber. The hostile reviews of Schiller's works in *Deutschland* were only the first shots of many, which, along with Friedrich Schlegel's 1796 review of the *Musen-Almenach* poem "Würde der Frauen" (Dignity of Women; *Deutschland* 2, 348–360), led Schiller to fire August Wilhelm Schlegel as contributor to *Die Horen*. This firing elicited an emotional response from both August Wilhelm and Caroline Schlegel on June 1, 1797, in which he asks for the opportunity to prove his loyalty and disavows his brother's critiques of Schiller, and she declares her unqualified admiration and love for Schiller (*NA* 37: 32), in stark contrast to the dim view of him presented in her letters. This attempt at reconciliation did nothing to prevent a thorough series of retaliatory *Xenien* by Schiller and Goethe published in Schiller's *Musen-Almanach* of 1797. A large number of the *Xenien* targeted the Schlegel circle, including all Schlegels, Bürger, Reichardt, and Forster (High 2004, 133–143) and called into question which of the hostile parties had raised the culture of the ancient Greeks to a form of cult worship—one of several narrow notions of Weimar Classicism—by labeling Friedrich Schlegel the key figure in a movement Schiller derides in his *Xenien* "Griechheit" (Greekness) and in "Die zwey Fieber" (The two Fevers) as "Gräcomanie" (Greco-mania), a replacement for the "Gallomanie" (Francomania) of Schlegel's waning enthusiasm for the French Revolution (*NA* 2: 348).

Inevitably, the Schlegels respond in kind: Friedrich Schlegel publishes back in an essay in Forster's defense in 1797, and writes in *Fragmente über Literatur und Poesie* (Fragments on Literature and Poetry, 1797): "Es giebt für die Kunst keinen gefährlicheren Irrthum, als sie in πολ [*Politik*] und Universalität zu suchen wie Schiller" (There is no more dangerous an error for art than to seek it, like Schiller, in politics and universality; Schlegel, 194) and "Keines Menschen Poesie ist weniger idealisch als Schillers" (No person's poetry is less ideal than Schiller's; Schlegel, 413). After his firing, August Wilhelm Schlegel promptly published a second critique of *Die Horen*, and in 1797, the Schlegels joined forces with Schleiermacher and Novalis to establish the journal *Athenaeum*, adding two further critical and anti-secularist voices to the mix. In "Apologie," the introduction to *Über die Religion* (On Religion, 1799), Schleiermacher addresses the "Verächter der Religion" (those who despise religion)—secularist writers like Schiller and Goethe—and launches an assault on Schiller's central unifying concept, "Freude" or "Glückseligkeit," as had Novalis in "Kann ein Atheist auch moralisch tugendhaft aus Grundsätzen seyn?" (Can an Atheist also be Moral out of Principal, 1789; Novalis, 20). Although Schiller was on average only some eleven years older than the *Athenaeum* contributors, the journal is often understood as the critical founding document of the forward-looking program of German Romanticism, created by a revolutionary youth movement that ironically simultaneously railed against Schiller as too political, too secularist, and not ideal enough, as well as against the imagined restrictions of the highly selective and poorly defined set of tendencies known as Weimar Classicism, all the while fairly worshipping Goethe, the author most identified with the concept. In fact, the notion of a theoretical clash between classical and modern movements is a serious oversimplification of a story that regards at its core a constellation of notably difficult characters. It is self-evident that one editorial principle of *Athenaeum* (like *Deutschland*) was to disgrace Schiller, his works, and his theories, one driven by a personal animosity that is—despite the hard feelings over Schiller's treatment of Bürger—largely absent from the Schlegels' comments prior to what August Wilhelm Schlegel called "den großen Haß" (the great hatred; *AWS Briefe*, 186) of 1796, which fueled a war of criticism and informed reception long after Schiller's death. For his part, Schiller appears to have moved on after expressing his disdain in the *Xenien*. Yet, even Friedrich Schlegel's criticism of Schiller had its limits; after fifteen years of seething resentment, in an 1812 lecture delivered in Vienna, Schlegel praised Schiller's entire oeuvre, concluding of the early dramas that Schiller was "erfüllt von jenen schwärmerischen Hoffnungen, von jener kühnen Opposition gegen alles Bestehende, welche der Revolution vorangingen" (full of those fanatical hopes and that bold opposition to all the existing circumstances that preceded the revolution; Schlegel 1841, 16: 460). Schlegel's preference for Schiller's early dramas expressed here represents perhaps the first attempt to create a Schiller of progressive and conservative phases, rather than recognizing that Schiller's early and late dramas were written in two distinctly different political and artistic eras, one focused more on liberation from native and internal forms of tyranny, and one focused more on foreign and external forms of tyranny.

Despite the time required for writing, teaching, and research, and despite his illness, Schiller's rate of production and versatility from 1789 to 1796 leave no room for theories of a revolution-inspired writer's block, nor do they indicate a sudden change of focus after the violence of the French Revolution, but the continuation of a shift that dates back years. On the contrary, Schiller's quantity and quality of production during the entire period from 1789 until the work on his late dramas and poetry is entirely in line with that of the remarkable run from 1781 through 1789, which already, according to Benno von Wiese, bordered "ans Unfaßbare" (on the incomprehensible; von Wiese, 351). As of his letter to Goethe of October 16, 1795, Schiller appears satisfied that he has achieved his most important goals as an aesthetic and political philosopher and is prepared to refocus on drama and poetry: "Soviel habe ich nun aus gewißer Erfahrung, daß nur strenge Bestimmtheit der Gedanken zu einer Leichtigkeit verhilft [...] Ich bin jetzt in der That froh, daß ich es mir nicht habe verdrießen lassen einen sauren Weg einzuschlagen, den ich oft für die poetisierende Einbildungskraft verderblich hielt" (I now know one thing from certain experiences, that only strict clarity of thoughts leads to adeptness [...] I am actually glad now that I did not let myself be discouraged from following a sour path, which I often held to be ruinous for the poetic imagination; *NA* 28: 79).

As Schiller begins work on his second series of dramas, the rebellious spirit of the early dramas later missed by Friedrich Schlegel remains glaringly evident, if Schiller understandably took aim at a more relevant target. As Schiller's universal-historical model had anticipated in *Abfall der Niederlande* in 1788, when the cycle of history repeats, similar contexts will call the victims of the most urgent form of oppression to similar acts of liberation. Since, by the late 1790s, the now mostly occupied and diminished German princes were no longer the prime movers of oppression, Schiller returns to the earliest source of his outrage, the Conqueror, now in the form of French occupation. Thus, it is not that Schiller's politics of autonomy had changed, but that the politics of enslavement itself had changed. Beginning with his condemnation of the French annexation of Mainz in 1792–1793, Schiller was a keen observer of the many French violations of the autonomy of the German states (High 2006, 231–232). On March 15, 1793, Schiller wrote to his publisher Göschen of the French: "Wir wollen hoffen, daß ihnen das deutsche Brod bald verleidet werden soll" (Let us hope that they will soon become sick of German bread; *NA* 26: 232). In early July 1796, the political became personal when French troops commandeered the Solitude residence in Stuttgart, where Schiller had studied, and where his family had sought refuge from the French. In a letter of July 20, 1796, Schiller's sister Christophina Reinwald details how the Schiller family packed their valuables but could not flee due to the father's terminally ill condition. She reports that on July 18 and 19, French troops plundered Stuttgart, poked the Schillers with rifles, and stole some of the clothing right off their bodies, and that she and her sister had spent a day hiding in a cave to avoid being raped (*NA* 36/1: 277–78). In a letter of July 21 and 22 (*NA* 36/1: 280), she describes further indignities of occupation, including the theft of a blind beggar's shoes. In his letter to Goethe of July 23 or 25, 1796,

Schiller describes the French takeover of the city: "Die Franzosen sind in Stuttgardt, wohin die Kaiserlichen sich anfangs geworfen haben sollen, so daß jene die Stadt beschießen mußten" (The French are in Stuttgart, where the imperial forces were initially supposed to have dashed, so that the former had to bombard the city; *NA* 28: 269). On July 25, Schiller heard from Karlsschule classmate and sculptor Johann Heinrich von Dannecker (1758–1841) that "Schwaben und Franken von Soldaten wimmeln" (Swabia and Franconia are swarming with soldiers); on July 31, 1796, Schiller writes to Goethe that he had no idea where his family was (*NA* 28: 275); and on August 15, 1796, Schiller wrote to Reinwald that his sister Christophina could not travel "ohne Gefahr der ärgsten Mißhandlungen" (without the danger of the most egregious assaults; *NA* 28: 286), later citing cases of "Roheit" (brutality) and "Vandalism der Franzosen" (vandalism of the French; *NA* 29: 193). In 1797, Schiller publishes a stinging series of Forster criticisms in the *Xenien*, concluding that Forster will land in metaphorical hell (the judgment of history) for his role in the occupation of German territories.

Ironically, just when Schiller's merely skeptical attitude toward the developments of the French Revolution had turned to outrage over the perpetual French invasions, he unexpectedly received the documents of his French citizenship on March 1, 1798, accompanied by a letter from the author, educational reformer, and fellow French citizen Joachim Heinrich Campe (1746–1818), and shared the news with Goethe the following day: "Gestern habe ich nun im Ernst das französische Bürgerrecht erhalten, wovon schon vor 5 Jahren in den Zeitungen geredet wurde" (Seriously, yesterday I finally received the French citizenship documents that were announced in the newspapers five years ago; *NA* 29: 214). Goethe took an ironic distance to the news in his letter of March 3, 1798, in which he playfully points out that everyone who had handled the documents, including Danton, Roland, and Custine, was dead: "Zu dem Bürger Decrete, das Ihnen aus dem Reiche der Toden zugesendet worden, kann ich nur in so fern Glück wünschen als es Sie noch unter den Lebendigen angetroffen hat, warten Sie ja noch eine Weile ehe Sie Ihre verewigten großen Mitbürger besuchen" (As for your citizenship documents from the realm of the dead, I can only congratulate you for being among the living when they arrived. Please do wait a while before you visit your great immortalized countrymen; *NA* 37/1: 257–258). Goethe is evidently responding to Schiller's ill-concealed enthusiasm over his own historical significance. Nonetheless, Schiller was clearly not alone in his interest in the documents: Duke Carl August requested that the documents be given to the library in Weimar, and, in his letter of March 26, 1798, Körner is curious to see the accompanying letter from the then Minister of the Interior Jean-Marie Roland (1734–1793; *NA* 37/1: 267), but dismisses the importance of the citizenship decree while expressing only annoyance with the French: "Die Pariser Ehrenbezeugung will zur Zeit nicht viel bedeuten. Das Comödianten Wesen dieser Menschen ist mir widerlich" (The Parisian honor does not count for much given the situation. The clownish nature of these people disgusts me; *NA* 37/1: 267–268). In a letter to Campe of March 2, 1798, Schiller tactfully suggests that he had earned this honor through nothing but his agreement in principle with the motto of the revolution (freedom, equality, fraternity), and carefully applied a condition to his acceptance in the form of an if/then sentence (Wertheim, 434): "[…] wenn unsre Mitbürger über dem Rhein diesem Wahlspruch immer gemäß handeln, so weiß ich keinen schöneren Titel, als einer der ihrigen zu sein" ([…]if our countrymen across the Rhine always act in accordance with that motto, then I cannot think of a better title than to be considered one of them; *NA* 29: 212). Clearly, by 1798, the French had failed to do so in Schiller's eyes. Thus, in precise doublespeak, Schiller confirmed his affinity with the original ideals of the revolution, while quietly distancing himself from its course and the current hegemonic program.

The reductive understanding of the term Weimar Classicism as a period of the wooden pursuit of form and its almost mythical national function stand in curious contrast to the reality on the ground in Schiller's Sachsen-Weimar during the composition of his last five completed dramas. As was the case with his relative caution in responding to the French Revolution, Schiller, who clearly responded to the phenomenon of Bonaparte, never mentioned him by name in any writing extant. Prior to the premiere of *Wallensteins Lager* in October of 1798, beginning in 1794, Bonaparte had already won twenty-six battles, and his success in Italy resulted in the expulsion of the Austrians and the occupation of Northern Italy, as well as both his invasion of Austria in 1797 and the strategic French occupation of Switzerland also in 1797, which occurred at his urging. Likewise, prior to the first performance of *Wallensteins Lager*, Bonaparte had conquered Malta in June of 1798 and won three battles in Egypt by July 21 of that year. The French invasion of Switzerland in 1798 and Bonaparte's coup in 1799 find resonance in Schiller's decision to work on the French liberation hero, Joan of Arc, in 1800, and to work at the same time on the drama of the Swiss liberation hero William Tell in 1802 (Wertheim, 446). In his letter to Goethe of March 13, 1798, Schiller cheers the Swiss resistance against France: "Man sagt hier daß die Franzosen bei Murten eine Schlappe bekommen. Es sollte mich herzlich freuen, denn auch ein kleines Glück, und gerade an diesem Ort, würde am Anfang besonders sehr gute Folgen für die Schweizer haben" (They say here that the French have suffered a failure to perform in Murten. That would make me happy to the bottom of my heart, because even a little success, and there, at the start, would have very good consequences for the Swiss; *NA* 29: 218).

The Napoleonic occupations are reflected in Schiller's late dramas: just as *Fiesko* is not about sixteenth-century Italy and *Don Karlos* is not about sixteenth-century Spain, neither are the late dramas about seventeenth-century Bohemia or fifteenth-century France. They are about the pursuit of happiness, and to that end of all ends, they are about the prerequisites of happiness, liberation, political autonomy, and personal autonomy. Likewise, in keeping with the Scottish reconciliation philosophy that informed Schiller's Karlsschule works, his historical writings, theoretical works, and the announcement of *Die Horen*, his dramas reveal a striking consistency in the belief in the negative influence of "Zwietracht" (discord) and the positive potential of "Eintracht" or "Vereinigung" (unity or unification) on matters of the most common concerns of morality, a phenomenon mechanized in the shared experience of the violation of autonomy that is coercion, war, and which appears most graphically in the portrayal of foreign occupation. Like his first four completed dramas, the final five each embark from a historical-political situation, each posing its own challenges in transforming a political fable into compelling drama, transforming the past into the present, and transforming historical truth into what Schiller called philosophical and artistic truth.

If Schiller had postponed his return to drama in some small part due to anxiety over the influence of his first four dramas, the success of the first of his final five dramatic works, *Wallenstein*, likely put his worst fears to rest. Written for the premiere of *Wallensteins Lager* at the newly rebuilt Weimar Theater in October 1798, Schiller's prologue demonstrates his clear intention to invoke the horrors of the Thirty Years' War as portrayed in his historical works by describing what is at stake on the 150th anniversary of its end in 1648, a period of relative peace ending in Bonaparte's wars of aggression: "Und jetzt an des Jahrhunderts ernstem Ende / [...] Um Herrschaft und um Freiheit wird gerungen" (And now, at the century's grim conclusion / [...] A struggle takes place between the power to rule and freedom). Schiller's timely implication is that the struggle between the "power to rule and freedom" refers to that between "gewaltiger Naturen" (powerful personalities; NA 8: 4)—Bonaparte and his opponents—and anyone who happens to be in their path, including foremost the German states. Like *Fiesko*, *Don Karlos*, and *Wallenstein*, power politics and cabinet intrigue likewise lie at the center of *Maria Stuart*, which Schiller conceived in 1793 and which premiered in Weimar on June 14, 1800 and focuses on the highly fictionalized portrayal of the brief period between Mary Stuart's death sentence and her execution, reaching its climax in an invented meeting of Mary Stuart and Elizabeth I; whereas Schiller's Maria Stuart had exploited her sexuality for personal autonomy and political gain, his Elizabeth accomplishes the same by declaring herself free of gender constraints: "Das Weib ist nicht schwach [...] / [...] Ich will in meinem Beisein / Nichts von der Schwäche des Geschlechtes hören" (Woman is not weak [...] / [...] I will, in my presence, / Hear no more of the weakness of the sex; NA 9: 52). The opening scene of *Die Jungfrau von Orleans*, which Schiller began just after the French invasions of southern German states in 1798 and which premiered on September 11, 1801, portrays the inhabitants of an idyllic, yet defenseless, shepherd village betrayed by opportunistic politicians, and in need of a hero to free them from the approaching tyranny of military occupation. The French heroine states the case for the right to a war of self-defense in poeticized Kantian moral terms herself—"Was ist unschuldig, heilig, menschlich gut, / Wenn es der Kampf nicht ist ums Vaterland?" (What is innocent, holy, humanly good, / If not the defense of the fatherland?; NA 9: 235). She demonstrates the same clarity of purpose—the removal of the conqueror—in Prologue, Scene 4: "Und wie die rasche Schnitterin die Saat, / Den stolzen Überwinder niederschlagen" (And, as the ripened corn the reapers mow, / Hew down the conqueror as he triumphs there; *NA* 9: 181). The political message in the context of 1801 is self-evident; if there is anything holy about Joan of Arc, then the French should be the first to recognize what it is—her calling to liberation from the conqueror.

Far from focusing on the great men of history, Schiller's late dramas mirror his early dramas in their complicated portrayals of highly problematic characters, an intention made clear in his letter to Wilhelm von Humboldt of March 21, 1796 regarding his character Wallenstein: "Er hat nichts Edles, er erscheint in keinem einzelnen LebensAkt groß. […] Seine Unternehmung ist moralisch schlecht, und sie verunglückt physisch. Er ist im Einzelnen nie groß und im Ganzen kommt er um seinen Zweck" (There is nothing noble about him, he does not appear great in any single action in life. His undertaking is morally bad, and it fails physically. He is never great in any particular detail and, on the whole, he does not achieve his intention; *NA* 28: 204). Similarly, the only thing great about Schiller's Maria Stuart is her sublime composure before her execution, a direct result of her frank admission of her complicity in the murder of her husband Darnley; in a hopeless situation of her own making, she finds strength in the promise of life after death in the last five acts of the life of a Catholic power politician lived at odds with Christian principles. Schiller's Elizabeth I is appropriately aware that her rival, Maria Stuart, is younger and considered to be more attractive, and Philipp II felt the same way about his, Don Karlos. While Schiller's Elizabeth I vacillates and accomplishes her highly problematic goal in an act of silence, his Wallenstein vacillates and fails silently, and his Johanna vacillates between a bizarre concept of faith and a clear liberation mission before committing to the latter and triumphing in death. Indeed, Schiller's heroines and heroes have much more in common than not, and a great deal in common with the complicated protagonists of his early dramas.

On April 29, 1802, shortly before the birth of their daughter Caroline Henriette Luise on October 11, 1802, Schiller and Charlotte Schiller, now with three children and financially secure, moved from their apartment in the Windischgasse in Weimar into what is now known as the Schiller House on the Weimar Esplanade, today Schillerstraße 12. Between the publications and premieres of *Die Jungfrau von Orleans* and *Die Braut von Messina*, Schiller received his title of nobility on November 16, 1802, just two and a half years prior to his death. The decidedly aristocratic form of recognition of Schiller's service to German culture during a dangerous period of Franco-German relations led to renewed expression of annoyance over Schiller's French revolutionary citizenship with the appearance of Carl August's annual *Hochfürstlich Sachsen-Weimar und Eisenachischen Hof- und Adreßkalender* on January 13, 1803. Schiller's revised entry reflected both his new title of nobility and included a second new and, for a citizen of Weimar, surprising title: "Herr D. Friedrich v. Schiller, Bürger von Frankreich" (Herr Dr. Friedrich von Schiller, Citizen of France).

The revision of 1803 was clearly unauthorized, as is evident from Privy Council Voigt's prompt report to Goethe, in which Voigt dismisses second-hand testimony from the printer that Schiller had delivered his calendar entry personally—"Wir wissen zwar wohl besser, wie es zugegangen ist" (We both know better how this came about; Jahn 1: 322)—adding that his only regret was that a misunderstanding could result in Schiller losing his new title of nobility. Since Schiller did not write the entry, someone else must have done so, and it follows from the context that Schiller was the victim of a prank that drew attention to the ideological gulf between the title "Bürger von Frankreich" of 1792 and the more recent title of nobility (High 2003). Schiller's final two dramas would leave no doubt as to his feelings about the human rights record of the most recent government of France.

Schiller published his final two completed dramas, *Die Braut von Messina* (The Bride of Messina, 1802) and *Wilhelm Tell* (1804)—the second and third of three consecutive dramas that embark from historical occupation situations—during the final three years of his life. Set during the eleventh-century Norman occupation of Sicily, *Die Braut von Messina* premiered on March 19, 1803. Early in the play, a member of Schiller's intentionally alienating chorus provides the intrusive narration of the back story as the prophecy of the demise of Messina appears to prove true: "Und jetzt sehen wir uns als Knechte / Untertan diesem Fremden Geschlechte" (And now we see ourselves enslaved / Subjects of this foreign race; *NA* 10: 28). A second chorus member corroborates: "Sklaven sind wir in den eigenen Sitzen, / Das Land kann seine Kinder nicht schützen" (We are slaves in our own lands, / The nation cannot protect its children; *NA* 10: 28). In addition to the innovative form and the occupation setting, Schiller once again portrays a main character's evolution from medieval to modern worldview and maturity, as well as the freedom to resist what appears to be fate; like Johanna before her, when the gods abandon Queen Isabella in her hour of need, she abandons the gods in order to defend her people on her own: "Warum besuchen wir die heilgen Häuser, / Und heben zu dem Himmel fromme Hände? / Gutmüthge Thoren, was gewinnen wir / Mit unserm Glauben" (Why do we visit the holy temples, / And raise pious hands to heaven? / Compliant fools, what do we receive / In return for our faith?; *NA* 10: 108). Nonetheless, the lack of unity and preponderant discord that first led to the occupation leads to the deaths of both heirs to the throne, and, with them, any hope of liberation, and political and individual autonomy. In the final scene of the play, Queen Isabella begs of her son, Don Cesar: "Lebe, mein Sohn! Laß deine Mutter nicht / Freudlos im Land der Fremdlinge zurück" (Live on, my son! Leave not your mother / Behind, joyless, in the land of the foreigners; *NA* 10: 122). Her plea goes unanswered, and so, it is not fate as actual nemesis, not the fulfillment of prophecy, but the belief in fate that dooms Messina.

Schiller wrote the opening scene of *Wilhelm Tell* just after the French march into Switzerland, which Schiller refers to as the "Unglücksfälle" (unfortunate events) in a letter to Cotta of August 7, 1802 (*NA* 31: 154). The play opens with a fisher boy singing of paradise among peace-loving shepherds, only to be interrupted by an Austrian police action. Imperial occupation forces pursue the rebellious lumberjack Baumgarten, who fought back when his wife was sexually assaulted by the emperor's castellan, a characteristic violent gesture of occupation recalling Schiller's story of his sisters hiding in a cave from French troops. According to his letter to Wilhelm von Wolzogen of October 27, 1803, Schiller was fully aware of the significance of the French occupation of Switzerland for the potential resonance of *Wilhelm Tell*: "[…] jetzt besonders ist von der schweizerischen Freiheit desto mehr die Rede, weil sie aus der Welt verschwunden ist" ([…] now in particular Swiss freedom is an even more popular topic, since it has disappeared from the earth; *NA* 32: 81). Like no other drama by Schiller, the play is repeatedly punctuated by inspirational speeches regarding inalienable rights, the right to self-defense, and the potential of unity on clear moral matters. It is difficult to avoid the conclusion that, by invoking three occupation settings in dramas published between 1801 and 1804, Schiller's target is Bonaparte, and he is certain that the play, a "Neujahrsgeschenk auf 1805" (New Year's Gift for 1805)—as advertised on the cover of the first edition—will unavoidably touch a nerve in some theaters and result in "Anstoß" (umbrage; *NA* 32: 124). His prediction was to prove prophetic, repeatedly: due to its portrayal of the justified murder of a tyrant, Joseph Goebbels and Adolph Hitler banned both the teaching and performance of *Wilhelm Tell* in 1941 (Ruppelt, 41). Despite his renewed success, Schiller remained critical to the end, expressing that, of the final five dramas, he was least satisfied with *Maria Stuart* and *Wilhelm Tell*, and less dissatisfied with *Wallenstein*, *Die Jungfrau von Orleans*, and *Die Braut von Messina*.

In a letter to Wilhelm von Humboldt of October 5, 1795, just as Schiller returned his attention to literary pursuits after the publication of *Ästhetische Briefe*, he had delivered a telling self-portrait in revealing a future marketing principle—artistic experimentation:

> Noch wollte ich, […] mich zugleich in einer neuen Gattung zu versuchen, eine romantische Erzählung in Versen machen […] Ich habe mich nach und nach in sovielen Fächern und Formen versucht, daß die Frage entsteht ob ich den Kreis nicht vollenden soll. Auch ist das Publikum wie es scheint auf diese Mannichfaltigkeit bey mir aufmerksam geworden, und sie scheint ein Ingrediens der Vorstellung zu seyn, unter der ich den meisten Lesern erscheine. Auf diesem Wege scheint also der Kranz zu liegen, der für mich zu erringen ist. (*NA* 28: 72)

> I still would like […] to try my hand at a new genre, to create a romantic story in verse […] Over time, I have experimented with so many subjects and forms that the question arises as to whether I should not complete the circle. The public, too, seems to have become aware of this versatility in my production, and it appears to be a factor in the image I project to most readers. Thus the wreath that I can yet earn seems to lie on this path.

It is remarkable that Schiller already saw his career in this light in 1795, given that his most experimental works of drama and poetry were yet to come. Indeed, for a dramatist who had experienced unusual streaks of success, Schiller's consistent experimentation with a variety of dramatic forms borders on reckless. Not only are the plots and characters in Schiller's dramas remarkably diverse, but, in stark contrast to prevailing definitions of Weimar Classicism, *Wilhelm Tell* marks the end of his most diverse run of dramas, in which the subtitles alone suggest a conscious focus on variety and inventiveness and an anti-programmatic approach to dramatic forms and functions: *Die Räuber. Ein Schauspiel*, which Schiller initially conceived of as "ein[ ] dramatische[r] Roman" (a dramatic novel; *NA* 3: 244); *Fiesko. Ein republikanisches Trauerspiel*; *Kabale und Liebe. Ein bürgerliches Trauerspieln*; *Dom Karlos, Infant von Spanien*, first *Ein Trauerspiel* in prose, which appeared later the same year as *Ein dramatisches Gedicht* (a dramatic poem) in iambic pentameter; *Wallenstein. Ein Trauerspiel* (A Play of Mourning); *Die Jungfrau von Orleans. Eine romantische Tragödie* (A Romantic Tragedy); *Die Braut von Messina oder Die feindlichen Brüder. Ein Trauerspiel mit Chören* (A Play of Mourning with Choirs); and, at first, *Wilhelm Tell. Tragödie* (A Tragedy; *NA* 10: 368), ultimately *Wilhelm Tell. Schauspiel. Zum Neujahrsgeschenk auf 1805*. Nonetheless, a common thread is clear: Schiller's aesthetic program is not only diverse in form, but also international by design. Defiant in exile in 1784, Schiller had opened the *Schaubühne* speech by declaring himself a "Weltbürger" (citizen of the world) and concluded the speech with the declaration that the greatest human experience is the awareness of the common potential for self-improvement and that this defines what it means "ein Mensch zu sein" (to be a human being; *NA* 20: 100). Schiller further articulates this position in a letter to Körner of October 13, 1789, writing: "Es ist ein armseliges kleinliches Ideal, für *eine* Nation zu schreiben" (It is a pathetic, petty ideal, to write for *one* nation; *NA* 25: 304). In *Über das Pathetische* (1793), Schiller labels the artistic focus on "Nationalgegenstände" (topics of national interest) and "Privatinteresse" (private interest) a sign of "barbarischen Geschmack" (barbaric taste; *NA* 20: 218–219). According to the 1797 poem, "Hofnung," the human condition is the universal pursuit of perpetual improvement: "Die Welt wird alt und wird wieder jung, / Doch der Mensch hoft immer Verbesserung!" (The world grows old and grows young again, / But the human being hopes always for betterment!; *NA* 1: 401). In the "Prologue" to *Wallensteins Lager* of 1798 and in the poem fragment, "Deutsche Größe" (On German Greatness, 1801), all human beings become siblings in the fight for reason and the civil rights of all peoples: "Freiheit der Vernunft erfechten / Heißt für alle Völker rechten / Gilt für alle ewge Zeit" (To fight and win the freedom of reason / Is to argue the rights of all peoples / And endures for time eternal; *NA* 2I, 431). True to his international mission, by his death on May 9, 1805, seven of Schiller's nine completed dramas were set in what are today the Czech Republic, England, France, Italy (2), Spain, and Switzerland, and only two were set in what are today German states, and both of those—*Die Räuber* and *Kabale und*

Liebe—feature individual struggles for autonomy against the backdrop of systemic international tyranny. As his fellow dissident and exile Heinrich Heine (1797–1856) put it, Schiller, who is often referred to as the German national poet, never aspired to any such distinction, but aspired to be a "Kosmopolit" (cosmopolitan), a practicing *Weltbürger*, neither foremost a Swabian nor a German, but foremost a *Mensch*.

On April 28, 1805, Schiller was on his way to a theater performance when he saw Goethe for the last time; Goethe was not well enough to accompany him, and Schiller fell ill that night. From May 6 until his death on May 9, Schiller was intermittently of clear mind or semi-conscious and delirious, reportedly speaking in Latin, speaking of war and soldiers (*NA* 42: 435)—or not (*NA* 42: 432, 725)—and mentioning either the dead author Georg Christoph Lichtenberg (1742–1799) or the Castle Leuchtenberg several times (*NA* 42: 435). According to Caroline von Wolzogen and Schiller's servant, Georg Gottfried Rudolph (1778–1840), an otherwise mostly incomprehensible Schiller had a religious conversion experience shortly before his death on May 9, 1805, a phenomenon Schiller had portrayed as the climax of atheist Franz Moor's nervous breakdown and sudden fear of judgment in *Die Räuber*. There are twenty-six eyewitness reports of Schiller's final days from eight sources. The reports by Rudolph and Wolzogen, and only theirs, are peppered with portrayals of visions, rays of light, sudden joy, and prayer. Of the four reports attributed to Rudolph, three are religiously informed (*NA* 42: 428–435). Of the nine reports by Caroline von Wolzogen, four strongly imply that Schiller experienced a religious awakening, three of which report that on May 7, two days before his death, Schiller exclaimed "Ist das euer Himmel? ist das eure Hölle?" (Is this your heaven? Is this your hell?; *NA* 24: 431). According to Rudolph, Schiller uttered "Judex" several times on May 9 (*NA* 42: 434). However, Rudolph and Wolzogen also write that Schiller had been deliriously reciting from his own works for the three days since May 6, foremost from the unfinished drama *Demetrius* (*NA* 42: 431, 434), which features the line: "Ist das euer Himmel? ist das eure Hölle?" Wilhelm von Humboldt, who knew both Schiller and Wolzogen well, expresses skepticism in his response: "Es ist zweifelhaft, ob er dies in eigener Wahrheit, oder wie im Stück gesagt" (It is not clear whether Schiller was stating this from his own point of view or as he had written it in the piece"; *NA* 42: 321). Of the thirteen firsthand reports by Charlotte von Schiller, Carl von Schiller, Luise von Göchhausen (1752–1807), Johann Heinrich Voß (1751–1726), Anton Genast (1765–1831), and Dr. Wilhelm Ernst Christian Huschke (1760–1828), none make any reference to religion. The final count of religious references and their uneven distribution provide reason for skepticism: Rudolph and Wolzogen make seven references to Schiller and religion in thirteen reports; everyone else who knew Schiller during his adult life make none in thirteen reports. Perhaps the most compelling testimony on the subject comes from Schiller's daughter Caroline, who sought and regretted finding "kein Zeugnis für das Christentum" (no evidence of Christianity; Renneke, 1103) in her father's writings. Based on the evidence, any effort to lend comfort, rehabilitate, or co-opt through post-deathbed conversion would have been offensive to the dramatist and philosopher who sarcastically described last-minute conversion as the "mächtiges Wunderwerk der Religion" (mighty miracle feat of religion; *NA* 20: 110) in *Philosophische Briefe* (1786). To the essayist who recognized "die Gerichtbarkeit der Bühne" (the justice of the stage; *NA* 20: 92) before that of the state and the church, to the poet who wrote that "Die Weltgeschichte ist das Weltgericht," "Judex" means judgment in the secular (moral and aesthetic) court of human history (High 2012, 163).

Schiller died on May 9, 1805, at the age of forty-five in Weimar, 180 miles from his birthplace in Marbach, some seventeen months before the fall of Prussia to Bonaparte on October 14, 1806. He had come a long way from his humble beginnings to international renown as a dramatist, historian, and philosopher, though the furthest he had ever traveled was to Berlin for a festival of his dramas in May 1804. He began in obscurity, became the foil to a tyrannical duke, met many of the leading thinkers of his age, and was courted by princes; he rose from a teenager who could only experience chamber music, symphonies, and operas at a state university Schubart described as a slave plantation to an author whose poetry inspired Schubert and Beethoven, and whose dramas inspired operas by Rossini, Donizetti, Verdi, and Tchaikovsky. Nevertheless, the inner circle of the philosophical poet who characterized his most resonant poem, "An die Freude," with the line "Diesen Kuss der ganzen Welt!" (This kiss is for all the world; *NA* 1: 169) was limited to a small number of those who not only witnessed but contributed to his happiness, as he wrote to Körner, Minna Körner, and Dora Stock in a letter of August 15, 1798: "[…] ich muß gestehen, daß Ihr, Humboldts, Göthe und meine Frau die einzige Menschen sind, an die ich mich gern erinnre wenn ich dichte und die mich dafür belohnen können, denn das Publicum, so wie es ist, nimmt einem alle Freude" (I must confess that you, the Humboldts, Goethe, and my wife are the only people who I like to think about when I write and who can reward me for what I write, for the public, such as it is, takes away all of one's joy; *NA* 29: 262). Shortly thereafter, in letters of January 31 and July 2, 1799, regarding performances of *Die Piccolomini* and *Wallensteins Tod*, it is evident how highly Schiller also valued the opinion of Charlotte von Kalb (Palleske, 248).

Schiller's education as a *Mensch* of letters began in an environment where actual autopsies were performed and proceeded to the literary performance of allegorical, anthropological, psychological, and philosophical autopsies that sought to understand the whole human being as physical and intellectual synthesis through dissection or dissolution—as in the "Leichenöffnung" (autopsy) of Christian Wolf's psychology in "Der Verbrecher aus verlorener Ehre" or the description of the philosopher as "Scheidekünstler" (chemist) in *Ästhetische Briefe*. Appropriately, his story ended with his own somewhat Gothic autopsy, performed by Huschke and Herder's son Emil Gottfried von Herder (1783–1855), who concluded that, although the immediate cause of Schiller's death had been acute pneumonia caused by tuberculosis, the whole had succumbed to multiple failures of its constituent parts. The autopsy demonstrated that Schiller's left lung was completely destroyed, his kidneys were almost dissolved, his heart muscle atrophied, and his spleen and bile were greatly enlarged; only the bladder and stomach were intact. Huschke concluded his report with a sober assessment: "Bey diesen Umständen muß man sich wundern, wie der arme Mann so lange hat leben können" (Under these circumstances, one must wonder how the poor man could have lived so long; *NA* 41/2: 535 footnote). Schiller was buried in a mass grave, the Kassengewölbe (Treasury Mausoleum) in Weimar, during the night of May 11–12, and later exhumed and reinterred in 1807 in the Weimar Fürstengruft (Ducal Mausoleum) in a midnight service attended only by Ernst von Schiller (1796–1841) and Goethe's son, August von Goethe (1789–1830). Goethe himself was too moved to attend. On May 3, 2008, for some reason, scientists assembled to verify Schiller's remains prior to the 250th anniversary of his death and announced that DNA tests had demonstrated that none of the bones reinterred in the Fürstengruft belonged to Schiller (see Hinderer). The coffin next to Goethe's in the tomb there now lies vacant.[1]

References

Alt, Peter-André. 2009. *Schiller. Eine Biographie*. 2 volumes. Munich: Verlag C. H. Beck.
Berger, Karl. 1894. *Die Entwicklung von Schillers Ästhetik*. Weimar: Hermann Böhlau.
Berghahn, Klaus L. 1992. "Gedankenfreiheit. From Political Reform to Aesthetic Revolution in Schiller's Works." *The Internalized Revolution. German Reactions to the French Revolution, 1789–1989*. Ehrhard Bahr and Thomas P. Saine, eds. New York & London: Garland Publishing. 99–102.
Besserer Holmgren, Janet. 2007. *The Women Writers in Schiller's Horen: Patrons, Petticoats, and the Promotion of Weimar Classicism*. Newark: University of Delaware Press.
Burwick, Frederick. 2015. "The Borderers (1796–1842)." *The Oxford Handbook of William Wordsworth*. Richard Gravil and Daniel Robinson, eds. Oxford: Oxford University Press. 152–168.
Carl August von Sachsen-Weimar. 1938. *Briefe des Herzogs Carl August von Sachsen-Weimar an seine Mutter Anna Amalia*. Alfred Bergmann, ed. *Jenaer Germanistische Forschungen* (30).
Coleridge, Ernest Hartley. 1895. *Letters of Samuel Taylor Coleridge*. Boston: Houghton Mifflin.
Conger, Syndy. 1987. "Another Secret of the Rue Morgue: Poe's Transformation of the Geisterseher Motif." *Studies in Short Fiction* (24). 9–14.
Conger, Syndy. 1980. "A German Ancestor for Mary Shelley's Monster: Kahlert, Schiller and the Buried Treasure of Northanger Abbey." *Philological Quarterly* (59). 216–232.

---

[1] I would like to thank the following scholars for their support in the research for and preparation of this manuscript: Norbert Oellers (Universität Bonn), Luke Beller and Glen Gray (Johns Hopkins University), Elaine Chen and Rebecca Stewart (Harvard University), Danna De Boer and Xochitl San Vicente (California State University, Long Beach), and Natalie Martz (University of Oxford).

Erdmann, Karl Dietrich. 1986. *Kant und Schiller als Zeitgenossen der Französischen Revolution.* London: Institute of Germanic Studies.
Glossy, Karl. 1915–1920. *Zur Geschichte der Theater Wiens.* Wien: C. Konegen.
Grimm, Reinhold and Jost Hermand. 1971. *Die Klassik-Legende.* Schriften zur Literatur. Vol. 18. Frankfurt am Main: Athenäum Verlag.
Hardenberg, Georg Philipp Friedrich Freiherr von. 1960/1981. "Kann ein Atheist auch moralisch tugendhaft aus Grundsätzen seyn?" *Novalis. Werke.* Stuttgart: Kohlhammer. 18–20.
Heine, Heinrich. 1977 [1836]. *Die Romantische Schule.* Helga Weidmann, ed. Stuttgart: Reclam.
High, Jeffrey L. 1995. "Schillers Plan, Ludwig XVI. in Paris zu verteidigen." *Jahrbuch der Deutschen Schillergesellschaft* (39). Ulrich Ott, Wilfried Barner, and Walter Müller-Seidel, eds. Stuttgart: Kröner Verlag. 178–194.
High, Jeffrey L. 2003. "'Herr D. Friedrich v. Schiller, Bürger von Frankreich'. Ein Eintrag im 'Hochfürstlich Sachsen-Weimar und Eisenachischen Hof- und Adreßkalender des Jahres 1803.'" *Zeitschrift für Germanistik* (3). Bern: Peter Lang. 650–652.
High, Jeffrey L. 2004. *Schillers Rebellionskonzept und die Französische Revolution.* Lewiston: Mellen Press.
High, Jeffrey L. 2006. "Schiller, 'merely political' Revolutions, the Personal Drama of Occupation, and Wars of Liberation." *Schiller: National Poet—Poet of Nations.* Amsterdamer Beiträge zur neueren Germanistik. Nicholas Martin, ed. Amsterdam: Rodopi. 219–240.
High, Jeffrey L. 2010. "Schillers Unabhängigkeitserklärungen: Die niederländische *Plakkaat van Verlatinge,* der 'amerikanische Krieg' und die unzeitgemäße Rhetorik des Marquis Posa." *Jahrbuch der Deutschen Schillergesellschaft.* Göttingen: Wallstein Verlag. 80–108.
High, Jeffrey L. 2011a [2008]. "Introduction: Schiller and the German Novella." *Schiller's Literary Prose Works. New Translations and Critical Essays.* Jeffrey L. High, ed. Rochester: Camden House. 1–8.
High, Jeffrey L. 2011b. "Schiller, Coleridge, and the Reception of the 'German (Gothic) Tale.'" *Colloquia Germanica.* 49–66.
High, Jeffrey L. 2012. "'Judex!' Blasphemy, and Posthumous Conversion: Schiller and (No) Religion." *Yearbook of the Goethe Society of North America.* Rochester: Camden House. 143–163.
High, Jeffrey L. 2013a. "Schiller, *Freude,* Kleist and *Rache* / On the German Freedom Ode." *Heinrich von Kleist—Style and Concept: Explorations in Literary Dissonance.* Dieter Sevin and Christoph Zeller, eds. Berlin: Walter de Gruyter. 123–145.
High, Jeffrey L. 2013b. "Friedrich Schiller, Secular Virtue, and 'The Gods of Ancient Greece.'" *Secularism and the Enlightenment.* Christopher Nadon, ed. Lanham, MD: Lexington Press. 315–324.
High, Jeffrey L. 2021. "'Prelude—Pre-Occupation Bonaparte: Historical and Literary Conquerors in Schiller's Life, Thought, and Works." Seán Allan and Jeffrey L. High, eds. *Inspiration Bonaparte? German Culture and Napoleonic Occupation.* Rochester: Camden House. 29–55.
Hildebrandt, Dieter. 2009 [2005]. *Die Neunte: Schiller, Beethoven und die Geschichte eines musikalischen Welterfolgs.* Munich: Hanser Verlag.

Hinderer, Walter. 2011. "Where is this Schiller now?" *Who is this Schiller now?* Jeffrey L. High, Nicholas Martin, and Norbert Oellers, eds. Rochester: Camden House. 99–115.
Hoock-Demarle, Marie-Claire. 1990. *Die Frauen der Goethezeit*. Munich: Wilhelm Fink Verlag.
Jahn, Otto. 1868. *Goethes Briefe an Christian Gottlob Voigt*. Leipzig: S. Hirzel.
Palleske, Emil, ed. 1879. *Charlotte: (Für die Freunde der Verewigten). Gedenkblätter von Charlotte von Kalb*. Suttgart: Verlag von Carl Krabbe.
Lukács, Georg. 1954. "Zur Ästhetik Schillers." *Beiträge zur Geschichte der Ästhetik*. Berlin: Aufbau Verlag.
Macor, Laura Anna. 2011. "Die Moralphilosophie des jungen Schiller. Ein 'Kantianer ante litteram.'" *Who is this Schiller now?* Jeffrey L. High, Nicholas Martin, and Norbert Oellers, eds. Rochester: Camden House. 99–115.
Mann, Thomas. 1960. *Gesammelte Werke in zwölf Bänden*. Oldenburg: S. Fischer Verlag.
McLynn, Frank. 1997. *Napoleon: A Biography*. New York: Arcade Publishing.
Mehigan, Tim. 2020. "Schiller after Kant: The 'Unexpected Science' of the *Briefe über die ästhetische Erziehung des Menschen*." *Kant-Studien*. 111 (2). 285–302.
Mehring, Franz. 1898/99. "Ästhetische Streifzüge." *Die Neue Zeit*. 17 (1). Stuttgart: Verlag von JHW Dietz. 314–320.
Mendelssohn, Moses. 1814 [1767]. *Phädon oder über die Unsterblichkeit der Seele*, David Friedländer, ed. Fifth edition. Berlin: Nicolai.
Moggach, Douglas. 2007. "Schiller's aesthetic republicanism." *History of Political Thought*. 28 (3). 520–541.
Moritz, Karl Philipp. 1784. "Schillers *Kabale und Liebe*." *Staats- und gelehrte Zeitung*. Berlin. Sept. 4, 1784. 831–833.
Oellers, Norbert. 1990. "Die Dame Luzifer zwischen Revolution und Literatur." *Acta Universitatis Wratislaviensis* 1115. 121–135.
Oellers, Norbert. 1996. *Friedrich Schiller. Zur Modernität eines Klassikers*. Michael Hofmann, ed. Leipzig: Insel Verlag.
Paulin, Roger. 2016. *The Life of August Wilhelm Schlegel: Cosmopolitan of Art and Poetry*. Cambridge: Open Book Publishers.
Plutarch. 1874. "Of Banishment." *Plutarch's Morals*. William W. Goodwin, ed. Boston: Little, Brown, and Company.
Reed, T. J. 1991. *Schiller*. Oxford: Oxford University Press.
Renneke, Pauline. 1904. "Eine Erinnerung an Schillers Tochter Caroline." *Montatsschrift für Stadt und Land*. 61. 1101–1105.
Roetzel, Lisa C. 1997. "Feminizing History." *Theory as Practice. A Critical Anthology of Early German Romantic Writings*. Jochen Schulte-Sasse, ed. Minneapolis: University of Minnesota. 361–381.
Ruppelt, Georg. 1979. *Schiller im nationalsozialistischen Deutschland: Der Versuch einer Gleichschaltung*. Stuttgart: Metzler.
Safranski, Rüdiger. 2005. *Schiller als Philosoph. Eine Anthologie*. Frankfurt am Main: Fischer Taschenbuch Verlag.
Saine, Thomas P. 1988. *Black Bread—White Bread: German Intellectuals and the French Revolution*. Columbia: Camden House.
Sharpe, Lesley. 1991. *Friedrich Schiller: Drama, Thought, and Politics*. Cambridge: Cambridge University Press.
Schiller, Charlotte von. 1860–1865. *Charlotte von Schiller und ihre Freunde*. 3 Volumes. Stuttgart: Cotta Verlag.

Schiller, Friedrich. 1943. *Schillers Werke. Nationalausgabe*. Julius Petersen et. al., ed. Weimar: Hermann Böhlaus Nachfolger.

Schiller, Friedrich. 2003. "Kallias or Concerning Beauty, Letters to Gottfried Körner." *Classic and Romantic German Aesthetics*. J. M. Bernstein, ed. Cambridge: Cambridge University Press. 145–183.

Schlegel, Friedrich. 1957 [1797–1801]. "Fragmente zur Litteratur und Poesie." *Literary Notebooks*. Hans Eichner, ed. Toronto: University of Toronto Press.

Friedrich Schlegel. 1841 [1814]. *Geschichte der alten und neuen Literatur. Vorlesungen gehalten zu Wien im Jahre 1812*. 16th Lecture. Berlin: Athenaeum.

Schmid, Gerhard. 1984. *Friedrich von Schiller, Bürger von Frankreich, Faksimile des Bürgerbriefs der Französischen Republik*. Weimar: Nationale Forschungs- und Gedenkstätte der klassischen deutschen Literatur.

Stäudlin, Gotthold Friedrich. 1792–1793. *Fortgesetzte Schubart'sche Chronik*.

Thomas, Calvin. 1901. *The Life and Works of Friedrich Schiller*. New York: H. Holt and Company.

Wertheim, Ursula. 1958–1959. "Schillers Auseinandersetzung mit den Ereignissen der Französischen Revolution." *Wissenschaftliche Zeitschrift Jena*. 8. 429–449.

Wiese, Benno Von. 1963. *Friedrich Schiller*. 2nd Edition. Stuttgart: Metzler.

Wilson, W. Daniel. 1999. *Das Goethe-Tabu. Protest und Menschenrechte im klassischen Weimar*. Munich: Deutscher Taschenbuch Verlag.

Wilson, W. Daniel, ed. 2004. *Goethes Weimar und die Französische Revolution. Dokumente der Krisenjahre*. Cologne/Vienna: Boehlau Verlag.

Wolzogen, Caroline Von. 1849. *Literarischer Nachlaß der Frau Caroline von Wolzogen*. Vol. 2. Leipzig: Breitkopf und Härtel.

CHAPTER 2

Schiller and His Philosophical Context: Pleasure, Form, and Freedom

Jennifer A. McMahon

INTRODUCTION

In this overview of the philosophical context of Schiller's thought, I have taken the view that there is no bird's-eye view where context is concerned. To gain an understanding of the milieu within which Schiller developed his philosophy, this chapter considers the way his background interests, such as theology, poetry, and literature, influenced the way he prioritized and ordered the philosophical ideas to which he had access. Reference to the dominant philosophical movements at the time, Rationalism, Sentimentalism and Empiricism, will be made in terms of those ideas which set the parameters of his thought either directly or by influencing those philosophers who did have a direct influence on his philosophy. Key among the work discussed will be the ethics and aesthetics of the British philosopher the Third Earl of Shaftesbury, and the German philosophers Moses Mendelssohn and Immanuel Kant. The work identified is chosen for its bearing on what can be considered the core of Schiller's philosophy, his key concepts of pleasure, form, and freedom.

Philosophical ideas can be influential not only when the ideas are accepted, but also when they are rejected. A rejected idea once it becomes a target for subsequent philosophy may influence that philosophy considerably. In some cases, some of Schiller's most significant contributions develop as alternatives to more influential views, such as his rejection of Kant's understanding of the

J. A. McMahon (✉)
University of Adelaide, Adelaide, SA, Australia
e-mail: jenny.mcmahon@adelaide.edu.au

© The Author(s), under exclusive license to Springer Nature Switzerland AG 2023
A. Falduto, T. Mehigan (eds.), *The Palgrave Handbook on the Philosophy of Friedrich Schiller*, https://doi.org/10.1007/978-3-031-16798-0_2

relation of the sensuous to rationality in the moral person. In what follows, Schiller's key concepts within their eighteenth-century context are presented, and their significance within this context is discussed by showing how he relates the sensuous to the rational through the following: "pleasure and morality" (Sect. "Pleasure and Morality"), "form and beauty" (Sect. "Form and Beauty"), and "freedom or nature" (Sect. "Freedom or Nature").

Before commencing, however, there is one caveat. The temptation to look back at Schiller through the prism of nineteenth-century Romanticism might be justified because his subsequent influence on Romanticism is universally accepted. However, I resist that temptation here. Schiller's philosophical context was removed from the kind of assumptions and orientation popularly associated with Romanticism, such as those which prioritized the individual's feelings over the interests of the community. And the understanding of beauty typical of German philosophy before and during Schiller's life is at quite some remove from notions that, while not in fact characteristic of Romantic artists, certainly came to be associated with Romanticism by the Anglo-American philosophers of art in the twentieth century. So setting that aside, we can now turn to the preliminary task of establishing how Schiller's preoccupations emerged before considering in the subsequent sections their philosophical context.

Locating Schiller in His Intellectual Milieu

Schiller writes in the fourth Kallias letter of February 19, 1793:

> the highest perfection of character in a person is moral beauty brought about by the fact that *duty has become its nature*. (*KAL* Bernstein 2003, 159)

It is worth pondering the way of being in the world that is reflected in that quote and Schiller's understanding of such terms as "morality," "beauty," and "nature." The attitude expressed there is certainly not inherent in the intentions and purposes of his ruler and benefactor the Duke Karl Eugen in whose duchy Schiller lived, the Duchy of Württemberg. The Duke's decisions regarding where and effectively what Schiller would study were forced upon him. Nor could Schiller's attitude to morality becoming one's nature be found in the way the Oligarchs operated within the various duchies within Germany at the time. And presumably their same autocratic impersonal style of leadership was repeated down through the chains of command within those duchies. But somewhere among Schiller's influences: parents, relatives, teachers, clergy and friends, or among literary sources, though presumably not the typical *Sturm and Drang* protagonists, Schiller developed a model of a person who exercised reason with feeling, accepted their duty with genuine care, and prioritized cooperation out of love rather than a calculation of personal benefit. As evidenced in his student writing, Schiller had thought that love was the true source of virtue (*Philosophische Briefe* in NA XX, 119; and Goebel 1924, 163-165). One learns to love what is good because one experiences the benefits of goodness and perfection. God is so beneficent that the world is constructed so that by seeking virtue and perfection one finds pleasure and happiness (an idea possibly derived from the 1725 treatise of the Irish philosopher Francis Hutcheson (1694-1746) (1993).

Early in his career Schiller was occupied by the classic question concerning the vocation of man. He began thinking that self-interest and morality were compatible as it was in each person's interest to love humanity, and hence be altruistic. But by the late 1780s and into the 1790s Schiller became more cynical. He came to think that egoism and love were incompatible: that some people acted on egoistic motives and others on love, and presumably each individual could act on either but, and this was the significant break with his earlier thinking: they could only do this at different times; that is, as a moral incentive egoistic motives could not be reconciled with love.

Schiller was already writing plays and poems in his student days and these interests no doubt played a role in the way he prioritized the ideas and concepts introduced to him during these years. But also obvious is the influence of theistic metaphysics on his early ethics. The influence of religion on German philosophy as elsewhere in the eighteenth century was substantial. Pietism and Calvinism were dominant in Germany, and Catholicism somewhat shunned within Schiller's duchy even though the Duke was himself a Catholic. This latter seemingly incidental piece of history did in fact have a significant impact on Schiller. It was standard of a higher academy/university at the time to offer theology, but it was not offered at the Karlschule which Schiller attended from 1773 to 1780. The Duke Karl Eugen was the founder and benefactor of the Karlschule, and while he had tight control over its curriculum, he did not have ultimate power. The Duchy was ultimately under the power of the old estates (a group of aristocrats and clergy) who were Protestant (Beiser 2005, 14), and they forbade the Duke introducing any religion into the academy for fear he would smuggle in Catholic ideas. Schiller had been summoned by the Duke to attend the Karlschule, so he had no choice in the matter. He eventually majored in medicine rather than what would have been his first choice, theology.

The Karlschule taught philosophical medicine which was concerned in large part with how the mind acted upon the body. In his student writings we see that Schiller thought emotions had an impact on physical states (Dewhurst and Reeves 1978). But it was not only through his medical studies that he would have developed this view. By the latter four to five years of Schiller's time at the Karlschule, fifteen hours a week were dedicated to the study of philosophy. Schiller had access to a broad range of writers including British, French, and German, including most notably the German philosopher Moses Mendelssohn (1729–1786). Mendelssohn's views on the relation between mind and body are helpful in understanding the way Schiller envisaged this relationship (Sect. "Form and Beauty").

Later in Schiller's student days, doubts about theology undermine his confidence in his own early ethics. The prevailing alternative to theology given the rise of empiricism and the scientific age, was materialism. The possibility that this might be the only option drove him to the Critical Philosophy of the immensely influential German philosopher Immanuel Kant, which offered an alternative to both theistic metaphysics and materialism (KAL, 175). Schiller also read Kant's essays. It is worth noting that in one essay, Kant gives religion a regulative rather than constitutive role, when he described it in terms of subjective principles serving objective ends (OT 136-137). Before adopting the terms of Kant's philosophy, Schiller's early writing in his poems, plays, and student dissertations suggests he already had his own model in view. However, once he attempted to describe and ground the model, it took him some time to refine the terms. He adopted Kant's system of the mind but through his own model emphasized and developed certain aspects which led to significant differences between their views on the role of sensibility in morality (Sect. "Form and Beauty"). In order to assist in understanding Kant's eventual major impact upon Schiller, it is worth considering that there were numerous influences on Kant's aesthetic theory including Mendelssohn but also the moral and aesthetic philosophy of the British philosopher the Third Earl of Shaftesbury (1671-1713) (Sect. "Pleasure and Morality").

It is not typical of artists and writers today to engage seriously with philosophy. It might be tempting to claim that academic philosophical writing has become too esoteric, remote, and difficult for the non-philosopher. But that same accusation was leveled at some philosophical writing in the eighteenth century and earlier. René Descartes and John Locke's analytical writing had been pilloried along these lines, and there were those who ridiculed the writing of Kant for remoteness and convoluted terms. The publisher Friedrich Nicolai who was a close friend and collaborator of Mendelssohn, satirized Kant's style of writing, and Kant responded to him with some animosity in a series of letters.[1] Even so, the intellectual climate in which philosophy developed at the time was created in part by essays written by artists and creative writers.

Consider that only those from a relatively privileged class including the children of clergy and medics would have the opportunity to attend higher academies and universities. The classical education offered, would have had common elements for all, including for those who eventually became philosophers, literary and art critics, dramatists, and novelists alike. This education facilitated communication across disciplines so that it was not unusual for creative writers to also engage in philosophical essay writing. For example, Johann Joachim Winckelmann (1717–1768), Gotthold Ephraim Lessing (1729–1781), Johann Wolfgang von Goethe (1749–1832), and Schiller joined in the disputes and debates on topics that impacted on their creative endeavors. And they did so not as debutantes but as seriously engaged philosophers, usually by collaborating with philosophers or as is the case with Schiller, by undertaking further study in philosophy. So, it might not have been as remarkable as it now seems for someone like Schiller who was already an acclaimed dramatist and writer,

---

[1] Kant, Immanuel. On Turning Out Books 1996 [1798]. In *Immanuel Kant: Practical Philosophy*, translated and edited by Mary J. Gregor. Introduction by Allen Wood. Vol.5. Cambridge: Cambridge University Press: 619-628 [AK 8: 433-437].

and had a sound philosophical education from his days at the Karlschule Academy (Beiser 2005, 16-19), to take a further three years out from his creative endeavors to study Kant's critical philosophy, which he did from 1793.

Pleasure and Morality

In the fifth Kallias letter of February 23, 1793:

> I hope to show by induction and by psychological means that a feeling of pleasure [*Wohlgefallen*] must flow from the combined concept of freedom and appearance, the harmony between reason and sense, which is the same as pleasure and which regularly accompanies the representation of beauty (KAL, 160).

Schiller learnt early through his studies in philosophical medicine at the Karlschule that the mind can shape experience (Dewhurst and Reeves 1978; Beiser 2005, 15-19). Schiller accepted the dominant view of the time that sensibility was distinct from rationality, but his studies, experience, and observation informed him that they could interact with significant results. This approach led him to an interest in some forms of British and Irish Sentimentalism such as found in the ethics and aesthetics of Shaftesbury, Hutcheson, and in some respects the Empiricism of David Hume.

Shaftesbury may be associated with the Sentimentalists due to his view that we know a moral truth through feeling, but he, like many other philosophers of the eighteenth century, wanted to recognize a rational foundation for feeling because moral incentive required a basis other than personal preference (2001, 77-81 [1714, 2.28-52]). At the time, reasons for action could be understood as "prudential" or moral. "Prudential" reasons focused on the means to secure self-benefits of various kinds. Moral reason, in contrast, involved making a judgment on the kind of ends to be preferred from the perspective which included serving other people's interests as well as one's own. A reason was moral if it was the kind of reason you would want all others to act upon irrespective of their particular circumstances. For example, as an owner of a company a reason to increase profits would not normally be a moral reason; however, if that owner wanted to make the company an effective benefit to the community for the sake of that community, then the reason to increase profits might be a moral reason (see Kant's Categorical Imperative in G 421). The problem concerns the incentive for moral action and how to facilitate it. The materialism that grew out of Empiricism suggested that actions were generated by self-interest; what else could motivate action apart from threat of reward or punishment?

Shaftesbury established a basis for moral incentive through a notion of intuitive reason as opposed to discursive reason. Intuitive reason was conceived as an exercise of reason which was more amenable to sensibility. But Schiller did not accept that only feeling understood as an exercise of reason was relevant to morality. In fact, Schiller thought the moral torpor of his age was due to the

Enlightenment's over emphasis on reason at the expense of sentiment. He also thought the terror of the French revolution was due to France's populace lacking well-rounded citizens in this regard, so their people were ill-equipped to create an ideal republic.[2] Shaftesbury had relied on two functions of reason, intuitive and discursive, to provide a systematic grounding to his conception of morality, but Schiller would see this as ultimately dividing a person against themselves, namely allowing reason to dominate sensibility. While Schiller would not accept Shaftesbury's view that the kind of feeling relevant to ethics was a feeling sourced in reason, there was common ground between them in that they were both intent on conceiving and arguing for a rationally grounded feeling.

The aim of understanding how feeling can be rationally grounded represents an important aspect of the context for Schiller's philosophy. The preoccupation with the role of feeling and appetite in our moral lives, and conversely, the role of reason in cultivating feeling and sensibility toward moral incentive, presents the backdrop to notions and attitudes to beauty in German philosophy of the eighteenth century. We know something is beautiful by how it makes us feel, but beauty is not a matter of personal preference. Schiller was convinced that beauty was an objective quality, and as such, he saw that the experience of beauty demonstrated the rational foundations of a kind feeling that would be relevant to understanding morality.

From his studies in medicine, combined with his studies in philosophy, Schiller had at his disposal a distinction between pathological feeling and practical feeling through Kant's distinction between pathological and practical love (Kant, G 399, MM 377-8). For Schiller, the problem required showing how bodily feeling could interact with mental volition. The aim was to explain how feeling could be enculturated so that it was something for which one could be held responsible. At the time German Rationalists held that someone ruled by feeling was likely to be someone in a state of nature, living by instincts, uneducated, and unpredictable, Jean Jacques Rousseau's attitude to nature notwithstanding (see Sect. "Freedom or Nature"). Schiller wanted to show how someone is lifted out of this state by cultivating rather than suppressing sentiment toward sociability. Aesthetic pleasure presented just such a possibility. Aesthetic pleasure would be characterized as practical rather than pathological.

In German philosophy during Schiller's time, the experience of beauty was an experience that orientated a person to the world in a morally enhancing life reaffirming way. For example, according to Johann Sulzer (1720–1779), a Swiss philosopher who worked in Berlin, beauty in appearance was the expression of inner character (Guyer 2014, 402), or according to Hutcheson, natural

---

[2] Frederick Schiller 2016 [1793]. Letters to Prince Frederick Christian von Augustenburg. In *Frederick Schiller On the Aesthetic Education of Man and Letters to Prince Frederick Christian von Augustenburg*, ed. Alexander Schmidt, trans. Keith Tribe, 113-179. London UK: Penguin, 119–129 (second letter to the Prince, July 13, 1793).

beauty is the mark of a benevolent creator, or as argued by the German philosopher and writer Karl Philipp Moritz (1756–1793), in an artwork beauty reflects the order and harmonious unity of the world (Guyer 2014, 410). Rationalists like the influential German philosopher Gottfried Leibniz (1646–1716) had earlier thought that beauty was perfection, and in this way, he could explain beauty as the object of reason (Wessell 1972). This gave beauty an objective basis, but it also removed from beauty the very characteristics that were of interest to Schiller. Schiller saw in beauty a way of explaining the rational nature or practical role of feeling. To this end, Schiller analyzed beauty as a quality rather than an objective property, so that he, like the German philosopher Alexander Baumgarten (1714–1762), could reveal the relational aspect of beauty. But Schiller prioritized the role of pleasure in our response to it, so the onus was on him to explain the difference between pathological and practical pleasure (KAL, 153).

Among understandings of aesthetic pleasure at the time was that it could be evoked by a kind of freewheeling but objectively focused mental activity (such as prompted by natural or artistic beauty) which pleased because it was stimulating (see discussion of Mendelssohn in Sect. "Form and Beauty"). In this way pleasure and mental activity could be enmeshed. The significance and meaning attributed to aesthetic experience through beauty from all philosophical schools of thought, Rationalist or not, always involved an intellectual involvement either in reflection or in the way one was engaged in order to experience beauty. And whether emotion or feeling was prioritized above objective properties, nonetheless, that something was beautiful was always understood as true or not for reasons independent of a particular individual's idiosyncratic choices. If the emphasis was on subjectivity, it was either implicitly or explicitly recognized as a case of inter-subjectivity, as such judgments were normative, if not objective.

Instead of adopting various amendments to the operations of reason as we see in Shaftesbury, Schiller creates a unified model of sensibility and reason by uniting pleasure and morality through the human love of sociability and community, an idea also proposed by the German philosopher Markus Herz (1747-1803) (Guyer 2014, 409) and eventually in Kant (arguably setting the groundwork in the "*Sensus Communis*" in CJ but non-controversially in MM). In Schiller, this orientation to morality is developed through experiences of beauty.

Form and Beauty

In the first Kallias letter of January 25, 1793, Schiller writes:

> The higher principle [that] subsumes beauty and morality under it, … is none other than existence out of pure form (KAL, 153).

In the fifth Kallias letter of February 23, 1793, Schiller writes:

> The form of beauty is a loose [*freier*] contract between truth, purposefulness, and perfection (KAL, 169).

Shaftesbury had characterized morality in terms which introduced an impartiality into moral feeling. In this way he thought he could maintain the impartial, abstract, and universal in morality without either having it descend into desire and self-interest on the one hand or remove feeling and hence moral incentive from it on the other. However, his critics thought the pleasure of moral action was a personal benefit and so undermined his claim of disinterestedness. To avoid this objection, those who employed his notion of disinterest in aesthetics such as Kant (CJ) treated the object of disinterested pleasure as something explained by the way the perception of the object engaged the mental faculties. This pleasure was disinterested not in how it felt but in terms of its object or what evoked it. Disinterested pleasure was evoked by a state of mind which held no interest in the ordinary sense of appetite, benefit, or utility (and this had been Shaftesbury's point also). Kant called the aspect of the object whose perception occasioned this state of mind, the "form of purposiveness." This was the object of an experience of beauty (CJ). Schiller's notion of the "form of the form of perfection" answered the same objection (KAL, 147).

During this early modern period, notions of "form" left over from pre-enlightenment days lingered. Form referred to the projection of meaning onto physical matter. The sensuous without this form was like an uncontrolled, chaotic, and godless void, and a creature embedded in such a natural state without form was like a creature at the mercy of sensations and appetite. Form was needed in order to be able to think, and grounded our capacity for understanding and reflection. Earlier philosophies had created positive connotations around the impartiality, abstraction, and distance from our animality implicated in this notion of "form," by explaining that the more we engaged in the world through "form," the closer we all came to sharing in the mind of God (cf. Plotinus 1966 [cAD270]).

While the enlightenment had certainly overtaken such beliefs (cf. Rousseau 1984 [1755]), traces of such ideas remained. The sensuous, that is the world as received through our sensations rather than shaped by reason, was determined by physical laws. From the perspective of the dominant German philosophy (and a significant British contingent), our sensuous experience in virtue of being caused by physical laws was determined by nature whether outside or within us. Our instinct and appetites were understood in these terms as not free. Only when instinct and appetite came under our volition as subject to the higher cognitive self, that is, the exercise of reason, that autonomy was possible. "Form" referred to that which was provided by the mind to establish the conditions of our autonomy. For Schiller, this projection involved the selection, prioritization, and ordering of aspects of experience, which, in turn, shaped experience in a manner akin to what we would now refer to as a constant feedback loop. That is, having reasoned on various occasions that one kind of behavior was preferred over another on moral grounds, the satisfaction experienced as a result would eventually establish this course of behavior as second nature. So, through repetition, the kind of experience that resulted from the imposing of form became second nature.³ In this way, experience took on a more rational aspect and with it our sensations, feelings, and appetites were educated.

This notion of form should not be confused with notions of form in twenty-first-century aesthetics. "Form" in eighteenth-century aesthetics referred to that aspect of the perceptual object provided by the mind, understood in terms of how it was configured or construed. But as the relevant aspect of the mind was conceived as above nature, this "form" took on connotations of freedom and morality.

Schiller proposed that aesthetic experience was a bridge between sensation (instincts and appetites) and reason with all its above-nature connotations. He thought of this bridge as the "play drive" (AE Letter 14). Through the play drive, appetites were suspended, and we subsequently found a new disinterested way of being in the world. In a sense then the way this play drive engaged us explained the enjoyment of the projection of form onto matter for its own sake. Other philosophers proposed other terms to describe the relation between sensibility and reason, and many like Schiller involved an account of beauty.⁴

Mendelssohn's account of beauty demonstrates a concept of form of particular relevance to us here. So as not to confuse the aesthetic experience with acquiring knowledge through cognition (his first faculty) or motivation to act through desiring (his second faculty), he introduced a third faculty and that was the faculty of approval (the aesthetic faculty). It has been suggested that in this respect he may have been influenced by the ideas of the British philosopher Edmund Burke (1990 [1757]) regarding the immediacy and experiential nature of beauty (Beiser 2005, 54-55). In any case, Mendelssohn emphasized that the aesthetic faculty was not concerned with finding truth or deciding on courses of action, but rather with enjoying those faculties which were concerned with truth and behavior. He called this aspect the formal aspect (2011 [1785] 41-47; Guyer 2014, 354-55; Beiser 2005, 240-3).

The standard Rationalist understanding of beauty which Mendelssohn had adapted had been that beauty was perfection. This was the view that a beautiful object involved cognition of the role that each part of the object played in achieving the purpose of that object (the teleological ends of the object). For example, the beauty of a tree rested on the cognition of the parts of a tree, and awareness of the role that each part played in its nature: the functions that the leaves, the branches, and the trunk served to secure water, oxygen, and nutrients for the tree are part of what constitutes the tree's aesthetic unity. But Mendelssohn pointed out that it was not that aesthetic pleasure is experienced in the object's perfection itself, but in the form of its perfection: the way the parts related to the whole, be it harmoniously or in surprising ways, while

---

³ See McMahon 2014, 54-62, for a discussion of second nature.
⁴ See McMahon 2020 for a brief history of beauty theory.

achieving perfect complementarity. This is the relevant experience of the way that perfection exercises cognition. Mendelssohn's point is that it is the form of that perfection rather than perfection itself in which aesthetic pleasure is experienced.

It cannot be emphasized enough that for Mendelssohn (and other aestheticians of the period) while the pleasure might be taken in the way the parts come together, nonetheless we can only experience this through cognition of those parts and the role they played in the whole. As such, "aesthetic form" evokes a pleasure in a complexity of elements including cognitive, sensuous, and presumably emotive engagement given aesthetic experience involved mixed sentiments according to Mendelssohn (Guyer 2014, 363). So aesthetic form involves our cognition of the relations between its components and what those components mean in relation to the whole can serve or obstruct aesthetic engagement. As such, Mendelssohn's notion of aesthetic unity or aesthetic form, nicely demonstrates the later eighteenth-century formalism of Schiller in that it encompasses, rather than setting in opposition, aesthetic cognitivism, and aesthetic formalism (e.g., Schiller's notion that beauty was the appearance of freedom or the form of the form of perfection). The later eighteenth-century formalism of Schiller engages not only a sensing but a knowing, whose end is appreciation of the feel of that sensing and knowing. But this engagement does not end in knowledge as was the more typical Rationalist view; rather it ends in appreciation, which, in turn, contributes to a life reaffirming orientation to the object which is beautiful in virtue of its aesthetic form.

Mendelssohn adopts a similar approach to Shaftesbury's conduit between aesthetic experience and morality when he applies his notion of the form of perfection to behavior. The form is found in the way behavior exhibits a moral purpose and so pleases on that basis. Similarly, other actions can be appreciated for the way they exhibit skill. In both these cases, it is not in the material content of their outputs or consequences that pleases but the form of the behavior or acts themselves. Most importantly, the form in each case requires understanding of a range of aspects of the behavior and skills in question. The harmony among parts could also apply to music and all the other art forms, as the form is constructed from quite complex elements of understanding.

The notion of aesthetic form derived from Mendelssohn has considerable explanatory power. For example, it explains our pleasure in fictional tragedy. Mendelssohn thought we could never find pleasure in anything that advertised our insufficiencies or failings. Because of this our pleasure in tragedy, evil or ugliness was something other than pleasure in the material or literal content. Instead, pleasure taken in fictional tragedy was pleasure in the way cognition or desires were stimulated by perfect renditions, interpretations, or representations. That is, we took pleasure in the dramatic depths conveyed by the tragic or evil characters, in the passions aroused or the perfection in the representation of the ugly. Hume had proposed an account of tragedy along similar lines. The pleasure in tragedy was in the way the tragedy was structured to arouse our emotions (1987 [1757]). But Schiller argued in his own essay on tragedy in

1791-92 that there are two sources of pleasure: our happiness and the fulfillment of moral laws. As tragedy does not please in virtue of our happiness, the source of the pleasure in tragedy must be due to its reflection of the way we exercise our freedom in mastering our passions and our sensuous nature. We witness this in the fate of the tragedy's protagonists (ESS 1-6). Schiller's account of tragedy can be seen to adapt aspects of both accounts in treating the form of beauty as the appearance of freedom in our actions.

Mendelssohn published his account of the aesthetic faculty in 1761 well before Schiller developed his own notion of the aesthetic as mediator between the sensuous and the cognitive. Mendelssohn's notion of the aesthetic as the formal aspect of cognition can be seen to adopt the idea of disinterested pleasure from Shaftesbury and Hutcheson, but to give it a firmer grounding by explaining it in terms of a system of the mind. Mendelssohn follows his own advice that he gave in a review of the work of the German philosopher Georg Meier (1718–1777) where he urges Meier to construct his account not by a priori principles alone, but through observation, hypothesis, and then confirmation in practice (Guyer 2014: 341). Mendelssohn had absorbed the methodological influences of empiricism and the new scientific age, and this can equally be said of Schiller.

Given the extent to which Kant's aesthetic theory would impact upon Schiller, it is worth noting that both Shaftesbury and Mendelssohn are likely to have significantly influenced Kant's characterization of aesthetic pleasure as disinterested, and its object as the "form of purposiveness." Their accounts certainly help explain aspects of Kant's aesthetics such as how disinterested aesthetic pleasure taken in the "form of purposiveness" evokes aesthetic ideas and involves the exercise of aesthetic judgment (CJ). Through the prism of their accounts, these aspects of Kant's aesthetic theory can be understood as complementary. The same link between form and beauty and the relevance to aesthetic form of cognitive content that one finds particularly in Mendelssohn's account, is taken up by both Kant and Schiller. In this light it is worth noting that the twentieth-century opposition between aesthetic formalism and aesthetic cognitivism which still has currency in certain quarters, should not be uncritically assumed to apply to eighteenth-century aesthetics.[5]

The form of behavior that is beautiful is a form that exhibits the moral law. The moral law encapsulates freedom as it is not given to us by nature but through our own reason. And the exercise of reason was understood at this time as above nature. Nature is not free, but we nonetheless project the appearance of freedom onto it when it seems to exhibit a form that reflects a unity generated by itself rather than imposed from the outside. To experience beauty is to perceive the appearance of freedom. When we do, we experience nature as beautiful. The possibility of freedom, conceived as the exercise of autonomy, was a central concern that reveals itself in many aspects of Schiller's creative and philosophical output. We have considered above how form and

---

[5] See McMahon 2017 for a discussion of standard formalism compared to Kantian formalism.

beauty are linked in Schiller's thought given his influences, and we turn now to what Schiller could have meant when he wrote that beauty was "the appearance of freedom" (KAL, 160).

Freedom or Nature

Schiller wrote in his second Kallias letter of February 8, 1793:

> But since this freedom is merely lent to the object by reason, since freedom as such can never be given to the senses and nothing can be free other than what is supra-sensible—in short, it is all that matters here that the object appears as free not that it really is so; thus this analogy of the object with the form of practical reason is not freedom indeed but merely freedom in appearance, autonomy in appearance. … a judgement of unfree effects according to the form of the free will, is aesthetic. The analogy of an appearance with the form of pure will or freedom is beauty (in its most general sense). Beauty is thus nothing less than freedom in appearance. (KAL, 151)

Non-philosophers today might think that by "freedom" we mean instant gratification and lack of responsibility. But in the eighteenth century, giving vent to unruled desires and inclinations was the mark of those enslaved by their passions. In contrast, self-control and taking responsibility demonstrated autonomy and freedom. Schiller's training and education had led him quite early to take as a given that duty, responsibility, and obligations to community were crucial to attaining happiness and living well. Hence, he had argued that a desire for happiness and pleasure was sufficient to motivate moral action. That is, moral action did not require a dour sense of duty, or some external factor such as a promise of reward or punishment. We have seen above that Schiller had to reconcile this satisfaction of a desire for happiness with the generally accepted view that self-interest did not constitute a moral incentive. He thought he achieved this in his early writing by arguing that ego, self-interest, and altruism were not only compatible but connected because we came to feel that altruism led to our own happiness (Beiser 2005, 20-22). But he came to see that the concept of the person by this account was governed by self-interest and, hence, unfree.

As discussed in Sect. "Form and Beauty" above, the idea of second nature served a crucial role in connecting happiness and duty for Schiller. He argued that doing one's duty would become a pleasure once duty became second nature. This might seem incompatible with a view he adopted from a teacher at the Karlschule. Jacob Friedrich Abel (1751–1829), a philosopher who taught Schiller, argued in a paper that extreme personalities and those with passionate ideas should be allowed to express themselves, as this benefits the community (cf. Mill 1910 [1859], 100-123). This idea seems to have influenced Schiller's early dramas, which included such personalities, and also confirmed his attitude to the important role of sensibility in the well-rounded person. But it was also an attitude that contrasted starkly with Schiller's own experience in his Karlschule years, given the lack of intellectual freedoms he was allowed, and which he saw around him in the oligarchical and feudal systems. It was as if the political oppression he witnessed around him became an indirect target for his philosophical work.

In eighteenth-century philosophy, aesthetic experience was conceived relative to a community rather than in terms of isolated individuals. One view which took a more Aristotelian than Kantian path was that a moral person is created within a community. Once a group of persons, as opposed to an isolated individual, had achieved the conditions for personal freedom, it could create the ideal republic. This was Schiller's view which set the relation between individual freedom and the ideal republic in converse order to that proposed by the French philosopher Jean Jacques Rousseau early in the eighteenth century ([1762]) and Kant (PP [1795]). The common ground though was that the ideal political system allowed citizens moral autonomy, and that this involved reason either dominating or alternatively interacting in some way with sensibility.

The belief in the importance of experiencing various perspectives also had a political voice during Schiller's time. There was a debate at the time in Germany regarding the undesirability of there being one dominant cultural institution. Instead, a range of such institutions were preferred to avoid a monopoly by any particular school of thought or political persuasion. They believed such institutions were necessary to avoid the anarchy of no cultural models, and apparently Goethe, who was a close friend and collaborator of Schiller's, was one of the defenders of this position (Schmidt 2016, 179 fn5; and Goethe 1795). This debate was fueled by a concern that a more base kind of art would dominate the attention of the public if alternatives were not provided to facilitate a more critical culture. But the critical culture in question did not require art with a political or determinate message which was considered rhetoric and, hence, bad art.[6] Schiller thought only art which expresses freedom was the appropriate art for an enlightened people, and freedom was expressed through the form of beauty (see endnote 2).

Aesthetic experience was of philosophical interest because of what it was thought to contribute to the happiness and well-being of a community. Art was meant to elevate rather than entertain. Schiller was no exception in believing that art that merely entertained was enervating and degenerate. He also believed that art which directed a determinate message at the audience was bad art. A precursor to the latter view were the views on art of Rousseau, who had argued that the arts in his time in Paris reflected and facilitated an affluent and degenerate society (2002 [1750]). This possibility was alive in the thought which reached Schiller but so were the distinctions between high and low pleasures, high and low art, and complex and popular beauty (KAL, 159; AE letters 26 & 27, and see endnote 2). According to Shaftesbury and many others such as Kant, aesthetic disinterested pleasure was an example of a high pleasure, and art which evoked it was high art, and Schiller agreed.

[6] See McMahon 2018 for an examination of the distinction between rhetoric and beauty.

High art engaged the right kind of pleasure, the kind that would serve to link the arts with morality through beautiful form. The conception of aesthetic pleasure that emerged in the eighteenth century was a pleasure that would lead us to negotiate nature and artworks in a way compatible with the highest levels of our humanity. It was not a pleasure that dulls the spirit and mind with physical excess and lazy wish fulfillment, but a pleasure that alerts us to the world's vivid colors and complexities. This is a pleasure that would wake the person up from their intellectual and emotional slumbers and lead them toward self-control rather than physical abandon.

While Schiller's philosophical milieu certainly included the ideas of Rousseau, he rejected Rousseau's famous treatment of the human being as essentially good. For example, Rousseau's notion of the noble savage was rejected by those like Schiller who believed the natural uncultivated human being was driven by pathological feeling, and so by definition lacked freedom. In order to be autonomous, one must exercise practical feeling, which requires enculturation through the kind of community involvement that exercises reason. Morality required such autonomy. However, German philosophers were more receptive to other ideas derived from Rousseau, particularly some of his notions regarding the conditions for the ideal Republic (1971 [1762]). During Schiller's time in Germany, a prevalent view was that aesthetic experience (of the practical feeling kind) orientated one outward toward community and created the right basis for a Republic of citizens who considered the good of the community as part of their own good.

Kant's moral philosophy was a major influence on philosophers during this period either as a model or a target.[7] Schiller accepted Kant's insistence that morality was sourced in reason alone, but unlike Kant, he did not treat morality as the highest good. Instead for him the highest good was a well-rounded human being which for him meant a person who enjoyed freedom both internally—free from compulsions and addictions—and externally—free from tyrants and other political oppression. A free human being was a person able to harmonize their sensibility and reason by "incorporating natural inclinations and feelings into their will" (this expression paraphrases Beiser 2005, 177). Only when sensibility and reason were in harmony was a person truly free. And this harmony was achieved, according to Schiller, through the experience of beauty. The experience of beauty provided the wherewithal to distance oneself from inclinations and feelings so that when the context was right, we could look critically upon, and make reasonable choices that were nonetheless responsive to, our sensuous natures.

---

[7] See Garve [1783] 2000 for the kind of criticisms leveled at Kant from the empiricist perspective and of which Schiller would have been aware, having had contact with Garve both directly and indirectly through the philosophical circles in which he moved. See also Sassen 2000. For a discussion of the differences between Kant and Schiller's moral theories, see Baxley 2010a, 2010b; and Deligiorgi 2020.

Concluding Remarks

Schiller's body of work, both creative and philosophical, demonstrates a lasting and committed preoccupation with the possibility of freedom in a world determined by physical laws. He thought freedom was achieved rather than granted both at an individual level and at the level of community (but the former was only possible in virtue of the latter). The experience of beauty played a crucial role in the way Schiller envisaged the possibility of freedom. Beauty models for us what it means to be neither compelled by external forces nor determined by physical laws. Beautiful objects exhibit a harmony in how they are constituted which is not determined or compelled by either internally generated laws, such as uncontrolled appetites, or externally imposed demands, such as promises, threats, or politically imposed constraints. "Form" makes something beautiful as it is the "form" that releases us (through the play drive according to Schiller, discussed in Sect. "Form and Beauty") from a material and determined existence into an autonomous and free existence by facilitating the cultivation of reason and morality. For Schiller, only by experiencing beauty can we accomplish the wherewithal to be free persons.

Morality was understood to be constituted by the exercise of reason, but the exercise of reason would not necessarily implicate moral choices. The freedom that reason would make possible was a freedom to choose and so one might choose immoral courses of action or to prioritize pathologically based feeling. One might choose in a particular situation to be guided by desire or appetite and this one can choose freely according to Schiller (GD 149-151). Reason is not morality. Reason requires some prompts in order to choose morality, and this is provided through the experience of beauty. Given beauty is freedom in appearance, beauty prompts us to exercise our freedom which we can only do through being moral persons. And this in turn involves the exercise of reason. Such are the key terms of reference that arguably set the parameters of Schiller's thought and provide the necessary conditions for the wealth of creative and philosophical ideas that his work continues to contribute to world culture.[8]

References

Baumgarten, Akexander Gottlieb. 1954 [1735]. *Reflections on Poetry*, trans. Karl Aschenbrenner and William B. Holther. Berkely and Los Angeles: University of California Press.

Baxley, Anne Margaret. 2010a. *Kant's Theory of Virtue*. Cambridge: Cambridge University Press.

Baxley, Anne Margaret. 2010b. The Aesthetics of Morality: Schiller's Critique of Kantian Rationalism. *Philosophy Compass* 5/12: 1084-1095.

---

[8] The research for this chapter was supported by the Australian Research Council Grant DP150103143.

Beiser, Frederick. 1992. Kant's Intellectual Development: 1746-1781. In *The Cambridge Companion to Kant*, ed. Paul Guyer, 26-61. Cambridge: Cambridge University Press.
Beiser, Frederick. 2005. *Schiller as Philosopher: A Re-Examination*. Oxford: Oxford University Press. DOI: https://doi.org/10.1093/019928282X.001.0001
Burke, Edmund 1990 [1757]. A Philosophical Enquiry into the Origins of Our Ideas of the Sublime and Beautiful, intro. and ed. A. Phillips. Oxford: Oxford University Press.
Deligiorgi, Katerina. 2020. Kant, Schiller, and the Idea of a Moral Self. *Kant-Studien* 111/2: 303-322.
Dewhurst, Kenneth and Nigel Reeves. 1978. *Friedrich Schiller : medicine, psychology and literature : with the first English edition of his complete medical and psychological writings*. Oxford: Sandford Pubs.
Garve, Christian [1783] 2000. The Garve Review. In *Kant's Early Critics: The Empiricist Critique of the Theoretical Philosophy*, ed. Brigitte Sassen, 59-77. Cambridge: Cambridge University Press.
Goebel, Julius. 1924. Schiller's Philosophische Briefe: A New Interpretation. *The Journal of English and Germanic Philology* 23/2: 161-172.
Goethe, Johann Wolfgang von. 1795. "Literary Revolutionaries", *Die Horen*, 2.5: 50-56. https://www.friedrich-schiller-archiv.de/die-horen/die-horen-1795-stueck-5/iii-litterarischer-sanscuelottismus/. Accessed 14th May 2020
Guyer, Paul. 2014. *A History of Modern Aesthetics Volume 1: The Eighteenth Century*. New York: Cambridge University Press.
Hume, David. 1987 [1757]. Of Tragedy. *Essays Moral, Literary and Political*, ed. E. F. Miller. Indianapolis: Liberty Classics.
Hutcheson, Francis. 1993 [1725]. *Inquiry into the Original of Our Idea of Beauty and Virtue*. The Hague: Nijhoff.
Kant, Immanuel. 1996. The Metaphysics of Morals (1797). In *Practical Philosophy*, trans. and ed. Mary J. Gregor, 363–602. Cambridge: Cambridge University Press [Ak 6].
Kant, Immanuel. 1996. Groundwork of the Metaphysics of Morals (1785). In *Practical Philosophy*, trans. and ed. Mary J. Gregor, 41-108. Cambridge: Cambridge University Press [Ak 4].
Kant, Immanuel. 1996. What Does It Mean to Orient Oneself in Thinking? (1786). Trans. Allen W. Wood. In *Religion and Rational Theology*, ed. Allen W. Wood and George di Giovanni, 7-18. Cambridge: Cambridge University Press [Ak 8].
Kant, Immanuel. 1996 [1798]. On Turning Out Books. In *Immanuel Kant: Practical Philosophy*, trans. and ed. by Mary J. Gregor, intro. Allen Wood, 619-628 [AK 8: 433-437]. Vol.5. Cambridge: Cambridge University Press.
Kant, Immanuel. 1996. Toward Perpetual Peace (1795). In *Practical Philosophy*, trans. and ed. Mary J. Gregor, 315-51. Cambridge: Cambridge University Press [Ak 8].
Kant, Immanuel. 2000. *Critique of the Power of Judgment* (1790). Trans. Paul Guyer and Eric Matthews. Ed. Paul Guyer. Cambridge: Cambridge University Press [Ak 5].
McMahon, Jennifer A. 2014. *Art and Ethics in a Material World: Kant's Pragmatist Legacy*. New York and London: Routledge.
McMahon, Jennifer A. 2018. Imagination. In *Social Aesthetics and Moral Judgment: Pleasure, Reflection, and Accountability*, ed. Jennifer A. McMahon, 66-87. New York: Routledge.

McMahon, Jennifer A. 2017. The Pervasive and Persistent in the Misreading of Kant's Aesthetic Formalism. In *The Palgrave Kant Handbook*, ed. Matthew C. Altman, 425-446. Basingstoke and New York: Palgrave Macmillan.

McMahon, Jennifer A. Beauty. 2020. In *The Oxford Research Encyclopedia of Literature*. Oxford University Press.

Mendelssohn, Moses. 2011 [1785]. *Morning Hours: Lectures on God's Existence*, trans. Daniel O. Dahlstrom and Corey Dyck. Dordrecht: Springer.

Mill, John Stuart. 1910 [1859]. On Liberty. In *Utilitarianism, Liberty and Representative Government*, intro. A. D. Lindsay, 65-170. London: J. M. Dent and Sons.

Peterson, Julius, ed. 1943f. Schillers Werke, *Nationalaugabe*, 42 vols. Weimar: Böhlausnachfolger.

Plotinus. 1966 [c AD270]. Enneads, trans. A. H. Armstrong. Cambridge MA: Harvard University Press.

Rousseau, Jean Jacques. 1971 [1762]. *The Social Contract*, trans. Maurice Cranston. Harmondsworth, UK: Penguin.

Rousseau, Jean Jacques. 1984 [1755]. *Discourse on the Origin and Foundations of Inequality Among Men*, trans. Maurice Cranston. London: Penguin.

Rousseau, Jean Jacques. 2002 [1750]. Discourse on the Sciences and Arts. In *The Social Contract and The First and Second Discourses*, ed. Susan Dunn, by Gita May, Robert N. Bellah, David Bromwich, and Conor Cruise O'Brien, 43-68. New Haven; London: Yale University Press.

Sassen, Brigitte 2000. Introduction: Major Trends in the Early Empiricist Reception of Kant's Critical Philosophy. In *Kant's Early Critics: The Empiricist Critique of the Theoretical Philosophy*, ed. Brigitte Sasson, 1-49. Cambridge: Cambridge University Press.

Schmidt, Alexander. 2016. Introduction and Notes. In *Frederick Schiller, On the Aesthetic Education of Man and Letters to Prince Frederick Christian von Augustenburg* [1795], trans. Keith Tribe. UK: Penguin Classics.

Shaftesbury, Third Earl. 2001 [1714]. *Characteristics of Men, Manners, Opinions, Times*, intro. Den Uyl. Indianapolis: Liberty Fund. https://oll.libertyfund.org/title/shaftesbury-characteristicks-of-men-manners-opinions-times-3-vols. Accessed February 22nd-26th 2021

Schiller, Friedrich. 1967. *On the Aesthetic Education of Man in a Series of Letters*. Transl. E. M. Wilkinson and L. A. Willoughby. Oxford: Oxford University Press.

Schiller, Friedrich. 1993. *Essays*, ed. Daniel Dahlstrom and Walter Hinderer. New York: Continuum.

Schiller, Friedrich. 2003. Kallias or Concerning Beauty: Letters to Gottfried Körner. Transl. S. Bird-Pollan. In *Classical and Romantic German Aesthetics*, ed. J. M. Bernstein, 145-184. Cambridge: Cambridge University Press.

Schiller, Friedrich. 2005. On Grace and Dignity. Transl. J. V. Curran. In Schiller's 'On Grace and Dignity' in its Cultural Context: Essays and a New Translation, ed. Jane V. Curran and Christophe Fricker, 123-170. Rochester: Camden House 2005.

Schiller, Frederick. 2016 [1793]. Letters to Prince Frederick Christian von Augustenburg. In *Frederick Schiller On the Aesthetic Education of Man and Letters to Prince Frederick Christian von Augustenburg*, ed. Alexander Schmidt, trans. Keith Tribe, 113-179. London UK: Penguin.

Wessell, Leonard P. Jr. 1972. Alexander Baumgarten's Contribution to the development of Aesthetics. *Journal of Aesthetics and Art Criticism* 30/3: 333-342.

CHAPTER 3

The Development of Schiller's Philosophical Attitude: Schiller's Philosophical Education

Laura Anna Macor

Schiller's philosophical attitude developed quite early on and remained constant thereafter, being unaffected by both intellectual and private events. This is mainly due to the education that he received at the Stuttgart *Karlsschule*, which was first and primarily, although not officially, an education in philosophy: according to then standards, philosophy was in fact regarded as the grounding discipline for any further training, and this meant that all students were taught courses in logic, history of philosophy, and ethics, independently of their special subjects being vocational. Schiller was no exception in this respect. In 1773 he was admitted to the *Karlsschule* as a student in law, and in late 1775, he turned to the newly introduced medical curriculum, which he apparently considered closer to his chief areas of interest, namely, philosophy, and literature. His favorite professor and later collaborator, Jakob Friedrich Abel, was a philosopher and prominent exponent of the late German Enlightenment in Württemberg, and Schiller's academic dissertations—written in 1779 and 1780 for the final examination—were not confined to physiology and its related fields, but addressed issues also (and most notably) in philosophy.

This chapter aims to reconstruct Schiller's initial experience of philosophy and the essential nature of his philosophical education, while also pinpointing the features that were to prove key and enduring in his subsequent thinking.

L. A. Macor (✉)
University of Verona, Verona, Italy
e-mail: lauraanna.macor@univr.it

Philosophy at the *Karlsschule*

The *Karlsschule* was founded as a military school by the duke of Württemberg Karl Eugen in 1770, being transformed into a full-fledged academy in 1773 and awarded the status of university by Emperor Joseph II in 1781. Closely connected to the founder's projects and ambitions, it was finally closed in 1794 by Karl Eugen's brother and successor Ludwig Eugen. In these twenty-four years of activity, it became one of the more progressive educational institutions in the German territories, combining practical instruction with theoretical teaching according to the model of the then faculty system: the degrees offered were vocational, but this did not preclude focus on other and more precisely philosophical and aesthetic subjects. Against an old-style narrative, therefore, Schiller did not spend his youth under the aegis of obscurantism—at least not in terms of cultural and intellectual stimuli—but was rather motivated to familiarize himself with the most recent and, in some cases, radical ideas of his time, and this was to influence his work well beyond graduation.

The design of the educational programs at the *Karlsschule* was first entrusted to the philologist and former teacher at the Ludwigsburg *Lateinschule*, Johann Friedrich Jahn (1728–1800), who served in this capacity until 1774. In keeping with his background and own personal convictions, Jahn credited the humanities with a fundamental role, not limited to specialist competencies but encompassing culture, history, and also philosophy as a tool for reasoning. Jahn gave courses not only in the Classical languages but also in metaphysics, logic, the history of philosophy, and morals following the *Elementa philosophiae rationalis* (*Elements of Rational Philosophy*, 1751) by Johann Christoph Knaus (1709–1796),[1] and, as far as theology was concerned, adhering to what it has become customary to term "neology," with Johann Friedrich Wilhelm Jerusalem (1709–1798) playing a central role. In terms of methodology, Jahn made the key ideas of the Enlightenment his guiding principles, championing "autonomous thought" (*Selbstdenken*) and independent judgment against mechanical rote-learning, and he did so to such an extent as to provoke criticism among his colleagues.[2] And yet, notwithstanding his commitment to the ideals of the Enlightenment and to the project of including philosophy within the education of future officers, Jahn's expertise was not in philosophy itself, but rather in philology and Ancient languages. Not by coincidence, therefore, was it that in 1774 he was transferred back to his previous position at the Ludwigsburg Latin School, and other professors took over his influential role, one above all.

Jakob Friedrich Abel (1751–1829) had been appointed in 1772, already before his theology studies at the University of Tübingen were complete, and

---

[1] This compendium rested on the system of Christian Wolff (1679–1754) and was officially used in Württemberg as a handbook for philosophy, and more particularly logic (cf. [Knaus], 1751); on this, see the recent reevaluation by Stašková 2021, pp. 82-97.

[2] For further details regarding Jahn's role, see Riedel 1995, pp. 389-390. On the key notion of *Selbstdenken*, one may still profitably read Dierse 1995.

was to become a leading figure not only at the *Karlsschule*—from 1786 to 1790, he also served as deputy president (the president being the Duke himself)—but also in Württemberg more generally, being appointed Professor of Logic and Metaphysics at Tübingen in 1790.[3] Over the eighteen years spent at the *Karlsschule*, Abel was helped in organizing and delivering instruction in philosophy by three colleagues. Two of them were already professors at Tübingen—more precisely, both had themselves taught Abel from 1768 to 1770—and moved to the nearby institution only for a year: August Friedrich Bök (1739–1815)—who was then extraordinary professor of philosophy at Tübingen—arrived in December 1774 and left in late 1775 or early 1776, having been made ordinary professor of Practical Philosophy, Rhetoric, and Poetry at Tübingen[4]; Gottfried Ploucquet (1716–1790), who held the Chair of Logic and Metaphysics in Tübingen, was assigned instruction in the relevant fields at the *Karlsschule* in 1778.[5] At the end of 1778, Kant's later opponent, Johann Christoph Schwab (1743–1821), was finally appointed Ploucquet's successor and in consequence became Abel's permanent colleague.[6]

In all this, Abel was and remained the leading figure, contributing crucially to shaping a new overall didactic vision, where philosophy was made into the grounding discipline for any vocational curriculum. On December 13, 1773, Abel sent the duke a sketch of the program, positing the central role of philosophy as a tool for making students "enlightened [*aufgeklärt*] and virtuous," and able to "think and reason" autonomously (Abel 1773, pp. 17, 23). On December 12, 1774, he insisted on his conviction that "most hours" needed to be devoted to philosophy, so that students could receive a "thorough and methodical" instruction, practice "rational reasoning," and thus become more capable of learning "the other sciences" as well. Not surprisingly, Abel described the "principal aim" of his teaching as generating "autonomous thought [*Selbstdenken*]" (Riedel 1995, pp. 391-392).

Evidently, Abel's intentions coincided with Jahn's, but he enacted them in a more vigorous and meaningful way. But that's not all. For Bök also shared this

---

[3] Abel's life and works, with a special focus on his teaching activity in Stuttgart and Tübingen, are dealt with by: Riedel 1995, pp. 284-285; Franz 2005, pp. 88-99; Macor 2011.

[4] Bök was professor to Hegel and Hölderlin at the Tübingen Faculty of Philosophy from 1788 to 1790, and author of the dissertation which both defended publicly in 1790 in order to obtain their master's degree; on all this and more generally on Bök's life, thought, and works, see Franz 2005, pp. 101-159, 405-504.

[5] Admitted to the Berlin Real Academy of Sciences as an external member in 1749, Ploucquet was the Swabian authority in the field of philosophy—and particularly for metaphysics and logic—over the entire period of his service at Tübingen (i.e., from 1750 until 1790, although for health reasons he stopped lecturing in 1782). On his characteristic way of combining mathematics and philosophy, see Franz 2005, pp. 27-69, 527-534; Ploucquet 1782/2006.

[6] Schwab is best known as the author of the anti-Kantian text *Welche Fortschritte hat die Metaphysik seit Leibnitzens und Wolffs Zeiten in Deutschland gemacht?* (*What progress has metaphysics made in Germany since the Time of Leibniz and Wolff?*), which was awarded the relevant prize of the Berlin Academy and was published in 1796. On Schwab's life and intellectual contribution to the philosophy of his time, see Riedel 1995, pp. 396-397; Franz 2005, pp. 512-513.

willingness to promote a more general level of practical wisdom for everybody as against a "mechanical" training rooted in obvious professional needs (Bök 1775b, p. 9) and supported a manner of teaching aimed at developing personal insight rather than merely passing on notions to be memorized. Not coincidentally, it was he who introduced a crucial change into the final examinations, bringing in the technique of disputation. This assessment device—widely used in most universities of the time—involved dividing students into groups of *Respondentes* and *Opponentes*, charged respectively with either defending or challenging the *Theses* (or *Säze/Säzze*) provided by their professors for the purpose of the examination. In so doing, students had to demonstrate knowledge of the subject being discussed, as well as the capacity to argue for and against any related issue, and this kind of polemics they had previously practiced in the second half of the year.[7] Tellingly, this applied not only to philosophy, but to all disciplines (including vocational ones), and was to remain in place until the institution's closure in 1794.

Critical thinking was clearly a priority, and philosophy was evidently viewed as an intellectual resource useful to all human beings, whatever their chosen professions.

In terms of philosophical trends, Abel, Bök, and Schwab shared a common interest in the key areas of the late German Enlightenment—namely, anthropology, empirical psychology, and aesthetics[8]—whereas Ploucquet's preference went to logic, ontology, and metaphysics. This, and more particularly the brevity of the latter's tenure, though, should not be taken as implying that logic was either marginalized or accorded less value—quite the contrary. Against a long-standing scholarly cliché, logic in fact played a crucial role either as the basis for any further knowledge according to Knaus' rationalist conception (itself based on Wolff's model), or again in being part of psychology, in keeping with the more recent trends of the so-called "popular philosophy" (*Popularphilosophie*). The latter option gained ground in the 1770s, endorsed only by Abel initially (cf. Abel 1773)—on this point he diverged greatly from Jahn—but swiftly winning the support of his new colleagues: Bök accorded psychology the first and introductory part of his 1775 theses, only afterward dealing with specific logical issues (cf. Bök 1775c), and Schwab did the same in an extant manuscript, likely dating from the first period of his activity at the *Karlsschule* and written together with Abel (Abel and Schwab 1778/1779). In the light of this, it can safely be claimed that logic was not banished or dismissed in favor of other disciplines but relocated in keeping with the accepted centrality of anthropology and psychology.[9]

---

[7] For the description of course content, allocation of hours, and overall organization of the 1775 philosophy lessons, see NA, 41, IIa, pp. 70-71.

[8] For a useful survey of ideas, authors, and trends in the late German Enlightenment, see Riedel 1995, pp. 402-450; Joeres 1997; Godel 2015; de Boer and Prunea-Bretonnet 2021. And additionally, see the relevant chapter in this volume by Jennifer A. McMahon.

[9] A comprehensive, updated, and innovative presentation of the trends underlying the instruction of logic at the *Karlsschule* is provided by Stašková 2021, pp. 41-97; Stašková 2022, pp. 17-20.

In terms of authors, the most widely read and discussed included not only the main protagonists of the German Enlightenment—Johann Joachim Spalding (1714–1804), Johann Georg Sulzer (1720–1779), Moses Mendelssohn (1729–1786), Christian Garve (1742–1798), and Johann Georg Heinrich Feder (1740–1821)—but also some key figures on the European scene such as Francis Hutcheson (1694–1747), David Hume (1711–1776), Adam Ferguson (1723–1816), Charles Louis de Secondat, baron de Montesquieu (1689–1755), Jean-Jacques Rousseau (1712–1778), and even Julien Offray de La Mettrie (1709–1751) and Claude-Adrien Helvétius (1715–1771)—the last two attracting bitter criticism.[10] In the late 1780s—so well after Schiller's graduation—Kant's philosophy entered the *Karlsschule* with Abel's two courses centered presumably on both the *Kritik der reinen Vernunft* (*Critique of Pure Reason*) and the *Kritik der praktischen Vernunft* (*Critique of Practical Reason*),[11] though this did not alter the predominantly pre-Kantian identity of the teaching on offer.

In 1790, Abel moved to Tübingen as Ploucquet's successor, and his position at the *Karlsschule* was filled by Christoph Gottfried Bardili (1761–1808), who remained Schwab's colleague until the school closed its doors in 1794.[12]

In conclusion, students at the *Karlsschule*—whatever the focus of their studies—received a thorough training in philosophy, both familiarizing themselves with the main trends of the German as well as the European Enlightenment, and practicing critical discussion on any relevant topic. The level of instruction was not to be out-matched, given that all members of the teaching staff had been educated at the University of Tübingen and—with the sole exception of Jahn—also served, or would do so in due course, at Tübingen's Faculty of Philosophy, where none other than Hölderlin and Hegel enrolled in 1788, joined by Schelling in 1790.

This, therefore, was the context of Schiller's introduction to philosophy.

Schiller's Education in Philosophy

Schiller was admitted to the *Karlsschule* in January 1773 and graduated in December 1780. Over these eight years, crucial changes took place, most significantly the switch from law to medicine in late 1775 as a consequence of Karl Eugen's reorganization of the available curricula, but one thing remained in place and continued steadily to take shape. This was philosophy. Schiller read

---

[10] It is impossible to list all authors that were directly studied, dealt with only partially, or simply mentioned in passing by all professors over the entire period of the school's existence. Useful information is provided by: Riedel 1985; Riedel 1995; Riedel 1998; Macor 2010, pp. 31-44, 74-78; Riedel 2011; Robert 2011, pp. 55-80; Burtscher 2013; Wübben 2022.

[11] Cf. Riedel 1995, p. 400. The first public mention of Kant's name and theories by Abel dates from 1786 (Abel 1786, p. VII), and from this point on his attention to Kant's work—with the notable exception of the short essays—showed no abatement. On all of this, see Macor 2011, pp. 42-45.

[12] On Bardili's contribution to the post-Kantian debate, see Paimann 2009.

philosophy every year—the only apparent exception being 1778—and became increasingly interested in moral-psychological, aesthetic, and religious issues, which ended up absorbing all his intellectual curiosity. This was due partly to his own intellectual priorities and preferences, and partly to the nature of the teaching on offer, at once thorough, pervasive, and inspiring.

In 1773 and 1774 Schiller received instruction in all disciplines from Jahn, who was no stranger to him, having introduced him to Ancient, and particularly Latin culture at the Ludwigsburg *Lateinschule* from 1769 to 1771.[13] As already anticipated, Jahn's philosophy lessons were based on Knaus' *Elementa philosophiae rationalis* (*Elements of Rational Philosophy*), which presented a rigorous explanation of all the relevant fields, following in the footsteps of Wolff with a special focus on syllogistic logic, and at the same time making the case for the essential role of experience in any further process of knowledge acquisition: "Experience is the mother of philosophy. For this reason, philosophers always give precedence to experience *[Experientia est mater philosophiae. Eam ob causam philosophi semper praemittunt experientiam]*" (Knaus 1751, p. 8). Evidently, Schiller's very first entry into philosophy did not take the path of an obsolete and antiquated methodology, fiercely averse to any form of inductivism, but entered directly the experience-oriented scene of his time. However important this may be—and indeed is—for the further development of Schiller's thinking in the context of late-Enlightenment anthropology, psychology, and epistemology up to his later encounter with Kant, this was not all. For Jahn's contribution to Schiller's education in philosophy was not confined to the dedicated weekly hours, but encompassed instruction in rhetoric, poetry, and Classical languages as well, which included reading and commentary on such authors as Cicero and Horace (cf. NA, 41, IIa, p. 44). Given Jahn's commitment to a protreptic and anything but merely philological way of sharing his specialist competencies, it can legitimately be claimed that Schiller received part of his philosophical training in lessons officially devoted to other disciplines.

In 1775 Schiller profited from the fifteen hours delivered weekly by Bök in logic, metaphysics, and rhetoric, gaining insights into the most recent anthropological debates. Schiller's close friend and fellow student, Friedrich Wilhelm von Hoven, recalls Bök's class as highly interesting, and stresses in particular the teacher's stature as a "self-thinking philosopher" (von Hoven 1840/1984, p. 46). For the final examinations due in December 1775, Bök wrote a series of fifty *Theses disputatoriae* (*Disputatory Theses*, cf. Bök 1775c), and the dissertation *De sensuum hominis externorum perfectione* (*The Perfection of the Human Being's External Senses*, cf. Bök 1775a), both of which testify to his predilection for the latest developments in the fields of psychology, ethics, and aesthetics. Schiller was familiar with these texts and their content, which issued from the lessons given over the whole year, and had moreover to study them in

---

[13] For details on Jahn's service at the Ludwigsburg *Lateinschule* and his capacity to generate his students' enthusiasm, see Alt 2009, pp. 75–79.

order to prepare for the mandatory exams. Indeed, he figures among the students admitted to participate in the public discussion of Bök's *Theses* according to the newly introduced technique of disputation (cf. NA, 41, IIa, p. 83), although the dissertation's printed version does not list his name (cf. Bök 1775a).[14]

In 1774 and 1775, Schiller also attended courses in law, especially Roman law, and these were not limited to technical matters, but included the ideas of modern authors genuinely committed and contributing to philosophy such as Wolff. Yet it seems that Johann Georg Friedrich Heyd (1748–1834)—at that time the only professor of law at the *Karlsschule*—did not promote autonomous reflection and progressive trends among his students, but rather upheld a passive and conservative attitude.[15] This might be a reason for Schiller's lack of interest and success in the field. But however frustrating his two years as a law student may have been, mandatory reading of the relevant texts cannot have failed to raise his awareness of some crucial questions, and these are the same political and ethical concerns that permeate Schiller's entire work, both theoretical and literary, both before and after the French Revolution.[16]

In 1776, 1777, and 1780, Schiller attended Abel's courses in psychology, aesthetics, ethics, and the "history of humankind" (Riedel 1995, p. 401), which is likely to have encompassed Enlightenment's philosophies of history with a special focus on the development of politics, the economy, and the arts. Ferguson's *Essay on the History of Civil Society* (1766)—translated into German in 1768 and explicitly mentioned by Abel in 1776—may have played a role in this (cf. Riedel 1995, p. 158). Accordingly, Schiller figures among the *Respondentes* of Abel's *Theses philosophicae* (*Philosophical Theses*, 1776), of his *Dissertatio de origine characteris animi* (*Dissertation about the Origin of the Spirit's Character*, 1776), and of his *Aesthetische Säze* (*Aesthetic Theses*, 1777). He must also have known or been familiar with the content of Abel's *Theses philosophicae* (*Philosophical Theses*, 1780) and *Philosophische Säze über die Religionen des Alterthums* (*Philosophical Theses on the Religions of Antiquity*, 1780), although he is not to be found in the relevant discussants' list (which is not surprising, given that in 1780 Schiller was not officially studying philosophy but was reading it out of his own interest). In 1778, Schiller received no formal instruction in philosophy, which means that he did not come into direct

---

[14] Both theses and dissertations were usually printed with a list on the (back) cover enumerating the students participating in the public disputation, the only exception being Bök's *Theses disputatoriae* (*Disputatory Theses*), which have remained in manuscript form with no explicit indication of the author's name. Wolfgang Riedel deserves recognition for vindicating their role as a valuable source for research into Schiller's education, although he first connected them with Abel (Riedel 1985, p. 18) and only later came to see that they should be ascribed to Bök (Riedel 1995, p. 394). They have finally been made available in Stašková 2021, pp. 65-71.

[15] On Schiller's education in law, which has only recently attracted scholars' attention, see Nilges 2012, pp. 37-60.

[16] For useful insights into Schiller's treatment of political and juridical issues in his literary and theoretical work, see: High 2004; Müller-Seidel 2009; Nilges 2012; Foi 2013.

contact with Ploucquet, but it seems that this was to change in 1779, since he is reported to have attended Schwab's lessons in logic, metaphysics, and the history of philosophy, which happened probably in the latter's first year of activity (cf. Riedel 1995, p. 401). Therefore, Schiller may also have come across topics and problems addressed in Schwab's *Dissertatio logica de methodo analytica* (*Dissertation in logic about the method of analysis*) and his *Theses e logica et historia philosophica depromptae, adjunctis aliquot metaphysicis* (*Theses taken from logic, the history of philosophy, and additionally metaphysics*, 1779). Here key aspects of logic, the theory of knowledge, and metaphysics are dealt with (Schwab 1779a; Schwab 1779b), and also a chronological survey from the Pre-Socratics to Wolff is provided (cf. Schwab 1779b, §§ 28-40).

Besides all these various texts, written expressly for the final examinations, Schiller also had the opportunity to listen to the public speeches delivered at the end of each academic year by a professor chosen from the teaching staff. These included Bök's *Rede von der Ordnung als der Seele der Erziehung* (*Speech Regarding Order as the Soul of Education*), Abel's *Rede, über die Entstehung und die Kennzeichen grosser Geister* (*Speech about the Genesis and Characteristics of Great Spirits*, 1776), and also his *Seelenstärke ist Herrschaft über sich selbst* (*Fortitude of the Mind is Dominion over Oneself*, 1777).[17] And in addition to all this, Schiller was confronted with philosophical issues in the lessons of Johann Jakob Heinrich Nast (1722–1807) and Balthasar Haug (1731–1792), who covered, respectively, the fields of Ancient languages and German language and style, including logic, poetry, and rhetoric. The former was Jahn's successor, sharing his interest well beyond the philological, and so it comes as no surprise that his academic writings addressed current theories about the origin of language in Herder's aftermath,[18] or that in 1777 he proposed a genuinely philosophical topic for the final ceremonial speech—namely the nature and degree of the passions' influence on human actions—albeit unsuccessfully.[19] Haug, on the other hand, was well versed in current aesthetics and a particularly strong supporter of Sulzer's ideas, as is proved by his *Säzze über Teutsche Sprache, Schreibart und Geschmack* (*Theses about the German Language, the Art of Writing and Taste*, 1779), in whose discussion Schiller demonstrably participated (cf. Haug [1779], pp. [2], 7).

Evidently, all aspects of Schiller's education and life at the *Karlsschule* centered around philosophy, even on festive occasions and with courses not officially aimed at delivering instruction in the field. This may explain why he chose to direct his final dissertation in a philosophical direction. And his decision caused him to engage with lively questions from the fields of anthropology and ethics, as well as religion and metaphysics, as is evident from two texts

---

[17] For a fresh evaluation of these speeches in terms of both content and form, with a special focus on Bök's, see Stašková 2021, pp. 128-143.

[18] Again, it is Stašková's achievement (2021, pp. 113-115) to have revisited Nast's teaching as a fruitful stimulus for Schiller's further development well beyond philology and translation from Ancient Greek.

[19] Cf. Riedel 1985, p. 56n.

submitted to his professors in late 1779 and late 1780 for his final examination.[20] The first was originally written in German and presented in Latin, but both versions are now lost. The extant manuscript is a fragmentary German transcription by an unknown hand, entitled *Philosophie der Physiologie* (*Philosophy of Physiology*), and may offer a faithful, even if incomplete, rendition of the original, or otherwise a translation from the Latin version back into German. Be that as it may, the surviving chapter—originally one of five—is sufficient proof of Schiller's intellectual priorities and the scope of his knowledge. The title itself is suggestive enough, clearly indicating an ambition to provide not a strictly scientific sketch, but a theoretical piece about physiological issues. Not coincidentally, the first chapter is devoted to spiritual life, and its first paragraph launches straight into a highly popular topic of German-Enlightenment religion, ethics, and philosophy, namely the highly familiar *Bestimmung des Menschen*.[21] So Schiller opens his medical dissertation with considerations on happiness, perfection, and the purpose of human life—following here the theologian Spalding and the philosopher Mendelssohn[22]—introduces physiology into his text while dealing with the relationship of body and soul, and finally goes back to philosophy, particularly to Sulzer's psychology, with the distinction between "thinking [*Denken*]" and "feeling [*Empfinden*]" (NA, XX, p. 28).[23]

This text was unanimously rejected by Schiller's professors, who did not appreciate his excessive confidence in dismissing medical authorities (be it a character trait or a consequence of his training according to Enlightenment principles—or even both), and so Schiller remained one more year at the *Karlsschule*, during which he tellingly chose to attend Abel's class in psychology again. By his own account, his main preoccupation in this additional and final year as a student lay at the boundary between "the philosophical and physiological disciplines," and this is why for his dissertation he hesitated over whether to focus on either "the great connection between the *animal* and the *spiritual* nature of the human being" or "the freedom and morality of the human being" (NA, XXI, p. 124). Being well aware that the former was more suitable—in terms of methods and questions—for the degree he was about to obtain, he wisely opted in this direction, submitting in late 1780 his final dissertation *Versuch über den Zusammenhang der thierischen Natur des Menschen mit seiner geistigen* (*Essay on the Connection between the Animal and the Spiritual Nature of the Human Being*).

---

[20] On these and all the other writings from Schiller's time at the *Karlsschule*, see the dedicated chapter in this volume by Jeffrey L. High.

[21] For a general survey of the history of this key term in eighteenth-century German philosophy, I refer the reader to my monograph, Macor 2013.

[22] Cf. NA, XX, pp. 10-12. On this tradition of thought, see Pollok 2010; Beutel 2014, pp. 75-86; Jurewicz 2018. For the young Schiller's position in all this, see Macor 2010, pp. 31-44.

[23] Sulzer has long been acknowledged as being crucial to Schiller's thought and literary work, and scholars nowadays agree on crediting the education at the *Karlsschule* with a key role in this respect, cf. Riedel 1993; Hinderer 2003; Pirro 2006.

The introductory remarks aimed at the duke signal at the outset the crucial role attributed to philosophy, which alone is able to raise medicine from the status of "a mechanical, bread-winning science [*mechanische Brodwissenschaft*]," where the "physician" possesses merely a "historical knowledge of the machine," that is, knowledge confined to "terminology and location" of the different parts of the body and the relevant diseases (NA, XX, p. 38). These considerations echo those of Bök's 1775 speech about vocational disciplines running the risk, if taught wrongly, of forming "mechanical" practitioners incapable of any further insight (Bök 1775b, p. 9), which permits the conjecture that Schiller shared his friend von Hoven's positive impression of the speech in question and, most of all, of the speaker himself (cf. von Hoven 1840/1984, p. 46). It might not be a coincidence than in 1789 the newly appointed professor at the University of Jena would draw the familiar distinction between "bread-scholar [*Brodgelehrter*]" and "philosophical head [*philosophischer Kopf*]" in a way that closely resembles his youthful reflections on medicine and philosophy (NA, XVII, pp. 361-363). In the light of all this, it comes as no surprise that the dissertation's two parts are devoted to the physical and the philosophical, respectively, with the second containing twenty paragraphs as opposed to five in the first. Moreover, Schiller includes quotations from Ferguson and his translator and commentator Garve (cf. NA, XX, p. 52; Ferguson 1772),[24] and also refers to his own first play, *Die Räuber*, giving a fictitious title and likewise a fictitious author (cf. NA, XX, p. 60).[25]

Clearly, Schiller considered his medical training not to be a distraction from philosophy, but rather an opportunity for doing philosophy in a challenging way. Our attention turns now to what he learned and achieved in so doing, and to whether all of this was to have a long-term impact on his own intellectual activity.

Key Features of Schiller's Philosophical Attitude

Schiller's education has long been acknowledged as being pivotal to his further development. This applies particularly to his education in philosophy, which made him familiar with topics and authors he never abandoned nor forgot in his ensuing career as poet, playwright, and historian. Most importantly, his education in philosophy gave him the intellectual tools to contribute crucially to the philosophy of his own time as well as ours by furthering a very specific stance on things and remarkably constant interests.

Schiller was raised as a child of the Enlightenment, and he remained such after entering what looked like a totally different scene in 1789. The Kantian and post-Kantian atmosphere in Jena and Weimar did not in any sense dent his

---

[24] For further insight into Garve's translation of Ferguson, see the new essay by Falduto 2021.

[25] For the mutual relationship between philosophy and medicine in the German Enlightenment, and particularly in the works of the so-called "philosophical physicians" (*philosophische Ärzte*), see: Košenina 1989; Zelle 2001; Garber 2015.

previous priorities, which on the contrary formed the basis for both his receptivity to Kant's criticism and his contribution to early Idealism. That is to say, Schiller owed to the years spent at the *Karlsschule* much more than his by no means insignificant knowledge of ethics, aesthetics, epistemology, and even logic, being prompted thereby to develop his own individual and distinctive theoretical identity.

The first aspect worth mentioning is Schiller's adherence to Jahn, Bök, and Abel's ideas around autonomous thought, which underlie even his appropriation of Kant's philosophy. In his letters to his Maecenas, Prince von Augustenburg (1793), Schiller introduces "[t]he revolution that has occurred in the world of philosophy," namely, Kant's "fruitful philosophy," and clarifies that this is not to be thought of as a new authority impeding individual thought (NA, 26, pp. 184, 186; Schiller 2016, pp. 116, 117). In fact, anything depending "upon the judgement of *pure reason*" must be of "especial interest to anyone who can think for himself [*Selbstdenker*]," since "every man who can think for himself [*jeder selbstdenckende Mensch*]" is called to contribute, being "a participant in this Court of Reason" (NA, 26, pp. 260-261; Schiller 2016, p. 122). In other words, Kant's criticism is an occasion, or rather the ideal occasion to practice autonomous thought, and this is how Schiller in point of fact proceeds in his rethinking of the relevant theories. So he insists on the personal nature of the arguments he is about to present in the letters to the prince, since "*[m]y* philosophy," "*my own* reflection" may be lacking in some points or even turn out unconvincing, but in no case "on account of its sectarian nature." Should it end up failing: "it will fail because of its fragility, and not seek to uphold itself by appeal to *authority* and external assistance," be it even that of "Critical Philosophy" (NA, 26, pp. 257-258; Schiller 2016, p. 119: my italics).[26]

But this is not all. The legacy of the eight years spent studying first law and later medicine, but most of all philosophy, also helped Schiller develop two further enduring intellectual traits. His thinking in fact quickly became, and remained, genuinely anthropological and earthly in nature, as will be shown in what follows by a comparison between the early and mature writings.

Schiller supported a holistic approach to the human being, aimed at doing justice to both the physical and the rational component, and consequently, he opposed any blind perspective, be it materialist or spiritualist. In the first paragraph of his *Versuch über den Zusammenhang der thierischen Natur des Menschen mit seiner geistigen* (*Essay on the Connection between the Animal and the Spiritual Nature of the Human Being*), the young Schiller reconstructs how the philosophers of the past dealt with the relationship between the body and the soul, and traces the relevant positions back to two fundamental and contrasting views. On the one hand, the body has been considered "the prison of the spirit," preventing any "so-called flight to perfection"; on the other hand, "every human perfection" has been identified with "the improvement of the

---

[26] I have expanded on this line of thought and interpretation in Macor (2023).

body," with "science and virtue" serving merely as "means to happiness" (NA, XX, p. 40). Both approaches are deemed "one-sided [*einseitig*]" by Schiller, who furthermore claims that "nothing is so dangerous for truth than one-sided opinions being rejected by one-sided opponents," for the reason that "a balance between both doctrines is the most advisable option in order to meet the middle line of truth more surely" (NA, XX, p. 40).

In the fourth letter on aesthetic education, the mature Schiller holds the same view, implementing moreover very similar expressions and even the same adjective: "[i]n a unilateral [*einseitig*] moral evaluation [...] reason is satisfied as long as its laws are unconditionally observed," whereas "in entirely anthropological terms [...] both form and content are of importance and living sensation also has a voice" (NA, XX, p. 316; Schiller 2016, p. 11). "Reason furthers unity, but nature furthers diversity," with "both" laying "claim to man," and so it will be "proof of a deficiency of upbringing if moral character can prevail only by sacrificing the natural" (NA, XX, pp. 316-317; Schiller 2016, p. 11). Clearly, sensation is not to be dismissed, and neither is reason, but in 1780 as in 1795 Schiller insists on stressing the rights of nature only because in Western culture it is customary to overestimate "the power of the spirit" and think of it as "independent of the body," rather than give due attention to the contribution of the senses, and this calls for a counterbalance (NA, XX, p. 40).

So, Schiller's philosophy, both early and mature, is anthropological in nature, in that it encourages a holistic consideration of the human being, being indebted to disciplines which are apparently alien to philosophy such as physiology and medicine.

Alongside this, or perhaps as a consequence of it, Schiller developed a decidedly earthly attitude toward things, eventually abandoning religion and metaphysics, and confining his reflections to human agency in this world. This is evident from his very first literary work, published shortly after graduation but written toward the end of his time at the *Karlsschule*. The play *Die Räuber* (*The Robbers*, 1781) testifies to a process of disenchantment which would reach its conclusion in the late 1780s—at the very latest in the *Philosophisches Gespräch* (*Philosophical Dialogue*, 1789) of *Der Geisterseher* (*The Spiritualist*, 1787–1789)—but initiated in 1780 if not earlier.

In Schiller's debut theater piece, both Franz and Karl Moor express doubts about the theoretical credibility and consistency of the immortality of the soul and the idea of eternal justice, which contradict the anthropological assumptions learnt by the young student of medicine. Franz explicitly recalls the teachings of "[d]octors and philosophers" about "how finely the motions of the mind are attuned to those of the machine that houses it" (NA, III, 38; Schiller 1979, p. 56), and it follows from this that "our being is but a motion of the blood, and when the last drop of blood has ebbed, with it go mind and spirit too," *pace* any faith in the "immortal soul" (NA, III, pp. 121–122; Schiller 1979, p. 145). Karl, in turn, refers to "fancy, wilful ape of our senses," which "spins strange shadows to deceive our credulous mind" trembling in front of the "single moment" that links together "[t]ime and eternity" (NA, III, pp. 109–110; Schiller 1979, p. 131). But there is more, since religion undermines ethics too. Franz says that "those who have come off badly in this life put their trust in eternity; but they will find themselves horribly cheated" (NA, III, p. 121; Schiller 1979, p. 145), and Karl seems himself to fall victim to this theoretical short circuit, as he claims that "there is something more" after death, "*for* I have not yet known happiness" (NA, III, p. 109; Schiller 1979, p. 131: my italics). The "economic calculation" underlying such view is explicitly unearthed in Schiller's unfinished novel *Philosophische Briefe* (*Philosophical Letters*, 1786), whose core is unanimously thought to have been written at the *Karlsschule*.[27] The protagonist Julius is committed to reflecting on his most urgent preoccupations—namely God, eternity, and virtue, which he considers essential to any philosophical construction and, most importantly, to any successful organization of daily life—but ends up surrendering to the egoistical nature of religious ethics. "The assumption of immortality [...] disfigures the high grace" of virtue "for ever," since "consideration of a future reward" goes against morality, and this calls for "a virtue enduring even in the absence of any belief in immortality" (NA, XX, p. 122).

In the light of this, it is of little surprise that the mature Schiller never mentions—let alone endorses—Kant's practical "rehabilitation" of the immortality of the soul and God's existence in the *Kritik der praktischen Vernunft* (*Critique of Practical Reason*, 1788), and clearly expresses his doubts about including Christian religion in *Die Religion innerhalb der Grenzen der bloßen Vernunft* (*Religion within the Boundaries of Mere Reason*, 1793; cf. NA, XXVI, pp. 219, 235). The Kantian Schiller speaks the same language as his younger self: "[o]ur moral duties do not bind us in the same way a contract would do, but absolutely. Virtues, which are performed only in return for future goods have no value," for "virtue possesses *inner* necessity, even if there were no other life" (NA, XXII, p. 178). The only role Schiller is ready to accord to religion is apparently that of "a surrogate of true virtue," for those who are unable to follow moral prescriptions out of pure conviction and thus need external aid (NA, XXVI, p. 331).[28]

Both the predilection for anthropology and the dismissal of religion are key features of Schiller's thinking in the last decade of the eighteenth century, and they identify the defining traits of what is justly considered his specific contribution to philosophy. For at heart his plea for an aesthetic education rests on these two premises, being the consequence of a desire to do justice to the whole human being as well as provide an alternative to an otherworldly conception of perfection.[29] All of this goes back to the years spent at the *Karlsschule*.

---

[27] On the novel's genesis and related details, see the dedicated chapter in this volume by Antonino Falduto. For Schiller's further analysis, or rather deconstruction of this "economy of virtue," see also Macor 2017.

[28] For a comprehensive investigation into religion, aesthetics, and anthropology in Schiller's both early and mature works, see Burtscher 2014.

[29] On the close connection between anthropology, religious disillusionment, and aesthetics, see the pertinent contributions in this volume by Wolfgang Riedel and Violetta Waibel.

References

Abel, Jakob Friedrich. 1773. Schreiben an Herzog Carl Eugen von Württemberg über die Neugestaltung des Philosophieunterrichts auf der Solitude. Nebst einem "Entwurf zu einer Generalwissenschaft oder Philosophie des gesunden Verstandes zur Bildung des Geschmacks, des Herzens und der Vernunft". 13. Dec. 1773. In Riedel 1995, 15-20.

Abel, Jakob Friedrich. 1786/1985. *Einleitung in die Seelenlehre*. Stuttgart/Hildesheim-Zürich-New York: Mezler/Olms.

Abel and Schwab 1778/1779. Gründe, warum die bißher in der Carls-Akademie üblich gewesene Ordnung, die philosophische Disciplinen vorzutragen, in etwas abgeändert worden ist, auf gnädigsten Befehl Seiner Herzoglichen Durchlaucht vorgelegt, von den Professoren der Philosophie Abel und Schwab. In Riedel 1995, 397-399.

Alt, Peter-André. 2009 (first edition 2000). *Schiller. Leben—Werk—Zeit*, vol. I, München: Beck.

Beutel, Albrecht. 2014. *Johann Joachim Spalding. Meistertheologe im Zeitalter der Aufklärung*. Tübingen: Mohr Siebeck.

Bök, August Friedrich. 1775a. *De sensuum hominis externorum perfectione*. Stuttgart: Cotta.

Bök, August Friedrich. 1775b. *Rede von der Ordnung als der Seele der Erziehung, am Stiftungsgedächtnistage der Herzogl. Würtembergischen Militärakademie, den 14. Dec. 1775 in Gegenwart Seiner Herzoglichen Durchlaucht und des Hofes gehalten*. Stuttgart: Cotta.

Bök, August Friedrich. 1775c. *Theses disputatoriae*. In Stašková 2021, 65-71.

Burtscher, Cordula. 2013. Schiller, Hume und die Religionspsychologie. Zu dem Gedicht *Resignation* und dem Bücherbestand der Karlsschule zu Schillers Schulzeit. *Philosophical Readings. Online Journal of Philosophy* 5: 50-62.

Burtscher, Cordula. 2014. *Glaube und Furcht. Religion und Religionskritik bei Schiller*. Würzburg: Königshausen & Neumann.

de Boer, Karin and Prunea-Bretonnet, Tinca, ed. 2021. *The Experiential Turn in Eighteenth-Century German Philosophy*. London-New York: Routledge.

Dierse, Ulrich. 1995. Selbstdenken. In *Historisches Wörterbuch der Philosophie*, vol. IX, ed. Joachim Ritter and Karlfried Gründer, 386-392. Basel: Schwabe.

Falduto, Antonino. 2021. Schottische Aufklärung in Deutschland. Christian Garve und Adam Fergusons *Institutes of Moral Philosophy*. In *Christian Garve (1742–1798). Philosoph und Philologe der Aufklärung*, ed. Udo Roth and Gideon Stiening, 33-54. Berlin-Boston: de Gruyter.

Ferguson, Adam. 1772. *Grundsätze der Moralphilosophie. Uebersetzt und mit einigen Anmerkungen versetzt von Christian Garve*. Leipzig: Dyck.

Foi, Maria Carolina. 2013. *La giurisdizione delle scene. I drammi politici di Schiller*. Macerata: Quodlibet.

Franz, Michael, ed. 2005. *"...im Reiche des Wissens cavalieremente"? Hölderlins, Hegels und Schellings Philosophiestudium an der Universität Tübingen*. Tübingen-Eggingen: Hölderlin-Gesellschaft and Isele.

Garber, Jörn. 2015. Anthropologie. In: *Handbuch Europäische Aufklärung. Begriffe, Konzepte, Wirkung*, ed. Heinz Thoma, 23-40. Stuttgart-Weimar: Metzler.

Godel, Rainer. 2015. Deutsche Aufklärung. In *Handbuch Europäische Aufklärung. Begriffe, Konzepte, Wirkung*, ed. Heinz Thoma, 86-90. Stuttgart-Weimar: Metzler.

Haug, Balthasar. [1779]. *Säzze [...] über Teutsche Sprache, Schreibart und Geschmack*. Stuttgart: Mäntler.
High, Jeffrey L. 2004. *Schillers Rebellionskonzept und die Französische Revolution*. New York: Edward Mellen Press.
Hinderer, Walter. 2003. Friedrich Schiller und die empirische Seelenlehre. Bemerkungen über die Funktion des Traumes und das "System der dunklen Ideen". *Jahrbuch der deutschen Schillergesellschaft* 47: 187-213.
Hoven, Friedrich Wilhelm von. 1840/1984. *Lebenserinnerungen*, ed. Hans-Günther Thalheim and Evelyn Laufer. Berlin: Rütten & Loening.
Joeres, Ruth-Ellen. 1997. The German Enlightenment (1720-1790). In *The Cambridge History of German Literature*, ed. Helen Watanabe-O'Kelly, 147-201. Cambridge: Cambridge University Press.
Jurewicz, Grażyna. 2018. *Moses Mendelssohn über die Bestimmung des Menschen. Eine deutsch-jüdische Begriffsgeschichte*. Hannover: Wehrhahn Verlag.
Knaus, Johann Christoph. 1751 *Elementa Philosophiae Rationalis Sive Compendium Logicae. In Usum Publicum Scholarum Wirtembergicarum Adornatum*. Stuttgart: Erhard.
Košenina, Alexander. 1989. *Ernst Platners Anthropologie und Philosophie. Der "Philosophische Arzt" und seine Wirkung auf Johann Karl Wezel und Jean Paul*. Würzburg: Königshausen & Neumann.
Macor, Laura Anna. 2010. *Der morastige Zirkel der menschlichen Bestimmung. Friedrich Schillers Weg von der Aufklärung zu Kant. Von der Verfasserin aus dem Italienischen übersetzt, auf den neuesten Stand gebracht und erweitert*. Würzburg: Königshausen & Neumann.
Macor, Laura Anna. 2011. Un capitolo svevo del tardo illuminismo tedesco. Per un profilo biografico e intellettuale di Jakob Friedrich Abel (1751-1829). *Historia philosophica. An International Journal* 9: 25-46.
Macor, Laura Anna. 2013. *Die Bestimmung des Menschen (1748-1800). Eine Begriffsgeschichte*. Stuttgart-Bad Cannstatt: frommann-holzboog.
Macor, Laura Anna. 2017. The Bankruptcy of Love: Schiller's Early Ethics. *Publications of the English Goethe Society* 86/1: 29-41.
Macor, Laura Anna. (2023). "Sapere aude". Schiller's *Letters to Prince von Augustenburg* and Kant's *Answer to the Question: What Is Enlightenment?*. In *The Forms of Knowledge. New Essays on Classical German Philosophy*, ed. Faustino Fabbianelli. Berlin-Boston: de Gruyter.
Nilges, Yvonne. 2012. *Schiller und das Recht*. Göttingen: Wallstein.
Müller-Seidel, Walter. 2009. *Friedrich Schiller und die Politik. "Nicht das Große, nur das Menschliche geschehe"*. München: Beck.
Paimann, Rebecca. 2009. *Das Denken als Denken. Die Philosophie des Christoph Gottfried Bardili*. Stuttgart-Bad Cannstatt: frommann-holzboog.
Pirro, Maurizio. 2006. Sulzers Physik der Seele und die Dramentheorien Schillers. *Zeitschrift für Germanistik* NF 16/2: 314-323.
Ploucquet, Gottfried. 1782/2006. *Logik*, ed. Michael Franz. Hildesheim: Olms.
Pollok, Anne. 2010. *Facetten des Menschen. Zu Moses Mendelssohns Anthropologie*. Hamburg: Meiner.
Riedel, Wolfgang. 1985. *Die Anthropologie des jungen Schiller. Zur Ideengeschichte der medizinischen Schriften und der "Philosophischen Briefe"*. Würzburg: Königshausen & Neumann.

Riedel, Wolfgang. 1993. Die Aufklärung und das Unbewußte. Die Inversionen des Franz Moor. *Jahrbuch der deutschen Schillergesellschaft* 37: 198-220.
Riedel, Wolfgang. 1995. *Jacob Friedrich Abel. Eine Quellenedition zum Philosophieunterricht an der Stuttgarter Karlsschule (1773-1782). Mit Einleitung, Übersetzung, Kommentar und Bibliographie.* Würzburg: Königshausen & Neumann.
Riedel, Wolfgang. 1998. Schiller und die popularphilosophische Tradition. In *Schiller-Handbuch*, ed. Helmut Koopmann, 155-166. Stuttgart: Kröner.
Riedel, Wolfgang. 2011. Aus den Anfängen der Projektionspsychologie. J. F. Abels *Von den Reizungen, die die tote Natur durch die beseelte erhält* (1784). Mit Abdruck des Abelschen Essays. In *Schiller im philosophischen Kontext*, ed. Cordula Burtscher and Markus Hien, 9-28. Würzburg: Königshausen & Neumann.
Robert, Jörg. 2011. *Vor der Klassik. Die Ästhetik Schillers zwischen Karlsschule und Kant-Rezeption.* Berlin-Boston: de Gruyter.
Schiller, Friedrich. 1979. *The Robbers* and *Wallenstein*, ed. Francis J. Lamport. London: Penguin Books.
Schiller, Friedrich. 2016. *On the Aesthetic Education of Man and Letters to Prince Frederick Christian von Augustenburg*, transl. Keith Tribe, ed. Alexander Schmidt. London: Penguin Books.
Schwab, Johann Christoph. 1779a. *Dissertatio logica de methodo analytica.* Stuttgart: Cotta.
Schwab, Johann Christoph. 1779b. *Theses e logica et historia philosophica depromptae, adjunctis aliquot metaphysicis.* Stuttgart: Cotta.
Stašková, Alice. 2021. *Friedrich Schillers philosophischer Stil. Logik—Rhetorik—Ästhetik.* Paderborn-Leiden: Fink/Brill.
Stašková, Alice. 2022. Die Logik der Rhetorik in Schillers philosophischen Schriften. Überlegungen mit Blick auf die Quellen der Karlsschule. In *Schillers Feste der Rhetorik*, ed. Peter-André Alt and Stefanie Hundehege, 11-27. Berlin-Boston: de Gruyter.
Wübben, Yvonne. 2022. Friedrich Schillers Psychologie-Lehrbücher. Rhetorische und logische Vermittlung psychologischen Wissens (Chr. Wolff, J. Chr. Gottsched, J. G. Krüger, G. Ploucquet, J. F. Abel). In *Schillers Feste der Rhetorik*, ed. Peter-André Alt and Stefanie Hundehege, 55-88. Berlin-Boston: de Gruyter.
Zelle, Carsten, ed. 2001. *"Vernünftige Ärzte". Hallesche Psychomediziner und die Anfänge der Anthropologie in der deutschsprachigen Aufklärung.* Tübingen: Niemeyer.

PART II

Schiller's Theoretical Writings

CHAPTER 4

Writings from Schiller's Time at the Karlsschule in Stuttgart (1773–1780)

Jeffrey L. High

Schiller studied at the Hohe Karlsschule between Ludwigsburg and Stuttgart beginning in 1773, at first struggling while majoring in Law and then improving markedly only as of 1775 in his study of Medicine, finally receiving his doctorate on December 15, 1780 after his third attempt at a dissertation and comprehensive examinations. While a student, Schiller wrote two philosophical speeches—"Rede über die Frage: Gehört allzuviel Güte, Leutseeligkeit und grosse Freygebigkeit im engsten Verstande zur Tugend?" (Speech on the Question: Does all too much Kindness, Sociability, and great Generosity necessarily Constitute Virtue?, 1779) and "Die Tugend in ihren Folgen betrachtet" (The Consequences of Virtue Considered, 1779–1780). Both speeches were assigned by Carl Eugen, Duke of Württemberg (1728–1793) and written in praise of Franziska von Hohenheim (1748–1811)—the Duke's mistress from 1772 to 1785, when she became his second wife—on consecutive birthdays. In addition to the two philosophical speeches, Schiller wrote one minor case study on the depression of a classmate, "Über die Krankheit des Eleven Grammont" (On the Illness of Cadet Grammont, 1780), and three medical dissertations: his rejected first dissertation, *Philosophie der Physiologie* (Philosophy of Physiology, late 1779); his second unsatisfactory submission, *De discrimine febrium inflammatoriarum et putridarum* (On the Difference between Inflammatory and Putrid Fever, November 1780); and his third, successful submission, *Versuch ueber den Zusammenhang der thierischen Natur des*

J. L. High (✉)
California State University, Long Beach, CA, USA
e-mail: Jeffrey.High@csulb.edu

© The Author(s), under exclusive license to Springer Nature Switzerland AG 2023
A. Falduto, T. Mehigan (eds.), *The Palgrave Handbook on the Philosophy of Friedrich Schiller*, https://doi.org/10.1007/978-3-031-16798-0_4

Menschen mit seiner geistigen (Essay on the Connection between the Animal Nature and the Intellectual Nature of the Human Being, November 1780).

THE KARLSSCHULE SPEECHES

"*Rede über die Frage: Gehört allzuviel Güte, Leutseeligkeit und grosse Freygebigkeit im engsten Verstande zur Tugend?*"

Textual Genesis: Schiller's first composition on moral philosophy was written for the occasion of the celebration of the thirty-first birthday of Baroness Franziska von Hohenheim, held at the Karlsschule, which, according to Hohenheim's diary (Hohenheim, 16), Schiller delivered on 10 January 1779, two months after his nineteenth birthday on November 10. The speech demonstrates the distinct influence of Schiller's professors, including Balthasar Haug's (1731–1792) teachings on classical rhetoric (Alt, 102–103), the Enlightenment works taught by Jakob Friedrich Abel (1751–1829), foremost evident in the intertextual presence of Moses Mendelssohn's (1729–1786) book *Phädon, oder über die Unsterblichkeit der Seele* (Phaedo, or On the Immortality of the Soul, 1767), an adaptation of Plato's seventh dialogue on the death of Socrates. Freely invoking foremost pagan characters in examples of true virtuous acts, the speech also features allusions to Christ's "Sermon on the Mount" and the Old Testament tale of Absalom, as well as references to Friedrich Gottlieb Klopstock's (1724–1803) ode "Für den König" (For the King, 1753) and his epic poem *Der Messias* (The Messiah, 1748–1773). Schiller's speech also invokes Ossian's (James Macpherson) "Temora" (Song 1, 1763) in his description of its central figure Cathmor. According to Johann Wilhelm Petersen (1758–1815), Schiller's classmate and the co-editor of Schiller's first journal, *Wirtembergisches Repertorium der Litteratur* (Württembergian Repertorium of Literature, 1782–1783), the heated baroque punctuation and underlining of key terms in Schiller's first speech demonstrate the stylistic influence of revolutionary Stuttgart poet, publisher, and organist Christian Friedrich Daniel Schubart (1739–1791), as well as the Scottish Common Sense virtue theory in Johann Joachim Spalding's (1714–1804) 1745–1747 translation of Shaftesbury's (1671–1713) *The Moralists, a philosophical Rhapsody* (1705), Gotthold Ephraim Lessing's (1729–1781) 1756 translation of Francis Hutcheson's (1694–1746) *System of Moral Philosophy* (1755), and Christian Garve's (1742–1798) 1772 translation of Adam Ferguson's (1723–1816) *Institutes of Moral Philosophy* (1769; Alt, 104–105). The manuscript resides at the Schiller National Museum/German Literature Archive in Marbach in a bound manuscript including twenty-eight additional speeches by other cadets (*NA* 21: 107).

Contents: Schiller's First Virtue Speech presents the case for what constitutes virtue in three sections, the first presenting Socrates as history's greatest role model for virtue, the second presenting the case against the merely superficial appearance of virtuous acts driven by ulterior motives, and the third on the importance of an inner struggle accompanying the difficult choice to act virtuously, even when acting virtuously is personally disadvantageous. These three subsections are followed by a lengthy and unsteady summary in which Schiller performs a balancing act between the appearance of piety and a spirit of heresy.

In the opening of §1 of the speech (paragraphs 1–6), Schiller, responding to an order from the duke to serve as "Lobredner" (laudatory speaker), coins a guiding construct for both his future critical thought and artistic production. Regarding the reciprocal relationship between inner freedom and happiness, in paragraph 1 and paragraph 2, Schiller poses the teleologically informed question: what distinguishes virtue from vice in the case of superficially laudable acts—"die schimmernde That vor dem Auge der Welt" (the glittering deed before the eyes of the world; NA 20: 3). Schiller finds the answer in "die innere Quelle der That" (the moral source of the deed; NA 20: 3), which he glosses as "Liebe zur Glückseligkeit" (love of happiness; NA 20: 3). As in his later writings, "der scharfsehende Verstand" (the sharp insight of reason [later *Formtrieb*; formal drive]; NA 20: 3), checking "Neigung" (impulse and inclination [later *Stofftrieb*; material or sense drive]; NA 20: 3), guides the moral decision-making process. Reason tests each choice according to whether it will lead to "höherer zu weiterumfaßender Glükseligkeit" (higher, more widespread happiness NA 20: 3) than its alternatives. To this moral formula, Schiller adds the measure of greater and lesser virtue: "Je heller also, je gewaltiger, je dringender die gegenseitige Neigung desto höherer Verstand—desto höhere Liebe—desto höhere Tugend" (The more vibrant, more powerful, more urgent the opposing inclinations, the greater the reason demonstrated—the higher love—the greater virtue; NA 20: 3). If the love of higher happiness (i.e., universal and moral happiness), which requires selfless conduct on the level of the individual, guides the subject in all choices between competing inclinations regarding virtue and vice, then the gravest and most extreme and thus most graphic moral act is the free choice to die in the name of virtue and freedom rather than to live an unfree life of enslavement (be the coercion external or internal). In paragraph 3, Schiller argues that the defining moment in the history of moral choice is Socrates' decision to choose death over coercion as a contribution to the freedom and happiness of all. According to Schiller's introductory formula, Socrates' "höchster Kampf" (greatest struggle; NA 20: 4) culminates in the reconciliation of competing inclinations of reason (toward higher happiness) and of the most basic of natural sensual drives (e.g., toward survival). Since there can be no more "entsezliche Freyheit" (terrible freedom), no clearer demonstration of self-determination or "höchster Verstand" (highest reason; NA 20: 4) than the choice between two inclinations that results in the most disadvantageous personal consequences, it follows that the choice of one's own death best demonstrates the reconciliation of duty and desire and the greatest possible freedom from sensual-physical coercion. In paragraphs 4–6, §1, Schiller concludes with a definition of virtue, which is also Schiller's formula for altruism: "Liebe zur Glükseeligkeit, geleitet durch den Verstand—Tugend ist das harmonische Band von Liebe und Weißheit!" (Love of happiness, guided by reason—virtue is the harmonious band that unites love and wisdom; NA 20: 4). The definition of virtue as the harmony of love and wisdom, which constitutes the thesis as well as the metaphorical leitmotif of the speech, appears another four times, at least once in each segment of the speech (*NA* 20: 4, 5, 6, 8).

In §2 (paragraphs 7–11), Schiller, like Shaftesbury and Hutcheson before him, strictly differentiates between the moral inspiration of a deed and its reception, and thus between true virtue and the mere appearance of virtue masking ulterior motives. To illustrate the political application of the idea that the end of virtue is happiness of the whole, Schiller contrasts Socrates' sublime reconciliation of reason and sensuality (ennobled reason)—the measure of totality of character—with a world history of tyrants and rebels, again, at least partially lifted from Hutcheson and Ferguson. The contrastive analysis of the actions of the tyrants and rebels demonstrates a lacking totality of character in each of them, which results in moral perversions marked either by a dangerously one-sided dictatorship of sensuality (here love) or of theoretical reason (here wisdom). Schiller proceeds to analyze these exempla according to the Socrates criterion, that is, whether or not their actions advanced the goal of humankind, namely happiness of the whole. The actions of the tyrants and rebels are divided into two clear categories: actions dominated by abstract reason unchecked by feeling, and actions dominated by sensuality unchecked by reason. The actions break down as follows in terms similar to those in Mendelssohn's description of the sophists—"Geiz, Ehrfurcht oder Wollust" (greed, awe, or lasciviousness; Mendelssohn, 7–8): 1) actions dictated by reason—François Ravaillac's regicide and Catiline's arsonist murder represent "verlarvtes Laster" (paragraph 10; vice in disguise; *NA* 20: 5); and 2) actions dictated by sensuality—Julius Caesar's entertainment of the masses with games and gifts represents "Herrschsucht" and "Ehrgeiz" (paragraph 8; hunger for power and ambition; *NA* 20: 5), while Augustus Caesar's desire to become immortal represents "wollüstiges Gefühl" (paragraph 9; lasciviousness; *NA* 20: 5), and Absolom's embrace of the lowest citizens represents "Durst nach Herrschaft" (paragraph 10; thirst for domination; *NA* 20: 5). According to Schiller's argument, acts that may appear to contribute to the happiness of the whole, such as rebellion against tyranny, often prove not to be motivated by virtue after all, but by selfish drives of the mind or the body that actually threaten the happiness of the whole. Throughout, Schiller restates his thesis, concluding of his tyrants and rebels that either, "Hier also war Güte die Larve des in der Tiefe der Seele laurenden Lasters" (paragraph 11; Thus here, kindness was merely masking vice lurking deep in the soul; *NA* 20: 5), or "Hier war die Güte mit Weißheit aber nicht mit Liebe im bund" (paragraph 11; Here kindness was in league with wisdom [reason] but not with love [feeling]; *NA* 20: 5).

§3, on moral resistance (paragraphs 12–16), represents one of the great masterpieces of Schillerian double-speak, a skill that was evidently as valuable at the Hohe Karlsschule as it would prove to be in Schiller's dealings with censors. Indeed, it is baffling why it took until 1788 for Schiller to be accused of outright blasphemy. Returning to his description of Socrates' decision to choose death before coercion as "höchster Kampf" (paragraph 3), Schiller introduces the measure of "Kampf der Seele" (paragraph 13; inner moral struggle; *NA* 20: 6) as the measure of virtue: "Die schönste That ohne Kampf begangen hat gar geringen Werth gegen derjeningen die durch großen Kampf errungen ist" (paragraph 13; The most beautiful deed done without struggle has precious little worth when compared to that which is achieved through great struggle; *NA* 20: 6). A person with all the trappings of wealth runs no risk in an act of charity, indeed, such a person is likely to gain from such an act, thus there is no "Gegengewicht" (counterbalance) to the "Neigung Wohlzuthun" (paragraph 13; inclination to do good; *NA* 20: 6), and the act is merely superficially good, but not virtuous. Following the order of considerations in his title, Schiller proceeds to address whether "Leutseligkeit" (sociability) necessarily constitutes virtue. According to the established formula, "jene Großer dort der seinen Adel seine Hoheit von sich legt" (paragraph 14; that particular person of importance there, who sets aside his nobility, his highness; *NA* 20: 6) and fraternizes with the common man, does not demonstrate virtue, because he lacks "das Gefühl *eigener innerer Erhabenheit*" (paragraph 14; the feeling of *one's own inner sublimity*; *NA* 20: 6) that would serve as a counterbalance to an empty act of sociability, since such an encounter likely serves only to inflate his pride: "So ist demnach allzuviel Güte und Leutseligkeit und große Freygebigkeit das harmonische Band von Liebe und Weißheit nicht;—so hat sie keinen Kampf gekostet; [...] Sie ist nicht *Tugend!*" (paragraph 15; Therefore, all too much kindness, sociability, and great generosity does not constitute the harmonious band between love and wisdom—for it cost no struggle [...] This is not *virtue!*; *NA* 20: 7).

In the conclusion (§4), it is difficult to overlook the subversive irony that the "Lobredner" Schiller showers both the Duke and his extra-marital partner Hohenheim with praise, though neither were popular with the students, and that he does so in terms that parallel his description of Socrates directly after he had disqualified self-serving gestures of sociability by the privileged toward the lower classes from the category of truly virtuous acts. The speech ends with a brazenly disingenuous vision of mourning, in which first "die Söhne der Zukunft" (the sons of the future) weep at Carl Eugen's funeral (a "Fest" or celebration), and then yet another future generation searches—evidently in vain—through the gravestones for those of "Wirtembergs trefflicher Carl" (Württemberg's worthy Carl) and "Franziska, die Freundin der Menschen" (Franziska, the friend, [or girlfriend] of humanity; *NA* 20: 9).

Philosophical Significance and Impact: Although the First Virtue Speech has been widely overlooked by scholars, it could hardly be more significant for Schiller's later literary, philosophical, and political thought. Schiller quietly lays the philosophical foundation for a life-long program to promote a reasoned, secular alternative to a faith-based role model, embarking from and concluding with the thesis that the destiny of humankind is happiness, and the path to happiness is virtue, both of which rely on what became the familiar Schillerian connection between moral rationalism and sensual foundation (Alt, 106).

What qualifies Socrates above all others as not only "den erhabensten Geist, den je das Altertum gebahr" (paragraph 3; the most sublime thinker whom the ancient world ever bore; *NA* 20: 3), but also the individual who accomplished the most sublime deed—"Erhabner nichts unter hohem, bestirntem Himmel vollbracht!" (Nothing more sublime was ever done under the great starry heavens; *NA* 20, 4)—is his rejection of belief in a reward in the afterlife—later, the *Augustenburg Letters* (1793), "ein Surrogat der wahren Tugend" (a surrogate for true virtue; *NA* 26: 330–31)—and his demonstration that dutifully giving one's only life without the comfort of a belief in the afterlife—as opposed to abandoning a dreary prelude to a blissful life after death—for the sake of the future happiness of others, is the most extreme test of virtue. Schiller returns to the singularity of this test in the subsequent paragraphs and in four later portrayals of Socrates' wisdom and his willingness to die for his principles in works on aesthetics and morality between 1786 and 1795: "Brief eines reisenden Dänen" (Letter from a Traveling Dane, 1786; *NA* 20: 106), *Über die tragische Kunst* (On Tragic Art, 1791; *NA* 20: 106), *Ästhetische Briefe* (Aesthetic Letters, *NA* 20: 338–339), and *Über Naive und Sentimentalische Dichtung* (On Naive and Sentimental Poetry, 1795; *NA* 20: 447).

The First Virtue Speech begins not only a decades-long pursuit of happiness through art intended to resonate and effect change in the sphere of public authority, but also the approach to moral philosophy and politics through the aesthetic. The enduring presence of Scottish Enlightenment eudaimonism and reconciliation philosophy in Schiller's thought is nowhere more evident than in the First Virtue Speech, which features the key concepts of disinterested virtue, the role of virtue in the perfection of the individual and civil society, and the means and end of happiness as the destiny of humankind. The parade of imbalanced tyrants and rebels presented in the text—Julius Caesar, Augustus Caesar, Ravaillac, and Catiline (*NA*, 20: 4–6), partially lifted from Hutcheson and Ferguson—very closely follow Shaftesbury's thesis that not all "good" acts are necessarily virtuous (Shaftesbury, *Characteristics*, volume II, part II, §I, 29–30); each stands in negative contrast to the stoic model of a ruler, Marcus Aurelius (*NA* 20: 8). The story of Absolom, the biblical son of King David, who conspired against his father and was killed during the coup attempt of his father, Officer Joab, has many of the elements of Schiller's dramas *Die Verschwörung des Fiesko zu Genua* (The Conspiracy of Fiesco at Genoa) and *Don Karlos*; Socrates' sublime composure and autonomy in the face of death parallels those of Marquis Posa in *Don Karlos*, Maria Stuart, and Johanna in *Die Jungfrau von Orleans* (The Maid of Orleans); Ravaillac's murder of a tyrant mirrors Fiesko's revolutionary hunger for power in *Fiesko*, and Catiline mirrors both Fiesko's hunger for power as well as Karl Moor's terror campaign in *Die Räuber* (The Robbers).

Already in the portrayal of Socrates' "entsezliche Freyheit" (paragraph 3) as the model of the dramatic sublime, Schiller establishes the paradigms for his later essays on drama theory and the sublime. A number of the features of the text call into question oversimplified views of Kant's influence on Schiller. The reconciliation philosophy model of the text's motto has essentially the same component and structures that mark his post-Kantian works, for example, in his 1784 speech, "Was kann eine gute stehende Schaubühne eigentlich wirken?" (What Effect Can a Good Permanent Theatre Actually Achieve?), Schiller expands the band between wisdom and love, and that between intellectual and animal nature, to address the "ästhetische[n] Sinn, oder das Gefühl für das Schöne" (aesthetic sense or sense for beauty), which makes possible "einen mittleren Zustand" (an intermediary state; NA 20: 90) or harmonic resolution of drives. In the final line of his Winter 1792–1793 Jena lecture on aesthetics, *Allgemeingültigkeit des Geschmacksurtheils* (Universal Validity of the Judgment of Taste): "Das Schöne ist das Mittelglied zwischen Sittlichkeit und Sinnlichkeit" (The beautiful is the mediator between morality and sensuality; NA 21: 81). The formula for the moral-aesthetic judgment of tyrants appears again in Schiller's *Philipp der Zweite, König von Spanien* (Philipp II, King of Spain, 1786), an adaptation of Louis Sébastien Mercier's (1740–1814) treatment of the same (1785), in which Philipp, like all rulers, is judged by the measure of his virtue and contribution to the happiness of the whole. In his best-selling history book, *Geschichte des Abfalls der Niederlande von der Spanischen Regierung* (History of the Revolt of the Netherlands against Spanish Rule, 1788), Schiller invokes the familiar condemnation of the conqueror of his second published poem, "Der Eroberer" (The Conqueror, 1777), in contrasting the revolutionary virtue of the Dutch with "schimmernden Thaten der Ruhmsucht und einer verderblichen Herrschbegierde" (glimmering deeds of the quest for glory and a destructive desire to dominate; NA 17: 10), both products of an imbalance of drives (see below).

Arguably, an important aspect if not the main focus of each of Schiller's subsequent theoretical treatises is the common sense conviction that both the end and the means—the regulative moral principle—of humanity is autonomy and happiness of the whole through autonomy and happiness of the individual, appearing as the end of all human pursuits in *Die Räuber* (III, 2; NA 3: 78); in *Die Schaubühne als moralische Anstalt betrachtet* (The Stage Considered as Moral Institution, 1784; NA 20: 88); in *Philosophische Briefe* (Philosophical Letters, 1786; NA 20: 107); in *Ueber die tragische Kunst* (On Tragic Art, 1790–1792). In *Ueber den Grund des Vergnügen an tragischen Gegenständen* (On the Reason for the Enjoyment of Tragic Objects, 1792; NA 20: 133), it is nature's end for humans that they be happy and in *Ueber Anmuth und Würde* (On Grace and Dignity, 1793; NA 20: 149), the "Glückseligkeitstrieb" (drive to pursue happiness; NA 20: 282) drives the human individual's decisions (NA 20: 282). It takes Schiller an entire two and a half sentences to get to the regulative idea of the *Ästhetische Briefe*, which is "happiness" (NA 20: 309). Schiller likewise revisits his analysis of the "moral source of the deed" repeatedly in both drama and theory, no more clearly than in his letter to Augustenburg of July 13, 1793 and in the *Ästhetische Briefe*, in which he describes the paradoxical gulf between the "Inhalt" (motivation), "Verhandlungsart" (act itself), and "Folgen" (consequences) of rebellion, employing the now sixteen-year-old "band that unites wisdom and love" again in the context of rebellion, specifically the French Revolution, which demonstrates the dictatorship of reason in its leaders and the dictatorship of sensuality in its followers. Where the abstract theoretical human being, Schiller concludes, is capable of rationalizing diabolical disregard for humanity, the sensual human being can fall no deeper than to an animal state (*NA* 26: 263), both due to a lack of "Totalität des Charakters" (totality of character; *NA* 20: 318).

"Die Tugend in ihren Folgen betrachtet" (The Consequences of Virtue Considered, 1779–1780)

Textual Genesis: As was the case with the first Karlsschule speech on virtue of 1779, Schiller's second came in response to an assignment directly from Duke Carl Eugen of Württemberg to write a speech in honor of Baroness Franziska von Hohenheim for the celebration of her (thirty-second) birthday on January 10, 1780, two months after Schiller's twentieth birthday on November 10, 1779. In contrast to the first speech, the second speech topic was assigned to only twelve cadets, and Schiller's speech was among those chosen to be delivered in person on Hohenheim's birthday. The source for the widely available print version of the speech is a bound manuscript that appears to have been written by Schiller's classmate Friedrich von Hoven (1759–1838), which was first published in 1839 (*NA* 21: 122). Here, more specifically than in the first speech, Schiller alludes to the works of the greatest "Weisen dieses Jahrhunderts" (thinkers of this century; NA 20: 32), his Scottish Enlightenment paradigms Shaftesbury, Ferguson, Hutcheson, and Adam Smith. Ferguson, in particular, who is also cited in a similar context in paragraph 2 of Schiller's first rejected dissertation, *Philosophie der Physiologie* (1779), prefigures Schiller's concept of an anthropological drive to progress from the animal nature of the human being toward a teleological concept of inevitable moral refinement. Schiller was likewise familiar with earlier iterations of this model evident in the thought of Gottfried Wilhelm Leibniz (1646–1716) and Christian Wolff (1679–1754; *NA* 21: 122), who also proposed a teleological development from the egoism of a state of nature toward an altruistic community of morally educated individuals.

Contents: The Second Virtue Speech comprises an essay of seven book pages, including an opening address to the duke (paragraph 1) followed by an introduction addressed to Hohenheim (paragraph 2); §1, "Folgen der Tugend auf das Ganze" (Consequences of Virtue for the Collective); §2, "Folgen der Tugend auf den Tugendhaften selbst" (Consequences of Virtue for the Virtuous Individual); and a closing address to Hohenheim (paragraph 15). In the opening address to the duke, Schiller specifically characterizes his speech as a response to the duke's assignment, and declares the topic entirely worthy of one who, surrounded by jubilating youth, appears to embody the motto—"*o daß ich alle glüklich machen könnte!*" (Oh, that I were able to make everyone happy; *NA* 20: 30). Following this dubious characterization of the duke—whose university the writer Schubart described as a "Sklavenplantage" (slave plantation)—Schiller introduces the parameters and operative terms of the speech, namely that the task alone warms a youthful heart to devotion to "den göttlichen" (the divine, *NA* 20: 30), due to the "Aussicht in ihre erhabene Folgen" (the prospects of its sublime consequences), namely "nur Vollkommenheit, nur Glükseeligkeit" (only perfection, only happiness; *NA* 20: 30). With this equation of perfection and happiness, Schiller delivers a second guiding construct for his thought looking forward—following love of happiness as the source of all moral action in the first speech—the secularist conviction that virtuous earthly happiness is the decidedly secular teleological end of the human being. Virtue makes the human being the "Abglanz der unendlichen Gottheit" (reflected glory of the infinite deity; *NA* 20: 30), which itself is a projection of human ideals; virtue is the most divine aspiration in that it mirrors the order of nature; and happiness arrived at through virtue is the highest conceivable form of human perfection.

In the introduction and address to Hohenheim (paragraphs 2–4), Schiller, who famously self-identified as a "Weltbürger" (citizen of the world) in 1784 (*NA* 22: 93), considers all human beings as "Bürger des grosen Weltsystems" (citizens of the great universe; *NA* 20: 30), declaring that the value of such a citizen can only be measured according to the positive or negative influence one exerts on the "Vollkommenheit dieses Systems" (perfection of this system; *NA* 20: 30). Since, according to Schiller, the harmony of the driving forces of the system self-evidently serves to promote the development of the sentient members of creation toward perfection (happiness), the morality of any given act can only be measured by the contribution to the "Vollkommenheit der geistigen Weesen" (perfection of the thinking beings; *NA* 20: 30–31), that is to say, to their happiness. In a rhetorical run reminiscent of the doublespeak in the First Virtue Speech, Schiller proposes that perfection is "Verherrlichung der Gottheit" (Glorification of the deity; *NA* 20: 31) and proceeds in the next sentence to define this concept of the divine not in Judeo-Christian terms, but as "Übereinstimmung mit den Eigenschaften der Gottheit" (correspondence to the characteristics of the deity; *NA* 20: 31), which he then defines as "Vollkommenheit der Geisterwelt" (perfection of the sentient-rational realm; *NA* 20: 31), which, in turn, does not require a god at all. Indeed, the "Weesen des Unendlichen" (nature of the infinite) again rings sufficiently and scientifically Deist, but in no sense religious, as the speech satisfies coercive religio-political expectations while driving the topic toward secular moral philosophy. Schiller then states with all clarity that his actual topic concerns beings "in der empfindenden und denkenden Natur" (in sentient and rational nature; *NA* 20: 31). The speech takes an important aesthetic turn when Schiller argues the case in terms of Ferguson's gravitation analogy: "Kraft dieses Gesezes wird uns das allezeit ergözen, was das Ganze vollkommener, das allezeit schmerzen müssen, was das Ganze unvollkommener macht" (By virtue of this law, we will always be delighted by what makes the whole more perfect, and will always experience pain at what makes the whole less perfect; *NA* 20: 31), which appears almost word for word in his first dissertation (*NA* 20: 11). The general consequence of virtue—happiness of the collective—contributes to a second, more personal, consequence, namely the happiness of the individual who acts virtuously.

Schiller summarizes §1 by introducing §2: a virtuous condition is that of a "weiser wohlwollender Geist" (wise sentient-rational being of good will; *NA* 20: 32) who can make other minds more perfect, the clearly less important consequence of which is that the former also attains happiness through an act of virtue.

In §1, "Folgen der Tugend auf das Ganze" (Consequences of Virtue for the Whole; paragraphs 5–9), Schiller embarks from Ferguson's gravitation analogy to argue that as in the realm of physics, so in the sentient-rational realm, the universal band of love bonds one human spirit to another. Love is the dynamic force of creation that drives the created, and that uplifts the individual "zum unendlichen Schöpfer" (to the infinite creator; *NA* 20: 32). Love unites the realm "aller denkenden Naturen" (of all thinking beings; *NA* 20: 32) under one organizing metaphorical moral and physical prime mover, here "Eines alli-ebenden Vaters" (One all-loving father; *NA* 20: 32). Schiller proposes that, as in the "Körperwelt" (physical realm) without the law of gravity; without love, the sentient realm would run riot "in anarchischem Aufruhr" (in anarchical turmoil; *NA* 20: 32). Just as love is the first drive after mere survival, the first effect of the interconnection of all thinking beings is "gegenseitige Ausbildung der Seelenfähigkeiten" (reciprocative formation of intellectual competencies; *NA* 20: 32) toward perfection, that is, happiness. Here, knowledge flows from one to another, sharp powers of reason correct crude conviction, the fire of youth is tempered by deliberate earnestness, and bilateral exchange of insights leads to mature reason, and ignites "Tugendliebe" (love of virtue; *NA* 20: 33). Thus, "Vollkommenheit der höheren Geisteskraft" (perfection of higher rational power; *NA* 20: 33) is the first consequence of the interconnection of all thinking beings through love. In paragraph 3 of §1, Schiller addresses the struggle between advancement and regression of humankind on the level of the individual, progressing from the love of parent to progeny, to that of the philosopher to an abandoned child, to a series of historical and legendary examples including Antonin, Trajan, Lykurgus, Montesquieu, Gellert, Haller, and Addison. Such examples that can enlighten a progression of human generations and races "mit dem Lichte der Wahrheit" (with the light of truth; *NA* 20: 33), that is, bring them closer to their sublime end, which has been established as happiness of the collective through happiness of the individual. Conversely, the vice of one individual (e.g., La Mettrie or Voltaire) can poison the minds of a thousand vulnerable individuals and cast a progression of human generations and races "in das barbarische Dunkel tierischer Wildheit" (into the barbaric darkness of animal savagery; *NA* 20: 33). In the final two paragraphs of §1 (paragraphs 8–9), Schiller returns to his function as laudatory speaker and restates the case in praise of the duke as the aforementioned father—a "vollkommener Geist" (perfectly sentient-rational thinker; *NA* 20: 34) who, himself inspired by "Allmächtige Tugend" (Almighty Virtue [herself]; *NA* 20: 34), transforms a "bildungslose[ ] Jugend" into the next Solon or Plato—who benefits from the virtuous support of the baroness. Here, as in the First Virtue

Speech and below, Schiller dedicates a conspicuous degree of attention to future generations gathered around the grave of the duke and the baroness: "Thränen des Danks auf Ihre Asche" (Tears of gratitude on your ashes; *NA* 20: 35).

In §2, "Folgen der Tugend auf den Tugendhaften selbst" (Consequences of Virtue for the Virtuous Individual; paragraphs 10–12), Schiller returns to a focus of the First Virtue Speech, the "Flittergold[] unwürdiger Thaten" (the tinsel of dishonorable deeds; *NA* 20: 35) masquerading as virtue. Since providence provides for happiness to result even from vice, Schiller concludes that the "innere Folgen" (inner consequences; *NA* 20: 35) of virtue, though unseen, result in clear sublimity of character and purpose that would force a conqueror like Alexander the Great to flee even in the midst of victory, or free the philosopher to be happy even when languishing in prison. Although Schiller argues here that many would act entirely immorally if the internal and external consequences of virtue were not heavenly and those of vice hellish, he quickly returns to the argument in the First Virtue Speech that a system of reward and punishment can only lead to a simulation of virtue. The inner consequences of virtue—"Ruhe der Seele" (composure of spirit), "Stärke des Geists" (intellectual fortitude), "Selbstgewisheit" (self-certitude), and an "unerschütterter Karakter" (unshaken disposition; *NA* 20: 35)—provide defense against all travails, and make possible freedom in the face of tyranny—be it in the form of internal coercion of drives or the external coercion of the villain. As was the case in the First Virtue Speech, Schiller provides exempla of such composure: a Regulus can cheerfully face a barbaric death while the Caesars of this world tremble beneath their crowns; Seneca has peace of mind while remorse hounds the tyrants; and when a tyrant like Domitian threatens the rule of law, every moral sensation will bear the menacing witness "des Rächers" (of the avenger), and conscience and the judgment of history "sich erheben" (rise up; *NA* 20: 36) against the wicked.

In the transitional final lines of §2 (paragraph 12) and in the closing paragraph of the speech (paragraph 13), Schiller delivers yet another characteristically dubious address to Hohenheim. The happiness that comes from an inner experience of virtue has the consequence that it selflessly "eine Welt um sich beglükt" (makes happy a world around oneself; *NA* 20: 36), placing the truly virtuous character in a sublime sphere high above "alle Lobsprüche" (any laudation; *NA* 20: 36). The precise logic of the final paragraph concludes in two short and pregnant sentences that everything Hohenheim in fact possesses—"Irdische Belohnungen" (earthly rewards), "Sterbliche Kronen" (mortal crowns), and Schiller's assigned task of delivering "die erhabenste Jubellieder" (the most sublime songs of joy; *NA* 20: 36) on two of her consecutive birthdays—is beneath the dignity of virtue, and, unlike true, historic acts of virtue, fade away in death, constituting Schiller's third curious invocation of her death in the two Virtue Speeches (*NA* 20: 9, 35, 36).

Philosophical Significance and Impact: As in the First Virtue Speech, Schiller's Second Virtue Speech draws heavily on the works of earlier philosophers from the ancient Greek as well as German and Scottish Enlightenment traditions. The tradition of Aristotelian eudaimonist virtue ethics, in which every action either contributes to the end of the happiness of the collective or does not, provides a common thread. The results of decisions and actions are not measured by utility, but by the moral source of the deed regardless of the results, as is frequently the case in Schiller's tragedies. In the First Virtue Speech and his first dissertation, *Philosophie der Physiologie*, Schiller had already grounded his moral aesthetics in Scottish terms closely resembling Ferguson's gravitation analogy. According to Ferguson, it is human nature to be attracted to that which causes pleasure and to be repelled by that which causes pain (*NA* 20: 11), and by this point, Schiller had also already cited Garve's translation of Ferguson's *Institutes of Moral Philosophy*, likewise in the first dissertation (*NA* 20: 30–36). The chain-of-being philosophy, reminiscent of Alexander Pope's (1688–1744) *Essay on Man* (1733–1734; Alt, 108), becomes a staple of Schiller's theoretical and poetic works, which repeatedly invoke the connection between the pursuit of happiness of the ant or the worm and the human being, notably in "An die Freude" (Ode to Joy, 1785/1786). The notion of perfection presented in the speech most closely resembles Ferguson's *An Essay on the History of Civil Society* (1767, published in German in 1768), in which Ferguson argues that even the "rudest state of mankind" distinguished itself through the "desire of perfection" (Ferguson I: 1, 13). Ferguson, like Shaftesbury and Hutcheson before him, equated the measure of perfection with the happiness achieved. Ferguson's *An Essay on the History of Civil Society* is informed throughout by the postulates, "to diffuse happiness, is the law of morality" (Ferguson I: 6, 62) and "the happiness of individuals is the great end of civil society" (Ferguson I: 9, 95), notions Schiller clearly adopts here.

The model of the sublime, as illustrated in the example of Socrates in the First Virtue Speech, returns in the portrayal of a series of exempla of historic acts of virtue. At its moral-aesthetic extreme, Schiller repeatedly cites the willingness to die for the freedom and happiness of others as an ideal of the sublime that later informed his treatises *Vom Erhabenen* (Concerning the Sublime, 1793) and *Über das Erhabene* (On the Sublime, 1794–96/1801). Schiller's aesthetic focus becomes most evident at the beginning of §2, in which he invokes the conqueror figure featured in his second published poem, "Der Eroberer" (The Conqueror, 1777), as well as the concept of the sublime addressed in the portrayal of the death of Socrates in the First Virtue Speech written in 1778. Indeed, although Socrates is not mentioned by name in the Second Virtue Speech, the descriptions of sublime sacrifice close with an allusion to the portrayal of his death, and the feeling of terrible and divine freedom that accompanies the experience of "einige Stralenzüge der Gottheit getroffen zu haben (to have touched just some rays of the deity; *NA* 20: 36)"—the rare ability to follow "zum Pfade der Seeligkeit ein zitternder Schein" (a quivering ray leading to the path of happiness; *NA* 20: 3) that leads an individual to choose freedom through reason regardless of personal consequences. This "hohe[ ] Bestimmung" (lofty destiny; *NA* 20: 33) of secular sublimity is a logical consequence of the natural drive to happiness, indeed, it is an act in accordance with "Vorsehung" (providence; NA 20: 35) as Schiller presents it, not as a religious concept, but as a function of secularist teleology and Common Sense anthropological psychology. Since all evidence indicates that the human being exists to be happy and thus free, the pursuit of happiness is the destiny of the individual and the collective.

Schiller's Second Virtue Speech is his first work of many to assert that the source and the consequences—the means and the ends—of virtue are "Vollkommenheit" (perfection) and "Glükseeligkeit" (happiness; NA 20: 30); the same pair appear in similar contexts in, among other texts, *Philosophie der Physiologie* (1779; NA 20: 11), in *Über Naiive und Sentimentalische Dichtung* (On Naive and Sentimental Poetry, 1795; NA 20: 427–428), and nowhere more clearly than in the fourteenth of the *Ästhetische Briefe*: "[…] es ist zufällig, ob unsere Glückseligkeit mit unsrer Vollkommenheit, oder ob dieser mit jener übereinstimmen werde" (it is random, whether our happiness corresponds to our perfection, or whether the latter corresponds to the former; NA 20: 354). Ergo, notions that Schiller meant anything more grand than human happiness by perfection ignore compelling evidence. Thus, Schiller's critique of Voltaire and La Mettrie is telling in the choice of disparaging terms, namely "unvollkommen" (NA 20: 33), for which the translation "imperfect" or "lacking" would constitute a surprising unwillingness to recognize Schiller's persistent equation of "Vollkommenheit" with "Glückseligkeit," and thus that their materialism is not only unhappy, but leads to unhappiness.

The concept of "gegenseitige Ausbildung der Seelenfähigkeiten" (reciprocative formation of intellectual competencies; NA 20: 32) toward perfection/happiness through reason—"Verfeinerung der Begriffe" (refinement of concepts; NA 20: 32)—appears in similar contexts as "richtigere Begriffe" in der *Schaubühne*-Speech of 1784 (NA 20: 97), in the Augustenburg Letter of July 13, 1793 as "Berichtigung der Begriffe" (revision of concepts; NA 26: 265), and in a letter to Goethe of October 16, 1795 as "strenge Bestimmtheit der Gedanken" (strict determinacy of thoughts; NA 28: 79; High 2004, 117). Schiller's warning in the speech that the French materialist thought of La Mettrie and Voltaire could cast back (*zurückstoßen*) the individual and the collective "in das barbarische Dunkel tierischer Wildheit" (into the barbaric darkness of animal savagery; NA 20: 33) bears a striking similarity to an excerpt of fifteen years later in the Augustenburg Letters—not only in phrase but in function and environment—in which Schiller describes the flawed attempt of the French to achieve political freedom as a result of an imbalance of sensuality over reason as having cast back (*zurückgeschleudert*) "dieses unglückliche Volk […] und ein ganzes Jahrhundert, in Barbarey und Knechtschaft" (this unhappy people […] and an entire century into barbarism and enslavement; NA 26: 262). The parallels run from the French contexts to the verbs (*zurückstoßen/zurückschleudern*), adjectives and nouns—*barbarische Dunkel* and *tierischer Wildheit* in 1780, *Barbar and Wilder* in the *Ästhetische Briefe*), and the eccentric use of the term "unglücklich" to cover two meanings, both unfortunate and unhappy, in an extended equation of perfection with happiness and imperfection with unhappiness. See the summary of Schiller's discourse on inner balance of character or imbalance of drives from 1779–1795 in the discussion of the First Virtue Speech above. Significantly, Schiller's theory of 1793—that religion, like popular taste or any form of heteronomy that coerces desired behaviors, can only serve as a "Surrogat der wahren Tugend" (surrogate for true virtue; NA 26: 330–331)—was already in place in 1780.

Schiller's Second Virtue Speech introduces a great number of philosophical terms and phrases central to and better known from his later literary works. Among the very large number of concepts present in his eudaimonist ode "An die Freude," one of the more striking examples regards the series of allegorical images portraying joy as the prime drive behind all human activity. In both the speech and the poem, everything in a mechanistic universe is held intact by the laws of nature—be they in the realm of physics (gravity) or individual sensuality and intellect—in the speech "Räder der Natur" (gears of nature; NA 20: 32) and in the poem: "Freude, Freude treibt die Räder / in der großen Weltenuhr" (Joy, joy, drives the gears / in the great clock of the cosmos; NA 1: 170). In both speech and poem, the realm "aller denkenden Naturen" (of all thinking beings; NA 20: 32) is united under one organizing moral and physical principal and prime mover, here, a kaleidoscope of metaphors for virtue, love, and joy, among them; in the speech, the concept "Eines alliebenden Vaters" (of One all-loving father; NA 20: 32) and in the poem: "Brüder—überm Sternenzelt / muß ein Lieber Vater wohnen" (Brothers—over the tent of stars / there must live a father dear; NA 1: 169). The concept of reciprocative formation of intellectual competencies in which the transfer of "Wonne des Freunds in die Seele des Freunds" (Joy of the friend into the soul of a friend; NA 20, 33) reappears in the joy of being "eines Freundes Freund" (a friend to a friend; NA 1: 169) in the poem. Schiller's concept of "Vorsehung," like that of, among others, Benjamin Franklin, John Adams, and Thomas Jefferson in their invocation of a phrase from Virgil's *Aeneid* to justify the US War of Liberation—"annuit coeptus"—to declare that providence approves of freedom and happiness, posits that since providence is a projection of human nature, it cannot do anything but corroborate. One aspect of the concept of providence in Schiller's speech plays a further important role in both "An die Freude" and in his tragedy *Don Karlos* (1787), namely, the idea that providence "ist eben so mächtig das Laster eines Einzigen in die Glükseeligkeit der Welt enden zu lassen, als sie diese durch Tugend glüklich machen kann" (is just as powerful to allow the vice of an individual to result in the happiness of the collective as it is to make the collective happy through virtue; NA 20: 35). Indeed, according to the poem, "durch den Riß gesprengter Särge" (through the cracks of blown-up coffins), one still sees joy standing "im Chor der Engel" (in the choir of angels; NA 1: 170). In *Don Karlos*, Posa delivers two variations of the same, arguing to Philipp II that the path to happiness through freedom includes the freedom of "des Uebels grauenvolles Heer" (the terrifying army of evil; *NA* 6: 192) to run amok throughout the cosmos, and the conviction that neither loss of life nor failure of mission are valid moral considerations when freedom and happiness are at stake: "Ob er vollende oder unterliege—/ Ihm einerlei!" (Whether he succeed or succumb—/ Should make no difference to him; *NA* 6: 268). In the same audience scene with Philipp II (*Don Karlos*, III, 10), Posa invokes the concept of happiness through virtue presented in the Second Virtue Speech literally twelve times. This trend regarding concepts from Schiller's Karlsschule speeches continues through Schiller's latest philosophical writings, as the parallels to the *Ästhetische Briefe* and *Über Naiive und Sentimentalische Dichtung* of 1795 indicate.

Both speeches ring entirely disingenuous in their praise of both the duke and Hohenheim, even more so in light of testimony from Schiller's classmate, Andreas Streicher—with whom he fled Württemberg—who preserved the following lines written by Schiller in 1783: "Was ihr an Reitz gebricht / hat sie an Diamanten" (What she lacks in charm / she makes up for in diamonds; Streicher, 233). There is a clear parallel between Streicher's report and the comment in act II scene 2 of Schiller's third drama, *Kabale und Liebe* (Intrigue and Love, 1784), in which the court servant reports that the duke gathers funds to buy his mistress diamonds by selling his subjects to England to fight in North America (*NA* 5: 28–29).

Philosophy in Schiller's Medical School Writings

Schiller changed subject majors from Law to Medicine in 1775, producing a total of three minor and three major works on philosophy, medicine, and psychology. An earlier minor work was a report on the religious conviction, moral constitution, dislikes, inclinations, hygienic habits, and relationships to faculty of classmates assigned to all cadets at the Karlsschule, "Bericht an den Herzog Karl Eugen über die Mitschüler und sich selbst" (Report to Duke Karl Eugen on the Classmates and on Myself), written in Fall 1774 when Schiller was still a Law student, and first published in 1841 (*NA* 22: 3–16). The second minor work was the "anatomische Schulaufgabe" (anatomical class assignment; *NA* 22: 352) "Beobachtungen bei der Leichen-Öffnung des Eleve Hillers" (Observations on the Autopsy of Cadet Hiller, 1778) that detailed Hiller's death due to pericarditis and tuberculosis. The third minor work was a report on a suicidal classmate suffering from "Hypochondrie" (psychosomatic depression), "Über die Krankheit des Eleven Grammont" (On the Illness of Cadet Grammont, June 26–July 21, 1780, first published in 1856), an early work of "Seelenkunde" (psychology). The three major works include Schiller's first, rejected dissertation, *Philosophie der Physiologie* (Philosophy of Physiology, Fall 1779), his second dissertation, *Versuch über den Zusammenhang der tierischen Natur des Menschen mit seiner geistigen* (Essay on the Connection between the Animal and the Intellectual Nature of the Human Being, November 30, 1780), and a third medical thesis written in Latin and submitted on November 1, 1780, *De discrimine febrium inflammatoriarum et putridarum* (On the

Difference between Inflammatory and Putrid Fever). Although it is rich in literary language and citations of, among other works, Shakespeare's *Hamlet* and Aesop's fable, "The Braggart," the Latin thesis focuses almost exclusively on the physical or animal processes regarding fevers, and is thus of substantially less interest philosophically.

Philosophie der Physiologie (Philosophy of Physiology, 1779)

Textual Genesis: Schiller's first, rejected dissertation was conceived in German as *Idee einer Physiologie*, which was translated into Latin and submitted as *Philosophia Physiologiae*. The Latin thesis was divided into five chapters, comprising a total of forty-seven paragraphs, according to the thesis advisor Johann Friedrich Consbruch's (1736–1810) review of November 6, 1779, of which only those few sentences cited by Consbruch remain. The final version was submitted in German as *Philosophie der Physiologie* on November 30, 1780, of which only a copy of the first chapter (eleven paragraphs) is extant from the personal collection of Schiller's classmate Karl Philipp Conz (1762–1827). The opening table of contents demonstrates a number of significant parallels to Schiller's final dissertation of November 1780 in addressing 1) Mental Life, 2) Nutritive Life of the Body, 3) Procreation, 4) The Relation between these Three Systems, and 5) Sleep and Natural Death (Dewhurst & Reeves, 149). The interdisciplinary focus on the relationship between the body and the psyche was common at the Karlsschule during this period due to Abel's seminars on related topics, as indicated by the dissertation titles of Schiller's classmates Immanuel Gottlieb Elwert and Friedrich von Hoven. The crux of Schiller's thesis regards an ongoing theoretical debate about the possibility of a "Mittelkraft" (transmutative force), which had been featured prominently in Haug's *Schwäbisches Magazin* between July and November of 1776. The transmutative force, located in what Albrecht von Haller (1708–1777) termed the "Nervengeist" (nerve spirit) within the nerve canals rather than in the brain, is neither body nor psyche, but communicates with both to produce ideas (Alt, 160). The thesis was rejected by Klein, Reuß, and Consbruch due to its often playful sense of humor, a flowery writing style that was deemed inappropriate for a medical dissertation, "der gefährliche Hang zum besser wissen" (the dangerous tendency to know it all; Klein), the author's "Feuer" (fire; Carl Eugen; *NA* 21: 114–115), and the disrespectful tone with which Schiller criticized Haller and other established medical authorities, whom he refers to as "metaphysische Donquixotte" (metaphysical Don Quixotes) and "die Geister der Toden in ihren Gräbern" (the spirits of the dead in their graves; *NA* 20: 16).

Contents: Chapter 1, "Mental Life," §1, "The Destiny of the Human Being," opens with a clearly stated regulative idea of the pursuit of an unachievable ideal of perfection that preempts any utopian readings (*NA* 20: 10; paragraph 1). Citing Ferguson as "Ein Weiser" (a wise philosopher; *NA* 20: 11; *NA* 21: 118), Schiller presents an early version of his later aesthetic drive theory: That which brings the human individual closer to their destiny will result in happiness, whereas that which distances them from this goal will result in pain. They will thus seek to avoid pain and pursue delight (*NA* 20: 11). Schiller indicates that all subsequent references to happiness and perfection regard the same state, thus both terms regard regulative ideas that are either rarely achieved or fleeting (paragraph 2). As in the First Virtue Speech, Schiller again declares of the destiny of the human being, "Diß ist Glükseeligkeit" (This is happiness; *NA* 20: 10–11), before establishing that the law of love demands that the human being is destined to promote the perfection of all individuals as part of the great system of nature, including animals (paragraph 3). Schiller further concludes that not only the happiness of one's fellow sentient being but also the experience of compassion for the pain of a fellow sentient being results in the happiness of the feeling subject (paragraph 4). Indeed, this is the end of every form of sensual pleasure. §2, "The Influence of Matter on the Mind," establishes that everything that takes place within the labyrinth of an individual being is a matter of psychology rather than physiology (paragraph 5). Schiller raises the question of how the psychological being interacts with the material world, concluding that while the material world is independent of feeling and subjective understanding, the individual is not, yet the separation of the two within the system of things would negate concepts of morality, freedom, and happiness (paragraph 6). Schiller addresses the concept of the experience of the miraculous, which he declares is a non-entity, since everything that happens in the physical and psychological world must be possible based on the inalterable relationship between the two (paragraph 7). He then posits the existence of a "Mittelkraft" (transmutative force) between the material world and the intellect, through which matter can change the intellect (*NA* 20: 13; paragraph 8–paragraph 9). §3 "Transmutative Force" argues that experience demonstrates that change within the individual is possible without any action, a phenomenon Schiller attributes to the transmutative force (paragraph 10–paragraph 11). In §4, Schiller describes how the process from matter to intellectual idea via the transmutative force is a process from the subject through the mechanical auxiliary forces and protective mechanical forces of each unique material organ, namely "Schützkräfte," that belong to what Schiller calls the "Bau" (material structure), while the material structure and the transmutative force taken together constitute the organ, which does not lie in the transmutative force but in the material construct (paragraph 12). That is to say, a chain of powers proceeds from material nature into the intellect: from sensation, to judgment, to material idea in the transmutative force, to a change in the mind that Schiller refers to as the "Idee" (idea; *NA* 20: 15; paragraph 13). In §5, "Categorization of the Perceptive Organs" (paragraph 14), the five organs of perception are divided into two main classes. The first is necessary for the perception of constructs, for which the senses of sight, hearing, and taste are responsible. The second class comprises two organs responsible for the senses of smell and feeling. Together these organs comprise the system of sensual perception.

Part 2: "System of Sensual Perception," §6, "Nerve, Nerve Spirit" (paragraph 15), dismisses a number of "Quixotic" theories of how nerves function and declares that the nerve is an infinitely fine, simple, and dynamic substance he calls the "Nervengeist" (nerve spirit), which constitutes the transmutative force (*NA* 20: 16), any change in which results in sensation. The nerve spirit is active in all organs, each of which has a different function and attitude toward the object and its own conduit through the nerves (paragraph 16). Schiller leaves the question of the difference between the machinations of the "Nervengeist" to future generations and turns to the subject of how objects come into contact with the transmutative force itself. §7, "The Attitude," addresses the mechanics of the sensual organs, beginning with the eye, concluding that the nerve spirits are not a function of the object but of the organ, here the eye itself, which paints the object through auxiliary forces such as membranes (paragraph 17). The protective powers are eyelids, eyebrows, tears, etc.; the eye is immediately responsible for the perception of characteristics such as light, darkness, color, and form, while the mind concludes the size and distance of an object through comparison with other senses (*NA* 20: 17). Similarly, the ear originally receives a sound in its highs and lows, and like the eye, through comparison with other senses, establishes elasticity, hardness, and distance of the origins. Schiller follows the same pattern in analyzing the senses from the most direct to the most basic, from taste (paragraph 18), smell (paragraph 19), to touch (paragraph 20), articulating the necessary mechanical powers of each as well as complex and simple functions, ultimately dividing these aspects into animal and intellectual aspects of the senses.

Part 3: "Material Thinking, § 8, "The Thought Organ, Material Imagination, Theories": The first principle of intellectual life is "Vorstellung" (perception, *NA* 20: 19), through the five organs addressed above, through which the material world impresses the mind. Schiller describes perception as a change of state in the mind through which the mind differentiates the "I" of the subject from the change in the environment (paragraph 22). The second principle of intellectual life, in the main task of perception, is the response to material conditions through "Denken" (thought; *NA* 20: 19). Citing Garve, Schiller defines perception as a simple act of a simple power set into motion by the nerve spirit through sensation, the work of which is concluded as soon as the sensation ends, and not necessarily requiring activity on the part of the "Verstand" (mind; paragraph 23). Temporary changes due to sensation remain the object of contemplation, introducing a new organ that is neither sense nor "Seele" (psyche; *NA* 20: 20), commonly referred to as "das allgemeine Sensorium" (the general sensorium), but which Schiller defines as the instrument of the mind, or "das Denkorgan" (the thought organ, brain), which maintains the sensation for contemplation (paragraph 24). Schiller introduces the first of two theories that explain how the thought organ and the imagination respond to the material ideas of sensation (paragraph 25), presenting a three-part thesis: I) "Are these impressions in the channels of the nerve spirit, or in the nerves, caused by the activity in the nerve spirit?" addresses the question of whether sensations are physically manifested in the channels of the nerve spirit, or if the flow of nerve spirits is so delicate that their flow does not erase impressions (paragraph 26), concluding that the theory of an "Eindruck" (impression) negates the very concept of the nerve spirit, thus sensations are a matter of constant movement, not permanent impressions, which he compares to scars. II) "Material ideas of the imagination constitute movements of the nerve spirit that are in harmony with those originally in the sensual spirits": The more active the entire system is, the more productive is the imagination (paragraph 27). Schiller concludes that the main concept is motion, which supports his theory of interaction between nerve spirit and "Seele" (psyche), and pursues the question of whether material ideas of the imagination are not oscillations of fibers stretched like the strings of an instrument which comprise the thought organ. III) Are the concrete ideas of the imagination oscillations emanating from fibers that are stretched like strings of an instrument, the sum total and relationship of which comprise the thought organ? The limitless variety of objects made visible by the light are created by only seven basic colors and yet these thought-fibers should somehow be able to perceive all of these sensual and intellectual perceptions? Nor has the art of dissection nor analogy for the moment nor anything in the entire physical construct of the human being contributed any solution to this question (paragraph 28). Schiller argues that its dynamic state, which ceases in death, explains why the thought organ has been found to be the least elastic and softest part of the human body. Schiller points out that Charles Bonnet's (1720–1793) hypothesis is a combination of all three of the theories above, but cannot be proven (paragraph 29).

§9, "Association: Application of the Theories," concludes that the concrete ideas of the imagination are not in a constant state of activity, and posits that additional causes activate dormant ideas and present them to the mind (paragraph 30). Chains of perception are based on sensual-intellectual association, which is based on relationships of time, place, or effect (paragraph 31). Schiller posits the primacy of the signifier, in this case a brook, which, upon entering the consciousness, sets off a chain of associations, possibly including a person who was standing at a tree by the brook or a sound that was heard near the brook, on and on until a new sensual idea interrupts the chain system and starts a new one. Analogical examples regard theories of resonant musical notes and colors, for example, that projecting light on a red object in a dark room will illuminate all other red objects, or playing a note on one piano will result in a second piano responding with a reproduction of the same note (paragraph 32). Schiller concludes the analogy by arguing that the first piano represents the sensual world, the air represents the nerve spirit, and the second piano represents the thought organ (paragraph 33). The nerve spirit transfers the vibrations from the sensual world to the mind, resulting in the "sinnliche Idee" (sensual idea; NA 20: 24), which in the mind will correspond to the mimicry of the second piano of the first piano, and so on as a mere echo of the idea (paragraph 34). For actual mental association to occur, corresponding fibers must already exist in the thought organ (paragraph 35). In a chain of association, the ocean can remind of a ship, and the ship can remind of the American War, only if one had previously experienced a ship or had knowledge of the

American War, once again revealing a flaw in Bonnet's theory. The "monstrous" consequence is that association is impossible without empirical knowledge (paragraph 36). Schiller concludes that even the simplest idea corresponds to its own spirit and its own channels, which are as constant as physical arteries themselves (paragraph 37). These channels are interconnected, and associations remain nonetheless exceedingly arbitrary, though the channels remain fixed, and the spirits do not mix. As a result, Schiller again criticizes Haller for proposing that fixed impressions can be set into motion by the mind through perception (paragraph 38), concluding that he cannot explain material associations through the mechanics of the thought organ because the thought organ is determined and eternal, while material association is infinitely complex and mutable (paragraph 39). Thus, the psyche cannot be the organizing principle of material association, since it would have to have access to all dormant ideas simultaneously.

§10, "The Influence of the Mind on the Thought Organ," posits that material association is the basis of thought—the guiding thread of the creative intellect, serving to unite, divide, compare, and contrast ideas, and thus direct the will to desire or rejection (paragraph 41). This argument would appear to result in the will being organically determined at the most basic level, thus limiting the freedom of will. The "Seele" (psyche) actively influences the thought organ. The psyche can focus more closely on select material ideas, resulting in stronger spiritual ideas through focused attention (paragraph 41). Thus it is the psyche that ascertains the motives and their strength. Schiller divides the will into two parts, the first of which dictates attention, and the final, which is a slave of the "Verstand" (intellect), dictates action. Freedom thus does not lie in the decision to act in accordance with what the intellect has recognized is best—because this is a moral law—but rather because one chooses what the intellect can determine is best. All morality of the human individual has its basis in attention, that is, in the active influence of the psyche on the material ideas in the thought organ. Those material ideas strengthened most by active focus can become residual and stand out deuteropathically before all others. They will affect the psyche more directly, and will play a more powerful role for the intellect in all associations and become a tyrant over the second will (paragraph 42). As a result, there are people who, in the end, mechanically commit moral or immoral acts due to a narrow focus of attention. Thus, all morality is a function of attention. The focused attention results in the most lively idea that clings to the psyche and rules over the intellect and the will. This is the source of all passions and dominant ideas, and at the same time, a warning to avoid both. If the psyche focuses attention on a number of ideas through association, it is said to be creating (*erdichten*); if the psyche concentrates on particular aspects of certain ideas and removes them from their contexts, it is said to be selecting (*absondern*). The psyche retains in the thought organ the ideas that have been placed in new chains of association by the creative synthesis and those that have been removed from their contexts by analysis. The capacity for attention—those ideas thought into new associations, and those removed from their associations by analysis—are captured in the thought organ, appearing to capture them in material forms because consciousness unites the ideas in memory. Therefore, as a result of attention, when one material idea deeply affects the mind, then a similar material idea will do the same, and the association will be more intense. Thus, the capacity for attention is responsible for imagination, recollection, analysis, creativity, and desire; and it is the active influence of the psyche on the thought organ that brings all of this about (paragraph 43). Consequently, the thought organ is the true tribunal of the intellect, each is subject to the other, and the intellect is dependent on the thought organ with the exception of attention. Schiller closes the section by addressing the potential for aberration as a result of a state of illness due to confusion of the spirits in the thought organ, which can turn the wise into fools and the most gentle individuals into furies, closing with examples of how the overexertion of an active intellect can destroy both intellect and memory, citing, for example, thinkers like Garve, Mendelsohn, and Swift, who overexerted the instrument of their intellect to the point that it is permanently out of tune (paragraph 44).

§11, "Sensations in Mental Life": The psyche is not only a thinking, but a feeling entity; the latter alone makes it happy, and the former alone makes it capable of happiness. It is a fact of creation that feeling is the state in which the psyche is aware of betterment or decline (paragraph 45). Feeling is distinct from perception in that the latter perceives itself as an external object and the former perceives itself. Schiller provides the sight of the sun and the stars, the sound of a brook or a harp or a raven cawing, as common changes of state caused by the perception of an external object (paragraph 46), and a series of comparatives and superlatives categorize visual and auditory responses to such impulses; sounds one enjoys are melodic and beautiful, and sounds one dislikes are ugly and discordant. According to the first law, which opened the essay, I can enjoy nothing but that which makes my current state more perfect, and can only dislike that which makes me less perfect (paragraph 47).

Philosophical Significance and Impact. Foreshadowing his third dissertation, Schiller seeks to counter the "materialistischen Medizinerzynismus" (materialistic cynicism of the physicians)—a parallel to the "Körpermaterialismus" (physical materialism; Safranski, 11) of his character Franz Moor in *Die Räuber*, who reduces every imaginable virtue to the mere satisfaction of a physical drive. Schiller's virulent assault on the materialism of Bonnet (*NA* 20: 22) finds telling parallels in his later critiques of Voltaire and La Mettrie in the Second Virtue Speech of January 1780, in which he contrasts what he characterizes as their resignation to imperfection with his own pursuit of happiness (*NA* 20: 33). In his attack on La Metterie's concept of the human being as a machine, as well as in his distaste for Rousseau's concept of the state as machine, Schiller was very early on the path to the individual becoming the state as in the *Ästhetische Briefe* and the "state as the perfect work of art" (Nilges, 13).

In the second paragraph of *Philosophie der Physiologie*, Schiller again defines the destiny of humankind as "Glükseeligkeit" (happiness; *NA* 20: 10–11), returning to the end of all human activity that remains in some form through the *Ästhetische Briefe*. Likewise, at the very outset, Schiller delivers the second of very many previews of what is to come in his philosophical and literary works by invoking a regulative idea that preempts any abstract utopian readings: "Ewigkeit ist das Maas der Unendlichkeit, das heist, er [der Mensch] wird ewig wachsen, aber es niemals erreichen" (Eternity is the measure of infinity, that means, the human being will grow eternally, but never achieve [the measure of infinity]; *NA* 20: 10). Note that Schiller's definition of the regulative idea here is a paraphrase of Mendelssohn's Socrates, who will play a role in Schiller's mature works on freedom and the subime: "[…] der Weg zu derselben [Vollkommenheit] ist unendlich, kann in Ewigkeiten nicht ganz zurückgelegt werden" ([…] the path to the same [perfection] is infinite, and cannot entirely be achieved in eternities; Mendelssohn, 188). The consistent primacy of the concept of perfection-as-happiness first becomes clear in the first dissertation, and though many have sought to dismiss this preoccupation as a phase, there is no evidence for this position and a great deal to the contrary; *Glückseligkeit* is, in fact, the stated end of aesthetic education in the first paragraph of the *Ästhetische Briefe* of 1795 (*NA* 20: 309). Schiller quickly describes the path via virtue to happiness intimately bound up with the "Bestimmung des Menschen," a contemporary key term foremost articulated by Spalding (Macor 2022), and transforms the term to his own radical dialectical ends to include an organic source to all moral action.

Schiller's articulate emphasis of feeling as the counterbalance of reason and matter has wide-reaching consequences for his oeuvre in the ensuing decades. He returns to the conviction that virtue, or happiness, love, loyalty ("Die Bürgschaft;" The Pledge, 1797) or hope ("Hofnung," 1797) are not empty illusions through the conclusion of his final drama. His insistence of the equality of every link in the chain of being is demonstrated in the presence of animal rights arguments both here, in the First Virtue Speech (*NA* 20: 11); in his final, successful dissertation (*NA* 20: 75); and in his discussion of the rational animal and the happy coexistence of the human being and nature in *Wilhelm Tell*. The first dissertation provides a preview of the theory of mutual recognition that appears in his mature philosophical writings—nowhere more prominently than in the *Ästhetische Briefe*—"Wir sind […] nicht mehr Individuen, sondern Gattung" (We are […] no longer individuals but constitute a species; Twelfth Letter; *NA* 20: 347)—and likewise informs his final dramas, in which denial of recognition through occupation awakens the oppressed to their inalienable rights. The reconciliation of matter and mind (and any number of ostensible polarities) is a declaration of an ideal of reconciliation of self and nature as well as self and other, based on the conviction that the rational animal can exist for only one purpose, namely to pursue the loftiest moral ideals of reason in harmony with nature. Schiller's portrayal of sensation and association in *Philosophie der Physiologie*, in which he combines elements of Gestalt Therapy and free association in his portrayal of the association between ocean, ship, and the US War of Liberation (*NA* 20: 24) became a psychological model for the relationship between inspiration and creative artist. Schiller's letter to Körner of December 1, 1788 (*NA* 25: 149), in which Schiller similarly describes the obscure process of artistic creation, was cited by Sigmund Freud (1856–1939) in *Die Traumdeutung* (The Interpretation of Dreams, 1899) as the inspiration for the psychoanalytical method of free association. As compelling as this citation is, a better model for free association is Schiller's first dissertation.

Professor Reuß, who shared Consbruch's criticism of Schiller's literary style and academic inconsistency, unwittingly described the text's primary virtue in his review: "*Philosophia Physiologiae* enthält den ganzen Umfang der Physiologie [...] in Verbindung mit philosophischen Abhandlungen, Säzen und Betrachtungen" (*Philosophia Physiologiae* contains the entire scope of Physiology [...] in connection with philosophical treatises, theorems, and observations; *NA* 21: 114–115). Schiller's reconciliation of philosophy and physiology, likewise evident in the Virtue speeches of 1779 and 1780, delivers a moral-aesthetic model that remains evident in his enduring 1787 drama *Don Karlos* and his criticism of the Enlightenment in the poem "Die Götter Griechenlandes" (The Gods of Ancient Greece, 1788), as it is in his latest aesthetic treatises of the mid-1790s, including the two essays on the sublime, the *Kallias* letters, and the *Ästhetische Briefe*. What Reuß describes here is an important moment in the history of aesthetics that Pugh has identified as Schiller's "fundamental role at the inception of this branch of philosophy" (Pugh, xii).

Versuch über den Zusammenhang der tierischen Natur des Menschen mit seiner geistigen (Essay on the Connection between the Animal and the Intellectual Nature of the Human Being, 1780)

Textual Genesis: After his first dissertation was rejected in 1779, Schiller submitted two further theses in November 1780, the Latin treatise on fevers rejected by Reuß, Consbruch, and Klein, and a third, successful dissertation, one of the first written in German at the Karlsschule, entitled *Versuch über den Zusammenhang der tierischen Natur des Menschen mit seiner geistigen*. The thesis was approved by the same medical faculty, and Schiller passed his medical exams in December 1780 and was assigned as regimental physician to the Stuttgart Grenadier Regiment of General Johann Augé (*NA* 23: 38). The influence of his professors and leading outside scholars is evident in the many parallels between Schiller's text and Abel's *Eine Quellenedition zum Phiolosophie Unterricht an der Stuttgarter Karlsschule (1773–1782)* (A Source Edition on Teaching Physiology at the Stuttgart Karlsschule 1773–1782), as well as Ernst Plattner's *Anthropologie für Aerzte und Weltweise* (Anthropology for Physicians and Philosophers, 1772). The criticism and praise delivered by Schiller's examiners ring ironic, given the career he chose, including "jene poetische Ausdrücke" (these poetic forms of expression) and an excessive tendency for "Einbildungskraft" (imagination; 124), among others. The thesis was subsequently published by Cotta in Stuttgart.

Contents: In §1, "Introduction," Schiller contrasts the description of the body as the prison of the spirit that binds it to the earthly and hinders its flight to perfection with the position that knowledge and virtue are not only the end but also the means to happiness, and that all perfection of the human being is gathered in the improvement of the body (paragraph 1). Schiller seeks to refute both arguments by pointing out that the former is only tolerated due to its idealistic focus on characters like Cato, Brutus, Seneca, and so on, while the latter is the result of ideological fanaticism, concluding that a balance between the two positions may provide a middle path toward truth (paragraph 2). Schiller concludes that historically too much weight has been given to the intellect as independent from the body, and declares his intention to establish the important and real contribution of the body's animal system of perception to the actions of the intellectual system of perception "Seele" (mind; paragraph 3).

Part A, "The Physical Connection," Chapter 1: "Animal Nature strengthens the Activity of the Mind," begins with §2, "The organ of psychological influences—of nutrition—of reproduction." Schiller embarks from an elementary thesis: the perfection of the human individual lies in the exercises of powers in consideration of the structure of the universe (paragraph 4). Since the most precise harmony is required between the totality of human power and the end of all human activity, the highest possible achievement of these powers lies in their mutual subordination to each other. But the activity of the mind (Seele) is connected through unknown necessity and manner to the activity of matter. Thus, changes in the physical world must be modified and refined by a class of intermediary organic powers, the senses, before they can awaken a perception. Therefore, other organic powers, the machines of voluntary physical actions, step between mind and world, in order to communicate the changes in the material world to the mind, and thus ultimately, operations of thought and perception must correspond to specific actions / motions of the inner sensorium, which combined constitute the organism of psychological activity. Matter is subject to eternal change, and exhausts itself through its own activity, while the simple entity, the mind, possesses permanence and stability (paragraph 5). Matter is unable to keep pace with mental activity, and thus, as matter, the organism and with it all function of the mind would be lost without the organic system of nutrition to maintain fading health through a constant chain of new creations. Finally, mortality would depopulate the planet due to an imbalance between loss and renewal, in the process precluding overpopulation through the loss of one generation and the rise of another (paragraph 6). In order to maintain contributive succession, a third system of organic powers is necessary, namely rejuvenation through reproduction. These three organisms constitute the human body. In the process, nothing new is *created*, and everything that is new is only possible through evolution.

§3, "The Body," describes the two main classes of organic powers, the first of which is the sensitivity of the nerves and the irritability of the muscles (contraction upon external stimulation), addressing the fact that the current state of science allows only an analogous description of the functions of nerves as the principle of sensitivity and motion through the transfer of a powerful fluid called the "Lebensgeister" (vital spirits; paragraph 7). The second class regards the laws of physics, including the mechanics of motion and the chemistry of the human body, and the vegetative or regenerative physical processes, of which Schiller concludes that vegetative and animal mechanics comprise physical life (paragraph 8).

§4, "Animal Life," posits that since attrition is more or less controlled by the mind, the same is necessarily true of physical renewal (paragraph 9); since the body is subject to the consequences of its constitution and surrounded by hostile forces, the power to protect the body and to create conditions beneficial to survival must lie in the mind. The mind must receive information on the negative or positive state of the organs and derive displeasure from a negative state and derive pleasure from a positive state, in order to remove or flee the former and prolong or pursue the latter. To this end, the organism is connected to the sensory powers and the mind is drawn into the interests of its body. This is more than organic ("Vegetation")—more than dead model, nerves, and the mechanics of muscles—now it is animal life. In a significant footnote, Schiller differentiates between the end of animal life and that of human life, explaining how, in the animal, means and end coincide, and that the animal senses pleasure in order to merely prolong animal life, while the human being experiences pleasure and pain in order to maintain animal life to the end of extending intellectual life, thus constituting the difference between animal and human being. Since animal life is essential for psychological health, it may not be damaged and thus the mind must be aware of physical life through an irresistible power (paragraph 10), and sensations of positive and negative animal states remain beyond the comprehension of the intellect, which would subject them to passions, sloth, or stupidity, and would require that the animal human being possess a complete knowledge of physiology beyond that of the most renowned scientists (Harvey, Boerhave, Haller). Therefore, the mind cannot have any *idea* of the state that requires change.

§ 5, "Animal Sensations," analyzes how, in contrast to those sensations that stem from rational operations, animal sensations arise as direct expressions of the current state of the organs, and direct the will to quick aversion or desire, without activating the sense of reason (paragraph 11). Responses to sensations that ensure preservation provide a pleasant affectation, and the painful affectation accompanies sensations that threaten the organism's collapse. Consequently, animal sensations have two sources: 1. the current condition of the machine, 2. the powers of sensitivity [sensory powers]. This explains why animal sensations move the mind to passions and actions irresistibly, and gain the upper hand against even the highest intellectual powers (paragraph 12). The power of abstraction and of philosophy over passions and opinions is unable to negate those of blind necessity, but can weaken and darken them through focused attention; for example, the stoic's ability to subordinate pain to higher perfection and general happiness, or the Roman youth Mucius, who earned release from captivity by thrusting his hand into fire without showing pain. Ultimately, although the mind through virtue and philosophy may provide happiness while facing a funeral pyre, it cannot protect the machine from the law of necessity that governs the lower needs of physical life—hunger, pain, and the elements— and each experience teaches human beings that they are something unfortunate between a beast and an angel (paragraph 13). Citing Heinrich Wilhelm von Gerstenbergs' (1737–1823) *Ugolino* (1768), Schiller describes how animal sensations overpower and forcefully bind the mind to the organism. In order to satisfy hunger and thirst, the human being is capable of deeds that terrify humanity, unwillfully becoming a traitor, a murderer, or a cannibal (paragraph 14). The powers of animal sensation are the strongest, and experience demonstrates that an excess of animal sensation has proven more destructive than a lack thereof (paragraph 15). The system of animal sensations and actions that ensure well-being marks the end of animal nature, but also provides the basis on which the constitution of intellectual instruments rests, and thus the first link in the connection of animal and human natures in determining the fragility and duration of intellectual activity itself (paragraph 16). § 6, "Moral Objections Against the Connection Between the Two Natures," concludes the first chapter by asking whether is it not absurd and unjust to entangle simple, necessary, and immutable animal nature with a human nature informed by an eternal vortex of vicissitude and self-aware necessity (paragraph 17).

Part B, "Philosophical Connection," Chapter d: Animal Drives Awaken and Develop Mental Drives":

§ 7 proposes the theoretical separation of the body from the intellect as the most certain method for explaining how intellectual drives develop, by analyzing how the human being proceeds to action, develops powers, and which steps are taken toward perfection (paragraph 18). The process requires that one ignore the actual development of the individual and look at the evolution of the entire human race, beginning with an abstract case: provided there is perception, volition, and a sphere of action and free transition between mind (*Seele*) and physical world, and between world and mind, how will the human being act?

§8, "The Mind Without Connection to the Body," traces the evolution of a concept by pursuing the sensation that first demonstrated that an action would lead to an improved state to the will to create a concept based on this experience, the prerequisite of both of which is the initial sensation (paragraph 19). Since there can be no sensation without a preceding idea, there can be no idea without an idea. Schiller's circular argument demonstrates that considering the intellectual nature of the human being without considering the animal nature of the human being bears no fruit, since it prescribes that either the human being was at birth and eternally intellectually active or will never be inspired to intellectual activity through sensation (paragraph 20).

§9, "In Connection," expands the attempt to connect the animal nature and the intellectual nature of the human being through the power of sensation (paragraph 21). The modification of the bodily instrument through sensation provides an impulse to the inner clockwork of the intellect and sets it in motion.

The transition from pain to aversion is the fundamental law of the mind, and all other operations are similarly automatic.

§10, "On the History of the Individual," follows the growth-stages of the "Seele" (mind) and the "Geist" (intellect): a.) early childhood, b.) youth, and c.) adolescence and adulthood (paragraph 22). a.) Citing Haller, Schiller describes the infant and young child as both more and less than animal; the human animal is in one sense more wretched than the animal, because it lacks instinct (paragraph 23; NA 21: 129). In both cases, animal and human, the pain of hunger causes protest with neither knowledge of the source nor the solution. Its nature is entirely passive; b.) Citing Haller and Garve, Schiller demonstrates that the youth is capable of reflection, but only regarding the satisfaction of animal drives, and every inclination proceeds from sensuality to the mind (work, love of parents, friends, and divinity), while all further objects remain dark and cold, only significant when they are connected to sensual reward, as intellectual means to an animal end (paragraph 24; NA 21: 129); c.) in the adolescent and adult, the frequent repetition of conclusions regarding what leads to pleasure and what to pain results in skills, and transference enables the discovery of beauty in what had been mere means—what was mere drive becomes inclination, the original end is forgotten, and the means itself becomes the end (paragraph 25), citing Mohammed's conversion of the Saracens as an example of teaching people the path toward wisdom (paragraph 26). In a lengthy footnote (*NA* 20: 52–53), Schiller cites Garve's explanation of the evolution from drives to simple ends to curiosity, which leads to enlightenment and the discovery that the ideas that promote the higher happiness, perfection, and virtue of the human individual and engagement with ideas of good will constitute the highest of all intellectual ends.

§11, "From the History of the Human Race," examines the universal history of the human race from birth to maturity, to demonstrate the validity of the preceding chapters (paragraph 27). Hunger and nakedness led the human being to become hunter, fisher, shepherd, farmer, and builder. Sensuality resulted in families, individual defenselessness brought together hordes, and thus arose social duties (paragraph 28). Soon the field could no longer support the tribe, and hunger scattered groups in distant lands and climates, teaching them new products, new refinements, and ways of responding to new environments. Traditions were handed down and refined. The human being learned to turn the powers of nature against themselves, to cast them in new relationships, and created the first simple and healing arts. What was at first art in service of the well-being of the animal became an increase in knowledge. In the fire where the primitive human being cooked fish, Börhaave discovered the mixture of bodies; with the knife with which the savage cut game, Lionet invented the knife that discovered the nerves of insects; with the compass for measuring hooves, Newton measured heaven and earth. Citing Ovid's *Metamorphoses*, Schiller describes how the force of an internally active nature combined with the meagerness of the initial environment led tribal leaders to think more daringly, and, under the direction of the stars, they sailed to new territories. New environments brought new dangers, new needs, and new challenges for the intellect (paragraph 29). The collision of animal drives pitted one horde against another, forged raw iron into sword, created adventurers, heroes, and despots. Cities were fortified, states created, and with the states arose the duties and rights of citizens, arts, numbers, lawbooks, clever priests, and gods. What were once needs were transformed into luxuries. Citing Virgil's *Aeneid*, Schiller traces cultural developments: veins are excavated, the ocean floor mined, trade and development flourish, East and West admire each other, foreign products are adapted to artificial environments, and the agricultural arts and products of three continents gather in one (paragraph 30). Artists learn to create works from nature, melodies soften the savage, beauty and harmony ennoble morality and taste, and art leads to science and virtue. Citing Schlözer, Schiller describes the removal of boulders, lakes and forests, and the creation of canals and irrigation systems that transform deserts into fields, and the intellect is refined by the refined climate. The state employs the citizens for the needs and comforts of life, and industriousness provides the state with security and peace both internally and externally, providing the thinker and the artist the leisure that led to Augustus Caesar's golden age (paragraph 31). The arts and sciences flourish, natural science and physics replace superstition, history reflects on the prehistoric world, and philosophy mocks the folly of the humans. As luxury degenerates into weakness and indulgence, bringing pestilence and pollution, the human being finds cures, and discovers cinchona bark, mercury, and poppy seeds. Chemistry discovers individual elements, alchemists enrich natural history, and Swammerdam's microscope reveals nature's secret processes. Necessity and curiosity refute superstition and discover nature's greatest masterpiece, the human being. The worst-case scenario of sickness and death thus brings about the greatest achievement, forcing the human being to learn its place (Schiller cites a maxim inscribed at the temple of Apollo at Delphi). The plague gives rise to Hippocrates and Sydenham, just like war produces generals, and the arrival of syphilis reforms medicine. The search for the appropriate enjoyment of sensuality, which was supposed to lead to the perfection of the mind, leads to the discovery that its recreational use, in fact, improves the reality of human life by necessitating a response to adversity (paragraph 32); the aberrations of the first end of nature—merchants, conquerors, luxury—accelerate a development that could have been more simple and regulated, but the human being had to first crawl in the dust like an animal before realizing that it is also capable of the flight of intellect; the body is thus the first impetus to activity, sensuality the first step toward perfection (paragraph 33).

Chapter B, b: "Animal Sensations Accompany Mental Sensations," §12, "Law," states that human understanding (*Verstand*) and all perceptions that come from its activity are extraordinarily limited. In order to provide understanding with greater impulse and to lead the will away from danger and toward perfection, both intellectual and animal natures are closely interconnected and communicate any change reciprocally. The fundamental law of combined natures states: The activities of the body correspond to the activities of the mind, and every surge in intellectual activities is always accompanied by a surge in bodily actions (paragraph 34). Therefore, intellectual desire is always accompanied by animal desire, and intellectual aversion is accompanied by animal aversion. Conversely, lethargy of the mind results in physical lethargy.

§13, "Intellectual Pleasure Promotes the Health of the Machine," concludes that any sensation that affects the entire mind shocks the entire construct of the body, from the most important (heart, arteries, nerves) to the least significant (body hair). Pleasurable sensations bring about a higher degree of harmonious activity—the heart beats free, blood flows gently or quickly, based on the pleasant or adverse nature of the impulse, and metabolism, secretion, and excretion proceed unhindered. Therefore, the state of the greatest temporary mental desire is also the state of the greatest physical well-being (paragraph 35). Even secondary activities are necessary for perfection; deriving from the confusion of all impulses, a total sensation of animal harmonies constitutes the most concentrated sensation of animal pleasure fused with and increased by higher intellectual or moral pleasure (paragraph 36). Thus, every pleasant emotion is the source of enumerable physical pleasures, a phenomenon evident in examples of the ill who were cured by joy; the victim of homesickness returns home and is transformed from near death into the picture of health; the dungeon prisoner who receives words of release; the malnourished sailor who hears the word "land"; the sight of a beloved person. This state of the mind responsible for deriving pleasure from every event and resolves every pain in the perfection of the universe is the most beneficial to the performance of the machine, and this state is virtue (paragraph 37).

§14, "Mental Pain Undermines the Health of the Machine," posits that, conversely, temporary unpleasant emotions are detrimental to physical health. Ideas experienced by an angry or terrified individual, which Plato called fever of the psyche, can be considered convulsions of the thought organ, which spread through the entire nerve system and destroy health by bringing vital spirits and bodily functions into discord. Thus, the state of the greatest mental anguish is the state of the greatest physical sickness (paragraph 38), in which the mind is informed of imposing ruin by a thousand obscure sensations and overwhelmed by a complete sensation of pain that stems from the original intellectual pain (paragraph 39).

§15, "Examples," examines the damage done to the physical constitution by chronic psychological pain, including forms of anger such as indignation, which can be comparable to the highest fevers (paragraph 40). Sufferers appear gaunt and pale, with deep-set eyes. Schiller cites Cassius in Shakespeare's *Julius Caesar* as an example of "Furcht, Unruh, Gewissensangst, Verzweiflung" (fear, restlessness, guilty conscience, despair; *NA* 20: 60); Gloucester in Shakespeare's *Richard III* as a victim of the uneasiness that comes from the very core of the human machine; and finally, the non-existent case history of Franz Moor—*Life of Moor. Tragedy by Krake*, in reality an early draft of *Die Räuber* Act V, Scene 1—who reduces all feelings to abstract concepts, and awakens pale and sweating from a nightmare vision of the afterlife in response to sensations too confused for the slow process of reason. Here, the ascending central image of a dream sets the entire system of dark ideas into motion and disturbs the function of the thought organ, causing an unusually intense feeling of pain that renders lame the entire nerve system (paragraph 41). The shudders that plague those about to commit a crime or who have committed a crime are identical to those of a patient suffering a fever; nightly tossing and turning is likewise accompanied by an increased pulse rate and a genuine fever caused by the sympathetic connection between mind and machine; for example, Lady Macbeth going to bed constitutes a case of phrenetic delirium. Even actors are affected by playing a role; Schiller cites Garrick's convulsions of gout after portraying Lear or Othello; the sympathy of audience members may result in convulsions and fainting (paragraph 42). Schiller concludes that, due to their vices, those plagued by foul moods, the villain who lives in a chronic state of hatred, and the envious person martyred by the perfection of others are the greatest enemies of their own happiness and health (paragraph 43).

In §16, "Exceptions," Schiller points out that even pleasant emotions have proved fatal, and unpleasant emotions have brought about miraculous cures (paragraph 44). When joy rises to the point of ecstasy, the action of the brain moves beyond harmony to convulsion, and can prove fatal, because it has crossed the line of natural emotion and health (paragraph 45). As for the second case, there are many examples of a moderate degree of anger breaking through the most chronic obstructions, or fear brought on by a fire healing chronic rheumatism and incurable paralysis (paragraph 46).

§17, "Lethargy of the Mind makes the Actions of the Machine more Lethargic," cites Haller's theory that mental activity during the business of the day can quicken the pulse in the evening, while mental lethargy can either weaken or even stop it (paragraph 47). A phlegmatic state is accompanied by a slow pulse, blood is watery and viscous, and abdominal circulation suffers. The lunatics described by Muzell demonstrated slow and laborious breath, had no drive to eat or drink nor for natural excretion, the pulse was irregular, and all bodily functions were slumberous and dull. The paralysis of the mind during terror or amazement, for example, is sometimes accompanied by a general suspension of all physical activity. Is the mind the cause of this state, or is it the body that paralyzes the mind?

§18, "Second Law," declares that what is true about the transference of intellectual sensations to animal sensations also applies in the opposite, the transference of animal sensations to intellectual sensations. Sicknesses of the body, often the natural consequence of overindulgence, are punished by physical pain, but the very foundation of the mind must also be attacked, such that the two-fold pain sharply encourages moderation (paragraph 48). Thus, a second law of mixed natures is that the general sensation of animal harmony is a source of mental pleasure, while animal displeasure should be the source of mental displeasure. Like two identically tuned string instruments, when a string on one is struck, the string on the other will reproduce the same note only somewhat weaker (paragraph 49). The remarkable sympathy that constitutes the human being as a single being comprised of heterogeneous principles is not a matter of mind and body, but rather the human being is the most intimate mixture of both.

In §19, "Intellectual Moods Follow Bodily Moods," Schiller cites Brother Martin in Goethe's *Götz von Berlichingen* (1773) in addressing the heaviness, the absence of thought, the moroseness that follows overindulgence, and likewise the miraculous effects of wine in those who drink with moderation (paragraph 50). Similarly, the good mood or sense of well-being that accompanies bright and healthy weather is partly a result of the association of ideas, but predominantly a consequence of the facilitation of the body's natural functions, which in turn results in a disposition for all activities of the intellect, an open heart for human sensibilities, and the practice of moral duties. Schiller's analysis posits that ancient cultural differences to some extent result from environment, while they are only one factor of many: the climate of Greece contributed to the appearance of thinkers and authors (Homer, Plato, and Phidias), while the weather of Lapland (Finland) did not. Schiller traces the development of German civilization from a landscape of forests and swamps inhabited by hunters to an era of moral development. Bodily disorders can also disrupt the entire system of moral sensibility and pave the way for the worst of passions (paragraph 51). Citing his own robber Moritz Spiegelberg (*Die Räuber,* II, 3), Schiller concludes that a human being who has been corrupted by sensual indulgence is more vulnerable to extreme behaviors than one who has maintained a healthy body: the best way to create a bandit is to corrupt both body and soul. Further examples include Catiline, who proceeded from libertine to arsonist, and Fiesco (Giovanni-Luigi Fieschi), who was a lech before he conspired to bring down the republic of Genoa, demonstrating that evil minds often inhabit sick bodies. In the case of malignant diseases, evidence of the sympathetic relationship between body and mind may be observed in early symptoms, such as the sudden transformation of the patient's character signaling the collapse of the mind as a result of a collapse of the body. Citing a "great physician" (possibly Schiller's professor Consbruch), Schiller describes the condition as "der Vorschauer (Horrores)" (preliminary horror; paragraph 52). Citing the parallel nervous breakdowns of Franz Moor (*Die Räuber,* V, 1) and Shakespeare's Winchester (*Henry VI,* Part 2, III, 3), Schiller concludes that once the disease has shown physical symptoms, the universal disorder of the machine demonstrates the reciprocal dependence of the mind and the body: just as the deep pain of the mind originated from the disorders of the machine, in reverse the mind helps render these physical disorders severe and universal.

§ 20, "Restriction of the Preceding Section," Citing Corinthians (15: 55–57), Schiller addresses common examples of the afflicted who rise above their suffering full of courage, and of the dying who face the death of the machine with sublime composure. In response, Schiller posits that wisdom is capable of protecting against the terrors of the organism, and that religious faith can likewise protect against the onslaught of the material, arguing that the preceding state of the mind dictates how one confronts changes in vital actions (paragraph 53). Schiller declares it an irrefutable truth that philosophy and a courageous mind uplifted by religion are capable of weakening the influence of animal sensation and to remove the mind from its coherence with matter. The thought of the deity, of the harmony of one's past life, and the anticipation of a happy future cast a bright light on every idea in the mind, while the mind of the fool and the nonbeliever is cast into the dark sensations of the mechanism (paragraph 54). Citing Addison's *The Death of Cato* (1712; V, 1), Schiller illustrates that when the philosopher and the believer experience pain, they can transform the feeling of bodily collapse into pleasure. The unusual cheerfulness of the mortally ill also has a physical cause, which occurs in conjunction with Hippocrates' description of fatal symptoms (paragraph 55). Namely, this cheerfulness is malignant. The nerves under attack by fever lose sensitivity, and the inflamed body parts cease to hurt with the onset of gangrene. Feeling is lost in the dead nerves and a fatal indolence appears to indicate recovery. The mind experiences the illusion of pleasurable sensation for having lost a chronic feeling of pain. Sympathy between the body and the mind ceases as soon as this connection is severed.

§21, "Further Outlooks Regarding the Connection," addresses insanity, sleep, stupor, epilepsy, and catalepsy, in which the free and rational intellect is subject to the despotism of the abdomen, as well as cases of hysteria and hypochondria, temperaments, idiosyncrasies, and consensus. Schiller notes that although it would be advantageous to demonstrate the truth based on medical experience at the sickbed, which is one of the main schools of the psychologist, it would go beyond the realistic parameters of the thesis (paragraph 56); he concludes that it has been established that animal nature is completely commingled with intellectual nature, and that this combination constitutes perfection (*Vollkommenheit*).

Chapter B, c: "Physical Phenomena reveal Mental Activity," §22, "Physiognomy of Emotions," analyzes the correspondence between the animal and the intellectual nature, which provides the basis for the field of physiognomy. This neural connection we are told results in sensations exposing the most covert emotions, for example, even the hypocrite is unable to mask passion. Every emotion can be recognized by its specific expressions, that is, its own peculiar dialect. Where noble and benevolent emotion beautifies the body, base and hateful emotions lend the body a bestial appearance. Thus, the mild appearance of the philanthropist is inviting to the needy, while the defiant look of the angry person repels, which constitutes the most indispensable guide to social interaction. The correspondence between physical appearances and emotions can be demonstrated in the attraction to the physical gestures of heroism and fearlessness, in the unattractiveness of the physical gestures of terror and fear—the attractive features caused by an old and sublime thought—and similar patterns follow for the experience of the infinite, mountains, storms and waves, and looking into a precipice (paragraph 57). The expression of hatred is repellent, the expression of love is attractive, and similar formulas regard the experience of pride, pettiness, fever, pain, and pleasurable reflections, which imbue the entire body with grace. Schiller concludes that these physical expressions are the result of a mechanical process of communication between the nerves and the mind that is no different than the relationship of paralysis to an injured ligament. It is possible for the recurrence of an emotion and sympathetic physical expressions for a psychic state to become habitual along with its physical expressions. If the emotion becomes an enduring characteristic, its sympathetic features will be etched into the machine and thus deuteropathically become organic, bringing about a perennial physiognomy of the individual that is all but inalterable, thus the mind shapes the body, and the experiences of youth may determine features for the remainder of life just as they inform moral character (paragraph 58). This phenomenon is observable in the lack of expression of the weak-minded, and can be extended to the emotions and characteristics described above. Regarding organic parts, for example, the shape and size of the nose, eyes, mouth, ears, and the color of the hair, and so on, it may be possible to draw certain limited scientific conclusions, though, to date, Lavater's work on physiognomy has only described prejudices and produced no valid scientific results (paragraph 59). In a footnote, Schiller draws attention to a further sympathetic relation between certain physical sensations and the mental associations they provoke, for example, a stomach cramp resulting in disgust and the recurrence of disgust reciprocally resulting in a cramp.

Chapter B, d: "Relaxation of Animal Nature is a Source of Perfection," §23, "It appears to act as a Hindrance," addresses the necessity of sleep. If the animal part of the human being provides all of the great advantages discussed above, it remains nonetheless ignoble, for the mind is slavishly bound to the activity of its tools, such that a periodic relaxation of the organism forces inactivity on the mind and periodically renders it inactive through sleep, which undeniably robs us of a third of our existence (paragraph 60). Further, our power of thought is extraordinarily dependent on the laws of the machine such that the former can impose a sudden stop to mental activity just when one is on the open path to truth. The intellect can barely stop to ponder an idea when the sluggish material being fails. The strings of the thought organ become slack at the slightest exertion; the body fails when it is needed most. What amazing steps the human being would make if it could think in a state of uninterrupted intensity? How could the human being reduce every idea to its ultimate elements, which the human being would pursue every phenomenon to its most hidden sources, if it could ceaselessly have them in mind? Why is this not the case?

§24, "Necessity of Relaxation," comprises a preamble to the concluding sections presented in five basic principles of the function of relaxation (paragraph 61): 1) The pleasurable experience was necessary to lead the human being toward perfection, therefore the human being is only perfectible because it experiences pleasure; 2) The nature of a finite being makes unpleasant sensations unavoidable, thus, although evil cannot be banned from the best of worlds, philosophers claim to find perfection in it; 3) The nature of a mixed being necessarily implies unpleasant sensations, because it is mostly dependent on them, therefore both pain and pleasure are necessary; 4) Every pain and every pleasure grows to infinite proportions; 5) Every pain and every pleasure of a mixed being aims at the destruction of that being.

§25, "Explanation," addresses the established law of the association of ideas: every feeling affects another feeling of the same kind and thus grows. The greater and more complex it becomes, the more associated feelings it arouses until it eventually dominates and occupies the mind entirely. Thus, every sensation is self-generating; every temporary state of the emotional faculty contains the beginning of a subsequent similar state of greater intensity (paragraph 62). Every mental sensation is associated with a similar animal sensation, to some extent dependent on nerve reactions. As the mental sensations increase, the nerve actions necessarily increase. Pathology teaches us that no nerve ever suffers in isolation, and every excess of focus here means a lack of focus there. Thus, every action of the nerves is self-generating. Just as nerve movements intensify mental sensations, mental sensations intensify nerve activity, forming a circle in which sensation must constantly grow. The activities in the machine causing the sensation of pain run counter to the harmonious tone that sustains them, that is, they constitute sickness. Sickness, however, cannot grow infinitely, therefore pain, which aims at the destruction of the subject, ceases with the total destruction of the machine. In the state of a pleasant emotion, the nerve activity is harmonious, favorable to the continued existence of the machine, and the state of the greatest psychological pleasure is the highest state of physical well-being, however, the pleasant emotion cannot perpetuate bodily health eternally (paragraph 63). To a certain degree, these neural actions are beneficial and truly constitute a state of health. If they exceed this point, they may bring about the highest level of activity and the highest momentary perfection, but they are then an excess of good health, which is no longer health. Health is only the good condition of natural processes that serves to perpetuate a future similar state. Therefore, an essential element of the concept of health is *permanency*. The body of the most debilitated lech achieves its highest harmony in the moment of excess, but such harmony is short lived, followed by a deep state of apathy, and is evidence of an unhealthy state. Consequently, exaggerated physical activity accelerates death as much as the greatest disharmony or the most acute sickness. Thus, both pleasure and pain draw us more quickly toward an unavoidable death, unless something exists that restricts their growth.

§26, "Merit of Relaxation": Precisely this limitation of the fragile machine, which appeared to provide arguments for its imperfection, serves to correct all of the malignant consequences of what the physical mechanism would otherwise inevitably bring about. Precisely this decrease and slackening of the organs prevents human strength from quickly wearing out, and does not allow for emotions to grow perpetually toward destruction (paragraph 64). Relaxation marks the phases of growth for every emotion, its climax and defervescence, providing the disturbed spirits time to recover their harmonious tone and the organs time for recovery. Therefore, the highest degrees of ecstasy, terror, and rage result in exhaustion, weakness, and fainting. Citing his own translation of

Shakespeare's *Macbeth* (II, 4): Schiller addresses the social function of sleep, during which the vital spirits return to the healthy balance necessary for continued existence; all of the tangled ideas and feelings, all of the strenuous activities that have tormented us during the day, are resolved in the total relaxation of the sensorium (paragraph 65). The harmony of the psychological process is restored and greets the newly awakened human being with more composure. Precisely this feature of the animal necessarily caused some who could have become happy to be sacrificed for the good of the public order and be forced to bear the oppression of hard labor. Many others, whom we tend to envy, probably without justification, had to torture their mental and physical powers with unceasing exertion in order to preserve peace in society at large. The same applies to the suffering of the sick and of unreasoning animals. Sleep seals the eye of grief, relieves the prince and the politician of the heavy burden of government, provides the sick vitality and brings peace to the harried soul, relieves the laborer from the voice of the overseer, and the abused animal from the tyranny of the human being (paragraph 66).

§27, "Division of the Connection": Finally, when the mind has achieved the end of its existence, the incomprehensible internal mechanism renders the body incapable of continuing as its tool. Wisdom itself in its economy created physical nature, such that despite constant compensation, attrition retakes the upper hand. Matter dissolves into its ultimate elements again, which now move through the kingdoms of nature in different forms and relationships to serve other purposes.

Philosophical Significance and Impact

Embarking from the position that materialist scientists and philosophers had been all too ready to limit the function of the body to that of a prison for the mind and the personality, Schiller's radical dialectical approach seeks not only to reconcile body and mind, animal and intellectual natures, but to demonstrate that it is in fact the body that makes moral improvement and happiness possible. Following the rejection of his first dissertation, Schiller's proposal for what would become his third dissertation announces the unusual divided approach "aus dem philosophischen und physiologischen Fach" (from the philosophical and physiological field; *NA* 21: 124). In an early version of his later aesthetic drive theory, Schiller states at the outset: "Was den Menschen jener Bestimmung näher bringt, es sei nun mittelbar oder unmittelbar, das wird ihn ergözen. Was ihn von ihr entfernt, wird ihn schmerzen. Was ihn schmerzt, wird er meiden, was ihn ergözt, danach wird er ringen" (That which brings the human individual closer to their destiny, either directly or indirectly, will make them happy. That which distances them from this goal will cause them pain. That which hurts them, they will avoid, that which delights them, they will pursue; *NA* 20: 11). For Schiller, as evidenced by the moral focus of his earliest and latest theoretical works, the pursuit of totality, harmony, and ultimately happiness through the reconciliation of drives was the unsolved problem of humanity. As a result, there are clear parallels between the earliest theoretical works that stretch far beyond the concrete references to Franz Moor and Fiesko, who are discussed as psychological case histories here (*NA* 20: 60). Schiller's discussion of pleasurable excess and the immoral pursuit of basic drives follows closely Shaftesbury's articulation of the problem in *Characteristics of Men, Manners, Opinions, Times* (1711): to the harmonious and whole individual, "low and sordid pleasures," even "when Will and Pleasure are synonymous"—are detrimental (Shaftesbury, *Characteristics*, volume II, part II, §I, 29–30).

The thesis regarding the imbalance of drives, which dates back at least to the First Virtue Speech and the first dissertation (*NA* 20: 11), appears repeatedly in Schiller's later theoretical works. In *Ueber Anmut und Würde* (On Grace and Dignity, 1793), Schiller articulates three possible states of the inner balance or imbalance of drives: 1) barbarism, the dictatorship of reason over feeling; 2) savagery, the dictatorship of feeling over reason; and 3) totality, the reconciliation of feeling and reason and of duty and inclination. All three ideas play significant roles in the *Ästhetische Briefe* in Schiller's analysis of the harmony of the *Form-* and *Stofftrieb* (Twelfth Letter; *NA* 20: 344–346). Already in the "Schaubühne" Speech of 1784, Schiller calls for the cultivation of "einen mittleren Zustand" (an intermediary state; *NA* 20: 90) which he refers to in the third of the *Ästhetische Briefe* as "den dritten Charakter" (the third character; *NA* 20: 315) or "mittlere Stimmung" (intermediary disposition; *NA* 20: 375). Schiller thus draws a line from the harmonious band of virtue in the First Virtue Speech of 1779—the mediator between sensual and moral nature—to the concept of the totality of the whole individual presented in the fourth of the Ästhetische Briefe. Here, through the moral education of the individual, a transition is created between the "Herrschaft bloßer Kräfte" (rule of mere might or state of nature/necessity) and the "Herrschaft der Gesetze" (rule of the laws of reason; *NA* 20: 315), resulting in "Totalität des Charakters" (totality of character; *NA* 20: 318). Although drive theories were proliferating around 1780, Schiller's version is among the earliest and most enduring, predating Johann Friedrich Blumenbach's (1752–1840) *Über den Bildungstrieb und das Zeugungsgeschäfte* (On the Formative Drive of the Generation Process, 1781) and Karl Philipp Moritz's (1756–1793) *Magazin zur Erfahrungsseelenkunde als ein Lesebuch für Gelehrte und Ungelehrte* (Journal of Experiential Psychology, as Reading for Scholars and Laypersons, 1783–1793). The final lines of Schiller's "Die Weltweisen" (The Worldly Philosophers, 1795)—reminiscent of his successful dissertation, are cited prominently in both Richard von Krafft-Ebing's (1840–1902) *Psychopathia Sexualis* (1886) and Freud's *Das Unbehagen in der Kultur* (Civilization and its Discontents, 1930). Likewise, the concept of perfection-as-happiness, which appears here in the fourth text in just over a year in its most articulate form, lays the groundwork for the *Spieltrieb* (play drive) in the fifteenth of the *Ästhetische Briefe*: the human being "ist nur da ganz Mensch, wo er spielt (is only fully human when at play; *NA* 20: 359).

Although it has often been pointed out that Schiller had read Lavater's *Physiognomische Fragmente* (1775–1778), there is little note of the fact that Schiller disapproved of Lavater's work in moral terms as directly contrary to his own theory of human freedom. In fact, far from employing Lavater's theories, Schiller deconstructed them in his portrayals of the brilliant and unattractive Franz Moor, the brilliant victim of racism Hassan in *Fiesko*, and the unattractive, yet moral and sensitive Christian Wolf in "Der Verbrecher aus verlorener Ehre" (The Criminal of Lost Honor, 1786)—tracing the challenges of all three characters to early-life trauma related to lack of personal, familial, and institutional recognition. Here, Schiller concludes that Lavater's attempts to interpret the physical forms of a range of unusual characters may in the end result in Lavater himself becoming a cartoon. The appearance of the psychosomatic phenomenon of homesickness central to Schiller's first novella, "Eine großmütige Handlung" (A Magnanimous Act, 1782), first appears here, as do the derivative metaphor of the sickly plant in a new climate (which appears repeatedly throughout Schiller's works), and the frequently invoked microscope and autopsy metaphors, both of which represent scientific insight into nature's most secret processes.

Too much is made of the intentionally elusive Deist references to God and the creator in Schiller's university works, which were written in a coercive environment in which superficial gestures of piety were policed by the duke himself. The logic of Schiller's decidedly anti-religious historical anthropology is particularly evident in the chronology of the appearance of his "clever priests," who necessarily pre-exist the "gods" they create (NA 20: 54), and in his clear habit of following his few mentions of God (singular) with an immediate reminder that there have been many gods (plural), for example, in "An die Freude," in which Schiller inverts the concept of divine judgment through verb tense as a purely human affair: humans judge first, after which God, a human projection, can do nothing but agree—"richtet Gott wie wir gerichtet" (God judges as we have judged; NA 1: 171). Once free of the religious constraints of the Karlsschule, and despite censorship, Schiller consistently characterizes the socio-political and anthropological function of religion as that of a temporary behavioral guide for an unenlightened populace—a "Surrogat der wahren Tugend" (surrogate for true virtue; NA 26: 330–331)—a transitional need he compares to the voluntary use of handcuffs by a violent mental patient in his letter to Prince Augustenburg of December 1793.

References

Abel, Jacob Friedrich. 1995. *Eine Quellenedition zum Phiolosophie Unterricht an der Stuttgarter Karlsschule (1773–1782)*. Wolfgang Riedel, ed. Würzburg: Königshausen & Neumann.

Alt, Peter-André. 2000 and 2004, *Schiller: Leben-Werk-Zeit: Eine Biographie*. 2 Volumes. Munich: Beck.

Beiser, Frederick. 2005. *Schiller as Philosopher: A Re-Examination*. New York: Oxford University Press.

Beiser, Frederick. 2008. "Schiller as Philosopher: A Reply to My Critics." *Inquiry*. 51 (1). 63–78.

Conti, Patricia. 2007. "Hunger and Love: Schiller and the origin of drive dualism in Freud's work." *International Journal of Psychoanalysis*. 88 (1). 167–182.

Cooper, Anthony Ashley, Third Earl of Shaftesbury. 1984. *Characteristics of Men, Manners, Opinions, Times*. John M. Robertson, ed. Indianapolis: Bobbs Merrill.

Dewhurst, Kenneth and Nigel Reeves. 1978. *Friedrich Schiller: Medicine, Philosophy, Literature*. Oxford: Sandford Publications.

Ferguson, Adam. 1969 [1773]. *An Essay on the History of Civil Society*. Fourth Edition. London: Gregg International Publishers.

High, Jeffrey. 2004. *Schillers Rebellionskonzept und die Französische Revolution*. Lewiston. Mellen Press.

High, Jeffrey. 2012. "'Judex!' Blasphemy, and Posthumous Conversion: Schiller and (No) Religion." *Yearbook of the Goethe Society of North America*. Rochester: Camden House. 141–161.

High, Jeffrey. 2013. "'Gehört allzuviel Güte, Leutseligkeit und grosse Freygebigkeit im engsten Verstande zur Tugend?': Socrates as Secular Jesus in Schiller's First Karlsschule Speech." *Reading Schiller*. Special Issue of *Philosophical Readings*. Laura Anna Macor, ed. 7–49.

Hohenheim, Franziska von. 1981. *Tagbuch der Gräfin Franziska von Hohenheim späteren Herzogin von Württemberg*. Faksimile-Ausgabe mit einem Vorwort v. Peter Lahnstein. Reutlingen. 16.

Humboldt, Wilhelm von. 1830 [1907]. "Ueber Schiller und den Gang seiner Geistesentwicklung." *Gesammelte Schriften*. Volume 6. Albert Leitzmann, ed. Berlin: Behr. 492–527.

Hutcheson, Francis. 1971 [1726]. *An Inquiry Concerning Moral Good and Evil*, in *An Inquiry into the Original of our Ideas of Beauty and Virtue*. Second Edition. New York: Garland Publishing.

Luserke-Jaqui, Matthias with Grit Dommes. 2011. *Schiller-Handbuch. Leben—Werk—Wirkung*. Stuttgart: Metzler.

Macor, Laura Anna. 2010. *Der Morastige Zirkel der menschlichen Bestimmung*. Würzburg: Königshausen & Neumann.

Macor, Laura Anna. 2011. "Die Moralphilosophie des jungen Schiller: Ein 'Kantianer ante litteram.'" *Who is this Schiller Now?* Jeffrey L. High, Nicholas Martin, and Norbert Oellers, eds. Rochester, NY: Camden House. 99–115.

Macor, Laura Anna. 2022. "Heinrich von Kleist, Johann Joachim Spalding and the *Bestimmung des Menschen*: Philosophy as a Way of Life?." *Heinrich von Kleist: Literary and Philosophical Paradigms*. Jeffrey L. High, Rebecca Stewart, and Elaine Chen, eds. Rochester, NY: Camden House.

Moland, Lydia L. 2017. "Friedrich Schiller." *The Stanford Encyclopedia of Philosophy*. Edward N. Zalta, ed. URL = <https://plato.stanford.edu/archives/sum2017/entries/schiller/>.

Nilges, Yvonne. 2018. "Schiller, Rousseau, and the Aesthetic Education of Man." *Aesthetic Reason and Imaginative Freedom*. Maria del Rosario Acosta Lopez and Jeffrey L. Powell, eds. Albany: State University of New York Press.

Plattner, Ernst. *1772. Anthropologie für Aerzte und Weltweise*.

Friedrich Schiller. 2004. *Sämtliche Werke in fünf Bänden*. Peter-André Alt, Albert Meier, and Wolfgang Riedel, eds. Volume 5. Munich: Hanser and dtv.

Spalding, Johann Joachim. 2006. *Die Bestimmung des Menschen*. Albrecht Beutel, Daniela Kirschkowski, and Dennis Prause, eds. Tübingen: Mohr Siebeck.

Streicher, Andreas. 1974 [1836]. *Andreas Streichers Schiller-Biographie*. Herbert Kraft, ed. Mannheim.

Wilkinson, Elizabeth. 1961. *Schiller: Poet or Philosopher?*. Oxford: Clarendon Press.

CHAPTER 5

What Effect Can a Good Permanent Theatre Actually Achieve? (1785)

Sandra Vlasta

In his so-called *Schaubühnenrede* [theatre speech], Schiller presents his theory of the theatre as a public medium: as one of the most important stately institutions, comparable to religion and the law but ultimately more effective than both. Theatre educates, it enables the audience to understand themselves and others, it is a place both for political criticism and for the formation of a national spirit. Ultimately, the theatre is the place where the human can feel its own humanity and from where an egalitarian society can begin. With regard to the development of Schiller's philosophical thoughts, we find, in his theatre speech, a first presentation of the "mittlerer Zustand" [middle state], later elaborated in his *Ästhetische Briefe* [1794; *Aesthetic Letters*].

Textual Genesis

Schiller's *Vom Wirken der Schaubühne auf das Volk* [*On the Theatre's Effect on the People*] speech was given on 26 June 1784 at a public meeting of the *Kurpfälzische Deutsche Gesellschaft* in Mannheim: a conservative language society that was dedicated to the study and advancement of the German language and its literature, of which Schiller had recently become a member. Through this speech, Schiller sought to present himself to the members of the society and to gain the position of its secretary. Schiller was well known in Mannheim at the time. His first play *Die Räuber* [*The Robbers*] had premiered in 1782 at

S. Vlasta (✉)
University of Genoa, Genoa, Italy
e-mail: sandra.vlasta@unige.it

the local *Hof- und Nationaltheater* [Court and National Theatre] that had been reopened as a modern theatre after major renovation in 1777. Schiller's plays, *Die Verschwörung des Fiesko zu Genua* [*Fiesco's Conspiracy in Genoa*] and *Kabale und Liebe* [*Intrigue and Love*], premiered in revised versions in January and April 1784 in Mannheim (they had premiered in Bonn and Frankfurt, respectively, in earlier versions). Already in September 1783, the theatre's director, Wolfgang Heribert Freiherr von Dalberg (who also directed the premiere of *The Robbers*), had offered Schiller a fixed-term contract as a playwright for a year. Thus, with his speech at the society the writer also wanted to position himself as the playwright of the local theatre in Mannheim.

Schiller's *Schaubühnenrede* was perhaps composed as an answer to questions that Dalberg had posed in May 1784 to the board of the Mannheim theatre, of which the playwright was also a member. Dalberg had asked about the nature of a national theatre, about how a theatre could become a national playhouse and if there already existed a German theatre that deserved this title (Schiller 1785, p. 194).

The speech also complements an earlier text by Schiller entitled *Über das gegenwärtige teutsche Theater* [*On Contemporary German Theatre*] (1782) in which he criticises the actual condition of the theatre as a mere place of amusement and uses similar arguments against the theatre as those deployed by Jean-Jacques Rousseau in his *Lettre à d'Alembert sur les spectacles* (1758; *Letter to M. D'Alembert on Spectacles*). At the time of the *Schaubühnenrede*, Schiller had become an active member of the theatre and therefore wrote from the perspective of an insider. Peter-André Alt underlines this development and states that the speech is part of Schiller's public profiling as an advocate of the theatre (Alt 2000, p. 383). Unlike his earlier lamentation about the poor conditions of the German theatre, Schiller now formulates his vision of an aesthetic education through drama and thus underscores his own role and its moral dignity. Schiller's new role is underlined in the print version of the *Schaubühnenrede*: whereas the first theatre essay was signed with an anonymous "U." (and not chosen for re-publication by Schiller), the later essay identifies the author as a member of the *Kurpfälzische Deutsche Gesellschaft* and as "herzogl. Weimarischer Rat" [Weimar ducal councillor].

Unlike earlier speeches delivered to the *Deutsche Gesellschaft*, Schiller's discourse was not published in the society's proceedings. Consequently, Schiller included it in the first (and only) issue of the *Rheinische Thalia* in March 1785, a journal edited by himself and published in Mannheim by Christian Friedrich Schwan. This first print version is entitled *Was kann eine gute stehende Schaubühne eigentlich wirken?* [*What Effect Can a Good Permanent Theatre Actually Achieve?*]. In 1802, Schiller included the speech in the fourth volume of his *Kleinere prosaische Schriften* [*Short prose writings*]. For this occasion, he changed the title once more to *Die Schaubühne als moralische Anstalt betrachtet* [*The Theatre Considered as a Moral Institution*] and discarded several passages, not least the original introductory part.

Contents

The speech is divided into three parts—an introduction, main part, and conclusion (see the useful scheme in Zelle 2011, p. 358). In the introduction (eliminated in the 1802 print version), Schiller poses his central question: "What effect can a theatre achieve?" (SW 5:819). The centre of his discussion revolves around two central themes. (i) The anthropological foundation of Schiller's view of the theatre—the "mittlere Zustand" (SW 5:821). (ii) Schiller's idea of the function of the playhouse, that is, its role as a higher court that exists parallel to and even above state jurisdiction and religion. He expands his main argument by adding further aspects in five subsections, the final one of which constitutes the conclusion of the speech.

To begin with, Schiller introduces his central question by addressing the hatred and the contempt that the four academic faculties at the time (theology, medicine, law, and philosophy) and other public institutions express towards art. In order to overcome the dislike between "truth" and "beauty" (SW 5:819), he proposes to reconcile them, suggesting that the stage is the enlightening and educational institution through which this can be achieved. He anticipates that his presentation of the theatre as a place of education will make it clear that it is indeed one of the most important state institutions. The final part of the introduction addresses Rousseau's above-mentioned criticism of the theatre as expressed in his *Lettre à d'Alembert* and puts it into perspective. Schiller argues that, just as Christianity cannot be held responsible for the atrocities committed in its name, art and the theatre should not be blamed for the failures of those who execute it badly. Thus, the last paragraph of the introduction represents a reversal of what Schiller himself had expressed only two years before in his essay on German theatre, *Über das gegenwärtige teutsche Theater*.

The main part of the speech (i.e. the first part in the 1802 print version) begins with a brief paragraph on Schiller's *Ausgleichsästhetik* (aesthetics of compensation), i.e. the balance between mind and body (*commercium mentis et corporis*) that can be found in a "mittlerer Zustand" (SW 5:821, middle state). In this "mittlerer Zustand", the two extremes of body and mind, sensual matter and morality are reconciled, and an equilibrium is established. This equilibrium, according to Schiller, corresponds to the aesthetic drive and the feeling for beauty (SW 5:821). It is, finally, the theatre where the formation of the mind as well as that of the heart ("die Bildung des Verstands und des Herzens", SW 5: 821-822) is united with the highest form of entertainment.

The following paragraphs are based on this anthropological thesis and are dedicated to the main argument of the speech, that is, Schiller's intention to implement the theatre with its particular jurisdiction as one of the highest state institutions. The stage is discussed in relation to the state, whose laws remain dead letters (SW 5: 824) and have a negative impact due to their limiting function. The theatre is furthermore discussed with respect to religion, which has a positive impact because it appeals to man's sensual matter and touches even the deepest recesses of his heart ("bis in die verborgensten Winkel des Herzens", SW 5: 822). In Schiller's enlightened times, however, religion has lost its force: as he states, art and in particular the stage have taken over its role and use the same means—imagination—to achieve more satisfying results. Whereas religion uses imagination to pose riddles without solving them, the theatre can show "Laster und Tugend, Glückseligkeit und Elend, Torheit und Weisheit" (SW 5:822; vice and virtue, bliss and hardship, foolishness and wisdom) in many colours and shades and resolves the riddles it has posed. In this manner, representations on stage have a stronger and longer-lasting effect than religion; theatrical jurisdiction may therefore replace the religious one.

Schiller's argument is not new: the idea of the theatre as a law-making institution had already been expressed by others in the eighteenth century: by Gotthold Ephraim Lessing in his *Hamburgische Dramaturgie* (7. Stück) and by Louis Sébastian Mercier, for instance. On the one hand, this idea is part of a strategy to legitimate the theatre. On the other hand, it is part of an enlightened criticism of the feudal state: the theatre becomes a place of moral jurisdiction and questions the political legitimation of the feudal state. The argument that the theatre is a law-making institution is part of a strategy in which morality and politics become two distinct entities and where morality is used to criticise (feudal) politics. As Reinhart Koselleck (1973) has shown, by suggesting a separation of morality from politics, the latter is criticised: moral law is thus seen as something higher than political law—it is pure whereas politics is immoral (Zelle 2011, p. 353). For Schiller, too, the worldly jurisdiction has power, but wrongly so, while the theatrical jurisdiction does not have power, but is right (Koselleck 1973). In what follows, Schiller underscores the dramatical effect of the theatre on the audience and rates it higher than both law and morality. He cites several well-known stage "criminals" (SW 5:823; Verbrecher), such as Medea, Lady Macbeth, and Franz Moor from Schiller's own play *The Robbers*, and stresses the lasting effect of their representations on stage (Schiller in fact talks about "Gemälde", pictures SW 5: 823, 824) that create everlasting deterrent memories that can easily be recalled.

In the next part, Schiller concentrates on tragedy and highlights its functions, namely the determent from vices and the incitement of virtues. In so doing, the tragedy, and with it the theatre, goes further than worldly justice. In the next moment of his argument, Schiller asserts that the theatre has educational functions in realms that law or religion does not touch at all, i.e. in the case of foolishness. This moves the discussion towards a different and distinct genre: the comedy. The means of the comedy are "Scherz und Satire" (SW 5:825; jokes and satire) and "Spott und Verachtung" (SW 5:825; mockery and scorn). Whereas "Scherz und Satire" enable us to laugh about our weaknesses, "Spott und Verachtung" might hurt our feelings and thus are disposed to have a much stronger effect on us. Accordingly, Schiller argues that compared to tragedies, comedies are the more effective genre.

All that said, Schiller is not unrestrictedly ambitious. He is well aware that Harpagon, the main character in Molière's play *The Miser* (1668), has not discouraged any usurer and that Sara's death in Lessing's *Miss Sara Sampson* (1755) will not scare off a single "Wollüstling" (SW 5: 827; voluptuary). Still, to Schiller, the theatre (like other literary genres) represents a school of general and practical wisdom. It conveys human nature through a concrete spectacle that enables the audience to understand people and the fullness of their characters in a way that would not be possible outside the confines of the theatre. In a similar vein, through plays, we are familiarised with different fates and are thus better prepared to accept predetermination and serendipity in our own lives. (Here, Schiller implicitly refers to elements of baroque poetics, such as *fortuna*, *constantia* and *consolatio*.) Accordingly, we see here Schiller's interest in the anthropological and psychological dimensions of theatre. In the next paragraph, he continues to talk about these aspects of the stage and refers to the motives for actions that are unfolded on stage. Here, Schiller introduces a historical perspective when he emphasises that the fact that humanity and tolerance ("Menschlichkeit und Duldung" SW 5:828) have found their way into courtrooms and the hearts of sovereigns is not least due to the theatre.

In the next part, Schiller touches upon further aspects of the theatre. The speech increasingly becomes a more heterogeneous list of reasons that are all bent on presenting the theatre as one of the pre-eminent state institutions. Fleetingly, Schiller mentions that the theatre is particularly instructive for those who rule as only in the playhouse they will hear the truth. The theatre thus becomes a sort of anthropologically motivated "mirror for princes" (Zelle 2011, p. 354). Eventually, the theatre is called a place for "die ganze Aufklärung des Verstandes" (SW 5:828, the complete education of reason). Schiller enumerates the different facets that contribute to this cultivation: the theatre enables comparison between peoples (anthropological) and centuries (diachronical). It elicits reflection upon stereotypes, on superstition, and it enables more accurate expression. One more time, Schiller gives a concrete example of the theatre's influence when he refers to the fact that tolerance towards different religions was prepared by plays even before Lessing's *Nathan der Weise* (1779; *Nathan the Wise*). He proposes that the theatre could have a similarly positive effect on child-rearing, a realm in which Schiller predicts a number of problems. Furthermore, the playhouse could be a place for the instruction of the people and the sovereigns could use it as a medium through which they could speak to their subjects—if they only knew how. Though for this to be the case, playwrights would need to be patriots.

The following paragraph is another climax of the speech, with regard to its content and its register. Here, Schiller turns to the theatre's possible impact on the spirit of a nation. He first gives a brief definition of the "Nationalgeist" (SW 5:830; spirit of a nation), which refers to the particularities with regard to opinions and predispositions that distinguish the individual nations from each other. Then he refers to ancient Greece as an example of a nation in which the plays dealt with patriotic themes and where one could feel both the Greek spirit in the theatre and the enormous interest the state had in the institution. Here, contrary to Lessing in his *Hamburgische Dramaturgie*, Schiller proposes a positive atmosphere of departure for the theatre: if only the playhouse could become a "Nationalbühne" (SW 5:830; national stage), then Germany would also become a nation. Schiller enumerates several schemes that would need to be undertaken in order to reach this aim: first, the playwrights would need to agree on the main aim of the theatre to be a national stage, and second, they would need to deal with national themes only in their plays.

In the final two paragraphs of the speech, rather than its didactical and juridical aspect, and with it, Schiller's criticism of current politics, Schiller takes up the anthropological groundwork from the main section. Like in the first part, Schiller refers to Jean-Baptiste Dubos' dictum about man's "ewiger Trieb nach Tätigkeit" (SW 5: 830; eternal drive for activity), on the one hand, and idleness on the other. Once again, Schiller gives several examples as to what might happen if these two extremes are not well balanced: if man gives in to sensuality alone, then he becomes an "animal" and eventually a threat to society's peace. Yet, a life of mind taken too far leads to an imbalance: scholars may become "dumpfe Pedanten" (SW 5:831; dull pedants). Since only art is able to unite the two extremes of man, Schiller again presents the theatre as the ideal place to find our "middle state". The final paragraph praises the theatre and enumerates some examples of how the two parts of man are united in the playhouse: "Die Schaubühne ist die Stiftung, wo sich Vergnügen mit Unterricht, Ruhe mit Anstrengung, Kurzweil mit Bildung gattet [...]" (SW 5: 831; The theatre is the institution where pleasure and instruction, rest and effort, and disport and learning unite). The theatre gives rise to the perfect balance between the individual parts and in doing so even has therapeutic effects: it may free us from grief, bad moods, and stress, and will give us back our real self. Here, then, Schiller unites the classical idea of the therapeutic effects of catharsis and Lessing's discourse on tragical catharsis as a compensation for emotional extremes. Again, this points to the balancing effect of the theatre that stimulates the elements that are missing: "Der Glückliche wird nüchtern, und der Sichere besorgt. Der empfindsame Weichling härtet sich zum Manne, der rohe Unmensch fängt hier zum erstenmal zu empfinden an" (SW 5:831; Those who are happy sober up and those who are confident become worried. The sensitive one becomes a man, the brute starts to feel for the first time).

Finally, Schiller refers to an aspect of the theatre that he calls a "triumph for nature" (SW 5:831; "Triumph für dich, Natur"): the shared social experience of the theatre enables a feeling of sympathy between men that overcomes boundaries of rank, class, and origin (SW 5:831). Theatre creates an egalitarian community through a collective forgetting of who we are (i.e. in the sociopolitical world) and where only the collective theatrical experience as well as our common humanity counts. As Helmut J. Schneider has underlined, this "Verbrüderung" (2020, 19; fraternisation) takes place in the space in front of the stage, i.e. in the auditorium rather than on stage. There, on the contrary, all the intrigues, pretences, and manipulations that divide society are in full swing. The collective experience of art enables us to overcome these divisions and to become a united people. This final thought promotes an egalitarian idea of society that, however, is not further elaborated and remains limited to the theatre.

Philosophical Significance and Impact

Schiller's *Schaubühnenrede* is an important document of eighteenth-century theatre and dramaturgy as well as a significant public document recounting the young author's anthropological ideas concerning classical aesthetics. What is more, the text in itself is an example of successful rhetoric as shown by its clear structure, the effective use of rhetorical figures, and the meta-level on which Schiller refers to the rhetorical aspects of the theatre.

With regard to theatre and dramaturgy in the eighteenth century, the speech displays a canon of well-known plays of the time, and Schiller illustrates his arguments with numerous examples. He refers both to his own work (*The Robbers*) and to plays by other writers from the history of the theatre (e.g. Euripides' Iphigenia in Aulis and Medea, Shakespeare's Hamlet, Macbeth, and King Lear) as well as from a contemporary repertory (e.g. Johann Christian Brandes' *Ariadne auf Naxos* [Ariadne on Naxos], Lessing's *Miss Sara Sampson*, and Friedrich Ludwig Schröder's *Berverley oder der englische Spieler* [Berverley or the English player]). In doing so, the speech documents the plays that were contemporaneously staged and thus familiar to Schiller's audience. The young author's self-confidence is also noteworthy: he mentions his own first play amidst those by classical authors and well-recognised contemporary colleagues. This of course is part of the self-positioning as an established (Mannheim) playwright that constitutes one of Schiller's overarching aims for his speech.

Furthermore, the text constitutes a summary of the thoughts on the role of the theatre in the eighteenth century and refers to the writings of Johann Christoph Gottsched, Gotthold Ephraim Lessing, Louis Sébastian Mercier, and others. In fact, the wording from the later title of the speech, *Die Schaubühne als moralische Anstalt* [*The Theatre as a Moral Institution*], has become a way of referring to Lessing's theatrical concept and, eventually, to any form of functionalising theatre in a moral and didactical manner. As was customary at the time, Schiller excerpts pieces from other writings without citing them. Besides the writings mentioned above, he draws heavily on Johann Georg Sulzer's article on "Schauspiel" [drama] from his *Allgemeine Theorie der Schönen Künste* [1771-1774; General Theory of the Fine Arts] and uses it as the anthropological basis of his own thoughts on the theatre. A second firm basis is Schiller's time as a student at the Karlsschule in Stuttgart, where he studied the anthropology of the so-called *philosophische Ärzte* [philosophical doctors]. The speech is a first document of the strong influence the study of these ideas had upon him.

By combining these sources and ideas, the *Schaubühnenrede* becomes the first text in which Schiller develops his own aesthetic theory, later elaborated in the *Ästhetische Briefe*. He explains the concept of the *mittlerer Zustand* (albeit briefly) which had appeared for the first time as the *Mittelkraft* [middle force] in his second and third dissertations. It later recurs in the *Letters* as the "mittlere" or "freie Stimmung" of the "ästhetischen" *Zustands* [*Über die ästhetische Erziehung des Menschen*, 20. Brief, SW 5:633; the middle or free disposition of the aesthetic state]. Again, Schiller's thoughts are inspired by different sources which he excerpts but does not quote (see Wolfgang Riedel (1985) for a documentation of them). As shown above, the speech, especially its final part, gives several examples of how art, and in particular the theatre, is the place where this *mittlerer Zustand* can be attained, and the text thus becomes a first practical example of Schiller's later *Ausgleichsästhetik* (aesthetics of compensation).

The idea of the theatre as an institution of (moral) jurisdiction that questions politics and the legitimation of the feudal state, shared by Schiller with other theoreticians of the theatre, has been pointed to as one of the most radical aspects of his speech. Still, as Zelle (2011, p. 353) states, this is only one relatively briefly addressed aspect of the speech and one should be careful not to overstate it. Rather, the speech illustrates Schiller's interest in the anthropological and psychological aspects of theatre. He builds on information acquired as a medical student in Stuttgart, merges it with his knowledge on the theatre and on philosophical aesthetics, and his experience as a playwright and theatre practitioner (to use an anachronistic term), and starts to create his own theory of aesthetics. In the speech, we see the first results of these considerations.

References

Alt, Peter-André. 2000. *Schiller. Leben—Werk—Zeit*. 2 volumes. Munich: C.H. Beck.
Koselleck, Reinhart. 1973 [1959]. *Kritik und Krise. Eine Studie zur Pathogenese der bürgerlichen Welt*. Frankfurt am Main: Suhrkamp.
Lessing, Gotthold Ephraim. 1767. *Hamburgische Dramaturgie*. Band 1. Hamburg: Cramer.
Mercier, Louis Sébastian. 1773. *Du théâtre ou Nouvel essai sur l'art dramatique*. Amsterdam: E. van Harrevelt.
Riedel, Wolfgang. 1985. *Die Anthropologie des jungen Schiller. Zur Ideengeschichte der medizinischen Schriften und der „Philosophischen Briefe"*. Würzburg: Königshausen und Neumann.
Schiller, Friedrich. 1785. Dramaturgische Preißfragen. *Thalia* vol. 1, no. 1: 194-199.
Schiller, Friedrich. 1782. Über das gegenwärtige teutsche Theater. *Wirtembergisches Repertorium der Literatur* vol. 1 (1. Stück).
Schneider, Helmut J. 2020. Der große Menschheitsaugenblick. Zu Schillers politischer Publikumsdramaturgie in *Don Karlos*. In Schillers Theaterpraxis, ed. Peter-André Alt and Stefanie Hundehege, 9-38. Berlin/Boston: de Gruyter.
Sulzer, Johann Georg. 1771-1774. *Allgemeine Theorie der Schönen Künste*. Leipzig: Weidmann und Reich.
Zelle, Carsten. 2011 [2005]. Was kann eine gute stehende Schaubühne eigentlich wirken? (1785). In *Schiller Handbuch. Leben—Werk—Wirkung*, ed. Matthias Luserke-Jaqui, 343-358. Stuttgart: Verlag J.B. Metzler.

CHAPTER 6

Philosophical Letters (1786)

Antonino Falduto

TEXTUAL GENESIS

The *Philosophical Letters* are divided into five parts. A text written in the form of an explanatory supplement to reminiscences (*Vorerinnerung*, SW 5: 336-337) serves as a preamble to the first (*Julius an Raphael*, SW 5: 337-340) and second letters (*Julius an Raphael*, SW 5: 340-342), addressed by Julius to Raphael. After, follows a short reply by Raphael (*Raphael an Julius*, SW 5: 342-343); and then follows a longer letter from Julius to Raphael (SW 5: 343-358, which also contains the so-called *Theosophie des Julius*, SW 5: 344-354) which ends the epistolary novel. In the manner of a prosecutor of this fictive epistolary, Gottfried Körner writes (1788) a literary piece for publication in the 1789 volume 7 of the *Thalia*, entitled "Raphael to Julius". This unexpected continuation of the fictive dialogue between the two young friends comes as a surprise to Schiller, who was not awaiting a resumption of the earlier discussion—a discussion which was held, as he notes, in a bygone stage of his life (see Schiller's letter to Körner dated April 15th, 1788).

We are informed, with certainty, about Schiller's project of writing this epistolary novel as soon as 1782. In fact, the lyric *Die Freundschaft* (*On Friendship*), which will be republished in the context of the so-called *Theosophy of Julius*, appears already in the published *Anthologie auf das Jahr 1782* (SW 1: 29-113). In the 1782 collection of poems, the lyric dedicated to the topic of friendship already appeared with the following supplementary information in the subtitle: "From Julius' Letters to Raphael, a still unpublished novel" ("*Aus den Briefen*

A. Falduto (✉)
Department of Humanities, University of Ferrara, Ferrara, Italy
e-mail: antonino.falduto@unife.it

© The Author(s), under exclusive license to Springer Nature Switzerland AG 2023
A. Falduto, T. Mehigan (eds.), *The Palgrave Handbook on the Philosophy of Friedrich Schiller*, https://doi.org/10.1007/978-3-031-16798-0_6

Julius an Raphael; einem noch ungedruckten Roman", SW 1: 91). Thus, the subtitle itself unconditionally proves that, at least as early as 1782, Schiller already has in mind the project of undertaking the composition of an epistolary novel, that will nonetheless remain just a project, as its fragmentary realisation shows.

It is a fact agreed upon and taken for granted in the context of the more recent philological research dedicated to the *Philosophical Letters* (in particular after and thanks to the extremely accurate philological study by Koopmann [Koopmann 1976]) that the *Theosophy of Julius* must be, chronologically, the first part of the text written by Schiller and around which the whole composition of the unfinished novel revolves (see also Riedel 1985: 153-154, and the commentary by von Wiese and Koopmann in NA XXI: 160; a slightly different perspective on the composition history of the *Philosophical Letters* is sustained by Beiser 2005: 33).

Nonetheless, against the temptation of thinking about a long evolutive process culminating with the publication of the unfinished novel, there is no way of distinguishing between a clearly attestable earlier core of the whole writing, to which later revisions are added, and it remains impossible to establish whether the manuscript of the *Philosophical Letters* lay some years untouched before Schiller publishes it in 1786, or whether Schiller revises it (and in which way) before the publication, and when and how long exactly. In his commentary to Schiller's writing (see SW 5: 1184), Wolfgang Riedel points at the difficulty of proving the conjectures that Raphael's stances towards and against metaphysical themes are newer additions subjoining the original version of the manuscript.

The topics treated in the *Philosophical Letters* attest to the proximity of the novel to Schiller's other works from 1782. In particular, there are overt overlaps between the *Letters* and lyrics published in the already mentioned *Anthologie auf das Jahr 1782*, as *Die Freundschaft* (SW 1: 91-93) and the odes dedicated to Laura show, namely: *Fantasie an Laura* (SW 1: 36-38), *Laura am Klavier* (SW 1: 41-43), *Vorwurf an Laura* (SW 1: 75-77), *Das Geheimniß der Reminiszenz: An Laura* (SW 1: 86-90), *Melancholie an Laura* (SW 1: 93-97; on the *Anthologie* themes, see Iffert 1926). The same is the case for the hymn *Der Triumf der Liebe* (SW 1: 60-66), a speech dating back to 1780, during Schiller's time in the Karlsschule (the so-called second Karlsschule speech: *Die Tugend in ihren Folgen betrachtet*, SW 5: 280-287), and the first section of Schiller's first medical dissertation from 1779 (*Philosophie der Physiologie*, SW 5: 250-268; on this dissertation, see for example Falduto 2020). Apart from the similarity concerning the topics treated, in the *Philosophical Letters* Schiller makes metaphysical arguments using the *pro-et-contra* methodology he acquired while at the *Karlsschule* (he also uses the methodology elsewhere in some of the works from his earlier years: for instance, *Der Spaziergang unter den Linden*, 1782, SW 5: 327-332; *Der Jüngling und der Greis*, 1782, SW 5: 332-334 [on this point, see Riedel 2011]). This methodology already constituted, at the end of the seventies, a literary arrangement for playing out different and divergent positions. As Schiller admits in a letter to Körner in April 1788, already by that point his method for literary textual composition consisted in using, from the philosophical writings he was acquainted with, only those materials that could be poetically transposed (this letter and useful remarks on it can be found in the commentary to Schiller's writing in SW 5:1192). And in fact, the focal subject matter of the *Philosophical Letters*—that is, a philosophical matter which had to be useful for stimulating humour and imagination—had become his favourite topic already by the end of seventies at the *Karlsschule* in Stuttgart.

CONTENTS

The *Philosophical Letters* narrate a crisis-inducing awakening from youthful metaphysical dreams in the style of an autobiographical analysis. In the *Letters*, the perspective of the younger correspondent, Julius, who represents Schiller through the development of his philosophical formation, is predominant. Only one letter is provided by Julius' older friend, Raphael, in whose lineaments scholars have recognised (i) Schiller's teacher at the Karlschule Jakob Friedrich Abel, (ii) his friend Christian Gottfried Körner, and (iii) the librarian from Meiningen Wilhelm Friedrich Hermann Reinwald.

The *Letters* can also be read backwards, from the last to the first. This is because the *Theosophy of Julius*, found in the middle of the last of Julius' letters, is the oldest text representing the former philosophical ideas of a younger pupil, while the first letters and the preamble are newer additions, which have the function of contextualising the older text. The scope is that of shedding light on the possible and practicable process of Enlightenment in the educational evolution of an intellectual.

At the beginning of the *Letters*, Julius presents himself as a passionate Neoplatonist immersed in metaphysical verve. His convictions are the object of the methodological doubt of his paternal friend and tutor, Raphael, who challenges Julius' philosophical enthusiasm. The fervid metaphysician Julius, who once expressed his profession of faith towards the possibility of approaching the supersensible (*das Übersinnliche*), confesses amidst the dialectic of the exchange that his courage is lost, and that he has doubts about the possibility of his own forces affording him the ability to attain knowledge of something beyond the sensory world. Raphael confesses that he had seen this crisis coming in his letter to Julius, reassures his friend about the fact that "to all souls, such as yours, this crisis is always impending" (SW 5: 342), and explains to his younger friend that the level he had reached before was not high enough, if compared with his real philosophical talent (cf. SW 5: 343). Thus, the letters are evidence of Julius' (i.e. Schiller's) past philosophical convictions, which are now overcome and now considered as illusory inventions and dreams. The letters constitute important evidence of the metaphysical universe of the younger Julius/Schiller. And these remembrances reconstruct the developmental history of Enlightenment in the microcosm of one individual.

At the beginning, Julius comforts himself in the nest of an innocent devoutness, in which he takes refuge in the answers he acquires from religion, and where happiness coexists and intermingles with the immaturity of a not yet independent thinker. But Raphael's teaching "has stolen my faith", Julius calls, and through a "cold wisdom" he "extinguished my enthusiasm" (SW 5: 339). Raphael's lesson pays tribute to the maxims of enlightened philosophy: "Believe no one but your own reason". And furthermore: "There is nothing holy but truth. Only what reason discerns is truth" (*ibidem*). Following Raphael's teaching, Julius cannot go back: his own "reason is now everything" to him, it now represents his "only guarantee for divinity, virtue, immortality" (SW 5: 340). This is the result to which he has arrived, as he confesses at the end of his first letter to his friend and mentor. At the end of the second letter to Raphael, Julius goes even further by confessing a most profound crisis: "I am not happy. My courage is lost. I do not trust my own forces" (SW 5: 342).

Raphael's answer, which is also the only letter by him contained in the *Letters*, makes no attempt to deny or avert Julius' crisis. Rather, he affirms the crisis as a necessary step in the process of untangling "truth and fallacy" and connecting "pleasure and virtue", which, until now, had both remained independent from one another. That said, the independence of pleasure and virtue has not hitherto been an obstacle for the young Julius to act morally: Raphael remained confident in Julius' morality because he knew Julius could be "good out of instinct, out of undefiled moral grace" (*gut aus Instinkt*, aus unentweihter sittlicher Grazie, SW 5: 343). Nonetheless, Julius' status as a person with the virtue of grace had been that of a minority: this is why the time comes for Raphael to initiate the supersession of reason over Julius' juvenile phantasy. In his youth, Julius himself personified the idea of a beautiful soul: though a beautiful soul does not err, it has nonetheless to be awakened from the dreams of fanciful imagination, in order to allow rationality and philosophical argument to assume the role of a guiding force—and in order to avoid the problems connected to the possibility of a beautiful soul leading a properly moral life (see Falduto 2021b).

As mentioned, the whole text up to this point, that is, the introductory "memory" (*Vorerinnerung*) together with the first two letters from Julius to Raphael and the following letter from Raphael to Julius, forms a sort of preparation which serves to introduce, in the last letter from Julius to Raphael, the juvenile philosophical work entitled *Theosophy of Julius* enclosed in the last epistle. In this manner, Schiller finds a way of giving testimony to his youthful beliefs and of comparing them with the present fortitude of reason's philosophical strength. The *Theosophy* is presented as an enthusiastic work, in which the "warmness" of the sentiments occupied the place of philosophical truth, in which Julius "searches for the laws of the spirits, swings up to the supersensible, but forgets to prove that they exist" (SW 5: 344).

By reading the *Theosophy of Julius*, we are afforded a glimpse into the philosophical laboratory of the young Schiller. In the *Theosophy*, Julius deals with the six concepts: (i) world and thinking being; (ii) idea; (iii) love; (iv) sacrifice; and

(v) God. Following the fifth section of the *Theosophy*, at the end of the second lyric quoted there as a conclusion to it, Julius' post-scriptum recapitulates in a few pages and, at the same time, retrospectively comments on his juvenile and criticism-subjected "philosophical" attempts. Julius tries to make the most of these bygone thoughts by abandoning his former positions but at the same time saving what can now be modified and reused in the new quest for discerning a way through the difficult process of Enlightenment. Through its overt negation of many points contained in the juvenile writing, the post-scriptum ultimately interrupts the dogmatic dreams of a Neoplatonist's metaphysics contained in the treatise.

Already the title, *Theosophy*, testifies of the influence of Schiller's lecturers at the Karlsschule on the metaphysical convictions of the younger Schiller/Julius. In this regard, the influence by Karl Friedrich Harttmann (1743-1815) in particular needs underlining. Harttmann teaches religion at the academy in Stuttgart in 1774-1775 and is a disciple of the theosophist Friedrich Christoph Oetinger (1702-1782), whose thought can be summarised by the opening of Julius' *Theosophy*: "The universe is a thought of God" (SW 5: 344; on Oetinger's role, see Riedel 1985: 155). According to the theosophical tradition and through some hermetical and pietistic intermediation, a mystical theory arises (see the commentary to Schiller's writing in SW 5: 1186), according to which the harmonisation and connectedness of the whole creation depend on its emanation from God. Schiller varies and develops a theory about the great chain of being (Košenina 2005: 360). A further capital influence upon the composition of the *Theosophy* is a Leibnizian one, mediated by the German *Popularphilosophie* best represented in the context of the Karlsschule by Jakob Friedrich Abel (1751-1829). In Schiller's years at the Karlsschule, Abel does not only divulge some of Leibniz' central theories: he also and most importantly plays the significant role of combining Leibnizian themes with the treatment of central trends derived from the Scottish Enlightenment. Abel is interested in sensualist moral philosophy and empiricism and, in his lectures on moral philosophy at the academy in Stuttgart, he allows the Scottish Enlightenment to play a decidedly significant role in his philosophical explanations and arguments. In the context of one of those lectures, Schiller has the occasion to read, among the others, the whole *Institutes of Moral Philosophy* by Adam Ferguson in Garve's translation—one of the texts which are of utmost importance for the development of Schiller as a young man of letters (see Falduto 2021a) and which are at the basis of the second part of the *Theosophy* by Julius with regard to the perfectibility (*Vervollkommnung*) theory (the other two texts are Moses Mendelssohn's *Phaedon* and Johann Joachim Spalding's *Reflections on the Vocation of the Human Being*; on the influence of the three texts see, among others, Riedel 1985: 160-173). All these features and philosophical influences can be clearly recognised from the very first part of the *Theosophy* onwards.

In terms of content, the first part of the *Theosophy* is dedicated to "The World and the Thinking Being". There, as mentioned, Julius defines the universe as one among the divinity's thoughts, and surmises that all thinking beings are called to retrieve unity with it. He states that all these beings are compelled to retrieve unity by "a law in this phaenomenon, a ground plan in this edifice" (SW 5:344). A series of concepts—harmony, truth, order, beauty, and excellence—are introduced in order to describe the observers joy of recognising herself as a rational being and, in this way, similar to the author of the creation himself: "There is no solitude in the whole of nature anymore: where I find a body, there I presage a spirit, where I notice movement, there I guess a thought" (SW 5: 345). The second section of the *Theosophy*, dedicated to the concept of "Idea", shows why the human being is attracted by other objects of the creation (and in this way, it introduces the next section dedicated to the concept of love): "Perception of beauty, of truth, of excellence, the excellent, is momentary possession of these qualities. Whichever state we perceive, we enter into it ourselves. The moment we think of them, we are the owner of a virtue, the author of an action, the inventor of a truth, the possessor of a bliss. We ourselves become the perceived object" (SW 5:346). Hence, "I desire the others' happiness because I desire my own" (SW 5:348). This procedure constitutes the grounding of benevolence (*Wohlwollen*) and love (*Liebe*). The recourse to benevolence constitutes the implementation of Leibniz' philosophy, overtly mentioned in this second section by the recourse to God's attributes discussed in the *Theodicy*, through Scottish ideas. A further important element contained in this section is a characteristic that will be reconsidered in later works on aesthetics by Schiller: the connection between God's and at the same time the artist's creation, on the one hand, and love, on the other hand (see Driscoll Colosimo 2007).

The third section of the *Theosophy*, dedicated to the concept of "Love", includes the lyric *On Friendship* (*Die Freundschaft*), pointing in this way at the necessary interconnectedness of these two concepts (love and friendship). This is a fact that is widespread in many literary and philosophical texts during the eighteenth century (Hinderer 2000). Love, defined as "the most beautiful phenomenon in the animate creation, the omnipotent magnet in the spiritual world, the source of devotion and of the most sublime virtue" (SW 5:348), is taken to be only a "reflection of the single primordial power, an attraction of the excellence grounded on a momentary exchange of personalities and beings" (*ibidem*). Against a materialistic tendency arguing for philosophical egoism, Schiller presents an altruistic conception of love, through which the human solitude, our perishability and finitude, are overridden by means of establishing again the divine primordial unity, which corresponds to the pristine elemental force from which God's creation in its absoluteness consists (Goebel 1924; Saße 1997). Julius is convinced of the fact that the return to the divine primordial origin can also be exemplified by means of his friendship with Raphael (SW 5: 349). And so, the first part of the lyric on friendship follows (*ibidem*: a second part of the lyric is to be found a few pages after, i.e. SW 5: 353). As mentioned, the treatment of the topic of friendship in the lyric, already published in the *Anthologie auf das Jahr 1782* (SW 1: 91), is also well testified in many other compositions on the so-called cult of friendship during the eighteenth century (Rasch 1936). Nonetheless, it is indeed of interest that even the lyric itself can also be defined as "a sort of poetic theosophy" (Düsing 1983). Against materialism—and, in this particular case, against Claude-Adrien Helvétius (Riedel 1985: 178-179)—Julius professes a harmonic view of the whole world based on its spiritual essence proved by friendship: "The human beings, who have come so far in finding beauty, greatness, and excellence in the small and the big in nature, and in noticing a great unity in its diversity, have already come much closer to divinity. The whole of creation flows into their personality. If each human being loved all human beings, each of them would own the world" (SW 5: 350).

Julius believes in the disinterested love made possible by friendship, which grounds his view of the world as a divine creation. In this way, in the fourth section dedicated to "Sacrifice", he implements his treatment of the topics of the preceding section and argues for human self-sacrifice as a consequence of the human refusal of egoism and solitude. Sacrifice is said to be due to the flowing together of the individuals into the whole of humankind through friendship and love (SW 5: 351-352). However, the complete assimilation of creator and creation takes place only in the fifth and final section of the *Theosophy of Julius* (SW 5: 352-354), which is constituted by the section dedicated to the concept of "God" and contains the second part of the lyric *Die Freundschaft* and a part of the lyric *Triumf der Liebe*. In this last section, examples from the hermetic and Cabbalistic tradition (Beiser 2005: 51) are coupled with Neoplatonic tendencies (mediated by the already mentioned Oetinger, SW 5: 1186-1187) and used for the explanation of the relation between God and the world God itself models. The concept of God is said to be identical with the one of nature: "All perfections in the universe are united in God. God and nature are two magnitudes, which are perfectly identical. [...] Nature is an infinitely divided God" (SW 5: 352). Love is defined as the attraction between all spirits, which are the products of nature's division. Through this attraction, "reproduced and extended into the infinite", the abolishment of the division and, with it, "God's production", should take place (SW 5: 353).

The *Philosophical Letters* is closed by considerations which return the reader to Julius' present (SW 5:354-358), in which the more mature Julius has abandoned the metaphysical fervour of his younger years, whilst still recognising that his juvenile philosophical credence has been able "to ennoble the heart and embellish the perspective of [his] life" (SW 5: 354). Julius can now critically comment on the concepts he believed in, by contrasting them with the assumption that, even if reason aims at "taking the measurements of the extrasensory, so that it applies the mathematics of its inferences onto the hidden physics of the superhuman (*Übermenschlich*)", a last proof is nonetheless still pending, "since no travellers have yet come back from those lands and reported their discoveries" (SW 5: 356).

The *Philosophical Letters* constitute evidence of the utmost importance of Schiller's philosophical reflections before his acquaintance with Kant's critical enterprise, in which the young man of letters still develops his thoughts exclusively in a literary form, rather than in a systematic one (Košenina 2005: 360-361; for further details on this see Mertens 2014, especially Part II).

Philosophical Significance and Impact

Even though the philosophical scholarship seems to have, for a long time, overlooked the *Philosophical Letters*, these writings constitute "undoubtedly the most remarkable work from Schiller's early philosophy" in so far as they provide a deep insight into Schiller's philosophical development, furnishing "both a confession and retraction, a statement and self-critique, of Schiller's early philosophical beliefs" (Beiser 2005: 29).

Still, on the history of their impact virtually nothing is known (Košenina 2005: 364). A possible explanation of the reason why the fragmentary the *Letters* have not been influential is, in all likelihood, connected to a fact already mentioned by Körner in the follow-up letter he writes through the protagonist Raphael in 1789 (*Thalia*, vol. 7—SW 5: 1189-1192). As Körner/Raphael points out himself, if the novel had to be continued at all, good argumentative answers would have to be provided against possible criticisms arising from Kant's philosophy. In fact, the *Philosophical Letters* argued for metaphysical models that became untenable in view of the theorisations contained in Kant's critical enterprise (Riedel 239-248): the defence of Julius' arguments and theses seemed to become impossible without an ongoing and thorough critique of Kant's critique of traditional metaphysics. Such an enterprise did not seem to be a viable option since, even though recognising some aporia in the critical philosophy after the period of his so-called Kant-Studies, Schiller repudiated most of the metaphysical premises he accepted in the context of the *Philosophical Letters*.

References

Beiser, Frederick (2005): *Schiller as Philosopher. A Re-Examination*. Oxford
Driscoll Colosimo, Jennifer (2007): "The Artist in contemplation: Love and creation in Schiller's *Philosophische Briefe*". In: *German Life and Letters*, vol. 60:1, pp. 18-39
Düsing, Wolfgang (1983): „»Aufwärts durch die tausendfachen Stufen«. Zu Schillers Gedicht Die Freundschaft". In: *Gedichte und Interpretationen*. Bd. 2: *Aufklärung und Sturm und Drang*. Hrsg. von K. Richter. Stuttgart. S. 453-462
Falduto, Antonino. 2020. ›Jenseits des Dualismus zwischen tierischer Natur und geistiger Natur: Kants Mensch 'in zwiefacher Qualität' und Schillers 'ganzer Mensch'‹. In *Kant-Studien*, 111(2): 248–268
Falduto, Antonino. 2021a. ›Schottische Aufklärung in Deutschland: Christian Garve und Adam Fergusons *Institutes of Moral Philosophy*‹. In: Udo Roth—Gideon Stiening (eds.), *Christian Garve (1742-1798). Philosoph und Philologe der Aufklärung*, Berlin/Boston: de Gruyter, pp. 33-53

Falduto, Antonino. 2021b. One more time on the alleged repugnance of Kant's ethics? Schiller's *Kallias letters* and the entirety of the human being. In *European Journal of Philosophy* 29(4): 795–810

Goebel, Julius (1924): "Schiller's *Philosophische Briefe*: A New Interpretation". In: *The Journal of English and Germanic Philology*, Vol. 23, No. 2, pp. 161-172

Hinderer, Walter (2000): „Konnotationen von Freundschaft und Liebe in Schillers Philosophischen Briefen und Hölderlins Hyperion". In: *Zeitschrift für deutsche Philologie (ZfdPh)*, Band 4, S. 498-516

Iffert, Wilhelm (1926): *Der junge Schiller und das geistige Ringen seiner Zeit. Eine Untersuchung auf Grund der Anthologie-Gedichte.* Halle a. d. Saale

Koopmann, Helmut (1976): „Schillers Philosophische Briefe—ein Briefroman?". In: *Wissen aus Erfahrungen. Werkbegriff und Interpretation heute. Festschrift für Herman Meyer*, hrsg. von A. v. Bormann. Tübingen. S. 192–216

Košenina, Alexander (2005): „Philosophische Briefe (1786)". In: *Schiller-Handbuch. Leben—Werk—Wirkung.* Hrsg. von Matthias Luserke-Jaqui unter Mitarbeit von Grit Dommes. Stuttgart. S. 359-364

Mertens, Marina (2014): *Anthropoetik und Anthropoiesis. Zur Eigenleistung von Darstellungsformen anthropologischen Wissens bei Friedrich Schiller.* Hannover

Rasch, Wolfdietrich (1936): *Freundschaftskult und Freundschaftsdichtung im deutschen Schrifttum des 18. Jahrhunderts. Vom Ausgang des Barocks bis zu Klopstock.* Halle a. d. Saale

Riedel, Wolfgang (1985): *Die Anthropologie des jungen Schiller. Zur Ideengeschichte der medizinischen Schriften und der Philosophischen Briefe.* Würzburg (in particular pp. 154-229)

Riedel, Wolfgang (2011): ›Schriften zum Theater, zur bildenden Kunst und zur Philosophie vor 1790‹. In *Schiller-Handbuch*, ed. Helmut Koopmann, 595-610. 2., verbess. Aufl. Stuttgart: Kröner

Saße, Günter (1997): »Der Herr Major ist in der Eifersucht schrecklich, wie in der Liebe«. Schillers Liebeskonzeption in den Philosophischen Briefen und in Kabale und Liebe, in: J. Lehmann—T. Lang—F. Lönker u. a. (eds.): *Konflikt, Grenze, Dialog. Kulturkontrastive und interdisziplinäre Textzugänge.* Frankfurt a. M., Berlin u. a. S. 173-184

CHAPTER 7

On the Cause of the Pleasure We Derive from Tragic Objects (1792)

Carsten Zelle

1.

In the summer semester of 1790, Schiller held a one-hour college course entitled *Artis tragicae theoriam* ("Theory of Tragic Art"), during which "many a luminous idea" on this subject (NA 26: 22, Letter to Körner, on May 16, 1790) emerged. He planned to develop a "theory on tragedy" from the material for these lectures and publish it in the 12th volume of the *Thalia* (NA 26: 43, Letter to Huber, September 30, 1790). However, the outbreak of Schiller's life-threatening illness at the beginning of January 1791, then a second episode in March, and the severe resurfacing of the illness in May which led to the rumour of Schiller's death, prevented the execution of the project and the essay going into press. On 7 November 1791, Schiller sent a "small essay" (NA 26: 109) to his publisher, Göschen, and on 4 December 1791, he informed Körner that he was working for the *Thalia* journal on an essay on aesthetics "concerning tragic pleasure", which exhibited "much Kantian influence" (NA 26: 116). There is agreement in the scholarship about the fact that the former essay "presumably" consisted in the writing of *On the Cause of the Pleasure We Derive from Tragic Objects* [*Über den Grund des Vergnügens an tragischen Gegenständen*], while the latter "probably" consisted in the writing of *On Tragic Art* [*Über die tragische Kunst*] (NA 21: 168, commentary).

On the Cause of the Pleasure We Derive from Tragic Objects appears in January 1792 in the volume number 1 of the *Neue Thalia* (Schiller 1792). For the

C. Zelle (✉)
Ruhr-Universität Bochum, Bochum, Germany
e-mail: carsten.zelle@rub.de

© The Author(s), under exclusive license to Springer Nature Switzerland AG 2023
A. Falduto, T. Mehigan (eds.), *The Palgrave Handbook on the Philosophy of Friedrich Schiller*, https://doi.org/10.1007/978-3-031-16798-0_7

subsequent reprint of the essay in the collection *Kleinere prosaischen Schriften* (Schiller 1802): (i) the terminology was made more precise on the basis of a more intensive reading of Kant that had taken place in the meantime; (ii) a passage that sought to distinguish Epos and Tragedy by recourse to the relationship between excited emotion and sublimity is deleted (FA 8: 238,$_{32}$–239,$_{8}$); (iii) and the formulation (found apparently offensive) that the "suffering of a criminal" amuses no less tragically than the "suffering [*Leiden*] of a virtuous person" (FA 8: 243,31 f.) is softened through the formulation "life [*Leben*] of a criminal" (all variants recorded NA 21: 169). The *Schriften* edition positions the essay after the later *Scattered Observations on Various Aesthetic Objects* [*Zerstreute Betrachtungen über verschiedene ästhetische Gegenstände*], shortened for the reprint, but still before *On Tragic Art* [*Über die tragische Kunst*]. It is important that the variance between the journal and the *Schriften* edition must be taken into account for the scope of the interpretation.

1.1

For the characterisation of the present work by Schiller and *On Tragic Art*, it is decisive that two significant events happen between the printing of the essays in January and March 1792 and the time of their conception during the course on tragedy in the summer of 1790, which Schiller offered "solely on the basis of [his] own experience and reason" (NA 26: 43, to Huber, 30 Sept. 1790): on the one hand, his life-threatening illness; on the other hand, his first dealings with Kant's *Critique of the Power of Judgment* (1790). Even though the University of Jena had been the "most important and most influential centre of early Kantianism in Germany" (Lange 1993: 121) since the penultimate decade of the eighteenth century, until then Schiller was acquainted only with Kant's writings published in the *Berlinische Monatsschrift* on the philosophy of history. A first reading of the third *Critique* begun while he was still ill, in February 1791. A second, thorough re-reading did not take place until the autumn of 1792. This would have a lasting influence on Schiller's aesthetics lectures in the winter of 1792/93, as well as upon his beauty-is-freedom-in-appearance formula from the contemporaneous *Kallias* letters to Körner, and his theory on the Pathetic Sublime. Schiller's reception of the third *Critique* is attested in his own copy of Kant's work (Schiller 1974). Schiller's study of the other two critiques happened in the winter of 1791/92.

The peculiar coincidence of a life-threatening illness, Schiller's Kant Studies, and his theory of tragedy points to an important biographical dimension of the formation of the theory. It has been interpreted as an "attempt at philosophical coping" with the illness, since the acquaintance with Kant's aesthetics of the sublime "could have become a welcome remedy for Schiller in the hopelessness of his seriously ill condition" (Darsow 2000: 117). Schiller dwelt "in the strangeness of life" (Staiger 1967: 427).

In terms of the history of the theory, the fact that the first confrontation with Kant's aesthetics lies between the collection of material for the treatise *On the Cause of the Pleasure We Derive from Tragic Objects* in the summer of 1790 and the writing of the treatise itself later (in 1791), confronts us with the problem of a discursive ambivalence. Then, in *On the Cause of the Pleasure We Derive from Tragic Objects*, Schiller formulates older, enlightened views in the new articulation-medium which is Kantianism. The traditional, dualistic anthropology of the Enlightenment, with its distinction between the animal and the spiritual nature of the human being, is reformulated in the terms of Kant's dualism of *mundus sensibilis* and *mundus intelligibilis*; the heroism of "strength of soul" in Kant's virtue rigorism; and the theory of mixed sensations in terms of the negative pleasure of the sublime.

In his public lecture *On the Part of Aesthetics that Deals with Tragedy* [*Publicum über den Theil der Aesthetik, der von der Tragödie handelt*], Schiller repeated several times that he did not consult any "aesthetic book", that is, a compendium on which his lectures were based, but rather he made "aesthetics on his own", and that he created moreover "a not uninteresting continuous material for the *Thalia*" (NA 26: 22, to Körner, 16 May 1790).

The question of the specific pleasure of tragedy is "obviously as old as this form of art itself" (Seidensticker 2005: 218). However, in the early modern period this question did not arise as long as the affective event was used for consolatory, cathartic, morally didactic, and so on purposes. With the new emotionalist approach to poetological and art theory discourse, this function is reconsidered. The "puzzle" concerning the reason why art never receives more applause than when it succeeds in arousing painful sensations leads Jean Baptiste Dubos in 1719 to the observation that a painful affect is always preferred to unbearable boredom ("ennui") (cf. Zelle 1987: 117-157). The different conditions of the literary field in France and the German-speaking territories blocked the reception of Dubos' emotionalism for almost half a century. It was not until 1760/61 that Dubos' *Reflexions critiques* (1719 et al.) appeared in German translation (cf. Zelle 1987: 304-315).

In 1755, Moses Mendelssohn took up Dubos' hypothesis in the *Beschluß* of the letters *On the sensations* [*Über die Empfindungen*]. He translated the problem into the terminology of the Wolffian "perfectionists" [Vollkommenheitsmänner] (FA 8, 277, to Körner, 25 Jan. 1793): the perception of perfection is associated with pleasure; that of imperfection, with displeasure. Mendelssohn did not arrive at a conclusive explanation of the problem of "painfully pleasant sensations" [schmerzhaftangenehmen Empfindungen] until 1771, when he separated the mixed sensation into its two components (cf. Zelle 1987: 315-358): the mixture of the "horrid delight" [schauervolles Ergötzen] arises from the unwillingness to imagine an imperfect, that is, terrible, evil, or painful object; and pleasure from the perfect way in which the recipient's imagination visualises it. Mendelssohn analyses the "horrid delight" [schauervolles Ergötzen] as a feeling of oneself, that is, as a feeling of the perfection of a subject in the face of the imperfection of an object. As a result, even "evil [...] becomes an element of perfection", that is, it occupies the soul and carries something pleasant with it (Mendelssohn 1771: 128 and

130). Mendelssohn's analysis of mixed sensations became influential for the late Enlightenment up to Kant and Schiller. Schiller had become acquainted with Mendelssohn's *Philosophical Writings* [*Philosophische Schriften*] at the *Karlsschule*, mediated by his philosophy teacher Abel. He refreshed his reading in the winter of 1782/83 and acquired the work in the 1777 edition for his library (cf. Zelle 1990b: 297). In view of the two transitional writings of January and March 1792, one is therefore well advised to read the Kantian signifiers as signified of late Enlightenment popular philosophy [Popularphilosophie]. At the same time, this and Schiller's figurative style, which Fichte already found objectionable, explain the hermeneutic obstacles for the understanding, which pose problems for a "rational reconstruction" of the emotional-psychological content of the writing *On the Cause of the Pleasure We Derive from Tragic Objects* (Köppe 2020, 91 f.).

2.

The paradox of tragic pleasure was one of the aesthetic themes in vogue in the second half of the eighteenth century. The author of the book *On Pleasure* [*Vom Vergnügen*] was able to state in 1788 that "much trouble [has] been taken to explain this phenomenon" (Villaume 1788: Part I, 124). In a parallel work, *On the Reasons for Pleasure in Sad Objects* [*Von den Gründen des Vergnügens an traurigen Gegenständen*], written in 1791 at the same time as Schiller's *Thalia* essay, the anonymous author states at the beginning that "much has already been written about this matter […]" (Anonymos 1791: 177). In fact, Christian Friedrich von Blanckenburg was able to add a three-column bibliography to the keyword "*Tragisch*" in the new edition of Sulzer's *General Theory of Fine Arts* [*Allgemeine Theorie der schönen Künste*] in 1794, enlisting those writings that dealt solely "with the pleasure of tragic, or sad, objects" (Sulzer 1792-1799: vol. 4, 555). In view of the large number of titles, Blanckenburg restricted his bibliography "to the most famous, and to those which have dealt with this matter in particular" (ibid.: 555 f.). Sixteen titles are listed, including the aforementioned Anonymous and writings by Hobbes, Hawkesworth, Dubos, Mendelssohn, Hume, d'Aguesseau, Campbell, Platner, Home, Fontenelle, Louis Racine and Hurd, as well as Schiller's essay in question here, and his treatise *On Tragic Art* [*Über die tragische Kunst*]. The number of titles could easily be multiplied (cf. Zelle 1990a: 85-91). And Schiller scholars have taken note of very few of them (cf. Zelle 1990b).

2.1

The writing furnishes in the first, general part (FA 8: $236_{,29}$–$241_{,29}$) "a concise theory of pleasure" (FA 8: 235) and clarifies in the second part ($241_{,30}$–$249_{,24}$) the particular pleasure which tragedy confers. Yet, in the guise of an introduction (FA 8: $234_{,1}$–$236_{,28}$), pleasure is (and indeed must be) highlighted in general as an immediate effect of art, since the earlier Schiller had already underlined the usefulness of art for morals, at least in relation to theatre. In the *Schaubühne* speech (1785), juridical, moral-didactic, and anthropological-psychological justifications had been piled up in an attempt to assert the high moral rank of theatre against Plato's condemnation of art in general (cf. Zelle 2005a), and Rousseau's condemnation of drama in particular (cf. Zelle 2009). Now, Schiller recants such an endeavour: "The well-meant intention to pursue the morally good everywhere as the highest end, which has already produced and sheltered many a mediocre thing in art, has also done similar damage in theory. In order to assign the arts a fairly high rank, in order to show them the favour of the state, the reverence of all human beings, they are driven out of their proper domain" (FA 8: 235). Respect for social status, favour for the state, and reverence to people had been the strategic goals that the playwright had pursued in the *Schaubühne* speech. As a professor of history in Jena, Schiller abandons these bastions in favour of "the frivolous purpose of amusement" [frivoler Zweck zu ergötzen] (ibid.) as the proper domain of art. With his role reversal, the accentuation of the purpose of art changes. A concept from Sulzer's *Allgemeine Theorie* is taken up, in which the keyword "*Ergötzend*" ("amusing") refers to that pleasant sensation that has no other purpose "than enjoyment [Genuß] itself" as its goal. Since what is "amusing" [das Ergötzende] can be both "estimable" [schätzbar] and "very contemptible" [sehr verächtlich], the artist must not stop there, he must combine with delight "the higher intentions of the useful [die höheren Absichten des Nützlichen]" (Sulzer 1792-1799: vol. 2, 97).

The acquittal of art from its direct service to morality leads Schiller to a more precise definition of the "delectation" [Ergötzen] or "pleasure" [Vergnügen] that art arouses, as well as of the relation between the directly delightful or pleasurable effect of art and its further moral purpose. With the "paltry merit of amusing [armseliges Verdienst, zu *belustigen*]", the pleasure that art affords "must not be put in the same class" (FA 8: 235). Rather, what is meant is a "free pleasure [freies Vergnügen]" that, in contrast to mere sensual feeling, is affected by the idea of a purposefulness, that is, is based on "moral conditions" (ibid.). With this distinction, Schiller follows Sulzer on the one hand; and on the other hand, he attempts to synchronise it with Kant's guidelines, since he had delineated the pleasure of the aesthetic judgement of taste by stating that it must be free of interest (CJ: § 2), that is, that it must be neither guided by the senses (ibid.: § 3), nor by concepts (ibid.: § 4). Although the connection to the senses is cut ("Sensual pleasure […] is excluded from the realm of fine art", FA 8: 237), the affinity to the "good" (CJ: § 4) is kept open. Art's direct tie to morality is replaced by an indirect one: Pleasure becomes the "means" [Mittel] through which art fulfils its moral "end" [Zweck] (FA 8: 236). At this stage, the intricate dialectic, that became characteristic of the relation between art's autonomy and social function around 1800, emerges. Only by being autonomous, that is, by not serving any particular purpose, be it political, moral, religious, or otherwise, can art fulfil its general task of promoting "the highest purpose of humanity to such a great extent" (FA 8: 235).

2.2

The first main part of the essay (a) takes a closer look at the concept of "free pleasure" [freies Vergnügen], (b) attempts to sort out the different types of pleasure, and (c) explores similarities and differences between the pleasure in the Sublime [das Erhabene] and in the Touching [das Rührende]. The intention behind this is to define the laws of the various arts by relating them more closely to the types of "delectation" [Ergötzen] they excite, that is, to link "a concise theory of pleasure [eine bündige Theorie des Vergnügens]" with a "complete philosophy of art [vollständige Philosophie der Kunst]" (FA 8: 235). Exemplarily, this enterprise is outlined in the present writing *On the Cause of the Pleasure We Derive from Tragic Objects*, as well as in the essay *On Tragic Art*. By contrast, the idea of demarcating the two genres of epic and tragedy by means of a complementary hierarchy of sublimity and emotion (FA 8: 238,$_{32}$–239,$_8$) is abandoned in 1802.

(a)
"Free, however [frei aber]": Schiller repeats and specifies the already mentioned difference between "delectation" [Ergötzung] and "amusement" [Belustigung]:

> I call it free, however, that pleasure in which the powers of the mind are affected according to their own laws, and where the sensation is produced by an idea; in contrast to the physical or sensual pleasure, in which the soul is submissively moved in accordance with a mechanism due to extrinsic laws, and the sensation follows directly from its physical cause (FA 8: 236 f.).

In the re-edited version of the work in 1802, Schiller modifies the formulation, still strongly influenced by the Wolffian-Baumgartenian psychology of the lower cognitive faculties, according to which in free pleasure "the powers of the mind are affected according to their own laws", by the terminology derived by Kant's *Critique of the Power of Judgment*, or more precisely, by its Analytic of the Sublime, in accordance with which, in free pleasure, "the mental powers, reason and imagination are active" (FA 8: 1291, commentary). But even this editing cannot hide the transitional character of the essay, since Kant had tied the pleasure that the aesthetic judgement of taste grants in the face of the "beautiful" to a free play of the understanding and the imagination, whereas the pleasure that the aesthetic feeling grants in the face of the "sublime", as a "negative pleasure", is tied to the contradiction of reason and imagination.

(b)
Schiller adopted Kant's distinction between an "Analytic of the Beautiful" (CJ: §§ 1-22) and an "Analytic of the sublime" (CJ: §§ 23-29) only later in his reflections, when he attempts to sort the different "sources" of free pleasure according to the classes of the Good, the True, the Perfect, the Beautiful, the

Touching, and the Sublime. Here, a Kantian distinction between "beautiful arts [schöne Künste]", which bring understanding and imagination into play, and "touching arts [rührende Künste]", which bring reason and imagination into contradictory play, comes to the fore (FA 8: 237 f.).

(c)
In this context, Schiller addresses the sublime and compares it to the touching, following, on the one hand, Kant's statements in the *Critique of the Power of Judgment* and, on the other hand, bringing in older conceptions relative to the mixed sensations. At the end of the seventeenth century, thanks to Boileau's rediscovery of the energetic conception of poetry in the treatise *On the Sublime* by Pseudo-Longinus, the Sublime became an aesthetic category, which since the beginning of the eighteenth century had not only been assigned a status equal to the Beautiful (Joseph Addison) but had also been juxtaposed with it (Edmund Burke). And yet, in Addison's work an extensive and an intensive version of the sublime had emerged, which was to be expanded during the eighteenth century. Sulzer summarises this conception for the late Enlightenment and distinguishes between the "Great [das Große]" (which expands the imagination or the power to feel) and the "Sublime [das Erhabene]" (which exceeds the recipient's expectation, irresistibly grips him and arouses surprise, admiration, and horror); Mendelssohn, on the basis of his extensive reception of Burke, connects the Sublime as the Sensually-Immeasurable of the Great and the Strength with the theory of mixed sensations and names pleasant dizziness and holy, sweet, or pleasant terror/horror as the effect of the sublime (cf. Zelle 1994).

For Schiller's reflections, Kant's explanation (CJ: § 14, A 43) of the opposing nature of emotion [Rührung] has a catalysing effect: he notes here and, in pencil, in his author's copy of the third Critique in the spring of 1791, how, with regard to sublimity, "pleasantness is only effected by means of instantaneous inhibition and the consequent even stronger outpouring of the vital force" (Schiller 1974: 133). Emotion [Rührung] and sublimity [Erhabenheit] are mixed sensations, where pleasure is felt only by means of displeasure, that is, a purposefulness associated with pleasure is felt only by means of a preceding purposelessness associated with pain. This mechanism of mixed sensation is incorporated into the anthropological conception of the human being as having a mixed nature, so that a pain contrary to purpose on the side of nature produces purposeful pleasure on the side of reason. Schiller projects the "ambivalence of feeling (pleasure/unpleasure)—anthropologically—onto the 'double nature' of the human being" (²SW 5: 1195).[1] This applies both to the "conflict" between imagination and reason in the "feeling of the sublime [Gefühl des Erhabenen]" (where the pain of the lower faculty "pleases the

---

[1] ²SW refers to the new edition of SW, which contains a newly written, revised, and supplemented commentary. The author of the commentary of the theoretical writings (vol. 5 of ²SW) is Wolfgang Riedel.

higher faculty [höhere Vermögen [...] ergötzt]", FA 8: 239,$_{25-28}$), and to the pleasure of emotion [Rührung] (where a purposeless "woe [Wehetun]" of (sensual) nature is "purposive for our rational nature", FA 8: 240,$_{10\,f.}$).

In Schiller's typical rhetoric, the mechanism outlined is used exuberantly for the indirect representation of morality and orchestrated as a conflict between nature and moral law in tragedy. Tragic art delights by showing the forces of nature (sensations, instincts, affects, passions, psychic necessity, fate, etc.) in conflict with the "whole power of the moral law": "The more terrible the adversaries, the more glorious the victory" (FA 8: 241,$_{23f.}$). This "abrupt opposition of reason and nature" leaves behind the "manifold efforts at a mediation" (FA 8, 1294, commentary on 241,$_{16\,ff.}$), which the anthropologically balancing concept of the "middle condition [mittlerer Zustand]" (FA 8: 188,$_{34f.}$) had still striven for in the *Schaubühne* speech. However, the collision between nature and moral law is still within the purview of the *Karlsschule* period. For the *commercium*-anthropology, which aimed at a balance, was diametrically opposed to a moral philosophy of "strength of soul" (cf. Riedel 1995, 436–440) based on unconditional autonomy (cf. Riedel 1992: 49). The early constellation prefigures, as it were, the late, elegiac pairing of two guides for life (October 1795), which also lies at the bottom of the system of aesthetic education in the writing *On the Sublime*.

2.3

In the second main part of the writing *On the Cause of the Pleasure We Derive from Tragic Objects*, the earlier developed theory of pleasure is used as an explanation for the pleasure derived from tragic objects. For Schiller, tragedy is neither "the most exciting form of poetry", as it was for Aristotle (Kommerell 1970: 99), nor the one that purifies the passions from their extremes by arousing them with pity and fear, as Lessing dietetically reinterpreted the Aristotelian catharsis in the 78th part of the *Hamburgische Dramaturgie* (1768/68). Rather, it is the dramatic genre that makes one feel the pleasure of purposeful reason, that is, freedom, by depicting the pain of nature that is contrary to its purpose. Lessing's model was still taken up in the conclusion of the *Schaubühne* speech (cf. FA 8: 200). It is now discarded or sublimated as an organisational structure of aesthetic, or more precisely, beautiful education. Rather, tragedy uses the mixed sensations which, due to a conflict between imagination and reason, sensuality and morality, "amuse through pain" (FA 8: 241,$_{32\,f.}$). Kant's concept (CJ: § 27, A 989) is taken up by Schiller in verb form to denote the opposite sentiment of sublimity, in which a sublime object is "purposive for reason, in that it *conflicts with* sensibility" and, in this way, it "delights" (FA 8: 239,$_{26}$, my emphasis).

In order to further illustrate this definition of tragedy in terms of aesthetics of effect, in the following remarks a taxonomy of conceivable cases will be explored, in which (a) some natural purposiveness is "sacrificed" for a moral expediency or (b) some moral purposiveness is "sacrificed" for another, higher-order moral expediency (FA 8: 241,$_{37}$). In doing this, Schiller, from the height of "autonomic reason [autonomische Vernunft]" apostrophised as the "palladium of freedom [Palladium der Freiheit]" (FA 8: 241,$_{13}$), makes a downright throwaway comment about nature. The natural world counts for nothing to him when it comes to the realm of freedom. He is prepared to reconcile himself with the painful "evil" [mit dem Übel aussöhnen], if only the "experience of the victorious power of the moral law" (FA 8, 242 f.) can provide us with that. A further engagement with Schiller's writings from the nineties will shed light on his wavering concept of nature, which always has a positive connotation in the tradition of moral-sense philosophy (Shaftesbury, Hutcheson) when it comes to the beautiful—but which loses value in the context of an ethics of the strength of soul and of Kantian virtue rigorism, and that has a negative connotation as soon as it comes to the Sublime.

(a)
In order to illustrate a tragic collision between natural purposiveness and moral purposiveness, the following examples are given: Huon and Amanda from Wieland's *Oberon* (1780) would rather die than acquire a throne through infidelity (FA 8: 242,$_{20}$–243,$_{4}$); Shakespeare's Coriolanus, according to Schiller, "violates the rules of prudence" in order to act in accordance with a "higher moral duty" (FA 8: 243,$_{5-30}$). However, the constellation is represented not only via examples of virtue, but also by reference to the "suffering of a criminal". For although his crime fills us with reluctance and pain, nonetheless his remorse, self-condemnation, and despair indirectly represent the moral law as the highest moving instance in his consciousness, through which, in such moments, he deprives himself of the pleasure of enjoying the reward of his crime. It is indifferent aesthetically whether the virtuous person in the first or second case sacrifices his life in order to act in accordance with the moral law, or whether the criminal in the third example kills himself in order to punish his violation of the law in himself, since respect for the moral law is aroused to the same degree in all three case studies—and, indeed, even more strongly in the last case, since here no conviction of right action facilitates the decision to die (FA 8: 243,$_{31}$–245,$_{19}$). Schiller's argument might seem to come close to an aesthetic justification of the criminal (cf. NA 21: 173, commentary; Koopmann 1977: vol. 1, 99). Nonetheless, it only repeats knowledge that was common in Enlightenment dramaturgy, insofar as Schiller, in the dialectical terminology of purposive purposelessness, only reformulates older literary-critical considerations, in which the independence of aesthetic judgement had been emphasised over moral evaluation. Thus, as Lessing bitingly writes in the 63rd *Litteraturbrief*: heroic virtue could be "morally good [moralisch gut]" but uninteresting and "poetically evil [poetisch böse]" (cf. Zelle 1989).

(b)
The tragic collision between some moral purposiveness and another, superior moral purposiveness, that is, the activation of moral pleasure through moral

pain, is initially acted out by Schiller in two cases. First, "that commandant" is recalled, who, faced with the alternative of "either surrendering the city or seeing his captured son lancinated before his eyes", unhesitatingly chooses the latter, "because duty towards his child is reasonably subordinated to duty towards his own country" (FA 8: 245,$_{34f.}$). Subsequently, we are reminded of the Corinthian Timoleon, whom Plutarch compared to the Roman Aemilius Paulus, because he was such an enemy of tyranny that he murdered his brother without hesitation when the latter wanted to raise himself to the position of sole ruler of his city (cf. FA 8: 246). That it is *nature* in both cases, that is, blood ties between father and son or between two brothers, that sets a *moral* purpose here, albeit of an inferior kind (the "natural instinct [Naturtrieb]" appears as "fatherly duty [Vaterpflicht]", brotherly love as a "moral feeling [moralisches Gefühl]", FA 8: 246), points once again at Schiller's iridescent concept of nature, which is visibly impregnated here by the British ethics of moral sense. In fact, the two examples quoted, regarding a certain moral purposiveness and another, higher-order moral purposiveness, orchestrate the collision between British and Königsberg moral philosophy, that is, between moral feeling and duty ethics. Although the "Unnatural" [das Naturwidrige] character of the deed at first arouses indignation, disgust, and horror, after a "stormy conflict of feelings" it draws us to "sweet admiration [süße Bewunderung]" and "respect [Achtung]" (FA 8: 246). In this way, they draw towards those affects that, on the one hand, are associated with heroic tragedy (e.g. in Mendelssohn's defence of admiration against Lessing's favouring of compassion in the *Briefwechsel über das Trauerspiel*, 1756/57), and on the other hand with the "moral feeling" highlighted by Kant—a feeling we perceive every time "the moral law directly determines the will" (CPrR: A 126). It seems as if Schiller, with his examples, were reanimating heroic tragedy, political tragedy, or Christian martyr drama, which Lessing had nevertheless declared dead (*Hamburgische Dramaturgie*, essay 1 and 2); though, in effect, the sovereignty of the modern subject, that is, an action of his own legislation, is established.

(c)
Finally, Schiller returns to the fascination with the sublime criminal, whose "highest coherence delights" us (FA 8: 247), although his actions are immoral and unlawful. This "too little noticed climax" of the essay (NA 21, 173, commentary) synthesises, like the corresponding passage a few pages earlier, elements of the preceding poetics and theory of mixed sensations. At the same time, these remarks denied the view that cases of "morally impeccable action" qualify for pleasure or a "'positive' emotion" (Köppe 2020: 103). The point of view of *"energy [Energie]" and "power [Kraft]"*, which had always played a role in rhetoric and the theory of the sublime (especially since Burke's addition of the "power" chapter to the second edition of the *Enquiry* in 1759), had led to Schiller's celebration of the villain in both the suppressed and the published preface to the *Räuber*. The skill of "voluntarily diverting" attention from the moral purposelessness of the villain, in order to enjoy "the pleasure

[…] that is made possible for us only through this exclusion" (FA 8: 248), quotes the Nero effect of "spoiled taste [verwöhnter Geschmack]" that Mendelssohn had introduced in the *Beschluß* of the letters *On Sensations* [*Über die Empfindungen*]. What then emerges is pure energy, with which the deeds are implemented in a planned manner against all opposition, including moral opposition. The sublime villain is a sort of power-genius of instrumental reason, which Lessing had already admired in Richard III, because (quoting Hume, since "*utility pleases*") we love "the Purposive [das Zweckmäßige] so much that it grants us pleasure, even independently of the morality of the purpose" (*Hamburgische Dramaturgie*, essay 79). Again and again, Lessing proves to be the "ancestor" (Meier 1992: 150) of Schiller—even if he was busy reading Kant.

2.4

A small final paragraph (FA 8: 249,$_{25}$–250,$_{20}$) sums up that the pleasure we derive from tragedy is produced in a double way (FA 8: 249,$_{29}$): through the "content" that has an influence on the "heart", and through the "form" that has an influence on the "understanding". The first effect is related especially to the "great multitude" who suffer it "blindly", the latter to the "connoisseur" who knows how to "see through" it. By interpreting the text, one must understand how to read the metaphors and sentence constructions that Schiller uses, in order to see through the order that they create, and the evaluations associated with them. In a chiasmus, extremes are juxtaposed, in order to balance them out in a middle position. Two receptive ways are contrasted, since the connoisseur, despite the successfulness of the effect, does not want to forgive the injured form; and the masses, despite perfect form, do not want to forgive the unsuccessful effect. Between these extremes, that is, that the "great multitude" is satisfied only by the content of the tragedy, the "connoisseurs" "merely by the form" (FA 8: 250), a middle position in the audience is addressed, which knows how to "happily defeat the adverse influence of both" extreme ways of reception. In the ability to strike the right balance lies the "glory of the character of the educated human being". A side blow is directed at French drama, which would have gone furthest with the cognizant "extreme" of observing "only the Beautiful [das Schöne]" form for all its emotion and sublimity (FA 8: 250). At the same time, the problematic of the artistic form of tragedy addressed in the concluding paragraph, which had hardly been considered before, points to the essay *On Tragic Art*, appearing in volume number 2 of the *Neue Thalia*.

3.

Compared to other theoretical writings, the transitional writings of January and March 1792 stand in a double shadow, namely in the shadow of the tragic treatises *On the Pathetic* (1793) and *On the Sublime* (1793/96; printed 1801), which in turn stand in the shadow of the great treatises (*On Grace and Dignity*, "*Aesthetic Letters*", *On Naive and Sentimental Poetry*). The National Edition sorts the corpus of so-called philosophical writings into "Smaller Writings after the Encounter with Kant", "Large Treatises", and "Further Smaller Writings". Among the others, *On the Sublime* is tucked away in the latter category, against the author's compositional intentions, which can be deduced from the arrangement of articles in his *Schriften* edition. Such a canonisation-effect is transferred, for example, to the Kröner *Schiller-Handbuch*, in which the contributions have been distributed according to the structure of the National Edition. Single articles are dedicated to the major treatises, and the rest, together with the tragic writings, are squeezed in under the heading "Smaller Writings after the Encounter with Kant" (Koopmann 2011). In the two hundred year old history of reception of Schiller's aesthetic essays, these tragic writings play only a subordinate role. In the corpus analysed by Lesley Sharpe (1995) for his study on two centuries of literary theory, they do not appear at all. Although Beiser (2005: 253-257) has briefly addressed Schiller's question of the "sources of tragic pleasure", it generally remains true that Schiller's work on the theory of tragedy has attracted little attention in the Anglophone world, and that it has even been ignored—what is particularly true of his "neglected theory of the pleasure we take in tragedy" (Hughes 2015: 417). It has not even been included in the current English translation of Schiller's *Essays* (ESS). The reception of the writing may be hindered, above all, by its forced rigorism, heightened by the exuberant rhetoric. To post-heroically conditioned ears, some pathetic formulations may even sound sadistic, inhumane, or terroristic (cf. FA 8: $242_{,37}$–$243_{,2}$, $243_{,19\,\mathrm{ff.}}$ und $245_{,32\,\mathrm{ff.}}$). An exception is constituted by Bert Brecht, who is "amused" by the way in which Schiller chases the immediate moral way of engaging theatre out the front door, in order to let the indirect moral purpose of tragedy back in the back door. Not without respect for this sleight of hand and with some self-irony, he notes, under the date 1 September 1948, in *Journal Schweiz*: "I am reading Schiller's *Pleasure from Tragic Objects* with amusement. He begins, like me in '*Organon*', with pleasure as the business of theatre, and, like me, he revolts against theories that want to harness the theatre for morality (and thereby ennoble it), but then immediately puts everything in order by saying that he cannot conceive of pleasure without morality, i.e., that the theatre does not satisfy morality by being pleasurable, but supposedly cannot be pleasurable at all if it is not moral. The Moral, then, must not be pleasurable, in order to be allowed into the theatre, but pleasure must be moral in order to be allowed into the theatre. I myself, of course, do something quite similar with learning, when I simply make it a pleasure of our time" (Brecht 1995: 273).[2]

German text translated into English by Antonino Falduto in connection with Bill Molyneux.

---

[2] The present article is a revised version of Zelle 2005b.

On the Cause of the Pleasure We Derive from Tragic Objects (1992)

Schema

Introduction	234,1- 236,28	Free pleasure as immediate effect of art: - refusal of the morally didactical function of art - refusal of mere amusement through art
1st main part: theory of pleasure	236,29- 241,29	"Concise theory of pleasure": (a) distinction: sensuous/free pleasure (b) taxonomy of pleasure and distinction of the arts in measure of the free pleasure, which art provides: beautiful arts/touching arts (c) touching emotion [*Rührung*] and sublimity [*Erhabenheit*] - feeling of the Sublime (Kant) - feeling of the Touching (Mendelssohn) - Community between both mixed sensations: Purposiveness (pleasure) through counterproductiveness (pain)
2nd main part: pleasure related to tragic art	241,30- 249,24	definition of the aesthetic effects of tragedy: delectation through pain – scenarios: (a) sacrifice of a purposiveness of nature in favour of a moral purposiveness. Examples: - Huon and Amanda - Coriolanus - Suffering of a villain (b) sacrifice of a moral purposiveness in favour of a superior moral purposiveness. Examples: - that commandant - Timoleon's patriotic duty (c) fascination of the villain
Conclusion	249,25- 250,20	The "double way" of tragic pleasure regarding content and form: the "cultivated human being" in the middle between the extremes of "great multitude" and "connoisseur"

References

Anonymos. 1791. Von den Gründen des Vergnügens an traurigen Gegenständen. *Neue Bibliothek der schönen Wissenschaften und der freyen Künste* 43, Stück 2, 177–185.

Brecht, Berthold. 1995. Journal Schweiz 1947/48. In *Werke. Große kommentierte Berliner und Frankfurter Ausgabe*, ed. Werner Hecht, Jan Knopf, Werner Mittenzwei and Klaus-Detlef Müller, vol. 27: Journale 2, 253–275, Berlin, Weimar, Frankfurt am Main: Aufbau Verlag, Suhrkamp.

Beiser, Frederick. 2005. *Schiller as Philosopher. A Re-Examination*. Oxford: Clarendon Press.

Hughes, Samuel. 2015. Schiller on the Pleasure of Tragedy. *British Journal of Aesthetics* 55/4: 417–432.

Darsow, Götz-Lothar. 2000. *Friedrich Schiller*. Stuttgart: Metzler.

Köppe, Tilmann. 2020. Schillers Theorien des 'tragischen Vergnügens' in "Über den Grund des Vergnügens an tragischen Gegenständen" und "Über die tragische Kunst". *Scientia Poetica* 24/1: 89–113.

Kommerell, Max. 1970. *Lessing und Aristoteles. Untersuchungen über die Theorie der Tragödie* [1940]. 4., unveränderte Aufl. Frankfurt am Main: Klostermann.
Koopmann, Helmut. 1977. *Friedrich Schiller*. 2 vols. [1966], 2., ergänzte und durchgesehene Aufl. Stuttgart: Metzler.
Koopmann, Helmut. 2011. Kleinere Schriften nach der Begegnung mit Kant. In *Schiller-Handbuch*. 2., durchgesehene und aktualisierte Auflage, ed. Helmut Koopmann, 611–624. Stuttgart: Kröner.
Lange, Erhard. 1993. Schiller und Kant. In *"Das Kantische Evangelium". Der Frühkantianismus an der Universität Jena von 1785–1800 und seine Vorgeschichte*, ed. Norbert Hinske, 121–130. Stuttgart-Bad Cannstatt: frommann-holzboog.
Meier, Albert. 1992. Die Schaubühne als eine moralische Arznei [!] betrachtet. Schillers erfahrungsseelenkundliche Umdeutung der Katharsis-Theorie Lessings. *Lenz-Jahrbuch* 2, 151–162.
Mendelssohn, Moses. 1974. Rhapsodie oder Zusätze zu den Briefen über die Empfindungen [2. Fassung 1771]. In *Ästhetische Schriften in Auswahl*, ed. Otto F. Best, 127–165. Darmstadt: Wissenschaftliche Buchgesellschaft.
Riedel, Wolfgang. 1992. Influxus physicus und Seelenstärke. Empirische Psychologie und moralische Erzählung in der deutschen Spätaufklärung und bei Jacob Friedrich Abel. In *Anthropologie und Literatur um 1800*, ed. Jürgen Barkhoff and Eda Sagarra, 24–52. München: iudicium-Verlag.
Riedel, Wolfgang. 1995. Einleitung. Weltweisheit als Menschenlehre. Das philosophische Profil von Schillers Lehrer Abel. In *Jacob Friedrich Abel: Eine Quellenedition zum Philosophieunterricht an der Stuttgarter Karlsschule (1773–1782)*, ed. Wolfgang Riedel, 377–450. Würzburg: Königshausen & Neumann.
Schiller, F.[riedrich]. 1792. Ueber den Grund des Vergnügens an tragischen Gegenständen. *Neue Thalia*. 1. Stück (= Januar), 92–125.
Schiller, [Friedrich]. 1802. Ueber den Grund des Vergnügens an tragischen Gegenständen. In: *Kleinere prosaische Schriften. Aus mehrern Zeitschriften vom Verfasser selbst gesammelt und verbessert*, Bd. 4, 75–109. Leipzig: Crusius.
Schiller, Friedrich. 1974. Vollständiges Verzeichnis der Randbemerkungen in seinem Handexemplar der Kritik der Urteilskraft. In *Materialien zu Kants Kritik der Urteilskraft*, ed. Jens Kulenkampff, 126–144. Frankfurt a.M.: Suhrkamp.
Schiller, Friedrich. 1998. Sur le fondement du plaisir pris aux objets tragiques. In *Textes esthétiques. Grâce et dignité et autres textes*, ed. Nicolas Briand, 99–110. Paris: Vrin.
Sharpe, Lesley. 1995. *Schiller's Aesthetic Essays. Two centuries of Criticism*. Columbia SC: Camden House.
Sulzer, Johann George. 1792–1799. *Allgemeine Theorie der schönen Künste* [1771/74]. Neue vermehrte zweite Aufl., 5 vols. Leipzig: Weidmann.
Staiger, Emil. 1967. *Friedrich Schiller*. Zürich: Atlantis.
Villaume, [Peter]. 1788 *Vom Vergnügen*, 2 vols. Berlin: Friedrich Vieweg der Ältere.
Zelle, Carsten. 1987. *"Angenehmes Grauen". Literaturhistorische Beiträge zur Ästhetik des Schrecklichen im achtzehnten Jahrhundert*. Hamburg: Meiner.
Zelle, Carsten. 1989. Ästhetischer Neronismus. Zur Debatte über ethische oder ästhetische Legitimation der Literatur im Jahrhundert der Aufklärung. *Deutsche Vierteljahrsschrift für Literaturwissenschaft und Geistesgeschichte (DVjs)* 63, 397–419.
Zelle, Carsten. 1990a. Über den Grund des Vergnügens an schrecklichen Gegenständen in der Ästhetik des achtzehnten Jahrhunderts (mit einem bibliographischen Anhang). In *Schönheit und Schrecken. Entsetzen, Gewalt und Tod in alten und neuen Medien*, ed. Peter Gendolla and Carsten Zelle, 55–91. Heidelberg: Winter.

Zelle, Carsten. 1990b. Schiffbruch vor Zuschauer. Über einige popularphilosophische Parallelschriften zu Schillers Abhandlungen über den Grund des Vergnügens an tragischen Gegenständen in den neunziger Jahren des 18. Jahrhunderts. *Jahrbuch der deutschen Schillergesellschaft* 34, 289–316.

Zelle, Carsten. 1994. Erhabene, das [17., 18. Jahrhundert: 1. Frankreich, 2. England, 3. Deutschland]. In *Historisches Wörterbuch der Rhetorik*, ed. Gert Ueding, vol. 2, 1364–1378. Tübingen: Niemeyer.

Zelle, Carsten. 2005a. Was kann eine gute stehende Schaubühne eigentlich wirken? In *Schiller-Handbuch*, ed. Matthias Luserke-Jaqui, 343–358. Stuttgart, Weimar: Metzler.

Zelle, Carsten. 2005b: Über den Grund des Vergnügens an tragischen Gegenständen. In *Schiller-Handbuch*, ed. Matthias Luserke-Jaqui, 364–374. Stuttgart, Weimar: Metzler.

Zelle, Carsten. 2009. 'Querelle du Théâtre'—literarische Legitimationsdiskurse (Gottsched –Schiller—Sulzer). *German Life and Letters* 62, 21–38.

CHAPTER 8

On the Art of Tragedy (1792)

Jens Ole Schneider

Textual Genesis

Schiller's essay *On the Art of Tragedy,* like the essay *On the Cause of the Pleasure we derive from Tragic Objects* [*Über den Grund des Vergnügens an tragischen Gegenständen*], has its origin in the lecture on the *Theory of Tragedy* [*Theorie der Tragödie*] from the summer of 1790. However, Schiller did not finish writing it until the winter of 1791/92. *Über die Tragische Kunst* appeared in the second issue of the *Neue Thalia* in March 1792. A continuation announced therein was never realised. The text was published in the *Kleinere prosaische Schriften* with very minor changes. It appeared immediately after the publication of the treatise *On the Cause of the Pleasure we derive from Tragic Objects* [*Über den Grund des Vergnügens an tragischen Gegenständen*], which indicates the related content of the two texts.

Contents

In contrast to the essay *On the Cause of the Pleasure we derive from Tragic Objects,* which was still focused on the notion of effect poetics, the essay *On the Art of Tragedy* develops the concept of effect *aesthetics,* that is, appeals to the emotional household of the spectator and focuses on the specifically theatrical means necessary to achieve this emotional effect (c.f. also Alt 2004, 89f.).

At the centre of the treatise stands a theory of compassion. In the first part of the treatise, Schiller treats compassion theoretically and develops it

J. O. Schneider (✉)
Friedrich Schiller Universität Jena, Jena, Germany
e-mail: jens.ole.schneider@uni-jena.de

© The Author(s), under exclusive license to Springer Nature Switzerland AG 2023
A. Falduto, T. Mehigan (eds.), *The Palgrave Handbook on the Philosophy of Friedrich Schiller,* https://doi.org/10.1007/978-3-031-16798-0_8

anthropologically. In the second part, Schiller discusses the technical means of drama that must be used to move the audience emotionally.

Schiller's anthropological definition of compassion refers, to some extent, to the emotionalist theory of art that emerged in the early eighteenth century, in particular to Dubos' *Reflexion critiques* (1719; German 1760/61), Mendelssohn's *Über die Empfindungen* (1761) and Sulzer's *Allgemeine Theorie der schönen Künste* (1771–1774). However, Schiller interweaves this theoretical tradition with a theory of the sublime derived from Kant. The sublime arises from a divergence of experience and contemplation: "Ein Meersturm, der eine ganze Flotte versenkt" is a catastrophe for the ship's crew. "[V]om Ufer aus gesehen" our "fühlendes Herz" is shocked at the sight of the shipwreck, but at the same time our imagination ("Phantasie") is greatly delighted (SW 5:372). The pleasure in tragic events competes with the selfish instinct for happiness. Those who see their bliss threatened can hardly feel tragic pleasure. Therefore, tragic pleasure can usually only be experienced by those who are not themselves involved in the tragic event. Nevertheless, some people can distance themselves from their bliss instinct in such a way that they feel pleasure in their tragic experience even in moments of greatest distress. The self-distance comes about through ethical consciousness. It is the "Lebensphilosophie" (SW 5:375), that is, ethics, which teaches us to see our self in a greater context and thus enables us to deal with ourselves as we would deal with strangers ("wie mit Fremdlingen umzugehen", ibid.). From such self-distance arises the privilege of feeling one's own suffering in the mild reflection of sympathy ("das Vorrecht, an sich selbst teilzunehmen und eigenes Leiden in dem milden Widerschein der Sympathie zu empfinden", ibid.). According to Schiller, this ability to feel pleasure in the mid of unpleasant experiences constitutes the utmost realisation of the human capacity for freedom. The free moral nature of man ("moralische Natur", SW 5:376) ensures that painful affects delight us in communication and in certain cases move us pleasantly ("[dass uns] schmerzhafte Affekte in der Mitteilung entzücken und […] in gewissen Fällen angenehm rühren", ibid.). Schiller also describes man's moral faculty as the cause of the pleasure that pity arouses in us. If pity is at first a form of suffering, an unpleasant sensory experience, it can nevertheless be felt as pleasant insofar as moral consciousness transcends the unpleasant sensory impression. Schiller also describes morality in active terms as "Trieb der Tätigkeit" (SW 5:377), as "sittliche[s] Handeln" (ibid.). This "Tätigkeitstrieb" (ibid.) can only unfold its full effect at the moment of a sad affect ("traurige[r] Affekt", SW 5:377), for it is in the confrontation with unpleasant sensory impressions that it unfolds its autonomous energy, enabling the subject to experience his perfect freedom ("seine […] vollkommene[ ] Freiheit", SW 5:377). Compassion is therefore a pleasurable experience because the subject experiences its freedom in it, the triumph of moral energies over the bliss instinct.

For Schiller, tragedy is the art that most evokes the pleasure of pity. In order to evoke pity in the audience, tragedy must meet various conditions. First, the displeasure at the cause of misfortune ("Unlust über die Ursache eines

Unglücks", SW 5:378) must not become too strong. It weakens our share, according to Schiller, if the unfortunate person whom we are to pity has plunged into his ruin through his own unforgivable fault. The self-infliction of a misfortune makes the person affected by this misfortune appear incapable of compassion.

In the same way, however, our compassion is clouded by the all too striking malice of the person who caused the misfortune. When the greatness of suffering ("Größe des Leidens", SW 5:379) is derived from the greatness of wickedness (Größe der Bosheit", ibid.), we feel only a flattened form of regret instead of pity. We feel pity somewhat more intensely when the misfortune is caused by the blind forces of nature and is not the result of human will. However, sympathy is only heightened tragically when we also feel sympathy for the person who caused the misfortune, because he himself is involved in the tragic event and has become the author of the misfortune against his inclination. Finally, sympathy is at its highest when the cause of the misfortune not only does not contradict morality, but is even possible through morality alone ("[wenn] die Ursache des Unglücks nicht allein nicht der Moralität widersprechend, sondern sogar durch Moralität allein möglich ist", SW 5:380). When the cause of the misfortune has moral reasons and the person affected by the misfortune is also affected for moral reasons, the feeling of pity reaches its purest intensity. For Schiller modern tragedy differs from Greek tragedy because the character suffers consciously caused for moral reasons. In Greek tragedy suffering is the consequence of blind fate, which also demands an immature submissiveness from the spectator, in modern times a tragic conception has emerged which understands misfortune as part of a teleological connection of things, a sublime order, a benevolent will. The modern spectator can feel a particularly heightened pity for the characters because he or she simultaneously has insight into the moral necessity of the tragic event.

The spectator's sympathy is a sensual experience, an approach to the original affect ("[den] ursprünglichen Affekt", SW 5:381), the experience of suffering of a character through sensual impressions. This sensual sympathy is the result of a particularly vivid representation of the character's suffering. Just as compassion can be weakened by too many disturbing simultaneous ideas and impressions, however, it can also be debauched to a degree that makes the pain predominant by too close an approximation to the original affect. Instead of morally supported pity, the spectator then experiences only a painful overwhelming that is unpleasant and unbearable for him. In order to prevent this unpleasant increase in pain, the tragic drama must, according to Schiller, contain a proper balance of sensuality and morality ("Sinnlichkeit und Sittlichkeit", SW 5:382). The purely sensual sympathy for the character's suffering must be accompanied by moral reflections so as not to end in blind pain. Ultimately, this is a matter of breaking the illusion. The theatrical illusion, which no longer allows the spectator to distinguish our own ego from the suffering subject, or truth from fiction, must be broken. Therefore Schiller prefers general truths or moral says that are interspersed at the right place in the dramatic dialogue.

Such interjections serve to grant the spectator moral reflection as well, despite all sensual overpowering, and thus allow him freedom of reflection.

Once the abstract goals of tragedy have been formulated, Schiller lists four central procedures through which these goals can be achieved. Here he refers in particular to Lessing's *Hamburgische Dramaturgie* and the interpretation of Aristotle's poetics of tragedy that it contains. First of all, Schiller states that the direct sensual experience of an event evokes greater compassion than the mere narration of such an event. Accordingly, he promotes a dramatic form that relies on the dramatic rather than the narrative mode, bringing actions to the stage for purposes of representation rather than relegating them to narrative character speech. Instead of putting reflections into the mouth of a speaking person, unmediated living presence and sensualisation ("[u]nmittelbare lebendige Gegenwart und Versinnlichung", SW 5:383) are necessary.

But in order to achieve a vivid impression of the character's suffering, this suffering must contain an element of "truth" or realistic content. This "reality effect" comes about because we also discover a part of the character's characteristics in ourselves: "Die Möglichkeit des Mitleids beruht nämlich auf der Wahrnehmung oder Voraussetzung einer Ähnlichkeit zwischen uns und dem leidenden Subjekt" (SW 5:384). In order to be able to empathise with the affect of a character, the conditions for this affect must be present in us. Only those who already know the character's states from their own experiences can feel sympathy for the character portrayed. In order to develop this potential for identification, tragedy must always refer to what is known to all, to what is generally "human" in human conditions ("das bloß Menschliche in menschlichen Verhältnissen", SW 5:385). The experiences portrayed must not be special or eccentric, they must be universally valid, generally relatable.

Thirdly, the depicted events must have a certain completeness for the audience. Both the inner processes of a character and the external circumstances must be depicted with such completeness and consistency that the audience cannot help but perceive the actions of the character as plausible and consistent. For Schiller, the impression of consistency only arises if the drama contains a causal structure, the completeness of the depiction is only possible through the linking of several individual ideas and feelings, which behave against each other as cause and effect and in their connection make up a whole for our knowledge. The completeness of a drama comes about through a series of individual sensualised actions, which combine to form the tragic action as a whole.

After all, the compassion in tragic drama must last in order to actually have an effect on the spectator. The illusion of the drama, through which an impression of suffering is created, must not let the spectator out of its clutches too quickly. The spectator must be temporarily deprived of his freedom to escape the illusion too soon ("der Freiheit beraubt werden, sich der Täuschung zu frühzeitig zu entreißen", SW 5:387). Therefore, it is not enough for sensual impressions to be increased to the greatest possible intensity, for the more violently the receiving faculty is stimulated, the more strongly the retroactive power of the soul expresses itself to defeat this impression. Since the tragedy must preserve the spectator's resistive impulses, the sensual affliction of the spectator must be interrupted again and again in between, in order to then return with all the greater intensity: Against weariness, against the effects of habit, the alternation of sensations is the most powerful means. The drama should precisely unfold the struggle of freedom against the compulsion of sensuality ("Zwang der Sinnlichkeit", SW 5:387) in the spectator, make the spectator assert his freedom again and again against the captivating sensuality of the representation. This struggle must be ignited throughout the drama: "In der geschickten Führung dieses Kampfes beruht eben das große Geheimnis der tragischen Kunst [...] (SW 5:387)". In order to maintain such tension throughout the drama, a proper dramaturgy of sensual effects is necessary. The drama must raise several strands of action that appeal sensually to the spectator in varying intensity and only at the end may these strands of action be brought together in a sensually heightened finale. The drama is thus a combination of plots, "[an] denen sich die Haupthandlung und durch sie der abgezielte tragische Eindruck vollständig, wie ein Knäuel von der Spindel, abwindet und das Gemüt zuletzt wie mit einem unzerreißbaren Netze umstrickt" (SW 5:387).

A tragedy that wants to do justice to these principles must fulfil six conditions: Firstly, it must imitate directly, place the event before the senses ("vor die Sinne gestellt", SW 5:388) and dispense with all narrative mediation. Secondly, in its imitation it must refer to an action and not merely represent states of mind ("Zustände des Gemüts") (SW 5:389), as lyric poetry does. Thirdly, tragedy must represent an event in its completeness, which means above all making the cause of an action visible on stage. Fourthly, tragedy must imitate an action worthy of compassion ("poetische Nachahmung einer mitleidswürdigen Handlung", SW 5:390). This means that it is not primarily guided by the historical correctness ("historische Richtigkeit", ibid.) of an element of action, but by its poetic function. Instead of a historical purpose ("historischer Zweck", ibid.), it pursues a poetic purpose ("poetischer Zweck", ibid.) (SW 5:390). Fifth, tragedy must represent an action which shows human beings in a state of suffering. Therefore, tragedy must depict human beings to the fullest extent of the word, and that means, above all, human beings capable of suffering. The characters portrayed in tragedy must neither be freed from the compulsion of sensuality ("von dem Zwange der Sinnlichkeit befreit", SW 5:391), nor must they renounce all morality ("von aller Sittlichkeit lossprechen", ibid.); they must be individuals with a capacity for sensory perception and moral consciousness, only then is the audience able to feel compassion for them. In this context, Schiller takes up Lessing's category of the "mixed character": the hero whose actions are neither purely good nor purely bad, who is neither purely sensually driven nor "reine Intelligenz" (ibid.). Finally, tragedy must combine all the elements mentioned; in the combination of means ("Verbindung der Mittel", SW 5:392) Schiller sees the actual "form" of tragedy. The tragic form can be set apart from the end. If the purpose of tragedy is to stimulate the affect of compassion ("den mitleidigen Affekt zu erregen", ibid.), its form consists in the imitation of a touching action ("Nachahmung einer rührenden Handlung") (SW 5:393). Finally, Schiller notes that this matching of form and purpose is present in very few tragedies in existence; most tragedies performed in contemporary times either have a tragic, that is, touching, form without pursuing a tragic purpose (and generating truly deep human pity), or they pursue a tragic purpose but do not make use of a tragic form. Such half-tragedies, however, meet with an audience frugality ("Genügsamkeit des Publikums", SW 5:393); the audience likes to be moved without a higher purpose and is rather averse to the "genius" combining form and purpose.

Philosophical Significance and Impact

In the eighteenth century, Schiller's writing was received primarily against the background of the late Enlightenment theory of mixed feelings. The reactions to the two Tahlia essays were not euphoric. Although reviewers praised the new and perceptive aesthetic considerations ("neue und scharfsinnige ästhetische Betrachtungen", Neue Nürnbergische gelehrte Zeitung 1792: 141), they lamented the lack of any truly new results. Particularly with regard to the concept of tragic compassion, Schiller couldn't claim to have opened up new vistas or to have penetrated more deeply into the essence of tragedy ("[kann] nicht behaupten, daß er neue Aussichten eröffnet habe, oder tiefer in das Wesen der Tragödie eingedrungen sey", Gothaische gelehrte Zeitungen 1792, 889).

Carsten Zelle, following the German studies of the early twentieth century (Rehm 1941; Kommerell 1941), rather emphasises the "Affinität Schillers mit dem Barockdrama" (Zelle 2005, 381) in particular the proximity to "Formen des Erlösungs- und Gnadenspiels, der Märtyrer- und Heroentragödie" (ibid.).

Nevertheless, Schiller's focus on the emotional and sensual impact of drama reveals the "anthropological turn" that, for Wolfgang Riedel, constitutes the "exemplarische Modernität des Philosophen und Ästhetikers Schiller" (Riedel 2006, 145). The moment of redemption and grace in his writing *On the Art of Tragedy* acknowledges the Baroque tradition, but also points ahead to Schopenhauer's aesthetics (cf. also Luserke-Jaqui 2018), which, like Schiller's aesthetic theory, further develops Kantian aesthetics. By emphasising the autonomy of art, Schiller's treatise also anticipated twentieth century theories of art, such as Theodor Adorno's aesthetic theory.

References

Alt, Peter André. 2004. *Schiller. Leben – Werk – Zeit*. Second volume. München: C.H. Beck, 89–92.

Kommerell, Max 1941. Schiller als Psychologe. In: Ibid.: *Geist und Buchstabe der Dichtung. Goethe – Schiller – Kleist – Hölderlin*. Frankfurt a. M.: Klostermann, 175–242.

Koopmann, Helmut. 1998. *Schiller-Handbuch*. Stuttgart: Kröner, 577–579.

Luserke-Jaqui, Matthias. 1994. Die Suche nach dem objektiven Begriff des Schönen. Von der Ästhetik Schillers zur Metaphysik des Schönen bei Schopenhauer. *Zeitschrift für Germanistik* 1, 24–34.
Riedel, Wolfgang. 2006. Die anthropologische Wende. Schillers Modernität. In *Friedrich Schiller und der Weg in die Moderne*, ed. Walter Hinderer. Würzburg: Königshausen & Neumann (Stiftung für Romantikforschung 40), 143–163.
Rehm, Walther. 1951. Römisch-französischer Barockheroismus und seine Umgestaltung in Deutschland. In Ibd.: *Götterstille und Göttertrauer. Aufsätze zur deutsch-antiken Begegnung*. München: Lehnen, 11–61, 329–337.
Zelle, Carsten. 2005. Über die tragische Kunst. In *Schiller-Handbuch*, ed. Matthias Luserke-Jaqui. Stuttgart/Weimar: Metzler, 374–382.

CHAPTER 9

Kallias, or Concerning Beauty (1793)

María del Rosario Acosta López

The *Letters Concerning Beauty*, or *Kalliasbriefe*, as they are better known within Schiller's scholarship, are a series of letters that Schiller exchanged with his good friend Gottfried Körner between January 25 and February 28, 1793. They were never published as an independent work by Schiller—unlike his letters to the Prince of Augustemburg, which Schiller edited for publication under the title *Letters on the Aesthetic Education of Humankind* (from now on *Aesthetic Letters*). This is why for a long time they were not considered part of Schiller's philosophical corpus (the NA groups them in a volume of his correspondence (NA 26) rather than in the volumes devoted to his philosophical writings (NA 20 and 21)). They contain, however, Schiller's first confrontation with Kant's aesthetics (as presented in the first part of the *Critique of the Power of Judgement*), and are therefore an important source for understanding not only Schiller's own stance on aesthetics—mostly on beauty—but also Schiller's aesthetical-political project that would be developed more fully a few years later in the *Aesthetic Letters*.

The *Kalliasbriefe* show the philosophical richness of Schiller's understanding of the "aesthetic" as an essential dimension of human existence, one separate from and perhaps even *more* ideal (i.e., truer to "human" nature) than a *mere* epistemological and a *mere* moral relationship to the world. They are also an important source for exploring some of Schiller's reactions to Kant's

M. d. R. Acosta López (✉)
UC Riverside, Riverside, CA, USA
e-mail: mariadea@ucr.edu

© The Author(s), under exclusive license to Springer Nature Switzerland AG 2023
A. Falduto, T. Mehigan (eds.), *The Palgrave Handbook on the Philosophy of Friedrich Schiller*, https://doi.org/10.1007/978-3-031-16798-0_9

practical project[1]—mostly his notion of freedom as autonomy—even though *Kallias* remains mostly an inquiry into what Schiller describes to Körner as an attempt toward the "deduction" of a "sensuous objective principle of taste" (KAL 146). In *Kallias* Schiller is thus exposing, for the first time after reading Kant, his own philosophical position regarding beauty through a number of definitions he "tests" throughout the letters, in anticipation of his friend's reactions, while also tacitly imagining a discussion with Kant.

Kant's *Critique of the Power of Judgement* is, indeed, Schiller's main philosophical reference throughout *Kallias*; he mentions Edmund Burke, Alexander Baumgarten, and Moses Mendelssohn at the very beginning, but it is clear that Kant's critical methodology is at the heart of Schiller's own mode of argumentation. One also needs to consider, however, that Schiller's approach to Kant's philosophy was already imbued with the kind of questions he had been exploring for years before he got in touch with Kant.[2] Even a cursory glance at his annotated copies of Kant's third critique shows how, for Schiller, what was most fundamental about this work were the passages where the connection between ethics and aesthetics is either explicit or can be traced.[3] This particular emphasis renders Schiller's reading a misreading of the Kantian project at times and leads him to place too much emphasis on notions Kant uses only in passing, while leaving aside others that are essential for understanding the role that the analysis of aesthetic judgments plays in Kant's system.

Rather than quarreling about whether Schiller properly understood Kant, what seems more productive for Schiller's scholarship is to seek in his occasional misreadings of Kant's aesthetics the creativity and richness of Schiller's own project.[4] More specifically, this chapter aims to uncover how Schiller's approach to Kant in *Kallias* is guided by one of his more pressing philosophical concerns at the time, namely, the question of whether art can be ethically and politically relevant without sacrificing its autonomy; hence, the question of how can aesthetic experience become the site for an ethical and furthermore a

---

[1] See most recently Antonino Falduto. 2021. One more time on the alleged repugnance of Kant's ethics? Schiller's *Kallias letters* and the entirety of the human being. *European Journal of Philosophy*, Vol. 29/4, 795-810.

[2] Laura Anna Macor has made an extraordinary effort to recover the originality of Schiller's thought, working thoroughly on Schiller's philosophical project before his reading of Kant. Cf. Macor. 2012. *Der morastige Zirkel der menschlichen Bestimmung. Friedrich Schillers Weg von der Aufklärung zu Kant.* Würzburg: Königshausen & Neumann.

[3] This material has been compiled in Jens Kulenkampff. 1974. *Materialen zu Kants 'Kritik der Urteilskraft,'* 126–144. Frankfurt am Main: Suhrkamp. There is not, to my knowledge, any systematic study of these annotations within Schiller's scholarship.

[4] For a careful reading of Schiller's *Kallias* following this same position, see particularly Dieter Henrich. 1982. Beauty and Freedom: Schiller's Struggle with Kant's Aesthetics. In *Essays in Kant's aesthetics*, eds. Ted Cohen and Paul Guyer, 237-257. Chicago: University of Chicago Press. See also Frederick Beiser. 2005. *Schiller as Philosopher*, Chapter 2. New York: Oxford University Press. An exposition of the aforementioned critical approach to Schiller that famously accuses Schiller of "dangerously" misinterpreting Kant and successfully institutionalizing this misreading for the history of philosophy is Paul de Man. 1996. Kant and Schiller. In *Aesthetic Ideology*, ed. Andrej Warminski, 129-162. Minneapolis: University of Minnesota Press.

political transformation precisely on the basis, and not at the expense, of its autonomy.[5]

Even though it is the *Aesthetic Letters* that fully develop this dimension of the argument, a reading of *Kallias* is necessary for a true understanding of the depth and richness of Schiller's later work. Schiller's attempts to define beauty throughout his *Kalliasbriefe* reveal the originality of his aesthetic project, the ethical and political undergirding his analysis, and how, as I've argued elsewhere, it is precisely in those places where Schiller seems to be "misreading" or at least "overinterpreting" Kant that something truly original opens up in Schiller's own philosophical engagement with aesthetics.[6]

In what follows, I offer an overview of Schiller's main arguments in *Kallias*, going over his six definitions of beauty, and the transitions that seem to take place from one to the other. Each definition allows access to an important side of Schiller's position on Kant's aesthetics while also revealing the development of his view concerning the foundations of beauty—the truly singular experience it awakens in us, the kind of comportment beautiful objects invite us to emulate, and the particular dimension it opens up for our existence, as well as the standpoint it provides for (a new form of) philosophical critique. Additionally, this chapter aims to show how Schiller's conception of beauty in *Kallias* prepares the way for his central notion of aesthetic freedom in the *Aesthetic Letters*. Schiller's final excursus on the beauty of art, which he attaches at the end of his last letter to Körner, will have to be left aside for the time being. Note, however, that what is said about beauty throughout *Kallias* is valid just as much for natural objects as for art—and that "nature," as becomes clear in some of the later letters, is redefined along the way to accommodate and explain *all* beautiful objects, whether they are produced by art or offered to us in our experience of nature.

---

[5] To understand why these questions are central to Schiller's aesthetics, one needs to go through his writings on theater throughout the decade of the 1780s, starting with his reactions to the harsh criticisms of *The Robbers*. Beiser reconstructs this story, as well as its philosophical implications for Schiller's project, in Beiser, *Schiller as Philosopher*, Chapter 6. See also María del Rosario Acosta López. 2008. *La tragedia como conjuro: el problema de lo sublime en Friedrich Schiller*, 75-105. Bogotá: Universidad Nacional de Colombia/Universidad de los Andes.

[6] Some of the main ideas presented here are part of previously published papers and book chapters. Much of the detailed description of Kallias is *verbatim* taken from María del Rosario Acosta López. 2016. The Resistance of Beauty. On Schiller's *Kallias Briefe* in Response to Kant's Aesthetics. *Epoche* 21: 235-249. See also, for an interpretation of the *Aesthetic Letters* resulting from my reading of *Kallias*, Acosta López. 2020. On an Aesthetic Dimension of Critique: The Time of the Beautiful in Schiller's *Aesthetic Letters*. In *Critique in German Philosophy*, eds. María del Rosario Acosta and J. Colin McQuillan, 89-110. Albany: SUNY.

Toward an Objective Ground for Aesthetics: From the Resistance of Beauty to its Self-Determining Power (Definitions 1 and 2)

Schiller starts his first letter to Körner situating his own investigation on the question of the beautiful in relation to what he describes as the current state of philosophical aesthetics. Between a "subjective sensual" approach to the beautiful, as it is represented by Burke among others, and a "rational objective" account of beauty, as developed by Baumgarten and Mendelssohn ("and the whole crowd of men who esteem perfection"), Kant's work in the *Critique of the Power of Judgment* "may have the great advantage of being able to separate the logical from the aesthetic," without falling back entirely into the empirical and immediate definition of beauty as a "mere affection of sensuousness" (KAL 146). By differentiating between a pure analysis of beauty and all those notions of beauty that "presuppose a concept of the object," Schiller writes: Kant's "subjective rational" aesthetics inaugurates a new possibility for aesthetics and its autonomy as a separate realm from logic and/or epistemology.

In Schillers viewpoint, however, in its attempt to avoid rationalists' objective epistemological claims, Kant's aesthetics have fallen prey to a different problem. Kant seems to have left almost entirely aside, Schiller argues, the question of the beautiful *object*. In doing so, he has also abandoned the possibility of arriving at any concept of beauty altogether. Schiller writes:

> This observation [that pure free beauty is and needs to be completely independent from any concept] seems to miss the concept of beauty completely. For beauty presents itself in *its greatest splendor* only once it has overcome [überwindet] the logical nature of its object, and how can this be done if there is no *resistance* [Widerstand]? (KAL 147, emphasis added)

In leaving almost entirely aside an analysis of the *beautiful object*, Kant has forgotten what he himself had started to explain in the third moment of the "Analytic of the beautiful." For Schiller, one of the key elements in Kant's analysis is the acknowledgment that, even though there is ultimately no determinate concept playing a grounding role in our experience of the beautiful, there still seems to be *something* that, in *resisting* conceptualization, occasions and triggers the (universal) subjective pleasure we call beauty. It is therefore true that beauty is ultimately connected to our experience of pleasure and that this experience is an experience of ourselves, and thus subjective. But, Schiller argues, "there must be something in the object itself" that allows us to speak of the object as beautiful. "I have the obligation to show this," he writes to Körner, "to show adequately that beauty is an objective quality" (KAL 152-153). Only then will aesthetics become "sensuous objective" (KAL 146).

By "objective" Schiller means here a sort of "ontological status for beauty," an aesthetics that can provide an explanation of how beauty does not only reside in the free play of the faculties (see CJ §9) but also somehow *in* the object, even though we might not be able to determine *a priori* and anticipate when an object will be experienced as beautiful, nor prescribe how that beauty might look—hence the emphasis on the sensuous *vis-à-vis* "rational" objectivity.[7] Schiller is here posing a criticism of Kant's project that will come back in the secondary literature on Kant's aesthetics again and again: following Kant's account, there is no way we can say why this object and not some other triggers in us the experience of the beautiful, which seems to leave unresolved the possibility of a rational ground for the question of taste. From a Kantian perspective, Schiller writes, "taste always remains empirical," thereby making it impossible to find an "objective principle of taste" (KAL 146) in Kant's account.[8]

Now, it is also interesting to note how in Schiller's case, the emphasis on the role of the object is connected to something he thinks plays a definitive role in Kant's argument and which Kant indeed introduces but then misses. Beauty, Schiller writes, can only present itself "in *its greatest splendor*" once resistance "to the logical nature of its object" has taken place. Thus, resistance becomes a *constitutive moment* of the experience of the beautiful in Schiller's reading—a resistance, at first, mostly to the very concept of perfection Kant is so adamant about excluding from the realm of pure aesthetic judgment (see particularly CJ §15). A resistance, one might also say, to any determination that ends up assigning a concept to the experience of the beautiful, as Kant himself explains throughout his analysis in emphasizing that judgments of taste are aesthetic, and thus, cannot rely on an objective ground (cf. CJ §1 to §5).

This is what gives way to Schiller's *first definition of beauty*: "the beautiful is only the form of form and that which we call its matter must be the at least formed matter. Perfection is the form of matter, beauty however, is the form of this perfection; it relates to beauty as matter does to form" (KAL 147). The first letter to Körner ends with the announcement of this definition, and much of what comes next is an attempt on the part of Schiller to explain what he means by this entanglement of the notion of resistance—which he has introduced as his own interpretation of Kant's definition of beauty as aesthetic-reflective—and the question concerning what he calls in his first definition "formed matter."[9]

---

[7] For a particularly clear account of how Schiller is using the notions of "sensuous" and "objective" here, see Beiser, *Schiller as Philosopher*, 54ff.

[8] This criticism of Kant on Schiller's part is very similar to the one he will pose to Kant in the context of his practical philosophy. For Schiller, Kant's notion of freedom is left with no real possibility for its actualization, since the only motivation for acting—and drive toward action—comes from sensibility, and Kant has deprived sensibility of any role, except for its self-negation, in the context of autonomy. See for this aspect of Schiller's critique to Kant, "On Grace and Dignity."

[9] Also, an emphasis on the question of resistance puts the experience of beauty for Schiller in closer connection to what for Kant takes place mainly and perhaps only in the experience of the sublime; resistance and "overcoming" are concepts that do not play a constitutive role in Kant's analysis of beauty, but for Schiller, aesthetic experience is always and already profoundly tied to theater as an artwork, and hence, to a kind of experience that is not entirely differentiated from a conflicted, agonistic, kind of pleasure.

Resistance is connected in the first place, for Schiller, to the very specific way in which the object *appears to us* when we experience it as beautiful. Following Kant's notion of disinterestedness (cf. CJ §2 to §5), Schiller writes:

> If the judgment of taste is to be absolutely pure, one must completely abstract from it the intrinsic (practical or theoretical) worth of the beautiful object, out of what matter it is formed and what purpose it might serve. *May it be what it will!* As soon as we make an aesthetic judgment of it, we only want to know if it is what it is through itself. (KAL 154)

It is interesting to note how Schiller takes up Kant's call for a *suspension* of all interest in the case of our judgments of taste. For Schiller, the fact that the pleasure of the beautiful is free from all determination, either prior to it (presupposed as an end, like in the judgment of the useful/good) or resulting from its experience (like the judgment of the agreeable which produces an interest in the existence of the object), means that, *in the case of the judgment of taste, we allow the object to show itself to us in its own way of being* ("May it be what it will!"). This is not, however, a *decision* we make in connection to the beautiful. Something in the object *resists* conceptualization; something *in* the object itself calls for it to be judged aesthetically as beautiful. This "something," Schiller writes, is "the being-determined-through-itself of the thing" (KAL 152).

One could say that here Schiller is following closely the steps Kant takes—perhaps inadvertently—in the Third Moment of the "Analytic of the Beautiful," where, from paragraph §10 to §15, Kant moves from speaking of beauty in terms of the "merely *formal purposiveness* in the play of the cognitive faculties of the subject" (CJ 107, Ak 5:222), and a corresponding "mere *form of subjective purposiveness*" as that which properly constitutes and is at the ground of our pure aesthetic judgments (cf. CJ 107, Ak 5:222), to speaking about the "purposiveness *of the form*" (CJ 108, Ak 5:223, emphasis added), which is then exemplified as the kind of *quality* belonging to the object (or its representation, Kant clarifies, leaving it open whether it is the one or the other), even though it (whatever it is) needs to be related *only to its form* and not to its *sensible qualities* (i.e., charm) (cf. CJ 110, Ak 5:225-226).

Rather than misreading Kant, Schiller seems to be following him to the letter in this move from the mere form of subjective purposiveness as the ground of our pleasure to this enigmatic idea of the form *of the* beautiful object that Kant mentions in passing, whose examples are also quite confusing (he mentions "ornaments" "like the borders of paintings, draperies on statues, or colonnades around magnificent buildings" (CJ 111, Ak 5:226), and which he does not develop further anywhere else in the text. This "something" in the object, which triggers in us the mere formal purposiveness in the play of the faculties, according to Kant, is, for Schiller, as quoted before, "the being-determined-through-itself of the thing" (KAL 152). This is how Schiller interprets Kant's description of the *form of the beautiful object* as a *purposiveness of the form*. There is something in the object, Schiller insists, that shows itself indeed to be purposive in relation to our own faculties and their own subjective purposiveness, since it immediately awakens this play of the faculties in us.

Schiller goes on to describe this purposiveness, this "appearance of self-determination," as "autonomy." This autonomy of the beautiful object is initially, for Schiller, how we try to make sense of its very particular way of displaying itself or *behaving* in our experience of it:

> Reason *lends* the object a capacity [Vermögen] to determine itself, a will, and then contemplates the object under the form of this will (not its will, since this would yield a moral judgment). Reason says of the object whether *it is what it is, through its pure will,* that is, through its self-determining power [Kraft]. (KAL 151, translation modified)

An emphasis on the disinterested character of beauty leads Schiller, as he clarifies to Körner, to propose an understanding of our aesthetic judgments in connection with the frameworks of our practical reason rather than our faculties for knowledge, as is the case in Kant. Resistance to conceptualization, understood in turn as self-determination on the part of the object, orients Schiller's argumentation (cf. KAL 150). Beautiful objects behave *as if* they were *free*, and thus, as if they were self-determining. In their resistance to being determined externally, they simultaneously display a *power* [Kraft] for self-determination that demands we understand them, and our relationship to them, *in analogy* to our concept of freedom.[10]

Schiller's *second definition of beauty* results from this first analogical relation. Beauty, Schiller writes at the end of his second letter, "is thus nothing less than freedom in appearance [Freiheit in der Erscheinung]" (KAL 152). This is not simply a different definition of beauty. It is rather entirely connected to, and even derivative of, the role resistance needs to play for an understanding of beauty. Freedom must therefore be understood here hand in hand with the notion of resistance to conceptualization (and to the concept of perfection). And this means resistance also describes the way freedom appears or manifests itself *in* beauty and *as* beauty.

For now, though, the notion of appearance remains entirely connected to the *analogical relation* to practical reason, and thus, to the idea that reason "borrows" a framework here to make sense of the very specific kind of experience that beauty produces in the subject. Schiller clarifies this to Körner before he finishes his second letter:

> But since this freedom is merely lent to the object by reason, since freedom as such can never be given to the senses and nothing can be free other than what is supra-sensible—in short, it is all that matters here that the object *appears as free* not that it really is so; thus this analogy of the object with the form of practical

---

[10] On the significance of this move on the part of Schiller as an original reaction to Kant's aesthetics, and as a sign of Schiller's own "modernism," see Jay Bernstein. 2008. Significant Stone. Medium and Sense in Schiller, *Internationales Jahrbuch des Deutschen Idealismus* 6: 162-182.

reason is not freedom indeed but merely freedom in appearance, autonomy in appearance. (KAL 151, emphasis added)

This exclusively analogical framework will change, however, in the third letter, where Schiller seems to be aware that the change of emphasis from the subject to the object in the analysis of aesthetic judgments entails a noteworthy displacement—at least, for now, as a change of standpoints. Instead of focusing exclusively *on beauty as a result of an operation of the subject's capacities [Vermögen], Schiller has now moved to speaking about beauty as also related to a force or a power [Kraft] displayed by the object*.[11] Schiller is very aware of this move, and his attempts to come to terms with its consequences occasion a series of definitions of the beautiful that will take him further away from Kant and toward his own notion of beauty and aesthetic freedom.

Toward an Aesthetic Viewpoint: From Freedom in Appearance to the Appearance of Freedom (Definitions 3 and 4)

Thus, beginning his third letter, Schiller makes it explicit to Körner that even though, and so far, his principle of beauty has been only subjective, there is indeed something in the object that is "noticed by reason" in our experiences of the beautiful; he must still thoroughly develop an "objective quality" (cf. KAL 152-153). He then moves, knowingly or not, from speaking of beauty as "freedom in appearance," to introducing a new expression that will determine an entirely different path for his notion of beauty:

> Thus, there is a *view of nature*, or *of appearances*, in which we demand nothing other than freedom from them and where our only concern is that they be what they are through themselves ... such a form in the sense-world which appears merely through itself, is an *exhibition of freedom* [Darstellung der Freiheit] ... Freedom in appearance is thus nothing but the self-determination of a thing insofar as it is available to intuition. (KAL 154, emphasis added)

Two points, at least, are worth underlining here. First, once again, beauty is no longer only connected to a concept we borrow from reason to make sense of the experience triggered in us by certain objects—where beauty is then

---

[11] In paying attention to these movements in Schiller's text, I am following Christoph Menke. 2013. *Force. A Fundamental Concept of Aesthetic Anthropology*, trans. Gerrit Jackson. NY: Fordham University Press, where he proposes to focus on the difference between faculty and force [Kraft, translated here rather as "power"] inaugurated by modern aesthetics in relation to a conception of the subject that opens itself to its own dissolution in aesthetic experience. Menke does not analyze the case of Schiller in his study. I would argue, however, in taking up Menke's framework, that Schiller is a key figure in the development of the importance of the concept of force as central to an alternative way of conceiving philosophy as aesthetics. And *Kallias* is a key moment to understand this development in Schiller's case.

freedom in appearance, and the object is merely interpreted *as if* it was free. Beauty is also now a sensuous *exhibition of freedom*, a comportment displayed by the beautiful object, which is therefore presenting and making perceptible its self-determining power.

Second, by speaking of beauty as freedom in appearance, the *very notion of appearance* has also been transformed in the process. Appearance not only refers here, on the one hand, to a sort of aesthetic semblance where objects appear *as if* they were free. In becoming the realm where freedom comes to be sensuously manifested and exhibited, it also now becomes the world (*a* world or a standpoint) *that beauty makes possible*: a viewpoint made possible precisely through the very singular resistance the question of beauty reintroduces in our relationship to the world—or, one should say, as we are about to see, in the relationship the world itself demands of us when experienced as beautiful.

The consequences of this shift in the meaning of appearance for Schiller's own aesthetico-political proposal will only become evident in the *Aesthetic Letters*. But it is in following *Kallias* that one can track these changes and become aware of their relevance for the later project. Appearance is the realm of beauty, indeed, but only because beauty opens up a realm of and a disposition toward freedom.[12] What "freedom" means here is also something that will become more and more clear along the way, through careful attention to the next two definitions of the beautiful.

If beauty represents a "view of nature" where we demand nothing but a display and an *exhibition of freedom*, then it cannot be treated as one experience among others but as one that opens up a different disposition toward the world around us; a standpoint for judgment where, rather than asking the world to accommodate to our own categories, we ultimately allow the world to show itself to us in its own terms. This is what Schiller decides to spell out in his *third definition of the beautiful*: "a form is beautiful if it demands no explanation, or if it explains itself without a concept" (KAL 155); beauty, Schiller continues, does not "impose [aufdringt]" a concept upon us" (cf. KAL 156, translation modified).

On the one hand, beautiful objects relate to us differently, without imposing a concept on us, and thus allow us to receive them "freely" through a different form of relationality. In the case of the beautiful, indeed, as Kant explains in the *Critique of the Power of Judgment*, we are summoned by the object into the act of mere contemplation [betrachten], in opposition, Schiller writes, to a tendency toward a theoretical kind of "observation" [beobachten] (cf. KAL 148). Even though beautiful objects do not allow us to determine them *from without*, we nonetheless, Schiller writes, "let ourselves be *invited* by the things

---

[12] Many misinterpretations of Schiller—and many of the criticisms of the dangers related to an "aestheticizing" gesture in Schiller's proposal—result from misreading what Schiller means by "appearance," particularly in the *Aesthetic Letters*. I have said more about this elsewhere, see María del Rosario Acosta López. 2010. La ampliación de la apariencia: la educación estética de Schiller como configuradora de un espacio compartido. In *Schiller, arte y política*, ed. Antonio Rivera, 49-90. Murcia: Edinum.

themselves to represent them [Wir lassen uns von der Dingen selbst zu ihrer Vorstellung einladen]" (KAL 148, translation modified).

On the other hand, beautiful objects, in their own resistance to conceptualization, place a specific demand on us that cannot go unnoticed. Schiller writes: "the thing itself, in its objective constitution, invites [einladet] us, or rather *requires* [nötigt] us to notice its quality of not-being-determined-from-the-outside" (KAL 161, emphasis added). This is one of the ways Schiller interprets Kant's analysis of the kind of claim or demand for universality that accompanies our judgments of the beautiful (see here CJ §6 to §8). It is not only that in our judgment we require of and demand agreement from others and assent to our own experience. According to Schiller, this is already *required and demanded by the object's very mode of appearing*. Once again, for Schiller, the focus of the analysis is not only the (subjective) conditions of possibility for the pleasure of the beautiful, but also, and moreover, the relation the object itself requires and demands of us given *the paradoxical (and forceful) combination it exhibits between the two sides of its resistance to conceptualization, namely, its (in)determinability and the appearance of its self-determination*.

And it is here also that we can go back to the lingering question of what "freedom" means if it becomes the grounding principle of beauty, that is, if it can be exhibited sensuously. Beauty leads us to conceive of freedom in connection to the world of appearances. This is the only way we can make any sense of that very particular experience the encounter with a beautiful object awakens in us. But this means, in turn, that in its connection to beauty, we can no longer think of freedom *only* in terms of a *capacity* for self-determination. Also, and most importantly, beauty requires that we begin to think of freedom in connection with the way this self-determining power [Kraft] of the object *displays itself* in the world in its appearing as beauty, and how its appearing therefore changes the way we think about freedom.

In its appearing and presentation to others, the beautiful object appeals to our disposition to let ourselves *be reached by* its very particular plea. Schiller writes: "This great idea of self-determination *reverberates* back [zurückstrahlen] at us from certain appearances of nature, and we call it beauty" (K 153, translation modified). It is almost as if the experience of the beautiful would simultaneously inaugurate and call for the need for its own grammars. A voice seems to be calling us back from out of beautiful objects, powerfully summoning us to hear its tones, inviting us to attune ourselves to its own melodies. Kant speaks beautifully in this context of "the cipher by ways of which nature figuratively speaks to us in its beautiful forms" (CJ 180). Schiller translates this, in turn, into the kind of language (or grammar, I would insist, since it is more about a change in *frameworks* than about the search for alternative concepts) that nature demands of us, different from and beyond a rational perspective, via the experience of the beautiful. This is indeed Schiller's *fourth definition of beauty*: "Self-determination of the rational is pure determination of reason, morality; self-determination of the sense-world is pure determination of nature, beauty." (KAL 156) If reason speaks the language of morality, beauty demands another view of nature altogether, and thus, an altogether different framework for understanding the kind of freedom that is at play in its phenomenality.[13]

Beauty makes freedom reverberate around it, it turns autonomy into a phenomenon that, rather than dealing exclusively with the "operation" of self-determination, turns this operation (and this subjective capacity, as mentioned above, cf. Schiller's second definition of the beautiful) into a power directed and extended toward others, toward the world around it. Schiller writes: "That is why the realm of taste is the realm of freedom –every object of natural beauty outside me is a happy citizen who calls to me: be free like me" ["Jedes schöne Naturwesen ausser mir ein glücklicher Bürger, der mir zuruft: Sei frei wie ich]" (KAL 173; translation modified). The language of beauty in Schiller's analysis becomes therefore a language of *exhortation*. Beautiful objects not only exhibit freedom. This exhibition becomes in itself an invitation to the actualization of freedom around them.

Thus, what is at stake is a notion of freedom intrinsically related in Schiller to the possibility of appearing to others and of inviting others to appear as well as self-determining beings. In its connection to freedom, beauty introduces a call, an invitation, to be perceived and judged on its own terms, under the criteria of another viewpoint entirely: neither a theoretical nor a practical standpoint, the experience of beauty opens up a completely different perspective that not only allows for the display of a singular behavior on the part of objects but that also demands a very specific relation/reaction from its audience. This is the viewpoint Schiller will ascribe much more clearly to the "aesthetic" in later works. Also, it is in tracing this path that we can understand how Schiller's *Kallias* is not only, on its own, an important source for reflecting on his genuine philosophical contribution, but also, a necessary step—and a crucial conceptual background—for interpreting Schiller's later writings. The final two definitions of beauty will help us make these connections even more explicit.

---

[13] At this point of *Kallias*, Schiller introduces his well-known story of the man who has been robbed in a road where various travelers go by; each one reflects, in their reactions, a different theory of the motivation for our actions. Kant's is famously represented—and caricaturized—by the traveler who against all his inclinations, and by offering to sacrifice all of his own needs, offers his help out of "pure duty:" "It will be difficult for me ... to separate myself from my coat, which is the only protection for my sick body, and to leave you my horse since my powers are at an end. But duty commands that I serve you." (KAL 157). Schiller is advancing here and testing what he will also formulate as a strong criticism to Kant's practical philosophy in "On Grace and Dignity." As much as beauty, in Schiller, has to do with the beauty of character and not only with our relation to beautiful objects, I'm leaving this reflection aside to follow only the arguments regarding the latter. The arguments regarding the former are much more strongly formulated in the aforementioned "On Grace and Dignity" and in the *Aesthetic Letters*, as well as in some of his texts on the sublime, written before and after his essays on beauty.

Toward Aesthetic Freedom: Formed Matter and the Power of Beauty (Definitions 5 and 6)

Let's retrace briefly some of the steps Schiller treads so far in his argument, via his first four definitions of beauty. There is a particular *power* enacted by beauty—one that coincides with the way beautiful objects "speak to us" and demand our attention, while inviting us—exhorting us—to "behave" like them. In their own way of appearing, beautiful objects not only show themselves as if they were self-determining, and thus, according to the ideas produced by our own reason, as if they were *free*, but even more, they seem to open a realm, a region of existence, where, according to Schiller, freedom comes to show itself in appearance. As he will put it later very clearly in the *Aesthetic Letters*, "beauty is the only way that freedom has of making itself manifest in appearance" (AE 155).

Schiller will go even further in the *Aesthetic Letters*, thinking of beauty not simply as one possible realm where we can come to a certain understanding of freedom but rather as the experience by way of which we *first* come to understand what freedom really is. This is related to his famous statement at the beginning of the *Aesthetic Letters*: "I hope to convince you that ... if we are ever to solve the problem of politics in practice we will have to approach it through the path of aesthetics, because it is *only through beauty that we make our way to freedom*" (AE 90, emphasis added). What seems to go so often overlooked in this statement is the complex role Schiller is assigning there to both beauty and aesthetics, as well as the notion of freedom that is at stake in this assertion. We need to return to the connections Schiller began developing in *Kallias* between beauty and resistance, and between resistance and freedom, in order to come to a better understanding of Schiller's project as a whole.

As I was suggesting before, this is a path that starts with Schiller's introduction of the concept of resistance as constitutive of the experience of the beautiful. It is also connected to the aesthetic dimension or standpoint that, according to Schiller, beauty opens up for us. Accordingly, let's have a closer look at these two sides of the argument in *Kallias* and interrogate the mode of relationship or comportment, the kind of freedom that grounds and is grounded on, this experience made possible by beauty.

So far, as we've seen, Schiller has been speaking of freedom in terms of "self-determination" and "autonomy." However, we've also seen that, when beauty makes freedom appear, it is not content only with being free itself. Like the noble nature Schiller speaks about in the *Aesthetic Letters*, "it must also set free everything around it ... We call that form noble that impresses the stamp of autonomy upon anything that by its nature merely serves some purpose (is a *mere means*)" (AL 155, emphasis added). This is the kind of power that Schiller assigns to the autonomy of the beautiful. By resisting being turned into a mere means to an end or into a mere product, as he points out in *Kallias* (cf. KAL 156), beauty is an experience that seems somehow to be able to interrupt the logic of productivity, of an economy of means toward ends, and thus, of the utilitarian imperative Schiller sees as pervasive in modern interpretations of rationality.[14]

For something like this to be possible at all, however, mere autonomy will not be sufficient. If there is to be a true interruption of the operative logic of means and ends (which for Schiller is entirely connected, ultimately, to a logic of coercion and domination) it is not sufficient to guarantee resistance to all external determination. Indeed, this resistance allows us to consider everything that attempts to externally determine the object as "*heteronomous and violent*" (KAL 165, emphasis added). This kind of resistance, however, pertains only to the form of the object and hence does not yet make of it a beautiful object: "this also goes for every strict mathematical figure which, nonetheless, may not be beautiful" (KAL 165). Beauty, Schiller writes, needs to take place in the "very territory of matter" (AE 156). It is not enough that form appears as self-determined. For beauty to be possible at all, Schiller writes, the form should not "exercise coercion on the very nature of the thing" (KAL 166). Beyond autonomy, then, for there to be beauty at all, matter *needs to have agreed and decided on its own form.*

Schiller speaks of this other essential moment of the beautiful as "heautonomy," (again, a Kantian term, taken from the Introduction to the *Critique of Judgment* (cf. Published Introduction, 72)). He describes it as "the *free consent* of the thing to its technique" (KAL 165). Hence, in the world of appearances opened up by beauty, "everything—even the tool that serves—is a free citizen, having equal rights with the noblest; and the mind, which would *force* the patient mass *beneath the yoke of its purposes*, must here first obtain its assent" (AE 178, emphasis added). This is the kind of freedom that is ultimately presented and exhibited in our encounter with beauty. And this means a freedom that cannot continue to be understood exclusively in terms of autonomy, since an attention to the beautiful object and its very singular comportment has shown that autonomy as such, in spite of its resistance to conceptualization, *is still the result of a hierarchical relation between form over matter.*

Thus, the need for freedom is understood in terms of heautonomy, whereby such a hierarchy seems to be put entirely into question by the introduction of a second kind of resistance, *that of matter claiming its own rights before the otherwise violent imposition of form.* Schiller goes so far as to describe this moment as the moment of a power capable of entirely suspending what otherwise would always be the result of a violent operation.[15] By rendering this violence and coercion superfluous, beautiful objects, both in art and in nature, have the

---

[14] See Schiller's descriptions in letter 6 of the *Aesthetic Letters* of what he calls "the character of our age" (AE 97ff).

[15] For a more careful explanation of how this is the case in Schiller, see the above quoted Acosta López, "The Time of the Beautiful...," 99ff.

capacity to display the inoperative effect of this very particular power.[16] Hence, Schiller's *fifth definition of the beautiful*: "Beauty is nature in artfulness [Kunstmässigkeit]." (KAL 162) By "nature," Schiller means here "what is through itself," and by "art [Kunst (one could also say 'technique')]" "what is through a rule." Thus, "nature in artfulness is what gives itself the rule—what is through its own rule. (Freedom in the rule, the rule in freedom.)" (KAL 163)

There is therefore something we come to understand about freedom when we think of it in connection to this perspective that beauty inaugurates and makes possible. In light of this perspective, according to Schiller, even autonomy seems *to appear* as a form of violence. Here one needs to pay attention to this appearance as a constitutive side of the question, since precisely it is only in its appearing, in its making itself *perceptible/sensible* in the phenomenal world, Schiller argues, that freedom as autonomy shows violence to be an essential trait of its operation. From an *aesthetic perspective*, Schiller writes, "the violence against our drives which practical reason brings to bear on our moral determination of will *appears* as something insulting and embarrassing. We never want to see coercion, even if it is reason itself which exercises it" (KAL 159).[17]

What beauty shows us, according to Schiller, and shows us precisely in the realm of appearance, is that a moral understanding of freedom, namely, freedom understood exclusively in terms of autonomy, is still caught in the framework that freedom itself is supposed to interrupt, namely, *a sacrificial framework* based on the logic of means to ends. As a suspension of this logic, we "regard every being in aesthetic judgment as an end in itself, [for] it disgusts us, for whom freedom is the highest thing, that something should be sacrificed for something else, and used as a means" (K 159). Hence, Schiller writes in the *Aesthetic Letters*, "there is thus no possibility of a moral transcendence

---

[16] There is another side of the story here that I must leave aside for the time being. Schiller moves in *Kallias* between at least two positions regarding the role of matter in the case of beauty. Besides the one I am emphasizing here which will, in the *Aesthetic Letters*, give way to a relationship of reciprocal effect and fragile balance between form and matter in the case of beauty, the relationship between matter and form also appears in *Kallias* at times as one of *a triumphant domination of form over matter*: one that, if successful (that is, if beautiful), can even hide the kind of coercion that form nonetheless needs to exercise over matter in order to "appear" beautiful, in order to "appear" free. In this case, appearance still means for Schiller something like mere semblance and beautiful objects appear as if free even if they are actually the result of a successful form of domination. There are passages in *Kallias* where this is clearly the case, and hence, where Schiller's notion of beauty becomes a perfect example of aesthetics as a very effective instrument for a form of *disciplinary power*, if not also as key for unveiling a dangerous and aestheticizing side of Schiller's project (Cf. e.g., Constantin Behler. 1995. *Nostalgic Teleology: Friedrich Schiller and the Schemata of Aesthetic Humanism*. NY: Peter Lang). This is, I believe, an ambiguity that survives throughout Schiller's work. I am indebted to the participants of my graduate seminar on aesthetics at DePaul University during the Fall and Winter quarters of 2015-2016 for emphasizing the importance of this side of the reading and how much can be concealed via the "secret" and the "mystery" Schiller wants to preserve for beauty *vis-à-vis* Kant's account. Thanks go particularly to Vilde Avistlaand, Amelia Hruby, and Jeta Mulaj.

[17] For an analysis of this side of Schiller's argument in *Kallias* in the context of his discussion with Kant's practical philosophy, see Falduto, "One more time...," *op. cit.*

(overcoming) of duty; but there is such a thing as an aesthetic transcendence (overcoming)" (AL 155).[18]

Here it is worth nothing not only the singularity of Schiller's philosophical position regarding the relationship between freedom and aesthetics but also that his account of beauty—both as an experience and as the reflection on the nature of this experience—is a key turning point for implementing this relationship. Schiller's aesthetic freedom, as made possible and opened up by the experience of the beautiful—and by this singular combination of nature and artfulness, as spelled out in his fifth definition—not only allows for a site, one might say, of *resistance* to and *suspension* of coercion as a source of violence, but even more so, for the *suspension of the philosophical categories* that give ground to said violence. This is why beauty, for Schiller, and more specifically art, have such critical *power*: not because they can tell us *how* to behave, but rather because, in the kind of experience they make possible and inaugurate for us, they bring about the possibility of putting on hold—and subjecting to critical examination—the frameworks and structures that otherwise determine us unknowingly in our historical present.[19]

Now, this does not mean that beauty itself, in its comportment, does not tell us something truly meaningful about the world. It is not only suspension that beauty offers, but also, as we've seen, resistance, and this means, as developed so far here, resistance not only as reaction but as power, resistance as heautonomy and thus, as the possibility for matter to agree to its own form, and thus of freedom to be conceived beyond the hierarchical structure of form *vis-à-vis* matter, reason *vis-à-vis* sensibility, autonomy *vis-à-vis* happiness.[20]

This is ultimately what one can read—between and behind the lines, but also by putting together all the steps we've given so far—in Schiller's *sixth and last definition of beauty* in *Kallias*: "Beauty is power [Kraft] limited through itself, self-restriction of its power" (KAL 171). As will become perhaps clearer in the *Aesthetic Letters*, beauty does not enter into a dialectical relationship with

---

[18] The details of these arguments concerning an aesthetic transcendence or overcoming of moral duty find their first clear formulation in Schiller's essay "On Grace and Dignity," which he wrote parallel to *Kallias* and the first drafts of the *Aesthetic Letters*. For a careful account of this argument in Schiller's philosophical work see Beiser, *Schiller as philosopher*, Ch. 7 213-237, and my own attempt to convey the nuances of the argument in María del Rosario Acosta López. 2008. ¿Una superación estética del deber? La crítica de Schiller a Kant. *Episteme* N.S. 28: 3-24. See also Laura Macor. 2019. Schiller on Emotions. Problems of (In)Consistency in His Ethics. In *Aesthetic Reason and Imaginative Freedom: Friedrich Schiller and Philosophy*, eds. María del Rosario Acosta and Jeffrey Powell. NY: SUNY.

[19] For a more careful development of this side of Schiller's philosophical contribution, see the aforementioned Acosta López, "The Time of the Beautiful…," op. cit., and Acosta López. 2021. Introduction to the *Letters on the Education of Humankind*, Bloomsbury Philosophy Library (DOI: 10.5040/9781350970588.009).

[20] The latter two pairs are categories that Schiller does not utilize in the context of *Kallias*, but that show how his argument regarding beauty in his letters to Körner is closely connected and thus also becomes relevant for his critique of Kant's practical philosophy in other writings, particularly in the *Aesthetic Letters* and in "On Grace and Dignity," respectively, corresponding in each case to his notion of aesthetic freedom and to the idea of a beautiful soul.

violence, opposing it face to face in the hopes of "overcoming" it, and thus reproducing the frameworks that govern its multiple forms of operating. Beauty rather seeks to *render this operation inoperative* by introducing a notion of power that does not need forceful coercion to exhibit freedom, while also facilitating the actualization of this freedom around it—in others and in the world.

The project of an aesthetic "overcoming" of duty, and how it translates into a critique of philosophy by philosophy and through the exercise of aesthetics, is ultimately Schiller's philosophical project. And it is in *Kallias* where Schiller begins to discover, in his reading of and reactions to Kant's third critique, how aesthetics can take us out of our traditional frameworks of thinking—a thinking that, otherwise, would be always already tainted with and caught within modern structures of power understood only as *coercion*. Beauty allows us to conceive of the relation between form and matter outside of their traditional metaphysical hierarchies. By doing so, it not only challenges our thought, demanding the need for new frameworks of sense that allow us to listen to beauty in its unique and singular tones; it further brings to light how violence is at the ground of the structures that frame all of our conceptions of experience, forcing us to come up with altogether new ways of conceiving freedom itself. It is beauty, Schiller writes, that first guides us in this way. Not because is sets us free, as Schiller is usually (mis)interpreted, but rather because it sets our thought into critical motion, not against or in abstraction from our sensibility, but precisely via the most truly sensible experience of all.

References

Acosta López, María del Rosario. 2008a. *La tragedia como conjuro: el problema de lo sublime en Friedrich Schiller*, 75-105. Bogotá: Universidad Nacional de Colombia/ Universidad de los Andes.

Acosta López, María del Rosario. 2008b. ¿Una superación estética del deber? La crítica de Schiller a Kant. *Episteme N.S.* 28: 3-24.

Acosta López, María del Rosario. 2010. La ampliación de la apariencia: la educación estética de Schiller como configuradora de un espacio compartido. In *Schiller, arte y política,* ed. Antonio Rivera, 49-90. Murcia: Edinum.

Acosta López, María del Rosario. 2016. The Resistance of Beauty. On Schiller's *Kallias Briefe* in Response to Kant's Aesthetics. *Epoche* 21: 235-249.

Acosta López, María del Rosario. 2020. On an Aesthetic Dimension of Critique: The Time of the Beautiful in Schiller's *Aesthetic Letters.* In *Critique in German Philosophy*, eds. María del Rosario Acosta and J. Colin McQuillan, 89-110. Albany: SUNY.

Acosta López, María del Rosario. 2021. Introduction to the *Letters on the Education of Humankind*, Bloomsbury Philosophy Library (DOI: 10.5040/ 9781350970588.009).

Behler, Constantin. 1995. *Nostalgic Teleology: Friedrich Schiller and the Schemata of Aesthetic Humanism.* NY: Peter Lang.

Beiser, Frederick. 2005. *Schiller as Philosopher.* New York: Oxford University Press.

Bernstein, Jay. 2008. Significant Stone. Medium and Sense in Schiller, *Internationales Jahrbuch des Deutschen Idealismus* 6: 162-182.
De Man, Paul. 1996. Kant and Schiller. In *Aesthetic Ideology*, ed. Andrej Warminski, 129-162. Minneapolis: University of Minnesota Press.
Henrich, Dieter. 1982. Beauty and Freedom: Schiller's Struggle with Kant's Aesthetics. In *Essays in Kant's aesthetics*, eds. Ted Cohen and Paul Guyer, 237-257. Chicago: University of Chicago Press.
Falduto, Antonino. 2021. One more time on the alleged repugnance of Kant's ethics? Schiller's *Kallias letters* and the entirety of the human being. *European Journal of Philosophy*, 29/4: 795-810.
Kulenkampff, Jens. 1974. *Materialen zu Kants 'Kritik der Urteilskraft,'* 126-144. Frankfurt am Main: Suhrkamp (there is not, to my knowledge, any systematic study of these annotations within Schiller's scholarship).
Macor, Laura. 2012. *Der morastige Zirkel der menschlichen Bestimmung. Friedrich Schillers Weg von der Aufklärung zu Kant.* Würzburg: Königshausen & Neumann.
Macor, Laura. 2019. Schiller on Emotions. Problems of (In)Consistency in His Ethics. In *Aesthetic Reason and Imaginative Freedom: Friedrich Schiller and Philosophy*, eds. María del Rosario Acosta and Jeffrey Powell. NY: SUNY.
Menke, Christoph. 2013. *Force. A Fundamental Concept of Aesthetic Anthropology*, trans. Gerrit Jackson. NY: Fordham University Press.

CHAPTER 10

On Grace and Dignity (1793)

Heiner F. Klemme

This essay appeared in the June edition of the *Neue Thalia* (vol. 3, no. 2), the journal edited by Schiller, as an offprint, and in the form of a standalone book (Leipzig). The latter two editions contain a dedication to Schiller's friend and patron Carl von Dalberg. Schiller added to the dedication a liberal translation of the following quotation, taken out of context from Milton's *Paradise Lost*: "What there though seest fair Creature is thyself" (Milton 2005, p. 118).[1] The essay was written in less than six weeks in May and June of 1793. After reading Kant's *Critique of the Power of Judgment* (1790), which he began in February 1791, and after his unfinished so-called *Kallias* letters to his friend Christian Gottfried Körner (January 25–February 28, 1793), Schiller began work on an independent aesthetic theory. The external occasion for composing "On Grace and Dignity," was the acute lack of contributions for the *Neue Thalia*. At the same time, he was working on the essay "On the Sublime," which also appeared in 1793 in the *Neue Thalia*. Like the *Kallias* letters, it features considerable overlap with "On Grace and Dignity." The *Kallias* letters are especially important for a deeper understanding of "On Grace and Dignity."

Let us turn briefly to the *Kallias Letters*, in which Schiller makes some preliminary remarks on the peculiarity of his theory of the beautiful. According to Schiller, theories of the beautiful can be categorized as follows: (1) "subjective

---

[1] Schiller renders this passage as follows: "Was du hier siehest, edler Geist, bist du selbst" (cf. Matuschek 2002, p. 79).

H. F. Klemme (✉)
University of Halle-Wittenberg, Halle, Germany
e-mail: heiner.klemme@phil.uni-halle.de

© The Author(s), under exclusive license to Springer Nature Switzerland AG 2023
A. Falduto, T. Mehigan (eds.), *The Palgrave Handbook on the Philosophy of Friedrich Schiller*, https://doi.org/10.1007/978-3-031-16798-0_10

sensible" (like that of Edmund Burke); (2) "subjective rational" (like that of Kant); (3) "rational objective" (like those of Alexander Gottlieb Baumgarten, Moses Mendelssohn, and "the whole crowd of men who esteem perfection"); or (4) "sensible objective" (KAL 146; SW 5: 394). The theory developed by Schiller himself is supposedly the sole genuine "sensible objective" theory and amounts to the following: "Beauty is thus nothing less than freedom in appearance" (KAL 152; SW 5: 400). Freedom and necessity do not contradict each other. A natural object is beautiful, if, in terms of its inner determination, it is perceived immediately (i.e., without a concept to explain it) in its appearance as what it wants to be. Even a tree has "its own nature, its personality" (KAL 165; SW 5: 415) in this sense. Where "*mass is completely dominated by form* (in the animal and plant kingdom) and by living forces (in the autonomy of the organic)," we perceive "everything to be beautiful" (KAL 164; SW 5: 413). External obstacles, violence, and coercion are opposed to beauty. A beautiful object either assumes or imitates the "form of practical reason" (KAL 150; SW 5: 398). Since freedom solely pertains to the supersensible, the object is not really free and only seems to be free. Thus, "this analogy of the object with the form of practical reason is not freedom indeed but merely *freedom in appearance, autonomy in appearance*" (KAL 151; SW 5: 400). We "lend" (KAL 151; SW 5: 399) the object freedom through our practical reason because the object appears to be determined "from within" (KAL 150; SW 5: 398).

It is striking that Schiller (in contrast to Kant in the *Critique of the Power of Judgment*) does not write that we judge the action *as if* it were free. It is not entirely clear why he does not adopt this expression, which is almost excessively employed by Kant. Perhaps it has something to do with Schiller's desire to emphasize the immediacy of our perception of the beautiful and thereby decidedly oppose Kant, who attempts to conceive of the beautiful within the context of a theory of pure aesthetic judgment of taste. Kant's theory does not "lend" the object freedom, but rather underscores the free play of the imagination and the understanding. Schiller aims toward a phenomenology of the beautiful, if you will, that stands closer to John Locke's "historical plain method" (*An Essay Concerning Human Understanding*, 1690, I,1.2) (which has its origin in medicine) than to Kant's transcendental philosophy. The metaphysical background of Schiller's concept of freedom is nevertheless Kant's transcendental idealism, i.e., the distinction between things in themselves and appearances. Schiller does not argue for his position, but describes what he takes our perception to demonstrate. Thus, the human being as a person is not subject to the universal mechanism of nature. Schiller is able to aesthetically judge the effects of nature, which in themselves are subject to the law of necessity, "according to the form of a pure[2] will" (KAL 152; SW 5: 400) because he avails himself of practical reason. Schiller does not explain how the relation of autonomy and heteronomy—of self-determination and natural necessity—is to be understood, nor

---

[2] The Cambridge translation of "free" has been changed here to "pure" following the German *Form des reinen Willens*.

does he clarify how beauty as an "objective property" is possible given that freedom can never be a property of nature. In principle, we should not have too great an expectation to grasp the phenomenon of beauty conceptually: "A form is beautiful, one might say, if it *demands no explanation*, or if it *explains itself without a concept*" (KAL 155; SW 5: 403).

In "On Grace and Dignity," Schiller continues his reflections on the theory of beauty with recourse to the concepts of grace[3] and dignity. He begins his essay by presenting and interpreting the Greek fable about the goddess of beauty (gr. Aphrodite, lat. Venus) from Book 14 of Homer's *Iliad*. Her girdle vests her with grace and has the power to procure love for her. She is accompanied by the graces.[4] Schiller elucidates the significance of the fable for his theory of beauty quite extensively before philosophically analyzing its main points. In his view, the fable attests that beauty (or charm) and grace (or the graces) are not identical. Grace is beautiful but not every beauty is also graceful. Animals can be beautiful but not graceful. Beauty is an objective characteristic of Venus, who remains beautiful even when she removes her girdle and gives it to Hera.

The first part of the essay (which does not have a proper title) serves to demonstrate that "grace is the expression of a beautiful soul," and the second part (titled "Dignity") that "*dignity* is the expression of a superior mentality" (GD 154; SW 5: 470). Grace accentuates freedom of the mind and of nature, dignity the aspect of the mastery of our mind over irrational nature. For Schiller, the two concepts complement each other. In addition to Kant, important authors upon whom Schiller draws and with whom he either critically or approvingly engages include Home (Lord Kames), Reinhold, Mendelssohn, Winckelmann, Sulzer, and Wieland. The concepts of grace and dignity were already widespread in aesthetic and moral-philosophical literature as Schiller discussed them. They are to be found in antiquity (*venustus et gravitas*) and were also treated in Early Modern aesthetics in connection or in combination with concepts such as charm (often synonymous with grace), power, and the sublime (often synonymous with dignity). Thus, in the German translation of Lord Kames' *Elements of Criticism*, published between 1763 and 1766, the terms "grace" and "dignity" were translated as *Anmut* and *Würde*. In 1769 Wieland published a poem with the title, "The Graces." Carl von Dalberg, to whom Schiller dedicates his work, explains in his *Principles of Aesthetics* (Erfurt 1791) that "power, united with grace," is "the highest ornament of beauty" (1791: 66). In another passage, he writes that aesthetics demands the unity "of strength with grace" (1791: 72). Von Dalberg claims further that "power determines inner essential worth, generates reverence, [and] satisfies the understanding. Temperance and grace, with regard to power, impart affection, love, [and] feed the heart" (1791: 67).

---

[3] "Grace" is the English translation of "Anmut" and "Grazie."
[4] In Greek mythology, the Graces, or "Charites," were three daughters of Zeus, namely Aglaie, Euphrosyne, and Thaleia (Apollodorus 1997, p. 29).

An understanding of Schiller's "On Grace and Dignity" is complicated by the high frequency of definitions and classifications he employs that are a testament to physicians and historians. Schiller's observations are, at their core, an account of what is the case. They do not seek to explain, but merely describe. They seek to describe how things in our perception aesthetically appear to us as persons. Justifications and deductions—as would be encountered by contemporary readers of Kant and of the tradition of the Leibniz-Wolffian school, which was heavily oriented toward concepts—are not to be found in Schiller's writings. His aesthetic theory is not aimed toward the distinctness of concepts but is based on intuitive evidence. It is no coincidence that Schiller first develops the significance of grace from a fable and only turns to the "philosophical investigation" in a second step. As a rationale for this methodology, he points out "that reason engaged in philosophy can boast of few discoveries that sense had not already *anticipated* and that poetry had not already *revealed*" (GD 127; SW 5: 437). In poesy and art, "anticipation" and "revelation" are sources of our knowledge almost equal to "reason engaged in philosophy." Without *mythos* there is no *logos*, for beauty and grace cannot be derived immediately from reason.

Schiller generally distinguishes his approach from alternative philosophical points of view by indicating that they are unsuitable for grasping the phenomenon of beauty, namely by virtue of the incommensurability of the effects of these alternative approaches with the phenomenon itself. An example of this is Schiller's criticism of Kant's moral philosophy. In the latter, "the idea of *duty* is presented with a severity that repels all graces and might tempt a weak intellect to seek moral perfection by taking the path of a somber and monkish asceticism" (GD 150; SW 5: 465). Methodologically, this is indeed consistent. Schiller attributes alternative approaches (such as that of Kant, on the one hand, and that of "course materialism," on the other) to the "circumstances of the time" (GD 150; SW 5: 465), which his own theory can apparently avoid. Schiller is the first to achieve an impartial view of what is beautiful. Thus, even Kant fails to do justice to this object of inquiry and misconstrues it in his presentation, although there can no longer be any disagreement about "the matter itself" (GD 150; SW 5: 465). The "matter itself" requires a presentation that "proceeds on purely objective grounds" (GD 150; SW 5: 465). "To the things themselves" is the battle cry of Schiller's aesthetics. He is the first to succeed in grasping the beautiful in its sensible objectivity.

Many passages of "On Grace and Dignity" point beyond aesthetic questions in the narrower sense. In addition to analogical references to politics and political science conveyed through the concept of freedom, Schiller takes a stand on a number of debates of the time, including: the relationship between nature and freedom, nature and mind, freedom and necessity, independence (autonomy) and heteronomy, soul and body, aesthetics and ethics, lordship and bondage, as well as those concerning the concept of the person and the vocation of the human being. Even his philosophy of love manifests itself in his work. In all of his remarks, Schiller presupposes (along with Kant) that the concept of freedom pertains to the supersensible and that the human being is characterized by two natures (freedom and sensibility) that can come into conflict. Grace and dignity signify phenomena that allow the dualism between freedom and nature to be harmoniously overcome.

In his interpretation of Greek mythology, Schiller refers to the "girdle of charm" (GD 125; SW 5: 435) with two distinct concepts of motion. *First*, he distinguishes between "static beauty" and the "*movable* beauty" (GD 125; SW 5: 434) of grace. Both kinds of beauty are objective. "Static beauty" is necessarily given with the person himself and remains as long as the subject exists. By contrast, the "*movable beauty*" of grace arises or vanishes by chance. If a person wears the girdle of grace, then grace is transformed into a personal characteristic. The person not only seems to be lovable; he really is "lovable" (GD 125; SW 5: 435). The effect of the girdle is not natural but "*magical*" because "its power extends beyond all natural circumstances" (GD 125; SW 5: 435). It is "*magical*" because it represents something expressed in nature "that lies outside nature in the realm of freedom" (GD 125; SW 5: 435). *Second*, Schiller designates grace as "beauty of movement" (GD 125; SW 5: 435). Movement is the sole alteration that an object can undergo without sacrificing its identity. Grace represents an "*extension*" (GD 126; SW 5: 436) of the concept of beauty. Indeed, the "magical power" of the girdle is also effective for the less beautiful and even the non-beautiful. It is restricted to the contingent movements of human beings. "Grace is a beauty not granted by nature, but brought forth by the subject itself" (GD 127; SW 5: 437).

Schiller begins his *philosophical* reflections on grace with elucidations of "static beauty," which he now calls "beauty of design (*architectonic beauty*)" (GD 127; SW 5: 438). The "*architectonic beauty*" of the human being is based on the necessary laws of effective natural forces. In this regard, the beauty of the human being is "a free natural effect" (GD 129; SW 5: 440). It is a beauty "in *outward appearance*" (GD 128; SW 5: 439). Nevertheless, even "*architectonic beauty*" is indirectly subject to the "idea of humanity" that stems from reason, i.e., a "technical perfection" of "human form," which represents a "*system of purposes*" (GD 128; SW 5: 438). "[R]eason's idea" can "never *distribute* beauty" to the "human form" but only "*sanction* it" (GD 129; SW 5: 440). This idea represents a necessary but not sufficient condition for architectonic beauty. "Beauty [...] has the peculiar characteristic that it is not simply represented in the world of senses but also arises in that world, that it is not only expressed but also created by nature" (GD 129; SW 5: 440). If the artist wishes to create something beautiful, he can only "achieve it insofar as he maintains the appearance of nature's having formed it" (GD 129; SW 5: 440–1).

Although beauty arises from the sensible world, reason has an interest in it. Beauty pleases reason. Reason does not find its ideas in the object but puts them as it were in the appearances, "treats something purely sensuous as more than sensuous," and thereby "makes transcendental use of this effect from the purely sensuous world" (GD 130–1; SW 5: 442). Following Kant's doctrine of two worlds, Schiller calls beauty "the citizen of two worlds, one *by birth*, the other *through adoption*" (GD 131; SW 5: 442). "Taste, as a faculty of judgment for beauty" (GD 131; SW 5: 442), steps between spirit and sensibility, between the intelligible and the sensible world, as an intermediary. It binds these two "natures into a happy union" (GD 131; SW 5: 442). As a result, Schiller maintains that the architectonic beauty of the human being is "*the sensuous expression of a rational concept*" (GD 131; SW 5: 443). In other words: "everything that is *objective* about beauty is given in *intuition alone*" (GD 131; SW 5: 443n).[5] Although the beauty of the human being surpasses all beauties in terms of degree, it is identical with other beautifies in terms of kind. It surpasses other beauties in terms of degree because the architectonic beauty of the human being is characterized by a natural necessity that is "supported by the necessity of the teleological basis that determines it" (GD 132; SW 5: 444).

"Nature on its own" (GD 133; SW 5: 445) can bring about the architectonic beauty of the human being. However, since the human being is at the same time a "person" and therewith can be "the cause and even the absolutely final cause of its condition" (GD 132; SW 5: 444), the human being never appears only as nature. "Its type of appearance is dependent upon the types of feeling and willing, that is to say, upon the conditions that it freely determines by itself, not those determined in accordance with the necessities of nature" (GD 132; SW 5: 444). Although the laws of nature persist, the mind is free. Schiller is aware of the difficulty of his position: how can one and the same appearance simultaneously be subject to the necessity of nature and the free power of choice of the human being as person? How are nature and freedom compatible? Schiller avoids offering a complex metaphysical-critical theory, as found in the *Critique of Pure Reason* and the *Critique of the Power of Judgment*. Instead he chooses formulations whose literary quality is able to express in its own way the harmonious coherence of nature and freedom, i.e., the purposiveness of nature and freedom. Although the alterations of creation, which nature "underwent under the rule of freedom, are effected *in accordance with* no laws but its own, nevertheless, they no longer emerge *from these* laws" (GD 133; SW 5: 445). With the mind (the soul) something decisive is added to the concept of architectonic beauty effected by nature: "the beauty of play" (GD 133; SW 5: 446), i.e., the free and independent movement of the human being. Schiller provides Kant's notion of the free play of the cognitive powers as the ground of pure judgment of taste with a realistic, inner-worldly interpretation that refers to nature. The free play of the imagination and the understanding results in the human being's free and self-determined movement in space and time; freedom manifests itself in this play. Schiller discusses grace against the background of this aesthetically grounded conception of freedom: "Grace is beauty of form under freedom's influence, the beauty of those appearances that the person determines. Architectonic beauty honors the creator of nature, grace honors those who possess it. The former is a *talent*, the latter, *personal merit*" (GD 133–4; SW 5: 446). If grace becomes habitual, then it can turn

---

[5] Translation modified.

into architectonic beauty. Only those movements that "correspond to a sentiment" (GD 135; SW 5: 447) can display grace.

Schiller distinguishes between three kinds of movement: *first*, movement based on "feelings" and "natural instinct" (GD 135; SW 5: 448); *second*, that which is based on the will of the person and the ends he sets; *third*, movement accompanied by "moral sentiment or moral attitude" (GD 136; SW 5: 448). Movements of the first kind cannot be graceful; movements of the second kind can be graceful only if they are connected to movements of the third kind. Grace "must always be natural, in other words, instinctive (or it must at least appear to be so) and the subject must not appear to be *conscious of possessing grace*" (GD 137–8; SW 5: 450). The human being comes to know his purpose through nature; however, he must fulfill this purpose through his own free choice. His development lies with the human being himself; it is a "personal expression" (GD 141; SW 5: 454). We experience what the human being has done "to fulfill this plan" (GD 141; SW 5: 454) from his countenance. We expect that the human being express his "moral person" (GD 144; SW 5: 457) in his character. The human being "should not simply reflect the beams of a foreign reason, as other sensuous beings do, even if it were divine reason; rather they should glow with their own light, like a sun" (GD 144; SW 5: 457). His "moral capacity" (GD 145; SW 5: 459) must reveal itself through grace. Beauty has a sensible cause but it must be, "or at least appear to be, a completely free result of nature" (GD 145; SW 5: 459). Schiller relies on a kind of preestablished harmony between sensibility and freedom. "One could say, then, that grace is a *favor* granted to the sensuous by the ethical, just as architectonic beauty can be regarded as nature *consenting* to a technical form" (GD 145; SW 5: 459). The supersensible ground in the disposition makes "grace expressive" (GD 146; SW 5: 460), the merely sensible ground in nature makes it beautiful.

Which moral sentiments "are most compatible with beauty as [it is] expressed?" (GD 146; SW 5: 461). "Ease," according to Schiller, is the "main characteristic of grace" (GD 146; SW 5: 461), such that violence is foreign to it. If nature reigns alone, "humanity disappears" (GD 146; SW 5: 461). Schiller distinguishes between three ways in which "a human being can relate to himself, that is, in which the sensuous part can relate to the rational" (GD 147; SW 5: 461): (1) the human being suppresses "the demands of his sensuous nature" (GD 147; SW 5: 461) in favor of his rational nature; (2) he subordinates his rational to his sensible nature; (3) sensible impulses "settle into harmony with the rules of the rational and human beings are at one with themselves" (GD 147; SW 5: 461). Schiller sides in favor of the third option. The beauty of play occurs whenever "*reason and sensuousness*—duty and inclination—*coincide*" (GD 149; SW 5: 463). He is prepared to accept, along with Kant, an objective difference between "actions from inclination and actions out of duty" (GD 149; SW 5: 464). However, grace does not turn on this distinction. For, according to Schiller, the human being is not intended to perform individual moral actions, "but to be an ethical being. *Virtue* is prescribed for him, rather than *virtues*, and virtue is nothing other than an 'inclination for duty'" (GD

149; SW 5: 464). Considered from the perspective of the human being (in the "subjective sense"), there is no opposition between duty and inclination because the human being not only "*may*, but *should* combine enjoyment with duty" (GD 149; SW 5: 464–5). Human beings ought to "obey their reason with joy. Not in order to discard it like a burden or shrug it off like a course covering, no, their purely intellectual nature is accompanied by a sensuous one so that the sensuous can agree as closely as possible with the higher self" (GD 149; SW 5: 465). Schiller once again draws on the concept of nature in this passage. Nature "made him a rational, sensitive being, that is, a human," and thereby obligated him "not to separate what it had bound together and, even in the purest expressions of his divine part, not to neglect the sensuous, and not to base the triumph of the one on the subjugation of the other" (GD 149–50; SW 5: 465).

Schiller's aesthetics culminates in the reconciliation of mind and nature, in the "ethical spirit" (GD 150; SW 5: 465) that has become nature. In order to indicate the harmony between the nature and reason—necessity and freedom—of the person independently formed in accordance with his purpose, Schiller seizes upon the concept of the "*beautiful soul*" (GD 152; SW 5: 468), commonplace in contemporary literature, and imparts to it a new moral-aesthetic significance. The *beautiful soul* "seals perfected humanity" and "has no other merit besides being" (GD 152; SW 5: 468). "It is in a beautiful soul that sensuousness and reason, duty and inclination are in harmony, and grace is their expression as appearance. Only in the service of a beautiful soul can nature possess freedom and at the same time preserve its form, since freedom vanishes under the control of a strict disposition and form under the anarchy of sensuousness" (GD 153; SW 5: 468–9). A beautiful soul also "spreads an irresistible grace" over subjects "lacking in architectonic beauty" (GD 153; SW 5: 469). Schiller correlates grace with gender: grace befits the female more than the male gender. "The physical form has to contribute to grace, as well as the character; the physical through its flexible ability to receive impressions and to be set in motion, the character through the moral harmony of feelings. In both, nature was more favorable towards woman than towards man" (GD 153; SW 5: 469; cf. Alt 2000: 109–10). Grace is the expression of the beautiful soul. According to Schiller, human beings have the task of "being a harmonious whole, and of acting with their full human capacity" (GD 154; SW 5: 470). But the beauty of their character, "the ripest fruit of humanity," is "only an idea that they can vigilantly strive to live up to, yet, despite all efforts, can never fully attain" (GD 154; SW 5: 470). Schiller takes the reason for this to reside in the human being's self-preservation, which nature provided for by means of the sensations of pain and pleasure. Even the "most strong-willed Stoic feels hunger just as acutely and loathes it just as strongly as the worm at his feet" (GD 155; SW 5: 471). In contrast to animals, human beings have "complete freedom to choose" (GD 155; SW 5: 471) whether they subject themselves to reason or the law of nature: "Animals *must* strive to free themselves from pain; humans can decide to hold on to it" (GD 155; SW 5: 471). The "will *alone* already elevates the human above animal nature; the *moral* will elevates him to divinity" (GD 155; SW 5: 471).

Schiller calls the concept of the will sublime and uses it as a segue to the second theme of his essay: "As grace is the expression of a beautiful soul, *dignity* is the expression of a superior mentality" (GD 154; SW 5: 470). The human being as a force of nature can freely choose insofar as he must follow neither the law of nature nor the law of reason. Schiller is an advocate of the unconditioned capacity for self-determination of the human being as person. Whether the human being becomes what he ought to become according to his purpose depends solely on what he himself wills. The human being can will to will. His will "is not free as a moral force, however; in other words, it *should* be accountable to the force of reason. It is *bound* to neither but *indebted* to the law of reason" (GD 155; SW 5: 472). The human being cannot make his desires disappear, but he can resist them, overcome them, and not allow them a determining influence on his will. "In the emotions, agreement with the law of reason is only possible by contravening the demands of nature" (GD 158; SW 5: 474). Because inclination does not take part in the action, the human being does not act "with *moral beauty*" but "with *moral greatness*" (GD 158; SW 5: 474). If the human being must overcome an emotion, resisting it, then the "beautiful soul" must "change into a *sublime* soul" (GD 158; SW 5: 474). Schiller designates the "moral strength" that controls impulses "spiritual freedom" and its expression in appearance "*dignity*" (GD 158; SW 5: 475). To be sure, this turn of phrase is to be understood metaphorically, since, strictly speaking, moral strength is incapable of representation in appearance by virtue of the fact that it belongs to the supersensible. Schiller also identifies dignity as "*peace in suffering*" (GD 160; SW 5: 476), as the "representation of intelligence in humans and the expression of their moral freedom" (GD 160; SW 5: 477), and thereby places it in the vicinity of Stoic ethics. The mind demonstrates its freedom in dignity, "its independence (autonomy)" proves itself to be "*ruler*" in the body, while it governs with "*liberality*" concerning grace, since in that case it must not overcome any opposition (GD 160; SW 5: 477). "Grace, then, lies in the *freedom of intentional movements*, dignity in the *mastery of instinctive ones*" (GD 160; SW 5: 477). We demand virtue of grace and dignity of inclination, we demand "grace from a person who places obligations, and dignity from someone who is placed under an obligation" (GD 162; SW 5: 479).

Schiller ends his essay with various reflections on the phenomenology of grace, charm, and dignity, of love and respect. Thus, he points out, for example, that the highest degree of grace is "*the enchanting*," while the highest degree of dignity is "*majesty*" (GD 168; SW 5: 486). He is evidently convinced that grace and dignity (the feminine and masculine elements in us) can be united in one and the same person. Dignity always manifests a particular limitation of desires and inclinations; grace "gives evidence of a peaceful, harmonious disposition and a sensitive heart" (GD 163; SW 5: 480). Grace is supported by architectonic beauty, dignity by strength. If grace and dignity are "*united* in the same person, then the expression of humanity is complete in that person, and he stands there, justified in the world of spirit and affirmed in appearance" (GD 163; SW 5: 481).

Schiller's conception of the beautiful and the sublime—aimed at harmoniously overcoming the dualism of nature and freedom and the representation of freedom—can be characterized as a thoroughly idealist position. "Freedom of reason" and "natural necessity" (GD 163; SW 5: 481) are ideally united in a person, as are respect and love. The object of love is sensible, its subject is "moral nature" (GD 166; SW 5: 483). It is "the *God* in us" (GD 166; SW 5: 483) who finds himself in sensibility in the emotion of love. The beautiful soul knows "no sweeter happiness than to see the sacred in itself imitated or realized and to embrace its immortal friend in the world of senses" (GD 166; SW 5: 484). The beautiful soul "seeks and appreciates" (GD 166; SW 5: 484) its own self in the appearance, in its object.

It is no coincidence that in the section on grace Schiller is critical of Kant's ethics, which has no room for grace because it constructs the concept of duty out of the opposition between freedom and nature. The categorical imperative, in terms of its structure, presupposes a typal difference between rational and sensible beings, which, as in the domain of Kant's aesthetics, can be overcome only within the framework of a theory of subjective reflection ("as if"). An objective theory of the beautiful that promises to accomplish more than this can be found in Schiller but not at all in Kant. On the other hand, Schiller refrains from any critical dissociation from Kant's ethics in the section on dignity, which Schiller conceives of as more of a "masculine" virtue that more closely approximates Kant's model of human volition characterized by conflict and difference. Apart from that, Schiller's conception of the sublime does not constitute any continuation of this doctrine in Kant, the latter of which has at its basis a fundamental discrepancy (between the person and violent nature incomprehensible to the imagination). Kant himself refers approvingly to Schiller's doctrine "in his masterfully written treatise" (Rel 6:23-4n; cf. 23: 98–101) in a footnote added to the second edition of his *Religion Within the Boundaries of Mere Reason* (1793), over which Schiller rejoiced. However, Kant does not appear to be willing to compromise on the matter at hand. Although, referring to Schiller, Kant emphasizes that "we agree on the most important principles," he indicates a crucial point that Schiller neglected in his criticism of Kant's position: while virtue allows for the "accompaniment of the *graces*" (Rel 6:23n), the concept of duty in itself cannot be explicated by the concept of grace. The concept of duty contains "unconditional necessitation" and therefore stands "in direct contradiction" to grace (Rel 6:23n). Virtue, on the other hand, is the "firmly grounded disposition to fulfill one's duty strictly" (Rel 6:24n). The virtuous human being nevertheless has "*grown fond*" (Rel 6:24n) of the good and observes his duty with a joyful heart.

Schiller's engagement with Kant is controversial to this day (Beiser 2005). Furthermore, Schiller's work served as an important impetus for the formation of an idealist aesthetics, of the autonomy of aesthetics, and—with its pathos of freedom—of German Idealism (Schilling 2005, 397–8). At times, "On Grace and Dignity" has also been seen as foundational to the idea of an aesthetic existence and way of life (Safranski 2004). Johann Wolfgang von Goethe saw in Schiller's treatise an attack on his "confession of faith" (Schilling 2005, 397), which Goethe took Schiller to misrepresent, and consequently rejected it. Schiller's work *On the Aesthetic Education of Man in a Series of Letters* (1794/95) would have a more sustained impact (Feger 2014).

German text translated into English by John Walsh.

References

Alt, Peter-André. 2000. *Schiller. Leben – Werk – Zeit*, vol. 2. Munich: C.H. Beck.
Apollodorus. 1997. *The Library of Greek Mythology*. Trans. and ed. R. Hard. Oxford: Oxford University Press.
Beiser, Frederick. 2005. *Schiller as Philosopher: A Re-Examination*. Oxford: Oxford University Press.
Dalberg, Carl von. 1791. *Grundsaetze der Aesthetik*. Erfurt.
Feger, Hans. 2014. Friedrich von Schiller. In *Grundriss der Geschichte der Philosophie. Heiliges Römisches Reich Deutscher Nation, Schweiz, Nord- und Osteuropa*, eds. H. Holzhey and V. Mudroch, 1356–1367. Basel: Schwabe.
Matuschek, Stefan. 2002. 'Was du hier siehest, edler Geist, bist du selbst.' Narziß-Mythos und ästhetische Theorie bei Friedrich Schlegel und Herbert Marcuse. In *Narcissus: Ein Mythos von der Antike bis zum Cyberspace*, ed. A. Renger, 79–97. Stuttgart: J.B. Metzler.
Milton, John. 2005. Paradise Lost. Ed. P. Pullman. New York: Oxford University Press.
Safranski, Rüdiger. 2004. *Schiller oder Die Erfindung der Deutschen Idealismus*. Munich/Vienna: Carl Hanser Verlag.
Schilling, Diana. 2005. Über Anmut und Würde (1793). In *Schiller-Handbuch, Leben – Werk – Wirkung*, ed. M Luserke-Jaqui, 388–398. Stuttgart: J.B. Metzler.

CHAPTER 11

Concerning the Sublime (1793) / On the Pathetic (1801)

Carsten Zelle

1.

Schiller began work for the journal *New Thalia* on the two essays "On Grace and Dignity" and "On the Pathos of Representation" in May 1793 (letter to Körner, May 27, 1793). In the early work on these essays, going back to the period of the *Augustenburger Letters* Schiller made use of materials he had developed in his lectures on aesthetics at the University of Jena in the winter semester 1792/93. Schiller's renewed investigations of Kant's *Critique of Judgment* also took place at this time (in October 1792) as well as, among other things, his reading of Edmund Burke's *Philosophical Investigations on the Origin of Our Concepts of the Sublime and the Beautiful* (1773, translated by C. Garve; English: 1757, 2nd ed. 1759), from whose second part individual examples of objects "appropriate to the sublime" (FA 8: 416) are drawn (e.g.: stillness, emptiness, solitariness, silence, terror, darkness). The essay was delivered in two portions. "Concerning the Sublime (Being an Extension of Some Kantian Ideas)" appeared in September 1793 (*New Thalia*, 3rd issue), followed by "Further Development of the Sublime" in August 1794 (*New Thalia*, 4th issue). At the conclusion of the latter a promise to provide additional material was made (NA 21: 188) but apparently not carried through, giving rise to speculation about whether the essay "On the Sublime", first published in 1801, was meant to fulfil this purpose. One part of the first portion, made up of the last 2/5 of the third issue of *Thalia* as well as the continuation in the fourth issue, was reproduced in 1801 without further editorial intervention under the now familiar title "On the Pathetic". Only the footnote in relation to Angelika

C. Zelle (✉)
Ruhr-Universität Bochum, Bochum, Germany
e-mail: carsten.zelle@rub.de

© The Author(s), under exclusive license to Springer Nature Switzerland AG 2023
A. Falduto, T. Mehigan (eds.), *The Palgrave Handbook on the Philosophy of Friedrich Schiller*, https://doi.org/10.1007/978-3-031-16798-0_11

Kaufmann (FA 8: 1362, commentary on 427,$_{33}$) was discarded. In terms of content "On the Pathetic" corresponds to the third section of the original essay as noted below. Today's Schiller editions of the essay amalgamate two different original texts, which is to say, they reproduce the first 3/5 of the essay "Concerning the Sublime" from the third issue of *Thalia* published in 1793, and present the other 2/5 of this portion appearing alongside the "Further Development of the Sublime" (published in the fourth issue of *Thalia* 1794) according to the *Schriften* version of this text and the 1801 title. This editorial convention not only disturbs the clarity of the relationship between the *Thalia* and the *Schriften* versions but also compromises above all the special significance that Schiller attached to the composition of the third part of the *Shorter Prose Works*. This special significance can be seen in Schiller's decision to put the essay "On the Sublime" before the reissued *Letters on the Aesthetic Education of Man* (in the *Horen* version of 1795) and the essay "On the Pathetic" after it. By these means the essay supplies further thoughts on "energetic" beauty (FA 8: 618) which Schiller had foreshadowed in the 16th *Aesthetic Letter* but not developed further in this work.

2.

Whilst Schiller's ruminations on beauty can be enlisted into the anthropological Mesotes discourse of his aesthetics of harmony, it is the discourse of the "strength of the soul" (FA 8: 423) which governs his "aesthetics of resistance" based in the sublime (cf. Zelle 1995: 147–219). Schiller's theory of the sublime rises to the status of an "emergency law of the aesthetic republic" (Zelle 1994c). The emotional intensity invoked by the tragedian aims at bringing to light a human "capacity for resistance" (FA 8: 423). The note written to Körner in May 1793 in relation to the *Thalia* essay then in preparation clearly supports the contention that Schiller's interest in the various manifestations of the sublime ultimately concerns the problem of "representing" (cf. Zelle 2007) the sublime. It is on account of its manner of visualization, i.e. through the priority accorded to dramatic representation over diegetic representation, that tragedy for Schiller appears as the form of art sui generis of the modern period, since the thematization of freedom can only be pursued by way of a negative mode of portrayal.

2.1

In his ruminations on the sublime Schiller stands alongside standard polebearers in the tradition of the sublime in the eighteenth century, namely E. Burke, M. Mendelssohn and J.G. Sulzer (cf. Zelle 1994a; cf. Zelle 1994b). However, this tradition, which continues subcutaneously, is being reshaped, as the subtitle of the *Thalia* essay alludes to, by Kant's "Analytic of the Sublime", to which the "Kantian" Schiller came to devote intense study (cf. Schiller 1974).

As with the beautiful, in regard to which imagination and understanding stand in a relation of "free play" (CJ: § 9, A 28), Kant holds the ground of determination of the sublime—the "struggle" of the imagination with reason—to be subjective (cf. CJ: § 27, A 98). At stake here is a condition of mind, not any attribute of an object. That a superior power is at work in the mind flows for Kant, in the case of the mathematical sublime, from the fact that the imagination is not capable of comprehending "magnitude in itself" (CJ: § 25, A 79) or, in the case of the dynamic sublime (CJ: § 28, A 103), from its not being able to represent the moment of being "physically overcome" by the terrible immensity of nature. In both cases reason finds itself exposed. Both magnitude and terror help this supersensible capacity of reason to come into itself: "in this way imagination and reason, through their struggle, set forth the subjective purposiveness [*Zweckmäßigkeit*] of the mind's powers: namely, the feeling that we have pure autonomous reason at our disposal" (CJ: § 27, A 98). By contrast, nature "diminishes" (ibid., § 26, A 95) and becomes "small" (ibid., § 27, A 96). If, however, the super-sensible capacity in the human being is sublime, what is nature from an aesthetic point of view? Nature is formless, i.e. ugly. Kant discovered in the vernacular way of talking about "sublime" nature a confusion (a "subreption", ibid, § 27, A 96; cf. ibid., § 23, A 75 f.), i.e. a metonymic mistaking of cause and effect insofar as sublimity is no predicate of immeasurable, colossal or powerful phenomena—these are rather considered raw, shapeless, fear-inducing or "horrible" (ibid., § 26, A 88)—but a feature of the reason which our mind "can render palpable to itself" (ibid., § 28, A 104) in relation to the appearances. Sublimity is the "self-directed feeling" of reason. As Schiller repeatedly emphasizes through verbatim reference to Kant in his "further application of certain Kantian ideas" and on the basis of examples found in Burke, the palpability of the sublime is rendered "appropriate [*tauglich*]" (FA 8: 415, 416; cf. CJ: § 23, A 75) by way of ugliness, chaos, untamed and unruly disorder and devastation. The aesthetics of the sublime and the aesthetics of ugliness are interdependent and behave in the manner of positive and negative poles in relation to each other (cf. Zelle 1996). The latter has critical force so long as it is accompanied by the former, i.e. as long as the sublime remains *negative*, which is to say, in Schiller's thinking, as long as it goes hand in hand with the highest aesthetic appreciation of the villain.

Since ideas of "reason", "taken literally and viewed logically [...] cannot be represented" (CJ: general note [at] § 29, A 114), Kant talks in connection with the sublime of a "merely negative presentation" (ibid., A 123), insofar as, through the effective mechanisms of a "negative pleasure" only "arising indirectly" (CJ: § 23, A 74 f.), it is possible for reason to "discover", "illustrate" or to "make palpable" or "alive". Kant again and again finds new verbal constructions for the rendering of the "self-affectation of reason" (Böhme and Böhme 1983: 224), whose status in scholarship varies from "quasi cognitive" (Crawford 1985: 181) to "non cognitive" (Lyotard 1991: 225).

2.2

The essay is divided according to rhetorical principles into three sections and, beyond this, is cued visually in the text through the typographic use of hyphens (scheme 1). The first of these sections (FA 8: 395–411,$_{11}$) provides a general definition of the sublime and, more particularly, brings two types of sublimity to discussion in relation to the theoretical and practical sublime, makes known their effective mechanisms and introduces the notion of security as the prerequisite for aesthetic pleasure. The second section (FA 8: 411,$_{12}$–422) effects a transition in the argument by way of a link to a more involved discussion of the practical sublime, represents the three "component parts" (FA 8:411,$_{26}$) which join forces in this manifestation of the sublime and derives from there a distinction between two "classes" which are then made the subject of detailed analysis: the contemplative sublime (FA 8: 412,$_{14}$–418,$_{26}$) and the pathetic sublime (FA 8: 418,$_{27}$–422,$_{10}$). This section comes to an end with a conclusion (FA 8: 421,$_{36}$–422,$_{10}$) which draws consequences for two "fundamental laws of all tragic art" from the ruminations on the pathetic sublime. These two laws are in turn made the basis of the third section (FA 8: 423–451,$_{26}$) which begins with a flourish and, as already mentioned, was reissued under the title of "On the Pathetic" in 1801. What is intended is a deductive procedure that moves from a general concept to the particularity of individual, poetically efficacious rules. The movement from a definition of two different types of the sublime (section 1), via the detailed investigation of these two forms leading to the formulation of two basic laws of tragic art (section 2) and then to its application with regard to two forms of optimally realized affectation specific to art (section 3) follows the logic of a tree diagram both, as it were, in regard to stem and branch (scheme 2).

Theoretical and practical sublime. Right at the start of the essay the indirect, two-stepped effective mechanism of the sublime is identified to which Schiller repeatedly recurs. This mechanism, in line with Schiller's credentials as a physician, is linked to a sensate/moral anthropology (cf. Riedel 1985) revealing the human to be a hybrid being. "*Sublime* is the name we give to an object in regard to which, when we seek to represent it, our sensual nature feels its limitations but our rational nature its superiority, its freedom from limitation" (FA 8: 395). The rhythmic succession according to which the sublime is "made known" (ibid.) through the registering of *physical* dependence and *moral* independence is repeated in formulaic fashion, since it is also the affectation process of the "pathetic sublime" introduced in the second section which bears on this succession and controls the effective mechanism discussed in the third section. As is the case with Kant scholarship (see above), so it is also the case in recent Schiller scholarship that the exact way in which freedom is involved in the process of affectation has drawn different responses. Does the sublime provide us with "a sense of our freedom" or a "*knowledge* of ourselves as rational beings?" (Beiser 2005: 257). Is such "awareness of our own super-sensible freedom"

(Hughes 2015: 421, cf. 423) or "consciousness of freedom" (ibid., 422) a matter of a "decidedly cognitive component" (Köppe 2020: 99), or it is rather the case that these two designations provide access to a range of connotative hues which prevent us from conceiving "awareness" and "consciousness" as synonyms, especially as the reference to a concept of cognition under the pretence of a "'rational reconstruction' of historical texts" (Köppe 2020: 92) leads to an open-ended discussion about the status of sensitive awareness which, in the eighteenth century, was pursued on a number of different fronts simultaneously.

As with Sulzer, who distinguishes a sublime relating to the "powers of representation" from a sublime that works on the "powers of desire" (Sulzer 1786: 85), and in agreement with Kant who distinguished the mathematical sublime from the dynamic sublime, Schiller also isolates two forms of the sublime: the "theoretical and the practical sublime" (FA 8: 396). The former is connected with the representation of the infinite, e.g. of an "ocean at peace" and has the effect of extending our "sphere", the latter with the representation of a danger, e.g. of an "ocean in storm" and has the effect of extending our "power [*Kraft*]" (FA 8: 398 f.). The examples adduced here are consistent with the discourse of sublime as it emerged with and after J. Addison in the eighteenth century (Zelle 1987a: pass.).

The tragedian is particularly interested in the practical sublime, on which we will concentrate attention in the following, since it is only here that a "true and complete independence from nature" can be experienced (FA 8: 399). This statement gains further emphasis and authority from Schiller's long quotation of Kant's expounding of the dynamic sublime in which reason's capacity to render palpable to itself in view of the awe-inducing power of nature is highlighted. "'Thus, as he [= Kant] concludes, nature may be called sublime because it brings the imagination to the point of representing those instances in which the mind can make palpable to itself the sublimity of its own calling [*Bestimmung*]'" (FA 8: 400; cf. CJ: § 28, A 104). The prerequisite for this, admittedly, is that the recipient should be in a position of physical security, i.e. that he is not really threatened and does not actually have any fear. It is a requirement for aesthetic "pleasure" in the sublime that one has "inner freedom of mind" (FA 8: 403), i.e. that terror is merely imagined but not actually suffered: "The sublime object must be terrible, but it must not evoke real fear" (FA 8: 403). It is somewhat macabre that Schiller cites certain verses of Lucretius (cf. Zelle 1997) in proof of this: "As sublime as a storm at sea appears to be when viewed from the shore, those who find themselves on the ship that the storm smashes to pieces are less in a position to reach an aesthetic judgment about it" (FA 8: 404). The emphasis given to inner freedom of mind and the sense of security required for aesthetic pleasure in the practical sublime suggest, far more than the Kantian model, a "Stoical trace" (Riedel 2007, 62) of an older ethics in which the soul's strength was to be disciplined—an ethics familiar to Schiller on account of his contact with Jacob Friedrich Abel, his philosophy teacher at the Karlsschule. Through his capacity to direct attention (cf. Riedel 1995, 439 f. und 572–574), the human being is able to free himself from the passivity imposed on him as a sensual being and to determine his own ends (cf. Abel 1777). In the same way, at the end of the first section, the practical sublime "discovers" a "capacity for resistance" or "becomes aware" of an "ideational [idealisch] [...] certitude [Sicherheit]" which "teaches" him to regard "the sensual part of our being, which is otherwise imperilled, as a foreign thing of nature that does not in the least concern our true persona, our moral self" (FA 8: 410 f.). Schiller had extolled in similar fashion in the preceding essay "On Tragic Art" (1772) "the high value of a life philosophy" which is capable of "treating ourselves like a foreign object [Fremdling]" (FA 8: 254). The way a capacity is to be trained to become a skill will provide the blueprint for the disciplinary mechanism later used in "On the Sublime" (1801).

Contempaltive and pathetic sublime. The second section draws from the definition of the practical sublime a consequence of importance for aesthetic action and deduces from it the "objects" through which it can be stimulated. For this to occur, an interplay of three elements is necessary: (1) an object of nature is presented in terms of its power; (2) the instance which receives this power is presented in its physical capacity for counter action as being without power; (3) the fact that being physically deprived of power can be fruitful, which is to say can lead to a surfeit of moral power in the recipient along this negative path (FA 8: 411). Two "classes" of objects are further distinguished.

With the *contemplative sublime* only the first component is brought to bear, i.e. only the "cause of suffering", but not "the suffering itself" (FA 8: 411) is revealed. The observer is on the one hand confronted with nature as a power in itself, but, on the other, the scenarios of catastrophe associated with it only play out in the realm of the imagination. Thus, that observer imagines, e.g. that a "rocky mass" (FA 8: 413) hanging above him could dash him to pieces. What is played through here is a series of familiar examples well known from the established discourse of the sublime which are considered "attuned to the sublime" (FA 8:416; cf. 415) or are "used" to bring forth the sublime (FA 8:415): darkness, emptiness, stillness, concealment, secrecy, mystery, i.e. the whole gamut serving as "ingredients of terror" (FA 8: 417) occurring among other things in the "Gothic novel" [Schauerroman] of the time.

With the *pathetic sublime* both the first and the second components are brought to bear, i.e. what is revealed by way of nature's power are both the "terror" and the suffering it induces in the human being (FA 8: 411). The power of nature is revealed not only as the cause of *possible* suffering, but, in the process of being "expressed" as something "really hostile" (FA 8: 418), as the cause of *actual* suffering (cf. Beiser 2005: 261). In the process of representing the second component, then, the observer is no longer afforded an element of choice. Rather, a whole set of optimally deployed rhetorical devices is used in order to compel a level of "sympathetic" compassion in the observer. The pathetic sublime is thus the result of the deployment of an all-moving means (cf. Ueding 1971: 75–78) that the tragic artist has at his disposal. In this regard, as was already the case in "On Tragic Art", a distinction is brought out between the "original" and the "mediated" affect (FA 8: 252 f.) or merely "sympathetic suffering" (FA 8: 419). Given that Schiller takes "*compassion*" to be a sad emotion which "we feel for another" (FA 8: 419), his concept of suffering differs in important ways from that of Lessing (cf. Zelle 2005b: 376 f.). In regard to suffering, a twofold distancing occurs. First, suffering itself does not occur but is merely represented through illusory effects and the invention of the imagination, which is to say it is received by "aesthetic" means (FA 8: 419). Secondly, "*compassion*" which is conveyed aesthetically and restricted to the world of sense must not prove to be overwhelming and turn into "*self-pity*", but rather, even "in the midst of the most violent affect", must be kept at a remove from the "self-pitying subject" and maintain the "freedom of its spirit" (FA 8: 419 f.). The entire set of effects discussed in the following, then, remains beholden to a freedom of aesthetic distance liberated from the burden of sensual impulse, although, at the same time, the artistry of the tragedian consists in allowing an oscillation between optimal distance and curtailment of distance by means of aesthetic illusion.

At the end of the second section where only the 1793 version of the text reaches a conclusion Schiller summarizes once more the two "main conditions" required for the pathetic sublime. First, the pathetic consists in "*suffering*", so that compassion is stimulated. Second, the sublime consists in "*resistance* to suffering" in order for the "inner freedom of mind" to be called forth into consciousness (FA 8: 422; cf. 426). The visualization of suffering in order to stimulate compassion is thus only a physical means for a higher goal associated with the portrayal of "moral independence" (FA 8: 422). Only through its end is the means justified. To represent mere passion (as in Gerstenberg's *Ugolino*) will be labelled "common" at a later stage of the essay (FA 8: 428). By taking dramaturgical compassion and a theory of the sublime to be complementary aspects of an anthropology which conceives of the human being as possessing both a sensual and a super-sensible nature, Schiller's conception of the pathetic sublime goes beyond Kant's "Analytic of the Sublime": "The paradigm of a sublime object […] shifts dramatically, from Alpine storms or volcanic eruptions to individual enduring through suffering" (Hughes 2015: 421).

On the Pathetic

The two "main conditions" underlying the effective mechanism of the pathetic sublime—"portrayal of suffering" and "portrayal of the super-sensible"—are taken up with studied emphasis in the first paragraph which ushers in the third section of the essay. It forms the beginning of the 1801 *Schriften* version which, under the title "On the Pathetic", begins with the following: "*Sensual beings* must *suffer* deeply and violently; pathos must be present so that rational beings can discover their independence and involve themselves in what is presented in an *active* way" FA 8: 423). Schiller's basic law of tragedy accords with a remark by Kant maintaining that the moral law "only makes itself known aesthetically through acts of sacrifice" (CJ: general note in reference to § 29, A 119). In his theory of tragedy, Schiller deduces from Kant's contention, that the sublime recurs not to any sensual form nor any natural power but only to an idea of reason, the notion that freedom can only be represented negatively. Accordingly, only "resistance [...] to the power of feeling [...] can make us cognizant of the free principle residing in us" (FA 8: 423). This "making cognizant" does not occur "in an abstract way in consciousness, but takes hold of our senses" (Schmitt 1992: 200).

A further subdivision applies as a result of these premises.

Initially in a sort of "querelle des anciens et des modernes", the complementarity of pathos stimulation and portrayal of resistance is investigated such that the tragic art of the Greeks is compared with the classical French tragedy and the bourgeois tragedy (cf. FA 8: 424 f.). As Schiller discusses, Greek art had known to allow their heroes both to feel sensual "suffering" and to be filled with moral "duty" (FA 8: 425), whereas the cool admiration of the tragédie classique ignored nature and the sentimental dramaturgy of compassion found in bourgeois tragedy had no conception of freedom.

Schiller goes on to distinguish the emotional construction of the "sublimity of *composure*", in which a sculptor or poet renders the super-sensible capacity of the human being palpable by showing how he maintains himself in the midst of suffering, from the "sublimity of an action" in which the poet indicates the idea of the super-sensible by showing how the human being decides to suffer (cf. FA 8: 440).

In a first step Schiller refreshes his premises. The portrayal of affect, i.e. the arousal of compassion, is not an end in itself. Schiller's theatre is not a theatre of terror or cruelty, it is a theatre of freedom. The pathetic is only "aesthetic" (FA 8: 428) when it is "sublime", i.e. when it conveys through the means of its representation of suffering the manner of resistance connected with a super-sensible capacity—"for everything sublime comes *only* from reason" (FA 8: 428). Neither suffering nor resistance to it can render freedom visible or conceivable. The pathetic sublime is an indirect or negative presentation of freedom. Kant's lexicon of terms can be found in the entire essay and especially at that point where it is ascertained that each appearance, whose final ground cannot be derived from the sensual world, is a "negative" or "indirect presentation of the super-sensible" (FA 8: 430).

The "super-sensible power of resistance" becomes intelligible when the struggle with affect is chiselled into stone or brought to the stage. In a subterranean way, Schiller's elaborations here flow into a wider comparison between the plastic arts and painting. The "struggle with affect" is distinguished from the cause of affect (FA 8: 429). Every animal being does this by seeking to remove the cause of a torment. Torment is only removed, however, insofar as a being has the power of *not* being nature.

In a second step, a comparison between Winckelmann's description of the Laocoon statue in the *Geschichte der Kunst des Altertums* (1764) and Vergil's epic treatment of the same in the *Aeneid* (II 199 ff.)[1] leads to a separation of the sublimity of composure and the sublimity of action. Lessing in *Laocoon* (1766), interpreting the medial and material effects and the reduction of affect in reference to the way in which the autonomy of the plastic material itself is asserted, used the distinction between the use of space in the plastic arts and the use of time in literature to make the observation that, in contrast with its epic treatment in Vergil, the Laocoon of the stone sculpture does not cry out, but only groans. Lessing's point against Winckelmann was to wrest the Greeks from the ethics of stoicism and free the dramaturgy from the emotion of admiration. By contrast, Schiller comes down on Winckelmann's side because Winckelmann reveals the struggle of intelligence with its suffering sensual nature. That Laocoon does not cry out like an animal but only sighs is an expression of his "'spirit armed with strength'" (FA 8: 434), as Schiller states, quoting Winckelmann. The pain Laocoon feels is contrasted with his composure and self-control. In such "disharmony" (FA 8: 432) one recognizes the autonomous spirit or the super-sensible principle that sets "a boundary to nature" (ibid.).

In contrast, Virgil is not interested in a description of the condition of mind. He is rather concerned to "penetrate" the reader of these verses "with terror" (FA 8: 435), i.e. to invest the reader, according to Schiller's analysis of compassion, with "compassionate terror" (FA 8: 419). The moment in Virgil's epic when the fearful sight of the snakes is no longer described but represented, i.e. when the snakes are about to attack Laocoon (*Aen.* II 212 f.), marks for Schiller the transition from the contemplative sublime to the pathetic. Whereas the Trojans take flight from fear, in order to preserve their lives, Laocoon hurries to the aid of his sons in fidelity to his "duty as a father" (FA 8: 439). It is significant that, at this point, Virgil talks of paternal *duty* and not of paternal *love*. At the same time this transition introduces a modification to the concept of the sublime, changing it from a subjective conception in Kant's sense to an objective conception, for when Laocoon suppresses the physical impulse to flight

---

[1] Schiller had already provided a free translation of the second book of the *Aeneid* under the title of *Die Zerstörung von Troja* in the *Neuen Thalia* 1792, 1. St., 3–78 (cf. SW 3: 392–424), in which the Laocoon episode is related from strophe 34 to 39, 27–30 (cf. SW 3: 401 f.).

out of a sense of duty, this decision illustrates the capacity for resistance in him, the capacity that invests "us with an attitude of respect" (FA 8: 439). Respect, as Kant had discussed, however, is a feeling in favour of the moral law (cf. CPrP A 130). The respect that reveals Laocoon to have dignity does not rest on any "subreption"; rather, in the process of responding with compassion, we share with him the quality of an inner capacity that goes beyond nature. Virgil's Laocoon is one, like Leonidas, who will later be used as an example (cf. FA 8: 442–444), "a person of great moral worth" who "*chooses* to suffer out of a sense of duty" (FA 8: 441).

The discussion of Laocoon finalizes in 1793 the first part of the essay "Concerning the Sublime" in the third issue of *Thalia*. Its "Further Development" in the fourth issue of *Thalia* moves from the "sublime of *composure*", which was a subject both for the sculptor and the poet because of the "co-existence" of its elements and because it was amenable to visual contemplation, to a more complete thematization of the "sublime of action" which is the preserve of the poet because its elements are subject to a principle of "succession" and can only be apprehended through "thought" (FA 8: 440). This distinction is based on the fact that the sublime of "composure" is *preserved* in suffering, whereas the sublime of "action" *decides* upon suffering. The difference here recurs to the contrast between passivity and activity.

In the context of what characterizes the human as a being who is not only free, but also who acts in accordance with freedom, Schiller introduces a separation between aesthetic and moral judgement allowing him to focus on the "sublime" criminal, a task already taken up in *On the Reason for Pleasure in Tragic Objects* (cf. Zelle 2005a: 371 f.), but a task which is then retracted in "On Tragic Art" (cf. Zelle 2005b: 377 f.). Conferring honour on the evildoer, who, aesthetically speaking, is a particularly attractive figure, establishes the rhetorical point of conclusion for the essay.

Aesthetic and moral judgement become opposed when Schiller uses the figure of chiasmus to state that the same object "when deployed aesthetically is not morally satisfying and when morally satisfying is not aesthetically useful" (FA 8: 442). Moral judgement, when it answers to a demand of reason, has imperative character. It thus obstructs aesthetic judgement, at whose base can be found the "*need of the imagination*" to exercise free play, and it restricts the "free drive of fantasy" (FA 8: 445). Thus, in the case of moral judgements drawn from individual examples occurring in reality, the recipient feels hemmed in, and with aesthetic judgements that align with general genre considerations, by contrast, feels expansive and free.

In this context we understand Schiller's reformulation of the Aristotelian insight (Aristot. *Poetics*, chap. 9)[2] that poetry is more philosophical than historiography because it imitates what is possible and not merely what is real. The promotion of aesthetic pleasure does not depend on historical truth, only on "*poetic* [...] truth" (FA 8: 448). In aesthetic judgement we are not interested in appropriating art for moral purposes, as occurs, e.g. with Sulzer, in the popular philosophy of the late Enlightenment, i.e. not in moral outcomes, but in the question of free action. To this end, the portrayal of each action is justified insofar as such an action expresses the power and strength of the will. "He [= the poet] is not concerned with the direction of this power" (FA 8: 447). For this reason, even the morally wayward can arouse aesthetic interest because, by virtue of their criminal behaviour in contrast to the virtuous, these characters put their own happiness, i.e. the principle of their nature, into question in view of the punishment that threatens them as sensual beings. For this reason, too, the "somewhat benign character" (FA 8: 451) often seems repugnant, but the "consistently evil character" (FA 8: 450) arouses "quivering admiration" (FA 8: 451). The demand for a "moral purposiveness in aesthetic matters" (FA 8: 451) is explicitly rejected. The "morally satisfying" is not always the "aesthetically apposite" (Berghahn 1980a: 203), as indeed Mendelssohn and Lessing (cf. Zelle 1986) had already emphasized. In the finding that concludes the essay "On the Pathetic" there is no trace, then, of the "moral trumpeter of Säckingen" (Nietzsche).

3.

Schiller's achievement consists in the fact that he connects the older discourse of sublimity, the late Enlightenment theory of mixed emotions and of pathos, with Kant's analytic of the sublime. Whereas in Kant, however, the sublime, as the "innate feeling" ("Selbstgefühl") of reason, remains tied to the immensity and terror of natural phenomena, in Schiller, invoking the concept of the pathetic sublime which he distinguishes from the contemplative sublime, the sublime is put in the service of a philosophy of tragic art. By linking the concept of the pathetic sublime with the pain of suffering and compassion, "at least a plausible interpretation of our pleasure in tragedy" (Hughes 2015: 428) is offered that still has philosophical currency today. Later theories such as those of Schopenhauer or Hegel show up "important limitation[s]" (ibid.) by contrast. At the same time Schiller insists on a separation between the value spheres of aesthetics and morality. Only aesthetic judgement is free. The sublime villain gains approbation as a tragic hero since it is not relevant for our aesthetic

---

[2] Caroline Beulwitz reported that Schiller's preparation for his lecture series *Artis tragicae theoriam* in the summer semester of 1790 involved reading Aristoteles's *Poetics* and often translating "passages from it" to her and her sister (NA 42: 129). However, a detailed discussion of the *Poetics* (in the translation of M.C. Curtius from 1753) did not take place until as late as 1797 (cf. Schiller's letter to Goethe, May 5, 1797).—The current article is a revised version of Zelle 2005c.

pleasure in the sublime whether actions are good or bad, insofar it is considered possible to speak of freedom in the context of actions performed against sensate nature (cf. Beiser 2005: 239).

In "post-heroic societies" Schiller's pathos, admittedly, has become "hollow". Georg Büchner was already repelled by the "affected pathos" of the "ideal poet", which is the reason he thought "so little of Schiller" (letter to his family, Straßburg, July 28, 1835). By contrast, Büchner's "aesthetic theory of 'realism' […] recurs to a type of poetics predating the poetics of autonomous compassion" (Schings 1980: 69). Büchner's charge here, however, has led to a highly critical portrait of Schiller that has "trodden him down flat" (Darsow 2000: 234), a portrait obscuring his ruminations on the sublime behind those of beauty, e.g. in the *Aesthetic Letters*. In this way, in his reading of "Concerning the Sublime", P. de Man deflates the "playwright" Schiller" in favour of the "philosopher" Kant, cavils at Schiller's argument, which he says is devoid of any "transcendental concern", calling it "entirely empirical, psychological", and turns him into an early "ideological idealist". In contrast to Schiller's "early idealism" de Man considers the "later *Letters on Aesthetic Education*" to reveal "a more balanced principle" (de Man 1997: 141, 143 und 146 f.). The long lack of interest in Schiller's concept of the sublime, which may be due to an overall retreat from emotion in general (cf. Meyer-Kalkus 1989; cf. Gessmann 2002; cf. Bär 2003) and scepticism towards the "rhetorician" Schiller in particular, has now been revised in view of the renaissance of interest in the sublime from the end of the twentieth century (cf. Pries 1994). Recent Schiller scholarship has recognized that Schiller's notion of aesthetic education "includes a grand pedagogy of the sublime" (Berghahn 1980b: 160). This pedagogy is central to an anthropology based on the capacity of the human to act against the senses; this anthropology, for its part, was still important in the early twentieth century when the human being was conceived as a creature "capable of saying no" (Scheler) (cf. Middel 2017). The new interest in the sublime in relation to Schiller can be seen in many recent translations which have provided research groups in individual nations with new stimulus. And yet it was still the case as late as 2015 that Schiller's "philosophical work on tragedy has received little attention in Anglophone aesthetics" (Hughes 2015: 417).

German text translated into English by Tim Mehigan.

On the Sublime (1793) / On the Pathetic (1801)

a. Structural Schema

Neue Thalia, 1793, 3. St., *Vom Erhabenen*, 320–394 [published mid-September 1793]	1. Section FA 8, 395–411,11	Establishment of concept of the sublime: • Comparison of two types of the sublime, the theoretical sublime (knowledge [*Erkenntnis*]) and the practical sublime (preservation of self) • Their effective mechanisms • Security as pre-condition for aesthetic pleasure	
	2. Section FA 8, 411,12–422,10	Partitio: classification of the practical sublime according to the three components that are operative in the representation of the sublime (objective and physical power, subjective and physical powerlessness, subjective moral superiority): • I. The contemplative sublime (412,14–418,26) (expression of power) • II. The pathetic sublime, (418,27–22,9) (expression of suffering in view of power) Conclusio: derivation of the fundamental laws of tragic art from the two main conditions underpinning the pathetic sublime (422,6–422,10)	
	3. Section FA 8, 423–451	Function of the pathetic (= expression of suffering) in tragic art: the expression of the suffering of the *suffering sensual being* facilitates the expression of the *rational free being* • Positioning of the correct expression of pathos in connection with Greek tragedy through a marking of difference from (a) The dramaturgy of admiration of *tragédie classique* (e.g. Corneille): no suffering nature—the protagonists are unfeeling (b) The dramaturgy of compassion in bourgeois tragedy [*bürgerlichen Trauerspiel*] (e.g. family portraits): no elevation of the spirit—merely the discharge of the tear ducts • Distinction of the *sublime of composure* from the *sublime of action* (a) Working out of difference through a comparison of the description of the Laocoon statue group by Winckelmann and the Laocoon description of Vergil (Aen. II 199 ff.)—Schiller endorses Winckelmann's position in relation to the Laocoon question in opposition to that of Lessing	

Neue Thalia, 1793, 4. St., *Fortgesetzte Entwicklung*, 52–73 [published late August 1794]		(b) Summary of difference:
		The *sublime of composure*: *holding firm* in suffering (plastic arts / poetry)
		The *sublime of action*: conviction to endure suffering (poetry), further examples of this:
		  e.g. Leonidas
		  e.g. Peregrinus Proteus
		  e.g. the sublime villain
		• Separation of morals and aesthetics:
		(a) The morally sufficient (the criterion *according to which* a decision against sensuality is made)
		(b) The aesthetically purposive (the criterion is *the fact that* a decision against sensuality is made)
		(Continuation at a future point in time.)
			Kleinere prosaische Schriften, Tl. 3. Leipzig 1801, 310–372

b. Stem Tree

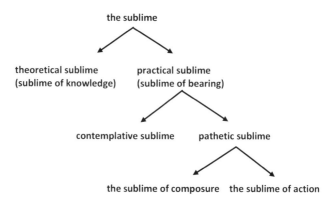

References

Abel, Jacob Friedrich. 1777. Rede [Seelenstärke ist Herrschaft über sich selbst]. In Jacob Friedrich Abel. 1995. *Eine Quellenedition zum Philosophieunterricht an der Stuttgarter Karlsschule (1773–1782). Mit Einleitung, Übersetzung Kommentar und Bibliographie*, ed. Wolfgang Riedel. 219–236. Würzburg. Königshausen & Neumann.

Bär, Jochen A. 2003. Pathos. In *Historisches Wörterbuch der Rhetorik*, ed. Gert Ueding, vol. 6: 689–717. Tübingen: Niemeyer.

Beiser, Frederick. 2005. *Schiller as Philosopher. A Re-Examination*. Oxford: Clarendon Press.

Berghahn, Klaus L. 1980a [^{1}1971]. Das Pathetischerhabene. Schillers Dramentheorie. In *Deutsche Dramentheorien I: Beiträge zur historischen Poetik des Dramas in Deutschland*, ed. Reinhold Grimm, 197–221. Wiesbaden: Athenaion.

Berghahn, Klaus L. 1980b. Zum Drama Schillers. In *Handbuch des deutschen Dramas*, ed. Walter Hinck, 157–173; 547–549. Düsseldorf: Bagel.

Böhme, Gernot, and Hartmut Böhme. 1983. *Das Andere der Vernunft. Zur Entwicklung von Rationalitätsstrukturen am Beispiel Kants*. Frankfurt am Main: Suhrkamp.

Crawford, Donald W. 1985. The Place of the Sublime in Kant's Aesthetic Theory. In *The Philosophy of Immanuel Kant*, ed. Richard Kennington, 161–183. Washington D.C.; Catholic University of America Press.

Darsow, Götz-Lothar. 2000. *Friedrich Schiller*. Stuttgart: Metzler.

De Man, Paul. 1997 [1983]. Kant and Schiller. In Paul de Man: Aesthetic Ideology, ed. Andrzej Warminski, 129–162. Minneapolis, London: University of Minnesota Press.

Gessmann, Martin. 2002. Pathos/pathetisch. In *Ästhetische Grundbegriffe. Historisches Wörterbuch in sieben Bänden*, ed. Karlheinz Barck et al., vol. 4: 724–39. Stuttgart, Weimar; Metzler.

Hughes, Samuel. 2015. Schiller on the Pleasure of Tragedy. *British Journal of Aesthetics* 55/4: 417–432.

Köppe, Tilmann. 2020. Schillers Theorien des ›tragischen Vergnügens‹ in *Über den Grund des Vergnügens an tragischen Gegenständen* und *Über die tragische Kunst*. *Scientia Poetica* 24/1: 89–113.

Lyotard, Jean-François. 1991. *Leçons sur l'Analytique du Sublime (Kant, Critique de la faculté de juger, §§ 23-29)*. Paris: Galilée.
Meyer-Kalkus, Reinhart. 1989. Pathos. In *Historisches Wörterbuch der Philosophie*, ed. Joachim Ritter et. al., vol. 7: 193–99. Darmstadt: Wissenschaftliche Buchgesellschaft.
Middel, Carina. 2017. *Schiller und die Philosophische Anthropologie des 20. Jahrhunderts. Ein ideengeschichtlicher Brückenschlag*. Berlin, Boston: de Gruyter.
Pries, Christine. 1994. Erhabene, das [Ende 18. Jh. bis 20. Jahrhundert]. In *Historisches Wörterbuch der Rhetorik*, ed. Gert Ueding, vol 2: 1378–89. Tübingen. Niemeyer.
Riedel, Wolfgang. 1985. *Die Anthropologie des jungen Schiller. Zur Ideengeschichte der medizinischen Schriften und der* Philosophischen Briefe. Würzburg: Königshausen & Neumann.
Riedel, Wolfgang. 1995. Zweiter Teil: Kommentar. In Jacob Friedrich Abel. 1995. *Eine Quellenedition zum Philosophieunterricht an der Stuttgarter Karlsschule (1773–1782). Mit Einleitung, Übersetzung Kommentar und Bibliographie*, ed. Wolfgang Riedel. 373–680. Würzburg. Königshausen & Neumann.
Riedel, Wolfgang. 2007. Die Freiheit und der Tod. Grenzphänomene idealistischer Theoriebildung beim späten Schiller. In *Friedrich Schiller. Der unterschätzte Theoretiker*, ed. Georg Bollenbeck and Lothar Ehrlich, 59–71. Köln, Weimar, Wien: Böhlau.
Schiller, Friedrich. 1974. Vollständiges Verzeichnis der Randbemerkungen in seinem Handexemplar der *Kritik der Urteilskraft*. In *Materialien zu Kants Kritik der Urteilskraft*, ed. Jens Kulenkampff, 126-144. Frankfurt am Main: Suhrkamp.
Schings, Hans-Jürgen. 1980. *Der mitleidigste Mensch ist der beste Mensch. Poetik des Mitleids von Lessing bis Büchner*. München: Beck.
Schmitt, Arbogast. 1992. Zur Aristoteles-Rezeption in Schillers Theorie des Tragischen. Hermeneutisch-kritische Anmerkungen zur Anwendung neuzeitlicher Tragikkonzeote auf die griechische Tragödie. In *Antike Dramentheorien und ihre Rezeption*, ed. Bernhard Zimmermann, 191–213. Stuttgart: M&P Verlag für Wissenschaft und Forschung.
Sulzer, Johann Georg. 1786. Erhaben (Schöne Künste). In Johann Georg Sulzer. 1786. *Allgemeine Theorie der Schönen Künste. Neue vermehrte Auflage*, vol. 2: 84–96. Leipzig: Weidmann.
Ueding, Gerd. 1971. *Schillers Rhetorik. Idealistische Wirkungsästhetik und rhetorische Tradition*. Tübingen: Niemeyer.
Zelle, Carsten. 1986. "Die Schaubühne hat ihre eigene Sittlichkeit." Zur Trennung von moralischem Urteil und ästhetischem Blick in der ersten Hälfte des 18. Jahrhunderts. In *Akten des VII. Internationalen Germanisten-Kongresses Göttingen 1985. Kontroversen, alte und neue*, ed. Albrecht Schöne, vol 8: 40–45. Tübingen: Niemeyer.
Zelle, Carsten. 1987. *"Angenehmes Grauen". Literarhistorische Beiträge zur Ästhetik des Schrecklichen im achtzehnten Jahrhundert*. Hamburg: Meiner.
Zelle, Carsten. 1994a. Erhabene, das [17., 18. Jahrhundert: 1. Frankreich, 2. England, 3. Deutschland]. In *Historisches Wörterbuch der Rhetorik*, ed. Gert Ueding, vol. 2: 1364-78. Tübingen: Niemeyer.
Zelle, Carsten. 1994b. Schiffbruch vor Zuschauer. Über einige popularphilosophische Parallelschriften zu Schillers Abhandlungen über den Grund des Vergnügens an tragischen Gegenständen in den neunziger Jahren des 18. Jahrhunderts. *Jahrbuch der deutschen Schillergesellschaft* 34: 289–316.

Zelle, Carsten. 1994c. Die Notstandsgesetzgebung im ästhetischen Staat. Anthropologische Aporien in Schillers philosophischen Schriften. In *Der ganze Mensch. Anthropologie und Literatur im 18. Jahrhundert. DFG-Symposion 1992*, ed. Hans-Jürgen Schings, 440–468. Stuttgart, Weimar: Metzler.

Zelle, Carsten. 1995. *Die Doppelte Ästhetik der Moderne. Revisionen des Schönen von Boileau bis Nietzsche*. Stuttgart, Weimar: Metzler.

Zelle, Carsten. 1996. Häßliche, das. In *Historisches Wörterbuch der Rhetorik*, ed. Gert. Ueding, vol. 3: 1304–26. Tübingen: Niemeyer.

Zelle, Carsten. 1997. Erhabene Weltuntergänge im Kleinen. Über Schiffbrüche und Schlachten vor Zuschauer – Bemerkungen zur Krise der Aufklärungsästhetik im Anschluß auf Lukrez' *De rerum natura*. In *Il gesto, il bello, il sublime. Arte e letteratura in Germania tra Sette e Ottocento*, ed. Emilio Bonfatti, 77–111. Roma: Artemide.

Zelle, Carsten. 2005a. Über den Grund des Vergnügens an tragischen Gegenständen. In *Schiller-Handbuch*, ed. Matthias Luserke-Jaqui, 364–374. Stuttgart, Weimar: Metzler.

Zelle, Carsten. 2005b. Über die tragische Kunst. In *Schiller-Handbuch*, ed. Matthias Luserke-Jaqui, 374–382. Stuttgart, Weimar: Metzler.

Zelle, Carsten. 2005c. Vom Erhabenen / Über das Pathetische. In *Schiller-Handbuch*, ed. Matthias Luserke-Jaqui, 398–406. Stuttgart, Weimar: Metzler.

Zelle, Carsten. 2005d. Über die ästhetische Erziehung des Menschen in einer Reihe von Briefen. In *Schiller-Handbuch*, ed. Matthias Luserke-Jaqui, 409–445. Stuttgart, Weimar: Metzler.

Zelle, Carsten. 2007. Darstellung – zur Historisierung des Mimesis-Begriffs bei Schiller (eine Skizze). In *Friedrich Schiller. Der unterschätzte Theoretiker*, ed. Georg Bollenbeck and Lothar Ehrlich, 73–86. Köln, Weimar, Wien: Böhlau.

CHAPTER 12

Detached Reflections on Different Questions of Aesthetics (1793)

Mirjam Schaub

Genesis and Context

The writing "Detached Reflections on Different Questions of Aesthetics" [*Zerstreute Betrachtungen über verschiedene ästhetische Gegenstände*] (1793) forms part of the fourth and final volume of the journal *Neue Thalia* (pp. 115–180) published by Friedrich Schiller and printed just before Friedrich Hölderlin's famous *Hyperion* fragment. In this fragment, Hölderlin's quote from Ignatio von Loyola's epitaph in the preface hints at Schiller's theme: the vital importance of the aesthetic estimation of magnitude *[ästhetische Größenschätzung]* in the perception of sublimity. Interestingly, Loyola favoured a focus on the smallest of things in order to identify sublimity precisely in them: *non coerci maximo, contineri minimo, divinum est*. Not to be confined by the largest, but to be contained in the smallest, is divinity, according to Loyola. Hölderlin expresses this as a more modern, more Christian *homo mensura* principle that contains both human restlessness and self-importance, in line with Hyperion's motto: "We are nothing; what we search for is everything" [*Wir sind nichts; was wir suchen, ist alles*—Hölderlin, *Hyperion* fragment, *Neue Thalia*, Vol. 4, 1793, p. 220].

If this is true, then the expectations placed on Schiller's *Zerstreute Betrachtungen* could not be higher. The detached quality of these writings is an

M. Schaub (✉)
University of Applied Sciences Hamburg, Hamburg, Germany
e-mail: mirjam.schaub@haw-hamburg.de

© The Author(s), under exclusive license to Springer Nature Switzerland AG 2023
A. Falduto, T. Mehigan (eds.), *The Palgrave Handbook on the Philosophy of Friedrich Schiller*, https://doi.org/10.1007/978-3-031-16798-0_12

admission and acceptance of an inability to achieve mastery over the material. Schiller does not appear to find this unpleasant, but instead regards it as appropriate for the matter in hand. After all, sublimity is particularly concerned with the failure of the aesthetic estimation of the magnitude of the sublime, starting with Edmund Burke's *Philosophical Enquiry into the Origin of our Ideas of the Sublime and Beautiful* (1757) and given further impetus by Immanuel Kant. In the third volume of the *Neue Thalia*, Schiller succinctly captures the problem of the enveloping of impotence in self-empowerment, taking the example of the sublime:

> Sublime we name an object, at whose conceptualization our sensuous nature feels its limits, but our rational nature its superiority, its freedom from limits; in the face of this we thus derive *physically* our brevity, which we surmount but *morally*, i.e., through ideas. Only as sensuous beings are we dependent, as rational beings we are free [*Erhaben* nennen wir ein Objekt, bey dessen Vorstellung unsre sinnliche Natur ihre Schranken, unsre vernünftige Natur aber ihre Ueberlegenheit, ihre Freyheit von Schranken fühlt; gegen das wir also *physisch* den Kürzern ziehen, über welches wir uns aber *moralisch* d. i. durch Ideen erheben. Nur als Sinnenwesen sind wir abhängig, als Vernunftwesen sind wir frey.—Schiller, "Vom Erhabenen (On the sublime)", in: *Neue Thalia*, Vol. 3, p. 320].

The publication of the "Reflections" spells out the "technical" reasons for this by outlining the crux of the issue of the aesthetic estimation of magnitude in minute detail.

However, let us return to the natural sequence, i.e., to the genesis and publication context of this text, which was published in 1793 by the *Georg Joachim Göschen'sche Verlagsbuchhandlung* company in Leipzig, in parallel with the *Hyperion* fragment. Schiller used this journal as a vehicle for his gradual reflections on Immanuel Kant's *Critique of the Power of Judgment*, which appeared in 1790. Each *Thalia* volume is divided into various sections which alternate between plays (and new translations of plays), historical aperçus, poems, sonnets, and aesthetic reflections, penned by authors as varied as Karl Philipp Conz, Johann von Kalchberg, Heimbert Paul Friedrich Hinze or Karl Heinrich Heydenreich, who are no longer remembered today.

The first volume of *Neue Thalia* (1792) contains the aesthetic reflections "Of the Cause of Pleasure We Derive from Tragic Objects" [*Ueber den Grund des Vergnügens an tragischen Gegenständen*] and "On the Tragic Art" [*Ueber die tragische Kunst*]. Schiller considers "tragic *emotion*" [*tragische Rührung*] and "the pleasure that we find in suffering" here (Schiller, *Neue Thalia*, Vol. 1, p. 120) as indices for a lively conflict between different moral purposes that cannot be ensured simultaneously or to the same degree. As the tragic conflict cannot easily be solved, the judgements and emotions of the observers switch sides and allegiances a number of times. In Schiller's writings, this conflict penetrates into the interior of morality as a result of the artistic treatment and allows this morality to take on a plastic form. In this way, the concept of propriety is also extended here for Schiller. By "awaken[ing] pity" (ibid. 190), the tragic provides pleasure to the same extent by preserving an aesthetic difference to reality, as predicted in David Hume's *Of Tragedy* (1757): "tragedy is an imitation; and imitation is always of itself agreeable". For Schiller, the tragic feeds particularly on the uplifting pain that directs the necessary attention to a higher and more general obligation (cf. ibid., p. 116), although this obligation "will seem to the crowd [*dem großen Haufen*] a revolting impropriety" (ibid., p. 119). It is noted here that Schiller himself is sympathetic to this contradiction. The idea of resistance famously remains embedded in his definition of beauty.

The third volume of *Neue Thalia* includes Schiller's influential essay "On Grace and Dignity" [*Ueber Anmuth und Würde*] (1793). In this essay, Schiller identifies grace as a very movable attribute that goes beyond fixed or merely architectonic beauty alongside Kantian pleasure in the beautiful; this attribute attaches itself to its accidental wearer in a malleable manner like a second skin and presents the wearer in the best of all lights: "Thus the girdle of charms [of grace] operates not by a natural effect", Schiller states, "but by a magical effect; that is to say, its virtue extends beyond all natural conditions" (Schiller, *Ueber Anmuth und Würde*, in: *Neue Thalia*, Vol. 3, p. 119). Even the ugliness of the figure can be completely forgotten as a consequence of the grace of movement, Schiller proposes. Just as in the case of the tragic, Schiller identifies a transition into the reasonable, the moral that is facilitated by the artfulness of expression and that acts upon our faculty of knowledge [*Erkenntnißvermögen*].

The fourth volume of *Neue Thalia* is itself divided into four subsections that are referred to as the fourth, fifth and sixth parts. Following on from *Scene from the life of Emperor Henry IV* [*Szene aus dem Leben Kaisers IV*] and a satirical poem by Johannes Daniel Falk about the *Battlefield at Mons* [*Schlachtfeld auf Mons*] Schiller proceeds in the "Fourth part" to deal with a *Continued consideration of the sublime* [*Fortgesetzte Entwicklung des Erhabenen*] as started in the third volume discussed earlier. A central position in this essay is occupied by an example of the growing rift between moral and aesthetic judgement, which Schiller uses as a basis for his graphic description of a forced transgression that constitutes the sublime by leaving the sensual perception behind to give rise to something intelligible. Interestingly enough, both rift and transgression as opposites to a smooth transition are not difficult to name or to qualify as such, but they are difficult to describe on the precise phenomenological level where they occur. The sublime thus becomes a crisis of expression. This prompts Schiller's ambition to put it right. He therefore refers to a well-known Cynic philosopher who lived in the first century A.D.:

> Consider the self-immolation of Peregrinus Protheus at Olympia. From a moral viewpoint, I cannot approve of this act, as I see impure intentions at work, for which the *duty* of self-preservation is neglected. When judged aesthetically, however, this act pleases me and it does so because it is testimony to great willpower to resist even the strongest of all instincts, namely the *urge* for self-preservation.

Whether it was a purely moral disposition or merely a more powerful sensory stimulus that suppressed the instinct for self-preservation of the idealist Peregrinus, this I do not take into account in my aesthetic judgement, where I no longer deal with the individual and move from the conditions of *his* will to the abstract principle of will, and where I consider human will as a faculty of the species relative to the entire force of nature (Schiller, *Fortgesetzte Entwicklung des Erhabenen*, in *Neue Thalia*, Vol. 4, p. 61f.).

In the "Fifth part" of the fourth *Thalia* volume, the *Zerstreute Betrachtungen* return to this topic with treatments of various aesthetic questions such as the agreeable, the beautiful, the good and the sublime, after which particular consideration is given to the aesthetic estimation of magnitude, e.g., with the mathematical sublime. As a result, the "Detached Reflections" can be divided into very distinct thematic parts: a short, compiling, recapitulating part that proceeds in a deductive-determining manner; this is followed by a desideratum—rhapsodically delineating, reflecting, but not actually casting judgement—based on the previous consideration of the transition from the natural into the intelligible.

It is not possible to say why the aesthetic estimation of magnitude was not dealt with earlier. If one were to give weight to a pessimistic interpretation, it may be conjectured that Schiller regarded his essay as too "technical", too incomplete in argumentative terms or too clumsy, with the result that he delayed its publication and was content to leave it unpublished. In a more optimistic interpretation, Schiller was waiting until Hölderlin's *Hyperion* fragment was completed before contributing an entire natural spectacle to support the aesthetic estimation of magnitude (an eminent failure of the latter), which up to then had only been considered in a cursory manner. In this interpretation, the "Detached Reflections" are intended to lend support to Hölderlin's *Hyperion* fragment.

Contents

(a) In the first part of the *Zerstreute Betrachtungen*, Schiller sets out his objective: he aims to classify the four basic "aesthetic attributes" (*ästhetische Prädikate*) [Schiller, *Zerstreute Betrachtungen*, in: *Neue Thalia*, Vol. 4, p. 122]—i.e., that which is felt and desired as agreeable, that which is thought of as good, that which is considered beautiful, and that which is marvelled at with fear and respect as being sublime. "All the properties by which an object can become aesthetic" (115) indirectly come into consideration for Schiller in this regard. However, why do certain things appear to be agreeable, but not beautiful; some as sublime, but nonetheless revolting, horrifying, abrupt, violent (cf. 124); others still judged to be beautiful or ugly; are found to be good or unsatisfactory, insofar as they are not "of no account to the moral judgement *(in der moralischen Schätzung gleichgültig)?*" (122). Schiller proposes that we can enjoy what we don't like or that we can like something that appals us intellectually; or conversely, that something can frighten us, but nonetheless stimulate and enchant us intellectually.

The purpose of art (*Zweck der Kunst*) is to provide pleasure, in Schiller's opinion, and it is clear that this objective is achieved in very different ways. To illustrate this state of affairs, Schiller begins with a rather schematic statement: that the above-mentioned aesthetic attributes—just as in Kant's philosophy—can be divided into four classes, of which only the beautiful and the sublime are exclusive to art. The classes are different from both subjective and objective viewpoints: subjectively different with regard to their ability to "produce on our passive and active faculties pleasures" (or not, as the case may be); objectively different in their "intensity" and in their "worth", as they "also are of an unequal use for the end of the fine arts" (*für den Zweck der schönen Künste auch von ungleicher Brauchbarkeit*) (all 115).

According to Schiller, the good pleases only reason, however, and is for that reason not one of the purposes of art, as the good "neither can nor ought to serve as a means of satisfying the wants of sensuousness" (*der Sinnlichkeit nicht als Mittel dienen*) (117). Schiller does not provide an argument here, but instead only perpetuates the familiar, centuries-old philosophical prejudice against the epistemic reliability of the sense organs (Cf. in this regard Schaub 2015). "On the other hand, that which is objective is altogether independent of *us*, and that which to-day appears to us true, useful, reasonable, ought yet (if this judgement of to-day be admitted as just) to seem to us the same twenty years hence" (118). The good is not sensed in an immediate manner as the agreeable, nor is it present in "mixed" form as the beautiful; it does not excite desires, nor inclinations; instead, it inspires only "esteem" in a reasonable subject—just as in Kant's philosophy (121). In short: the good must be neither imagined nor felt in order for it to exist.

Conversely, the agreeable is not worthy of art, as it pleases the senses merely through its materiality, but not through its form (cf. 116). The agreeable does not reveal any knowledge about an object, nor is it based on any such knowledge. Our judgement "changes as soon as our state, with regard to its object, has changed" (118). Just as in Kant's thinking (cf. Kant, *Critique of Pure Reason*, B 207–218), Schiller also quotes the familiar example of our highly fluctuating perception of temperature depending on our needs, which regards warm air as a blessing only when it is frosty, but not when it is warm.

Schiller concludes his deliberations with a sentence that is typical of him:

the agreeable exists only because it is *experienced*, and that the good, on the contrary, *is experienced* because it exists [*Das Angenehme [...] ist nur, weil es empfunden wird; das Gute hingegen wird empfunden, weil es ist*]. (119)

Schiller also considers the intermediate position of the beautiful: its sensing side tends to the agreeable, its observing, reflecting side tends to the good. The beautiful "pleases through the medium of the senses", but also "pleases reason, on account of its form". While the good pleases "by its form being *in harmony with reason (vernunftsgemäße Form)*", the beautiful does so merely "by its form having some relation of *resemblance with reason [vernunftsähnliche Form]*" (116).

For Schiller, the commonality between the agreeable and the beautiful lies in the pleasing, which is based on appearance and thus on sensuous mediation, without any link to knowledge about the nature of the associated objects. However, pleasing by the beautiful is to be described in terms of reason, as:

> The beautiful is not only pleasing to the individual but to the whole species; and although it draws its existence but from its relation with creatures at the same time reasonable and sensuous, it is not less independent of all empirical limitations of sensuousness, and it remains identical even when the particular constitution of the individual is modified. (119f.)

That is the theory. Nonetheless, it is evident in Schiller's thinking, in contrast with Kant, that even the good as an aesthetic concept is a relative notion in changing constellations, e.g., as it expresses appropriateness to the "theoretical and practical laws" of reason (cf., 120). However, this "and" (which is an inclusive *oder* in the German original text) captures the potential for conflict that is inherent here. In Schiller's opinion, these conflicts are exacerbated by the interaction between the four different aesthetic attributes:

> The difference separating the agreeable, the good, and the beautiful being thus established, it is evident that the same object can be ugly, defective, even to be morally rejected, and nevertheless be agreeable and pleasing to the senses; that an object can revolt the senses, and yet be good, i.e., please the reason; that an object can from its inmost nature revolt the moral senses, and yet please the imagination which contemplates it, and still be beautiful. It is because each one of these ideas interests different faculties, and interests differently. (121)

In the following passage, Schiller directs precisely this manifest paragone debate between the aesthetic attributes noticeably towards the fourth element that has not been given much attention up to this point: the sublime:

> The inclination to the pathetic—an inclination common to all men—the strength of the sympathetic sentiment—this force which *in nature* makes us wish to see suffering, terror, dismay, which has so many attractions for us *in art*, which makes us hurry to the theatre, which makes us take so much pleasure in the picturing of great misfortune,—all this bears testimony to a *fourth source of aesthetic pleasure*, which neither the agreeable, nor the good, nor the beautiful are in a state to produce. (130f.)

Schiller almost stealthily approaches the issue of the sublime by presenting an example that, when carefully considered, turns into a natural spectacle, to a veritable scenario, that follows no smaller goal than the (re-)production of the sublime in fantasy: the idyllic scene that Schiller creates in the imaginations of readers of *Thalia* couldn't be more "attractive" [*reizvoller*], as he speaks not just of being surrounded by "a beautiful landscape, illuminated by the purple light of evening"; no, everything comes together here "in charming the senses [*unsere Sinne zu ergötzen*]", the "play of lights", the sound of a nearby waterfall, the "song of the nightingales" (122). This passage of the essay has the effect of words of encouragement directed at the author himself, "the mellow outlines" of the objects have the effect that "the mind is rejoiced by the easy and rich flow of the ideas, the heart by the sentiments which overflow in it like a torrent" (123).

Let us examine what this results in. Schiller quickly changes the scenery, from evening to night, from a mild breeze to a thunderstorm. He masterfully depicts the embarrassing silence, the booming thunder, blinding lightning. A "terrible spectacle" undoubtedly draws us in to the same extent that it "wounds and repulses our senses". As long as the fear of being struck oneself doesn't gain the upper hand, as long as "all liberty of judgment [*Freyheit des Urtheils*]" (124) remains intact, he states, the attraction remains dominant. Why is this so?

Instead of attempting a discussion of the dynamically sublime in nature and about fear in line with Kant's thinking, we shall now proceed, somewhat surprisingly, to the mathematical sublime and to its impact due to its sheer magnitude. Interestingly, this is systematically positioned behind and not before the dynamically sublime in Schiller. This could be a first indication that Schiller continues to position the mathematical sublime in nature by being more interested in the sublimity of magnitude than in the infinite—as in the case of Kant. Schiller introduced the sheer sublimity of magnitude—inductively—in the manner of a veritable thought experiment and navigates the imaginations of his readers. Thus, one can think of a green landscape with a barren hill that is large enough to block the pleasant view. Schiller does not waste a single line on this unfortunate situation, and instead allows the hill to become planted and to take on a threatening inclination, without changing its basic proportions, so "that we could expect it every minute to crash down", and this "terror" makes the mountain "still more attractive" (126).

The support from the mountain beneath this will negate precisely this effect; if terracing is added or it is "artificially decorated with plantations", this will have the opposite effect and will ruin the overall impression. (Schiller's artificial decorations probably refer to fountains and other water features, in line with his frequent negative remarks about French garden landscaping.)

Schiller then undertakes a methodical reflection on how a pleasing view can be created from a neutral or unpleasant view by means of sheer growth (enlarging). In this context, imaginary mountains for comparative purposes create a deflationary effect; i.e., an imaginary comparative scale tends by its very nature to reduce the impression created by size as an absolute—and as a result also reduces the aesthetic pleasure drawn from this perception (cf. 128).

At this point, Schiller returns to the terror of tragedy. Just like Burke, who in turn quotes John Milton's *Paradise Lost*, Schiller mines Greek mythology, with the Furies or Erinyes emerging from "infernal regions" to pursue a criminal, with their "heads covered with serpents in the place of hair" (which greatly offends our taste), as they hunt down Orestes, the infamous matricide, in the name of "the anger of justice" (ibid. 128). However, according to Schiller, the poet with the certainty of the practitioner, the crime itself is "able to please us in a work of art". Medea, Clytemnestra, Orestes—Schiller identifies all of these characters who "fill our soul with horror and with pleasure" (129) as evidence.

Schiller attaches importance to the observation that common animals such as an ox, dog or horse "are raised to the rank of aesthetic objects" if they are stimulating enough. Attentiveness (which turns into respect) plays a role in pleasure here (cf. 130). Schiller interprets this as evidence for the existence of "something objective" in our reactions (131), which either "oversteps […] the power of comprehension of our senses, or their power of resistance". In German, the difference is clearer than in the misleading English translation: the successive perception by all five senses is—close to Kant's terminology—always "apprehension", as *sinnliche Fassungskraft* translates the Latin term *apprehensio*, in contrast to the (normally) simultaneously occurring conceptual summing up or framing by the faculty of reason as "comprehension". Both of these aspects are familiar from Kant's treatment of the sublime. Schiller again takes up the idea of resistance, and subsequently gives more careful attention to the role of failing *apprehension* than to the failing *comprehension*, as Kant does.

Schiller's psychological reasoning, which always includes both forms of the sublime, is as follows: (1) A sublime object is an object "which appears to upraise itself as an enemy, even against our existence—which provokes us, so to say, to combat, and makes us anxious as to the issue". (2) Schiller differentiates between two forms of the sublime that are in conflict with our sensuous nature, (a) a knowledge-stimulating form ("the sublime of knowledge"), approximately comparable with the mathematically sublime in Kant's philosophy, and (b) a form that stimulates powerlessness and evokes the power of comparison (i.e., "the sublime of force"), approximately comparable with the dynamically sublime of nature in Kant. (3) For Schiller, the main reasons for the "aesthetic value [*ästhetischer Werth*]" of the sublime are the disturbing experience of a (nameless) horror or of an (incomparable) magnitude. (4) After nerve-racking anxiety, "our mind falls back on itself by reflection", which almost automatically results in "a higher consciousness of its independent strength and dignity" (132), similar to Kant's self-empowerment idea. (5) As a consequence of these particular effects, Schiller suggests that one should think more in terms of the "elevated" (133) than the sublime. (6) Schiller is in unison with Kant only with regard to the effect, but not the genesis of the sublime. Schiller proposes a slightly different explanation than Kant for the self-empowerment of reason.

(b) In the following, longer section on the aesthetic estimation of magnitude, Schiller provides various examples for the failure of the aesthetic estimation of magnitude [*ästhetische Größenschätzung*]. In order to be able to ascribe sublimity—of both the dynamical and mathematical natures—at all, the estimation of magnitude must also fail, not only in Kant's but also in Schiller's thinking. But Schiller is pursuing various aims in this regard. On the one hand, he wishes to illustrate using practical examples why an object that is great because of its dimensions becomes *aesthetic* only through fantasy, while this object appears sublime *only by means of an operation of reason*:

> The idea of the absolute certainly requires a more than ordinary development of the higher faculty of reason, a certain richness of ideas, and a more rigorous acquaintance on the part of the individual with his noblest self. He whose reason has undergone no cultivation at all, will never know how to make a supra-sensual use of the grandness of the senses. (170)

Schiller proposes a baton change between abstract, mathematical consideration and sensuous-concrete consideration:

> The power of imagination thus relinquishes its intuitive business, and the mind begins its discursive (here, actually symbolic) work. Number must assist where perception no longer suffices, and thought must subdue, where the eye's vision can no longer become master. (155)

However, the power of the imagination and the intellect only appear to combine productively in the case of the sublime; ultimately, they increase the disharmony between these two poles for Schiller, regardless of whether this is desirable or not.

Schiller's illustrative example for this ultimately fruitless replacement of sensuous with logical units begins with the estimation of the magnitude of soldiers standing in an orderly fashion. Even if they were standing in a clear formation and even if 1000 were mathematically divided by ten two times to yield groups of ten that are easy for our senses to take in, their "immediate representatives", in this case the soldiers, would "themselves have vanished into darkness" (157) as part of this operation. That which is represented by the concept "loses itself in darkness or disappears" (156). As a result, the "logical profusion" of mathematical exactness also results in an "aesthetic impoverishment [*ästhetische Armuht*]" (157).

The problem begins with *how* the power of imagination evaluates all sensuous magnitudes by dividing them into smaller units, i.e., by treating them as a continuous *quantum* (cf. 135). This estimation of magnitude has a physiological limit, he believes: more than around ten different countable units are difficult to compare, to consider in detail and to remember. Assume that the "maximum of sensuous comprehension is ten" without losing sight of any of the ten—this may be a "subjective base-measure", but it exists "in all human beings" (with "sameness"), and "every quantum in Nature [is] estimated" according to this base-measure (Schiller, *Zerstreute Betrachtungen*, in: *Neue Thalia*, Vol. 4, 1793, p. 153f). In Schiller's thinking, anything we perceive beyond this limit is necessarily taken in as a *magnum*, i.e., as something that cannot be sensibly divided into smaller units and is therefore *potentially sublime*. Thus, the difference between a quantum and a magnum is explicitly not a category-based one, but instead merely a gradual difference, determined solely by the physiological limit of the apprehending human senses. With this, Schiller makes use of both inflationary and deflationary concepts of the sublime; he reduces its aesthetic significance by increasing its occurrences quantitatively; the crisis of expressing the sublime here clearly becomes a problem of the limits of the power of imagination.

The mere combination of a quantum with another, Schiller continues, leads to the formation of a magnum relative to this quantum:

> Held up against its own measure, every magnitude is a magnum, and still more so, held up against the measure of its own measure, compared with which its own measure is itself again a magnum. But, just as this process operates in a descending manner, it also applies in the ascending direction: every magnum is small as soon as we think of it contained in another, and where is the limit here, since we can again multiply any number series, however large, by itself? (137)

According to Schiller, it is no great achievement to collect thousands of impressions individually, one after another, if you have enough time to analyse them. But this is precisely why the aesthetic estimation of magnitude fails in the case of the sublime; it is a "difficult task (*schwere Aufgabe*)" "to recognize the consciousness strewn into all these thousand mental images of units as self-identical, to grasp a thousand different apperceptions in a single one" (154f.).

Schiller's conclusion is not surprising: the "clarity of intuition" of the power of imagination remains "confined" to small numbers (up to 10); no matter how much "discursive progression" the mind achieves, "the power of imagination never expands its real wealth (as far as the simultaneity of perception is concerned)" (ibid. 160). This physiological "maximum of comprehension" thus determines "the ultimate base-measure" [*das letzte Grundmaaß*] in the "mathematical estimation of magnitude" [*mathematische Größenschätzung*]. This is naturally limited "by the constraints of our subjectivity" (153).

In one important detail, Schiller does not follow Kant's explication of the phenomenon.

In Kant, the *apprehension* of sensuous impressions is dependent on our power of imagination, but our *comprehension* is dependent on our reason, i.e., on assignment among already existing concepts. In Schiller, both operations are tasks for the power of imagination: the necessary comprehension is supplemented by the intuition" of the power of imagination in the moment when the aesthetic estimation of magnitude takes place. When liberated in this manner, reason is present as an unrelenting instructor that unapologetically insists on the creation of "unity" and "totality" from the numerous, detached impressions:

> Reason insists, in accordance with its necessary laws, upon absolute totality of perception, and without letting itself be rebuffed by the necessary limitation of the power of imagination, the mind requires from it a complete summation of all the parts of a given quantum in one simultaneous mental image. The power of

imagination is thus compelled to exhaust the entire scope of its comprehensive capacities, but because it nevertheless does not complete this task to the end, and, all exertions notwithstanding, cannot extend its scope, the power of imagination sinks back into itself exhausted, and sensuous man experiences with painful disquiet his limitations. (161f.)

In contrast with Kant, Schiller even views it as the task of the power of imagination to counteract logical abstractness in a concrete manner by attempting "to restore the sensuousness of the mental image out of the logical representation provided by number-concepts, and so to grasp length with breadth, simultaneity with succession in one intuitive act "(161). He adds:

> But is it an external force, which gives him this experience of his limitations? Is it the fault of the measureless ocean, or the infinite star-sown heaven, that I become self-conscious of my impotence while representing their greatness? Whence, in that event, do I know, that their greatness exceeds the reach of my representation, and that I can obtain no totality of their image? Do I, indeed, know of these objects, that they are supposed to constitute a totality of a mental image? I could only know this by virtue of my mental image of them, and in no other way, and yet it is presupposed, that I cannot imagine them as a totality. They are thus not presented to me as a totality, and I myself am the very one, who first put the concept of totality into them. I thus already have this idea in me, and I myself, the thinking being, am the very one, by which I, the being who makes representations of images of the intellect, am vanquished. In contemplating these great objects, I indeed experience my *powerlessness*, but I experience it through my *strength*. I am not vanquished by Nature, *I am vanquished by mine own self*. (162f.)

Not abstract infinity, but instead a concrete totality, a completeness in the form of a comprehensive force encompassing the human capacity for imagination—for Schiller, this is the key to transforming the powerlessness of the power of imagination into a triumph of reason: "It is required of the power of imagination, that it summon up all its resources of comprehension to set forth the representation of the Absolute, toward which Reason unremittingly presses" (169). In this regard, Schiller's focus is less on the well-known Kantian primacy of the principle of reason, but instead rather on the consequences for the constitution of the feeling and thinking subject. His attention is directed to not just towards a (phenomenal) "I" that fluctuates along with its fluctuating impressions, but also to an "I" that is interested in wanting to understand. An "I" that experiences the failing intuition of the power of imagination through a magnum's process of becoming expressive in the moment of the impossible "representation" of a quantum:

> Thus, I want to dissolve images of the intellect, which I already have, into a single one, and cannot do it, and I am pained, that I cannot. But in order to experience, that I cannot fulfill a requirement, I must at once have the idea of this requirement and that of my incapacity. But this requirement is present: totality of the parts in the act of comprehension, or unity of my 'I' in a certain series of

transformations of my 'I'. Thus, I must only imagine, that I cannot generate in consciousness a mental image of the unity of my 'I' in all these transformations; but precisely in so doing I do produce this idea. Precisely in so doing, I think the totality of the whole series, and that I want to think it, for I can want nothing of which I do not already have an idea. I thus already bear within myself this totality which I seek to represent, just because I seek to represent it. Greatness, therefore, is in me, not outside me. It is my eternally self-same Subject, persistent through every change, finding itself once more in every transformation. I can continue the act of apprehending into infinity: this means nothing else, than that, in endless transformations of my consciousness, my consciousness is self-identical, the entire infinity lies in the unity of my 'I'. (164f.)

Schiller also makes it clear why he—in contrast with Kant—identifies the role of the power of imagination in the failure of comprehension and dramatises this, with the aim of triggering the contradictory and conflictual moment in the experiencing of the sublime through maximum contrast with the capacity of reason:

The sublimity of the magnitude is therefore no objective property of the object to which it is attributed; it is purely the effect of our own subjectivity, occasioned by that object. It arises in *one part* out of the imagined incapacity of the power of imagination of the mind to achieve the totality demanded by Reason in portraying magnitude, *partly again* from the imagined capability of Reason to make such a demand. On the first is based the *repulsive*, on the second the *attractive* power of great magnitude and of the Sensuous-Infinite. (167)

In Schiller's thinking, reason orchestrates this conflict in the manner of a conductor.

Philosophical Significance and Impact

Certain passages in the *Zerstreute Betrachtungen* read like notes on Kant's *Critique of the Power of Judgment* jotted down with the left hand while Schiller was already restlessly leafing through the rest of the book with his right hand, thinking ahead, pushing things forward, and coming up with new and different practical examples, for better and for worse. Schiller thus expands the reason for and frequency of the occurrence of sublimity significantly by emphasising the limits of the power of imagination in the aesthetic estimation of magnitude by means of a categorical continuum including both quanta and magna. Schiller minimises the aesthetic overestimation of these elements here; ultimately, he deflates this concept. This finding is also supported by Schiller's wry closing remark that heights and depths (*profundus*) are not equally terrifying. After all, to fall from a height, one must first have climbed high; on the other hand, a conception of terrifying nature accompanies the depths indirectly, as can be confirmed by peering into the water at the bottom of a dark well. Schiller often works with comparisons of this type, which always serve to demystify the sublime by an act of comparison alone (Cf. 178). In this way, he very much follows the Kantian argument that the mathematical sublime is the greatest of all, i.e., that which evades measurement and thus also comparability.

The impression of the epigonal deceives according to Schiller, extending the thinking of Kant. Upon closer examination, Schiller remains true to his original intention to render the three Kantian powers—those of the mind, reason, and imagination—even more physiological, physical, vital, and even libidinous. The role of the mind in the particular experiencing of the sublime dramatises the contentious conflict between reason and the *imagination* as vital forces. The mind demands unity/comprehension in the manner of an impresario and thus acts equally on the power of imagination and on the will to think.

If one wishes, one can already see Schopenhauer's *The World as Will and Representation* (1819) opening up as a possibility between the lines:

> It is indeed the object which changes me, but I, the conceiving Subject, am what makes the object into an object, and through its generation, changes itself. In all these transformations, however, there must be something which does not change, and this eternally immutable principium is precisely the pure and self-identical "I," the ground of the possibility of all objects, in so far as they become represented to the intellect. Whatever of greatness lies in the idea, lies in us, who bring forth these ideas. (165f.)

Statements such as "the entire infinity lies in the unity of my 'I'" later find an echo in G.W.F. Hegel's reflections on the difference between good and bad infinites. Later ideas from Hegelian aesthetics, on the form-content penetration of classical art, can also be identified in an embryonic stage in Schiller's writing.

The *Zerstreute Betrachtungen* contain a number of examples that do not appear in Kant in the same form, but that Schiller works on and exhausts himself on. His often-used dramaturgical tool of juxtaposition leads Schiller onto dangerous territory—not just theoretically, but also in practical terms. At a remove of 228 years, we can be amused about his broadsides against French and English landscape gardeners as justifiable mockery of uncontrolled plants and of excessive devotion to rules, but his mixture of civility and wildness is somewhat disturbing. Both sides do not emerge with much credit in Schiller's writing: anyone who, like an "unnerved weakling" [*entnervter Weichling*], suffers from an overwrought fantasy and at the same time from a sufficiently independent reason will seek "succor from the consolatrix of all weak men, the *rule*". "If he cannot stand up straight to the greatness of Nature, then Nature must climb down to his small powers of comprehension" (both 171f.). On the other hand, Schiller makes derogatory and stereotyping remarks about the "crude savage", as "the savage can dwell in the lap of most sublime Nature, and amidst the symbols of the Infinite, without thereby being awoken from his bestial slumber, without revering even from afar the great spirit of Nature, which speaks to a feeling soul out of the sensuous-immeasurable" (171).

One has to ask where Schiller got this dangerous nonsense from. Hölderlin's painful scepticism with regard to the interpretation and existence of these feeling souls is very much to be preferred. In this way, simple-mindedness and insight are never very far away in the *Neue Thalia*: by lucky coincidence, Hölderlin addresses the insufficiencies of some of Schiller's accounts, by musing: "I ask the stars and they fall silent, I ask the day, and the night; but they don't answer. From myself, when I ask myself, emerge mystical proverbs, dreams without meaning" (*Hyperion* fragment, *Neue Thalia*, Vol. 4, 1793, p. 220).

German text translated into English by Patrick Sheehan.

Reference

Schaub, Mirjam: "Die Krux des Sinnlichen aus philosophischer Sicht – und die Folgen für die Ästhetik", in: Philosophisches Jahrbuch, Vol. II/2015, Freiburg: Alber 2015, p. 387–404

CHAPTER 13

Letters on the Aesthetic Education (1795)

Tim Mehigan

TEXTUAL GENESIS

Only six letters and the beginning of a seventh letter survive from ten original letters that Schiller composed to his patron Prince Friedrich Christian von Schleswig-Holstein-Augustenburg in 1793. These "Augustenburg Letters" represent the first draft of a project that was to become the *Letters on the Aesthetic Education of Man*. As a letter to Körner attests, Schiller intended these letters to be published at a later date, perhaps in combination with other writings on the same topic. Their original purpose was twofold: first, to convey gratitude for the unexpected beneficence of an annual pension at a time when Schiller was plagued by ill-health and limited means; second, to "road-test" his own reading of the Kantian philosophy—a philosophy whose ground-breaking significance for aesthetics and morality had struck Schiller from his first acquaintance with Kant's *Critique of the Power of Judgment* (1790).

During the year or so in which these letters were composed Schiller appears to have had no notion of going beyond Kantian precepts, claiming to follow the main thrust of Kant's philosophy "as far as the rudiments of ethics are concerned" (Schiller, *Aus den Briefen*, [December 3, 1793], 154). This intention is noticeably weakened in the *Aesthetic Letters* where Schiller notes a discrepancy between "the letter and the spirit" of Kant's project (SW 5: 608). In truth such distance was already present in the "Augustenburg Letters", where differences are discernible in regard to the category of taste, which for Schiller, in

T. Mehigan (✉)
School of Languages and Cultures, University of Queensland,
St. Lucia, QLD, Australia
e-mail: t.mehigan@uq.edu.au

© The Author(s), under exclusive license to Springer Nature
Switzerland AG 2023
A. Falduto, T. Mehigan (eds.), *The Palgrave Handbook on the Philosophy of Friedrich Schiller*, https://doi.org/10.1007/978-3-031-16798-0_13

line with a view expressed in a letter to Körner in the same year (January 25, 1793; K 394), reaches forward to an "objective" claim, but which Kant in the *Critique of Judgment* does not allow to be more than subjective. Schiller calls taste "everything that allows aesthetic play, and can only be judged by a panel of connoisseurs"; taste, accordingly, is everything "necessary and eternal within human nature" (letter to Prince von Augustenburg, July 13, 1793; cf. Pollok 2019, 232).

That Schiller's intersubjectively premised view of aesthetic judgement was soon to find itself at odds with Kant's "rigoristic" ethics is witnessed in Schiller's essay "On Grace and Dignity" (1793). This work constitutes an important stepping-stone from the "Augustenburg Letters" to the *Aesthetic Letters*. In this essay, Schiller expresses dissatisfaction with Kant's moral philosophy insofar as Kant holds that inclination (*Neigung*), with its wellspring in sensuality, has no direct part to play in duty (*Pflicht*). Later in the essay Schiller introduces the notion of the "beautiful soul", a spiritual entity whose defining attribute is that its action "knows" no separation between the aesthetic and the moral. The moral actions of such a soul, accordingly, overlook the fact of ontological separation between these two domains and for that very reason are held to be beautiful.

If Schiller meant the beautiful soul to provide clinching evidence for a shortfall in the Kantian account of duty, he was sorely mistaken. Kant, in a long footnote in the second edition of his treatise *Religion within the Bounds of Reason Alone* (1794), took Schiller's objection to his account of duty to be non-substantive "if only we make ourselves clear to each other" (Kant IV, 669–70). Kant contends that both he and Schiller in fact had equivalent moral commitments, notwithstanding Schiller's evocative account of the beautiful soul in "On Grace and Dignity". Kant presses this point in the footnote, insisting that when grace is involved it arises in view of, and as an accompaniment to, "morally-directed reason" (670). This could only mean that inclination can neither be coincident with duty nor its cause. If Schiller understood matters differently, then—this is Stiening's view (2019, 4–5)—he had plainly misunderstood Kant's moral philosophy. Kant sets out the proper view in the footnote, noting that "virtue, i.e., the firmly founded conviction that one must do one's duty to the letter, is providential in its consequences—more than anything that nature and art in the world can achieve" (ibid: my translation). Stiening's version of this exchange, however, misses the very frisson at work in Schiller's misprision in regard to Kant's moral theory. The "takeaway" from the recondite discussion about difference between the poet and the philosopher is surely less that Schiller found Kant's remarks to be justified, less that he expressed regret about misapprehending Kant's moral theory, and sooner that his difference from Kant required further exploration and a more nuanced account of their respective positions. Kant's reply to Schiller thus added fuel to an already brightly flickering fire.

Schiller returned to the "Augustenburg Letters" in mid-1794, with the *Letters on the Aesthetic Education of Man*, appearing in three instalments in

Schiller's new journal *Die Horen* in January, February and June 1795. These *Letters* can be read as Schiller's response to Kant's renewed insistence in his treatise *Religion within the Bounds of Reason Alone* that sensuality can play no direct part in morals, that reason alone inspires virtue, though virtue may be accompanied by gracious "consequences" in the art that celebrates it. Since the last part of Kant's remarks is not left free of condescension towards poetry in the area of morals, it may have particularly irked Schiller. Schiller might well have read such comment in the context of a far older dispute between philosophy and poetry variously alluded to in Plato's Socratic writings. In this "ancient quarrel"—a spectral presence throughout the *Aesthetic Letters*—philosophy formally disavows the claim of poetry to say anything of final value about moral truth. If Schiller was indeed so irked by Kant's footnote, his disagreement was now as much with the terms of settlement of the ancient quarrel as it was with Kant's moral thought.

One further aspect must be noted by way of introduction to Schiller's *Aesthetic Letters*. During Schiller's long immersion in the critical philosophy—a process of deep reading which began in 1791 after the appearance of Kant's third *Critique* and took on new seriousness in early 1793 after Schiller received his pension from the Prince of Schleswig-Holstein-Augustenburg—a historical event of supreme importance was unfolding across the border from Germany in France. This was the French Revolution, which started life as a parliamentary revolt of deputies in 1789 and had already moved through its constitutional phase to a period of escalating violence and terror by late 1792. As his poetical works reveal, Schiller had been something of a revolutionary himself in his early years (though one notably averse to violence). When the full force of the Jacobin revolt arrived to confirm the failure of the reform phase of the Revolution, Schiller's earlier fervour for the cause of political change built from Enlightenment principles was thrown into question. These factors left their imprint on the argument of the *Aesthetic Letters*, constituting the direct grounds for proclaiming the existence of a "political problem" that the "aesthetic path" predicated on beauty was invoked to solve (SW 5: 573). It is above all this political problem—the problem of unbridled political violence that the Age of Enlightenment had spawned and which its moral precepts had not made unthinkable—that, for Schiller, scratched at the old wound of man's uncomfortably accommodated dualism and demanded a new solution to it.

When Schiller returned to the "Augustenburg Letters" in 1794 in response to this problem, he soon discovered a new source of potential disagreement with Kant. While Kant's promotion of a rigorous form of morals, fit, as Schiller noted in the essay "On Grace and Dignity", more for the "knaves of the house" than its children (SW 5: 466), now looked more reasonable, even such stern morality had patently not met with success in guiding the revolutionaries towards the state of enlightened civility. Watching events in France take their disastrous course, Schiller concluded that a philosophy of moral enlightenment could not reform a tragically riven humanity.

This insight had consequences for the educative mission of the *Letters*. Whereas Schiller had understood the task of education in the "Augustenburg Letters" in terms of *Bildung*, the "self-formation" of intellectually curious subjects later formalised as a program of teaching and research by Wilhelm von Humboldt (Humboldt 1843), Schiller in the later *Letters* preferred a more forceful term for education, that of *Erziehung*, a term referring to the serious business of rearing children and making them fit for life. By conferring on such education, a programmatic status in the title of the new work, Schiller sought to unify two seemingly disparate purposes: first, the settling of accounts with Kant regarding the question of art's relation to morality; second, a cogent response to the "political problem" that did not fully come into view until the later months of 1793 and early 1794 when the Terror reached its zenith.

Contents

The *Aesthetic Letters*, as mentioned, were released in serialised form in three instalments in *Die Horen* in 1795. A minor amount of reworking of the text of the *Letters* occurred for the collected edition of Schiller's works published in 1801. Schiller's use of the epistolary form is only partly accounted for with reference to the genesis of the *Aesthetic Letters*—namely, that they originally "really" were letters penned by a grateful subject to his patron. For it is also apparent that the epistolary form lends itself to a set of intentions that aims neither at a philosophical treatise nor a poetical work but rather an amalgam of the two. The interests of poetry and the interests of philosophy meet, as it were, on the neutral ground of the letter, enabling stylistic and content shifts to occur without injury to the appearance and function of the whole. The internal structure of the *Letters*, indeed, indicates a clear progression from the cultural and historical discussion of the first nine letters, through philosophical discourse in the middle letters (Letters 10–16), where Schiller professes to derive from the transcendental approach a "pure intellectual concept of beauty", to a concluding section where political and anthropological argument holds sway (Letters 17–27). The result of these shifts, as Riedel (2004, 1221) notes, is not any new theory of beauty or an objective account of beauty (such as that sought in the *Kallias* Letters), not any new theory of taste in the manner of Kant's third *Critique*, nor even a theory of art from the viewpoint of its creative production. Rather, the *Letters* highlight a reflective approach to the aesthetic domain reminiscent of Winckelmann's art criticism in the mid-eighteenth century that approaches art from the viewpoint of those who experience it (for further discussion of this approach: Mehigan 2020).

On this ground of aesthetic experience, far below the exigencies of formal presentation, can be found the underlying drivers of Schiller's argument. For it turns out that the nature of aesthetic experience is not primarily a philosophical question, but one that concerns what human beings value, what makes them really "tick". Schiller finds in the attributes of aesthetic experience less a proposition to augment or oppose Kant's claim that moral judgement must be restricted to the autonomy of the rational will, nor convincing evidence that sensuality shapes this will and must be included in any account of the moral ends of human beings. While these latter aspects remain consistent with Schiller's interests and outlook, they represent its ostensible goals but not its final purpose. Much closer to Schiller's heart and the real goal of the *Letters* is a vision of human beings that rises above the tragic internal division that marks them—a humanistic vision commentators like Safranski (2016), with some justification, call a species of idealism. The *Letters* aim to use the full resources of philosophical, historical, cultural and anthropological argument to make this vision come to life. The means by which to do so is provided by art—not an art of modest reach in line with Kant's theory of aesthetic taste, but, going beyond Kant, art as intellectually and sensually lived experience, art, indeed, as an expression of the highest feeling for life of which human beings are capable.

Letters 1–10

The first instalment of *Letters* begins this project in reference to recent events in France. It is not the Revolution as such that constitutes the "political problem" from which these letters take their point of departure, for Schiller's sympathies had lain from the outset with the cause of political freedom on which the Revolution was premised. It is the annulment of this freedom that Schiller is concerned with—an annulment, as Schiller sees it, that had occurred under Robespierre's Jacobins during the Reign of Terror. In this unfreedom of the Jacobin revolutionaries Schiller locates a point of commencement for his inquiry, in contrast to the earlier "Augustenburg Letters", for which Kant's "revolution in the philosophical world" (AGL 49) had sufficed as grounds for initiating correspondence with Schiller's patron. This new point of departure for the *Letters* has consequences for their internal arrangement, for the philosophical inquiry with which the "Augustenburg Letters" began is now relegated to the middle part of the *Letters*. Not only this: when Schiller calls art "a daughter of freedom" (572) in the second letter, his concern is not primarily with philosophy so much as with the social position of art in his age—an age in which spiritual and religious affiliations recede under a process of rising secularisation and in which the sciences command ever greater regions of intellectual activity and "knowledge" and progressively narrow the remit of the aesthetic (ibid). The "political problem" with which Schiller declares himself concerned at the start of the *Aesthetic Letters* thus accrues a second motivation at least as serious as the first, namely, the need to find a basis for the return of art and art-based thinking to the forefront of modern life. The decision to foreground the question of freedom in the discussion of art in the second letter (cf. 573), from this angle, represents both a concession to moral arguments of Kantian provenance, whose main discussion is put back to the middle grouping of *Letters*, as well as recognition that only a general argument about art's value in modern society can hope to gain traction at the present moment of "sunken humanity" (572).

In the third letter a new problem is brought into view. As Edmund Burke had already argued in his *Reflections on the Revolution in France* (1790), the Revolution had nearly taken away that which it had professed to reform. As true as this observation was, Schiller clearly wants something more than the position espoused by conservatives like Burke that revolutions have a deleterious impact on the ancient contract of a present society with its predecessor formations. As a modern man and social reformer, Schiller finds greater cause for optimism than Burke in the prospect of social and moral improvement, but, as he concedes in the third letter, the new moral character of man must first be brought into being (575). How to achieve such a development of character without doing permanent injury to its present constitution, how, in short, to reform and conserve *at the same time*, is the crux of the political problem Schiller isolates in the early stages of the *Letters*. The solution to this problem, as Schiller opines at the end of the third letter, lies with the production of a "third character" (576), one that would secure transition from the lawless state of nature, where only brute force can reckon with success, to the state of civil society, where respect for the rule of law has become a universal commitment.

While it is already clear that Schiller wishes to position art as the vehicle for production of such a character, his concern in the fourth and fifth letters is still with the consequences of the division at the heart of human nature. In the fourth letter, for example, Schiller characterises the will of common humanity as sitting squarely between the Scylla of principles and the Charybdis of feelings—as if it were a matter of a choice between the two. Schiller's design only becomes evident when contrasting the primitive (*Wilder*), who chooses feeling over principles, with the barbarian (*Barbar*), who destroys feeling for the sake of principles—an attitude perhaps even more malign in its consequences than its alternative (cf. 579). Schiller's purpose here is unmistakable: the contrast, which is drawn from a study of recent events in France, is merely a placeholder for the debate he means to resume with Kant. An implication of this shadow-framing of that debate is that, while the position of the primitive can certainly not be endorsed, rigid insistence on the rule of principles, the viewpoint of the barbarian, equally misses something essential about the human character. To this end, Schiller concludes the fourth letter with reference to the "totality" of character traits that must be appealed to if the *Notstaat*, the state born of necessity, the original state of man, is to carry forward to the *Staat der Freiheit*, the higher state of the human being that honours the basal principle of freedom [for a valuable discussion of Schiller's theories of the state, see Löwe and Stiening (2021)].

It can immediately be concluded, then, that Schiller's theories of political formation run out into a republicanism with the principle of freedom at its centre. Schiller develops this political approach in the sixth letter with the recognition that freedom—the freedom of the individual to develop fully her innate qualities—is unequally distributed in society (582). Schiller's credentials as a thinker in the Marxist tradition are thus clearly underlined (cf. Ross 2017, esp. 34–42). Schiller's endorsement of the republican tradition, nevertheless, is by no means straightforward. Republicanism is the view that the state, once put in its best form (i.e., as a free and independent republic), must be regarded as the first concern of political life, for it is from the state that the capacity to foster enlightened citizens is derived. Yet as Schiller notes in the seventh letter, following Rousseau's diagnosis of the poor state in which eighteenth-century civilisation finds itself (1755), "the state as it is constituted at present has caused the [current] evils" (588).

There are two immediate consequences arising from this view, both important for the development of Schiller's argument as a whole. The first—of great interest to the Romantics—is that Schiller does not endorse the rationalist position that culture (and civilisation) stand apart from nature and are in some sense superior to it. Schiller instead subordinates culture (and morality) to nature, thereby committing the anthropology he will develop in the final section of the *Letters* to the logic of pure immanence. The second consequence concerns Schiller's treatment of distant antiquity, for he by no means considers Greek republicanism in every respect the *non plus ultra* of human social development. Certainly, as he says in the sixth letter, Greek culture in its heyday is greatly to be admired, constituting "a maximum" (586)—but patently not *the* maximum. Here Schiller's credentials as a historian are underlined, because historical analysis reveals that Greek culture went past its summit for very good reason. Though this ancient culture was built around reverence for the tenets of beauty, the cultivation of taste at this time was still in its infancy. Art did not, and perhaps could not, remain central to it. As Schiller observes, clearly meaning Plato though not mentioning him by name, even better minds denied "the arts of the imagination admittance to the [ideal] republic" (597). If the study of history reveals that art cannot easily be sustained as the lynchpin of social and political life, another path must be tried to demonstrate art's indispensable value to humanity. This other path is opened up in the *Letters* by way of transcendental critique—the attempt to derive "the pure rational concept of beauty [...] from the possibility of the sensual-rational nature" of human beings (600). Put another way, Schiller not only intends to put the idea of beauty and the concept of humanity in touch with each other; he determines that the one entity entails the other in a relationship of interdependence.

Letters 11–16

While Kant is barely mentioned in the first grouping of letters, the movement into transcendental argument in the second grouping would appear to make good on Schiller's statement at the start of the *Letters* that his inquiry "mainly [rests] on Kantian principles" (570). An early footnote in this section makes the link to Kant explicit by referring to the intention of "transcendental philosophy" to separate form and content for the sake of a better appreciation of the difference between accident and necessity. Schiller defends this philosophy against the charge that it conceives of materialism as a barrier to intellectual inquiry, since this charge is not borne out in the "spirit" of Kant's philosophy even if it is occasionally to be found in its letter (607–8). Although these footnoted comments speak to a level of rapport with the Kantian system, they equally suggest some distance from Kant. The distinction between the letter and spirit of Kant's philosophy invokes such distance, even if indirectly.

Throughout the middle section of the *Letters* new influences on Schiller's argument are felt. While still broadly Kantian in outlook, these influences are no longer wholly attributable to Kant. In the 11th letter, for example, Schiller introduces a distinction between "person" (*Person*) and "condition" (*Zustand*) to ground his transcendental inquiry: the enduring aspect of (mental) life, on one side, and the factor of perennial alteration in the physical condition of that life, on the other. The dualism that emerges from this distinction is directed less at observing Kant's signature division between intuition and understanding and more in obeisance to K. L. Reinhold's dichotomy of *Form* and *Stoff* or "matter" (cf. Bondeli 2019), where, in regard to the latter, a physical aspect is implied. While Kantian enough in his own philosophy to derive this contrast from the mental capacity for representation (ibid.), Reinhold nevertheless puts, as it were, flesh on its bones when conferring on both the status of a *Trieb* ("drive" or "impulse"). Thus, when Schiller returns to the distinction between "person" and "condition" at the end of the 11th letter, *Stoff* (à la Reinhold) is already a physical force driving the agency of person towards ever greater contact with reality, *Form* already a countermanding drive inside the person that constrains and patterns such contact (cf. 603). A plausible confluence is thereby suggested between two entities hitherto—which is to say, under the Enlightenment dispensation—held to be incongruent. This confluence proves vital for the construction of Schiller's eventual synthesis of the two entities through the means of aesthetic education (cf. Ziolkowski 1998: 133). In Reinhold, then, Schiller finds a psycho-philosophical disposition even more amenable to his own purposes than that which he had found in Kant.

Nevertheless, the dialogue between form and sense faces many obstacles. For one thing, as Schiller concedes, there is the undeniable factor of ontological difference: inclination, on the side of sense and matter, directly engages the here-and-now, whereas moral pronouncements, issuing from the realm of ideas, hold forever. In any clash of executive with legislative powers, as Kant's thought prescribes, the legislative authority of the moral trumps the aesthetic reach of the executive. In the 13th letter, perhaps for this reason, Schiller departs from this contest of unevenly matched powers by providing for a third drive, the *Spieltrieb* or "play drive". Schiller introduces this third drive with care, preserving the connective thread of his affiliation with Kant's theory of aesthetic judgement by denying it the status of a "fundamental drive" (*Grundtrieb*). Yet a drive it remains, invested with the capacity to arbitrate between the ontologically distinct realms of form and sense with the purpose of drawing out the best energies from both. This is not achieved by subordinating sense to form—the approach that applies under the Kantian approach.

Schiller instead launches an argument that allows a maximum of inclination to be brought to bear against a maximum of reason—for the sake of fidelity to both. How does he achieve this outcome?

An answer is provided at the beginning of the 14th letter by way of the concept of *Wechselwirkung* or "reciprocal action", a term Schiller borrows from the philosophy of Fichte. Reciprocal action, Schiller explains, is action that works on the base drives of form and sense by turns, "grounding and delimiting" both while allowing each drive to achieve "its highest expression (*Verkündigung*) by means of the action of the other" (611). Reciprocal action makes its appearance in Schiller's aesthetic theory to solve the issue of the partial suppression of the life force—the spectre that Kant's moral theory raises. Schiller considers this life force necessarily invested in both sides of a divided humanity, which is to say, in sensual inclination as well as reason. A restriction involving one aspect of this life force, Schiller reasons, risks impairment to the life force in general—a potentially disastrous result for the enterprise of freedom on which all conscious human activity depends. The play drive intervenes in this high-stakes drama of opposing forces facilitating, first, a coming together of the two drives, while, secondly, coordinating and preserving the energetic action of each drive in its own domain. The value of the principle of reciprocal action lies with its respect for the free expression of both drives in accordance with the never fully knowable "intuition of humanity" (612). Schiller's claim here is that the fate of humanity need not rest, as Kant imagines, on a necessary curtailment of inclination in the name of duty. If the world-facing sense drive banishes autonomy but inculcates suffering, and the form drive, for its part, restricts suffering dependence on the world in order to preserve autonomy and moral necessity (613), the play drive acknowledges the worth of both endeavours, fostering harmony between the two through a hitherto "unexpected" (618) meeting of human ends, one that implicitly moves beyond the tragic vision bequeathed to posterity by Greek antiquity (on this "unexpected science", cf. Mehigan 2020).

The alternative vision Schiller sketches for the denizens of a new age is brought into view in the 15th and 16th letters. In this vision of a future state of the human being, homage is paid to the operation of the life force. The object of the sensual drive, Schiller now says, is "life in its most extended meaning", the object of the form drive "living form" (614). To these instantiations of the life force Schiller then adds beauty, which he calls "the consummation of humanity" (615), a concept already understood by the ancient Greeks to be vitally connected with play. The play Schiller has in mind is not frivolous play in the vernacular meaning of that term, but the serious play of the artwork. The activity of such play realised in the production of art as well as in the experience of the artwork brings about nothing less than the true purpose of humanity, for, as Schiller famously observes in the 15th letter, "humanity (*der Mensch*) only plays in the full meaning of this word when it is human and is only fully human when it plays" (618).

Letters 17–27

In the final grouping of letters Schiller descends, as he puts it, "from the region of ideas to the arena of visible reality" (622). It is in this arena that the project of education announced in the title of Schiller's inquiry as an answer to the political problem with which the inquiry began is finally articulated. At this point in the *Letters*, it is incumbent on Schiller to explain how the formal insights of the middle section of letters gain traction in the realm of concrete human experience, in respect of which, as with any work of education, questions of practice are front and centre. A metaphysical approach might respond to this need by transposing the reconciliation of drives through play to a "higher" realm of ideas. The elevation of humanity by way of beauty would be brought to light, in this case, in a theoretical realm where the true, the good and the beautiful would co-mingle. Schiller, however, professes no interest in such a solution, and his "transcendental" approach renders it, in any case, moot. The transcendental approach, for its part, while eliminating the "two worlds" issue of metaphysics, must still explain how a brokering of opposites under the aspect of beauty is practically grounded in the here-and-now and secures its successes. Schiller's response to this desideratum in the 18th and 19th letters is ingenious and has accrued significance in the history of philosophy, providing the groundwork for Hegel's dialectic. Schiller stabilises the connection between form and sense—the two "eternally" opposed drives in humanity—in reference to the new notion of *Aufhebung* or "sublation". As he explains:

> [B]eauty binds [*verbindet*] the two opposed conditions [of sense and form] and thereby cancels [*hebt ... auf*] their opposition. However, since both conditions remain eternally opposed, they are not bound in any other way than by being sublated [*aufgehoben*]. (SW 5: 625, my translation)

While reciprocal action allows the distinctiveness of individual drives to be realised, the mechanism of sublation under the aegis of the play drive allows the varying determinations of beauty these drives promote to be secured (Schiller calls such determinations "melting beauty" and "dynamic beauty", though perhaps there are also others). These determinations represent concrete contributions to the "aesthetic culture" (635) of humanity. Aesthetic culture, to this extent, again looking ahead to Hegel, is historical culture and vice versa.

In a key passage in the 20th letter, Schiller finally reclaims the true goal of his inquiry—a response to Kant's moral law—by adducing the dynamic agency of a medial voice or mood he calls *Stimmung*. In a passage that is professedly only an augmentation of Kant's moral theory but could equally be regarded as its refutation, emotion is shifted onto the plane of rational thought not because of the primacy of the latter over the former, but because sensuality and reason, individually and together, are optimised and brought to their highest fulfilment. Driving this fulfilment, as with Schiller's thought more generally, is the indispensable factor of human freedom. Schiller thinks of the medial agency, for this reason, as a free modality (*eine freie Stimmung*). The condition of "real and active determinability" it brings about is then called the "aesthetic condition" (633). The aesthetic condition, precisely because its disposition is open and determinable, is in turn susceptible to influence and therefore education, though, admittedly, such open "determinability" could serve poorer ends as well as better ones. The focus of "aesthetic education" naturally falls on the positivity of the latter, and in this regard the "true work of art" (638) is a talisman. Schiller underscores art's connection to the "ideals of aesthetic purity", though, as he also points out, such ideals are never actually attained, at best only approximated (ibid.; Frank's thesis of "endless approximation" in regard to the goals of early German Romanticism is thus anticipated in Schiller [cf. Frank 1998]).

In this last section of the final grouping of letters, Schiller is at pains to describe the pitfalls as well as the virtues of aesthetic culture. As Schiller maintains of the mid-zone of the aesthetic condition in the 21st letter (SW 5: 635), no warrantable knowledge is discovered, no belief ratified. Nor do things look better in the domain of morality, for here it is equally the case that no single moral duty in the aesthetic condition is spelled out, no head indubitably cured of its prejudices (635). The value to be had from a program of aesthetic education pertains solely to the esteem and dignity that accrue to the individual person (ibid). For the allure of warrantable knowledge and the certainty of a moral principle, then, Schiller offers something less tangible but perhaps ultimately of greater worth: a vision of individuals in possession of the secret of their own value—a "poetic" learning more than a "philosophical" one (cf. 636).

Reviewing the last letters in Schiller's essay on aesthetic education, Pollok, following Sharpe (1995), is moved to pose this vital question: "Did art become the goal of our development, or is it a means to an end?" (Pollok 2019, 220). Put another way, how does Schiller finally settle the question of art's purpose as a social and moral activity? A study of the *Letters* suggests two contrasting ways of responding to this question (cf. Tauber 2006). The first way is consistent with the Kantian view that art is a means to a moral end, and, in the final analysis, no more than that. In the final letters, where Schiller lays out a map of human progress over time and thus something like a conceptual anthropology, Schiller provides encouragement for the Kantian view through his characterisation of the challenge that human beings face in life: they must transit from "sensual dependence to moral freedom" through beauty (654); there is "no other way to make the sensual human being rational except by making him aesthetic first of all" (641). These statements suggest amity with Kant's position that art provides vivid illustration of the indispensability of the moral law without its commanding an independent capacity to make moral pronouncements. The contribution art can make to morality, accordingly, is strictly limited.

The second response to the question of art's value and purpose becomes transparent over the final stretches of Schiller's inquiry. This response maintains that art is the vanishing point of all human endeavour (cf. Bykova 2020, who reads the *Letters* in this spirit). In the 23rd letter, for example, Schiller refers to the transition from the "suffering condition of emotion to the active [condition] of thought and will [...] through an intermediate condition of aesthetic freedom" (641). Yet this "intermediate" condition is not said to lapse or be replaced by any other mode or condition. In this vein, Schiller notes in the 25th letter that the task at hand is "no longer a question of how the human being moves from beauty to truth, which according to its faculty is already found in the former, but how the human being follows a path from a lower [*gemeinen*] reality to aesthetic reality" (655). This path to aesthetic reality is considered "decisive" for human beings. It is made possible by a crucial step into "aesthetic semblance" that, in turn, allows a program of aesthetic education to be brought into being (656–7). While aesthetic education might appear optional, a choice among many approaches to the education of humans, Schiller conceives of it as the motor of cultural development and the driver of the interests of humanity—nothing, in short, that can be ignored or left by the wayside. Thus, if the first way of determining art's value and social purpose proceeds along a philosophical route, the second in its main outline is poetical and no longer observes the protocols and commitments of philosophical argumentation—nor means to.

In view of these conflicting reports in the *Letters* about the purpose of aesthetic judgement and aesthetic experience, the question of whether art in Schiller's argument is the goal of human social development or merely a means to a better moral outcome for humanity appears unresolved. The reader of the *Aesthetic Letters* is entitled to reach the conclusion that Schiller himself remained undecided, or else was unable to finish the bridge from aesthetics to ethics he had set about constructing. In his last responses to Kant in the *Letters* there is seemingly still hedging and qualification: aesthetic semblance is "permitted" in the moral world "insofar as semblance desires neither to represent reality nor be represented by it"; aesthetic semblance can be trusted "not to endanger the truth of morals" (660). As this hedging suggests, Schiller is unable to answer Kant on Kant's own ground, which is to say, to provide a cogent philosophical response to Kant's moral rigorism.

Yet this finding does not exhaust the obligation Schiller feels to his own position, nor does it provide a satisfactory response to the "political problem" with which his inquiry began. This task is acquitted in the final letters in the form of an anthropological and political argument that discusses the requirements for a free society. Here the ordering of essentials undergoes a striking modification. While the "dynamic state (*Staat*)" only makes society "possible" and the "ethical state" only renders moral necessity available, it is now the "aesthetic state (*Staat*)" that appears in the third position at the endpoint of human aspirations, for only this state can make society "real (*wirklich*)" (667). A paradoxical outcome is thus highlighted at the end of the Schiller's inquiry:

art, which is made from semblance and illusion, is revealed to be more productive of reality in its consequences than other forms and capacities, because only the appearance of beauty—the beauty the artwork necessarily cultivates in order to be art—has the capacity to make wholes and thus also whole societies. As Schiller notes, doubtless with a sideways glance towards Kant, "all other forms of communication divide society" (667). That the "aesthetic state" not only augments the work of the "ethical state" in accordance with the governorship of the human, but is destined one day to replace it, is the clear implication of Schiller's final letter on "aesthetic education".

Philosophical Significance and Impact

Detailed consideration of the impact of Schiller's *Letters on Aesthetic Education* on later thought would run to many hundreds of pages. This impact, accordingly, can only be briefly sketched here.

The significance of the *Letters* has been broadly of three types. The first concerns the value the *Letters* have held for theorists of education, starting with Wilhelm von Humboldt, one of several high-calibre interlocutors with whom Schiller engaged during his years in Jena. Humboldt's philosophy of education, for which the notion of *Bildung* ("formation" or "self-formation") is pivotal (von Humboldt 2017), is indebted to the account of free energetic selfhood that Schiller developed in the *Aesthetic Letters*. Later educationalists such as the American philosopher John Dewey also drew inspiration from the *Letters*. Dewey's major work *Art as Experience* (2005/1934), one of the most important contributions to educational theory in the last one hundred years, could not have been written without Schiller's foundational work on aesthetic education in the *Letters*. The contributions of more recent philosophers of education such as Gert Biesta have emerged out of the rich heritage bequeathed to posterity by Schiller, Humboldt and Dewey (e.g., Biesta 2014).

A second type of influence concerns the construction of Schiller's argument in the *Letters*. Such influence may be looked upon as mainly methodological. Of many later philosophers to have drawn lessons from Schiller from this quarter, as indicated above, was Hegel (1970/1807), whose use of dialectic was adapted directly from Schiller's transcendental method in the middle grouping of letters. Others to have made a formal use of Schiller's argument in the *Letters* include Nietzsche, whose dichotomy of Dionysus and Apollo in *The Birth of Tragedy* (2021/1872) is reminiscent of Schiller's contrast between form (as rational intellect) and sense (or sensuality). The similarities here pertain especially to the central role commanded by art as the driver and mediator of human experience.

A third level of influence concerns what might be called Schiller's "philosophical attitude" in the *Letters*. Schiller may be looked upon, in this context, as a pioneer of the "continental" style of philosophical argumentation, an approach which views thought and philosophy as embedded in, and dependent upon, both language and history. If this contribution to the tradition of continental philosophy is given credence, Schiller must be included in the pantheon of thinkers who have exercised influence on all later moderns. Among those who have expressly acknowledged such influence are hermeneutic philosophers such as Hans-Georg Gadamer (2004/1960) and philosophically oriented psychologists such as Carl Jung (1921). The list of writers with philosophical interests whose work recurs to Schiller directly or indirectly is long, beginning with the German Romantics in the early nineteenth century (see discussion in this volume) and extending through to J. M. Coetzee in the early twenty-first century. Coetzee's Jesus trilogy (2013–19), which is vitally concerned with the question of aesthetic education, may be taken as evidence of Schiller's continuing importance for the thought of today.

References

Biesta, G.J.J. 2014. *The Beautiful Risk of Education*. Boulder: Paradigm Publishers.
Bondeli, Martin. 2019. In: Gideon Stiening (ed.): *Friedrich Schiller: Über die Ästhetische Erziehung des Menschen in einer Reihe von Briefen*. Berlin/Boston: 2019.
Burke, Edmund. 2003 (1790). *Reflections on the Revolution in France*. Ed. Frank M. Turner. New Haven: Yale UP.
Bykova, Marina F. 2020. "Friedrich Schiller and the Aestheticization of Ethics." In: Elizabeth Millán Brusslan (ed.): *The Palgrave Handbook of German Romantic Philosophy*. Cham, Switzerland: Palgrave Macmillan, 157–176
Coetzee, J.M. (2013–19). *The Childhood of Jesus/The Schooldays of Jesus/The Death of Jesus*. London: Vintage.
Dewey, John. 2005 (1934). *Art as Experience*. London: Penguin.
Frank, Manfred (1998). *"Unendliche Annäherung". Die Anfänge der philosophischen Frühromantik*. Berlin: Suhrkamp.
Gadamer, Hans-Georg. 2004. *Truth and Method*. London/New York: Continuum.
Hegel, G.W.F. 1970 (1807). *Phänomenologie des Geistes*. Frankfurt: Suhrkamp.
Humboldt, Wilhelm von. 2017. *Schriften zur Bildung*. Ed. Gerhardt Lauer. Stuttgart: Reclam.
Jung, C.J. 1921. *Psychologische Typen*. Zürich: Rascher Verlag.
Löwe, Matthias, and Stiening, Gideon (eds). 2021. *Ästhetische Staaten: Ethik, Recht und Politik in Schillers Werk*. Baden-Baden: Nomos Verlagsgesellschaft.
Mehigan, Tim. 2020. "The 'Unexpected Science' of the *Briefe über die Ästhetische Erziehung des Menschen*." In: *Kant-Studien*. Vol. 111, no. 2, 285–302.
Nietzsche, Friedrich. 2021 (1872). *The Birth of Tragedy: Out of the Spirit of Music*. London: Penguin Classics.
Pollok, Anne. 2019. "A Further Meditation and the Setting of Limits: The Concept of Aesthetic Semblance and the Aesthetic State." In: Stiening, Gideon (ed.): *Friedrich Schiller: Über die Ästhetische Erziehung des Menschen in einer Reihe von Briefen*. Berlin/Boston: 2019, 219–235.
Riedel, Wolfgang (ed.). 2004. *Friedrich Schiller: Sämtliche Werke*. Vol. 5. München: Deutscher Taschenbuchverlag.

Ross, Nathan. 2017. *The Philosophy and Politics of Aesthetic Experience: German Romanticism and Critical Theory.* Cham: Palgrave Macmillan.

Rousseau, Jean-Jacques. 1992 (1750). *Discourse on the Sciences and Arts and Polemics.* Dartmouth: Dartmouth College Press.

Safranski, Rüdiger. 2016. *Schiller oder: Die Erfindung des Deutschen Idealismus.* Frankfurt am Main: Fischer Taschenbuch.

Sharpe, Leslie. 1995. *Schiller's Aesthetic Essays: Two Centuries of Criticism.* Rochester NY: Camden House.

Stiening, Gideon (ed.). 2019. *Friedrich Schiller: Über die Ästhetische Erziehung does Menschen in einer Reihe von Briefen.* Berlin/Boston.

Tauber, Zvi. 2006. "Aesthetic Education for Morality: Schiller and Kant." In: *Journal of Aesthetic Education.* Vol. 40, no. 3, 22–47.

Ziolkowski, Theodore (1998). *Das Wunderjahr in Jena. Geist und Gesellschaft 1794/95.* Stuttgart, Klett-Cotta.

CHAPTER 14

Concerning the Necessary Limits in the Use of Beautiful Forms (1795)

Anne Pollok

The essay "On the Necessary Limits in the Use of Beautiful Forms" is a combination of two shorter pieces published in the 9th and 11th piece of Schiller's *Horen* in 1795.[1] Whereas the first piece deals with the dangers of merely beautiful forms regarding theoretical knowledge, in the latter piece Schiller discusses the sometimes negative impact of beautiful forms in morality.[2] The former concerns the theoretical, the second the practical dimension of an adequate aesthetic education. Together, they are also supposed to strengthen Schiller's stance in the so-called *Horenstreit* with Fichte: here, Schiller seeks to show to what degree a beautiful packaging of philosophical thoughts is beneficial (which would be: his style in the *Aesthetic Education*), and when it merely masks a rather problematic stance (as Schiller accuses Fichte of proposing in his submission to the *Horen: Ueber Geist und Buchstab in der Philosophie. In einer Reihe von Briefen*, which in turn accuses Schiller of misusing his aesthetically pleasing presentation to hide conceptual insecurities). I will not discuss the *Horenstreit* in much detail, as it is the topic of another paper (see here Chap. 28). I rather wish to show, first, in what sense Schiller's position in "On the

---

[1] The final, combined version first appeared in Schiller's *Kleineren prosaischen Schriften* in 1800.
[2] This piece is closest to Wilhelm von Humboldt's critique of a Kantian rigorism that he published in Schiller's *Neue Thalia* in 1792.

A. Pollok (✉)
Johannes Gutenberg Universität Mainz, Mainz, Germany
e-mail: apollok@uni-mainz.de

Necessary Limits" supports and extends the exposition of the notions of aesthetic semblance and the aesthetic state in the *Aesthetic Education*. By drawing the limits of the usage of beautiful forms to make a content more amicable to us, Schiller clarifies the boundaries of beautiful semblance, a concept that oscillates between an idea of "beautifying crude reality" and indeed "masking ulterior motives." Only the latter, which Schiller excludes now more explicitly from aesthetic use supports manipulation rather than the emergence of an adequately educated human being. Hence, the first question I ask is: do the necessary limits that Schiller establishes in his essay succeed in clarifying the use and function of aesthetic semblance?

The second question I will ask here is rather different. In "On the Necessary Limits," Schiller also limits women to the area of "taste" instead of knowledge, thus relegating learned women to the sidelines of any serious literary discussion, marking them as mere "dilletantes" (and negating the concept of a female academic altogether). Can we read this essay, then, as an argument for a gender-specific structuring of the literary market?

Semblance and the Supposed Absoluteness of the Aesthetic State

In Letter 26 of the *Aesthetic Education* Schiller announces that he will treat the necessary limits of beautiful form separately, so as to offer a more in-depth discussion of cases in which beauty usurps truth and goodness to their mutual harm. As Schiller states in Letter 26, it is a true sign of culture once we can afford to be impervious toward reality and take an interest in aesthetic semblance and play (see AE 656), as it shows our external freedom from material needs, but also an inner freedom of mental strength: first, because we can create something for the sake of itself; second because we are and stay aware of the artificiality of semblance, even while we are thoroughly immersed in it. Schiller thus distinguishes beautiful semblance from logical semblance, only the latter as a deception that explicitly aims at presenting a (mutilated) reality as truth. Sometimes, reason becomes overzealous and tries to ban each and any sort of semblance from our world (we might want to think of Plato's argumentation in the *Republic*[3])—and hence, so Schiller, it is important to deal with the necessary limits of semblance in particular elsewhere. This "elsewhere" is "On the Necessary Limits."

Beautiful forms are a particular kind of *Wechselwirkung*, a mode of interplay between the two drives, sense and formal drive (*Stoff- und Formtrieb*) he introduced in the "transcendental" part of the *Aesthetic Education*, Letters 10–16. In their harmonious interaction they both fulfill their original determining

[3] As Schiller did in Letter 10, AE 597.

function, but also allow the respective other drive to determine what they themselves left undetermined. In such a coordination, everything is indeed determined, but this determination is not visible or palpable: it feels natural, purposive, and hence, free. It is beautiful semblance that masks this mutual determination.

In "On the Necessary Limits" Schiller deals with one issue that emerges from the necessity of this interplay. Since this interplay comes with a feeling of completion,[4] this very feeling might become the ground on which we want to decide on the truth of a statement, or the moral adequacy of a certain action. However, the feeling shall not be the determining ground in order to see the truth and do good, but the truth and the good themselves should be. Truth, ultimately, generates from a lawful harmony of perceptions (NL 670), distinct concepts, and principles (NL 672). We can still seek to present a true content beautifully (and maybe also in a popular manner), even though the final ground for the truthfulness of our claims lies in the content, not its form. For the good, Schiller reiterates Kant's standpoint according to which the emotional state does not matter as long as the act is done out of respect for the law (NL 670 and 688). But, as in the *Aesthetic Education* (and also in earlier works such as *Über Anmuth und Würde*[5]), Schiller was unhappy with an all-too rigorous interpretation of Kant's position, according to which a human being would have to suppress their emotions completely, as only in contradistinction to their feelings such a human being would ever act morally (which would be the conception of the "sublime human being" in the Letters, see #23, AE 645). Instead, Schiller advocates a propensity to act out of the moral law that also is enjoyable for the agent: the *edle Mensch*, the noble soul, who not only seeks personal happiness, but wants to improve her whole world (AE 644). Ideally, the noble soul is a being perfectly combining reason and sensibility, not one that must subject the latter to the former. However, as he stresses in the "Necessary Limits," the final say should be with morality or truth—as otherwise the delicate harmony established by aesthetic play destabilizes our higher faculties and turns into a hidden dictatorship of the sensible apparatus. Or, in other words, we might end up becoming barbarians after all, who mask their baser drives behind a fancy facade.

In this sense, as Schiller argues in the *Aesthetic Education*, the adequate application of beautiful semblance is indeed an indicator of the level of our culture. We enjoy a specific form of appearance—but, if we are of the appropriately cultured mind, we prefer aesthetic semblance over mere illusions that hide the object just to delight the eye. Such a joy in illusions is all-too short-lived. It is misguided, as it does not really help us to deal with reality but instead lures us to avoid it altogether. Schiller argues that aesthetic semblance is of higher

---

[4] An excellent discussion on the desire for wholeness is by Gardner 2018.
[5] See here Chap. 2.7

worth than mere illusion in that it stems from a beautiful *form*[6] (and not for the merely sensually pleasing absence of coercion): form does not negate matter, but elevates it to a true unity with the intellect. Beautiful form hence balances appearance and reality; it allows for a more complete experience, where sensibility and reason, but also the imagination are involved.

However, Schiller is quite aware of the fact that a stress on aesthetic semblance has its dangers. Beauty is Janus-faced: it can be used to highlight something, balance something out, but also to hide. In a letter to Friederike Oeser from the 13th of February 1769, Goethe calls beauty "cross-eyed" (see WW 328): it gives birth to truth and untruth simultaneously. Thinkers of the Late Enlightenment such as Sulzer and Mendelssohn read semblance (*Schein*) and illusion (*Täuschung*) synonymously and stress the beneficial effects of such illusions that offer the possibility of enjoying emotions without having to experience their real causes (e.g. we weep for the dead on the stage without losing a loved one). Kant's famous distinction between noumena and phenomena stresses the difference between appearance (phenomenon) and illusion: the appearance of all objects of possible experience is guided by the laws of our faculty of representation (*Vorstellungsvermögen*) and hence is as true as our recognition of any noumenon can be. Illusion, on the other hand, is restricted to the realm of art: it offers us appearances that claim to be something different (e.g. a two-dimensional painting can offer the illusion of three-dimensional depth). These we can (and should) enjoy disinterestedly: not for the sake of their reality, but for their form. As Schiller himself was aware, a concentration of the appearance or form of things has its dangers. In Letter 10 of the *Aesthetic Education*, he references the lure of illusion[7] that might cause a deterioration into decadence. In Letters 15 and 26, however, Schiller references the term "semblance" positively.[8] As long as we are concerned with the appearance and form of things, we view them aesthetically. In particular the stress on form bends the view back onto ourselves, in a way, as the capacity to recognize form is due to the power of our reflective power. Our joy in form is our joy in ourselves as form-giving agents: this joy cannot be decadence, but the true emergence of an important aspect of our humanity, as it allows us to access the intellectual realm—and bind the sensible and intelligible together.

---

[6] Shape 1995, 161–162 offers a wonderful definition of form: "By form Schiller means the artistic shaping of the material such that it is the vehicle for a response to the world, a sense of how the world is experienced, in a way that allows the observer the opportunity to perceive and contemplate that response. The subject matter is consumed (or abolished, to translate more literally) but the art object has sensuous reality and through its form conveys to us a particular sense of life."

[7] Schiller uses the terms *Schönheit, reizende Einkleidung der Wirklichkeit, Erscheinung*, and, with the most negative connotation, *Politur* (AE 598–99), but not the later *Schein* in letter 10. For a comprehensive overview, see WW 328–30.

[8] Letter 15 *freieste und erhabenste Schein* (AE 618).

The Whole Human Being: Human Vocation Versus Pure Morality

In the *Aesthetic Education*, Schiller leaves open how this free use is still guided by laws (and by which laws in particular). In "Necessary Limits", he now ventures to discuss this aspect. Right at the beginning, Schiller argues that such a limitation must be privy to the one general goal of all human endeavors—"to gain knowledge and to act according to it" (NL 670). Schiller once again reaches back to the Enlightenment's discussion of the "human vocation," calling for an encompassing development of our higher faculties with decisive help from the lower ones. We should therefore take note, with Gardner (2018, 240–41), that Schiller reaches this overarching view of freedom (both within reason and within nature) through a more encompassing view, which is reflected in the various "non-equivalent distinctions" (ibid.) which Schiller offers throughout the *Aesthetic Education*. The "Necessary Limits" are an apt continuation of this method, as he here clarifies the various styles of writing (or presenting in general) that cover all forms of meaningful transmission of content, harmonizing or at least mediating between the concrete and abstract, freedom and necessity, form and content, thinking and feeling, concept and intuition, proof and result. The continuous (and sometimes somewhat nausea-inducing) oscillation in between these dualisms is on purpose and should not be overcome, turning into angelic morality or wise learnedness alone. It is true that in NL Schiller urges to ultimately give the key to our thoughts and actions to reason and morality. But at the same time, he insists on the power and importance of the so-called lower faculties: our body, sensibility, sensuality even, and also our nature. While he first concentrates on the adequate mediation of philosophical thought (thus defending his own philosophical style against the likes of Fichte, see Sect. 2), it also becomes clear that he defends the importance of aesthetically relevant "mutual action"—*Wechselwirkung*—as a mode of being that is adequate for us as humans.[9]

Schiller also distinguishes the style of writing according to the occasion—whether the author aims at a popular or a learned presentation, or whether he[10] wants to aesthetically please the audience. The limits of beautiful form of course differ in respect to these goals. Whereas a learned presentation must aim at clearly presenting concepts and allowing for a rational understanding that can follow (and re-create) all reasons given for the overall argument, thus aiming at a proof of necessity, a popular presentation rests on an emotional impact, where we are not given clear and exact reasons, but reach the presenter's conclusion by a feeling of assent. Popular writing aims at presenting the material as possible and desirable (NL 677). The distinction between these two is expressed by

---

[9] For a similar argument albeit concerning a different set of texts see Deligiorgi 2013, in particular p. 75.

[10] For the time being, the choice of the male pronoun is deliberate. Schiller allows the female writer on certain occasions, but, as I will argue in part 5, these are rather limited.

the German distinction between the merely rhetorical *Überredung* versus rational *Überzeugung*: the aim to merely cajole you into believing a certain instance versus the aim to rationally convince you.

However, Schiller makes it quite clear that popular presentation does not need to fall prey to the negative judgment that we connect with mere cajoling, as a popular presentation—to be not only convincing, but also good—should also fulfill the criteria of beauty: the presentation must be more than merely didactic, but has to combine "*sensibility in its expression*" and "*freedom in its motion*" (NL 674). This pretty much covers what Schiller had called, as early as in the *Kallias Letters*, "freedom in appearance" (*Freiheit in der Erscheinung*, KL 409). A sensible presentation offers a concrete, lively picture instead of a bare, abstract concept—in this way, such a presentation is richer (in that it offers something concrete that is thoroughly determined), but also more limited (in that the reach of a concept is broader, see NL 675). In such an engaging presentation, so Schiller, the imagination is relatively free. Generally, imagination seeks completely determined perceptions and wants to present the full image within a concrete case; it wants to "give a body to the abstract" (NL 672). This inclination is what the popular author feeds. However, this does not allow him just to gloss over everything: even he has to know the fundamental structure of things, and must first analyze what he sets out to present. But in contrast to the learned author he has to hide this analysis in his presentation (see NL 672–75) to allow the imagination of his listeners or readers to roam freely within the offered material.[11] The freedom of the imagination (here, Schiller presents it even as an *arbitrariness*, see NL 672–73, 675) has to step back in the learned presentation to allow the reader or listener to understand and follow the reasonable connections between concepts and arguments. The clear advantage of the popular presentation is that it is engaging and concrete, colorful and rich for the imagination; this renders it, however, only reproductive, and somewhat poor and one-sided for our reason (NL 675). Only the beautiful presentation could help out here, in that it would cloak the reasoned parts in beautiful illusionary dresses—but then again, this is not desirable in each and every aspect, as it could make us too used to linking a beautiful outside to a true inside.

Truly beautiful diction (NL 676) is of course hard to reach, as it offers the imagination all the connection that it seeks, but also leaves it free to roam among these connections at its own inclination. In contrast to popular presentation, a beautiful diction does not seek to present its content as real, but only as possible (NL 677); it has to regard our sensations and emotions (so that we come to wish for the truth of a thing, but are ultimately satisfied with a creation that stimulates our imagination alone). In this sense, beautiful diction is adequate when we do not have a heightened *interest* in the truths of its presentation (NL 677)—as beautiful (and popular) diction only lends us a cognition,

---

[11] Or at least seemingly freely—as Iris Murdoch stressed in an interview with Bryan Magee in 1978, philosophy clarifies, literature mystifies.

but does not justify us having it. This is the reason why Schiller does not want all too engaging and beautiful presentation of content for the education of the youth (NL 679), as the students should be aware of the dutiful and sometimes painful tiny steps that need to be taken in order to arrive at a justified conclusion. This is also the reason why he asks his friendly supporter, the Duke of Augustenburg, to suffer through a more or less scholarly presentation of his ideas regarding the aesthetic education: an education which shall allow beautiful semblance its necessary place in our lives, but which in itself is not necessarily beautiful (and easy) at all. In the end, the proof for an aesthetic education cannot be beautiful in itself, but Schiller must justify why beauty is of such importance.

In the "Necessary Limits," Schiller thus explains and justifies the seeming paradox why his *Aesthetic Education* is not as nicely written as one might expect a poet to do, and also why his insistence on a full development of our sensible and imaginative capacities is not tantamount to replacing the textbook by the novel in the education of the youth. With this, Schiller also takes a public stance against Fichte.

Disagreement with Fichte and Beautiful Education

The actual disagreement with Fichte—as much as Schiller references Fichte's works in the *Aesthetic Education*[12]—begins after its publication, with Schiller's rejection to publish his colleague's *Ueber Geist und Buchstab in der Philosophie. In einer Reihe von Briefen* in the *Horen*. It is quite obvious just by the title that Fichte intended this piece as a continuation of Schiller's work—or we should better say: as a correction, as Fichte rejects Schiller's dualism of drives in order to return to his original theory, which takes the "I" not as one part of the equation, but as an absolute as the highest principle that expresses itself by the different drives, and that becomes visible by the *Wechselwirkung* between these. For Fichte, the I is not the person (as for Schiller, see AE, Letter 11), but the "determined I" which has its ground in the "absolute I." Both "person" and *Zustand* are accidents (*Accidenzen*) of the absolute I; whereas Schiller conceptualizes the I as one part of the equation, facing the material, passive, determining *Stofftrieb*, and their mutual action/*Wechselwirkung* allowing for a true harmony of nature and reason/will.

But as Beiser argues very convincingly,[13] the dispute with Fichte starts as early as Letters 4 and 13, in which Schiller develops his view of culture in contradistinction to Fichte. He hides this contrast by first directing us toward his problem with Kant's insistence that reason shall trump sensibility in all moral issues, using Fichte's term *Wechselwirkung* in a positive light, and also in highlighting two of Fichte' works that are important for our understanding of

---

[12] See on this, Chap. 5.3 with further references.
[13] Beiser 2005, 144–47, in contradistinction to Hans-Georg Pott: *Die schöne Freiheit*. München: Fink 1980.

Schiller's stance: the *Wissenschaftslehre* of 1794 and the *Vocation of the Scholar* (1794). Whereas Fichte defended a view on culture that turned upon the development of our rationality as a truly universal attribute—which ultimately elevates the individual up into the universal, a single infinite being—Schiller's approach is indebted to his anthropologically inclined predecessors such as Sulzer and Mendelssohn.[14] Taking up the thought he developed in early writings such as his second dissertation, Schiller assumes that the highest point in culture is reached when we developed *all* our capacities. This means also that we must include our sensibility instead of suppressing and eradicating it. Not the complete overcoming of nature in order to be the free angel, but the perfect inclusion of nature within our rationality is Schiller's (and not Fichte's) goal (see Beiser 2005, 146).

But Schiller's rejection of Fichte has a material, as discussed, and a formal dimension. While we only have sketches of the rejection letter that Schiller sent to Fichte and which sparked the *Horenstreit*, we know that Schiller reasons as follows: Fichte's doctrine of three drives seems arbitrary, as it lacks a reasonable justification (a *Einteilungsgrund*, GA III/2, 334). Moreover, Fichte omits the sense drive (sinnlicher Trieb; which fits well to the aforementioned structure of cultural development designed to supersede sensibility); and, lastly, function and range of the aesthetic drive in Fichte's view remain unclear. But additionally, Schiller rejects Fichte's piece on formal grounds: he diagnoses an unhealthy mixture of scientific-philosophical and artistic presentation that hinders any comprehension. Schiller, in the "Necessary Limits," preemptively tries to showcase the dangers of inadequate styles of presentation, and give a typology of adequate styles for different goals. If the whole human being should be addressed, brain and heart, reason and sensibility must both be engaged. This necessitates a careful balance between scholarly and popular presentation, allowing for both abstraction and imaginative representation.

Fichte had criticized Schiller's concept of imagination in the *Letters*, claiming that Schiller tried to make imagination think.[15] In the "Necessary Limits" Schiller indeed seems to accept this difference between understanding and imagination—and calls for their necessary *cooperation* relative to the respective aim of the genre. Apart from the imagination's tendency to individualize the universal, Schiller also stresses its genuine productive quality for rational understanding. A representation that combines understanding with imagination captures us—through sensuous expression and the freedom of its movement (NL 674). It is free because it hides the lawfulness of the inner relation of ideas and thus avoids a reduction to a fixed set of such ideas. It offers a sensible presentation in that the universal is presented in the particular, without confining the richness of the universal, nor abandoning the distinctiveness of the individual.

---

[14] See on this Pollok 2010, 8–9, 241–43, 351–53 and Pollok 2020, 282–83.

[15] Fichte writes in a letter from June 27, 1795: "You chain the power of imagination—which can only be free—and want to force it to think—which it cannot do." FW I,2, p. 399, see Martinson 1996, 206 and Allen Wood: *Fichte's Ethical Thought*, Oxford 2016, 1–28.

Both aspects reiterate Schiller's main ideas in the last two letters: the imagination gives us aesthetic semblance that covers sensible and rational necessity, and that enables the representative function of an individual form to capture and educate us about more universal issues without us even realizing this. This holds true for a beautiful presentation if and only if the creator of said presentation can combine (through ratiocination or creative genius) the truth of content with the perfection of form. And hence, we cannot just trust any beautiful form to educate us, but must limit the usage of beautiful form by reference to the adequacy of its creator. Clearly, Schiller thought of himself of being capable of this, whereas he had his doubts in regard to Fichte (whom he critiques mainly for the lacking foundation—that the packaging also left something to be desired is an unfortunate side effect).

Left by itself, the imagination would just jump from impression to impression, resulting in chaos and confusion. True beauty, as Schiller argues in the "Necessary Limits," is a cooperation between understanding and imagination: it is grounded in "strict determination, the most exact differentiation, and the greatest inner necessity" (Martinson 1996, 209), none of which, however, is forced onto the artist, but springs from their mind naturally (NL 680). Thus, we are closer to the final mediation between imagination and reason that Schiller envisions in the preparation of humanity for its true destiny, as a true community of free souls, in the *Aesthetic Education*. What Schillers offers is a "spelling out" of how exactly beauty can offer a comprehensive account on truth. The crux of the issue is, now, that beautiful presentation is not the same as didactic presentation: the former puts the stress on the comprehensive view of the whole that engages the imagination, the latter guides the student through the structure of this comprehensive view.

However, beauty is not supposed to be excluded from the classroom altogether, as students should be encouraged to communicate what they have learned in an imaginative way (NL 682–83). Only that knowledge that we can bring to life through our artful presentation is a knowledge that we truly have: they are not only part of our reason, but of our will and life as well.

Beauty and Goodness

The problem is heightened in the area of morality, as "belletristic power of choice" (*belletristische Willkürlichkeit*, NL 687) of thinking might lead to mistakes and obscures the mind, but arbitrariness in our maxims is *evil* (NL 688). If we allow taste to become the determinate factor in our maxims, we ultimately resign the will to our feelings and sensibility.

Schiller stresses the problematic difference between our conscience that presents our maxims as a *feeling* of duty, and taste, which can operate outside of such maxims—but still impresses on the mind a feeling for a certain decision, which is just not based on our respect for the law, but our enjoyment of beautiful form (or a mere feeling that we tend to heighten as a "feeling of reason"). Again, as in the *Aesthetic Education*, Schiller situates this problem within the (modern) barbarian, who got used to act in accordance to a supposedly dutiful feeling, but ended up misusing the concept of duty to fulfill more base needs. Schiller illustrates this in the conflict of perfect and imperfect duties, a concept taken from modern natural law à la Pufendorf, Grotius, and Thomasius, perfected by Mendelssohn and Kant, according to which our duties can be ranked from those that are necessitated to those that we can fulfill out of love (or more strongly, that cannot be prescribed by an external force), or which need a previous assent to become perfect duties (for particular cases between particular people). Some people, so Schiller, convince themselves that they have to go against one duty in order to fulfill a higher one. But what they actually do is that they harm an imperfect duty for a perfect one—they ultimately gave in to their baser proclivities at the expense of a true duty. But instead of realizing this, they blind themselves to such harmful developments and insist on the necessity of a well-rounded feeling for *and* knowledge of their duties, or, to speak with Schiller, they insist on aligning an affect with the (moral) "feeling" of respect (*Achtung*, NL 690). These are the cases where the barbarian just masks their inclinations by a pretend-duty, allowing for even baser sins—and sins that are evil, due to our awareness of them as such—than the somewhat innocent, artless, or thoughtless brutality of the savage.

Schiller appreciates necessity and chance, but he agrees with Kant that arbitrary, non-essential aspects shall not become the necessary condition of the good. In other words: that something feels right is not enough, and hence mere beauty cannot make us moral all by itself—the aesthetic education is still in need of the support by nature, and by mature and responsible artists.

With this, Schiller also problematizes an ordinary understanding of the term "respect"—respect for the law is indeed a feeling connected to reason, but it is also a feeling that is dangerously close to others, such as love, which cannot ascertain the moral worth of an action. Schiller here argues against a justification of means by ends: "the ideal of political happiness can be realized by the horrors of anarchy; we can get rid of laws to make way for better ones; we should not hesitate to make current generations miserable for the sake of future ones"[16] (NL 692). Reasoning like this is never going to work; we rather try go beyond reason and be more reasonable than reason itself (ibid.). This trait is particularly bad because it works unconsciously—we delude ourselves into thinking this way *as being reasonable*, and become unable to return to a proper sense for "respect."

Once again we are faced with a problem here: even though Schiller proposes an aesthetic education, it is quite clear that in most cases the educator has to be very careful in their use of beautiful forms, so that they are employed adequately (see on this Liebsch 2017, 25, 209–11). The interconnection of

---

[16] We have to say that in particular for this last one, nowadays the moral dilemma strikes us rather the other way: current generations cannot stop indulging themselves since they just cannot feel the need to spare anything for future generations. But this is another issue that Schiller could not quite have anticipated.

beautiful semblance and artistic genius cannot be the main topic here, but we should remember that the ultimate limit is set by a true artist who truly discovers the idealizing and lightening mode of art.

> Yes, thank [the muse] that she plays the moody image
> Of truth over to the cheerful realm of art.
> She destroys the illusion which she herself created
> honestly, and she plants her semblance
> onto truth, not aiming to hide her.
> Life is serious, yet art is cheerful.[17]

The Problem of the Dilettante: Schiller's Attempt at Keeping the Women at Bay

Still within his discussion of the theoretical benefits of a limitation of beautiful form, Schiller references the fair sex, which may have access to truth in general, but only through the medium of beautiful form, not through reason or science (NL 683). Whereas for men, for whom form comes second after content, a woman "does not excuse a neglect of form even for the richest content" (NL 683). She is governed by beauty (even though she might not govern beauty herself) and only appreciates truth through its medium. This, of course, entails that she could never appropriately justify said truth, but would only ever judge in the court of the sentiments (ibid.). Schiller's description oscillates between praise and condescension here: on the one hand, women are creatures of beauty and have a keen grasp of this important mode of being. On the other, they can never adequately discern the reasons for a particular truth—and hence, they never really obtain nor grasp this truth by its roots.[18] By Schiller's reasoning, some might be able to present content beautifully, but only intuitively so. After all, the female popular or beautiful author obtains her talent by mere luck, not through careful observation and thinking.

Schiller's insistence that women are not able to write anything deeper than popular novels makes him part of a common trend in the second half of the eighteenth century: part of a tribe of learned men fending off a discourse

---

[17] My translation of the famous portion of the prologue in *Wallensteins Lager* (1798), NA 8, 6.
[18] Here, Schiller is not far from Fichte's stance, who sharpens the distinction by allowing woman only one sort of popular writing, and that is in the area of women's literature. To be more concrete, woman authors should limit themselves to the field of the "vocation of woman," see Becker-Cantarino 2000, 53–54 with reference to the last chapter of Fichte's *Grundriss des Familienrechts* (Addendum to *Grundriss des Naturrechts*, 1796).

initiated in Germany by women such as Dorothea Christiane Erxleben,[19] and continued by woman writers such as La Roche, but more pressingly by Amalia Holst and Marianne Ehrmann, to name just a few. Instead of indirectly controlling woman authors by a censoring male editorship (as Martin Wieland did with La Roche's *Fräulein von Sternheim*, 1771) excluding them by censoring them, Schiller opts here to exclude women directly from the inner circles of "true authorship" with a more principled stance—a stance that takes a rather shaky detour to the female "inner organisation."

One important source for Schiller's views are without doubt Wilhelm von Humboldt's essays "On the difference of the sexes and its influence on organic nature" (1794), and "On Female and Male Form" (1795); both appeared in *Die Horen* as well—and in their discussions of these texts, they referenced them together as *Über die Weiber*.[20] In these essays, Humboldt offers a somewhat naturalistic take on the female versus male character, insinuating that their respective determinate features are formed already by way of conception: male power is creative and determining, female power is receiving and passive. Both aspects depend on one another and complete each other.[21] What we seek, then, is a harmony between these forces—and of course, we may hear Schiller's dichotomies when Humboldt references male depth and female grace and abundance, male reason and female sensibility. In both Humboldt's essays and "On the Necessary Limits," the presentation oscillates between a call for a harmonious *Wechselwirkung* between "male" reason and "female" sensibility, and a quite different call for male superiority and an appropriate limitation of female power. The harmony, in the end, does not indicate equality. Same as the ultimate purpose of "Necessary Limits"—to allow for beautiful form, but only within the limits of reason, marking reason as the ultimate criterion—here the "female" aspect of artistic creation, moral action, and scientific research is

---

[19] Who is the first woman in Germany to receive a doctorate (in medicine), and who published her *Thorough Examination of the Reasons that keep the Female Sex from Studying* (1742). We should note here that such books had a rather short life, as their reception was absolutely lacking. Only a few decades later, a grandson would not even remember that the book was written in German, not Latin (see Corey Dyck, "On Prejudice and the Limits of Learnedness: Dorothea Christiane Erxleben and the *Querelle des Femmes*", in: *Women and Philosophy in Eighteenth Century Germany*. Ed. C.D. Oxford 2021, 51–71, 52).

[20] Note that "Weib" can be understood derogatively. However, the reference to "Weib" instead of "Frau" is part of the tradition of discussing the role of the woman as partner and mother, both of which can also be included in the connotation of "Weib." This makes it not a *simple*, or *straightforward* derogatory misogynistic term, but it still is not neutral: it was meant to put woman in 'her place'. Another indicator of Schiller's stance are his poems, for instance "The Power of Woman" (Macht des Weibes), "The Dignity of Women" (Die Würde der Frauen), "The Famous Woman" (Die berühmte Frau), and "The Virtue of Woman" (Die Würde des Weibes); but here is not the place to discuss them all.

[21] The claim for wholeness, or harmony, is decisive here: "Nature's striving aims at something boundless. (*etwas Unbeschränktes*)" which can only come about by a cooperation of forces (not by them canceling each other out). Humboldt also calls this mode of cooperation *Wechselwirkung*. I cite from the electronic version of Die Horen by the Schiller Archiv: https://www.friedrich-schiller-archiv.de/die-horen

acknowledged only to be ultimately limited to its sphere. Women are allowed to follow their supposed nature, but nothing more, whereas it falls upon men to supervise their "weaker" counterpart.

Schiller's own comment on the female character in his *Robbers* (1781), Amalie, is an interesting, and tellingly ambivalent instance of his judgment of female characters. In an anonymous review on his own drama, Schiller assumes that the author was not able to find a middle way of expression, but chose the heroic and powerful overall—which forced him to paint the female figure in such an overdone passive way that this irks even the "reviewer", aka Schiller himself. Overall, he states, we would expect the softly suffering, pining girl—but then he surprisingly ventures on that the character in the play is *too* passive: a criticism that does not quite fit with the girlish (and this comes with the connotation: passive) character he declared to be missing just a sentence earlier. Be it as it may, here Schiller wants the female lead to be more active and resourceful: she should not only fight people off, but move, make plans herself, decide on how to move on. Once Amalie's love interest is back in the picture, her character gains traction in the later part of the play. But this highlights the ambivalent power of *Wechselwirkung* that I mentioned earlier: a female character might even develop a certain strength, a certain power of action—but the source of this power is male, in that it is always tied to the relation to her lover: Amalie shines only through Karl, not on her own.

A similar move we can detect in the reflections on dilettantism that Schiller developed together with Goethe. Women as dilettantes can be reproductively imaginative (no pun intended); they can imitate "true" artists to produce popular works. However, these works only look like art, but lack art's originality and splendor. To be a good dilettante, you need to recognize your inferior talent. As long as women stay within their realm of popular literature and literary advices for their fellow women, they are fine. Moving beyond the necessary limits of female authorship, so Schiller's verdict, would be tantamount to being evil.

Conclusion

The short essay "On the Necessary Limits in the Use of Beautiful Form" overall has two main goals and two somewhat hidden side goals. It should clarify the limits of beauty in regard to our presentation and grasp of the truth and the good. In a more hidden move, it represents Schiller's defense of his style in the *Aesthetic Education*, in contradistinction to Fichte. Yet more subtly, Schiller here instantiates the female dilettante as the only acceptable version of a woman author, therewith setting the limits of gender in the application of beautiful form per se.

References

Anne Pollok, "Die schöne Seele. Ansätze zu einer ganzheitlichen Anthropologie bei Mendelssohn, Garve und Schiller", *Christian Garve (1742–1798). Philosoph und Philologe der Aufklärung*. Ed. Udo Roth, Gideon Stiening (Berlin, Boston: De Gruyter, 2020), 267–285.

Anne Pollok, *Facetten des Menschen: Zur Anthropologie Moses Mendelssohns*. Hamburg: Meiner 2010.

Barbara Becker-Cantarino: *Schriftstellerinnen der Romantik. Epoche – Werk – Wirkung*. Munich: Beck 2000.

Frederick Beiser, *Schiller als Philosopher: A Re-Examination*. Oxford 2005.

Katerina Deligiorgi, "Schiller's Philosophical Letters: Naturalising Spirit to Moralise Nature", in: *Philosophical Readings* 5 (2013), 63–78.

Leslie Shape, *Schiller's Aesthetic Essays: Two Centuries of Criticism*. Columbia 1995.

Sebastian Gardner, "The Desire of the Whole in Classical German Philosophy", in: *Begehren/Desire*, ed. by Dina Emunds and Sally Sedgwick. New York: De Gruyter, 2018, 233–256.

Steven D. Martinson, *Harmonious Tensions: The Writings of Friedrich Schiller*. Newark/London 1996.

CHAPTER 15

On Naïve and Sentimental Poetry (1795/96)

Gideon Stiening

INTRODUCTION

While working on *Letters on the Aesthetic Education of Man*, Schiller was already devising and drafting an essay that derived a special theory of poetry and literature from the principles of his general aesthetics. He would go on to present this literary theory to the public in three parts in *Die Horen*, in November and December 1795 and January 1796, respectively. In 1800, he published a slightly modified version of the essay in its entirety under the title "On Naive and Sentimental Poetry" (SW 5:694–780). In this text, Schiller offers a literary theory that, on the basis of a theoretical and practical anthropology, enables historical differentiations and literary-theoretical specifications that allow for literary-critical judgments. In doing so—as in "On Grace and Dignity" and the *Aesthetic Letters*—he uses Kantian terminology to elaborate what is ultimately an anti-Kantian poetics insofar as it claims to be able to grasp and judge literature by bringing it under concepts. Furthermore, Schiller again ties poetry to a cultural-ethical educational mission, against Kantian reservations (KdU § 59).

PRECONDITIONS IN THEORETICAL
AND PRACTICAL ANTHROPOLOGY

Schiller's essay is divided into three sections, the first of which deals with the naive, the second with sentimental poetry, and the third with the relationship between the two poetic genres as well as certain anthropological preconditions of his literary-theoretical argumentation. It has often rightly been observed

G. Stiening (✉)
University of Munich, Munich, Germany

© The Author(s), under exclusive license to Springer Nature
Switzerland AG 2023
A. Falduto, T. Mehigan (eds.), *The Palgrave Handbook on the Philosophy of Friedrich Schiller*, https://doi.org/10.1007/978-3-031-16798-0_15

(Koopmann 1998, 628 f.; Zelle 2005, 451; Janz 2008, 1421 f.) that Schiller by no means had the final line of argumentation and structure of this theory in mind when writing the first part, and thus the text represents a work in progress. Nevertheless, the essential systematic elements of this literary theory are present, unchanged, in all three sections.

Before reconstructing the course of the text's logical argumentation, we must first consider the central anthropological premises underlying Schiller's theory of poetry. It is not until the third part of the text that Schiller advances to these presuppositions, which he provisionally describes in terms of a "remarkable psychological antagonism" (769). Schiller explicitly describes this fundamental dualism in the manifestations of the human soul as historically invariant (Wiese 1959, 531) insofar as it has existed "from the beginning of culture" to its "end" (with only a few exceptions). Access to these types of soul, described as anthropological constants, is presented as a process of abstraction: "One best arrives at the true concept of this contradiction if one [...] abstracts from both the naive and the sentimental character what each possesses of the poetic" (770). As a result, one obtains two souls, or types of character, which, according to Schiller, have fundamentally different relations to the reality that surrounds them from both a cognitive and a practical point of view—namely, the cognizing and acting person is either an empiricist and a realist or a rationalist and an idealist:

> Of the former, then, from a theoretical point of view, nothing remains but a sober spirit of observation and a firm attachment to the uniform testimony of the senses; from a practical point of view, a resigned submission to the necessity (but not the blind necessitation) of nature: an acquiescence to what is and what must be. Nothing remains of the sentimental character (from the theoretical perspective) but a restless spirit of speculation that insists on the unconditioned in all knowledge; from the practical perspective, a moral rigorism that insists on the unconditioned in acts of the will. He who belongs to the first class can be called a *realist*; he who belongs to the second, an *idealist*. (770)

With the foundations of his literary theory, Schiller thus again reproduces the great contrast between empiricist and rationalist epistemology and ethics that had preoccupied much of the eighteenth century (Cassirer 1991 II). In doing so, he emphasizes that these relations to the world cannot be reconciled; i.e., one can be either an empiricist and a realist or a rationalist and an idealist. At the same time, he also makes clear that neither position can claim sole representative status, because only from both positions can the "concept of reason of mankind" (770) be fully grasped. Therefore, despite the one-sidedness of the individual "systems" (776), their deficiencies are complementary, such that on the one hand they completely capture the "rich content of human nature" (777), while on the other hand the "ideal of human nature is distributed among both but is fully attained by neither" (778).

It is in the sufficient and complete distinction between naive and sentimental poetry that the dualistic characteristics of theoretical and practical anthropology are realized—characteristics that, in the opposition between epistemological empiricism and rationalism on the one hand and between ethical realism and idealism on the other, once again bring to the fore the contentious theoretical constellation of the pre-critical Enlightenment. On the basis of an ahistorical anthropology, Schiller introduces cultural-historical differentiations that by no means lay the basis for a Hegelian philosophy of history (cf. Szondi 1978) but rather carry over to literary history the form of a philosophy of history that identifies individual with social history, as developed for example by Isaac Iselin (1784) and Christoph Meiners (1793).

Structure and Course of the Argumentation

As mentioned above, the text is divided into three sections, the argumentative course of which will be reconstructed in the following.

The Naive

In the first part (694–716), Schiller develops the ethical-aesthetic concept of the naive and the corresponding concept of naive poetry, thus engaging with a concept that was well known and intensely debated in pre-critical philosophical Enlightenment aesthetics and of which, among others, Mendelssohn, Sulzer, and Wieland offered greatly influential accounts. In considering the naive, all three Enlightenment theorists were concerned with a phenomenon that is of considerable importance for the justification of a (relatively) secular ethics: an ethical disposition that is owed not to reflection, and thus to practice, but to nature, and thus to feeling—a disposition that is therefore natural and found above all in children and 'primitive' peoples and which can therefore serve as evidence of nature as a source of ethical normativity, which, along with reason, gradually replaced the divine authority of God during the long eighteenth century (Bayertz 2015). The "noble simplicity" that, according to Mendelssohn, is a necessary characteristic of naivety (Mendelssohn 2009, I, 210) precisely expresses this dimension of an unreflective and thus natural moral disposition, which is also associated with the concepts of 'innocence' and 'grace'. In their article "Naive" in the *General Theory of the Fine Arts*, Sulzer and Wieland use the phenomenon of natural morality to establish a connection between literature and the ethical educational mission that was essential to Enlightenment theory before *Sturm und Drang* and Kant:

> The naive is not a small class of aesthetic material; it is not only pleasing but can even cause delight. For this reason, works of taste in which thoroughly naive feelings and manners appear are highly valuable, insofar as they support and strengthen the taste for the noble simplicity of a thoroughly good and amiable nature. (Wieland 1997, vol. I, 353)

It is the taste for natural virtue that, since at least the 1750s, had represented the distinctive task of an emotionalistic ethics and aesthetics and took a special interest in the naive. Schiller likewise took an interest in unreflective and thus 'undisguised' virtue—a disposition he had celebrated in *On Grace and Dignity* (Stiening 2020). Nevertheless, he had to explicate and defend his ethics and aesthetics against the challenging background of Kantian objections to the direct instrumentalization of poetry for ethical purposes. Not only had Kant— to the great chagrin of late Enlightenment ethics and aesthetics—demoted all forms of eudaimonism in moral theory, but the close connection between aesthetics and ethics (as conceptualized and practiced in Gottsched's rational and Lessing's emotive theory of poetry, for example) was replaced, in the concept and idea of the "symbol of morality" (KdU § 59), with a precondition-rich indirectness, which had led not to an ethical disposition as its goal but to a precondition of taste based on the autonomy of aesthetic judgment (Recki 2008, 207 f.).

Against these tendencies—some *Sturm und Drang* authors had likewise called for the separation of aesthetics and ethics—Schiller once again focuses on the significance of art and literature for the formation of an ethical and cultural-political disposition, a notion that first becomes concrete in his work on the naive. This phenomenon initially arises independently of its literary form, however: Schiller cites examples from nature, such as landscapes, but also from human nature, such as the behavior of children and the "morals of country folk" and of antiquity (694). Nevertheless, the concept is not applied to such natural objects directly but only when they show themselves to be superior to 'culture' in their natural morality—'culture' here meaning culturally induced, i.e., considered or learned, actions. This superiority reveals itself when one acts ethically with integrity, without being forced to do so by others or by one's own understanding of one's duties. 'Naivety' therefore always refers to the ethical quality of human behavior or action, which is called superior because it does not have to be coerced, i.e., by one's own reason or that of others. Schiller sets out the decisive anthropological preconditions for this type of judgment in the first part of his treatise. With regard to the effect of (beautiful) nature on the moral sensibilities of the observer, he writes:

> Nevertheless, nature will always have something of this effect even on those most lacking in feeling, because the *predisposition* to morality, which is common to all men, is already sufficient for it, and we are all driven to it *in the idea*, however great the distance between our *deeds* and the simplicity and truth of nature. (696)

Without this natural "predisposition to morality", we can neither conceive of nor explain the pre-reflective and thus noble naivety that can be observed in "children and childlike peoples" (696). However, the predicate 'naive' is the product of the reflective figure of an observer of such actions, not the actions themselves. It is certainly possible for naive actions to be performed consciously, and thus Schiller distinguishes—with considerable difficulty—between the "naive of surprise" and the "naive of disposition" (699). Nevertheless, this predicate can only be given by a judge who already holds normative views of his own and who lacks such naivety. Schiller interprets this distance between the judge and the one judged to be naive both anthropologically and culturally insofar as the former must be neither a child nor a member of a 'pre-civilized' society but rather an adult who lives in a culturally shaped society. The famous formula: "They *are* what we *were*; they are what we *ought* once again *to become*!" (695) reveals not only the cultural-*historical* distance between the judging person and the naive—and thus natural, i.e., non-coercive—form of a moral feeling, but also the cultural-critical devaluation of all rational (*and thus*, on this interpretation, coercive) ethics, the latter tradition being associated not only with Wolff but also with Kant.

Schiller repeatedly makes it unmistakably clear that he associates the naive mode of thought and action with a moral disposition that comes about without external or internal constraint, i.e., without rational norms, which he rejects as "crutches of weakness", as the "taskmaster of perversity" (704). The 'naive man' acts—as with grace—out of "instinct" and thus from his inclination; he always already *wants* to do what he *ought* to do (on this see Stiening 2020) and thus is not subject to any constraint. This does not mean, however, that the natural moral disposition does not conform to the laws of ethical normativity. On the contrary, Schiller emphasizes that the naive way of thinking and acting follows an "inner necessity", interpreted as "moral greatness" (699 f.) (and thus not as a theoretical natural law). Insofar as this practical necessity is accompanied by the affect of inclination, such that ought and will are identical for the one who is naive, Schiller can speak of his "beautiful humanity", insofar as 'beautiful', for Schiller, is to be understood in terms of a correspondence between the needs of nature and the demands of practical reason (cf. Tschierske 1988, 375 ff.).

As a preeminent example of the identity of nature and morality, the figure of the "genius" is introduced in the course of the first section (704 ff.). Here, the genius—who can only be naive, as Schiller claims in this section (704)—differs from the naive thought and action of the child or of 'primitive' peoples in that, although he also acts according to his inner inspiration or "feeling", in doing so he does not merely conform directly to ethical norms but rather creates new, and indeed eternal, laws. In this, for Schiller, the genius is an ancient *deus*:

> The genius must undertake the most complicated of tasks with unassuming simplicity and ease; the egg of Columbus applies to every ingenious decision. Only by prevailing over the intricate art with simplicity does the genius establish himself as a genius. He proceeds not according to recognized principles but according to flashes of insight and feelings; but his ideas are the inspirations of a god (everything done by healthy nature is divine), his feelings are laws for all ages and for all generations of men. (704 f.)

Although, damaged by civilization, the observer of the naive mourns the immediate identity of moral perfection and happiness and must strive for it anew as an ideal, Schiller also identifies a decisive shortcoming of the naive attitude: its lack of freedom. Although it is true that both the naive person in general and his specific manifestation, the genius, are free from inner and outer constraint insofar as they follow ethical maxims out of inclination and are thus happy and good at the same time, this way of thinking and acting lacks a central element of the culturalized human being for Schiller: freedom of will and action. Only when the identity of will and ought, the unity of morality and happiness, has become a product of free will can one speak of an ideal of humanity. The culturalized human being must ultimately abandon the status of naivety in order to be good and happy through free will; he must become sentimental.

Sentimental Poetry

It is not until late in the section on "the naive", which begins as more of a moral-theoretical treatise than a poetics, that Schiller turns to the figure of the naive poet. In connection with his counterpart, the sentimental poet, Schiller defines both forms of poetry at the beginning of the second chapter (716–751) as follows:

> The poet, I said, either is nature or he will *seek* it. The former makes for the naive, the latter for the sentimental poet. (716)

Not only does Schiller discuss poetry at the very beginning of this chapter, but he also reduces the naive to 'nature' and the sentimental to the search for it—as he did toward the end of the first section (712)—with 'nature' here again unmistakably implying the forms of natural morality (as was also the case in the first section). The naive poet has the related identity of will and ought, happiness and morality, directly at his disposal, whereas the sentimental poet has lost this unity, although he is aware of this loss and undertakes to overcome it. Both modes of poetry—which, incidentally, are exhaustive of the forms that poetry can take, on Schiller's view—are thus oriented toward a specific relationship between the two traditional *teloi* of human action: happiness *and* morality, and in particular their identity. Schiller explicitly points out the close connection between poetic ability and the "moral drive" (716), such that one can and must speak of a re-ethicization of literature conceived against *Sturm und Drang* and the Kantian theory of aesthetic judgment.

It is only in this chapter that Schiller's distinction—more cultural-critical than cultural-historical—between the ancient and the modern poet comes into play, but again on the basis of a universal, i.e., supra-temporal, practical anthropology:

The latter path, which the modern poets take, is after all the same path that man in general must take, both individually and as a whole. Nature makes him one with himself, art divides and disunites him, and through the ideal he returns to unity. (718)

Since the ideal must remain unattainable, however, modern man (like the poet) will never attain the perfection of the ancients (who take the place of 'primitive' peoples in this chapter), which means nothing other than that modern man will only approximate that immediate identity of nature and morals, of happiness and morality, whereas this identity was immediately available to the ancients, albeit without free will. However, since the idea of progressive development toward freedom belongs to man as an anthropological constant (718), the loss of natural unity is as necessary as the need to be good and happy.

Schiller would apply this basic anthropological framework, which constitutes man both as an individual and as a species, to historical classificatory schemes, thus sketching out a normatively overlain, and ultimately cultural-critical, historical anthropology. Moreover, the abstract schema of unity, separation, and striving in vain to re-establish that unity also affects these elements of his general theory of literature and the specific 'genre theory' that he develops in the course of the chapter. Even in his somewhat sharp literary criticism, this schema plays a defining role.

First, however, Schiller maintains that his schema of anthropological development is to be applied to an appropriate theory of literature:

> The same that is said here of the two different forms of humanity can be applied to the two kinds of poet corresponding to them. (718)

This premise leads to the argument that, from the standpoint of the aesthetics of production, the naive poet not only draws his productions from his nature, i.e., his feelings, but also, from the standpoint of the aesthetics of the work, seeks to establish a unity between the work and reality in the concept of imitation. Even from the standpoint of the aesthetics of their reception, the works of the naive poet form a unity insofar as they give rise to one and the same feeling, which can be distinguished only by degree in the individual works (720).

By contrast, the sentimental poet creates his works in the execution of the insurmountable difference between the ideal and reality—and this again in ethical terms: "The sentimental poet is therefore always concerned with two conflicting conceptions and feelings, with reality as the limit and with his idea as the infinite, and the mixed feeling he arouses will always testify to this twofold source" (720 f.).

Sentimental poetry is thus constituted by an always contrastive correlation between the ideal and reality, where the ideal consists in the recovery of natural morality—albeit out of free will. This correlation can take place in different ways and in this respect conditions the different types of sentimental poetry:

satire, elegy, and idyll. Schiller explicitly states (728 f., note) that he associates these terms not with designated literary genres but with types of sentimental poetry, understood as a basic genre. Quite consistently, he therefore defines satire as follows:

> The poet is satirical if he takes as his subject alienation from nature and the contradiction between reality and the ideal (in their effect on the mind, both amount to the same thing). [...] In satire, the real as a deficiency is contrasted with the ideal as the highest reality. (721 f.)

Satire, then, is primarily concerned with a reality in which human actions and beliefs are not grounded in a moral disposition—as natural actions and beliefs. Satirical portrayals can take two forms: pathetic satire, in which the "dreadful experience of moral depravity" is brought to light (723), and playful satire, in which a lack of natural morality is bathed in the gentle light of humor. The latter is particularly difficult because it must be carried out not by a cynical character who merely mocks the absence, indeed the unattainability, of the ideal but by a "beautiful heart" (724) who immediately perceives the ideal of natural morality as true—and is thus singularly close to the naive soul.

Schiller distinguishes satire, as the primary manifestation of sentimental poetry, from elegy, which he defines as follows:

> Should the poet so oppose nature to art and the ideal to reality such that the representation of the former predominates and pleasure in it becomes the ruling sentiment, I call him *elegiac*. (728)

Elegy is therefore primarily concerned with the ideal (of natural morality), which it constitutively opposes to a morally depraved reality. This genre of sentimental poetry likewise has two manifestations: elegy in the narrower sense, in which sorrow may "flow only from an enthusiasm awakened by the ideal" (728), and the idyll, which consists in a representation, ultimately remote from reality, of a realized ideality. The latter can only be poetized in ancient or modern pastoral poetry, the most significant manifestations of which were the idylls of Salomon Geßner and, above all, John Milton's *Paradise Lost* (749).

Schiller enriches these passages of his treatise with a wealth of literary examples, which are also evaluated (negatively and positively) from a literary-critical point of view according to the standards of his literary theory. In the end, the idyll is distinguished as the most significant realization of sentimental poetry, including from a normative point of view:

> The concept of the idyll is the concept of a fully resolved struggle, both in the individual human being and in society, of a free union of inclination and the law, of a nature purified to the highest moral dignity; in short, it is nothing other than the ideal of beauty applied to real life. Its character consists, therefore, in the fact that *all opposition between reality and the ideal*, which had furnished the material for satirical and elegiac poetry, is completely annulled, and therewith all conflict

among the feelings ceases. *Tranquillity*, then, would be the prevailing impression of this kind of poetry, but the tranquillity of perfection, not of idleness; a tranquillity that flows from the equilibrium, not the stagnation, of powers, that flows from fullness, not from emptiness, and is accompanied by the feeling of an infinite capacity. (751)

Schiller has greater difficulty integrating the idyll, thus characterized, into his fundamentally dualistic literary theory, in part because it must frame the sentimental "opposition between reality and the ideal" as having been overcome (751), and this would be intrinsically naive under the conditions of free will, i.e., modernity. It is these passages on the idyll that are difficult to integrate into Schiller's fundamentally dualistic anthropology and theory of poetry (cf. Gethmann-Siefert 1984, 72 ff.).

The Relationship Between Naive and Sentimental Poetry

In the third section of his treatise on naive and sentimental poetry (751–789)—a distinction that he considers both necessary and, for a systematic concept of literature, sufficient—Schiller attempts to determine the relationship between the two types more precisely. It quickly becomes apparent that the historical assignment of naive poetry to antiquity and sentimental poetry to modern times cannot be sustained insofar as both—ultimately anthropologically based realizations—are historically invariant and can therefore be found in antiquity as well as in modern times. Moreover, the concept of genius is no longer applied only to the naive poet; rather, in this section, Schiller also speaks more frequently of the "sentimental genius" (754, 759, and elsewhere).

First, however, he makes clear that, in their complementary interplay, the two genres of poetry that he developed from and related to anthropology sufficiently and fully represent the concept and function of literature: "To give humanity its most complete expression is, however, the common task of both, and without it they could not be called poets at all" (752). Because both poetic genres fully capture the concept of literature, however, Schiller can subsequently elaborate on the respective achievements and limitations of naive and sentimental poetry in terms of each other's merits and shortcomings: where the naive poet is "whole in himself" (752), the sentimental poet strives for that harmony in and with himself first and foremost; where the naive genius remains bound to the representation of sensuous reality, the sentimental genius can soar up to a greater object, namely the "infinity of the idea" (753); where the naive and hence pre-reflective genius remains dependent on his nature, i.e., his happy intuition, the sentimental genius can and must rely on the achievements of his reflection (753–755).

Nevertheless, both genres of poetry are in danger of leaving the path of true poetry precisely because of their respective features. It is these at times lengthy passages, in which Schiller details the deviations of the two genres of poetry from the norms set for them, that he uses to exemplify literary criticism.

Homer, Shakespeare, and Lessing are not exempt from this often biting criticism (757), which documents his excessive pretension. Their transgression consists in the fact that they, like all naive geniuses, confused "true nature" with "actual nature" in the representation of reality (or neglected this distinction altogether). Schiller distinguishes these two concepts of nature as follows:

> Actual nature is every outburst of passion, however crude; it may also be true nature, but it cannot be truly *human* nature; for this requires the participation of the independent faculty in every pronouncement, the expression of which is always dignity. Actual human nature includes all moral baseness, but it is to be hoped that true human nature does not; for the latter cannot be other than noble. (755)

Consequently, naive genius, bound to the representation of reality, must not deign to give shape to the commonness of moral depravity—Schiller speaks of "common nature" (759)—because it would thereby fail in its task: the representation and generation of a "pure" ethical disposition as moral feeling. Without a doubt, these later passages reveal the highly normative aspects of Schiller's poetics, which is more reminiscent of Gellert and Lessing than he may have wished.

Sentimental poetry is likewise in danger of straying to the extent that it distances its task—the representation of the ideal—so far from reality that it leads to "overextension" and "rapture". Schiller's concern in this critique is to distinguish the clearly defined ideal of the unity of happiness and morality in a moral sentiment corresponding to free will from literary creations with other or imprecisely defined goals. To this end, Julie and St. Preux, Werther and Lotte, and even some of the protagonists of Wieland's novels, are invoked (762)—figures who pursued ideals that could no longer be tied to reality, in part because they propagated the 'supererogatory actions' that were also criticized by Kant. In addition, Schiller distinguishes as 'political' poetry that pursues ideals that can no longer be tied to the sensibility of representation that is essential to all poetry (762). The *telos* of the representation of an ethical ideal, which Schiller views as the purpose of all sentimental poetry, may only assume such degrees of abstraction that are still executable within the framework of poetic sensibility.

Before concluding his treatise with the remarks on theoretical and practical anthropology already reconstructed above, Schiller provides an excursus on the Horatian maxim according to which poetry should "benefit and delight" (764–769). Here, he once again documents his strict dissociation from the pure hedonism of literary reception on the one hand, which fails to recognize the cultural-historical achievements of poetry, and from the pure intellectualism of preoccupation with the ethical ideal on the other, which lacks the necessary ties to reality—two critical dissociations that constitute an implicit criticism of Kant (cf. 766 f.). Consequently, a true appreciation of genuine literature cannot be expected from either the working class, which seeks only recreation, or the contemplative class, which reflects a type of moral ennoblement that is remote from reality. Just as he does at the end of the *Aesthetic Letters*, Schiller relies on a special "popular class" that, in the constant mediation of work and contemplation, can completely transcend the correlative constellation of naive and sentimental poetry and reach the "ideal of beautiful humanity" (768 f.).

Reception and Critical Appraisal

Schiller's last major theoretical treatise was swiftly and intensively received (cf. Zelle 2005, 471–573; Janz 2008, 1441–1444). For the most part, the comments were overwhelmingly positive. Goethe, in his own sardonic way, established the thesis that Schiller's treatise had prompted the emergence and development of Romanticism. Moreover, Schiller's biographizing of the difference between the naive and the sentimental poet (with which he sought to capture the differences between Goethe and himself) has influenced research to the present day (cf. Wiese 1959, 530 ff.; Koopmann 1998, 632 ff.). Zelle (2005, 473) rightly notes that, following the nineteenth- and early twentieth-century preoccupation with the *Aesthetic Letters*, as of 1945 the various scholarly disciplines began to devote themselves more intensively, and quite profitably, to Schiller's poetics. Surprisingly, however, this discussion was again interrupted with the important handbook articles by Koopmann (1998) and Zelle 2005; more recent references, which tend to be ephemeral (Kaufmann 2019, 576–581), have been unable to change this.

Too little attention has been paid to the fact that Schiller's treatise on literary theory further developed his fundamental critique of Kant, already presented in *On Grace and Dignity* and the *Aesthetic Letters* (Beiser 2005, 169–190). Furthermore, his connection to pre-critical Enlightenment aesthetics (Sulzer, Gellert, Lessing)—in particular Schiller's theses on the conceptual determinability of art and literature and his emphatic proof of the ethical valence and thus cultural-critical significance of poetry, both of which cannot be reconciled with Kant and are clearly intended as critiques of him—remains to be examined. What ultimately remains to be considered is the position and function, in both *naive and sentimental poetry*, of the more decisive perspective of theoretical and practical anthropology, as opposed to the long, overemphasized schematic perspective of cultural history.

German text translated into English by Carolyn Benson.

References

Bayertz, Kurt. 2015. Ethik/Moral. In *Handbuch Europäische Aufklärung. Begriffe, Konzepte, Wirkung*, ed. Heinz Thoma, 181–192. Stuttgart, Weimar: Metzler.

Beiser, Frederick. 2005. *Schiller as Philosopher: A Re-Examination*. Oxford: Clarendon Press.

Cassirer, Ernst. 1991. *Der Erkenntnisproblem in der Philosophie und der Wissenschaft in der neueren Zeit*, 4 vols. Darmstadt: wbg.

Gethmann-Siefert, Annemarie. 1984. *Die Funktion der Kunst in der Geschichte. Untersuchungen zu Hegels Ästhetik*. Bonn: Brouvier.

Iselin, Isaak. 1784. *Geschichte der Menschheit*, 2 vols., new edition with a biography of the author. Carlsruhe: Schmieder.

Janz, Rolf-Peter. 2008. Kommentar. In Friedrich Schiller, *Theoretische Schriften*, ed. Rolf-Peter Janz, 1125–1605. Frankfurt am Main: DKV.

Kaufmann, Sebastian. 2019. *Ästhetik des Wilden. Zur Verschränkung von Ethno-Anthropologie und ästhetischer Theorie 1750–1850*. Basel: Schwabe.

Koopmann, Helmut. 1998. Über naive und sentimentalische Dichtung. In *Schiller-Handbuch*, ed. Helmut Koopmann, 627–638. Stuttgart. Kröner.

Meiners, Christoph. 1793. *Grundriß der Geschichte der Menschheit*. Lemgo: Meyersche Buchhandlung.

Mendelssohn, Moses. 2009. Betrachtungen über das erhabene und das Naive in den schönen Wissenschaften. In Mendelssohn Moses, *Ausgewählte Werke. Studienausgabe*, 2 vols., vol. 1, ed. Christoph Schulte, Andreas Kennecke, and Grażyna Jurewicz, 195-213. Darmstadt: WBG.

Recki, Birgit. 2008. Die Dialektik der ästhetischen Urteilskraft und die Methodenlehre des Geschmacks (§§ 55–60). In *Immanuel Kant. Kritik der Urteilskraft*, ed. Otfried Höffe, 189–210. Berlin: Akademie.

Stiening, Gideon. 2020. "Womit aber hatten es die Kinder des Hauses verschuldet, daß er nur für die Knechte sorgte?" Schillers Auseinandersetzung mit Kants 'Rigorismus'. In *Kant-Studien* 111: 269–284.

Szondi, Peter. 1978. Das naive ist das Sentimentalische. Zur Begriffsdialektik in Schillers Abhandlung. In Peter Szondi, *Schriften II*, ed. Jean Bollack et al., 59–105. Frankfurt am Main: Suhrkamp.

Tschierske, Ulrich. 1988. *Vernunftkritik und ästhetische Subjektivität. Studien zur Anthropologie Friedrich Schillers*. Tübingen: Niemeyer.

Wieland, Christoph Martin. 1997. Naiv (Schöne Künste). In Christoph Martin Wieland, *Von der Freiheit der Literatur. Kritische Schriften und Publizistik*, 2 vols., vol. 1, ed. Wolfgang Albrecht, 351–363, Frankfurt am Main: Inseln.

Wiese, Benno von. 1959. *Friedrich Schiller*. Stuttgart: Metzler.

Zelle, Carsten. 2005. Über naive und sentimentalische Dichtung. In *Schiller-Handbuch*, ed. Matthias Luserke-Jaqui, 451–479. Stuttgart, Weimar: Metzler.

CHAPTER 16

On the Sublime (1801)

Carsten Zelle

1.

In the absence of "direct evidence" (NA 21: 328, *Kommentar*) allowing us to pinpoint the origin of the short text "On the Sublime" (*Über das Erhabene*), it is not possible to say with certainty when it was written. The factors that affect the assessment of these origins concern the interpretation of the essay, the evaluation of the status and importance of the concept of the "sublime" and arguments maintaining a "see-saw-pattern" in the development of Schiller's aesthetics (Brooks 1988: 92; Brooks 1995: 92 [!]). While questions concerning the genesis of the essay accordingly remain open and "controversial" (NA 21: 328, *Kommentar*), any attempt, despite these circumstances, to assign an origin to the text will inevitably involve the provision of an interpretation that necessarily is prejudicial towards other views. To put it bluntly, how we date the text varies depending on whether the interpreter chooses to give weight to a reading of Schiller as an author of *reconciled* or of *endorsed* contradictions. Interpreters interested in reconciliation, utopia and the like try to position "On the Sublime" in close proximity to Kant's *Critique of the Power of Judgment*, i.e., to come up with as early a date for the essay as is possible and to downplay the essay's status as an early exercise in the appropriation of Kantian thought—in contrast to the (supposedly) more mature position set out in the *Aesthetic Letters* (cf. Barnouw 1980: 510).

The conjecture by the editors of the *Nationalausgabe*, according to which "On the Sublime" might "have been composed sometime between 1794 and

C. Zelle (✉)
Ruhr-Universität Bochum, Bochum, Germany
e-mail: carsten.zelle@rub.de

1796" (NA 21: 328, *Kommentar*) and "was probably revised" (NA 21: 329, *Kommentar*) before going to press in 1801, has recently been reassessed (cf. Koopmann 2011: 617) and taken to be valid in Anglophone scholarship (cf. Beiser 2005: 238 and 257; cf. Hughes 2015: 420). "Despite this, doubts remain" (^{2}SW 5: 1260, *Kommentar*).[1] While the treatise is linked to Schiller's writings on tragic pleasure, tragedy and the sublime (cf. Zelle 2005b–d) on the one hand, it presupposes, on the other hand, the *Horen* version of the *Letters on the Aesthetic Education*, which remained a fragment. The remarks on the sublime or energising beauty, already mentioned in the "enclosure" (*Einschluß*) to the Augustenburg letter dated November 11, 1793 (FA 8: 519 f.) and promised as a continuation of the investigation in the *partitio* of the 16th aesthetic letter (FA 8: 618), were never followed up (cf. Zelle 2005e). A renewed consideration of the question of how we date the essay points to the fact that the composition of this writing between 1796 and 1801 can be taken to be "probable" and was most likely composed between 1796 and 1799, i.e., in the context of the *Wallenstein* trilogy (Barone 2004: 114). Meanwhile, more recent interpretations consider "On the Sublime" to be a "late writing" (Riedel 2007: 60) on the basis of which Schiller gives us "an epilogue and conclusion to his earlier efforts on theoretical subjects" (^{2}SW 5: 1261, *Kommentar*). Since no new philological facts allowing for a definitive assessment have come to light, all pronouncements about its genesis remain a matter of speculation.

The essay appeared in May 1801 in the third volume of the *Shorter Prose Works* (*Kleinere prosaische Schriften*) with the additional remark "unprinted" ["(*ungedruckt*)"—Schiller 1801]. It was published for the first time in this volume—alongside a series of texts already published elsewhere and reprinted here. The essay was followed in the volume by the copy-edited reprint of the *Aesthetic Letters* published in the *Horen* and the last section of the essay "Concerning the Sublime" [*Vom Erhabenen*], previously published in the *Thalia* and now newly entitled "On the Pathetic" (→ 2.8). The flanking of the aesthetic education through the sublime and pathetic expressed by the composition of this volume was disturbed in later Schiller editions by other decisions of the editors and has been invisible ever since.

2.

The fact that Schiller brings together the three aforementioned writings in one volume indicates they attain consistency only as a whole. Since the *Aesthetic Letters* were interrupted following the deduction of the "rational concept of beauty" (*Vernunftbegriff der Schönheit*, FA 8: 592) and the investigation of the "effects of melting beauty" (*Wirkungen der schmelzenden Schönheit*, FA 8: 618), and since the flagged book version that was to be supplemented with further letters (cf. letter to Cotta, June 2, 1795; NA 27: 192) also did not

---

[1] SW refers to the new edition of SW, which contains a newly written, revised and supplemented commentary. The author of the commentary of the theoretical writings (vol. 5 of ^{2}SW) is Wolfgang Riedel.

come into being, the version of the text published for the first time in 1801 has been regarded as a "direct substitute for parts no longer composed" in the *Aesthetic Letters* (NA 21: 330, *Kommentar*), i.e., as a substitute for the missing statements concerning "energizing beauty" announced in the 16th letter. In its closing stages (see below), the essay specifically states that the sublime must be added to the entirety of aesthetic education so that views suggesting that Schiller seems "not to have seen" the connection between his writing on education and that on the sublime (FA 8: 1448, *Kommentar*) contradict the letter of the text itself.

Whereas the *Aesthetic Letters* are based on a triadic or dialectical model, on whose basis the sensuous/moral dualism founded on Schiller's "complete anthropological appraisal" (FA 8: 565) is balanced by the "play" of a "middle condition", in "On the Sublime" this dualism is treated as a "contradiction" (*Widerspruch*, FA 8: 828), i.e., formulated in Kant's words as a "conflict" (*Widerstreit*, CJ: § 27, A 98). At this point all concepts of mediation have been omitted. "Sensibility" and "reason" (FA 8: 828), "physical" and "moral [...] culture" (FA 8: 823), "physical" and "moral human being" (FA 8: 828) stand, as it were, "forehead to forehead" (FA 8: 837).

Following the suggestion of a French translator (Hartmann 1997: 101), I divide "On the Sublime" into six sections.

2.1.

Already the first section (paragraphs 1 to 6, FA 8, $822,_1$–$824,_5$) deals with the concept of death. "This point, i.e., death as a boundary of freedom, is the theoretical focus of Schiller's last philosophical effort" (Riedel 2007: 59). How does a mortal being know that it is free? The problem is exposed by juxtaposing two quotations: a truism in the form of a proverb and a statement taken from a drama. In the play *Nathan the Wise* (1779; I 3), the title character says to the dervish: "Kein Mensch muß müssen" [*No human being must abide*] (FA 8, 822), while the "proverb" [*Sprüchwort*[2]] points out that there is a remedy for everything "except for death" (*ibid.*). Death, a factor which makes the human being understand its subjection to the laws of nature, overturns the anthropological concept of human being, which according to a *complete* view of it possesses a *mixed* nature.

From the time of the medical writings through the early *Playhouse* speech [*Schaubühne*] right up to the mature aesthetic letters and the late writing, the philosophical physician Schiller never wavers from this basic anthropological model. The dual, sensuous-moral human being differs from the animal being in that it is determined not only by drives but also by reason. Practical reason becomes a differentiating criterion insofar as the human being is a being "that wills", in contrast to all other beings. The "will is the character of humankind"

---

[2] Schiller is referring here to an insight developed in the historical literature of dietetics: *contra vim mortis non est medicamen in hortis* (*Regimen sanitatis Salernitanum*, De Salvia, cap. 60).— The present article is a revised version of Zelle 2005g.

(ibid.). It is the animal being that is able to say no (Scheler). This results in an "exceptional position" (Riedel 2007: 60) ensuring that the human being stands out before all other living beings. "For this very reason, nothing is so unworthy of a human being as to suffer violence, because violence nullifies that being" (FA 8: 822). Violence is at odds with the dignity of a human being. Schiller's idealism, which some consider to be inessential (cf. de Man 1997: 146), comes into its own at precisely this point. If this were not the case (as Schiller might be taken to say), we would be unable to justify why torture, for instance, contradicts human rights (UN resolution, December 9, 1975). Torture destroys the human being and dissolves the human image of itself (cf. Peters 1985: 221 f.). Although the human being as a physical, i.e., sensuous being, is mortal, it is nonetheless free, as a metaphysical, i.e., moral, being, "conceptually [*dem Begriff nach*] to annihilate" death by making itself its "own action" [*eigene Handlung*], i.e., not by suffering, but rather by willing such an act (nowadays, one would say by "accepting" it). Such a "voluntary submission" is described by means of the moral-philosophical term "resignation to necessity" [*Resignation in die Notwendigkeit*], or the religiously imbricated term "surrender to the divine counsel" (*Ergebung in den göttlichen Ratschluß*; FA 8: 823 f.). In the modern era this attitude, in consequence of the dwindling validity of ecclesiastical institutions, is hardly ever taught. In this regard the *Playhouse* speech (*Schaubühne*, 1785) underscored the specific "jurisdiction" of the playhouse, whose importance was a consequence of the undermining of religious authority (cf. Zelle 2005a: 352).

2.2.

At this point in the argumentation, "On the Sublime" ties in with the concept of aesthetic education. It turns out that the analysis, hitherto limited to the concept of beauty, remained unsatisfactory. The corresponding second section, leading to an initial juxtaposition of the beautiful and the sublime (paragraphs 7–10, FA 8: 824.26–826.24), begins with the restrictive term "admittedly" (*zwar*). "Admittedly" (ibid., 824,26) the formation of the feeling of the beautiful makes one, to a certain extent, independent from nature, i.e., insofar as one is not affected by "matter", but rather by the "forms" of art—and thereby senses a "free satisfaction" [*freies Wohlgefallen*] that allows one to feel "the undeniable inner plenitude of life" (FA 8: 824 f.). However, the beautiful remains bound to the matter in which it is embedded. Bringing together the determination of the moral and of the sensuous into playful harmony proved to be advantageous in the *Aesthetic Letters* in the context of the discussion about the medial condition. However, in this context, it now becomes a disadvantage. In fact, insofar as sensibility always remains in "play" in the beautiful, no matter how sublimated it might be, the "contentment experienced in the aesthetic condition still remains dependent on nature as a power" (FA 8: 825).

Because it is a "characteristic of good and beautiful, but at all times weak, souls" that with moral and aesthetic concerns "too much is conceded to matter", one must turn to the "more sprightly affect" that boosts the mind and fortifies it "in its strength" (FA 8: 825). The difference between the feeling of the beautiful and that of the sublime with regard to weakness and strength engages with Kant's distinction between "melting" [*schmelzend*] and "courageous" [*wacker*] affects (cf. the "General Remark on the Exposition of Aesthetic Reflective Judgements" following § 29: CJ, AA 5: 266f., transl. 149f.) and, here and there, is drawn into the critique of sentimentalism (*Empfindelei*). The parable of the "two genii" illustrates this distinction (FA 8: 826). The prose paragraph corresponds to the epigram *Beautiful and Sublime* [*Schön und Erhaben*], presumably written at the beginning of October 1795 and published in the same year in the 12th volume of the *Horen* (and reprised in 1805 under the title *Die Führer des Lebens*). The symbol of the "two genii" stands for the "aesthetic education" involving beauty and sublimity (FA 8: 519), i.e., the "twofold" or "double beauty" of melting and energising beauty in which, according to the *Aesthetic Letters*, the "ideally beautiful" appears empirically (FA 8: 616). The distiches summarise the complete programme of aesthetic education in a nutshell (cf. SW 1: 244).

After reading the epigram, Herder had interpreted the "chasm,/where at the sea of eternity the mortal stands shuddering" [*Kluft [...], / Wo an der Ewigkeit Meer schaudernd der Sterbliche steht*] as a "grave" and asserted that the sublime genius is not only of importance at the moment of death "by the grave", but must already stand "supportively by the side" of the beautiful genius during life (see Herder's letter dated October 10, 1795; NA 35: 375). In order to avoid such misunderstandings, a clarification arrives when the epigram is transformed into a prose parable in the ninth paragraph of the essay "On the Sublime". Instead of a "chasm" at the point where Herder saw a "grave", "the dangerous places" appear "where we act as pure spirits and must lay everything corporeal aside" (FA 8: 826). In such situations, the beautiful genius' "earthly wing" fails and the "strong arm" of the sublime genius is needed to carry us over the "heaviest depths" (ibid.). Schiller's metaphorical imagery is guided by a set of problems through which Kant, in the *Critique of the Power of Judgment* (KU: Introduction, AA 5: 176; transl. 63; cf. Pries 1995), sought to bridge the great "incalculable gulf between the domain of the concept of nature as the sensible and the domain of the concept of freedom as the supersensible".

2.3.

The "dizzying depths" alluded to in the parable denotes the difference between the sensible and the supersensible found in the human being according to the anthropological perspective advanced by the philosophical physician Schiller. This countervailing fate manifests itself in the "feeling of the sublime" presented in the third section (paragraphs 11–15, 826.25–830.8). It is felt as a "mixed feeling" of "woe" [*Wehsein*] and "delight" [*Frohsein*] revealing "that the laws of nature are not necessarily also ours" (FA 8: 826 f.). Schiller took over the term "delight" [*Frohsein*] from Mendelssohn, who used it to translate the English word "delight" in the context of a theory of mixed sensations where Burke had used it to describe the relative pleasure that comes from the release of pain in contrast to pure pleasure (cf. Zelle 1987: 355). Delight, which can increase to the point of enchantment, is therefore said to be "actually not pleasure [*Lust*]", although "preferred by far to all pleasure experienced by finer souls" (FA 8: 826). Since, to account for sharply divergent feelings later described as "terrible pleasure" (*schauerliche Lust*, FA 8: 832), it cannot be that the object upholds opposite relations to the recipient at the one time, it must be the recipient who upholds "two sharply opposed relations" to the object at one and the same time. That recipient—a sensuous being—feels "woe" [*Wehsein*]. Since this is so, the feeling of "delight" [*Frohsein*] must have a different explanation.

Thus, the "delight" in being in "woe" points to an "independent principle in us [...], free from all sensuous stirrings" (FA 8: 827). Through the mixed feeling of the sublime we "experience" (ibid.) reason. The composite quality of the human being and that of sensation are thus related. We can see, then, that this essay, like those before it, essentially follows Kant's analytic of the sublime according to which the *feeling of the sublime*, a "negative pleasure", is the agency through which the mind makes "tangible [*fühlbar*]" its freedom from nature (CJ: § 23, A 74 f. and § 28, A 104).

A "double aspect" (FA 8: 827) is further distinguished within the sublime corresponding to Kant's distinction between mathematical and dynamic sublime. The theoretical sublime had already been distinguished from the practical in "Concerning the Sublime" [*Vom Erhabenen*] (1793/94). Through what is now called the sublime of the "power of comprehension" [*Fassungskraft*], the subject discovers something "unequivocally great" in itself in view of the "terror" of nature that transcends everything "sensuous-infinite". In view of this "terror", the subject experiences through the "vital force" of the sublime that the "will of the human being" is in its own hands, although, as a sensuous being, it is subject to "physical necessity" (FA 8: 827). The concept of the "sublime of the power of comprehension" used here, which refers to Kant's mathematical sublime, must not be confused with the terminology used in "On the Pathetic" [*Über das Pathetische*]. There, both the sublime of the "comprehension" that preserves itself in suffering and the sublime of the "act" that chooses to suffer refer to the dynamic sublime (see above, 2.8. "Concerning the Sublime" [= *Vom Erhabenen*] (1793)/"On the Pathetic" [= *Über das Pathetische*] (1801)).

Crucial here is the fact that the determinations of the sublime are subjective, i.e., no properties of objects are designated, but rather a human capacity is discovered that would otherwise have remained unknown to us. This subjectivist version that Kant calls "subreption" (CJ: § 27, A 96) leads, in the fifth section, to a negative concept of nature and a disillusioned concept of history, in which, since the turn of the millennium, the actual radicality and extreme modernity of this late writing has been recognised (cf. Riedel 2002, 2007).

2.4.

After highlighting the experience of reason as an achievement of the sublime, the fourth section draws conclusions in a second comparison of the beautiful and the sublime (paragraphs 13–16, FA 8: 828.1–830.36). The sublime uncovers what the concept of beauty presupposes. The transcendental deduction of the beautiful in the 11th to the 15th aesthetic letters would hang in the air if it were not supplemented by "On the Sublime". This addition "could prove to be a *supplément* in Derrida's sense—calling into question the basis of the conception to be supplemented" (Hofmann 2003: 98). Since sensibility and reason conform in the beautiful, one would "never experience that we are determined and capable of proving ourselves to be pure intelligences" (FA 8: 828). One would not know that, in the "aesthetic condition", reason is also "at play". The sublime must be added, in order to reveal what the beautiful presupposes. "On the other hand, in the sublime, reason and sensibility do not fit together, and the magic with which it grips our mind lies precisely in the contradiction between the two" (FA 8: 828). Since the physical and the moral human being are "here most sharply separated from each other" (ibid.), it is here that morality first becomes recognisable. The sublime does not only complement aesthetic education in terms of the empirical bearing of its straining effect, as the first parable of the two genii had explained in the second section: it must be added to the transcendental deduction in order to make it complete.

Through the sublime, the modern subject steps out of the order of nature towards itself. In order to illustrate that the sublime provides "an exit from the sensible world, where the beautiful would always like to keep us imprisoned" (FA 8: 830), a further parable is told, namely a scene from Fénelon's *Adventures of Telemachus* (published in French in 1699; translated into German first in 1700—and repeatedly later): "Beauty, in the form of the goddess Calypso, has enchanted the courageous son of Ulysses and, through the power of her charms, keeps him imprisoned on her island for a long time. For the longest time he thinks he is paying homage to an immortal deity, since he is only in the arms of voluptuousness. But a sublime impression suddenly seizes him in the shape of Mentor: he remembers his better, higher destination, throws himself into the waves and becomes free" (FA 8: 830). The parable shows the crisis in which the subject's ability to harmonise its cognitive dissonances is threatened and shattered. Schiller's interest in the sublime is not motivated solely by the Stoic "armouring of character" (à la Theweleit), but rather also by the situation of decision. The transitional terminology dominating the *Aesthetic Letters* with regard to the beautiful is abandoned in this context. The sublime is a breakthrough experience that tears the independent spirit away from the sensible world "not gradually (for there is no transition from dependence to freedom) but rather suddenly and by a shock" (FA 8: 830). The suddenness, with its eventful perceiving structure is a significant mode of the sublime, as already Pseudo-Longinus noted (*Peri hypsous*: 1,4). This explains why the return of the sublime at the end of the twentieth century has led to the accentuation of "suddenness" as a genuine aesthetic category (e.g., Bohrer 1981).

By means of his Telemachus parable, Schiller re-actualises the decisionistic figures in the Prodicus fable of Hercules at the crossroads, which had lain fallow since the Anacreontic aesthetics of the "rational" viz. "philosophical physicians" in favour of a positively valorised "middle condition" (cf. Zelle 2005h: 100–103). The connotations associated with the beautiful are now upended and turned towards the negative. The beautiful is no longer the embodiment of an "immortal deity", as it appeared embodied by Juno Ludovisi (FA 8: 615) in the 15th aesthetic letter, i.e., the beautiful is no longer the appearance of freedom, but rather of "voluptuousness". In Schiller's parable, in the figure of Mentor, the goddess Athena appears in the role of the sublime genius who becomes the guide in "dangerous circumstances".

One should even go a step further. From a mythological angle Calypso is a goddess of death. According to the etymology of her name, she is a "veiled" goddess. Her beautiful appearance has twice "bewitched'" Telemachus (FA 8: 830). He is soon in danger of succumbing to a double deception. Calypso, i.e., apparent beauty, is not freedom, but rather voluptuousness—and voluptuousness heralds death. Freedom no longer takes the veiled form of the enchanting beauty of Calypso. Death, i.e., the principle of nature, hides behind such voluptuousness. Through this contrast, by painting Telemachus's sublime act in a good light ("he throws himself into the waves and becomes free"), the parable completely obscures the beautiful and, at the same time, hides in a deceptive way the "beautiful appearance" that the 26th aesthetic letter had sought to legitimise in the face of Plato's condemnation of art (cf. FA 8: 664–666).

The instability of these evaluations, which change abruptly depending on whether they are argued in the context of the beautiful or of the sublime, have been interpreted as symptoms of Schiller's "Platonism" mediated by Kant (cf. Pugh 1991, 1996). This results in a typical, unresolvable contradiction, insofar as the Platonic doctrine of ideas is equally dominated by "the separation between 'idea' and 'appearance'" as well as "the link between the two". "We cannot understand the theoretical sense of the separation, of the χωρισμός [*chōrismós*], without understanding the meaning of the participation, of the μέθεξις [*méthexis*]" (Cassirer 1922/23: 21). The tension between *chorismos* and *methexis*, between separation and participation, between diremption and reconciliation, controls the aporetic argumentation through which Schiller, on the one hand, divides beauty and sublimity, but through which he, at the same time, aims at reuniting both categories in the "ideally beautiful" (FA 8: 828), as this was called earlier in this late writing, when taking up the terminology from the 16th aesthetic letter (cf. FA 8: 616 and 618). The change from one aesthetic category, i.e., that of beauty, to the other, i.e., that of sublimity, leads to the change from methectic to choristic viz. tropic argumentation, and to the associated change of sign or evaluation, i.e., towards that aforementioned conceptual "boat swing" that impressively demonstrates the sudden transformation of Calypso from the embodiment of "beauty" to her embodying "voluptuousness" (and death).

2.5.

The second parable suggests that the "beautiful soul" is not only a weak girl, but also a "light" one. When the beautiful soul is a paramour and freedom towards the sublime is the *higher* destination—compared to the freedom conferred by the beautiful—trust in nature and history is extinguished. The objects of the sublime thematised in the fifth section (paragraphs 17–23, 830.37–836.14) are denoted accordingly. Nature is "wild bizarreness", "bold disorder", "lawless chaos", in which no "wise plan" but rather "mad chance" reigns, which "mocks all rules" (FA 8: 833 and 835). Like the angel in Benjamin's ninth historical-philosophical thesis, history is the return of the same, i.e., a heap of rubble and the trail of horror "of an all-destroying and re-creating, and again destroying transformation" (FA 8: 837). The illusory concept of history associated with black nature forms the necessary reverse side of the sublime. As happened in Kant's philosophy, where, on the basis of "subreption", the sublime of the subject was confused with the "grisliness" of the object appropriate to the indirect representation of freedom (CJ: § 27, A 96 and § 23, A 76), so it is also the case in Schiller's "On the Sublime" that sublimity and horror viz. ugliness relate to each other like positive and negative poles. Nature, both the great, infinite, "*incomprehensible*" nature (unlimited distances, incalculable heights, vast oceans, etc.) and the terrible, destructive, "*corrupting*" nature, is called "sublime" only insofar as it serves to discover our "high demonic freedom" (FA 8: 831).

The concept of history is naturalised in this context. "World history is a sublime object" (FA 8: 835) only insofar as our "independence" (FA 8: 837) from natural forces thereby becomes recognisable, but not within that history. By calling history "sublime", Schiller implies it is abominable. In this way, he "revokes" (Riedel 2002: 207) the universal-historical concept that, in his inaugural lecture in Jena (1789), he had initially shared with Schlözer and Kant, and adopts the "meta-narrative" (Lyotard) of Enlightenment philosophy of history (cf. Pugh 1993). From this angle it is evident why Hegel takes up Schiller's malleable concept of beauty and why, also, the sublime from this point of view commands conspicuously less importance.

2.6.

In contrast to the arbitrariness of the powers of nature and history—now returning to the starting point of the essay—Schiller advises the reader to assume a resigned attitude in order "to endure what one cannot change and surrender with dignity what one cannot preserve!" (FA 8: 836). Accordingly, the crucial sixth section positions the sublime within the programme of aesthetic education (paragraphs 24–28, 836.15–840.6). Here the discussion concerning "strength of soul" advocated by Abel in the *Karlsschule*—a "genuinely Stoic concept" aiming at the *ultima ratio* of "Stoic preservation of autonomy" (Riedel 2002: 206)—once more comes to the fore. The ability to "morally disembody oneself before any physical power does it" (FA 8: 836) must now be practised—and to this end "the artificial unhappiness of the pathetic" (FA 8: 837) is the best remedy. The image of "moral disembodiment" has been understood in two ways: passively, as an act of resignation, or actively, as an act of "Stoic free death (*mors voluntaria*)" (Riedel 2007: 66).

In the same way as the bourgeois tragedy of Schiller's time sought to arouse the capacity to empathise, Schiller's dramaturgy of the pathetic also aims at practising a "capacity" (*Fertigkeit*, FA 8: 837) to treat serious misfortune as artificial and, this way, aesthetically to gain distance from it. "It is the task and the purpose of tragic art to develop our sensitivity towards the sublime in such a way that our mental resilience is stiffened into an attitude" (Berghahn 1980: 207). Schiller chooses a medical image to convey this purpose of training resistance through aesthetics. The pathetic is conceived as an "inoculation [*Inokulation*] of inevitable fate", whereby it is "robbed of its malignancy and the attack on the same is directed towards the strong part of the human being" (FA 8: 837). The *Philosophical Letters* [*Philosophische Briefe*] (1786) had already raised the medical metaphor of "inoculation" [*Einimpfung*] (FA 8: 216) alongside a dietary metaphor of hardening, in order to be immune or immunised in the face of situations of crisis.

The explanations about the aesthetic strengthening of the will through pathetic inoculation (cf. Zumbusch 2012: 113–130) fill out the concept of "energizing beauty" that the *Horen* version had announced but left open. The code words "enervation" [*Erschlaffung*] and "lustiness" [*Rüstigkeit*] (FA 8: 839) recall the tensing/relaxing model that is familiar to the reader from the *partitio* of the 16th aesthetic letter. If on the one hand the beautiful "renders outstanding service to the human being" by keeping the material and formal drives in a state of free play and the sublime "renders outstanding service to the pure demon" in the human being, the former, on the other hand, must be accompanied by the latter "in order to make aesthetic education a complete whole" (FA 8: 838). Only when the beautiful and the sublime "consort with each another" (FA 8: 838), i.e., only when the two aesthetic categories are conjoined and united and mutually complement each other can the programme of aesthetic education reach completion.

In view of the overall organisation of the 1801 volume, we are now in a position to appreciate the full significance of "On the Sublime" in relation to the *Aesthetic Letters*. The earlier *Horen* version of the *Letters* had the status of a fragment in view of the intention of the author to continue it at a later date (cf. Zelle 2005e: 410 f.). As the later volume suggests, the position accorded to the minimally amended 1801 version of the *Letters* relative to the two companion essays on the sublime was now accorded its proper significance in Schiller's aesthetics.

3.

In the context of criticism at Schiller's time, besides the "fragmentary" *Aesthetic Letters*, which, despite the "philosophical darkness" they evoked in the readers, "recommend themselves through many new and true things", "On the Sublime" was received as a "splendid contribution to aesthetics" ([Lenz] 1802). The complementarity of the two writings expressed in the arrangement of essays in the volume was also immediately recognised with reference to the passage just quoted from the final section of the treatise "On the Sublime". It stands with respect to the *Aesthetic Letters* "in approximately the same relationship as the last essay of the second volume to the penultimate one" (Anonymous writer 1801: 367). The analogy was meant to suggest that the *Aesthetic Letters* were flanked and limited by "On the Sublime" in the same way as "On Grace and Dignity" [*Über Anmut und Würde*] was flanked and limited by the treatise *On the Necessary Limits in the Use of Beautiful Forms* [*Über die notwendigen Grenzen beim Gebrauch schöner Formen*] in the second volume of the *Shorter Prose Works* [*Kleineren prosaischen Schiften*] from 1800 (cf. Zelle 2013). At the same time, the anonymous reviewer raises the question of the relationship between the beautiful and the sublime in Schiller's aesthetic writings. According to him, "only in relation to aesthetic education can the sublime be given precedence over the beautiful, but not in relation to the ideal" (Anonymous writer 1801: 368).

Schiller's treatise offers an important contribution to the aesthetics of the sublime in modern times, which has long been obscured by the dominance of a historiography of aesthetics fixated on the beautiful and has received little attention even in the scholarship on Schiller (cf. Sharpe 1995, index). "The problem of the sublime has always been in the shadow of the question concerning the nature of the beautiful and of art, or it has been treated as a part of the theory on tragedy" (Düsing 1967: 1). While the commentary of the so-called bigger treatises extensively documents the history of their impact, such information is lacking in the case of the writings on the pathetic and the sublime, even though this information is certainly available (see above).

Access to "On the Sublime" was precluded for a long time because the philosophy in it was "sublime, yet sterile" (Dürrenmatt 1959: 432). At the end of the 1950s on the 200th anniversary of Schiller's birth, that beauty had to "allow itself to be accused of the very finest arts of seduction" (Staiger 1959: 416) before the "tribunal" of the sublime argued against its purpose and efficacy. Conversely, the "negative" moment of the sublime, seemingly close to existentialism, which accentuated the dimension of finitude and nothingness (Weischedel 1960: 344), allowed Schiller's "nihilistic" earnestness to be used against nineteenth-century thinking premised on the elevating effects of beauty (Wais 1959: 428). It has been argued again in recent times that Schiller's late work "marks the beginning of post-metaphysical reflection on human existence in German philosophy as a 'being to death'", insofar as it turns "old European heroic stoicism" into "modern heroic nihilism" (Riedel 2007: 69 and 71).

The philosopher Ernst Bloch was fascinated by the sense of the "upright gait" animating Schiller's conception of the will in reference to the "character of human species". This "is a perspective with a plan worth listening to", because in the opening sentences of "On the Sublime" the "best in Enlightenment" is encountered (Bloch 1961: 14.). In Germany, this judgement was met partly with approval (cf. Mayer 1966: 314), partly with scepticism. However, Schiller's "Aesthetics of Resistance" not only contained the "draft of a morally justified resistance" emphasised by Bloch, but also held within it the "behavioural doctrine of the sublime" on account of its Stoic dimension which also included the "offer of a retreat" to hibernate in "apolitical humanism" (Alt 2000: 97).

After an initial "rehabilitation of the sublime" (Weischedel 1960) in the context of existentialism, it was only the "post-modern" question concerning the possibility of an artistic "representation of the unrepresentable" (Lyotard 1982) based on Kant's concept of "negative representation" (cf. Lyotard 1991: 185–188) that led to a new interest in Schiller's theory of the sublime, which had been stopped until then by a one-sided reading of the *Aesthetic Letters* with its focus on the beautiful. This led to the conclusion that the *Aesthetic Letters* were not the entirety of his theory of art, but that the beautiful "only depicts a partial area of the human being, the unconstrained agreement of his faculties. For the representation of the conflict of the faculties, the sublime is needed" (FA 8: 1400, *Kommentar*). With the sublime, the beautiful in Schiller's aesthetics gains an antagonist that was posited as an "emergency legislation in the aesthetic state" (Zelle 1994), in opposition to the reconciliatory approach that had turned Schiller into a utopian and, what's more, an uninteresting classical author. At the turn of the millennium, such "innovative lines of research" brought about interpretations of Schiller as a "forerunner of a self-critical modernity that is aware of the aporias of an aesthetics of reconciliation", thus reclaiming him as a "contemporary of our epoch" (Hofmann 2003: 194). The renewed interest in Schiller's theory of the sublime since the 1980s is also underpinned by a series of relevant translations (e.g., Schiller 1966, 1989; ESS; Schiller 1997) or reprints of older translations (e.g., Schiller 1859, 1997), which, in each case, triggered further research impulses in their relevant fields. A comparative study of these impulses remains a critical desideratum. Nevertheless, the old question about the relationship between the sublime and the beautiful in Schiller's aesthetic theory, which the anonymous reviewer already raised in 1801 (see above), remains open. "How is the sublime to be reconciled with an aesthetics, with gaiety, with a freedom of mind that should belong to art and to the reception of art?" (Schings in Wittkowski 1982: 409). Should we understand the relationship between beauty and sublimity in Schiller's double aesthetic as a "complementarity" (²SW 5: 1261), as suggested by the first parable of the two genii, or does the sublime hold "the last word" (Zelle 2005g: 479) over the beautiful as the better destination in Schiller's late writing, as suggested by the second parable of Telemachus's divinely inspired decision? If we project the determinations of the sublime into the philosophy and history of art, which the treatise "On Naive and Sentimental Poetry" [*Über naive und sentimentalische Dichtung*, 1795/96] outlines (cf. Zelle 2005f), the sublime can be taken to anticipate a divided modernity. The fact that sentimental poetry shapes the divergence between ideality and reality leads Schiller to include essential characteristics of the sublime in the determination of sentimental art (cf. Zelle 1995: 179–184, 207–219). The alienated present is aesthetically mastered by means of the sublime. By contrast, the "world of modernity has no longer an adequate expression in the aesthetics of the beautiful. […] In the fractured world of modernity, art should not present a picture of harmony to a disharmonious real world, but rather include disharmony in its representation. Reluctance [*Unlust*] must be regarded as an essential constituent of sentimental art and literature" (Hofmann 2003: 127f.). This is one of the reasons why not only Hegel (*On Wallenstein—Über Wallenstein*, 1800/1801) responded to Schiller's Wallenstein with incomprehension. While Greek tragedy cathartically "passes through" pity and fear and puts one in a state of mind "that makes a prosperous happy human life", Schiller's drama distresses the spectator and leaves her alone with "pusillanimity", "bitterness" and "fearfulness" (Süvern 1800: 16, 161 and 157). The Greek, however, is no reference point for Schiller's art anymore. He responds to Süvern's criticism of *Wallenstein* by alluding to the tension model of energising beauty viz. sublimity: "Our tragedy has to contend with impotence, inertness, the lack of character of the spirit of the age, and with a mean way of thinking; therefore, it must show strength and character, it must try to shake the mind, to elevate it, but not to suspend it. Beauty is for a happy generation; however, an unhappy one must try to stir itself sublimely" (letter to Süvern, July 26, 1800; NA 30: 177).

The "grief" (Lyotard 1987: 296) about the present justifies the interest in the sublime found today. The post-modern revival of the sublime may have fallen quiet in recent years. Still, it has revealed to contemporary aesthetics a deeper historical dimension that had previously been lost sight of, leading to an understanding of aesthetics in terms of *aisthesis*. And by referring to the questions of aesthetic experience, rhetorical performance, presence and intensity, it has identified central problem-fields for contemporary literary theory.

German text translated into English by Antonino Falduto in connection with Tim Mehigan.

On the Sublime (1801)

Schema

1.	Paragraphs 1–6 (822,₁-824,₅)	Starting point: "Kein Mensch muß müssen" [*No human being must abide*]—death negates the sensuous, not the moral being—what a human being also is
2.	Paragraphs 7–10 (824,₆-826,₂₄)	First distinction between Beautiful and Sublime: (First parable) "Two Genii" *Complementarity* of Beautiful and Sublime
3.	Paragraphs 11–12 (826,₂₅-827,₃₇)	Feeling of the Sublime: "mixed feeling" of "woe" [*Wehsein*] and "delight" [*Frohsein*] reveals the "independent principle", i.e., the human being as autonomous rational being. Two modes of the Sublime: – Sublime as power of comprehension [*Fassungskraft*] – Sublime as life force [*Lebenskraft*]
4.	Paragraphs 13–16 (828,₁-830,₃₆)	Second distinction between Beautiful and Sublime:: – Beauty: interaction of sensibility and reason – Sublime: antagonism of sensibility and reason, through which the human being is proved as "pure intelligence" – (second parable) "throws himself into the waves and becomes free" *Superiority* of the Sublime—compared with the Beautiful, it is the better vocation
5.	Paragraphs 17–23 (830,₃₇-836,₁₄)	Objects of the Sublime: – "Sublimity" of nature: (a) great, infinite nature (b) terrible, destroying nature – "Sublimity" of the history of world history (= disenchanted, modern imagine of history)
6.	Paragraphs 24–28 (836,₁₅-840,₅₆)	Position of the Sublime in the context of aesthetic education: "sublime" education must accompany "beauty" education, in order to make a "complete whole" out of it.

References

Alt, Peter-André. 2000. *Schiller. Leben – Werk – Zeit*, vol. 2. München: Beck.

Anonymous writer. 1801. [Rez.] Leipzig, b. Crusius: *Kleinere prosaische Schriften* von Schiller, aus mehrern Zeitschriften vom Verfasser selbst gesammelt und verbessert. 2ter Theil 1800. 3ter Theil 1801. [Leipziger] *Jahrbuch der neuesten Literatur* vol. 1, no. 45: 355–360; no. 46: 361–368; no. 47: 377–384 [recte: 369–376].

Barnouw, Jeffrey. 1980. The Morality of the Sublime. *Studies in Romanticism* 19: 497–514.

Barone, Paul. 2004. *Schiller und die Tradition des Erhabenen*. Berlin: Erich Schmidt.

Beiser, Frederick. 2005. *Schiller as Philosopher. A Re-Examination*. Oxford: Clarendon Press.

Berghahn, Klaus L. 1980 [¹1971]. Das Pathetischerhabene. Schillers Dramentheorie. In *Deutsche Dramentheorien I: Beiträge zur historischen Poetik des Dramas in Deutschland*, ed. Reinhold Grimm, 197–221.Wiesbaden: Athenaion.

Bloch, Ernst. 1961. *Naturrecht und menschliche Würde*. Frankfurt am Main: Suhrkamp.

Bohrer, Karl Heinz. 1981. *Plötzlichkeit. Zum Augenblick des ästhetischen Scheins*. Frankfurt am Main: Suhrkamp.

Brooks, Linda M. 1988. Sublime Suicide: The End of Schiller's Aesthetics. In *Friedrich von Schiller and the Drama of Human Existence*, ed. Alexej Ugrinsky, 91–101. New York, Westport CT, London: Greenwood Press.

Brooks, Linda Marie. 1995. *The Menace of the Sublime to the Individual Self. Kant, Schiller, Coleridge, and the Disintegration of Romantic Identity*. Lewiston, Queenston, Lampeter: Mellen.

Cassirer, Ernst. 1922/23. Eidos und Eidolon: Das Problem des Schönen und der Kunst in Platons Dialogen. *Vorträge der Bibliothek Warburg* 2: 1–27.

De Man, Paul. 1997 [1983]. Kant and Schiller. In Paul de Man: *Aesthetic Ideology*, ed. Andrzej Warminski, 129–162. Minneapolis, London: University of Minnesota Press.

Dürrenmatt, Friedrich. 1959. Mannheimer Schiller-Rede [1959]. In *Schiller. Zeitgenosse aller Epochen. Dokumente zur Wirkungsgeschichte Schillers in Deutschland*, ed. Norbert Oellers, 2: 430–439. München: Beck 1976.

Düsing, Wolfgang. 1967. *Schillers Idee des Erhabenen*. Phil. Fak., Diss. Köln.

Hartmann, Pierre. 1997. *Du sublime (de Boileau à Schiller): suivi de la traduction de ›Über das Erhabene‹ de Friedrich Schiller*. Strasbourg: Presses Université de Strasbourg.

Hofmann, Michael. 2003. *Schiller. Epoche – Werk – Wirkung*. München: Beck.

Hughes, Samuel. 2015. Schiller on the Pleasure of Tragedy. *British Journal of Aesthetics* 55/4: 417–432. doi: https://doi.org/10.1093/aesthj/ayv029.

Koopmann, Helmut. 2011. Kleinere Schriften nach der Begegnung mit Kant. In *Schiller-Handbuch*. 2., durchgesehene und aktualisierte Auflage, ed. Helmut Koopmann, 611–624. Stuttgart: Kröner.

[Lenz, Karl Gotthold]. 1802. [Rezension] Kleinere prosaische Schriften von *Schiller*. Aus mehrern Zeitschriften vom Verf. selbst gesammelt und verbessert, *Dritter Theil*. Leipzig, bey Crusius, 1801. *Allgemeine deutsche Bibliothek* 71: 123.

Lyotard, Jean-François. 1982. Presenting the unpresentable. The sublime. *Artforum* 20: 64–69.

Lyotard, Jean-François. 1987 [frz. 1983] *Der Widerstreit*. München: Fink.

Lyotard, Jean-François. 1991. *Leçons sur l'Analytique du Sublime (Kant, Critique de la faculté de juger, §§ 23-29)*. Paris: Galilée.

Mayer, Hans. 1966. Schillers Ästhetik und die Revolution (Der Moralist und das Spiel) [1966]. In *Das unglückliche Bewußtsein. Zur deutschen Literaturgeschichte von Lessing bis Heine*, 292–314. Frankfurt am Main: Suhrkamp ²1986.

Peters, Edward. 1991 [engl. 1985]. *Folter. Geschichte der Peinlichen Befragung*. Hamburg: Europäische Verlagsanstalt 1991.

Pries, Christine. 1995. *Übergänge ohne Brücken. Kants Erhabenes zwischen Kritik und Metaphysik*. Berlin: Akademie Verlag.

Pugh, David. 1991. Schiller as Platonist. *Colloquia Germanica* 24: 273–295.

Pugh, David. 1993. How Enlightened Are Schiller's Aesthetics? In *Impure Reason. Dialectic of Enlightenment in Germany*, ed. W. Daniel Wilson, Robert C. Holub, 166–184. Detroit: Wayne State University Press.

Pugh, David. 1996. *Dialectic of Love. Platonism in Schiller's Aesthetics*. Montreal, Kingston, London, Buffalo: University of Toronto Press.

Riedel, Wolfgang. 2002. "Weltgeschichte ein erhabenes Object". Zur Modernität von Schillers Geschichtsdenken. In *Prägnanter Moment. Studien zur deutschen Literatur der Aufklärung und Klassik. Festschrift für Hans-Jürgen Schings*, ed. Peter-André Alt et al., 193–214. Würzburg: Königshausen & Neumann.

Riedel, Wolfgang. 2007. Die Freiheit und der Tod. Grenzphänomene idealistischer Theoriebildung beim späten Schiller. In *Friedrich Schiller. Der unterschätzte Theoretiker*, ed. Georg Bollenbeck and Lothar Ehrlich, 59–71. Köln, Weimar, Wien: Böhlau.

Schiller, [Friedrich]. 1801. *Kleinere prosaische Schriften. Aus mehrern Zeitschriften vom Verfasser selbst gesammelt und verbessert*, Dritter Theil, Inhalt, unpag. Leipzig: Crusius.

Schiller, Friedrich. 1859/1997. *Du Sublime* (trans: Adrien Régnier). Arles: Edition Sulliver.

Schiller, Friedrich. 1966. *Naive and Sentimental Poetry and On the Sublime. Two Essays* (trans: Julius A.[nthony] Elias). New York: Ungar.

Schiller, Friedrich: 1989. *Del Sublime – sul patetico – sul sublime* (trans: Luigi Reitani). Milano: SE.

Schiller, Friedrich. 1997. Sur le sublime (trans: Pierre Hartmann). In Pierre Hartmann. 1997. *Du sublime (de Boileau à Schiller). Suivi de la traduction de ›Über das Erhabene‹ de Friedrich Schiller*, 171–182. Strasbourg: Presses Université de Strasbourg 1997.

Sharpe, Lesley. 1995. *Schiller's Aesthetic Essays. Two centuries of Criticism*. Columbia SC: Camden House.

Staiger, Emil. 1959. Schillers Größe [1959]. In *Schiller. Zeitgenosse aller Epochen. Dokumente zur Wirkungsgeschichte Schillers in Deutschland*, ed. Norbert Oellers, 2: 412–423. München: Beck 1976.

Süvern, Johann Wilhelm. 1800. *Über Schillers Wallenstein in Hinsicht auf die griechische Tragödie*. Berlin: Buchhandlung der Königlichen Realschule.

Wais, Kurt. 1959. Das Echo Schillers in der Welt [1959]. In *Schiller. Zeitgenosse aller Epochen. Dokumente zur Wirkungsgeschichte Schillers in Deutschland*, ed. Norbert Oellers, 2: 423–430. München 1976.

Weischedel, Wilhelm. 1960. Rehabilitation des Erhabenen. In *Erkenntnis und Verantwortung. Festschrift für Theodor Litt*, ed. Josef Derbolav and Friedhelm Nicolin, 335–345. Düsseldorf: Schwann.

Wittkowski, Wolfgang. 1982. Schlußdiskussion (Leitung: Lawrence Ryan). In *Friedrich Schiller. Kunst, Humanität und Politik in der späten Aufklärung*, ed. Wolfgang Wittkowski, 403–410. Tübingen: Niemeyer.

Zelle, Carsten. 1987. "Angenehmes Grauen". Literaturhistorische Beiträge zur Ästhetik des Schrecklichen im achtzehnten Jahrhundert. Hamburg: Meiner.

Zelle, Carsten. 1994. Die Notstandsgesetzgebung im ästhetischen Staat. Anthropologische Aporien in Schillers philosophischen Schriften. In *Der ganze Mensch. Anthropologie und Literatur im 18. Jahrhundert. DFG-Symposion 1992*, ed. Hans-Jürgen Schings, 440–468. Stuttgart, Weimar: Metzler.

Zelle, Carsten. 1995. *Die Doppelte Ästhetik der Moderne. Revisionen des Schönen von Boileau bis Nietzsche*. Stuttgart, Weimar: Metzler.

Zelle, Carsten. 2005a. Was kann eine gute stehende Schaubühne eigentlich wirken? In *Schiller-Handbuch*, ed. Matthias Luserke-Jaqui, 343–358. Stuttgart, Weimar: Metzler.

Zelle, Carsten. 2005b. Über den Grund des Vergnügens an tragischen Gegenständen. In *Schiller-Handbuch*, ed. Matthias Luserke-Jaqui, 364–374. Stuttgart, Weimar: Metzler.

Zelle, Carsten. 2005c. Über die tragische Kunst. In *Schiller-Handbuch*, ed. Matthias Luserke-Jaqui, 374–382. Stuttgart, Weimar: Metzler.

Zelle, Carsten. 2005d. Vom Erhabenen / Über das Pathetische. In *Schiller-Handbuch*, ed. Matthias Luserke-Jaqui, 398–406. Stuttgart, Weimar: Metzler.

Zelle, Carsten. 2005e. Über die ästhetische Erziehung des Menschen in einer Reihe von Briefen. In *Schiller-Handbuch*, ed. Matthias Luserke-Jaqui, 409–445. Stuttgart, Weimar: Metzler.
Zelle, Carsten. 2005f. Über naive und sentimentalische Dichtung. In *Schiller-Handbuch*, ed. Matthias Luserke-Jaqui, 451–479. Stuttgart, Weimar: Metzler.
Zelle, Carsten. 2005g. Über das Erhabene. In *Schiller-Handbuch*, ed. Matthias Luserke-Jaqui, 479–490. Stuttgart, Weimar: Metzler.
Zelle, Carsten. 2005h. Anakreontik und Anthropologie. Zu Johann Arnold Eberts *Das Vergnügen* (1743). In *Anakreontische Aufklärung*, ed. Manfred Beetz and Hans-Joachim Kertscher, 93-105. Tübingen: Niemeyer.
Zelle, Carsten. 2013. "Der Geschmack im Vortrag der Wahrheit" – zu den Gefahren ästhetischer Erziehung und philosophischer Schreibweise im Anschluß an den Augustenburger-Brief vom 21. November 1793. In *L'éducation esthétique selon Schiller. Entre anthropologie, politique et théorie du beau*, ed. Olivier Agard and Françoise Lartillot, 45–66. Paris: L'Harmattan.
Zumbusch, Cornelia. 2012. *Die Immunität der Klassik*. Berlin: Suhrkamp.

PART III

Schiller's Philosophical Topics

CHAPTER 17

Schiller and Philosophical Anthropology

Wolfgang Riedel

CONCEPTUAL HISTORY

"Philosophical anthropology" is an unusual lemma for a Schiller handbook. In the context of the philosophical terminology in the German language, this term refers to a current of twentieth-century thought emerging from the reflections by Max Scheler, Helmut Plessner and Arnold Gehlen (cf. Fischer 2008). At the time, the term constituted a philosophical attempt to register in a decisive way the impact of the empirical and experimental natural sciences in areas ranging from sensory physiology through to evolutionary theory, and with particular reference to the new biology—and thereby to integrate this advance in the history of knowledge into philosophical reflection. In this context, the question concerning "the human being" was of capital importance, especially as a question regarding the human being's position in the continuum of natural history in general, and in the continuum of animal evolution specifically. The philosophical investigations dedicated to the question regarding the human being were no longer to be conducted without reference to human biology (these researches even referred to "philosophical biology": Plessner 1928:4f.). "Anthropology" lent itself, like no other, as a term to describe the bridge between philosophy and empirical research. Admittedly, this was the case only in German, since in other languages its meaning stresses more the ethnological than the biological sphere, that is, it leads in the direction of social and cultural rather than the natural sciences. Hence, what in German has been

W. Riedel (✉)
University of Würzburg, Wuerzburg, Germany
e-mail: wolfgang.riedel@uni-wuerzburg.de

© The Author(s), under exclusive license to Springer Nature Switzerland AG 2023
A. Falduto, T. Mehigan (eds.), *The Palgrave Handbook on the Philosophy of Friedrich Schiller*, https://doi.org/10.1007/978-3-031-16798-0_17

called *Völkerkunde* or *Kulturanthropologie*, in English and French was simply referred to as "*anthropology*"/"*anthropologie*".

Still, the German usage of the term leads directly back to the origins of its conceptual history. "Anthropology" was no classical denomination but rather a neo-Latin coinage dating back to the sixteenth century (Magnus Hundt, *Anthropologium de hominis dignitate, natura et proprietatibus*, 1501; Galeazzo Capella, *Anthropologia*, 1533; Otto Casmann, *Anthropologia*, 1594–1596; cf. Hartmann/Haedke 1963; Marquard 1971; Benzenhöfer/Rotzoll 1991). It aimed at a science of the human being that no longer left the "two natures" ("*spiritualis et corporea*") in the hands of two different disciplines, that is, philosophy and medicine, but rather aimed at integrating them into an overarching doctrine of the whole human being ("*de homine toto*") (cf. Hartmann/Haedke 1963:47f., 51ff.). With regard to the latter, especially German conceptual history, this early undertaking took on an exemplary character. This still applies to twentieth-century "philosophical anthropology" and especially to eighteenth-century "anthropology" in Germany—and, thus, also to Schiller (Linden 1976; Schings 1977; Riedel 1985, 1995, 2004, 2006; Zelle 2001; Košenina 2016).

Nonetheless, early modern conceptual history had long been the preserve of medical historians (from Hartmann/Haedke 1963 to Benzenhöfer 1993). Its close link to physiological empiricism drove away philosophical interest—and this remains a subject-specific bias to this day. In fact, the more ambitious the concepts of mind or of reason became, the more unwelcome the focus on the body remained. A classic case of this aversion in German philosophy is Kant's *Anthropology from a Pragmatic Standpoint* (1798; Ak 7). Although based on lectures from the 1770s onwards, it only appeared at the end of the century when German Enlightenment anthropology was already on the wane. Therefore, Kant's verdict on anthropology and its affinity with the "physiological knowledge of the human being" took on the appearance in the history of philosophy of a kind of eulogy: The "study of what nature makes of the human being" remains a "pure waste", since it is of little help to the human being in its actions; philosophically meaningful is only the "pragmatic" study of the human being (*pragmatische Menschenkunde*), which sets out what the human being, "as a free-acting being, makes of itself, or can and should make of itself" (Ak 7:119). Following his ethos of unconditional self-determination, Kant thus removes the concept of anthropology from its traditional field, that is, nature, and assigns it to culture (Marquard called this a "turn to the world of life (*Wende zur Lebenswelt*)"—Marquard 1965:126, 1971:365).

Kant had a certain success in the history of philosophy (see Heidegger's critique of "Philosophical Anthropology"), but not in the history of knowledge. On the contrary, the pressure of empirical natural science on the conception of what a human being is taken to be only increased. In German philosophy, outsiders such as Schopenhauer (whose theory of the will was directly connected to the state of biology at that time, cf. Riedel 1996:49f.) and Nietzsche (who took philosophy to be "thought tied to the margins of the body (*Denken am Leitfaden des Leibes)*", as "physiology", ibid.:203) passed on the legacy of pre-Kantian to post-Kantian anthropology, also and especially to the "philosophical anthropology" (ibid.:166, cf. Gehlen 1938). Kant, however, successfully prevented the historical and philosophical reappraisal of the anthropology of the German Enlightenment: this desideratum, persisting already for many decades (Hinske 1965:413; cf. Marquard 1971:364), has remained unanswered, not least because of Marquard himself (among the few exceptions are Linden 1976; Caroll 2018). The consequence has been that this research lacuna has only been filled by historians of German and European literature (cf. Riedel 1985, 1994; Barkhoff/Sagarra 1992; Schings 1994; Galle 2001; Garber/Thoma 2004, Macor 2008, 2013; Caroll 2018:XIVf.).

"Anthropology" in German Enlightenment

Christian Wolff divided the doctrine of the human being, according to the Cartesian model, into two sections: psychology, as the doctrine of the soul conceived as immaterial substance (*vis repraesentativa/substantia simplex*, i.e., the Cartesian *res cogitans*) (Wolff 1720), and physiology, as the doctrine of the bodily machine, belonging purely to matter (*res extensa*) and its functions (Wolff 1725). In the context of this dualism, a "natural" bridge between the two could not be plausibly conceived (cf. Specht 1966, 1976). Instead, use was made of theology, with recourse to models such as "pre-established harmony". The great lexica of the early Enlightenment dealt with the topic in a similar way: the medical faculty was responsible for the treatment of the aspects dedicated to the body, the philosophical faculty for those aspects dealing with the mind. The term "*anthropologia*" came into play only as a synonym for human physiology and not in its comprehensive meaning (Zedler 1732–54 II:522 [1732]; Walch 1733 I:106f.).

However, this situation did not last. On the one hand, the concept of organic bodies changed. Microscopes brought about such a stupendous change in the understanding of developmental processes of embryos and microorganisms that physiology switched from being a mechanistic to an epigenetic paradigm and began to find that organisms, even and especially the "spiritless" ones, had a capacity for autonomous productivity, which we now call autopoiesis or self-organisation (Abraham Trembley, *Mémoires pour servir a l'histoire d'un genre des polypes d'eau douce*, 1744; Caspar Friedrich Wolff, *Theoria generationis*, 1759; cf. Riedel 2017:353–381 [2000]). At the same time, experiments on decapitated frogs proved the independence of physical movements from mental authorship and control (Johann Georg Zimmermann, *Dissertatio physiologica de irritabilitate*, 1751; Albrecht von Haller, *De partibus corporis humani sensibilibus et irritabilibus*, 1752). The physiological "animism" of Georg Ernst Stahl (*Theoria medica vera*, 1707), which was disseminated after 1700 and had assumed the soul to be accountable in all respects, thus also became obsolete. From this, it followed that, around 1750, the human body could no longer be conceived as a "dead" machine that could be brought to life only through "ensoulment".

On the other hand, the rationalist concept of mind or soul also lost plausibility. The Wolffian psychology was a pure pneumatology, which defined its object by immateriality, immortality, possession of reason and unconditional freedom of will (*Psychologia rationalis*, 1739). It was assisted by a *Psychologia empirica* (1732), which was to verify what had been proven pneumatologically "*per experientiam*" (§ 5). But this handmaiden of *psychologia rationalis* turned out to be its gravedigger. The empirical evidence contradicted the mental-metaphysical premises, and empirical and experimental natural research became the guiding principle of knowledge ("*man verfährt hiebey, wie in der Physik mit den körperlichen Dingen, welche man durch Erfahrung und Versuche kennenlernt*"/"one proceeds here, as in physics, with the physical things which one gets to know through experience and experimentation"). This paradigmatic shift immediately called for a new nomenclature such as "experimental physics of the soul" (*Experimentalphysik der Seele*; Johann Georg Sulzer, *Kurzer Begriff aller Wissenschaften*, ²1759, § 204/Sulzer 2014:140; Johann Gottlieb Krüger, *Versuch einer Experimental-Seelenlehre*, 1756). Closer to the original was the later "empirical doctrine of the soul" (*Erfahrungsseelenkunde*; Karl Philipp Moritz, *Magazin zur Erfahrungsseelenkunde*, 1783–1793), though the original name continued to be used (*Allgemeines Repertorium für empirische Psychologie und verwandte Wissenschaften*, 1792–1801).

Probably the most important "empirical psychologist" of the German Enlightenment was Sulzer (Pross 1994; Riedel 2017:3–34 [1994]; Grunert/ Stiening 2011). His psychological treatises, published from 1751 onwards in the yearbooks of the Berlin Academy of Sciences, were available from 1773 under the title of *Vermischte philosophische Schriften*. The consequence of this paradigmatic shift, that is, the depotentiation of reason and freedom of the will in the context of the interaction of mental powers, is clearly evident in these works, especially in the theorem of the non-identity of representing (*Vorstellen*) and sensing (*Empfinden*) (*Über den verschiedenen Zustand […] des Vermögens, sich etwas vorzustellen und des Vermögens zu empfinden*, Sulzer 1973:225–243 [1763]), as well as in the theory of uncontrolled, compulsive reactions, actions and—*avant la lettre!*—parapraxis (*Erklärung eines psychologischen paradoxen Satzes: Dass der Mensch […] selbst gegen dringende Antriebe und überzeugende Gründe handelt und urtheilet*, Sulzer 1773:99–122 [1759]). As Sulzer argues, the "dewolffianisation" of the concept of soul is discharged through two doctrines (Riedel 2017:9ff.). Firstly, human acts of will, decisions and actions are in most cases not determined by rational reasons, but rather by sensations (of pleasure and pain or displeasure) and by affects (such as hope, fear, etc.) (Sulzer 1773:241ff., 213ff.). Secondly, many psychic and mental processes do not take place voluntarily, but rather involuntarily, especially the activities of the imagination (*imaginatio involuntaria*) and the process of association. Moreover, they do not take place consciously and in the clear awareness of one's own believing and willing, but in a space of "obscure ideas" (*dunkle Ideen/ideae obscurae*) at a remove from reason and below the transparent space of "clear" ideas (Sulzer 1773:110ff.). In particular, the latter may be considered a prototype of modern psychologies of the "unconscious".

In all this the reception of Western European philosophy already played a role, above all the psychology of the pre-rational of Montaigne's *De la force de l'imagination* (*Essais*, 1588, XX; dt. 1753–1754) and Condillac's *Traité des sensations* (1754) as well as the Anglo-Saxon sensualism and anti-innatism of Locke's *Essay Concerning Human Understanding* (1698, [4]1700, dt. 1757) and Hume's *Treatise of Human Nature* (1739–1740)—and here in particular its association theory (*Essay*, II.33 [[4]1700]; *Treatise*, I.1.4). Particularly Hume's *Treatise* may have been a silent generator of the empirical turn as regards the conception of human being in the German Enlightenment—something which in historical retrospect is often underestimated.

Transformed in this way, physiology and psychology moved closer together again, and the question of their interaction, the *commercium mentis et corporis*, took on new urgency, this time under anti-metaphysical auspices. The theory of "natural influx" between body and soul (*systema influxus physici*) now dominated the field, even though its causality could not be explained (Riedel 1985:22ff.). Thus, medically, the assumption of the dependence of the highest mental forces on physiological conditions and, philosophically, the doubt about "innate ideas" (*ideae innatae*) prevailed. Even the organ mediating this interaction was taken to be identified: the brain and nervous system (Robert Whytt, *Essay on the Vital and Other Involuntary Motions of Animals*, 1751; Albrecht von Haller, *Elementa physiologiae corporis humani*, 1757–1766, vol. 4–5). This was localised as centrally as possible ("Gehirnmark", *interius cerebrum, corpus callosum*: Platner 1772:44–48; Abel 1995:255f. [1779]), or at least at the "origin of all nerves" (Haller 1781: § 370ff.; cf. Abel 1995:607f.). The eighteenth-century neurology at its outset, and its theorising concerning questions such as the one regarding the exact *sedes animi/Sitz der Seele* ("seat of the soul"), the cerebral, physiological equivalents of the ideas (*ideae materiales/materielle Ideen*, "material ideas", precursors of today's *neuronale Korrelate*, "neuronal correlates"), and the way neural conduction of sensitive stimuli happen, might still be speculative. Still, undeniable evidence such as the connection between brain traumata and disturbance of the faculty of thinking cancelled any doubt about the fact that the brain was not only the physiological place but also the "natural" switching point of the *commercium*.

The expression and consequence of this new interweaving of physiology and psychology was the programmatic idea of the "philosophical physician" (Schings 1977:11–40; Riedel 1985:11–17). Neither medicine nor philosophy could grasp the human being as a whole. Since "knowledge of the physical human being cannot be separated from knowledge of the spiritual human being" ("*Känntniß des körperlichen Menschen von der Känntniß des Menschen, wiefern er Geist ist, nicht getrennt werden*", cf. Riedel 1769:127), then "the philosopher must be a doctor and the doctor a philosopher" ("*der Philosoph Arzt, und der Arzt Philosoph seyn*", Hißmann 1777:22). No wonder that, from the 1760s at the latest, voices were raised that brought back the term

"*Anthropologie*". Johann Bernhard Basedow's *Philalethie*, for instance, which is a pedagogical compendium from 1764, summarised all philosophical knowledge on this side of theology under the term "anthropology" (Basedow 1764 I:1–412). A draft of Herder's writing dedicated to a *Philosophie zum Besten des Volks* ("Philosophy for the Best Interests of the People", 1769), written only a few years later, contains a dictum that possibly only paraphrases Basedow, but that, at the same time, reads like a somnambulistic oracle about the spirit of the times: "*Philosophie wird auf Anthropologie zurückgezogen*" ("philosophy is reduced to anthropology", Herder 1985–2005 I:103; cf. Pross 1987:1133ff.).

From 1770 onwards, writings appeared that established the style of thinking described above in the late German Enlightenment, above all Ernst Platner's *Anthropologie für Aerzte und Weltweise* (*Anthropology for Physicians and the Worldly Wise*, 1772), which tried to abolish the separation of "anatomy and physiology", on the one hand, and "psychology", epistemology ("logic") and "moral philosophy", on the other hand, by recurring to an "anthropology" that considers the two natures of the human being "*in ihren gegenseitigen Verhältnissen, Einschränkungen und Beziehungen zusammen betrachtet*" ("in their mutual respects, limitations and relations"—Platner 1772:XVIf. cf. reprint 2000:303–324, afterword by Košenina; Naschert/Stiening 2007). The essential feature of this anthropology is the *systema influxus physici* (Platner 1772:35ff., 90ff.,192ff., 235ff.,282ff.), and specifically the dependence of mental operations on cerebral ones, on the processing of "material ideas" (117ff.). In contrast, *ideae innatae* are rejected ("alle Ideen entstehen zuerst durch die sinnliche Empfindung"/"all ideas first arise through sensuous sensation", 49). The soul may be an "immaterial" being (22ff.), but it and its faculties, including *Urtheilskraft* (the power of judgement) and *Genie* (genius) (192ff., 282ff.), are to be thought of as indissolubly embedded and bound into organic functional contexts. The idea of a completely self-sufficient and autonomous human mind becomes a chimera. Here, human mind and reason set out to become "weak" variables, quite in the sense of a *pensiero debole*, as we know it as an anti-transcendental concept from recent philosophy (Vattimo/Rovatti 1983). This is precisely the historical-philosophical significance of the Enlightenment influxionistic anthropology. Or rather, to use Kondylis's Schmittian hermeneutics of the history of ideas as a battlefield of perpetuating "friend-foe relationships" (Kondylis 1981:20–24), this is precisely where its specific and specifically effective "polemical" contour lies, even presented as unpolemically as in Platner's work. It immediately becomes clear why the transcendental philosopher Kant had to reject it *in limine*. If he did not want to damage his "strong" concepts of reason, power of judgement and freedom of the will, he could only conceive of his own anthropology as strictly non-influxionistic. He called it "pragmatic". Thus, the difference between Platner and Kant in the history of anthropology lies here, and not in the *Wende zur Lebenswelt* (turn to the world of life, to the environment, which is possible also in an influxionistic way).

Even where there is no reference to anthropology in the title, there are motives and convictions that can be moved closer to Platner's work, notwithstanding some divergences in particular questions, but broadly the same. This is the case for Franz Karl von Irwing's *Erfahrungen und Untersuchungen über den Menschen* (1772–1785), Christoph Meiners's *Kurzem Abriß der Psychologie* (1773), Melchior Adam Weikard's *Der philosophische Arzt* (1773–1775, ³1790), Jacob Friedrich Abel's *Dissertatio de origine characteris animi* (1776), Johann Nicolaus Tetens's *Philosophischen Versuchen über die menschliche Natur und ihre Entwicklung* 1776–1777), Michael Hißmann's *Psychologischen Versuchen* (1777), Dietrich Tiedemann's *Untersuchungen über den Menschen* (1777–1778), Johann Georg Heinrich Feder's *Untersuchungen über den menschlichen Willen* (1779–1786), Johann Carl Wezel's *Versuch über die Kenntniß des Menschen* (1784–1785) and Abel's *Einleitung in die Seelenlehre* (1786), but also for the 1770 still well-read work by Johann Friedrich Zückert, *Medicinischer und moralischer Abhandlung von den Leidenschaften* (1764, ³1774), or in Carl Friedrich Flögel's *Geschichte des menschlichen Verstandes* (1765, ³1778).

In the face of the pan-European development (and perhaps with the contemporaneous literary and cultural trend of *Empfindsamkeit* in mind), Kondylis proposed with some success the catchphrase "*Rehabilitation der Sinnlichkeit*" (rehabilitation of sensibility) for the main philosophical concern of the Enlightenment (Kondylis 1981:19). This hit the nail on the head. However, for the German Enlightenment specifically, "rehabilitation of anthropology" would perhaps be even more appropriate. In this way, the "long lines" of the relevant history of knowledge in the German-speaking world would become more visible. For, the questions of late Enlightenment anthropology do not represent something historically lost or "pre-critically" obsolete. On the contrary, they constitute a new beginning, the origin of a paradigm of thought and research that is still alive today. Often pushed aside and never settled, these questions return again and again, *cum variatione*. The twentieth century also knows "philosophical physicians" in the German-speaking countries, first of all, Sigmund Freud and Viktor von Weizsäcker. Both psychoanalysis (specifically Freud's late non-clinical writings from *Jenseits des Lustprinzips* from 1920) and Weizsäcker's "medical anthropology" (*Stücke zu einer medizinischen Anthropologie*, 1926; *Der Gestaltkreis. Theorie der Einheit von Wahrnehmung und Bewegung*, 1940; *Grundfagen medizinischer Anthropologie*, 1948; cf. Weizsäcker 1986–2005, vol. 5, 4, 7) go into philosophical detail and deal with "the whole human being" and, as a consequence, with the problem of the *commercium* in its always new perspectives.

The same is the case at the end of the century, during the "decade of the brain" (1990–2000), in which the alliance of physicians (neurologists), (empirical) psychologists and philosophers (with anthropological interests or even medical expertise) that was so characteristic of Enlightenment anthropology returned in a concentrated form—in Germany, for instance, already through the trio of opinion leaders of the time: Ernst Pöppel for psychology (Pöppel 1993), Gerhard Roth for philosophy (Roth 1994) and Wolf Singer for experimental brain research (Singer 2002). The fact that, at the time, the history of science increasingly turned to the beginnings of brain physiology before and around 1800 (Breidbach 1997; Hagner 1997) fitted into the picture. It was recognised that a focal point of anthropological self-questioning, which persistently intrigues the modern mind, was breaking open here.

Reception of the New Anthropology at the Hohe Karlsschule

Medical empiricism and influxionistic anthropology in the German late Enlightenment also reached the *Hohe Karlsschule* in Stuttgart. Indeed, there they became the ruling doctrine (Riedel 1985:17–37; Riedel 1995:416–436, cf. MPL:89–108). Jacob Friedrich Abel, the academy's leading philosophy professor from 1772 to 1790 (Riedel 1998), was completely devoted to it. Although he did not adopt the term "anthropology", he did undertake the concepts advocated by Sulzer to Platner, which are listed hereinafter in no particular order: (a) combination of the doctrines of the soul and of the body: "*psychologia nisi cum physiologia iungatur semper insufficiens manet*" (Abel 1995:31 [1776]); (b) *Systema influxus physici*: "*Wer weiß es nicht, daß alle Seelenkräfte des Menschen auf eine außerordentliche Weise vom Körper abhangen*" ("who does not know that the human mental powers depend on the corporeal ones"—*Rede über die Entstehung und die Kennzeichen grosser Geister*, 1776: Abel 1995:186; *Dissertatio der origine characteris animi*, 1776: ibid.:148ff., *De influxu corporis*); (c) critique of the *ideae innatae* (Abel 1995:49 [1777], Abel 1786, § 9); (d) psychology of "association" (*Adsoziation*—Abel 1995:39f. [1777]; (e) principle of pleasure and displeasure as a control factor on the soul: "*anima vult conservare & augere omne jucundum, removere omne injucundum*" (Abel 1995:50 [1777], 55 [1778]); (f) theory of *ideae obscurantissimae* (Abel 1995:81 [1780]), ditto dissertation of Abel's pupil (and Schiller's friend) Wilhelm von Hoven: *Versuch über die Wichtigkeit der dunkeln Vorstellungen in der Theorie der Empfindungen* (von Hoven 1780; cf. Riedel 2017:152ff. [1992]); (g) theory of material ideas (*materielle Ideen*) and their power on the trains of thought, both as basis for memory and associations and for fix ideas and other cognitive constraints: "*disceptatio de impressionibus cerebro contentis, summi momenti est*" (Abel 1995:49 [1777]), more broadly explicated in the mentioned *Dissertatio de origine characteris animi* (ibid.:148ff.).

Abel was not an isolated figure in the debate, the Tübingen supervisor's critique notwithstanding, that is, the metaphysician and logician Gottfried Ploucquet (Riedel 1995:395f.). The philosophical colleagues August Friedrich Böck and Johann Christoph Schwab sang the same tune (ibid.:427): "*actio animae in corpus et corporis in animam physica et realis est*" (Böck, *Theses disputatoriae*, 1775); "*influxus physicus nullo ideoneo argumento refutari potest*" (Schwab, *Dissertatio logica de methodo analytica*, 1779). Ditto the physicians.

Both faculties actualised the ideal of the "philosophical physician" in cooperation. The head of the medical faculty, Johann Friedrich Consbruch, was a strenuous influxionist (Alt 2000 I:150ff.) and repeatedly proposed for the academic anniversary speeches topics in accordance with his interests, for instance, in 1777, *Von dem Einfluß der Organisation deß Hirns auf das Genie* (Riedel 1985:21f.).

New impulses such as French materialism were added, first through La Mettrie's *L'homme machine* (1748) and afterwards especially by Claude Adrien Helvétius (cf. Krebs 2006). In Germany, La Mettrie had difficulties; he was held to be too radical, but even graver was the fact that the paradigm of the machine, which is to be found in the title of his work, became obsolete after 1750 (Durner et al. 1994; Riedel 2018:252ff.). At any rate, at the Hohe Karlsschule, Helvétius was the materialist of the hour. Abel dealt extensively with his works *De l'esprit* (1758, dt. 1760) and *De l'homme* (1773, dt. 1774), which had been both translated into German (Abel 1995:435, 525f., 614ff.). Much of what was contained in those works, such as strict sensualism and anti-innatism, or the control of the soul by affects and sentiments of pleasure and displeasure (here called "*sensibilité physique*"), was not new to him, but, still, the radical conclusions that Helvétius drew from it, especially the doctrine of the absolute dominance of egoism in the human soul based on the *sensibilité physique*, were genuinely new. In his opinion, this went too far (Abel 1995:135 [1782]). Instead, he took over from Helvétius the idea of an expansion of the spectrum of influence derived from the sensualistic genesis of all mental dispositions and contents to include social influence, that is, the shaping of the soul through education and milieu. By means of the addition of this "*influxus circumstantiarum externarum*" (ibid.:166ff. [1776], 549f.), the influxionism taught by Abel was complete. Empiricism, influxionism, empirical psychology and anthropology, the convergence of philosophy and medicine—in this intellectual world, the intellectual socialisation of the young Schiller—the second following that of his family—now occurred. And as conventional and religious as the first had been (the boy's and his parents' original wish was theology, Oellers 2006:167ff.), this second socialisation drew him deeply into the process of Enlightenment. Already with the change to medicine dictated by the feudal lord, the "polemical" (in Kondylis's sense) potential of this process was activated.

At the *Hohe Karlsschule*, philosophy was a main subject in the context of medical studies and from 1776 Schiller belonged to the circle of Abel's pupils (Riedel 1995:391, 401). For the final examination, he wrote three *Probschriften* or dissertations, one purely medical on febrile diseases (*De discrimine febrium* […], 1780, SW [2004!] 5:1056ff.; cf. Alt 2000 I:172ff.; Robert 2011a:55ff.) and two further writings, which completely followed the ideal of the "philosophical physician" and built a bridge to philosophy: *Philosophie der Physiologie* (*Philosophy of Physiology*, 1779, SW 5:250–268), which has only survived in fragmentary transcriptions, and *Versuch über den Zusammenhang der thierischen Natur des Menschen mit seiner geistigen* (*Attempt on the Connection of the Human Being's Animal Nature with Its Spiritual One*, 1780, SW 5:287–324).

Only the last one secured him the degree. The writing on febrile diseases was regarded as too superficial (Riedel 1985:3), and the lost *Philosophia physiologiae* did not meet with approval either. It began metaphysically/pneumatologically from the concept of "spiritual life", and only then came to the physiological assumption and finally to its end, that is, to "death" (SW 5:250, *Plan*). However, to "spiritual life" was already guaranteed "eternity" in § 1, on the vocation of the human being (§1, *Bestimmung des Menschen*); the soul would also continue to "grow" postmortem and thus approximate "God-likeness" in "infinite" time (ibid.). Schiller followed here a bestseller of the German Enlightenment (1748, [10]1774, [11]1794): Johann Joachim Spalding's *Die Bestimmung des Menschen* (Spalding 2006; cf. Riedel 1985:166–173; Macor 2013). The theological Neoplatonic *topos* of an *ascensio ad deum* and its Leibnizian variant (*Monadologie*, 1714, § 83f.), the determination of the human soul, conceived as an "*image de la Divinité*", to imitate (*imiter*) the archetype as well as to finally be united in a community with it ("*une maniere de Societé avec Dieu*"), were linked by Spalding as part of Protestant Enlightenment theology ("neology") to a popular compensatory formula that was intended to satisfy the "metaphysical need" for both the theological and the philosophical. *Conditio sine qua non* of these "expectations of eternity" was the pneumatological concept of soul, which was still philosophically current— see Moses Mendelssohn's also widely read *Phaedon oder über die Unsterblichkeit der Seele* from 1767 (Riedel 1985:160ff.; Macor 2013:182ff.). But to make this the basis of a medical dissertation on the *commercium*, which was to receive the placet of experientially oriented physicians, was a bold act. It was even more risky, of course, to present to them the speculative positing of a substance-transcendent "middle force" (*Mittelkraft*/vis transmutatoria) with all kinds of secondary forces "in the nerve" as an answer to the riddle of bodily/mental interaction, which did without any support in physiological observation (SW 5:253ff.; cf. Riedel 1985:61ff., 2011:585ff.). For Consbruch, this was a reversion to the *qualitates occultae* of the ancients (Riedel 1985:101), so that the work was rejected as too empirical.

Schiller understood and approached the matter in a completely different manner in his second attempt (Riedel 1985:106ff., 2011:588ff.). The *Attempt on the Connection of the Human Being's Animal Nature with Its Spiritual One* does not start with the mind, but with the body, and in the first part (*Physischer Zusammenhang*/physical connection) it first lays down a physiological foundation before discussing in the second part (*Philosophischer Zusammenhang/* philosophical connection) the interaction of the bodily/mental interactions (Falduto 2020). In this way, Schiller now builds anthropology from the bottom-up, inductively as it were, consistently following the empiricist motto *hypotheses non fingo*. He reports the well-known observations of psychophysical coincidences and parallelisms, but no longer proposes causative "forces" for his explanation. Instead, he formulates two "fundamental law[s] of the mixed natures" (*Fundamentalgesetz[e] der gemischten Naturen*, SW 5:306, 312), but these are understood as purely empirical, that is, they are limited to fixing the recurrent regularity of body-mind synchronicities in general propositions. Even with regard to the concept of "sympathy" (ibid.) between bodily and mental states, which is used in this context, no *qualitas occulta* is introduced, but rather a medically familiar term is used to designate simultaneous but locally separate symptoms (Riedel 1985:121ff.). Only in the final paragraph does Schiller allow himself to go beyond the limits of empirical knowledge by writing down some cautious allusions to the concept of immortality (SW 5:323f.). Since this now passed muster for academics in medicine, the work was accepted.

SCHILLER AS ANTHROPOLOGICAL THINKER

The step taken between 1779 and 1780 from a theologically/pneumatologically based metaphysical anthropology to the empirical one asserted by the influxionists and the "philosophical physicians" was a radical conceptual break and a distinctive crossroads in Schiller's intellectual biography (cf. MPL:307–372, *The Intellectual Legacy of Medicine and Psychology* [1976]). In the quasi-autobiographical *Philosophical Letters* (1786), Schiller took the painful awakening from the dreams of metaphysics as occasion for the composition of an epistolary novel, which remained a fragment, though one that aimed at narrating the process of "Enlightenment" as a successful passage through critique and crisis (SW 5:336–358; cf. Riedel 1985:145–248). The juvenile protagonist Julius, a Neoplatonic enthusiast of the kind Wieland might have invented, falls into the mills of "doubt" under the influence of his friendly mentor Raphael (a literary copy of Abel) and confronts the idea that his original metaphysical convictions, communicated in the novel in the form of an internal essay (SW 5: 344–354, *Theosophie des Julius*), might merely be wishful thinking and illusion: "My heart sought a philosophy, and phantasy sublated its dreams. [...] A bold attack by materialism destroys my creation" (344); "Possibly [...] the whole framework of my conclusions was an insubstantial dream" (354; cf. 1185 regarding the long unclear interconnection between essay and postscript).

Further texts from these years also deal with this experience of disillusionment, mostly in dialogue form. The pro-et-contra method learned in the context of his philosophical studies becomes a literary arrangement aiming at playing out different positions: *Der Spaziergang unter den Linden* (1782), *Der Jüngling und der Greis* (1782), the "philosophical conversation" in the *Geisterseher* (1789) (SW 5:327ff., 332ff., 160ff.; cf. Riedel 2011:604ff.) or also the philosophical poem *Resignation. Eine Phantasie* (1786, SW 1:130–133), a brilliant enactment of the rejection of the belief in immortality (Riedel 2017:121ff. [1996]). The resignation *in metaphysicis*, worked out step by step, as it were, in these literary roles, leads Schiller close to intellectual attitudes that will be called pessimism or nihilism in the nineteenth century (Panizzo 2019). However, Schiller does not embrace these attitudes (neither does he use these terms). I would also hesitate to apply to Schiller the quasi "objectified", value-neutral term of "nihilism", as proposed by Kondylis as the vanishing point of the disenchantment dynamic of the European Enlightenment (Kondylis 1981:490; Panizzo 2019:40f.), even though Schiller's thought follows precisely such a line of development. Even if it is correct to point out the line of connection that few appreciate running from Schiller to Nietzsche (and also to Georg Büchner, who, however, saw this line as little as Nietzsche), it would be wrong to define this proximity too narrowly. Franz Moor unquestionably represents a brute experiment in nihilism (sadism was also spoken of time and again, ibid.:9, 93ff.)—but this remains a negative experiment (Schings 1982). Schiller, once he became a philosopher of the Enlightenment, remained so his whole life. The same path of thought that had led him to a sceptical attitude in matters transcendent to experience, and, at the same time, taught him the reality principle in matters immanent to experience. Morally and politically, he had thus become a convinced realist at early age, to whom nothing human or inhuman could be alien, but who, because of it, was not willing to give up the fact of his equivalent distance to wishful thinking and misanthropy.

From empirical psychology Schiller had acquired not only theories of "material ideas" (SW 5:259), "obscure ideas" (310) and involuntary "association" (994), but also a "phenomenalistic" conception of human cognition. If nerve stimulations and, as their result, a material signal in the brain lie at the origins of our representations, these cannot be immediate "images of things, but merely their necessarily [namely physiologically] determined and coexisting signs [...] Neither God nor the human soul nor the world are what we really hold them to be", but rather are only a "conventional illusion" (355). Something similar was to be learned, for example, in Adam Ferguson's *Institutes of Moral Philosophy* (1769), which was well known to Schiller through Garve's translation (Ferguson 1772:75–79; cf. Riedel 1985:215ff.).

With regard to the immanent world of experience, the mere sign character of the perceptual and representational "images" was not harmful, as long as the correlations between nerve stimulation, *idea materialis* and representational image remained secure. In the case of transcendent representations, however, this link to the sensory periphery and neuro-cerebral stimulative conduction is missing and the production of ideas becomes freer, more subjective and autogenous. If anthropological self-reflection starts here, religious ideas are threatened with psychologisation. Hume's *Natural History of Religion* (1757, German transl. 1759), which Abel introduced to the Karlsschule, provided the pattern for tracing back human assumptions about the afterlife not to reason, but rather to projections of affect—"hopes and fears" (Hume 1992 IV:315; Hume 1759:27; Abel 1995:89 [1780]) or "*Hoffnung*" and "*Schrecken*" (SW 1:132). Loosely based on Xenophanes B15, Schiller sums up the anthropomorphic inversion according to which the human being creates its gods in "its own image" (SW 5:652), and not vice versa: "If you gave to a crystal the faculty of representation, [...] its divinity [would be] the most beautiful form of crystal" (SW 5:165).

In the context of the doctrine of the impulses, Schiller took over from Helvétius and Abel the doctrine of the power of "self-interest" in the soul, even in matters seemingly remote from egoism such as familiar and sexual love (Abel 1995:614ff.). Furthermore, especially as a playwright and shaper of characters, he became a "connoisseur of human nature" of the calibre of the French moralists (to whom Helvétius owed his part), who vivisected the "inner workings" and the "most secret operations" of the "soul" (*Räuber*, opening speech, 1781, SW 1:484f.) as only La Rochefoucauld ever could (cf. Robert 2011b; Kruse 2003). This is the case particularly in the rapturous analyses that he gave, not only of the "*Mißmenschen*" (ibid.) such as Franz Moor, but also, and until his late work, of the enthusiasts among his heroes, who were drawn with sympathy and, at the same time, with a cold gaze: Karl Moor, Ferdinand von Walter, Marquis Posa, Mortimer and Johanna. And this is also the case for the lucid "psychoanalyses" of power and its owner: Fiesko, Philipp, Kardinal Großinquisitor, Wallenstein, Burleigh, Boris Godunow and Demetrius. Schiller's psychology in his dramas set the standard for the psychological realism that was to dominate the German-language stage from Kleist and Büchner onwards.

However, as in Abel's case, the following holds again: egoism's predominance is upheld; egoism's supremacy is not (this is also the decisive difference between them and Nietzsche, who, instead, directly followed Helvétius, cf. Riedel 1996:214ff.). However, even before he encountered Helvétius, Schiller had already been influenced by the dualistic theory of the impulses issuing from Rousseau and the Scottish moral philosophers (Riedel 1985:176ff.; Abel 1995:525f.). The human being's natural egoism, accordingly, was balanced in equal measure by a natural and pre-rational counterforce, which had many names at the time: *moral sense* (Shaftesbury), *benevolence* (Francis Hutcheson), *sympathy* (Adam Smith), *pitié* (Rousseau), "*Gesetz der Geselligkeit*" (in the German translation of Ferguson 1772:80), "*Wohlgewogenheit*" (Spalding 2006:85), "*Wohlwollen*" (Abel 1995:56f. [1778]) and, in Schiller himself, "*uneigennützige Liebe*" (SW 5:351, *Theosophie des Julius*). Hence, he did not take Helvétius's "black psychology" as an anthropological principle or even as a maxim of the "ought", but rather only as an instrument for analysing real relations, that is, the imperfections of the human "being".

Similarly, Schiller also detects in the cognitive sphere—perception, imagination, memory—the influence of the unconscious and involuntary production of ideas, which has been proven by empirical psychology, balanced by a likewise empirical faculty of the soul, and which can already be verified by self-observation, to prefer certain representations rather than others, and to push aside disturbing ones—what was called *attentio* or "*Aufmerksamkeit*" in the "scholastic philosophy" (*Schulphilosophie*) (SW 5:266, *Philosophy of Physiology*). The concept reached the *Karlsschule* via Charles Bonnet's *Essai analytique sur les facultés de l'âme* (German transl. 1770/71) and its critique of Condillac's radical sensualism (Abel 1995:573). Perhaps, also Herder's treatise on the origin of language (*Abhandlung über den Ursprung der Sprache*, 1772) that was also directed against Condillac played a role, since its "discretion" (*Besonnenheit*) theorem was based on the phenomenon of "attention" (*Aufmerksamkeit*—Herder 1985–2005 I:722).

However, this ability was already relevant for Abel, not only in a cognitive but also in a moral sense, as an empirically validated potential of the soul to be able to act not only against sensations, but also against impulses. In this way, the *attentio* becomes the empirical support of moral autonomy or "strength of soul" (Abel 1995:219ff. [1777]). At this point, neo-Stoic thought—widespread in German Enlightenment and fundamental for Abel's ethics—was incorporated. In addition to Zückert 1774 (§§ 66ff., 81ff.) and Garve, who translated Cicero's *de officiis* (*Abhandlung über die menschlichen Pflichten*) in 1783, Thomas Abbt's book *Vom Verdienste* (1765, ²1766) and its chapter *Von der Stärke der Seele* (cf. Abel 1995:570ff.) should be mentioned here. Schiller also adopted this specific link between psychology and ethics: "All human morality has its ground in attention" (SW 5:266). And, with an enlightened version of neo-Stoicism adopted early on, he never wavered from trust in the freedom of the will as the anchor point of his ethical convictions in contrast to the impulses exerted from the drives. This was the case from the philosophy of his youth (see, in addition to the quoted essay *Philosophy of Physiology*, the chapter of the *Theosophie* dedicated to sacrifice/*Aufopferung*, SW 5:351f.) to the late theory of the tragic and the sublime (*Über das Pathetische*, 1793, SW 5:529ff.; *Über das Erhabene*, 1801, SW 5:793ff.; cf. Piñeiro Costas 2006; Riedel 2017:304ff. [2007]). The view maintaining a "neo-Stoic change of mind" around 1790 (in contrast to Richter/Mojem 2021) is not sustained.

The avoidance of a system is characteristic of Schiller's thinking. He followed Shaftesbury's *bon mot* "the most ingenious way of becoming foolish, is *by a System*"—whether he knew it or not. Abel was already a practising eclecticist (Riedel 1995:411ff.), and Schiller also kept his thinking flexible according to the motto "the best of everything". In the context of German Enlightenment, neither of them belongs to the system-loving Leibnizians, but rather to the system sceptics close to Thomasius, who preferred open thinking forms rather than closed ones, and did not shrink from provisional solutions and bricolage in the construction of their theory (ibid.:415). The association law and "attention", egoism and altruism, or even affect dependence and strength of soul may be theories that conflict with one another; however, by combining them, one comes surprisingly close to empiricism. The later, in the context of anthropology called "symbiosis appetite" (*Symbiosenappetit*, Marquard 1971:366), has its historical basis in its early alliance with eclecticism.

The transition from anthropology to the philosophy of history can also be read as an eclectic experiment, as Schiller performed it in 1789 in the inaugural Jena lecture *What is [...] Universal History?* (SW 4:749ff.) and in *The Artists* (SW 1:173ff.), among the others following Kant's *Idea for a Universal History with a Cosmopolitan Aim* (1784, Ak 8:15–32). Schiller took seriously the compatibility of sceptical realism and historical-philosophical optimism, but he did not in the end adhere to the latter since he understood how the empirical course of history led one astray during the "fall back into barbarism" (i.e., through the turn of the French Revolution into the *Grande Terreur*, see the second one of the *Augustenburg Letters*, 13.7.1793, NA 26:262; *On the*

Sublime, 1801, SW 5:802ff.; cf. Riedel 2017:279ff. [2001]). This was also the case for his relationship with the secret society of the *Illuminati*, which was also present at the *Karlsschule* (thanks to Abel) in 1781–1785. As *Don Carlos* and the associated *Letters* (1788, SW 2) show, Schiller certainly dealt with the idea of realising Enlightenment in politics via a "march through the institutions" and a "reform from above". However, since he recognised (as Abel himself did) that the arcane methods of the revolutionaries exactly mirrored the power relations they criticised (which brings us back to the question of egoism), he kept his distance from them (Schings 1996; Riedel 2017:103ff. [2003]).

Thus, Schiller's thought was relatively mature when he began to deal with Kant's *Critiques* in February 1791 (cf. Beiser 2008:37ff.). It is not a new start, but rather an addition of new materials to an already-solid foundation. Schiller had already carried out, on a phenomenalistic path, Kant's newly formulated focus on cognitive references in the *Critique of Pure Reason*, which was compared with a "Copernican revolution" (it is not intuition, "*Anschauung*", which conforms to the "constitution of the objects", but rather "the object [… which conforms to] the constitution of our faculty of intuition", KrV, B XVI–XVII). However, it was not a matter of the nature of the "transcendental *a priori*", but rather a matter of the "endemic forms of human neurophysiology", in which natural history ("the planet") "gives us the idioms of our concepts" (*die Idiome unsrer Begriffe überliefert*, SW 5:355). Since Kant's inversion was already clear to him from an empirical point of view, the first *Critique* did not turn his world upside down, but it rather only clarified "internally" the conditions of possibility of the forms of thought themselves. The same applied to ethics. Schiller acknowledged the categorical imperative as a principle of "morality" (*Sittlichkeit*) solely out of "respect for the law of reason" (cf. the third one of the *Augustenburg Letters*, dated 3.12.1793, NA 26:322). However, at the same time, he saw that this only applies "in theory", not "in the application" of it, since "human nature" could "never be expected" to "act uniformly and persistently as a pure mental nature, without interruption and relapse" (ibid.:330, 332). Against Kant's condemnation, Schiller unwaveringly persists in asking the question about what nature makes out of a human being.

From this it follows that Schiller would become an aesthetician. Historically and factually, the philosophical aesthetics founded by Alexander G. Baumgarten (*Aesthetica*, 1750–1758) is a sibling of empirical psychology and anthropology (Zelle 2001:5). The latter appeared at the same time and both followed the transformation of Wolffian rationalism, in Baumgarten as "*gnoseologia inferior*" (§ 1)—as a theory of "sensuous knowledge" (*aisthesis*) mediated not by *ratio* but by *physis*. The aesthetic problem was already an anthropological one, and also Schiller's path to aesthetics did not lead him out of anthropology but, on the contrary, into it. Indeed, his theory of beauty and the arts, especially drama, constantly reaches beyond aesthetic-poetic questions in the narrower sense, extending to questions of political intervention (*Augustenburg Letters*, 1793) in the form of a critique of Enlightenment rationalism (*Letters on the Aesthetic*

Education of the Human Being, 1795) to a theory of the modern attitude to life (*On Naive and Sentimental Poetry*, 1795–1796) or to a post-metaphysical "philosophy of life" (*On Tragic Art*, 1792, SW 5: 375; *On the Sublime*). These are all questions and intentions that pertain to the field of anthropology and especially to that of "pragmatic" anthropology. Schiller's "turn to aesthetics" simultaneously, and quite precisely, therefore, accomplished a "turn to the lifeworld", to anthropology as "lifeworld philosophy" (*Lebensweltphilosophie*), which Marquard wished to be Kant's preserve (Marquard 1965:126, 1971:365). However, Schiller carried out this turn while retaining the physiological aspects of anthropology that Kant had rejected. And it is exactly in this respect that the difference (following Kondylis' terminology: the "polemical" difference) between Schiller and Kant and between Kant's conception and Schiller's conception of philosophical anthropology is found—a difference of importance in the history of ideas.

The clearest sign of this is to be found in the *Letters on the Aesthetic Education of the Human Being* and in the *Augustenburg Letters* (cf. Riedel 2017:225ff. [2013]). In the face of an Enlightenment that only appealed to people's heads and therefore did not reach their hearts, these letters call for the "complete anthropological esteem" (*vollständige anthropologische Schätzung*), in which "sensation", "feeling" and "nature" (*Empfindung, Gefühl, Natur*) also have a voice together with "reason" (SW 5:577). "*Connection of the Human Being's Animal Nature with Its Spiritual One*": Schiller brings into position here the *homo-totus*-anthropology in an Enlightenment-critical way (cf. Falduto 2020, 2021). A lack of cultivation of sensation and instinct, on the one hand, and a reductive perspective through rationalism only, on the other hand (580), would have caused Enlightenment and Revolution to fail—and the latter to regress into de-humanisation. "Training the faculty of feeling" (nothing else is here meant by "aesthetic education") is therefore "the most urgent need of the time" (592). Only in the "*totality*" of his "character" (579), only as *homo totus*, can the human being achieve humanity, or hope to strive for it. The ideal of a "condition" (*Zustand*)—or "aesthetic condition" (633, 641f.), one maximally relieved of inner and outer pressures in which the connection between the two human natures is realised in a completely "free" and "light" way, that is, as a "play" (616ff.) and consequently also considered as an unconstrained connection of "freedom", "equality" and "beauty"—forms a "state" (*Staat*) as the union of different people, and thus called "aesthetic" in that sense (667ff.). Nonetheless, this ideal, which is based upon an illusion, is not, according to Schiller, the goal of the aesthetic education. In fact, as an exceptional condition, it may confer on existence a "beautiful appearance" (*schöner Schein*), preferably in privileged social enclaves ("selected circles"), but it can never become a rule (669). Therefore, the philosophical point of the *Aesthetic Letters* is not the vision of a possible target condition to be reached (this was variously entertained in other theories at the time), but rather the choice of the right anthropological starting point for an enlightened policy of humanisation, namely a point of departure in human sensibility and animal nature. Even though the *Letters* end with the "beautiful" utopia of an "aesthetic State", they are still supported, in the last paragraph, by the insight that this utopia merely formulates a "need" (669), and that, in reality, as Kant puts it (Ak. 8:23), the "crooked wood" the human being is made of finds its best possible realisation in a striving for the next best.

Schiller's aesthetic theory unfolds from this point towards the side of the beautiful. The complement to this, entirely in accordance with the "double aesthetics of modernity" (Zelle 1995:147ff.), is provided, again, also in anthropological and pragmatic terms, by the theory of the "sublime". For not all situations in life make possible the beautiful "harmony" (SW 5:667) between the human being's two natures—and many situations even compel it to abandon the aforementioned harmony in favour of an asymmetrical predominance of reason (i.e., Abel's "strength of soul"), in view of insight into ethical duties or physical and other further external necessities. In such cases, the individual is required to step out of its own "nature". Schiller calls this act of elevation above animal nature "*idealistic*", since he knows that it is not "*realistically*" possible (*Über das Erhabene*, SW 5:793)—certainly not up to the end. At the end of the life cycle of animal nature stands the great humiliator of spiritual nature—death. In death the power of reason perishes. "No human being must abide" (*Kein Mensch muß müssen*), Schiller quotes Lessing's *Nathan*, but everyone must die, that is, everybody must do what each "does not want to" (792f.). Here, in each person's own death, lies the focus on the lifeworld that characterises Schiller's aesthetics of the sublime, which thus becomes a classical Stoic *meditatio mortis* (Riedel 2017:301ff. [2007]; Riedel 2022). In the face of death nothing but the intelligible abstraction from corporeality remains in order for this to annihilate physical annihilation "according to the concept", in this separation of the spirit (794). This is thought in a very dialectical way. In fact, the unconditional "must" that death demands of us cannot be denied, but rather only subverted, as it were, through its acceptance, as "resignation to necessity", through the transformation of the compulsion of nature into a "work of free choice" (ibid.). Schiller calls this "moral self-disembodiment" (*moralische Selbstentleibung*, 805). Only in the paradoxical acceptance of nature's heteronomy, which retains the last word precisely at this point, can reason's autonomy still be saved: "Death cannot be evil because it is something general" (Schiller 1805 orally, cf. Wolzogen 1990 II:288). Schiller's anthropological realism does not omit this extreme. The difference from Goethe, for instance (*den Tod statuiere ich nicht*, i.e., "I do not allow death", Goethe 1972:289 [1825]), could not be greater.

In this *meditatio mortis*, Schiller is not concerned to seek consolation through "ideas of religion". These ideas are not validated with regard to affective and projective psychology as mere "soothing reasons for our sensibility" (*Vom Erhabenen*, 1793, SW 5:498). The enlightened mind is able to deal with them only in the mode of the *as-if*, and it is precisely in this sense that they become the subject of Schiller's aesthetics, especially in the *Kallias Letters* (1793, SW 5:394ff.), in the *Matthisson Review* (1794, ibid.:992ff.), in the poem infused with the philosophy of religion, namely *Die Götter Griechenlandes*

(1788, ²1800, SW 1:163ff.), and in the work *Über naive und sentimentalische Dichtung* (694ff.). The common theme of these three treatises is the aesthetic interest in external nature, be it a single natural being or a natural ensemble (nature as landscape). The source of all three works may have been Abel's theory of nature's ensoulment, which Schiller had already appropriated (Abel 1784; cf. Riedel 2017:63ff. [2011], 206ff. [2009]): "Nature charms and delights us only through that which we confer on it" (Letter to Caroline von Beulwitz and Charlotte von Lengefeld dated September 12, 1789, NA 25:292). It is not its "mere" existence that stimulates our "feeling of pleasure", but rather the idea projected onto it and, thus, "represented" by it, that we love in nature (*Naive und sentimentalische Dichtung*, SW 5:694f.). The *Matthisson Review* calls this act of projection a "symbolic operation" (998). And the *Kallias Letters* also allow natural beauty to arise in the mind of the observer: The "bird in flight" (413f.), which according to the Cartesian understanding of animals in the eighteenth century is to be considered a "heteronomous" event, that is, "determined" by natural causality, takes on the anthropomorphic appearance of "autonomy", of "similarity to freedom" (*Freiheitähnlichkeit*, 398–404), as soon as we "lend" it our freedom and it becomes for us a "symbol of freedom" (414). This is precisely what the key term of these letters, "freedom in appearance" (*Freiheit in der Erscheinung*), means (400).

Against this background, the cultural-historical difference between "naive" and "sentimental" can immediately be read as a religious-psychological one. Naïve culture was not disunited from nature only because it had not yet "lost nature in humanity" (711) but also because it had conceived of nature as animate and saw itself reflected in this pantheon of spirits and gods, namely a world full of subjectivities. Therefore, ancient polytheism—as the "birth of a happy imagination, not of brooding reason, like the church faith of the newer nations" (ibid.)—is "beautiful" for the modern observer (*Die Götter Griechenlandes*, SW 1:163). However, according to Schiller, after passing through monotheism, the observer has already left behind the anthropomorphic inversion as the pivot point of the world's disenchantment and, consequently, sees the "outside" only in a de-subjectified, soulless matter, as "de-deified nature" (ibid.:164, 168). After becoming a "representation" of the observer, the "gods" belong only to one's own inwardness and imagination (SW 5:652). Naive culture "believes" in the result of its projections and does not yet "know" its origin; the enlightened-sentimental culture knows it and no longer believes in its result (it "no longer bends its knee", Hegel 1835/42 I:110). Sentimental consciousness counterbalances the disenchantment of nature through secondary re-ensoulment—however, since it is something that is principally *known*, this only succeeds as an aesthetic and poetic act in the *as-if* mode (SW 5:399) of the "beautiful appearance", that is, of an appearance that is neither completely wrong nor completely right, but indispensable.

We see here that Schiller, as an anthropologist, is by no means thinking antihistorically. And he does not only include, as is the case here, the cultural-historical dimension, but also the natural-historical one. The "temporalisation of the natural", ever-present in 1800 (*Temporalisierung des Natürlichen*—Darwin was still far away, but the "chain of beings" was already theoretically temporalized, cf. Lovejoy 1936:242ff.; Lepenies 1976), takes on immense power as a question about the "natural" transition from the animal to the human. Kant had already transferred the method of humanistic myth's allegoresis to the Old Testament (i.e., of extracting a narratively disguised rational core from mythological narratives—Francis Bacon, *De sapientia veterum*, 1609) in order to accomplish the creation of the human being and the expulsion from the garden of Eden (Genesis, 1–3) with a reading compatible with the Enlightenment. The "voice of God" thus becomes "instinct", that is, the "call of nature", which "all animals obey", and human non-compliance with the divine command becomes the human being's "first attempt" to "become aware of its own reason" and make use of it (Kant, *Muthmaßlicher Anfang der Menschengeschichte*, 1786, Ak 8:107ff.). Schiller follows this view in *Etwas über die erste Menschengesellschaft nach dem Leitfaden der mosaischen Urkunde* (1790, SW 4:767ff.). Anthropogenesis began as a result of the "fall" from the "guiding bond of instinct" (equivalent to "God's voice in the Eden") as the "daring" of freedom and self-determined morality. It was not to be regarded as an event of guilt and atonement, but rather "the happiest [...] event in human history" (769), a "positivisation of the fall" (*Positivierung des Sündenfalls*, Marquard 1981:57ff.). The paradisiacal innocence is "naturalised" into the innocence of the animal, which is embedded in nature through the couple instinct/reflex just as firmly and securely as this has been taken to be the case since Uexküll's *System Environment Biology* (*Umwelt und Innenwelt der Tiere*, 1909).

More original is the anthropogenetic invention of the primal scene in the third of the *Augustenburg Letters*, which derives the abandonment of the animal condition from the sublimation of sensibility itself (cf. Riedel 2017:239ff. [2013]). When the human animal's purview, which had always been determined purely by actual "need", became capable (even if only partially) of a "free contemplation" detached from greed and fear (a distance that will become constitutive in the later life of that animal), this purview becomes part of its relating to the world. The objects of instinctive wanting and flight from reflex took on a certain distance. The relation to these objects became "liberal", temporarily relaxed, and stress-free: "space between human being and appearances occurs" (NA 26:311f.). In this position of distance, which arose from a modification of sensibility itself (*aisthesis*) without any involvement of reason (this is the difference from Herder), and which is thus already pre-rational, Schiller recognises the natural ground for enabling both the sublimation of drives, which gradually "refined the raw stock of nature" (306), and the development of reason in general, that is, the "free contemplation" liberated from acute interest that was the very first thing serving to develop our rationality (312).

Even though these reflections remain vague, they are nevertheless audacious. They have little in common with the theological ideas of divine "guidance" of the humanisation process developed half a generation earlier in

Herder's *Älteste Urkunde des Menschengeschlechts* (1774–1776—Herder 1985–2005, vol. V:602ff.) and Lessing's *Erziehung des Menschengeschlechts* (1777–1780). Schiller aims at thinking anthropogenesis in purely anthropological terms. In doing so, he also goes further than Herder in composing the origin of language (*Abhandlung über den Ursprung der Sprache*, 1772). In fact, precisely here, "the human being's reasonableness (*Vernunftmäßigkeit*)" and its capacity for independent reflection (*Besonnenheit*) are always presupposed as a point of difference naturally bound to creation and the genuine character of the species (Herder 1985–2005, vol. I:716ff.), whereas Schiller precisely seeks a natural-historical point of mediation, that is, the transition from animal to human *aisthesis*.

The late Schiller is thus closer to the future of anthropology, especially to post-Darwinian anthropology, than to its past (cf. Midell 2017; Riedel 2017:244ff. [2013], 2019:19ff.). The idea that cultivation cannot be achieved through the domination of reason over drives, but only through the sublimation of the drives themselves will be encountered in Freud. The idea that the human being, even though it is a nature-based organism, is at the same time a habitual distance-seeking being, *habituelles Distanzwesen*, in Simmel and Plessner; the idea that the "openness to the world", or, in Schiller's terminology, *freye Betrachtung*, is based on the disengagement of reflex and instinct, will come up in Scheler and Gehlen (cf. Probst 1994); the idea that detached, free (and in this sense "aesthetic") observation opens up the "space of thought" (*Denkraum*), will be seen in Aby Warburg; the idea that the concept of play represents an anthropologism of the highest order, in Buytendijk, Huizinga and Gehlen; and the idea that post-metaphysical thinking must also "allow death" will recur in Heidegger. "Philosophical anthropology" always recognised Herder as its early precursor (Gehlen 1940:90ff.); Schiller is at least to be accorded a place next to him.

German text translated into English by Antonino Falduto in connection with Tim Mehigan.

References

Abel, Jacob Friedrich. 1784. 'Von den Reizungen, die die tote Natur durch die beseelte erhält'. In: Riedel 2017:73–86.

Abel, Jacob Friedrich. 1786. *Einleitung in die Seelenlehre*. Stuttgart: Mezler [sic]. – Reprint 1985. Hildesheim/Zürich/New York: Olms.

[Abel 1995:] *Jacob Friedrich Abel. Eine Quellenedition zum Philosophieunterricht an der Stuttgarter Karlsschule (1773-1782). Mit Einleitung, Übersetzung, Kommentar und Bibliographie*, ed. Wolfgang Riedel. Würzburg: Königshausen & Neumann.

Alt, Peter-André. 2000. *Schiller. Leben – Werk – Zeit*, 2 vols. München: Beck.

Barkhoff, Jürgen, and Sagarra, Eda (ed.). 1992. *Anthropologie und Literatur um 1800*. München: Iudicium.

Basedow, Johann Bernhard. 1764. *Philalethie. Neue Aussichten in die Wahrheiten der Vernunft bis in die Grenzen der glaubwürdigen Offenbarung*, 2 vols. Altona: Iversen.

Beiser, Frederick. 2008. *Schiller as Philosopher. A Re-Examination*. Oxford: Clarendon Press.
Benzenhöfer, Udo. 1993. *Psychiatrie und Anthropologie in der ersten Hälfte des 19. Jahrhunderts*. Hürtgenwald: Pressler.
Benzenhöfer, Udo, and Rotzoll, Maike. 1991. 'Zur "Anthropologia" (1533) von Galeazzo Capella'. In *Medizinhistorisches Journal* 26: 315–320.
Breidbach, Olaf. 1997. *Die Materialisierung des Ichs. Zur Geschichte der Hirnforschung im 19. und 20. Jahrhundert*. Frankfurt/M.: Suhrkamp.
Caroll, Jerome. 2018. *Anthropology's Interrogation of Philosophy from the Eighteenth to the Twentieth Century*. Lanham: Lexington Books.
Durner, Manfred, et al. 1994. *Wissenschaftshistorischer Bericht zu Schellings naturphilosophischen Schriften 1797-1800*. Stuttgart: Frommann-Holzboog.
Falduto, Antonino. 2020. 'Jenseits des Dualismus zwischen tierischer Natur und geistiger Natur: Kants Mensch 'in zwiefacher Qualität' und Schillers 'ganzer Mensch''. In *Kant-Studien*, 111(2): 248–268.
Falduto, Antonino. 2021. 'One more time on the alleged repugnance of Kant's ethics? Schiller's *Kallias letters* and the entirety of the human being'. In *European Journal of Philosophy* 29(4): 795–810.
Ferguson, Adam. 1772. *Grundsätze der Moralphilosophie*. Uebersetzt und mit einigen Anmerkungen versehen von Cristian Garve. Leipzig: Dyck. – Reprint 1986. Hildesheim: Olms.
Fischer, Joachim. 2008. *Philosophische Anthropologie. Eine Denkrichtung des 20. Jahrhundert*. Freiburg/Br.: Alber.
Galle, Roland. 2001. 'Entstehung der Psychologie'. In *Die Wende von der Aufklärung zur Romantik 1760-1820*, ed. Horst A. Glaser and György M. Vajda, 315–335. Amsterdam: Benjamins.
Garber, Jörn, and Thoma, Heinz (ed.). 2004. *Zwischen Empirisierung und Konstruktionsleistung: Anthropologie im 18. Jahrhundert*. Tübingen: Niemeyer.
Gehlen, Arnold. 1938. 'Die Resultate Schopenhauers'. In A.G., *Gesamtausgabe*, ed. Karl-Siegbert Rehberg, vol. 4, 25–49. Frankfurt/M.: Klostermann 1983.
Gehlen, Arnold. 1940. 'Der Mensch. Seine Natur und Stellung in der Welt'. In A.G., *Gesamtausgabe*, ed. Karl-Siegbert Rehberg, vol. 3. Frankfurt/M.: Klostermann 1993.
Goethe, Johann Wolfgang. 1972. *Goethes Gespräche*, ed. Wolfgang Herwig, vol. 3.2. Zürich et. al.: Artemis.
Grunert, Frank, and Stiening, Gideon (ed.). 2011. *Johann Georg Sulzer (1720-1790). Aufklärung zwischen Christian Wolff und David Hume*. Berlin: Akademie Verlag.
Hagner, Michael. 1997. *Homo cerebralis. Der Wandel vom Seelenorgan zum Gehirn*. Darmstadt: Wissenschaftliche Buchgesellschaft.
Haller, Albrecht von. 1781. *Grundriß der Physiologie für Vorlesungen*. Berlin: Haude & Spener.
Hartmann, Fritz, and Haedke, Kurt. 1963. 'Der Bedeutungswandel des Begriffs Anthropologie im ärztlichen Schrifttum der Neuzeit‹. In *Sitzungsberichte der Gesellschaft zur Beförderung des gesamten Naturwissenschaften* 85: 39–99.
Hegel, Georg Wilhelm Friedrich. 1835/43. *Ästhetik*, ed. Friedrich Bassenge, 2 vols. Berlin: Aufbau 1976.
Herder, Johann Gottfried. 1985–2005. *Werke in zehn Bänden*, ed. Günter Arnold et al. Frankfurt/M.: Deutscher Klassiker Verlag.

Hinske, Norbert. 1965. 'Kants Idee der Anthropologie'. In *Die Frage nach dem Menschen. Festschrift für Max Müller*, ed. Heinrich Rombach, 401–424. Freiburg/München: Alber.

Hißmann, Michael. 1777. *Psychologische Versuche. Ein Beytrag zur esoterischen Logik*. Frankfurt/Leipzig: o.V. – Jetzt auch in M.H., *Ausgewählte Schriften*, ed. Gideon Stiening and Udo Roth. Berlin: Akademie Verlag 2012.

Hoven, Wilhelm von. 1780: *Versuch über die Wichtigkeit der dunkeln Vorstellungen in der Theorie der Empfindungen*. Stuttgart: Cotta.

Hume, David. 1759. *Vier Abhandlungen*, trans. Friedrich G. Resewitz. Quedlinburg/Leipzig: Biesterfeld. – Reprint 2001, ed. Heiner F. Klemme. Bristol: Thoemmes Press.

Hume, David. 1992. *The Philosophical Works*, ed. Thomas H. Green and Thomas H. Grose, 4 vols. Reprint Aalen: Scientia.

Kondylis, Panajotis. 1981. *Die Aufklärung im Rahmen des neuzeitlichen Rationalismus*. Stuttgart: Klett-Cotta.

Košenina, Alexander. 2016. *Literarische Anthropologie. Die Neuentdeckung des Menschen*. Berlin/Boston: de Gruyter.

Krebs, Roland. 2006. *Helvétius en Allemagne ou la tentation du matérialisme*. Paris: Honoré Champion.

Kruse, Margot. 2003. *Beiträge zur französischen Moralistik*, ed. Joachim Küpper. Berlin/New York.

Lepenies, Wolf. 1976. *Das Ende der Naturgeschichte. Wandel kulturelles Selbstverständlichkeiten in den Wissenschaften des 18. und 19. Jahrhunderts*. München: Hanser.

Linden, Mareta. 1976. *Untersuchungen zum Anthropologiebegriff des 18. Jahrhunderts*. Frankfurt/M.: Lang.

Lovejoy, Arthur O. 1936. *The Great Chain of Being. A Study of the History of an Idea*. Cambridge/London: Harvard University Press [13]1976.

Macor, Anna. 2008. *Il giro fangoso dell'umana destinazione. Friedrich Schiller dall'illuminismo al criticismo*. Pisa: Edizioni ETS.

Macor, Anna. 2013. *Die Bestimmung des Menschen (1748-1800). Eine Begriffsgeschichte*. Stuttgart-Bad Cannstatt: Frommann-Holzboog

Marquard, Odo. 1965. 'Zur Geschichte des philosophischen Begriffs "Anthropologie" seit dem Ende des achtzehnten Jahrhunderts. In O.M., *Schwierigkeiten mit der Geschichtsphilosophie. Aufsätze*, 122–144, 213–248. Frankfurt/M.: Suhrkamp 1973.

Marquard, Odo. 1971. 'Anthropologie'. In Ritter 1971-2007, I:362–374

Marquard, Odo. 1981. 'Felix culpa? – Bemerkungen zu einem Applikationsschichksal von Genesis 3'. In *Poetik und Hermeneutik IX: Text und Applikation*, ed. Manfred Fuhrmann et al., 53-71. München: Fink.

Midell, Carina. 2017. *Schiller und die Philosophische Anthropologie des 20. Jahrhundert*. Berlin/Boston: de Gruyter.

Naschert, Guido, and Stiening, Gideon (ed.). 2007. *Ernst Platner (1744-1818). Aufklärung zwischen Philosophie, Medzin und Anthropologie*. Hamburg: Meiner.

Oellers, Norbert. 2006. 'Schiller und die Religion'. In *Friedrich Schiller und der Weg in die Moderne*, ed. Walter Hinderer, 165–186. Würzburg: Königshausen & Neumann.

Panizzo, Paolo. 2019. *Die heroische Moral des Nihilismus. Schiller und Alfieri*. Berlin/Boston: de Gruyter.

Piñeiro Costas, Trinidad. 2006: *Schillers Begriff des Erhabenen in der Tradition der Stoa und Rhetorik*. Frankfurt/M.: Lang.

Platner, Ernst. 1772. *Anthropologie für Aerzte und Weltweise. Erster Teil.* Leipzig: Dyck [mehr nicht ersch.]. – Reprint 2000, ed. Alexander Košenina. Hildesheim/Zürich/New York: Olms.

Plessner, Helmuth. 1928. 'Die Stufen des Organischen und der Mensch. Einleitung in die philosophische Anthropologie'. In H.P., *Gesammelte Schriften*, ed. Günter Dux and Odo Marquard, vol. 4. Frankfurt/M.: Suhrkamp 1981.

Pöppel, Ernst. 1993. *Lust und Schmerz. Über den Ursprung der Welt im Gehirn*, 2. ed. Berlin: Siedler.

Probst, Peter. 2004. 'Weltoffenheit'. In Ritter 1971-2007: XII,496–498.

Pross, Wolfgang. 1987. 'Herder und die Anthropologie der Aufklärung'. In Johann Gottfried Herder, *Werke*, ed. Wolfgang Pross, vol. 2, 1128–1229. München/Wien: Hanser 1987.

Pross, Wolfgang. 1994. '"Meine einzige Absicht ist, etwas mehr Licht über die Physik der Seele zu verbreiten." Johann Georg Sulzer (1720-1779)'. In *Helvetien und Deutschland. Kulturelle Beziehungen zwischen der Schweiz und Deutschland in der Zeit von 1770-1830*, ed. Hellmut Thomke et al., 134–148. Amsterdam: Atlanta.

Richter, Sandra, and Mojem, Helmuth. 2021. 'Ermahnungen an einen Freund. Verschollener Schillerbrief [1790]'. In *Frankfurter Allgemeine Zeitung*, 5.4.2021.

Riedel, Friedrich Just. 1769. ['Rez. von J.H. Feder, *Logik und Metaphysik [...]*, Göttingen 1769]. In *Philosophische Bibliothek* 1.3:125-163.

Riedel, Wolfgang. 1985. *Die Anthropologie des jungen Schiller. Zur Ideengeschichte der medizinischen Schriften und der "Philosophischen Briefe"*. Würzburg: Königshausen & Neumann.

Riedel, Wolfgang. 1994. 'Anthropologie und Literatur in der deutschen Spätaufklärung. Skizze einer Forschungslandschaft'. In *Internationales Archiv für Sozialgeschichte der deutschen Literatur*. Sonderheft 6, Forschungsreferate 3:93–157.

Riedel, Wolfgang. 1995. 'Weltweisheit als Menschenlehre. Das philosophische Profil von Schillers Lehrer Abel'. In Abel 1995:377–450.

Riedel, Wolfgang. 1996. *"Homo Natura". Literarische Anthropologie um 1900*. Berlin/New York: de Gruyter.

Riedel, Wolfgang. 1998. 'Abel, Jacob Friedrich (von)'. In *Die Deutsche Literatur. Biographisches und bibliographisches Lexikon in sechs Reihen*, ed. Hans-Gert Roloff et al., Reihe IV.A, 1:49–65. Stuttgart-Bad Cannstatt: Frommann-Holzboog.

Riedel, Wolfgang. 2004. 'Erster Psychologismus. Umbau des Seelenbegriffs in der deutschen Spätaufklärung'. In Garber/Thoma 2004:1-17.

Riedel, Wolfgang. 2006. 'The Anthropological Turn: Schiller, a Thinker at the Threshold of Modernity'. Trans. Andrew Cusack. In *Yearbook Germanistik in Ireland* 1:9–27. – Auch in *Nineteenth-Century Literature Criticism*, vol. 370, *Friedrich von Schiller*, ed. Catherine C. DiMercurio et al., 129–134. Farmington Hills: Gale Cengage / Columbia: Layman Poupard 2019.

Riedel, Wolfgang. 2011. 'Schiller und die popularphilosophische Tradition', 'Schriften der Karlsschulzeit', 'Schriften zum Theater, zur bildenden Kunst und zur Philosophie vor 1790'. In *Schiller-Handbuch*, ed. Helmut Koopmann, 162–174, 582–594, 595–610. 2., verbess. Aufl. Stuttgart: Kröner.

Riedel, Wolfgang. 2017. *Um Schiller. Gesammelte Studien zur Literatur- und Ideengeschichte der Sattelzeit*, ed. Markus Hien et al. Würzburg: Königshausen & Neumann.

Riedel, Wolfgang. 2018. 'Künstliche Menschen. Die Entstehung der Lebenswissenschaften und ihre Gespenster: Olimpia The Creature Homunkulus'. In *Technik und Science Fiction in der Vormoderne*, ed. Brigitte Burrichter and Dorothea Klein, 247–283. Würzburg: Königshausen & Neumann.

Riedel, Wolfgang. 2019. *Ästhetische Distanz*. Würzburg: Königshausen & Neumann.

Riedel, Wolfgang. 2022. 'Wie zu sterben sei. Zur *meditatio mortis* bei Schiller'. In *Schiller-Studien* 1 (2022). Special Issue *Schillers Krankheiten. Pathographie und Pathopoetik*, ed. Helmut Hühn, et al.: 107–133.

Robert, Jörg. 2011a. *Vor der Klassik. Die Ästhetik Schillers zwischen Karlsschule und Kant-Rezeption*. Berlin/Boston: de Gryuter.

Robert, Jörg. 2011b. 'Eine Analytik der Selbstliebe - Schiller und die Moralisten'. In *Literatur und Moral*, ed. Volker Kapp and Dorothea Scholl, 339–357. Berlin: Duncker & Humblot.

Roth, Gerhard. 1994. *Das Gehirn und seine Wirklichkeit. Kognitive Neurobiologie und ihre philosophischen Konseqenzen*. Frankfurt/M.: Suhrkamp.

Schings, Hans-Jürgen. 1977. *Melancholie und Aufklärung. Melancholiker und ihre Kritiker in Erfahrungsseelenkunde und Literatur des 18. Jahrhunderts*. Stuttgart: Metzler.

Schings, Hans-Jürgen. 1982. 'Schillers "Räuber". Ein Experiment des Universalhasses'. In H.-J.S., *Gesammelte Aufsätze*, 229–247. Würzburg: Königshausen & Neumann 2017.

Schings, Hans-Jürgen (ed.). 1994. *Der ganze Mensch. Anthropologie und Literatur im 18. Jahrhundert*. Stuttgart/Weimar: Metzler.

Schings, Hans-Jürgen. 1996. *Die Brüder des Marquis Posa. Schiller und der Geheimbund der Illuminaten*. Tübingen: Niemeyer.

Singer, Wolf. 2002. *Der Beobachter im Gehirn. Essays zur Hirnforschung*. Frankfurt/M.: Suhrkamp.

Spalding, Johann Joachim. 2006. *Kritische Ausgabe*, ed. Albrecht Beutel et al., vol. I.1, *Die Bestimmung des Menschen* (^{1}1748–^{11}1794). Tübingen: Mohr Siebeck.

Specht, Rainer. 1966. *Commercium mentis et corporis. Über Kausalvorstellungen im Cartesianismus*. Stuttgart-Bad Cannstatt: Frommann-Holzboog.

Specht, Rainer. 1976. 'Influxus physicus. Influxionismus'. In: Ritter, Joachim, et al. (Ed.). 1971–2007. Historisches Wörterbuch der Philosophie, 13 vols. Basel: Schwabe, vol. IV:354–356.

Sulzer, Johann Georg. 1773. *Vermischte philosophische Schriften*. Leipzig: Weidmanns Erben & Reich. – Reprint 1974. Hildesheim/New York: Olms.

Sulzer, Johann Georg. 2014. *Gesammelte Schriften. Kommentierte Ausgabe*, ed. Elisabeth Décultot et al., vol. 1, *Kurzer Begriff aller Wissenschaften (1745/1759)*. Basel: Schwabe.

Vattimo, Gianni, and Rovatti, Pier Aldo (Ed.). 1983. *Il pensiero debole*. Milano: Feltrinelli.

Walch, Johann Georg. 1733. *Philosophisches* LEXICON, 2 vols. 2. Aufl. Leipzig: Glebitsch.

Weizsäcker, Viktor von. 1986–2005. *Gesammelte Schriften*, ed. Peter Achilles, et al. Frankfurt/M: Suhrkamp.

Wolff, Christian. 1720. *Vernünfftige Gedancken von* GOTT, *Der Welt und der Seele des Menschen*. Halle: Renger.

Wolff, Christian. 1725. *Vernünfftige Gedancken von dem Gebrauche Der Theile in Menschen, Thieren und Pflantzen*. Franckfurt/Leipzig: Renger.

Wolzogen, Caroline von. 1990. *Gesammelte Schriften*, 2 vols., ed. Peter Boerner. Hildesheim: Olms.
Zedler, Johann Heinrich (ed.). 1732-54. *Grosses vollständiges UNIVERSAL LEXICON Aller Wissenschaften und Künste*, 68 vols. Halle/Leipzig: Zedler. – Reprint 1961-64. Graz: Akademische Verlagsanstalt.
Zelle, Carsten. 1995. *Die doppelte Ästheik der Moderne. Revisionen des Schönen von Boileau bis Nietzsche.* Stuttgart/Weimar: Metzler.
Zelle, Carsten (ed.). 2001. *"Vernünftige Ärzte". Hallesche Psychomediziner und die Anfänge der Anthropologie in der deutschsprachigen Frühaufklärung.* Tübingen: Niemeyer.
Zückert, Johann Friedrich. 1774. *Von den Leidenschaften.* 3. Aufl. Berlin: Mylius.

CHAPTER 18

Schiller's Aesthetics: Beauty Is Freedom

Violetta L. Waibel

> *Aesthetic culture with civic virtue with political freedom hand in hand.*
> —Schiller (November 11, 1793; to the Prince of Augustenburg, 34;
> transl. LG)

Friedrich Schiller's aesthetics aims at a comprehensive concept directed at the education of the whole person, appealing to the senses as well as to the mind. To shape nature into a culture of beauty, and to do so under the condition of the morality of the individual, but always in the perspective of a politically well-formed structure of human community, this is what the passage from Schiller's letter from November 11, 1793, to the Prince of Augustenburg expresses. Freedom is a key concept for Schiller, one that profoundly shaped his thinking, poetry and work. These are the facets of freedom of action—political freedom—that Schiller still has very clearly in mind before—and then with and after—the events of the French Revolution of 1789. He also means moral freedom as the autonomy of pure practical reason, as Schiller will experience and adopt from Kant's moral philosophy, as well as artistic freedom as a free play of forces that is and produces beauty. Freedom is the idea, the formula, the perception of beauty that Schiller's artistic and theoretical concept can encapsulate in a single word. This multi-perspectivity of Schiller's aesthetics probably has to do not least with the path he travelled to become a poet and dramatist. He first began studying law in what was then Württemberg in 1774, received philosophy lessons from Jakob Friedrich Abel, then became a medical doctor

V. L. Waibel (✉)
University of Vienna, Vienna, Austria
e-mail: violetta.waibel@univie.ac.at

(he began studying in 1776), and gained recognition very early on as a playwright and author with *Die Räuber* (*The Robbers*, 1781). His escape from Württemberg, prompted by the conflict he got into with his superiors in his role as a military doctor on the one hand and as a playwright on the other, led him via various stations to Leipzig in 1785 (to Christian Gottfried Körner) and finally to Jena. Here in 1789, at Goethe's initiative, he received an associate professorship in universal history at the university, after his *Geschichte des Abfalls der vereinigten Niederlande von der spanischen Regierung* (*History of the Revolt of the Netherlands*, 1788)—which took the quest for civil liberty as its paradigmatic theme—had attracted very considerable attention.

In addition to other important historical writings, such as *Geschichte des dreißigjährigen Krieges* (*History of the Thirty Years' War*, 1791 to 1793), he continued to work on his own dramas, such as *Wallenstein* (1800), *Maria Stuart* (*Mary Stuart*, 1801) and *Wilhelm Tell* (*William Tell*, 1804), which are among his most important artistic works. In addition, he distinguished himself early on as a poet and as a storyteller and continued to do so until late in his life. He also produced a series of stage adaptations of authors such as Euripides, Gozzi, the French Picard, Racine and Diderot for the court theatre in Weimar (1799 to 1805), where he worked together with Goethe. Moreover, he was active in the National Theatre in Mannheim under the direction of Wolfgang Heribert von Dalberg as early as 1783–1784; he additionally adapted Shakespeare's Macbeth and stage works by Goethe (although not always to his satisfaction), and others. In various periods of his life, he also made translations of Virgil.

For the artist Friedrich Schiller, these many different experiences—as a lawyer, physician, playwright, poet, essayist, historian, philosopher and dramatist—played an important role. Schiller's aesthetic work must be understood against the backdrop of these diverse fields of activity. When it comes to his aesthetics, his philosophical aesthetic writings in particular play a significant role and are still closely associated with his name today. It is only fair to say that it is the diversity of approaches and aspects that have enabled the perspectivity of Schiller's aesthetics in its various directions and the richness of his dramatic, poetic, philosophical-aesthetic work.

As a professor at the University of Jena, Schiller lectured not only in his field of universal history but also on aesthetics, which emerged from his intensive study of Kant's aesthetics in particular. In 1787, even before he received the professorship, he began to study Kant's first shorter writings, which had appeared in the *Berliner Monatsschrift*. Leading up to this, he had made the acquaintance of Johann Gottfried Herder, Christoph Martin Wieland and Karl Leonhard Reinhold in Weimar, who drew his attention to Kant. Schiller's aesthetics can be divided into a before and an after of his reading of Kant, which can be seen in his aesthetic philosophical writings as well as in his literary works, especially the dramatic works.

Already in *Don Carlos* (1787) the proud free spirit Marquis of Posa is seen as a character who acts in the spirit of Kant's moral philosophy. Later, in

Wallenstein (1799), it is Max Piccolomini who acts entirely in the spirit of the Kantian ethos; *Die Jungfrau von Orléans* (*The Maid of Orleans*, 1801) is drawn with character traits that meet the moral requirements of Kant.

Schiller's study of Kant's main aesthetic work, *Kritik der Urteilskraft* (*Critique of the Power of Judgement*), was first documented in February 1791, relatively soon after the work's publication. Schiller suffered a violent attack of illness in May 1791, and, according to tradition, he said a silent goodbye to his family and friends, brought to the belief that he was dying as a result of breathing difficulties. His wife Karoline took this opportunity to read the passages from *The Critique of the Power of Judgment* that mention immortality (Wilpert 2000, 165). Possibly the addition at the end of § 91 of *The Critique of the Power of Judgement* is what is meant. In it, Kant reflects on the three postulates of pure practical reason with regard to the question of a moral ultimate purpose of the world and the role of "God, freedom and immortality of the soul" (Kant, *CJ* Ak 5, 473), as Kant explicitly states. This episode, if it really happened, underlines the great importance that Kant and especially the *Third Critique* had for Schiller. After his recovery, Schiller started intensively reading and studying Kant's moral philosophy and *The Critique of the Power of Judgement* (Wolzogen 1830/1990, 83).

For Schiller, Kant's *Third Critique* is the one text that has always been at the centre of his philosophical studies. In his correspondence with Christian Gottfried Körner from January 25 to February 28, 1793, Schiller's critical attempts to establish an objective concept of beauty emerge against Kant's subjective concept of beauty, which can only be justified as a special form of the human ability to judge. This correspondence is known today as *Kallias, or Concerning Beauty*. The attempt to objectively justify beauty against Kant is considered unsuccessful (Beiser 2005, 72; Pieper 1997, 138–142), although Schiller himself still speaks of objective beauty in his subsequent essay *Ueber Anmuth und Würde* (*On Grace and Dignity*). Even before Schiller begins his expositions on beauty in letters to Körner, in the letter to him dated May 25, 1792, Schiller speaks of the fact that, intending to write the planned "aesthetic letters", he not only reread Kant's *The Critique of the Power of Judgement* but also planned to read Baumgarten beforehand and wondered whether Sulzer could be useful (Schiller, to Körner, May 25, 1792, NA 26, 140–142). This probably refers to Alexander G. Baumgarten's (1714–1762) founding document of aesthetics, the unfinished *Aesthetica*, published in two volumes in 1750 and 1758, as an independent discipline, if not as an independent science. Johann Georg Sulzer (1720–1779) wrote the encyclopaedic work on the fine arts, *Allgemeine Theorie der schönen Künste* (*General Theory of the Fine Arts*, First Edition 1771–1774), which Schiller consulted again and again. On January 11, 1793, Schiller reported that he already owned writings on aesthetics by "Burke, Sulzer, Webb, Mengs, Winkelmann, Home, Batteux, Wood, Mendelssohn, together with 5 or 6 bad compendia" (Schiller to Körner, January 11, 1793, NA 26, 174; transl. LG). Körner extends the reading list on January 18, 1793, to include "Hogarth on the line of beauty, Hagedorn

Reflections on Painting, Dubo's Réflexion sur la peinture et la poésie, Lessing's Laokoon, Herder's Critical Forests, The New French Encyclopaedia, Reynolds' Lectures in the English Academy of Arts, D'Argenville Lives of the most famous painters, Vasarie Vie des peintres etc., Sandrart's Academy of Arts, The most excellent Travels in Italy, such as: la Lande, Volkmann, Moritz" (Körner to Schiller, January 18, 1793, NA 34, 218; transl. LG).

Schiller worked through this considerable reading list to a remarkable extent, as the very illuminating study on Schiller's aesthetics by Jörg Robert (2011) shows. It is clear that the reading of Kant's *The Critique of the Power of Judgement* and the intention to convey his new thoughts on beauty to his friend in a series of letters was the decisive moment for Schiller to deal intensively with the aesthetics of the time. These letters to Körner are known today as *Kallias oder über die Schönheit* (*Kallias, or Concerning Beauty*), the title that Schiller mentioned to his friend Christian Gottfried Körner on December 21, 1792, for the publication that was to appear at Easter 1793. It was meant to be a critical examination of Kant's notion of beauty. The work, which was based on Schiller's lectures on aesthetics in the fall term of 1792–1793 and the correspondence with Körner between January 25 and February 28, 1793, survived as a fragment but was not known to the reading public of the time.[1]

However, Schiller studied not only the aesthetics of Kant, Sulzer, Baumgarten and many others but also Kant's moral philosophy. It was obvious for him to examine beauty, sublimity and morality within the context of the emotional world generated by the most important genre of literature for him, tragedy (see Berghahn, 1981). Tragedy plays such an important role for Schiller—after all, he is the author of a series of dramas that unmistakably document the spirit of Kant's moral philosophy, a philosophy criticised as being rigid but also held in high esteem (Waibel 2021). Schiller's reflections linking the sublime and the tragic can be found, for example in *Ueber den Grund des Vergnügens an tragischen Gegenständen* (*On the Reason Why We Take Pleasure in Tragic Subjects*, 1790–1792), *Ueber die tragische Kunst* (*On the Art of Tragedy*, 1792), *Ueber das Erhabene* (*Concerning the Sublime*, 1793–1801) and *Ueber das Pathetische* (*On the Pathetic*, 1783–1801).

Schiller rewrote Kant's idea of beauty and the sublime into an anthropology with the aim of educating people aesthetically. Even before Schiller immersed himself in Kant's aesthetics and moral philosophy, the study of which paved the way for his main aesthetic writings, *Ueber Anmuth und Würde* (*On Grace and Dignity*, 1793), *Ueber die Erziehung des Menschen in einer Reihe von Briefen* (*On the Aesthetic Education of Man in a Series of Letters*, 1795) and *Ueber naive und sentimentalische Dichtung* (*On Naïve and Sentimental Poetry*, 1795–1796),

---

[1] Schiller's aesthetic lectures from the winter term 1792–1793 are preserved in a transcript (Nachschrift) written by Christian F. Michaelis. See Christian Friedrich Michaelis' transcript *Fragmente aus Schillers aesthetischen Vorlesungen vom Winterhalbjahr 1792-93*, in: NA 21, *Philosophische Schriften. Zweiter Teil* (Fragments from Schiller's Aesthetic Lectures of the Winter Term 1792–1793, in: NA 21, Philosophical Writings. Part Two), edited by Benno von Wiese with the assistance of Helmut Koopmann. Weimar 1987, 66–88 and ibid. 383–388.

he already reflects on the role that the theatre can play in the realisation of a freer, better society and in the comprehensive education of bourgeois individuality.

THE STAGE AS A PUBLIC PLACE TO MIRROR AND ENACT FREEDOM

Friedrich Schiller was a playwright and, at the same time, a theatre poet with dramaturgical duties at the National Theatre in Mannheim (which Schiller later also did for the Court Theatre in Weimar, where Goethe was artistic director). In his treatise, *Die Schaubühne als eine moralische Anstalt betrachtet* (*The Stage as a Moral Institution*), published in 1785 in his *Rheinische Thalia*, he was already interested in the significance and effectiveness of art on the stages of public theatres, focusing especially and above all on tragic art.

Schiller delivered this lecture at a public meeting of the German Electoral Society in Mannheim in 1784.[2] As early as this point, the poet states his belief in a politically aesthetic education of the human being in the broadest sense. He writes:

> He who first made the remark that a state's firmest pillar is religion—that without it the laws themselves lose their power—has perhaps, without wanting to or knowing it, defended the theatre from its noblest side. It is precisely this inadequacy, the fluctuating quality of political laws, which makes religion indispensable to the state, that also determines the moral influence of the stage. Laws, he wanted to say, revolve only around negating duties—religion extends its demands to real action. (Schiller, StMI, NA 20, 91; transl. LG)

The role that Schiller assigns here and several times in the text to religion and the theatre stage is quite surprising for us today, namely that of being a stabilising factor in relation to the state, its institutions and in relation to the fluctuation of the "political laws". Year 1784, when this is delivered, and 1785, when this is published, is admittedly a time when the rule of law of Western democracies has not yet become a reality. Even the French Revolution with its far-reaching positive as well as negative consequences has not yet taken place. Consequently, the Declaration of the Rights of Man and of the Citizen did not yet exist, nor did the *Déclaration des droits de l'homme et du citoyen* of 1789 in the wake of the French Revolution. But Schiller, with his legally trained eye, and other intellectuals of the time, looked to America and the Virginia Bill of Rights of 1776, which had already declared that all men were free, all power emanated from the people, and government was to serve the general welfare, protection and security of the people (see Pohanka 1776/2009). It is noteworthy that even before the French Revolution and before the intensive reading of

---

[2] For the more precise circumstances of the lecture and the changing titles of the printings, see the article on this writing by Carsten Zelle, in: *Schiller Handbuch. Leben—Werk—Wirkung*, (The Schiller Handbook. Life—Work—Impact), ed. by Matthias Luserke-Jaqui, Stuttgart Weimar 2005, 343–358, and Schiller, NA 21, 139–145.

Kant's works (around 1790), Schiller demonstrated a deep sense of freedom, justice and public spirit in his early dramatic as well as theoretical writings. This was thanks to his legal education, his historical research in the context of his work on *Don Carlos*, but also his readings of Rousseau.

It is worth remembering that Schiller grew up in Württemberg, ruled by the despotic monarch Duke Karl Eugen (1728–1793), who was known for his pomp and extravagance, his egoism and the exploitation of the people of his estates. Because of *The Robbers* (1781), Schiller had to flee, as mentioned, and was confronted with great uncertainties for many years until he took up his professorship in universal history in Jena in 1789. The striving for freedom, the instinctive sense of recognising one's enemies and obstacles and the will to place freedom before the eyes of every rational being grew out of Schiller's very personal experiences. This is how he emphatically phrases it:

> What a reinforcement for religion and laws when they enter into alliance with the theatre, where there is contemplation and living presence, where vice and virtue, happiness and misery, foolishness and wisdom pass before one's eyes in a thousand paintings, tangible and true, where Providence unravels its riddles, untangles its knots before one's eyes, where the human heart confesses its slightest impulses on the tortures of passion, all guises fall, all make-up is washed away, and truth, incorruptible as Rhadamanthus, holds court. [...] As surely as visible representation has a more powerful effect than dead letters and cold narration, so surely does the theatre have a deeper and more lasting effect than morals and laws. (Schiller, StMI, NA 20, 91/93; transl. LG)

Schiller continues:

> But its great sphere of activity is far from over. The theatre, more than any other public institution of the state, is a school of practical wisdom, a guide through civic life, an infallible key to the most secret paths into the human soul. (Schiller, StMI, NA 20, 94; transl. LG)

These considerations of Schiller's are an important and early key to his work as a dramatist as well as an aesthete, in which the idea of an aesthetic education of the human being already manifests itself. This education approaches not only reason but the whole human being in a different way than philosophical moral education.

In 1790 Schiller began work on a piece entitled *Ueber den Grund des Vergnügens an tragischen Gegenständen (On the Reason Why We Take Pleasure in Tragic Subjects)*, which appeared in the *Neue Thalia* in 1792, that is, after the serious illness and first involvement with Kant's writings. A central theme here is also the reflection on the relation between art and moral education.

Since human beings normally seek to avoid or repress pain and suffering, Schiller's line of questioning about the reason why we take pleasure in tragic subjects makes sense. The purpose that nature provides for humankind is its happiness, even though humankind itself, that is, humans as rational beings, have to disregard their sensual longings, if happiness and moral commandments contradict each other. This thought itself shows that Schiller is already developing his reflections here in the framework of Kant's moral philosophy (Schiller, PTS, NA 20, 134).

Schiller makes it clear that works of art written for the purpose of moral instruction generally fail as works of art, since this is not the purpose of art. A treatise on moral philosophy would be better for that. And yet it is the tension between the longing for happiness on the one hand and the moral value of the behaviour of dramatic characters in difficult, challenging situations on the other that, with all its tension, offers an important part of the pleasure of tragic subjects, as Schiller points out. He speaks of a "free pleasure" ("freien Vergnügen"), when the mental powers, that is, reason and imagination, are set into action, and sensations are produced not by blind necessity but by imagination. Here his thinking, schooled in Kant's philosophy, becomes apparent when he states that pleasure in a work of art is caused by "whatever is the object of free pleasure, namely the taste in the arrangement that delights our intellect, not the physical stimuli themselves, which only delight our sensuality" (Schiller, PTS, NA 20, 135; transl. LG). These words echo Kant's distinction between the pleasant and the beautiful and the sublime. Speaking of the arrangement that delights the intellect reads like a distant allusion to Kant's free play of imagination and understanding (Kant, CJ, § 9, Ak 5, 217–218). As sources of free pleasure, Schiller lists "the good, the true, the perfect, the beautiful, the touching, the sublime" (Schiller, PTS, NA 20, 136; transl. LG), clearly going beyond Kant's aesthetic conception.

These predictors of human behaviour will be elaborated on by Schiller and examined in more detail below. The true, the perfect and the beautiful stimulate above all the intellect and the imagination to be active, and they have their place in the fine arts, while the charming, the touching (*Reiz* and *Rührung*) and the sublime occupy reason and find expression in the arts that move the heart. The last two, that is, the touching and the sublime, arise at the same time from a mixture of pleasure and displeasure, of purposiveness and contrapurposiveness. Schiller observes that the pain experienced in emotion and in the sublime has an inherent contrapurposiveness, because humans, by their nature, want to experience joy and pleasure. But the experience of pain, which is triggered by these two feelings, is now in turn accompanied by a purposefulness and with it by pleasure, because the mind is stimulated to activity. Human freedom is manifested in the fact that, although humans must experience pain and suffering, free spirits nevertheless seek to prove themselves morally in the face of adversity. Schiller is convinced that: "No purposiveness concerns us as closely as moral purposiveness, and nothing exceeds the pleasure we feel over this moral purposiveness" (Schiller, PTS, NA 20, 139; transl. LG). The moral force is most strongly felt and recognised when the spirit is challenged to fight for moral integrity. The form of art that is best able to portray this is tragedy:

> That kind of poetry, then, which affords us moral pleasure in the highest degree, must for that very reason make use of mixed feelings, and give us pleasure through pain. This is preferably done by tragedy, and its field encompasses all possible cases in which some natural purposiveness sacrificed to a moral purposiveness, or even a moral purposiveness to another that is higher. (Schiller, PTS, NA 20, 140; transl. LG)

Morality is not the purpose of tragedy, and it shouldn't be the purpose of any other form of art. When the subject is humans, the reflection of their circumstances, their conflicts with each other, then it is also about individuals who act morally better or worse. Unlike moral philosophers, playwrights are interested not only in drawing morally exemplary characters but also in creating a vivid moral image of various stronger and weaker characters that they want to put on stage.

Schiller, however, clearly opposes the confusion of truthfulness, completeness and continuity of the tragic plot with historical accuracy and attention to detail. It is the privilege of writers to take the historical events on which they base a drama, if necessary, and arrange them according to the purpose of their art (Schiller, AT, NA 20, 166/167).

The "results" that matter to Schiller in terms of the tragic—which he elaborates as the conditions of tragic emotion—he summarises in this way:

> *Firstly*, the object of our pity must belong to our sort, in the whole sense of this word, and the action in which we are to take part must be a moral one, i.e., understood under the domain of freedom. *Secondly*, the suffering, its sources and its degrees, must be fully communicated to us in a sequence of interrelated events, and *thirdly*, it must be presented to the senses, not indirectly through description, but directly through action. Art unites and fulfils all these conditions in tragedy. (Schiller, AT, NA 20, 164; transl. LG)

Schiller's Aesthetics of Autonomy as Purposiveness Without Purpose and the Education Towards Freedom: A Contradiction?

Schiller's aesthetics was influenced most significantly by Kant's aesthetics. If the latter is first and foremost an aesthetics of reception of the beautiful and sublime based on the theory of judgement and transcendental philosophy (although it also provides a decisive theoretical foundation for the autonomy and self-regulation of art), Schiller's aesthetics, with the questions it raises, is an aesthetics of production determined by the dramatist's practice and guided by aesthetic anthropological questions—an aesthetics that resolutely wants to see stage events oriented towards enlightened moral philosophy. In this way, he is also concerned with an aesthetic of autonomy that embraces freedom and self-determination in several senses. The autonomy, the regulation of the self, is an expression of an art that sets the content and form of art itself, instead of moving within the canon of a traditional rule aesthetics. The autonomy of art does not mean a lack of rules, but a decisive individualisation of artistic subjectivity and the will to create art, which sometimes means a break with tradition and yet can also be a dialogue with it.

Schiller's theoretical and artistic work was concerned with freedom in a variety of dimensions. This freedom also means that with his aesthetic writings he has made contributions to the philosophy of aesthetics, and this in a form of writing that, stylistically speaking, are not philosophical treatises in the strict sense, especially if one were to measure them against the philosophical style of argumentation of a Kant, or, in the older tradition, a René Descartes, Baruch de Spinoza, Christian Wolff, Gottfried Wilhelm Leibniz or David Hume. Schiller's aesthetic essays certainly follow an argumentation, an inner structure of thoughts, but are also characterised by an associative, sometimes even erratic line of thought. Various things have been said and written about internal contradictions, concerning terminology as well as the definition of guiding ideas. Schiller embraced philosophical thought to a great extent, but he is not a systematist in the strict sense, even though he has been elevated to the rank of philosopher by authors such as Frederic Beiser (Beiser 2005). This claim is entirely justified if philosophy determines the essential contents that were so important to Schiller—as an author during the High Enlightenment—as an author supporting the idea of freedom that defines humanity. Schiller's philosophical-aesthetic works stand for their own. They are not only self-reflections of the artist on the way to his works of art, but have their own autonomy, for Schiller for the most part published them himself. On the other hand, the theoretically aesthetic essays are nevertheless closely related to Schiller's literary works. For Schiller, as an Enlightenment philosopher and playwright, the theatre soon became a place of (indirect) moral education.

"Poetry thereby attains a higher dignity, in the end she becomes once again what she was in the beginning—*the teacher of humanity*; for there is no more philosophy, no more history, poetry alone will survive all the other sciences and arts" (Hegel, *eine Ethik* ..., / *The Oldest System-Programme of German Idealism*, 1995, 200). Poetry, the art of verse, as a teacher of humankind, "in the end she becomes once again what she was in the beginning", it says in a text, where the author could be Hegel, but this is not clear—it does not originate from Schiller, but is probably deeply influenced by his programme of an aesthetic education of humankind. Obviously, this is a vision of the future in which poetry is intended to play a role that it already had in its primordial beginning. The text also states provocatively: "for there is no more philosophy, no more history, poetry alone will survive all the other sciences and arts" (Hegel, *eine Ethik* ..., / *The Oldest System-Programme of German Idealism*, 1995, 200). It is very likely that Schiller did not know this text, called *Älteste Systemprogramm des deutschen Idealismus* (*The Oldest System-Programme of German Idealism*), probably written in 1797. However, its authors were probably well acquainted with Schiller's aesthetic writings. Still, it is not only a line from Schiller that points to the near future of this famous text, but also a line back to an author who was an important inspiration for Schiller's aesthetics. Johann Georg Sulzer praises the arts of rhetoric highly, which could have been of great interest to Schiller:

> One cannot challenge rhetoric's (Beredsamkeit) prominence among the fine arts. It is evidently the most perfect means of making people more understanding, more well-mannered, better and happier. It was through it that the first sages gathered the scattered people into social life, made manners and laws popular to them; it was through it that Plato, Xenophon, Cicero, Rousseau, became teachers of men. (Sulzer *Schöne Künste* [*Fine Arts*] 1, 1771, Artikel Beredsamkeit [Article on Rhetoric], 147; Robert 2011, 267; transl. LG)

With regard to both Schiller's *On the Aesthetic Education of Man* and the aforementioned *Älteste Systemprogramm (The Oldest System-Programme of German Idealism)*, the following consideration of Sulzer is also highly noteworthy:

> True politics finds in rhetoric the most important means of making the state happy. External coercion does not make good citizens: through it the state is a lifeless machine that survives no longer than as long as an external force exerts pressure; through rhetoric it acquires an inner living force by which it continues unceasingly. In the hands of a wise ruler it is a magic wand that transforms a desolate region into a paradise, makes a sluggish people industrious, a cowardly one courageous, an ignorant one understanding. If it assists the philosopher, reason and understanding spread over a whole people; if it lends its help to the moralist, the attitudes of righteousness, honesty and magnanimity take the place of immorality, selfishness and all pernicious passions: through it, then, a wild, nefarious, sacrilegious people becomes civilised and virtuous. (Sulzer 1771, *Schöne Künste* [*Fine Arts*] 1, Beredsamkeit [Rhetoric],148; transl. LG)

Sulzer goes on to explain that any wise legislator and ruler cannot be indifferent to the art of rhetoric, since it is of the utmost importance for the education and cultivation of the people in a state. These are words that must have appealed to Schiller very much, if he read them, which is quite likely.

Schiller's essay *On the Aesthetic Education of Man in a Series of Letters* appeared in 1795 in a series of three instalments in the *Horen* edited by Schiller himself. It contains the programme for the implementation of the aesthetic educational mission. Schiller's idea is to make the present State of Need (Staat der Not), he diagnoses, superfluous and to establish a State of Freedom (Staat der Freiheit) or an Aesthetic State (Ästhetischen Staat) (though Schiller's terminology varies). For future human beings, Schiller demands a complete education and development of all the sensual and rational powers of humankind instead of merely one-sided moral and technically practical education. Schiller writes in the fourth of his aesthetic letters:

> Every individual human being, one may say, carries within him, potentially and prescriptively, an ideal man, the archetype of a human being, and it is his life's task

to be, through all his changing manifestations, in harmony with the unchanging unity of this ideal. This archetype, which is to be discerned more or less clearly in every individual, is represented by the *State*. (Schiller, AE, NA 20, 316; OUP, 17)

Schiller understands the state ("Staat") as something general, surpassing individual reason, which all individuals must cultivate within themselves. Schiller goes on to express this idea further:

> One can, however, imagine two different ways in which man existing in time can coincide with man as Idea, and, in consequence, just as many ways in which the State can assert itself in individuals: either by the ideal man suppressing empirical man, and the State annulling individuals; or else by the individual himself *becoming* the State, and man in time being *ennobled to the stature* of man as Idea.
>
> It is true that from a one-sided moral point of view this difference disappears. For Reason is satisfied as long as her law obtains unconditionally. But in the complete anthropological view, where content counts no less than form, and living feeling too has a voice, the difference becomes all the more relevant. Reason does indeed demand unity; but Nature demands multiplicity; and both these kinds of law make their claim upon man. (Schiller, AE, NA 20, 316–317; OUP, 19)

Here Schiller explains that one must do justice to the "the complete anthropological view" and "the State should not only respect the objective and generic character in its individual subjects; it should also honour their subjective and specific character". Schiller points out that the rationality of reason is important for literature and poetry, but that it must be contained within the many moments of aesthetic experience in art—if one wants to create a work that is as lively as it is full of spirit and that elevates people. One can say that Schiller specifically condenses the aesthetic idea that Kant sees present in the beauty of a work of art (but also in the beauty of nature) in such a way that it represents the whole human being. Kant defines spirit as the principle that places the forces in the human being in a purposeful relationship to each other that is as playful as it is stimulating:

> Now I maintain that this principle is nothing other than the faculty for the presentation of aesthetic ideas; by an aesthetic idea, however, I mean that representation of the imagination that occasions much thinking though without it being possible for any determinate thought, i.e., concept, to be adequate to it, which, consequently, no language fully attains or can make intelligible.—One readily sees that it is the counterpart (pendant) of an idea of reason, which is, conversely, a concept to which no intuition (representation of the imagination) can be adequate. (Kant, CJ § 49, Ak 5, 313/314)

How is it possible that art (literature in particular) on the one hand should fulfil the role of a teacher of humanity, and on the other hand—although it sets the forces in motion in a purposeful way, at the same time, as Kant so aptly formulated—purposefulness is realised without purpose, and that also means without moral instruction? The author and tragic poet Schiller is convinced that the claims and duties of morality are not only felt to be contrapurposive to the sensible human nature, but can at times also be experienced pleasurably. It is literature in which the contradiction of forces is staged as an analogy to life and in this way playfully brings people into contact with their better-known and lesser-known inner forces and impulses, and this in the deepest sense of the word.

What is remarkable is that not only Schiller but already Kant in the *Critique of the Power of Judgment* speaks of a play of forces. Most famous is the free play of imagination and intellect in the perception of a beautiful object, which establishes the general communicability of beauty and thereby lifts the experience of beauty out of the realm of private sensation into a sphere of intersubjectivity and generally valid common sense:

> The powers of cognition that are set into play by this representation are hereby in a free play, since no determinate concept restricts them to a particular rule of cognition. Thus the state of mind in this representation must be that of a feeling of the free play of the powers of representation in a given representation for a cognition in general. Now there belongs to a representation by which an object is given, in order for there to be cognition of it in general, *imagination* for the composition of the manifold of intuition and *understanding* for the unity of the concept that unifies the representations. This state of a *free play* of the faculties of cognition with a representation through which an object is given must be able to be universally communicated, because cognition, as a determination of the object with which given representations (in whatever subject it may be) should agree, is the only kind of representation that is valid for everyone. (Kant, *CJ*, § 9, Ak 5, 217)

This play of forces thematised by Kant, this specific free play of imagination and intellect, is taken up and transformed by Schiller in order to elaborate more precisely its suitability for the play on stage—the drama, the comedy or the tragedy.

But how is the freedom of play compatible with the idea of aesthetic education? Art as an end in itself that obeys no external agenda, and the claim that art can or must serve as an instance of aesthetic, moral, civic education, suggests a self-contradiction. In Kant's expositions on the purposefulness of beauty, which at the same time is necessarily thought to be without purpose, Schiller was able to find an important figure of thought for his concern. In *The Critique of the Power of Judgment*, Kant distinguishes between free and adherent beauty. On the one hand, Kant clearly states: "There can be no objective rule of taste that would determine what is beautiful through concepts" (Kant, *CJ*, § 17, Ak 5, 232)/ On the other hand, it is nevertheless possible for things to be beautiful that are not simply beautiful in themselves (free beauty), but that are defined by purposes. This is particularly evident in buildings, churches and other products designed for a specific purpose. But it is also true for human beings as rational beings that they are ends in themselves. Kant makes an important distinction, in order to pacify the possible "disputes about beauty between judges of taste" according to which "the one is concerned with free beauty, the other with adherent beauty, the first making a pure, the second an applied judgment of taste" (Kant, CJ, § 16, Ak 5, 231). In the one case, one judges according to what one has in one's senses, while in the other case according to what one has in one's thoughts.

Kant seems to hold the idea that there are transitions, perhaps even fluid transitions, between pure beauty and adherent beauty determined by ideas when he gives a very remarkable hint for understanding the purity of judgment of taste: "A judgment of taste in regard to an object with a determinate internal end would thus be pure only if the person making the judgment either had no concept of this end or abstracted from it in his judgment" (Kant, CJ, § 16, Ak 5, 231).

In this way, Kant concedes that there are objects that are subjected to a merely aesthetic judgement of taste, but in which concepts in the form of ideals, a sensually oriented normal idea (Normalidee) and an idea of reason oriented towards purpose are nevertheless mixed in. In judging, therefore, it is possible, consciously or unconsciously, to refrain from the purpose of a beautiful object, assuming that there is a purpose. Kant goes on to develop the idea of beauty adherent to the form of the human being and in this context also reveals that there are objects other than the human being, such as artefacts like houses or churches, and also works of art that can be attributed to this non-pure kind of beauty. Human beings, acting intentionally and according to purposes, are at the same time the only ends in themselves, namely as morally virtuous beings. Kant accordingly writes:

> Only that which has the end of its existence in itself, the *human being*, who determines his ends himself through reason, or, where he must derive them from external perception can nevertheless compare them to essential and universal ends and in that case also aesthetically judge their agreement with them: this *human being* alone is capable of an ideal of *beauty*, just as the humanity in his person, as intelligence, is alone among all the objects in the world capable of the ideal of *perfection*. (Kant, CJ, § 17, Ak 5, 233)

Kant explicitly distinguishes between two aspects of the human form, the normal idea (*Normalidee*) of the human being, which can be determined from the purely sensory means of its form, and the rational idea, with which the purpose of humanity is presented. But the human being as an end in itself must not be understood merely as sensual beauty, for then one would deny the "humanity in his [own] person", and, that is to say, one would disregard the human being as an intelligible being, whose end in itself is morality and consequently freedom. In this way, the normal idea ("Normalidee"; Kant, CJ, Ak 5, 233) is joined by an idea of reason, which is the visible expression of the morality that defines human beings. This does not call for judging the morality of a person, but for judging the sensory traces of morality in the appearance of a person through the free play of the faculties.

In Schiller's letters *On the Aesthetic Education of Man*, two theoretical contexts are of particular interest here, which Schiller develops starting from Kant and going further in teaching through literature by means of freedom in play. First, he unfolds a theory of *impulses* that allows us to go beyond Kant and think of the subject's powers as spiritual-mental and sensual-bodily desires. Schiller outlines an impulse for formal and material based on Kant's two branches of knowledge: understanding and reason on the one hand and sensuality on the other. The bridging of both is what he calls the play-impulse, which is—no coincidence—reminiscent of the free play of imagination and understanding in Kant's judgement of beauty. Second, this impulse theory linking sensuality and intellect, derived not least from the theories of Karl Leonhard Reinhold and Johann Gottlieb Fichte, makes possible the outline of a transcendental poetology, combined with a rudimentary theory of the developmental genesis of the human being on the basis of theoretical moments that Schiller calls passive and active determination and passive and active determinability.

Freedom in and Through the Play of Faculties: Beauty as Active Determinability

The aesthetic education of the human being, which Schiller envisions in his letters *On the Aesthetic Education of Man* aims both at the formation of aisthesis, the training and sensitisation of the faculties of the senses in the Greek sense of the word, and at an aesthetic education in a modern meaning of the formation of the senses for beauty and harmony. Schiller calls for the training of as many faculties as possible, both intellectual and sensorial, through the mediating power the impulse of play, which is not a separate *impulse* alongside the source of reason (*formal impulse*) and sensuality (*material impulse*). Schiller shows himself to be a Kantian when he holds on to the two sources of perception and concept with the dualism of the *material* and *formal impulses*. The impulse of play is play because it represents the connection between the *formal* and material *impulses* and has to establish a successful balance between the forces of reason and sensuality. In the letters 19 to 23, Schiller develops a model of how the formation of all faculties through the stimulation of the impulse of play is to be carried out in greater detail (Waibel 2013).

The two impulses represent tendencies of an unbalanced upbringing in human beings, in which sometimes the sensual nature is suppressed in favour of the rational nature, and sometimes vice versa. Aesthetic education aims to establish a balance through which the natural and rational powers and aspirations of the human being are developed in a balanced relationship. Schiller speaks of an interaction between the material and the formal "impulse", a term that, as he expressly emphasises, he found in Johann Gottlieb Fichte's *Grundlage der gesammten Wissenschaftslehre* (*Foundation of the Entire Wissenschaftslehre*, GA I 2, 131).

Now, since Schiller agrees with Kant that the basic impulses arise from different sources, their interaction cannot just be brought about instantaneously and directly. He writes about the material impulse and the formal impulse, meaning the sensual impulse and the rational impulse, that "their tendencies do indeed conflict with each other" but "not in the same objectives" (Schiller, AE, 13th Letter, NA 20, 347; OUP, 85). With Fichte, Schiller imagines the intended interaction of the two impulses as follows:

> Subordination there must, of course, be; but it must be reciprocal. [...] Both principles are, therefore, at once subordinated to each other and co-ordinated with each other, that is to say, they stand in reciprocal relation to one another: without form no matter, and without matter no form. (This concept of reciprocal action, and its fundamental importance, is admirably set forth in Fichte's Fundaments of the Theory of Knowledge, Leipzig, 1794.) (Schiller, AE, 13th Letter, NA 20, 348, Note; OUP, 85; see Waibel 1997)

With the two impulses, Schiller also sees temporality and empiricism, as well as extra-temporality, reason and normativity brought into a relationship and mediated by the play impulse:

> The sense-drive demands that there shall be change and that time shall have a content; the form-drive demands that time shall be annulled and that there shall be no change. That drive, therefore, in which both the others work in concert (permit me for the time being, until I have justified the term, to call it the play-drive), the play-drive, therefore, would be directed towards annulling time within time, reconciling becoming with absolute being and change with identity. (Schiller, AE, 14th Letter, NA 20, 353; OUP, 97)

If the state is reached in which the play impulse mediates the two basic tendencies in humans, sensuality and form, consequently life and form are conveyed as "living <u>form</u>", which manifests itself as beauty. "For", Schiller writes, "to mince matters no longer, man only plays when he is in the fullest sense of the word human being, and he is only fully a human being when he plays" (Schiller, AE, 15th Letter, NA 20, 359; OUP, 107).

What it means, more precisely, to transform this impulse theory into a living form in literary works is described by Schiller in the letters 19 to 23, which are as systematically challenging as they are dark, and whose systematic content will now be summarised in a highly condensed form.

At the beginning of the 19th letter, Schiller claims: "We can distinguish in man as such two different states of determinability, the one passive, the other active, and—corresponding to these—two states of passive and active determination. The explanation of this proposition will offer the shortest way of reaching our goal" (Schiller, AE, 19th Letter, NA 20, 368; OUP, 129).

Schiller distinguishes four states here, two of which are understood as active and two as passive, that is, as self-active and as receptive. Furthermore, determinability as the mere possibility of being determined is contrasted with determination. Schiller has pointed out with regard to reciprocal determination that he found this theorem in Fichte; however, there is no mention of Fichte in connection with determinability. However, it was Fichte again who had made determination and determinability the central terms of his construction of the imagination in *Foundation of the Entire Wissenschaftslehre* (Fichte, GWL, GA I 2, 345ff; Waibel 2000, 301–318).

The explanation of these four states of mind, as announced by Schiller, is presented in more detail in the following letters, even if it is not recognisable right away. It becomes apparent that the impulses mentioned earlier, the material and the formal impulse, return as "passive", receiving and "active", creating, self-acting "determination" and "determinability". According to both Fichte and Schiller, the spirit is continuously found in states of being determined and of determining. A determination is passive if it can be attributed to sensuality, that is, to receptivity, and if it manifests itself through feelings, perceptions and views that happen to a subject rather than being intended. In this, Schiller shows himself closer to Kant, for Fichte attributes a high degree of activity to sensuality. For Schiller and Kant, active determinations are those actions that come about through thought and judgement and are attributable to the intellect or reason.

But what are determinabilities? In the literal sense of the word, these are states that make it possible to be determined before a determination occurs. In Fichte's construction of the imagination, it is proposed that the productive power of imagination, which constitutes views, oscillates and hovers between determinability and determination (see Fichte, GWL I 2, 359–361). Every view is a determination, a fixation of the mind on a particular, single mental state. If the determinations obtained were not open to renewed determinability, another view would not be possible. The oscillating and hovering of the imagination between determinability and determination, between the infinite and the finite, as Fichte also says, makes possible sequences of different views, sequences of images and series of ideas. Unlike Fichte, Schiller does not speak of an oscillation or hovering of the power of the imagination, but of determinability and determination.

Schiller calls the state of the human spirit before any determination "undeterminacy", which is blank infinity. Here we are obviously dealing with passive determinability (Schiller, AE, 19th Letter, NA 20, 368). One might indeed wonder how to imagine such a condition. In remarkable proximity to some trains of thought of Fichte's *Foundation of the Entire Wissenschaftslehre*, Schiller asserts that only through negation of infinity does one arrive at a position, at a definite placement: "[O]nly through the surrender of our unconditional determinability that we achieve determination" (Schiller, AE, 19th Letter, NA 20, 369; OUP, 129). It must be "through some autonomous act of the mind [*Thathandlung*; F/Act; VLW] the negating were referred to something positive, and from no-position op-position were to ensue. This activity of the psyche we call judging or thinking; and the result of it we call *thought*" (Schiller, AE, 19th Letter, NA 20, 369; OUP, 129–131).

Into the empty infinity, into the mere determinability of the spirit, a thought enters. Schiller borrows from Fichte's concept of subjectivity with his "absolute F/Act" ("*absolute[n] Thathandlung*") (Fichte, GWL I 2, 260f.; see Breazeale 2021, 103). The still completely indeterminate absolute ego is the agent and carrier of all possible active spontaneity of the human spirit and so seems to Schiller to be suitable for making passive determinability conceivable. This model of subjectivity, presented very briefly by Schiller in the style of Fichte, is linked to the task of liberating individuals from their self-alienation, their one-sidedness and divisiveness, in order to renew the centre of the human being and freedom or to awaken it in the first place (Schiller, AE, 19th Letter, NA 20, 370).

Schiller links the coexistence of the material impulse and the formal impulse, of sensuality and reason, of passive and active determination, with a genetic representation of the development of the two natures in human beings. Human beings first develop their sensual nature, and only later their rational nature (Schiller, AE, 19th Letter, NA 20, 373). Schiller emphasises that by freedom he does not mean the self-acting spontaneity of intelligence, but that freedom which is based on the blended nature of the individual. Ideally, the will achieves aesthetic freedom and accordingly the impulse to play.

The negative, passive determinability now also comes with an active counterpart. Schiller imagines the aesthetic state, which is active determinability, as a complete openness to what can evolve from this state. It is a freedom that has broken away from old ties and determinations in order to determine itself anew and to be determined. This openness and aesthetic freedom in a state of active determinability is caused by the contemplation of a work of art, just as it is a condition of the production of works of art. "If, therefore, the latter—indetermination through sheer absence of determination—was thought of as an *empty infinity*, then aesthetic freedom of determination, which is its counterpart in reality, must be regarded as an *infinity filled with content*: an idea which accords completely with the results of the foregoing inquiry" (Schiller, AE, 21. Brief, NA 20, 377; OUP, 145).

This is what Schiller states: "It is, then, not just poetic licence but philosophical truth when we call beauty our second creatress" (Schiller, AE, 21. Brief, NA 20, 378; OUP, 147). Beauty itself, which puts one in the state of aesthetic mood, is neither physical, nor moral, nor thinking, nor active in any other way. But it is the condition for initiating determinations that embrace the whole human being with all his or her strengths.

> If, then, in *one* respect the aesthetic mode of the psyche is to be regarded as *Nought*—once, that is, we have an eye to particular and definite effects—it is in another respect to be looked upon as a state of *Supreme Reality*, once we have due regard to the absence of all limitation and to the sum total of the powers which are conjointly active within it. (Schiller, AE, 22nd Letter, *NA 20, 379*; OUP, 151)

The active determinability is called active because in it, all forces are active and present. If Fichte had reason in mind with the act of the absolute ego, Schiller, with this transcendental poetology, is concerned with absolute freedom and openness in the aesthetic state of the play of all forces, and not merely with the spontaneity of reason.

Schiller's enthusiasm for the aesthetic state as such, which puts the whole human being and all his or her powers into action, collapses again in the last letters when, surprisingly, he gives preference to the primacy of reason, as Kant and Fichte do. His innovative approach of bringing material and form into an interrelationship, of seeing and treating them as equals, turns into the opposite when sensuality—as the "fearful kingdom of forces"—is juxtaposed with the "sacred kingdom of laws", which is obviously the realm of reason. "[T]he aesthetic impulse to form is at work, unnoticed, on the building of a third joyous kingdom of play and of semblance, in which man is relieved of the shackles of circumstance, and released from all that might be called constraint, alike in the physical and moral sphere" (Schiller, AE, 27th Letter, NA 20, 410; OUP, 215). Ultimately, in Schiller's concept a one-sided supremacy of reason also triumphs, which forces are to be rendered subordinate to—even in works of art. Schiller's programme is fascinating, but in the end it falls back into a nonsensical sensuality.

Schiller systematically expands Kant's concept of the free play of imagination and intellect in § 9 of the *Critique of Judgement*, to a play of all the human forces. In Kant's view, free play emerges from the receptive as well as active faculties in the contemplation of a beautiful object. Schiller's aesthetic condition of active determinability emerges from the contemplation of a work of art, but is also a prerequisite for the production of a work of art.

"*To bestow freedom by means of freedom* is the fundamental law" of the aesthetic realm (Schiller, AE, 27th Letter, NA 20, 410; OUP, 215). The aesthetic freedom of the creative artist is the freedom that, according to Schiller's aesthetic education, gives freedom, namely to those who allow themselves to be put into a state of aesthetic, free determinability by works of art.

Why Schiller, on the one hand, elaborates this impressive aesthetic of a free, open state of active determinability—thereby giving the artistic work the highest dignity of the aesthetic idea—but then opens the doors of art to the idea of reason, which is apparently no longer tacitly present in the aesthetic idea, is regrettable to note. Perhaps freedom of thought, granting freedom politically and morally, was too much in Schiller's outgoing eighteenth century. "Marquis von Posa", the Knight of Malta, friend of Don Carlos, fighter for the freedom of the Netherlands, is an invention of Schiller, who stands opposite the Spanish king, Philip II (1556–1598). Posa, the personification of freedom and reason, which Giuseppe Verdi made glow in the name of freedom—and not Don Carlos, the Infante of Spain—forms the beating heart of freedom in Schiller's "dramatic poem" *Don Carlos, Infante of Spain*:

It seems to me that what is objected to against this character, from the age in which I let him appear, speaks more for him than against him. According to the example of all great minds, he emerges between darkness and light, an outstanding isolated phenomenon. The moment of his formation is that of the general fermenting of minds, the struggle of prejudices with reason, the anarchy of opinions, the dawn of truth—from time immemorial the birth of extraordinary individuals. The ideas of freedom and human nobility, which a fortunate coincidence, perhaps a favourable upbringing, threw into this purely organised receptive soul, astonish him by their novelty and affect him with all the force of the unfamiliar and the surprising; even the secret under which they were probably communicated to him must have increased the strength of their impression. (Schiller, *Letters on Don Carlos, 2nd Letter*, NA 22, 140; transl. LG)

The figure of Marquis von Posa embodies the philosophy of reason and human rights, which gained public attention through the American Declaration of Independence. As such, he contrasts the idea of political freedom, civil rights and humanity with the very different reality of the king's court. Schiller sees in Marquis von Posa the boldest ideal of a republic of men, general toleration and freedom of conscience, where could it be born better and where more natural than within the vicinity of Philip the Second and his Inquisition?

All the Marquis' principles and favourite sentiments revolve around republican virtue. Even his sacrifice for his friend proves this, for self-sacrifice is the epitome of all republican virtue.

The moment when he appeared was precisely the moment when there was more talk than ever of human rights and freedom of conscience (Schiller, *Letters on Don Carlos, 2nd Letter*, NA 22, 141, transl. LG).

Schiller portrays King Philip II as touched and fascinated by the Marquis, who in turn plucks up the courage to win Philip II over to the ideas of political freedom:

> Become A King of million kings [VLW].[3]
> [He approached boldly, while directing firm and fiery looks at the KING]
> I wish the exhortation of the thousands
> Whose destinies depend on this great hour
> Could crowd into my words and raise the gleam
> Beginning in your eyes, into a blaze!
> Tear from your face the evil mask of Godhead,
> Beneath whose eyes we perish. Be the image
> Of truth and everlastingness. For never
> Has any mortal man possessed so much,

---

[3] Don Karlos, 3. Akt, 10. Auftritt, Vers 3200-3216, NA 6, 191: "Werden Sie/ Von Millionen Königen ein König" is inadequately translated to "And make your citizens a million kings" in the Oxford translation by Hilary Collier Sy-Quia and Peter Oswald from 1999. This translation does not reflect the original meaning of the verse. Thus, an alternative translation was provided here.
I would like to thank Bernadette Maul for her thorough editing.

> To do such good with. All the kings of Europe
> Honour the name of Spain above all others.
> A single word of yours can suddenly
> Create the world anew. Give us the freedom
> To think.
> (Don Carlos, Act Three, Scene X, Verse 695–708, NA 6, 191).

German text translated into English by Linnea Gustavsson.

References

Beiser, Frederick. 2005. *Schiller as Philosopher. A Re-Examination.* Oxford: Oxford University Press.
Berghahn, Klaus L. 1981. Nachwort. In *Friedrich Schiller: Vom Pathetischen und Erhabenen. Ausgewählte Schriften zur Dramentheorie*, ed. Klaus L. Berghahn, 133–157. Stuttgart: Reclam.
Breazeale, Daniel. 2021. Editor's Introduction. In *J. G. Fichte: Foundation of the Entire Wissenschaftslehre*, ed. Daniel Breazeale, 1–47. Oxford: Oxford University Press.
Fichte, Johann Gottlieb. 2021. *Foundation of the Entire Wissenschaftslehre.* Trans. D. Breazeale. Oxford: Oxford University Press.
Hegel, Georg Wilhelm Friedrich. 1984. eine Ethik… In *Mythologie der Vernunft. Hegels 'ältestes Systemprogramm' des deutschen Idealismus*, eds. Christoph Jamme, Helmut Schneider, 11–14. Frankfurt am Main: Suhrkamp.
Hegel, Georg Wilhelm Friedrich. 1995. The 'Oldest System-Programme of German Idealism'. Trans. T. Carman. *European Journal of Philosophy* 3,2: 199-200.
Kant, Immanuel. 2000. *Critique of the Power of Judgment* (1790). Trans. P. Guyer and E. Matthews. Ed. Paul Guyer. Cambridge: Cambridge University Press.
Körner, Theodor. 1997. Brief von Körner, 18. Januar 1793 (Nr. 188). In *Schillers Werke, NA 34, I: Briefwechsel. Briefe an Schiller. 1.3.1790-24.5.1794*, ed. Ursula Naumann. 218–219.
Michaelis, Christian F. 1987. Fragmente aus Schillers aesthetischen Vorlesungen vom Winterhalbjahr 1792-93. In *Schillers Werke, NA 21: Philosophische Schriften. Zweiter Teil*, ed. Benno von Wiese with the assistance of Helmut Koopmann, 66–88 and 383–388.
Pieper, Heike. 1997. *Schillers Projekt eines menschlichen Menschen. Eine Interpretation der "Briefe über die ästhetische Erziehung des Menschen von Friedrich Schiller".* Lage: Jacobs.
Pohanka 1776/2009: Virginia Bill of Rights, 1776. In: *Dokumente der Freiheit*, ed. Reinhard Pohanka, 55–75. Wiesbaden: Marix 2009.
Robert, Jörg. 2011. *Vor der Klassik. Die Ästhetik Schiller zwischen Karlsschule und Kant-Rezeption.* Berlin/Boston: De Gruyter.
Sulzer, Johann Georg. 1771. *Allgemeine Theorie der Schönen Künste.* Bd. 1. Leipzig: M. G. Weidemanns Erben und Reich.
Waibel, Violetta L. 2013. *Die Schönheit als zweite Schöpferin des Menschen. Schillers Idee des „Spieltriebs" und der „aktiven Bestimmbarkeit" in den Briefen 'Über die ästhetische Erziehung'.* Beitrag für die Festschrift von Konrad Liessmann zum 60. Geburtstag

im April 2013. In *Intellektuelle Interventionen: Gesellschaft, Bildung, Kitsch*, eds. Katharina Lacina and Peter Gaitsch. Wien: Löcker - http://www.loecker-verlag.at/docs/ViolettaL.Waibel.pdf (accessed 26 April 2021).

Waibel, Violetta L. 1997. Wechselbestimmung. Zum Verhältnis von Hölderlin, Schiller und Fichte in Jena. In *Fichte und die Romantik. Hölderlin, Schelling, Hegel und die späte Wissenschaftslehre. 200 Jahre Wissenschaftslehre – Die Philosophie Johann Gottlieb Fichtes. Tagung der Internationalen J.G.Fichte-Gesellschaft (26. September – 1. Oktober 1994) in Jena. Fichte-Studien Bd. 12*, ed. Wolfgang H. Schrader, 43-69. Amsterdam: Rodopi. Concurrently: http://sammelpunkt.philo.at/id/eprint/2708/1/Fichte_Wechselbestimmungen_14022006.pdf

Waibel, Violetta L. 2000. *Hölderlin und Fichte 1794–1800*. Paderborn: Ferdinand Schöningh.

Waibel, Violetta L. 2021. Feelings, Morality, Human Beings seen Holistically. A Dialogue between Kant and Schiller. In: Antonino Falduto and Jens Timmermann (eds.): *The Early Critique of Kant's Moral Philosophy*. Special Issue of *Studi Kantiani*, Anno XXXIII (2020), 87-99.

von Wilpert, Gero. 2000. *Schiller-Chronik 1933–2009. Sein Leben und Schaffen*. 2. Auflage. Stuttgart: Reclam.

von Wolzogen, Caroline. 1990. *Schillers Leben, verfaßt aus Erinnerungen der Familie, seinen eignen Briefen und den Nachrichten seines Freundes Körner, 2 Teile* (1830). Ed. Peter Boerner. Hildesheim: Olms.

Zelle, Carsten. 2005. Was kann eine gute stehende Schaubühne eigentlich wirken? In *Schiller Handbuch. Leben – Werk – Wirkung*, Matthias Luserke-Jaqui, 343-358. Stuttgart: J. B. Metzler.

CHAPTER 19

Schiller on Morals

Jörg Noller

In Schiller's philosophical works, his ethics is not presented as a separate, clearly defined theory. None of his works is devoted solely to moral philosophy. Rather, in Schiller's philosophy, ethics, aesthetics, anthropology, and theory of human freedom are intimately interwoven. For this reason, the systematic significance of Schiller's ethics needs to be reconstructed.[1]

Schiller is concerned with ethical questions throughout his entire philosophical work. Two works are of special importance for a reconstruction of Schiller's ethics: His *On Grace and Dignity* (1793) and *On the Aesthetic Education of Man in a Series of Letters* (1795). Besides that, we can find interesting conceptions of morality and virtue in Schiller's early philosophical writings that can be traced back to his pre-Kantian *Karlsschule* period (1779–1786). It is especially important to consider these lesser-known texts because they show Schiller's original thoughts on ethics and virtue from the very beginning.

From a general systematic point of view, Schiller's ethics is about unifying the rational and sensible nature of man. His ethics can be therefore called an *ethics of harmony* or a *compatibilist* conception of ethics, which is to be distinguished from an ethics of duty. Because Schiller uses aesthetic terminology to describe and express morality, we can call his ethics an *aesthetic compatibilism* (Noller 2021). Schiller's ethics of harmony can further be described as a

---

[1] For a similar reconstruction, however, with regard to his theory of freedom, see Noller (2020a, b, 2021).

J. Noller (✉)
University of Munich, Munich, Germany
e-mail: Joerg.Noller@lrz.uni-muenchen.de

teleological and *perfectionist* ethics (Beiser 2005, 187) that leads to an *evolution theory* of morality: Morality, according to Schiller, needs to be developed by harmonizing sensibility and reason. As such, Schiller holds an *anti-reductionist* conception of morality that can also be called a *holistic* account of ethics.

Schiller is not so much concerned with the justification and deduction of morality, but rather with the formation and expression of a moral character and a moral society. We can therefore call Schiller's ethics an *expressivist ethics* and a kind of *virtue ethics*. Schiller's ethical interest is already obvious in his early, pre-Kantian writings. In his later writings that are influenced by Kant's philosophy, Schiller uses the notion of the human will, of heautonomy, of love, virtue, grace, and of beauty to further illustrate and elaborate his ethics (Noller 2020a, b, 2021).

Morals in Schiller's Pre-Kantian Writings

Already in his early philosophical writings, Schiller conceives of morality as a unity of the sensible and rational human nature. These writings include his first Karlsschule *Speech about the question: Does too much goodness, kindness and great generosity in the narrowest sense of virtue?* (*Rede über die Frage: Gehört allzuviel Güte, Leutseeligkeit und große Freygebigkeit im engsten Verstände zur Tugend?*) (1779), his second Karlsschule speech on *Virtue considered in its consequences* (*Die Tugend in ihren Folgen betrachtet*) (1780), and his third dissertation *Essay on the connection between the animal nature of man and his spiritual nature* (*Versuch über den Zusammenhang der thierischen Natur des Menschen mit seiner geistigen*) (1780).

Throughout his early works, Schiller often uses the term "Tugend" (virtue), in order to refer to a harmonious state of the human individual. He defines virtue as "the harmonious bond of love and wisdom" (NA XX, 4). Here we can see that Schiller attempts to unify sensibility and reason as two constitutive principles of human nature. Also his perfectionist ethics becomes obvious when he writes that "we can appreciate or condemn every moral action only according to the degree according to which it has contributed more or less to the perfection of the spiritual beings" (NA XX, 30–31). Schiller defines virtue as "[t]hat state of a thinking mind by which it becomes most capable of making minds more perfect, and by perfecting them to be blissful itself" (NA XX, 31). This means that Schiller's ethics is not only about a moral individual but also about a moral society in which individuals coexist in freedom.

In his third dissertation, *Essay on the connection between the animal nature of man and his spiritual nature*, Schiller formulates "a fundamental law of mixed natures", that is, of human beings with rationality and sensibility, which reads as follows: "The activities of the body correspond to the activities of the mind" (NA XX, 57). According to this correspondence thesis, Schiller describes the "condition of virtue" as "that condition of the soul which shows how to derive pleasure from every event and to dissolve every pain into the perfection of the universe" and argues that it "must also be most conducive to the workings of the machine [of our body]" (NA XX, 58). Schiller criticizes that "too much has been written on the own account of the mental power, in so far as it is thought to be independent of the body, with disregard of the latter" (NA XX, 41). Against this reductionist rationalist view, he attempts to "explore the higher moral purposes that are achieved with the help of animal nature" (NA XX, 41). Because of his correspondence thesis, morality cannot be fully realized by only referring to our rational nature. Rather, both our rational and sensible nature must, since they basically correspond to each other, be developed and realized in intimate unity and harmony.

Morals in Schiller's Post-Kantian Writings

Schiller's philosophical reception of Kant's ethics is not so much an adoption of his theory but rather reformulation of Schiller's earlier, pre-Kantian thoughts on morals by means of concepts that Kant's philosophy brought into the philosophical discourse. These concepts are, among others, the concept heautonomy, of beauty, and of play.

On Grace and Dignity

Schiller's ethics takes shape in opposition to Kant's moral philosophy and his conception of the autonomy and autocracy of reason (Gauthier 1997; Deligiorgi 2006; Baxley 2008, 2010; Falduto 2021). Schiller especially criticizes Kant's opposition of sensibility and reason in moral action:

> In Kant's moral philosophy, the idea of *duty* is presented with a severity that repels all graces and might tempt a weak intellect to seek moral perfection by taking the path of a somber and monkish asceticism. However much this great philosopher tried to defend himself against this misinterpretation, which, to his serene and free spirit has to be the most outrageous one, he himself, it seems to me, has provided strong grounds for it (although, for his purpose, this was unavoidable), in his strict and harsh opposition of the two principles that have an effect on the human will. (GD 150; NA 20:284)

Against Kant, Schiller emphasizes the unity and coordination of sensibility and reason in an individual subject, and not the suppression of one nature to the other: "Human beings do have the task of establishing an intimate agreement between their two natures, of always being a harmonious whole, and of acting with their full human capacity. But this beauty of character, the ripest fruit of humanity, is only an idea that they can vigilantly strive to live up to, yet, despite all efforts, can never fully attain" (GD 154; NA XX, 289). Therefore, Schiller substitutes the categorical imperative of pure practical reason by an alternative imperative, the imperative of human harmony and of unity. This conception of morals is opposed to a conception according to which reason controls human sensibility and demands that "the impulses of the sensuous settle into harmony with the rules of the rational and human beings are at one with themselves" (GD 147; NA XX, 280). Schiller calls this state of unity within an individual rational and sensible being a "beautiful soul": "It is in a beautiful soul that sensuousness and reason, duty and inclination are in harmony."

According to Schiller's expressivist conception of morals, "grace is their expression as appearance" (GD 153; NA XX, 288). An ethics of duty, as Kant proposed it, cannot be stable in Schiller's opinion since it does not fully do justice to the very human condition as a unity of reason and sensibility. Morality must therefore be a kind of human life form:

> Only when it gushes forth *from mankind as a whole* as the combined effect of both principles, *when it has become his nature*, is the ethical spirit secure, since, as long as the ethical spirit still employs *force*, the natural impulse has to respond to it with *strength*. The enemy who has merely been *laid low* can get up again, but the one who is *reconciled* has been truly overcome. (GD 150; NA 20:285)

Schiller's perfectionist ethics demands the unity of sensibility and reason: "[T]he ethical perfection of the human being can only become clear precisely because of the part played by the inclination in moral actions" (GD 149; NA 20:283). Schiller does not so much focus on individual actions or maxims but the moral character: "The human being is not destined to perform individual ethical actions but to be an ethical being" (GD 149; NA XX, 283).

Against Kant, who had conceived of morality and duty as the subordination of inclinations by pure practical reason (see CPrR, Ak 5:74), Schiller defines virtue as "an inclination for duty" (GD 149; NA XX, 283). In opposition to Kant, Schiller's ethics demands that "humans not only *may*, but *should* combine enjoyment with duty; they should obey their reason with joy" (GD 149; NA XX, 283). This different conception of virtue that is based on Schiller's harmony model of morals[2] is also expressed in his famous distich on "Scruples of Conscience": "Gladly I serve the friends, but alas I do it with inclination, / And so it often bothers me that I am not virtuous" (NA I, 357). Virtue, according to Schiller, does not rule out inclination but rather demands it. However, virtue is more than just a mixture of reason and inclination. Rather, both principles of human nature need to be balanced and united, and this is the very idea of Schiller's conception of normativity and morals.

Schiller's ethics of harmony can be further understood in terms of his conception of will (Noller 2020b). He generally defines the human will as "a suprasensual faculty" that "is not so subject either to the law of nature or to that of reason that it does not have complete freedom to choose whether to follow the one or the other" (GD 155; NA 20:290). Schiller argues for a general conception of will that can be used in a moral and immoral way: "The will of man" is according to Schiller "a noble concept, even when one does not

---

[2] For Schiller's harmony model, see Roehr (2003, 134) and Baxley (2010, 1087).

consider its moral application". The will, as Schiller puts it, "stands between these two jurisdictions, and it alone decides which law to accept" (GD 155; NA 20:291). It is therefore the "capacity of choice" (AE 17; NA 20:316). In order to be free, human persons demand "an intimate agreement between their two natures, of always being a harmonious whole" (GD 154; NA 20:289). This "intimate agreement" can be understood in terms of harmonious structure of first-order desires and second-order volitions in which the individual "resonance frequency" of the person is realized.[3] The will is the principle of unity that encompasses and harmonizes reason and sensibility in freedom.

In order to develop his expressivist harmony model of ethics, Schiller opposes Kant's conception of the autonomy and autocracy of reason with his conception of heautonomy (Baxley 2003, 2008; Schindler 2008, 2012; Noller 2016, 254–255). Heautonomy means the individual, harmonious volitional self-determination that expresses the entire human nature as a both rational and sensible being. Schiller's notion heautonomy can be interpreted as the key concept that allows us to reconstruct his ethics of a both sensible and rational subject that harmoniously integrates the demands of both nature and reason (Noller 2021). Schiller conceives of individual freedom and beauty as a harmony and unity: "Just as *freedom* lies in the centre between anarchy and the suppression of law, we now find *beauty* in the middle between *dignity*, that is to say, the expression of dominant mind, and *lust*, as the expression of dominant impulse" (GD 148; NA 20:282). Schiller determines the life form of morality as the state of play: "When neither *reason dominating the sensuous*, nor *sensuousness dominating reason* is compatible with beauty of expression, then (as there is no fourth alternative) the state of mind *in which reason and sensuousness*—duty and inclination—*coincide* will be the condition under which the beauty of play occurs" (GD 148; NA 20:282). In playing, we are dynamically balancing and harmonizing our two natures, and thereby expressing morality.

Kant's conception of moral motivation through the feeling of respect proves to be a paradigmatic point of reference for Schiller's critique of Kant's autocracy model of morals (Baxley 2010). Schiller contrasts Kant's concept of respect, which "is forced", with the state of love, which he characterizes as a "free emotion" (GD 166; NA 20:303). According to Schiller, morality is not realized by the oppression of individuality, but is rather an *expression* of it. More precisely, love is an expression of a will that is essentially harmonious and unified. Like his concept of will, Schiller's conception of love allows him to conceptually grasp the unity of the sensible and rational nature of man. As Harry Frankfurt has pointed out,

[t]he heart of love [...] is neither affective nor cognitive. It is volitional. That a person cares about or that he loves something has less to do with how things

---

[3] For the notion of a "resonance effect", see Frankfurt (1971, 16): "When a person identifies himself *decisively* with one of his first-order desires, this commitment 'resounds' throughout the potentially endless array of higher orders."

make him feel, or with his opinions about them, than with the more or less stable motivational structures that shape his preferences and that guide and limit his conduct. What a person loves helps to determine the choices that he makes and the actions that he is eager or unwilling to perform. (Frankfurt 1994, 433–434)

As Frankfurt argues, Love is "in a way reflexive" and therefore characterizes second-order volitions. It is in the state of love that a person maintains her "volitional unity" (Frankfurt 1994, 444).

Besides the feeling of love, the concept of beauty serves as the paradigm for Schiller's harmony model of morals. According to Schiller, "beauty" is to be regarded as "the citizen of two worlds, one *by birth*, the other *through adoption*. It receives its existence in the sensuous world and *achieves* citizenship in the world of reason", whereby it "transforms the sensuous world, in a certain way, into a realm of freedom" (GD 131; NA 20:260). Schiller's harmony model of morals does not conceive of nature as something that needs to be controlled or even oppressed by reason. Rather, nature must be cultivated and united with reason. Schiller's harmonistic concept of ethics follows Kant's aesthetic concept of freedom insofar as, according to it, "the judgment of taste must rest on a mere sensation of the reciprocally animating imagination in its *freedom* and the understanding with its *lawfulness*", which corresponds to the "free play" of the human epistemic capacities (CPJ Ak 5:287). Schiller describes the harmonic state of the will as that of a "*beautiful soul*" in which "nature possess[es] freedom and at the same time preserve its form, since freedom vanishes under the control of a strict disposition and form under the anarchy of sensuousness" (GD 153; NA 20:288).

On the Aesthetic Education of Man

In his *Letters on the Aesthetic Education of Man*, Schiller develops an evolution theory of morality and therefore distinguishes between different drives that "exhaust our concept of humanity" (AE 185; NA 20:347) (Noller 2020b). Schiller's distinction of these volitional structures does not follow the Kantian opposition between autonomy and heteronomy. Rather, he conceives of both drives as the basis of the realization and expression of morality:

> I have no qualms about using this expression [scil. "drive"] collectively, both for that which seeks to follow a law and for that which seeks to satisfy a need, although it is otherwise restricted to the latter only. Just as rational ideas become imperatives or duties as soon as they are placed within the limits of time, so these duties become impulses as soon as they are related to something specific and real. (NA 21:243–244)

Schiller argues that only in a certain harmonious relationship between nature and man's reason can a truly moral activity arise, since an imbalance would not permit the self-distancing of the will with regard to its first-order desires:

"*Exclusive* domination by either of his two basic drives is for him a state of constraint and violence, and freedom lies only in the co-operation of both his natures" (AE 119; NA 20:365). He deprives the capacity of pure practical reason of its *principium executionis*, which he transfers to the capacity to choose: "Reason has accomplished all that she can accomplish by discovering the [moral] law and establishing it. Its execution demands a resolute will and ardour of feeling" (AE 49; NA 20:330). However, both drives do not exist independently of each other. In this way, the human person would be divided, which Schiller aims to avoid. Rather, both drives must stand mutually in a relationship of subordination: "Both principles are, therefore, at once subordinated to each other and co-ordinated with each other, that is to say, they stand in reciprocal relation to one another: without form no matter, and without matter no form" (AE 85n.; NA 20:347n.).

Schiller describes the complex personal drive structure as follows: The "sensuous drive" (AE 139; NA 20:374), or the "material drive"—as Schiller reformulates the finite and empirical nature by analyzing the *real* side of his concept of freedom—"proceeds from the physical existence of man, or his sensuous nature" and "set[s] him within the limits of time" (AE 79; NA 20:344). Here the material drive, as it were, "presses for reality of existence" (AE 81; NA 20:345). Each drive is characterized by its specific intentionality and its object. Schiller calls the object of the material drive "life, in the widest sense of this term" (AE 101; NA 20:355). As a "life impulse" (*Lebenstrieb*) (AE 139; NA 20:374), this drive represents the volitional structure directed towards the preservation of the individual. While the material drive constitutes the empirical and finite dimension of the person, the formal drive has "*form*" as its object, inasmuch as it "includes all the formal qualities of things and all the relations of these to our thinking faculties" (AE 101; NA 20:355).

However, both drives are not only in a synchronous relationship of coordination but also in a genetic one of *evolution*, which motivates his programme of an aesthetic moral education. Schiller conceives a developmental theory of morality on the basis of nature: "The sensuous drive awakens with our experience of life (with the beginning of our individuality); the rational drive, with our experience of law (with the beginning of our personality); and only at this point, when both have come into existence, is the basis of man's humanity established" (AE 137; NA 20:373). Harmonious morality, as Schiller puts it, "arises only when man is a *complete* being, when *both* his fundamental drives are fully developed" (AE 139; NA 20:374). Nature thus represents the *real* basis of morality, out of which, as the last stage of volitional evolution, truly human morality emerges. Schiller locates morality genetically in relation to nature: "Since nature *gives* purpose to human beings but places the fulfillment of that purpose in their will, the present relationship of their condition to their purpose cannot be a work of nature, but must be their own work. The expression of this relationship in their constitution thus does not belong to nature but to themselves, that is, it is a personal expression" (AE 141; NA 20:273).

In opposition to Kant, reason and sensibility are not mutually exclusive principles of human nature but can rather be brought into unity. Since the form-drive and the material drive are directed towards "opposite ends", they "cancel each other out, and the will maintains perfect freedom between them" (AE 135; NA 20:371). Schiller understands the mutual relation of both drives not as a mere opposition, but as a harmonious coordination, which he calls "play-drive". In the dynamic state of play-drive, the form-drive and the material drive "act in concert": "it will, therefore, since it annuls all contingency, annul all constraint too, and set man free both physically and morally" (AE 97; NA 20:354). The state of such a harmoniously integrated will, in which first-order desires harmonize with second-order volitions, is "to be looked upon as a State of *Supreme Reality* (*höchste Realität*), once we have due regard to the absence of all limitation and to the sum total of the powers which are conjointly active within it" (AE 151; NA 20:379), so that "through the use of his freedom"—through specific spontaneity—"it is now up to the mind (*Geist*)[4] to make use of its tools" (GD 133; NA 20:263).

The play or the game—both expressed by the German word "Spiel"—is not so much a "*limitation*" as an "expansion" of man (AE 195; NA 20:358), or as Schiller puts it in his famous dictum: "man only plays when he is in the fullest sense of the word a human being, and *he is only fully a human being when he plays*" (AE 107; NA 20:359) Playing does not mean a morally meaningless or indifferent activity (Noller 2020b, 348). In playing, "the material constraint of natural laws and the spiritual constraint of moral laws" are abolished in an aesthetic state of "higher concept of Necessity, which embraced both worlds at once; and it was only out of the perfect union of those two necessities that for them true Freedom could proceed from which" (AE 109; NA 20:359). Schiller understands inner necessity not as a kind of fatalism that makes freedom and morality impossible. Rather this kind of necessity is a state of "real and active determinability" (AE 141; NA 20:375), that is, as a unity of determination and contingency, which—in contrast to metaphysical or logical necessity—is an expression of harmonious morality. In playing, the form-drive and the material drive are preserved, so that this state "is not just lawlessness but rather harmony of laws, not arbitrariness but supreme inner necessity" (AE 125; NA 20:367).

Schiller distinguishes this free state of inner necessity from that of the necessitation of reason in Kant's conception of autonomy and respect by referring to Kant's notion of heautonomy.[5] Schiller thus argues, as it were, with Kant against

---

[4] There are different ways to translate Schiller's notion of "Geist". Wilkinson and Willoughby translate it with "spirit", whereas Curran translates it with "mind". Since the German word "Geist" can be understood in terms of "spirit" and "mind", I will use both English words to refer to Schiller's notion of Geist.

[5] Cf. Kant's concept of heautonomy as individual self-determination versus universal self-determination: "The power of judgment thus also has in itself an a priori principle for the possibility of nature, though only in a subjective respect, by means of which it prescribes a law, not to nature (as autonomy), but to itself (as heautonomy) for reflection on nature" (CPJ Ak 5:185–186). For the notion of heautonomy in Schiller, see Schindler (2012, 67).

Kant, for the concept of heautonomy refers to the capacity of aesthetic *judgement*: "The perfect can have autonomy insofar as its form is purely determined by its concept; but heautonomy is possible only in beauty, since only its form is determined by its inner essence" (KAL 169; NA 26:210). The play-drive is a "middle disposition", "in which sense and reason are both active", and "in which the psyche is subject neither to physical nor to moral constraint, and yet is active in both these ways" (AE 141; NA 20:375). It is in playing that the human individual realizes and expresses its vocation as a moral being. The mind (*Geist*), understood as the self-reflective will, and expressed by beauty, is the basis of Schiller's compatibilist notion of morals. Schiller's compatibilist concept of the mind thereby adopts an analogous position to Kant's concept of the power of judgement, "which in the order of our faculties of cognition constitutes an intermediary between understanding and reason", "as the intermediary between the faculty of cognition and the faculty of desire" (CJ, Ak 5:168), without being able to be reduced to natural causality or causality of reason.

Harmonious morality, as Schiller understands it in terms of beauty, acquires its determination not "in the *exclusion of certain realities*, but in the *absolute inclusion of all realities*, that is, therefore, not limitation but infinity" (AE 125; NA 20:367). The greater the diversity of first-order desires can be harmoniously integrated into the unity of a will, the more sustainable morality is. As such, Schiller's harmony model of ethics entails an intersubjective dimension: "A noble nature is not content to be itself free; it must also set free everything around it" (AE 167 n., NA 20:386n). A free person thus transfers her inner-harmonious volitional structure to an interpersonal community, which she places in a common "resonance frequency": "He is to set up a world over against himself because he is Person, and he is to be Person because a world stands over against him" (AE 353; NA 20:353).[6]

Schiller further develops this idea of an intersubjective, compatibilist spread of harmony within the framework of his theory of an aesthetic state, which he distinguishes from the dynamic and the ethical state (Moland 2021; Noller 2021, 439–440). This difference can be further analyzed in terms of morality in such a way that, as one passes through all three states as stages, more and more human freedom and morality is realized and harmoniously expressed. Schiller argues that the moral state is "the most fruitful of all in respect of knowledge and morality" (AE 151; NA 20:370). While in the dynamic state human coexistence is regulated by rights, so that "it is as force that one man encounters another, and imposes limits upon his activities", which corresponds to the stage of legality, the ethical state regulates human coexistence by duties insofar as "[m]an sets himself over against man with all the majesty of the law, and puts a curb upon his desires", which corresponds to the stage of duty (AE 215; NA 20:410). Schiller assigns the modality of possibility to the dynamic state, and the modality of necessity to the ethical state. The aesthetic state,

---

[6] For a discussion of the relationship between individuality and multiplicity, see Beiser (2005, 140–141).

however, is distinguished by the modality of reality, in the manner of a synthesis of both states. It consists in the fact that the human being appears not as an object of forces, laws or commandments, but as a moral "Gestalt," that is, "as an object of free play". Schiller explains the harmonious intersubjectivity of the aesthetic state through his concept of taste (*Geschmack*), which can be understood in terms of *virtue*:

> Taste alone brings harmony into society, because it fosters harmony in the individual. All other forms of perception divide man, because they are founded exclusively either upon the sensuous or upon the spiritual part of his being; only the aesthetic mode of perception makes of him a whole, because both his natures must be in harmony if he is to achieve it. All other forms of communication divide society, because they relate exclusively either to the private receptivity or to the private proficiency of its individual members, hence to that which distinguishes man from man; only the aesthetic mode of communication unites society, because it relates to that which is common to all. (AE 215; NA 20:410–411)

As in the case of the principles of reason and sensibility in an individual, so in society we need a unity of the opposed dynamic and ethical states. The aesthetic state unifies the dynamic and ethical state and realizes harmony in society:

> Every other state into which we can enter refers us back to a preceding one, and requires for its termination a subsequent one; the aesthetic alone is a whole in itself, since it comprises within itself all the conditions of both its origin and its continuance. Here alone do we feel reft out of time, and our human nature expresses itself with a purity and *integrity*, as though it had as yet suffered no impairment through the intervention of external forces. (AE 152; NA 20: 379)

In the aesthetic state, the moral state is not destroyed or abolished but rather mediated and sublated in a more comprehensive state in which its normativity is still preserved. The aesthetic state is not indifferent towards the normativity of morality but rather realizes a second-order normativity for it unites morality with human nature. Schiller's concepts of love, play, and the aesthetic state are in this respect less emotional states than volitional structures that describe specifically human freedom and morality in nature, history, and society. Even if Schiller does not conceive of freedom primarily in moral terms, his aesthetic compatibilism nevertheless has a normative dimension. We can understand it in terms of an educational ideal that, in the final analysis, closely links the dynamics of sensible-rational harmony with the normativity of morality.

References

Baxley, A. M. (2003). Autocracy and Autonomy. *Kant-Studien* 94(1): 1–23. doi:https://doi.org/10.1515/kant.2003.003.

Baxley, A. M. (2008). Pleasure, freedom and grace: Schiller's "completion" of Kant's ethics. *Inquiry* 51(1): 1–15. doi:https://doi.org/10.1080/00201740701858886.

Baxley, A. M. (2010). The aesthetics of morality: Schiller's critique of Kantian rationalism. *Philosophy Compass* 5(12), 1084–1095. doi:https://doi.org/10.1111/j.1747-9991.2010.00350.x.

Beiser, Frederick. 2005. *Schiller as philosopher. A re-examination.* Oxford: Oxford University Press.

Deligiorgi, Katerina. 2006. Grace as guide to morals? Schiller's aesthetic turn in ethics. *History of Philosophy Quarterly* 23(1): 1–20.

Falduto, Antonino. 2021. One more time on the alleged repugnance of Kant's ethics? Schiller's *Kallias letters* and the entirety of the human being. In *European Journal of Philosophy* 29(4): 795–810.

Frankfurt, H. G. 1971. Freedom of the will and the concept of a person. *The Journal of Philosophy* 68(1): 5–20. doi:https://doi.org/10.2307/2024717.

Frankfurt, Harry G. 1994. Autonomy, necessity and love. In *Vernunftbegriffe in der Moderne: Stuttgarter Hegel-Kongress 1993*, ed. Hans Friedrich Fulda, Rolf-Peter Horstmann, 433–447. Stuttgart, Germany: Klett-Cotta.

Gauthier, Jeffrey A. 1997. Schiller's critique of Kant's moral psychology: Reconciling practical reason and an ethics of virtue. *Canadian Journal of Philosophy* 27(4): 513–543.

Moland, Lydia L. 2021, Friedrich Schiller. In *The Stanford Encyclopedia of Philosophy* (Summer 2021 Edition), ed. Edward N. Zalta. https://plato.stanford.edu/archives/sum2021/entries/schiller/.

Noller, Jörg. 2016. *Die Bestimmung des Willens: Zum Problem individueller Freiheit im Ausgang von Kant.* 2nd edition. Freiburg/München: Alber.

Noller, Jörg. 2020a. From Autonomy to Heautonomy: Reinhold and Schiller on Practical Self-Determination. *Idealistic Studies.* doi:https://doi.org/10.5840/idstudies2020821116.

Noller, Jörg. 2020b. ‚Heautonomy': Schiller on freedom of the will. *European Journal of Philosophy* 20(2): 339-353.

Noller, Jörg. 2021. Die Stimmung des Willens: Schillers ästhetischer Kompatibilismus. *Deutsche Zeitschrift für Philosophie* 69(4): 529-552.

Roehr, Sabine. 2003. Freedom and autonomy in Schiller. *Journal of the History of Ideas* 64(1): 119–134.

Schindler, David. 2008. An aesthetics of freedom: Schiller's breakthrough beyond subjectivism. In *Yearbook of the Irish Philosophical Society*, ed. F. Long, 84–109. Maynooth: Irish Philosophical Society.

Schindler, David. 2012. *The perfection of freedom: Schiller, Schelling, and Hegel between the ancients and the moderns.* Eugene, OR: Cascade Books.

CHAPTER 20

Schiller on Politics and Political Theory

Daniel Stader

In October 1989, few weeks before the fall of the Berlin wall, the Schwerin state theatre visits the *Volksbühne* in East Berlin for a guest performance of Schiller's *Wilhelm Tell*. The production was by "costume, stage set and stage action located in the presence of the GDR" and by this means had "provided a tremendous actuality to Schiller's text" (Piedmont 1995: 213). The stage was constantly set in a bright light, even during scenes set in the evening or at night (cf. ibid.: 217), so the most secret and hidden action would be visible under the best conditions. This presentation of what had been covered, concerning the rulership as well as hidden conspiracy and protest against it, by giving it artistic voices and images was an aesthetic fulfilment of the political claim of *glasnost*. This relocated staging provoked spontaneous applause with verses like "Who will want to live here without freedom" or "Tear down the walls!" (SW 2: 989, 1014, cf. Schuller 2009: 138f.), and "'[t]he theatre raved with enthusiasm at the end of the performance'" (Piedmont 1995: 213). It is not only this response to a performance of one of Schiller's plays that leaves no doubt about their political potency.

Schiller is not an author of political theory, but nonetheless a political author. Schiller's account is holistic. His focus doesn't spot on separated disciplines, such as natural law, pure morals, and sheer aesthetics, but the actual interaction of society, statehood, and human behaviour and its grounding, history, as well as (sentiments of) beauty and art. This holistic approach demands a "complete

D. Stader (✉)
Martin-Luther Universität-Halle-Wittenberg, Halle (Saale), Germany
e-mail: daniel.stader@phil.uni-halle.de

anthropological view" (AE: 19), and seeks not to answer the question of the potential of particular human faculties or social institutions, but to approach the riddle of men with all their drives, influences, and conditions. Therefore, Schiller hasn't written a separable political theory, but his anthropological take has a comprehensive and ineradicable political dimension. However, due to his holistic perspective, this political dimension is simultaneously inseparably entangled with moral and aesthetic domains as it is situated in concrete historical contexts.

Some Basic Assumptions: Theses on Schiller's Realm of Politics

The arrangement of Schiller's work to bring out its political dimension demands structural guiding by premising its basic assumptions, supplemented by some remarks on the shifts of Schiller's understanding of the political realm:

1. The first assumption concerns nature and purpose of man. Schiller's anthropological account on the inner drives that determine human nature is based on two contrasting twists. With the first one, Schiller accompanies Kant against Rousseau. The latter claimed, especially in his *First* and *Second Discourse*, that the virtues and the destiny of man lied exclusively in his nature. Under the inconvenient sociocultural conditions of the actual civilized world, it all came down to cultivating this original disposition in the best possible way. Kant countered Rousseau by claiming that man is determined by his double nature: Besides natural disposition, he is provided with reason and therefore destined to determine himself. By self-cultivation, man "ought to achieve the purposes of humanity by reason, wherefore his animality was equipped by instinct with the mere disposition" (R 1515, Ak 15: 859). So far, Schiller agrees: Destiny of human species is to be achieved by reason, insofar as reason provides the possibility of freedom for self-determination. But Schiller draws further consequences from the idea of man's double nature. While Kant understands the rule of reason as humankind's destiny, Schiller states that both natures, the sensuous and the intellectual, demand for fulfilment. Man's destiny can't solely lie in one of his natures, because "nature gave the human being notice of his obligation not to separate what it had bound together and, even in the purest expressions of his divine part, not to neglect the sensuous, and not to base the triumph of the one on the subjugation of the other" (GD: 150). Demanding unification of both natures, Schiller does not work with a transcendental, but with an anthropological notion of freedom (cf. AE: 137), and consequently understands alienation[1]—and harmonization—as a historical process and therefore a "'political' problem" (Marcuse 1962: 170).

[1] For the problem of alienation, which is no doubt also a political one, see the Chap. 35, *Schiller and Marx on Alienation*, in this volume.

2. This historical process includes political needs of the genus as a social species. Considering its development, these political needs themselves are object of continuous shifts. To understand and outline the structure of that process and its needs, Schiller joins the ranks of a long historical tradition of analogizing the individual and the species. It is already Plato's *Republic* that understands a political collective as an emergence that is structurally dependent on the individuals who constitute it. As "the same three forms or dispositions found in the city also exist in each one of us" (Plato 1979 435e: 102), the threefold division of the individual soul into the rational, the spirited and the appetitive part is corresponding the social division into a ruling, a guarding, and a producing class in the city. Thus, justice means in either case "that each of his parts tends its own business in regard to ruling and being ruled" (ibid. 443b: 111). Aristotle denies such a direct influence from inherent structures of the soul on outer structures of the political realm, but nonetheless draws analogies between the despotic (which is analogue to the reign of soul over body) and the constitutional political reign (that equals the reign of intellect over appetite, cf. Aristotle 2016 1254b: 7). In a more covert way, Kant's philosophy of history also structures the development of the species analogously to the individual's. The perfection of the species "has great similarity with the age of man, and the interim period until perfection is like the interim period of the maturity of nature and the civil maturity of a man, i.e. the age of youth" (Ak 25: 1197). Schiller draws both analogies: the simultaneous relationship of the inner drives and faculties of the individual with the political rulership (cf. GD: 146–148 and Eagleton 1990: 113f.), and also the development of the use of one's faculties in relation to historical progress of political reign. Thinking of both in similar structures, the (changing) conception of one always relates to the other.

3. Talking of the use of one's faculties already reveals the anthropological perspective that has already been mentioned. Even if Schiller establishes the aesthetic education and the aesthetic state as ways to achieve the last ends of the individual and the state, it is not a realm on its own. Schiller accents that there are only two original drives that affect man, and that there is no third, aesthetic drive. The aesthetic can only institutionalize itself as "a third character" (AE: 15) or play-drive, which is a relationship in the functioning, a merging use of the original two, and therefore is in line with the level of Kant's anthropology, which does not deal with human faculties themselves, but with the use of faculties, or, "what *he* [man] as a free acting being makes of himself, or can and should make of himself" (Anth, Ak 7: 119). For Schiller, the aim of moral as well as political freedom is only to be achieved by generating such a third character as in individual and as a people, because it "might prepare the way for a transition from the rule of mere force to the rule of law, and which, without in any way impeding the development of moral character, might on the contrary serve as a pledge in the sensible world of a morality yet

unseen" (AE: 15). The aesthetic education of man serves that purpose of being the key to build the "most perfect of all the works to be achieved by the art of man: the construction of true political freedom" (ibid.: 7). Schiller's both individual and collective need to develop such an aesthetic character results partly in the merging of moral and political sphere, especially when it comes to the person of a political ruler.

Besides that, Schiller's political thought is also underlying some shifts: (a) One ongoing catalyst of problems and focus of Schiller's political account is the French Revolution, which he enthusiastically welcomes, and its aftermath, especially the execution of Louis XVI, which disgusts him (cf. NA 26: 183, Alt 2007: 27–30). (b) Schiller's work is also driven by a methodological shift from psychology to anthropology, which enables his general theory on the aesthetic education of man as generic history in the first place. After 1792, Schiller replaces his "psychological study of political patterns of behaviour and thought by an anthropological frame analysis, that itself founds the new program of an aesthetic education of the social emancipated individual" (Alt 2002: 108). (c) Dependent on those shifts is the change of Schiller's political orientation from welfare to liberty and the focus from the education of the ruler to the education of the people.

Politics in Theory: Education, Character, and the Aesthetic State

For Schiller, statehood is the natural form of human society. The social life of human beings is constituted by laws out of need, so "compulsion organized it [the state] according to purely natural laws before *he* could do so according the laws of Reason" (AE: 11). It is the opposite of this natural, positive, physical state or state of compulsion (which are the same due to Schiller's "loose use of terms", Wilkinson and Willoughby 1967: xlv) and the moral state or state of reason, which determines Schiller's conception of politics and history as termini that represent man's double nature. The natural state is a state institutionalized by force, whereas a state of reason is the ideal of a conscious self-determination by laws. Referring to the categories of modality of Kant's *Critique of Pure Reason* (cf. B106), Schiller emphasizes that "physical man does *in fact* exist, whereas the existence of moral man is as yet *problematic*" (AE: 13). In his theoretical writings, Schiller examines the needs of such a self-determined moral state and how to establish it.

In a letter to the Duke of Augustenburg, Schiller outlines his understanding of the requirements of such a development in the context of criticising the excesses of the French Revolution. A people cannot simply give itself a new constitution and dismiss its monarch to provide a state of reason and determine itself. According to Schiller, the outcomes of the French Revolution have shown "that the human race has not yet outgrown guardianship, that the liberal regiment of reason comes too early where one can hardly cope with resisting the brutal violence of animalism, and that he is not yet ripe for *civil* freedom who still lacks so much for *human* freedom" (NA 26: 262). The subsequent conception of the needs of historic progress follows Kant. Kant doubts that revolution as a historical means is quite promising using an argument, which might as well be the motto of Schiller's account on political history: "A revolution may well bring about a falling off of personal despotism and of avaricious or tyrannical oppression, but never a true reform in one's way of thinking; instead, new prejudices will serve just as well as old ones to harness the great unthinking masses" (WE, Ak 8: 36). Quite similar, Schiller puts the people's capacities to use its freedom and its need for political rulership in proportion:

> All reforms that are to endure must start from the way of thinking, and where there is corruption in the principles, nothing healthy, not benign, can germinate. Only the character of the citizens creates and maintains the state, and makes political and civil freedom possible. For if wisdom itself descended in person from Olympus and introduced the most perfect constitution, it would have to hand over the execution to men. (NA 26: 264)

Political progress in self-determination of humankind depends on the character of the people, that is, its ability to make use of its freedom in a reliable way. Political and civil liberty can only be build "on the firm foundation of a refined character, one will have to begin by creating citizens for the constitution before one can give the citizens a constitution" (Ibid.: 265). It is this dependence of the state on the character of its people and its belonging individuals that explains in the first place why Schiller, in his work on the art of political freedom, goes into such detail about the education of man's inner drives. This idea of a political need for education is highly influenced by Mirabeau's *Travail sur L'Education Publique* (cf. Johnston 1984). The anthropological key concept of character refers to political and moral, individual and collective forms of acquiring the ability to use and to relate one's faculties at the same time. Being deployed on all of those levels, it entails the structural analogy between the development of the individual and of the people/the species, which similarly are in need for education to build a character that is capable of freedom in a reasonable way. At this point, Schiller faces a problem in either case: How is such a progression of character-building possible if "the character of the citizen is depending on the constitution as well as the latter rests upon the character of the citizen"? (NA 26: 265, cf. AE: 45). Whether the perfection of individual or state should be primary had already been asked by Kant in his lectures on anthropology with a slight tendency to answer in favour of the education of the individual exclusively in an early lecture (cf. Ak 25: 691, 1202). Analogously, the individual itself "would first have to be wise to love wisdom" (AE: 51), and seemingly couldn't strive for a use of and self-determination by reason unless it was already reasonable. On both levels, Schiller presents the aesthetic education as a solution to this circles.

What does the aesthetic in aesthetic education refer to? According to the analogous multilevel of Schiller's approach, it has multiple meanings. Firstly, the aesthetic describes the middle sphere or stage of human's development "which both the individual and the species as a whole must pass": "Man in his *physical* state merely suffers the dominion of nature; he emancipates himself from this dominion in the *aesthetic* state, and he acquires mastery over it in the *moral*" (Ibid.: 171). Besides, these stages "are also to be distinguished in each single act of perception" (ibid.: 183). Secondly, the aesthetic refers to the means of education: Especially concerning the political level, to break the reciprocal dependency of political constitution and the acquiring of character of the people, "we should, presumably, have to seek out some instrument not provided by the State, and to open up living springs which, whatever the political corruption, would remain clear and pure. [...] This instrument is Fine Art" (Ibid.: 55), because "it is only through Beauty that man makes his way to Freedom" (Ibid.: 9). Thirdly, the aesthetic names the end of education: The individual acquirement and refinement of character ought to create a "beautiful soul" (GD: 152), and correspondingly the species has "to concern itself with that most perfect of all the works to be achieved by the art of man: the construction of true political freedom" (AE: 7). In Schiller's *Fiesco*, the old Doria will also refer to his state as "the most beautiful artwork of government" (SW I: 684).

The aesthetic as a stage is based on the premise of the double nature of man. Being inherent to each single act of perception, to the ideal development of each individual, and to the species as a whole, it shows not only the continuity but also the dependence of political possibilities on the human condition in general anthropological and specific historical regard. Shifting the perspective from faculties (senses and reason) to drives (sensuous or material and formal drive), Schiller highlights the functional mechanism of the faculties' activity. While the sensual drive strives for impressions that are as diverse and changing as possible, the formal drive seeks to create unity and stasis. This corresponds to the diversity and vicissitude of sensual experience and needs on the one hand and the striving of reason for lawfulness in the theoretical and practical sense on the other. According to Schiller, each perception, each individual, and each state start their existence with mere sensations, sensual experiences/needs, or natural forces, and are meant to be recognized as lawful and self-determined by laws of reason. The transformation from one to the other would be the aesthetic stage, for here both drives are challenged into activity.

The simultaneous activity of both drives, with their different functions and demands, is required for education, as it enables to use one's reason in the first place as well as to create a balance of both of the drives. The balanced connection of their activity spawns what Schiller calls the "*play-drive*", which is "directed towards annulling time *within time*, reconciling becoming with absolute being and change with identity" and "will endeavour so to receive as if it had itself brought forth, and so to bring forth as the intuitive sense aspires to receive" (AE: 97). In that way, the play-drive "deprives feelings and passions of their dynamic power, it will bring them into harmony with the ideas of reason; and to the extent that it deprives the laws of reason of their moral compulsion, it will reconcile them with the interests of the senses" (Ibid.: 99).[2] Schiller's term of beauty defines this exact harmony of the matter with the form, "it is at once a state of our being and an activity we perform" (Ibid.: 187). The simultaneous activity has the role of initiating the use of reason: One has to learn to generalize in theoretical and practical way by abstracting from the diverse sensuous material, and one can do this only by bringing forth one's own forms. It is through play that humans learn how to use their reason; "there is no other way of making sensuous man rational except by first making him aesthetic" (Ibid.: 161). But the equilibrium of the drives is not limited to that moment of transformation; an educated formal drive, a reason capable of self-determination, is not meant to dominate the soul recklessly but has to integrate the sensual drive. While man comes into being with the necessity of physical determination, it is only after gaining the capability of self-determination through reason that he is free in Schiller's anthropological understanding. Only by this free choice within "the opposition of two necessities" (ibid.: 137), "when *both* his fundamental drives are fully developed" (ibid.: 139), one can reach a truly aesthetic balance meaning "a middle disposition in which sense and reason are both active *at the same time*" (Ibid.: 141).

This intra-subjective relational activity, which doesn't seem to be a matter of politics at first glance, is in fact crucial to Schiller's understanding of the political realm and its progress. Firstly, because the aesthetic education is the means to build and refine character, and the character's quality determines the possibilities of a state's constitution. Hence, art is a specific engine of education and freedom. Secondly, because the intra-subjective relationship of sensuousness and reason equals the relationship of a people and its legislator. Concerning man's double nature, "[o]ne can think of three ways altogether in which a human can relate to himself, that is, in which the sensuous part can relate to the rational" (GD: 147): the domination of sensuousness, the domination of rationality, or the harmony of sensuous impulses and rational demands. It is no figurative speech, when Schiller identifies the intra-subjective relationships with political ones:

> When a monarchic state is run in such a way that, although everything proceeds in accordance with the will of one person, the individual citizen can still persuade himself that he is living according to his own lights and simply following his inclinations, one calls this a liberal government. However, one would be very hesitant to give it this name if *either* the ruler imposed his will against the citizen's inclinations or the citizen imposed his inclinations against the will of the ruler; since, in the first instance, the government would not be *liberal*, and in the second it would not be a *government*. (Ibid.: 145f.)

The first of these relationships between the two natures in the human is reminiscent of a *monarchy* in which the ruler's strict surveillance bridles every free

---

[2] See Chap. 18, *Schiller's Aesthetics: Beauty and Freedom*, in this volume.

stirring; the second is like a wild *ochlocracy*, in which the citizen, by refusing obedience to the rightful supremacy, fails to gain freedom, just as the human constitution, by suppressing moral self-motivation, fails to become beautiful; instead, he becomes a victim of the more brutal despotism of the lowest classes, just as form falls victim to mass. Just as *freedom* lies in the centre between anarchy and the suppression of law, we now find *beauty* in the middle between *dignity*, that is to say, the expression of dominant mind, and *lust*, as the expression of dominant impulse. When neither *reason dominating the sensuous*, nor *sensuousness dominating reason* is compatible with beauty of expression, then (as there is not fourth alternative) the state of mind *in which reason and sensuousness*—duty and inclination—*coincide* will be the condition under which the beauty of play occurs. (Ibid.: 148)

Without going into further detail of the intra-subjective relationships, it is necessary to elucidate the relationships of government and citizens. In a historical comparing lecture published in 1790, when Schiller still put the ruler at the heart of political conception, he describes political legislation analogously to what is later called formal drive:

It has always been a giant step of the human spirit to treat as a work of art that which until now had been left to chance and passion. The first attempt at the most difficult of all arts must necessarily be imperfect, but it always remains estimable because it was made at the most important of all arts. [...] The legislators will continue to practice crude experiments for a long time, until the happy equilibrium of the social forces finally presents itself to them of its own accord. [...] The legislator alone works on a self-acting resisting material—human freedom. Only imperfectly can he bring into fulfilment the ideal which he has still so purely conceived in his brain, but here the attempt alone is worthy of all praise, if it is undertaken with disinterested benevolence and completed with expediency. (SW 4: 818)

Here, Schiller argues closely to Mandeville in the preface to his *Fable of the Bees*, which is written in order to "extol the wonderful Power of Political Wisdom, by the help of which so beautiful a Machine is rais'd from the most contemptible Branches" (Mandeville 1924: 6, cf. SW 5: 821). Speaking of the legislator as the formal drive, it is a generic law he has to put the people under. On the other hand, the people consists of individuals, with different abilities, interests, and demands—inclinations—whose diversity is not meant to be equalized and suppressed by law, just as the sensuousness of the individual itself: "The State should not only respect the objective and generic character in its individual subjects; it should also honour their subjective and specific character, and in extending the invisible realm of morals take care not to depopulate the sensible realm of appearance" (AE: 19). Contrary to the actual artist, the politician works not only with mere material but also with humans that are ends in themselves. The state as a work of art has to serve the people as an end, because it is not an end in itself: "The state is a work of man, man is a work of the unattainable great nature. The state is a creature of chance, but man is a necessary being, and by what else is a state great and venerable but by the powers of its individuals?" (NA 25: 146f.).

The formal self-determination of the individual and of the state refer to the same source: the law of reason. Ideally, this law of reason is in harmony with the individual sensuous drive, respectively the subjective specifics and inclinations of the people, meaning the diverse abilities and the ideas of happiness of its individuals. The state as a work of art has to provide what Schiller once called "the fundamental principle on which all states must rest: to give oneself the laws to be obeyed, and to fulfil the duties of the citizen out of insight and out of love for the fatherland, not out of slavish fear of punishment, not out of bilious and flaccid submission to the will of a superior" (SW 4: 832). The political-historical question now is: How is a transfer from a provisory, unjust natural state of force to a moral state possible? The key concept has already been mentioned: character, for "[a]ll improvement in the political sphere is to proceed from the ennobling of character" (AE: 55). Schiller is totally affirmative to "any attempt on the part of a people grown to maturity to transform its Natural State into a Moral one" (Ibid.: 13). It is the right of every people to give itself a constitution that enables for self-determination by reasonable laws. Indeed, a successful transformation demands several conditions, and the crucial condition is character. The transformation of a state requires a seemingly impossible feat:

> When the craftsman has a timepiece to repair, he can let its wheels run down; but the living clockwork of the State must be repaired while it is still striking, and it is a question of changing the revolving wheel while it still revolves. For this reason a support must be looked for which will ensure the continuance of society, and make it independent of the Natural State which is to be abolished. (Ibid.)

The unification of feelings and rationality to a harmonious whole of the beautiful soul enables the individual to "leave affect to guide the will without hesitation and is never in danger of standing in contradiction of its decisions. For this reason the actions of a beautiful soul are not themselves ethical, but the character as a whole is so" (GD: 152). The fact that the character as a whole includes the "development of man's capacity for feeling" (AE: 53) thereby contradicts the popular thesis, which is that education of character equals the education of judgement in Kant's understanding (cf. Habermas 1990: 48, Aigner 2012: 141), because Kant classifies judgement after all as an upper faculty. Schiller's conception of character assumes the plasticity of feeling. This presupposes the possibility to educate inclination itself and thereby to strengthen the character's reliability. This specific topic seems to be conceptualized closer to Baumgarten's "*aesthetic exercise*" (Baumgarten 2007: 39) than to Kant's aesthetic judgement. For a successful transformation of the state, the people's unifying character has to guarantee that the abolishment of natural force is accompanied by proactive lawful behaviour and doesn't lack substitution:

> The setting up of a moral State involves being able to count on the moral law as an effective force, and free will is thereby drawn into the realm of cause and effect, where everything follows from everything else in a chain of strict necessity. [...] If, therefore, we are to be able to count on man's moral behaviour with as much certainty as we do on *natural* effects, it will itself have to *be* nature, and he will have to be led by his very impulses to the kind of conduct which is bound to proceed from a moral character. (AE: 17)

According to Schiller's metaphor of the craftsman, the successful "changing of the revolving wheel while it still revolves" would only be possible if the clock-hands were already capable of moving themselves. The people has to have a reliable character before it can give itself a liberal constitution, before it can replace the natural state by a moral state. This condition of a successful transformation ("*Wholeness* of character must therefore be present in any people capable, and worthy, of exchanging a State of compulsion for a State of freedom" Ibid.: 23) explains, according to Schiller, why the French Revolution failed: "The attempt of the French people to assert its sacred human rights and to achieve political freedom has only revealed its incapacity and unworthiness" (NA 26: 262). The French people lacked that kind of character that would have guaranteed an adherence to the very human rights during the transformation of its state it wanted to enact as a state principle in the first place. The French Revolution was born just out of theoretical, philosophical insight in the right of a people to give itself a constitution, but wasn't covered by a practical character that lived up to respective demands (see the sixth to eighth of Schiller's *Letters*, AE: 32–53 or SW 5: 1015; Humboldt has a likewise view, cf. Aigner 2012: 182f. and for a similar interpretation cf. Habermas ²1980: 92). Related to that point of view, Schiller's friend Johann Benjamin Erhard goes a step further and considers a revolution legitimate if the people is superior to the government in the capacities for self-government on the one hand, or if the government denies the means to appropriate capacities "to make itself mature": "Therefore, if one wants to prevent the people from enlightening itself, it is right to rise up, and if these obstacles arise from the constitution, to abolish the constitution" (Erhard 1970: 92, for Schiller's relationship to Erhard, see Alt 2002: 127, 130f. and Müller-Seidel 2009: 28–33). Even if Schiller is not as radical as Erhard, he refuses to be as reactionary as Burke with his *Reflections on the Revolution in France* (cf. Wilkinson and Willoughby 1967: xviii, to Burke's influence on Schiller in general cf. Subramanian 2007). The people indeed has the right to abolish the constitution of a natural state, but it ought to have the necessary political skills before it can acquire them in the political freedom it seeks. This idea of a failure of the transformation of the state, which doesn't already do what it aims at, finds expression in plenty of Schiller's plays. The people should already be capable of moral self-determination that is grounded in an aesthetic character, before it can dismiss the state as a natural force that protected the individuals from each other as mere animals. Because the natural state as a mere force is not able to create such a moral character, it has to be educated in a non-governmental sphere: by art. This function shows contrary to several accusations against Schiller, that art is not meant as compensation of social deficits, that "aesthetic education was not conceived by Schiller as a kind of escape from the world but as a means of fitting every individual to turn outwards towards the world and exercise responsibility in it" (Sharpe 1991: 2). This is quite similar to Habermas' understanding of actual education of children in a special social institution, "in the protected space of an educational field largely unburdened by major social tensions", where children learn to act without the burden of actual social sanctions and are "coming of age under the care of presumed maturity" (Habermas 1961: 257). Likewise, the "aesthetic mode of the psyche which first gives rise to freedom" takes place "in the favoured zone where activity alone leads to enjoyment, and enjoyment alone to activity, [...] where imagination ever flees actuality yet never strays from the simplicity of nature" (AE: 191). With the outsourcing of the aesthetic education of the political sphere, Schiller confirms the thesis of Koselleck, that "Criticism set itself apart from the State as non-political, yet subjected it to its judgment" (Koselleck 1988: 114): "The jurisdiction of the stage begins where the territory of the secular laws ends" (SW 5: 823, cf. e.g. AE: 55, 197 and Koselleck 1988: 98–102). The aesthetic education of the people and its means, art, are at the same time non-political—as they only directly aim at the moral character and the ability for self-determination—and political—for they are meant to enable the people to supersede the political authority of the natural state in the long run, and makes the people weary from force that keeps it from using its capacity of self-determination. It is not mere intellectual or transcendental freedom Schiller's aesthetic education is about, "but freedom *in* the reality" (Marcuse 1962: 171).

Last but not least, it is necessary to examine what has been thought to be an inconsistency in Schiller's objective of state development: "The divergence consists in the fact that what was introduced at the beginning as a *means* to an end, as just seen, becomes an *end in itself* at the end" (Sandkaulen 2005: 49, cf. Janz 1998: 623, and for a resemblant discussion, Wilkinson and Willoughby 1967: xliii–xlviii). Of course, this concerns the phenomenon that Schiller starts his *Letters* aiming at the moral state, and ends them with the aesthetic state as an ultimate purpose of the species. Proponents of this divergence as a theoretical inconsistency explain it from shifts of intention during the piece-by-piece composing of the *Letters* in an extensive period of time. In the beginning, Schiller reduces the actual natural state as historical continence for man in regard "to the highest end which Reason now decrees in him as Person. This is the origin and justification of any attempt on the part of a people grown to maturity to transform its Natural State into a Moral one" (AE: 13). It may seem that the aesthetic is a mere means, when Schiller points out that "there is no other way of making sensuous man rational except by first making him aesthetic" (Ibid.: 161). But at the end, Schiller prefers the "*aesthetic* State" as superior to the "*ethical* state" for exclusively conferring a "*social character*" (ibid.: 215). But firstly, the political aim of a moral state is not degraded, but complemented with the aesthetic state. A mere moral state, a self-imposed liberal constitution does refer to the monophony with the reasonable character of its people, but not with the actual harmony with its nature. Secondly, it is not only that the aesthetic state develops and emerges in the character of the people outside of the political sphere of a natural state and that it enables successful change of the political constitution. It also transcends the political sphere, which by constitutional law only determines *what* has and has not to be done, by reconciliation of the human's double nature into harmony of *how* something is done, and embraces the political sphere of laws as a sphere of sociability. In fact, Schiller's analogy of the individual and the people (or even the species) is that adequate, that the missing pieces at the end of the *Letters* may be extrapolated with the statements of *On Grace and Dignity*. According to that, an ideal aesthetic state would be the state whose laws are followed not only out of insight by the citizen's own reason but also by his sensuous affection and originated in his whole nature:

> Only when it gushes forth from *mankind as a whole* as the combined effect of both principles, *when it has become his nature*, is the ethical spirit secure, since, as long as the ethical spirit still employs *force*, the natural impulse has to respond to it with *strength*. The enemy who has merely been *laid low* can get up again, but the one who is *reconciled* has been truly overcome. (GD: 150)

Inside of such an aesthetic state, the moral state would be the guardian of law in regard to "either the particular limits of the subject or those of mankind in general" (ibid.: 161) for such a harmony. The political government would have "*only entrusted* sensuousness [i.e. figuratively the citizen] with the helm, it will take it back the moment that instinct tries to abuse its power" (ibid.:158). Thus, the aesthetic state included a strict reasonable moral state that guarded its lawfulness.

Political Intentions in Practice: The Case of Schiller's Plays

To show the political implications of Schiller's idea of aesthetic education, I take a brief look at its practice by highlighting some political topics of exemplary plays. They ought to educate people playfully, for "[t]he seriousness of your principles will frighten them away, but in the play of your semblance they will be prepared to tolerate them; for their taste is purer than their heart" (AE: 61, cf. 217). Taste, "as a faculty of judgment for beauty, steps in between spirit and sensuality and binds these two mutually disdainful natures into a happy union—just as it gains the respect of reason for the *material* and inclines sense toward the *rational*", and finally "transforms the sensuous world [...] into a realm of freedom" (GD: 131). Consequent maxims, even of a villain, are admired for illustrating the strength of human will in general: "Where else can it come from that we push away the half-good character with reluctance and often follow the very bad one with shuddering admiration?" It is because "vices which testify to strength of will announce a greater disposition to true moral freedom than virtues which borrow a support from inclination" (SW 5: 536). Here Schiller agrees with Kant, who prefers evil character to lack of character because changing maxims is easier than acquiring a character in the first place (cf. Ak 25: 631, 650f., 823). By sensuous means, the stage has to illustrate rational ideas and universal laws by specific cases and to form them into experience; that's what distinguishes the dramatic stage from the mainly sensual religion (cf. SW 5: 822). Schiller chooses to take most of his material from history itself, because despite the eternity of the principles of reason, "man is not just Person pure and simple, but Person situated in a particular Condition" (AE: 75). The historical topics of Schiller's plays reveal the historicity of contemporary conditions of actions and the supratemporal demands of principle-based action; they are at the same time affirmative and alienating, moreover politically innocuous at first: "Under the cover of history can be hidden, what can't be imparted to the contemporaries as present" (Müller-Seidel 2009: 85).

Schiller's earlier plays seem to be addressed to the prince himself, and have often been related to mirrors for princes in their intended functioning. Especially *Fiesco* has been referenced to Niccolò Machiavelli's *The Prince*, a work that deals with taking over princely power and the *virtù* of the prince (cf. Alt 2009a: 344, Aigner 2012: 38–45; for an interpretation of Schiller's *Letters* as an answer to Machiavelli's *Prince* cf. Subramanian 2007: 120f.). In this regard, the early plays still stick to an older understanding of politics, that is centred around the action of the prince—political criticism then is moral criticism of the ruler or conspirators (and is still based on a psychological account, cf. Alt 2002: 104f.), but not of absolute rule itself. This concerns *The Robbers*, *Fiesco*, or *Intrigue and Love* and goes along with an Aristotelian understanding of the purpose of the state, being welfare or happiness of the people, not its liberty (in German enlightenment popular via Christian Wolff's *Deutsche Politik*): "The highest and last demand which the philosopher and legislator of a public institution just can make is the promotion of universal happiness" (SW 5: 819; for Kant's critique of such a paternalistic government as despotism cf. TP, Ak 8: 290f.). From that outdated perspective, Schiller focuses on illustrating failure as educational critique. So in *The Robbers*, the failure of the relationship of father and son represents the failure of political paternalism (cf. Müller-Seidel 2009: 66f.) due to a weak prince, and an affective, immature people. This already indicates Schiller's idea of character, for the prince and the people are similarly unable to govern themselves prudently and firmly, so both are susceptible to manipulation (by Franz Moor as representation of an increasingly nihilistic materialism), which destroys their social order. *Fiesco* then introduces one of Schiller's favourite political topics: tyrannicide (cf. Müller-Seidel 2009: 34–59), but can't live up to expectations of its subtitle *A Republican tragedy.* Still, political power depends on the moral character, the resoluteness, or recklessness of rulers or conspirators. This is what Luhmann counts as traditional understanding of rulership in contrast to modern understanding of politics: "The rightness of political action ensues not just simply from the rights of the one who is acting; it is not more synonymous with application of law or legitimacy. It consists of the watchful realization of an own ratio, the raison d'état […]" (Luhmann ²1998: 88). The considerations of *Fiesco*—to become prince or to make Genoa a republic—depend on his virtue and his mental state, not on the reflection of political conceptions or legitimacy (cf. Koopmann 1998: 357). The play leaves with just one central political statement: when the tyrannicide becomes arbitrary, it is not better than tyranny itself. While *Fiesco* wants to invade absolutism with his virtue, in *Intrigue and Love* the powerful nobility invades the bourgeois family as a place of sociability. The double rift between the involved runs between the nobility and the bourgeoisie, but at the same time between virtuous and non-virtuous. In a political sense, the powerless are at the mercy of the powerful, but even more crucial, the virtuous are at the mercy of the non-virtuous despite social status. Here Schiller anticipates what he will point out in his *Letters*: a functioning society is founded in the character of its members, without regard to their social rank.

Don Carlos then turns away from a paradigm of absolutism by addressing the demand for freedom of the Flanders from the Spanish crown. Posa with his promotion of this demand has often been interpreted as Schiller's mouthpiece, but Schiller himself reflected and problematized the means of Posa in his *Letters on Don Carlos*. As implemented by Posa, the legitimate request for freedom undermines itself by choosing means that contradict the request. Here, Schiller representatively criticizes secret societies like the Illuminati, which claim to induce enlightenment and abolish absolutism, but ground themselves on absolute hierarchy (cf. SW 2: 257 and the remark ibid.: 1233). Posa chooses a "subordination of friendship to the more important [i.e. political, liberal] interest" (ibid.: 238), and therefore manipulates his friend, who "was regarded by him only as the *only indispensable tool*" (Ibid.: 243). He sacrifices truthfulness and his personal bond to his political agenda, and therefore undermines the sincerity of the latter itself. The means already erodes the end, for maxims of action have to be universal: "By practical laws, not by artificial births of theoretical reason man is to be guided in his moral action" (Ibid.: 260). Particularizing use of practical laws of moral action contradicts the term of the law and reduces it to interest, and for Schiller equates the idealist and the despot,

> because the object of both endeavours resides *in* them, not *outside* them, and because the one who models his action on an inner mental image is almost as much in conflict with the freedom of others as the one whose ultimate goal is *his own ego*. True greatness of mind often leads no less to violations of other people's freedom than egoism and imperiousness, because it acts for the sake of the action, not for the sake of the individual subject. (Ibid.: 259)

The history of society, politics, freedom, or rulership cannot "*shorten* its way" (ibid.: 261) by great deeds, because real change depends on the condition of character, and Posa fails the respective test. Schiller levels the difference of political and moral action, which was often taken to account by rulers to justify themselves, as Frederick II did when he distinguished (even in a pejorative way) "private morality" from "the morality of princes" (Friedrich der Große 1913: 2). Again, Schiller's lesson is: Political change has to match the laws it wants to establish; it already has to be what it aims at, because it has to rely on a character that precedes the political change.

The first dramatical work after the happenings of the French Revolution and Schiller's extended trip into philosophy leads into the 30 Years' War and combines Schiller's idealized antique tragedy and the need for tangible material. *Wallenstein* is an exemplary individual that illustrates human history as literally fatalistic. Schiller "consistently transferred the metaphysical categories of Attic tragedy to the immanence of history" (Alt 2009b: 457). Fate is transformed from a metaphysical into a historical category, and its nemesis relies on individual action ("That is just the curse of the evil deed / That it, procreating, must always give birth to evil", SW 2: 398) as well as the historical-political condition of the species (cf. Alt 2002: 107). Showing the greatness of history just by denying catharsis serves the educational mission, for "Man grows with his greater purposes" (SW 2: 271): "By pointing to the dark side of history, the drama deepens the awareness of its open structure and teleologically based perfection, which obliges to work on its more humane appearance" (Alt 2009b: 463). The historic setting of *Mary Stuart* can also not be considered a coincidence, but contemporarily negotiates the arrest and the execution of Louis XVI (cf. Johnston 1998: 60–62, Nilges 2009: 87). Schiller shows the conflict between Elisabeth and Mary amongst political claims to power, moral misconduct, and personal interests, leaving no doubt that this spheres are not divided, but inevitable merged. The play is structured by court proceedings, but their impartiality and their purpose of justice are constantly thwarted by Elisabeth with her absolute sovereignty "that is cast in a highly dubious light here" (Alt 2009b: 501). Her role is criticized by Mary, who "has, one might say, read Locke and Montesquieu in reclaiming a judiciary that remains strictly divorced from the executive—Elizabeth and her interests" (Nilges 2009: 85). Beyond that, Elisabeth inverts the purpose of political liberty when she laments over the "slavery of the people's service" and being object of public opinion, keeping her from being "free on this Throne" (SW 2: 655), which illustrates the anachronism of absolute power under advanced historical conditions, ending in tragedy. Initially, Schiller planned his *Wilhelm Tell* as a tragedy as well, but in fact, "it was his only play that did not end tragically" (Knobloch 1998: 490), and it is no coincidence that it is his only play where tyrannicide is carried out successfully. Solely by being set in Switzerland, it refers to Rousseau and therefore embodies the right to resistance against Kant, for dead-end tyranny sets the people back into state of nature (cf. ibid.: 493–496 and Rousseau 2002: 214–216). But Tell himself commits murder not as a political act of resistance, but as a "private matter" (NA: 32: 89) of protecting his family: "Tyranny must first become so intolerable that resistance and self-defence are forced upon even the non-political, unbiased citizen" (Johnston 1998: 64). At the end of his dramatical work, Schiller comes to a conclusion about the last resort of tyrannicide: even if it is inevitably a political act, it is only legitimate as an act from moral motivation without own political intentions; it is meant to end tyranny, but not to found a new rulership or even constitution. Consequently, Tell refuses a political role and leaves the founding of the constitution to the confederation, and the confederation hereby keeps its moral integrity: "Blessed are you, for you have not stained with blood / Our spotless victory!" (SW 2: 1016).

The plot and the promoted values of *Wilhelm Tell* result in numerous censorial interventions regarding the first performances concerning especially the *Rütlischwur* as confederate vote for the right to resistance; Schiller himself cancelled the last act at the premiere (cf. Alt 2009b: 570f.). The consistent political direction, which can also be read as affirmative to the American independence, has played several political roles and was object of numerous political usurpations. In the first years of Nazi Germany, it was the most performed of Schiller's plays, and parts of it were required reading in schools (cf. Ruppelt 1979: 41). Further, the Nazis promoted the aestheticization of politics and especially the "aestheticization of the working world" by setting the "'beauty of work'" (Reichel [2]1992: 235) against class struggle, to unify and redefine the people's efforts under a national dictatorship. Nonetheless, a coherent reframing of Schiller as a national poet and precursor of Nietzsche's will to power (based on *On the Sublime* with its strong notion of will as human condition, cf. Kaiser 2007: 232) failed just like a "monoparadigmatic reorientation of the interpretation of Schiller does not succeed between 1933 and 1945" (Ibid.: 230). It is the conditionality of Schiller's understanding of the state, the fact that politics always is in service of sociability and the individual, that makes it incongruous for such an absorption of a totalitarian state: "The state is never an end in itself, it is only of importance as a necessary condition for the achievement of mankind's end, and this end of mankind is none other than the cultivation of all powers of man" (SW 4: 815; for the influence of this text on the Scholl siblings cf. Wilkinson and Willoughby 1967:xvi, fn.). The totalitarian consideration of "human beings as means and not as ends" is exactly the opposite of the purpose of a state and tears down "the foundations of natural law and of morality lawfully" (SW 4: 816). For the state, to abandon its purpose means to set back the relation of government and people into state of nature, and allows tyrannicide in the last resort as a moral act of self-defence. Hitler rants about Schiller's ineptitude as a national dramatist who would draw a line of tradition to the Holy Roman Empire: "Schiller, of all people, had to glorify this Swiss sniper" (Hitler 1980: 43). On June 3, 1941, the tyrant himself prohibits any performance of *Wilhelm Tell* on stage just as its reading in school (cf. Ruppelt 2005: 41).

References

Aigner, Susanne. 2012. *Friedrich Schiller und die Politik: Schillers politisches Denken im Wandel der Zeit*. Marburg: Tectum Verlag.
Alt, Peter-André. 2002. "Arbeit für mehr als ein Jahrhundert": Schillers Verständnis von Ästhetik und Politik in der Periode der Französischen Revolution (1790–1800). In *Jahrbuch der deutschen Schillergesellschaft* 46, eds. Wilfried Barner et al., 102–133. Stuttgart: Alfred Kröner Verlag.
Alt, Peter-André. 2007. Ästhetische Revolution, schwieriger Staat, ferne Nation: Schiller und die Politik. In *Würzburger Schiller-Vorträge 2005*, ed. Jörg Robert, 27–45. Würzburg: Könighausen & Neumann.
Alt, Peter-André. 2009a. *Schiller: Eine Biographie. Band I: 1759–1791*. München: Verlag C.H.Beck.
Alt, Peter-André. 2009b. *Schiller: Eine Biographie. Band II: 1791–1805*. München: Verlag C.H.Beck.
Aristotle. 2016. Politics, in: *Aristotle's Politics: Writings from the Complete Works: Politics – Economics – Constitution of Athens*, ed. Jonathan Barnes, intr. Melissa Lane, 1–225. Princeton/Oxford: Princeton University Press.
Baumgarten, Alexander Gottlieb. 2007. *Ästhetik. Band 1*, ed. and trans. Dagmar Mirbach. Hamburg: Meiner.
Eagleton, Terry. 1990. *The Ideology of the Aesthetic*. Cambridge, Massachusetts: Basil Blackwell.
Erhard, Johann Benjamin 1970. Über das Recht des Volks zu einer Revolution. In *Über das Recht des Volks zu einer Revolution und andere Schriften*, ed. Hellmut G Haasis, 7–98. München: Carl Hanser Verlag.
Friedrich der Große. 1913. *Die Werke Friedrichs des Großen. Zweiter Band: Geschichte meiner Zeit*, ed. Gustav Berthold Volz, trans. Friedrich v. Oppeln-Bronikowski. Berlin: Reimar Hobbing.
Habermas, Jürgen. 1961. Pädagogischer "Optimismus" vor Gericht einer pessimistischen Anthropologie: Schelskys Bedenken zur Schulreform. In *Neue Sammlung. Göttinger Blätter für Kultur und Erziehung* 1, 250–278.
Habermas, Jürgen. ²1980 [¹1971]. *Theorie und Praxis: Sozialphilosophische Studien*. Frankfurt am Main: Suhrkamp.
Habermas, Jürgen. 1990. *The Philosophical Discourse of Modernity: Twelve Lectures*, trans. F. Lawrence. Cambridge, Massachusetts: The MIT Press.
Hitler, Adolf. 1980. *Monologe im Führerhauptquartier 1941–1944. Aufgezeichnet von Heinrich Heim*, ed. Werner Jochmann. Hamburg: Knaus.
Janz, Rolf Peter 1998. Über die ästhetische Erziehung des Menschen in einer Reihe von Briefen. In *Schiller-Handbuch*, ed. Helmut Koopmann, 610–626. Stuttgart: Alfred Kröner Verlag.
Johnston, Otto W. 1984. Mirabeau and Schiller on Education to Freedom. *Monatshefte* 76/1: 58–72.
Johnston, Otto W. 1998. Schillers politische Welt. In *Schiller-Handbuch*, ed. Helmut Koopmann, 44–69. Stuttgart: Alfred Kröner Verlag.
Kaiser, Gerhard. 2007. Das Finstere in klassischen Zeiten: Vom literaturwissenschaftlichen Umgang mit Schillers theoretischen Schriften zwischen 1933 und 1945. In *Friedrich Schiller: Der unterschätzte Theoretiker*, eds. Georg Bollenbeck and Lothar Ehrlich, 215–236. Köln/Weimar/Wien: Böhlau Verlag.

Knobloch, Hans Jörg. 1998. Wilhelm Tell. In *Schiller-Handbuch*, ed. Helmut Koopmann, 486–512. Stuttgart: Alfred Kröner Verlag.
Koopmann, Helmut. 1998. Die Verschwörung des Fiesko zu Genua. In *Schiller-Handbuch*, ed. Helmut Koopmann, 354–364. Stuttgart: Alfred Kröner Verlag.
Koselleck, Reinhart. 1988. *Critique and Crisis: Enlightenment and the Pathogenesis of Modern Society.* Cambridge, Massachusetts: The MIT Press.
Luhmann, Niklas. ²1998 [¹1989]. Staat und Staatsräson im Übergang von traditionaler Herrschaft zu moderner Politik. In *Gesellschaftsstruktur und Semantik: Studien zur Wissenssoziologie der modernen Gesellschaft. Band 3*, 65–148. Frankfurt am Main: Suhrkamp.
Mandeville, Bernard. 1924. *The Fable of the Bees: Or, Private Vices, Publick Benefits. The First Volume*, ed. F. B. Kaye. Oxford: Clarendon Press.
Marcuse, Herbert. 1962. *Eros and Civilization. A Philosophical Inquiry into Freud.* New York: Vintage Books.
Müller-Seidel, Walter. 2009. *Friedrich Schiller und die Politik: 'Nicht das Große, nur das Menschliche geschehe'*. München: Verlag C.H.Beck.
Nilges, Yvonne. 2009. Maria Stuart – Politik und Gerechtigkeit. In *Zum Schillerjahr 2009: Schillers politische Dimension*, ed. Bernd Rill, 81–90. München: Hans-Seidel-Stifung e.V.
Piedmont, Ferdinand. 1995. 'Reißt die Mauern ein!' Schillers 'Wilhelm Tell' auf der Bühne im Jahr der 'deutschen Revolution' 1989. *German Studies Review* 18/2: 213–221.
Plato. 1979. *The Republic*, ed. and trans. Raymond Larson. Wheeling, Illinois: Harlan Davidson Inc.
Reichel, Peter. ²1992 [¹1991]. *Der schöne Schein des Dritten Reiches: Faszination und Gewalt des Faschismus.* München/Wien: Carl Hanser Verlag.
Rousseau, Jean-Jacques. 2002. The Social Contract. In *The Social Contract* and *The First and Second Discourses*, ed. Susan Dunn, 149–254. New Haven/London: Yale University Press.
Ruppelt, Georg. 1979. *Schiller im nationalsozialistischen Deutschland: Der Versuch einer Gleichschaltung.* Stuttgart: J.B. Metzlersche Verlagsbuchhandlung.
Ruppelt, Georg. 2005. *Hitler gegen Tell: Die "Gleich- und Ausschaltung" Friedrich Schillers im nationalsozialistischen Deutschland.* Hameln: Niemeyer.
Sandkaulen, Birgit. 2005. Schönheit und Freiheit: Schillers politische Philosophie. In *Schiller im Gespräch der Wissenschaften*, eds. Klaus Manger and Gottfried Willems, 37–55. Heidelberg: Universitätsverlag Winter.
Schuller, Wolfgang. 2009. *Die deutsche Revolution 1989.* Berlin: Rowohlt.
Sharpe, Lesley. 1991. *Friedrich Schiller. Drama, Thought and Politics.* Cambridge et al.: Cambridge University Press.
Subramanian, Balasundaram. 2007. Die 'Ästhetischen Briefe' als 'Fürstenspiegel' der politischen Moderne: Zum Einfluß Edmund Burkes auf Schiller. In *Friedrich Schiller: Der unterschätzte Theoretiker*, eds. Georg Bollenbeck and Lothar Ehrlich, 87–121. Köln/Weimar/Wien: Böhlau Verlag.
Wilkinson, Elizabeth M., Willoughby, L. A. 1967. Introduction, in: *On the Aesthetic Education of Man in a Series of Letters*, eds. and trans. Elizabeth M. Wilkinson and L. A. Willoughby, xi–cxcvi. Oxford: Clarendon Press.

CHAPTER 21

Schiller's Philosophy of History

Andree Hahmann

A discussion of Schiller's Philosophy of History must address two questions: First, does Schiller have a philosophy of history at all? Second, if so, is it more than a popularized form of Kant's philosophy of history? The first question arises in part from a more general concern about Schiller's philosophy that has been expressed variously by scholars in recent centuries. At the heart of this concern lies the fact that Schiller is conceived primarily as a poet, and one wonders how a poet can be a philosopher at the same time. The second question is based on Schiller's open admiration for Kant and the overall presence of Kantian themes and phrases in Schiller's theoretical work.

This chapter will answer both questions. The first part argues that Schiller worked out a philosophy of history that shaped his approach to history as we find it both in the published lectures and in his major historical writings. The second part emphasizes important differences between Schiller's approach to history and Kant's. It will be shown that essential aspects of Schiller's philosophy of history can not only be traced back before his first engagement with Kant, but are also consistent with his overarching aesthetic-philosophical project.

Schiller's Philosophy of History

Some scholars claim that Schiller has not proposed a philosophical account of history comparable to his philosophical letters or his work on aesthetics. His two major historical works appear to be unaffected by any philosophical views

A. Hahmann (✉)
Tsinghua University, Beijing, China
e-mail: ahahmann@mail.tsinghua.edu.cn

(Malter 1995, 281–282, Schmidt-Biggemann 1995, 273–274, 280). Rather, we find limited reflections on the philosophy of history only in a few short texts. More than that, most of the views expressed in these texts are simply variations on Kant's thought (Kaufmann 1940, 65; Schieder 1960, 31). But if this were the case, we would have to conclude that Schiller has no philosophy of history of his own. It is therefore not surprising that Frederik Beiser in his otherwise groundbreaking work on Schiller's philosophy does not address the philosophy of history as a separate but devotes only some lines to Schiller's "study of history" (2005, 39). In what follows, I will show that, contrary to these assumptions, Schiller actually proposed a unique view on history that is based on what can rightly lay claim to be called a philosophy of history. We will then see that Schiller's approach assumes a fairly independent position within late German Enlightenment. In fact, important features of later idealistic views of history are already prefigured in Schiller's philosophy of history.

Philosophy of History and Universal History

Admittedly, Schiller did not devote an entire book to his philosophy of history. This does not mean, however, that he did not develop his own philosophical account of history. It should be noted that Kant also did not present his account of history in a single work, but developed his philosophy of history in a series of short texts aimed at a wider audience. There are several reasons for this. Firstly, the historical themes aroused the interest of a general audience concerned with the ideas of the Enlightenment.[1] Of crucial importance to what was considered the great project of the Enlightenment is the idea of man's unique determination.[2] This determination requires the special education of man, nicely depicted in Lessing's influential essay on *The Education of the Human Race* (1780). In this essay, Lessing connects the educational project with what is called a universal history, that is, the idea that one has to "consider the entire sequence of human beings, during the entire course of the ages, as a single man who lives perpetually on and learns something all the time" (Blaise Pascal, taken from Abrams 1973, 201). In Germany, influential versions of this idea were presented, aside from Lessing, by Schlözer, Iselin, Herder, Gatterer, Tetens, and Kant. As mentioned above, Kant is considered particularly important for the development of Schiller's conception of universal history. However, although there is an evident impact of Kant's account of history on Schiller, we must not lose sight of other possible sources for Schiller's conception of universal history. I will return to this later.

---

[1] The Berlinische Monatsschrift was founded in 1783 by Friedrich Gedike and Johann Erich Biester, with whom Kant had been in correspondence since 1779. The letters show that Kant's choice of topics for the journal was partly based on Biester's wishes.
[2] A popular version of this idea goes back to Johann Joachim Spalding's *Betrachtung über die Bestimmung des Menschen*, Greifswald 1748.

Kant's first publications on history can be seen against the backdrop of the work of his former student Herder. In fact, it is difficult to disentangle the relationship between Kant's and Herder's development of philosophy of history (Schmidt-Biggemann 1995, 267–269). Herder admired Kant's lectures on anthropology, which in turn already encapsulated central ideas of Kant's mature philosophy of history. Important for us is that Kant commented in a series of reviews on the first and second part of the books of his former student Herder (*Ideen zur Philosophie der Geschichte der Menschheit* 1784–1791). What Kant found particularly objectionable about Herder's account of history was that Herder proceeded without principle and thus without philosophical guideline but rather emphasized the role of chance in his presentation (*Review of J. G. Herder's Ideas for the philosophy of the history of humanity. Parts 1 and 2* AA 8: 54–55). As becomes clear from Kant's *Idea for a Universal History with a Cosmopolitan Aim*, what a philosophy has to accomplish is to order the seemingly irregular course of human history in order to make history fruitful for the overriding objective of philosophy, namely to contribute to the realization of the determination of man (*IUH*, AA 8: 25; 27; 29; 31). With the *Conjectural Beginning of Human History*, published in 1786, Kant then also presented an explicit counter-proposal to Herder. Central to Kant's essays are above all two assumptions, which are spelled out differently in his texts on history: First, the claim—put at the beginning of the earlier-published *Idea for a Universal History with a Cosmopolitan Aim*—that the history of free actions is as an appearance also subject to a certain regularity that can be assessed teleologically (*IUH*, AA 8: 17, 19). This natural purpose is said to consist in the perfect development of human predispositions, since predisposition is determined by nature to completely develop (*IUH*, AA 8: 18; 19, 21; 30. See also AA 8: 115, 308). However, this development presupposes a liberal political constitution (*IUH*, AA 8:22, 28. See also *Review of J. G. Herder's Ideas for the philosophy of the history of humanity. Parts 1 and 2* AA 8: 64; *PP* AA 8:366). Consequently, to establish this political constitution becomes the ultimate end of the natural development of man (*MM*, AA 6: 355; see Hahmann 2013, 2018).

Secondly, Kant assumes that this natural realization of the human predispositions cannot happen in the individual, but only in the whole species (*IUH*, AA 8:18). To achieve this end, nature employs a special means, namely natural antagonism. This idea can be traced back to the 1770s and was developed in different ways by Kant in his writings. In the end, however, it refers to a kind of "unsociable sociability" (*IUH*, AA 8:20–21), according to which man's striving is, on the one hand, to socialize with fellow humans, but, on the other hand, also to isolate himself from the very others. The result is discord among the people and eventually war (*Conjectural Beginning of Human History* AA 8: 119–120, 121; *TP* AA 8: 310; *PP* AA 8: 365).

The influence exerted by Kant's ideas on the systematics of history become evident, for example, in Reinhold, who was particularly concerned with the scientific status of history itself. Reinhold claims that, in order to call history a science, it will be necessary to give it a systematic form. Otherwise, it would remain a mere collection or aggregate of historical facts. To provide this form to history is one of the main objectives of a philosophy of history, or, rather, it constitutes the essence of philosophy of history (*Briefe über die Kantische Philosophie* vol. 1, 1790: 34–35).

This brings us eventually back to Schiller. We know that Schiller's engagement with Kant has been heavily influenced by Reinhold (Heinz 2007). In fact, it was Reinhold who sparked Schiller's interest in Kant's philosophy in the first place as Schiller confessed in a famous letter to his friend Körner.[3] For our purposes, it is noteworthy that Schiller was particularly interested in Kant's philosophy of history since his first contact with Kant's philosophy. Two things follow from this: Firstly, Kant's work in the philosophy of history undoubtedly helped to shape Schiller's own conception of philosophy of history.[4] However, this does not mean that Schiller blindly adopted Kant's approach, and it does not justify to downplay Schiller's own contribution at all. We will come back to this in the second part of the chapter. Secondly, and even more importantly for the moment, we have to bear in mind the importance of systematic form to universal history. Against this background, it is not surprising to note that similar to Kant and Reinhold, Schiller also emphasizes the systematic form that history must take and he also believes that philosophy of history has to establish this system. This becomes evident most of all in Schiller's inaugural lecture delivered after his appointment as professor of philosophy[5] in Jena. From this lecture emerged the text *Was heisst und zu welchem Ende studiert man Universalgeschichte*, which is considered Schiller's most important and explicit contribution to philosophy of history (published in Teutscher Merkur, November 1789).[6]

The importance that Schiller lays on systematic form becomes evident at the beginning of the text. There Schiller famously distinguishes between the bread-and-butter scholar on the one hand and the genuine philosophical head on the other (SW 4:750–754). At this point, we cannot consider all possible aspects of

---

[3] Letter to Gottfried Körner, 29 August 1787: "Only in October do his lectures begin, which have Kant's philosophy and beautiful sciences as their content. Against Reinhold you are a despiser of Kant, for he claims that after 100 years Kant must have the reputation of Jesus Christ. But I must confess that he spoke sensibly of it, and already got me started with Kant's little essays in the Berliner Monatsschrift, among which the *Idea for a Universal History* gave me extraordinary satisfaction. That I will read and perhaps study Kant seems to be certain."

[4] This has already been noted by Reinhold in a letter to Kant (14 June 1789, AA 11: 62).

[5] Although Schiller is often conceived as professor of history, this is not true, at least in the strict sense. In fact, he was appointed extraordinary professor of philosophy, which has been emphasized by his colleagues in Jena who refused to accept Schiller as a historian at the faculty. See Muhlack (1995), 9.

[6] This text is followed by *Die Sendung Moses* (Thalia, Heft 10, 1790), *Etwas über die erste Menschengesellschaft am Leitfaden der Mosaischen Urkunde* (Thalia, Heft 11, 1790), and *Die Gesetzgebung des Lykurgus und Solon* (Thalia, Heft 11, 1790).

Schiller's comparison.[7] However, we can clearly see that with the help of this example Schiller contrasts synthetic activity with mere analytic thinking. The former is related to philosophy, whereas the latter exhibits a rather limited view on the underlying subject. Taken literally, *synthesis* means to combine distinct elements, whereas *analysis* is a decomposition or division of what is already combined. A crucial condition of this procedure is the idea that everything in the world is actually interrelated or connected to which Schiller points in various writings (SW 4:752, 773; SW 5:281, 283–284, 289). For Schiller, a real philosophic head aims at this overarching coherence (SW 4:764; SW 5:284).[8] Consequently, a philosophical or synthetic mind can never be satisfied with mere fragments. His findings remain fragments, however, if the individual pieces are not combined, or, as Schiller puts it in his inaugural lecture, synthesized (SW 4:752–753).

One must notice that Reinhold already pointed out in his discussion of history that history remains to be a mere collection or aggregate of unrelated facts if it is not united from a specific point of view. Reinhold takes this perspective as a unifying principle to combine what is as such separated, and it is only in virtue of this principle that a system can emerge. Schiller not only emphasizes this thought in his inaugural lecture but also stresses the systematic combination of facts at various places in his oeuvre, but especially in his historical writings (Kaufmann 1940). It becomes clear therefore that Schiller agrees with both Kant and Reinhold that it is a major task of a philosophy of history to create a systematic unity that distinguishes a philosophical view on history, that is, universal history from a collection of historical facts. And if we agree with Reinhold that this is also what essentially constitutes a philosophy of history for Schiller and his contemporaries, we must admit that Schiller indeed proposed a philosophy of history insofar as he accomplished to constitute a universal history based on principles. To assess therefore Schiller's philosophy of history, we need to consider his system more thoroughly. In the following, I will argue that Schiller's systematic constitution of history is determined by a teleological perspective.

Providence in History

One of the major tenets of Enlightenment accounts of history, which is still most problematically discussed, is the relationship between history and teleology. According to a frequently raised objection, Enlightenment thinkers naively assumed that history must be conceived as a teleologically ordered sequence of

---

[7] Prüfer (2002), 114–115, identifies a former, more personal motivation and points to Körner, who in a letter from 1785 complains about his "Brotstudium". Others point to institutional reasons for Schiller's distinction and his aim to criticize the traditional division between the lower faculty, that is, philosophy, and the higher faculties, theology, medicine, and law, at German universities (Muhlack 1995, 27–28).

[8] See also SW 4:846: "Reason cannot endure in an anarchic world. Always striving for harmony, it would rather run the risk of unhappily defending order than desisting with indifference."

events. At first sight, this seems to apply to Schiller as well. He frequently appeals to this teleological order in nature that emerges from seemingly chaotic events and helps to develop human predispositions and talents (Alt 2008, 532–533). Similar to Kant, Schiller calls this purpose in history either providence, reason, fate, or simply nature. We can find many examples of how Schiller employs the idea that divine providence is governing human fate and thus the course of world history all over Schiller's historical writings (SW 4:764, 766, 767, 768, 776, 784, 787–788, 847, 850; SW 5:250–251, 285). However, we should not immediately infer from the usage of these terms that Schiller simply and naively adopted the view that history is guided by an overarching purpose. As I will show in this section, it is not so much the uncritical application of theological assumptions but rather underlying systematic considerations that are responsible for Schiller's teleological approach to history. In other words, systematicity as such requires a superordinate teleology in history because only this teleological assumption can provide a systematic organization of what appears to be chance events.

How exactly can teleological principles help to give history a systematic form? First of all, it is important to note that the concept of providence unites three different aspects of history: first, the idea of progress; second, that good arises from evil; and third, the idea of an overarching order. That history need not necessarily be seen as progressive is evident and emphasized by Kant, who points out that alternatively there could be improvements in small matters but all in all considered things remain the same (*IUH* AA 8: 17, 25). At least in the *Idea for a Universal History*, Kant leaves it at this statement and expresses his conviction that the philosopher must choose the side of providence. Schiller adds to this thought by noting that human societies reveal distinct levels of development (SW 4:754). According to Schiller, "it is a wise hand" (SW 4:754) that draws our attention to this fact in order to demonstrate that human societies naturally develop, and it is on the basis of these observations that the historian is enabled to determine the origin and course of this development.

The second idea, that good emerges from evil, is important in propelling the development of society. Similar to Kant, Schiller claims that this development depends on contrary conditions, either within human society (SW 4:813) or between different states where hostility plays an essential role as incentive to establish a juridical condition (SW 4:755, 766, 849). In *Etwas über die erste Menschengesellschaft*, for example, the development of human societies is triggered by opposing forces of nature (SW 4:769–770). It is only through war that man can reach a position to completely develop his "reason and *Sittlichkeit*" (*morality*, SW 4:770). For Schiller, however, the fact that good can emerge from evil is also demonstrated by the fate of individuals who can turn the evil that befalls them to their own good or the good of their people, as we can see from the example of Moses. It is through providence, also called foresight or fate in this chapter, that Moses was taken from the Hebrews and enjoyed an Egyptian education which in turn was necessary to develop the capability and will to accomplish to save the Hebrew people from Egyptian slavery (SW 4:787–788).

The two preceding ideas finally culminate in the idea that the purpose of nature consists in creating political order or "to guide freedom by the bonds of necessity" (SW 4:766).[9] The opposite state to this would be "lawless freedom", which is at the same time a state of war (SW 4:755, 776, 805, 850). According to Schiller, however, this condition has been overcome by continuing peace prevailing in Europe at that time (SW 4:756–757). The reason for this state of peace sees Schiller in the balance of European powers established by providence or the "spirit of order" (SW 4:851). For Schiller, this balance brought about an enduring but fragile state of peace in Europe as late as 1789, that is, shortly before the outbreak of warfare that would shake Europe as a result of the French Revolution.

If we look more closely at these passages, it becomes clear that Schiller uses providence as a methodological device to structure historical facts and sometimes also to fill historical gaps. Apparently, historical documents are often scarce, especially regarding the oldest development of human societies. This can put the historian in a problematic position. In order not to be left with a mere aggregate or assemblage of historical facts, the universal historian has to appeal to reason to establish a systematic presentation (SW 4:763, 771):

The Mosaic document leaves us here and skips a period of 15 or more years to show us the two brothers as already grown up. But this intervening period is important for human history, and if the document leaves us, reason must fill the gap. (SW 4:771)

Reason is equipped with many tools to fill these gaps. Not only does it infer from effects to causes (SW 4:761), but it can also proceed according to analogy or take from various sources to establish a systematic whole (SW 4:764). In this special case, it means that Schiller also employs Greek sources to explain what remains unclear in the biblical tradition (SW 4:780; 782). The choice of material and the inferences by analogy, however, are guided by a teleological view on history, which allows the universal historian to make use of these various sources in view of an overarching teleological structure of events or "to transform what he sees related as cause and effect into a combination of means and purpose" (SW 4:764). We can see therefore that it is not so much the unquestioned adoption of theological assumptions but rather systematic aims that made Schiller employ this approach to history. In other words, systematicity as such requires a superordinate teleology in history, which allows for systematically organizing the seemingly random historical events. Or, as Schiller puts it:

He begins to remove one phenomenon after another from the domain of blind chance, from freedom from law, and to fit it as a link into a harmonious totality (which to be sure, exists only in his imagination). (SW 4:764, translation taken from [1972], 332)

---

[9] See also SW 4:776: "It is usually only through the consequences of disorder that people arrive at the introduction of order, and lawlessness usually leads to laws in the first place."

This last point deserves our special attention. It also makes clear that Schiller does not naively assume that history is actually teleologically ordered. On the contrary, Schiller is well aware of the subjective status of providence (Reed 2011, 272). It is the historian himself who conceives of history as if it were determined by a superordinate plan:

> Thus he transplants this harmony from himself to the nature of things; that is, he imports a rational purpose into the course of the world, and a teleological principle into world history. (SW 4:764 translation taken from [1972], 332)[10]

This superordinate plan of nature which constitutes a systematic whole provides the means to order the seemingly random facts presented by the historical sources. And only in view of this systematic whole is it worth calling history a science. In a nutshell then, the harmonious order of historical facts is produced by the universal historian who applies a teleological method of reason in order to satisfy the systematic standards of philosophy of history.

Two points follow from this observation. First of all, Schiller's teleological assumptions that underly his historical writings must not be conceived as an expression of the "passionate strength of his own will" (Kaufmann 1940, 8) but derive from methodological considerations shaped by his philosophy of history (Dann 2005, 74). Secondly, this philosophy of history is essentially constructivist insofar as the historian has to establish a systematic whole that rightly deserves to be called universal history.[11] We have seen that Schiller agrees in this method both with Kant and Reinhold. They are also well aware that in order to find any sense in history we have to make it.

Schiller and Kant

Let us now turn to the second question and see whether Schiller blindly follows Kant in his philosophy of history. As mentioned above, some scholars go so far as to claim that Schiller's approach is basically little more than a variation on Kantian themes and thoughts (Malter 1995, 283). This judgement can draw on several observations. We have seen that Schiller's first contact with Kant's philosophy was through Kant's texts on history. Moreover, in a famous letter Reinhold mentions to Kant that he won Schiller over to Kant's project (letter to Kant, 14 June 1789, AA 11: 62). Aside from the systematic claims

---

[10] See also SW 4:764: "This impulse strives for harmony and irresistibly nags the philosopher to assimilate everything around him to his own rational nature and to transform every phenomenon in his experience into the highest reality he knows—into thoughts" (translation taken from [1972], 332).

[11] Schiller's constructivist approach is nicely depicted by his friend Wilhelm von Humboldt, Werke, Bd. II, S. 381–382: "Schiller used to claim that the historian, if he had absorbed all the factual information through precise and thorough study of the sources, must still first construct the material thus collected into a history out of himself [...]." See also Schiller's letter to Caroline von Beulwitz, 10 December 1788 (NA 25:154).

discussed in the first part of this chapter, there are many terminological similarities between Kant's and Schiller's approach to history. For example, Schiller seems to have adopted from Kant the important distinction between the philosophical head and the bread-and-butter scholar in his inaugural lecture (Kant, *IUH* AA 8: 30). But nowhere else does Schiller's debt to Kant become as clear as in *Etwas über die erste Menschengesellschaft nach dem Leitfaden der mosaischen Urkunde* (SW 4:767–783). It has been pointed out that Schiller not only modelled the text according to Kant's *Conjectural Beginning of Human History* but also took over central claims from his predecessor. But while all this is clearly the case, it does not follow that Schiller did not make a unique and original contribution to philosophy of history: First of all, it should be noted that the same or similar observations also apply to Reinhold and Fichte, who are also heavily influenced by Kant. Moreover, it is still unclear whether Schiller's engagement with Kant is not essentially shaped by Reinhold's perspective on Kant (Heinz 2007).[12] We also know that Schiller cannot be counted among the blind followers of Kant's philosophy from his critical discussion of other aspects of Kant's thought, most importantly Kant's so-called rigorism in ethics (Hinderer 2005, 37). But even more strikingly, Kant's own thoughts on history are not only problematic to locate within his overall philosophical system, but he also seems to have adopted many of his basic ideas from other Enlightenments thinkers, such as, Lessing, Schlözer, and Herder. Although it is almost impossible to determine who took what from whom, it simply cannot be excluded that Schiller draws from the same sources when he developed his philosophy of history and later adds Kantian material to his original project.[13] In fact, I will show below that we have good reason to believe that Schiller is pursuing a philosophical project of his own that not only clearly sets him apart from Kant (and Reinhold) but also fits in well with his overall literary production.

The Ends of History

So far, we have only pointed out that providence serves as a teleological perspective (Reinhold, *Briefe über die Kantische Philosophie* I:34: "gemeinschaftlichen Gesichtspunct") or guideline (Kant, *IUH*, AA 08:17: "Leitfaden") necessary to establish a system. But until now, the exact purpose that providence promotes has been left open. In this section, we will see that Schiller's and Kant's philosophies of history diverge most clearly in this point. As mentioned above, Kant's philosophy of history must be seen in the overall context of the Enlightenment question of the determination of man. It was briefly mentioned that Kant first addressed this topic in his lectures on anthropology,

---

[12] Notice also that *Die Sendung Mose* draws on Reinholds, *Die Hebräischen Mysterien oder die älteste religiöse Freymaurerey*.

[13] Or as Reed (2011), 273, puts it: "Schiller was already on the way to Kant's position before he ever read the essays."

from which his philosophy of history emerged. Although the exact details of Kant's determination of this purpose are still under dispute, it is clear that for Kant the final end of nature is related to the moral development of man. To this end, juridical conditions must be created, which in turn promote the cultural development of man and serve as a prerequisite for the moral final destination. Looking at history, understood in a broad sense as the proper sphere of moral action (Kant, *IUH*, AA 8:17 and Schiller, SW 4:749), helps to promote this goal by pointing people towards it and thus strengthening their will and determination to achieve it. What is more, this end provides the focal point of the historian, needed both for the selection of his material and to establish the necessary order to conform to scientific requirements.

At first sight, Schiller agrees with Kant in determining the overall purpose of nature, although there are slight differences in terminology and emphasis. Similar to Kant, Schiller also stresses the importance of the juridical state as a means to fulfill the determination of man, that is, the complete development of all human predispositions.[14] Moreover, Schiller seems to have adopted Kant's terminology when he calls this condition "the highest good" (SW 4:815). For Schiller, the highest good includes "Sittlichkeit" (morality) paired with "Kunstfleiß" (artistic diligence), "Wissenschaften" (sciences), and "Fortschreitung des Geistes" (progress of the spirit, SW 4:817), which taken together constitute true happiness.

We can set the differences aside for the moment. What is important for us to note is that Schiller also derives a subordinate end from the overall determination of man. The exact relationship between these two ends is difficult to grasp in Kant. We have already seen that the final end of creation, that is, the moral development of man presupposed specific legal requirements that Kant also calls the highest political good. In his *Critique of the Power of Judgment*, Kant takes the latter to be the last end of nature ("letzter Zweck der Natur") and the former the final end of creation ("Endzweck" AA 5:431; see Geismann 2006). Although Schiller agrees with Kant in assuming two distinct purposes in nature, at closer inspection we can see that both of these ends differ crucially from what can be found in Kant. Schiller strangely emphasizes the present state of affairs and demands that the universal historian takes this present state of affairs as the focal point of his systematic research. Accordingly, he wants the universal historian to concentrate primarily on those events that had an influence on the current world state. In other words, the historian should only concern himself with events that are apparently relevant to the production of the current state of affairs understood as an overall end of all preceding history. What determines therefore Schiller's teleology is the actual state of affairs. To put it differently: Schiller takes the current point of human development as an endpoint for all proceeding events, which were thus destined to produce the actual state

---

[14] SW 4: 815: "The state itself is never an end, it is only important as a condition under which the end of humanity can be fulfilled, and this end of humanity is none other than the development of all the predispositions of man, progress." See also SW 4: 831, 832–833.

as their final end (SW 4:760–761, 766; see Mann 1959, 1124 and Frick 1995, 99). With this in mind, the current state of affairs provides the starting point of the universal historian to look for past events that had the highest impact on the development of world history and finally brought about or fundamentally contributed to the determination of the current world state.[15]

This is a highly remarkable claim, not only because it nicely depicts Schiller's above-mentioned constructivist approach to universal history. We can also see more clearly how the teleological principle helps to establish a system from isolated facts by the application of causal laws that are effective in history (SW 4:763). It is precisely in the way Schiller applies these causal principles that it becomes most evident how his universal history departs from world history, understood as the sum or collection of all historical facts. For universal history, neither proceeds mechanistically, that is, according to a blind sequence of causes and effects, nor does it abolish these very laws. On the contrary, Schiller repeatedly emphasizes how important causality and the observation that similar causes produce similar effects are for a historian (SW 4:763). Yet, universal history and world history, taken as this unspecified sequence of events, diverge in a most important aspect: A universal historian picks out peculiar events from a present-day standpoint. As Schiller stresses, these events even seem to be causally isolated in their own time and happen without any preceding notice. Yet they have the greatest impact on the following time. He illustrates this idea with the help of an example, namely the birth of Jesus Christ which is a most important fact for universal history (SW 4:763). A further example of an event that greatly influenced the development of world history is the constitution of the Judaic state (SW 4:783). Against the backdrop of these events, we can clearly see how history understood in the widest sense and universal history necessarily break apart: The former has no means to approach this type of events properly: "[…] neither in the age in which it appeared, nor in the people among whom it came into being, can one find […] a satisfactory explanation of its appearance" (SW 4:763, translation taken from [1972], 331). Consequently, these events can only be understood as mere chance events. Accordingly, from the point of view of history understood in the widest sense, which takes into account all historical facts in equal measures, history presents itself as a fragmentary or chance assemblage of events. As seen above, Schiller takes this stance towards history to be unworthy of a real philosophic mind, who in turn will connect these events in a rational system—which forms a coherent whole (SW 4:763).[16]

To come back to the twofold teleological structure mentioned above: similar to Kant, Schiller also assumes an overarching philosophical purpose in

---

[15] SW 4:762: "World-history therefore proceeds upon a principle which directly reverses the world-order itself. The real series of events descends from the origin of things to their most recent state, while the universal historian moves in the opposite way from the most recent state of the world up to the origin of things" (translation taken from [1972], 331).

[16] Frick (1995, 84) points out that Wilhelm von Humboldt closely follows Schiller in this point.

addition to this actual state which eventually also shapes the view on the present state of affairs and thus the perspective of a universal historian. But two things must be noted. Firstly, this philosophical purpose does not replace the historical perspective but complements it. Secondly, Schiller once more fundamentally departs from the path embarked by his famous predecessor in how he conceives of this ultimate end of creation. Kant points out that the final purpose ("Endzweck") under which everything else must be subsumed is the complete moral development of man included in the highest good. This development, although one can detect some drawbacks, follows a forward-leading succession. Schiller, on the other hand, agrees with Kant to a large extent about the nature of this ultimate end, but disagrees with him about the path that leads to it. Schiller also assumes that it is the purpose of man "to educate himself as a human being" (SW 4:750), whereby above all the liberative moral aspects are important. However, how he conceives of history is not so much a straightforward development but more a dialectical model of distinct stages. I believe what has led Schiller to this assumption is a problem that Kant simply did not recognize as a problem since his major interests were exclusively devoted to morality. For Kant, ancient philosophers did not properly distinguish between both aspects of the highest good, that is, morality and happiness. Consequently, morality has been mixed up with happiness. From this perspective, however, the ancient world did not become aware of the holy nature of morality. Kant emphasizes that the idea of pure morality was first introduced by Christianity (CPrR, AA05: 127–128). Accordingly, if we take complete moral development as the endpoint of history, we can see clear progress from ancient to Christian and thus even medieval thought. In Schiller, however, who equally emphasizes the importance of art and science for the overall development of human "Sittlichkeit" (morality), a completely different picture emerges. Without question, the ancient world provided the finest example of a highly developed art only to fall down into pieces and decline for centuries. Only recently can art and sciences claim to have reached a level comparable to antiquity (SW 4:829–830). This is the crucial observation that Schiller has in mind when he sets out his view on universal history.[17] Accordingly, the history that he outlines is not so much linear but appears to be circular, at least at first sight. For it is here that we can see Schiller's second striking innovation that sets him apart from Kant. Indeed, Schiller's view on history is not circular but dialectical and the objective endpoint of historical development is a return of the dialectical movement to itself, that is, to its ancient starting point, but not to negate the departure but in order to "aufheben" and

[17] SW 4:766: "By unravelling the fine gears by which the silent hand of nature has been developing the powers of man since the beginning of the world, and by indicating with precision what has been gained in each period for this great plan of nature, it [universal history, A. H.] restores the true standard of happiness and merit which the prevailing delusion has falsified differently in each century. It cures us of the exaggerated admiration of antiquity and of the childish longing for times past; and by drawing our attention to our own possessions, it does not make us wish back the vaunted golden ages of Alexander and August." See also SW 4:845; SW 5:582.

culminate in a more advanced state. Take, for example, *On the Aesthetic Education of Man in a Series of Letters*, in which Schiller contrasts Greek with modern humanity (SW 5:582, 436–437) or how he presents the three stages of natural harmony, cultural division, and the ideal of the future of humankind in *On Naïve and Sentimental Poetry*: "They *are*, what we *were*; they are, what we *should become* once more. We were nature like them, and our culture shall lead us along the path of reason and freedom back to nature" (SW 5:695, translation ESS 181; see also SW 5:581; Abrams 1973, 213). In this model, Schiller introduces the "aufheben" in a synthesis, and thus prepares Hegel's later approach to history (Abrams 1973, 212–213; Hinderer 2005, 35–36, 39–41; Kaufmann 1940, 6–7):

> Beauty unites [...] two conditions *which are diametrically opposed* and can never become One. It is from this opposition that we have to start. [...] In the second place [...] beauty *unites* these two opposed conditions and thus destroys the opposition [hebt also die Entgegensetzung auf]. Since, however, both conditions remain everlastingly opposed to each other, there is no other way of uniting them except by sublating[18] them [als indem sie aufgehoben werden]. [...] both these conditions totally disappear in a third without leaving any trace of division behind in the new whole that has been made. (SW 5:625, translation AE 123–125)

For Schiller, the history of civilization is distinguished into three stages: a natural, an aesthetic, and a moral stage, whereby the third stage incorporates and preserves the values of both the natural and the aesthetic stages (Abrams 1973, 213). Given that the first stage finds its finest example with the ancient Greek world and especially Greek art, it is not surprising that Schiller most clearly worked out this view on history in his late aesthetical essays. But this does not mean that he changed his view on history or abandoned fundamental earlier assumptions that shaped his philosophy of history as some assume (Koopmann 1995, 69–72; Frick 1995). On the contrary, Schiller makes ample use of this threefold developmental scheme in various historical writings. For example, we can trace back Schiller's dialectical understanding of history at least to *Etwas über die erste Menschengesellschaft nach dem Leitfaden der Mosaischen Urkunde* (Abrams 1973, 209).[19] We can add to this that Schiller worked out his historical texts in line with this dialectical method too (Muhlack 1995, 15; Schieder 1960).

In the next section, I will show that basic features of Schiller's overall philosophical view on history reach back as early as his academic writings from the *Karlsschule*. Moreover, we find fundamental aspects of Schiller's philosophy of history equally in his medical, poetic, and theoretical work.

---

[18] Wilkinson and Willoughby translate as "destroying" which however does not properly capture the dialectical process described here by Schiller.

[19] SW 4:768: "He should learn to revisit the state of innocence which he now lost, through his reason, and come back as a free rational spirit to where he had started from as a plant and as a creature of instinct [...]." See also SW 4:771; 845.

Philosophy of History and Schiller's "Lifetime-Project"

It has been noted that Schiller's engagement with history goes back to his earliest writings composed at the *Karlsschule* (Hinderer 2005, 34). In these texts, Schiller mentions two important sources of his historical approach: Schlözer and Garves commentary on Ferguson (SW 5:300–301; Dann 2005, 77; Koopmann 1995, 61). In his second medical dissertation, Schiller quotes from Schlözer's conception of universal history, through which he is introduced to the universal history of the whole human race (SW 5:303–306). Schlözer remains an important point of reference for Schiller, who also refers to Schlözer in his later work. For instance, Schiller uses Schlözer's text in the preparation of the lectures in Jena (NA, 25: 387; see Muhlack 1995, 10). In Schlözer, we already find the idea that it is the aim of a universal historian to transform the aggregate of historical facts into a system (*Vorstellung seiner Universal-Historie* I, § 9–10, 14–19) that is determined by a teleological perspective or plan:

> The universal historian raises them [the great world events] out of the already prepared material of innumerable special histories [...] selects them purposively, and arranges each history in a relation to the other parts and to the whole plan: this gives them their form. (*Vorstellung seiner Universal-Historie*, I. § 8, 13–14)

Above we identified this objective as the fundamental feature of a philosophy of history. We can see now that this view is not unique to Kant or Reinhold but also shows up in other important inspirations of Schiller's work. As indicated at the beginning, we cannot rule out either that Kant and Schiller have drawn from similar sources or that these ideas belong to a common set of conceptions and ideas shared by many thinkers in late Enlightenment thought. A further important source of Schiller's philosophy of history can be seen in Herder. Both thinkers share a strong fascination for natural philosophy. In Schiller's case, this fascination also goes back to his medical training. Schiller's later repeated parallelization of natural and political developments perhaps also stems from this background (Peter Hanns Reill 2006, 69). In any case, in his first theoretical texts we can see not only a clear idea of the goal of historical development but also the idea that the study of history itself must be subordinated to this superior goal (SW 5:250–251, 281–285, 302–306). As Walter Hinderer notes in his discussion of Schiller's early anthropological texts: "Schiller's first dissertation, Philosophie der Physiologie, already contains in nuce the ideas of his later writings" (2005, 35).[20] To put it differently, in his later work, Schiller elaborates on his early understanding and advances his view

---

[20] Hinderer (2005), 42: "Although Schiller's theoretical ideas were stimulated by 'the philosophy of the physicians' [...], popular philosophy [...], and the writings of Garve, Kant, Reinhold, Herder, and Fichte, he developed a basic view of the human being quite early that later changes only in its questions, its methodology, and above all in the differentiation of its terminology." As I will briefly indicate in the following, Schiller's basic aims, nicely captured by Hinderer in terms of the ancient claim to assimilate to the divine, remain the same and constitute what deserve to be called his lifetime project.

but he does not completely transform it, as one might expect if we assume that Schiller's philosophy of history is nothing more than an adaption of Kant's thought.

The fact that Schiller's preoccupation with history cannot be attributed solely to his reading of Kant is also made clear by the function Schiller assigns to the study of history and how it fits into his overarching project. In his inaugural lecture, Schiller claims that the occupation with universal history is not only an attractive and useful activity but it also has therapeutic effects on individuals and even whole societies. Through enlarging the historical perspective, it displays the grand picture of the times and nations before one's eyes. Consequently, the perspective of universal history will have an effect on the rash decisions of the moment and can even help to transcend egotism. For it not only connects the individual with his past but also opens her view to the future, by extending the brief existence of human beings. Thus, universal history can bridge the gap between self-love and freedom, or the individual and the species (SW 4:765). This way it allows for real education and progress of humankind. This is in fact no small task that Schiller attributes to universal history. Instead, this is actually, so to speak, Schiller's lifetime project as becomes clear both from his earliest and latest writings (Frick 1995, 87).

Contrary to other scholars, who believe that Schiller's own development, but above all his works on history, is determined more by coincidental circumstances, I conclude therefore that Schiller's philosophy of history remains remarkably constant over his intellectual development. What others framed as "ruptures" (*Brüche* Frick 1995, 97) in Schillers relationship with history, I would call development or change in emphasis, often related to the genre in which Schiller expresses his thought. History, for Schiller, remains not only an important source of inspiration, from which he takes the ideas of his poetic work, as he confessed to Goethe (Letter to Goethe, 5 January 1798, *NA* 29:183). We now see that these works are consistent with his overarching goal. The only difference is the means Schiller uses when he pursues this goal. Applying Schiller's own method, one could also say: what seems random in itself comes together to form a harmonious whole in view of this overarching goal of achieving man's determination.[21]

Conclusion

I want to conclude my discussion by returning to our two initial questions: Does Schiller have a philosophy of history? I believe we can vigorously affirm this question both with respect to how Schiller's contemporaries Kant and Reinhold conceive of a philosophy of history and its major objectives but also in light of Schiller's own engagement with history. Is it more than a popularized form of Kant's philosophy of history? Although it is tempting to view eighteenth-century philosophy exclusively through Kantian lenses, Schiller,

---

[21] See once more Humboldt's judgement about his friend (Werke, Bd. II., 384).

like Reinhold and Fichte, offers a good example of how Kant's contemporaries both responded to and reshaped Kant's thought, ultimately adapting it to their own ends. But in contrast to his peers Reinhold and Fichte, Schiller's contribution to the development of German idealism is still largely undervalued. I believe that his philosophy of history in particular offers a good example of how his thoughts paved the way for the great idealistic systems of the philosophy of history.

REFERENCES

Abrams, H. M., Natural Supernaturalism. Tradition and Revolution in Romantic Literature, Norton Library: New York 1973.
Alt, Peter-André, Natur, Zivilisation, Narratio. Zur triadischen Strukturierung von Schillers Geschichtskonzept, in: Zeitschrift für Germanistik 18.3 (2008), 530-545.
Beiser, Frederick, Schiller as Philosopher. A Re-Examination, Oxford 2005.
Frick, Werner, Der Maler der Menschheit. Philosophische und poetische Konstruktionen der Gattungsgeschichte bei Schiller, in: Schiller als Historiker, hrsg. von O. Dann, N. Oehlers und E. Osterkamp, Stuttgart, Weimar 1995, 77-107.
Dann, Otto, Schiller the Historian, in: A Companion to the Works of Friedrich Schiller, ed. by Steven D. Martinson, Rochester 2005, 67-86.
Geismann, Georg, "Höchstes politisches Gut" - "Höchstes Gut in einer Welt". Zum Verhältnis von Moralphilosophie, Geschichtsphilosophie und Religionsphilosophie bei Kant, in: Tijdschrift voor Filosofie, 68 (2006) 23-41.
Hahmann, Andree, Pflichtgemäß aber töricht! Kant über Spinozas Leugnung der Vorsehung, in: Das Leben der Vernunft. Beiträge zur Philosophie Kants, ed. by D. Hüning, S. Klingner, C. Olk, Berlin, Boston 2013, 477-505.
Hahmann, Andree, Naturzustand und Naturgarantie in Kants Schrift *Zum ewigen Frieden*, in: *... jenen süßen Traum träumen. Kants Friedensschrift zwischen objektiver Geltung und Utopie*, hrsg. von D. Hüning und Stefan Klingner, Baden-Baden 2018, 65-90.
Heinz, Marion, "Die Harmonie des Menschen mit der Gottheit" – Anthropologie und Geschichtsphilosophie bei Reinhold und Schiller, in: Friedrich Schiller. Der unterschätzte Theoretiker, ed. by G. Bollenbeck und L. Ehrlich, Köln, Weimar, Wien 2007, 27-37.
Hinderer, Walter, Schiller's Philosophical Aesthetics in Anthropological Perspective, in: A Companion to the Works of Friedrich Schiller, a.a.O. 2005, 27-46.
Humboldt, Wilhelm von, Werke in fünf Bänden, ed. by A. Flitner and K. Giel, 3rd ed. Darmstadt 1979.
Koopmann, Helmut, Das Rad der Geschichte. Schiller und die Überwindung der aufgeklärten Geschichtsphilosophie, in: Schiller als Historiker, a.a.O. 1995, 59-76.
Malter, Rudolf, Schiller und Kant, in: Schiller als Historiker, a.a.O. 1995, 281-291.
Mann, Golo, Schiller als Historiker, in: Merkur 13/142 (1959), 1120-1137.
Muhlack, Ulrich, Schillers Konzept der Universalgeschichte zwischen Aufklärung und Historismus, in: Schiller als Historiker, a.a.O. 1995, 5-28.
Prüfer, Thomas, Die Bildung der Geschichte. Friedrich Schiller und die Anfänge der modernen Geschichtswissenschaft, Köln, Weimar, Wien 2002.

Reed, T. J., So Who Was Naïve? Schiller as Enlightenment Historian and His Successors, in: Who Is This Schiller Now? Essays on His Reception and Significance, ed. by J. L. High, N. Martin, N. Oelers, Rochester 2011, 271-283.
Reill, Peter Hanns, "Schiller, Herder, and History" in: Schiller und die Geschichte, ed. by. M. Hoffmann, München 2006, 68-78.
Reinhold, Carl Leonhard, Briefe über die Kantische Philosophie, vol. 1, Leipzig 1790.
Schieder, Theodor, "Schiller als Historiker", in: Historische Zeitschrift 190 (1960) 31-54.
Schiller, Friedrich 1972 [1789]. "The Nature and Value of Universal History: An Inaugural Lecture." *History and Theory* 11, no. 3: 321-334.
Schlözer, Ludwig August, Vorstellung seiner Universal-Historie. Göttingen, Gotha 1772.
Schmidt-Biggemann, Wilhelm, Geschichtsentwurf und Erziehungskonzept, in: Schiller als Historiker, a.a.O. 1995, 267-280.

CHAPTER 22

"Upward to Freedom": Schiller on the Nature and Goals of Aesthetic Education

Robert B. Louden

If sense's pleasure and sense's pain,
  Entangled around the heart of man,
  Entangled by a thousand knots,
  Drag him down into the dust,
  Who will protect him? Who will save him?
  The arts, which draw him
  Upward to freedom on golden rings,
  Charmed by refinement that
  Hovers him between earth and heaven.
  (Schiller to Prince Frederick Christian August von Augustenburg, July 13, 1793)[1]

---

[1] According to Alexander Schmidt, these verses "were presumably taken from earlier, now lost versions of Schiller's poem 'The Artists' of 1788–1789" [Friedrich Schiller, *On the Aesthetic Education of Man* and *Letters to Prince Frederick Christian Augustenburg*, trans. Keith Tribe with an Introduction and Notes by Alexander Schmidt (London: Penguin Books, 2016), 178 n. 3].

R. B. Louden (✉)
University of Southern Maine, Portland, ME, USA
e-mail: louden@maine.edu

By all accounts, *On the Aesthetic Education of the Human Being* [*des Menschen*][2] *in a Series of Letters* (1795) is Schiller's most important and influential philosophical work. And—despite the frequently commented-on ambiguities and perplexities of the text[3]—since the term "aesthetic education" features prominently in the title of the book, we can start confidently by claiming that Schiller's educational theory is one that places a premium on *aesthetic* education. Indeed, he is usually read as holding that aesthetic education is the *only* kind of education that will enable human beings to achieve their full potential as individuals as well as to eventually live together in a just and humane society. Aesthetic education, according to Schiller, is a necessary condition for human development. As he writes in the 2nd Letter: "if one is ever to solve … [the] problem of politics in practice one will have to approach it through the path of the aesthetic, because it is only through beauty that one makes one's way to freedom" (AE, 9).[4]

But why does Schiller place so much weight on aesthetic education? (What does he think aesthetic education will accomplish? Why is it so important to him?) And what exactly does he mean by "aesthetic education?" These are the main questions that I shall address in the present chapter.

---

[2] In my earlier work as one of the translators and editors for *The Cambridge Edition of the Works of Immanuel Kant*, I was encouraged to render "*Mensch*" as "human being," and I have decided to do so in the present chapter as well. However, this is by no means a perfect solution, and in order to avoid straying too far from Schiller's German I have still used the singular male pronoun "he" in conjunction with "human being." But I do think Schiller means to say that aesthetic education is necessary for *all* human beings—women as well as men. Cf. Tribe and Schmidt's "Note on the Text," *On the Aesthetic Education of Man*, xlii.

[3] This is by no means a new issue. William von Humboldt, in a letter to Schiller of August 15, 1795, writes: "Someone said to me, after the usual tribute of praise, that he did not understand your work [viz., *On the Aesthetic Education of the Human Being*] and that its obscurity is of a worse sort than, for example, Kant's. For one reads Kant with great difficulty and stops doubtfully at every sentence; but, once one has struggled through, he knows distinctly what he has read. In the case of your work the reader readily accepts each individual sentence, and thinks he has understood everything equally well; but if he asks himself afterward what he has read, he does not know how to articulate it" [as cited by Dieter Henrich in "Beauty and Freedom: Schiller's Struggle with Kant's Aesthetics," in *Essays in Kant's Aesthetics*, eds. Ted Cohen and Paul Guyer (Chicago: University of Chicago Press, 1982): 237–257, at 237].

[4] References to Schiller's *Aesthetic Education* (AE) are cited in the body of the text by page number in Friedrich Schiller, *On the Aesthetic Education of Man in a Series of Letters*, trans. Elizabeth M. Wilkinson and L.A. Willoughby (Oxford: Clarendon Press, 1967). This edition includes the German text as well as an English translation. I have sometimes made minor changes in Wilkinson and Willoughby's translation, and in making these changes I have often been influenced by Keith Tribe's more recent translation (see n.1). Strictly speaking, the "only" in "only through beauty" is not explicitly in the original German. But it is implied: only through beauty can humans arrive at freedom.

Why Aesthetic Education?

Because the *Why?* question is a bit easier to answer than the *What?* question, I shall start with it. And I have already hinted at least a part of Schiller's answer to it. He believes that aesthetic education is necessary in order for human beings to achieve their full potential as individuals as well as to eventually live together in a just society. In the present section, I shall expand on this summary statement.

Many of the earlier letters focus on problems in the political arena engendered partly by the downward turn of the French Revolution. "Expectantly the gaze of both the philosopher and the man of the world [*des Weltmanns*] are fixed on the political scene, where now, it is believed, the very fate of humanity is being debated" (AE, 2nd Letter, 9). The political problem, Schiller believes, can only be solved by means of aesthetic education, a process that will involve, among other things, "transforming a work of need [*Not*] into a work of one's free choice [*seiner freien Wahl*],[5] and of elevating physical necessity to a moral necessity" (AE, 3rd Letter, 11). For some (viz., the "savage [*Wilder*]"), whose "feeling rules his principles", this necessary transformation will entail listening more to reason; for others (viz., the "barbarian [*Barbar*] who "scorns and dishonors nature"), it will involve listening more to feeling (AE, 4th Letter, 21). But in both cases what is needed is a more balanced life, one that Schiller calls "the complete anthropological valuation [*vollständigen anthropologischen Schätzung*],[6] where both form and content count and living sensation [*Empfindung*] also has a voice … Reason furthers unity, but nature furthers diversity; both lay claim upon the human being" (AE, 4th Letter, 19). Only "beauty [*die Schönheit*]" can lead human beings back from this "twofold straying," and only "beautiful culture [*die schöne Kultur*]" can "enchain nature in the savage, and set it free in the barbarian" (AE, 10th Letter, 63).

But Schiller is not merely reacting to the Reign of Terror. There is a deeper problem in modern society that also concerns him. The core problem is one of

---

[5] Schiller subscribes to a strong libertarian conception of free will. For instance, in "On Grace and Dignity" (1793), he defines the human being as "a *person*, a being, that can in *itself* be the cause and even the absolutely final cause of its condition and which can change in accordance with reasons which it draws from itself" [Jane V. Curran and Chrisophter Frickers, eds., *Schiller's "On Grace and Dignity" in its Cultural Context: Essays and a New Translation* (Rochester: Camden House, 2005), 131; cf. 132]. See also his claim in the 11th Letter of AE that "the person must therefore be its own ground" (AE, 73). And later in "On Grace and Dignity" Schiller emphasizes that this capacity to be one's own cause is uniquely human: "In animals and plants, nature not only gives the destiny [*Bestimmung*] to them; *she alone carries it out.* In humans, however, she only gives the destiny to them, and leaves them to fulfill it *themselves.* It is this alone that makes them humans" (141). Or, as remarks more succinctly at the beginning of his essay "Concerning the Sublime": "all other things must; the human being is the entity that wills" [Friedrich Schiller, *Essays*, ed. Walter Hinderer and Daniel O. Dahlstrom (New York: Continuum, 1993), 70–85, at 70].

[6] As Hinderer and Dahlstrom note, "Schiller's philosophy of art thus constitutes a kind of anthropological aesthetics, involving a program of education that is both personal and sociopolitical precisely because it is aesthetic" ["Introduction," in Schiller, *Essays*, vii–xxv, at ix].

alienation and fragmentation: "we see not merely individuals, but whole classes of human beings, developing but one part of their potentialities, while of the rest, as in stunted growths, only faint traces remain" (AE, 6th Letter, 33). Furthermore, it is "culture itself [*Die Kultur selbst*] which inflicted this wound upon modern humanity" (AE, 6th Letter, 33)—more specifically, the increased specialization of modern knowledge and work. As a result, "the human being himself [*der Mensch selbst*] develops into nothing but a fragment; perpetually in his ear the monotonous sound of the wheel that he turns, he never develops the harmony of his being, and ... he becomes nothing more than the imprint of his occupation, his specialized knowledge [*Wissenschaft*]" (AE, 6th Letter, 35).[7] But this fragmentation is a specifically new and modern condition, one that has not always affected humanity. In particular, we do not find it among the ancient Greeks. The Enlightenment's "reputation for education [*Ausbildung*] and refinement ... can avail us nothing against the natural humanity of the Greeks ... The Greeks put us to shame not only by a simplicity that is alien to our age; they are at the same time our rivals, indeed our models" (AE, 6th Letter, 31).[8]

Schiller's claim that art can somehow solve the most fundamental problems of modernity has understandably inspired many readers, particularly those influenced by the Frankfurt School. Marcuse, for instance, in *Eros and Civilization*, writes: "Schiller's *Letters on the Aesthetic Education of Man* ... aim

---

[7] As Jürgen Habermas remarks, Schiller's critique of alienated labor and bureaucracy "reminds us of the early Marx" [*The Philosophical Discourse of Modernity: Twelve Lectures*, trans. Frederick G. Lawrence (Cambridge: MIT Press, 1987), 46]. But according to Frederick Beiser, this diagnosis of modern alienation also tracks back to Scottish author Adam Ferguson (1723–1816) [*Schiller as Philosopher: A Re-Examination* (Oxford: Clarendon Press, 2005), 161].

[8] Schiller's poem "Die Götter Griechenlands" (The Gods of Greece, 1788) is perhaps the most famous expression of his longing for ancient Greece. ["Schöne Welt, wo bist du? Kehre wieder/ Holdes Blütenalter der Natur!"—in Friedrich Schiller, *Gedichte*, (Wiesbaden: Insel Verlag, 1955), 32]. And some commentators have argued that his views about aesthetic education stem from Plato. Herbert Read, for instance, claims that "Schiller alone" among Plato's "followers" has "taken seriously" "the thesis ... that art should be the basis of education" [Herbert Read, *Education through Art* (London: Faber, 1943), 1; see also 278]. But while Plato and Schiller both do argue in favor of an education grounded in aesthetics, ultimately the differences in their views outweigh the similarities. In the *Republic*, Socrates argues that artists must be carefully "supervised" so that they do not "represent a character that is bad, illiberal, and graceless" (401b). Schiller does not advocate censorship of the arts. Socrates also holds that "musical training is most important," in part "because rhythm and harmony permeate the innermost element of the soul, affect it more powerfully than anything else's, and bring it grace" (401d). Schiller does not place music above the other arts. Socrates also holds that poets must be banned from the ideal city (see 595b)—except for those who write only "hymns to the gods and eulogies of good people" (607a). Poets are not banned from Schiller's aesthetic utopia. However, the biggest difference is that Schiller advocates aesthetic education in part as a means to individual freedom ("it is the aesthetic mode [*Stimmung*] of the soul that first gives rise to freedom"—AE, 26th Letter, 191), whereas in the *Republic* art is used as a tool not to promote individual freedom but rather the common good (see 420b) and the binding of citizens together (see 462b). For further discussion, see David Pugh's chapter on "The Rational and Aesthetic State" in *Dialectic of Love: Platonism in Schiller's Aesthetics* (Montreal: McGill-Queen's University Press, 1996), 287–366.

at a remaking of civilization by virtue of the liberating force of the aesthetic function."[9] And Habermas, in *The Philosophical Discourse of Modernity*, praises Schiller's *Letters* for their portrayal of "an aesthetic utopia that attributes to art a virtually social-revolutionary role ... Art itself is the medium for the education [*Bildung*] of the human race to true political freedom."[10]

The fragmentation of modernity has also contributed to moral regress, and part of what Schiller hopes to accomplish through aesthetic education is "the transformation of the state according to moral principles" (AE, 4th Letter, 17). Although a qualified supporter of the Enlightenment[11] ("the human being has at last awoken from his long indolence and self-deception"—AE, 5th Letter, 25), he holds that the technical and intellectual advances made possible by the forces of Enlightenment have not led to moral advances. As a result, at present "the *moral* possibility is lacking" for "making true freedom the foundation of political association"—the present generation is "unprepared to receive it" (AE, 5th Letter, 25). Aesthetic education will (somehow!) make this necessary moral progress a reality.

Realizing a just society, achieving one's potential, overcoming alienation, moral progress, freedom—Schiller clearly has multiple answers to the question, "*Why* aesthetic education?" But when viewed together, these various goals would seem to place an insurmountable burden on Schillerian aesthetic education. How can it possibly achieve all of these objectives? However, before addressing this question in detail, it behooves us to gain a clearer understanding of what exactly Schiller means by "aesthetic education," and this is my aim in the next section.

But there is also an important subsidiary question to the *Why?* issue that deserves comment first. "Is aesthetic education the means or the ends of the process described by Schiller?"[12] That is, does aesthetic education acquire its

---

[9] Herbert Marcuse, *Eros and Civilization: A Philosophical Inquiry into Freud* New York: Vintage Books, 1962), 164. For some criticisms of Marcuse's appropriation of Schiller, see Paul Guyer, "Marcuse and Classical Aesthetics," *Revue internationale de philosophie* 2008 (246.4): 349–365.

[10] Habermas, *The Philosophical Discourse of Modernity*, 45. Schiller provides readers with a faint glimpse of his aesthetic utopia in the final, 27th, Letter, when he contrasts "the *dynamic* state of rights" and "the *ethical* state of duties" with "the *aesthetic* state" (AE, 215). In the latter, human beings "stand to one another only as the object of free play. The fundamental law of this realm is *to give freedom by means of freedom* ... The dynamic state can make society [*die Gesellschaft*] possible . . .; the ethical state can make it (morally) necessary . . .; only the aesthetic state can make it real" (AE, 215). But to what extent is Schiller's aesthetic state a democracy? In the final paragraph of the text (which appeared as a footnote in the first edition of 1795), he asks: "But does such a state of beautiful appearance [*Staat des schönen Scheins*] exist, and where can it be found? As a need, it exists in every finely tuned soul; as a fact one is likely to find it only in a few select circles [*in einigen wenigen auserlesenen Zirkeln*]" (AE, 219). This elitist strand in the aesthetic state casts doubt on Albert Reble's claim that Schiller is "inspired by an aspiration to national education [*von einem volkserzieherischen Wollen beseelt*]" [*Geschichte der Pädagogik*, 19th rev. ed. (Stuttgart: Klett-Cotta, 1999), 200].

[11] In the 8th Letter Schiller acknowledges that "the era is enlightened [*aufgeklärt*]," but he then asks "why, then, are we still barbarians?" (AE, 49–51).

[12] Schmidt, "Introduction," *On the Aesthetic Education of Man*, vii.

significance for Schiller solely because it is an allegedly necessary means to important ends, or is it also important for its own sake? Is aesthetic education merely a means to a number of ends, or is it also an end in itself? These questions are also implied, I think, in the following remark by Eva Schaper: "it is not altogether clear when he speaks of 'aesthetic education' whether it is education to the aesthetic, understood as the ideal state for man to attain, or *through* which ordinary living can be enhanced, made easier and, indeed become 'the good life'."[13]

I believe that Schiller views aesthetic education as both a means and an end in itself, though his declarations concerning the former are admittedly a bit easier to locate in the text of AE. Indeed, most of the present section up until now amounts to an explication of the various goals that Schiller believes will be achieved by aesthetic education.

But Schiller, like Kant, also views the human being as "an end in itself [*Selbstzweck*]," and, like Kant, he also believes it is to the Enlightenment's credit that it has "finally" started to "honor" human beings in this manner (AE, 5th Letter, 25). However, according to Schiller, human beings are not fully human beings until they have experienced beauty and transformed themselves through aesthetic education. As he stresses in the famous 15th Letter, beauty consists of "mere play" (AE, 105), and it is "exactly play and play *alone* that makes the human being complete [*vollständig*]" (AE, 105). "The human being should *only* play with beauty, and he should play *only with beauty* … The human being plays only when he is a human being in the full sense of the word [*in voller Bedeutung des Worts*], and *he is only a complete human being when he plays*" (AE, 107).[14] In other words, Schiller values aesthetic education as both means and end. He advocates an education *to* as well as *through* the aesthetic.

---

[13] Eva Schaper, "Towards the Aesthetic: A Journey with Friedrich Schiller," *British Journal of Aesthetics* 25 (1985): 153–168, at 156; cf. 153. The questions are also implied (albeit a bit more obliquely) in the following remark of Brian O'Connor: "The switching perspectives of immanent and teleological analyses make for a challenging feature of Schiller's text" ["Play, Idleness and the Problem of Necessity in Schiller and Marcuse," *British Journal for the History of Philosophy* 22 (2014): 1095–1117, at 1099.

[14] In his stress on the centrality of play in education, was Schiller perhaps influenced by Johann Bernhard Basedow and his experimental school, the Philanthropin? As one author notes, "*learning through playing*: this is the main point of his [viz., Basedow's] method" [Albert Pinloche, *Geschichte des Philanthropinismus*, trans. J. Rauschenfels and A. Pinloche (Leipzig: Friedrich Branstetter, 1896), 31]. Wilkinson and Willoughby raise this question in a footnote to Schiller's discussion of "*praktische Philanthropie*" (AE, 88, 90), concluding that Schiller "has something far wider in mind" (AE, 248) than Basedow's school. I concur. Schiller no doubt was aware of Basedow's influential school and its learning through play orientation, but Basedow and Schiller have different reasons for emphasizing the importance of play. Basedow emphasizes play simply because he believes it makes learning easier and more enjoyable, whereas Schiller emphasizes it because he believes that through play humans actualize freedom and achieve their humanity. For further discussion of Basedow and the Philanthropin, see my *Johann Bernhard Basedow and the Transformation of Modern Education: Educational Reform in the German Enlightenment* (London: Bloomsbury, 2021).

What Is Aesthetic Education?

One of the central challenges facing anyone who sets out to understand Schiller from the perspective of educational theory is that—unlike other Enlightenment-era philosophers who wrote on education such as Locke, Rousseau, Basedow, and Kant—Schiller says virtually nothing about curriculum, texts, educational institutions, or even pedagogy. His entire philosophy of education rests on his not-easy-to-fathom remarks about "aesthetic education."

One might think that by "aesthetic education" Schiller means simply an education via contact with and reflection on various forms of art—poetry, drama, music, painting, and so on. But it is not quite this simple, in part because he sometimes uses "aesthetic" in a pre-Baumgartian sense—namely, to refer not the philosophy of art and/or beauty, but rather to the science or study of sensation. Part of what Schiller is after when he advocates aesthetic education—particularly education for "the civilized classes" (AE, 5th Letter, 27) who constitute his main readers—is fundamentally a kind of education that places more weight on feeling and sensation and less on understanding and abstract reasoning. This is because "the enlightenment of understanding that the refined classes not unjustly praise ... has tended to reinforce corruption through principles [*Verderbnis durch Maximen*]" (AE, 5th Letter, 27). But what he essentially advocates for everyone is an education that balances the roles of sensation and understanding in human life, and he believes that aesthetic education—an education focusing on the felt experience and intellectual appreciation of beauty, beauty in nature as well as in artworks—is the best way for humans to obtain this balance. As Paul Guyer puts it: "Schiller's claim is ... that it is the experience of beauty that will induce this balance in us, and thus what we need is to be educated to experience beauty."[15] Or, as Schiller himself remarks a bit more obliquely in the 18th Letter: "there must be a *middle* condition between *matter* and *form*, between passivity and activity, and beauty transports us to this middle condition" (AE, 123).

In the following key passage from the 13th Letter, he elaborates on this desired middle condition and the freedom and "fullness of existence" that result from it:

> His education [*seine Kultur*] will therefore consist: *firstly*, in procuring for the receptive faculty the most manifold contacts with the world, and, within the purview of feeling [*des Gefühls*], intensifying passivity to the utmost; *secondly*, in securing for the determining faculty the highest degree of independence from the receptive, and, within the purview of reason [*der Vernunft*], intensifying activity to the utmost. When both these aptitudes are conjoined, the human being will combine the greatest fullness of existence [*der höchsten Fülle von Dasein*] with the highest independence and freedom [*die höchste Selbständigkeit und Freiheit*]. (AE, 87)

---

[15] Paul Guyer, *A History of Modern Aesthetics*, 3 vols. (Cambridge: Cambridge University Press, 2014), I: 485.

However, in order to better understand this passage it is necessary first to clarify some of Schiller's basic terms. Behind Schiller's plea for balance and harmony in human life is his belief that there exist two fundamental and opposing human drives: a *sinnlicher Trieb* or sensuous drive,[16] and a *Formtrieb* or formal drive. As he remarks at the beginning of the 12th Letter:

> We are impelled by two contradictory forces [*zwei entgegengesetzte Kräfte*], which, since they drive us to the realization of their object, may be termed drives [*Triebe*]. The first of these, which I call the *sensuous* [*sinnlichen*] drive, proceeds from the human being's physical existence, or his sensuous nature ... The second of the two drives, which one can call the *formal drive*, proceeds from the human being's absolute existence, and endeavors to place him in freedom, bring harmony to the variety of his appearance, and affirm his person amid all changes of condition. (AE, 79–81)

Schiller paints with a very broad brush when he describes these two drives. The sensuous drive is essentially an urge towards matter and stems from our physical or animal nature. It is passive, temporal, focuses on concrete particulars, and receives impressions from the outer world. The formal drive, on the other hand, stems from our inner rational and spiritual nature. It is active, atemporal, and seeks to bring order and form to the outer world through laws ("the first drive only furnishes *cases*, the second one gives *laws*"—AE, 12th Letter, 81). The sensuous drive only results in personal or subjective validity, while the formal drive gives us objective validity: "Feeling [*das Gefühl*] can only say: this is true *for this subject* and *in this moment*, ... but if the thought [*der Gedanke*] is once stated: *that is*, then it decides forever [sic.] and eternity" (AE, 12th Letter, 83). However, as Schiller reminds readers later, neither of these two drives is meant to dominate over the other, and they must learn to achieve a state of peaceful co-existence and harmony within each human being: "Nature is not meant to rule the human being exclusively, nor should reason rule him conditionally. Both systems of rule should remain completely independent from one another, and yet be perfectly as one" (AE, 24th Letter, 181). As many other commentators have pointed out,[17] Schiller's two drives are reminiscent of Kant's distinction between sensibility and understanding (perhaps with an extra dash of his distinction between phenomena and noumena also thrown in for good measure). But here, as elsewhere, in appropriating Kant Schiller is also introducing some changes.

As we have seen, Schiller posits two contradictory forces in human life, yet he insists that they should also be in perfect concord with one another. But how is this possible? As he himself announces at the beginning of the 13th Letter, "these two drives exhaust the concept of humanity, and a third *fundamental drive* [*Grundtrieb*] is simply an unthinkable concept [*ist schlechterdings*

---

[16] Sometimes Schiller refers to this first drive simply as the *Stofftrieb* (see, e.g., AE, 13th Letter, 93).

[17] See, e.g., Beiser, *Schiller as Philosopher*, 139; Guyer, *A History of Modern Aesthetics*, I: 485.

ein undenkbarer Begriff]" (AE, 85). "Unthinkable" or not (and here we arrive at what surely counts as one of more ad hoc moves in the entire text of AE), in the 14th Letter Schiller introduces readers to "a new drive" with which the other two drives "work in combination." "This drive," he announces, in which both of the other two drives "work in alliance, ... I call the *play drive* [*Spieltrieb*]" (AE, 97).

The play drive (its mysterious origin notwithstanding) is clearly the linchpin in Schiller's concept of aesthetic education. For the basic object of this third drive is "all the aesthetic qualities of appearances [*Erscheinungen*], what, in a word, one calls *beauty* in the widest sense of the term" (AE, 15th Letter, 101). It is by way of the play drive that humans find balance and harmony in their lives, and the play drive's focus on beauty is what enables them to realize freedom and achieve their destiny and vocation (*Bestimmung*).

One qualification in Schiller's discussion of beauty that deserves comment is his distinction between "melting (*schmelzende*)" and "energetic (*energetische*)" beauty. First introduced in the 16th Letter, he insists that while "ideal beauty is indivisible and simple," "in experience *there is* a melting and an energetic beauty" (AE, 113). Why the two types of beauty? Schiller's extremely terse answer comes in the 17th Letter: "Melting beauty ... is for tense souls; energizing beauty for relaxed souls" (AE, 119). Here as elsewhere, Schiller's appropriation of Kant's aesthetics is evident: energizing beauty is reminiscent of the Kantian sublime.[18] But his main motive for introducing this distinction between two types of beauty seems to be simply the desire to make beauty big enough to do its work on a wide range of human beings: some people need more exposure to melting beauty because they are too tense, while those who are too relaxed will benefit from more exposure to energetic beauty.

"Beauty is ... nothing less than freedom in appearance," Schiller announces in one of the *Kallias* letters, shortly after declaring that "I am speaking here mostly as a Kantian."[19] And a very close relative of this claim appears later in a footnote to the 23rd Letter of AE: "Beauty is ... the sole possible expression of freedom in appearance" (AE, 167). What exactly does he mean by this key

---

[18] Wilkinson and Willoughby claim that "the identity of energetic beauty and the sublime was refuted by Böhm" (AE, xlii n.1). "Identity" is of course too strong, but in the Enclosure to Schiller's letter to Prince von Augustenburg of November 11, 1793, one can see multiple uses of the term "sublime" that are quite similar to Schiller's later usage of "energetic beauty" in AE. For details, see R. D. Miller, *A Study of Schiller's "Letters on the Aesthetic Education of Man"* (Harrogate: The Duchy Press, 1986), 102–110. See also Tribe and Schmidt's edition of *The Aesthetic Education of Man*, 138–144, 174 n.1. Beiser, on the other hand, in his discussion of "The Two Forms of Beauty," claims that "Schiller's account of the forms of beauty and their effects is essentially an application of the medical theories of [Scottish physician] John Brown, which were very popular in Germany in the eighteenth century" (*Schiller as Philosopher*, 148). And Guyer argues that it recalls "Burke's physiological account of the effects of the beautiful and sublime in Part IV of his *Enquiry*" (*A History of Modern Aesthetics*, 1: 486).

[19] Schiller, "Kallias or Concerning Beauty: Letters to Gottfried Körner," in *Classic and Romantic German Aesthetics*, ed. J. M. Bernstein (Cambridge: Cambridge University Press, 2003), 145–183, at 152, 148.

assertion? Beauty is freedom in appearance because (as Kant remarks in his *Critique of the Power of Judgment*) "the beautiful prepares us to love something, even nature, without interest" (KU 5: 267). When we truly experience the beautiful, we do so without any ulterior motives or utilitarian aims. We are not trying to get anything out the experience other than the appreciation and enjoyment of the object for its own sake. In making aesthetic judgements about beauty, we thus learn how to love something for its own sake. In all true instances of the aesthetic experience of the beautiful, there is a freedom and autonomy from all external constraints and considerations present. Kant makes an analogous remark in his *Metaphysics of Morals* when he refers to the human disposition "to love something (e.g., beautiful crystal formations, the indescribable beauty of plants) even apart from any intention to use it" (MS 6: 443). Here too, we see the same emphasis on independence from external constraints. But this human experience of beauty also takes place within the realm of appearances—we are enjoying something tangible, whether it be an indescribably beautiful plant in the realm of nature or an artwork created by a genius. The freedom we experience in aesthetic experience thus gives us a glimpse—indeed, a concrete experience of—our noumenal freedom.[20] Or, as Schiller puts it, beauty is "the consummation [*Konsummation*] of one's humanity" (AE, 15th Letter, 103). Art draws us "upward to freedom on golden rings" (Schiller to Augustenburg, July 13, 1793), and "it is only through beauty that one makes one's way to freedom" (AE, 2nd Letter, 9).

Two Problems

Although there is certainly more to say about Schiller's challenging concept of aesthetic education, in this chapter I have tried to focus on two essential issues—namely, what it is and why it is important. And I have tried to do so without getting bogged down in the multiple accusations of inconsistency and unclarity that commentators have brought against AE over the years. I have tried to read Schiller charitably, primarily in order to make sense out of his position, but also in an effort to make things manageable for the reader. However, in closing I would like to briefly discuss two important criticisms of Schiller's account. The first is a charge of circularity. Guyer writes:

> He seems to be inconsistent, sometimes suggesting that it is the experience of beauty that activates the play drive and allows us to enjoy its beneficial effects which are necessary for all moral and political progress, but sometimes suggesting that it must be a sheer act of the will that keeps both the form and the sense-drives

---

[20] As Schiller remarks in the opening lines of his essay, "On the Pathetic" (1793): "The ultimate purpose of art is to depict what transcends the realm of the senses and the art of tragedy in particular accomplishes this by displaying morality's independence, its freedom, in the throes of passion, from nature's laws" (in Schiller, *Essays*, ed. Hinderer and Dahlstrom, 45–69, at 45).

within their proper limits, thereby creating the space within which both aesthetic experience but also moral and political progress can take place ... In other words, Schiller's theory seems circular: Moral progress is said to presuppose aesthetic experience, but the possibility of aesthetic experience itself seems to presuppose a moral decision.[21]

If we read Schiller literally, he does appear to be guilty as charged. In the 13th Letter, for instance, he writes:

> It must be an act of freedom [*eine Handlung der Freiheit*], an activity of the person which, by its moral intensity, moderates that of the senses and, by mastering impressions, robs them of their depth only in order to give them increased surface. Character must set bounds to temperament ... Personality must keep the sensuous drive within its proper bounds, and receptivity, or nature, must do the same with the formal drive. (AE, 93; cf. Guyer, I: 487)

Similarly, right after a famous passage where he calls beauty "our second creator," because it "makes humanity a possibility for us," he immediately adds that we must use "our free will [*unserm freien Willen*]" to make this possibility a reality (AE, 21st Letter, 147–149). In these passages, Schiller seems to be saying that an act of free will is necessary in order to lead human beings to beauty.

But in other passages, several of which we have cited earlier in this chapter, Schiller says the opposite—namely, that it is the experience of beauty that gives birth to freedom. Passages in this second group include the line in the opening epigraph for his essay where Schiller says that the arts draw the human being "upward to freedom," his remark in the 2nd Letter that "it is only through beauty that one makes one's way to freedom" (AE, 9), and his claim in the 13th Letter that the experience of beauty will lead to "the highest independence and freedom" (AE, 87). In these as well as still other passages,[22] he appears to be stating that it is beauty that leads humans to freedom, rather than vice versa.

However, when we read Schiller more charitably (and in my earlier remarks concerning the first reference to the play drive in AE, I hinted that consistency is not his strong suit), he can be acquitted of the circularity charge. I believe his considered view is that while an act of free choice is needed to consciously direct one's attention to the beautiful, repeated experiences of and reflections on beauty heighten and strengthen one's freedom, transforming it from a bare capacity to a central feature of one's character. The capacity for free will is innate in humans (as Schiller puts it, nature "gives"[23] it to humans), but it is up

---

[21] Guyer, *A History of Modern Aesthetics*, I: 487.
[22] For example, at the end of the 19th Letter he says that the harmony achieved by the two opposing drives "gives *freedom* its origin [*Ursprung*]" (AE, 137).
[23] "On Grace and Dignity," 141.

to us to exercise, cultivate, and fully actualize this capacity through experience with and reflection on beauty.

It is also worth noting that a close relative of the circularity charge has also been used to criticize Kant's educational theory. How can a philosophy that stresses the central importance of autonomy—freely giving principles to oneself—even find room for education? As Johann Friedrich Herbart remarks, in his 1804 review of Kant's *Lectures on Pedagogy*:

> How did Kant imagine moral education? As an effect of transcendental freedom? Impossible, for the concept of the latter comes to an end, as soon as one thinks it is not entirely free from every causal nexus. Transcendental freedom does what it does by itself; one cannot hinder it through anything, one cannot help it through anything. It discovers maxims; what the teacher says to it is immaterial ... One cannot influence transcendental freedom ... In this way Kant and his followers describe transcendental freedom to us;—and in this way they destroy all pedagogy.[24]

In more recent years, Lewis White Beck has echoed this charge in his claim that "the teacher ... cannot make the child moral; only the child himself can do that ... Kant ... does not even seem to see that his strict moral philosophy has, and can have, no place for moral education."[25] But the common-sense reply to this charge is simply that Kantian education is an education *towards* autonomy.[26] Kantian moral education does not give us autonomy; rather, it helps us strengthen our innate capacity for autonomy. Similarly, Schillerian aesthetic education does not give us free will, because we already have it. Rather, it helps us to further develop and increase our innate capacity for freedom.

The second criticism is one I touched on earlier, towards the end of section "Why Aesthetic Education?". Won't aesthetic education be crushed by the tremendous weight that Schiller places on it? How can aesthetic education possibly achieve all of the ambitious goals that he claims flow out it? Is aesthetic education in fact a necessary means for human development, moral and political progress, overcoming alienation, and freedom?

Numerous counterexamples indicate that the short but correct answer to this last question is, "no." The world is filled with individuals who have benefitted from an excellent aesthetic education but who remain morally bankrupt. And some individuals who have not enjoyed the advantages of aesthetic education have still managed to become moral saints. But before we gloat too much over Schiller's defeat, we should remind ourselves that when it comes to moral

---

[24] Johann Friedrich Herbart. Review of *Immanuel Kant über Pädagogik*, ed. Friedrich Theodor Rink. *Göttingische gelehrte Anzeigen* 26 (February 18, 1804): 257–261, at 261.

[25] Lewis White Beck, *Essays on Kant and Hume* (New Haven: Yale University Press, 1978), 201.

[26] I discuss this issue in more detail in my essay, "'Total Transformation': Why Kant Did Not Give Up on Education," *Kantian Review* 21 (2016): 393–413.

education, there are no guarantees. None of humanity's manifold efforts over the centuries to "make virtue something acquired by teaching"[27] have proven to be solid successes. Unfortunately, there appear to be no proven necessary means to human moral development (other than those necessary for the continuation of human life itself—e.g., food, water, and shelter).

Here also, a version of the "aesthetic experience is necessary for moral development" fallacy is also present in Schiller's hero, Kant—"the immortal author of the Critique, to whom fame is due for having reestablished healthy reason out of philosophical reason."[28] For Kant, the experience of the beautiful—a concept which, he holds, "is valid only for human beings [*nur für Menschen*]" (KU 5: 210)—is also held to be a necessary means to morality. As he remarks in a *Reflexion*: "The culture of taste is a preparatory exercise for morality [*Vorübung zur Moral*]" (Refl 993, 15: 438). Beauty is—for humans, but perhaps not for other creatures who are built differently than us—"a symbol of morality" (KU 5: 351), and, as noted earlier in our discussion of beauty and freedom, the human experience of "the beautiful prepares us [*bereitet uns vor*] to love something, even nature, without interest" (KU 5: 267). This capacity to love something for its own sake is a key feature of genuine moral judgements, and the disposition "to love something ... even apart from any intention to use it," he adds in the *Metaphysics of Morals*, "greatly promotes morality or at least prepares the way for it [*die Moralität sehr befördert, wenigstens dazu vorbereitet*]" (MS 6: 443).

Kant's defense of the claim that, for humans, aesthetic experience is a necessary means for moral development is just one of several unexpected examples in his work of what I have elsewhere called "humans-only norms"[29]—namely, norms that are based on purported general facts about human nature, rather than (as Kant holds is true with genuine moral norms) norms that "must hold not merely for human beings but for *all rational beings in general* [*alle vernünftige Wesen überhaupt*]" (GMS 4: 408; see also 410n., 412, 426, 431). Humans-only norms are impure, a posteriori, and empirical, whereas official Kantian moral norms are pure, a priori, and non-empirical.

But, again, on this point Kant and Schiller are both wrong. Not all human beings who experience the beautiful will become morally good agents. The art-morality connection is much more tenuous than this. So where does this leave

---

[27] Plato, *Meno* 70a.
[28] Schiller, "On Grace and Dignity," 149.
[29] See my "Kant the Naturalist," *Journal of Transcendental Philosophy* 1 (2020): 3–17, and "Humans-Only Norms: An Unexpected Kantian Story," in *Kant on Morality, Humanity, and Legality: Practical Dimensions of Normativity*, ed. Ansgar Lyssy and Christopher Yeomans (New York: Palgrave Macmillan 2021). Guyer, however, while criticizing Schiller for holding that aesthetic experience is a necessary means to human moral development, claims that Kant does not commit this error. "Kant recognized ... limits on the significance of the cultivation of taste for moral development ... in no case does he argue that the support that morality can get from aesthetic experience is indispensable" (*A History of Modern Aesthetics*, I: 489–490).

us? Aesthetic education will not necessarily make us morally better, it will not necessarily usher in a just and humane society, and it will not necessarily erase the fragmentation of modern life. But it will "make one graceful, if one is properly trained" (*Republic* 401d-e), and it will make one more aware of, and more appreciative of, the myriad forms of beauty in nature as well as in the artworks created by one's fellow human beings. Art deepens and intensifies the way one looks at life. Isn't this enough?[30]

---

[30] I would like to thank Richard Eldridge and Robert Lehmann for helpful comments on an earlier draft of this chapter.

PART IV

The Relevance of Schiller's Philosophical Thought in the Context of His Entire Work

CHAPTER 23

The Role of Philosophy in Schiller's Plays

Giovanna Pinna

PHILOSOPHICAL ANTHROPOLOGY: *THE ROBBERS*

Schiller's debut as a dramatic poet is under the sign of philosophy. In his first play, *Die Räuber* (1781), the relationship between dramatic elaboration and philosophical reflection is explicit: one could almost say that it is an exposition of philosophical issues through the inverted mirror of the drama. The various doctrines with which Schiller came into contact during his medical studies at the Karlsschule—the materialism of Helvétius and La Mettrie, the philosophy of moral sense, Platner's anthropology, the Stoic doctrine of the fortitudo animi—are not simply an ideal background for the play; they are part of the construction of the characters and the action. Evidence of the fact that in the young Schiller literary creation was originally interconnected with philosophical themes is also found in his third medical dissertation (*Über den Zusammenhang der tierischen Natur des Menschen mit seiner geistigen*, 1780), in which passages from the as-yet-unpublished *Die Räuber* are quoted, with a reference to a fictitious title, *Life of Moor, Tragedy by Krake* (SW:5, 308 and 309 ff.). The 'voluptuary Fiesco', the main character of Die *Verschwörung des Fiesko zu Genua* (1783), is also mentioned there as an example of the interdependence between corruption of the soul and corruption of the body (SW:5, 314; MPL 277; see Alt I, 210). Furthermore, Schiller attached to his first tragedy two prefaces (one of which was suppressed) and a *Selbstbesprechung*, in

G. Pinna (✉)
University of Molise, Campobasso, Italy
e-mail: giovanna.pinna@unimol.it

which he sought to illustrate his idea of tragedy as a critical analysis of the moral world through the representation of the deviations, perversions and temptations of the individual. The subject of dramatic art is the contradictions of human action, and its method is '*die Seele gleichsam bei seinen geheimsten Operationen zu ertappen*' (*Vorrede*, SW:5, 484).

In his dissertation, Schiller does not use examples from medical practice but from dramatic literature to demonstrate the thesis of the commercium mentis et corporis: Cassius, worn out by sleepless nights in Shakespeare's *Julius Caesar*; Lady Macbeth, 'walking in her sleep in a case of phrenetic delirium' (GW:5, 309; MPL 273), in whom remorseful conscience causes a feverish state that consumes the body; allusions to Richard III, the model for the character of Franz Moor. In the play, these themes are most evident in the moment of the catastrophe, in which unconscious fears and the terror of death, amplified by the dream, produce a feverish state and intense physical discomfort (*Räuber* V/1). Significantly, it is above all through the character of Franz, 'who had been previously cunning enough to annihilate humanitarian feelings by reducing logic to a bare skeleton' (GW:5, 309; MPL 272), that Schiller dramatises the philosophical issues that most concerned him at the time: the mixed nature of human beings, sensory and rational, the criticism of materialism as a perversion of rationality, and the rejection of the utilitarian conception of the social pact. In constructing his characters, Schiller works through the mechanism of inversion (Riedel 1993). Franz, in particular, is a negative version of the doctor-philosopher, using his science and his skill as a psychologist not to cure, but to ruin the body through the spirit, and his argumentative capacity to demonstrate the groundlessness of the moral order based on transcendent principles. He himself declares the destructiveness of his intellect: 'You see I have my wits about me too, but my wit is the bite of scorpions' (*Räuber* I/1; GW:1, 496; transl. 29).

The model of the relationship between soul and body adopted by Franz in the play can be traced back to La Mettrie's *homme machine*. The latter model denied the idea of the soul as an autonomous spiritual principle and, in contrast to Descartes' mechanistic dualism, attached great importance to the sphere of instincts and emotions. The cognitive relevance of the emotions will remain a topic of reflection for Schiller even after his encounter with Kant's critical philosophy, from the perspective of an integration between impulses and the activity of reason. But Franz Moor is interested in destroying the vital force through passions, not in enhancing it (Guthke, 52 ff; Alt I, 293 ff.). He knows how to make use of what doctors and philosophers' have taught him, namely 'how finely the motions of the mind are attuned to those of the machine that houses it' (*Räuber* II/1; SW:1, 522; transl. 56), as when he subtly manipulates his father's feelings in order to wrest the right of primogeniture, that is, wealth and power, from his brother Karl. In reporting on his brother's disordered life, he describes the alleged physical consequences of his moral debauchery, emphasising the fact that 'moral suffering erodes the vital forces, the overburdened spirit destroys its armour', and thus induces in a state of weakness in his father's ageing body. Paradoxically, the state of psychophysical prostration that precedes his anything but heroic suicide will make him experience directly the fragility of the 'bodily machine' in the face of the 'dunkle Vorstellungen'. This notion, borrowed from Sulzer, refers to the subconscious sphere and is the negative counterpart of the healthy body-psyche relationship, in which physical stimuli help the development of cognitive abilities (S. Hinderer 2003).

Medical anthropology is not the only terrain in which der 'spekulativischer Bösewicht' Franz (Letter to Dalberg 12.12.1781, FA:11, 33) moves at ease. In the *Selbstbesprechung*, Schiller recognises that his character's interest lies in his philosophical education: 'Dann sind auch die Räsonnements, mit denen er sein Lastersystem versteht, das Resultat eines aufgeklärten Denkens und liberalen Studium' (GW:1, 627). These arguments are mainly directed towards the refutation of the philosophy of universal love set out in the *Theosophie des Julius* (Schings 1980; Riedel 1993) and its metaphysical presuppositions: the existence of God as a perfect being from whom the universe proceeds by emanation, through the infinite diversification of the original unity, the immortality of the soul and the principle of sympathy between beings as a universal cohesive force.

Franz's materialistic-utilitarian critique, explicitly stated in his monologues or in disputes like the one with Pastor Moser (*Räuber* V/2), is also directed against the notion of family relations as the positive foundation of social order. Paternal love in his eyes is nothing more than a fiction masking natural sexual drives: 'Can I acknowledge any love that does not rest on respect of my person? Could respect for my person exist, when my person could only come into being through that for which it must be a condition? And what is so sacred about it all? The act itself through which I was created? As if that were anything but the animal gratification of animal desires?' (*Räuber* I/2; SW:1, 502; transl. 34). Nature is not the source of harmony among human beings, but of the instinct to overcome the other. The drive towards self-preservation is the only principle that Franz recognises as the basis of interpersonal relations which, deprived of all emotional content, become pure relations of force: 'Each man has the same right to the greatest and the last; claim destroys claim, impulse destroys impulse, force destroys force. Might is right, and the limits of our strength our only law' (*Räuber* I/1; SW:1, 500; transl. 33). There are therefore no moral obstacles to his plan to get rid of his father and brother, nor to the regime of terror he imposes on his subordinates.

In the play, the principle of egoism, which can be traced back to Hélvetius, has a twofold moral and sociopolitical significance. It not only is the radical alternative to the Platonic metaphysics set out in the *Theosophie des Julius* but also contrasts with the idea that there is a natural tendency of individuals to create a social pact that aims at the common good while safeguarding the freedom of the individual. Franz, 'der philosophische Antagonist des Julius' (Riedel 1993), represents in this sense the perversion of the principles of natural law and, more generally, of rationalism, in such a way as to constitute a sort of 'dialectic of the Aufklärung'.

The questioning of his philosophies is entrusted to the dramatic development, which shows the overthrow of the 'system of egoism' advocated by Franz both in the failure of his criminal designs and in the collapse of his psychic resilience. The dialectical contrast between rationalist scepticism and the idea of a moral basis for action emerges in the dual function of the concept of conscience (Gewissen). In general, conscience consists of a feeling associated with a moral conviction, which influences the decision whether to perform an action or not. In eighteenth-century culture, however, the concept had marked theological-normative roots. Franz, for whom conscience is nothing more than a deception induced by religious belief, uses it to manipulate his victims, knowing that they are conditioned by it (S. Godel 2015). As for himself, while on the one hand he sees it as an obstacle to rational decision and approaches superstition ('Conscience—yes, indeed!—an excellent scarecrow, to keep the sparrows from the cherry trees'! *Räuber* I/1, GW:1, 500 f; transl. 33), on the other hand he unconsciously fears it and wants to exorcise its possible effects. Paradoxically, it is precisely the manifestation of the repressed conscience, now understood as an inner court, that determines Franz Moor's intellectual and psychological collapse. The atheistic critique of the moral order turns ultimately into a 'philosophy of despair' (*Räuber* V/1; SW:1, 605).

The principles underlying Franz's action are the opposite of the philosophy of love expressed in the Shaftesbury-influenced *Philosophische Briefe* (Cassirer 2004; Beiser 2005, 21f.). The dramatisation of the concept of love as a principle of universal order follows the same pattern as the above: it is expressed ex negativo, by showing the selfish consequences that its absence produces in the two brothers (s. Schings 1980). The lack of love is at the origin of Franz's feeling of revenge against nature, which had been only a stepmother to ihm: 'She gave me nothing; what I can make of myself is my affair' (*Räuber* I/1; SW 1:500; transl. 33). Karl, on the other hand, favoured by nature, reacts to the loss of paternal love caused by his brother's intrigues, by choosing to become an outlaw, turning spurned love into universal hatred (*Räuber*, IV/3). In both cases, love is intrinsically connected to its opposite. Of this dialectic of love, prefigured in the play, Schiller was to provide a theoretical exposition years later, in the essay *Über die notwendigen Grenzen beim gebrauch schöner Formen* (SW: 5, 690 ff.; s. Macor 2011).

Moral Principles and Political Order: *Don Carlos*

The relationship of the individual to the moral order of society is the dominant theme of the philosophy underlying *Die Räuber*. The two brothers are specular images of the conflict between the subject's desire for self-assertion and the conditions of reality (see Sautermeister 1991, Alt I, 295 ff., Guthke, 46f.). The more specifically political element of the drama, the critique of a still-feudal system of domination, is present in the construction of the characters, but remains in the background compared to the anthropological-moral interest, the same interest that animated Schiller's first theoretical writings. It is in later dramas, *Die Verschwörung des Fiesko zu Genua* (1783) and above all *Don Karlos* (1787), that the focus shifts to the relationship between moral principles and political action. If the reading of Plutarch's *Parallel Lives*, mediated by Abel's teaching (Luserke-Jaqui 87 ff.), plays an important role in the conception of the 'greatness' of the tragic character, the dramas that precede the experience of the French Revolution are influenced by the theories of republicanism. The problem explored in plays like *Fiesko* is whether and to what extent moral principles that are conceived in relation to the individual can apply to political action and, consequently, how the private and the public spheres, which in principle should both be based on the principle of benevolence (Wohlwollen), interact (see Maier 1987, Stachel 2011). Schiller does not provide an unequivocal answer to this question, not least because of his indecision between family drama and 'republican drama' (as the subtitle states), but he anticipates the problem of the abstractness of moral principles that will occupy him in his engagement with Kant's practical philosophy.

Don Karlos was also born as a family drama, but in the course of its tormented elaboration, the focus progressively shifted to the question of the amount of freedom granted to individuals by the state and the border between moral intention and political action. The conflict between Philip II and his son Karlos, with the sentimental colouring given by the son's passion for his stepmother, lost its centrality in favour of the political-intellectual confrontation between Philip and the Marquis of Posa, standard-bearer of republican virtues. Schiller himself accounts for this shift in focus in his *Briefe über Don Karlos*, with an explicit reference to Montesquieu as the philosophical basis of the play (SW:2, 258). Although Schiller probably read the *Esprit des Lois* soon after the drama's conclusion, Montesquieu's theories on the republican state were known to him through Adam Ferguson's *Institutes of Moral Philosophy* (Ayrault 1948; Bresky 1961; Riedel 1985, 125).[1] In the play, the key character, the Marquis of Posa, is the spokesman of an anti-absolutist conception, according to which the power of the sovereign is legitimised by the will of the citizens, who can exercise their 'free opinion' (Meinungsfreiheit) while accepting the relations of domination. Of course, Schiller's republicanism does not correspond to a modern idea of democracy, but rather to a form of oligarchy, that is, a state organisation based on restricted representation (Nilges 2011). Posa calls himself a 'citizen of everywhere' and initially refuses to collaborate with Philip II because this would put him in the position of a subject, forcing him to renounce the guiding principle of his existence, love for humanity, which presupposes the principle of equality.[2] The anachronism of Posa's ideals, still unsuited to the context of the time, is intentional and, one could say,

---

[1] A. Ferguson, *Institutes of moral Philosophy*, Edinburgh 1769 (*Grundsätze der Moralphilosophie*, übersetzt mit einigen Anmerkungen versehen von Christian Garve, Leipzig 1772).

[2] Significantly, Posa's words literally recall those of Schiller himself in the advertisement for the journal 'Rheinische Talia' in 1784: 'Ich schreibe als Weltbürger, der keinem Fürsten dient', in reference to his break with the Duke of Württemberg and subsequent flight after the publication of *Die Räuber*. See SW:5, 855.

programmatic, both in terms of the political function of dramatic writing and in the progressive-enlightenment vision of history. 'This century/ is far from ripe for my designs. I live/ Among the citizens that are to come' (*Don Karlos* III/10, 3177–3178; transl. 112), says Posa: his position is that of someone who looks upon the current situation from a future more civilised era, which will succeed the dark times of absolutism. 'Kinder centuries' that will bring a 'milder wisdom', where 'the happiness of citizens/ will thrive upon the greatness of their lords' (*Don Karlos*, III/10, v.3150–3151; transl. 124). In the scenario that Posa describes to the king to convince him to grant Flanders its freedom, the historian's view of the development of Europe in the following two centuries is combined with a utopian cosmopolitanism that survived only in Schiller's future philosophical development.

Posa's idealism does not make him a positive hero tout court. His dramatic nature lies precisely in the intrinsic contradictory nature of his action: after having championed the republican cause, he deludes himself that he can use Philip himself to obtain the autonomy of Flanders and create the conditions that make possible the maximum freedom of the individual in the state ('Give us the freedom/To think', *Don Karlos* III,10, v. 3213–3214), so that political realism ends up prevailing over principles (see Malsch 1988).

From the Stage to Philosophy and Back: *Kant Studies*

The *Don Karlos* had left Schiller highly dissatisfied with the very concept of dramatic form, as the *Briefe über don Carlos* testify. It was only in October 1796 that he resumed work on a drama centred on the character of Wallenstein, a project dating from the early 1790s, which took its cue from his historiographic work on the Thirty Years' War. Between the two dramas lies the study of Kant's philosophy and the writing of his aesthetic essays. Schiller's intense reflections on Kant's Third Critique had led to the theoretical considerations on tragedy of the early 1790s. As he wrote to his friend Körner in 1792, 'um der Ausübung selbst willen philosophiere ich gerne über die Theorie; die Kritik muß mir jetzt selbst den Schaden ersetzen, den sie mir zugefügt hat' (25.5. 1792; FA: 11, 603). Philosophy was assigned the role of critical observer and regulator of the play of the imagination.

The end of the 'philosophical' period marks the transition from the first to the second phase of Schiller's dramatic production. On the one hand, his reflection on transcendental subjectivity and his reflections on Kant's ethics had changed the theoretical coordinates on which his literary activity was based. On the other hand, he had become convinced that he could provide a more adequate response to the spiritual needs of the post-revolutionary era through an artistic representation of the conflict between the self-determination of individuals and the objectivity of the historical world.

The conception of freedom as the autonomy of reason remains at the heart of both Schiller's philosophical writings and tragedies, but he seeks to develop a more articulate vision of the relationship between reason and sensibility. The critique of Kant's rigour found in *Über Anmut und Würde* marks in some ways a point of no return in the evolution of Schiller's ideas, although he did not question in principle the cogency of Kant's moral law and acknowledged Kant's merit in having overcome a utilitarian-egoistic view of reason. What does not convince Schiller in Kant's position is that freedom is understood as the dominion of reason over the sensitive constitution of the subject ends up, a position that ends up contradiction itself, since freedom entails the oppression of one part of the human being over the other (s. Falduto 2021). While it is indeed true that 'the demands of the sensuous (…) are *completely* rejected in the sphere of pure reason and moral legislation, they have an ineliminable function' in the realm of appearance and in the actual fulfillment of ethical obligations' (SW:5, 464; GD, 149). Although the morality of the individual action depends on its correspondence to the law of reason, what determines the moral character of an individual is the fact that in him the moral principle acts not against inclination, but in accordance with it. Beyond the aesthetic consequences (the definition of grace), Schiller's argument implies a critique of the dualistic Kantian model, in which rationality is affirmed through the subjugation of sensory impulses. To the rigid opposition between sensibility and reason, Schiller opposes the idea of a dynamic relationship between the parts, which tends towards a point of equilibrium. The search for a possible integration between the moral-rational sphere and the sphere of impulses and feelings has an anthropological matrix that has never been erased and whose basic approach goes back to the years of his medical-philosophical apprenticeship. Schiller, who in his first dissertation had tried to offer a 'physiological' explanation of the interaction between body and psyche through the concept of an 'intermediate force' (Mittelkraft) residing in the nervous system, remains faithful to a holistic view of the human being. The original question of the relationship between body and psyche, already found in the *Räuber*, was reconfigured, in the philosophical essays of the 1790s, in critical-transcendental terms through the concept (borrowed from Fichte) of *Wechselwirkung*, as the focus shifted towards the discussion of how emotions and impulses enter into relation with the moral-rational foundation of the person.

Schiller's doubts on Kant's moral conception, which were made explicit in the *Letters on Aesthetic Education* (see Beiser 2005, 184–190), had a significant influence on his decision to dedicate himself exclusively to literary activity and, more specifically, on the design of his 'classical' tragedies, beginning with *Wallenstein*. In short, Kantian ethics, insofar as it is oriented towards an ascetic (mönchisch) ideal of the affirmation of the moral will against sensibility, no longer appears to Schiller as instrument capable of accounting for the complexity of the motivations of human action. As he wrote to Goethe, since for Kant the human being has 'einen positiven Antrieb zum Guten so wie zum sinnliche Wohlseyn', the morally wrong choice should be traced back to a 'positiven inneren Grund zum Bösen', since the positive cannot be taken away (aufgehoben) through a simple negation (to Goethe 2.08.1799, FA:12, 471). In reality, Schiller observes, the two Triebe cannot be placed on the same level, and morally wrong choices are not necessarily motivated by a principled option for evil, but may derive from a choice in favour of a morally inferior duty because it is connected to an affection, or be the result of omission or, again, of an inability to decide. In *Über die notwendigen Grenze beim Gebrauch schöner Formen*, he had precisely investigated the ambiguity of the relationship between moral duty and inclination, particularly evident in the affirmation of 'imperfect duties', which depend on the individual's arbitrariness and make the good of the individual prevail over the general interest, for example, or social decorum over the affirmation of truth. Moreover, Kant's ethics of duty excludes tragic conflict insofar as the autonomous will that follows the categorical imperative does not come into conflict with empirical objectives (Feger 2007).

In contrast, for the tragic poet, who does not have to explain the relationship between the two spheres in speculative terms and has the advantage of being able to remain 'im Reich der Erscheinungen', it is rather the opaque motivations, 'die dunklen Stellen in der Natur der Menschen', that are interesting as the source of the passions and the motivation of the behaviour of human beings as a whole (to Goethe 2.08.1799, FA:12, 471). Speculative thought must give way to tragic art in the effort to grasp the meaning of the dialectic between nature and history. It is indeed the imagination, as a faculty capable of accessing the unrepresentable, the dark and frightening dimension of our natural foundation, that performs this task and makes the results visible through art. What Schiller is interested in, unlike Kant, is the phenomenology of the relationship between moral foundation, inclination and action, and in this sense he understands tragedy as a representation of the possibilities for the affirmation of freedom through contrast with the objective limitations of reality. The emphasis is on possibility, so that the tragic hero does not have to be moral, but simply bring out a disposition to act morally (s. *Über das Pathetische*).

Drama As a Theory of Action: *Wallenstein, Mary Stuart*

After the conclusion of *Über naive und sentimentalische Dichtung*, Schiller thus came to the conviction that philosophical speculation is no longer the appropriate instrument for exploring the contradictions of real existence and decided to continue his reflection on man through tragedy. On the other hand, he also believed that tragedy needed to be redesigned in terms of its fundamental structure. From 1796, during *Wallenstein*'s reworking phase, Aristotle's *Poetics* became the essential point of reference for the development of a new model of tragedy. Although there is no shortage of references to Aristotle in the writings of the early 1790s on tragic art and the pathetic sublime, these are conventional references, echoed in Lessing's *Hamburgische Dramaturgie* and the polemic against classical French theatre (Reinhardt 1976). Schiller now set out to derive the structural principles of Greek tragedy from his reading of Aristotle in order to amend the faults of his own previous theatrical production. This study revolved around two essential points: the concept of action (Handlung) and the possibility of using the concept of destiny in modern tragedy. Regarding the concept of action, it is first of all necessary to distinguish two different and interconnected meanings, which concern, respectively, dramatic structure and dramatic content, one could say the philosophical content, of tragedy. Action characterises the drama in poetic-formal terms; it corresponds to Aristotle's mythos. It is the concatenation of events, says Schiller, and not the nature of the characters that arouses the spectator's interest and determines the aesthetic quality of the tragedy. In contrast to Lessing, Schiller attaches more importance to the phobos (Furcht) produced by the events than to the emotional participation in the suffering of the characters (eleos, Mitleid). Sophocles' *Oedipus Rex*, as a 'tragic analysis', for example, seems to him to be particularly effective because the idea of the inevitability of the event enhances the effect of fear on the spectator (to Goethe 2.10.1787, FA:12, 331). The fact that the mournful outcome of the event is already known contributes to the tragic nature of the play, underlining the inevitability of the causal sequence of events.

The attention to the structure of the drama, however, is connected in the post-philosophical phase of the elaboration of *Wallenstein* and *Maria Stuart* to a redefinition of the role of the tragic hero, which in turn has to do with a conception of the subject centred on the idea of the will (Willen) as freedom of choice between good and evil. Action thus has also to do with the practical realisation of the self's potential. In *Über Anmut und Würde*, the concept of person is defined by the will to modify the existing through action: 'The act by means of which he brings this about is mostly called a *action* and those of his accomplishments that flow from such an action are, by contrast, called his deeds. A human being, then, can nly prove himself a person by his deeds' (SW:5, 454; GD, 141). The psychological and moral characteristics of the individual characters lose the relevance they had in the early tragedies and the focus is on the decision-making processes. Action is not a consequence of character, but rather character is defined through action (see Kommerell 147f, Ette 2011). The case of Wallenstein is emblematic of this transformation. Schiller's problem was to give poetic substance to a political-historical story centred on a morally dubious figure who is hardly likely to arouse the sympathy of the spectator. He therefore makes the tragic pathos revolve on the futility of individual attempts to halt the course of events. To a remark by his friend Körner, who saw Max Piccolomini as the true centre of the tragedy, on account of his noble character and sentimental attractiveness, Schiller responds by programmatically observing that '*das moralische Gefühl (hat) niemals den Helden zu bestimmen, sondern die Handlung allein, insofern sie sich auf ihn allein bezieht oder allein von ihm ausgeht*' (to Körner 13. 7.1800, FA:12, 518). Since tragic development is a dynamic system of actions in which the intentions of the acting subjects collide with the objective conditions of the historical world, the aesthetic interest of the character Wallenstein lies in being the centre and catalyst of this system of actions and reactions, to which a plurality of actors contribute.

At the basis of the dramatic construction, there is thus a phenomenology of action whose structural elements can be traced back to the 'psychological antagonism' between a 'realist' and an 'idealist' attitude. According to Schiller, it is this antagonism, more than the casualness of particular interests, that determines the unsurpassably conflicting nature of human relations (s. SW:5, 769–770). This typological opposition between realism and idealism, formulated in the concluding part of *Über naive und sentimentalische Dichtung*, is for Schiller can be used to interpret the actions of the characters in *Wallenstein*. In 1796, Schiller wrote to Wilhelm von Humboldt that the character of Wallenstein is 'echt realistisch' and appeared to him as the experimental confirmation of the 'ideas about realism and idealism' set forth in the essay (21.3.1796; FA:12, 161). The term "realism" defines a mode of action based on the recognition of the existing, independently of a unifying ethical view. In the theoretical sphere, the realist adopts an empirical attitude, knows phenomena in their individuality but does not arrive at conceiving the whole. In the practical sphere, he pursues self-assertion by exploiting the possibility offered by reality and by manipulating objective situations. Schiller compares this way of proceeding to the action of nature, which only acquires meaning as a whole. Similarly, the moral autonomy of the realist is not manifested in the individual act, but in the totality of his actions (See Barnouw 1977).

In contrast, the realist's opposite and complementary type, the idealist, takes 'his knowledge and motivation from pure reason'. Assuming an agreement between the laws governing the objective world and 'the laws of the human spirit', the idealist's action is marked by a moral rigour that tends to disregard the complexity of experience. One could say that the idealist evaluates circumstances by following the principium individuationis, while the idealist has as a methodical rule the subsumption of the particular into the universal. While in *Über naive und sentimentalische Dichtung*, the two anthropological types are analysed in their positive and negative characteristics, in the tragedy; Schiller represents their limits by showing the failure of subjective intention in the face of the necessity of events. Wallenstein's Machiavellian tacticism, which actually leads to inaction, is counterbalanced by the self-destructive outcome of the loyalty to moral principles of the idealist Max Piccolomini. While the former character evidences the conflict between the individual and the world, in Max, whose actions are marked by an ideal vision of duty, the contrast is between two duties and two loyalties, to Wallenstein and the emperor, respectively. This is not, however, a collision of two ethical powers in the sense of Hegel's interpretation of Antigone, since Max's loyalty to Wallenstein is accompanied by a strong affection for this 'almost father'. In general, in Schiller's historical tragedies, the opposition between realism and idealism takes the form of a collision between politics and morality. In this sense, Elisabeth in *Maria Stuart* is also an embodiment of political realism who relies on omission to achieve an end that she cannot control in all its implications. Schiller stages the failure of both the realist and the idealist in their attempts to influence the unstoppable concatenation of historical events. In the late tragedies, the traditional scheme of the conflict between duty and inclination, which recurs in the theoretical writings and accords with the Kantian setting of the pathetic sublime, is replaced by different types of collision, which often take the form of a confrontation between opposing legal instances. This is the case of the contrast between Ottavio Piccolomini and Wallenstein, in which the reasons for the preservation of the balance guaranteed by the traditional political order, argued by Ottavio, are opposed to the demands for the cessation of the destruction of war, of which Wallenstein is the bearer, albeit for reasons of personal power.

In *Über das Erhabene*, Schiller reformulates the opposition idealism-realism, relating it directly to the tragic mechanism. The individual can try to assert his will—he writes—'either *realistically*', when he 'opposes violence with violence, (...) or *idealistically*, when he withdraws from nature and thus, as concerns himself, overcomes the concept of violence'. But since in reality 'the forces of nature can be controlled or diverted only up to a certain point' (GW:5, 793; transl. 194), the will ends up submitting to circumstances. The paradoxically tragic outcome of the idealistic denial of the dependence from reality is its acceptance, as in the case of Max Piccolomini's near-suicide (see Riedel 2007). The late tragedies reflect this metaphysical resignation, which correlates with the abandonment of a finalistic view of history. The enlightened belief in historical progress, which Schiller had adopted since the time of the Jena prologue, albeit tempered by a harsh critique of the effects of civilisation, gave way to the idea that 'the world, as an historical subject matter, is basically nothing but the conflict of natural forces among themselves and with man's freedom' (SW:5, 803; transl. 207). History is nothing more than the account of the defeats that independent reason has suffered at the hands of nature, in which all human emotions must be included' (SW:5, 803; transl. 207).

Instead of a utopian integration of nature into history, Schiller confronts us with an irresolvable antagonism between nature and freedom, a tragic resignation to the possibility that the order that man seeks to trace in the events of universal history will coincide with a rational meaning.

Between Stoicism and Pessimism

In addition to the definition of the structure of the tragic event, the reading of the Aristotelian *Poetics* contributed decisively to Schiller's reflection on Greek tragic models, which in the previous phase had been much less relevant compared to the tragédie classique and Shakespeare. From this comparison, which he considers very productive in terms of the formal organisation of the dramatic text, Schiller nevertheless derives the conviction that there is an unbridgeable cultural gap between the tragic vision of the Greeks and that of the moderns. After a long search for 'a subject for tragedy of the type of *Oedipus Rex*', he had come to the conclusion that the constituent elements of Sophocles' tragedy, above all the function of the oracle, could not be reproduced in a 'less fabulous' age (to Goethe, 2.10.1797; FA: 12, 330–331). The fundamental difference lies in the conception of the modern subject: whereas Oedipus' breaking of the law is predetermined by fate and involuntary, the plays *Wallenstein* and *Maria Stuart* focus on individual responsibility and decision (See Feger 2006). If on the one hand a person manifests himself through his acts (Taten), on the other hand the exercise of the freedom of the will presupposes the moment of decision. To decide means to draw lines of demarcation, to define one's relationship with objectivity, to transform subjective intention into reality. The tragic paradox of the Wallenstein, a leader, a man of action par excellence, is that the precipitation of events towards catastrophe is produced, or at least favoured, by his sudden inability to connect intention and action, in short to decide. In the so-called *Achsenmonolog*, he looks incredulously at the consequences of his ambition, which had led him to enter into negotiations with the Swedish enemy to block the action of the imperial army and establish his own kingdom in Bohemia. Used to coldly calculating his moves and unscrupulously using people, he discovers that he no longer has power over what his will has initiated:

> My deed was mine while it lay in my breast.
> Released from this sure corner oft he heart,
> Ist mother-ground, out into life abroad,
> It belongs to those perfidious powers no
> Mere human hand can never hope to tame
> (*Wallensteins Tod*, I,4; vv.186–191; transl. 157)

There is a Hamletic trait in Wallenstein's soliloquy, but the doubt does not concern the metaphysical nature of things, the moral conscience, but the criteria and assumptions of practical action. In Schiller's tragic universe, self-reflection is always connected to will and action. 'My general, you've forced me to grow up./ Until today I had no need to find/ My path myself or choose my own direction', exclaims Max Piccolomini when he learns of Wallenstein's real intentions, who up to that moment he had believed to coincide with the truth and the right path. The realisation of the centrality of power relations deprives Max of his innocence: 'Now fort he firts time you return me to/ Myself, and I am forced to make a choice/ Between you and the prompting of my heart' (*Wallensteins Tod* II/2, 711–718; transl. 174). Awareness of moral autonomy implies the impossibility of evading the decision, which the idealist Max tragically combines with self-sacrifice, subjecting himself to an abstract conception of moral duty. In *Maria Stuart*, too, the decision, or rather the non-decision, plays a significant role in determining the tragic mechanism. Elizabeth, faced with the decision to execute Mary Stuart's death sentence, as requested by the court and the parliament, chooses not to decide: she signs the sentence, but refuses to give precise orders regarding its delivery, ultimately placing the responsibility for the execution on the officer to whom the document had been entrusted (*Maria Stuart*, IV/11). She thus tries to separate the effect of the action from its intention, rejecting the moral responsibility for the act. In this attempt to evade the judgement of her own conscience, Elisabeth represents the tragic reversal of the ethos of autonomy.

Recent scholarship (Riedel 2007, Neymeyr 2008) has drawn attention to the presence of Stoic elements not only in Schiller's theoretical writings but also in his tragedies.³ The Stoic doctrines with which Schiller had come into contact through Seneca and Cicero and Abel's teaching, centred on the theme of fortitudo animi (Seelenstärke) and the control of emotional states (Alt 2000, I, 108–113), certainly had an influence on Schiller's aesthetic reflection, contributing to the transformation of Kant's dynamic sublime into the practical, that is, pathetic, sublime. The pathetisation of the concept of the sublime in Schiller is in fact connected to the idea that the consciousness of the supersensible is activated by the combination of two factors, the 'lebhafte Vorstellung des Leidens' and the 'Vorstellung des Widestandes gegen das Leiden' (SW. 5, 512). Schiller progressively shifts the axis of the discourse on the sublime from the experience of the supersensible to its representation, so that the pathetic sublime becomes the foundation of a conception of tragedy that in part still looks to classical models of neo-Stoic inspiration such as Corneille's *Cid*, described as 'the masterpiece of tragic theatre' in *Über die tragische Kunst* (SW:5, 380). From the definition of the pathetic sublime follow the two 'fundamental laws' of tragic art, the first being the Darstellung der leidenden Natur and the second the Darstellung der moralischen Selbständigkeit im Leiden (SW:5, 512). Crucially for Schiller, the affirmation of autonomy is aesthetically interesting insofar as it manifests itself through suffering and brings the human being onto the stage in all its complexity.⁴

The above theoretical line is mostly embodied in the first phase of his dramatic practice. In the early works, the Stoic legacy appears especially in the motif of heroic sacrifice. Seneca (as a philosopher) in particular is cited in *Die Räuber* as the spokesman of the doctrine according to which authentic freedom is manifested through contempt for death and the denial of the instinct of self-preservation (*Räuber* III, 2. SW:1, 565 ff.). The reference is couched in ironic overtones, signalling a partial distancing, yet the drama does indeed end with a typically Stoic gesture: a self-sacrifice that is at the same time an affirmation of one's own autonomy. The robber Karl decides to face death by giving himself up to justice to reaffirm the moral order that his criminal deeds had attempted to destroy. The value of the act lies in its voluntariness, and self-sacrifice is nothing other than the affirmation of the individual's freedom of choice.

The principles of Stoic ethics, according to which control of the passions allows human beings 'to meet the reversals of fate with constantia and even to overcome the fear of death' (Neymeyr 2008), are also relevant in the construction of the character of Maria Stuart, the incarnation of the pathetic sublime. From her first scene, in which she exhorts the governess to control her indignation at the deplorable conditions of her captivity, the Queen of Scots expresses

---

³ This aspect had been little considered in the past, with the exception of Max Kommerell (Kommerell, 186f.).
⁴ In this, contrary to Barone's assertion, Schiller's conception does not substantially diverge from the neo-Stoic view of the tragic hero, which does not imply the idea of apatheia in the sense of the absence of passions (s. Barone 303). See on this Neymeyr (2008), 898.

in words and demeanour her refusal to submit to the suffering and humiliation of her status as a prisoner (I,1, vv. 154–156). Sustained by the awareness of having been falsely accused of high treason, Mary ends up showing her inner autonomy and her dignity as queen with the serene acceptance of the inevitable unjust death sentence (Alt 2000: I, 506 ff.).

It would, however, be misleading to assume that there was a constant and unified influence of Stoicism on Schiller's dramatic production. Despite its undoubted relevance for the theoretical definition of the sublime-tragic, this does not mean that this conception is directly applicable to the late tragedies. Indeed, the writings on the sublime, with the exception of *Über das Erhabene*, occupy an intermediate position in the development of Schiller's idea of the tragic, since they express to a great extent an a posteriori reflection on the setting of the early dramas, albeit through the new philosophical instrumentation of Kantianism.[5]

Schiller's 'cryptostoicism', which probably helps to explain his initial lack of interest in Greek tragedy (Ette 2012), takes a back seat precisely when Schiller begins to seriously engage with Greek tragedy through Aristotle. I refer here to the philosophical side of Stoicism. A different issue, which cannot be dealt with here, is Schiller's reception of Seneca's dramatic production, which focuses on the analysis of passions. This was a turning point for Schiller's conception of modern tragic subjectivity. Themes such as the disciplining of the passions and sacrifice become secondary to the configuration of the characters in the late tragedies, and motifs also linked to the Stoic tradition such as suicide become associated with a resigned pessimism (Riedel 2007) and the inability of the characters to dominate unconscious drives.

Exemplary in this sense is the suicide of Don Cesar in *Braut von Messina*. The character's motivations can hardly be traced back to an idealistic affirmation of the individual's moral self-determination (s. Guthke: 2005, 277). After killing his brother, Don Manuel discovers that Beatrice, the girl they both love, is actually their sister. The tragic climax is triggered by the revelation of her identity, which alters the meaning of actions and interpersonal relationships. The discovery of consanguinity does not cancel Don Cesar's passion, but makes it morally abject, opposing an impassable wall to his existential aspirations. He expresses remorse for the act he has carried out only after realising that it makes it impossible for him to obtain Beatrice's love. The dominant feelings are jealousy and an envy that goes beyond death: 'Er lebt in deinem Schmerz ein selig Leben—he says to Beatrice—Ich werde ewig todt sein bei den Todten' (vv. 2813–2814). The motivation for suicide remains morally ambiguous. In fact, if on the one hand he expresses the need for the reconstitution of a moral order doubly distorted by the incestuous character of love passion and by fratricide,

---

[5] Here I follow the thesis of the late elaboration of *Über das Erhabene*, which was published in 1801. Probably begun in 1793, there are numerous elements that suggest a later reworking, not least the revision of the relationship between the tragic and the sublime. On this Zelle (1995), 189 ff.; Pinna (1999), Riedel (2002), Barone (2004), 112 ff.

on the other hand the decisive impulse to commit suicide seems to come from an irrepressible narcissistic impulse. The final part of the play is an analysis à la Racine of the disturbances and deviations of a stratified subjectivity, in which a fundamental role is played by a pre-Freudian vision of the subconscious.

ON MYTH AND HISTORY: THE LAST YEARS

Braut von Messina is probably the most explicitly 'philosophical' of Schiller's late tragedies. Its programmatic and experimental character is underlined in the preface (*Über den Gebrauch des Chors in der Tragödie*), which can be considered the last of Schiller's theoretical writings. The investigation into the intrinsically antithetical structure of personality, on which the action hinges, is only part of the aesthetic project that inspired the composition of the drama, whose formal novelty is represented by the reintroduction of the chorus. Schiller's intention is to test on stage some questions already addressed in his aesthetic essays, such as the function of art in modern culture and the use of symbolic and mythological instruments in artistic representation. The chorus, unusually divided in two parts,[6] is entrusted first of all with the task of re-establishing a connection between the individual sphere, that is, the affections and the related moral conflicts, and the public sphere, characterised by the exercise of power and relations of domination. In modern tragedy, the chorus is necessarily, says Schiller, a 'künstliches Organ', a simulacrum of collectivity through which it is possible to recreate through reflexive mediation the connection between individual interests and collective ethos that in Greek tragedy was given naturally and immediately (SW: 2, 819). This instrument borrowed from classical tragedy serves to place a story with archetypal traits in the perspective of historical change, a dimension, therefore, specifically modern. It is possible that Schiller was reacting to the questions posed by the idealists on the essence of tragedy and the possibilities of the tragic in modernity. It is significant, from this perspective, that the writing of *Braut von Messina* followed Schiller's exchange with Schelling about *Über das Erhabene* (s. Courtine 1990, 99–102). One could say, schematising a little, that this aspect of Schiller's conception of the chorus is a literarily problematic attempt to affirm through tragedy a non-formalistic vision of morality, almost an anticipation of ethics in the Hegelian sense. But the theme of the relationship between individual and community, as well as the historical dimension of the actions of individuals, enters into the construction of the tragic through the mediation of myth, as for example with the ironic reduplication of the motif of the oracle. In many ways, a similar mythologisation of history is to be found in *Wilhelm Tell* and *Die Jungfrau von Orléans*.

Secondly, the chorus serves to establish a distance from ordinary experience and to undermine the illusion of naturalness of what takes place on stage. The

---

[6] The two parts of the chorus are respectively the armed followers of the two enemy brothers and the inhabitants of Messina. In the last part of the play, however, they appear as a whole.

un-actual solemnity of choral singing brings the abstract dimension of space and theatrical action to the fore, since in order to grasp 'the spirit of nature', poetry must leave the terrain of natural reality, the domain of both the intellect and the senses. Nietzsche wrote in the *Birth of Tragedy*, commenting sympathetically on the considerations on the chorus expressed in the Preface to the *Braut*, that Schiller 'considered it a living wall that tragedy draws around itself, in order to shut itself off in purity from the real world and to preserve its ideal ground and its poetic freedom'. In this way, Schiller struggles 'against the common concept of the natural, against the illusion commonly demanded of dramatic poetry' (Nietzsche 1999, 38).

The instance of denaturalisation (of which the modern chorus is supposed to be an instrument) can be seen as the application to tragedy of the conception of aesthetic appearance (ästhetischer Schein) set forth in the 26th Letter on Aesthetic Education. Here Schiller shifts his attention to the theory of reception, recalling the Aristotelian doctrine of catharsis: 'The Chorus thus *purifies* tragic poetry, while separating reflection from the action, and by means of this separation, supplies reflection with poetical power' (SW:2, 821; transl. 155). But beyond the controversial function of the chorus, the fundamental issue for Schiller is the relevance of the cognitive dimension of the effect of tragic representation. The emotional response to the events depicted, compassion and fear, must be purified by reflection in order for the 'energetic beauty' of tragedy to achieve its purpose of placing the individual in a condition of freedom from the objective constraints of reality.

The return to dramatic writing after the 'philosophical pause' was in fact understood by Schiller as the verification of the possibility of art to operate in the post-revolutionary social context (Barnouw 1972). The critical function of drama is based on this combination of emotional shock and distancing. In a letter to Johann Wilhelm Süvern, regarding the specifically modern character of *Wallenstein*, Schiller states: 'Our tragedies would be obliged to struggle against the powerlessness, the flabbiness, the characterlessness of the time, against our base way of thinking; our tragedy must show force and character, it must shake our mind and elevate it, not relax it. Beauty is for a happy generation, but an unhappy one must be moved by the sublime' (to Suvern, 26.06.1800).

References

Alt, Peter-André 2000. *Schiller. Eine Biographie*. I, II. München: Beck.
Ayrault, Roger. 1948. Schiller et Montesquieu, *Etudes germaniques* 3: 233-240
Barone, Paul. 2004. *Schiller und die Tradition des Erhabenen*. Berlin: E. Schmidt.
Barnouw. Jeffrey. 1972. Das Problem der 'Aktion' und Wallenstein,. *Jahrbuch der deutschen Schillergesellschaft* 16: 330-408.
Barnouw, Jeffrey. 1977. *Über den Realismus Wallensteins und Schillers. Mit einer Kritik der Hegelschen Deutung*, in: F. Heuer, W. Keller (hg), *Schillers Wallenstein*, Darmstadt, WBG 1977, 396-421.

Beiser, Frederick. 2005. *Schiller as Philosopher. A Re-Examination.* Oxford. Clarendon Press.
Bresky, Dushan. 1961. Schiller's Dept to Montesquieu and Adam Ferguson. *Comparative Literature* 13, 239-253.
Cassirer, Ernst. 2004. *Schiller und Shaftesbury*, in E. C., *Gesammelte Werke*, ed. B. Recki, Hamburg: Meiner 2004, vol. XVIII, 333-352.
Courtine, Jean François. 1990. Tragédie et sublimité. L'interprétation spéculative de l'OEdipe Roi au seuil de l'idéalisme allemand. In: Id., *Extase de la raison. Essais*, 75-111. Paris: Galilée.
Ette, Wolfram. 2011, Wallenstein. Das Drama der Geschichte. *Deutsche Vierteljahrsschrift für Literaturwissenschaft und Geistesgeschichte* 85: 30-46.
Ette, Wolfram. 2012. Die Tragödie als Form philosophischer Selbsterkenntnis. In: *Handbuch Literatur und Philosophie*, ed. Hans Feger, 87 – 122. Stuttgart / Weimar: J. B. Metzler.
Falduto, Antonino. 2021. One more time on the alleged repugnance of Kant's ethics? Schiller's *Kallias letters* and the entirety of the human being. In *European Journal of Philosophy* 29(4): 795–810
Feger, Hans. 2006. Die Entdeckung der modernen Tragödie. Wallenstein – Die Entscheidung. In: *Friedrich Schiller. Die Realität des Idealisten*, ed. Hans Feger, 289-286. Heidelberg: Winter.
Feger, Hans. 2007. Erhaben ist das Tragische. Kant-Schiller-Schelling. In: *Positive Dialektik. Hoffnungsvolle Momente in der deutschen Kultur*, ed. Jost Hermand, 49-80. Oxford-Bern-Berlin: Peter Lang.
Godel, Rainer. 2015. Gewissen und Gewissheit in Friedrich Schillers Dramatik. In: *Gewissen. Interdisziplinäre Perspektiven auf das 18. Jahrhundert*, ed. Simon Bunke and Katharina Mihailova, 223-236. Würzburg: Königshausen & Neumann.
Guthke, Karl. 2005. *Schillers Dramen. Idealismus und Skepsis*, Tübingen: Francke.
Hinderer, Walter. 2003. Friedrich Schiller und die empirische Seelenlehre. Bemerkungen über die Funktion des Traumes und das "System der dunklen Ideen". *Jahrbuch der deutschen Schillergesellschaft* 47:187-213.
Kommerell, Max. 1956. *Schiller als Gestalter des handelnden Menschen.* In: id. *Geist und Buchstabe der Dichtung*, 132-174. Frankfurt a. M.: Klostermann.
Macor, Anna Laura 2011. Die Moralphilosophie des Jungen Schiller. Ein 'Kantianer ante litteram', in: *Who is this Schiller now? Essays on His Reception and Significance*, ed. Jeffrey L. High, Nicholas Martin and Norbert Oellers, 99-115. Rochester: Camden House.
Maier, Albert. 1987. Der Zuschauer am Zügel. Die ästhetische Vermittlung des Republikanismus in Schillers Die Verschwörung des Fiesko zu Genua. *Jahrbuch der deutschen Schillergesellschaft* 31: 117-136
Malsch, Wilfried. 1988. *Moral und Politik in Schillers "Don Karlos"*. In: *Verantwortung und Utopie. Zur Literatur der Goehezeit*, ed. Wolfgang Wittkowski, 238-250. Tübingen, Niemeyer.
Neymeyr, Barbara. 2008. "Seelenstärke" und Gemütsfreiheit". Stoisches Ethos in Schillers ästhetischen Schriften und in seinem Drama Maria Stuart, *Jahrbuch der deutschen Schillergesellschaft* 52: 897-825.
Nietzsche, Friedrich. 1999. *The Birth of Tragedy and other Writings*, Cambridge: Cambridge University Press.

Nilges, Yvonne. 2011. Schiller und die Demokratie. In *Who is this Schiller now? Essays on His Reception and Significance*, ed. Jeffrey L. High, Nicholas Martin and Norbert Oellers, 205-216. Rochester: Camden House.
Pinna, Giovanna. 1999. Il sublime in scena. Sulla teoria schilleriana della tragedia. *Strumenti critici* 16: 175-203.
Reinhardt, Hartmut. 1976. Schillers Wallenstein und Aristoteles. *Jahrbuch der deutschen Schillergesellschaft* 20: 268-337.
Riedel, Wolfgang. 1985. *Die Anthropologie des jungen Schiller*, Würzburg: Königshausen & Neumann.
Riedel, Wolfgang. 1993. Die Aufklärung und das Unbewußte. Die Inversionen des Franz Moor. *Jahrbuch der deutschen Schillergesellschaft* 37: 198-220.
Riedel, Wolfgang. 2002. "Weltgeschichte ein erhabenes Objekt". Zur Modernität von Schillers Geschichtdenkens. In: *Prägnanter Moment. Studien zur deutschen Literatur der Aufklärung und Klassik*. Festschrift für Hans-Jürgen Schings, ed. Peter-André Alt et al., 193-214. Würzburg: Könighausen & Neumann.
Riedel, Wolfgang. 2007. Die Freiheit und der Tod. Grenzphänomene idealistischer Theoriebildung beim späten Schiller. In *Schiller. Der unterschätze Theoretiker*, ed. Georg Bollenbeck and Lothar Ehrlich, 59-71. Weimar: Böhlau.
Sautermeister, Georg. 1991."Die Seele bei ihrer geheimsten Operation ertappen". Unbotmäßiges zu den Brüdern Moor in Schillers *Räubern*. In: *Kulturelles Erbe zwischen Tradition und Avantgarde*, ed. Thomas Metscher and Christian Marzahn, 311-340. Köln-Weimar-Wien: Böhlau.
Schings, Hans-Jürgen. 1980. Philosophie der Liebe und Tragödie des Universalhasses. "Die Räuber" im Kontext von Schillers Jugendphilosophie. *Jahrbuch des Wiener Goethe-Vereins* 84: 71-95.
Stachel, Thomas. 2011. 'Ein unbestechliches Gefühl für Recht und Unrecht. Schiller und der Moral Sense. In: *Schiller im philosophischen Kontext*, ed. Cordula Burtscher and Markus Hien, 29-39. Würzburg: Königshausen & Neumann.
Zelle, C. 1995. *Die doppelte Ästhetik der Moderne. Revisionen des Schönen von Kant bis Nietzsche*.Stuttgart: Metzler.

Translations

The Robbers, transl. Francis Lamport. London: Penguin 1980.
Don Carlos and Mary Stuart, transl. With notes by Hilary Collier Si-Quia, with an Introduction by Lesley Sharpe. Oxford-New York: Oxford University Press 1996
Wallenstein: A Dramatic Poem. Translated by Flora Kimmich. Open Book Publishers 2017.
Naive and Sentimental Poetry- On the Sublime, transl. by Julius A. Elias. New York: Ungar 1966.
Über den Gebrauch des Chors in der Tragödie. On the Use of the Chorus in Tragedy, transl. by Guido Avezzù, with an Introduction by Stephen Halliwell. *Skenè. Journal of Theatre and Drama Studies* 1:2015, 135–166.

CHAPTER 24

The Role of Philosophy in Schiller's Poetry

Matthew Feminella

INTRODUCTION

From his poignant allegory of the Belt of Venus in *On Grace and Dignity*, to his use of figures from Greek mythology to examine the Kantian sublime, Schiller writes philosophy with a poet's sensibility. Yet the relationship between philosophy and poetry in Schiller's writing hardly flows in a single direction. Just as his philosophy exhibits an undeniably poetic tone, so too does his poetry bristle with philosophical premises, themes, and references. Often this poetic engagement with philosophy manifests quite explicitly, such as his allusion to Rousseau in "The Words of Faith" ("Die Worte des Glaubens") "Man was created, and man is, *free*, / No matter if born in chains" ("Der Mensch ist frei geschaffen, ist frei / und würd er in Ketten geboren").[1] Other times it manifests as a figurative representation of his own philosophy of history. Schiller's poetry even occasionally muses on the value of doing philosophy altogether.

The ease with which Schiller shifts between writing poetry and philosophy conceals a historically fraught relationship that can be traced back to ancient Greece. Plato's *Republic* condemns literature and poetry as unphilosophical third-rate derivatives of the ideal forms. By contrast, Aristotle in *The Poetics* considers poetry to be more philosophical than historical, since poetry operates according to general principles rather than particularities. Philosophers of antiquity frequently turned to poetic verse to expound philosophical themes.

[1] All translations of Schiller's poetry are my own prose translations unless otherwise noted.

M. Feminella (✉)
University of Alabama, Tuscaloosa, AL, USA
e-mail: mfeminella@ua.edu

Lucretius provides one of the more comprehensive accounts of Epicureanism in *On the Nature of Things*, a poem he composed in dactylic hexameter, the standard verse for epics. In Schiller's century, poets such as Alexander Pope and Albrecht von Haller frequently turned to meter as a medium for philosophical thought. In *Pope a Metaphysician*, Gotthold Ephraim Lessing and Moses Mendelssohn sought to uncouple what they viewed as the two distinct enterprises of poetry and philosophy. While the philosopher strives for clarity and precision and works systematically, the poet eschews such a slavish adherence to the rules of order and utilizes aesthetic means to create an emotional resonance in the reader. Lucretius' *On the Nature of Things* is indeed philosophy, but it is no poem (Lessing 1985). According to this line of thought, since poetry and philosophy are two distinct areas of discourse with their own rules, any attempt to justify judging a poem by a philosophical standard and vice versa would prove to be a fruitless endeavor.

What does it mean to view Schiller's poetry in its philosophical context? Is it to demonstrate the process by which Schiller transforms philosophical concepts into verse? Or is it to reveal how Schiller's poetry intervenes in his own theoretical writings as well as in contemporary philosophical debates? The following will examine a selection of his poetic works regarding its broad philosophical context. Though it is no surprise that Schiller would gravitate toward aesthetics considering his vocation as poet and playwright, one prominent theme that emerges from much of this analysis is how Schiller's poetry grapples with the role of art and aesthetics in light of the dominant rationalizing tendencies of the Enlightenment. His poetry offers a reflection on how the recognition of aesthetic modes of engagement can restore harmony in an alienated world.

Ode to Joy

Published in 1786 in the journal *Thalia*, "Ode to Joy" ("An die Freude") teems with unrestrained enthusiasm in which the world's failings and contradictions are surmounted through Joy or *Freude*. Joy appears as a ubiquitous and somewhat mysterious metaphysical force with multiple manifestations, most notably the principle of harmony. Only a few years prior, Schiller depicted in his "On the Contemporary German Theater" ("Über das gegenwärtige teutsche Theater") the state of the German theater as beset with polarizing oppositions in desperate need of reconciliation. Though a specific concern for the theater is absent from "Ode to Joy," the same tendency to harmonize oppositions or discrepancies persists. When Joy enters the realm of the prevailing social hierarchy, it abolishes forms of stratification and injustices. Not only does Joy eliminate past transgressions and obligations as "Our book of debts is nullified" and "all sinners shall be forgiven" ("Unser Schuldbuch sei vernichtet"; "Allen Sündern soll vergeben") (FA 1:412–413), but it also engenders a radical egalitarianism in which "beggars become the brothers of princes" ("Bettler werden Fürstenbrüder") (FA 1:410). Manifestations of Joy's power of reconciliation also extend to disparate planes of existence, as it possesses the ability to bridge the gulf between heaven and earth. Previous transcendent realms become accessible as Joy enables the search for the creator—"Seek him over the canopy of stars / Above the stars he must dwell" ("Such ihn über Sternenzelt / Über Sternen muss er wohnen") (FA 1:411)—with the underworld meeting the same fate as the book of debt as "hell no longer exists" ("die Hölle nicht mehr sein") (FA 1:413). This harmonization continues on the level of disparate religious traditions. The lyrical voice freely mixes imagery from ancient Greek mythology—his apostrophe Joy is a "Daughter of Elysium" ("Tochter aus Elisium") (FA 1:410)—and the Judeo-Christian tradition "choir of angels" ("Chor der Engel") (FA 1:411). Although the theme of unity figures prominently, the use of gendered language reveals that not all are included in this union. Joy creates a universal brotherhood in which figures of femininity are considered either a prize to be enjoyed—"whoever wins a fair woman" ("wer ein holdes Weib errungen) (FA 1:410)—or as a mediating force between Joy and its recipients "All beings imbibe Joy / on the breasts of nature" ("Freude trinken alle Wesen / an den Brüsten der Natur") (FA 1:410).

At the same time that it unites opposites, Joy permeates the universe as an invisible force of movement. "Ode to Joy" issues a critique of a mechanistic Enlightenment understanding of the world as operating according to the principles of physics. While the world may appear as an immense "world clock" ("Weltenuhr") (FA 1:411), in reality the hand of Joy originates the clock's motion. Joy is both an inexplicable and hidden driving force in a mechanistic model and also a force of attraction in an organic one, in which "it lures flowers from their seeds" ("Blumen lockt sie aus den Keimen") (FA 1:411). Joy's ubiquitous presence is also demonstrated beyond the confines of the terrestrial: it is responsible for the movement of the sun and even yet to be discovered planetary bodies in space. Such a conceptualization of physical motion would appear to stand somewhat at odds with the principle of harmony that is exhibited by Joy. While Joy as harmony unites otherwise distinct realms, it simultaneously highlights the great discrepancy between its boundless magic and the limitations of technology to gain access to undiscovered realms: "it rolls spheres into spaces / which the seer's tube does not know" ("Sphären rollt sie in den Räumen, / die des Sehers Rohr nicht kennt!) (FA 1:411). While Joy can make possible a union with the Godhead, grasping the vast expanse of the heavens appears for the moment out of reach for humanity.

The poem represents an early manifestation of the tripartite structure of history that undergirds much of Schiller's poetry and philosophy. In this structure, an ideal world order of the past is hypothesized that stands in contrast with a fallen present and gestures to the promise of a restoration of the lost ideal. "Your magic binds again / what the sword of fashion split" ("Deine Zauber binden wieder, / Was der Mode Schwert geteilt") (FA 1:410) presupposes a historical rupture that Schiller would later in his *Aesthetic Education of Man* attribute to the emergence of culture (*Kultur*). In envisioning this radical break with the past, "Ode to Joy" simultaneously reveals the artificial accretions embedded in the current system as well as explores the process for reconstituting the previous order.

By 1800, Schiller would come to distance himself from "Ode to Joy," referring to it in a letter to Christian Gottfried Körner as a "a bad poem" ("ein schlechtes Gedicht") that "denotes a stage of education, which I absolutely had to leave behind in order to create something respectable" ("bezeichnet eine Stufe der Bildung, die ich durchaus hinter mir lassen mußte um etwas ordentliches hervorzubringen.") (FA 12:538). As he regarded the work as a mark of his immaturity, Schiller would only come to recognize that its value resides in its popularity as a folk poem ("Volksgedicht") (FA 12:538). The poem would later undergo revisions for the edition of his collected poetry. Alterations made do not so much reflect his philosophical period of the 1790s, but rather political events that transpired between the two publications. Though far from calling for a revolution of the existing political order, the poem's original text would have been read quite differently in the aftermath of the French Revolution. Some of the alterations made when it was published again veer away from the specific political implications of its egalitarian language of the first ("Bettler werden Fürstenbrüder" becomes "Alle Menschen werden Brüder") (FA 1:248). The final stanzas were also removed that would evoke the abuses of the prevailing ruling authority, such as "Salvation from the tyrant's chains" ("Rettung von Tirannenketten") (FA 1:413). Despite Schiller's own repudiation of its merits, it remains one of his most enduring poems, as Beethoven incorporated the later version into his Ninth Symphony.

The Gods of Greece

Published originally in Wieland's *Der Teutsche Merkur* in 1788, Schiller's "The Gods of Greece" ("Die Götter Griechenlandes") breaks with the relentless optimism of "Ode to Joy" and instead strikes an elegiac tone that accentuates the divergence between an idealized world of Greek mythology and the modern human predicament. Through a veritable flood of figures from Greek mythology, many of which would come across as obscure for even an educated reader, the poem envisions a lost era of the past when the world of Greek gods, rather than inhabiting a separate space, cohabitated with the imminent realm of humanity. From "Tantalus' daughter remains silent in this stone" ("Tantals Tochter schweigt in diesem Stein") (FA 1:286) to "Philomela's pain in this grove" ("Philomelens Schmerz in diesem Hain") (FA 1:286), Greek divinities imbued the surrounding landscape with their sublime presence. The conventional dichotomy between immanence and transcendence, sacred and profane, divine and human, had little meaning in this idealized past, "since the gods were still more human / and humans more divine" ("Da die Götter menschlicher noch waren, / Waren Menschen göttlicher") (FA 1:291). Such a division occurs with the advent of modernity, when the gods departed a world that no longer has use for them ("unnütz einer Welt") (FA 1:290) and can maintain its own integrity ("Sich durch eignes Schweben hält) (FA 1:290). Understanding the Greek gods as existing in the past and in the present only as a memory gives rise to the lyrical speaker's longing for the irretrievable past. The divergence between the lost world of Greek mythology and modern humanity is expressed precisely in the modern reinterpretation of the sun:

> Where now, as our wise men say,
> Only a fireball soullessly turns,
> Back then did Helios steer his golden chariot
> In silent majesty
> Wo jetzt nur, wie unsre Weisen sagen
> Seelenlos ein Feuerball sich dreht,
> Lenkte damals seinen goldnen Wagen
> Helios in stiller Majestät (FA 1:286)

The disparity between the awe-inspiring grandeur of the sun's enchanted past and a present that conceptualizes it merely according to its material properties accentuates the sense of loss. In highlighting the division between the idealized past and modern alienated state, the lyrical speaker displays strong criticism of the perceived Enlightenment tendency to establish the truth by reducing phenomena to their component parts. The figure of the modern expert—often held as an object of ridicule in Schiller's poetry—has evacuated the celestial bodies of their sense of wonder and sublimity leading to an irredeemable abasement. Rather than science providing human beings with a deeper connection to the objects of its inquiry, "The Gods of Greece" reveals that attempts by science to provide clarity and truth invariably result in the estrangement between the human and the celestial.

"The Gods of Greece" disputes not only the alleged achievements of science, which has disenchanted the miracles of the heavens, rendering them lifeless hunks of matter, but in what would become the poem's most controversial aspect, Christianity as well. Christianity provides no suitable substitute for the loss of the mythopoetic understanding of the world, since in the modern world the divine fails to summon the sense of wonder and harmony: "No divinity reveals itself to my view" ("Keine Gottheit zeigt sich meinem Blick") (FA 1:290). Allusions of Christianity as a supplanter of the poetic world of the Greek gods become particularly salient in the following passage:

> Back then no gruesome skeleton
> Approached the bed of the dying.
> A kiss took the final life from the lips,
> Silent and sad did the spirit lower
> His torch
> Damals trat kein gräßliches Gerippe
> Vor das Bett des Sterbenden. Ein Kuß
> Nahm das letzte Leben von der Lippe,
> Still und traurig senkt' ein Genius
> Seine Fackel

As in the case of the soulless sun, the lyrical speaker likens the departure of the gods to the stark contrast between life and death. In this case, even death itself has been robbed of any pleasantries of the kiss and the extinguished torch and replaced with a dreadful skeleton to signify death. The lyrical speaker highlights how the new Christian paradigm works in metaphors that, instead of aestheticizing the experience of death, thereby rendering it comfortable, only exacerbate its horrors and the emptiness of the world.

Schiller's mourning of the lost world of the Greeks simultaneously laments what can be read as the loss of prominence of the poet in interpreting the world, a theme that would routinely occur in his later poetry. The poet's task of aestheticizing the world, in which the "artistic overlay of poetry" ("der Dichtkunst malerische Hülle") (FA 1:285) is more vital than the truth it conceals, is a theme that would be often repeated in his subsequent poetry. "The Gods of Greece" thus conceptualizes a unique role for the poet—or rather the artist in general, in which the artistic works of Pindar the poet, Arion the musician, and Phidias the sculptor served as conduits that harmonize the immanent and transcendent realms. For modernity, it is only in the poet's "fairyland of song" ("in dem Feenland der Lieder") (FA 1:290) that the traces of this beautiful world remain.

Schiller was far from the first to grapple with the notion of a modernity alienated from the ancient Greek mode of engaging with the world. Writing decades earlier, Johann Joachim Winkelmann and more contemporary for Schiller, Ludwig Ferdinand Huber, exerted an influence on him in this regard (Alt 2000). Through the undisputed idealization of ancient Greece that pervades through so much of his poetry, only the Greek gods and a few select artists appear to inhabit this space. Ancient Greece as the simultaneous birthplace of Western philosophy finds no such ideal depiction. It remains an open question whether the lyrical speaker includes the Greek philosophical tradition as a culprit in the predicament of modernity, as Nietzsche would come to explore in the figure of Socrates in *The Birth of Tragedy*. Although mapping a strict historical framework onto the poem would be incongruent with its own proclivity to idealize the past, it is fitting that the three artists mentioned, Pindar, Arion, and Phidias, had passed away long before the ascent of Plato and Aristotle.

After its publication, "The Gods of Greece" was heavily criticized for its alleged irreverent attitude toward Christianity and celebration of paganism. This unexpected reception effectively prompted Schiller to reevaluate his understanding of the relationship between art and the world. Dismayed at the fact that his poem was subject to societal expectations, Schiller wrote to Körner, "I am convinced that every work of art is only accountable to itself, that is its own rule of beauty, and is subject to no other demand" ("ich bin überzeugt, daß jedes Kunstwerk nur sich selbst d.h. seiner eigenen Schönheitsregel Rechenschaft geben darf, und keiner andern Foderung unterworfen ist") (FA 12:363). It is here that scholars have noted that Schiller articulates a notion that would structure so much of his poetry and thought for the remainder of his life: aesthetic autonomy (Beiser 2005). Increasingly, would Schiller distance himself from claims that orient work of art in relation to the world or a means to some other societal end, for which it would be evaluated for a variety of reasons external to it, such as its monetary or pedagogical value, or in the case of Schiller's "The Gods of Greece," its religious implications. Rather, Schiller began to view the work of art as an end in itself subject to its own aesthetic rules.

Just as "Ode to Joy" underwent substantial revisions to remove some of its more scandalous content, so too did "The Gods of Greece" appear in a revised version that purged the offending passages. The second version reflects a shift to aesthetic matters, with the concept of beauty taking on a more prominent role—perhaps not surprising considering that the revision of "The Gods of Greece" took place simultaneously with the writing of the *Kalliasbriefe*. Schiller however would not completely repudiate the original version as he would with "Ode to Joy." In the second volume of his collected poetry, he would reprint the original version "for the friends of the first edition" ("Für die Freunde der ersten Ausgabe") (FA 1:285).

The Artists

If Schiller's experience with the reception of "The Gods of Greece" induced him to reconceptualize his notion of the work of art in favor of the concept of aesthetic autonomy, then "The Artists" represents its poetic articulation. Schiller's role as a philosopher and poet cannot be divorced from his role as a historian, as his poetry often unveils a philosophy of history. "The Artists" can be described as an encomium to the role art plays in human history. Such cultural histories were a well-established practice by Enlightenment thinkers Jean-Jacques Rousseau, Johann Gottfried Herder, and Immanuel Kant (Alt 2000). Human beings are born with an aesthetic sensibility which they can cultivate into art. The poem notes the tendency to forget art in light of other qualities, such as the diligence and skill that the lowly bee and worm display with greater expertise, but as the lyrical speaker observes "Art, O human, you alone possess" ("Die Kunst, O Mensch, hast du allein") (FA 1:208). In its apology for the role of the artist, the poem takes aim at captivating notions—the most conspicuous being reason itself—that compete for human attention.

> What first, after thousands of years passed,
> Aged reason invented,
> Lay in the symbol of Beauty and Grandeur
> Already revealed to the child-like understanding
> Its sweet image tells us to love virtue,
> A tender sense opposes vice,
> Before even a Solon wrote the law
> The faint blossoming slowly carried on.
> Before the daring concept of infinite space
> Stood before the thinker's mind,

> Who gazed up to the starry stage,
> And had already felt its presence?
> Was erst, nachdem Jahrtausende verflossen,
> Die alternde Vernunft erfand,
> Lag im Symbol des Schönen und des Großen
> Voraus geoffenbart dem kindischen Verstand.
> Ihr holdes Bild hieß uns die Tugend lieben,
> Ein zarter Sinn hat vor dem Laster sich gesträubt,
> Eh noch ein Solon das Gesetz geschrieben,
> Das matte Blüten langsam treibt.
> Eh vor des Denkers Geist der kühne
> Begriff des ew'gen Raumes stand,
> Wer sah hinauf zur Sternenbühne,
> Der ihn nicht ahndend schon empfand? (FA 1:208–209)

Some themes present here easily find resonance with "The Gods of Greece." Two moments in human history are similarly contrasted, with the earlier—oriented on art—considered in a privileged position in relation to the latter—oriented on reason. Yet, as a whole "The Gods of Greece" represents a static worldview: There exists no prospect for a return to the mythopoetic past, no promise of a future containing untold contingencies. "The Artists," on the other hand, is grounded in the Enlightenment view of history predicated on progress, in which the continual unfolding of human history leaves open the possibility of a return to the unity of art and truth. Furthermore, unlike in "The Gods of Greece," reason does not represent a threat to the enchanted world that leaves a variety of lifeless objects in its wake. Reason, later synonymous in the poem with the spirit of scientific inquiry, is more of a redundancy, merely confirming what the human aesthetic sensibility already knew, as in the case of science postulating the infinite of space only after it was already intuited in an aesthetic sense. The poetic diction—the heavens conceived as a "stage" on which the stars are observed—further attests to this primacy of art and superfluousness of reason. Beauty is presented here as not only obviating much of scientific inquiry but also erecting a framework for ethical interaction that renders externally mandated behavior—Solon's legislative contributions in Athens—unnecessary as it produces internally the desire to adhere to virtue and avoid vice. Though making a case for beauty through highlighting its capacity to morally educate would appear to contravene the notion of aesthetic autonomy that was beginning to take hold of Schiller's thought, the spirit of the message claims that beauty and art are at least equal to those other areas of discourse which they are often subjected to.

Within Schiller's philosophy of history, there is a tragic moment when artists find themselves usurped by a newcomer: the arrival of science and the modern world. Science arrives with "new drives" ("neuen Trieben") that strive to measure and standardize nature according to human weights "menschlichen Gewichten" (FA 1:215). "The Artists" alludes to the coming of the Enlightenment: "There one saw millions of chains fall / and instead of slaves spoke now of human rights" ("Da sah man Millionen Ketten fallen / Und über Sklaven sprach jetzt Menschenrecht") (FA 1:218). The infatuation with the Enlightenment features as its protagonist the figure of the "scientist" ("Forscher"), who "with a quick hand reaches towards the crown" ("mit rascher Hand schon nach der Krone greift") (FA 1:218). While preceding science and culture and even enabling its development, art is superseded by science, relinquishing its crown and being permitted to dwell in "the position of first slave" ("den ersten Sklavenplatz") (FA 1:218) under the hegemony of science. The irony of witnessing the liberation of peoples only for art itself to be reduced to a servant of the spirit of scientific inquiry serves as a further apology for the burgeoning concept of aesthetic autonomy.

The ascendency of science appears as less of an agonizing defeat and more of a temporary setback. In contrast to "The Gods of Greece," in which a reconciliation between the mythopoetic realm of the Greek gods and modern scientific inquiry appears out of reach, "The Artists" ends with a more optimistic and didactic message for the modern artist not to permit the Enlightenment's allure to take hold and let one forget art's foundational contribution to the progress of human history (Malles 1996). The lyrical speaker addresses the role of the artist to not only reclaim its lost position but also restore the preexisting harmony between the two. Beauty for the poetic speaker originally provided the exclusive access to the "land of knowledge" ("der Erkenntnis Land") (FA 1:208), and one of the recurring themes in "The Artists" is that beauty and truth/knowledge are not necessary antagonisms but rather ought to work in tandem: "What we experience here as beauty / will one day approach us as truth" ("Was wir als Schönheit hier empfunden, / Wird einst als Wahrheit uns entgegen gehn") (FA 1:209).

Such concerns about the integrity of the work of art are also bound up in the genesis of "The Artists" itself. Readers of early drafts such as Wieland and Körner noted that the poem resembled more versified philosophy than true poetry. While the philosophical poem could boast of a long-established tradition in the eighteenth century through such luminaries as Alexander Pope and Albrecht von Haller, the suggestion that poetical elements of "The Artists" would come secondary to the delivery of its philosophical content is at odds with the very message of the poem: art as an equal and independent partner to reason. Just as the "The Artists" envisions a future in which art will be recognized once again as the purveyor of truth, so too did Schiller seek to weave the poetic aspects and philosophical content so as to give the poetic qualities of "The Artist" the upper hand. August Wilhelm Schlegel would later defend the poetic content of "The Artists." It makes little sense to pose the question "did it really happen that way?" ("ist das auch wirklich so geschehen?") to a poem that strives not to come to terms with the facts of history, but instead has the objective of idealizing them (Schlegel 1790). If one were to follow Schlegel and consider idealism to be the hallmark justification of poetry, one wonders whether the inverse argument would hold true for Schiller's theoretical writings. If commitment to idealism thwarts the argument of versified philosophy, are his theoretical writings to be considered a prose version of his poetry?

The beginning of Schiller's so-called philosophical period is usually marked after the publication of "The Artists" when he set aside writing poetry in favor of a philosophical study. During his six-year hiatus from poetry, Schiller engaged extensively with Kantian philosophy and published his great aesthetic treatises: *On Grace and Dignity*, *On the Aesthetic Education of Man*, and *On Naïve and Sentimental Poetry*. It is sensible to question the category of a "philosophical period" when applied exclusively to the first half of the 1790s, as doing so would misrepresent the high degree of continuity in regard to philosophical content present in both his theoretical texts and his poetry in the late 1780s. Schiller's commitment to aesthetic autonomy was born out of his poetic engagement in works such as "The Gods of Greece" and "The Artists" well before he read Kant's *Critique of Judgment* (Beiser 2005). Furthermore "The Artists" in many ways provides the blueprint for *The Aesthetic Education of Man* with its construction of a tripartite interpretation of human history.

The Realm of Shadows

The Year 1795 would come to mark the beginning of a productive literary output for Schiller as he returned to writing poetry. Despite this extended lapse, "The Realm of Shadows," published in *Die Horen*, in many ways picks up exactly where he had left off and repeats many of the themes from "The Artists" and "The Gods of Greece." Once again, Schiller employs Greek mythology as figure for the ideal and situates the current state of humanity as falling invariably short of that same ideal, which is the true realm of the aesthetic. "The Realm of Shadows" exhibits a similar antithetical structure as "The Gods of Greece" through its oscillation between "When" ("Wenn") and "But" ("Aber") stanzas that contrasts the opposing realms.

Despite the similarities, "The Realm of Shadows" elaborates on these themes in ways not attended to in his previous poetic period. What was considered temporal unfolding of human history now becomes spatially conceptualized in the dualism between the realm of the senses and the supersensible realm of freedom. In contrast to "The Gods of Greece," in which the gods exist only in the past and in poetry, here they reside on an ideal plane, whether "in the sphere of beauty," "in silent shadowlands of beauty" or "or in the merry regions" ("in der Schönheit Sphäre"; "der Schönheit stille Schattenlande"; "in den heitern Regionen") (FA 1:428). "The Realm of Shadows" furthermore exhibits little sense of nostalgia for a departed world that renders the current state of alienation all the more acute. Longing for the ideal is not depicted as a kind of nostalgic loss—the two realms are not temporally situated, rather spatially—but rather a more general lack: the ideal—as the name indicates—exists as an absolute perfection with none of the disadvantages of the present human condition. Humans are depicted as dualistic beings oscillating between satisfying their material and immaterial aspects, with little apparent hope of reconciling the two. The lyrical speaker professes fantasies of being corporeally unbounded in a realm where time knows no meaning. Forms of violence, pain, competition, and struggle disappear as the realm of the ideal is conceptualized as a place where the dialectic of human existence finds its end in a synthesis in which dissolution of oppositional forces brings drives to rest.

> Dissolved in the tender reciprocity of love,
> United in the free association of grace,
> Rest here the reconciled drives,
> and vanished is the enemy.
> Aufgelöst in zarter Wechselliebe
> In der Anmut freiem Bund vereint,
> Ruhen hier die ausgesöhnten Triebe,
> Und verschwunden ist der Feind. (FA 1:428)

At the same time, "The Realm of Shadows" exhibits traces of Schiller's lengthy exploration of Kant from the previous several years. Though the poem is often interpreted in regards to Kantian aesthetics (Baumanns 2009), the "grandeur of the law" ("Des Gesetzes Größe") (FA 1:428) as a paradigm of virtue calls to mind Kantian moral philosophy—namely the categorical imperative. If this is indeed the case, "The Realm of Shadows" provides a unique interpretation of its implications. For Kant, the categorical imperative provides a means for determining the moral goodness of human action. For all its attempts to abstract human interest from a system of morality predicated on exceptionless obligations, Kant makes it clear that the moral law constitutes a practical and achievable standard. This is demonstrated by several quotidian examples Kant cites in his *Groundwork of the Metaphysics of Morals*, such as the shopkeeper who acts out of self-interest and not out of duty to the moral law when choosing not to exploit his customers' ignorance for financial gain (G 4:397). In contrast, the lyrical speaker of Schiller's poem views the representative of the ideal in the moral law as imposing a standard to which human virtue is unable to live up. The moral law in "The Realm of Shadows" is hardly posed as a goal for which human beings should strive, and there exists a strong sense of futility in light of its lofty principle: "No creature has reached this goal" ("Kein Erschaffner hat dies Ziel erflogen") (FA 1:429).

While Schiller likely had Kant in mind when composing these lines, perhaps a more apt interlocutor is Martin Luther. For Luther in *Freedom of a Christian*, every human invariably falls short of the ideal standard set by the Ten Commandments. Rather than merely informing us of a code of ethics, the Ten Commandments for Luther serve as a reminder of humans' inability to find redemption through their own actions, a realization that should ideally lead them to place their spiritual salvation in the hands of God (Luther 1962). Similarly, in "The Realm of Shadows" there exists no redemption in the imminent realm, which appears to only function as a foil to redirect attention to the ideal realm of freedom. The "dreadful chasm" ("grauenvollen Schlund") of the immanent realm, in which "no anchor finds ground" ("kein Anker findet Grund") (FA 1:429), only becomes traversable when it becomes the filled abyss of the transcendent one.

The contrast between "when" and "but" stanzas ends in a scene of transfiguration with allusions to the myth of Hercules, in which a worldly figure is welcomed into the realm of the ideal. One wonders if during this process the transfigured would express the same nostalgia for the lost past as in the "The Gods of Greece." Would not the loss of the human attributes—such as feeling pain and engaging in competitive struggle—become once again alluring in the dull tranquility of the higher realm? Is it not the earthly deeds of Hercules that receive aesthetic recognition and remembrance, and not his eventual arrival on Mount Olympus? The poem would indicate otherwise. Whereas in the worldly existence "the cheeks of joy become pale" ("der Freude Wange werde bleich") (FA 1:429), the transfigured is greeted by a rosy-cheeked goddess with a goblet, a symbol for liveliness, frivolity, and celebration. Far from a realm of dreary shades, the poem depicts a synthesis of the ideal with the former embodiment. The figure of Hercules as the offspring of both a divine and mortal parent, who ends his mortal existence as a god on Mt. Olympus, is a fitting embodiment of this synthesis.

Unlike many of the poems that underwent revisions before being published in his collected poetry, "The Realm of Shadows"" would also lose its title, first becoming "The Realm of Forms" ("Das Reich der Formen") before settling on "The Ideal and the Life" ("Das Ideal und das Leben"). In a letter to Schiller, Wilhelm von Humboldt alluded to some potential confusion among the readers who would associate the image of shadows with the notion of death. One might add to Humboldt's objection the philosophical tradition of the shadow. Though some interpretations of Schiller's poetry and philosophy have highlighted their Platonic tendencies (Pugh 1996), Plato's own allegory of the cave employs the image of the shadow as a representation of the debased imminent realm. Any careful reading of the "The Realm of Shadows" would reveal, however, the opposite: the image of the shadow is resignified as the realm of the ideal in a reversal of the Platonic dichotomy between the sensible and the supersensible. Schiller's own poetry provides precedent for this unique metaphorical usage. As we have already encountered, the image of the shadow occurs often in "The Artists," bearing the same meaning. Instead of a derivative of reality, in these cases shadows are viewed as a pure form, an abstraction from which an object's idiosyncrasies have been removed. Nevertheless, Schiller evidently felt that this use of shadow in the title was expendable and in the final version it appeared as "The Ideal and the Life."

The Worldly Wise

As discussed, many of Schiller's major works of poetry can be viewed as variations on the theme of lamenting the apparent loss of or disconnect of the modern world from the mythopoetic sensibilities of an idealized Greece, a worldview that holds numerous advantages over the developments of modern thought. Schiller maintained this focus in "The Worldly Wise," yet instead of critiquing the general mode of scientific inquiry or the mechanistic Newtonian paradigm, the poem singles out the alleged achievements of philosophy. Originally published in *Die Horen* in 1795 as "The Deeds of the Philosophers" ("Die Thaten der Philosophen"), "The Worldly Wise" unveils an anxious vision of the world in which philosophers can only offer the world specious axioms on the nature of things. Scarcely a single philosophical discipline escapes the scathing and often ironic rebuke of the lyrical speaker, as the poem runs the gambit through metaphysics, epistemology, moral philosophy, and political philosophy. "The Worldly Wise" begins with attempting to name and thus know the enigmatic binding force holding together an otherwise fragile world on the verge of collapse. Appearing outside the purview of science and thus becoming a focus of metaphysical speculation, such arcane knowledge remains obscure, leading the lyrical speaker to resort to figuratively conceptualizing a world that would "otherwise break into shards" ("sonst in Scherben ging") (NA 1:245), if not for Zeus' intervention.

Attempts by philosophy to provide a better explanation for any number of fundamental principles falls flat. "The Worldly Wise" takes aim at the field of metaphysics for possessing only the ability to confirm the basic intuitions of our senses, telling us what we already knew.

> Yet whoever studies metaphysics
> He knows that whoever burns doesn't freeze
> Knows that wet things are moist
> And that bright things illuminate
> doch wer Metaphysik studiert,
> Der weiß, daß wer verbrennt, nicht friert
> Weiß, daß das Nasse feuchtet
> Und daß das Helle leuchtet. (FA 1:245)

Yet this does not mean that the epistemology promoted by this poem privileges the senses. Both Empiricism and Rationalism, represented in references to John Locke and Rene Descartes, are simultaneously dispensed with for their inability to conceive of "genius and heart" ("Genie und Herz")." As antitheses to founders of two opposing philosophical paradigms, the lyrical speaker positions Homer and his epics. As in "The Artists," "The Worldly Wise" privileges the domain of poetry over the modern intellectual achievement on the basis of two points: the poetic impulse precedes it ("Eh noch Weltweise waren") (FA 1:245) and modern philosophical inquiry not only fails to exceed poetry but also comes up short of matching its exploits ("Was *Lock'* und *Des Cartes* nie gedacht") (FA 1:245). Though the lyrical speaker highlights two philosophers over a 100 years removed from Schiller's own time, the speaker makes no effort to differentiate them from more contemporary philosophical schools, implying that even Kant is subject to these criticisms. When compared to multifaceted achievements of poetry, the notion of progress proves illusory.

Questions regarding epistemology and what holds the world together eventually give way to the realm of politics and ethics. Here again philosophy is satirized for rendering otherwise intuitive and obvious phenomena, such as the strong triumphing over and subjecting the weak, into needlessly complex "systems of morality." Citing two political philosophers, Samuel von Pufendorf and Johann Georg Heinrich Feder, the lyrical voice pronounces the necessity of human interdependence to achieve great goals. In a distilled version of social contract theory, these two philosophers are depicted as attaching great importance to the human ability to collaborate. The capacity to collaborate permitted humans to depart from the state of nature, in which humans had originally acted in isolation like a lone wolf. Issuing such pronouncements from their lecterns, the poem depicts Pufendorf and Feder as just as isolated and out of touch as the life of the lone wolf. As both a seventeenth-century philosopher and a contemporary of Schiller are mocked in the same breath, "The Worldly Wise" once again calls into question the value of philosophical contributions and their ability to build upon one another to achieve progress.

By the poem's end, the lyrical speaker has effectively issued a damning verdict of the contributions of the philosophers. Philosophers deliver superficial observations that fail to reach more fundamental aspects of the inner workings of the universe. Philosophical inquiry has produced nothing that could match the achievements of poetry and human intuition and amounts to a gratuitous complication. In the final lines, the poem shifts from satire to elaborating on the initially mentioned principle that structures the universe.

> But since, what a professor says,
> Doesn't quite get to the center of things,
> So nature practices its maternal duty,
> And ensures, that the chain never breaks,
> And that the bracelet never snaps.
> Till the day when philosophy
> Secures the structure of the world,
> It maintains its machinery
> Through hunger and through love.
> Doch weil, was ein Professor spricht,
> Nicht gleich zu allen dringet,
> So übt Natur die Mutterpflicht,
> Und sorgt, daß nie die Kette bricht,
> Und daß der Reif nie springet.
> Einstweilen bis den Bau der Welt
> Philosophie zusammenhält
> Erhält sie das Getriebe
> Durch Hunger und durch Liebe. (FA 1:246)

As discussed in "The Gods of Greece" and "The Artists," the truth claims of science—despite its ability to illuminate otherwise obscure phenomena—pale in comparison to the enchanted worldview of the poet. This sentiment continues in "The Worldly Wise," though the achievements of philosophy are even further demoted. While science can at least reveal the sun to be a soulless fireball—though the speaker's point is that such knowledge is not worth gaining—the quest of philosophy proves inept at reaching any of its goals. The world of essences remains elusive, especially for philosophical approaches mentioned above. Though the lyrical speaker conceives of a future in which philosophy assumes a role as an organizing force for conceptualizing the universe, this observation should be considered ironic. Philosophy's spotty track record offers little assurance that it could make good on its many promises. Instead, other forces—hunger and love—are granted this faculty. Over a 100 years after its publication, the final lines of "The Worldly Wise" would exert their influence in the realm of Psychoanalysis. Sigmund Freud cites hunger and love as the "two most powerful motive forces" in "Screen Memories" (Freud 1989). Even late in his career, Freud would continue to reference the influence of Schiller—referring to him as a "poet-philosopher"—and his poem on *Civilization and its Discontents*, with hunger and love representing two manifestations of his theory of drives: the former revealed in the self-preservation of the individual, the latter in the preservation of the species (Freud 1989). Thus, while "The Worldly Wise" appears to cast doubt on the value of philosophy, in the use of love and hunger it instead envisions a mode of philosophical engagement that spotlights the importance of passions—particularly those predicated on desire—as motivating forces in human behavior.

The Metaphysician

The final poem considered here does not hold the same place of prominence in Schiller's canon of poetry as the previous ones. Nevertheless, "The Metaphysician" offers a thoughtful reflection on the duties of philosophy through a cautionary tale detailing the folly of a castle-building philosopher. The poem opens with the voice of Hans Metaphysikus gazing from his tower at the "little humans" ("Menschlein") (FA 1:114) living below and toward the heavens for which he strives. This philosopher attributes his elevated position to his art. The story of the metaphysician distracted by the heavens is as old as metaphysics itself, with Thales of Miletus falling into a well because of his preoccupation. Whether Schiller has a particular philosopher in mind as an object of ridicule is left open—possible contemporary candidates could include Kant and Fichte.

Hans Metaphysikus stands next in a long line of disparaged experts in Schiller's poetry, dwelling effectively in a kind of ivory tower. In contrast to "The Worldly Wise," "The Metaphysician" directs its critique less on the enterprise of metaphysics, but rather on the metaphysicians themselves. In the second part of the poem, when the voice of the lyrical speaker emerges (who ultimately has the poems final word), Hans Metaphysikus is described as a "little big man" ("Kleiner großer Mann") (FA 1:114), effectively one who lives in a perpetual state of contradiction. His name itself, Hans Metaphysikus, is based on the same principle of incongruity: the sublimity of the last name juxtaposed with a one-syllabled generic and informal "Hans," thus establishing him as a figure of ridicule. Such a character would not be out of place in a mid-eighteenth Saxon comedy of types (*Sächsische Typenkomödie*), in which a character's name reveals a thinly veiled satire of a particular vice or character flaw.

So much of "The Metaphysician" thematizes the discovery of the correct direction for the philosopher's gaze. Two options present themselves initially. Inclined to look below, Hans Metaphysikus is so far removed from worldly affairs that human beings appear to him only as barely visible abstractions, which itself triggers the reorientation of the metaphysician's gaze to the heavens. The lyrical speaker proposes a third option in which the vision should be instead redirected once again toward the surface of the earth, though not for the sake of the indistinguishable human beings below, but rather for what becomes visible from his state of elevation: the valley.

This poem appears at first to lend itself to readings that highlight unjust disparities in the social hierarchy that were salient in the earliest version "Ode to Joy": a caricatured philosopher who not only casts down a "noble" ("vornehm") (FA 1:114) glance upon the rest of world but also neglects the processes which created his position of prominence in the first place: "*Wovon* ist er? – *worauf* ist er erbauet?") (FA 1:114). As such, it would pose similar questions as Bertolt Brecht's poem "Fragen eines lesenden Arbeiters." Yet the poem does not seek to question whether such towers of distinction should exist, but rather the assumptions of those who inhabit them. Hans Metaphysikus initially conceives of the tower as an escape into the realm of the ideal without much regard for the world he abandons. Yet as the lyrical speaker reveals, the tower's purpose lies in the creation of a dialectical relationship between itself and the valley. The redirection of the philosopher's gaze toward his origins—the valley—enables a mode of aesthetic contemplation that was not possible before the tower's construction. As such, "The Metaphysician" should not be read as a critique of striving for the glorified realm of idealism present in "The Realm of Shadows" in favor of materialist concerns. Rather, the poem operates as a satire revealing that the errors of metaphysics reside in the metaphysicians themselves, whose lofty vision has made them forget their true purpose.

Yet what is this true purpose and how is it made manifest in the dualism between the images of the tower and the valley? A quick digression into another one of Schiller's binary pairs of naïve and sentimental poetry will provide some clarity here. For Schiller, the naïve poet exists harmoniously with his surroundings and without such modern antagonisms as reason versus emotion. This poet needed no recourse to idealism since idealism was his reality. The sentimental poet, however, exists in a state of alienation. Confronted with his irretrievable past, the sentimental poet's task is to elevate his reality to the ideal. In this confrontation, the sentimental poet has at his disposal a novel mode of aesthetic engagement: reflection and self-consciousness, since it is only through alienation from the naïve that it exists as an object of contemplation. In this relationship between the naïve and sentimental, gazing backward in reality leads forward, revealing an object of aesthetic contemplation present in the naïve but inaccessible: the valley. As such, the poem views the role of metaphysics in terms of the larger project of aesthetic education. Playing on the ambiguity in the word "erbauen," both to build and to edify, the tower of the metaphysician is conceptualized as a harbinger of aesthetic education, if only the philosopher would understand its true purpose.

References

Alt, Peter-André. 2000. *Schiller: Leben – Werk – Zeit*. 2. vol. Munich: Beck.
Baumanns, Peter. 2009. "Der Schönheit stille Schattenlande". Zur Topographie in Schillers Gedicht *Das Ideal und das Leben*. Text & Kontext: Jahrbuch für germanistische Literaturforschung in Skandinavien. 31:31–53.
Beiser, Frederick. 2005. *Schiller as Philosopher: A Re-examination*. Oxford: Oxford University Press.
Freud, Sigmund. 1989. The Freud Reader, ed. Peter Gay. New York: W. W. Norton & Company.
Lessing, Gotthold Ephraim. 1985. *Werke und Briefe in zwölf Bänden*, ed. Conrad Wiedemann, Wilfried Barner, and Jürgen Stenzel. Frankfurt: Deutscher Klassiker Verlag.
Luther, Martin. 1962. *Martin Luther: Selections from his Writings*. New York: Anchor Books.
Malles, Hans-Jürgen. 1996. Fortschrittsglaube und Ästhetik. In: *Interpretationen: Gedichte von Friedrich Schiller*. Stuttgart: Reclam.
Pugh, David. 1996. *Dialectic of Love: Platonism in Schiller's Aesthetics*. Montreal: McGill-Queen's University Press.
Schlegel, August Wilhelm. 1790. Ueber die Künstler, ein Gedicht von Schiller. In: *Akademie der schönen Redekünste*. 1: 127–179.

CHAPTER 25

The Role of Philosophy in Schiller's Prose

Matthew Cipa

In this chapter, I consider the ways in which Schiller's literary prose contains resonances of the ideas he would develop in his later, fully fledged philosophical works. I draw on two examples of Schiller's prose. The first is a short story written in 1782, *A Magnanimous Act from Most Recent History* (henceforth referred to as *A Magnanimous Act*), which follows two brothers who are in love with the same woman. The older brother eventually marries the woman, though in her dying moments she reveals that she was actually in love with the younger brother. The second, longer work *The Spiritualist. From the Memoirs of Count von O*** (henceforth referred to as *The Spiritualist*) (1789) follows a first-person recounting by the titular Count von O** of an attempt to convert a German Prince from Protestantism to Catholicism. The work's complex structure and style—involving letters between different characters, long monologues, recollections of characters, and a variety of narrators—matches its wide-ranging concerns involving religion, politics, the individual citizen, and moral aspects of existence. The philosophical concepts I consider are drawn from two major essays from Schiller's philosophical period after 1791—*On Grace and Dignity* and *On the Aesthetic Education of Man in a Series of Letters* (henceforth referred to as *Aesthetic Letters*).

The logic informing my use of literary works from what could be construed as Schiller's "pre-critical" phase in concert with philosophical works from his "critical" period is as follows. Primarily, it rests on my conviction that

M. Cipa (✉)
University of Queensland, St. Lucia, QLD, Australia
e-mail: m.cipa@uq.edu.au

philosophical concepts from Schiller's Kantian phase in the 1790s are in principle already discoverable in the pre-critical prose works. The advantage of proceeding in this way is to suggest the plausibility of an unbroken line in Schiller's intellectual development, notwithstanding the fact, as this volume will also demonstrate, that Schiller's decision to expend effort on the critical philosophy in his mature years represents a distinct phase in his career as a writer. Though the distinctiveness of this Kantian phase speaks in one sense for itself, in another sense it is apt to be overdetermined. In the following, therefore, I argue that it is possible to treat Schiller's Kantian writings in a somewhat un-Kantian way—not in terms of a "pre-critical" before and a "critical" after, as with Kant, but in terms of a wider project that had already been laid out in essential outline before Schiller's decision to gain close acquaintanceship of the critical philosophy.

I begin by situating the present work in the context of the question of free will and Schiller's understanding of aesthetic education, especially as it relates to Schiller's theory of three drives: the form drive, the sense drive, and the play drive. I then turn to consider Schiller's views on duty, inclination, and grace to outline how, according to Schiller, we cannot consider any work of art in isolation from art's necessary role in the formation and development of the citizen and civilised society. I conclude with a discussion of the ideal of art as it relates to what Schiller calls the beautiful soul, and also test the extent to which Schiller's Kantian thought is present in the pre-critical prose works I address in this chapter.

Aesthetic Education, Free Will, and the Three Drives

For Schiller, the importance of our experience of art does not just involve art's ability to offer lessons, moments to reflect on, and periods of leisurely enjoyment. Instead, Schiller holds that in order for individuals (citizens) to move from a state of nature (lacking moral sense) to the state of civility (possessing morality), we must move through an aesthetic condition—it is through art and the experience of it whereby we are educated (morally formed and developed) in line with the aims of civilised society (Mehigan 2020: 297). I will pursue art's connection to society and the individual-as-citizen in the following section. Here, I explore how free will connects to aesthetic education. That is, in what ways does art allow us to freely participate in its educative formation of our moral character, such that we can contribute to the development of civil society? As is often the case, there is an ambiguity in what we are "to do" with art which is sometimes motivated by the content and form of the particular work itself. Rather than undermining the role of aesthetic education, the various ambiguities that form part of an aesthetic experience with an artwork can be crystallised by freely working through and reflecting on them in terms of our own sense of morality with an end to contributing to the development of a civilised society. A prior question, however, can be asked of the conditions that shape the sorts of moral actions that should lead to such an end.

Free will involves our capacity to choose how to act and to enact our agency in the world. This is a matter developed at much greater length and more specificity in the *Aesthetic Letters* than in *On Grace and Dignity* (Roehr 2003: 127). Schiller's approach to free will is made clearer through his theorising of three drives: the sense drive, the form drive, and the play drive. The sense drive "determines human beings as material beings, through sensation…making them subject to temporal change living in a realm of mere facts" (Ibid.: 127–128). The form drive "aims to transform human beings into persons according to the unchangeable laws of their rational nature" (Ibid.: 128). To the play drive, Schiller assigns a mediating role between the other two drives that involves "their [the sense and the form drives] reciprocal relation, their community" (Ibid.: 128). These three drives emphasise a prior, metaphysical concern with human nature especially as it relates to free will.

The theorisation of these drives has important implications for how Schiller conceives of the human person. As mentioned, the sense drive regards the needs and imperatives of the individual as a living, *embodied* existence. Existing within time and with a physical dimension, individuals are susceptible to, and experience change across, the lifespan. As such, the needs for fulfilment revolving around the embodied dimension of our existence will also shift and change in different ways across time. In this domain of our lives, we are driven and impelled, unsurprisingly, by the senses. There is, if not a degree of selfishness, certainly a dimension of self-interest, of preservation. The sense drive can be likened, therefore, to the so-called lower, but nevertheless fundamental, aspects of our existence—its concerns lie with those very things that we require to continue existing.

On the other hand, the form drive involves the attributes of our existence that remain constant in spite of any bodily, physical change wrought by the needs of the sense drive. That is, regardless of any kind of change there is an aspect of human nature—the human *form*—that remains constant despite any physical change through time. Motivated by the principles of reason—of the rational nature of humanity—the form drive needs to be, if not truncated, kept in check at various points so as to ensure and so as not to deny the needs of the embodied and physical existence of the individual.

If there is a constant and perennial tension between the sense and the form drives—and one, as is contended here, that predates Schiller's reference to them in the *Aesthetic Letters*—how are we expected to navigate such a dynamic, to achieve harmony between and across the two? Schiller suggests that developing such balance—ensuring the reciprocity and stability that emerges out of the sensate attention to each drive—is the achievement of the play drive. Rather than subsuming one under the other, the play drive has a mediating role. Instead of being slaves to or dominated by one of the drives, the play drive ensures not just balance, but as mentioned earlier, reciprocity, community, or the working *together* of the drives in concert. There is a sense therefore where the play drive has a stake in the sense and the form drives. The play drive presupposes a profound understanding of the nature of humanity in the individual, whereby the object of experience that provided such knowledge becomes inextricably tied to such accomplishment. For Schiller, this is no less than the experience and contemplation of beauty itself.

I will return to the role of beauty in the final section of this chapter. For now, though, we can begin to see how free will, aesthetic education, and in particular the play drive might intersect. If an understanding of humanity is tied to the object that provided such understanding, then the relation to art is clear in that art has a necessary role in developing (educating) the individual-as-citizen in terms of the ideals of civilised society. However, art is of course complex. As an object of experience, it features ambiguities in its content or the telling (emplotment) of such content. The place of free will in this context, then, is twofold. Firstly, it is to be found in the tension between the sense and the form drives that is the purview of the play drive, and, secondly, free will is also involved in the active and reflective participation in our experience of art such that we are able to be educated by it.

There is also a literary potential in this approach, since the first two drives rest largely on the level of character, especially character development. We can imagine a story that illustrates the changing motivations and priorities of a character—or three, in the case of *A Magnanimous Act*.

A Magnanimous Act and the Three Drives

Despite the title, there are in fact three magnanimous acts which generate the philosophical thrust of this short story. The context for each is as follows: neither brother initially knows about the other's love of the woman, and the woman makes a conscious decision to conceal each brother's feelings from the other (for much of the story, at least). This fact of the story alone provokes interesting moral questions, particularly regarding the woman's actions: What are the motivations for her concealing such critical information? Is it an attempt to ensure the stability of the relationship between each brother, or is the woman trying to avoid a potentially difficult situation? Or is she motivated by something else entirely? This moral ambiguity is central to the rest of the story. Schiller, even in setting up the plot, doesn't resort to clear-cut moral motivations of characters—he aims to recreate the confusing, complex, and challenging moral realities of the ordinary world. Rather than conceptual abstraction, he brings the concepts to the very forefront of lived experience. As such, the moral ambiguity is heightened in its embodiment in three moments of practical action.

The first magnanimous act belongs to the older brother—the truth of the brother's feelings for the woman have been revealed, and so he leaves Germany (the story's setting) and moves to Holland. However, the despair created by his unrequited love and displacement from the woman's very existence is too much to bear, and he moves back to Germany in a state of near-fatal melancholy and into the woman's loving embrace. The second magnanimous act is committed by the younger brother—sacrificially foregoing his love for the woman, he moves to the East Indies to live in isolation, where he imparts to his brother that he is committed to a new mode of existence, thereby allowing the couple to happily enjoy the rest of their lives together. They marry; however, after only one year the woman is diagnosed with a terminal disease, and after withering away in illness confesses on her deathbed to her closest friend that she had always possessed a greater, deeper love for the younger brother. This introduces the story's third and final magnanimous act.

The effects of each act can help inform our understanding of the others. We are told—and in the context of the story we have no reason to disbelieve—how agonising the despair generated by separation was for the older brother. In retrospect and in light of the woman's confession, we can then infer the effect the younger brother's self-imposed exile had on the woman. It is notable that each act (not just in terms of the story's title) is framed as magnanimous—a grand, selfless gesture, one of deep generosity and of unreserved consideration of the Other. However, the effects of these acts hardly seem to align with magnanimity at all, and so Schiller's penchant for moral ambiguity and complexity can be seen as a characteristic feature of the story.

Evaluating these characters in terms of the sense and the form drives, we can consider what impels them to act, illustrating precisely the earlier point that the drives concern the ontological character of human nature and existence, thereby informing the specifically moral concerns that emerge out of this in terms of duty, inclination, and grace (which I will note in the following section). Part of the moral ambiguity that characterises *A Magnanimous Act* is precisely how the three magnanimous acts can be situated in conversation with the sense and the form drives. The openness of the motivations for these acts is given some clarity when we as readers consider why each character acts "magnanimously" when they do: Were they being motivated by form, that is, the principles of reason, or impelled forward by the sense drive? To take one example: Is the older brother's moving to Holland, and then back to Germany in a state of despair, indicative of the form drive's overwhelming of the sense drive (that he is being motivated by reason, impelling him to dutiful behaviour), or is the reverse the case (he is swept up in and unable to overcome his embodied, physical needs)? Yet the openness and, as mentioned, reflection provoked by the story lies precisely in the fact that their acts are cast as magnanimous—as supposedly generous, selfless grand gestures. As such, the very form of this particular story embodies two of the drives just mentioned.

The ambiguity of the characters' motivations and the deterministically tragic texture of the plot suggests the absence of the play drive rather than its presence. However, this does not preclude potential readers from enjoying a profound experience with the work. Experiencing *A Magnanimous Act* under the aesthetic condition—that is, in terms of aesthetic education—and perhaps especially in this case due to the story's illustrations of the nature of the human predicament (or at least elements of such a predicament), we are provided a unique insight into our own existential situation. That it has been artistically rendered is one reason that, for Schiller, art uniquely produces the moral sensibility that characterises our actions in the world. It is through a willing contemplation and reception of artistically expressed possibilities that we learn certain lessons and gain specific insights which cannot be attained outside of experiences with art. However, we shouldn't expect a single aesthetic experience to produce this effect, nor should we understand Schiller to tie aesthetic education solely (or even primarily) to personal intellectual illumination in the individual-as-citizen. The necessary stage of moral formation that aesthetic education provides should develop and form citizens with an end to acting and behaving in the world in the interests of a civilised society. It is this issue to which I now turn.

Aesthetic Education and the Individual-as-Citizen

As already discussed, the social aspect of aesthetic education is realised when the subject makes a free commitment to an ethical course of action, that is, when the subject acts autonomously. It is not merely a case of the individual locating moral content in a particular work and deploying the experience for some kind of isolated personal gain. It is that, for Schiller, the aesthetic condition forms the necessary stage in development from nature to civilised society. As such, it is in and through aesthetic education that the individual-as-citizen recognises and voluntarily aligns himself in line with the ends of civilised society: aesthetic experiences with art, then, are themselves social, public, and intersubjective. This is in part due to the nature of society, but it is also in part due to the nature of the aesthetic condition that leads to civilised society itself. In the context of the present discussion, we the readers understand the realities of the Other in our thoughts and feelings via our experiences with art. Our moral formation and subsequent moral actions do not occur in a vacuum, but in the complex nature of reality where we must enact our will as well as contend with the wills of others and the pressures and demands of society itself. While the previous section sought to address the terms of our freely acting in the world, here I am concerned with how negotiating potential possible courses of action is understood in Schiller's work. As such, I situate the concerns of this section within Schiller's arguments on grace, duty, and inclination.

I will return to the concept of grace in a moment, as integral to appreciating Schiller's particular understanding of grace is an awareness of two underlying concepts—inclination and duty—that he takes over from his reading of Kant. Inclination consists of what an individual is *disposed* to do in a given situation, whereas duty consists of what an individual *should* do in a given situation. In the Kantian tradition, duty follows from the presumption that rational acts are autonomous acts, and that the moral law (that is determined by our reason) tells us that we ought to act in a particular way.

There are three important points worth noting from the outset. First, inclination is not equivalent to desire. While desire speaks to an object or state in which one consciously aspires or seeks to achieve, inclination instead refers to the actions and tendencies to which an individual is naturally disposed. There is definitional or conceptual room here, then, to entertain the possibility that one's inclination can be trained or cultivated in a way which has it increasingly resemble duty—that part of one's moral formation for acting responsibly and productively in the world is by closing the gap, so to speak, that exists between an individual's inclination and duty at any given moment.

This leads to the second point, namely that there is a basic tension between inclination and duty. It is easy to imagine a particular moral predicament where one feels *inclined* to act in a certain way, while simultaneously understanding or knowing that one *should* act in a way different to that inclination. Part of the way in which an individual navigates their way to a more morally rich, responsible, and productive existence is by reflecting on one's experiences and consciously choosing to act dutifully in the world—as mentioned, to consciously act in such a way that the gap between inclination and duty is reduced. Another way is to attentively reflect on the predicaments and actions of others—especially those of whom we experience in works of art.

The third point regards the fact that the very way in which one understands inclination and duty—even in the general sketch I have offered thus far—lends itself to a narrative form. Understanding how to act in the world involves assessing our own or someone else's capacity, tendency, and choice in effecting one's agency. Further to this point, it is clear that the individual is not an isolated being, but a necessarily social one caught up in a particular social, political, and cultural milieu. Assessing and evaluating the moral sensibility or character of an individual, therefore, involves not just appreciating the individual, but the individual's existential situation in which they find themselves. Moreover, as Schiller suggests, our duties and inclinations cannot be developed in line with the ends of civilised society *without* the necessary stage of aesthetic education. It is in the aesthetic condition that the individual-as-citizen does not just better understand what the ends of civilised society actually are, but how we should act so as to achieve them.

We can return to the example of *A Magnanimous Act* to consider duty and inclination, especially in light of the (perhaps pseudo-) magnanimous act of each character. Schiller adopts a critical and reflective approach to the acts of each character: the younger brother's move to the East Indies not only intensifies his desolation but works as the catalyst of the woman's death; the woman's decision not to interfere in the brothers' acts towards each other removes the possibility of happiness for her and one of the brothers (Martin 2008: 192–193). It is unclear whether or not each character's defining act is governed more by duty or inclination. In the most morally optimistic sense, regardless of whether each character acted more in accordance with inclination or duty, all three characters share a flawed understanding of what is required in each's particular predicament.

This interpretation also reaffirms the social aspect of moral action—there is, in the case of *A Magnanimous Act*, a clear tension between what is best for the Self versus the Other. Each character has in front of them distinguishable and potential courses of action; and while even this as compared to the ordinary world is somewhat simplistic, the fact that there is still an ambiguity in the motivations and moral sensibility of each character's actions highlights the complex dynamic between an individual's attempt to navigate between duty and inclination. *A Magnanimous Act*, then, gives life to something with which we all are familiar—perhaps not the nuances particular to the romantic entanglement between the woman and the two brothers, but certainly the experience of being inclined to act in a particular way, feeling that one has a duty to act in a way that may be different to one's inclination, and having one's reflective participation in a course of action dramatically influenced by the knowledge one has of the situation at hand. Furthermore, there will always be external pressures that influence one's chosen course of action: the forces of society influencing and malforming the moral development of the individual (Mahoney 2008: 237). An individual—in a work of literature or the real world—may demonstrate an understanding of how they should act, and even be inclined to do so, however given external pressures feel compelled to act in some other way. While this is likely understandable, it points to a lack of conviction and strength of character—a moral flaw that is also illustrated in the characters of *A Magnanimous Act*.

Navigating the opposition between duty and inclination is achieved through grace, which involves the conjoining of duty and inclination. Through grace, one's sensory, embodied existence is united with moral nature and law whereby "duty arises as if out of inclination" (Ştefan-Sebastian 2014: 173). Grace is the quality in which the so-called gap separating duty and inclination closes, whereby one involuntarily—one is inclined to—acts in terms of duty. For Schiller, the presence of grace necessitates that one attends to duty in a particular way. In unifying duty and inclination through grace, there is an ease or effortlessness to acting morally in the world. To act according to duty begrudgingly, with hesitation or resignation, would not suggest the presence of grace in that individual's actions (Deligiorgi 2006: 8). Inherent to grace therefore is an authenticity, located in the involuntary taking-up of duty, that demarcates it from something like showing-off or attention-seeking. Notably for Schiller, the ease, effortlessness, and authenticity of grace is interpreted and read in the external physical signs of the individual—in the very bodily way in which duty is met. As such, central to detecting grace's presence is its embodiment in "gestures, facial expression, tone of voice, or general demeanor" (Ibid.: 8).

It is worth briefly noting the structural echo between duty, inclination, and grace with the three drives already discussed: two competing aspects of an individual's existence (duty and inclination, the sense drive and the form drive) that can be unified or harmonised by a third attribute (grace in the former instance, the play drive in the latter). However, we should be cautious about equating too strongly the particular nature of each concept with its apparent correlate. As mentioned, if the three drives relate to the ontological conditions of existence, the concepts of duty, inclination, and grace are concerned with articulating the realities of our moral predicament—how we should act in a particular circumstance, and the ends for which such action occurs.

We can turn to an example from *The Spiritualist* to better understand grace. At a crucial point in the Prince's story, he has wandered by himself into a side-chapel of a church where he finds himself enraptured by a Grecian woman. Our access to this part of the story is multiply mediated—it is conveyed to us in a letter to the titular Baron as part of a recollection of the Prince's telling of it to another individual. There are two parts to this encounter I would like to highlight. The first conveys the Prince's experience moving from outside the church to inside, and the second regards the moment he is seized by the appearance of the woman. In translation, the first part reads as follows:

> The church was quite empty—a cool, ominous darkness enfolded me as I left the dazzling, sultry sunlight outside. I found myself alone in the wide vaulted space, as silent and solemn as a grave. I went to the centre of the cathedral and abandoned myself to the fulness of this impression; gradually the grand proportions of the majestic building became clearer to my eyes, and I lost myself in grave but pleasing contemplation. The evening Angelus rang out above me, its sound echoed gently away under the vaults as it did in my soul. (Schiller *The Spiritualist* 2008b: 127)

The second part, again in translation, reads:

> Everything was dark around us, only a single window admitted the fading daylight into the chapel, the sun shone no more but on that figure. In expressible grace—half kneeling, half lying—she was prostrating herself before an altar—the boldest, fairest, most perfect shape, unique and inimitable, the most beautiful outline in nature. Black was the robe which gathered about the most enchanting body and the most delicate arms, and fell about her in spreading folds like a Spanish cloak; her long, light blond hair, braided into two broad plaits that had loosened themselves by their weight and escaped the cover of her veil, flowed far down her back in exquisite disorder—one hand touched the crucifix, and she sank down to rest gently on the other. But where can I find words to describe the heavenly charms of her face, where an angel's soul shone forth in all its glory as if seated on a throne? The evening sun played upon it, and its ethereal gold seemed to surround her like a halo in a painting. (Ibid.: 127)

In these evocative, sensorially rich passages, the connection to grace (beyond the use of the word in the second example) in Schiller's sense should be quite clear. It is notable that in setting up the encounter with the woman, the Prince, in making his way from outside the church to inside, moves from "dazzling, sultry sunlight" to the "cool, ominous darkness" that enfolds him in the "silent" and "solemn" church. The sense of light, heat, and immersion in this movement from outside to inside prefigures the experience of the woman, the shift from one qualitative environment of experience to its polar opposite heightening the effect of the woman's presence on the Prince. The sensuous aspects of the outside world have a cacophonous and overwhelming nature; yet, in their particular embodiment in the woman, they attain an exceedingly pleasant character. Making his way from the outside of the church to the side-chapel where the Prince is stopped in his tracks, completely swept away by the woman's beauty, the Prince's own countenance and physical presence is imbued with the contemplative, soulful, and even transcendent essence of his surrounds.

The Prince's account of the woman highlights in vivid detail not just the physical attributes which stole his attention but also their nature. The woman's embodied presence is not just impressive to the Prince in its own right, but in the context of Schiller's philosophy this suggests the ease and effortlessness with which grace is present in the woman. In recounting the story to his interlocutor, the Prince even has to clarify that the Grecian woman was not a painting or apparition. The force of the woman's effect is made more vivid to readers in that the experience being conveyed to us is the first-person recounting of it by the Prince (via another character). Tied up in the Prince's description therefore is not just the appearance of the woman, but the impact it had on him.

The reader's alignment with the Prince's experience is central to *The Spiritualist*, whereby we are given evocative accounts of the circumstances that contextualise his actions, inviting us to empathise with rather than condemn him (Mahoney 2008: 236). Across the entire work of *The Spiritualist*, the pressures applied to the Prince so as to motivate his religious conversion grow, and he is beset by greater and greater moral challenges. However, this feature of *The Spiritualist* has particular resonance with specific moments, such as the one mentioned earlier where Schiller conveys what it is like not just for the Prince to experience grace, but what it can be like to be seized by the grace of another. We can consider grace in another way: through its absence in the Prince, again conveyed through Schiller's evocative account of his interior experiences and the constant stream of social engagements used to wear him down and bend his behaviour to the whims of other characters (Mahoney 2008: 241).

The Prince's existence begins to spiral out of control, his inclination and duty articulated through the chaos of a confused haze. Importantly, while this is conveyed from the inside of the Prince's experience, readers are also informed as to the way in which his situation and its effects on him are rendered in the Prince's physical presence and demeanour. As is characteristic of Schiller's prose works, therefore, the moral ambiguity heightens as the novella develops. And this too applies to the Grecian woman, when we learn that she—a woman who consumes the Prince's attention and time long after the moment of his seeing her for the first time—is revealed to be a plant as a means of trying to motivate his conversion.

These comments make clear the importance of concepts such as duty, inclination, and grace in Schiller's oeuvre. For Schiller, when duty and inclination coincide more or less naturally in the actions of a character, that character can be said to have acted with grace. Yet grace is recognised in a work of art not just as a conceptual feature of that work but also in the minor, narrative features of the work's description—that is, the means by which the author has rendered the character's countenance and demeanour, the qualities of the character's gestures and behaviour, and so on.

The historical-social milieu of *The Spiritualist* is illustrative of this final point in particular. The experience of the Grecian woman may well have struck the Prince so profoundly precisely because much of the Prince's world lacks the beauty and grace that she possesses. The so-called moral quality of *The Spiritualist's* setting—clearly rendered as a likeness of the then real-world counterpart—is imbued with its own moral ambiguity that plays into the themes and form of the story. This combines with certain recurring elements, relevant to the work's plot occurring during Carnival time, which heighten the work's sensory aspects and establishes the sense of uncertainty which pervades the novella (Mahoney 2008: 236). With so much hidden in the world of *The Spiritualist*—the motivations that prod the Prince into different circumstances and the wide-ranging narrators and literary forms of the story which reinforce the instability of the truth of the world of the work—what makes the Grecian woman notable once again is the fact she is in plain view. This, of course, is then completely undercut with absolute and virtuosic irony on Schiller's part when it is later revealed that her attributes of grace and beauty have been co-opted to motivate the Prince's religious conversion.

The very form of the work itself embodies ambiguity—it manifests the Herculean task of unlocking the nature of things, the critical pieces of knowledge that shape how we come to understand the limits and capabilities of our free will, and how we are to enact that will in the world. Schiller's use of *Schlüssel* (key) and *Decke* (veil, cover) to refer to the "unlocking" or "unveiling" of the truth is used in tandem with a host of narrators of varying unreliability to create an experience whereby it is impossible to know the truth of the events of the story (Mahoney 2008: 236). The aesthetic experience arising from such a work, therefore, does not just give rise to reflection but demands it: reflection on the extent to which we as individuals are willing to engage with and experience beauty, the extent to which we are willing to exercise our will to try and maintain a graceful balance between duty and inclination, which Schiller suggests is fundamental to our existence, and thereby whether or not—or how often—we realise our fullest possible potential. I will develop the idea of beauty and its connection to art in the final section; however, first it is worth revisiting the central concerns of *The Spiritualist* with the interests of this section—the role of aesthetic education in forming the citizen—in mind.

The ambiguities inherent in *The Spiritualist* do not erode the value of aesthetic education. Characters might be misguided, morally ambiguous, their intentions for acting in particular ways hidden, or their embodied existence not rendered especially clearly. In such circumstances, our experience with these sorts of works can still contribute to our moral formation. Schiller's literary prose works often take on a reflective and provocative quality, requiring readers to think through possibilities and contingencies alongside or through concrete examples. Such cases can produce a deep and rich formation of one's character as a result of the demanding nature of the engagement. Perhaps most potently, works like *The Spiritualist* combine representing citizens acting in a society while negotiating the different societal and individual demands of life, with a phenomenologically evocative account of the experiences, thoughts, and feelings of certain characters (such as the Prince) from their first-person perspective. In our close attention to such works and the characters depicted in them, readers are tasked with investing, totally, in the Other being brought to life. We are given access to subjectivity in a way not available in our experience of others in the ordinary world, and this augments the representation of their actions in the world of the work. Experiencing these different elements of *The Spiritualist* in the aesthetic condition offers a unique and necessary means of morally forming and developing the citizen. It clarifies and refines a sense of the ideals of civilised society and prepares the individual-as-citizen experiencing the work to act in line with those ideals—gracefully, whereby duty and inclination merge with the goods of society as their end—in the ordinary world of experience.

THE BEAUTIFUL SOUL AND THE IDEAL OF ART

While the ambiguities in behaviour and narrative form in works like *A Magnanimous Act* and *The Spiritualist* may resist moral clarity on the part of the reader, it can still *clarify* and educate, providing understanding that is necessary to our development as citizens and the attainment of a civilised society. As mentioned earlier, it is the play drive to reach as its achievement the contemplation of beauty through a total understanding of an aspect of human nature, whereby the object that produces such understanding is inextricably tied to the understanding it provides. That this is no doubt difficult to accomplish does not, for Schiller, make it an impossibility.

For Schiller, the beautiful soul acts instinctively and without forethought or guile—action, then, does not require the help of intellectual concepts or any strategising about how to act. That is, the beautiful soul is one who has harmonised or unified the potentially opposing tendencies of duty and inclination as expressed in the individual's embodied existence, manifesting in appearance and action the presence of grace. The beautiful soul is a concept developed in Schiller's Kantian phase and can be considered ideal in the sense of a transcendental idea rather than idealistic in the pre-critical sense of conformity to a particular ideal. At this point, I return to the motivations for considering literary works from Schiller's pre-critical phase with the intent of searching for the presence of concepts from his critical period. In the texts considered thus far, I suggest that, especially in *The Spiritualist*, the beautiful soul is suggested in its absence and as such not developed to the point of its being philosophically significant. The absence of such philosophical development is nevertheless not unimportant. On the contrary, it can indicate some important things about Schiller's intellectual work.

The varying ways in which Schiller's philosophical work and literary tendencies are woven together (that is, some philosophical ideas being developed in prose and some not) helps to reinforce the point that Schiller is not strictly or properly Kantian: the connection Schiller's prose works have to authentic socio-historical settings and the sorts of plotlines he develops indicate the seriousness with which he takes the implications of certain moral/philosophical ideas, but the shifts in his struggles with (predominantly) Kantian ideas denotes that his intellectual development is not linearly congruent with Kant's.

Taking both analyses together lends support to an argument I have developed throughout the chapter whereby there is a mutual influence of philosophy and literature that exists in Schiller's output. While the scope of the chapter is contained to his literary prose works, when we consider Schiller as a thinker, it is not just his essays we must pay attention to but also his poems, plays, and short stories. The more literary dimension to Schiller cannot be excluded from our consideration of him as a philosopher.

Second, and relatedly, the shifts in Schiller's intellectual convictions unfold throughout his prose works as much as his philosophy, and so we can better understand Schiller's intellectual struggle by looking to his literary output as well as his philosophical works. I hold that the absence of a philosophically significant depiction of the beautiful soul in the pre-critical work I consider lends support to such an argument, too. The pre-critical prose articulates a certain moment in Schiller's struggle with a Kantian philosophical system—a system that Schiller absorbs into his own philosophical framework. Despite this, there is undoubtedly still a presence, however nascent its depiction, of what is to come as he moves into his critical period.

The works I consider suggest Schiller's unwillingness to yield to the rigours of a full-blown Kantianism. Briefly touching on another of Schiller's literary works will help to further this point. *The Criminal of Lost Honour: A True Story* (1786) examines the psychological motivations and qualities of an innkeeper's son. Christian Wolf, the story's protagonist, turns to minor crimes to purchase gifts for the woman he loves and who he is trying to impress. He suffers disproportionately harsh punishments for these crimes, and, angrily disillusioned, seeks revenge for the circumstances which have befallen him. The story balances the psychology of Christian with the extent to which he is responsible and how external societal forces shape his conduct and perhaps mitigate his guilt. Even in this summary of the story, and in light of the preceding discussion, the story's concerns with the balance of duty and inclination are perhaps even more at the forefront than the other two works of prose I have considered at greater length. Nevertheless, and as is the case with *The Spiritualist* as well, there is not just the absence of a true, beautiful soul, but an absence of a philosophically cogent case of such a concept in the story's narrative and characters. It is not just a story, as with the other examples, that provokes complex moral questions to readers, but is also a story that illustrates Schiller's own wrestling with these very questions and the (Kantian) philosophical concepts which underpin them. Moreover, and in combination with the prose works given greater consideration earlier in the chapter, we can begin to see how the beautiful soul connects in important ways to Schiller's sense of aesthetic education.

An individual may be precluded from possessing the beautiful soul due to a lack of grace, but a lack of grace may not always be due to moral weakness or a lack of formation or sensibility. Circumstances may conspire against the individual—it may be that one simply isn't able to involuntarily walk the path of duty in a given moral predicament. On the face of things, this existential complexity characterised by the absence of the beautiful soul seems much truer to life than would its presence and, as such, in the context of Schiller's literary work, the reader is left "more unsettled and more reflective" (Rainer qtd. in Martin 2008: 192).

Furthermore, Schiller highlights the aesthetic experience of art as a central way in which to activate the play drive wherein we realise our highest possible potential. This is an important point for the concerns of the present chapter. If (1) the contemplation of beauty is the way in which we activate the play drive, (2) this awakening allows us to realise our potential, and (3) art is a central way in which to contemplate beauty in the first place, it should be unsurprising that Schiller places such importance on the educative and formative role of our experience with art of all kinds. In reading a work we might experience beauty and activate the play drive, enriching the very sense of our human nature and thereby enabling us to realise our full potential. However, in an aesthetically educative sense, we might also read or experience a work of art that deals with characters contemplating beauty, thereby allowing us to reflect on the value and nature of contemplation itself. This is certainly the case in the Prince's perception of the Grecian woman mentioned earlier. Alternatively—and this is characteristic of certain Schiller stories—we might be struck by a lack of beauty, which can involve characters themselves voicing and living out such concerns. This feature of a lack of beauty or a lack of the experience and contemplation of beauty can be included on the part of the author to awaken in readers an association with our own world. Once again, then, we can see how not just ambiguities but also an absence of those qualities to which we should aspire can serve to educate our moral sensibility, shaping the way in which we act in the world (should we be freely open to such an effect). As such, we can recognise once more why Schiller sees the experience of art in the aesthetic condition as a necessary means of moving from the state of nature to the state of civility.

In conclusion, in the literary works considered in tandem with certain concepts gleaned from Schiller's later philosophical writings, it is clear that philosophy is an essential aspect of understanding his prose works. Part of the reason this is the case is that Schiller's philosophy has a peculiarly literary character. The way in which he conceives of duty, inclination, grace, the beautiful soul, and the three drives (the sense drive, the form drive, and the play drive) lends itself to literary form. As such, for Schiller, the philosophical is a subset of the literary—literature is an all-encompassing form whereby ethics and aesthetics cannot be easily teased apart (if at all). This underpins the idea of aesthetic education, which is a necessary stage through which we must pass in order to attain a civilised society. What I have shown is that Schiller's literary output, composed at least in part as the nascent expression of the philosophical ideas he would look to develop in the guise of philosopher later in life, is concerned with the most visceral, the most animated, and, indeed, the most human dimensions, problems, and tasks of human experience, as well as articulating Schiller's own intellectual struggles with these very issues.

REFERENCES

Deligiorgi, Katerina. January 2006. Grace as Guide to Morals? Schiller's Aesthetic Turn in Ethics. *History of Philosophy Quarterly* 23.1: 1–20.

Mahoney, Dennis F. 2008. *Der Geisterseher:* A Princely Experiment or, the Creation of a "Spiritualist." In *Schiller's Literary Prose Works*, ed. Jeffrey L. High, 234–250. Rochester: Camden House.

Martin, Nicholas. 2008. Playing with the Rules: Schiller's Experiments in Short Prose Fiction, 1782–1789. In *Schiller's Literary Prose Works*, ed. Jeffrey L. High, 188–201. Rochester: Camden House.

Mehigan, Tim. 2020. Schiller after Kant: The "Unexpected Science" of the *Briefe über die ästhetische Erziehung des Menschen*. *Kant Studien* 111. 2: 285–302.

Roehr, Sabine. January 2003. Freedom and Autonomy in Schiller. *Journal of the History of Ideas* 64.1: 119–134.

Schiller, Friedrich. 2008a. A Magnanimous Act from Most Recent History (1782). Transl. Ian Codding. In *Schiller's Literary Prose Works*, ed. Jeffrey L. High, 9–11. Rochester: Camden House.

Schiller, Friedrich. 2008b. The Spiritualist. From the Memoirs of Count von O** (1789). Transl. Francis Lamport. In *Schiller's Literary Prose Works*, ed. Jeffrey L. High, 67–149. Rochester: Camden House.

Ștefan-Sebastian, Maftei. 2014. Schiller's Aesthetic Freedom and the Challenges of Aesthetic Education. *Procedia – Social and Behavioral Sciences* 163: 169–178.

PART V

Kant, the Kantian Tradition, and Schiller

CHAPTER 26

Schiller and Kant on Grace and Beauty

Paul Guyer

At least among philosophers, the most frequently quoted of the *Xenien*, a compilation of satirical distiches that Friedrich Schiller and Johann Wolfgang von Goethe published in 1796, is the following:

Scruples of Conscience
I like to serve my friends, but unfortunately I do it by inclination
And so often I am bothered by the thought that I am not virtuous.
Decision
There is no other way but this! You must seek to despise them
And do with repugnance what duty bids you.[1]

This is often taken as meant to be a biting criticism of Kant. Some have rather held that it is meant to be a parody of poor readers among Kant's critics,[2]

---

[1] Translation quoted from Wood (1999), p. 28. As a piece of poetry, I prefer the translation by A.B. Bullock, quoted by Hastings Rashdall in *The Theory of Good and Evil* and in turn quoted from him by H.J. Paton:
Gladly I serve my friends, but alas I do it with pleasure.
Hence I am plagued with doubt that I am not a virtuous person.
Sure, your only resource is to try to despise them entirely,
And then with aversion to do what your duty enjoins.
But here I have used Wood's translation because his use of "inclination" rather than "pleasure" brings out better the issue we are about to discuss.
[2] See Beck (1960), p. 231n63.

P. Guyer (✉)
Brown University, Providence, RI, USA
e-mail: paul_guyer@brown.edu

and given that the *Xenien* jabbed at many in the contemporary literary world but were in part at least meant to defend the younger Jena philosophers—Fichte and the emerging Schelling—from shallow Berlin critics such as Friedrich Nicolai,[3] there may be something to be said for this interpretation.[4] In any case, whether Schiller and Goethe were lampooning them or joining them, there were certainly plenty of critics who thought that Kant was committed to precisely such a ridiculous conclusion. Thus, in his ill-tempered screed *On Mister Kant's Moral Reform*, Gottlob August Tittel first crudely paraphrased Kant's position in the following terms, obviously transforming one of Kant's thought-experiments in *Groundwork* I meant to lead to a clear formulation of the moral principle from cases of agents who *could* act on it without inclination into a requirement that a morally worthy agent *have no* inclination in favor of what morality demands: "In the case of a good will, the human being always acts from duty. Thus—not on account of any use. Also, not—merely in accord with duty, but from inclination; but also contrary to his inclination, only because it is his duty to so act, as for example an unhappy person preserves his life without loving it." Tittel then responds, "The moral worth of a human being consists in the fact that in him duty has become his dominant inclination. The strength of this inclination elevates his worth. The more reservations or stimuli lie in the way, which this inclination conquers, all the stronger must it be" (Tittel 1786, p. 12). Tittel might seem to contradict himself, first rejecting Kant's alleged view that the good will has to overpower inclination and then arguing that moral worth is to be measured precisely by the strength of resistance to inclination, but what he means is that moral worth consists in having an *inclination* in favor of duty that is stronger than all other *inclinations* and capable of overpowering them, and this he takes to be a criticism of Kant.

This seems an unfair criticism of Kant, who in *Groundwork* I was certainly not attempting to give a completely realistic picture of the actual motivation of a morally worthy person but rather was offering narrowly defined thought-experiments, examples of cases in which persons could be imagined to be acting with moral worth but without any inclination in behalf of their actions, from which it would follow that the fundamental *principle* of morality, the criterion for distinguishing between right and wrong, cannot depend on inclination, and must instead directly concern only the form of our maxims rather than the matter of our happiness. Tittel's larger argument is directed precisely against that position, so it cannot be argued that in general he simply

---

[3] See Boyle (2000), pp. 400–401.
[4] But note that Schiller and Goethe were also capable of poking fun at Kant's followers as well:
Kant and His Interpreters
But how can a single rich man provide nourishment for so many beggars!
When kings build, the charnel houses have plenty to do.
(My translation from Schiller 1996, volume 3, p. 145.
The *Xenien* spared no one.

misunderstood Kant. But in taking Kant to be intending to provide a complete phenomenology of morally worthy motivation in *Groundwork* I, he was being unfair to Kant.

But whether in the notorious distich Goethe and Schiller meant to be parodying a critic like Tittel or to be taking his side, in his famous essay *Anmut und Würde* ("On Grace and Dignity") of 1793 (GD), thus seven years after Tittel's little book but three years before the poem, Schiller offered what seems to be a more subtle criticism of Kant's position on the role of feelings in moral motivation. The argument of this essay is complex, however, and by no means directed solely against Kant's ethical theory, so it will take a moment to reach the point of dispute between Schiller and Kant, if in fact there really is one. Schiller begins with a debate in aesthetics rather than ethics, and initially his target seems to be Henry Home, Lord Kames, rather than Kant. Indeed, Kames's 1762 *Elements of Criticism*, widely popular in Germany,[5] includes a chapter (11) entitled "Dignity and Grace," so although Schiller reverses the order of Kames's title, it is also clear that Kames is more than just an ancillary target for Schiller. In that chapter, Kames first states that "These terms must belong to sensitive beings, probably to man only" (Kames 2005, vol. I, p. 245). Schiller agrees with this, although from his point of view, on this issue entirely Kantian, both dignity and grace will belong to humans as the only sensitive *and rational* beings with whom we are acquainted. Kames further argues that "we never attribute dignity to any action but what is virtuous" and that the term "dignity" is further "appropriated" to express the human being's "SENSE of the worth and excellence of his nature: he deems it more perfect than that of the other beings around him; and he perceives that the perfection of his nature consists in virtue, particularly in virtues of the highest rank." He states further that "to behave with dignity, and to refrain from all mean actions, is felt to be, not a virtue only, but a duty" (Kames 2005, vol. I, p. 246). Acting with dignity is thus acting in a way that expresses the agent's own sense of his moral worth, and it is a duty for human beings to so act. Of course, for Kames, as a moral sense theorist, the dignified person does not merely act with a sense of his own worth, but duty and virtue are defined by our moral sense, not by any form of pure reason. Schiller will take the part of Kant rather than Kames on this score.

Having devoted the bulk of his chapter, which is in any case not one of the longer ones in the *Elements of Criticism*, to dignity, Kames then devotes two pages to grace. He says first that it is displayed externally, and in particular to sight; this is in line with his initial definition of beauty in general as in the first instance a quality for sight and only secondarily for the other senses (Kames 2005, ch. III, vol. I, pp. 141–142). He then argues that unlike beauty, which

---

[5] According to Jane Curran, Schiller "consulted the third German edition of 1790–1793, with commentary by Georg Gottlob Schatz" (GD, p. 134n5.) I have not been able to identify this edition. There are Heinrich Home, *Grundsäzte der Kritik*, letzte verbesserte Auflage, translated by Johann Nicolaus Meinhard (Leipzig: Dyck, 1790–1791, and Wien: Schrämbl, 1790). There can be no doubt that Schiller had ready access to Kames's work.

can be found in static objects, grace "is undoubtedly connected with motion; for when the most graceful persons is at rest, neither moving nor speaking, we lose sight of that quality as much as of colour in the dark" (Kames 2005, ch. XI, vol. I, p. 251). In particular, grace "is too deep for any cause purely corporeal," and instead lies in motions "which indicate mental qualities, such as sweetness, benevolence, elevation, [and] dignity"; "Collecting these circumstances together, grace may be defined [as] that agreeable appearance which arises from elegance of motion and from a countenance expressive of dignity" (Kames 2005, ch. XI, p. 252). Thus, for Kames grace and dignity are hardly mutually exclusive, but grace is a feature of the appearance of motions stemming from moral qualities of mind and above all from dignity. For him, grace is the appearance of dignity in the motions of a human agent. Thus, dignity is a purely moral notion, while grace is more of an aesthetic concept, although like other Britons of the eighteenth century Kames did not use the term "aesthetic" that Alexander Gottlieb Baumgarten had introduced into German.

In a general way, Schiller is in complete agreement with Kames that grace is an expression of the moral quality of an agent, but it is not an expression of dignity as he defines it. At the same time, his ultimate ideal of human perfection is that grace and dignity should coincide. Schiller deals with grace first, and in the course of his analysis his target shifts from Kames to Kant. He contrasts grace first with beauty, then with "static" beauty, then with "architectonic" beauty. But the key idea remains the same: beauty under its several names is an enduring feature of an object, while grace is a "movable beauty, a beauty that can appear in a subject by chance and disappear in the same way," or "beauty of movement" (GD, p. 125; NA 253). As Kames had held that grace is "elegance in motion," thus far there is no difference between him and Schiller. Next, Schiller argues that "if grace is a prerogative of human development, then none of those movements that humans have in common with merely natural beings can lay claim to it," for example the rippling of curls in a head of beautiful hair (GD, p. 126; NA 254). Again, there is still no difference with Kames, nor is there when Schiller adds that this is because grace is an expression of the moral quality of the graceful agent, or in his Kantian language, an "expression of purpose" (GD, p. 128; NA 257). His analysis diverges from Kames's, however, when he argues, now drawing on the central notion of Kant's aesthetics that beauty lies in a free play that appeals to and unifies our sensible and intellectual capacities, that grace "is always only beauty of the physique that *freedom sets in motion*" (GD, p. 134; NA 265), that it must be connected to both the intentional expression of moral purpose and yet to motions that are entirely natural to human beings, and therefore locates it in "*sympathetic* movements" (GD, p. 135; NA 266), or movements that "accompany moral sentiment or moral attitude" (GD, p. 136; NA 266), that is, in the unintended accompaniments of intentional actions. As Schiller explains, "Whatever is left undetermined by either will or purpose can be sympathetically determined by the emotional state of the person and serve as the expression of that state." Thus, grace is the natural accompaniment of actions dictated by reason, and expresses the harmony between nature and reason. In particular, a person's "sympathetic" movements are the best expression of his real intentions and moral character because while intentional movements can easily be faked, their unintended accompaniments cannot be: for example, "one can deduce from a person's words how he would *like to be viewed*, but what he *really* is must be guessed from the mimic gestures accompanying the speech, in other words, from the movements *that he does not will*" (translation modified) (GD, p. 137; NA 268). This is a subtlety that is not present in Kames's account, and is part of what Schiller means when he says later that he "takes up characteristics of dignity into grace...His observations are usually correct, and the rules he *initially* forms from them, true; but one should not follow him further than this" (GD, p. 164n; NA 301): dignity is strictly an expression of the morality and rationality of an agent, but the motions that Kames had correctly identified as constituting grace must be natural, and therefore must be the unintended accompaniments of intended action rather than the intended movements of the action themselves.

Schiller also criticizes Kames for assuming "too *narrow* a meaning for the idea of grace" when he argues that it disappears entirely when a person is at rest (GD, p. 134n; NA 264). Schiller's objection is that a person's movements, intentional or sympathetic and graceful or not, leave enduring traces on her physiognomy: "The rigid features were originally nothing other than movements that through frequent repetition became habitual and left lasting traces" (GD, p. 134; NA 264). Schiller's original training as a physician gave him a stronger sense of the intimate connection between mind and body than many of his philosophically trained contemporaries had.

This would seem like a minor point, but it is part of Schiller's inexplicit criticism of Kant's conception of the "ideal of beauty." In the Analytic of the Beautiful in the *Critique of the Power of Judgment*, Kant had argued that an ideal of beauty would be a uniquely maximal sort of beauty, that such an ideal would have to be in some way fixed by a concept or idea even though beauty is never *determined* by a concept, and that the only candidate for such a role is the idea of human morality itself, the capacity of the human beings "to determine his ends himself through reason" (CJ, §17, Ak 5:233). From this, he concluded that the ideal of beauty can be found "only in the *human figure*" as "the expression of the *moral*," as the "visible expression of moral ideas, which inwardly govern human beings" (CJ, §17, Ak 5:235). In fact, Kant's account is doubly problematic: he treats the ideal of beauty as a species-wide ideal for human beings, but of course some human beings are moral and some are not—although all have the capacity to be moral, in Kant's view, some choose not to be—and therefore only some human beings will express morality in their outward appearance; and, but for the exception noted in Schiller's criticism of Kames, the expression of morality will not lie in the fixed form of a human figure or face, which is a product of nature alone, but in an individual's graceful movements, the unintended accompaniments of intended actions that are the product of reason and nature together. The "human form is expressive" of individual morality "only in those appearances that accompany and serve to express its moral attitude" (GD, p. 140; NA 272), not in the natural beauty of an individual and certainly not in some beauty of form common to the entire human species. "We are thus not satisfied when a human form presents to our eyes the universal concept of humanity or perhaps the degree to which *nature* has fulfilled it in the individual...In the former case one can easily see that nature *planned* for a human being, but only in the second case does it emerge whether it *actually* became one" (GD, p. 141; NA 273). This cannot be a criticism of Kames, because he had said no such thing; it is a criticism of Kant, who tried to find the expression of human morality in the architectonic beauty of the species when it can lie only in the graceful movements of the individual.

Thus far, Schiller seems to be arguing only with Kant's aesthetics, not with his moral theory. And when he proceeds beyond a mere analysis of the concept of grace to explain what he takes to be the expectation or even demand for grace, he makes it clear that this issues not from our expectation of morality alone but from our demand for beauty:

> Human beings, as appearance, are also an object of the senses. Where the *moral* feeling finds satisfaction, the *aesthetic* feeling does not wish to be reduced, and the correspondence with an idea may not sacrifice any of the appearance. Thus, however rigorously reason demands an ethical expression, the eye demands beauty just as persistently.

To be sure, these two demands have to be conjointly satisfied, because they are to be satisfied in one and the same object:

> Since both these demands are made of the same object, although they come from different courts of judgment, satisfaction for both must be found in the same source. The frame of mind in which a human being is most able to fulfill his moral purpose must permit the type of expression that is also most advantageous for him as simple appearance. In other words: moral capacity must reveal itself through grace. (GD, pp. 144-5; NA 277)

This double requirement, Schiller goes on to argue, can be satisfied only when the person who is to satisfy the demands of both morality and aesthetics (the person as object, who presumably might be the same as the subject who is making both a moral and an aesthetic judgment on the object, but who will typically be numerically distinct) satisfies something like the Kantian condition of free play between intellect and sensibility, the condition by which Kant defines the aesthetic but which Schiller has now extended to the relation between aesthetics and morality: "When neither *reason dominating the sensuous*, nor *sensuousness dominating reason* is compatible with beauty of expression, then...the state of mind *in which reason and sensuousness*—duty and inclination—*coincide* will be the condition under which the beauty of play appears" (GD, p. 148; NA 282). Now it may seem as if Schiller has by his lengthy argument reached the same point that Tittel quickly asserted against

Kant, namely that duty and inclination must coincide, but it might also seem that he has cast this demand not as a purely moral demand but as a demand of our dual sensuous and rational, our aesthetic and moral character, and thus that while superficially agreeing with Tittel, he has in fact offered Kant a defense— for Kant should have no objection to an aesthetic demand for grace, or for the idea that while morality alone may have no interest in inclination coinciding with duty, our dual moral-aesthetic nature might well have such an interest. But Schiller continues to emphasize that the demand for grace is a demand that originates in our whole, complex nature, not in our capacity for morality alone: it is nature, not morality, that gives "the human being notice of his obligation not to separate what it had bound together and, even in the purest expressions of his divine part, not to neglect the sensuous, and not to base the triumph of the one on the subjugation of the other" (GD, p. 150; NA 284). Schiller also puts the point in terms of his famous concept of the "beautiful soul": "One refers to a beautiful soul when the ethical sense has at last so taken control of all of a person's feelings that it can leave affect to guide the will without hesitation and is never in danger of standing in contradiction of its decisions"; but he makes it clear that the demand for a "beautiful soul" is an aesthetic demand, or a jointly aesthetic and moral demand, but not a demand of morality alone: "It is in a beautiful soul that sensuousness and reason, duty and inclination, are in harmony, and grace is their expression as appearance" (GD, pp. 152–153; NA 287). The demand for grace is not a demand of duty alone.

Schiller concedes that Kant has laid himself open to the criticism of insisting on a necessary opposition between duty and inclination, that "the idea of *duty*...repels all grace," which might "tempt a weak intellect to seek moral perfection by taking the path of a somber and monkish asceticism," but argues that Kant was "incensed" by the "moral state of his time, as he found it in theory and practice," to exaggerate this contrast. Only thus, Schiller suggests, could Kant counter the hedonistic utilitarianism that is always a temptation for people and was being encouraged by the "inappropriately accommodating" and "lax" philosophers around him (GD, p. 150; NA 285). But his position remains that the demand for grace in our performance of duty, thus for harmony between duty and inclination, is a demand of our dual nature, not of our moral nature alone. Moreover, when he turns from grace to dignity, his position seems to become, just like Kant's position, that in case there is a conflict between the demands of duty and of inclination—which, given the frailty of human nature, there inevitably will be—then inclination must give way to duty, and the person must act with dignity, the "expression in appearance" of "control of impulses through moral strength" rather than the appearance of harmony between impulse and duty (GD, p. 158; NA 294). Schiller's concept of dignity is not the same as Kant's: for Kant, dignity is a strictly moral concept, that of the absolute value of humanity or the *capacity* for rational free being in human beings (G, Ak 4:434–435),[6] while for Schiller it is a phenomenological,

---

[6] See Kant, *Groundwork*, 4:434–435. For a careful analysis of Kant's concept of dignity as a term expressing the unconditional value of humanity rather than as the property that itself has unconditional value, see Sensen (2011).

perceptual, or aesthetic concept, the concept of the *appearance* of the actual triumph of morality over contrary impulse in a particular individual. (Kant does refer at least once to a "certain sublimity and *dignity* in the person who fulfills all his duty," which is part of Schiller's conception of dignity, but he does not refer to the sensible appearance of such a person's fulfillment of duty, which is the other part of Schiller's concept; G, Ak 4:440.) But he does not seem to disagree with Kant's position that human beings do not always do their duty gladly, and that when they do not, then we must settle for dignity rather than grace:

> Human beings do have the task of establishing an intimate agreement between their two natures, of always being a harmonious whole, and of acting with their full human capacity. But this beauty of character, the ripest fruit of humanity, is only an idea that they can vigilantly strive to live up to, yet, despite all efforts, can never fully attain.
>
> The reason they cannot reach it is the unchanging outlines of their nature; the physical conditions of their existence hinder them. (GD, p. 154; NA 289)

In this case, it seems, humans must at least achieve dignity, a claim that Schiller illustrates with his own take on a common topic in German literary life of his time, the famous Roman statue of the Trojan priest Laocoön and his sons being destroyed by Neptune's serpents. Unlike Johann Joachim Winckelmann, he does not think that the composure of the priest's face in contrast to the struggle of his body represents a merit of Greek culture as a whole, and unlike Gotthold Ephraim Lessing, he does not think it represents a concession to the laws of beauty in a visual medium like sculpture as contrasted to a verbal medium like epic poetry (where Virgil's Laocoön, *vox clamantes ad sidera*, can scream all he wants). In his view, Laocoön's composed face represents his individual "*peace in suffering*, in which dignity actually consists," the visible expression of the moral freedom of an individual who knows he is doing the right thing regardless of the consequences even for his beloved children as well as himself (GD, p. 160; NA 296). Schiller uses the iconic statue to illustrate his conception of dignity as the appearance of the best moral condition that human beings as conceived by Kant can sometimes, although not always, achieve. As he puts this last point, now using Kant's term "humanity" to designate the combined rational and sensuous character of human beings rather than their free and rational character alone, "In general, the law is valid here that humans should do everything with grace that can be carried out within humanity, and everything with dignity that requires going beyond humanity" (GD, p. 162; NA 298).

This would seem to be the final step in Schiller's argument, and nothing to which Kant would object. But he does not quit while he is ahead, and makes two further claims. First, he makes the epistemological claim that only grace, not dignity, offers conclusive evidence of a person's commitment to morality:

Dignity alone displays a certain restriction of desires and inclinations whenever we encounter it. Only the grace associated with it can establish beyond doubt whether what we take to be control is not actually a dullness (hardening) of sensibility and whether it is really one's own moral activity and not rather the preponderance of another emotion, deliberate exertion, that holds the outbreak of the present one in check. Grace gives evidence of a peaceful, harmonious disposition and a sensitive heart. (GD, p. 163; NA 300)

Second, essentially returning to his previous conception of the beautiful soul, Schiller argues that only the union of grace with dignity satisfies our complex conception of human perfection rather than our strictly moral conception of human virtue:

If grace, supported by architectonic beauty, and dignity, supported by strength, are *united* in the same person, then the expression of humanity is complete in that person, and he stands there, justified in the world of spirit and affirmed in appearance. The two legislations are in such close contact here that their boundaries flow together. (GD, p. 163; NA 300-1)

But his position still seems compatible with Kant's, namely that although our overall conception of human perfection, grounded in our distinct interests in moral achievement on the one hand and aesthetic pleasure on the others, demands the union of dignity and grace, morality alone demands that if there is a conflict between duty and inclination, then duty must trump inclination, and dignity without grace must manifest itself in appearance. Of course, it is nice when duty and inclination coincide, but if they do not, then duty must be done. Schiller's claim about the complete expression of humanity does not conflict with this, and his epistemological claim that only grace gives adequate evidence of a complete commitment to morality does not contradict the normative claim that in case of conflict duty must trump inclination, thus dignity must appear without grace.

In the Vigilantius transcription of Kant's lectures on the metaphysics of morals, within the first few days of a course that began on October 14, 1793, Kant is reported as digging his heels in, taking just the position that a critic like Tittel imputed to him, and seeing no common ground between himself and Schiller, for here he insists that there is *always* a felt conflict between duty and inclination:

It is also certain that every obligation is forthwith associated with a moral constraint, and that it is contrary to the nature of duty to *enjoy* having duties incumbent upon one; it is necessary, rather that man's impulses should make him disinclined to fulfill the moral the laws.

It is not just contingent whether our inclinations would move us to actions contrary to the moral law, and thus contingent whether there is a conflict between duty and inclination; Kant insists here that it is inevitable. This leads to a rejection of what Kant takes to be Schiller's position in *Grace and Dignity*:

Assuming that man's fulfillment of the moral laws can be accomplished only under a necessitation, it cannot therefore be claimed, as Schiller does in his *Thalia*,[7] where he takes issue with the Kantian critique of reason, that such fulfillment has a certain *grace*[8] about it, though otherwise, by man's nature, the necessitation requires obedience to the moral laws; if we wish, with Schiller, to assume a worth arising therefrom, it is nothing more than man's respect for the moral law, and that provides no ground for supposing a grace that attracts us to fulfilling it. That is contradicted by the authority of the laws, which enjoins absolute obedience, and awakens resistance and struggle, which we perceive in fulfilling them.

Kant continues that a person may take reflexive or second-order pleasure in the fact *that* it has become easy for him to fulfill duty by the strength of his own will, but denies that a person can simply enjoy doing his duty without any such further reflection:

> It is true that we can find pleasure in virtue and the contemplation of it, but only by the time, and for the reason, that we have already become equipped to fulfill duties, and it is thus easy for us to follow the prescriptions of reason; we thereby take satisfaction in our actions, and in the strengthening of our will to comply with the prescriptions of reason...Finally, even psychological experience tells against Schiller's view: *We would do many things, if only they did not have to be done from duty*...It would be good if men were so perfect that they fulfilled their duties from a free impulse, without coercion and law; but this is beyond the horizon of human nature.(LE, Ak 27:490-1)

Kant evinces no recognition either that Schiller was criticizing his conception of the ideal of beauty in aesthetics but attempting to defend Kant in moral philosophy or that in his discussion of dignity, at least in its initial phase, Schiller was actually agreeing with him that assuming human beings could always fulfill their duties with grace is unrealistic. Later in the lectures, he says that "Schiller is right to this extent, that [moral] worth lies in the intellectual nature of the determination to duty," but he still insists that there will always be a felt conflict between duty and inclination: "But the moral law also engenders worth through the very compulsion that fetters us in obedience" (LE, Ak 27:623). In other words, it is not enough for moral worth to be motivated by the moral law and that motivation has to be in conflict with one's inclination for one to deserve the accolade of moral worth. Kant does not appear to be making an epistemological argument, that it is only in the case of a conflict with inclination that we can *know* that someone is being motivated by the moral law; his claim seems to be the normative point that it is only when an agent has to overcome contrary inclination that he deserves esteem—but no need to worry, for the human agent always will have inclinations contrary to morality to

---

[7] Schiller's journal, in which he first published *Anmuth und Würde*.

[8] In his translation of the lectures, Peter Heath translates *Anmuth* as "charm" rather than "grace." For the sake of consistency with the rest of my discussion, I am translating it as "grace." See Kant, LE, p. 259.

overcome. Toward the very end of the lecture notes, finally, Kant reverts to Schiller one more time, and here acknowledges Schiller's claim that "we must couple virtue with grace," but he still supposes that there will inevitably be conflict between grace and virtue (here indicated by the Latin words *decorum* and *honestum*), and that in such a case "strict duty" must always be preferred to grace or *decorum* (LE, Ak 27:707).

Kant's response to Schiller in a note added to Part One in the second edition of *Religion within the Boundaries of Mere Reason* is more complex. Kant appends this note to a discussion of rigorism, to which it is not actually relevant, for he defines rigorism as the position that there is no intermediate between good and evil, and then argues that although there may be *actions* that are morally indifferent, neither good nor evil, agent's *fundamental maxims* can be only either good or evil, as he will subsequently put it, the maxim to subordinate self-love to morality in any case of conflict or the maxim to subordinate morality to self-love in any case of conflict.[9] The footnote on Schiller concerns rather whether or not there must be a conflict between duty and inclination in moral motivation. Kant does not immediately reject Schiller's position wholesale; rather, he begins by saying that "Since we are however at one upon the most important principles, I cannot admit disagreement on this one, if only we can make ourselves clear to one another." But then he seems to take the same negative stance toward what he supposes to be Schiller's position that he took in the Vigilantius lectures, saying that "the concept of duty includes unconditional necessitation, to which grace[10] stands in direct contradiction," although he is willing to concede that "the glorious picture of humanity, as portrayed in the figure of virtue, does allow the attendance of the *graces* [*Grazien*], who, however, maintain a respectful distance when duty alone is at issue." Presumably the graces are the personification of grace, and thus, although Kant is attempting to be more conciliatory to Schiller in this public forum than he was in the relative privacy of his classroom, he is still insisting that grace cannot be too closely connected to duty, thus that there can never be an immediate inclination to fulfill duty and a feeling of complete freedom from conflict in so doing. "These same attendants of Venus Urania become wanton sisters in the train of Venus Dione as soon as they meddle in the business of determining duties and try to provide incentives for them," Kant adds, although Schiller certainly did not say that grace, sympathetic movements, or inclination could determine what our duties are and indeed did not even suggest that inclination could become an incentive for the fulfillment of duties the content of which is determined by reason. His position was really only that the involuntary grace of an agent's voluntary movements would prove that his moral motivation was genuine and not faked.

---

[9] The discussion of rigorism is at Rel, Ak 6:23–24, the subsequent characterization of the two possible fundamental maxims at 6:36.

[10] In this case, George di Giovanni translates *Anmuth* as "gracefulness"; again I am using "grace" for the sake of consistency. See Kant, Rel, p. 72n.

However, Kant now takes a break (marked by a one-em dash), and suddenly seems to agree with Schiller that something like grace can and must serve as *evidence* of genuine virtue: "if we ask, 'What is the *aesthetic* constitution, the *temperament* so to speak of *virtue*: is it courageous and hence *joyous*, or weighed down by fear and dejected?' an answer is hardly necessary. The latter slavish frame of mind can never be found without a hidden *hatred* of the law, whereas a heart joyous in the *compliance* with duty (not just complacency in the recognition of it) is the sign of genuineness in virtuous disposition." Kant continues that a "firm resolve to improve in the future...encouraged by good progress, must needs effect a joyous frame of mind, without which one is never certain of having gained also a *love* for the good" (Rel, Ak 6:23-4n). Kant's position by the end of the note thus seems to be that human agents *can* have a firm resolve to make continuous progress in being good and that their grace—grace in Schiller's sense, not in the sense of a divine gift—can be conclusive evidence of this. In this regard, Kant seems in the end to go further than Schiller, who seemed to suppose that even though our ideal of perfection demands grace as well as dignity, we can never realistically suppose that human beings can always accompany dignity with grace, and sometimes will have to settle for dignity— the manifestation of the struggle to be good in the face of contrary inclinations—alone.

It might seem strange for Kant to go further than Schiller on this point, that indeed he has been carried away, but this conclusion is in fact entirely consistent with the central argument of the *Religion*, namely that since evil is imputable it must be the product of freedom, but if it is the product of freedom, it means that human beings are also free to choose good rather than evil, and thus can effect a moral conversion from evil to good: radical evil implies the possibility of radical goodness (Rel, Ak 6:37). Indeed, the argument of the *Religion* may out-Schiller Schiller. At the same time, there does seem to be one tension between Kant's position in the footnote and his position in the remainder of the *Religion*. In the note, he seems to be adopting Schiller's position that grace and only grace (but again in Schiller's sense, not in the Christian sense, which is actually expressed by a different term, *Gnade*, and which Kant will discuss throughout the *Religion*) can be adequate evidence of the firmness of resolve to make continuous moral progress. In the body of the work, however, Kant seems to argue both that our moral conversion can be *complete*, not a mere firm resolve to make moral progress, but also that because our exercise of our absolute freedom to be good rather than evil is noumenal, not something for which we can have evidence in experience; in fact, we have neither the possibility nor the need of having adequate evidence for the true condition of our will (that is, *Willkür*, the capacity of choice, which is the aspect in which the will is free). In fact, Kant argues, only God (assuming he exists) can have adequate evidence of a human's real moral disposition, not the human being himself.

More precisely, Kant argues that because of the inescapably temporal character of human self-representation, human beings can represent their moral conversion to themselves *only* in the form of continuous moral progress, continuous progress in submitting their inclinations to the fundamental maxim of morality, even though their moral conversion is in fact complete and can and indeed must be known to be so by God. As Kant puts it:

> According to our mode of estimation, [to us] who are unavoidably restricted to temporal conditions in our conceptions of the relationship of cause to effect, the deed, as a continuous advance *in infinitum* from a defective good to something better, always remains defective, so that we are bound to consider the good as it appears to us, i.e., according to the *deed*, as *at each instance* inadequate to a holy law. But because of the *disposition* from which it derives and which transcends the senses, we can think of the infinite progression of the good toward conformity to the law as being judged by him who scrutinizes the heart (through his pure intellectual condition) to be a perfected whole even with respect to the deed (the life conduct). And so notwithstanding his permanent deficiency, a human being can still expect to be *generally* well-pleasing to God, at whatever point in time his existence be cut short. (Rel, Ak 6:67)

So, contrary to Schiller, Kant believes that a complete moral conversion *is* possible, not mere progress in morality, and thus one would think that grace, or the complete joyousness of heart that he describes in the footnote to Part One, should be available to human beings along with dignity, which Schiller actually denied. At the same time, Kant thinks that because of the distinction between the phenomenal and noumenal character of human beings, even complete moral conversion can *appear* to human beings only in the form of continuous *progress* toward morality, which is closer to what Schiller seems to have held possible, and that only God can know that a human being has in fact undergone moral conversion, a conclusion that the thoroughly secular Schiller did not suggest at all. And this in turn undercuts Kant's adoption of Schiller's suggestion that the aesthetic quality of grace in a person's conduct might be both possible and necessary evidence of his completion of moral conversion. For Kant, no such evidence should be either possible or necessary for human beings.

So Kant's position on the harmony of inclination and duty in his controversy with Schiller in 1794 seems unresolved or at least unclear. But this is not Kant's last word on the possible role of feeling in moral motivation. In the *Metaphysics of Morals*, not the classroom lectures of 1793–1794 but the book of that name finally published in two parts in 1797, Kant returns to the subject of moral feeling, as he calls it there as an "aesthetic precondition of the mind's susceptibility to the concept of duty." Here Kant seems to present an unconflicted position on the possibility and indeed necessity of moral feeling, or several kinds of moral feelings, in the empirical manifestation or phenomenology of moral motivation. Yet since this very late work of Kant did not have the degree of influence in its time as his earlier works, because the next generation of philosophers led by Fichte and Schelling had begun to stake out their own positions on many issues before this book even appeared, Kant's late incorporation of moral feeling into his account of moral motivation has not always been appreciated.

Kant does not return to the abstract question of free will in the Doctrine of Virtue, the second part of the *Metaphysics of Morals*, which enumerates those of our duties that as a matter of morality itself cannot be coercively enforced, and therefore can be enforced only by the individual's own commitment to the moral law (unlike the duties of right enumerated in the Doctrine of Right, which can be judicially enforced). This is of course in Kant's view a commitment made by the choice of the free will (*Willkür*), but that is now taken as settled, and Kant instead focuses on virtue in a double sense, the specific non-coercively enforceable duties or virtues such as self-perfection and beneficence to others, and the general virtue that is itself the motivation to fulfill these particular duties. Kant describes virtue in this general sense as "the strength of a human being's maxims in fulfilling his duties." But he immediately continues that "Strength of any kind can be recognized only by the obstacles that it can overcome, and in the case of virtue these obstacles are natural inclinations." Virtue "is a self-constraint in accordance with a principle of inner freedom" (MM, Doctrine of Virtue, Introduction, Section IX, Ak 6:394), namely the moral law, but since it has to overcome natural inclinations, it cannot simply be the determination of the noumenal will to act only in accordance with the moral law, but must be a force in the natural, phenomenal world where those inclinations lie, or a force that bridges the gulf between the noumenal and the phenomenal world—the medium through which the determination of the noumenal will is effective in the phenomenal world. The same can then be said about the "aesthetic preconditions of the receptivity of the mind to concepts of duty in general" that Kant describes several sections later (MM, Doctrine of Virtue, Introduction, Section XII, Ak 6:399)[11]: there may be a transcendental, noumenal act that can be described simply as the determination of the will by the moral law, or the determination of the will to make the moral law its fundamental maxim—nothing Kant says suggests that he is taking back this cornerstone of his philosophy—but these "aesthetic preconditions" are conditions in the phenomenal world through which the duties of virtue are fulfilled in that

---

[11] Mary Gregor translated Kant's German section title, "Ästhetische Vorbegriffer der Empfänglichkeit des Gemüths für Pflichtbegriffe überhaupt" as "Concepts of what is Presupposed on the Part of Feeling by the Mind's Receptivity to Concepts of Duty as Such" (MM, p. 528). I have preferred the literal translation "aesthetic" to her "on the part of feeling" because among what Kant is about to discuss, one item, namely conscience, cannot be properly called a feeling, although it is empirical, something that we in some sense properly call "aesthetic"; and I have translated "Vorbegriffe" as "preconditions" not only because Kant refers to them in Latin as *praedispositio*[*nes*], for which that seems a good translation, but also because he is not about to engage in conceptual analysis, but in psychological explanation. Finally, it should be noted that Kant's use of the term *Gemüth* here suggests that he talking about the mind as a phenomenon in the natural world, not in any other sense.

world.[12] Kant further says that "Every determination of choice [*Willkür*] proceeds *from the representation of a possible action to* the deed *through the feeling of pleasure or displeasure*," which is a "state of feeling" (MM, Doctrine of Virtue, Introduction, Section XII, Ak 6:399; second emphasis added). This makes it clear that for Kant, at least at this late stage of his thought, however pure the determination of the noumenal will may be, *the empirical etiology of every action involves feeling*, thus even action that is at some level motivated by respect for the moral law itself *must also, in the phenomenal world, involve feeling*. Kant is now not talking about a contingent coincidence of inclination and duty, or postulating a special feeling or expression of grace as a *sign* of moral motivation, but rather maintaining that feeling is a normal part of moral motivation at the empirical level.

Specifically, Kant identifies four aesthetic preconditions, namely "moral feeling," "conscience," "love of human beings," and "respect," and of each of these says that our duty is not to create it out of whole cloth, since if we did not at least have a predisposition to it, we would not be able to be "put under obligation at all"—we would not be susceptible to concepts of duty *aesthetically* or in the empirical world, and would be as good as "morally dead"—but instead "to *cultivate* it and strengthen it" (MM, Doctrine of Virtue, Section XII, 6:400). The identity of and relations between these four aesthetic preconditions are not obvious. In the *Critique of Practical Reason*, Kant had identified only a single "moral feeling," namely the feeling of respect at the moral law, a complex feeling involving both an unpleasant feeling at the striking down of self-conceit and an exhilarating feeling of pleasure at the recognition that it is one's own pure practical reason that is striking down one's self-conceit (see CPrR, Ak 5:72–73; for the identification of respect with moral feeling, see 5:76), but here moral feeling and respect are being distinguished from each other, so must refer to different things. And although love of human beings certainly sounds like a feeling, at least if it is what Kant calls "pathological" love, conscience is not exactly a feeling at all, but rather "practical reason holding the human being's duty before him for his acquittal or condemnation in every case that comes under a law" (MM, Doctrine of Virtue, Introduction, Section XII, 6:400). I suggest the following interpretation of the four aesthetic preconditions.[13]

"Moral feeling" is identical with what Kant previously called respect: it is our general awareness at the empirical, felt level of "the constraint present in the thought of duty," it is a precondition—as Kant calls it—of the fulfillment of particular duties in the phenomenal world and of everything that might involve, and it is to be cultivated and strengthened, although Kant does not say

---

[12] More precisely, these aesthetic preconditions are the only conditions through which fulfillment of the duties of virtue can be enforced in the empirical world; duties of justice can be enforced through external, politically instituted juridical and penal sanctions, but *can* also be enforced through the inner—although not noumenal—"aesthetic preconditions." See Kant, MM, Introduction, 6:219–220, and Doctrine of Virtue, Introduction, Section II, Ak 6:383.

[13] I have argued for this interpretation at length in Guyer (2010); pp. 130–151.

much about how this is to be done except that it is to be done "through wonder at its inscrutable source"—focusing our attention on the source of the moral law in pure reason will somehow strengthen our motivation to act in accordance with this law.[14] That means in turn that strengthened moral feeling in this general sense is an indispensable factor in the phenomenal motivation to cultivate the *other* aesthetic preconditions, which are further, more proximate causes of the fulfillment of duty at the phenomenal level. Conscience, the next of the four "preconditions," does not seem like a feeling at all, but more like the disposition to bring particular proposed actions or their maxims before the bench of the moral law for judgment, particular possibilities of action that suggest themselves in and only in the natural world and that must be judged in the natural world. We have a disposition to conscience, but it too must be strengthened through our general moral feeling, presumably through the motivation to do whatever is necessary to be moral that this feeling strengthens and the recognition that the development of conscience is so necessary. Love of other would then be feelings that specifically motivate beneficence and gratitude to others, or what Kant later in the text calls "sympathetic feelings" (MM, Doctrine of Virtue, §§34–35, Ak 6:456–457), and such feelings too would be both cultivated with the encouragement of moral feeling in the first sense but also subjected to the constraints of conscience, checking whether acting on feelings of love or sympathy would in fact be appropriate in specific circumstances—Kant says that we have a "conditional" duty to cultivate sympathetic feelings as a "means to promoting active and rational benevolence" (MM, Doctrine of Virtue, §34, Ak 6:456), presumably because although we need to cultivate our sympathetic feelings as the proximate cause of beneficence, helping others is not in fact morally appropriate or permissible in every circumstance (helping a thief), so these feelings, even when properly cultivated, or precisely when properly cultivated, sometimes also have to be checked. Finally, by the aesthetic precondition of respect Kant now means not the general feeling of respect for the moral law but rather "*self-esteem*," respect for "one's own being," which is "the basis of certain duties, that is, of certain actions that are consistent with [one's] duty to himself" (MM, Doctrine of Virtue, Introduction, Section XII, Ak 6:402–403). Thus, just as the feeling of love for others is the proximate cause for fulfillment of (non-juridical) duties to others, so the feeling of self-esteem is the proximate cause for fulfillment of specific duties to oneself (all of which are non-juridical, because their violation does not directly hinder the freedom of others and thus does not give others, in the collective person of the state and its juridical system, the right to enforce them coercively). The fulfillment of duties to oneself is also a distal, if not proximate, cause of the

---

[14] Grenberg (2013) argues that phenomenological "awareness" is the source of our knowledge of the content of the moral law. I do not find that a plausible interpretation of Kant, but I do think that Grenberg's notion of focused awareness could be used in the interpretation of the cultivation of the motivation to obey the law, the content of which is given (for Kant) by pure reason rather than by anything merely empirical.

fulfillment of duties to others, since one needs to cultivate some talents, for example, not only for one's own sake but also in order to be able to benefit others when that is necessary or appropriate. And the feeling of self-esteem can be cultivated with the impetus of the general moral feeling as well as constrained when necessary by conscience.

Kant has thus concluded his moral philosophy not with Schiller's account of grace but with a complex account of the role of a variety of moral feelings or "aesthetic preconditions" in the phenomenal etiology of moral motivation. Unfortunately, the battle lines over the role of feelings in Kant's moral philosophy had been drawn as soon as the *Groundwork* had been published, long before this account was published, and it was neglected by Kant's immediate successors and for many generations to come.

References

Beck, Lewis White Beck, 1960. *A Commentary to Kant's* Critique of Practical Reason. Chicago: University of Chicago Press.

Boyle, Nicholas, 2000. *Goethe: The Poet and the Age,* Volume II: *Revolution and Renunciation*. Oxford: Clarendon Press.

Grenberg, Jeanine, 2013. *Kant's Defense of Common Moral Experience: A Phenomenological Account*. Cambridge: Cambridge University Press.

Guyer, Paul, 2010. "Moral Feelings in the *Metaphysics of Morals*." Pp. 130-51 in Lara Denis, ed., *Kant's* Metaphysics of Morals: *A Critical Guide*. Cambridge: Cambridge University Press.

Kames, Henry Home, Lord, 2005. *Elements of Criticism,* sixth edition, edited by Peter Jones. 2 vols. Indianapolis: Liberty Fund.

Sensen, Oliver, 2011. *Kant on Human Dignity.* Berlin and New York: Walter de Gruyter.

Tittel, Gottlob August, 1786. *Über Herrn Kants Moralreform*. Frankfurt and Leipzig: Gebrüder Pfähler.

Wood, Allen W., 1999. *Kant's Ethical Thought*. Cambridge: Cambridge University Press.

CHAPTER 27

Karl Leonhard Reinhold's Influence on Schiller's Reception of Kant

Martin Bondeli

On 14 June 1789, Karl Leonhard Reinhold wrote the following to his teacher, Immanuel Kant:

> *Schiller*, my friend, and as I am convinced after intimate acquaintance with him, one of the best living minds, harkens to your teachings through my mouth. The universal history he will create is designed according to your *plan*, which he has grasped with a purity and a fire that has made him all the dearer to me. (RKA 2:134–135)

Indeed, this allusion to Reinhold's influence on Schiller's reception of Kant is no exaggeration. Reinhold, who taught at Jena from the autumn of 1787 to the end of 1793, had recommended Kant to Schiller, who gave his inaugural address on universal history at the University of Jena in May 1789. More than this, however, Schiller's reading of Kant's critical philosophy was guided significantly by Reinhold's writings, and he oriented his own philosophical-aesthetic thinking in line with the practical part of Reinhold's post-Kantian system of Elementary Philosophy. In particular, this orientation relates to Reinhold's findings regarding aesthetic pleasure as the basis of the theory of the faculty of taste and regarding the doctrine of drives and freedom as part of the theory of the faculty of desire. Of course, this is not to say that other contexts and authors were not important to Schiller's 'Kant studies'. It is clear, for

M. Bondeli (✉)
University of Berne, Bern, Switzerland
e-mail: martin.bondeli@philo.unibe.ch

example, that Schiller's engagement with Kant's analysis of beauty in the *Critique of the Power of Judgement*, which began around 1791 and intensified from 1793 onwards, was initiated by his friend Christian Gottfried Körner. Körner also read Reinhold's work and thus contributed to the spread of a form of Kantianism that was influenced by the founder of the Elementary Philosophy.

Schiller's First Encounter and Unsteady Friendship with Reinhold

Of great significance to Schiller's approach to Kantian philosophy were his personal encounters and conversations with Reinhold. The first of these was a meeting in August 1787. Shortly after his arrival at the *Weimarer Gelehrtenhof* in the summer of 1787, Schiller travelled to Jena and stayed with Reinhold for 2 weeks, the latter having just been appointed professor of philosophy. Schiller recounted this encounter to Körner on 29 August 1787:

> In comparison to Reinhold, you are an enemy to Kant: he maintains that one hundred years hence Kant will have the reputation of Jesus Christ. But I must avow that he spoke of him with great understanding and has already induced me to commence reading Kant's short treatises in the Berliner Monatsschrift, among which his idea of a universal history gave me great satisfaction. That I will continue to read Kant, and perhaps study his works, is, I think, more than likely. Reinhold told me that Kant will soon publish a critique of practical reason, or on the will, and afterwards a critique of taste. You can look forward to it. (NA 24:143; cf. transl.: Simpson 1849)

That a Kantian-Reinholdian spark had ignited Schiller at this meeting is undeniable. According to the subsequent brief correspondence (see RKA 1:254–255, 259–260), both had found the conversation pleasant and stimulating and were eager to engage in further discussion. Reservations were also apparent, however, at least on Schiller's part, who immediately wrote to Körner of a perceived polarity in his dealings with Reinhold, hinting at the character differences that separated him from the latter and that would likely make a closer relationship with him difficult:

> Reinhold can never become my friend, nor I his, although he fancies so. We are quite opposite beings. His intellect is cold, deep and clear-sighted—mine is not, nor can I appreciate him; but his imagination is poor and circumscribed, and his spirit narrower than mine. [...] He never could be capable of great virtues or great crimes, either in imagination or in reality, and that is unfortunate. (NA 24:144; cf. transl.: Simpson 1849, slightly modified)

For Schiller, it was not primarily Reinhold's contrasting temperament but his kinship and professional relationship with Christoph Martin Wieland that would later prove to be an obstacle to maintaining an untroubled friendship (see Roehr 2003a). Schiller—who, following a reading of *Don Carlos*, had been given the honorary title of Weimar Court Councillor by Karl August, sovereign Duke of Saxe-Weimar—had hoped to find permanent employment and earn a middle-class living in the city of Goethe, Herder, and Wieland. An opportunity presented itself when Wieland proposed the restructuring of his renowned journal *Der Teutsche Merkur* (December 1787: 286–287). Schiller was to be involved in editing the *Merkur*, which was seeking to broaden its readership. In exchange, there was to be a merger between the *Merkur* and Schiller's journal, *Thalia* (see NA 24:165–166). Schiller accepted this proposal with optimism, believing it would 'secure [his] entire livelihood' (NA 24:171). For financial reasons, however, the project did not come to fruition, and it was Wieland's son-in-law Reinhold—who, in addition to his professorship, also held a leading position at the *Merkur*—whom Schiller held responsible for the failure and did not spare from hostile remarks (see NA 25:168).

After the Weimar administration offered Schiller the prospect of a professorship in universal history at Jena at the end of 1788, the personal relationship between the two returned to normal, and it was clear that Schiller's interest in Reinhold, who had won respect and fame for his *Letters on the Kantian Philosophy*, increased from that point on (on the origin and significance of the letters, see RGS 2/1, IX–LXVI). Reinhold, for his part, had raised the possibility of Schiller's securing a position at Jena at their first meeting (see NA 24:148) and now welcomed the idea of having him as a future colleague. The years following Schiller's appointment—a professorship that was officially affiliated with philosophy rather than history—saw productive collaboration between the two on a professional level. A philosopher by profession, Reinhold played the part of the systematically versed and instructive Kantian. Schiller, by contrast—who had ambitions as a playwright but, as a graduate of the Karlsschule in Stuttgart, was also highly receptive to philosophical-anthropological discourse—appropriated Kantian-Reinholdian ideas on morality and aesthetics, all with great skill, flexibility, and a certain subversiveness. For a time, the two encountered each other regularly at meetings of a professorial council that included seasoned Kantians such as Gottlieb Hufeland, Carl Christian Erhard Schmid, and Christian Gottfried Schütz, editor of the *Allgemeine Literatur-Zeitung*. When Schiller fell seriously ill and ran into financial hardship in 1791, Reinhold revealed his caring side. He conveyed his colleague's predicament to his friend and pupil Jens Baggesen (see RKA 3:297–298), who secured a three-year pension for Schiller from the Danish Hereditary Prince Friedrich Christian von Augustenburg and Count Ernst von Schimmelmann (see RKA 3:318–319; see also Schulz 1910:69–71). This was to give Schiller the opportunity to delve into his Kantian aesthetic work, to communicate the results of his studies in letters to the Danish hereditary prince, and to make them accessible to a wider public in the newly founded journal *Die Horen* (first issued in 1795). As Schiller had predicted, he and Reinhold never did establish an intimate friendship, even further down the road. Over time, however, the two managed to develop a stimulating collegial relationship and a mutual esteem.

The Reception of Reinhold's Texts: Not a One-Way Street

It was a good two years following his first encounter with Reinhold before Schiller would engage with Kantian philosophy in anything more than a sporadic fashion. The discussion in the Jena circle evidently encouraged him to familiarise himself with the latest writings of his colleagues, alongside the relevant works by Kant. A letter to Körner from April 1789 shows that Schiller was acquainted with Reinhold's *On the Previous Fate of the Kantian Philosophy*, published in the *Merkur* (see NA 25:241). In another letter to Körner, written in 1790, Schiller acknowledges the newly published first volume of Reinhold's *Letters on the Kantian Philosophy* and Schmid's *Attempt at a Moral Philosophy*, a standard work on Kant's practical philosophy (see NA 26:26). Körner, who detected in Reinhold's thinking 'many connections' to his own views (NA 33/1:152), referred Schiller to the older version of the *Letters*, and then also to Reinhold's 'treatises on pleasure', which concerned a theory of taste (NA 33/1:283). Yet Schiller had already had access to the first four texts from the *Merkur* version of the *Letters* (published from August 1786 to February 1787) as early as March 1787 (see RKA 1:206–207). A letter from the end of October 1789 also reveals that Schiller had been in possession of Reinhold's *Essay on a New Theory of the Human Faculty of Representation* since that time as well. Schiller had received Reinhold's 'new philosophical work as a gift' (NA 25:311) after sending Reinhold a printed copy of his inaugural address at Jena. The *Essay*—in which, after discussing the question of the first principles of cognition, morality, and natural law, Reinhold develops a prototype of his system of Elementary Philosophy in two extensive books (see RGS 1:123–366)—was considered a success even beyond Jena, catching the attention of both Schiller and his friend Körner, whose opinion on the 'Reinholdian book' Schiller requested (NA 25:324; NA 33/1:415–416). In January of 1792, Reinhold was pleased to report to Baggesen that Schiller had 'already carefully studied more than half of the *Essay*' (RKA 4:36). Of Reinhold's many other publications, Schiller then apparently acquired the second volume of the *Letters*, which were made available to the public at the Michaelmas Fair in 1792 (see RGS 2/2, VII). In the essay *On Grace and Dignity*, published in *Thalia* in 1793, reference is made to the theory of the will and of freedom contained in this volume (see SW 5:472, note). It is likely that Schiller had also read Reinhold's 1791 programmatic essay *On the Foundation of Philosophical Knowledge*, in which the Elementary Philosophy is elevated to the status of the ultimate development of the theories of Leibniz, Locke, Hume, and Kant (see RGS 4, 40–47, 66–68). This is indicated by Schiller's remark that he was now studying Kant's philosophy with 'great eagerness' and that he intended to take on 'Locke, Hume, and Leibniz' at the same time (NA 26:116).

Interestingly, this relationship was not one-sided. Reinhold, too, had been following his colleague's work for some time, and more closely since 1789. He was an avid reader of Schiller's poetic texts and was familiar with many essays from *Thalia*, including the *Philosophical Letters* (see RKA 1:207), in which, in 1786 and 1789, Schiller had published examples of his mainly pre-Kantian anthropological and metaphysical thinking. Reinhold was therefore curious to find out which paths Schiller intended to take in his treatment of Kantian aesthetic questions. In early 1792, Schiller gave him a copy of the essay *On the Cause of the Pleasure We Derive from Tragic Objects*, also published in *Thalia* (see RKA 4:24, 36). Reinhold is likely to have taken great interest in Schiller's essays on the ideas of the sublime and the pathetic published from 1793 onwards, the important *On Grace and Dignity*, and the series of letters *On the Aesthetic Education of Man* (1795). Unfortunately, in the course of 1793, personal encounters between Reinhold and Schiller became less frequent (see RKA 5:69), and, following Reinhold's relocation to the University of Kiel in the spring of 1794, the two were rarely in direct contact.

Under the Spell of Reinhold, Illuminist and Enlightenment Philosopher

Due to his training as a Catholic priest and his later conversion to the Lutheran faith, which instilled in him a firm, moral-religious disposition, Reinhold bore little resemblance to the heroic figures that Schiller so admired and portrayed in his dramas. As Schiller soon came to appreciate, however, Reinhold had other qualities and virtues. Not only was he an accomplished authority on Kant, but his interpretation of Kant's teachings was original and innovative, bridging the gap between philosophy and the fine arts and sciences. According to a later distinction, he viewed himself as an 'independent thinker' rather than a mere 'parroter' of Kant's thought (RGS 5/2:93). Equally important, Reinhold was also a theoretical and practical Enlightenment philosopher par excellence. In his youth in Vienna, in addition to his teaching activities with the Order of the Barnabites, he held high rank in the officially banned Masonic order of the Illuminati, disseminating Enlightenment pamphlets directed against the church orthodoxy, partly openly and partly under an assumed name. He maintained his commitment to the Masonic order while in Jena and, together with Hufeland, managed its local membership. Shortly after arriving in Kiel, he was called upon to reorganise illuminist Freemasonry within the German territories as a whole (see RGS 6/1: Introduction). Against this background, Reinhold was also keen to understand Kant's critical philosophy as the cornerstone of an illuminist Enlightenment and global transformation. From the mid-1780s on, he expressed the conviction that Kant's *Critique of Pure Reason* would usher in a new age of humanity, even speaking of a new 'gospel of pure reason' (RKA 1:153). After 1789, he announced that Kantian philosophy was the intellectual and cultural counterpart of the political revolution in France.

The only slightly younger Schiller, for his part, had also long been a progressive thinker of his time. He had come into contact with Enlightenment thought during his years as a student in Stuttgart, and from that point on he counted various illuminist figures among his acquaintances, including his good friend Körner and his philosophy teacher, Jacob Friedrich Abel (see Schings 1996). We can therefore presume that, following his arrival in Weimar and Jena, Schiller developed a certain fascination with Reinhold—the illuminist Enlightenment philosopher—and with his Kantian spirit of revolution and renewal. In this context, it cannot be ruled out that, inspired by Reinhold, Schiller took his involvement in the Illuminati movement beyond the level of intellectual sympathy. Schiller's *Mission of Moses*, published in *Thalia* in 1790, is worthy of mention in this regard. This account of the origin and spread of the Mosaic religion is a retelling of Reinhold's Masonic text *The Hebrew Mysteries, or the Oldest Religious Freemasonry*, published in 1788, as Schiller explains in a note referencing this text and citing Reinhold's Masonic pseudonym, 'Bruder Decius' (see SW 4:804). One is given the impression that, by engaging with this subject matter and referring to the text's secret author, Schiller wished to signal his ties to Reinhold's illuminist circle at Jena. It should also be noted that those in Reinhold's circle who lobbied for financial support for Schiller—Baggesen and Prince von Augustenburg—also saw themselves as an illuminist network. Interestingly, in the correspondence between Baggesen and Augustenburg, Schiller is referred to by the pseudonym 'Enceladus' (Schulz 1910:179, 182). Whether Schiller became a full member of the Illuminati at the time or kept to the role of sympathiser and literary accompanist is a task for future research. In any case, it is worth noting that Reinhold and his illuminist entourage provided Schiller with ample material with which to continue writing the secret society novel he had begun in 1786, *The Ghost-Seer*, and that Schiller, in criticising the obscurantist tendencies within Freemasonry, agreed with Reinhold's rationalist reorientation of the Illuminati movement.

Kant's Philosophy of History as a Common Starting Point and Disagreement on the Question of a Morality of Benevolence

A strand of thought that was attractive to both Reinhold and Schiller was Kant's philosophy of history. In contributions to the *Berlinische Monatsschrift*, especially the essays *Idea for a Universal History with a Cosmopolitan Aim* (1784) and *Conjectural Beginning of Human History* (1786), Kant had argued that the process of history should be understood as the human being's emergence from an original state of harmony with nature and reconstructed in line with the idea of human society's gradual ascent to a world of freedom and rational morality. When referring to the ideas of the creation and the beginning of the world, a distinction was made between the 'history of *nature*' as the '*work of God*' and the 'history of *freedom*' as the '*work of the human being*' (Ak 8:115; AHE 169), so as to situate the latter as the proper focus and aim of history. The vision of a higher, final harmony was not rejected altogether, but this final state was only to be achieved along a path of emancipation from the constraints of nature—constraints which become apparent with the awakening of freedom and reason. With regard to the question of overcoming the constraints of nature, there was talk, among other things, of 'the human being' as 'an *animal which*, when it lives among others of its species, *has need of a master*' (Ak 8:23; AHE 113)—a statement that at the time outraged philosophers of history such as Herder, who were optimistic about nature.

For his part, from the mid-1780s onwards, Reinhold was occupied with the goal of establishing a satisfying relationship between reason and faith on the basis of Kant's philosophy of history. In his essay *Sketch of a Theogony of Blind Faith*, published in *Der Teutsche Merkur* in 1786 and included in *Letters on the Kantian Philosophy* in 1790, he offered a basic outline of the beginning, progress, and final end of human history, in which the ascent to a world of freedom and rational faith—which involves overcoming the constraints of nature—is at the same time described as the path of the individual human being, who develops from an 'infant at the breast of nature' and from a 'pupil of nature' to a 'child', 'youth', and 'man' (RGS 2/1:241–242; LKP 223). The relationship between nature and reason is viewed primarily as a relation between forces. Whether the world of freedom and reason is achieved depends on the 'force' of reason, its 'strength' or 'weakness'. The main task of the Enlightenment philosopher is thus to strengthen moral reason and to curtail sensibility, which has united itself with blind faith and a weak reason. As a suitable means for this task, Reinhold recommends the advancement of scientific and moral culture, while at the same time emphasising the beneficial 'influence of taste on scientific and moral culture' (RGS 5/1:119–132).

As indicated, from 1787 onwards, Schiller also read Kant's essays on the philosophy of history in the *Berlinische Monatsschrift* with great enthusiasm. In 1790, in the essay *Remarks on the First Human Society on the Basis of the Mosaic Record* (published in *Thalia*), he then formulated his own view—in a Kantian spirit—on the rhythm of the process of history on a large scale. Schiller's text deals only marginally with the biblical story of creation and paradise; its real focus is the development of the human being. In it, Schiller describes the human being as having been a 'pupil of nature' in his 'infancy', guided by a divine natural instinct. It is precisely through 'falling away from his instinct' that the human being then entered the world of reason and freedom. Due to his 'weak reason', he initially fell victim to numerous errors and confusions before gradually, enabled by a strengthened reason immersed in art and morality, 'working his way upward to a paradise of knowledge and freedom' (SW 4:767–769). Quite a few of Schiller's turns of phrase in this essay are reminiscent of Kant, Herder, and Reinhold, the motif of the strength of reason echoing above all the latter. In all this, it should not be forgotten that Schiller was able to draw on resources in both anthropology and the philosophy of history from his German dissertation *On the Connection between the Animal and the Spiritual Nature in the Human Being*. Even as a student in Stuttgart, he had been concerned with the representation of historical periods, and he based his outline of the structure of the process of history on a basic human pattern. Following Christian Garve's notes in his translation of Adam Ferguson's *Institutes of Moral Philosophy*, Schiller proposed a classification of historical periods based on the stages of the individual human being (see SW 4:299–301).

Like Reinhold, Schiller's historical thinking evinces a general optimism regarding progress and reason. Schiller is far more strongly inclined towards sentimentality regarding nature, however, and is moved far more intensely by a longing for the world of the Greek gods. He hopes for the progress of enlightened reason, not primarily through a strengthening of the sciences and moral culture, but through the reawakening of a moral-aesthetic spirit of the sublime. Reinhold's appeal to the beneficial influence of aesthetic taste on science and morality is therefore welcomed, although it is surpassed by the thesis that the aim of humanity will only be achieved 'when scientific and moral culture once again melt into beauty' (NA 25:200). Schiller also puts a different emphasis than Reinhold on the relationship between reason and sensibility. His vision of a final end of history, which hinges on the ideal of the union of nature and reason, has a Stoic and Kantian tinge. According to Reinhold, unity can only be achieved under the primacy of moral reason. Schiller, by contrast, favours a union of nature and reason according to the model of equilibrium and reciprocity between the material and the spiritual. Even if we are to think of it as integrative, the dominance of the rational over the animal nature of the human being is out of the question for Schiller.

Schiller thus essentially restates what he had already articulated in his dissertation. The ultimate aim of the history of the individual human being and of humanity in general is to be understood as a state in which both animal and rationally guided needs are satisfied. Once again, this would seem to accord with what Garve writes in his notes to Ferguson's *Institutes of Moral Philosophy*. Schiller approvingly quotes a passage (see SW 5:301–302) that culminates in the assertion that human 'benevolence'—physical and mental, subjective and intersubjective—is a 'state of spiritual perfection' (See Ferguson 1792:324). In 1786, in the *Philosophical Letters*, Schiller situated these final thoughts on the spirit of benevolence within the framework of a metaphysics of perfection: 'I desire the happiness of others, because I desire my own. Desire for the happiness of others we call benevolence, *love*' (SW 5:348). Understood in this way, benevolence is to be expressly conceived of as an unselfish relation, such that one can 'admit it frankly; I believe in the reality of an unselfish love' (SW 5:351).

With regard to this point from the *Philosophical Letters*, it is important to note that Reinhold explicitly distanced himself from a morality of benevolence and thus deliberately opposed Schiller's conclusions regarding the philosophy of history. In a previously published (1791) text from the second volume of the *Letters on the Kantian Philosophy*, Reinhold argues that a morality of benevolence falls short compared to the new, much esteemed rational-moral view of the source of our duties and rights found in Kant's philosophy. Reinhold first refers critically to Rousseau, who sought and found the ground of morality in the feeling of sympathy, 'in the capacity to be moved by the sight of the suffering of others' (RGS 2/2:40). He goes on to say that 'a famous German moral philosopher' believed he had 'derived the ground from this very feeling, from *benevolence*, or the capacity to derive pleasure from the wellbeing of others' (RGS 2/2:40–41). Reinhold's target here is clearly Garve, who, in his comments on Ferguson, placed 'benevolence' and the ability 'to find pleasure in the happiness of others' above the moral feeling of respect (Adam Ferguson 1792:101, 336–337). Reinhold is thus also giving a nod to Schiller, whom he later explicitly associates with Garve (see RGS 2/2:298). Reinhold makes clear that, in a philosophy of history modelled on Kant, one cannot avoid formulating the ultimate aim of reason and freedom in the spirit of Kant's doctrine of morality. With diplomatic restraint, he also shares that Garve—who in the course of the 1780s, together with Feder, had made scathing remarks about the *Critique of Pure Reason*—was not exactly popular in the camp of Kant's friends. Kant himself had already famously put Feder's circle of so-called popular philosophers in their place around 1783. In 1793, in the essay *On the Common Saying*, he then explicitly rebutted Garve, who had claimed that the 'purity' of morality on which Kant insisted was unattainable (Ak 8:284). Reinhold was presumably aware of Schiller's appropriation of Garve's moral philosophical views, if not as a result of reading Schiller's dissertation, which he likely had to submit in order to obtain his teaching qualification at Jena (in this regard, see NA 25:122, 163), then certainly from conversations among the professors at Jena.

Pleasure as the Basis of the Faculty of Taste and Demarcating Limits in the Relationship Between Morality and Aesthetics

A remarkable intellectual fellowship, which nonetheless led to differences of opinion concerning the question of the relation between morality and aesthetics, arose between Reinhold and Schiller when it came to the concept of aesthetic pleasure. Reinhold, who in his first years of teaching at Jena lectured primarily on Kant and aesthetics (including on Wieland's epic poem *Oberon*), had published the study *On the Previous Concepts of Pleasure* (RGS 5/1:133–170) in 1788 and 1789. Engaging with the relevant theories of pleasure of the time, Reinhold sides with the view that aesthetic pleasure should be understood on the basis of a distinctive relation between subject and object. Unlike in cognition and desire, in aesthetic pleasure the active subject relates to an object with an approving feeling of light and lively engagement. The object, for its part, contributes to this feeling insofar as in it, at the level of a pure, clear intuition, can be found the rule-governed yet free structure of the unity of the manifold. In the course of further conversation, Reinhold suggested that the beautiful and the sublime ought to be understood as two types of pleasure, with pleasure serving as an intermediary between the two. In addition, with regard to the question of classification, he considered it useful to start from the generic concept of 'pleasure in general', to divide it into 'mere pleasure' (on the subjective side) and 'delight' (on the objective side), and to link this to a distinction between the agreeable, the beautiful, and the morally good (RGS 2/2:166–167). Furthermore, the judgement of taste, which discursively expresses aesthetic approval or disapproval, and which is to be distinguished from the judgement of the understanding, which is based on truth, should be able to extend to all kinds of pleasure in general, and thus also to the agreeable. Finally, in terms of the broader system, it was declared that pleasure was to be understood as the foundation of the faculty of taste. This step simultaneously decreed the independence of the faculty of taste and emphasised its distinction from the faculties of cognition and desire. The function of the faculty of taste, which is an intermediary between cognition and desire and thus promotes both a sense of truth and moral sense, was also emphasised. Within the architectonic of the system of Elementary Philosophy—which consisted of a basic theory of the faculty of representation, along with a theory of the faculty of cognition and a theory of the faculty of desire constructed on its basis—this revaluation and determination of the function of the faculty of taste did not lead to any significant changes. That is to say, a third branch of the system was not constructed alongside cognition and desire.

It cannot be overlooked that Reinhold's intention in the essay from 1788 and 1789 was to apply Kant's results to the doctrine of taste and in this way to assist Kant in completing the *Critique of the Power of Judgement*. This project failed, especially since Kant was in no way agreeable to placing pleasure at the pinnacle of aesthetics. On the contrary, Kant downgraded this concept. 'Pleasure', Kant wrote in § 3 of the third *Critique*, was a subjective state in which 'enjoyment' was essential, as opposed to the 'pleasing' that is relevant to a judgement of taste (Ak 5:207). This led to a controversy behind the scenes, in which Reinhold defended his view on the matter (see Bondeli 2017:20–23).

Schiller, who gave a lecture on theories of tragedy in 1790, apparently had no objection to following Reinhold in placing the concept of pleasure at the centre of the faculty of taste and artistic activity. In the essay *On the Source of the Pleasure We Derive from Tragic Objects*, published in January 1792, this concept is considered essential to characterising art and to distinguishing it from morality. Thus, Schiller explains that 'pleasure' is an indirect end of morality, whereas 'for art' it is the direct, 'highest', or 'chief end' (SW 5:377). Like Reinhold, Schiller endeavours to identify different types and domains of pleasure. This is meant to show that the feeling of pleasure manifests itself in sensible and spiritual ways, in connection to nature and morality, morality and immorality, and in the tension between lively activity, joy, and happiness, on the one hand, and suffering, pain, and sorrow, on the other. At the level of spiritual and free pleasure, the 'sources of pure pleasure' are to be grasped in terms of and divided into the following classes: 'good, true, perfect, beautiful, affecting, and sublime'. In terms of the faculty of the soul as a whole, we must bear in mind that 'reason' concerns itself with the 'good', 'the understanding with the true and the perfect; the understanding and the imagination with the beautiful; and reason and the imagination with the affecting and the sublime' (SW 5:377).

From the very beginning, Schiller gives decisive weight to reflection on the relationship between art and morality. Art must be based on 'moral conditions' and must 'make its way through morality', if the stage of spiritual and free pleasure is to be reached (SW 5:359). But this is only a necessary, not a sufficient, condition. Moral art is the 'appraisal of art', but not yet the 'perfection of art' (SW 5:360). If art is elevated to morality, and if the purpose of art is thus primarily moral, 'then it loses that on account of which it alone is powerful, its freedom, as well as that on account of which it is so universally effective—the allure of pleasure' (SW 5:359). When Schiller then includes 'moral pleasure' (SW 5:367) in his considerations, he does not intend it as an oxymoron. In this case, it is rather to be understood either as a pleasure of an imperfect kind or as a kind of artistic pleasure in which there is a correspondence between morality and perfect art.

Schiller goes on to examine the relationship between art and morality in further detail by incorporating the idea of the Kantian moral law. In doing so, he argues that it is 'not only obedience to the moral law' that gives us the 'representation of moral purposiveness', but also 'anguish over its violation' and the accompanying sequence of feelings of 'sadness', 'remorse', and 'self-condemnation' (SW 5:366). Here, Schiller expresses the conviction that the 'tragic emotions' that arouse pleasure in suffering and compassion have their origin in a 'feeling of moral purposiveness' (SW 5:369). Schiller also sides with a horizon-broadening view which in substance concerns the incentive to moral action. In his opinion, 'respect for the moral law' should be presented such that it is comprehensible both as an overcoming of counterforces and as a 'source of moral pleasure' (SW 5:367). It is clear that Schiller is here primarily referring to the aesthetic concept of the sublime; the moral fitness of beauty, of the beautiful soul, is not at issue. On the whole, Schiller takes the view that the pleasure we derive from tragedy is advantageous when it comes to elaborating a conception of morality along Kantian lines. However, the pleasure taken in tragedy is compatible with the Kantian conception of morality only to the extent that it approximates pleasure taken in the moral law, in its spirit of attentiveness and unselfishness. The more the human being is able to escape the dictates of his 'self-interested drives' and to free himself from the exclusive 'gratification of the drive for happiness' (SW 5:375), the more moral and rational his tragic feelings.

In the following months, Reinhold also apparently read and assessed *On the Source of the Pleasure We Derive from Tragic Objects*, which he had received in the spring of 1792. In the seventh letter of the second volume of *Letters on the Kantian Philosophy*, which dates to late autumn 1792, there are at any rate passages that raise the same points Schiller had discussed regarding the relationship between pleasure and morality. Reinhold stresses that the concept of unselfishness corresponds to the lawlike and universal character of the moral law and must not be confused with notions of public utility, sympathetic feeling, or social pleasure. 'Moral pleasure' can only ever be 'self-interested' (RGS 2/2:171). Reinhold further urges us to distinguish between the determining ground, the incentive, and the end of morality and to bear in mind that moral pleasure can belong neither to the determining ground, nor to the incentives, but only to the determination of the end of morality. Pleasure can '*provide neither the subjective nor the objective determinant of moral action*' (RGS 2/2, 181). In short, moral pleasure belongs not to the foundation, but to the conclusions of morality. Finally, Reinhold points out that a morality based on moral pleasure does not take into account the concept of the 'will' and the freedom of the will, which is necessary for moral judgement and for the question of '*imputation*' (RGS 2/2:170).

Schiller is likely to have referred to Reinhold's more recent clarification of the concept of pleasure and the distinction between the moral faculty and the faculty of taste. Indeed, some of Schiller's statements in On *Grace and Dignity* (1793) can be interpreted as a reaction to Reinhold's objections. Schiller clearly heeded Reinhold's remark on the will and the freedom of the morally capable human; as the essay repeatedly states, when it comes to the human being, in addition to nature and reason, the 'authority' that we call the '*will*' must also be taken into account. Indeed, special attention must be paid to the '*will*, which, as a supersensible faculty, is not subject to either the law of nature or that of reason in such a way that it does not have complete freedom to choose whether to comply with the one or the other' (SW 5:471). Schiller also apparently followed Reinhold's advice in distinguishing between different authorities and levels in Kant's conception of morality. At any rate, he is here operating with Kantian-sounding distinctions between ought and is, disposition and act, approvingly declaring that 'moral legislation' is to be regarded as a matter of 'pure reason' alone and that the 'claims of sensibility' must in this case be '*completely* repudiated' (SW 5:464). With that said, at least in the realm of moral motivation, he does not at this point wish to abandon his previous standpoint, which privileges aesthetics. It is in this sense that he affirms that, in addition to 'moral sense', it is equally necessary to satisfy 'aesthetic sense', which goes hand in hand with reality and the use of our moral faculty, and which thus ultimately helps morality to secure greater and more enthusiastic acceptance. An action that conforms to morality in this way '*satisfies*' my 'moral sense (reason)' and '*enraptures* my aesthetic sense (imagination)' (SW 5:529).

In a later step, Schiller will ultimately make a concession to the Kantian on this last point as well, emphasising that 'respect for the law' is the only true moral incentive (NA 26:322). The role of aesthetics thus consists in cultivating human nature such that it does not stand in the way of this incentive. That Schiller is prepared to make this concession has to do with the fact that he is considering not only the usefulness of aesthetics for morality, but also the limits, in terms of influence, within the relationship between aesthetics and morality. In this context, Schiller is considering the possibility of bringing the standpoint of aesthetics more fully to bear, even independently of any close connection to the moral standpoint. Ultimately, he recognises that there is good reason to place the aesthetic standpoint above the moral standpoint when it comes to the end of a free, fully integrated human life.

THE DOCTRINE OF DRIVES AND THE DOCTRINE OF FREEDOM ACCORDING TO REINHOLD'S THEORY OF THE FACULTY OF DESIRE

While Reinhold did not further elaborate the theory of taste in his Elementary Philosophy after 1793, Schiller gradually approached the pinnacle of his philosophical-aesthetic reflections in the following years and remained interested in discussing the findings of his interlocutor, who was then teaching in Kiel. This is particularly evident in the series of letters *On the Aesthetic Education of Man*, published in the journal *Die Horen* from January to June 1795. Schiller conceived of this text as a further, novel contribution to the moral-aesthetic thinking that had emerged as a result of interpretations of the 'practical part of Kant's system' (SW 5:571). Schiller also speaks to Körner of Reinhold's 'Elementary Philosophy', which he presupposes in this context (NA 27:178). In his exposition of the basic human drives and human freedom of the will, Schiller evidently adhered to parts of Reinhold's theory of the faculty of desire, replicating Reinhold's specifications but with his own aesthetic recalibrations.

In the concluding section of *Essay on a New Theory of the Human Faculty of Representation*, Reinhold developed the Kantian ideas of morality, the moral law, and moral community on the basis of a doctrine of drives. The notion of a drive, in the sense of a force that strives for the realisation of ideas and the fulfilment of moral duties, is thus assigned a key role. On closer inspection, what is at stake is a drive that is to be divided into 'two essentially distinct and essentially connected basic drives'—into 'the *drive to the material* and the *drive to the form* of the representation' (RGS 1:356; VNT 276)—and which on this basis finds expression both in the realm of physical and aesthetic sensibility and in the realm of moral reason. With regard to its effects in the realm of moral reason, the sensible drive to material is described as being 'satisfied only when there is some *given*' and thus as being '*self-interested*', while the drive to form, which corresponds to the moral law, is satisfied 'only through *action* per se' and is thus '*unselfish*' (RGS 1:356; VNT 276). With regard to moral ends, the two drives are interpreted as the demand to realise the cosmological and theological ideas of '*interaction*' and '*absolute community*' (RGS 1:364ff.; VNT 283–284). As Reinhold argues in accordance with Kant's practical postulate of the highest good, a moral world is to be brought about in which, on the condition that the unselfish drive is given primacy, the self-interested drive is also given its due, and thus the 'COMPLETE *good of the human being*' is satisfied (RGS 2/2:257). Reinhold thus calls for the harmonisation of the basic drives via subordination and integration.

The distinction between the self-interested and the disinterested drive is subsequently also constitutive of the morally relevant understanding of the will and freedom of the will that Reinhold defended from 1789 on and further elaborated in the context of writing the second volume of *Letters on the Kantian Philosophy*, where he claimed to have explicated the foundation of practical philosophy. According to Reinhold's conception, human freedom of the will can be defined as the ability of the willing person to decide, completely independently, in favour of either the demands of the self-interested drive (sensible inclination) or the demands of the unselfish drive (the moral law). If the two demands are understood as grounds with which we are confronted as volitional beings, they are grounds that merely induce action rather than constraining it. It is ultimately we alone who decide which grounds to accept and are in this (and only this) respect responsible for our decisions. This implies that, for the willing person, there is a prior independence not only from sensible impulses but also from the moral law. The faculty of free will is thus to be regarded as an authority within us that is different from the moral law, which—in contrast to natural laws—applies to us as a law of freedom and is given to us by the fact of practical reason. In short: 'The *freedom of the will* is to be distinguished from the *self-activity of reason*' (RGS 2/2:137). This also means that both the moral will, which conforms to the law, and the immoral will, which contradicts the law, are to be described as free. In this sense, '[b]oth the *pure* will and the *impure* will are therefore nothing other than the two equally possible modes of action of the *free* will' (RGS 2/2:188). Morally relevant freedom must therefore be distinguished from moral freedom: the former concerns freedom of the will and the latter the moral aim for which we must strive. Finally, it is clear that Reinhold's interpretation of freedom of the will, which he holds up against the interpretation of the Kantian concept of moral freedom proposed by his colleague Schmid (*intelligible fatalism*), must show the extent to which we are justified in relating freedom of the will to the notions of indifference, decisionism, and a self-contained ground of personality (where personality is reflected in a free and binding conscience). In this regard, Reinhold takes issue with the '*equilibrists*' (RGS 2/2:191–192), arguing that while their assertion of the complete independence of the will is correct, their notion of equilibrium must be rejected, since it is associated with a barrier to decision-making or with a blind faculty of choice.

As a student, Schiller had engaged with questions concerning the basic human material and spiritual drives, and in this context he had also given thought to the fact that the interaction of material and spiritual forces is presumably due to the existence of a '*mediating force*' (SW 5:253). However, it was only in writing the series of letters *On the Aesthetic Education of Man* that he developed a doctrine of drives relevant to the areas of morality and aesthetic creativity. The extent of his departure from the Kantian-Reinholdian taxonomy and terminology that took place in the meantime is unmistakable. The account of drives that Schiller develops in the twelfth and thirteenth letters gives the impression of being a version of the doctrine of drives that we find in Reinhold's theory of the capacity for desire, only stripped of its strict systematic form, made more precise in parts, and given new facets (for more on this, see Bondeli

2019). Like Reinhold, Schiller considers a 'drive' in general to be a force that pushes for the realisation of representations. Drives are said to play a role both in the realisation of ideas and in the demand of 'duty' and 'observance of the law', being of importance both objectively, in relation to force or law, and subjectively, in relation to the 'satisfaction of a need' (Horen 1795 II, 63, note). Like Reinhold, Schiller then assumes two opposing basic drives, the *'sensuous drive'* (later also called the 'material drive'), corresponding to the 'sensible nature' of human beings, and the *'formal drive'*, corresponding to the rational nature of human beings (Horen 1795 II, 64, 66; SW 5:604f.; OAE 79, 81).

Finally, a remarkable parallel emerges with regard to the aforementioned fact that Reinhold's doctrine of drives ends with the idea of absolute community. Immediately after characterising the two basic drives, Schiller interprets the formal drive as the author of a theoretical law that makes objectively valid cognition possible, as the legislator of a practical law that provides us with the objective determining ground of moral action, and finally as the originator of a *'unity of ideas'* that encompasses these laws (Horen 1795 II, 67; SW 5:606; OAE 83). Following Reinhold, Schiller thus also makes the formal drive the matrix of a totalising completion of rational cognition.

Far more intensely than Reinhold, Schiller reflects on the way in which the two basic drives can be appropriately conceived: as both wholeness and harmony. The idea of subordination proposed by Reinhold is considered unsatisfactory. Instead, an equilibrium, a coordination, or even a relation of mutual limitation and recognition between the two drives is considered. The idea of a mediating third drive is also offered up for discussion, although it is immediately rejected with the remark that a 'third *basic drive*' is 'a completely unthinkable concept' (Horen 1795 II, 69; SW 5:606f.; OAE 85). Yet in the fourteenth letter, Schiller takes a different view. The previously introduced play drive is proposed as a drive that is awakened by the material drive and the formal drive. In this sense, it is a mediating third drive, but not a basic drive. Owing to its mediating role, a self-referential unifying structure is ascribed to the third drive, such that it can be read as a new, first, and proper attempt adequately to conceive of the unity of the two basic drives. With this endorsement of a mediating third drive, Schiller once again sets himself apart from Reinhold's Kantian way of thinking, offering his own distinctive aesthetic perspective on the matter. According to Schiller, in the realm of morality, the domestication of sensibility by reason is unavoidable; in the realm of aesthetics, by contrast, sensibility and reason can be kept in playful interaction, and thus in harmony. This is not to say that morality should be replaced by aesthetics or that it should become a hybrid 'aesthetic morality' or 'moral aesthetics'. Rather, this is meant to convey the idea that aesthetics has different priorities than morality within the spectrum of our moral-aesthetic way of life.

Schiller was not unprepared for Reinhold's idea of freedom of the will, as various aspects of the theme of freedom had occupied him long before his time in Weimar and Jena. However, it was only with the turn to Kantian philosophy that he was able to break away from traditional anthropological-metaphysical conceptions of freedom and to formulate a morally relevant conception of freedom of the will from a moral-aesthetic perspective. The lasting influence of Reinhold's theory of free will is unmistakable: the appropriation of the 'dignified theory of the will in the second part of Reinhold's letters' (SW 5:472, note) made evident in *On Grace and Dignity* is implicitly continued in the letters *On the Aesthetic Education of Man*, with Schiller arriving at an aesthetic transformation of Reinhold's concept of free will as a result (siehe Röhr 2003a, b; Noller 2015:236–260; Bondeli 2020). In the nineteenth letter, Schiller states in addendum that he wishes to distinguish between two types of human freedom. The 'first order' of freedom is a type of freedom that 'necessarily appertains to man considered as an *intelligent being*, and which can neither be given unto him nor taken from him'—a freedom that is displayed by the human being in 'acting rationally at all'. Freedom 'of the second order', by contrast, is based on the 'mixed nature' of the human being and is displayed by the human being's 'acting rationally within the limits of matter, and materially under the laws of reason' (Horen 1795 VI, 61; SW 5:631, note; OAE 137). At this point, Schiller adheres to Reinhold's distinction between intelligible freedom on the one hand, which exists alongside the moral law as the law of freedom, and mixed freedom of the will on the other, which concerns the human being's dual nature as a sensible-intelligent being. Moreover, and again in line with Reinhold, an argument is made for the complete independence of the free will. The 'will of man', we read in the fourth letter, 'stands completely free between duty and inclination, and no physical compulsion can, or should, encroach upon this sovereign right of his personality. If, then, man is to retain his power of choice [...], this can only be brought about through both of these motive forces, inclination and duty, producing completely identical results in the world of phenomena' (Horen 1795 I, 17; SW 5:576; OAE 17). In the eighth letter, in the spirit of Reinhold's striking distinction between the autonomously deciding will and the given law of practical reason, an appeal is made to the will's power of action. The 'resolute will' is to execute what 'reason' 'discovers and establishes' as the law (Horen 1795 I, 39; SW 5:590f.; cf. OAE 49). In the nineteenth letter, it is attested that the will is able to maintain its 'perfect freedom' between the two basic drives (Horen 1795 IV, 58; SW 5:630; OAE 135). Deepening and sharpening the comparison, it is significant that Schiller arrives at an understanding of the balance of power between the drives and the will and takes up the equilibristic notion of '*equilibrium*' that Reinhold had criticised (Horen 1795 II, 90; SW 5:619; OAE 111). Thus, in the nineteenth letter, Schiller explains that in this equilibrium between the material and the formal drive, a state exists in which the 'two compulsions' against the will disappear, and the 'will' acts 'as a *power* (power being the ground of all reality) *vis-à-vis* both drives' (Horen 1795 VI, 58; SW 5:630; OAE 135). The will is thus free precisely because it derives absolute, self-sufficient power in the case of equilibrium between the drives. Whereas Reinhold discusses the equilibrist view in order to immediately transpose it to an as yet undeveloped interpretation of the freedom of indifference, Schiller retains the idea of equilibrium, which, he assumes, located at the natural level of the human being, is a necessary condition for the transition to a new, spiritual-aesthetic level of free decision-making.

The essential point of contention when it comes to the concept of freedom of the will, however, again concerns the relationship between morality and aesthetics. Reinhold advocates a freedom that exists within (and given) morality; Schiller's attitude, on the other hand, is characterised from 1795 onwards by the novel insight that 'it is only through beauty that man makes his way to freedom' (see Horen 1795 I, 12; SW V:573; OAE 9). Schiller's chief aim is thus no longer moral freedom but aesthetic freedom. In this sense, Reinhold's conception of a will that is completely autonomous, has ethical attributes (and is thus in particular involved in the demands of conscience and responsibility), and is ultimately bound to moral life, whereas the will described by Schiller, while also completely autonomous, is fuelled by aesthetic notions of equilibrium and harmony and is related to the goal of aesthetic consciousness and the aesthetic life. Schiller's free will thus turns out, at base, to be the play drive, which is not only the intermediary between the formal drive and the material drive but also a self-perfecting mediating activity. On the whole, Schiller's reflections are marked by the conclusion that it is primarily the aesthetic, not the moral, life for which we should strive. And with this it is likely that Schiller's personal struggle was brought to an end. The future blueprint for life should be aesthetic, indeed poetic.

Lastly, it cannot be overlooked that the ramifications of moral and aesthetic freedom are reflected in the socio-political thought of our two protagonists. Around 1795, Reinhold forged plans for the founding of a 'moral federation', which was to realise the Kantian idea of free morality (see at length RGS 6/1). Schiller, on the other hand, was around this time considering an '*aesthetic* state', a social circle 'where conduct is governed by beauty', where the idea of free play can manifest itself, and where bestowing '*freedom by means of freedom*' is the fundamental law (Horen 1795 VI, 120; SW 5:667; OAE 215).

German text translated into English by Carolyn Benson.

Glossary

Angenehm	Agreeable
Anschauung	Intuition
Antrieb	Impulse
Befriedigung	Satisfaction
Begehrung	Desire
Begehrungsvermögen	Faculty of desire
Bestimmungsgrund	Determining ground
Bloße Vergnügen	Mere pleasure
Einbildungskraft	(Power of) imagination
Endziel	Ultimate aim
Endzweck	Final end
Erhabene	Sublime

(*continued*)

(continued)

Erkennung	Cognition
Forderung	Demand
Formtrieb	Formal drive
Gefallen	Pleasing
Gefallen (das)	Pleasing
Genießen	Enjoyment
Genießen (das)	Enjoyment
Geschmacksvermögen	Faculty of taste
Gleichgewichtigkeit	Balance
Glückseligkeit	Happiness
Hauptzweck	Chief end
Lehre	Doctrine
Mitleid	Sympathy
Rührend	Affecting
Sachtrieb	Sensuous drive
Selbstgrund	Self-contained ground
Stofftrieb	Material drive
Trieb	Drive
Triebfeder	Incentive
Uneigennützigkeit	Disinterestedness
Vergnügen überhaupt	Pleasure in general
Vermögen	Faculty
Vernunfterkenntnis	Rational cognition
Verstand	Understanding
Vollkommen Geistes	Spiritual perfection
Vorstellungsvermögen	Faculty of representation
Wohlgefallen	Satisfaction
Wohlstande	Well-being
Wohlwollen	Benevolence
Zwang	Constraint
Zweck	End

References

AHE = *Anthropology, History and Education*, The Cambridge Edition of the Works of Immanuel Kant, Eds. Paul Guyer, Allen Wood. Conjectural Beginning and Idea for Universal History trans. Allen Wood. CUP 2007.

RGS = Karl Leonhard Reinhold. 2007ff. *Gesammelte Schriften. Kommentierte Ausgabe*. Ed. by Martin Bondeli. Basel: Schwabe. TRANSLATIONS: Reinhold, Karl Leonhard. Essay on a New Theory of the Human Capacity for Representation. Trans. Tim Mehigan and Barry Empson. De Gruyter 2011; Reinhold, Karl Leonhard. Letters on the Kantian Philosophy. Ed. Karl Ameriks, Trans. James Hebbeler. CUP 2005.

RKA = Karl Leonhard Reinhold. 1983ff. *Korrespondenzausgabe der österreichischen Akademie der Wissenschaften*. Ed. by Reinhard Lauth, Kurt Hiller, Wolfgang Schrader, from 2007 by Faustino Fabbianelli, Ives Radrizzani et. al. Stuttgart-Bad Cannstatt: Frommann-Holzboog.

Bondeli, Martin. 2017. Reinhold im Anschluss an Kant über Geschmack, Moral und moralische Religion. In *Kant und die Folgen. Die Herausforderung in Ästhetik. Ethik und Religionsphilosophie*, ed. Rudolf Langthaler, Michael Hofer. Wiener Jahrbuch für Philosophie XLVIII. Wien:11-33.

Bondeli, Martin. 2019. Sachtrieb, Formtrieb und die Suche nach einem harmonischen Verhältnis der beiden Grundtriebe. Schillers Triebkonzept im Ausgang von Reinholds Trieblehre (Brief 12 und 13). In. Gideon Stiening (Ed.): *Friedrich Schiller: Über die ästhetische Erziehung des Menschen in einer Reihe von Briefen*, ed. Gideon Stiening. Reihe *Klassiker auslegen*. Bd. 69. Berlin, Boston: de Gruyter: 125-140.

Bondeli, Martin. 2020. Schillers zwei Arten der Freiheit. Eine ästhetische Transformation von Reinholds Theorie der Willensfreiheit. In *Kant-Studien* 2020, 111/2:1-21.

Die Horen. 1795. Die Horen: Eine Monatsschrift, ed. by Schiller. Vol. I-VI (1795). Tübingen.

Ferguson, Adam. 1792. Adam Fergusons Grundsätze der Moralphilosophie. Translated and annotated by Christian Garve. Leipzig: Dyckische Buchhandlung.

Noller, Jörg. 2015. *Die Bestimmung des Willens. Zum Problem individueller Freiheit im Ausgang von Kant*. Freiburg /München. Karl Alber.

Röhr, Sabine. (2003a). Zum Einfluß K. L. Reinholds auf Schillers Kant-Rezeption. In *Die Philosophie Karl Leonhard Reinholds*, ed. Martin Bondeli, Wolfgang H. Schrader. Amsterdam, New York: Rodopi: 105-121.

Röhr, Sabine. (2003b). Freedom and Autonomy in Schiller. In *Journal of the History of Ideas* 64:119-134.

Schings, Hans-Jürgen (1996). *Die Brüder des Marquis Posa. Schiller und der Geheimbund der Illuminaten*. Tübingen: Max Niemeyer.

Schulz, Hans (Ed.) (1910): Timoleon und Immanuel. Dokumente einer Freundschaft. Briefwechsel zwischen Friedrich Christian zu Schleswig-Holstein und Jens Baggesen. Leipzig: S. Hirzel.

Simpson, Leonard. 1849. *Correspondence of Schiller with Körner*. Vol. 1. London: Richard Bentley, New Burlington Street.

CHAPTER 28

The Controversy Between Schiller and Johann Gottlieb Fichte

Emiliano Acosta

> *Einer, das höret man wohl, spricht nach dem andern, doch keiner*
> *Mit dem andern; wer nennt zwei Monologen Gespräch?*
> —(Das philosophische Gespräch)

The controversy between Schiller and Fichte is usually confined to the so-called *Horen-Dispute* (*Horenstreit*): this is the epistolary polemic in the summer of 1795 between both thinkers initiated by Schiller's rejection for publication in his recently founded and short-lived journal *Die Horen* (1795–1797) of Fichte's article "Concerning the Spirit and the Letter in Philosophy in a Series of Letters".[1] Accordingly, this controversy is reduced to the thematic axes of the *Horen-Dispute*: the theory of drives and the causal interaction

---

[1] Fichte published this article a few years later in the journal he edited with F. Niethammer: "Ueber Geist und Buchstab in der Philosophie. In einer Reihe von Briefen", in: *Philosophisches Journal einer Gesellschaft Teutscher Gelehrten*, Bd. IX, H. 4, (1800), pp. 199–232 and 291–305. There is an English translation: "On the Spirit and the Letter in Philosophy", in: Simpson, D. (ed.) *German Aesthetic and Literary Criticism: Kant, Fichte, Schelling, Schopenhauer, Hegel*. Cambridge: Cambridge UP, 1984, pp. 74–93. Quotation from Fichte follows (üGB) the edition by I. H. Fichte in: *Fichtes Werke* Bd. VIII. Berlin: De Gruyter, 1971, pp. 270–300.

E. Acosta (✉)
Vrije Universiteit Brussel, Brussel, Belgium
e-mail: emiliano.acosta@ugent.be

© The Author(s), under exclusive license to Springer Nature Switzerland AG 2023
A. Falduto, T. Mehigan (eds.), *The Palgrave Handbook on the Philosophy of Friedrich Schiller*, https://doi.org/10.1007/978-3-031-16798-0_28

(*Wechselwirkung*) between concepts and images as the style appropriate for an exposition of philosophical ideas for a broad public.

Nevertheless, the *Horen-Dispute* represents the tip of the iceberg in the philosophical disagreement between Schiller and Fichte. In the second part of the fragment of a draft for his last letter concerning the rejection of publication, Schiller explained to Fichte that their real divergence concerns neither style nor their conceptions of the aesthetical drive. The real problem behind all their arguments is that they have two totally different and irreconcilable ways of thinking and feeling (GA III/2: 366). The issue in their correspondence is thus a symptom of a more fundamental difference. The controversy between Schiller and Fichte after Kant and after the French Revolution is sooner a confrontation between two ways of resolving the Kantian antinomy between freedom and necessity. As such, it represents one of the foundational moments of so-called German idealism.

This chapter offers an introductory analysis of this controversy.[2] Section 1 presents a brief commentary on the relation of Schiller and Fichte with Kant concerning Schiller and Fichte's attempts at overcoming Kantian philosophy by developing a new way of making philosophy. Section 2 offers an outline of the *Horen-Dispute*, and in Sect. 3, the philosophical controversy between Schiller and Fichte is presented and discussed.

With Kant Beyond Kant

In their attempt to reconcile freedom and reason with nature and ideality with reality, Schiller and Fichte developed different dialectical devices. In the case of Fichte: a dialectic that operates according to both a *radicalization* of the Kantian primacy of practical reason and the principle of absolute identity. In the case of Schiller, a dialectic guided by what I would like to call the primacy of aesthetical reason and by the postulate of an original irreducible duality in human nature. Both thinking devices resolutely do not follow basic rules of the Kantian transcendental doctrine of method set out in Kant's first *Critique*: for instance, that assumptions in the field of practical reason cannot directly be used in theoretical philosophy (KrV B 804), that apagogic proofs cannot be used in transcendental philosophy (KrV B 817), and that philosophy must not make use of mathematical methods of demonstration, namely that a priori cognition of concepts is the proper method of philosophy, not a priori construction of concepts by means of intuition (KrV B 872).

With the help of Kant, and convinced of the need to critically re-think his legacy, both thinkers took their leave of the Kantian world—although both constantly tried to convince the public that they are the real Kantians, since they understood Kant better than Kant understood himself (see for instance SW 5: 608 fn. and GA I/4: 221–223). At the same time, they established the foundations of so-called German idealism. The dispute between Schiller and

---

[2] For a more detailed study, see Acosta (2011).

Fichte opens up a new conceptual and methodological space, wherein the crucial questions of the Kantian philosophy are reformulated in such a manner that the Kantian legacy can no longer provide any effective or convincing response to them.

Neither Schiller nor Fichte hesitated to show respect and admiration for Kant. But they also did not vacillate in making clear that the Kantian system needed updating. The Kantian method of exposition and deduction never satisfied Fichte. He is in no doubt about the fact that Kant changed his life, or rather, as Fichte confessed to F. A. Weisshuhn between August and September 1790, that Kant *gave* him a life, a creed to survive with dignity as a free being in a determinist universe (GA III/1: 167–168). Kant woke him up from the dogmatic slumber of determinism. Nevertheless, the love and admiration for Kant did not prevent him from admitting in a letter to Weisshuhn, probably from November 1790, that the Kantian style of writing and explaining was unnecessarily obscure and needed to be improved upon (GA III/1: 188–190).

Fichte suggests in a letter to H. Stephani from December 1793 that the core ideas of Kantian philosophy have to be presented following a method of mathematical evidence or geometric demonstration (GA III/2: 28). This methodological translation of Kant's transcendental philosophy—which like every translation is unavoidably a betrayal—is his own philosophy: the doctrine of science (*Wissenschaftslehre*). The first publication of his own system of transcendental philosophy is the 1794/95 *Foundations of the Entire Doctrine of Science*. At that time, Fichte had already been appointed as Reinhold's successor to the Chair of Philosophy at the University of Jena and was recognized by sympathizers as well as enemies of transcendental philosophy as the new Kant or, as Jacobi called him a few years later in his *Letter to Fichte*, the "Messiah of speculative reason" (GA III/3, 227).

Schiller is, philosophically speaking, also a convert. Like Fichte and most of their generation, the young Schiller was a kind of Spinozist in the German way, for whom "God and Nature are two magnitudes that are exactly the same" (*Theosophy of Julius*, SW 5:352). The Kantian philosophy changed his mind and vocabulary completely. He learned to think, question, and argue in a different way. The *Kallias-Letters* is the best testimony of Schiller's conversion to Kantianism (see for instance SW 5: 395–400 and 432).

But in 1795, Schiller distanced himself from Kant and developed a capacity for critically and autonomously thinking the issues of beauty, freedom, and nature. At the beginning of his *On the Aesthetic Education of Man in a Series of Letters* (hereafter: *Aesthetic Letters*), Schiller very carefully tells the reader what separates him from Kant: he will not repeat the Kantian methodological mistakes that made Kant blind for what he now wants to investigate: beauty as a principle and imperative and the realm or kingdom of semblances as the only world in which man can freely and totally develop all his faculties (SW 5: 571, 609–611fn. and 668–669).

The Horen-Dispute

As already mentioned, Schiller initiated this polemic with his letter from probably June 24, 1795, by notifying Fichte that his article had been rejected for publication in Schiller's journal. The original letter is lost. Fichte sent it back to Schiller together with his answer, for he assumed that Schiller did not have any transcription of it (GA III/2: 340). Maybe the impulsive tone of the letter made Fichte suppose that the letter was a kind of impromptu, written without being planned, and that Schiller did not take the time to amend it or erase the considerable number of arguments *ad hominem* in the letter. Contrary to what Fichte thought, three drafts of this letter have been preserved (GA III/2: 329–335). The drafts are from June 23 and 24.

Fichte sent the first part of *A Series of Letters concerning the Spirit and the Letter in Philosophy* on June 21 (GA III/2, 325–326) and on the next day the rest of the text, namely the end of the second letter and the third letter (GA III/2: 328). The drafts of Schiller's notification of his decision, written between June 23 and 24, provide testimony not only that it took Schiller less than 24 hours to come to the conclusion that the article could not be published, but also that he committed two days to the task of composing the right words for such a difficult notification and the best possible objective arguments for the rejection, so Fichte would not have the impression that the decision was arbitrary (GA III/2, 335). Later, in the draft of his last intervention in this dispute, Schiller regrets having spent so much time over this task (GA III/2, 365).

After communicating the unhappy decision and confessing how sorry he felt about it, Schiller points out the reasons why the article cannot be published (GA III/2: 333–335). Neither the content nor the treatment of the topic satisfies him. Systematicity, clarity, and sharpness he finds wanting. A good exposition, according to Schiller, must follow the dynamic of a causal interaction (*Wechselwirkung*) between image and concept and not merely consist of an alternation between these two registers based on the arbitrariness of the author. Schiller emphasizes in the drafts, and very likely in the final version of the letter as well, both words: causal interaction and alternation. The causal interaction or reciprocal effect is one of the most fundamental concepts in the 1794/1795 version of Fichte's system and Schiller refers to Fichte in his *Aesthetic Letters* when he uses it in his deduction of "pure of concept of the human being" (SW 5: 600) in order to explain the way in which the antagonism between the original drives in man, formal and sensuous drive, must be solved (SW 5: 607fn.). It seems that Schiller emphasized these words to be sure that Fichte would comprehend the point. The message is clear: the father of the concept of causal interaction did not actually know how to use it or never understood what causal interaction is in the first place.

Schiller is right when he reproaches Fichte that the title is confusing, since the article does not discuss at all what the title announces, namely: the spirit and the letter in philosophy. Fichte's use of the term "spirit" is ambiguous: sometimes in opposition to letter and sometimes in opposition to the lack of creativity in the arts. Moreover, in the article, there is no mention of philosophy at all. Instead, it is an essay on the aesthetic drive, on the artist and the arts that, without mentioning it, criticizes Schiller's view of the aesthetic drive as presented in letters 10 to 16 of his *Aesthetic Letters*. These letters, the second part of the *Aesthetic Letters*, were published in the second issue of 1795 of *Die Horen* which Fichte surely had read.

The form of the title of the rejected article, "concerning" (*über*) + topic + "in a series of letters" (*in einer Reihe von Briefen*), is the same as the title of Schiller's *Aesthetic Letters*. Some expressions Fichte uses in the rejected article recall passages in Schiller's writing. Fichte writes, for instance, about an "aesthetic education" as a means to elevate man to freedom (üGB 287). For this reason Schiller explains to Fichte that the publication of his version of the aesthetic drive is inappropriate for a journal that already has published on the same topic. Furthermore, Schiller confesses he would have tolerated the fact that Fichte wrote a refutation or a confirmation of his drive theory, but, in his view, Fichte's version of the aesthetic drive is almost unreadable and does not make any sense.

According to Schiller, Fichte's classification of the drives into a knowledge drive, a practical drive, and an aesthetic drive is erratic, arbitrary, and unclear. He laments that Fichte did not make use of his own theory and, more specifically, of his concept of a material or sensuous drive (*Stofftrieb* in this letter, *sinnlicher Trieb* in the *Aesthetic Letters*, SW 5: 604), since without the presupposition of this drive "it is impossible", according to Schiller, "to bring together in one class the drive towards multiplicity and the drive towards unity" (GA III/2: 334).

The rejection of the article, the unfriendly explanation of the objective reasons for it, and the disrespect towards his person were something totally unexpected for Fichte. Since, as he writes in his answer from June 27, he thought that because Schiller praised his philosophical talent,[3] and had invited him to be part of the editorial board of *Die Horen*, he was allowed to rectify or fill the conceptual gaps in Schiller's *Aesthetic Letters* (GA III/2: 336). Fichte was aware that Schiller used his name and needed his contributions in order to gain more readers for the journal. In the presentation of his journal, Schiller introduced him, together with Jacobi, Goethe, Gentz, and Garve, among others, as one of the significant personalities of the German academic and literary world of the time who would contribute to the journal.[4] But the *Horen-Dispute* shows that Fichte was wrong in assuming he had *carte blanche* as an invited author.

In his letter from June 27 (GA III/2: 336–340), Fichte does not accept Schiller's verdict about his article. He gives for each argument of Schiller a

---

[3] The epigram "Fichte und Er" serves as example of Schiller's admiration of Fichte as philosopher: ""Freilich tauchet der Mann kühn in die Tiefe des Meeres,/Wenn du, auf leichtem Kahn, schwankest und Heringe fängst".
[4] *Die Horen*, (1795) 1. Bd. 1. St., p. VIII.

counterargument, sometimes referring to his philosophy in general, sometimes referring to the rejected writing, and sometimes, as Schiller did, with arguments *ad hominem*. Fichte does not seem to have any hope about the possibility of convincing Schiller that the article deserves to be published. Hence, he proposes a third person to intervene as a judge to settle this conflict between their irreconcilable ways of conceiving the aesthetical dimension of human life.

With respect to a conceptual reconstruction of the *Horen-Dispute*, the most important points of Fichte's answer concern the concept of causal interaction and the theory of drives, since both pre-announce the real philosophical controversy between Schiller and Fichte, which will be presented in the next section of this chapter. To Schiller's criticism about the lack of causal interaction between images and concept, Fichte answers by attacking back: he never found in Schiller's writings the causal interaction Schiller misses in the rejected article. Schiller uses, according to Fichte, too many images and does not clarify them with abstract concepts but adds new images. So, Schiller uses images where he must make use of concepts. In this passage of Fichte's letter, his proposal for a productive collaboration between concepts and images, however, seems to be the alternation Schiller criticized, since Fichte states that images must come *before* or *after* the concept and not instead of it (GA III/2: 338–339). Fichte's answer shows that they have different conceptions of causal interaction and/or reciprocal effect.

Concerning the defence of his own drive theory against Schiller's criticism (GA III/2: 338), Fichte argues that Schiller's advice to include the sensuous drive in Fichte's theory ignores two things. First, that there cannot be a drive towards existence or a sensuous drive on the same ontological level as the three drives of Fichte's theory, since such a drive presupposes existence, something the subject can be aware of *thanks* to the theoretical and practical drives, and matter (*Stoff*) arises from the limitation of the spontaneity of the subject, thus, not from its activity. Secondly, the conscious experience of matter—or as Fichte put it, the presentation of matter in the mind—is an effect of what Fichte calls the drive to knowledge. So, according to Fichte, Schiller should subordinate the sensuous drive to Fichte's knowledge drive.

In the rejected article, Fichte considers the theoretical, practical, and aesthetic drives as specifications of one and the same drive. The aesthetic drive is deduced as the condition of possibility of the division of the original drive into theoretical and practical (üGB 281). This is something Fichte already affirmed in his *On Stimulating and Increasing the Pure Interest in Truth*—an article Schiller did accept for publication for the first issue of *Die Horen*.[5]

Schiller's criticism of Fichte's theory of drives because of the absence of the sensuous drive is based on his own drive theory in his *Aesthetic Letters* that, unlike Fichte's drive theory, departs from the premise that there is no original *single* drive, but two original drives (*Grundtriebe*): the formal and the sensuous

---

[5] Fichte, J. G., "Ueber Belebung und Erhöhung des reinen Interesse für Wahrheit", in: *Die Horen*, (1795) 1. Bd. 1. St., pp. 79–93 (GA I/3: 83–90).

drive (SW 5: 606). At the very origin of human nature, there is thus already an irreducible duality of drives, which is a specification or further development of the original duality of person and condition as the highest concepts in man (SW 5: 601). The aesthetic drive for Schiller is not an original drive, but an element required to make possible harmony between form and matter, reason and nature, and freedom and necessity in the human being. The duality and the antagonism between the formal and sensuous drive, which Fichte neglects with his thesis of the unicity of all drives in an original one, is for Schiller constitutive for the human being and cannot be reduced to a higher or more fundamental drive.

In the series of letters which the *Horen-Dispute* consists of there is no immediate answer of Schiller to this letter. Fichte had to write again in August in order to receive an answer from Schiller. Fichte's second letter is lost, but it is assumed that he reiterated his answer to Schiller or asked that he answer the letter of June 27. Schiller's answer is also lost. A fragment containing two drafts, from 3 and 4 August, is the only document about Schiller's last letter concerning his polemic with Fichte (GA III/2: 360–368). In these drafts, Schiller does not accept Fichte's proposal for a third person as a judge. As mentioned, at the beginning of this chapter, he considers that a solution for this discussion is impossible, because of the profound discrepancy in their ways of thinking and feeling. He is convinced that there is no going back on his decision. It seems at this point that he has already decided to stop the scientific and editorial collaboration with Fichte in *Die Horen*.

The next letter we still have in the correspondence between Fichte and Schiller is Fichte's short letter dated January 18, 1799 (GA III/3, 177). This is the time of a new dispute in Fichte's life: the *Atheism-Dispute*, the accusation of atheism against Fichte that ended with his dismissal from the University of Jena. Fichte asks Schiller to read his *Appellation to the Public*, a composition arguing against the confiscation of his own journal, the *Philosophisches Journal*, because of the charge of atheism. Schiller answered on January 26 in a very friendly fashion. He expresses support for Fichte and condemns the confiscation (GA III/3: 184). The *Horen-Dispute* seems to be totally forgotten by both. After the rupture with Schiller in 1795 and despite of having said during the *Horen-Dispute* that Schiller never understood his philosophy, Fichte told his students—as documented in the student transcripts of his lectures on the doctrine of science between 1796 and 1799, the so-called *Doctrine of Science nova method*—that his concept of causal interaction or reciprocal effect (*Wechselwirkung*) has been "best understood by Mr. Councillor Schiller in his *Letters on the Aesthetic Education* in *Die Horen*" (GA IV/3: 372).

The Philosophical Ground of the Controversy

Behind the confrontation between Fichte and Schiller in the *Horen-Dispute* concerning the aesthetic drive and the concept of causal interaction a more fundamental confrontation between them was taking place: the confrontation between, as Schiller suggested, their ways of feeling and thinking, which refer to their dialectic devices, mentioned above in Section "With Kant Beyond Kant". Fichte's theory of drives conceives the plurality of drives according to the principle of absolute identity: all drives are actually manifestations of the one and the same drive. Plurality can and ought to be reduced to an original unity. In the case of the drives, this unity is the original drive, which is essentially practical, since, as Fichte suggests in the rejected article, all drives are basically practical (üGB 279). Here Fichte's primacy of practical reason appears as that which determines the kind of unity the drive theory needs. Fichte had presented this idea of the one and the same original and practical drive, from which all other drives are developed, not only in his *On Stimulating and Increasing the Pure Interest in Truth*, his contribution to the first issue of *Die Horen* (GA I/3: 84), but also in paragraph 5 of his *Foundation of the Entire Science of Knowledge*, which is concerned with the practical dimension of the I (GA I/2: 418). The drive is the result of a specification of the I in its ceaseless attempts at accomplishing what practical reason orders: becoming the totality of reality. Fichte calls this imperative of reason "Kant's categorical imperative" (GA I/2: 396n.). Fichte postulates a practical principle as the principle of practical and theoretical philosophy—something Schelling also does in his 1795/96 *New Deduction of Natural Law* (Schelling 1980).

Fichte follows Reinhold's conviction that the Kantian philosophy needed a principle that gives it the systematic unity Kant did not provide (Breazeale 2022). But unlike Reinhold, who sought this principle in theoretical philosophy and formulated it as the principle of consciousness (1790: 167), Fichte's principle is a practical one (see for instance GA III/2, 314–315 and 386). Fichte's solution, following the method of geometrical construction supported by intuition Kant rejected for transcendental philosophy, is a transgression and at the same time a radicalization of Kant (Acosta 2019). For he extends the realm of application of concepts of Kant's practical philosophy to the domain of theoretical philosophy. He is convinced that his solution is nothing but a reorganization of the elements of the Kantian philosophy, a reorganization Kant, in Fichte's view, did not *dare* to undertake. This is an example of how Fichte's translation of the Kantian philosophy, his doctrine of science, is a betrayal of Kant, since according to Kant, transcendental philosophy must respect the limits between the theoretical and the practical.

Fichte's introduces his radicalized version of the categorical imperative, conceived as an imperative of absolute unity demanding that the I ought to become the totality of reality, in order to explain the dialectic between I and Not-I, two Fichtean terms that respectively refer to freedom/reason/activity/infinitude and necessity/nature/passivity/finitude.

According to Fichte, self-consciousness is a living contradiction between the I and the Not-I that ceaselessly produces syntheses that generate again and again new contradictions in its attempt to definitively cancel the difference between I and Not-I, and this is why reason is essentially practical (GA I/2, 65, *Rezension Aenesidemus*). This contradiction is solved in the concept of reciprocal determination or causal interaction (*Wechselwirkung*) between I and Not-I in his *Foundation of the Entire Science of Knowledge*. This concept shows the basic structure of Fichte's dialectics: the dialectical movement begins with the affirmation of absolute unity and identity, from which the Not-I emerges as the representative of the negation, duality, and difference everyone finds in his/her thinking by reflecting on the activity of mind. An absolute affirmation of the Not-I would signify the annihilation of the I. This according to Fichte is absurd, because it contradicts the self-evident fact that there is rational life. This *reductio ad absurdum* allows Fichte to postulate the subordination of the Not-I to the I, namely the integration in the I of this strange element the I spontaneously but with no consciousness of it at all produces as the only possible solution of the contradiction that affirms the freedom of the I which the categorical imperative presupposes. In solving this contradiction, the I is thus following the imperative of the absolute unity of reason—what Fichte called, as already mentioned, the Kantian categorical imperative. In Fichte's reciprocal effect or causal interaction only one of the elements in the contradiction is active: the I. It initiates the movement, it produces and solves the difference and the contradiction, and it is eventually the very place where the whole dialectic movement occurs. This is why the first formulation of this reciprocal determination corresponds with the third axiom of his 1794/1795 system that reads as follows: the I posits *in itself* I and a Not-I in reciprocal determination (GA I/2, 280–282).

Schiller's aesthetic drive, which he calls the interplay drive (*Spieltrieb*) in his *Aesthetical Letters*, represents the conclusion of the first dialectical movement of his deduction of the "pure concept of the human being" (SW 5: 609) as the harmony between the formal and the sensuous drives and of beauty as the element in which the human being can get knowledge of his real nature and destination (SW 5: 613–615). This dialectical movement initiates with the affirmation that the pure concept of the human being consists of only two elements: person and condition (SW 5: 601). Schiller explains that there is no higher concept unifying both. There is no place for Fichte's absolute I as origin and principle of the human being in Schiller's thinking. A dialectic developed from the postulate of the absolute unity and autonomy of the rational in the human being, according to Schiller, is a one-sided view of human reality that produces a one-sided idea of reality.[6]

The deduction departs thus from an original duality. Schiller then reformulates this duality in terms of contradictory forces attempting to oppress and subordinate each other. In this confrontation of forces, one of them is always oppressing the other. Either an excess of rationality or an excess of sensibility governs the human being. In both cases, man cannot be free. The Fichtean concept of reciprocal effect appears within Schiller's conceptual space as an example of the oppression and subordination he tries to solve. These forces

---

[6] Epigram "Ein sechster" is an example of this criticism of Schiller: "Ich bin ich und setze mich selbst, und setz ich mich selber/Als nicht gesetzt, nun gut! Setz ich ein Nicht-Ich dazu".

presuppose drives as their conditions of possibility. These are the formal drive, in the case of rational power, and the sensuous drive in the case of the power of sensibility. Since both drives are specifications of the original duality in the human being, this antagonism is as such unresolvable and both drives must be considered as the only original drives in the human being. A possible solution without a third element, Schiller's idea of the perfect being as a being where person and condition are an eternal unity (SW V: 601), would result in the annihilation of the human being and so in the impossibility of demonstrating that central function of beauty for the realization of man Schiller is trying to argue for in his *Aesthetic Letters*. This *reduction ad absurdum* allows Schiller to postulate a third drive consisting in a non-original drive directed to the production of a harmonic interaction between the original drives: this is the interplay drive. Schiller understands this harmony as causal interaction (*Wechselwirkung*) between person and condition, freedom and necessity, infinity and finitude, and reason and nature.

In order to understand the originality of Schiller's proposal, it is important to bear in mind that the aesthetic drive does not solve the original antagonism—since this antagonism is *per definitionem* unresolvable—but displace the problem to another space, the realm of semblance, where the aesthetical solution can be postulated as a possible one. Furthermore: the proof of the impossibility of a solution to the original antagonism in man is the argument that allows Schiller, by means of an apagogic argument, to postulate the need of both the action of an aesthetic drive and his idea of beauty as "the consummation of man's humanity" (SW 5: 615). Schiller reiterates this way of arguing in the case of his aesthetic state: the impossibility of resolving the political problem is the point of departure for his postulation of an apolitical realm, the aesthetic state, as the only place in which human beings can interact as free beings in reciprocal recognition as equals (SW V: 667–669). The aesthetic state is thus an aesthetic solution for a political problem based on the acceptance of the impossibility of a political solution.

The concepts of man as harmony of the antagonist drives, man in the "aesthetic condition" (SW 5: 631) or the "noble soul" (SW 5: 644fn.), and the aesthetic state as the most human way of human interaction are examples of the way in which Schiller understands causal interaction. It is true that Schiller explicitly acknowledges that he takes this concept from Fichte's philosophy (SW 5: 607fn), but the *Aesthetic Letters* show that Schiller redefines this Fichtean concept within his own dialectic. This is something most of the scholarship on the relation between Schiller and Fichte has overlooked, since it is usually said that Schiller *applies* to his deduction of the pure concept of man Fichte's concept of reciprocal effect. Consequently, this relation is explained as the influence of Fichte on Schiller (Acosta 2011: 12–27). But this is an interpretation based on a genetic fallacy, since it is presupposed that the provenance of this concept explains its meaning. Nevertheless, unlike Fichte, Schiller thinks of causal interaction as a relation initiated by both opposites. Man is not essentially, as Fichte affirms, an I. The I for Schiller is one of two original elements in the pure concept of man (SW 5: 601–602). Whereas Fichte thinks of the subject as an I with a body, Schiller considers mind and body as ontological equals. Schiller's causal interaction is, accordingly, the interaction between two original elements, both constitutive for the nature of subjectivity.

This explains why the movement in Schiller's concept of causal interaction starts from both sides of the contradiction. In this regard, Schiller's reformulation of *Wechselwirkung* anticipates the dialectic dynamic of Hegel's concept of self-consciousness as reciprocal recognition in his *Phenomenology of Spirit* (HW 3: 145). But unlike Hegel's account, the double movement of Schiller's dialectic is ordered and guided by an imperative of reason, which Schiller, unlike Fichte, considers as aesthetical. The primacy of aesthetical reason is what gives Schiller's concept of causal interaction its specification. This primacy can be seen in Schiller's reformulation of the imperative of reason, which reads as follows:

> Reason, however, declares: The beautiful is to be neither mere life, nor mere form, but living form, i.e., Beauty; for it imposes upon man the double law of absolute formality and absolute reality.
>
> [Nun spricht aber die Vernunft: das Schöne soll nicht bloßes Leben und nicht bloße Gestalt, sondern lebende Gestalt, das ist, Schönheit sein; indem sie ja dem Menschen das doppelte Gesetz der absoluten Formalität und der absoluten Realität diktiert]. (15th letter, transl. p. 107, SW V, 617)

In the conflict between person and condition incarnated in the antagonism between formal and sensuous drives, the causal interaction, which the aesthetic drive (*Spieltrieb*) is directed to, functions as a reciprocal limitation of the antagonistic forces. But this reciprocal limitation that follows the imperative of aesthetic reason implies, as in the case of a matter and form in a piece of art, a kind of cross-fertilization of reciprocal contamination between both original drives and between reason/freedom and nature/necessity, since the limit of sensibility "must be an act of freedom, an activity of the person" (SW 5: 610) and the limit of the person must be the "plurality of sensations" (SW 5: 611).

Schiller's concept of causal interaction is a limitation in the sense of a management of man's powers aiming at the realization of *all* powers in man—not only the faculties related to the rational in man. The causal interaction must guard and secure the respective realms of each drive. This according to Schiller is the task of culture (*Kultur*):

> Its business [sc.: of culture] is twofold: first, to preserve the life of Sense against the encroachments of Freedom; and second, to secure the Personality against the forces of Sensation. The former it achieves by developing our capacity for feeling, the latter by developing our capacity for reason.
>
> [Ihr Geschäft [sc.: of culture] ist also doppelt, erstlich: die Sinnlichkeit gegen die Eingriffe der Freiheit zu verwahren; zweitens: die Persönlichkeit gegen die Macht der Empfindungen sicher zu stellen. Jenes erreicht sie durch Ausbildung des Gefühlvermögens, dieses durch Ausbildung des Vernunftvermögens]. (13th letter, transl. p. 87, SW V, 608)

Schiller's concept of the causal interaction does not have the structure of a causal interaction in general, but, according to the primacy of aesthetic reason, of a *beautiful* interaction. This causal interaction is beautiful when their opposites are thought from the principle of duality. Neither should the sensuous impulse be subordinate to the rational, nor the rational impulse to the sensuous: no subordination at all is tolerated. Rather, it is mutual subordination that must be brought about, which, however, cannot be reduced to an original unity. In Fichte's causal interaction, on the contrary, one of the opposites, namely the rational, has primacy. If the other side of Fichte's interaction, the Not-I, were absolutely independent and autonomous, then the postulate of the freedom of the I, which is a requirement of the primacy of practical reason in Fichte's philosophy and at the same time a regulative idea in Fichte's concept of causal interaction, must be given up.

Unlike Fichte, Schiller develops a dialectic logic that produces syntheses, which do not subsume the original opposites or neutralize their effects, but which constitute a new element that is situated between the opposites and not above them: the interplay drive between the formal and the sensuous drive, the aesthetic state between the rational and the nature state, for instance. The synthesis of Schiller's dialectic logic, therefore, instead of neutralizing the constitutive difference of the contradiction, not only affirms it, but introduces a new element raising the number of members in the opposition from two to three. The third element does not synthesize the opposition in itself, but adds a new difference: the difference between the new element and the original ones.

The analysis of Schiller's deduction of the interplay drive and his concept of causal interaction shows that Schiller's dialectic procedure basically consists of (i) identifying a conflict and formulating it as an antinomy in the Kantian sense: a contradiction between two elements; (ii) demonstrating the impossibility of a synthesis between them without a third term; (iii) creating a space or identifying the space between the two opposites: the difference; (iv) redefining from the difference the opposites; (v) suspending the pretension of absolute validity of each opposite element; (vi) resolving the contradiction outside the original place, thus, within the space the new element is created; and, finally, (vii) establishing a new demarcation of the fields of validity and action of the original opposites.

In this controversy, Schiller and Fichte are already establishing the foundations of so-called German idealism. By means of deconstructing Kant, reformulating the antinomy between freedom and nature, developing new ways of thinking, and proposing alternatives to the Kantian transcendental philosophy—Fichte departing from a radicalization of the primacy of practical reason, Schiller from a primacy of aesthetical reason—they show to their contemporaries that it is not only possible but necessary to transform and subvert the Kantian legacy.

Schiller and Fichte's concepts of the aesthetic drive and of reciprocal determination or causal interaction are the result of very different logical devices that are incompatible with each other. Their difference has to be understood in terms of a contradiction. The principle of absolute unity negates the principle of duality, and vice versa. The authority that orders and guides the dialectic movement is therefore either the primacy and the imperative of practical reason or the primacy and imperative of aesthetic reason. They cannot govern together. Neither cedes authority to the other.

This is why for both thinkers a civilized discussion about the very nature of the aesthetic drive and the very meaning of causal interaction is impossible. Every form of compatibility would result in the disappearance of one of the opposites. Applying Fichte's concept of causal interaction to Schiller's concept of the human being would, for instance, result in the reduction of the original duality in human nature to the absolute unity of the I. It would also imply giving prevalence to the rational in mankind. Mankind as the object of research would consequently disappear and give its place to the rational being as Fichte conceived it. A deduction of the need for an aesthetic drive for the arts and an aesthetic education for the realization of human destiny could no longer be substantiated. A negotiation or a dialogue aiming at reconciliation or agreement implies that the parties at least partly must abandon their principles. This is something philosophers have no idea about. They do not listen to one other. They never dialogue with one other. They usually misunderstand, mistranslate, and betray one other. A real philosophical discussion is not a debate between scholars but rather, as the controversy between Schiller and Fichte suggests, a confrontation between two monologues.

References

Acosta, Emiliano (2011): *Schiller versus Fichte. Schillers Begriff der Person in der Zeit und Fichtes Kategorie der Wechselbestimmung im Widerstreit*. Fichte-Studien-Supplementa 27, Leiden: Brill.

Acosta, E. (2019): "Observaciones acerca del estudio de la relación entre Kant y Fichte". pp. 9–17 in *Anuario Filosófico*. 52 (1).

Breazeale, Daniel (2022): "Freedom and Duty: Kant, Reinhold, Fichte". pp. 118–137 in: James A. Clarke and Gabriel Gottlieb, eds., *Practical Philosophy from Kant to Hegel. Freedom, Right, and Revolution*. Cambridge: Cambridge University Press.

Hegel, Georg Wilhelm Friedrich Hegel (1970): *Werke in 20 Bänden*. Frankfurt a. M.: Suhrkamp (HW)

Reinhold, Karl Leonhard (1790): *Beyträge zur Berichtigung bisheriger Missverständnisse der Philosophen*. 1. Bd. Jena: Johann Michael Mauke.

Schelling, F. W. J. (1980): *New Deduction of Natural Right*, pp. 221–252 in: Schelling, F.W.J., *The Unconditional in Human Knowledge. Four Early Essays (1794–1796)*, trans. by F. Marti, Lewisburg, PA: Bucknell University Press, 1980.

Schiller on the Aesthetics of Morals and Twentieth-Century Kant Scholarship and Philosophy

Katerina Deligiorgi

Our philosophical moral vocabulary expresses a predilection for depth.[1] The familiar characterisation of moral agency as critical and reflective agency has its roots in the thought that work is needed both to discover what is genuinely morally demanded and to understand what moves people to think and act as they do. Our theories seem to prepare us to confront the moral fogginess of things. In such context, advocating on behalf of appearances, the moral significance of movement, voice, and facial expression, is bound to perplex. This chapter focuses on just such a philosophical outlier, Schiller's defence of grace (*Anmut*) in *On Grace and Dignity*, which appeared in 1793 in *Neue Thalia*.[2] 'Grace' refers to a quality we notice immediately in a person's 'voluntary movements' (GD 171, NA 20b: 254). Graceful demeanour is an 'expression of moral feelings' (GD 171, NA 20b: 254), Schiller contends, explaining that in perceiving grace, we witness a moral accomplishment, the 'coincidence' between the inner and outer person which is the ultimate moral aim:

---

[1] A version of the essay originally appeared in the *History of Philosophy Quarterly* 2006 vol. 23:1:1–20. It is reprinted here with significant stylistic alterations to fit it with the requirements of the present volume.

[2] The translation I provide is based on an anonymous version published originally in 1875, and frequently reprinted subsequently, by George Bell and Sons, in London.

K. Deligiorgi (✉)
University of Sussex, Brighton, UK

© The Author(s), under exclusive license to Springer Nature Switzerland AG 2023
A. Falduto, T. Mehigan (eds.), *The Palgrave Handbook on the Philosophy of Friedrich Schiller*, https://doi.org/10.1007/978-3-031-16798-0_29

> The frame of mind that is best suited to the fulfilment of man's moral destiny must find the most favourable expression in man's outer appearance. In other words, his ethical accomplishment must be revealed in grace. (GD 193, NA 20b: 277)

These claims are bound to puzzle a contemporary audience. To make sense of Schiller's argument about grace, it is necessary to start, in Sect. 1, by placing it in its proper philosophical context, specifically his criticism of the role of inclinations in Kant's moral philosophy. It is then possible to present the positive moral ideal Schiller proposes under the concept of 'grace' in Sect. 2. Section 3 examines the details of the argument and reaches some conclusions about the value of his distinctive moral vision.

The Value of Inclination

Schiller's central argument in *On Grace and Dignity* is widely recognised as one of the 'classical objections' (Allison 1990, 180) to Kant's conception of moral agency. On a typical interpretation, Schiller's aim is 'to correct the unduly harsh picture that Kant paints of the moral life by emphasising the proper role in this life of the sensuous, emotive side of human nature' (Allison 1990, 181).[3] While it is true that Schiller seeks to defend a model of moral agency that incorporates what Kant excludes, talk of 'sensuous' and 'emotive' is rather vague. Having clearly in view what Schiller finds missing from the Kantian picture is essential to understanding how he employs the concept of grace.

The resonant formulations Schiller uses to present his criticisms make the task of identifying precisely their object surprisingly tough:

> Either man suppresses the demands of his sensuous nature, in order to behave conformably with the superior demands of his rational nature; or else, he does the opposite and subjects the rational part of his being to the sensuous part, that is to the sheer forces of natural necessity that rule all appearances alike. (GD 195, NA 20b: 280)

The pulling and pushing of the soul in different directions is a potent image of struggle, which, as Schiller claims later, has no possible positive outcome as it leads either to moral severity, resulting from the subjugation of sensuous nature, or to moral laxity, resulting from surrendering to natural demands. The general message is easy to grasp. Note, however, the elusive nature of the basic diagnosis. What are the parties to the struggle? The term 'rational nature' suggests that reason is a natural force within the person competing with other natural forces. By contrast, talking of the 'rational part' of one's being indicates receptivity to the demands of a possibly supernatural force. The 'sensuous part' is easy enough to associate with the domain of emotions, desires, and

---

[3] Allison reflects an interpretative tradition established by Henrich (1954–1955) and (1982), Wildt (1982), and Prauss (1983).

affects—what is sometimes referred to as 'inner nature', though a more austere interpretation, suggested towards the end of the quote, where 'sensuous' describes human beings simply as part of nature understood as the realm of appearances ordered conformably with causal necessity. The interpretative possibilities revealed in this preliminary analysis show that to understand Schiller's argument and the deeper concerns that motivate his criticism of Kant, we need to dig deeper.

Schiller positions himself from the start as a sympathetic critic. He praises Kant, 'the immortal author of the Critique', for restoring 'healthy reason' to moral philosophy (GD 198, NA 20b: 282). However, as he quickly points out, Kant's restoration of reason to moral philosophy took a problematic form. Kant presents the idea of duty with a harshness 'that could easily tempt a feeble mind to seek for moral perfection in the sombre paths of an ascetic and monastic life' (GD 200, NA 20b: 284). The trouble is not just with the occasional misunderstanding of Kant's theory, however. Schiller hints at a systematic misrepresentation of 'the principles of the philosopher' 'by himself and also by others' (GD 198, NA 20b: 282), resulting in the deprecation of inclination and of pleasure: 'inclination is a very dubious companion to moral sense, and pleasure a suspect accessory to moral determinations' (ibid.).

The references to inclination and to pleasure suggest that Schiller may be making a point about the ineffectiveness of a morality of purely rational imperatives. Later in the text, he claims that since pleasure and pain 'are the only springs which set the instincts in motion' obedience to reason should itself be 'an object of inclination' (GD 282, NA 20b: 298). Schiller develops such an argument in *On the Aesthetic Education of Man*, where develops an empiricist model of psychology predicated on the idea the 'drives' (*Trieben*) (see AE 17f, NA 20: 315f, AE 49f, NA 20: 330f) in order to show how Kant's moral theory can be practically effective (AE 5, NA 20: 310).[4] The problem with imposing this reading on the present text is that it indicates a rather radical disagreement with Kant, for whom the practicality of reason is a core tenet. Kant presents human beings as fully capable of acting on laws that are independent of nature and 'have their ground in reason alone' (G 113, Ak 6: 452). Aside from the earlier quote about pleasure and pain, there is no indication that motivation is an issue here for Schiller. Rather his chief concern is with the severity, rather than the ineffectiveness, of moral reason, which he portrays as a powerfully constraining force, comparable to a monarchy 'where strict surveillance of the prince holds in check all free movement' (GD 197, NA 20b: 282).

What does Schiller mean exactly when he talks about the severity of reason's moral rule? One possibility is that he sees Kantian ethics as encouraging a certain moralist disregard for happiness. Judging from the account of moral struggle Schiller uses to make vivid the effects of reason's rule, it is clear that his concern is with the plight of the moral who appears doomed to a life of self-denial or permanent inner conflict:

---

[4] See Schaper (1979), and Roehr (2003).

[The moral agent] pushes away all that is sensuous in him and only through this separation from matter does he attain a feeling of his rational freedom. But because sensuous nature puts up an obstinate and vigorous resistance, he must exercise considerable force and great effort, in order to contain his desires and to reduce to silence the energetic voice of instinct. (GD 196, NA 20b: 280)

It is not right, Schiller concludes, that man should 'sacrifice his sensuous part, not even for the sake of the purest manifestations of the divine in him', the triumph of the one should not 'be founded on the ruins of the other' (GD 199, NA 20b: 284). The problem with Kant's moral theory then would be that it pays no heed to the natural human desire for happiness. This interpretation is plausible. The criticism itself, however, less so. For one thing, the disinclined agent can find himself in the state of frustration, discontent, even wretchedness, Schiller depicts, confronted with *any* kind of rule, anything that presents itself with the force of necessity. More importantly, there is ample evidence in Kant's work, including in remarks directly addressed to Schiller, that unhappiness is not a necessary companion to virtue. In the second edition of *Religion within the limits of reason alone*, Kant vigorously denies that duty should be performed with a heavy heart, he insists that the 'temperament' of virtue is 'joyous' not 'fear-ridden and dejected'.[5] This remark fits with Kant's overall strategy which is to acknowledge the desirability of joining together happiness and morality and illustrate their compatibility in his theory, for instance in his treatment of the distinctive pleasures of morality, while at the same time underlining the independence of morality from happiness.[6] The requirement for independence follows from Kant's analysis of the characteristic modality of genuinely moral demands, which in turn, explains the role of pure reason in the account, as the ground of the distinctive necessity of morality.

It is possible, however, to read Schiller's comments about the 'sensuous' as having a more precise reference in Kant's theory, namely inclination. This interpretation makes better textual sense, has philosophical merit, and is useful for understanding the positive argument about grace. Textual evidence comes from the passage in which Schiller praises Kant's vindication of the autonomy of morality by providing it with an independent ground in reason. 'To be altogether sure that inclination has not interfered with the demonstration of the will', Schiller writes, 'it is preferable to see it as at war rather than in accord with the law of reason. ... In this respect, I believe I am in perfect agreement with the rigorists in morals' (GD 198–9, NA 20b: 282–3). The problem is that the

---

[5] 'Now if one asks, What is the *aesthetic character*, the temperament, so to speak, of *virtue*, whether courageous and hence *joyous* or fear-ridden and dejected, an answer is hardly necessary. This latter slavish frame of mind can never occur without a hidden *hatred* of the law. And a heart which his happy in the *performance* of its duty (not merely complacent in the *recognition* of thereof) is a mark of genuineness of the virtuous disposition' (Rel 19, Ak 6: 23–4).

[6] See, for example, Kant treatment moral 'contentment' [*Zufriedenheit*] in CPrR 234–5, Ak 5: 118–9; and the role of aesthetic pleasures in the cultivation of virtue in MM 588, Ak 6: 473–4 and Rel 42–4, Ak 6:47–9).

rational grounding of duty leaves inclination with no positive role. To get clarity on why failure to recognise the moral value of inclinations is a problem, it is useful to consider examples from contemporary treatments of the topic.

The first example comes from Marcia Baron's essay, 'Kantian Ethics'. Baron seeks to correct certain persistent misrepresentations of the concept of duty, especially the idea that a duty-based ethics fosters 'rigidity and moral complacency' (Baron 1996, 51).[7] She illustrates the problem of moral complacency, with Flannery O'Connor's short story, 'The Geranium', in which an old man goes to live with his dutiful daughter and family. The daughter's conception of her duty is capacious enough to include the social duties of conversation:

> Sometimes when the daughter and Old Dudley were alone in the apartment, she would sit down and talk to him. First she had to think of something to say. Usually it gave out before what she considered was the proper time to get up and do something else, so he would have to say something. He always tried to think of something he hadn't said before. She never listened the second time. (Baron 1996, 51)

The spare prose and short sentences convey very well the misery of these stunted conversational efforts. Yet it is difficult to fault the daughter's behaviour from a strictly moral perspective. She does her duty: she is 'seeing that her father spent his last years with his family and not in a decayed boarding house'. Baron observes that the person who is 'dominated by thoughts of duty will be insensitive' (Baron 1996, 52). This may be true, but then sensitivity is not and cannot be itself a duty. If we value the capacity to attend to the particulars of a situation, then we need to think differently about moral psychology, that is, not exclusively in terms of obligation. This is central to Schiller's insistence that inclination should be part of the moral picture. Schiller is not saying that duty is destructive of affective bonds, but rather that a shape of life in which all that is left is duty is dreary. This thumbnail sketch of the dutiful daughter does not show her to be angry, bitter, or resentful; she does not have to do battle with contrary inclinations. She is neither sorrowful nor joyful. She merely acts in accordance to, and, for all we know, out of, duty. But this 'merely' stands for an impoverished moral life.

The second example comes from Rae Langton's discussion of the relation between Kant and Maria Herbert. Langton uses Herbert's letters to develop an internal criticism of certain features of Kantian ethics. It is the inner landscape that Herbert's letters reveal that concerns us here. Her first letter asks for Kant's advice on whether full honesty is advisable in all contexts, including romantic friendship. The second letter describes how the friendship initially suffered as a result of her frank confession, but also her subsequent loss of interest in the man's renewed offers of affection: 'My vision is clear now. I feel

---

[7] Baron aims to exculpate Kant's ethics of the idea that 'as long as one does one's duty, one has done all that can morally be expected of one' (Baron 1996, 51). However, the idea of duty which is precisely about what we can reasonably expect of each other is foundational for Kant. This is why other desirable elements such as smiling disposition, for example, are not duties.

a vast emptiness extends inside me and all around me—so that I almost find myself to be superfluous, unnecessary. Nothing attracts me. I'm tormented by a boredom that makes life intolerable. Don't think me arrogant for saying this but the demands of morality are too easy for me' (Langton 1992, 493). Herbert's letter grants us a rare insight into a moral life in the process of being drained of life. As Langton comments, this is a desolate moral landscape; the letter is 'chilling in its clarity, chilling in its nihilism' (Langton 1992, 494). Herbert states explicitly that she has no desires or inclinations: 'nothing attracts me'. This absence of inclination, which renders morality 'too easy', describes a process of disengagement from the world, a withering away of the attachments of self and society. The void of inclination does not necessarily fill with a more vivid impression of moral personality; it can lead rather to a depletion of self and unbearable boredom.

The last example, though less extreme serves as a complement to the previous two. It comes from Peter Railton's discussion of a state he calls 'alienation' (Railton 1988, 94). Railton gives the example of John, a model husband who, upon being congratulated for the exquisite care he takes of his wife, replies: 'I've always thought that people should help each other when they're in a specially good position to do so. I know Anne better than everyone else does, so I know better what she wants and needs. Besides, I have such affection for her that it's no great burden' (Railton 1988, 94). Railton also tells the story of Helen, who having been a loyal friend to Lisa, accepts the latter's thanks with words to the effect that friendship is a reciprocal relation and that 'this is what friends are for' (Railton 1988, 95). Neither Helen nor John is portrayed as a specifically Kantian agent. They are designed rather made to represent a broad category of agents who possess a capacity successfully to disengage themselves from the particulars of the situation in which they find themselves. John and Helen are of course constructs, but as such, they convey highly effectively the spookiness of the perfectly deliberative self. Railton traces our uneasiness with John and Helen to the 'estrangement between their affections and their rational, deliberative selves; an abstract and universalising point of view that mediates their responses to others and to their own sentiments' (Railton, 1988, 97). For these two individuals, inclinations pose no problem because they are kept at a tidy distance, thoroughly mediated and perfectly groomed by the deliberative self.

The kind of moral life reduced to mere outline shown in the first two examples or a life of detachment illustrated in the last example are reflected in Schiller's warning that a moral life that excludes inclination resembles 'a drawing whose hard strokes exemplify what the rule demands' (GD 203, NA 20b: 287). The remedy Schiller proposes makes inclination integral to moral agency. In this alternative, 'reason and the senses, duty and inclination are in harmony' (GD 197, NA 20b: 282), a harmony that manifests as grace. [8]

---

[8] Schiller's point should not be confused with mere affirmation of nature instead of reason: 'where pure nature reigns humanity disappears' (GD 195, NA 20b:280), its rule is 'a wild ochlocracy' (GD 197, NA 20b:282).

The Ideal of Harmony

Schiller's central argument, then, is that the richer conception of moral life that can be glimpsed in Kant's own writings cannot be realised, if we focus only on what is obligating for us, that is, on duty alone at the expense of inclination. How Schiller describes his solution is in terms of inner harmony which is reflected externally in grace.

When Schiller first introduces the concept of grace, he says very little about the issues of moral psychology that have concerned us so far. His principal task is to distinguish grace from beauty and virtue. Grace, he argues, is powerfully and immediately attractive like beauty (GD 169, NA 20b: 252). Whilst beauty is a natural gift, however, grace is 'an expression of moral feelings' (GD 171, NA 20b: 254) and thus a quality that shows personal 'merit' and 'honours those who possess it' (GD 181, NA 20b: 264). For this reason, grace can only be attributed to the human form, when we consider human beings as moral rather than as purely natural creatures. Further, unlike beauty which is 'fixed', grace is a 'kind of moveable beauty' observed in someone's gestures, facial expression, tone of voice, and generally the 'voluntary movements' characteristic of someone's demeanour (GD 169–171, NA 20b: 252–4). Though grace has this element of voluntariness it differs from virtue, which is acquired through training.[9] The principal feature of grace is 'ease' (GD 195, NA 20b: 280). Not only is obvious effort contrary to grace, but the deliberate imitation of graceful behaviour, once the artifice is detected, ceases to charm us. Whilst grace is not pure nature, it charms us precisely because it appears as something involuntary, not contrived, and hence as a visible manifestation of the person's soul: 'as soon as we observe that grace is artificial, our heart suddenly closes. ... Spirit suddenly becomes matter, and the heavenly Juno is but a shape in the clouds' (GD 186, NA 20b: 270). To get a sense of how these different elements compose a single concept, it is useful here to make a detour through Goethe's *Wilhelm Meisters Lehrjahre*, a work begun in 1777, under the title *Wilhelm Meisters theatralische Sendung*, but revised and completed under Schiller's influence in 1794.

Halfway through the book, the young Wilhelm writes a letter to his friend Werner to explain why he has decided to become an actor. This letter touches upon issues that are directly relevant to our topic. Wilhelm explains to his friend that his aim in life has always been to cultivate, or educate (*ausbilden*) himself. He adds that had he been a nobleman he would not need to strive for this, but because he is a bourgeois he must 'make his own way' in the world (Goethe 1959, 233). It is in this contrast between bourgeois and nobleman that the theme of appearance emerges. 'In Germany', Wilhelm continues, 'a certain generalised and, so to speak, personal culture is only possible for the

---

[9] The concept of grace does not track interpretations of Schiller's position that emphasise the significance of training in achieving inner harmony; see Allison (1990, 80ff), Prauss (1983, 240–308), and Wildt (1982, 158–162).

nobleman. A bourgeois can achieve great merit and at most cultivate his spirit; his personality, however, will be lost, try as he may'. The nobleman's demeanour when he goes about ordinary things has 'a certain imposing grace', while with serious and important matters he deals with 'a kind of charming light-heartedness'. This equanimity is linked to the concept of appearance: 'Whereas the nobleman gives everything through the presentation of his person, the bourgeois gives nothing through his personality and is not supposed to do so. The former may and should "appear to be"; the latter must only "be"'. Here we have a series of links: culture, personality, graceful demeanour, appearance. These interconnections, Wilhelm suggests, are the product of a harmonious development of one's nature: 'The bourgeois must develop specific skills to make himself useful, and it is taken for granted beforehand that his nature is not and should not possess harmony, because in order to make himself useful in one way, he must neglect everything else' (Goethe 1959, 234). The contrast is one between striving to shape one's identity, to find a place in the world, to achieve something and be judged for one's achievement, in short to *be* someone, and a more nebulous and loosely defined set of qualities that bespeak a lack of effort but also a knack for getting things right, an unproblematic but honourable and attractive 'appearance'. Finally, Wilhelm confesses: 'I have an irresistible propensity for precisely this harmonious development of my nature denied me by my birth' (Goethe 1959, 335).

Wilhelm is critically concerned with giving shape to his personality. He argues that this is a bourgeois concern, because the notion that one shapes oneself and thus becomes who one is does not arise typically for someone who is born into a role and a nexus of relations that determine his or her identity. We can detect in Wilhelm's search for self-definition what Robert Pippin defines as the characteristically modern ambition to establish 'what is truly mine', 'a compelling norm, wholly unto oneself, in a wholly self-legislated, self-authorized way' (Pippin 1997, 7). What is interesting about Wilhelm's interpretation of this goal, however, is that he wants to pursue it in a way that appears to go against it: by appealing, that is, to pre-modern ideals of belonging, to roles and structures that are not self-chosen, but inherited, given, and accepted as such. There is a structural paradox to the framing of this goal, to which he is alert when he admits that he seeks to achieve precisely what is denied him by birth, and, by implication, only obtainable by birth.

Closer examination of the content of Wilhelm's aspirations should enable us to circumvent this paradox. The noble ideal he describes is precisely that, an ideal. Its characteristics include a harmonious personality, ease in the performance of one's tasks, and consideration for the appearance of things. So, there is more to it than the privileges of birth; though a noble birth may turn out to be a necessary condition for the flourishing of these characteristics, it is not presented here as a necessary ingredient of the ideal. To gain a better sense of Wilhelm's aspiration, it is useful to think about what these characteristics are intended to oppose. In announcing his attraction for the noble ideal, Wilhelm repudiates the bourgeois ideal, which is essentially one of effort and application: the bourgeois sets himself tasks and pursues them, finds what he is good at and applies himself to it, formulates goals and strives to achieve them; in the process he shapes himself and his world. In a different context, Ivan Nagel describes the historical emergence of the individual who 'by an act of clenched will, subdues an indifferent or unfavourable outer world' and whose ethic 'transfigures sour drudgery into the solipsistic ecstasies of duty and discipline' (Nagel 1991, 35).[10] Looking at Wilhelm's hopes in this broader context, we see the beginning of a different sensibility emerging, one that takes on the bourgeois—or, as Pippin would say, modern—challenge of self-determination, while seeking to get away from its requirements of struggle and confrontation.

If we return now to Schiller's text, with Wilhelm's letter in mind, we can begin to see certain affinities in the shapes of life both describe. First, there are certain clear parallels between noble and graceful behaviour, such as the capacity to appear in certain ways and to do so without effort. Secondly, both are presented as worthy objects of aspiration. The content of this aspiration is the achievement of harmony, by which we are given to understand a kind of fit among different expressions of oneself, of one's desires, talents, aspirations, but also a fit between self and environing world. Harmony is what is visible in the ease and charm of appearance. But if it is an object of aspiration, we are entitled to ask, how it is to be realised. For Wilhelm, the problem is that he seeks to achieve a shape of life that by his own admission is granted rather than achieved. This is not the question of birth, which we addressed earlier, but rather a question of whether a task-like, and hence bourgeois, approach is suitable to the pursuit of Wilhelm's noble ideal. A similar problem arises for the reader who is attracted by Schiller's idea of grace. Insofar as grace is the visible imprint of our moral personality it is, as Schiller says, a merit. Yet, the exercise of the will that we ordinarily presuppose when we judge something to be meritorious spoils grace. Grace must appear natural, or it is no longer grace. Goethe's solution in the novel is given through Wilhelm's theatrical vocation: the self Wilhelm seeks he can find only in the theatre, by literally assuming a role and acting out a given personality. Schiller's solution is given through his aesthetic turn in ethics.

Schiller's aim is to formulate a coherent moral account that allows for a positive conception of the role of inclinations. The question is how we are to understand this role. We know that the view he seeks to correct is that morality is a matter of mastering contrary inclinations. It is plausible to think that he is sympathetic to the view—expressed by Kant in his post-*Groundwork* writings—that appropriately cultivated inclinations can support righteous actions. The

---

[10] Nagel's topic is the Mozart's 1791 opera, the *Magic Flute* (1791). He argues that it expresses a view of happiness that has nothing to do with the rewards of 'self-exertion' in world 'far away from Luther and Kant' (Nagel 1991, 35).

point of cultivation is to ensure that inclination serves rather than sabotage the purpose we seek to pursue, or the character we seek to shape. To recognise the moral value of inclinations is also to cease to consider them only as potential saboteurs, but also as potential supporters of our moral aims as they are in themselves. He concedes that there are moments in which inclinations do not offer any steer when we should advert to pure reason, orientating ourselves by its commands. His praise of spontaneity, his description of the ease, effortlessness, and charming naturalness of grace has the purpose of directing his readers to consider what a positive conception of inclination might look and feel like. What he seeks to describe is a model of moral agency from which inner struggle is entirely absent; harmony denotes a state of being in accord with oneself. What we recognise and admire when we respond to grace is a person who 'trust themselves to be guided by the voice of instinct with a certain confidence that they are not in danger of being led astray' (GD 202, NA 20b: 287).

While Schiller writes eloquently the appeal of inner harmony and its external pull, he is remarkably reticent about the path to its achievement. On reflection, it is not difficult to see why: if the aim is not to groom inclination so as to appear in a certain way, that is, under the perfect direction and jurisdiction of the deliberative self, then an element of passivity, of not trying, must be admitted as part of the notion of inner harmony. Grace is a moral possibility for us, only if we let go the burden (and perhaps illusion) of the heroic—or, on Wilhelm's account, prosaic—perspective of moral world-shaping. But there is another obstacle to the pursuit of grace. Grace describes not merely the inner state of the subject, but also an inter-subjective relation: it is recognised by others who are delighted by it and attracted to it. Less obviously, but in a similar fashion, the agent who seeks to align his actions in accordance with the moral law also places himself in relation to others in a certain way. The difference is that, in the latter case, the emphasis is on the deliberative process, on the reflective and psychological capacities of the individual, who then delivers his decision to the world through his action. The distance or separation from the world that is needed for this deliberative process has its mirror-image in the inter-subjective fit described by grace. Although this is an understated concern in *On Grace and Dignity*, the link between soul and society is unmistakeable: inner harmony has as its correlate a harmonious, unforced relation to the environing world. There is, in other words, a social dimension to Schiller's insistent and dramatic descriptions of the divided self. Harmony describes also a non-agonistic relation to the social world. We are now in position to recognise the full magnitude of the task: to attain harmony, we need not only a certain trust in inclinations, the element of passivity that cannot be forced, but a certain trust in the world in which we find ourselves. This is perhaps the greatest difficulty confronting Schiller's ideal, for this is a world without guarantees that our trust is well-placed, that our inter-subjective relations are in good order, or that our intentions will successfully be recognised in our actions.

The Significance of Grace

Schiller's concept of grace has been shown to depend on a 'thick' conception of agency with distinctive intra-subjective and inter-subjective aspects. The obscurity of the psychological mechanisms that produce the form of harmony that is visible in grace can, retrospectively, be seen as integral to Schiller's aesthetic turn: the reconciliation of inclination and duty is precisely what we witness, and what charms us, when we are in the presence of grace. But, on the other side, it is unclear whether there is anything we can do to achieve grace for ourselves. This is a deep problem.

On the one hand, grace is presented an attractive model of moral agency, and, on the other hand, making grace the aim of our strivings is performatively anomalous, because grace is antithetical to effortful exertion. Imitating the graceful, and so camouflaging the exertion, destroys what we seek to achieve, because as soon as the imitation is detected, the performance ceases to charm, because it is not grace but its imitation. It is impossible to have 'be graceful!' as a moral command. This makes sense: everything Schiller says about the perfect inner accord with oneself, the reconciliation of inclination and duty, the fit between self and world, the very vocabulary of trust he uses in this context, bespeak precisely an antithesis of effort. At the same time, this harmonious state seems unobtainable. To be charmed by grace is not to be graceful. The way forward is to appreciate that charm here signifies experiencing a kind of normative pull, a compelling force that has moral significance without having the form of a moral imperative. There is no need for a command because the attraction to grace, which is an attraction to harmony, is itself a compelling force. The experience of grace seems to open, however obscurely, a path to harmony. To unpack the dynamics of this relation between subjects it is essential to get clearer about what is going on within the subject who embodies Schiller's ideal of moral agency. Granted, inner harmony is a moral quality, but if our attraction to grace has moral valence, then we need a precise account of the how inner states are outwardly expressed. The basis of Schiller's vindication of the moral value of appearances rests on this.

Schiller presents an argument about 'sympathetic movements' to explain the connection of inner and outer: 'when a person speaks, we also see his eyes, his face, his hands—often the whole person speaks to us—and it is not rare that this mimic part of the conversation is the most eloquent part' (GD 183, NA 20b: 266). Sympathetic movements are not purely instinctive nor strictly speaking, involuntary: 'it is what happens when something involuntary mingles with the voluntary act' (GD 183, NA 20b: 266). This account has clear application to grace. Grace appears when 'the mind finds an outer expression of its will and feelings in sensuous nature, so that nature aligns itself perfectly with the will and gives the most eloquent expression of feeling' (GD 194, NA 20b: 279). Schiller's account of sympathetic movement is not widely discussed in the literature. One notable exception is Jeffrey Gauthier who sees Schiller's notion of sympathetic movement as part of a 'theory of action'. Distinguishing between instinctive, voluntary, and sympathetic movement, Gauthier argues that the latter are 'habitual and thus involuntary, but nevertheless possess the capacity to express the will since they are "concomitant" with its aims' (Gauthier 1997, 533). Sympathetic movements are thus seen as uniquely endowed with the capacity to 'express the inner intention of the agent, and so to act as the vehicle of character and will' (Gauthier 1997, 534).

Despite Gauthier's hardening of Schiller's distinctions for the purpose of producing a 'theory of action', his interpretation is not implausible. It makes, however, for an unconvincing theory. If we take it as a piece of empirical psychology, it leaves unanswered precisely the question we ask of it, namely, to know how exactly different moral dispositions map onto movement, facial expression and the like. To baptise a movement 'sympathetic' is no more that to attribute to it a co-operative character. If, on the other hand, this is an exercise in transcendental psychology, then we are no further with it than we are with the Kantian position concerning the ultimate inscrutability of the interaction between the noumenal and phenomenal worlds. There is an alternative interpretation of Schiller's argument that fits better with what he says and also serves better his purposes. His account of sympathetic movement should be seen not in terms of psychology, but metaphysics. What Schiller is writing about is not a theory of motion but a theory of appearances. Looking first at a passage in Kant's *Metaphysics of Morals*, and then to an early essay by Iris Murdoch should help clarify this point.

It seems that the better we understand Schiller's argument, the further we move away from Kant. Schiller's aesthetic turn reveals itself to have profound implications as to how we shape our aspirations and how we experience their normative pull. The appeal of grace is clearly very different from the respect, indeed 'awe', which accompanies our awareness of the moral law. In fact, our present questioning of the moral status of grace is indicative of the effort it takes us to think about the proximity of aesthetics and ethics. It is therefore useful to remember that Kant attempts to do this in the *Metaphysics of Morals* where he discusses the possibility of an 'aesthetic of morals'. Such an aesthetic, he argues, would treat of the feelings that accompany the constraining power of the moral law, such as 'disgust, horror, etc., which make moral aversion sensible' (MM 207, Ak 5:406). Kant further considers the association of grace with virtue and welcomes manifestations of 'agreeableness, tolerance, mutual love, and respect (affability and propriety, *humanitas aesthetica et decorum*)' (MM 265, Ak 5:474). However, even while bringing to the attention of his audience the importance of aesthetic moral features, Kant speaks of them as a 'beautiful illusion resembling virtue', and sharply distinguishes between truth, that is, real virtue, and beautiful appearances that approximate it but are not identical to it (MM 265, Ak 5:473). The crucial element in Schiller's aesthetic turn is the value he places on appearances. Schiller is not simply asking that we recognise the aesthetic element of morality (our attraction to grace), or the moral element of aesthetic pleasure (grace bespeaks a moral personality). Rather he claims that appearances possess cognitive primacy: a person's countenance, their behaviour, the shape they give to their actions and interactions with others, are not deceptive illusions but a field rich with moral *knowledge*.

Schiller's aesthetic turn is of a piece with the normative content of the ethics of grace: his criticism of the reductive conception of agency he finds in obligation-based ethics has its counterpart in the expansion of the domain of moral phenomena he seeks to bring to our attention. Finally, then, his response to what he considers unsatisfactory in the Kantian picture takes the form of a vindication of appearances, rather than a search for the true inner self. A similar vindication can be found in Iris Murdoch's early essay, 'Vision and Choice in Morality', in which she attempts to show the limitations of what she calls the 'modern' view of the moral life as a 'series of overt choices, which take place in a series of specifiable situations' (Murdoch 1956, 34). To counteract this reductive tendency, Murdoch draws attention to what she calls the 'texture of a man's being'. This quality, she argues, 'is shown by their mode of speech or silence, their choice of words ... in short the configurations of their thought which show continually in their reactions and conversation' (Murdoch 1956, 39). The concept of a 'texture of being' is particularly useful in the present context because it captures the range of phenomena that Schiller describes when he talks about sympathetic movements. It also captures the idea that each movement is not an isolated fragment but forms part of a whole, what Murdoch calls 'a total vision of life', or, as Schiller expresses it, 'the destiny of man is not to accomplish isolated moral acts but to be a moral being' (GD 199, NA 20b: 283).

Piecing together these references we can summarise Schiller's argument on grace as follows. The appearances that are morally significant, the graceful quality in someone's demeanour, speak to us only if we let them. We could ignore them, train ourselves to doubt them, and, having put them aside, judge others by searching into their motives, deeper feelings, dispositions of the will, or practical deliberations. Such searches cut us off from the moral knowledge contained in what is directly in front of our eyes. The argument on grace is a particular case of a general thesis that 'the manner in which [man] appears depends upon the manner in which he feels and wills' (GD 179, NA 20b: 262), or conversely, that reasons, feelings, and desires are the sort of things that cannot fail to appear. Appearances can deceive, but even deceptions and disappointments are made visible as they affect the texture of one's moral being. So by inviting us to attend to the embodied expression of moral harmony, Schiller encourages us to reconsider our suspicion of appearances and so indirectly perhaps move closer to grace.

References

Allison, Henry E. 1990. *Kant's Theory of Freedom*. Cambridge: Cambridge University Press.

Baron, Marcia. 1996. 'Kantian ethics'. *Three methods of ethics*. M. W. Baron, P. Pettit, M. Slote eds. Oxford: Blackwell.

Gauthier, Jeffrey A. 1997. 'Schiller's critique of Kant's moral psychology: reconciling practical reason and an ethics of virtue'. *Canadian Journal of Philosophy* 27:4: 513–544.
Goethe, Johann Wolfgang. 1959. *Wilhem Meisters Lehrjahre*. München: Wilhelm Goldmann.
Henrich, Dieter. 1954–1955. 'Das Prinzip der kantischen ethik'. *Philosophische Rundschau* 2:29–34
Henrich, Dieter. 1982. 'Beauty and freedom: Schiller's struggle with Kant's aesthetics'. *Essays in Kant's aesthetics* eds. Ted Cohen and Paul Guyer. Chicago: University of Chicago Press.
Langton, Rae. 1992. 'Duty and desolation'. *Philosophy* 67:262: 481–505.
Murdoch, Iris. 1956. Symposium: 'Vision and Choice in Morality', Aristotelian Society, *Dreams and Self-Knowledge*, Suppl. Vol. XXX. London: Harrison and Sons.
Nagel, Ivan. 1991. *Autonomy and Mercy. Reflections on Mozart's Operas*. Cambridge, MA: Harvard University Press.
Pippin, Robert R. 1997. 'Avoiding German Idealism: Kant, Hegel and the Reflective Judgment Problem' Idealism As Modernism Cambridge: Cambridge University Press. 129–153.
Prauss, Gerold. 1983. *Kant über Freiheit und Autonomie*. Frankfurt: Klostermann.
Railton, Peter. 1988. 'Alienation, consequentialism, and the demands of morality'. *Consequentialism and its Critics*, Samuel Scheffler ed. Oxford: Oxford University Press.
Roehr, Sabine. 2003. 'Freedom and autonomy in Schiller'. *Journal of the History of Ideas* 64:1: 119–126.
Schaper, Eva. 1979. *Studies in Kant's aesthetics*. Edinburgh: Edinburgh University Press.
Wildt, Andreas. 1982. *Autonomie unde Anerkennung: Hegels Moralitätskritik im Lichte seiner Fichte-Rezeption*. Stuttgart: Klett-Cotta.

PART VI

Schiller's Philosophical Legacy

CHAPTER 30

Schiller and the Birth of German Idealism

Hans Feger

Friedrich Schiller's significance for philosophy was established in an irrefutable way by the Neo-Kantians. Following Kuno Fischer's brilliant lectures in Jena in 1858 under the title of "Schiller as Philosopher" and Friedrich Albert Lange's development of the "standpoint of the ideal" from Schiller's philosophic poetry in the last part of his *Geschichte des Materialismus* (1866, 2nd edition 1873/75), many thinkers including Karl Vorländer (1894), Eugen Kühnemann (1895), Bruno Bauch (1905), Wilhelm Windelband (1905) and Ernst Cassirer (1916, 1975) underscored the value of Schiller's philosophy and also made clear that his philosophy cannot be approached independently of his poetry and his dramatic work. While Rüdiger Safranski's biography (2004) finds the vital impulse for the emergence of German idealism from this melding of Schiller's philosophy and poetry, the seminal studies of Dieter Henrich (*Grundlegung aus dem Ich*, 2004) and Manfred Frank (*"Unendliche Annäherung". Die Anfänge der philosophischen Frühromantik*, 1997) on the origins of German idealism did not indicate that Schiller had contributed in an essential way to German idealism. This contrast in the evaluation of Schiller's credentials in this regard can be drawn back to the fact that the relationship between idealism and realism in Schiller is not determined, as with Kant, in relation to the concept of knowledge, but from the viewpoint of beauty and the sublime, which combine reason and nature in such a way that idealizes reality. The centrepiece of Schiller's philosophy is the poetic imagination. To this extent, Schiller anticipates in a basic way the later movement of philosophical Romanticism (see also Feger 1995, Feger 2006)

H. Feger (✉)
Free University Berlin, Berlin, Germany
e-mail: hdfeger@zedat.fu-berlin.de

© The Author(s), under exclusive license to Springer Nature Switzerland AG 2023
A. Falduto, T. Mehigan (eds.), *The Palgrave Handbook on the Philosophy of Friedrich Schiller*, https://doi.org/10.1007/978-3-031-16798-0_30

Early Anthropology

Already in early writings composed during Schiller's study of medicine (*Philosophie der Psychologie*, 1779, *Abhandlung über die Fieberarten*, 1780, *Versuch über den Zusammenhang*, 1780) the hypothesis of a so-called medial power ("*influxus physicus*" after Johann Friedrich Consbruch) is encountered in relation to which physical and psychological processes, body and soul, medicine and philosophy exert reciprocal influence on one another. Influenced by Johann Kaspar Lavater's physiology, Ernst Platner's und Jakob Friedrich Abel's anthropology, Johann Georg Sulzer's "physicality of the soul" und Karl Philipp Moritz's experientially premised inquiry into the soul (*Erfahrungsseelenkunde*), Schiller examines psycho-physical interactions which are not rationally explicable, since, as such, they can be neither matter nor spirit, but must be drawn back to some medial agency that tends to overcome such dualism. This "anthropological turn" (cf. Riedel 1985) as Schiller's speculative point of departure has direct consequences extending to *Anmut und Würde* (1793), *Die Räuber* (1781) and *Wallenstein* (1799). What is decisive for the emergence of a philosophy in the narrower sense, however, is the step Schiller takes in discovering this medial power in the double role played by the power of the imagination which, according to Kant's dictum, is found as an "ingredient" (AA, IV 89) in both perception and knowledge. This ingredient connects the two natures of the human being.

Against this background the *Philosophische Briefe* (1786)—according to its structure a fragmentary epistolary novel—represent an attempt to undermine the rational belief of the Enlightenment by arguing that the psychic constitution of human beings is unable to confer any final authority on reason. Schiller finds in the pious naivety to which the "excesses of brooding reason" (*Ausschweifungen der grübelnden Vernunft*) also belong a theodicy which arises from the natural events of the world ("this God is revealed through a world of worms" [*dieser Gott ist in eine Welt von Würmern verwiesen*]) and only reaches completion in the utopia of universal love (*Theosophie des Julius*, A: I/3 114–139; B 119–151, SW 5: 344–358). With this theory of perfection going back to Shaftesbury and Ferguson on one side and Garve and Mendelssohn on the other, Schiller polemicizes against Mandeville and Helvetius who see the organization of human relations in terms of self-interest. In basing such a powerful anthropological theory of inclination on altruistic sympathy, Schiller's direct target is Shaftesbury's theory of "moral sense" according to which the human being possesses an innate moral (*sittlich*) instinct. Religion interests him in this context only insofar as it works through sensation and, at the same time, works on that part of common humanity maintained through the sensual. In his address *Was kann eine gut stehende Schaubühne eigentlich wirken?* (1785, SW 5: 818–831) he even contends in areas where religion diminishes or is overtaken by religious enthusiasm that art must take the place of religion, because art not only determines morality on the outside but also, in areas where "the jurisdiction of the stage extends into even the most obscure corners of the heart" (*Die Gerichtsbarkeit der Bühne fängt an, wo das Gebiet der weltlichen Gesetze sich endigt*; A 10; B 7, SW 5: 823), can bring religious sentiment to bear with even greater effect than religion. In this way Schiller reverses the traditional manner of distinguishing the two. While the images of religion are drawn on a canvas of fantasy, in art, where they are made efficacious through the *productive* imagination, they are "palpable and true" (A 9; B 7, SW 5: 822). The power of the imagination forms the centrepiece of Schiller's philosophy. This leads him to draw philosophical consequences from his engagement with Kant—consequences which, without meddling with the basic structure of Kant's theory of knowledge, go beyond the dualism of intuition and thought in Kant and contains a stimulus essential for the emergence of German idealism.

History of Philosophy and Historiography

Schiller's career as a writer began in 1782 after the great success of the first performance of Schiller's drama *Die Räuber* in Mannheim. Thereafter followed with great rapidity *Die Verschwörung des Fiesko zu Genua* (1783), *Kabale und Liebe* (1784) und *Don Karlos* (1787)—all of them dramas based on history. The historical studies of the Dutch rebellion and the history of the Thirty Years' War represent important studies underpinning his later professional work as a historian and associate professor in Jena. In 1787 Schiller read the historically focused philosophical essays of Kant in the *Berlinische Monatsschrift*. These were attempts based on the theory of "unsocial sociability" (*ungesellige Geselligkeit*) (AA, VIII 20) to answer the question of the drivers of history which Kant had posed in 1784 in his essay *Idee zu einer allgemeinen Geschichte in weltbürgerlicher Absicht*. Kant interprets the antagonism driving human beings to exit the state of nature as constituting an important stimulus for the view that the historical process is teleologically directed. To the same degree that the danger of war and destruction is diminished, so it is that the innate attributes and skills of humanity are developed and directed incrementally and with ever greater sensitivity towards the observation of lawful practice. Even if Schiller, in contrast with Kant, seeks out the basis for this rational and practical lawfulness in a putatively unpolitical art, nevertheless it is also the case that this teleologically informed view of history exerted a significant degree of influence on his historical works (*Geschichte des Abfalls der vereinigten Niederlande von der Spanischen Regierung* 1788; *Geschichte des dreyßigjährigen Krieges* 1791/1792). In his inaugural lecture as Associate Professor for History at the University of Jena *Was heißt und zu welchem Ende studirt man Universalgeschichte?*, which he gave in 1789, the year the French Revolution took place, Schiller provides the first original response to Kant's *Idee zu einer allgemeinen Geschichte in weltbürgerlicher Absicht* by engaging with Schlözer's *Universalhistorie* und Herder's *Ideen zur Philosophie der Geschichte der Menschheit*. From the teleology of nature, which Kant understood to unfold according to a hidden plan of history, Schiller crafted a teleology of human reason.

Reception of Kant's Aesthetics

Schiller studied Kant's *Kritik der Urteilskraft* from February 1791 as a result of a suggestion both by Christian Gottfried Körner, a close friend since 1785, and above all by Karl Leonhard Reinhold, whose *Briefe über die Kantische Philosophie* (1786/1787) had brought Kant's critical philosophy to a wider audience. Proceeding on the basis of Kant's third *Critique*, Schiller hoped now to be able to work his way "into the critical philosophy bit by bit" (letter to Körner of 3rd of März 1791, *Briefe* III 136) and obtain new impetus for his own poetic projects which had not been moving ahead. In the same manner as Hölderlin, Novalis and Friedrich Schlegel, Schiller read into the Kantian system in the reverse order in which the *Critiques* had been written. A new phase in Schiller's writing career thus commenced with study of Kant's philosophy and a so-called Kant crisis. In a letter of 9 February 1793 to Prince Friedrich Christian von Schleswig Holstein Augustenburg, Schiller talked in terms of the "foundation of a theory of art" and even of his own "aesthetic system" (*Briefe* III 248–250), and in a letter of October 1794 to Goethe he made an open commitment to "Kantian belief" (*Briefe* IV 48). The *Kritik der Urteilskraft* marked a significant turning point for Schiller. The formula that beauty is a "form of purposiveness ... without representation of a purpose" (*Form der Zweckmäßigkeit ... ohne Vorstellung eines Zwecks*) (AA, V 236) introduced the Copernican turn in philosophy into aesthetics. In the autumn of 1793, he read this work a second time and, in the winter of this year, based a private lecture on aesthetics given before an audience of 25 people on the work. It was not until five years later, after reading the *Kritik der praktischen Vernunft* and parts of the *Kritik der reinen Vernunft*, that he resumed his poetic activity. He was only now in a position to incorporate the basic idea of Kant's practical philosophy into his literary production, as the "Wallenstein" project demonstrates so impressively.

From 1791, under the influence of Kant's aesthetic writings, Schiller composed a number of fundamental contributions to aesthetics in quick succession: *Über den Grund des Vergnügens an tragischen Gegenständen* and *Über tragische Kunst* (1791, published in 1792), then die *Kallias-Briefe* (1793, not published until 1847), *Über Anmut und Würde* (1793), *Vom Erhabenen* and *Über das Pathetische* (1793), *Über den moralischen Nutzen ästhetischer Sitten* (1793) and finally the *Briefe an den Augustenburger* (1793), which in revised form appeared under the title *Über die ästhetische Erziehung des Menschen in einer Reyhe von Briefen* in 1795. The last of these writings *Über naive und sentimentalische Dichtung* appeared in 1796.

Even his first writings on tragedy which Schiller composed under the influence of Kant's Analytic of the Sublime reveal a remarkably independent, if not to say, at times idiosyncratic, reception of Kant's thinking. Kant derives the sublime from a "mixed feeling" consisting of reluctance (*Unlust*), when the boundaries of the imagination are exceeded, and desire, when through reversion to supersensible determination even this incapacity takes on a positive determination (AA, V 257–260, KU § 27). Schiller transfers this process of subreption to the conflictual schema of tragedy and derives from it an aesthetic of the sublime. The genesis of the sublime as Kant analyses it contains for Schiller those attributes and features which are constitutive of a theory of tragedy. The advantage of this appropriation of Kant's thinking is immediately apparent when one considers that Schiller succeeds in relating the long tradition of mixed feeling in compassion found in Burke, Mendelssohn and Lessing to Kant's theory of "negative desire" for the sublime and thereby anchors it to the sensual-moral double nature of the human being. The moral purposiveness of tragic pleasure is no longer examined empirically and psychologically but is derived transcendentally anthropologically from the human experience of the agency of self as a sensual-moral double being. In contrast to the feeling of beauty, the mixed feeling of the sublime carries human beings beyond the sensual world and extends in a utopian direction. There is a "contrary effect in nature" (*Zweckwidrigkeit in der Natur*) whereby human beings suffer and, through this very suffering, can gain *aesthetic* access to the sphere of supersensible determination in which they are "no longer directed to suffering" (*A* 104; *B* 87, SW 5: 363). With this change from an aesthetic theory of sensual knowledge to an aesthetics which is focused on the self-knowledge of the human being, nature is given a utopian dimension.

In point of fact, this is already the main idea Schiller discovers in Kant. With this study of Kant's aesthetics a utopian concept of nature is brought into view that is of fundamental significance for the realization of human being itself. In the play drive, whose lawfulness Schiller obtains from a study of Kant's free play of the power of the perception (*Erkenntniskräfte*) (AA, V 217), the concept of humanity is elevated to a state of perfection. The totality involved here is communicated through the idea of beauty. Under the influence of Kant's subjectification of aesthetics, Schiller's earlier, mainly physiologically oriented, anthropology changes into a utopian anthropology in which, right up to Schiller's final writings, poetry accrues the status of "bestowing on humanity an expression of the highest possible perfection" (IV/12 3; *B* 60, SW 5: 717).

With such a utopian understanding, however, Schiller finds himself in a latent conflict with Kant who, for his part, only wishes to allow an anthropology to be a philosophy of the lifeworld or a form of "acquaintance with the world" (*Weltkenntnis*) "from a pragmatic point of view". This understanding is pragmatically oriented because it no longer wishes to speculate physiologically on "what nature makes of the human being" but only on "what the human being as a freely acting being makes of itself or can and should make of itself" (*was er als freihandelndes Wesen aus sich selber macht oder machen kann und soll*; AA, VII 119). In the attempt at overlaying this pragmatic anthropology with an aesthetic utopia Schiller generates conflict with the objective reference in pure aesthetic judgement. For this reason, he writes to Körner on 21 December 1792: "I have suddenly understood the nature of beauty in a new light and believe that I can win you over to my theory. I now believe myself to have found the objective concept of beauty which *eo ipso* qualifies as an objective principle of taste and which brought Kant to despair" (*Briefe* [III 232]). Nevertheless, every attempt to objectify aesthetic judgement is bound to contradict the basic idea of Kant's aesthetics which contends that no object in and of itself can be beautiful or sublime. And yet it is precisely this anti-Kantian objective concept of beauty in the *Kallias-Briefe* which Schiller—in accordance with Kant—believes himself able to make "completely a priori legitimate proceeding from the nature of reason" (*Briefe* [III 237], SW 5: 394).

THE OBJECTIVITY OF BEAUTY

The idea Schiller pursues here is as astounding as it is simple. He follows Kant in the estimation that judgements of taste are based on the "reflection of the subject about its own situation (of desire or reluctance)" (*Reflexion des Subjekts über seinen eigenen Zustand [der Lust und Unlust]*; AA, V 286). Pure judgements of taste do not rest on general prescriptions or rules according to which something can be demonstrated to be beautiful or not, but are anchored in the reflective power of judgement of each individual subject. But from this Schiller does not draw the consequence that the last word about the objective constitution of objects has been spoken or that there is something missing in subjectification. Rather, he understands subjectification as the highest level of objectivity. In aesthetic reflexion a position is reached which liberates nature and cancels out the eccentric relation of the understanding towards nature—a relation through which beauty *of its own accord* comes towards the subject. Kant's subjectification of aesthetics is consistent with a natural philosophical dimension that Schiller himself does not yet fully grasp and yet this is a dimension he is brilliant equipped to respond to. In the *Letters to the Augustenburger* he has the following to say about this hesitant and yet at its core groundbreaking remodelling of Kant's philosophy: "Beauty, too, it seems to me, must rest on eternal principles just as truth and law do, and the original laws of reason must also be the laws of taste" (*Briefe* III 249). If one is of a mind to view Schiller as the vanguard of German idealism, it is precisely speculations like this about *aesthetic* reason assuming a core reference to objects that point the way forward in this respect.

One must remember here that beauty is not only to be understood as subjective semblance, but is also interpreted as an object that from within itself calls forth this semblance, even that its autonomy is an *objective* condition of the object itself ("*Heautonomie*") which persists even when—as Schiller actually thinks—"the representing subject is entirely thought away" ("*das vorstellende Subjekt ganz hinweggedacht wird*", *Briefe* III 275, SW 5: 416). The *Kallias-Briefe* (1793), which emerge from correspondence with Körner, investigate how objects of nature and art must be composed in order to be suitable for the promotion of a symbolic intuition of freedom. Thus it can be contended on one side in an entirely Kantian manner: "Beauty or, rather, taste views all things as objects in themselves and does not tolerate any circumstance where one serves the other as a means or bears the yoke of the other" ("*Die*

Schönheit oder vielmehr der Geschmack betrachtet alle Dinge als Selbstzwecke und duldet schlechterdings nicht, dass eins dem andern als Mittel dient oder das Joch trägt", Briefe III 280, SW 5: 421). On the other hand, this "subjective principle translates into an objective principle" (*"subjektive Prinzip doch ins objektive hinübergeführt"*, Briefe III 259, SW 5: 403) insofar as beautiful things in and of themselves must show their self-determination and independence from goals, rules and conceptual determinations. A wavy line is beautiful because it is free in its movement; a container is beautiful when it hides its character as instrument; the flight of a bird is beautiful when it follows its nature. Ideas and intuitions are connected in the beautiful object in such a way "that both share *one* rule of perception [*Erkenntnisregel*] with each other" (*Briefe* III 256, SW 5: 401). In aesthetic reflection the object itself is suddenly released from its contingency as the nature of or as the "person of the thing" (*Person des Dings*; Briefe III 269, SW 5: 411). This, indeed, is precisely what is meant by the famous formula "beauty in appearance" (*"Freiheit in der Erscheinung"*, Briefe III 256, SW 5: 401). It is not the "sensual appearing of the idea" (Hegel) which is meant, but the lucky happenstance that occurs when aesthetic intuition comes across self-determination as an "analogy of the pure determination of the will" (*"Analogon der reinen Willensbestimmung"*, Briefe III 256, SW 5: 401).

It is only on account of this anchoring of aesthetic semblance to nature that Schiller is entitled to say that beauty is an object which demands a *new* subject, namely the human being insofar as they are *entirely* human. From this human being a new creation emerges which is a further development and intensification of first nature. The formula "freedom in appearance" is above all a natural philosophical speculation through which the ground of human freedom, which otherwise cannot be conceived, is grasped aesthetically in nature. From this point all other deviations from the Kantian philosophy then take place.

Consequences

(1) The direct result of Schiller's approach is a new understanding of being. Whilst Kant's aesthetics is developed from a theory of knowledge, Schiller—like Hölderlin—bases aesthetics on practical philosophy. Schiller was occupied with this notion right up to his late text *Über den moralischen Nutzen Ästhetischer Sitten* (1796): "The human being is not destined to carry out individual moral actions, but to become a moral being" (*"Der Mensch nämlich ist nicht dazu bestimmt, einzelne sittliche Handlungen zu verrichten, sondern ein sittliches Wesen zu sein"*, A 179–180; B 294, SW 5: 464). It is above all the conciliatory aspect of Schiller's aesthetics—its status as a theory dedicated to overcoming the dualism of the human and nature—which constitutes the most significant correction of Kantian aesthetics. Indeed, in relation to Kant's concept of teleology, Schiller formulates an inverse teleology which, while

starting with the hardwired dualism typical of Kant's system, runs in the opposite direction and then overcomes this dualism through the notion of aesthetic education. In the Matthisson reviews of 1794 there is this passage: as far as reason is concerned the appearance of beauty is "a symbol of its own actions, the dead letter of nature becomes a living language of the spirit, and the external and internal eye read the same document of the appearances in an entirely different way" ("*ein Sinnbild ihrer eigenen Handlungen, der tote Buchstabe der Natur wird zu einer lebendigen Geistersprache, und das äußere und innere Auge lesen dieselbe Schrift der Erscheinungen auf ganz verschiedene Weise*", SW 5: 1000). And in *Anmut und Würde*, a text extolled by Kant—in spite of a certain amount of criticism of it—as "written in a masterly hand" (AA, VI 23), Schiller shows that in the lusty feeling of beauty a different type of freedom is revealed than that of self-determined action. In contrast to the fulfilment of duty, the "beautiful soul" shows that reason and morality, duty and inclination can go together. While the former is "the autonomy of the will as the practical freedom of action" ("*die Autonomie des Willens als der praktischen Freiheit des Handelns*") und the idea of duty is put forward with such severity that "all the graces are frightened away" ("*die alle Grazien davon zurückschreckt*", *A* 181; *B* 296, SW 5: 465), the latter is the freedom of the imagination in its playful interaction with the understanding. What is crucial here is that Schiller explicates the postulatory character of practical reason not conceptually as an object of a merely theoretical culture, but in terms of *images*—and this is done precisely in opposition to Rousseau and Shaftesbury. A moral action is beautiful when it appears as a result of the workings of nature. Here Schiller—in contrast to Kant—considers an action performed from an inclination issuing in beauty to be consistent with the indicators of morality. "One speaks of a beautiful soul when the feeling of ethical civility in regard to the full compass of human sensations has reached assurance that it can transfer the guidance of one's will with confidence to the emotions and thereby never run the risk of standing in contradiction with the choices arising from them" ("*Eine schöne Seele nennt man es, wenn sich das sittliche Gefühl aller Empfindungen des Menschen endlich bis zu dem Charakter versichert hat, dass es dem Affekt die Leitung des Willens ohne Scheu überlassen darf und nie Gefahr läuft mit den Entscheidungen desselben im Widerspruch zu stehen*", *A* 186; *B* 303, SW 5: 468). The idea of aesthetic education points up how moral principles can be made habitual through an autonomous art whose function is to create culture such that "coercion" (*Nötigung*) is no longer needed to guarantee the plausibility of these principles.

(2) An indirect consequence is that Schiller's aesthetics becomes a theory of art which, while it emerges from the arena of philosophy, only gains its full philosophical relevance and significance when it is applied to the

arts. This is in stark contrast with Kant, whose *Kritik der Urteilskraft* is concerned with the unity of philosophy and with the need which a philosophy, divided in itself in its own area, cannot supply in its own domain and which leads it to reach for aesthetics as a type of knowledge accessed at the margins. Schiller's idea of aesthetic reason cancels out the romantic notion of philosophy and substitutes it with a notion of poetry—a notion which excited both Hölderlin and Friedrich Schlegel and even led the former to formulate the intention of writing his own "New Letters on Aesthetic Education". A perspective comes into view in this respect which leads Hegel in his *Lectures on Aesthetics* (1835–1838) quite correctly to remark that "Kantian subjectivity and conceptual abstraction are broken open; an attempt is made to go beyond these terms in order to find unity and harmony in an artistic grasping of the nature of truth" ("*die Kantische Subjektivität und Abstraktion des Denkens durchbrochen und d[er] Versuch gewagt [wird], über sie hinaus die Einheit und Versöhnung denkend als das Wahre zu fassen und künstlerisch zu verwirklichen*", Werke—Suhrkamp Ausgabe: XIII 89/ Hotho-Nachschrift). For these two diametrically opposed positions Schiller's aesthetics provides the main point of reference.

(3) A less remarked-upon line of influence leads from Schiller's anthropologization of Kantian transcendental imagination to Schelling's formulation of art as the acme of philosophy. It is exactly this anthropology which functions as a crucial connecting thread to the nature philosophy and art philosophy of the young Schelling. Through the integrative play of aesthetic reason Schiller, taking a holistic conception of reason as a point of departure, succeeds in going beyond Kant and conceiving the aesthetic condition as a condition of endless plenitude in which the determination of the nature of the human being is experienced and looks ahead to its own completion. While Schelling, on the basis of these considerations, however, ascribes to art the function of referencing the metaphysical domain, "since art, in its totality, when organized as a system ... is no longer conditioned by a dualistic ontology according to which our world is a lesser world separated from a higher world" ("*da Kunst, im Ganzen eines Systems geordnet ... nicht mehr von einer dualistischen Ontologie geprägt [ist], derzufolge unsere Welt als geringere von der Hinterwelt geschieden bleibt*", Schulz 1985: 270), Schiller reduces it in socio-anthropological terms to a form of decentred modern world experience from which criteria for the study of moral and aesthetic behaviour emerge. More information about these criteria can be gleaned from the *Briefe über die ästhetische Erziehung des Menschen* which, on account of its programmatic character, can be regarded as perhaps Schiller's single most important statement about aesthetics.

Aesthetic Education

In the *Briefe über die ästhetische Erziehung des Menschen* as well as in *Über naive und sentimentalische Dichtung*, "aesthetic reason" becomes the means for Schiller to launch a critique of alienation from the viewpoint of the idealizing function of the power of the imagination. The kernel of this critique of alienation is the notion of aesthetic education. This notion seeks to address the problem of how nature develops historically, namely, through a process of historical re-transformation of culture into nature. The self-alienation of human beings is caught up in this process, becoming itself reversed (inversion). Only art has the critical potential to overcome the hostility to nature in Schiller's present. It does this when the "naïve" principle of nature is regained through the striving of "sentimental poetry" for its "ideal". Motivating this critique is the French Revolution which Schiller considers having failed morally even though he condones the values that inspired it. Thanks to a notion of aesthetic education advanced as an artistic ideal, Schiller considers it possible to bring about a bourgeois revolution without incurring the risk of the excesses of the French Revolution. This programme aims at positioning aesthetic education as a preparation for political reason. Schiller's revolution of the spirit requires a concept of education which will provide support for the laws of morality.

In order to solve this "problem encountered in experience, [one must] take a path through the aesthetic [question]" ("*Problem in der Erfahrung zu lösen, durch das ästhetische den Weg nehmen*", *A* 12; *B* 53, SW 5: 573): Schiller sets his sights on art as the way to achieve a cosmopolitan bourgeois society. The Marxist interpretation of Schiller on this point made the basic mistake of assuming that aesthetic education is at root a-political (cf. Lukács 1954). In contrast to Kant, Schiller understands the antagonism of social forces not only as a blind means of nature serving the development of human capacities but also as a prominent instrument of culture. Schiller's theory of tragedy is based on the same antagonism whereby the disjuncture of ideal and real is never transcended but constantly reintroduced on the quiet. The agonistic drive—as a wound of culture—brings about the further development of humanity and, as Schiller discusses, pressed past even those successful instantiations of identity in the Greek character. This drive must, however, itself be overcome at a higher stage of art representing the entire human being. Against this background of antagonistic contrary drives in the modern era, Schiller looks towards those special features of art which will serve as a basis for going beyond the present state of reality.

Political Aesthetics

The rational state is unable to ground any better type of humanity using the means of politics and law and, as such, is part of the evil it wants to dispense with. This rational state has no capacity to develop through the means of aesthetic play a totalizing utopia. The attempt to come up with improvements to the state based on principles invoked in the French Revolution was ultimately not able to redefine the relationship between art and reality. "If it were a fact that the most extraordinary case came about that reason could pronounce on political matters which would respect and treat the human being as an end in itself, would put law onto a high throne and make true freedom the basis for the house of state, then I would gladly take permanent leave of the muses and entrust all my energies to that most splendid of works of art, the monarchy of reason. But it is precisely this assumption that I dare to cast into doubt" (*"Wäre das Faktum wahr, wäre der außerordentliche Fall wirklich eingetreten, dass die politische Gesetzgebung der Vernunft übertragen, der Mensch als Selbstzweck respektiert und behandelt, das Gesetz auf den Thron erhoben, und wahre Freiheit zur Grundlage des Staatsgebäudes gemacht worden, so wollte ich auf ewig von den Musen Abschied nehmen, und dem herrlichsten aller Kunstwerke, der Monarchie der Vernunft, alle meine Thätigkeit widmen. Aber dieses Faktum ist es eben, was ich zu bezweifeln wage"*, Briefe an den Augustenburger, Briefe III 332). The political aesthetic which makes its presence felt here takes on the unpolitical appearance of a non-binding artistic ideal of beauty. But the subversive side of this ideal, invoking the aesthetic judgement of the human being, aims at bringing about a "revolution in the way human beings avail themselves of their senses [*Empfindungsweise*]" (27th letter; A: II/6 112; B 290, SW 5: 662) such that humans are "made *absolutely immune* to the arbitrary quality of the human will". What Schiller uncovers in the play drive and what he wishes to direct "not at the citizen of the state in the human being, but the human being in the citizen of state" (*nicht auf den Staatsbürger in dem Menschen, sondern auf den Menschen in dem Staatsbürger zielen*; Über das Pathetische; B 367, SW 5: 534) is this pure rational concept of beauty as a necessary condition of humanity. The cultural and pedagogical alternative to the French Revolution is contained here in the tightly woven bond of political critique and idealized humanity. Schiller ponders the fulfilment of an "aesthetic state" without borders that exists "according to its need [...] in every finely tuned soul", although, indeed, one is "only likely to find it in the form of the *pure church* or the *pure republic* in a few elite circles" (*"wohl nur, wie die reine Kirche und die reine Republik in einigen wenigen auserlesenen Zirkeln finden"*, 27th letter; A: II/6 123–124; 308–309; SW 5: 669; original emphasis).

The aesthetic state thus activates the aesthetic condition as an arena of play in which the human being "acts rationally within the confines of matter and materially under the laws of reason" (*"in den Schranken des Stoffes vernünftig und unter den Gesetzen der Vernunft materiell handelt"*, 19th letter; A: II/6 61; B 211, SW 5: 631) and accords to this condition the status of a preparatory consciousness in which the harmony of the human being within itself is realized through a process of anticipation. In this way, while linking up with Kant, Schiller goes beyond him. For Schiller the play drive enacts the conditions of possibility of an ideality which escapes the agonistic sphere generated by the conflictual base drives in modern life. The transcendental and anthropological derivation of the play drive does not refer to a type of facticity, however composed, but to a potentiality which cannot make its way to experience except through the independence of art. If there were cases where human beings "experienced things from two aspects at once and could become *aware of their freedom* and *feel their being* simultaneously, then one could say in such cases that they would be able to access a *complete intuition of their humanity*, and the object which led to this intuition would become for them a *symbol of a determination they had carried out themselves*, and consequently (because such is only given in the totality of time) would serve to *represent the eternal*" ("*diese doppelte Erfahrung zugleich machte, wo er sich zugleich seiner <u>Freiheit bewusst</u> würde und sein <u>Dasein empfände</u>, wo er sich zugleich als Materie fühlte und als Geist kennenlernte, so hätte er in diesen Fällen ... eine <u>vollständige Anschauung seiner Menschheit</u>, und der Gegenstand, der diese Anschauung ihm verschaffte, würde ihm zu einem <u>Symbol seiner ausgeführten Bestimmung</u>, folglich (weil diese nur in der Allheit der Zeit zu erreichen ist) zu einer <u>Darstellung des Unendlichen</u> dienen*", 14th letter; *A* I/2 79; *B* 159–160, SW 5: 612; original emphasis).

Translated into the language of the drives this means that the reception of beauty unleashes a new (play-)drive in the human being according to which the two basic drives—the form drive and the material drive—are connected such that they lose their opposition to each other. Schiller thus describes a totally new *experience of freedom*. Harmony and totality are a form of (aesthetic) freedom because they cancel out the coercion to which the human being is subject when only one drive—in isolation from the other—is allowed to rule. Aesthetic freedom has nothing in common with Kant's practical freedom (26th letter). Almost as an aside Schiller introduces a new way of conceiving the human being—a way rich in its implications—according to which the human being is a *goal of itself* (*Zweck seiner selbst*), and thereby leaves behind the Kantian understanding of the human being as an end *in itself* (*Zweck an sich selbst*). Schiller abandons the Kantian thesis that the human being is an end *in itself*, because the autonomy of will cannot merely be seen as a means to realize an intention. In place of this thesis Schiller introduces the demand that the human being as an *individual* person is a goal of itself and, as such, is also obliged to realize itself, that is, when understood as the personal identity of the actor. The humanistic demand for the unfolding of the entire human being leads in his view to the point where the aesthetic conception of freedom is put above the moral conception of freedom. The constitutive role of beauty underpinning the realization of a complete human nature consists in the communication of a (double) experience arising from the beautiful in which the human being is both *conscious of its freedom* and *senses its being*. In the 25th letter Schiller calls this the "capacity for union of both natures, the realisation of the infinite in the finite" ("*Vereinbarkeit beider Naturen, die Ausführbarkeit des Unendlichen in der Endlichkeit*", *A:* I/6 100; *B* 270, SW 5: 654). The appearance of the beautiful neither compensates reality with an ideal nor takes away the earnestness of practical reality, morality and politics. Rather, it puts ahead of this earnestness and this reality an image of what human beings could *be* if they valued the multitude of possibilities lying before them and yet grasped themselves as being different from these possibilities. The paradox of "giving freedom through freedom" (*"Freiheit zu geben durch Freiheit"*, 27th letter; *A:* II/6 120; *B* 303, SW 5: 667)—since time immemorial a bone of contention for every process of rational thought—expresses its full dialectical quality here.

The aesthetic drive to education thereby works "unnoticed through a third, joyous realm of play and semblance, in which this drive releases human beings from the burden of all hitherto existing relationships and delivers them from anything that could be called compulsion, either in the physical or the moral domain" (*"unvermerkt an einem dritten, fröhlichen Reiche des Spiels und des Scheins, worin er dem Menschen die Fesseln aller Verhältnisse abnimmt und ihn von allem, was Zwang heißt, sowohl im Physischen als im Moralischen entbindet"*, 27th letter; *A:* II/6 120; *B* 302, SW 5: 667). With this drive Schiller overcomes the core idea of a subjectivity giving power to itself. "What meets the standard of the good is now a type of teaching where one moves from the known to the unknown. This type of teaching is beautiful insofar as it is Socratic, i.e., when through questioning of the head and the heart of the listener the same truths are elicited. In the case of the former, convictions are formally demanded through the understanding, in the second case they are enticed from it" (*"Gut ist eine Lehrart, wo man vom Bekannten zum Unbekannten fortschreitet; schön ist sie, wenn sie sokratisch ist, d.i. wenn sie dieselben Wahrheiten aus dem Kopf und dem Herzen des Zuhörers herausfragt. Bei dem ersten werden dem Verstand seine Überzeugungen in forma abgefordert, bei dem zweiten werden sie ihm abgelockt"*, *Briefe* III 283, SW 5: 423). This aesthetic idealism acquires a utopian dimension as a result of a deeper insight into the nature of reality. Such idealism is invested from the beginning with a movement "in which a subjectivity which gives its own power to itself is brought to an actual understanding of itself through the experience of its impotence" (Walter Schulz: *Die Vollendung des Deutschen Idealismus in der Spätphilosophie Schellings*, 1955, 6–7).

When this happens, it becomes possible to understand becoming in terms of a *movement* through freedom. In order to preserve identity in such a process of movement and not to sacrifice it, necessity takes the form of becoming. What is at stake here is that "time must be sublated *in time*, becoming must be conjoined with absolute being, change with identity" (*"die Zeit in der Zeit aufzuheben, Werden mit absolutem Sein, Veränderung mit Identität zu vereinbaren"*, 14th letter; *A:* I/2 79; *B* 161, SW 5: 612–13). And, thus, Schiller's view of the historical possibilities of the French Revolution indicates precisely that moment of repentance which emerges from the overcoming of the temporality of history. This repentance becomes aware of the fact that it has fallen victim to the attempt to overcome (false) necessity. Such repentance signals the fact that it wants to take reality back to the condition of possibility lying before the moment of change in the process of becoming. In this sense Schiller wishes to "re-do" the French Revolution. For Schiller, then, the Revolution is an event which, although it marks the failure of freedom and the rational state to be fully realized, pinpoints precisely those elements which could bring about its ultimate success.

German text translated into English by Tim Mehigan.

REFERENCES

Bauch, Bruno. 1905. "Schiller und die Idee der Freiheit". In: *Kant-Studien* 10: 346–372.
Cassirer, Ernst. 1916. *Freiheit und Form. Studien zur deutschen Geistesgeschichte.* Berlin.
———. 1975. *Idee und Gestalt. Fünf Aufsätze* (Berlin 1921). Darmstadt: Wissenschaftliche Buchgesellschaft.
Feger, Hans. 1995. *Die Macht der Einbildungskraft in der Ästhetik Kants und Schillers.* Heidelberg.
———. 2006. (Ed.): *Friedrich Schiller. Die Realität des Idealisten.* Heidelberg.
Kühnemann, Eugen. 1895. *Kants und Schillers Begründung der Ästhetik.* München.
Lukács, Georg. 1954. *Beiträge zur Geschichte der Ästhetik.* Berlin. 438.—Vgl. 11–96.
Riedel, Wolfgang. 1985. *Die Anthropologie des jungen Schiller. Zur Ideengeschichte der medizinischen Schriften und der «Philosophischen Briefe».* Würzburg.
Safranski, Rüdiger. 2004. *Friedrich Schiller oder Die Erfindung des Deutschen Idealismus. Biographie.* München 2004.
Schulz, Walter, 1985. *Metaphysik des Schwebens. Untersuchungen zur Geschichte der Ästhetik.* Pfullingen.
Vorländer, Karl. 1894. "Ethischer Rigorismus und sittliche Schönheit". In: *Philosophische Monatshefte* 30: 225–280; 371–405; 534–577.
Windelband, Wilhelm. 1905. "Schillers transzendentaler Idealismus". In: *Kant-Studien* 10: 398–411.

CHAPTER 31

Schiller and Early German Romantics (Kleist, Hölderlin, Goethe)

Tim Mehigan

INTRODUCTION

It is customary to locate the beginnings of the movement of Romanticism in Germany in a type of elevated disagreement with the aims and ideals of eighteenth-century Enlightenment. If this characterization of German Romanticism is accepted, it would make Schiller, an unequivocal supporter of the goals of the Enlightenment in his early to middle period, an unlikely source of inspiration for the Romantics. Schiller's (albeit nuanced) advocacy for rationalist causes in the works of this period would not appear to square well with Romantic ideals in which feelings and desires accrue value precisely because they eschew the primacy of reason in assignations of value. The perspective shifts markedly, however, when Schiller's Kantian writings are considered, especially those writings in which Schiller advertises some measure of disagreement with Kant's moral theory. In the essay *On Grace and Dignity* (1793) and the longer treatise *Letters on the Aesthetic Education of Man* (1795), for example, Schiller develops a series of arguments which, while outwardly still committed to Kant's moral theory, undertakes a move in an independent direction. In the later *Aesthetic Letters* especially, Schiller not only sets out the case for a

T. Mehigan (✉)
School of Languages and Cultures, University of Queensland, St. Lucia, QLD, Australia
e-mail: t.mehigan@uq.edu.au

© The Author(s), under exclusive license to Springer Nature Switzerland AG 2023
A. Falduto, T. Mehigan (eds.), *The Palgrave Handbook on the Philosophy of Friedrich Schiller*, https://doi.org/10.1007/978-3-031-16798-0_31

sensually rich orientation towards the domain of morals foreign to Kant's understanding, but also describes how this orientation is made potent through the agency of art. It was in the significance Schiller attached to art as an agency of the good that the interest of the German Romantics predominantly lay—notwithstanding the high regard that Schiller's dramatic work commanded by the late 1780s nor the reputation Schiller already enjoyed as the most important German playwright since Klopstock.

If the connections Schiller set about forging between aesthetic and moral judgement were alluring for the German Romantics, the case for "aesthetic education" brought forward in the *Aesthetic Letters* was equally so. In the *Augustenburg Letters* (1793)—letters Schiller wrote to his patron that may be looked upon as the first draft of the *Aesthetic Letters*—Schiller had already conceived education in terms of the organic "(self-)formation" (or *Bildung*) of the learner. In the later *Letters*, now invoking the more peremptory notion of *Erziehung*, Schiller put this notion of formation in service to the goals of mankind. In the final letters, Schiller argued that the final state of the human being is not just a "moral state", as Kant had envisaged, but an "aesthetic state"—a state built on the proposition that beauty has harmonizing effects capable of addressing the discord found at the very root of humanity. Not only this. Art's capacity to unify the mental and emotional dualism intrinsic to the human condition also had a hitherto unforeseen political application. Leveraging this potential in the *Aesthetic Letters*, Schiller put forward art as a political response to the events of the age—events that had seen the overturning of the feudal order in France, the execution of the monarch, and the emergence of a violent terror under the Jacobin revolutionaries. The direct motivation for presenting the political case for art was a shortfall in the rationalist account of morality, of which Kant's moral law was a prime example. The revolutionaries in France had clearly taken no heed of any such moral law. What was needed in view of this shortfall in the uptake of rational morality, Schiller reasoned, was a more balanced approach to the problem of the divided nature of human beings—a nature that saw human responses tugged towards excessive "inclination" on one side and excessive rule-induced dogmatism on the other. The Romantics took Schiller to have worked out precisely such a balanced approach to the human being and thereby opened the way for the emergence of a better humanity.

The Romantics also felt drawn to Schiller's account of cognitive and emotional dissonance in the human being. As Schiller contended in the middle section of the *Aesthetic Letters*, the factor of perennial mutability represented the "condition" (or *Zustand*) of outer life. The resources of *Person*, as it were on the inside, arose in response to the social-psychological need of individuals to confer order on such mutability. In the tension between the alteration of the world and the need to institute forms of order at the level of the person to deal with it, Schiller had discovered a formula that neatly captured the drama of inner and outer life as many Romantics experienced it. In Ludwig Tieck's stories *Der blonde Eckbert* (Eckbert the Blond) (1797) and *Der Runenberg* (The

Mountain of Runes) (1801), for example, the protagonists walk a tightrope of inner feeling that takes them to the edge of madness—or into madness outright. If the mystery of inner states remains uncomprehended in these stories, no satisfactory experience of outer life appears possible. In other signature works of German Romanticism a similar problematic is evident. For the focalizing figure in E.T.A. Hoffmann's *Der goldne Topf* (The Golden Pot) (1814), for instance, success in the outward trappings of professional life on one side and in the voluntary state of love at the level of inner experience on the other are sharply opposed. Only the elemental force of beauty can overcome the disjuncture that separates these states. A similar schism of outer and inner life is encountered in *Undine* (1811), Fouqué's story of a water sprite who owes her very existence to the love of a mortal, and in *Aus dem Leben eines Taugenichts* (From the Life of a Good-for-Nothing) (1826), Eichendorff's whimsical tale about a useless boy devoted to his fiddle but otherwise incapable of making his way in the world. The cancelling of the cognitive dissonance from which the boy suffers in this latter story does not consist in the abandonment of his fiddle for a respectable profession, but, at a much more profound level, in locating a point where poetry and the world might be brought into harmony. In these typical scenarios of Romantic literature, art is not just make-believe, but a virtual storyboard in which the complex task of finding a balance for the conflicted ends of the human being is enabled. As Schiller argues in the *Aesthetic Letters*, it is this capacity of art to identify the conflicts that belabour human experience as well as the ways of overcoming them that the true value of artistic experience is found.

Overall, then, Schiller's account of the importance of art for the societies of the future as well as the significance of the artist as the agency to lead into this future represented something of a new "evangelium" for the Romantics. In crafting this evangelium, Schiller had not broken with Kant's new critical philosophy outright, but rather provided a way of imagining the further service it could provide. In one fell swoop, Schiller had purged reason of its moralistic tone yet retained (a sensualized) moral reason; linked reason to a more complete understanding of the freedom of the human being and thereby given both—the "new" reason of critical philosophy and the "new" morality with its freshly minted aesthetic admixture—a logical underpinning. Schiller's ideal of aesthetic education, in which the revised account of reason and the new emphasis on freedom come together, duly became the idealism of the Romantics (cf. Beiser 1998). Novalis described this idealism, famously, as "progressive universal poetry" (Novalis). Beiser paraphrases Novalis's new platform for knowledge and experience in the following terms: "to make us aware of the magic, mystery, and wonder of the world; ... to educate the senses to see the ordinary as extraordinary, the familiar as strange, the mundane as sacred, the finite as infinite" (Beiser 1998: 294). Schiller's *Aesthetic Letters* fitted this Romantic search for wonder, mystery, and fulfilment as hand to glove.

In what follows, Schiller's importance for the Romantic generation is discussed in relation to three writers and thinkers whose work arose in close connection—and by no means always consonance—with Schiller's thought. Nor is this surprising: disagreement, however it presents, is as much an indicator of influence as its converse. This is certainly true of the leading Romantic intellectual Friedrich Schlegel, who after a period of tension and hostility only affirmed the true extent of Schiller's impact on him after Schiller's death.

The authors discussed in the following are Friedrich Hölderlin, Heinrich von Kleist, and Johann Wolfgang Goethe—writers of a broadly Romantic disposition who, nevertheless, often stood apart from the Romantic mainstream. Of the three, Hölderlin and Kleist give prominence to philosophical concerns, absorbing key influences from Kant as well as Schiller. Goethe, by contrast, drew writerly influences from Schiller rather than philosophical ones, though it is also true that his acceptance of a philosophical objection Schiller had raised with him led to friendship between the two and brought about the literary experiment that was to become Weimar Classicism. This friendship will be considered at the end of these remarks. As a prelude to discussing Hölderlin, Kleist, and Goethe, I turn first to the short text *The Oldest System Program of German Idealism*, one of the founding documents of German Romanticism. It would not be pressing the point too far to suggest that this important text could not have been written without prior knowledge of Schiller's Kantian writings.

THE OLDEST SYSTEM PROGRAM OF GERMAN IDEALISM

The *System Program* is a draft text composed in 1795–1796 which was later discovered among Hegel's papers. It appears to have been the work of three friends and graduates of the Tübingen Seminary, viz. Hegel, Schelling, and Hölderlin, more or less equally.[1] Consistent among the varying outlooks of these thinkers and present already in the early text itself is the insight that philosophy is needed to ground the claims of a literary-philosophical "idealism", the forerunner of what would later be dubbed "romanticism". The philosophy considered in the text to stake out this idealism, more than any other, is the new Kantian philosophy. Yet, as Reinhold had argued in his *Versuch einer neuen Theorie des menschlichen Vorstellungsvermögens* (New Theory of the Human Capacity for Representation) (1789), a work purporting to be an exposition of Kant's critical philosophy, that philosophy was in need of a foundation. If Reinhold could be believed, the Kantian philosophy, while proceeding from a powerful set of principles established in the subjective viewpoint, did not finalize the Copernican "revolution" it had laid out on its own ground. As the authors of the *System Program* suggest—most of whom had attended Reinhold's lectures in Jena (cf. Frank 1997)—that finalization had to be imagined as a forward movement from metaphysics to ethics and the eventual replacement of metaphysics with a newer, updated and more complete ethics.

---

[1] As Lacoue-Labarthe and Nancy note, however, the text, though found among Hegel's papers and in Schelling's hand, appears to have been composed under the direct influence of Hölderlin (Lacoue-Labarthe and Nancy 1998).

The passage towards such an ethics could not be fashioned *ex nihilo*, as Schiller had already suggested in the *Aesthetic Letters*. Any such attempt would risk the recurrence of the same "political" problem that had surfaced in the tilt into violence during the French Revolution. This argument had important instructional value for the authors of the *System Theory*, for Schiller had identified a problem of continuity that would first have to be addressed if ethics was to be secured as the mainstay of future societies. Since such continuity could not be expected from ethics on its own ground, a separate instance—an intervention from a different quarter—was needed. In Schiller's argument that intervention is provided by art. Schiller mobilized this intervention in reference to a source argument about aesthetic judgement in Kant's *Critique of the Power of Judgment*, but he extended that argument in new ways. In his third *Critique* Kant had found in "aesthetic judgment" an ally for the work of ethics, but he did not consider art to be a substitute for it. Hesitating to observe the same demarcation, Schiller favoured a much more robust account of art than Kant had contemplated. In Schiller's argument, aesthetics is not merely the handmaiden of ethics and morality, but an independent agency or capacity akin to a separate faculty that enabled ethical claims to be grounded and advanced.

Schiller's main innovation in his aesthetic writings consisted in the caveat he attached to the work of ethics in *its* domain. It is not enough, he contended, that an ethical precept should issue its demand through direct appeal to a "moral law". This was so because human beings have a "mixed" nature: their disposition is stretched between two conflicting sets of interests so fundamental in nature and so powerful in their effects that Schiller determined each to be constituted as a "drive" (or *Trieb*). The problem for rational moralities in Schiller's estimation is that their prescriptions spoke to one of these drives, the rationally motivated "form drive", more than to the other—the "sense drive" with its seat in physical sensation. Given this lopsidedness, moral prescriptions would have to be augmented from a different quarter if they were properly to command the attention of human beings. Such augmentation is supplied in Schiller's approach by beauty, an independent "fact" (SW 5: 655) in the world possessing both a sensuous and a rational dimension and as such able to make appeal to both. Since beauty makes its appearance when the "play drive" is engaged, art—speaking to both base drives in human nature simultaneously—is able to bring a moral investment to bear, even as it also observes the autonomous principles of its own operation. It followed, Schiller contended, that ethics can only gain traction as a force in the world if art and aesthetic judgement first achieve success in corralling the fractious elements in the human being. They achieve this by bringing the form drive and the material or sense drive into alignment—effectively erecting a bridge between these two aspects of human experience through the "condition" of "aesthetic semblance". As Schiller observed in the *Letters*: "Among the most important tasks of culture is … that of making the human being aesthetic, because it is only on the basis of the aesthetic condition, and not on the basis of man's physical condition alone, that the moral condition is able to develop" (SW 5: 643).

Romanticism comes alive on the back of this intention to construct a bridge between aesthetics and morality—a task begun by Schiller but, in the estimation of the authors of the *System Program*, not completed by him. The completion of the bridge is imagined in the *System Program* as a marriage of Plato and Kant—an unusual one, given Kant's "critical", that is, professedly non-metaphysical, approach. As the argument of the *System Program* suggests, Plato is needed to overcome the difficulty attending Kant's moral theory, which, as Schiller presents it, lies with the fact that morality has no power to make appeals to the social collective from within its own domain. By contrast, art in Schiller's account is tied to wider social interests from the beginning. While the direction of movement of the social collective over time cannot be finally known in Schiller's theory except as an "intuition" of humanity (SW5: 612), its progression can be understood through cultural and historical analysis, which is to say, as an anthropology (cf. Riedel 2017; Mehigan 2020). Hegel's phenomenology of spirit and Marx's dialectical materialism have their origins in this insight. Sensing the promise of a fruitful dialogue between philosophy and art in such an anthropology, the authors of the *System Program* conclude that "the philosophy of the spirit is an aesthetic philosophy. ... Poetry thereby accrues a higher dignity, it becomes again what it was in the beginning—the *teacher of humanity*" (HW 557, original emphasis).

The Oldest System Program of German Idealism, from this angle, is clearly indebted to Schiller in important respects. The restitution of links between philosophy and art by way of an argument about the pivotal importance of aesthetic judgement in ethics could be taken as a bridge between the two domains of art and morality—domains largely kept apart since antiquity on the strength of philosophy's eminence in moral matters. This was a bridge across which most later Romantics were to pass—the philosophically minded early Romantics such as Hölderlin, Hegel, Schelling, Friedrich Schlegel, and Novalis no less than Coleridge, Byron, Keats, Shelley, and the later Wordsworth in the Anglophone cultural setting. Only the sceptically minded Prussian writer Heinrich von Kleist questioned core tenets of the Romantic ethos and the plausibility of such a bridge. Significantly, Kleist's challenge to the Romantics was brought forward as a challenge to the validity of Schiller's sensualizing of Kantian ethics. This challenge to Schiller's arguments was never successfully rebutted during the era of Romanticism and is still a source of philosophical interest today. Kleist's dissident position regarding the central claims of Romanticism will be considered later in these remarks.

Hölderlin

Friedrich Hölderlin (1770–1843) can be reckoned among the most important writers of the Romantic generation. Inspired, as Schiller was, by Kant's investigation of "aesthetic judgment" in The *Critique of Judgment*, Hölderlin commenced study of Kant's philosophy in 1790. His rich—albeit fairly one-sided—correspondence with Schiller began a few years later in 1794.[2] Though marked by long pauses and enthusiastic restarts, both of which clearly taxed Hölderlin and the forms of decorum he was obliged to observe as an unheralded junior writer, this correspondence lasted until 1801. Perusal of this correspondence suggests that Hölderlin did not just feel great admiration for Schiller, but also found in him the kind of older writer and thinker on whom to model his own intellectual development. In a letter to his friend Neuffer in the autumn of 1794, Hölderlin supplies key information about a specific work that had provided Hölderlin with intellectual stimulus and served as the starting point for his own attempts to write about "aesthetic ideas":

> The basic idea is that the essay should contain an analysis of beauty and the sublime, according to which the Kantian analysis is simplified, and on the other hand more multifaceted than Schiller provided in his work on Grace and Dignity, which [for its part] also attempts to take a step beyond limits set by Kant, but a step that is smaller in my opinion than the step he should have taken. (HW 713, my translation)

In these remarks, Hölderlin expresses support for Schiller's challenge to the Kantian edifice in matters of aesthetics. Yet, as Hölderlin also points out, Schiller's discussion leaves the thrust of Kant's ethics unchallenged. A half-objection only is registered in Schiller's critique—the objection that Kant's rule-bound moral law tends to infantilize those it was intended for. As Hölderlin recognizes of the 1793 essay, Schiller did not break with Kant's critical project on any substantive point of ethics or aesthetics. At the same time, Schiller's references to the beautiful soul in the same essay suggest a role for art that is no longer consistent with the type of reformed virtue ethics in favour of which Kant had spoken in both the *Critique of Practical Reason* and the *Critique of Judgment*. So long as art in that account is restricted to providing examples of estimable conduct, it is bound to discharge no more than an ancillary function in the area of morals. Yet is it not also the case—as Schiller's discussion of the beautiful soul implied—that art's importance extended beyond this function of communicating examples of "right" conduct, particularly if the beautiful soul did not just serve the cause of exemplary behaviour but was itself a *force majeur* in ethical life that had the power to compel, to inspire, to teach, and thereby to usher in a quite different conception of how one might live in the world?

Hölderlin's reference in the letter to Neuffer to Plato's *Phaedrus* suggests precisely the kind of ethical reach of aesthetic ideas that Schiller had glimpsed but, at least on the evidence of *On Grace and Dignity*, not fully acted upon. The reference to Plato also indicates thatHölderlin's preoccupation with the Greeks, a signature aspect of his thought, can be distinguished even from that of Winckelmann a half century before. Winckelmann's discovery of a principle of restraint in Greek art governing the ethical bearing of subjects (Winckelmann

---

[2] Hölderlin first met Schiller a year before in 1793.

1756) had served to maintain the separation of the ancients from the culture of the moderns. Yet Hölderlin was not content to put Greek art and culture in all matters on a pedestal and thereby to affirm the putative "inimitability" (ibid.) of that art and culture. Though Greek excellence could not be challenged in many areas, it was sometimes important *not* to follow the Greeks slavishly, especially in matters of rule legislation in art. Supporting such a project is Schiller's insight in the *Aesthetic Letters*, first, that it is "one of the most important tasks of culture to ... make human beings aesthetic" (SW 5: 643), and second, Schiller's suggestion in the *Letters* that the Greeks had only journeyed part of the way along this path and not fully realized their "aesthetic republic". In the Böhlendorff letter, Hölderlin deploys a similar aesthetico-cultural approach to Schiller to find a solution to a pressing problem of education. In devising this solution, also like Schiller, Hölderlin works out a cultural way forward for the Germans.

This is how Hölderlin puts things in a letter to Casimir Böhlendorff of June 1801:

> It sounds paradoxical. But I contend once more and present it for your examination and use: that which is actually a nation's strength [*das eigentlich Nationelle*] always becomes the lesser gift in the process of development [*Bildung*]. For that reason, the Greeks are less the masters of divine pathos since this was already innate in them; on the other hand, they are excellent with respect to the gift of depiction [*Darstellungsgabe*], beginning with Homer. ... For us it is the other way round. That's why it's so dangerous to abstract rules of art solely and alone because of Greek excellence ... that which is one's own must just as well be learned as what is foreign. On that account the Greeks have become indispensable to us. Yet it remains the case that we will not approach them regarding our own national excellence, because, as just stated, the *free* use of one's *own* is the most difficult thing. (HW 788, my translation)[3]

Hölderlin's thinking in this passage is clearly indebted to Schiller's *Aesthetic Letters*. As Hölderlin contends, following Schiller's lead on the centrality of aesthetic education, education proceeds by absorbing the great examples of the past. To achieve this, educators and artists are obliged to place the need to learn from the past above anything innately possessed. On these assumptions, however, any gifts in one's own cultural make-up are shifted aside or overlooked altogether. To correct this imbalance, any project dedicated towards

---

[3] "Es klingt paradox. Aber ich behaupt es noch einmal, und stelle es Deiner Prüfung und Deinem Gebrauche frei: das eigentlich Nationelle wird im Fortschritt der Bildung immer der geringere Vorzug werden. Deswegen sind die Griechen des heiligen Pathos weniger Meister, weil es ihnen angeboren war, hingegen sind sie vorzüglich in Darstellungsgabe, von Homer an ... Bei uns ists umgekehrt. Deswegen ists auch so gefährlich, sich die Kunstregeln einzig und allein von griechischer Vortrefflichkeit zu abstrahieren ... das Eigene muß so gut gelernt sein wie das Fremde. Deswegen sind uns die Griechen unentbehrlich. Nur werden wir ihnen gerade in unserm Eigenen, Nationellen nicht nachkommen, weil, wie gesagt, der *freie* Gebrauch des *Eigenen* das Schwerste ist" (HW 788).

mastery of foreign excellence must also direct attention to what is original or excellent in one's own national make-up. In the case of the Germans, such innately possessed excellence is "clarity of expression"—something, as Hölderlin tells us, which the Greeks, for their part, had to learn from the Greek gods, their great teachers. Since intellectual matters between the Greeks and the Germans are now reversed (the Germans possess innately what the Greeks had to acquire, and vice versa), the Germans must now do two things simultaneously: devote attention to Greek excellence as well as *relearn* what is excellent in their own make-up. Hölderlin concludes that the *free* use of what one innately possesses is an accomplishment of supreme difficulty (HW 789). It follows that it would be folly—Hölderlin says "dangerous"—to obey the artistic rules laid down by the Greeks in all matters of art. The focus for the Germans should now lie less with directing attention to the foreign and more with the cultivation of innately held areas of excellence such as the—neglected—gift of artistic depiction.

The Böhlendorff letter, then, indicates how Hölderlin—an original thinker in his own right—profited from the example of Schiller. Schiller, it could be said, pointed Hölderlin back towards the importance of "clarity of expression"— a gift amply on display in the *Aesthetic Letters*. Another level of indebtedness to Schiller may be found in the concept of beauty—a pivotal concept for both authors. In the fragment *Reflexion*, Hölderlin considers the awakening of beauty in the human being to provide a way of feeling and intuiting the whole, claiming that "all knowledge begins with the study of beauty" (HW 503). The link between knowledge and beauty is reminiscent of a similar claim about the rational content of beauty found in Schiller's *Aesthetic Letters*. In the middle section of the *Letters*, for example, Schiller sets out to arrive at a "pure rational concept of beauty" (SW 5: 600). On the assumption that this rational concept of beauty is plausibly derived, he then explains that the "aesthetic condition", which only comes about through engagement with the beautiful, registers the presence of both "knowledge" (*Erkenntnis*) and morality (*Moralität*) insofar as the latter entails the former (SW 5: 637).[4] This argument reaches its highpoint in the final letter when Schiller contends that the vanishing point of human cultural development is not, as Kant had maintained, the "moral state", but in fact the "aesthetic state (*Staat*)" (SW 5: 667). This re-ordering of affairs in Schiller's account is premised on the view that beauty as a principle of order must be understood to work in unison with the principle of reason. Leaning heavily on Schiller with respect to art's social and cultural importance, Hölderlin then reaches the conclusion that "all religion in its essence is poetic" (HW 539). With a statement that leverages Schiller's insights but now goes beyond

---

[4] In a later record of Schiller's lectures on aesthetics Schiller clarifies the distinction in question, finding that morality can be looked upon as "vernunft*mäßig*", "*according to* reason", whereas beauty is "vernunft*ähnlich*", which is to say, "*similar to* reason" (SW 5: 1040). A somewhat different impression about the relation between beauty and reason is raised in the *Aesthetic Letters*, at least over its final stretches.

them, Hölderlin maintains that the "providential relation" (*höheres Geschick*) obtaining between humans and their world comes into being not through any rational purposiveness on its own, nor any argument redounding to the force of the passions on its own. Rather, it is poetry from which the mythic quality of religion is made and from which it draws its special status and binding power (cf. Hölscher 2006).

This vision of the significance of poetry is conveyed in Hölderlin's sublime riverine poems and the elegiac masterpiece "Brot und Wein" (Bread and Wine). These poems resulted from a concentrated period of philosophical reflection beginning with Kant's notion of aesthetic judgement and carried further by Schiller's later Kantian writings. It was these Kantian writings that clarified for Hölderlin what could be claimed for art—or should be. Hölderlin's understanding of the vital significance of poetry had its source in Schiller's "derivation" of the rational concept of beauty. The prophetic dimension of such poetry—the question Hölderlin puts in "Brot und Wein" in terms of "the function of the poets in troubled times" (*Wozu Dichter in dürft'ger Zeit?*) (HW 120–25)—is indebted to the vision of the "aesthetic state" Schiller unfolds in his final "aesthetic letter". While Hölderlin brings art and myth together in entirely new ways, it would be fair to say that the intellectual buttressing needed to arrive at such a conception of art is properly and unequivocally Schillerian.

Kleist

If Hölderlin presents the clearest example in the emerging Romantic generation of the positive impetus flowing from Schiller's Kantian writings, the case of the Prussian Heinrich von Kleist (1777–1811), a more unruly spirit and a writer less clearly aligned with Romanticism, shows that Schiller's legacy was also received critically, if not to say with scepticism, in that generation. Like Hölderlin, Kleist was a student of Kant's philosophy, though he did not obtain the kind of independent purchase on the critical philosophy that Hölderlin and his friends Hegel and Schelling from the Tübingen seminary were able to acquire. Kleist's early career was spent not in a religious academy with a philosophical orientation but in the Prussian army. He did not come into contact with the new Kantian philosophy until he had left the military and progressed to tertiary study at the University of Frankfurt (Oder) in his hometown in 1798. While he was clearly made aware as a student of law in Frankfurt an der Oder of the critical philosophy, Kleist appears not to have appreciated the full import of this philosophy until he undertook independent study of Kant in late 1800 or early 1801. His intellectual encounter with Kant, when it properly arrived, occasioned the kind of collapse of mental frameworks later attributed to Kant's teachings by Heine (Heine 1997; cf. discussion in Mehigan 2011). By the same token, when Kleist became aware of Schiller's Kantian writings (scholarship is yet to determine precisely when this awareness occurred), he could not find in them anything resembling his own disastrous response to Kant, and thus one might surmise that Kleist had come to the view that Schiller could not properly have understood the revolutionary nature of Kant's teachings. However this may be, it seems that Kleist could not locate in Schiller's Kantian writings what he was looking for—a new position according to which the implications flowing from Kant's critical philosophy could be accommodated. As letters to his bride Wilhelmine von Zenge and his half-sister Ulrike von Kleist attest, Kleist suffered a severe emotional and intellectual crisis as a result of his encounter with Kant's philosophy: "My sole and […] highest goal [has] sunk away" (KSW 2: 634, my translation). Critics have found much melodrama in this sentiment and not a little miscomprehension of Kant (see Ensberg 1999). Yet these later judgements themselves mistake what it meant for a denizen of the late eighteenth century—one schooled in the habits of Prussian exactitude and Wolffian rationality—to take the Copernican turn with the critical philosophy and assess what, if anything, could be salvaged from the old habits of understanding and old ways of being in the world.

Kleist's literary career began after—and perhaps as a result of—this traumatic encounter with Kant or Kantianism. This fact alone makes it seem even more inevitable that Schiller's own responses to Kant's philosophy acquired great significance for Kleist. Kleist's reaction to those responses is set out in several short stories that discuss the merit of Schiller's notion of the "beautiful soul" and an essay, *Über das Marionettentheater* (On the Puppet Theatre) (1810), that engages directly with Schiller's essay *On Grace and Dignity* and specifically with the claim that grace and dignity function as reliable markers of ethical experience. The tendency of the tribunal Kleist convenes about these responses is to come out against Schiller and, by default, in favour of Kant. Certainly, it is the case that Schiller could not become for Kleist the sort of teacher he undoubtedly was for Hölderlin. By the same taken, such a conclusion is apt to obscure the fact that the need to ask questions of Schiller's Kantian writings drove Kleist to some of his most original and thoughtful writing. In the case of the short stories, this writing consists of a series of finely woven narrative "essays" on elementary problems in epistemology, and, in the case of the essays, issues an ethics of Kantian provenance must face in the kind of post-religious settings that were beginning to be encountered in Kleist's day and are widespread in ours today. Kleist's genius, first, is to look forward to a time when the deistic claims staked out in the ethical domain for a rational religion (the project Kant announces in the *Religion within the Bounds of Mere Reason*) no longer gain traction. Kleist also appears to anticipate, second, a development in German letters that was not to see the light of day until a new tradition in thought—that of hermeneutics—had made its appearance. Hans-Georg Gadamer, a leading twentieth-century exponent of this manner of thought, is right to pinpoint Kleist's importance for this tradition in the latter stages of his major work *Truth and Method* (2004), just as it is also plausible to assign importance to Schiller in the early part of that work. As Gadamer's "book-ending" of the tradition of hermeneutics reveals, Schiller can be positioned at the beginning of a new type of world-making that Kleist, at the end of it, can be said in a certain sense to conclude. Kleist's capacity to stay within the orbit of Schiller's Kantian reception while still exercising criticism of it might even be taken in support of Benjamin's view that art criticism (Benjamin 2008) just as much as art must be understood as integral to the movement of Romanticism.

The Beautiful Soul

Schiller's discussion of the beautiful soul is introduced in a later section of his essay *On Grace and Dignity*. This is Schiller's definition:

> One speaks of a beautiful soul when the feeling of ethical civility [*das sittliche Gefühl*] in regard to the full compass of human sensations [*Empfindungen*] has reached assurance that it can transfer the guidance of one's will with confidence to the emotions [*Affekt*] and thereby never run the risk of standing in contradiction with the choices [*Entscheidungen*] arising from them. (SW 5: 468, my translation)

Schiller makes two claims in this passage for the beautiful soul—an established trope of eighteenth-century thought. The first is that the activity of the beautiful soul has a social and moral (*sittlich*) component. The moral interest of the wider social collective is apparent in the activity of this soul. This already suggests the existence of a channel running between beauty and morality—a channel which Schiller deepens in the later *Aesthetic Letters*. A second claim for the beautiful soul is registered through the observation that the emotions need not conflict with the freedom of the will but may in certain circumstances operate in harmony with them. When such harmony applies, the will need not be called upon to provide service but can be entrusted directly to the emotions. In that case, the emotions would do, practically speaking, "moral work". Kleist tests both these claims in his stories.

In *Das Erdbeben in Chili* (The Earthquake in Chile) (1807), for example, a community of beautiful souls comes about spontaneously after an earthquake razes most of the city of St. Jago to the ground. Following Rousseau's presentiment in the *Discourse on Inequality* that civilization is inherently decadent, the state of original human nature, by contrast, virtuous, beautiful souls on the model laid out by Schiller come together after the earthquake in a secluded valley beyond the city to provide mutual support and assurance. Kleist compares the human spirit that rises like a Phoenix from great suffering and general social destruction to a "beautiful flower" (KSW 2: 152). Only one among this embryonic new society is moved to express alarm, however, when a plan is hatched to send a small party from this "valley of Eden" (149) back to the town to give thanks in the Dominican church for the gift of survival. After a carefully choreographed depiction of a humanity which has arrived at the point of Schillerian beauty, Kleist vents his spleen on such idealistic sentiment that so misconstrues the true "Hobbesian" nature of human relations. Apocalyptic scenes follow the discovery that Donna Josephe and Jeronimo—lovers whose relationship had provided insult to the social mores of the old society—are among the party of beautiful souls. Only Don Fernando, the leader of this party, and the lover's child (but not Don Fernando's own child), survive the violent fury meted out to them. Kleist's question to Schiller appears to be this: the beautiful soul may "naturally" express the true interests of the social and moral collective, but what if its moral presentiments are ruinous to the interests of life? Can we, under these circumstances, trust them?

In *Die Verlobung in St. Domingo* (The Betrothal in St Domingo), a story that was among the last Kleist wrote before his early death in 1811, criticism of the thesis of the beautiful soul is taken even further. In this story Kleist finds no capacity of beautiful souls to, in Schiller's words, "triumph over the fragility of nature" (SW 5: 469). Rather, they—along with those they seek to protect—succumb to circumstances whose enmity has cast whites against blacks and coloureds. Before, as Kleist puts it, the mestiza Toni breathes out the last of "her beautiful soul" to her white lover Gustav, who in a confused rage had turned his pistol against her shortly before, she utters the words "you should not have mistrusted me" (KSW 2: 193). Kleist's point appears to be that the beautiful soul has no capacity to establish a level of intersubjective understanding strong enough to overcome the fragility of mortal life. In Kleist's view—but not in Schiller's!—language and concepts, the order of nature and the order of society do not fall together, and no "guidance" for the will issuing from the province of sensuality appears possible.

Kleist convenes a final tribunal on these matters in his famous essay *On the Puppet Theatre*. The subject of this essay is the proposition about grace in Schiller's essay *On Grace and Dignity*, specifically the claim that "where grace occurs, the soul is the principle of movement, and in that soul is found the basis [*Grund*] of the beauty of movement" (SW 5: 437). Kleist's ironic treatment of this claim consists in attributing the graceful movement in Schiller's account to a lifeless puppet—or a puppet whose movement originates with the hidden agency of a "Maschinist" (i.e. a person who works a machine). The true author of the puppet's movements, by these means, remains unclear. Deepening this lack of clarity, Kleist further embeds his treatment of Schiller's claim in a dialogic setting in which the first-person narrator is engaged in conversation with a certain "Mr C", a noted dancer who enthusiastically promotes the untestable claim that the puppet, by virtue of an inner "centre of gravity", moves with a grace that a human dancer "may learn a good deal from" (KSW 2: 339). Mr C, indeed, effectively holds a post-humanist foil to Schiller's humanist claim that mechanical principles and mathematical calculations are enough to steer the puppet towards the execution of perfect movement. In this proposition, *Geist* (mind or spirit), otherwise notoriously subject to error in view of the biblical fall, are no longer called on to offer service. False emotion, in the form of affected movement can similarly be eliminated, so long as strict alignment with the centre of gravity of the puppet is purportedly maintained. Kleist's irony—an unmistakeable sideways dig at Schiller—attaches to the view that the original fall from grace in the biblical account could be annulled by the vacant consciousness of a puppet or, in another example, a trained exhibit from the realm of nature in the form of a fencing bear. Neither the basic proposition about the puppet nor any of the minor examples adduced by Mr C, however, are unambiguously ratified in Kleist's essay. Kleist leaves us, instead, with a reference to the fictional structure of storytelling and speculation about the need "to eat again from the tree of knowledge in order to fall back into the state of innocence" (345).

GOETHE

Johann Wolfgang Goethe (1949–1832) was the dominant literary figure in Europe in the last decades of the eighteenth and the early decades of the nineteenth century. In the question of literary guidance and impact, it is usually Goethe who is taken to have provided influence rather than received it. This was certainly the case over much of his literary career—with two notable exceptions. The first concerns the early inspiration Goethe took from Herder—inspiration that in Goethe's "storm and stress" period led to his unrivalled early love poetry and his first novel *Die Leiden des jungen Werthers* (The Sorrows of Young Werther) (1774). The second exception pertains to the decade after 1794 when Goethe and Schiller established a literary-philosophical alliance that lasted until Schiller's death in 1805. This friendship was of such cordiality and value for both writers that it has been looked upon as expressing a special undertaking—a literary collaboration now known as "Weimar Classicism". The reference to "Weimar", however, is somewhat misleading. In truth, this friendship began in Jena when Goethe and Schiller overcame their earlier guardedness with each other and made common cause around Schiller's *Horen* project—the project that was to witness the publication of Schiller's *Letters on the Education of Man* (1795) and Goethe's *Unterhaltungen deutscher Ausgewanderten* (Conversations of German Emigrés) (1795).

As Goethe's many letters to Schiller from September 1794 to late 1795 reveal, Goethe derived great profit from Schiller's capacity as a thinker. The feedback Goethe liberally solicited and generously obtained from Schiller during this period helped put his *Wilhelm Meister* project on a sound intellectual footing. In Schiller Goethe found an interlocutor of equal sophistication and a philosophic critic of even greater acuity than himself. Goethe's prominent discussion of *Bildung* ("[self-]formation") as a literary-philosophical concept in that project and in its progenitor novel *Wilhelm Meisters theatralische Sendung* (Wilhelm Meister's Theatrical Mission) (1785) had been paralleled by Schiller's deployment of the same concept both in the "Augustenburg Letters" (1793) and, less directly, the *Aesthetic Letters* (1795). Goethe's novel *Wilhelm Meister's Apprenticeship* and Schiller's *Aesthetic Letters* thus have their seed in intellectual ground long tilled by both writers. A degree of reciprocal influence may confidentially be ascribed to both—Schiller's embrace of the term deriving from Kant's principle of moral autonomy, Goethe's betraying an affiliation with morphological principles of natural growth and flourishing reminiscent of Rousseau's concept of nature (cf. Rousseau 1992).

It was this common intellectual ground that proved decisive in establishing a friendship between the two after a long period of reticence and distance. The circumstances leading to the forging of friendship between the two are instructive. Both attended the same natural scientific talk in Jena on the 20th of July 1794 (Schiller held a teaching post at the University of Jena; Goethe lived in nearby Weimar and regularly visited the university town). Reconstructing events from a study of Goethe's diaries, Ziolkowski (1998) relates how the two chanced to encounter each other upon leaving the venue. In conversation after the talk Goethe referred to his morphological study of plants as arising from concrete "experience" (*Erfahrung*). With Kantian precepts in mind and critical philosophy at his fingertips after an already protracted study of Kant, Schiller contradicted Goethe, finding the principle to which Goethe appealed better described as an "idea" (*Idee*)—a speculation, a transcendental idea from Kant's perspective, which in the absence of sufficient empirical testimony about its operation could not hope to be more than a conjecture about how the natural order is composed. It is likely that Goethe did not appreciate the full significance of Schiller's objection. It is not unreasonable to assume that Goethe understood Schiller's reference to an "idea" in a Platonic sense—a lesser charge, from Goethe's vantage-point, in view of his reverence for antiquity, his own metaphysical leanings and his relative ignorance of Kant's transcendental method. At any rate, as Ziolkowski reports, Goethe accepted Schiller's rebuttal and the friendship was sealed on a point of intellectual rapprochement. Goethe later noted in his diary that he and Schiller had come together in the context of the never-ending "competition" between subject (Goethe) and object (Schiller) (quoted in Ziolkowski 1998: 99).

From Schiller's perspective, the nature of the difference elaborated in this comment was not straightforward and indeed merited a longer treatment. This was supplied in the essay *On Naive and Sentimental Poetry* (1795–1796), where Schiller characterized the general difficulty in approaching reality in terms of two contrasting input factors, one, grounded in sensation, taking reality as its point of reference and its "limit", the other, based in ideas (*Vorstellungen*), taking its cue from the idea of limitlessness and "the eternal" (SW 5: 720–1). This was a characterization that recurred to the dualism of "form" and "sense" already expounded by Schiller in the *Aesthetic Letters*. While this dualism of "mixed feeling" (721) held for all human beings, it shook out into two quite different stances when applied to poetry. Schiller called these two stances "naive" and the "sentimental" and thought of his own approach to poetry in terms of the latter and Goethe's in terms of the former (for an extended discussion of this essay, see 2.12 in this volume).

As Schiller discusses in the essay, the first type of poet—the "naive"—gains access to their material in a direct, even guileless, way. The poetry of the naive poet is governed by the task of imitating what appears before their mind's eye. These poets have "no choice" but to take the objects around him as they find them (720). Differences between the two types of poets and the two "orders" of poetry become obvious when the standard of nature is applied. With the naive poet, nature is directly intimated; the poet is directly "nature" itself. With the "sentimental" poet, by contrast, nature is not given immediately to the self, but must be made evident by way of a patient and disciplined search or inquiry (716). Given, as Schiller then notes, that human beings no longer live in thrall to nature, since, in the continuing development of culture over time, art has "laid its hand" (716–7) on human beings, the naive poet in Schiller's imagining must be reckoned among those few souls still capable of being governed directly by the living power of nature. That Goethe himself was to be reckoned among such rare souls—souls tutored by nature in unimpeachable ways—underscores the supreme regard Schiller felt for his friend and collaborator in the final decade of his life.

References

Beiser, Frederick C. 1998. "A Romantic Education. The Concept of *Bildung* in Early German Romanticism." In: *Philosophers on Education. New Historical Perspectives*. Ed. Amélie Oksenberg Rorty. London and New York: Routledge: 284–299.

Benjamin, Walter. 2008. *Der Begriff der Kunstkritik in der deutschen Romantik*. Frankfurt am Main: Suhrkamp.

Eichendorff, Joseph. 2012 (1826). *Aus dem Leben eines Taugenichts*. Stuttgart: Reclam.

Ensberg, Peter. 1999. "'Das Gefäß des Inhalts: Zum Verhältnis von Philosophie und Literatur am Beispiel der 'Kantkrise' Heinrich von Kleists." In: *Beiträge zur Kleist-Forschung*. Ed. Wolfgang Barthel and Hans-Jochen Marquardt. Frankfurt an der Oder: Kleist-Gedenk-und Forschungsstätte: 61–123.

Fouque, Friedrich de la Motte. 1977 (1811). *Undine. Ein romantisches Märchen*. Munich: Winkler.

Frank, Manfred. 1997. *"Unendliche Annäherung." Die Anfänge der philosophischen Frühromantik*. Frankfurt am Main: Suhrkamp.

Gadamer, Hans-Georg. 2004 (1960). *Truth and Method*. London/New York: Continuum.

Goethe, Johann Wolfgang. 1774. *Die Leiden des jungen Werthers*. Leipzig: Weygand'sche Buchhandlung.

———. 1991 (1795). *Unterhaltungen deutscher Ausgewanderten*. Stuttgart: Reclam.

———. 1986 (1795–1796). *Wilhelm Meisters Lehrjahre*. Stuttgart: Reclam.

———. 1986 (1785). *Wilhelm Meisters theatralische Sendung*. Stuttgart: Reclam.

Heine, Heinrich. 1997 (1833–1834). *Zur Geschichte der Religion und Philosophie in Deutschland*. Stuttgart: Reclam.

Hölderlin, Friedrich. 1977. *Werke, Briefe, Dokumente*. Munich: Winkler. (cited above as HW with volume number and page reference).

Hölscher, Stefanie. 2006. "Schiller and Hölderlin: From Beauty to Religion." *Publications of the English Goethe Society* 75/2: 83–94.

Hoffmann, E.T.A. 2021 (1814). *Der goldne Topf. Textausgabe mit Kommentar und Materialien*. Stuttgart: Reclam.

von Kleist, Heinrich. 1983. *Sämtliche Werke und Briefe*. 2 vols. Darmstadt: Wissenschaftliche Buchgesellschaft (cited above as KSW with volume number and page reference).

Mehigan, Tim. 2011. *Heinrich von Kleist: Writing after Kant*. Rochester: Camden House.

———. 2020. "The 'Unexpected Science' of the *Briefe über die Ästhetische Erziehung des Menschen*." *Kant-Studien* 111/2: 285–302.

Lacoue-Labarthe, Philippe and Jean-Luc Nancy. 1998. *The Literary Absolute: The Theory of Literature in German Romanticism*. Stony Brook: SUNY Press.

Reinhold, K.L. 1789. *Versuch einer neuen Theorie des menschlichen Vorstellungsvermögens*. Prague and Jena: C. Widtmann and I.M. Mauke.

Riedel, Wolfgang, 2017. "Philosophie des Schönen als politische Anthropologie. Schillers Augustenburger Briefe und die Briefe über die ästhetische Erziehung." In: W.R.: *Um Schiller. Studien zur Literatur und Ideengeschichte der Sattelzeit*. Eds Markus Hien, Michael Storch and Franziska Stürmer. Würzburg: Königshausen & Neumann: 225–277.

Rousseau, Jean Jacques. 1992 (1750). *Discourse on the Sciences and Arts and Polemics*. Dartmouth: Dartmouth College Press.

Tieck, Ludwig. 2018. *Der blonde Eckbert. Der Runenberg. Textausgabe mit Kommentar und Materialien*. Stuttgart: Reclam.

Winckelmann, Johann Joachim. 1756. *Gedanken über die Nachahmung der griechischen Werke in der Malerei und der Bildhauerkunst*. Dresden and Leipzig. Im Verlag der Walterischen Handlung.

Ziolkowski, Theodore. 1998. *Das Wunderjahr in Jena*. Stuttgart: Klett-Cotta.

CHAPTER 32

The Neo-Kantians and Schiller's Transcendental Idealism

Frederick C. Beiser

THE OTHER SIDE OF THE TRACKS

It is a tale often told, and one that has never lost much in the retelling. Scholars never cease to ponder the Schiller-Kant relationship, which continues to be controversial. It is not hard to see why. Schiller once said that he only wanted to follow the spirit of Kant's philosophy, even if, on a few minor points, he would depart from its letter.[1] But he also did not hesitate to contradict Kant explicitly on major points, attempting, for example, to build an objective aesthetics in direct conflict with Kant's teaching about the subjectivity of aesthetic judgment. How can we bring both these points together to form an intelligible account of the Kant-Schiller relationship? Scholars have been working on this for generations. There is no simple solution.

Amid all this confusion and uncertainty at least one thing is clear and certain: that almost all the controversy about Schiller's relation to Kant revolves around one part of Kant's philosophy, namely, his ethics and aesthetics, or what

---

[1] See the *Ästhetische Briefe,* NA XX, 309; and Schiller's December 3, 1793, letter to Prince von Augustenberg, NA XXVI, 322. NA designates the *Nationalausgabe* of Schiller's *Werke,* eds. Lieselotte Blumenthal and Benno von Wiese (Weimar: Hermann Böhlaus Nachfolger, 1943ff). Roman numerals refer to volumes, Arabic numerals to pages. All references to Schiller will be to this edition.

F. C. Beiser (✉)
Syracuse University, Syracuse, NY, USA
e-mail: fbeiser@syr.edu

© The Author(s), under exclusive license to Springer Nature Switzerland AG 2023
A. Falduto, T. Mehigan (eds.), *The Palgrave Handbook on the Philosophy of Friedrich Schiller,* https://doi.org/10.1007/978-3-031-16798-0_32

Kant would call his "practical philosophy". But what about his "theoretical philosophy", his work in epistemology and metaphysics? What, indeed, about his signature doctrine, "transcendental idealism"? Kant's doctrines in theoretical philosophy are the foundation of his philosophy, and his aesthetics and ethics presuppose them. So this naturally raises the question about Schiller's relationship to Kant's *theoretical* philosophy. This should be just as important as his relationship to Kant's practical philosophy. But the relationship on the theoretical side has been as underinvestigated as that on the practical side has been overinvestigated. To what extent did Schiller follow Kant's theoretical philosophy? Did he accept his transcendental idealism? Seldom have these questions been properly investigated. If there is little controversy about them that is because so few have tried to answer them.

Whence this negligence? The obvious explanation is that Schiller simply did not write about Kant's theoretical philosophy. Scholars have not investigated this topic, it seems, just because his texts say so little about it. And for Schiller's silence there is also an obvious explanation: Schiller's lack of interest and competence in the field of epistemology. Scholars have taken note of Schiller's admission that he had little appetite for the intricacies and subtleties of epistemological issues.[2] For this lack of interest in epistemology they have developed different explanations. Some explain that Schiller was not a philosopher at all but an expositor or popularizer of Kant;[3] others contend that he was really more a secret metaphysician than an epistemologist.[4] Whatever the reason, Schiller's relationship to Kant's theoretical philosophy is a non-subject simply because Schiller himself never wrote about or developed that relationship; we are absolved, therefore, from not writing about it.

But these are poor excuses. The problem with them is that, even though Schiller wrote little about Kant's theoretical philosophy, and even if he had little love for epistemology, his ethics and aesthetics still *presuppose* the principles of Kant's epistemology. The basis for Schiller's philosophy was Kant's critical philosophy, whose results and implications were woven into the fabric of his ethics and aesthetics. There is still a *logical* connection between Schiller's ethics and aesthetics and Kant's theoretical philosophy, even if it is never made explicit. It is the task of the Schiller scholar to make this connection clear.

That Schiller's relationship to Kant extends even to his theoretical philosophy is no new discovery. It was recognized long ago, beginning in the late nineteenth century, by several neo-Kantian philosophers: Friedrich Lange (1828–1875), Wilhelm Windelband (1848–1915), and Ernst Cassirer

---

[2] See Schiller to Goethe, January 7, 1795, NA XXVII, 116; and December 17, 1795, NA XXVIII, 132.

[3] See Paul de Mann, 'Schiller and Kant', *Aesthetic Ideology* (Minneapolis: University of Minnesota Press, 1996), pp. 146–7, 154–5.

[4] David Pugh, *Dialectic of Love: Platonism in Schiller's Aesthetics* (Montreal: McGill-Queen's University Press, 1996), pp. 107, 113, 245, 323–4. This approach is also taken by Lesley Sharpe, *Schiller's Aesthetic Essays: Two Centuries of Criticism* (Columbus, S.C.: Camden House, 1995), p. 27.

(1874–1945).[5] With great care and finesse, they investigated Schiller's relationship with Kant's transcendental idealism. They saw this relationship as especially important because they believed, perfectly correctly, that transcendental idealism is the *foundation* for Schiller's ethics and aesthetics. Without transcendental idealism, they argued, Schiller's aesthetics and ethics would lose its guiding inspiration and would lapse into either dogmatism or skepticism, the two great enemies of criticism.

The aim of this article is to examine and appraise Cassirer's, Lange's and Windelband's accounts of Schiller's relationship to Kant's theoretical philosophy. This should help to shed some light on the underinvestigated half of Schiller's relationship to Kant.

Cassirer on Schiller's Adoption of Transcendental Idealism

One of the most interesting accounts of Schiller's relationship to Kant's theoretical philosophy is that of Ernst Cassirer.[6] To explain why Schiller was attracted to Kant's philosophy, Cassirer takes us back to the philosophy of the young Schiller, and specifically to the philosophy he sketched in his *Philosophische Briefe*. Schiller published this philosophy in 1786, several years before his first encounter with Kant in 1790.[7]

The *Philosophische Briefe* is a fictional correspondence between a young philosopher, Julius, and his older teacher, Raphael. Julius has learned from Raphael that he must first of all trust his reason, and that before he believes anything he must first weigh it before reason's tribunal. "All things in heaven and on earth have no worth, no validity, except insofar as my reason acknowledges it", Julius writes (112). But this rigorous and uncompromising use of his reason has left Julius disconsolate. All his former beliefs, which gave him security and a sense of place in the world, have lost their rationale. "Our philosophy is the unhappy curiosity of Oedipus, who did not cease to investigate until the terrible oracle resolved itself" (112). To advise his unhappy student, Raphael asks Julius to send him his papers; only then will he know how much his early philosophy passes the test of reason. Obeying his teacher's wishes, Julius rummages through his old papers and eventually finds a text that contains a convenient summary of his early beliefs. This remarkable text, which is entitled "Theosophie des Julius", is the centerpiece of the conversation.

---

[5] On the neo-Kantian interpretation of Schiller, see my *Schiller as Philosopher: A Re-Examination* (Oxford: Oxford University Press, 2005), pp. 4, 268–70.

[6] See Ernst Cassirer, 'Die Methodik des Idealismus in Schillers philosophischen Schriften', *Idee und Gestalt*, Zweite Ausgabe (Berlin: Cassirer Verlag, 1924), pp. 81–113. See also his chapter 'Schiller' in *Freiheit und Form: Studien zur deutschen Geistesgeschichte* (Berlin: Cassirer Verlag, 1916), pp. 269–303. The first essay is reprinted in Ernst Cassirer, *Gesammelte Werke, Hamburger Ausgabe*, ed. Marcel Simon (Hamburg: Felix Meiner Verlag, 2001) IX, 316–345.

[7] Schiller published it in the *Thalia*, Band I (1786), 100–139. Reprinted in *Nationalausgabe* XX, 107–129, which is the edition cited in parentheses here.

Young Julius's theosophy is an eclectic *mélange* of ideas from neo-Platonism, Shaftesbury and Leibniz. "The universe", we are told in the first sentence, "is a thought of God" (115). After this thought was realized in the creation, it has been the task of all thinking beings to recover and understand it. They must explain "the rule in the machine, the unity in the composition, the law in the phenomena". Julius then introduces the ancient idea of the *liber naturae*, the idea that nature is the secret language of God. According to this idea, "everything inside and outside of me is a hieroglyph ... the laws of nature are ciphers, which the thinking being [i.e. God] has joined together to make them comprehensible to the thinking being" (116). This language is "the alphabet by means of which all spirits, and the most perfect spirit, communicate with one another" (116). The task of the individual is to interpret this secret language, so that he knows what God is communicating to him and others. To explain how we understand this language, Julius appeals to some ideas from the neo-Platonic tradition. To comprehend anything, Julius explains, we must internalize it and make it part of ourselves. This internalization does not mean that we make the thing like us but that we make ourselves like the thing. "Intuition of the beautiful, the true and excellent is a momentary taking possession of these qualities. ... We become the felt object" (117). We know what a thing means for us when we become part of it and change ourselves accordingly. Behind this process of understanding is the moving power of love, which makes us internalize the object, and so understand it from within.

It was a happy philosophy that Julius had outlined in his "Theosophie". He could feel comforted in its anthropocentric view of the universe, according to which God loved him and spoke to him through his creation. Pleasure came from the perception of perfection, as Leibniz had taught, and since the universe was filled with perfection, the mere contemplation of it gave great happiness. "This philosophy has ennobled my heart, and beautified the perspective of my life", Julius wrote (126). But there still remained a troubling question: even though this philosophy makes one happy, is it true? Raphael had already planted this doubt in Julius, who found it impossible to uproot. He confesses to Raphael: "I searched according to the laws of the mind—I elevated myself to the infinite; but I forgot to show that they [these laws] are really true. A bold attack of materialism would destroy my creation" (115). Even the neo-Platonic epistemology Julius had sketched in his "Theosophie" would not help him resolve these doubts. For how did we know that our internalization of the object was anything more than a projection of our imagination, a creation of our fantasy? Julius had constructed his theosophy on the assumption that there is an affinity between his imagination and the universe itself; but he had offered nothing to justify that assumption. No wonder that he now was in a crisis.

It was in this context, a few years later, that Schiller studied Kant.[8] He had already read Kant in the late 1780s when he read his essays on history; but, because of its notorious difficulty, he had put off reading the first *Kritik*, the

---

[8] On Schiller's encounter with Kant, see *Schiller as Philosopher*, pp. 37–46.

Kritik der reinen Vernunft. It was not until the Spring of 1791 that he began to study Kant properly. He first read the *Kritik der Urteilskraft*; and it was only in early 1792 that he studied the *Kritik der reinen Vernunft* itself. What he discovered there he later revealed to Körner in his famous letter of February 18, 1793: "Certainly, no greater words have ever been spoken of a mortal human being than these Kantian ones, which are at the same time the content of his whole philosophy: determine yourself!"[9]

This idea of self-determination was central to not only Kantian ethics but also its epistemology. In fact, Kant first developed this idea not by thinking about ethics but by pondering the problem of knowledge. The problem of how a representation conforms to an object to provide knowledge only made sense to Kant by emphasizing the creative activity of the subject in making the standards of objectivity. If, *per contra*, the standard of objectivity was an object existing completely independent of the subject, then knowledge would be impossible; that is because the subject cannot jump outside its consciousness to see if it conforms to something completely independent of it. Such reflections were the basis of some of Kant's most fundamental epistemological principles: the idea that the understanding is the lawgiver of nature; and his paradigm of knowledge, according to which the self knows a priori only what it creates. Indeed, the whole Copernican Revolution came from these reflections; for the leading idea of that Revolution, as Kant crudely explains it,[10] is that truth consists in not the conformity of a representation with an object but in the conformity of an object with a representation.

It was in virtue of these principles, Cassirer argues, that Schiller was now in a position finally to resolve Julius's early crisis.[11] The skeptics and materialists could no longer destroy Julius's philosophy, for they had shown themselves to be hidden dogmatists who had questionable presuppositions of their own. They had assumed that truth consists in the conformity of a representation with its object; and when they found they could never confirm that a representation conforms to an object existing independently of it—where this object is a thing-in-itself—they concluded that there could be no knowledge at all. Kant's Copernican revolution obviated this problem by proposing a very different paradigm of knowledge: not the correspondence of a representation with a thing-in-itself but the conformity of a representation with the universal and necessary laws of the understanding. Since these laws are universal and necessary, they serve as an objective standard of knowledge; they alone ensure the knower against all arbitrariness and idiosyncrasy; hence there is no need to get *per impossible* beyond the circle of our representations.

Cassirer writes as if the Kantian paradigm of knowledge saved Julius from his intellectual crisis because it showed him that there is no need to fear skepticism

---

[9] NA XXVI, 191.
[10] Kant, KrV, B xvi–xvii.
[11] Cassirer, 'Methodik des Idealismus', pp. 95–6.

or materialism.[12] The objections against his early philosophy were hollow, he argues, because they were based upon a misconceived paradigm of knowledge, which requires that representations somehow correspond with their objects, which are things-in-themselves. All this is well and good. Cassirer is correct that the Kantian paradigm dispelled these dogmatic objections. But there is still a problem lingering with Julius's theosophy. The crisis was not over. For many of the ideas of his early metaphysics—the idea of God, the *liber naturae*, the concept of perfection—still required justification from other sources. Even worse, these ideas are metaphysical, going beyond the boundaries of possible experience; they therefore fell foul of the Kantian standards of knowledge: possible experience. Once Schiller accepted the Kantian principles, he also had to endorse the Kantian limits on knowledge. For these principles make it necessary to accept that we know only objects in possible experience. If we know only what we create, and if what we create are only appearances, then knowledge is indeed limited to appearances, the realm of experience. So, Julius's metaphysics, measured by Kantian standards, was doomed.

But this was a conclusion Schiller was now ready to accept. For, after his discovery of Kant in the early 1790s, Schiller had essentially abandoned Julius's metaphysics. There were elements of it that he would still try to save—viz., the idea of love—but he would now make them conform to critical guidelines; in other words, they would have to be *regulative* principles, useful guides to enquiry but forfeiting any claims about existence. But if Julius's metaphysics had to go, the Kantian epistemological principles would remain, providing the framework for Schiller's new more Kantian philosophy.

Despite this *non sequitur*, Cassirer's account of Schiller's intellectual development succeeds in showing the central role of Kant's epistemology in moving Schiller away from his early philosophy. The principle of self-determination, which Kant first developed in an epistemological context, would later prove crucial for Schiller's ethics and aesthetics. It should be clear then: the separation of Schiller's ethics and aesthetics from Kant's epistemology is a misleading abstraction, contrary to the facts of Schiller's philosophical development.

LANGE AND THE POETRY OF THE THING-IN-ITSELF

It was not only the principle of self-determination that tied Schiller's ethics and aesthetics with Kant's epistemology. There was another link between these domains: the concept of the thing-in-itself. Shortly after the publication of the *Kritik der reinen Vernunft* in 1781, the thing-in-itself had become the most notorious concept of Kant's epistemology. It was the great stumbling block to its reception. Friedrich Heinrich Jacobi had famously written that without the thing-in-itself, he could not enter the Kantian system; but that with it, he could

---

[12] Cassirer, 'Die Methodik des Idealismus', p. 95.

not remain inside it.¹³ Jacobi's dictum expressed an apparently inescapable dilemma. The thing-in-itself is *necessary*: it alone explains the finitude of human cognition; and it alone explains the cause of all our representations. But the thing-in-itself is also *impossible*: it lies beyond all possible experience, which circumscribes the limits of knowledge.

Nowhere in the corpus of his ethical and aesthetic writings does Schiller have anything to say about the Kantian thing-in-itself. All the paradoxes seemed to have escaped him, or at least not interested him. For some, this has been reason to think that Schiller simply had little interest in epistemology. Better, then, to discuss Schiller's ethics and aesthetics, to leave Kant's theoretical philosophy aside.

However, what if there lay within Schiller's ethics and aesthetics an implicit solution to the problems raised by the thing-in-itself? What if it were only a matter of making this solution explicit? In that case the connection between Schiller's ethics and aesthetics and Kant's epistemology would be restored. It so happens that this connection was made explicit long ago by one of the most fascinating figures of the neo-Kantian movement: Friedrich Lange.¹⁴ If there were any neo-Kantian philosopher who made Schiller the poet of the movement it was Lange. The neo-Kantians, Schiller enthusiasts down to a man, had been citing Schiller for generations before Lange; but it was Lange who elevated Schiller to a pivotal role in Kant' epistemology. Schiller became the pied-piper whose charming flute beguiled and vanquished the monster of the thing-in-itself.

Lange's views on the thing-in-itself appeared in his *Geschichte des Materialismus*.¹⁵ His views on this issue changed considerably between its first (1866) and second editions (1873–1875). In the first edition, Lange attempted to defend the *existence* of the thing-in-itself. The examination of our faculty of knowledge shows us, he argued, that what appears in our experience is relative to our faculties, so that what we know is determined by our specific physiological constitution. Hence the world will appear differently to creatures with different physiologies. What appears so differently to all these different creatures,

---

¹³ Friedrich Heinrich Jacobi, 'Beylage. Ueber den transcendentalen Idealismus', *David Hume über den Glauben, oder Idealismus und Realismus. Ein Gespräch*. See *Werke* (Leipzig: Fleischer, 1815), II, 289–310.

¹⁴ On the role of Lange in the neo-Kantian movement, see my *The Genesis of Neo-Kantianism* (Oxford: Oxford University Press, 2014), pp. 357–421.

¹⁵ Friedrich Albert Lange, *Geschichte des Materialismus und Kritik seiner Bedeutung in der Gegenwart* (Iserlohn: J. Baedeker 1866). The second edition, which was much enlarged, appeared in two volumes, the first in 1873 and the second in 1975. See *Geschichte des Materialismus und Kritik seiner Bedeutung in der Gegenwart, Zweite verbesserte und vermehrte Auflage* (Iserlohn: Baedeker, 1873–75). The two volumes have different titles: Band I: *Erstes Buch, Geschichte des Materialismus bis auf Kant;* Band II: *Geschichte des Materialismus seit Kant*. All references in parentheses above, unless otherwise noted, are to the second edition.

their "common unknown source", is the thing-in-itself.[16] In the second edition, however, Lange argues expressly that the limitations Kant had placed on knowledge did not allow him to postulate the existence of the thing-in-itself. If all knowledge is limited to possible experience, as Kant preached tirelessly in the first *Kritik*, then he cannot claim that the thing-in-itself exists, given that the thing-in-itself transcends all possible experience. And so Lange wrote: "That there are things that have a spaceless and timeless existence Kant could not prove from his own principles, for that would be a transcendent, even if negative, knowledge of the properties of thing-in-themselves, and such knowledge is completely impossible according to his own theory" (36). Why Lange had changed his views is not clear. In a long endnote,[17] he points out the important role of Hermann Cohen in getting him to change his views, though he also said the change in them was "already prepared by his own studies".

Although Lange now saw the difficulty in postulating the existence of the thing-in-itself, he still did not banish the concept entirely. Taking his cue from the "Amphibolien" and "Phaenomena und Noumena" chapters of the *Kritik*,[18] Lange stressed that the thing-in-itself was only "a limiting concept" (*Grenzbegriff*), that it designated "a completely problematic something" (II, 49). A limiting concept is not descriptive, that is, its content does not refer to an entity; rather, it is an imperative, prescribing that a concept be used only within a definite range of things. Such a concept involves no claim to existence at all.

Although much of the inspiration for Lange's idea of a limiting concept came from Kant, Lange gave it a different meaning from his predecessor. Both Lange and Kant would refer to limiting concepts as "ideas" in the Kantian sense. In the Kantian system an idea designates something unconditioned, something that can never be given in experience and that serves as an ideal of excellence or perfection. Among the ideas were God, the soul, or the cosmos as a whole. For Kant, these ideas were objects of belief, though they had a strictly *problematic* status, that is, one could not make dogmatic assertions about their existence. For Lange, however, these ideas were only the antiquated baggage of the metaphysical tradition. Kant included them in his system only as a concession to Christian orthodoxy. That was a concession that Lange himself was not willing to make. The only legitimate ideas, in his view, were those that had a strictly ethical or aesthetic meaning; these ideas did not refer to anything that exists; they were not even true or false; rather, they were strictly normative in their significance. Among Lange's ideas, therefore, were the sublime and the beautiful.

---

[16] *Geschichte des Materialismus* (1866), pp. 267–8. See also Lange's March 14, 1867, letter to Dohrn, in A.O. Ellissen, *Friedrich Albert Lange. Eine Lebensbeschreibung.* (Leipzig: Baedeker, 1894), pp. 258–9.
[17] *Geschichte des Materialismus* (1873), II, 130–1, note 35.
[18] KrV, B, 310-311, B 342–344.

Through his reconception of a limiting concept, Lange could redraw Kant's famous distinction between noumena and phenomena. Kant saw this distinction as one between kinds of entities; even though noumena had a problematic status, they could still exist. Phenomena were objects of the senses; and noumena were objects of the intellect. But Lange saw this distinction between kinds of discourse. Phenomena stood for discourse about experience; noumena were norms and values, ideals that we create through our own activity. Lange sometimes called noumena "fictions", as if they were creatures of imagination alone; but this was misleading because it suggested that they could be arbitrary or fanciful. To correct this impression, Lange insisted that his aesthetic and moral ideas were universal and necessary, that is, they were ideas that no intelligent being would or could disown.

The point of Lange's distinction between noumena and phenomena was to save a place for religion in the modern world. Though Lange had no sympathy for the old theism or even enlightenment deism, he still believed that religion had an important role to perform in keeping alive the feelings for "the realm of the ideal". If religion was eradicated, then the state would have to take over the role of the educator of humanity, which was a recipe for dictatorship. But if we cannot abolish religion, we can still reform and transform it. The agent of that reformation and transformation for Lange should be art. Art is a pleasant form of communication accessible to the public; and it does not involve all the questionable claims to truth of metaphysics. Everything that we feel in religion, Lange is convinced, is ultimately translatable into poetry without loss of meaning, and without involving all the suspicious beliefs of dogma, metaphysics, or myth.

Lange was demanding a lot of poetry in asking it to transform religion. It would have to inspire people through its idealism; yet it would have to avoid all the symbols and clichés of the past. Was any poet capable of doing this? Lange was convinced that there was indeed such a poet. That poet was no less than Schiller. It is in Schiller's philosophical poetry, he claims, that one finds the highest ideals expressed with the greatest feeling and imagination (II, 545). His poetry combines the deepest feeling with the clearest intellectual precision, providing a model for the discourse of a new religion. It was under Schiller's hand that the "dreams and shadows" of religion could be elevated to the ideal (II, 62).

Such was Lange's faith in Schiller that he wrote a book on his philosophical poetry. He had worked on this book for nearly a decade, but he had never published it, though it was in proof stage at his death. The book was eventually published posthumously by his biographer, A.O. Ellissen, as *Einleitung und Kommentar zu Schillers philosophischen Gedichten*.[19] The purpose of the book was to serve as a teacher's guide to help Gymnasium students read Schiller's more difficult philosophical poems. This was Lange's way of realizing Schiller's ideal of an aesthetic education.

---

[19] Friedrich Albert Lange, ed. A.O. Ellissen, *Einleitung und Kommentar zu Schillers philosophischen Gedichten* (Bielefeld: Velhagen & Klasing, 1897).

Remaining True to Kant by Contradicting Him

In 1905, to mark the centenary of the great poet's death, Wilhelm Windelband gave a lecture on Schiller.[20] Windelband was a voice to reckon with, because he was a prominent figure in the neo-Kantian movement.[21] He was the leader of the so-called Southwestern school, which was centered around the universities in Heidelberg, Straßburg, and Baden. The title of Windelband's lecture accurately specifies its content: "Schillers transcendentaler Idealismus". Those who thought of Schiller as a poet, or only as a philosopher of ethics and aesthetics, would have found the title surprising. But that, of course, was precisely Windelband's point: he wanted to show that transcendental idealism played a central role in Schiller's ethics and aesthetics. The foundation of his work in these fields, Windelband insisted, lay in Kant's epistemology.

It was one of Windelband's most famous dicta that "to understand Kant means to go beyond him".[22] It was in that spirit that he wrote of Schiller: "Schiller can be considered a genuine Kantian where he believed to go beyond Kant" (214). Windelband meant that Schiller was only developing Kant's principles even when the consequences appear to violate the letter of Kantian doctrine. We shall soon see that was particularly the case with regard to the principles of transcendental idealism.

Windelband is very plain and quick in stating what he means by Schiller's transcendental idealism. The core of transcendental idealism, he explains, is Schiller's "fundamental conviction" "that there is for consciousness no other reality, no other 'objects', than what it produces from its own rational activity". (216). Windelband was referring, of course, to the principle behind Kant's "new method of thought": "that we know of things a priori only what we ourselves have put into them".[23] Since for Kant a priori knowledge is the basis of all knowledge, and since we know a priori only what we create, it follows that the world we know is the world we create. This doctrine was the very spirit of the critical philosophy for Schiller, who would make it the basis for all his thinking. And so Windelband writes: "The transformation of the world into objects of consciousness is the decisive act of the critical philosophy. And this decisive point Schiller had seen as clearly, and grasped so strongly, as Fichte. It is the basic tone upon which all of Schiller's philosophical accomplishments are tuned" (216).

Windelband suggests that there is another formulation for Schiller's leading principle. "If we call the spontaneity of the mind in producing its objects 'freedom'", he writes, "then it would also be true in this sense—but only in this

---

[20] 'Schillers transzendentaler Idealismus', in 'Präludien. Aufsätze und Reden zur Philosophie und ihrer Geschichte', Neunte Auflage (Tübingen: J.C.B. Mohr, 1924) I, 212–229. All references in parentheses above are to this text.
[21] On Windelband's role in the neo-Kantian movement, see *The Genesis of Neo-Kantianism*, pp. 492–530.
[22] The 'Vorwort' to the 1883 edition of *Präludien*, p. iv.
[23] KrV, B xviii. Cf. B xiii–xiv.

sense!—that freedom is the central concept of Schillerian thinking just as much as Kantian and Fichtean thinking" (216). As the interjection makes clear, Windelband thinks that this is a rather special sense of freedom, having little to do with politics. It is the sense of freedom involved "in the production of the object from the spontaneity of consciousness" (216–17). But what sense of freedom is this?

Windelband's answer to this question is complicated. "The general formula of autonomy, which expresses the essence of transcendental idealism", he writes, "contains a multiplicity of meanings which are intertwined in Kant's doctrine, and according to the emphasis on the one or the other they give a different color to the basic idea of the production of the object through the spontaneity of consciousness" (216–17). There are three chief meanings, Windelband explains, that we can give to the "consciousness" to which we attribute "the autonomous production of the object". This consciousness can be (1) "the individual, (2) humanity, or (3) 'consciousness in general'" (217). What exactly Windelband means by each of these meanings requires some explanation. But he writes that it is only their connection that comprises "the whole of the critical horizon", which appears in a very different light depending on which meaning is emphasized.

If we stress the first meaning, Windelband explains, then "the idea of personality" moves into the forefront of transcendental idealism (217). What does Windelband mean by "personality"? He does not explain its meaning in any detail; but we can give it a definite sense because it was a technical term in Kant's system. "Personality", according to the *Kritik der praktischen Vernunft*, is "the capacity of a being who is subject to the pure practical laws that are characteristic of its reason".[24] These practical laws, Kant goes on to explain, are those that are given by the agent himself as a rational being. This seems to be what Windelband has in mind when he paraphrases "the idea of personality" as "the self-legislation of the will, the self-determination of action, the self-formation of life" (217). It is "the ideal of a disposition which recognizes no other values in the world other than those posited by itself".

Schiller first gave the idea of personality more an aesthetic than an ethical meaning, Windelband reminds us (218). Hence in the *Kallias Briefe* he defines beauty as "freedom in appearance" or "autonomy in appearance". The object that appears to our senses appears beautiful to us if we think that it follows the laws of its own nature, or if it appears to move according to its own efforts alone, such that it is not subject to any constraint by something outside itself. As a principle of transcendental idealism, autonomy in appearance did not apply simply to particular objects, viz., painting, sculptures, but to experience as a whole. The whole world of nature then became beautiful, a work of art. Hence Windelband wrote about Schiller's "aestheticization of the transcendental idealism" (219).

[24] KpV, V, 87.

Windelband detected a problem, however, in Schiller's equation of autonomy with individuality. If autonomy is only "the prerogative of the individual aesthetic personality", then one loses "the feeling for universal lawfulness" (220). Autonomy is then in danger of becoming complete subjectivity. It was a failing of Schiller, Windelband writes, that he had no feeling for "the supersensible substrate of humanity", which accounted for "the universal communicability" of aesthetic experience (220).

Nevertheless, Windelband still thinks that Schiller avoided the danger of subjectivism (220–1). This is because his attempt to develop an aesthetics went in the opposite direction of subjectivism. In his *Kallias Briefe* he attempted to develop an "objective" aesthetics, according to which beauty signifies properties in the object itself. There had to be some difference in objects themselves to account for the difference in their "aesthetic utility" (*Verwertbarkeit*), Schiller argues. The justification for a judgment that an object is beautiful had to involve some account of the qualities of the object.

Schiller thought his objective aesthetic to be in contradiction with Kant, who had stressed the complete subjectivity of aesthetic judgment, that is, that the feeling of pleasure aroused by beauty designated no feature of the object.[25] Windelband, however, maintains that Schiller's objective aesthetics is still in keeping with the Kantian spirit. This is because the objective aesthetic did not invalidate transcendental idealism; the differences in objects themselves were still only differences in their *perceivable* qualities, that is, in their qualities as *appearances*. Schiller was giving the objective qualities no status as properties of things-in-themselves. So now we can see the point of Windelband's dictum: it is precisely when Schiller seems to deviate from Kant that we can see how much he affirmed him; if he went beyond Kant in developing an objective aesthetic, the terms in which he understood its objectivity were still transcendental (222).

The second meaning Schiller gave to consciousness in Kant's transcendental idealism, Windelband maintains, is "humanity", or what he also calls "the anthropological". Kant regarded it as the distinctive characteristic of a human being that it is both rational and sensible; it stood between two worlds: the purely intellectual or rational, which determines the principles of morality; and the sensible or phenomenal, which is governed by the laws of nature. These domains could often be in conflict: the commands of reason demanded obedience even if it were contrary to the desires and emotions of sensibility; and the desires and emotions of sensibility could arouse temptation and so undermine the commands of reason. Schiller called for harmony between these domains, so that our sensible nature does not resist our rational but fulfills its commands effortlessly and with pleasure. The ideal was "*Pflicht aus Freude*", as Schiller once put it. This standpoint where reason and sensibility harmonize, where duty and inclination work together as one, Schiller called "the complete anthropological perspective".[26] Although Windelband is not so explicit, this is where he derives his term "anthropological" to refer to the second meaning.

---

[25] *Kritik der Urteilskraft* §1, V, 203–4.
[26] *Ästhetische Briefe*, NA XX, 316. Schiller's exact phrase is "*die vollständigen anthropologischen Schätzung*".

What this second meaning of "consciousness" has to do with Kant's transcendental idealism is not too difficult to determine. As much as Kant insisted upon a sharp distinction between reason and sensibility in his ethics, he stressed their interplay in his epistemology. It was one of the famous dicta of the *Kritik der reinen Vernunft* that the concepts of the intellect are empty without the intuitions of sensibility, and that the intuitions of sensibility are blind without the guidance of the intellect.[27] The interplay between these faculties is an ideal of theoretical reason as much as practical reason. The complete anthropological perspective is already implicit in the first *Kritik*; in referring to an anthropological perspective, Schiller was only making this explicit.

The third and final meaning Schiller gave to consciousness, Windelband says, is "consciousness in general" (*Bewusstsein überhaupt*). This is another Kantian codeword, one which refers to consciousness as it is governed by the universal and necessary laws of understanding and sensibility.[28] It designates not any particular person who is conscious but to the product of consciousness as such, to intelligibility and meaning. As such it is not the subjective but the intersubjective. To use a word to which Windelband would later give much currency, consciousness in general is "the normative". To refer to it as "consciousness in general" is somewhat misleading because a norm has validity whether or not someone is conscious of it. But Windelband wanted to give a place to normativity in the structure of the psychological language of the first *Kritik*, and "consciousness in general" seemed to come close to that.

Windelband admits that Schiller had only a vague understanding of the normative. He glimpsed it, but only through a glass darkly. Of course, he would talk about the ideal realm all the time, which he would refer to quasi-Platonically. This realm had "truth", a "logical value", even if it did not exist in any prosaic sense (226).

The world according to transcendental idealism, Windelband was ultimately saying, is the world of intersubjective norms. These norms have validity even if they do not necessarily exist. Since it is also not necessary that someone be conscious of a norm, there is also no necessary reference to something subjective in the world of norms. The norms can be valid even if they are not attached to any subject, be it individual or universal. But if that is the case, one might well ask, how transcendental idealism is idealism at all? We are on the very cusp of an "objective idealism" here, where the ideal does not mean subjectivity in contrast to objectivity but the archetypical in contrast to the ectypical. This was just another way in which Schiller's transcendental idealism leads to the later idealism of Schelling and Hegel. All this seems very far from Kant; but Windelband would just say: "To understand Kant is to go beyond him".

---

[27] KrV, B 75.
[28] See *Prolegomena zu einer jeden zukünftigen Metaphysik*, §20, IV, 300.

CHAPTER 33

Schiller's Horen, Humboldt's Rhodian Genius, and the Development of Physiological Ideas in Mythical Form

Elizabeth Millán Brusslan

Schiller, as this volume amply demonstrates, made important contributions to the field of philosophy. I will focus upon a small area of his legacy, located in an unexpected area, namely in his relation with Alexander von Humboldt (1769–1859), a natural scientist, explorer, and Renaissance thinker of the period. Humboldt was not a philosopher, and as Beiser's seminal study of Schiller illustrates, it has taken us (especially in the Anglophone world) a long while to appreciate Schiller *as* a philosopher (see Beiser 2005). What can I illuminate about the field of philosophy with a focus on the relation between Humboldt, who is not a philosopher, and Schiller, whose philosophical contributions have long been neglected? What I hope will emerge from my examination are: (1) evidence of the central role Schiller played, both as editor and thinker, on intellectual developments of the period; (2) insights about the status of nature in the work of both Schiller and Humboldt; and (3) the central role that life force (*Lebenskraft*) played in their views of nature.

To present the role that Schiller played in Humboldt's work, I shall focus on a particularly puzzling chapter of *Views of Nature/Ansichten der Natur*, "Life Force or the Rhodian Genius: A Tale"/*Die Lebenskraft oder der rhodische*

E. Millán Brusslan (✉)
DePaul University Chicago, Chicago, IL, USA
e-mail: emillanb@depaul.edu

Genius: Eine Erzählung (hereafter *Rhodian Genius/Life Force* essay). This chapter of *Ansichten* was the only chapter that had been previously published. Humboldt had been invited by Schiller to write this piece for his journal, *Die Horen*. The letter of invitation came on June 13, 1794. Humboldt replied affirmatively to the invitation on August 6, 1794, apologizing for his delayed reply (Jahn and Lange 1973, 346–347). In order to appreciate this curious allegory and the light it sheds on the relation between Schiller and Humboldt, we must consider the intellectual interactions taking place not only between Humboldt and Schiller but also their connections to Goethe and the early German Romantics. These interactions will lead us to the historical context necessary to understand not only the text but also Schiller's wide-ranging intellectual role in the period. An account of the genesis and publication of Humboldt's *Rhodian Genius/Life Force* essay will take us to a closer examination of the role that mythology, physiology, and the blending of the borders between art and the natural sciences played during the late 1800s.

JOURNALS AND THE TASK OF THE EDITOR IN THE AGE OF GOETHE AND SCHILLER

Goethe and Schiller stand together immortalized in Ernst Rietschel's (1804–1862) statue at the center of Weimar. In their lifetimes, Goethe and Schiller shaped the culture of German-speaking lands, not only through their writings on nature and art and their prolific literary work, but also in their role as editors of journals that helped to set the intellectual tone of the period. Schiller's journal, *Die Horen* (1795–1797), and Goethe's *Propyläen* (1798–1800), though short-lived, were important literary vehicles of the period and provided a forum that brought scientists, historians, philosophers, and poets into conversation with one another. According to Ilse Jahn and Fritz Lange, editors of the *Jugendbriefe Alexander von Humboldt* 1787–1795, in the letter that Schiller sent to Humboldt inviting him to contribute to *Die Horen*, Humboldt was told that the journal would deal with everything that can be treated "with taste and philosophical spirit." Schiller mentions philosophical investigations and historical and poetic presentations of topics for the journal: natural scientific investigations were not explicitly mentioned. Yet, in his lone contribution to *Die Horen*, Humboldt certainly pushed the boundaries of art and natural investigation of a scientific bent (Jahn and Lange 1973, p. 347). Such a collaboration between an empirically minded thinker such as Humboldt, one dedicated to the methods of the natural sciences, and a figure like Schiller, rooted in the humanities, with training in medicine, should not come as a surprise. The late 1700s and early 1800s were years of intense and innovative intellectual development in German-speaking lands; the arts flourished and aesthetics developed as a serious branch of philosophy. Philosophers, scientists, and artists collaborated without the borders to which we have become all too accustomed. Part of this collaborative spirit arose out of necessity, as certain fields had not yet defined their borders. As John Reddick points out, "[w]e need to appreciate the real enormity of the problems faced by life-scientists in the half-century or so before Darwin did for biology what Newton had done for physics almost two centuries earlier; even the very word 'scientist'—not coined until 1834 (by William Whewell)—is an anachronism that tends to beg essential questions" (Reddick 1990, p. 330). Humboldt dealt with the problem of science's disarray by carving out new spaces for his areas of inquiry. Even if, during the time of Humboldt's writing, the term 'scientist' had not come into its present-day use, and even if the fields in which he was working had not yet been sharply defined, he was seen as a "scientist" by figures such as Goethe, Schiller, and Schlegel. In part, something as simple as his use of instruments and data collection sealed his identity as a scientist. Yet, as Humboldt himself was aware, the data collected by means of those instruments could not tell us the full story of nature's meaning. If we were to come to a full understanding of natural phenomena, we needed not only to measure the phenomena of nature, but also to approximate them aesthetically.[1]

In the company of the "twin giants of Weimar Classicism," the Schlegel brothers shaped culture in a decidedly romantic way in Jena. Much in the style of Schiller and Goethe, the Schlegel brothers also founded a journal, *Das Athenäum* (1798–1800), the central literary vehicle of the early German Romantic Movement. Both Schiller and Goethe, while openly critical of certain aspects of Romanticism, shaped the early German Romantic Movement in important ways. In the summer of 1796, Friedrich Schlegel left Dresden in order to join his brother, August Wilhelm, in Jena. August Wilhelm had been invited there by Schiller to work on Schiller's journal *Die Horen*. Jena quickly became the center of early German Romanticism. Count Carl August of Weimar was the chief administrator of the University and was liberal concerning matters of the human sciences. This made the University in Jena an intellectually progressive place. At the time, Kant's critical philosophy fueled most innovation in the field. In Jena, Kant's philosophy was taught by Karl Leonhard Reinhold, Gottlieb Hufeland, and Carl Christian Erhard Schmid. One of the most important journals of the time, the *Allgemeine Literatur-Zeitung* was published in Jena. These two factors coupled with Jena's proximity to Weimar, a cultural center, attracted a broad range of thinkers, over which Schiller had a formative influence.[2]

Schlegel did little to ingratiate himself to Schiller. While prominent thinkers of the period, such as Hegel, lauded Schiller's contributions to philosophy and literature, Schlegel's reviews of Schiller's work were filled with irony and stinging criticisms. Especially harsh was Schlegel's criticism of Schiller's poem, "The Worth of Women," which appeared in Schiller's journal *Musenalmanach* in 1796. In that review, Schlegel ridiculed Schiller's celebration of the domestic

---

[1] For an excellent discussion of the blending of the aesthetic with the empirical in Humboldt and Schiller's influence on this blending, see Tresch (2010). I thank Michal Dettelbach for bringing my attention to this important essay.

[2] For more on the group of scholars assembled in Jena during this period, see Zielkowski (1998).

functions of women, and even claimed that the text was not even worthy of being classified as a poem, writing: "In the strict sense, this piece cannot be counted as a poem: neither the material nor the unity are poetic. Indeed, it benefits when one inverts the rhythm mentally and reads the entire piece, stanza by stanza, backwards. Even here the presentation is idealized; only in a reversed direction, not upwards but backwards, rather deeply below the truth. Men like these should have their hands and legs tied up, for such women leashes and cape cloth would be fitting" (*KFSA* 2, p. 6).[3] Despite his harsh criticisms of some of the conservative views he perceived in Schiller's work, Schlegel did acknowledge his indebtedness to Schiller's essays on aesthetics, especially "On Naive and Sentimental Poetry."[4] However, Schlegel's polemic with Schiller made it difficult for him to remain an active and financially supported member of the Jena intellectual community, for Schiller controlled the most important journals in Jena. During his time in Jena, Schlegel had contributed to the Berlin-based journals *Lyceum der schönen Künste* and *Deutschland*, both edited by the Berlin *Aufklärer* C.F. Reichhardt.[5] Seeking more opportunities to publish his work, in 1797, Schlegel left Jena for Berlin, hoping for better opportunities and a more progressive intellectual climate.

In Berlin, Schlegel and his brother founded *Das Athenäum*. *Das Athenäum* was in part a reaction against what Schlegel viewed to be the conservative mood of journals such as those edited by Reichhardt and against some of the conservative views that Schlegel attributed to Schiller. The journal of the early German Romantics was progressive: the Schlegels wanted their journal to be open to innovative articles at both the level of form *and* content. Friedrich Schlegel even went so far as to proclaim that all contributions which were polemical and "sublimely impudent" (displaying "*erhabene Frechheit*") would be included, that is, all contributions which were "too good" for other journals (Letter to his brother, cited by Eichner in *KFSA* 2, XLII).

It is noteworthy that three of the most important literary vehicles of the period had names that summoned the glory of the Ancient world—the title of Schiller's journal summoned the *Horai* or Hours, the three daughters of Zeus and Themes; Goethe's *Propyläen* summoned the ancient entryways of the classical world; and the *Athenäum* conjured to modern readers the ancient Greek capital. Although Goethe, Schiller, and the early German Romantics had their

---

[3] My translation. Strenge genommen kann diese Schrift nicht für ein Gedicht gelten: weder der Stoff noch die Einheit sind poetisch. Doch gewinnt sie, wenn man die Rhythmen in Gedanken verwechselt und das Ganze strophenweise rückwärts liest. Auch hier ist die Darstellung idealisiert; nur in verkehrter Richtung, nicht aufwärts, sondern abwährts, ziemlich tief unter die Wahrheit hinab. Männer, wie diese müßten an Händen und Beinen gebunden warden; solchen Frauen ziemte Gängelband und Fallhut.

[4] For more on Schlegel's love-hate relationship with Schiller, see Eichner's introduction to *KFSA* 2. For the pivotal role that Schiller played in the development of early German Romanticism, see Lovejoy (1948).

[5] For more on Schlegel's relation with Reichhardt, see Beiser (1992, pp. 253–260).

intellectual differences, the following sentiment expressed by Goethe was shared by all of them:

> Should the title *Propylaea* call to mind the gateway through which one had to pass to reach the Athenian citadel, Minerva's temple, we shall not protest. But we hope we will not be accused of presumptuously attempting to compete in these pages with so magnificent a work of art. What we wish to convey by this title is at most something that might have taken place there: discussions and conversations which perhaps would not have been unworthy of those hallowed halls.
>
> Do not thinkers, scholars and artists in their best moments dream of living in that land, among a people whom nature endowed with the perfection we seek and never attain, a people who in the course of time were able to develop a culture that had harmony and continuity, in contrast with our own which seems so fragmented and transitory? (... *eine Bildung in schöner und stätiger Reihe entwickelt, die bei uns nur als Stückwerk vorübergehend erscheint* ...) What modern nation does not owe its artistic heritage to the Greeks, and, in certain respects, who owes more than the Germans? (Gearey 1994, p. 79/Steinhagen 1999, p. 82).[6]

Goethe speaks in one collective voice for himself and the collaborators of his journal. As John Gearey tells us:

> The *we* of the Introduction is a plural, not an editorial *we*. Goethe worked together with a group who would later call themselves the Weimar Friends of Art; Heinrich Meyer, artist and art historian, professor at the Weimar art academy, and closest collaborator; Wilhelm von Humboldt, the philologist and statesman; Friedrich August Wolf, classical philologist at Halle; and Schiller, more as a consultant than as contributor. (Gearey 1994, p. 248, note 1)

The list of collaborators for the journal reflects the impressive level of collaboration that is a mark of this period of intellectual development in Weimar and surrounding towns. A deep and fruitful friendship with art was forged. The yearning for the "beautiful continuity and harmony" of the ancient Greeks that is expressed in the opening volume of *Propylaea*, a nostalgia for the lost "Golden Age" that might just be recovered with the proper cultural center, marks the period to which Schiller, Goethe, and both the Schlegel and Humboldt brothers belonged. The longing for "the perfection we seek and never attain" is a central feature of the period. Alexander von Humboldt's fusion of the scientific (quantifiable) aspects of nature with the aesthetic (qualitative) aspects of nature, which we shall observe in the details of his *Rhodian Genius/Life Force* essay, is intimately connected to the eternal yearning for the "beautiful continuity and harmony" referenced in the opening statement of Goethe's journal.

---

[6] *Essays on Art and Literature*, John Gearey, ed. (Princeton: Princeton University Press, 1994), pp. 78–90 at p. 79. J.W. Goethe, *Einleitung in die Propyläen*, in Harald Steinhagen, ed., *Schriften zur Kunst und Literatur* (Stuttgart: Reclam, 1999), pp. 82–101, at p. 82.

A prominent idea shaping the cultural vision of this period was the belief that art could unify the fragmented, modern society and return culture to the "beautiful harmony" invoked in the *Propyläen* statement. As Goethe, Schiller, and the Schlegel brothers turned their attention to art and the fate of culture throughout the late 1700s and early 1800s, they each took a decidedly ancient turn. And we find traces of this turn in Humboldt's work, not only the *Rhodian Genius/Life Force* essay he wrote for Schiller's *Die Horen*, but also in the title of his final publication, *Kosmos/Cosmos*. As Humboldt writes in *Cosmos*:

> [T]he word Cosmos, which primitively, in the Homeric ages, indicated an idea of order and harmony, was subsequently adopted in scientific language, where it was gradually applied to the order observed in the movements of the heavenly bodies, to the whole universe, and then finally to the world in which this harmony was reflected to us. ... Pythagoras was the first who used the word Cosmos to designate the order that reigns in the universe, or entire world. (Humboldt 1845, pp. 68–69)

In a note, Humboldt extends his etymological analysis of the word "cosmos" telling us that, "in the most ancient, and at the same time most precise, definition of the word, [it] signified *ornament* (as an adornment for a man, a woman, or a horse); [...], it implied the order or adornment of a discourse" (Humboldt 1845, p. 69).[7] The matter of naming his last work was not a simple one for Humboldt. As Herman Noack points out, Humboldt claimed that his brother, Wilhelm, was supportive of the title, *Kosmos*, whereas he remained unconvinced, perhaps because of his own humility (Noack 1976, p. 47). In a letter dated October 24, 1834, Humboldt wrote: "I know that *Cosmos* is quite lofty and not without a certain degree of affectation, but the title expresses heaven and earth in a one word catch phrase [...]. My brother is also in favor of the title *Cosmos*, I wavered for a long period."[8] Humboldt's *Cosmos* takes us back to the ancient Greek meaning of the word, "cosmos," for it is a work that takes ornament seriously, opening space in the investigation of nature for the delights and pleasures we take in the order of nature; presenting the scientific *and* the aesthetic order of nature. The aesthetic order of nature is on a register different from the order attained by calculations and measurements. In Humboldt's work the aesthetic order of nature introduces freedom, in particular, a freedom from the mastery imposed by the scientific order. Like Goethe, Humboldt emphasized that to understand nature in its unity, one had to keep an eye on its "beautiful continuity and harmony"—both measurement and

---

[7] For a more recent discussion of the word "cosmos" and its connection to our understanding of order and our place in the world, esp. as it bridges science and religion, see Toulmin (1984).

[8] "Ich weiss, dass Kosmos sehr vornehm ist und nicht ohne eine gewisse Afféterie, aber der Titel sagt mit einem Schlagworte *Himmel und Erde* [...]. Mein Bruder ist auch für den Titel Kosmos, ich habe lange geschwankt" (Cited in Noack 1976, p. 47). Petra Werner's book title plays on Humboldt's reference to heaven and earth, and her study is an excellent analysis of *Cosmos*. See Werner (2004).

aesthetic appreciation were necessary to keep said continuity and harmony in sharp focus.

Humboldt's commitment to both the empirical aspects of the phenomena of nature and their aesthetic dimensions connects his work to Schiller's and to early German Romanticism. The vastness of the romantic territory has caused some problems with how to characterize the various Romanticisms and the role of various individuals within the movement. In the tale of Humboldt's connections to Romanticism, the figures who are handled most problematically are Goethe and Schiller. From the German perspective, they are most certainly *not* romantics, but rather pillars of Weimar Classicism. From the perspective of the British, however, Goethe and Schiller often heralded as the leaders of Romanticism. Arnd Bohm provides a good account of the reasons for the frustrating confusion surrounding Goethe and Schiller's role in Romanticism:

> Anyone attempting to compare or correlate the histories of German and English literature in the period between 1750 and 1850 can quickly become frustrated by the incommensurable categories deployed in the respective camps. Students of German literature who are used to thinking in terms of the succession *Aufklärung* (Enlightenment), *Sturm und Drang* (Storm and Stress), *Klassik, Romantik*, and *Vormärz* (Literature up to March 1848) encounter an entirely different sequence in English. There one finds categories such as the age of Johnson, the age of Sensibility, Gothic, Romantic, and Victorian. The one term that might seem familiar is Romantic. But even there difficulties immediately arise, not least because the English participants did not use the term Romantic of themselves. Complicating matters more is the fact that many critics schooled in the English tradition disregard their German colleague's distinctions and consider Goethe to be a Romantic writer. (Bohm 2004, p. 35)

Bohm most diplomatically stresses that "dismaying" as the view of Goethe and Schiller as romantic writers might be to those who "are used to thinking of Goethe and Schiller as the pillars of a period of such stellar achievement that is has earned the accolade German Classicism, the view from a more distant outlook is not without merit" (Bohm 2004, p. 35). The term "romantic" for the early German Romantics did indeed develop out of a concern for carrying on the famous ancient modern debate in terms that were suited to the contemporary developments in literature. Friedrich Schlegel first used the adjective "romantic" to denote a certain class of writings from a certain period in the history of literature: romantic poetry was opposed to classical poetry, it was subjective and artificial (*künstlich*), whereas classical poetry was objective and natural. In 1797, Schlegel published an essay (written in 1795), "Über das Studium der griechischen Poesie" which lauded the value of the objective standard of the Greek world, while scorning developments in modern literature. Yet soon after the publication of this essay, Schlegel distanced himself from his earlier *Objektivitätswut* and announced his romantic turn. As he writes in Lyceum/Critical Fragment 7,

> My essay on the study of Greek poetry is a mannered prose hymn to the objective quality in poetry. The worst thing about it, it seems to me, is the complete lack of necessary irony; and the best, the confident assumption that poetry is infinitely valuable—as if that were a settled thing. (*KFSA* 2, pp. 147–48/Firchow 1991, p. 1)

Schlegel's use of the term "romantic" pushed the debate between the ancients and the moderns from a merely chronological debate about the progress of culture. In this emphasis on culture's progress we find a decidedly political thrust to romantic thought, one that is found in the work of Humboldt and Schiller as well.

The Transformative Power of a New Mythology: Humboldt's Life Force and Schiller's Aesthetic Empire

As the air of reform left in the wake of the French Revolution swept over Europe, a desire for innovation in all areas of life was enlivened. The early German Romantics saw their intellectual work as part of project to transform society and the very disciplines of poetry, philosophy, and even science. As we saw above, the appeal to the Greeks and to mythology was part of their project of social transformation. Michael Dettelbach provides a detailed account of the intellectual reception of the French Revolution in the circle around Goethe and Schiller in Jena. Dettelbach situates Humboldt's work within the context of empire that was taking shape during this period. Dettelbach argues that Humboldt's global physics and Schiller's aesthetic empire are "complementary visions of a future Germany." Dettelbach convincingly locates the roots of this shared vision in the constellation of thinkers orbiting around Goethe and Schiller. As he writes:

> Perhaps no group had such a clear and developed consciousness of the empire's dissolving legal and institutional structure and the implications of this dissolution for German nationhood, or talked as much about it, as the loose horde of government officials, young bureaucrats, academics, and literati assembled around Schiller and Goethe in the 1790s. In one way or another, despite their famous and often bitter differences, Fichte, Schelling, the Humboldt brothers, the Schlegels, were devising recipes to reconstitute German nationhood and translate the empire. (Dettelbach 1996, p. 273)

As we shall see, Humboldt's global physics and Schiller's aesthetic empire fuse in the essay Humboldt wrote for Schiller's *Die Horen*. Life forces appear in mythical garb, blending the aesthetic empire summoned by Schiller and the global physics that was central to Humboldtian science.

The perceived loss of empire central to this period gave rise to a nostalgic look back to the "beautiful continuity and harmony" summoned in the opening statement of Goethe's journal. Such nostalgia prompted many thinkers of the period to a call for a new mythology that would restore lost cultural order.

One of the most important texts calling for a new mythology was a curious document first published in 1917. Indeed, along with Schlegel's famous *Athenäum* Fragment Nr. 116, the so-called, *Oldest Programme for a System of German Idealism* (1796) is often appealed to as kind of manifesto of the early German Romantic Movement, although not one of the contributors to *Das Athenäum* is a candidate for its authorship.[9] The text was published anonymously in Hegel's handwriting, but its authorship continues to be a matter of debate, with Hegel, Hölderlin, and Schelling each in contention for authorship. Given that the text swings from the use of "I" to "we," some scholars suggest the text was jointly authored.

The matter of this text's authorship remains a debated topic. As Martin Gammon points out:

> [S]ince Pöggeler's landmark defense of Hegel as the author of the fragment in 1969, most commentators have taken his account to be definitive (albeit with some significant dissent). One major consequence of Pöggeler's defense, however, has been a dramatic reappraisal of Hegel's early view of art, in light of this fragment's call for a new "aesthetic philosophy." (Gammon 2000, p. 145)

Gammon explores this reappraisal in his article, "Modernity and the Crisis of Aesthetic Representation in Hegel's Early Writings," making a strong case for rejecting Hegel as the author of this fragment. Gammon rejects Hegel as the author of this fragment due to Hegel's view that ancient mythology could not be resurrected to address the pressing cultural problems facing modernity, in part, because "modernity lacks an inherent 'sensuous certainty' (*sinnliche Gewissheit*), which was the precondition of Greek mythological presentation" (Gammon 2000, p. 148).

The text found in Hegel's handwriting sets out a program for the development of an aesthetic philosophy, a philosophy that the more mature Hegel had no interest in developing.[10] What brims from the imperatives articulated in its lines is the revolutionary spirit that shaped the young thinkers who hoped to transform their society and unify the disparate social groups found with it. The program announced in the text is program for a new mythology, one that will unify society by presenting a set of symbols legible to all members of society, one that would help to create a new cultural center, and so help develop social cohesiveness, a sense of unity. As Rüdiger Bubner has pointed out, this short text has been analyzed so exhaustively, that we can compare the literature on it to a forensic report. I will not repeat those findings here, or track all of the fascinating paths that are to be found in the short, but highly suggestive text.

---

[9] See Mittman and Strand (1997, pp. 47–71) and Seyhan (1992). Philippe Lacoue-Labarthe and Jean-Luc Nancy begin their study, *The Literary Absolute. The Theory of Literature in German Romanticism*, with a discussion of this text, using it as a kind of "overture" to the early German Romantic Movement.

[10] I have developed this point in an article demarcating the lines between German Idealism and early German Romanticism. See Millán (2014, pp. 389–408).

My interest lies in the call for the development of social cohesiveness that the author(s) locate in the aesthetic realm, for this call to make ideas aesthetic was one that is relevant to the story of Humboldt's presentation of nature and to Schiller's concern with the development of an aesthetic culture:

> Until we make ideas aesthetic, that is, mythological, they are of no interest to the *people*, and vice versa: until mythology is rational, it will be an embarrassment to philosophy. Thus, those who are enlightened and those who are not must finally make common cause, mythology must become philosophical, to make the people rational, and philosophy must become mythological, to make philosophy sensuous. Then eternal unity will reign among us. Never again the arrogant glance, never again the blind shuddering of the people, before its wise men and priests. Only then will *equal* development of *all* of our powers await us, for the particular person as well as for all individuals. (Bernstein 2003, pp. 186–7)[11]

The project of establishing social unity is described as the "greatest task of humanity," and it will be carried out by an aesthetic revolution of sorts. The idea of beauty taken in the "higher Platonic sense" is that which will unify all, which is why the "philosopher must possess as much aesthetic power as the poet." The call for a new mythology is an aesthetically inspired critique of the state, which seeks through the establishment of a new mythology to establish a new sense of harmony, of social cohesiveness. For Humboldt, the Enlightenment goals of order and progress will be achieved through an emphasis on empirical observation and measurement, balanced with an aesthetic appreciation of nature. Humboldt takes the aesthetic revolution into the realm of the natural sciences.

Like the author (s) of the *Programme for a System of German Idealism*, Schlegel sees his society as one that is decaying, breaking apart. Schlegel (with the voice of Ludovico) opens his *Speech on the New Mythology/Rede über die Mythologie* with the following lament:

> I call on you my friends, to ask yourselves, with the same earnestness with which you revere art: Shall the power of enthusiasm continue to be splintered (*versplittert*) even (*auch*) in poetry, and finally fall silent alone, when it has fought itself weary against the hostile enemies? Shall the highest and the holiest remain forever nameless and formless? (Schulte-Sasse et al. 1997, p. 182 / KFSA 2, pp. 311–312)[12]

The reference to the "splintered" condition of modernity brings to mind Goethe's words in describing the offering of his journal, *Propyläen*. The search for a culture developed in beautiful continuity and harmony guides Goethe's journal. Schlegel also believes that a new mythology will offer to modernity just such a beautiful continuity and harmony. Without social cohesiveness, art

---

[11] The essay has been translated into English as *Oldest Programme for a System of German Idealism*, in Bernstein (2003, pp. 185–87).

[12] Translated as *Speech on Mythology*, in Schulte-Sasse (1997, pp. 182–188 / KFSA 2, pp. 311–322).

will indeed fall victim to "namelessness and formlessness," in a word, to chaos, for there will be no tradition available to provide a context, a context crucial for critical discussion; there is no dialogue possible without the unity that makes such exchange possible. Schlegel's *Speech/Rede* continues in this mood of alarm, with a feeling of nostalgia for a unity (or, though Schlegel does not use Goethe's term, beautiful continuity) that has been lost. In modern society, there is no more community, unity, continuity, but rather just a collection of individuals, isolated parts with no sense of the whole. What is missing is a tradition, that which helps to create a sense of cohesiveness vital to societies:

> The modern poet must work this all out from within and many have done it magnificently—each, however, alone until now; each work anew, as if creating from nothing. (Schulte-Sasse et al. 1997, p. 182/*KFSA* 2, p. 312)

These lines from his *Speech/Rede* reveal that Schlegel believed that the creation of artists took place within a tradition, and that historical consciousness of that tradition formed an important element of the creative process and to the very meaning of works of art. Mythology, he argues, will help to correct the excessive isolationism plaguing society:

> Our poetry, I maintain, lacks a midpoint as mythology was for the poetry of the ancients and modern poetic art's inferiority to classical art can be summarized in the words: we have no mythology. But I would add that we are close to attaining one, or rather, it is time that we try earnestly to take part in producing one. (Schulte-Sasse et al. 1997, p. 182/*KFSA* 2, p. 312)

We do well to keep Gammon's insight in mind: for Hegel the harmonizing center of ancient Greek culture was found in an inherent, "sensuous certainty," something lacking in modernity. In contrast, Schlegel understands the unifying center of the ancients to be more closely aligned with a sense of tradition, and he believes that the modern writers *can* create a tradition that would give them just the sense of a unity that is needed to establish the beautiful continuity needed to bring society into a cohesive whole. Schlegel's appeal to the ancients as providing a model of unity for a modern culture that he saw as splintering apart was an appeal made by several of the leading intellectuals of the period. As it was for the Greeks, Schlegel sees mythology as something that will help bring modern society together into some sort of cohesive whole. This new mythology is an aesthetic mythology, and in an aesthetically infused culture the relation between philosophy and art becomes a most intimate one. Let us now consider the consequences of Humboldt's acceptance of the fusion of mythology and art especially for his view of nature and how this embrace of an aesthetic mythology connects Humboldt and Schiller. To explore these matters we shall turn to the lone essay Humboldt wrote for Schiller's journal, *Die Horen*, an essay he would include in his collection, *Views of Nature/Ansichten der Natur*.

The Rhodian Genius: Humboldt's Search for Nature's Beautiful Harmony

Humboldt published three editions of *Ansichten der Natur*, the first in 1807, shortly after his return from his voyage to the equinoctial regions of the earth (1799–1804), another in 1826, and a third in 1849, which included material from his voyage in Russia. The preface to the first edition makes explicit Humboldt's indebtedness to Schiller and highlights their affinities on views of nature, freedom, and the aesthetic. Humboldt's preface ends with these lines from Schiller's *Bride of Messina*:

> On the mountains is freedom! The breath of decay/Never sullies the fresh flowing air;/Oh! Nature is perfect wherever we stray;/'Tis humanity that deforms it with anguish (Bohn, x, translation altered)/ Auf den Bergen ist Freiheit! Der Hauch der Grüfte/Steigt nicht hinauf in die reinen Lüfte;/Die Welt ist vollkommen überall,/Wo der Mensch nict hinkommt mit seiner Qual. (*Ansichten*, x)[13]

Humboldt developed an intellectual relationship with Schiller during his time in Jena, and the *Rhodian Genius/Life Force* essay was just one fruit of their intellectual exchange. As Humboldt tells us in the preface to the second edition of *Ansichten*:

> I oversaw the second edition of *Views of Nature* in Paris in in the year 1826. Two articles—an essay "Concerning the Structure and Action of Volcanos in Various Regions of the Earth" and "The Life Force, or The Rhodian *Genius*"—were added at that time. During my long stay in Jena, Schiller, in memory of the medical studies of his youth, enjoyed discussing physiological matters with me. My work on the disposition of stimulated muscle and nerve fibers through contact with chemically differing materials often led our discussions in a more serious direction. The short article on life force originates from this time. Schiller's fondness for the "Rhodian *Genius*," which he accepted for publication in his journal *Die Horen*, gave me the courage to have it printed again. (Humboldt 2014, p. 27)

Humboldt goes on to tell his readers that his brother, Wilhelm, felt that the allegory was out of tune with the cultural sensibilities of the time, writing:

> In a letter that has just recently been published (Wilhelm von Humboldt's *Briefe an eine Freundin*, part II, p. 39), my brother gently touches upon the same matter, but aptly adds: "The development of a physiological idea is the goal of this essay. At the time in which it was written, there was more love than one would find now for such a half-poetic adornment [*halbdichterische Einkleidungen*] of serious truths." (Humboldt 2014, p. 27)

---

[13] For a detailed account of the ways in which the mountains figure prominently in the work of both Humboldt and Schiller, see Dettelbach (1996).

In light of Humboldt's own comments on the genesis of the text, it is clear that to understand the *Rhodian Genius* we need to understand how Humboldt's concern with physiology is related to his embrace of poetry. This text is a strong example of Humboldt the scientist, going beyond the "charts and graphs" of empiricism to embrace freedom and beauty. Certainly the "halbdichterische Einkleidungen" of serious truths to which Wilhelm makes reference in his description of his brother Alexander's *Rhodian Genius* pose a hermeneutical challenge to readers, especially if those readers are philosophers. With his claim that "the development of a physiological idea is the object of the essay," Wilhelm brings the essay into productive conversation with much of Humboldt's corpus, and he helps to lift the veil cloaking the "ernsthafter Wahrheiten" (serious truths) to be found in the whimsical essay. Michael Dettelbach sees the "physiological scaffolding" in Humboldt's works as central to his eventual authority as a philosophical traveler and experimental philosopher. Dettelbach argues this point in his article, "The Stimulations of Travel: Humboldt's Physiological Construction of the Tropics," where he writes: "It is well known that Humboldt conceived of his tropical sojourn principally as an exercise in comparative physiology and anatomy, an opportunity to investigate the influence of inanimate nature on the animate plant and animal creation" (Dettelbach 2005, p. 45). Dettelbach makes a strong case for the influence of physiology on the work that came out of the voyage from 1799–1804. As he tells us:

> Humboldt's account of the American tropics is pervaded by physiology, especially close attention to his own physiological and aesthetic responses to outside stimuli—a trait shared with many diarists and letter writes of the late eighteenth century. This physiological scaffolding was put in place in the decade before he left for America, as an experimental philosopher and Prussian official. (Dettelbach 2005, p. 45)

Certainly, a "physiological scaffolding" connects the *Rhodian Genius/Life Force* text to the rest of Humboldt's corpus, for the text is an allegorical presentation of nothing less than vital force, the force animating all physiological activity. Dettelbach, argues that, "attending to the effects of the tropics on one's own physiology (including aesthetic effects) was critical to establishing one's authority as a philosophical traveler" (Dettelbach 2005, p. 45). Dettelbach links Humboldt's work on physiology to his view of nature, a view, "focused on the reactions of the irritable human living body to the fluctuating physical forces that make up nature" (Dettelbach 2005, p. 45). While not an account of the tropics, the *Rhodian Genius/Life Force* is perhaps the most explicitly aesthetic and physiological text in Humboldt's corpus, a text presenting an allegory of the forces at play in physiology. The same techniques Humboldt develops in this essay are used in the other chapters of his *Ansichten/Views of Nature* to provide his readers with *Naturgemälde* or physical portrait of the Latin American landscape.

In the *Rhodian Genius* essay, we are introduced to the eponymous genius through a painting. As we are told:

> Among the countless paintings that the Syracusans had collected with assiduous diligence from their mother country, there was but one that had for a full century attracted the attention of all passersby. Even when the Olympian Jupiter, or Cecrops, founder of Athens, or the valor of Harmodius and Aristogieton wanted for admirers, still throngs of people stood crowded around this picture. Whence came this affection? Was it a rescued work of Apelles, or had it come perhaps from the school of Callimachus? No; dignity and grace indeed radiated from the picture, but in the blending of colors, in character and style as a whole, it could not measure up to several of the others works in Poikile. (Humboldt 2014, p. 261)

With no pendant to guide the viewer, to offer clues to its meaning, the riddle of its meaning and the mystery of its force of attraction remained unsolved:

> No one even knew in what temple it had originally stood, for it had been saved from a stranded ship, and only the ship's other cargo hinted that the picture had come from Rhodes. (Humboldt 2014, p. 261)

Humboldt valued historical context, and he uses the lack of such context to emphasize how isolated the painting remains, how uprooted from its meaning. What the viewers of the painting can ascertain are the forms to be found on the painting. We are told that "the human expressions of longing and sorrow—all seemed to strip them of anything heavenly or godlike and bind them to their earthly homeland" (Ibid.). The gaze of the figures is "directed to a Genius, that, surrounded by a bright shimmer, floated in their midst" (Humboldt 2014, p. 262). On the shoulder of the genius is a butterfly and in his right hand, a flaming torch. The butterfly and the flame will make an appearance in Goethe's "Selige Sehnsucht" with the theme of the life force and our own human finitude. Nature is a collection of infinite vital forces, and we, humans, are left to *Sterben und werden* (dying and becoming).[14] In Humboldt's portrait of this process of life and death, the human figures deferentially gaze upon the Genius, who appears other-worldly, in command of the forces of nature (symbolized by the butterfly on his shoulder and the flaming torch in his right hand). When a new shipment of art treasures sails into the Aegean Sea, those in search of the meaning of this captivating painting are given a clue, for in a shipment of art treasures from Rhodes the pendant to the Rhodian Genius is found. In the companion painting:

> Again, the Genius stood in the middle, but without the butterfly and with his head bowed, the extinguished torch pointed earthward. The circle of youths and maidens were now almost falling over him in many an embrace; their glance was

---

[14] For an excellent analysis of how life force is revealed in Goethe's work, especially in his "Selige Sehnsucht," see Mehigan and Banki (2020).

no longer solemn and obedient, but bespoke a condition of wild abandon, the fulfillment of a long-nurtured desire. (Humboldt 2014, p. 262)

Both paintings are sent to Epicharmus, the philosopher of the school of Pythagoras, a figure, who,

> seldom visited the court of Dionysians, not as if excellent men of all of the Greek colonial cities did not gather there, but because such close proximity to princes robs even the most intellectual men of both their intellect and their freedom. He occupied himself constantly with the nature of plants and animals, with the harmonic laws that govern how celestial bodies in vast spaces and snowflakes and hailstones in small ones take the form of spheres. (Humboldt 2014, pp. 262–63)

It is Epicharmus (a figure quite like Humboldt himself), the student of life forces, finding an order in nature that is more noble than the artificial order of human culture who is able to see that the paintings, with their depictions of the Rhodian Genius at two different points in the development of his *Lebenskraft*, are representations of life and death, of the movement and shift of life force from the Genius to his followers, a life force that may shift direction, but which is boundless and infinite. As we have seen from Humboldt's own account of the genesis of this essay, his most prominent early essay, "Versuche über die gereizte Muskel und Nervenfasser," was an exploration of *Lebenskraft* in a non-allegorical way, and it was a discussion about that essay with Schiller that led him to his "little allegory on vital force." Humboldt's allegory is a fusion of scientific method with literary whim, all with an eye back to the Greeks. The *Rhodian Genius/Life Force* essay was inspired by Humboldt's discussion with Schiller, and it is flavored with the belief that a turn to the Greeks would yield important guidance for modern culture. Yet, while the *Rhodian Genius/Life Force* essay brings Humboldt and Schiller together, it is also the site of differences between their approaches to nature, differences that would draw the attention of twentieth-century thinkers.

Schiller linked *Lebenskraft* to a central aesthetic experience: our experience of the sublime. As Emily Brady convincingly argues, Schiller's notion of the sublime "provides the groundwork for locating an aesthetics of nature in [his] philosophy" (Brady 2013, p. 93). In his 1801 essay, *Concerning the Sublime/Über des Erhabene*, nature and its great vital force (*Lebenskraft*) are presented within the context of our human limits and the infinite force of nature. Nature in its boundlessness confronts us with our limits, and talk of minding the limits of our mastery is used by Schiller to clarify the dual nature of the sublime:

> The sublime object is of a dual sort. We refer it either to our *power of apprehension* and are defeated in the attempt to form an image of its concept; or we refer it to our *vital power* and view it as a power against which our own dwindles to nothing. But even if, in the first case or the second, it is the occasion of a painful awareness of our limitations, still we do not run from it, but rather are drawn to it by an irresistible force. … We gladly permit the imagination to meet its master in the

realm of appearances because ultimately it is only a sensuous faculty that triumphs over other sensuous faculties; but nature in her entire boundlessness cannot impinge upon the absolute greatness within ourselves. (Schiller 1966, pp. 198–99/cf. Schiller 1993, p. 74)

While Humboldt, as Schiller knew from their conversations about Humboldt's experiments on nerves and his essay for *Die Horen*, connected *Lebenskraft* and physiology, and then used the connection between *Lebenskraft* and sensibility to build a connection to the aesthetic realm, Schiller uses *Lebenskraft* to take us directly to the sublime and a discussion of human cognition. Ultimately, for Schiller, it is the human subject who dominates over the forces of nature. Both Humboldt and Schiller are using our experience of nature to take us to a consideration of our own limits and the joy of abandoning limits. Ultimately, both thinkers are propelled by life force to the aesthetic realm. Indeed as Dettelbach argues in his essay, "The Stimulations of Travel: Humboldt's Physiological Construction of the Tropics," "vital force" is the root of sensibility (Dettelbach 2005, p. 54). Vital force or life force (Lebenskraft) linked Humboldt's work in America to the realm of both natural science and aesthetics. As Dettelbach observes: "The relationship between feeling and measurement, between aesthetic appreciation and exact science in Humboldt's work is … not accurately termed a synthesis. Instead feeling and measuring were closely identified, even continuous activities, and the display of 'tropical' sensibility was an integral part of Humboldt's credibility as a scientific observers" (Dettelbach 2005, p. 58). Humboldt's presentation of nature involves a balance between that which can be mastered, in Humboldt's case with careful empirical measurement, and that which is the source of delight, or that which cannot be measured at all, part of the "realm of freedom" which is the essence of Humboldt's view of nature. In Schiller's presentation of nature in *Concerning the Sublime* (1801), the presentation of nature takes place as the limits of our cognitive faculties (the powers of apprehension) are balanced with that which is beyond mastery, taking us to the realm of freedom, where the ideas of the sublime and of beauty find their home. Their projects are similar, yet Schiller and Humboldt define this home for beauty and the sublime in distinct ways. Humboldt's realm of freedom is nature itself, whereas Schiller's idea of freedom is rooted in the human subject, a subject which eclipses nature itself.

Concluding Remarks

Adorno, an intellectual heir of German Romanticism, would later diagnose the problems for natural beauty that arose from Schiller's view of nature and freedom:

> Natural beauty vanished from aesthetics as a result of the burgeoning domination of the concept of freedom and human dignity, which was inaugurated by Kant and then rigorously transplanted into aesthetics by Schiller and Hegel; in accord

with this concept nothing in the world is worthy of attention except that for which the autonomous subject has itself to thank. The truth of such freedom for the subject, however, is at the same time unfreedom: unfreedom for the other. ... Perhaps nowhere else is the desiccation of everything not totally ruled by the subject more apparent, nowhere else is the dark shadow of idealism more obvious, than in aesthetics. (Adorno 1970, pp. 62, 98–99)

Adorno goes on to claim that Humboldt, "occupies a position between Kant and Hegel in that he holds fast to natural beauty yet in contrast to Kantian formalism endeavors to concretize it" (Adorno 1970, pp. 71, 112). In concretizing nature, Humboldt granted freedom to nature rather than placing nature under the dominion of the subject. Even if Schiller is guilty of some of the moves Adorno attributes to the German Idealists, to his credit, Schiller's *Die Horen* was a publication which gave voice to an essay that lifted the "dark shadow of idealism" allowing readers to see nature as a realm of freedom with a life force not subject to the limits of human subjectivity.

References

Adorno, T.W. 1970. Ästhetische Theorie. Frankfurt: Suhrkamp. English edition: Adorno, T.W. 1997. Aesthetic Theory (Trans. Hullot-Kentor, Robert). Minneapolis: University of Minnesota Press.

Beiser, Frederick. 1992. *Enlightenment, Revolution, and Romanticism. The Genesis of Modern German Political Thought, 1790–1800*. Cambridge, MA: Harvard University Press.

———. 2005. *Schiller as Philosopher.* Oxford: Oxford University Press.

Bernstein, J.M., ed. 2003. *Classic and Romantic German Aesthetics.* Cambridge: Cambridge University Press.

Bohm, Arnd. 2004. Goethe and the Romantics. In *The Literature of German Romanticism*, ed. Dennis F. Mahoney, 35–60. Rochester, NY: Camden House.

Brady, Emily. 2013. *The Sublime in Modern Philosophy. Aesthetics, Ethics, and Nature.* Cambridge: Cambridge University Press.

Dettelbach, Michael. 1996. Global physics and aesthetic empire: Humboldt's physical portrait of the tropics. In *Visions of Empire: Voyages, Botany, and Representations of Nature*, eds. David Philip Miller and Peter Hanns Reill, 258–292. Cambridge: Cambridge University Press, 1996.

———. 2005. The Stimulations of Travel: Humboldt's Physiological Construction of the Tropics. In *Tropical Visions in an Age of Empire*, eds. Felix Driver and Luciana Martins, 43–58. Chicago: University of Chicago Press.

Firchow, Peter, trans. *Friedrich Schlegel. Philosophical Fragments*, foreword by Rodolphe Gasché. Minneapolis: University of Minnesota Press, 1991.

Gammon, Martin. 2000. Modernity and the Crisis of Aesthetic Representation in Hegel's Early Writing. In *Hegel and Aesthetics*, ed. William Maker, 145–169. Albany: SUNY Press, 2000.

Gearey, John, ed. 1994. *Essays on Art and Literature.* Princeton: Princeton University Press.

Humboldt, Alexander von. 1845. Kosmos. Entwurf einer physischen Weltbeschreibung. Stuttgard: Kottascher Verlag. English edition: Humboldt, A.v. 1997. Cosmos. A

Sketch of the Physical Description of the Universe. Trans. E.C. Otté, Introduction, Nicolas A. Rupke. Baltimore: The Johns Hopkins University Press.

———. *Views of Nature*. 2014. Trans. Mark W. Person. Edited by Stephen T. Jackson and Laura Dassow Walls. Chicago: University of Chicago Press.

Jahn, Ilse and Lange, Fritz, eds. 1973. *Die Jugendbriefe Alexander von Humboldt 1787–1795*. Berlin: Akademie Verlag.

Lacoue-Labarthe, Philippe and Nancy, Jean-Luc. 1988. *The Literary Absolute. The Theory of Literature in German Romanticism*. Trans. P. Barnard and C. Lester. Albany: SUNY Press.

Lovejoy, Arthur. 1948. Schiller and the Genesis of German Romanticism. In *Essays in the History of Ideas*, 207–227. Baltimore: The Johns Hopkins University Press.

Mehigan, Tim and Banki, Peter. 2020. Goethe's Philosophy of Nature. In *The Palgrave Handbook of German Romantic Philosophy*, 375–397.

Millán, Elizabeth. 2014. The Aesthetic Philosophy of Early German Romanticism and Its Early German Idealist Roots. In *The Palgrave Companion to German Idealism*, ed. Matthew Altman, 389–408. New York: Palgrave/Macmillan.

Mittman, Elizabeth and Strand, Mary R. 1997. Representing Self and Other in Early German Romanticism. In *Theory as Practice. A Critical Anthology of Early German Romantic Writings*, Jochen Schulte-Sasse et al., eds., 47–71. Minneapolis: University of Minnesota Press.

Noack, Herman. 1976. Naturgemälde und Naturkenntnis: Alexander von Humboldts *Kosmos* in problemgeschichtlicher Rückschau. In *Universalismus und Wissenschaft im Werk und Wirken der Brüder Humboldt*, ed. Klaus Hammacher, 46–74. Frankfurt a.M.: Vittorio Klostermann.

Reddick, John.1990. Georg Büchner and Naturphilosophie. In *Romanticism and the Sciences*, eds. Andrew Cunningham and Nicholas Jardine, 322–340. Cambridge: Cambridge University Press.

von Schiller, Friedrich. 1966. *On the Sublime*. Trans. Julius A. Elias. New York: Frederick Ungar.

———. 1993. *Concerning the Sublime* Trans. Daniel Dahlstrom. In *Essays*, eds. Walter Hinderer and Daniel O. Dahlstrom. New York: Continuum.

Schulte-Sasse, Jochen et al., eds.1997. *Theory as Practice. A Critical Anthology of Early German Romantic Writings*. Minneapolis: University of Minnesota Press.

Seyhan, Azade. 1992. *Representation and Its Discontents. The Critical Legacy of German Romanticism*. Berkeley: University of California Press.

Steinhagen, Harald, ed. 1999. J.W. Goethe, *Einleitung in die Propyläen* in *Schriften zur Kunst und Literatur*, 82–101. Stuttgart: Reclam, 1999.

Toulmin, Stephen. 1984. Cosmology as Science and as Religion. In *On Nature*, ed. Leroy S. Rouner, 27–41. Notre Dame, IN: University of Notre Dame Press.

Tresch, John, 2010. Even the Tools will be Free: Humboldt's Romantic Technologies. In *The Heavens on Earth. Observations and Astronomy in Nineteenth-Century Science and Culture*, eds. David Aubin, Charlotte Bigg, and H. Otto Sibum, 242–284. Durham: Duke University Press, 2010.

Werner, Petra. 2004. *Himmel und Erde, Alexander von Humboldt und sein Kosmos*. Berlin: Akademie Verlag.

Zielkowski, Theodore. 1998. *Das Wunderjahr in Jena. Geist und Gesellschaft 1794–95* Stuttgart: Klett-Cotta.

Friedrich Schiller and Georg Wilhelm Friedrich Hegel

Valerio Rocco Lozano

Friedrich Schiller's influence is certainly one of the most important factors in understanding the philosophy of G. W. F. Hegel. It has therefore been widely studied, both in general and in terms of its impact on several aspects of Hegelian philosophy: logic (Pöggeler 1981), aesthetics (Böhler 1972), philosophy of nature (Hoffheimer 1985), philosophy of religion (Acosta López 2007), and philosophy of spirit (Acosta 2012; Kain 1982; Schindler 2012). Some of Hegel's most important passages, such as the well-known final verses of *The Phenomenology of Spirit*, are quotations or reformulations of Schiller's texts, which has also given rise to numerous studies on this—more localised—influence on specific comments on Hegel's works (Kojève 2007). As for Hegel's *Lectures on Aesthetics*, in their different versions, mentions of and implicit references to Schiller are so abundant and significant that any critical edition of them is already, to a large extent, an analysis of the general influence explored here. In this regard, consider the relevance in Hegelian aesthetics of the notion of *Schein* (appearance) rooted in Schiller's work, or Schiller's decisive contribution (comparable only to that of Hölderlin) to forging his image of ancient Greece in general (Taminiaux 1967), and of its tragedy in particular (Aranzueque 2011; Pöggeler 1973). Finally, it should be noted that studies on Schiller's presence in Hegel's works tend to concentrate on the latter's mature

V. Rocco Lozano (✉)
Autonomous University of Madrid, Madrid, Spain
e-mail: valerio.rocco@uam.es

production, from his time in Jena to the lectures and writings produced whilst living in Berlin.

For all these reasons, the remainder of this article will limit its exploration of the relationship between Schiller and Hegel to a less studied and very specific area: the philosophy of history, and in particular the influence of the Roman world—and its republicanism—on the two authors. The research set out here will also be limited to a specific time frame: the early production of Hegel, in the *Gymnasium* years, in which Schiller's influence was absolutely decisive.[1] The final part of the study will address a specific case of the political usage of Roman history in terms of republicanism: the rapes of Lucretia and Virginia. As we will see, these two specific episodes are fundamental in some of Schiller's dramas, which are in turn decisive in shaping the republicanism of young Hegel.

The two works on which we will focus here, to study Schiller's influence on Hegel (Schiller's *Fiesco* and Hegel's *Unterredung zwischen Dreien*) have strong political contents and, despite their literary rather than strictly philosophical form, are fundamental to understanding a crucial element in modern philosophy of history: the importance of Latin classics, both among the French revolutionaries themselves and the intellectuals who witnessed the great *Begebenheit* of 1789, in shaping an emancipatory symbology through which the great aspirations of a generation could be driven in search of a profound change in political institutions and, more importantly, in the way of thinking (cf. Highet 1957: 393). If the main purpose of this whole era, which could be called the *Age of Criticism*, was oriented precisely towards transforming the *Denkungsart* of the people (cf. Duque 1997: 32ff), the protagonists and interpreters of this endeavour undeniably found references in Roman history. The reasons for this return to Rome as an inspiration for the revolutionary process are manifold, and because of their complexity they cannot be fully addressed in the study presented here.

However, it is important to highlight for the purposes of this research that, even before the outbreak of Revolution, for intellectuals of different generations—such as Schiller and Hegel—in search of new political ideals that could guide their cravings for social change, the Roman Republic was the main model used. The reason for this choice is clear, and largely summed up in Rousseau's decisive influence,[2] with his determined praise for the political regimes of Rome and Sparta, marked by a sober and virile conception of virtue, in contrast to Athens and all those states that would have opted more for "good words" over "good deeds" (Montaigne 2007: I, XXV).

---

[1] In this sense, it is interesting to note how the most systematic research on the role of Classical Antiquity in Hegel (Desmond 2020), with a whole section (97–104) devoted to the influence of Schiller, concentrates considerably more on the role of Greece (with respect to Rome) and on late works (in relation to his youthful output).

[2] Regarding Rousseau's influence on the formation of a Roman republicanism before the French Revolution, and in particular in the young Hegel, cf. Rocco 2013.

This expression of a series of political conceptions through a reference to the language and history of Rome is found in the *Unterredung zwischen Dreien* (Hegel 1989: 37–39), a text written in May 1785 and of great symbolic value, as the first of Hegel's text which has survived into the present day. The subject of this writing is a conversation between Octavian, Mark Antony, and Lepidus about their plans to seize power in Rome following the murder of Caesar by the conspirators. The decision to write on this subject was surely due to the strong presence of several classical authors, in this case Latin, who addressed genuinely political issues, in the education received by Hegel at the *Gymnasium Illustre*.[3]

Fascinated by the ideas of Republican *libertas* and stoic *virtus* learned in his lessons on Roman history and literature, the young Hegel writes an impetuous text, full of enthusiasm and love for these notions. However, it is far from a naive text, despite what we might think, given the author's age (just 15 years old). The proof of this is the indirect means, *sub-contrario*, by which Hegel praises the freedom of the Roman Republic. Indeed, instead of glorifying its defenders directly—especially Brutus, as was customary at the time—Hegel depicts the ideas and projects of the enemies of *Libertas*, describing them in such negative tones that the reader's sympathy for the Republican ideas that they intend to destroy is instantaneous. Octavian's doubts about Mark Antony's plans to re-establish absolute power after Caesar's assassination serve in fact to clarify, indirectly, that the Republican regime was marked by a freedom that the Romans would not easily renounce (cf. Hegel 1989: 37). As the future Augustus gives voice to another doubt, expressing the general feeling of the people of Rome rather than his own opinion, he is forced to recognise the great moral stature of his adversaries, the murderers of Caesar: "but a Brutus, or a Cassius, are well above the Plebeian sphere" (Hegel 1989: 37). This passage allows Hegel to praise, this time directly, the heroes of Republican *libertas*.

In contrast, the future members of the triumvirate—and, in particular, Mark Antony—are depicted in the text as usurpers of power. Indeed, they show aristocratic contempt towards the people, believing that they can corrupt them with the classic formula of *panem et circenses*: just as the soldier is on the side of the triumvirate, "the same will happen, in the case of the low plebe, with a few words, some wheat and public spectacles" (Hegel 1989: 38). The members of the triumvirate lack the fundamental *virtus* of *loyalty*. Even as they are joining forces to overthrow the Republican regime, each man is secretly planning to eliminate the others to seize power solely for himself. Firstly, Mark Antony tells Octavian of his intention to rid himself of Lepidus as soon as they seize power: "Should we allow this sterile head (*unfruchtbaren Kopf*) to one day participate in world domination?" (Hegel 1989: 38). Faced with this suggestion, Octavian is reluctant, declaring his respect for Lepidus as a soldier. Do we find here a

---

[3] For a study of the influence of Latin classics on Hegel's education, cf. Rocco 2011: 11–117.

relative salvation of the future *princeps*, perhaps an implicit admiration felt by Hegel for this majestic character, despite his liberticidal actions? Although there have been strong interpretations[4] in this regard, there may be another way to read the text, and in particular its conclusion.

In fact, Hegel, the adolescent student, knows very well which forms of behaviour he should attack, and at the end of the text, Octavian is represented as equally despicable as the other two. In fact, in an intense and dramatic inner monologue, the future Augustus shows that his defence of Lepidus was not sincere, but rather was uttered so that Mark Antony would trust him and not suspect him when the time came for him to seize absolute power:

My neck has known no master and is not accustomed to drawing beneath the shelter of an arrogant dominator. I will let him [Antony] romp in his lechery and wait patiently on the side-lines. When his physical and emotional strength slumbers, when he is unprepared, only then will I raise my forehead, let him see my own greatness, and then ... *aut Caesar, aut nihil*. Either he must be prostrate before me in the dust, or I will choose death over an ignominious life. (Hegel 1989: 39)

The typically republican language of non-submission to slavery is here perverted by the future Augustus: his neck has never bowed down before a master (certainly by virtue of his aristocracy, but also because of the prevailing freedoms in the Republic) and he will not kowtow to Anthony's aspirations for absolute domination. However, the purpose of this opposition is not the preservation of the *libera respublica Romanorum*, but the dream of becoming *princeps* himself, or die trying, which is summed up in a phrase possibly taken from Herder[5]: "Either Caesar, or nothing". The conspiracy between the three is revealed to be devoid of ideological foundation and political legitimacy, and is represented as a struggle for personal power, in which the main victim is the freedom of a Republic deeply admired by the young Hegel.

Having briefly summarised the content of the text, one may wonder about the influences that inspired it, in addition to the most obvious and widely studied ones, such as the Roman historiographic sources and Shakespeare's *Julius*

---

[4] This is how the *Unterredung* has been interpreted by H. S. Harris: "Octavius [...] is clearly Hegel's hero" (Harris 1972: 31). Harris takes to be sincere the defences of Lepidus and Cicero put forward by the future Emperor and considers that expressions of non-subjection to slavery are a sign of "idealization of Republican freedom".

[5] This is the opinion of the editors of volume 1 of *Gesammelte Werke*, identifying these words with a slogan by Cesare Borgia, recorded by Herder as "aut Caesar aut nihil, aut nuncuam aut!" in his *Ueber die Seelewandrung. Drittes Gespräch* (cf. Hegel 1989: 548–549).

Caesar.[6] In addition to these, we find a work apparently removed from the Roman theme: Schiller's drama *Fiesco* (1783) set in Genoa under the rule of the Doria family.[7] This work was read and analysed by Hegel at the *Gymnasium* for a somewhat trivial reason, which probably has nothing to do with its theme or the fact that the subtitle is "A Republican Drama" (Schiller 2015: 1; NA 4: 5).

Indeed, there is the interesting case that *Fiesco* was dedicated to one of Hegel's teachers, Jacob Friedrich Abel.[8] Schiller had studied his bachelor's degree in Stuttgart, where Abel was his favourite teacher and Schiller was in turn Abel's favourite student. This may have played a part in the fact that Hegel "worked closely" (cf. Ripalda 1978: 136 *in note*) on a play by Schiller that had little resonance elsewhere. Abel, who would be Hegel's teacher again in Tubinga, had maintained a fairly close relationship with him since Stuttgart.[9]

As to when Hegel actually read *Fiesco*, there may be some doubts that it is appropriate to dispel or at least try to rebut beforehand. According to Rosenkranz, in 1786 Hegel wrote a "fragment attempting an analysis of the republican drama *Fiesco*" (Rosenkranz 1977: 13). On the basis of this testimony (the only one remaining on his reading of this work) it might appear that, if Hegel drafted this text—unfortunately now lost—in that year, 1786, he might not have known it a year earlier, in May 1785, when *Unterredung* was written. This is not necessarily the case, however, because the fact that Rosenkranz refers to an "attempt at analysis" indicates, first of all, that it might not be a mere *Exzerpt* such as the ones Hegel wrote whilst he was reading other works, but a more reflective and more difficult composition, which might, secondly, explain why it remained an "attempt". Such an analysis would probably require prior knowledge of the work, so it does not seem unlikely that at

---

[6] "The ideal of the great 'narrator, poet, creator' was, for the *Sturm und Drang* generation, Shakespeare. [...] He was absolutely the ideal of a Promethean genius, upon whom they bestowed divine attributes. [...] Along with Lenz's ideas about the theatre, which were so far ahead of his time, Goethe's open letter 'On Shakespeare's Day' (1771) and Herder's composition 'Shakespeare' are the most revealing documents of the reverence felt towards Shakespeare that characterised the protagonists of *Sturm und Drang*. The colossal stature of Shakespeare's genius was his ideal and the assurance that his ambitious dreams could be realised" (Ruhle 1997: 41). Given this view of the author of *Julius Caesar* at the time of Hegel's education, the praise he often expresses towards him as an educator of the English people is not surprising. Cf., for example, a text from *The positivity of the Christian religion*: "The characters in Shakespeare's works, on account of their veracity, made a deep impression on the English people and formed a world of fantastic images, apart from the fact that many of those characters are known from history. As a result, the people, when seeing exhibitions of academic paintings, fully understand and enjoy the Shakespearean Gallery, in which the best artists compete" (Hegel 1978: 145).

[7] For an excellent interpretation of this work cf. Graham 1974: 9–44.

[8] On the figure of Abel, who first taught at the Karlsschule in Stuttgart and later at the *Stift* in Turbinga, as a fundamental mediator in the enlightened ideas of the young Schiller, cf. Macor 2010: passim, and especially pp. 31–36.

[9] Hegel himself, in a *Journal* entry dated 14 July 1785, expresses the great admiration he felt for Abel, since he considered it an honour and a privilege even to walk alongside him (Cf. Hegel 1974: 15).

the time of writing the *Unterredung* Hegel would have worked "closely" (as Ripalda argues) on *Fiesco*. In any case, even if we do not admit that Hegel might have read the work in 1785, we must acknowledge that Abel possibly spoke to him during his visits to the *Gymnasium Illustre*, in private conversations such as the one that took place on 14th July 1785, which Hegel recorded in his *Journal*. Indeed, as stated before, it was probably at the suggestion of this professor that Hegel became aware of Schiller's drama, described by Villacañas as "a sparkling mirror of republican heroism in the fire of theatre" (Villacañas 1993: 229).

Hence, having clarified the reasons for and circumstances surrounding his reading of this work, we might ask ourselves in what sense did the story about the Count of Lavagna, set in the sixteenth century, influence Hegel's writing about the murky episodes in the transition from the Republic to the Principality.

Firstly, the similarity of the theme, that is, the conspiracy of a group of Republicans to overthrow the Doria family, bears an influence. However, Schiller's text is politically ambiguous: the tyrants (Andrea and Gianettino) are surrounded by a heroic aura which the conspirators lack, presented instead as evil, in the case of Sacco and Calcagno, or proud, as is the case with Fiesco himself: "A romantic prefers a great and noble (in both senses of the word) soul to the people, unable to live more than representatively and as a slave" (Ripalda 1978: 137 *in note*).

The second and most important connection that this play has with Hegel's *Unterredung* are the continuing references to Rome, right from Sallust's quotation about Catilina that opens the *Vorrede*: "*nam id facinus in primis ego memorabile exsistimo sceleri atque periculi novitate*" (NA 4: 5).[10] The republican jargon of the Renaissance conspirators is the same as in the works of Roman writers, philosophers, and politicians. This fact is very important if we recall that, according to many scholars, the references of French revolutionaries to ancient Rome were due to the fact that they knew virtually no other example of republican political rhetoric and terminology (cf. Highet 1957: 393). Schiller, commenting on a sixteenth-century conspiracy, has the same problem, so he constantly draws on clichés from Latin literature. In the words of Ripalda:

Schiller's *Fiesco*, despite his political indecision, and in part also because of it, becomes embroiled in tirades full of "republic" and "republicans", "tyranny" and "tyrants", "freedom" and "virtue". The ideal model in which all this enthusiastic vocabulary is measured is pre-imperial Rome, authentic and "virtuous". The *ex ergo* is a quote from Sallust about Catilina. Virginia and Appius Claudius, Octavian, Brutus and Portia all conspire at decisive moments. (Ripalda 1978: 137)

Therefore, mainly for this reason, Schiller's *Fiesco* must be seen as a component of the influences that shaped young Hegel when he was writing the *Unterredung*, and an example of that cultural environment which, in Germany,

---

[10] "I consider this crime firstly because of the singularity of evil and danger".

before the outbreak of Revolution, already presented aspirations for profound change through the allusion to Roman history.

Marcela Vélez studied the importance and endurance of *Romanitas* throughout Schiller's political and philosophical evolution, highlighting the Roman elements present in *Fiesco*.[11] In the second part of this contribution, I would like to focus on one of these elements, that is, a concrete example that runs through European intellectual history and is a recurring element in cases of revolutionary political ideology: sexual violence against women as a metaphor for the violation of freedom.

In *Fiesco*, Gianettino Doria, Genoa's tyrannical ruler, is responsible for a double violation, which sparks indignation and rebellion among the people. Firstly, a political violation, a prevarication in Lomellino's election as an attorney, and secondly, the rape of a woman, Berta, who contemplates committing suicide following her assault and the curse levelled at her by her own father. As we will see below, this episode is incomprehensible without references to the Roman historical examples of Virginia and Lucretia: the link between the three events is masterfully expressed by Schiller in the words spoken by Verrina, Berta's father: "One who puts Genoa under the yoke can surely also force a girl?" (Schiller 2015: 28; NA 4, 33). In the dialogue between father and daughter, when she reveals that she has been raped by a masked man wearing a green cloak, whom Verrina immediately recognises to be Gianettino, references to the historical account of Virginia are more than evident. The Genoese noble takes his sword and sets upon his daughter, in a clear imitation of Virginius's desperate gesture when he kills his daughter to free her from disgrace at the hands of Appius Claudius, the powerful Decemvir:

VERRINA *(after a pause, laughing bitterly)*. Quite so, quite so. You milksop, Verrina.—The little villain lays hand on the sanctuary of the law—that was too feeble a transgression for you.—He had to reach into the sanctuary of your bloodlines— *(Leaps up)*. Quick! Call Nicolo—Lead and powder!—But wait! I've thought of something different—better—Fetch me my sword, say an Our Father. *(His hand on his forehead)*. But what am I doing?
BERTA. I'm frightened, Father.
VERRINA. Come. Sit down beside me. *(With meaning)*. Tell me, Berta—Berta, what did that old Roman do, grey like ice, when they also found his daughter—how should I put it—also found his daughter so attractive? Tell me, Berta: What did Virginius say to his mutilated daughter?
BERTA *(shuddering)*. I don't know what he said.
VERRINA. You silly thing—He didn't say a word. *(Stands up suddenly, seizes a sword)*. He reached for a slaughtering knife.
BERTA *(frightened, rushing into his arms)*. Dear God! What are you about to do?
VERRINA *(casts the sword aside)*. No! There's yet justice in Genoa! (Schiller 2015: 25–26; NA 4, 31–32)

[11] Cf. Vélez 2017.

In scene VIII of Act V, in Berta's subsequent disconsolate reflections, alone and waiting for the result of the conspiracy against the tyrant, we see the ghost of Lucretia, who committed suicide, unable to live with the dishonour brought upon her after she was raped by Sextus Tarquinius.

References to the tales of Virginia and Lucretia would not be merely anecdotal in *Fiesco*; they would not be just another example of the work, if we follow Villacañas' interpretation, according to which "Fiesco can be both the great private and public man, only because love within the piece is governed through the institution of marriage" (Villacañas 1993: 233). Republicanism is not merely a public matter; it is born of a complex dialectic between the emotions and the realm of political action:

Fiesco never knows whether he is fighting for the Republic or for the sake of his vanity [...]. But the result is the same: the private man and the public man demand mutual destruction or common salvation. Love or ambition for glory—what is the difference?—must die within the revolutionary. But what then will become of political action, stripped of life and soul? How will it emerge, without a generous passion at its foundation? If those powerful affections die, either the revolution will not succeed due to a lack of strength, or its triumph will bring forth new oppression through a lack of goodness. Schiller already knew this outcome in his early dramas. (Villacañas 1993: 226)

That is why the reference to the rape of virtuous women is so relevant in Schiller's drama: because the indignation that an event like this provokes is one of the strongest drivers of human passions, which can then be directed towards a political objective. And this, as we shall see, will be crucial in Hegel's philosophy of history. The dual public-private dimension of the Republican hero finds its trigger, which spurs him into action, in that ultimate crime, which begins as a most intimate and private matter and then erupts into public anger, into the violent action of the crowd. Indeed, Verrina himself bemoans that fate should have used his daughter's rape to spark a political coup to overthrow Gianettino: "If I understand your sign correctly, Eternal Providence, you want to free Genoa by my Berta" (Schiller 2015: 29; NA 4, 34). He then casts a terrible curse upon his daughter, which fills those gathered there with horror, and he does so precisely to inflame the souls of his friends, so that they do not hesitate to overthrow the rapist:

Genoa's lot has been thrown in with my Berta's. I have delivered a father's heart over to my civic duty. Who among us is weakling enough to delay Genoa's deliverance, now that he knows that his cowardice will cost this innocent lamb endless sorrow?—That was no fool's blathering, by God.—I have taken an oath and shall show my child no mercy until one of the Dorias lies stretched on the ground, in his death throes, even if I have to think up new forms of torture, like a hangman, and if I have to smash this innocent lamb on a cannibal's rack.—They're trembling.—White as a ghost, they leer at me.—I repeat, Scipio: I hold her hostage to your tyrannicide. By this cherished thread I bind you, me, and all of us to our duty. Genoa's despot must fall, or the girl will despair. I shall not recant. (Schiller 2015: 30; NA 4, 35)

And finally, Borgognino, who is in love with the raped woman, clearly expresses the close links between political duty and the restitution of honour: "Berta and Genoa will be free on one and the same day" (Schiller 2015: 31; NA 4, 35).

Certainly, the connection between the psychological-moral element (horror at the sexual violence committed against an innocent girl) and the political element (with the analogy between the rape of women and violation of the homeland) was inspired by the main sources through which we know about the historical episode. Indeed, Livy had been very clear that the rape of Lucretia, experienced by herself, by her father, and by her husband fundamentally as a private matter, disconnected from the political situation of the time, was used *pro domo* by Brutus, who took advantage of the indignation of the people to spearhead the rebellion that expelled Tarquin the Proud and killed his son. Precisely in order to provoke a popular uprising, Lucretia's body is put on public display, removing her corpse from the private domain of family grief, confined to the *domus*:

They bore Lucretia's body from the house to the forum, where they drew a large crowd that was scandalized by the extraordinary turn of events, as anyone would be. Each man expressed his personal sense of outrage at the rape the prince had committed. And not just the father's grief moved them, but Brutus also, when he rebuked them for tears and useless complaints when what they should be doing as men and Romans was to take arms against those who had dared such violence. (Livy 1998: 68)

The clear distinction between the psychological-moral and political element (presented in the reactions of two different characters) continues in the speech given by Brutus, according to Livy:

He spoke of the violence and lust of Sextus Tarquin, of the unspeakable rape of Lucretia and her wretched death, of the bereavement of Lucretius Tricipitinus and the cause of his daughter's death, which for him was more unworthy and more pitiable than the death itself. He mentioned also the arrogance of the King himself and how the plebs had been forced underground to dig out trenches and sewers: the men of Rome, victorious over all their neighbours, had been turned into drudges and quarry slaves, warriors no longer. (Livy 1998: 69)

Livy himself is quite clear in stating that Brutus used the wrath of the people, caused by moral outrage, to direct it towards a political goal:

After saying these things and, I am sure, even more shocking ones prompted by his outrage of the moment, which are not easy for writers to capture on paper, he brought his listeners to such a pitch of fury that they revoked the king's power and ordered the exile of Lucius Tarquinius, together with wife and children. (Livy 1998: 69)

Livy also provided the inspiration for the connection between the rape of Lucretia and that of Virginia. When introducing the story of the latter, he points out:

A second outrage took place in the city, originating in sexual passion and ending as ignobly as that which drove the Tarquins from the city and their throne, when Lucretia was raped and died: the same fate befell the decemvirs as the kings and the same cause precipitated their fall from power. (Livy 1998: 185)

The commoner Virginia, desired by the decemvir Appius Claudius, is claimed as a slave by the latter, eager to ravish her. In this episode, a number of legal tricks were introduced, which robbed the young woman's father, Virginius, of any possible retribution. Once he understands that his daughter's fate is sealed, he kills her in the middle of the Forum, so that she is not dishonoured by the powerful magistrate, thereby giving Virginia, according to Livy, the only freedom available to her. Also in this case, the young woman's body is put on public display to cause indignation:

Icilius and Numitorius lifted up the corpse and displayed it to the people; they bewailed Appius' wickedness, the girl's fatal beauty, and the necessity that had driven her father to commit such act. [...] The men's talk, and particularly that of Icilius, centred wholly on the loss of the tribunes' power and of the right of appeal to the people, as well as on the indignity suffered by the nation at large. (Livy 1998: 189–190)

Having briefly recounted the two historical episodes of Virginia and Lucretia, we can return to late eighteenth-century Germany. Firstly, it is important to note that the sources that might have inspired Schiller—also in his *Philosophische Briefe*, published in 1786 but written over the previous years, in which he speaks of the "lechery of Tarquinius Sextus" (NA 20, 128–129)—were not exclusively classical ones, that is, Titus Livy and Book II of Cicero's Republic.[12] Nor did he draw solely from the patent influence of Shakespeare's poem *The Rape of Lucretia*, which in turn draws heavily from the same sources.[13] Indeed, there are a number of works that, in the eighteenth century, both in France and in Germany, had rescued accounts of the rape of Lucretia for mainly political purposes, which were anti-monarchical and anti-Christian, as we shall see.[14]

The anti-Christian aspect of bringing the story of Lucretia back to light can only be understood if we look back to the harsh and rather unacceptable criticism of St. Augustine. In his *De Civitate Dei*, clearly to oppose the justification of honour-driven suicide on the part of stoicism, but also to solve the social problem surrounding the growing imitation of Lucretia's action by hundreds of Roman women raped during the barbaric incursions, the Bishop of Hippo states that surely the heroine must have stabbed herself through feelings of guilt at having experienced a certain pleasure during the rape (Saint Augustine 2012: 22). This Augustinian condemnation of Lucretia was strongly attacked

---

[12] Cf. Cicero 1829: 99–100.

[13] Cf. Shakespeare 1977: 3–214.

[14] The fundamental work that explores the evolution of Lucretia's image in modern literature is by Galinsky (Galinsky 1932). For the centuries immediately preceding the Enlightenment in Germany see Schmidt 2008.

by Pierre Bayle in his *Dictionnaire historique et critique* (Bayle 1820), and re-emerged, as we will see, in the midst of the German Enlightenment, although now applied to the historic case of Virginia.[15]

However, during the Enlightenment and the revolutionary period, these Roman heroines, and especially Lucretia, were frequently praised as political icons of extreme rebellion and resistance to tyranny. Lessing himself, whose attitude, as we will see, was very ambiguous in the case of *Emilia Galotti*, wrote a tragic sketch entitled *Das befreite Rom*, with Lucretia as the main character, although unfortunately only a general outline of the work and two pages of text have been preserved (Lessing 2003: 777–779). In addition, we should also mention the famous case of the novel outline dedicated to the Roman heroine written by J. J. Rousseau, of which he speaks in *Confessions* (1.5) and of which only the first two acts have survived.[16] Equally interesting are two other dramas dedicated to Lucretia, written fifty years apart, significantly at the beginning and at the culmination of the Enlightenment. In 1740, Johan Elias Schlegel wrote his tragedy in prose, *Lucretia*, which remained unfinished.[17] It emphasised the political aspect of the historical example of Lucretia, with a series of what we might term *ante litteram* "gender" slogans and demands, such as the phrase given to Servia, the mother of the unfortunate suicide victim: "[W]eep for the chastity of all Roman women. These tyrants, who turn our men into sacrifices, who make our sex the slaves of their vices" (Schlegel 1773: 32). Furthermore, he has Brutus give an impassioned defence of regicide, in which, once again, the private theme of honour gives rise to a public-political stance:

By whom are we unhappy but by our king? If we expect his death, another monster will take his place. [...] You must not let the Tarquin reign any longer, Collatin. Thus [through my killing] thou hast turned thy shame to thy honour; thus hast thou smelt thyself; thus hast thou saved virtue!. (Schlegel 1773: 43)

This play, along the same lines, concludes with the following words, full of republicanism: "Awake, Rome, you who were born to rule! Set thyself free! Drive out thy tyrants and rule thyself!" (Schlegel 1773: 44)

Unsurprisingly, half a century later, in 1793, just shortly after the expulsion of the tyrants, in the same year as the regicide, a tragedy penned by R. Piquenard appeared, entitled *Lucrèce ou la royauté abolie*,[18] in which, once again, the people were encouraged to overthrow tyrants who were so depraved that they might rape such a chaste woman as Lucretia, just as they had subverted the laws in their own interest. Tarquin, the expelled king who allied himself with the ancient enemies of his homeland, represented a very tempting historical antecedent to justify the French monarch's treason, caught fleeing abroad and subsequently executed by guillotine.

---

[15] For a review of Bayle cf. Donaldson 1982: 58ff.
[16] Published in Dufour 1906: 218–244.
[17] Cf. Tietz 1999: 79.
[18] Cf. Tietz 1999: 83.

However, it is important to note that, just as the authors mentioned previously strongly emphasised the public, revolutionary component of the Roman heroine's actions, in another central work of the *Aufklärung*, *Emilia Galotti* by Lessing (performed in 1772), in which the historical reference is clearly Virginia (which Schiller had quoted together with Lucretia in the aforementioned passage of *Fiesco*), something different happens; in fact, all political content of the rape is deliberately omitted, restricting the story of the raped heroine to psychological drama, confined to the private sphere, similar to Shakespeare's poem about the rape of Lucretia. This was recognised by Lessing himself in a letter to Nicolai in 1758:

For he [Lessing himself] distinguished the story of the Roman Virginia from everything that made it interesting for the whole city; he believed that the fate of a daughter who is killed by her father, who values her virtue more than her life, was tragic enough in itself, and capable of shaking the whole soul, even if no overthrow of the whole state constitution followed. (Lessing 1987: 267)

Indeed, in *Emilia Galotti*, the father kills his daughter, but does not create any political scandal, and decides to submit to the prince's judicial authority. In the end, the author even casts doubt over the heroine's moral status, in a way that is strongly reminiscent of St Augustin's stance towards Lucretia. Indeed, Lessing wonders if Emilia perhaps asked her father to kill her because she feared, deep down, she might be attracted by the seductive prince.

This example of Lessing shows us that references to the rapes of Lucretia and Virginia did not necessarily encompass, in themselves, a political dimension, and indeed Manfred Tietz has emphasised the extent to which, not only in *Emilia Galotti*, but also in some works by Spanish enlightened writers such as Moratín or Feijoo, the potentially subversive and revolutionary facet was deliberately omitted.[19] It is precisely for this reason that it is even more interesting that Schiller—who, for example, cites *Emilia Galotti* in a work just two years before *Fiesco* (*Ueber das gegenwaertige teutsche Theater*)—wanted to exploit in his "republican drama" all the revolutionary potential of this and other symbolic elements from the Roman political tradition.[20] Soon these elements will bear their most tangible fruits in that "Revolutionaries must be Romans", with which Saint-Just, quoted by Marx (Marx 1956: 164) faultlessly defined one of the aspirations of the protagonists of the great *Begebenheit* of 1789.

But if we go even further in the analysis of Schiller's Fiesco, and as a hypothesis, we might understand that the examples of Lucretia, and especially of Virginia, could have inspired another fundamental passage in one of Schiller's youthful works, the end of his *Trauerspiel The Robbers*, in which Karl Moor

---

[19] Tietz 1999: 72ff.

[20] For example, another classic theme of Roman republicanism, that is, tyrannicide, is dealt with by Schiller in his 1804 *William Tell* (NA 10).

suddenly kills his beloved Amalia.[21] After deciding to abandon his fellow troublemakers to join her, and after the robbers refuse to let their captain leave, he tries to use rhetoric to soften the villains' hearts, and he resorts, as in the cases we saw in Livy, to exposing the woman's body, although in this case whilst she is still alive:

(Takes the handkerchief from Amalia's neck and discovers her bosom). Gaze on this beauteous sight! If ye be men! Felons! have ye hearts of stone?—Behold me here! I'm young—I've felt the power of love! I was beloved! betroth'd!—I had reached the gate of paradise! (Schiller 1792: 215; NA 3: 233)

But since the robbers laugh at his pleas, he understands that the only way to give her freedom, and at the same time to have Amalia all for himself, perhaps freeing her from horrific assaults by his former companions, is to stab her to death.

Now she is mine! She's mine!—Or that hereafter is but the dream of fools!—I have foil'd my destiny!—In spite of fate, I have brought home my bride:—And with this sword, have seal'd our wedding vows—Thousands of years shalt pass, and seasons roll, e'er the bright sun shall witness such a deed.—*(To Amalia with tenderness.)* Was it not sweet, my Amalia, to die thus by thy bridegroom's hand?

Amalia. (Stretching out her hand to him). Oh most sweet! *(She dies).* (Schiller 1792: 216–217; NA 3: 234)

Note that it had previously been Amalia herself who had pleaded for death at the hand of her beloved, bringing her case closer to the historical example of Lucretia, who also, according to Livy, had at first asked her relatives to kill her, due to her physical frailty. We should also note that over the body of Amalia, Karl Moor can break his oath and regain his freedom, breaking away from the group of robbers to which he had been bound. The death of the beloved woman now gives grounds for individual liberation, just as in *Fiesco* it justifies the collective liberation of a city from its ruling tyrant.

In conclusion, the example explored in the last part of this study, examining the political role played by the figures of Virginia and Lucretia in modernity, provides further proof of the relevance that the symbolic recoveries of Roman history played in the time immediately preceding the Revolution, and which was later forged in the neo-Roman essence of this event in France. As we have seen, some years before 1789, in Germany, in the early productions of Hegel and Schiller, in their enthusiasm for republicanism, for the realisation of genuine political emancipation in the face of all forms of tyranny and despotism, inspiration had already been taken from Rome. We should not forget that in the initial motto of Schiller's *The Robbers*, as well as in the personal album of young Hegel from the Gymnasium (precisely on the day Louis XVI was

---

[21] It should be noted that the passage quoted only appears in the *Trauerspiel*, whereas the *Schauspiel* version of *The Robbers* does not include it.

executed), we find a resounding Latin phrase summing up this spirit: "*In Tyrannos!*".[22]

The case of Lucretia and Virginia, analysed in their adaptations in Schiller's dramas, also allows us to highlight another important influence in Hegel: the connection between the arbitrariness of the psychological-moral element of individuals and the political (theoretically rational) level of the objective spirit is a constant throughout Hegel's philosophy of history. Indeed, from the *Unterredung* of his youth, with its vicious characterisation of the conspirators, to the *Lectures on the Philosophy of History* from his time in Berlin, human passions, with their vices and baseness, are the driving force behind the greatest historical and political changes.[23] And, interestingly, also in the Berlin Lectures, when dealing with this subject in a general and introductory way, Hegel resorts to the transition between the Roman Republic and the autarchy established by Caesar.[24]

The thread running through Roman republicanism, which is decisive in both Schiller and Hegel, as we have seen in the examples studied, allows us to shed new light not only on the works of both authors, but also on the influence of the former on the latter, in a field as relevant to their thinking as the philosophy of history, as well as for their contribution to the political transformation of their own time.

---

[22] Cf. D'Hondt 2002: 72. This phrase is important because it is found in Lipsius' commentary to the famous Virgilian verse "*discite justitiam moniti*", which Hegel himself used in his translation of the *Confidential Letters* of Cart (cf. Hegel, 2014: 402). Lipsius words are the following: "These punishments upon tirants and spoilers of the whole world, most necessarily be inflicted sometimes, that they may bee mirrors to admonish vs, *That it is the eie of iustice which behouldeth all things.* Which also may crye out to other princes and people: *Learn iustice now by this, and God above despise no more*" (Lipsius 1594: 82). It should also be noted that there is an influential Huguenot treaty, published in Basel in 1579, entitled *Vindiciae contra Tyrannos*, and which is very significantly signed under the pseudonym "Junius Brutus".

[23] Cf. Hegel 1953: 26–27: "When we contemplate this display of passions and the consequences of their violence, the unreason which is associated not only with them, but even—rather we might say specially—with good designs and righteous aims; when we see arising therefrom the evil, the vice, the ruin that has befallen the most flourishing kingdoms which the mind of man ever created, we can hardly avoid being filled with sorrow this universal taint of corruption. And since this decay is not the work of mere nature, but of human will, our reflections may well lead us to a moral sadness, a revolt of the good will (spirit)—if indeed it has a place within us. Without rhetorical exaggeration, a simple, truthful account of the miseries that have overwhelmed the noblest of nations and polities and the finest exemplars of private virtue forms a most fearful picture and excites emotions of the profoundest and most hopeless sadness, counter-balanced by no consoling result. We can endure it and strengthen ourselves against it only by thinking that this is the way it had to be—it is fate; nothing can be done".

[24] Cf. Hegel 1953: 27–28: "Caesar, without changing the form of the constitution, became the sole ruler of the state. In accomplishing his originally negative purpose—the autocracy over Rome—he at the same time fulfilled the necessary historical destiny of Rome and the world. Thus he was motivated not only by his own private interest, but acted instinctively to bring to pass that which the times required."

REFERENCES

WORKS BY FRIEDRICH SCHILLER

NA 3—Schiller, Friedrich. 1953. *Schillers Werke*, vol. 3: *Die Räuber*. Weimar: Böhlau. English edition: Schiller, Friedrich 1792. *The Robbers. A Tragedy*, trans. Lord A. Fr. T. Woodhouselee. London: G. G. J. & J. Robinson.

NA 4—Schiller, Friedrich. 1983. *Schillers Werke*, vol. 3: *Die Verschwörung des Fiesko zu Genua*. Weimar: Böhlau. English edition: Schiller, Friedrich. 2015. *Fiesco's Conspiracy at Genoa*, trans. F. Kimmich. Open Book Publishers, 2015, http://www.jstor.org/stable/j.ctt15m7n82. Accessed 16 March 2022.

FURTHER LITERATURE

Acosta, Emiliano. 2012. "Schiller y el reconocimiento del otro en su otredad". *Pensamiento*, 256: 225–247.
Acosta, López, María del Rosario. 2007. "Tragedia como libertad y teodicea. Acerca de una relación entre Schiller y Hegel". *Estudios de filosofía*, 36: 175–206.
Augustine, Saint. 2012. *The Works of Saint Augustine*, vol. I/6: *The City of God (De Civitate Dei)*. New York: New City Press
Aranzueque, Gabriel. 2011. "Historia y catástrofe. Tragedia y reconciliación en Schiller y Hegel". *Pensamiento*, 67: 5–31.
Bayle, Pierre. 1820. Lucrèce. In *Dictionnaire historique et critique*, 492. Paris: Desoer.
Böhler, Michael. 1972. "Die Bedeutung Schillers für Hegels Ästhetik". *Publications of the Modern Language Association of America*, 87.2: 182–191.
Cicero. 1829. *The Republic*. New York: Carvill.
D'Hondt, Jacques. 2002. *Hegel*. Barcelona: Tusquets.
Desmond, William. 2020. *Hegel's Antiquity*. Oxford: Oxford University Press.
Donaldson, Ian. 1982. *The rapes of Lucretia. A Myth and its Transformation*. New York: Clarendon Press.
Dufour, Théophile. 1906. "Pages inédites de Jean-Jacques Rousseau. Deuxième serie". *Annales de la Société Jean-Jacques Rousseau*, 2: 153–270.
Duque, Félix. 1997. *La estrella errante*. Madrid: Akal.
Galinsky, H. 1932. *Der Lucretia-Stoff in der Weltliteratur*. Breslau: Prietbasch.
Graham, Ilse. 1974. *Schiller's Drama: Talent and Integrity*. London: Meuthen.
Harris, Henry Silton. 1972. *Hegel's Development, I: Toward the Sunlight: 1770–1801*. Oxford: Oxford University Press.
Hegel, Georg Wilhelm Friedrich. 1953. *Reason in History*, Liberal Arts Press: New York
Hegel, Georg Wilhelm Friedrich. 1974. *Dokumente zu Hegels Entwicklung*, ed. Johannes Hoffmeister. Stuttgart: Fromman-Holzboog.
Hegel, Georg Wilhelm Friedrich. 1989. *Frühe Schriften I (Gesammelte Werke, 1)*, ed. F. Nicolin and G. Schüler. Hamburg: Felix Meiner.
Hegel, Georg Wilhelm Friedrich. 2014. *Frühe Schriften II (Gesammelte Werke, 2)*, ed. F. Nicolin, I. Rill and P. Kriegel. Hamburg: Felix Meiner.
Highet, Gilbert. 1957. *The Classical Tradition: Greek and Roman Influences on Western Literature*. New York: Oxford University Press.
Hoffheimer, Michael. 1985. "The influence of Schiller's Theory of Nature on Hegel's Philosophical Development". *Journal of the History of Ideas*, 46.2: 231–244.

Kain, Philip. 1982. *Schiller, Hegel and Marx. State, Society and the Aesthetic Ideal of the Ancient Greece*. Kingston/Montreal: McGill-Queen's University Press.
Kojève, Alexandre. 2007. "Sur deux vers de Schiller". *Revue Internationale de Philosophie*, 61: 215–230.
Lessing, Gotthold Ephraim. 1987. *Werke und Briefe*, vol. 11/1: *Briefe von und an Lessing 1743–1770*. Frankfurt am Main: Deutscher Klassiker Verlag.
Lessing, Gotthold Ephraim. 2003. *Werke und Briefe*, vol. 3: *Werke 1754–1757*. Frankfurt am Main: Deutscher Klassiker Verlag.
Livy. 1998. *The Rise of Rome. Books One to Five* (trans: Luce, T. J.). Oxford: Oxford University Press.
Macor, Laura Anna. 2010. *Der morastige Zirkel der menschlichen Bestimmung. Friedrich Schillers Weg von der Aufklärung zu Kant*. Würzburg: Königshausen & Neumann.
Marx, Karl. 1956. *The Holy Family or Critique of critical Critique*. Moscow: Foreign Languages Publishing House.
de Montaigne, Michel. 2007. *Les Essais*. Paris: Gallimard.
Pöggeler, Otto. 1973. *Hegels Idee einer Phänomenologie des Geistes*, Freiburg/München: Alber.
Pöggeler, Otto. 1981. "Schillers Antagonismus und Hegels Dialektik". In *Konzepte der Dialektik*, ed. W. Becker and W. K. Essler, 42–45. Frankfurt a. M.: Klostermann.
Ripalda, José María. 1978. *La nación dividida*. México: FCE.
Rocco, Valerio. 2011. *La vieja Roma en el joven Hegel*. Madrid: Maia.
Rocco, Valerio. 2013. "La tensión entre Romanitas y cristianismo en Rousseau y su influencia en el joven Hegel". In *El legado de Rousseau 1712–2012*, ed. J. López and A. Campillo, 223–224. Murcia: Universidad de Murcia.
Rosenkranz, Karl. 1977. *Hegels Leben*. Darmstadt: Wissenschaftliche Buchgesellschaft.
Schindler, David. 2012. *The Perfection of Freedom. Schiller, Schelling, and Hegel between the Ancients and the Moderns*. Eugene: Cascade.
Schlegel, Johann Elias. 1773. *Werke*, vol. 2. Kopenhagen und Leipzig: Proft und Rothe.
Schmidt, Claudia. 2008 *Die Figur der Lucretia in der deutschen Literatur des 16. Und 17. Jahrhunderts*. Magdeburg: Grin.
Taminiaux, Jacques. 1967. *La nostalgie de la Grèce à l'aube de l'idéalisme allemand*. Den Haag: Nijhoff.
Tietz, Manfred. 1999. La figura de Lucrecia *la romana* vista por la Ilustración alemana y española. In *La Ilustración en España y Alemania*, ed. R. Mate and F. Niewöhner, 71–93. Barcelona: Anthropos.
Vélez, Marcela. 2017. "Variaciones en el juicio de Schiller acerca de la revolución: un viaje de Roma a Grecia". *Philosophical Readings* IX.2: 13–20.
Villacañas, José Luis. 1993. *Tragedia y teodicea de la historia. El destino de los ideales en Lessing y Schiller*. Madrid: La balsa de la Medusa.

CHAPTER 35

Schiller and Marx on Alienation

Gabriel Rivero

The reception of Schiller's philosophy by left-wing thinkers in the nineteenth and twentieth centuries can be characterised by its ambiguity.[1] In the arguments of single authors one finds arguments both for and against Schiller. On the one hand, Schiller's sharp criticism of the political and social situation of his time was continually appreciated in the Marxist tradition. On the other hand, Schiller's focus on aesthetics was widely deemed idealistic and, in turn, judged as an escapist and bourgeois form of criticism. Indeed, it could plausibly be asserted that the 'idealism' of his theory was a permanent point of objection.

In the twentieth century specifically, this ambiguity can be seen manifest in the reception of Schiller by important authors in the Marxist tradition. Notably, it can be seen in the way Franz Mehring interpreted Schiller as an ideal for the working class (cf. Oellers 1976, 161), and in the way Georg Lukács' and Leo Kofler's positively appraise Schiller for his treatment of the problem of reification (cf. Lukács 2013; Kofler 1968). Nonetheless, these authors

---

[1] In his magnificent work *Schiller as Philosopher* Frederick Beiser almost exclusively highlights the critical position of Marxism on Schiller, leaving aside the positive aspects of the reception developed in this tradition (cf. Beiser 2005, VIII, 11, 12). A critique of this approach is given by Violeta Weibel in her review of Beiser's book (see Waibel 2008, 52). For a reply to this objection see Beiser 2008, 63–78, particularly 76–77. Considering this discussion, the term 'ambiguity' offers, in my opinion, the most appropriate way to characterise Schiller's reception in the Marxist tradition. For more details about Schiller's reception in the twentieth century, see Matuschek 2009, 231–239.

G. Rivero (✉)
Martin Luther University Halle-Wittenberg, Halle, Germany
e-mail: gabriel.rivero@phil.uni-halle.de

© The Author(s), under exclusive license to Springer Nature Switzerland AG 2023
A. Falduto, T. Mehigan (eds.), *The Palgrave Handbook on the Philosophy of Friedrich Schiller*, https://doi.org/10.1007/978-3-031-16798-0_35

simultaneously maintain that Schiller's idealistic tendencies signify an important limitation of his social and political criticism.

The same ambiguity is noticeable in Schiller's nineteenth-century reception; in, for instance, Arnold Ruge's and Theodor Echtermeyer's *Der Protestantimus und die Romantik* (1839), in which they compare Schiller and Goethe. Somewhat reprovingly, they argue that Goethe is exclusively oriented towards the subjectivity of beauty and morality. In a manner of approval, they argue that Schiller understands the aesthetic as a means of transforming reality—that is, the union of nature and spirit, and freedom and necessity—thereby orientating him towards the objectivity of aesthetics. However, despite this appraisal, Ruge and Echtermeyer maintain that Schiller's philosophy ultimately remains merely an ideal (cf. Oellers 1970, 362–367).

In Marx's and Engels' *Oeuvre*, allusions and references to Schiller are not rare. The same ambiguity mentioned above can also be observed in their work. The young Engels refers to Schiller with great enthusiasm. In his letter to Wilhelm Graeber on 30 July 1839, he describes Schiller superlatively as the 'greatest liberal poet' and the precursor of a new epoch following the French Revolution (cf. Marx/Engels 2010b, 468). Years later, however, this adulation changes dramatically. In his critique of Karl Grün's book on Goethe, Engels reprovingly suggests that Schiller's work, unlike Goethe, took an idealistic and escapist turn.[2]

With regard to Marx, there are some important biographical considerations that, prima facie, signify notable indications of Schiller's importance for the development of his philosophical system. The first is related to Marx's education in secondary school (*Gymnasium*) in Trier. During his time their humanist education was of outstanding importance, and the presence of classical authors, like Schiller, dominated the syllabus (cf. Heinrich 2018). In the year 1835, Marx, at the age of seventeen, took his final examinations (*Abitur*), which, among other subjects, comprised the composition of three essays on three topics: Latin, religion and German. Of these three essays, the essay written in relation to German—*Reflections of a Young Man on the Choice of a Profession*—is notable for its Schillerian influence. There, Marx stresses the importance of human being's capacity for choice, which, in his view, constitutes the kernel of the human essence. The young Marx argues that, 'To man [...] the Deity gave a general aim, that of *ennobling mankind* and himself' (Marx/Engels 2010a, 3; *my emphasis*); and, in contrast to animals—whose sphere of activity is exclusively determined by nature—the means of achieving this finality is left to free human choice (the self-determination of human being). Moreover, Marx attempts to show how choice of profession and self-determination are necessary conditions for the achievement of perfection and human dignity: '[W]orth

---

[2] Marx/Engels (2010d, 259): 'Goethe was too universal, too active a nature, too much a man of flesh and blood to seek refuge from this wretchedness in a Schillerian flight to the Kantian ideal; he was too keen-sighted not to see how ultimately such a flight amounted to no more than the exchange of a prosaic form of wretchedness for a grandiloquent one.'

can be assured only by a profession in which we are not servile tools, but in which we act independently in our own sphere' (Marx/Engels 2010a, 7). The various references to the concepts of ennoblement (*Veredlung*) and self-improvement/perfection (*Vervollkommung/Vollendung*) have been considered confirmation of Schiller's presence in Marx's early thought and, in particular, as the early developmental stages of his theory of alienation (cf. van Herpen 1983). As a second and supplementary relevant biographical aspect, the young Marx's intellectual relationship with his father may also be considered important, in so far as Heinrich Marx was an admirer of Schiller's work and mentioned him in a letter to Marx as an ideal worthy of emulation (cf. also van Herpen 1983, 341).

However, harsh criticism of Schiller by Marx can be found in his later years. A clear example of this are Marx's comments on Ferdinand Lassalle's drama *Franz von Sickingen*. In a letter from April 1859, he highlights the manifest influence of Schiller as a negative dimension of the drama. Marx contrasts Shakespeare's style with that of Schiller, associating the idealistic, subjective and bourgeois tendencies in Lassalle's book with the latter. He wrote:

> Then you would automatically have had to 'Shakespearise' more, whereas your principal failing is, to my mind, 'Schillering', i.e., using individuals as mere mouthpieces for the spirit of the times. Have not you yourself—like your Franz von Sickingen—succumbed, to some extent, to the diplomatic error of regarding the Lutheran-knightly opposition as superior to the plebeian-Münzerian? (Marx/Engels 2010e, 420)[3]

Despite this negative assessment, implicit references to Schiller are found in Marx's later and principal work, *Capital*, as is rightly indicated by Thomas Kuczynski in his edition of the first volume (cf. Marx 2017, 107, 140, 337, 357, 509, 526). Additionally, van Herpen interprets some passages of the third volume of *Capital* in terms of their similarity to Schiller's ideas about human nature and production (cf. van Herpen 1983, 342). These facts clearly suggest that despite Marx's criticisms, the presence of Schiller's work was a continuum in his thought.

Let us, then, next inquire: Which philosophical aspects of Schiller's theory may have influenced Marx and his critical social theory? It does not seem possible to find passages in Marx's *Oeuvre* in which he explicitly discusses Schiller's works in detail, which is the case, for instance, in Marx's explicit discussions of authors such as Epikur, Aristotle, Hegel or Feuerbach, and others. Nonetheless, there are thematic congruencies with respect to the problem of alienation (*Entfremdung*) from which Schiller's influence on Marx can be reconstructed.

Looking back, the term alienation was already alive in Schiller's time. First, in an economic sense, where the meaning denoted the mercantile transaction

---

[3] Continuing with his critique, Marx writes in this letter: 'To come down to details, I would censure the sometimes excessive preoccupation of individuals with themselves—the result of your predilection for Schiller'. Ibid.

of objects between persons. The German term '*Entfremdung*' can be understood as the translation of this economic concept of alienation, as Zedler's dictionary seems to affirm in its entry '*Alienare*': Zedler defined this term using the German verbs '*veräussern*', '*entfremden*', '*verkaufen*', and exclusively referred it to the exchange of property of a thing (cf. Zedler 1731–1754, 1211). In this sense, for example, Kant expresses the impossibility of a person being alienable, since a person or personality should not be treated as a thing.[4] Second, in a politico-legal sense, where alienation was considered the transfer of the unlimited natural freedom of the subject for the sake of an institution (the state), which limited and guaranteed legal freedom by means of public law (cf. Lukács 1973, 826–828).

It was Hegel's philosophy that gave the term a new and broader meaning. Instead of limiting alienation to particular spheres, such as the economic or politico-legal, Hegel put the concept at the centre of his *philosophical* system. For this reason, with regard to the Marxian origins of the term alienation, most scholars have deemed Hegel the starting point of the Marxian evolution (cf. Sayers 2013). Not only does the centrality of alienation in the *Phenomenology of Spirit* seem to justify this assumption, Marx's detailed critique of Hegel in his *Philosophical Economic Manuscripts* (1844) seems to provide further support for the correctness of that interpretation. However, other scholars assess Schiller's influence on Marx as a decisive factor (cf., for instance Kofler 1964, 24; Herpen 1983; Henning 2015, 62–71; Habermas 2019, 59–64).

The common approach to the problem of alienation seems to address the question solely from an anthropological and subjective perspective. This anthropological approach usually focuses on two fundamental aspects of alienation: the one-sided development of the faculties of human being, and the negative effects of the modern specialisation of labour. I will focus on alienation not so much from an anthropological perspective, but rather from a political and juridical perspective. From this perspective, I claim that Schiller's account of alienation can be better understood in the specific context of a politico-juridical debate about the relation between the right of mankind (*Recht der Menschheit*) and state (*Staat*), which emerged in Germany at the end of the eighteenth century, following the French Revolution.

With the French Revolution, the question of the relationship between the natural liberty of human being and the state is placed at the core of the political discussion: Should the civil laws of a state be based on the natural freedom? What is the relationship between the concepts of human being and citizen? What this debate ultimately focuses upon is the relationship between private individuals and the political state, that is, the relationship between private and political human being. Thereafter, a discussion about the relationship between individual and species-being, individual man and society, mankind and citizenship, and the particular and the universal occurs. I endeavour to understand Schiller's conception of alienation in continuity with these political debates

---

[4] See Refl. 7884, Ak 19: 545: 'Personalitas non est alienabilis'.

emerging from the French Revolution.[5] More specifically, to understand Schiller's concept of alienation, I will home in on the split between the individual and its species-being. This reconstruction does not primarily refer to the dichotomy of human faculties (drives), but mainly to a disjunction between individual human being and citizen.

If we look at Marx's early writings, it transpires that he describes the problem of alienation in similar terms to the aforementioned. In particular, the writings *Contribution to the Critique of Hegel's Philosophy of Law* and *On the Jewish Question* state the problem of alienation in Schillerian terms: as a conflict between particular and universal spheres, that is, private human being (individual) and political human being (species-being, state). In these writings, it is seen how Marx comprehends the modern political state as a sphere of social life, in which human life appears as an abstract division between the *bourgeois* (private human being) and the *citoyen* (political human being). Based on this concordance in the terms used to formulate the problem of alienation, I claim that the influence of Schiller on Marx can be affirmed, particularly in relation to the work *On the Aesthetic Education of Man in a Series of Letters* (1795).

In asserting this influence, I intend to provide an interpretation of Schiller's concept of alienation, focusing on the following three specific aspects. First, a *historical* aspect: Schiller's conception of alienation has to be interpreted in historical continuity with problems that arose in connection with the reception of the French Revolution towards the end of the eighteenth century in Germany. Second, a *systematical* aspect: accordingly, Schiller's *Letters* must be placed in the intellectual context of the German Enlightenment and are to be considered as an 'essentially political work'.[6] The fundamental aim of Schiller's work is the realisation of individual and political freedom by means of a criticism of the division between individual and political human being. Lastly, *the historical reception*: following the two already mentioned aspects, it can be seen that the same fundamental formulation of the problem of alienation is noticeable in the young Marx up until the year 1843.

Schiller on Alienation

Mankind and State: Conservative and Radical Positions

In the light of events in France, one of the most discussed topics in the German milieu of the late eighteenth century was the relevance of natural freedom and a rational right of mankind in the formation of a state. In this regard, two main groups can be distinguished in German political philosophy at that time: conservatives and radicals. The conservatives denied any relevance of natural

---

[5] Beiser refers to the political context in Germany and claims also that the main aim of the *Letters* is related to the German discussion between conservatives and radicals. Cf. Beiser (2005, 129–134).

[6] Cf. Beiser (2005, 120): 'the *Briefe* is an essentially political work'. See also ibid.: 123–134. See also Stiening (2019, 49–62).

freedom and the right of mankind for the specific historical formation of the state. They argued that freedom, understood as an a priori rational principle, can by no means prove its real effectiveness for the development of civil laws. Rather, it is the empirical development of societies that conditions the content of law. Therefore, the rational concept of mankind has no significance for the concept of citizen. On the contrary, the radicals affirmed the unavoidable importance of the concept of mankind and its rational right as the fundamental concept of citizen and political institutions. They claimed that the moral and rational faculty of man is given before any political and social formation, and so, freedom has to be understood as a rational and natural capacity of man, which establishes the basis for a state and its laws in accordance with human nature.

In this regard, a series of articles were published at the beginning of the 1790s in the *Berlinesche Monatsschrift* in which the role of the concept of mankind for the formation of the civil law and the state was keenly discussed. From a conservative point of view, Justus Möser, for instance, argued in his article *Ueber das Recht der Menschheit, als den Grund der neuen Französischen Konstitution* in June 1790 that the formation of a state is similar to the formation of a cooperation or association, in which property (not natural freedom) defines the membership of such an association. According to this account, it is not the abstract idea of an individual right of human being, but rather a contract based on relations of property that defines the state (cf. Möser 1790, here 499–500). In a similar way, Johann Erich Biester stated in an article of August 1790 the following:

> The right of mankind (*Recht der Menschheit*) and civil constitution (*bürgerliche Verfassung*) have [...] nothing at all to do with each other. The latter is based on contracts, institutions, laws, and is intended primarily to secure property, of which all the sheer mankind (*bloße Menschheit*) knows nothing. (Biester 1790, 211)

The radicals evidently pursue the opposite claim. This can be seen, for example, in Karl von Clauer's article *Noch ein Beitrag über das Recht der Menschheit* from November 1790. In reply to Biester, he defines human being as a moral being endowed with reason, through which he is capable of action. The right of mankind is, according to this definition, the ethical condition of human being, through which it has rights and obligations independent of all social and political agreements and contracts (cf. Clauer 1790, 443). From this idea, he drew the conclusion: '*The human being was earlier than the citizen*; and the civil laws must be directed absolutely according to the human being and his innate moral condition' (Clauer 1790, 452, *my emphasis*).

A series of famous translations and books were also devoted to this issue, for instance: Gentz's German translation of Edmund Burke's *Reflections on the Revolution*, the translation of Thomas Paine's *Right of Man*, as well as the controversy between August Wilhelm Rehberg and Johann Gottlieb Fichte about the right to revolution. Like Möser and Biester, Rehberg claims in his work

Untersuchungen über die französische Revolution (1793) that the idea of mankind has no relevance for the formation of the legal state (cf. Rehberg 1793, 44). The definition of the concept of citizen is thus independent of the concept of human being (*Mensch*). Furthermore, Fichte gives a direct answer to Rehberg in his writing *Beiträge zur Berichtigung der Urtheile des Publicums über die französische Revolution*. In clear contrast to Rehberg, Fichte asserts the following: 'If I am to be able to enter into a contract at all, I must enter into it as a human being. As a citizen I cannot' (Fichte 1971/[1]1793, 135). Again, the relationship between the rational concept of individual human being and the political citizen is at the centre of the discussion.

But how does this debate relate to Schiller's *Letters* and the topic of alienation? The *Letters* themselves can be interpreted as Schiller's reaction and reply to the discussion between conservatives and radicals. Most specifically, when he deals with the problem of the state as the question of the objective representation of human being. It is precisely in the formulation of this problem, as will be seen below, that Schiller develops notions that bear a significant relationship to the concept of alienation.

Schiller's Letters as a Political Work: A New Approach to the Problem of Alienation?

Concerning the concept of alienation, it is wise to first refer to its treatment in Schiller's 6th *Letter*, wherein he offers a critical consideration of social and cultural life (cf. Matuschek 2009, 164–165). Several of the most crucial aspects for understanding alienation are presented in this letter in all clarity, and it is precisely here that Schiller exposes—amongst other topics—the mechanisation of life and the fragmentation of human capacities at the hands of labour specialisation (cf. NA 20:321–328, AE:32–43). That said, taking this letter in isolation, it may be suggested that Schiller's approach is somewhat unoriginal. For example, Adam Ferguson had already pointed out many of the negative aspects of the division of labour in the development of society. Therefore, it seems necessary to take a step back in order to comprehend the originality and particularity of Schiller's account. In my view, the innovative character of his theory becomes salient when the 3rd and 4th *Letters* are taken into account. In so doing the relationship between the *Letters* and the intricacies of the political discussion between conservatives and radicals will also become increasingly clear.

Whilst in the 1st *Letter* Schiller expounds the problem of the aesthetic and the arts, the 2nd *Letter* critically raises the question of the political and social situation determined by the French Revolution. The 3rd *Letter* presents the dualism between the state of nature/state of need (*Naturstaat/Notstaat*) and the state of reason/state of freedom (*Vernunftstaat/Staat der Freiheit*). In this way, the first three *Letters* reveal the connection between aesthetics, political circumstance and forms of state. On this basis it is seen that Schiller was primarily concerned with the following two problems: firstly, to find a form of state in which *freedom* is real (i.e. the realisation of the state of freedom), and secondly, to establish the *conditions for the transition* from state of nature to state of freedom—avoiding an anarchic breakdown along the way (cf. Stiening 2019, 57–58.).

For Schiller, the French Revolution had made clear that the question of a legitimate juridical order (state) should not be reduced to an empirical issue (i.e. to the right of the strongest). Rather, the Revolution showed that the state is an issue of reason and rational legislation: 'A question which was formerly answered only by the blind right of the stronger is now, it appears, being brought before the tribunal of pure reason[.]' (NA 20:312). In terms of the dispute between conservatives and radicals, it can now be appreciated that Schiller takes the radical side in so far as he champions the significance of pure reason and, consequently, the right of mankind as a necessary idea for the formation of a state of freedom. In this regard, he affirms the following:

> *Every individual human being* [*Mensch*], one may say, carries within him, potentially and prescriptively, an ideal man, the archetype of a human being [*reinen idealistischen Mensch*], and it is his life's task to be, through all his changing manifestations, in harmony with the unchanging unity of this ideal. (NA 20:316, AE:18; *my emphasis*)

As is apparent, Schiller considers the 'great task' of human life to consist in the achievement of a unity of the pure human being (the objective and universal form) with the empirical human being (the temporal and subjective form). At this point, it becomes clear why the question concerning the form of state assumes an essential role in rendering this unified idea of the human being possible and real:

> This *archetype* [*Dieser reine Mensch*], which is to be discerned more or less clearly in every individual, is *represented by the State*, the objective and, as it were, canonical form in which all the diversity of individual subjects strive to unite. (NA 20:316, AE:18–19; *my emphasis*)

From this basis, the question of which way the pure human being can be represented by the state arises. Schiller sees two ways of achieving this objective unity:

> One can, however, imagine two different ways in which *man existing in time* can coincide with *man as Idea*, and, in consequence, just as many ways in which the State can assert itself in individuals: either by the ideal man suppressing empirical man, and the State annulling individuals; or else by *the individual himself becoming the State*, and man in time being ennobled to the stature of man as Idea. (NA 20:316, AE:19; *my emphasis*)

Beginning with the division between objective and subjective spheres and the necessity of accomplishing a unity between them for the realisation of freedom, it becomes apparent with the consideration of this latter quotation that Schiller was also *critical* of the radical position. Regarding the first way of unity, he affirms that the enlightened understanding of the state represented by the French Revolution became merely an abstract and ideal statement, with no relevance to (any) particular individuals. In this regard, in his *Augustenburger Brief* of July 1793, Schiller mentioned explicitly the right of mankind (*'seine heiligen Menschenrechte'*)[7] and judged it upon its abstract and one-sided understanding in the French Revolution as one of the causes of the disastrous situation that ensued.

It could be said that the mere *abstract unity of reason* can only be obtained by means of the suppression of the real and temporal sphere; this means that the objective state suppresses individuals and the *variety of nature*. Accordingly, the *nature of human being* (the particular human being, the variety) and the *reason of human being* (the universal, political human being, the unity) emerge as antagonistic entities. One could then affirm that this abstract form of the state—based only on an ideal right of mankind—is a form in which *bourgeois* and *citoyen* appear as two separated realities.[8] It is exactly this divisiveness that alienation consists in.

By means of this one-sidedness and abstractness, Schiller identifies two kinds of alienated characters: the savage or the uncultivated human being, whose principle of action lies merely in nature; and the barbarian or the human being of Enlightenment, who acts according to reason alone, without any relation to his nature (cf. NA 20: 318; AE:21). The savage cannot be free because nature determines him and his action. The barbarian is also unfree but, unlike the savage, his situation is even more despicable: 'the barbarian derides and dishonours Nature, but, more contemptible than the savage, as often as not continues to be the slave of his slave' (NA 20:318, AE:21). The mere objective, namely the mere moral, unity of reason leads to self-alienation, in which not the state of freedom, but the 'moral state of nature' (*moralischer Naturstand*) is realised.

In Schiller's view, the overcoming of these two breeds of alienated human being, in which nature and reason appear divided, is possible through the formation of the '*whole character of man*' (cf. NA 20:318, AE:23). Though he does not proffer a mere psychological and individualistic solution to this division by focusing only on the question of the natural and rational faculties; rather, in the 5th *Letter*, he also sets forth a socially oriented understanding of the problem through a discussion of economic situation and social class. The lower class acts in accordance with the drives of nature and in so doing breaks from society, and the civilised class—in only cultivating an observance of abstract morality—also arrive at a form of unsociability. Due to the 'mere

---

[7] Cf. Schiller (2010, 137).

[8] Cf. NA 20:318, AE:21: 'If [...] in the character of a whole people the subjective man sets his face against objective man with such vehemence of contradiction that the victory of the latter can only be ensured by the suppression of the former, then the State too will have to adopt towards its citizens the solemn rigour of the law, and ruthlessly trample underfoot such powerfully seditious individualism in order not to fall a victim of it'.

nature' (*bloße Natur*) and 'brutalisation' (*Rohigkeit*) represented by the first class, as well as the 'perverseness' (*Verkehrtheit*) and 'unnaturalness' (*Unnatur*) existent in the civilised class, the organic and species-being oriented and free life relapses into a system of egoism, antagonism and fragmentation (cf. NA 20:319–320, AE: 26–29).

Reconsidering the broader historical context of the discussion, the specific question about alienation in the 6th *Letter* can be considered a consequence of standpoints that were raised in the 3rd, 4th and 5th *Letters*. Beginning with a comparison between the idea of humanity in Modernity with that of ancient Greece, Schiller characterises modern life, in the 6th *Letter*, as a dispersion of individuals without relation to their species-being.[9] The human being in Greek culture is the 'whole man', while the human being of Modernity is nothing more than an isolated fragment. The impossibility of experiencing the full character of human being leads—in social terms—to the mechanisation of life:

> Everlastingly chained to a single little fragment of the Whole, man himself develops into nothing but a fragment; everlastingly in his ear the monotonous sound of the wheel that he turns, he never develops the harmony upon his own nature, he becomes nothing more than the imprint of his occupation or of his specialized knowledge. (NA 20:323, AE:35)

In political terms, the same impossibility leads to an opposition between individuals and the state. Schiller wrote, in this regard:

> Thus, little by little the concrete life of the Individuals is destroyed in order that the abstract idea of the Whole may drag out its sorry existence, and the *State remains for ever a stranger to its citizens* since at no point does it ever make contact with their feeling. (NA 20:324, AE:37; *my emphasis*)

Here it can be seen quite clearly how Schiller ascertains, in terms of alienation, the division between the state and the individual human being. It can also be noticed how he, despite his affirmative position on the pure idea of human being, differs from modern theories of the social contract and, too, from the standpoint of the radicals. The social contract theory assumes the idea of natural freedom and supports the necessity of limiting it through the objective institution of state; that is, it supports the idea of a restriction on subjectivity by the objective sphere. Schiller, by contrast, does not assume the idea of a natural state (*status naturalis*) which must be limited by a social or legal state (*status civilis*). Since this modern division seems to be foreign to his thought, Schiller assumes the pre-modern conception of a pre-established harmony between subjective and objective right (cf. Bach 2019, 65, 76), by means of

---

[9] NA 20: 322, AE:33: 'How different with us Moderns! With us too the image of the human species is projected in magnified form into separate individuals—but as fragments, not in different combinations, with the result that one has to go the rounds from one individual to another in order to be able to piece together a complete image of species.'

which the human being *as a whole* will be realised. 'Men have awoken from their long lethargy and self-deception, and by an impressive majority they are demanding the restitution [*Wiederherstellung*] of their inalienable rights' (NA 20:319; AE:25). It is this restitution that demands a new form of the state to overcome the one-sidedness of the abstract idea of mankind.

With this in mind, the second way of unity that Schiller proposes in the 4th *Letter* can be understood in his affirmation that the *individual has to become state*. Then, the state as a unity with the 'man as idea' should represent individuals ('man in time'), and be, therefore, only the interpreter of their legislation.[10] Only in this way will the temporal human being be ennobled (*veredelt*) to the 'man as idea'—the *variety* of *nature* will be harmonised with the *unity* of *reason*, and the unity of the individual human being with the political and universal human being will be made real. This presupposes, in Schiller's view, the formation of the '*whole character of man*'. But how is the formation of such a unity and whole character possible? The 7th *Letter* gives a conclusive answer to this question in negative terms: 'CAN we perhaps look for such action from the State? That is out of the question' (NA 20:328, AE:46). This indicates the limitations of the modern political state in relation to the formation of the whole human being. The development of the whole character is an aesthetic issue to be solved, through the accomplishment of freedom and a new state, by the arts.

In sum, Schiller's conception of alienation is associated with the *atomistic, rationalising, mechanising* and *depoliticising* features found in modern human life. The first refers to the dissociation between individual and species-being, the second to the abstractness of reason, the third to the division of labour, and the fourth to the separation between individual and state. In contrast to these alienating propensities, Schiller proposes the recovery of the character of human being as a whole, which solidifies the unity between individuals and species-being, the unity of nature and reason, the harmonious development of drives and the objective representation of individual human beings by the state.

In specific relation to these atomistic and depoliticising features, some aspects of the young Marx's conception of alienation turn out to be suggestively concordant with Schiller's account. Even more so when it is considered that Marx, like Schiller, regards these two fragmenting aspects as impediments to the realisation of human being as a whole.

---

[10] See NA 20:317, AE19: 'The State should not only respect the objective and generic character in its individual subjects; it should also honour their subjective and specific character, and in extending the invisible realm of morals take care not to depopulate the sensible realm of appearance.' See also NA 20:318, AE:21: 'But just because the State is to be organization formed by itself and for itself, it can only become a reality inasmuch as its parts have been turned up to the idea of the whole. [...] Once man is inwardly at one with himself, he will be able to preserve his individuality however much he may universalize his conduct, and the State will be merely the interpreter of his own finest instinct, a clearer formulation of his own sense of what is right.'

Marx on Alienation: Contribution to the Critique of Hegel's Philosophy of Law and on the Jewish Question

In what follows, I will suggest that the aforementioned dissociation between individual and species-being and the antagonism between individual and state are present as principal features of alienation especially in two of the young Marx's works, namely in the unpublished *Contribution to the Critique of Hegel's Philosophy of Law* (1843) and in *On the Jewish Question* (1844). In my view, a more detailed examination of these texts reveals that Marx, like Schiller in the 4th *Letter*, seems to propose two ways of establishing unity between individuals and the state. Moreover, as in Schiller's criticism, the idea of the whole man plays a dominant role.

Focusing on the paragraphs 261–313 of the *Grundlinien der Philosophie des Rechts*, Marx offers, in his *Contribution*, a critical commentary of Hegel's conception of the state. He begins his treatise with an exposition of Hegel's definition of state in paragraph 261. According to Hegel, for the (real) spheres of the family and civil society, the state is an *external necessity* as well as an *end in itself* (cf. Hegel 1970, 407–408). In this characterisation, an antagonism between the particular sphere and the general sphere is assumed, that is, between a particular interest of individuals and a general interest of state. Understood as external necessity, the state is referred to, in relation to family and civil society, as 'subordination' and 'dependence' of a universal and objective idea. But at the same time, as an immanent finality, the state should also represent the instance of realisation of the particular sphere and its interest (the realisation of freedom).

In Marx's opinion, Hegel's solution to this antagonism between external necessity and immanent finality provides only a mere logical and idealised mediation, in which the external necessity appears, exclusively, as a determining element. Notably, Marx defines the idealistic and abstract unity between the universal and the particular as an '*imposed*, illusory identity' (Marx 2010c, 6). One of the consequences of such an 'imposed identity' is manifest in the suppression of the particular, rendering it a mere means for the realisation of the abstract idea. 'The real subjects, namely, civil society, family [...] become *unreal* objective elements of the idea with a changed significance' (Marx 2010c, 8). In this sense, the main critical point refers to a mediation between the universal and the particular spheres.

Marx's remarks reveal that his objections to Hegel are most specifically directed towards the abstractness and sheer one-sided affirmation of an objective idea; hence, the defects of his account are essentially due to an inversion of the relation of subject and predicate (cf. Marx 2010b, 23), which result in the objectivisation and 'logical mystification' of the idea.[11] In other words, a way of unity by which real and empirical relations appear only as an idealised phenomenon of 'essential relations'. It could be affirmed that this objection resembles Schiller's description of the first way of unity, in which the individual was abrogated by the state. Moreover, it is precisely this phenomenon of modern political state as oppressive element that Marx suggestively mentions here in connection with the concept of alienation (*Entfremdung*).[12] The reason for that is, in Marx's view, the following: '[T]he citizen, the *man* of the particular interest as opposed to the general, the *member of civil society*, is looked upon as a fixed individual, whereas the state also confronts the citizens in fixed individuals' (Marx 2010c, 42). This means that the conditions of alienation are connected with a one-sidedness of the general and abstract idea, as well as with the solidification of individuals as mere atomistic pieces. This split between individuals and species-beings is precisely what Schiller called the state of nature (*Naturstaat*).

If Marx's critique of Hegel is notable here for its parallelism with Schiller's statement, then it becomes even more remarkable when Marx seems to agree with Schiller's thesis that *the individual must become a state* in order to overcome the condition of oppression. Although Schiller is not mentioned, Marx asserts in his criticism of Hegel something similar to Schiller's view: 'Hegel starts from the state and makes man the subjectified state; democracy *starts from man and makes the state objectified man*' (Marx 2010c, 29; *my emphasis*). This quotation resembles Schiller's description of the second way of accomplishing unity described in the 4th *Letter*, and suggests on the basis of its criticism of Hegel that the state has to start from the individual human being ('man in time') in order to guarantee its freedom as objective human being ('man as idea'). The same idea can be found extended, when Marx writes about the 'genuine state':

> In the genuine state it is not a question of the opportunity of every citizen to devote himself to the general estate as one particular estate, but the capacity of the general estate to be *really general*—that is, *to be the estate of every citizen*. (Marx 2010c, 50; *my emphasis*)[13]

Furthermore, the division between individuals and species-being and its consequences with regard to alienation are portrayed by Marx in extenso in his

---

[11] Marx (2010c, 8): 'The idea is made the subject and the actual relation of family and civil society to the state is conceived as its internal imaginary activity. Family and civil society are the premises of the state; they are the genuinely active elements, but in speculative philosophy things are inverted' (Marx 2010c, 8).

[12] Marx (2010c, 6): 'Hegel has further developed one side of the dual identity, namely, the aspect of the estrangement within the unity'.

[13] See also Marx (2010c, 10): 'The transition is thus derived, not from the particular nature of the family, etc., and from the particular nature of the state, but from the general relationship of necessity to freedom'.

text *On the Jewish Question*. The main purpose of that work is to show the limitations of Bruno Bauer's concept of political emancipation. Bauer's proposal reveals its limited character, in so far as it only offers a criticism of the Christian state, but not of the state as such (cf. Marx 2010c, 149–150). In this sense, Marx exhibits how political emancipation leads to the liberation of the state by separating itself—as a modern and secular institution—from religion. Nevertheless, he claims, the same process of emancipation from religion does not occur in the sphere of individuals. Rather, the state can only achieve its own emancipation through a displacement of religion from the objective sphere to the subjective sphere, thus leaving the existence of religious consciousness unaffected (cf. Marx 2010c, 151, 155 and 167).

In Marx's view, the perfect political state not only evades opposing the existence of religion, but rather consolidates it at the level of individual consciousness. Accordingly, the modern political state must introduce a necessary division between the individual human being (*bourgeois*) and the political and general human being (*citoyen*) in order to guarantee the emancipation of the state. 'Man, as the adherent of a particular religion, finds himself in conflict with his citizenship and with other men as members of the community' (Marx 2010c, 154). Consequently, the political emancipation of the state from religion implies a phenomenon of *decoupling* the particular sphere (individual) and the general sphere (species-being, citizen), through which the life of man appears dissociated and with different contents.

> Where the political state has attained its true development, man—not only in thought, in consciousness, but in *reality*, in *life*—leads a twofold life, a heavenly and an earthly life: life in the *political community*, in which he considers himself a *communal being*, and life in *civil society*, in which he acts as a *private individual*[.]. (Marx 2010c, 154)

The political emancipation of state and the religious consciousness of individuals are, therefore, the manifestations of a decoupled consciousness; they are the manifestations of a secular narrowness, which is grounded on the state itself. In other words: political emancipation is the consciousness of a free state without free individuals. Marx calls this human condition in the political state alienation.

> It is indeed estrangement [*Entfremdung*] which matters in the so-called Christian state, but not man (Marx 2010c, 158). […] Political democracy is Christian since in it man, not merely one man but every man, ranks as sovereign, as the highest being, but it is man in his uncivilised, unsocial form, man in his fortuitous existence, man just as he is, man as he has been corrupted by the whole organisation of our society, who has lost himself, been alienated, and handed over to the rule of inhuman conditions and elements—in short, man who is not yet a real species-being. (Marx 2010c, 159)

It can be argued that this description of alienation in the political state exhibits certain similarities with Schiller's figure of the barbarian, since the abstractness of the idea of human being is also denounced here. In separating the spheres, the political emancipation of the state establishes a solidification of them, in light of which individuals can only appear to each other as atomistic, egoistic and antagonistic pieces. In Marx's view of this, the individual human being 'regards other men as a means, degrades himself into a means, and becomes the plaything of alien powers' (Marx 2010c, 154). That is, an individual who is recognised and idealised as sovereign, but nevertheless 'who is not yet a real species-being'—in Schiller's terminology, the human being is a *fragment* (*Bruchstück*).

This shows the limitations of the political state with regard to human emancipation. In so far as political emancipation from religion presupposes not a theological dichotomy (God-Human Being relationship) but a secular dichotomy (Human Being-State/*bourgeois-citoyen* relationship),[14] the modern state maintains the condition of alienation as a twofold life. In this regard, Marx extends his remarks from religion to the right.

In Marx's view, the modern state, based on the idea of mankind, dissociates the right of individual human being from civil rights. Then, through political emancipation, the 'twofold life' exists concurrently as *droit de l'homme* and *droit du citoyen*. The private human being (the natural basis of right) is the right of the fragmented, and egoistic human being. Marx sees the definition of freedom in the French Constitution from 1793—'liberty [...] is the right to do everything that harms no one else'—as the confirmation of this atomistic character of the right of mankind. This right of freedom represents neither a *connection* of human beings nor the realisation of their freedom; rather the right of *dissociation* of human beings and, consequently, the restriction of their freedom (cf. Marx 2010c, 162–163).[15] Similar to Schiller's appraisal of the right of mankind and the French Revolution, Marx recognises political emancipation as progress (Marx 2010c, 155), but he also highlights its limitations: the political state remains a state of alienated individuals. This remark shows how Marx does not assume the modern division between *status naturalis* and *status civilis* on the grounds that this divisiveness renders human being only a partial human being: either the natural egoistic individual (*bourgeois*), or the abstract political and universal human being (*citoyen*). In Marx's words: '[T]he modern state itself disregards *real man* or satisfies the *whole* of man only in imagination' (Marx 2010c, 181).

---

[14] Marx (2010c, 159): 'The members of the political state are religious owing to the dualism between individual life and species-life, between the life of civil society and political life. They are religious because men treat the political life of the state, an area beyond their real individuality, as if it were their true life. They are religious insofar as religion here is the spirit of civil society, expressing the separation and remoteness of man from man.'

[15] See also ibid.: 'It is a question of the liberty of man as an isolated monad, withdrawn into himself'.

Hence, the overcoming of the limited political emancipation demands, what Marx calls *human emancipation*, and this form of emancipation requires the whole man and its real unity as individual and species-being.

> Only when the real, individual man re-absorbs in himself the abstract citizen, and as an individual human being has become a species-being in his everyday life, in his particular work, and in his particular situation, only when man has recognised and organised his '*forces propres*' as social forces, and consequently no longer separates social power from himself in the shape of political power, only then will human emancipation have been accomplished. (Marx 2010c, 168)

Final Remarks

The foregoing considerations have shown that there are important convergences between Schiller's and the young Marx's account of alienation. Both authors coincide in a criticism of the modern state and the theory of the social contract. Both authors see here a division, to use Schiller's terminology, between the 'man in time' and the 'man as idea', which results in a one-sidedness of the abstract idea of human being and his right. Both also coincide in the statement that the atomisation and depoliticisation of the individual are the result of the division of the particular subject from its species-being. In both cases, the complete character of human being, the 'whole man', provides the way for overcoming the state of alienation.

Despite Marx's criticisms of Schiller in his late period, the first drafts of a theory of alienation by young Marx show a remarkable concordance with Schiller's own reflections on the subject. Here, then, the possibility arises for a more exact determination on the often suggested, but rarely demonstrated, influence of Schiller on Marx. The continuity between conservative-radicals, Schiller, and Marx, which I proposed on the basis of a discussion about the right of mankind and the state, is intended as a contribution to this demonstration.

References

Bach, Oliver. 2019. Natur—Mensch—Staat. Zu Schillers politischer Theorie. In *Friedrich Schiller: Über die Ästhetische Erziehung des Menschen in einer Reihe von Briefen*, ed. Gideon Stiening, 63–80. Berlin/Boston: De Gruyter.
Beiser, Frederick. 2005. *Schiller as Philosopher*. Oxford: Clarendon Press.
Beiser, Frederick. 2008. Schiller as Philosopher: A Reply to My Critics. *Inquiry* 51/1, 63–78.
Biester, Johann Erich. 1790. Nachschrift zu dem vorstehenden Aufsatz. *Berlinische Monatsschrift* (August): 209–220.
von Clauer, Karl. Noch ein Beitrag über das Recht der Menschheit. *Berlinische Monatsschrift* (November 1790): 441–469.

Fichte, Johann Gottlieb. 1971 (¹1793). *Beiträge zur Berichtigung der Urtheile des Publicums über die französische Revolution*. Fichtes Werke, Bd. VI. Berlin: Walter de Gruyter.
Habermas, Jürgen. 2019. *Der philosophische Diskurs der Moderne. Zwölf Vorlesungen*. Frankfurt am Main: Suhrkamp.
Hegel, Georg Friedrich Wilhelm. 1970. *Grundlinien der Philosophie des Rechts*, Werke, Bd. 7. Frankfurt am Main: Suhrkamp.
Heinrich, Michael. 2018. *Karl Marx und die Geburt der modernen Gesellschaft. Biographie und Werkentwicklung. Band I: 1818–1841*. Stuttgart: Schmetterling Verlag.
Henning, Christoph. 2015. *Theorien der Entfremdung. Zur Einführung*. Hamburg: Junius Verlag.
Herpen, Marcel H. van. 1983. Schiller und Marx. Die unbekannte, erste Entfremdungstheorie von Marx. *Kant-Studien* 74/3: 327–342.
Kant, Immanuel. 1900. *Gesammelte Schriften*. Berlin: Walter de Gruyter.
Kofler, Leo. 1968. *Perspektiven des revolutionären Humanismus*. Hamburg: Rowohlt.
Kofler, Leo. 1964. *Der proletarische Bürger. Marxistischer oder ethischer Sozialismus*. Wien: Europa Verlag.
Lukács, Georg. 2013. *Geschichte und Klassenbewusstsein*. Bielefeld: Aisthesis Verlag.
Lukács, Georg. 1973. *Der junge Hegel*. Frankfurt am Main: Suhrkamp.
Marx, Karl. 2017. *Das Kapital. Kritik der politischen Ökonomie. Erster Band Buch I: Der Produktionsprozess des Kapitals*, ed. Thomas Kuczynski. Hamburg: VAS: Verlag.
Marx, Karl/Engels, Friedrich. 2010a. *Collected Works*, vol. 1. Lawrence & Wishart Electric Book.
Marx, Karl/Engels, Friedrich. 2010b. *Collected Works*, vol. 2. Lawrence & Wishart Electric Book.
Marx, Karl/Engels, Friedrich. 2010c. *Collected Works*, vol. 3. Lawrence & Wishart Electric Book.
Marx, Karl/Engels, Friedrich. 2010d. *Collected Works*, vol. 6. Lawrence & Wishart Electric Book.
Marx, Karl/Engels, Friedrich. 2010e. *Collected Works*, vol. 40. Lawrence & Wishart Electric Book.
Matuschek, Stefan. 2009. *Kommentar*. Friedrich Schiller, Über die ästhetische Erziehung des Menschen. Frankfurt am Main: Suhrkamp, 125–262.
Möser, Justus. 1790. Ueber das Recht der Menschheit, als den Grund der neuen Französischen Konstitution. *Berlinische Monatsschrift* (Juni): 499–505.
Oellers, Norbert. 1970. *Schiller—Zeitgenosse aller Epochen. Dokumente zur Wirkungsgeschichte Schillers in Deutschland. Teil I: 1782–1859*. Frankfurt am Main: Athenäum Verlag.
Oellers, Norbert. 1976. *Schiller—Zeitgenosse aller Epochen. Dokumente zur Wirkungsgeschichte Schillers in Deutschland. Teil II: 1860–1966*. München: Verlag C.H. Beck.
Rehberg, Wilhelm August. 1793. *Untersuchung über die Französische Revolution nebst kritischen Nachrichten von den merkwürdigsten Schriften welche darüber in Frankreich erschienen sind*. Hannover/Osnabrück: Christian Ritscher.
Sayer, Sean. 2013. *Marx and Alienation. Essays on Hegelian Themes*. New York: Palgrave Macmillan.
Schiller, Friedrich. 2010. *Über die ästhetische Erziehung des Menschen in einer Reihe von Briefen. Mit den Augustenberger Briefen*, ed. By Klaus L- Berghahn. Stuttgart: Reclam.

Stiening, Gideon. 2019. "Der Versuch eines mündig gewordenen Volks". Schillers allgemeine und besondere Revolutionstheorie. In *Friedrich Schiller: Über die Ästhetische Erziehung des Menschen in einer Reihe von Briefen*, ed. Gideon Stiening, 49–62. Berlin/Boston: De Gruyter.

Waibel, Violeta. 2008. How Shall We Read Schiller Today? *Inquiry* 51/1, 50–62.

Zedler, Johann Heinrich. 1731–1754. *Grosse vollständiges Universal-Lexikon aller Wissenschaften und Künste, welche bishero durch menschlichen Verstand und Witz erfunden und verbessert worden*, Band I. Halle-Leipzig.

CHAPTER 36

Schiller and Critical Theory

Claudia Brodsky

> *Wie verwahrt sich aber der Künstler vor den Verderbnissen seiner Zeit, die ihn von allen Seiten umfangen? ... Gleich frei von der eiteln Geschäftigkeit, die in den flüchtigen Augenblick gern ihre Spur drücken möchte, und von dem ungeduldigen Schwärmergeist, der auf die dürftige Zeit den Masstab des Unbedingten anwendet ... strebe [er] aus dem Bunde des Möglichen mit dem Notwendigem das Ideal zu erzeugen ... präge es in die Spiele seiner Einbildungskraft und in den Ernst seiner Taten ... und werfe es schweigend in die unendliche Zeit*
> —(Schiller, *Briefe über die ästhetische Erziehung der Menschen*, Letter 9).

> *Was ich etwa mit der Forderung konfrontiert, wie man wörtlich sagte, "Kultur zu messen," so besann ich dem gegenüber mich darauf, dass Kultur eben jeder Zustand sei, dass eine Mentalität auschliesst, die ihn messen möchte*
> —(Adorno, "Meine Wissenschaftliche Erfahrungen in Amerika").

> *Kultur ist der Zustand, welcher Versuche, ihn zu messen, ausschliesst*
> —(Adorno, "Thesen zur Kunstsoziologie").

To inquire after the relationship of Schiller's theoretical writings to contemporary critical theory is to inquire about no less than the future of the relation between aesthetic and social thought. Long classified as an "idealist" endeavor

C. Brodsky (✉)
Princeton University, Princeton, NJ, USA
e-mail: claudiab@princeton.edu

© The Author(s), under exclusive license to Springer Nature Switzerland AG 2023
A. Falduto, T. Mehigan (eds.), *The Palgrave Handbook on the Philosophy of Friedrich Schiller*, https://doi.org/10.1007/978-3-031-16798-0_36

to defend a now "anachronistic"[1] view of the "autonomy" of art defined by a traditional historical conception of the German Enlightenment,[2] Schiller's aesthetic theory was first brought into prominent contemporary relation with Marxist social thought by Frederic Jameson, who, reframing its purported idealism as a mode of potentially revolutionary utopianism, clearly identified the echoes of Schiller's distinctively social view of aesthetic activity in the potentially liberatory workings of Eros upon the political imagination described by Marcuse. Comparing the relationship of Schiller's thought to Kant's, and of Marcuse's to Freud's, by way of a four-part analogy between "hypothetical" and "necessary" "conditions" of conception, on the one hand, and the "possible" or "extant" social and psychic "states" that constitute their respective objects, on the other, Jameson importantly observes:

> Marcuse's position with regard to Freud is in many ways markedly similar to that of Schiller in the face of Kantian critical philosophy. The latter had set itself the task of exploring the conceptual preconditions of what already exists, of formulating the necessary conditions of possibility of the experiences of sense perception and of beauty, of free will. Schiller ... continues to deduce conditions of possibility: but these are now the preconditions not of an existing but of a hypothetical state. Schiller wishes to determine ... how much man's psyche would have had to have been constructed for a genuinely free and harmonious personality to become one day a real possibility ....
>
> In much the same way, where Freud's instinctual theory is designed to explain the structure of real and existent mental phenomena, of hysteria and the neuroses and psychoses, Marcuse's use of that theory has a more speculative and hypothetical cast: for it aims at describing the conditions of possibility of a society from which aggression will have been eliminated and in which libidinally satisfying work will be conceivable.[3]

The theory of the possible existence of reciprocally mirroring, "harmonious" "personalit[ies]" and "societ[ies]" that Jameson attributes to Schiller and Marcuse in this, his earliest seminal work in dialectical theoretical criticism,

---

[1] For a theoretically oriented refutation of that historicist interpretation, see Reingard Niethersole, "... die Triebe zu leben, zu schaffen, zu spielen": "Schillers Spieltriebkonzeption aus gegenwärtiger Sicht," in *Schiller heute*, Hrsg. Hans-Jörg Knobloch u. Helmet Koopman (Tübingen: Stauffenberg Verlag, 1996), pp. 167–88 (167). Niethersole underscores the centrality of "play" to Schiller's (neo-Kantian) triadic division of *Stoff*-, *Form*- and *Spieltriebe* to rebut the view of the "apparent anachronism" of any such "separation of aesthetic from nonaesthetic activity," arguing instead for the "actuality" of Schiller's conception evident in Wittgenstein's concept of "Sprachspiel" and Derrida's "Spiel der *différance*," and what he terms the larger "deconstructive or poststructuralist conception of the world as constituted in and through and through language" (167–68; see also 176–78, 181–83, 186–88). Translations from the German throughout this essay my own.

[2] *Ibid.*, pp. 168–69, 174–75. See also, Peter Horn, "Die 'Tochter der Freiheit' und die 'Tendenz' zur Autonomie der Kunst" in Schillers "Über die Ästhetische Erziehung des Menschen" und Schopenhauers 'Die Welt als Wille und Vorstellung'" in *Schiller heute*, pp. 59–73, for a recapitulation of Kant's separation of the "realm of the aesthetic" from the concerns of epistemology and ethics insofar as it provides the basis for Schiller's view of an "autonomous" realm of art "not easily reconciled," Horn adds, with particular relevance for the present argument, "with the order of the state" (62–65).

[3] Frederic Jameson, *Marxism and Form* (Princeton: Princeton University Press, 1971), "Marcuse and Schiller," pp. 83–116 (114–115).

makes the case for the contemporary efficacy of Utopian thinking, in the face of unyielding historical contradiction and the systematic co-optation of all practical thinking, that will remain a central tenet of Jameson's ongoing analyses of both theoretical and literary texts. Loosely linking Utopian thinking to dialectical criticism itself, and speculatively stipulating its "concrete" usefulness, in prose as moving of that of its own closest theoretical model, Bloch,[4] within the increasingly dilated context of "late" capitalism, Jameson will continue to detect the shaped evidence of its impulse in the present, in scrupulous analyses of its manifestations within "real and existent" (social and economic, rather than psychic) contemporary formations, as well its conscious and unconscious representation in international developments in literature and theory. At the source of that present, for Jameson, is the pivotal figure of Schiller, playwright of real historical-political conflict, sympathizer with contemporary revolutionary movements, and theorist of an "idea of freedom" manifested in aesthetic *forms*. Embracing an extraordinary array of social objects and experiences glimpsed anew, in nearly Benjaminian fashion, by way of their synchronic juxtaposition, Jameson "reads" across these individual contextual frames a kind of *historically mimetic* history of the changing styles and implicit allegorical contents of literary and other cultural forms. The logic that links these temporal cross-sections in classical, structuralist fashion,[5] are the dialectical relations

---

[4] The excellent discussion of Bloch in *Marxism and Form* directly succeeds that comparing Marcuse and Schiller. Exemplary of the dialectical criticism by which Jameson, following Lukács and Auerbach, identifies formal stylistic traits with real historical change, the highpoints of the exegesis of Bloch are themselves exegeses of literature: of a "Marxism [i.e., Bloch's] that springs not from Hegel but from Goethe"—that is, Faust's "genuinely concrete and indeed profoundly political vision" of "'a free people standing on free ground'" (140) for whose sake he recognizes he would, and, in so doing, *does* tell "the moment" "to linger"—and, most eloquently and surprisingly, of what Jameson characterizes as "the Utopian impulse" of a work never associated with the term, Proust's *Recherche*. Beneath the "psychology" and "decaying" "distorting" rituals of social "snobbery" of Proust's characters (152–54), he argues, lies the always temporally expansive yet formally contained structure of the unique Proustian period we read. Demonstrating his own extraordinary ability to read, in a truly philosophical way, the deep structures of grammar and syntax animating the thematic superficies of each specific literary text, Jameson describes Proust's social universe *à huis clos* as a sentential realm of ever-expanding temporal experience: "Thus Proustian composition, and the reading of Proust, is itself a figure of the experience of eternity, of the experience of Utopian adequation, and for the first time also that empty space within the novel of the artist, that empty canvas which is his putative work of art, is filled (in the Proustian superposition of the experiences in the fallen world, and their expression, from beyond the end of the novel, from beyond the end of that world, by the narrator) by the concrete time of verbal expression" (155–56). In a manner only indirectly implied by Bloch, Jameson here equates the "concrete" with "verbal expression" itself. For a directly related conclusion, regarding the explicitly verbal fusion of verbal with concrete at the architectonical highpoint of *Faust*, see Part One of my *In the Place of Language. Literature and the Architecture of the Referent* (NY: Fordham University Press, 2009).

[5] Jameson's imaginative "method" for constructing revealing historical homologies, here and elsewhere, owes to the singularly literary perception of narrative coherence born of synchronic tensions that he shares with Lévi-Strauss. As indebted to Hegel as to Saussure, Levi-Strauss' replacement of positive "mythological" identities by functional differences first made meaningful in dialectical relation, perhaps best encapsulates Jameson's analytic approach to revealing the structural contours of capitalism within culture. Cf. Claude Lévi-Strauss, *La pensée sauvage* (Paris: Plon, 1962; Eng. tr. 1966, 2021).

whose ongoing diachronic dynamic suggests their resolution in a "Utopian future."[6] Jameson describes the utility of "the Utopian idea" that his own writings, perhaps more than those of any other contemporary theorist, have made an international tenet of social thought, far outstripping its association with Marcuse and Bloch, or Schiller before them, as follows:

> For where in older society (as in Marx's classic analysis) Utopian thought represented a diversion of revolutionary energy into idle wish-fulfillments and imaginary satisfaction, on our own time the very nature of the Utopian concept has undergone a dialectical reversal. Now it is practical thinking which everywhere represents a capitulation to the system itself, and stands as a testimony to the power of that system to transform even its adversaries into its mirror image. The Utopian idea, on the contrary, keeps alive the possibility of a world qualitatively distinct from this one and takes the form of a stubborn negation of all that is.[7]

This is an extraordinary claim, whose own powerful aesthetic effects continue to carry extraordinary consequences for the practical, conceptual, and imaginative—which is to say, political—lives of all those affected by it. While it may well be too obvious, it is obviously not too early to observe that the greater, or more "stubborn[ly]" pure of pragmatic, not to say referential concerns the utopianism of the stance so affected, the greater, more violently at odds with extant reality the pure pragmatism of the fascism that crushes it, and more easily the ever-manufacturable technologies for annihilating the real are implemented. For having already removed both the real and the power to reference it from the realm of necessary consideration, "Utopian thinking," by the light of its own "qualitative distinct[ion]," can define its efficacy solely in function of its ideal "negation" of the facts and circumstances of this world, that is, up until the moment when these latter prove their value *in retrospect*, that is, in being reconceived within the "dream" of a fully "aesthetic metapolitics" as objects worthy of present "melancholy," if not "mourning,"[8] having already been destroyed. More "Kantian"

---

[6] "Thus, for example, [Marcuse's] ingenious hypothesis [in *Eros and* Civilisation] of a 'maternal super-id' is designed to show how in a Utopian future the apparently contradictory claims of the pleasure principle and of some form of social morality might be harmonized and justified by the topology of the instincts themselves" (*Ibid.*, p. 115).

[7] Jameson, *Marxism and Form*, p. 111.

[8] In contrast to Jameson's material-historical view, see Jacques Rancière's casting of Schiller as lead proponent of such an aesthetic "metapolitics" of sentiment, itself based on the surreal proposition of a "total revolution of the sensible," in "Aesthetic Revolution and Its Outcomes," *New Left Review* 14, March/April (2002): 133–51 (133–136 in particular) and *The Politics of Aesthetics*, trans. Gabriel Rockhill (London: Continuum, 2004 [*Le partage du sensible*, 2000]), pp. 7–41 (pp. 27, 30, 33, 36, 37). Offering contradictory accounts of "art *replacing* politics as a configuration of the sensible world," on the one hand, and a "metapolitics *of* the aesthetic which *frames the possibilities* of art," on the other, Rancière concludes: "Aesthetic art promises a political accomplishment that it cannot satisfy and thrives on that ambiguity. That is why those who want it … to fulfill its political promise are condemned to a certain melancholy" (151). On the "mourning" and "nostalgia" for a utopian "lost paradise of incarnate presence," see p. 150 and *The Flesh of Words. The Politics of Writing*, tr. Charlotte Mandell (Stanford U Press, 1998 [orig. Fr. ed., *La chair des mots*, Paris 1998]).

than the most starry-eyed gazer upon "the star-filled skies above," such a happy embrace of annihilation in the name of utopianism, to be looked back upon melancholically, but never remorsefully, is certainly entirely less Kant-*like*, in that Kant's writings on political theory and history are as resistant to conflating political action, carried out, by definition, within this world, with a mode of mental transportation into another world, as they are to all other wishful assertions of "the thing itself" by which the worldly modalities of life and law are not changed but ignored in favor of the "pure" pursuit of a utopian conception of the "moral law within" (the second of the two sources of "awed respect" famously coupled at the close of the Second Critique).[9]

I will return later to this anticritical strain of Marxian aestheticism, more "idealist" or "Kantian" than Kant would ever aspire to be, as it surfaces in a bluntly pragmatic question posed by Benjamin of Adorno, and the unequivocal practical data of existence and annihilation that Adorno is compelled to report, in unconditional empirical terms, in response. Aligned with that unvarnished acknowledgment of material fact, Adorno's decidedly nonutopian consideration of the interaction between the opposing ends of art and society may share more with Schiller's theoretical orientation of dramatic theater upon the encompassing historical context of the *polis* or "state,"[10] than with a futurist, sensationalist, or any other unmediated reframing of Schiller's, or, for that matter, Marcuse's uncompromising insistence on the essential role of aesthetic *form*. For just as Marcuse's singular emphasis on the "revolutionary" "necessity" of aesthetic "form" to any

---

[9] Kant, *Kritik der praktischen Vernunft. Werkausgabe*, 12 Bde., Hrsg. Wilhelm Weischedel (Frankfurt: Suhrkamp, 1977) A 289, VII: 300: "Zwei Dinge erfüllen das Gemüt mit immer neuer und zunehmenden Bewunderung und Ehrfurcht, je öfter und anhaltender sich das Nachdenken damit beschäftigt: *Der bestirnte Himmel über mir, und das moralische Gesetz in mir*" (emphasis in original) [Two things fill the mind with ever new and increasing admiration and awe, the more often and more steadily (the power of) reflection occupies itself with them: *the starry sky above me and the moral law within me*].

[10] See Letters 1 through 4 of Schiller's *Briefe über die ästhetiche Erziehung des Menschen*, and the excellent discussion by Elizabeth Wilkinson and L. A. Willoughby of the political-philosophical motivation of Schiller's aesthetic orientation toward staging "die Erscheinung der Freiheit" in the "sensory" mode of historical dramaturgy in their accompanying monograph to the Oxford dual-language edition of the *Briefe*: *On the Aesthetic Education of Man in a Series of Letters* (Oxford: Clarendon, 1967 [4th ed. 1989]), pp. xiv–xxix, esp. (all further citations from the *Briefe* from this edition, with modifications of translations provided). Wilkinson and Willoughby observe that, convinced that the "clue to the whole history of human freedom is to be found in the fact that we are creatures of sense, before we become creatures of reason," Schiller the artist chose decidedly against taking "the way of a political quietest" in either his dramatic or aesthetic-theoretical work (p. xiv). In Letter 2, see esp. Schiller's coinage of the term "political theater" ("politischer Schauplatz") in direct analogy with the general sensory realm of the aesthetic he calls the "theater of the fine arts" ("Schauplatz der schönen Künste"): for Schiller, both are based on the understanding that the "way" to "resolving the political problem in experience" passes through "the aesthetic ... en route to freedom" ("dass man, um jenes politisches Problem in der Erfahrung zu lösen, durch das ästhetiche ... den Weg nehmen muss ... durch welche[n] man zu der Freiheit wandert" [p. 8]). See also Letter 3: "[Man] wakes from his sensory slumber, recognizes himself as a human being, looks around himself and finds himself—in the state" ("Er kommt zu sich aus seinem sinnlichen Schlummer. erkennt sich als Mensch, blickt um sich her und findet sich—in dem Staate" [p. 10]).

subject's active ability to "negate" "established reality," and concomitant critique of any purported "historical materialism" that substitutes its own ideological conflation of base with superstructure for art's "formal autonomy,"[11] must reject all promises of utopia premised upon amorphous aestheticization, so the Weimar playwright of political history aims in practice and theory to provide formal representations of the necessary "revolution" within "human nature."[12] Schiller defines that "revolution" in the distinctly productive terms of a turn away from both the "instinctual" "animal" capacity for "material accumulation" and distinctly human proclivity to substitute a "surplus of things" for "freedom," toward the "fulfillment" of the "equality" that the "free" "making" and "disinterested" "contemplation" of "autonomous [aesthetic] semblances" of "things" introduces into the world of actual social relations.[13] Similarly, when both Marcuse and Schiller underscore the necessarily "subjective" nature of the encounter with autonomous

---

[11] See Herbert Marcuse, *The Aesthetic Dimension. Toward a Critique of Marxist Aesthetics* (Boston: Beacon Press, 1978 [*Die Permanenz der Kunst. wider eine bestimmte Marxistische Ästhetik*, München, 1977]), pp. 3, 8–11, 52–53, 57, *et passim*.

[12] While Wolfgang Düsing has argued that, after Kant's "analysis" of the "subjective" basis of "judgments of taste," the "representational" object of art for Schiller is no longer "nature" but human "subjectivity" itself, that view, I think, mistakenly conflates subject and object, and theory and practice, in a way neither theorist does. In theorizing a general, non-rule based, "free" verbal capacity within the subject to predicate unknown pleasurable (or unpleasurable) objects as "beautiful" (or "sublime"), Kant does not propose a "subjectivization" of the object of judgment—quite the contrary, that object remains a practical object of sensuous perception, and, in Kant's examples, it is most commonly a given natural object appearing, as does any cognitive object, outside us, but one whose encounter is now shorn of any cognitive concept. Likewise, in theorizing the "revolution" that the experience of aesthetic objects can bring about in "human nature," Schiller is in no way proposing that aesthetic objects are themselves "expression[s] of subjectivity." They are instead, as Schiller—like Adorno later, and Plato originally—categorically states, "semblances" (*Scheine*) of things they are not, the experience of which *negates*, for him, as for Adorno, the ideological role assigned "art" within already reified social relations: the same reason for which Plato instead *banishes* poets from the state. See Wolfgang Düsing, "Ästhetische Form als Darstellung der Subjektivität. Zur Rezeption Kantischer Begriffs in Schillers Ästhetik," in *Schillers Briefe über die ästhetiche Erziehung*, Hrsg. Jürgen Bolten (Frankfurt: Suhrkamp, 1984), pp. 185–228 [185–86, 195, 216–17, esp. For Düsing's surprising assertion, that Schiller was "influenced" by the "anthropological and psychological" aesthetics of Burke, whose false reduction of the aesthetic to an experience of bodies by bodies Schiller explicitly criticizes for its equation of "beauty" with "mere life," (see his note to Letter 15, p. 102*) and implicitly associates with the program of the "political and pedagogical artist" who uses art to achieve its destruction, see p. 187; Schiller, *Briefe*, Letter 4, p. 18).

[13] See Schiller, *Briefe*, Letter 27, pp. 204–218 (pp. 204–206, p. 218, esp.), Schiller's argument *opposing* the "freedom" intrinsic to "human nature" to the "craving" for "surplus" material accumulation in Letter 27 is remarkably similar to that of Rousseau's Second Discourse, published and banned a few decades earlier, with the salient difference that whereas Rousseau famously situates the origin of inequality in the division between "being and appearing" ("être et paraître") and attributes its rapid development to the attraction and subsequently enforced acquisition of the semblance of power attaching to aesthetic appearances, Schiller considers the aesthetic "the sole mode of communication" capable of "uniting" an otherwise artificially divided society ("nur die schöne Mitteilung vereinigt die Gesellschaft")., p. 235). See J.-J. Rousseau, *Discours sur l'origine et les fondements de l'inégalité parmi les hommes*, ed. Jacques Roger (Paris: Flammarion, 1971 [orig. pub. 1755]).

aesthetic form,[14] and "call" the effect of that "dialectical"—or in Schiller's terms, "reciprocally effective" ["Wechselwirkung"[15]]—encounter "beauty," it is no *beau ideal* that they have in mind. Rather, the "quality of Beauty" that brings with it "the promise of liberation," or what Marcuse, in one of his most original and potent formulations, calls "political Eros,"[16] is a sensuous form that must first be "wrested from established reality,"[17] just as for the historical dramatist, that "concept" which, "in the widest sense of the word," we "call" "the Beautiful," designates the complementary capacities of a "form" to "live in our feeling" and of "life" to "form itself in our understanding," not because form is immaterial but, rather, a particularly productive "material thing."[18]

The "subjective" experience of beauty is accordingly no mere distraction from "the real," but the necessary "contradiction" of "an established reality"[19] whose "enlightened" developments in "philosophy and science" and dissipation of "false conceptions" through "free inquiry" *coexist*, on Schiller's uncannily foreboding account, with the "compulsive" "prejudice" of "barbarians."[20] No flight into an otherworldly, properly neither social nor antisocial, aesthetic nor anti-aesthetic utopia, but the realization of a kind of action that, on Marcuse's account, "can become a material force,"[21] the "material thing" of aesthetic experience is for neither pre- nor post-Marxist thinker a prosthetic for an historically absented idea, but, one could say instead, a kind of "base structure" for history itself.

Before examining the relation of Schiller's aesthetic theory to Adorno's, including his anti-Platonic critique of the nascent "culture industry" of eighteenth-century Weimar, if we are to understand the critical difference between Schiller's aesthetic theory and the utopian idealism with which it has been conflated in recent decades, the bases of the distinction that Jameson draws between Marcuse's and Schiller's utopianism merit investigation. Stipulating that the very possibility of "the Utopian idea" itself is based on an (unequivocally Kantian) "idea of freedom," among whose "stubborn" sources of regeneration across centuries and genres he counts Schiller, Jameson first makes the contrary case for the apparently nonutopian, "realist" thrust of Marcuse's thinking, admitting, "[t]o be sure there

---

[14] Of the counterproductive "devaluation" of "subjectivity" by schematic "Marxist aesthetics," Marcuse comments: "The schema implies a normative notion of the material base as the true reality and a political devaluation of nonmaterial forces, particularly of the individual consciousness and subconscious and their political function. ... The subjectivity of individuals ... tends to be dissolved into class consciousness. Thereby a major prerequisite for revolution is minimized, namely the fact that the need for radical change must be rooted in the subjectivity of individuals themselves, in their intelligence, and their passions, their drives and their goals" (*The Aesthetic Dimension*, pp. 3–4).

[15] Marcuse, *The Aesthetic Dimension*, p. 29; p. 102
[16] Marcuse, *The Aesthetic Dimension*, p. 64.
[17] Marcuse, *The Aesthetic Dimension*, p. 46.
[18] Schiller, *Briefe*, Letter 15, p. 100.
[19] Marcuse, *The Aesthetic Dimension*, p. 9, 11, 41.
[20] Schiller, *Briefe*, Letter 8, pp. 48–50.
[21] Marcuse, *The Aesthetic Dimension*, p. 3.

is always the possibility that such a society is precisely impossible, ... that we do not find ourselves in a prerevolutionary, let alone a revolutionary, situation, and that the total system may yet ultimately succeed in effacing the very memory of the negative,[22] and with it of freedom, from the face of the earth," before concluding: "this final alternative, which the a priori model leaves open for us, is itself the source of Marcuse's realism."[23] He then proceeds, however, to turn the tables on this "realistic" possibility—of a definitive negation of the negative—by commenting, in a remarkably Schillerian (and Marcusian) tenor, on the personal "pleasure" he takes in "contemplat[ing]" his own aesthetic linkage of three "profoundly different," but narratively homologous historical "shapes" in which "the idea of freedom" emerges from apparent oblivion: those of the contemporary social "philosopher in exile," the eighteenth-century "historian-playwright" at home in his already antiquated "feudal-state," and the manifestly anti-idealist, anti-colonialist, communist-turned-anarchist "poet" and theorist of surrealism,[24] as they reinvent the "form" that Jameson attributes to antihistorical, utopian thinking. Introducing Schiller as the opening figure of this extraordinarily extensive description of comparable historical "shapes," Jameson observes:

> Yet whatever the outcome, it pleases me for another moment still to contemplate the stubborn rebirth of the idea of freedom, in three such profoundly different shapes, at three such profoundly different moments in history: its reinvention by the historian-playwright, dreaming the heroic gestures of political eloquence in his tiny feudal city-state open to the fields, stimulated by the news of revolutionary victories there where in a few years the shock of Napoleonic armies will cause the earth to tremble; by the poet stalking his magical fun-park for the neon omens of objective chance, behind the hallucinatory rebus of the street scene never ceasing to hear the pop gun volleys of the vicious, never-ending military pacification of colonial empire; by the philosopher, in the exile of that immense housing development that is the state of California, remembering, reawakening, reinventing—from the rows of products in the supermarkets, from the roar of the

---

[22] Jameson's commendation of Marcuse's recognition of the critical necessity of negation to freedom compels us to recall, with regard to his admiration for Schiller, that it was Kant who first introduced the (now as then) "revolutionary" notion of "the negative" into philosophy. Kant's new methodological proposition, that the "critical" negation of purely sense-dependent presuppositions, while appearing "merely negative" in comparison with such apparently positive self-evidence, is instead uniquely productive of "real" positive value, because designed *not* to replace one (necessarily fictitious) "a priori model" of the real with another. See Kant, *Kritik der reinen Vernunft* B vii, xi, xiv, xv, xvi, xxii, xxx, *Werkausgabe*, III: 20, 22–25, 28, 33, for Kant's repeated definition of his "critical" introduction of the emphatically "*negative*" ("*negativ*") into philosophy as a "revolution in mode of thinking" ("Revolution der Denkart").

[23] Jameson, *Marxism and Form*, p. 115.

[24] Jameson's early interest in Bréton, as in the manifesto perhaps best understood as the successor to his own, Deleuze and Guattari's *Anti-Oedipe: le capitalism et la schizophrénie* [1972]), may owe not only to the poet-theorist's lifelong refusal to accept any version of a status quo, whether participating in the politically charged meeting in Paris of the International Congress of Writers in 1935, or collaborating soon thereafter on a new surrealist manifesto with Trotsky when sent to Mexico as cultural ambassador of France, but to the deep appreciation for Bréton expressed decades later by Lévi-Strauss, whose structuralist view could hardly be more opposed to the surrealist conception of "automatic" artistic production, but with whom he formed a close friendship during their shared years of refuge from fascism in New York City.

freeways and the ominous shape of the helmets of traffic policemen, from the incessant overhead traffic of the fleets of military transport plans, and, as it were from beyond them, in the future—the almost extinct form of the Utopian idea.[25]

This vividly detailed chronicle of distinct historical and material contexts connected by a series of syntactic parallelisms composes one of the most moving periods Jameson has written. Presenting in seamless narrative form a series of brutal conflicts imagistically frozen in time, the visual immediacy of whose aesthetic "shapes" belies a pastness to which we could not otherwise be privy, this panoptical view of concrete historical manifestations of an invisible idea comprises Jameson's own lushly cinematic "récit de Théramène." By linking the actual lived experience of three great thinkers in situ not to any similarities of situation (indeed, underscoring their differences), but to "the idea of freedom" that, on this view, lay at the root of both their historical greatness *and* dissimilarity, Jameson here, like Marcuse in his unequivocal insistence upon the "transhistorical" "emancipatory" power of aesthetic form,[26] appears more than willing to be misconstrued as an "idealist," closer in "aesthetic ideology" to Schiller—whose theory of opposing sensuous and formal *Triebe* "sublated"[27] by a "uniting" *Spieltrieb*[28] defined a dialectic born of aesthetic activity—than to the theories of art shaped by either Hegel's dialectical history of consciousness or the dialectical materialism of Marx. For neither the pro-revolutionary classical dramatist whose theoretical reflections transpose aesthetic experience from the stage to the state, nor anti-Stalinist emigré critic of the capitalist conflation of culture with consumption, nor American Marxist analyst of literary style as

---

[25] Jameson, *Marxism and Form*, p. 116.

[26] Marcuse, *The Aesthetic Dimension*, pp. 6–9, 11, 22, 52–53. Marcuse's radical disassociation of the "emancipatory" "potential" of aesthetic form from any subject's class-based sense of "false immediacy" ("Marxist theory is not family research" [19, 66]; "Revolutionary art is supposed to speak 'the language of the people'. ... But who are 'the people'?" [33]; "The tyranny of form is indeed tyranny in as much as it suppresses the immediacy of expression. But what is here expressed is false immediacy: false to the degree it drags along the unreflected mystified reality" [42–43]) and defense of the ability of any "subjectivity" to "step out of the network of exchange relationships and exchange values," a capacity represented, for him, by the "idea of the Beautiful" long "rejected" as a "central category of '*bourgeois* aesthetics'" alone (62, 4), are especially pertinent to the contemporary theoretical reception of Schiller. See pp. 16, 30–35, 42–43, 64–66, esp. See also Marcuse, *Eros and Civilization. A Philosophical Inquiry into Freud*. (Boston: Beacon Press, 1966), Part Two esp.

[27] Schiller's *Formtrieb* and *sinnliche Trieb* clearly derive from Kant's hypothesis of the specifically *cognitive* unity of two simultaneous mental activities: the independent or *a priori* intellectual act of formation applied in "real time" to the experience of contingent or *a posteriori* sensations. Unlike Schiller's aesthetic "play," however, Kant's mediating "play of understanding and imagination" in acts of *aesthetic judgment* does not "join" or "unite" two opposing drives but rather sets those two faculties of mind into dynamic motion (Schiller, *Briefe*, Letter 14, pp. 96, 98.)

[28] While Schiller's main exposition of the three drives occurs in Letters 12 to 16, the *Spieltrieb* is first introduced in Letter 14 as a "new drive" necessitated specifically by the opposing temporal requirements, for change and permanence, of the sensuous and formal drives, respectively. See Schiller, *Briefe*, p. 96). See Marcuse's new integration of Schiller's *Spieltrieb* into the Freudian model of the psyche, in *Eros and Civilization. A Philosophical Inquiry into Freud*. (Boston: Beacon Press, 1966), Part Two esp.

critically legible symptom of dialectical history, would find any material, let alone cognitive or ethical basis for subordinating the ideational to the sensational, let alone for canceling our very ability to think by conflating the two. Impossibly asserting its own magical surpassing of both conscious and unconscious intellectual processes, such a sensationalist ideology is one that even Bréton, champion of the surreal collision of sensation and psyche, would find beneath consideration, *below* not above the real.

In the immediate wake of Kant's theory of our general capacity to "judge" perceptible forms shorn of concepts, Schiller was first to underscore the objecthood and materiality *of* such forms,[29] further theorizing the relation between the "living" aesthetic formation of matter and its "revolutionary," "social" effect.[30] Its explicit integration of the social and material dimensions of art not only distinguishes Schiller's aesthetic theory from the aesthetic "idealism" of a Schelling with whose ideology it is commonly conflated.[31] It also effectively decouples the idea of aesthetic form from that of a utopianism to which it remains just as "stubborn[ly]" attached, not only in Jameson's own

---

[29] See Schiller, *Briefe*, esp. Letter 12, p. 80: "form is never made manifest except in some material" ("alle Form nur an einer Materie ... erschient." See also Letter 14, p. 98, on the coordination of otherwise opposed sense and form-drives in a play drive capable of "integrating form into matter" ("Form in die Materie ... bringt") and Letter 15, p. 100: "The object of the sense-drive ... is called *life*. ... The object of the form-drive ... is called *form*. ... The object of the play-drive ... may therefore be called living form" ("Der Gegenstand des sinnlichen Triebes ... heisst *Leben* ... Der Gegenstand des Formtriebes ... heisst *Gestalt* ... Der Gegenstand des Spieltriebes ... wird also *lebende Gestalt* heissen können").

[30] Schiller, *Briefe*, Letter 27, pp. 204, 214: "If want necessitates the assembly of men into societies, only beauty can impart to man a social character" ("Wenn schon das Bedürfnis den Menschen in die Gesellschaft nötigt ... so kann die Schönheit allein den einen *gesellgien Charakter* erteilen.") Cf. Marcuse, *The Aesthetic Dimension*, p. 53: "The work of art can attain political relevance only as autonomous work. The aesthetic form is essential to its social function."

[31] In *The Aesthetic Ideology* (Minneapolis: University of Minnesota Press, 1996), pp. 129–62, De Man describes Schiller's recasting in "On the Sublime" of Kant's mathematical and dynamic modes of sublime experience into the opposing categories of the infinite and physically threatening, or "theoretical" and "practical" sublime, as symptomatic not only of the "playwright" Schiller's "pragmatic" interest in the "staging" of human "psychology," but all our daily interests in translating the "transcendental" or truly "philosophical" questions of how and what we can know into "pragmatic" ones based instead on the principles of self-preservation, self-representation, and self-identity, themselves based on a circular presumption and promotion of principles of verisimilitude. While de Man is somewhat less critical of the later, "more complex" *Letters* (147), his argument, that the *Letters'* organization of our experience into opposing *Triebe* synthesized in an aesthetic *Spieltrieb* is a purely "tropological" one modeled on chiasmus and reversibility (158), rather than a properly "dialectical" one (147–48, 151) requiring "negation" (157) and "materiality" (132, 159) is successful, he would be the first to admit, *only* insofar as *it omits* to mention Schiller's inclusion of the necessity of "negation" and "the material" to the very possibility of any relation between the "sinnlicher Trieb" and "Formtrieb," a necessity not unlike that of the popularly unwelcome introduction of "negation" into philosophy by Kant. See this essay, note 22, for Kant's explicit acknowledgment of both the distaste for the "negative" he anticipates his *Critique* will elicit from the public, and the absolute necessity of negation to any "critical" understanding of our capacities for knowledge and moral action. (For an extensive analysis of the necessary negative condition of the mediating capacity for aesthetic judgment, see my *The Linguistic Condition. Kant's Critique of Judgment and the Poetics of Acton* [London and New York: Bloomsbury, 2021). On the "materiality" of form and necessity of "negation" to thinking in Schiller, see citations from the *Letters*, notes 29 and 34 this essay.

enormously and deservedly influential thinking but in the reception of Schiller, by critics of very different, explicit and implicit political convictions, that Jameson so powerfully extends here.[32]

For while Schiller's and Marcuse's aesthetic theories are both profoundly motivated by the radical potential of art to act, in Marcuse's terms, as a necessarily "estranging form" capable of "contradicting" any "affirmative ideological function" and prescribed aesthetic content,[33] and, in Schiller's, as "an autonomous semblance" able to "negate" "given" intellectual conceptions and, with them, the apparently autonomous "aims" of a "material world" over which we are doomed to exercise only similarly instrumental dominion,[34] they also both conceive of that very form as a mode of "seeming," *Schein*: a "fictitious appearance" or "aesthetic imitation." Such seeming is an appearance of something else, some extant material thing or perceptible action somewhere, rather than of nothing nowhere. The other, indeed "alternate" reality it presents resides in its "stylized" "representation" of the "truth of our experience" within and of the world, rather than a purely fictive conception of another world, an entirely imaginary state not only bearing no relationship to the reality of human experience and action, but representing no material part of it.[35]

Now the first notion of such a purely ideational, "utopian" state is, of course, as old as philosophy itself, the entire history of whose development Marx

---

[32] Walter Muller-Seidel's recent *Friedrich Schiller und die Politik. "Nicht das Grosse, nur das Menschliche geschehe"* (München: C. H. Beck Verlag, 2009), provides a telling exception to this general rule. Analyzing Schiller's dramatic *oeuvre* in view of the playwright's overriding concern with the "human," whose epitomization in Kant's transhistorical figure of the never entirely rectifiable *krumme Holz* of human nature was rapidly distorted into a pretext for its own inherently contradictory "nationalist sacralization," Müller-Seidel draws a straight line from the humanist philosophy of *Die Horen* and resulting conception of the *Kulturnation* centered in Weimar, to *Nationsstolz* based on cultural achievements, to nationalist pride taken in the efficient taking of human life—including praise for the "humanity" of Joseph-Ignace Guillotin's killing machine and "scientific" propaganda on behalf of the "human" benefits of utilizing poison gas in warfare—leading, ultimately, to the ensuing *Menschlichkeitskatastrophe* of world war that quickly lay the groundwork for full-scale genocide. For Müller-Seidel, Schiller's unsurpassed "modernity" lies precisely in his early understanding of the "tragedy" of this appropriation of "humanism," which, long preceding the twentieth-century transmutation of the latter into full-scale "barbarism," was shared to an equal extent, in Müller-Seidel's view, only by Hölderlin among Schiller's contemporaries. See Müller-Seidel, pp. 326–341 esp.

[33] Marcuse, *The Aesthetic Dimension*, pp. 10–11, 72.

[34] See Schiller, *Briefe*, esp. Letter 19 (on "Negation" as necessary to "thought," an autonomous or "absolute Tathandlung des Geistes" [pp. 128–130]; Letter 26; and Letter 27, in which Schiller underscores the representational basis of autonomous semblance by describing the unbalanced relationship between semblance and reality as follows: "Fear not for reality and truth if the elevated conception of aesthetic semblance that I proposed in the previous letter were to become universal. ... On the part of semblance, as it has been here understood, there is little to worry about as concerns reality: much more is to be feared for semblance from the side of reality. Chained to the material world, man had long allowed semblance to serve only its aims" [p. 204]).

[35] See Marcuse, *The Aesthetic Dimension*, pp. 1, 3, 6–9, 11, 13, 18, 23, 27, *et passim*. See Schiller, *Briefe*, esp. Letters 19–27.

challenged all theoretical materialist thought, most famously, to leave behind.[36] Something there is about thinking, however apparently idealist or anti-idealist and materialist, that loves to imagine a place that requires none, a utopia.[37] The question of materialism's own ideational basis is itself of course only as "new" as the newest animistic "ontology" conflating material "being" with "feelings" (most recently, those of "things themselves," described, conveniently, to mirror our own) and as old as the successive theories of Epicurus, Lucretius, Spinoza, and La Méttrie, whose materialist theories differed significantly only in the magnitude of their imagined vehicles, the sensuous models of either mechanically autotelic or divinely defined matter they conceived: that of atoms in random motion and collision, of God as rational Substance of a Nature whose laws are thus just as sensuously embodied as their affective extension into physical entities, and of the closed loop of the individual bodily machine. None of these sensuous bodies *is* a theory of materialism; each is the illustration of a necessarily *ideational* hypothesis, serving to figure that hypothesis to our cognizing imagination.[38] For the cognition of an hypothesis about physical bodies and actions is a cognition of nothing, unless mediated by a sensory vehicle: the fate of all rational hypotheses, when not strictly mathematically logical in the classical non-physical sense, is to require some form of sensuous representation that, if purported to be simultaneously systematic in scope, must necessarily be imaginary in origin—a theoretical part, taking the shape of a body, of the theory itself, on whatever scale the theorist conceives it. Thus, where a pure or unmediated "idealism" meets an equally purely material or unmediated "materialism"—where Leo Strauss, avowedly "apolitical" patron saint of "conservative values," anti-universalism, and illiberal, esoterically embedded hierarchies of knowledge, shares common "headspace" with Gilles Deleuze, contemporary mythologist of exocentric micro-anarchies expanding without trace across space, itself conceived as an infinitely figuratively repopulatable biosphere of political action without politics—seems to be the fully imaginary, ideational "space" of the purely functional and anti-idealist machine. The first theorist to imagine such a machine whose frictionless workings would be ensured by an external organizing "Idea," be it the vertical Straussian idea

---

[36] "Die Philosophen haben die Welt nur verschieden *interpretiert*, es kommt darauf an, sie zu verändern" (Thesis 12 of the *Thesen über Feuerbach* [1845]).

[37] With apologies to Robert Frost.

[38] However inaccurate his own tropological identification of Schiller's aesthetic theory with a full-scale "ideology of Kant's critical philosophy," de Man's critique of the *aestheticizing* basis of all supposed pragmatisms or realisms that, masquerading as theories with some immediate purchase on the real, inevitably "result in a total loss of contact with reality, in a total idealism," is precisely the crux of the present analysis of all "utopian" alternatives to the necessarily heterogeneous axes of any actual theory, that, contemporarily ascribed to Schiller, and of increasing popularity, under semblance of "materialist theory," in the purely descriptive practices of "political" utopianism today, all repeat [began with] Plato's original imagining of a purely ideational utopian state, whose proud, purely pragmatic functionalism—dream of every self-crediting "philosopher-king" granted total sovereignty over the state machine—is its every real component's nightmare. See de Man, *The Aesthetic Ideology*, pp. 142, 146.

of an autocratic, intellectual and moral governing elite or Deleuzian idea of homogenous, self-replicating "rhizomes," "folds," and other nonhuman "outsides without insides" imagined in eternal procession across a purely horizontal plane, is, of course, Plato, whose "utopian" theory of the perfectly functioning state, it is always worth recalling, *was not one to begin with*, but instead followed illogically upon a failed attempt to define a very different form of functioning—one, as it is soon discovered, without adequate sensory or imaginary, let alone mechanical embodiment—called "justice."

Even the topic of "justice" (δική, δικαιοσύνη) appears to surface only incidentally in the course of πολιτεία, the extended dialogue long mistranslated as the *Republic*,[39] when a conspicuously trivial dinner conversation concerning the joys of old age (and, on Socrates' suggestion, the role of wealth in enabling them) includes the citation, by its elderly host, Cephalus, the most self-satisfied (and indeed wealthy) among its participants, of a pointless if "delightful" Pindaric homily regarding "hope" which happens to mention "justice" in the context of a formulaic epithet: "'Hope,' a delightful Pindaric saying has it, nurtures the soul of "those who live their life in justice and piety" (ἂν δικαίως καὶ ὁσίως τὸν βίον [I: 331a4]). The "blessings of riches" to "a decent ['good' or 'lenient'] (επιεικει) man" (I: 331b2), Cephalus continues, is that he "has no occasion to defraud or deceive others for his own benefit," and is able to pay off his debts before dying. Socrates' responds with a question that, grasping, apparently arbitrarily, upon one word in the Pindaric truism, turns the till then trivial tenor and vehicle of the discussion inside out: "Well said Cephalus, but as concerning justice, what is it? To speak the truth and pay one's debts? No more than that?" (I: 331c2–4).[40]

The series of materialist rabbit holes that then ensues, as each dinner conversationalist frames his own suggested definition of justice beginning with the rudimentarily mechanical one of paying off one's debts, is rapidly dispatched as insufficient to the task by Socrates, but not before that initial version of justice as rewarding like with like leads to a series of other identitarian suggestions

---

[39] The Greek πολιτεία originally denoted nothing resembling the practical architecture of a particular kind of state or city (πόλις) but rather the abstract condition and special legal status of individual bodies that we now call "citizenship" within any polity. For while πολιτεία took on the meaning of *Republic* pursuant to Cicero's far more widely circulated *De Re Publica* ["On Public Things or Matters"], itself written, by one of those backwards ironies of historical revisionism, as a kind of sequel to the work the meaning of whose title its own replaced, "justice," the concept upon which this, Plato's longest dialogue (till its amendment by *The Laws*), and of all by far the most figurative, had trained a first spotlight, was not merely obscured by that later titular translation. Rather, that now canonical *mistranslation* unwittingly imitates, as does the dialogue's history of readers, what was lost in the original to begin with—the concept of "justice," replaced by the verbal sleight-of-hand, carried out by Socrates in plain sight, of its "large print" transformation into the autocratically ruled state—just as the detailed prescription of parts assigned within the fixed *content* of that smoothly functioning state machine has been confused with the changing historical forms and reflective critical function of political *theory*.

[40] Plato, *Republic* Vol. I (Cambridge, Mass.: Loeb Classical Library, 1978), p. 18 (with modifications of English translation provided).

(including that of different "justices" accorded "friends" and "enemies") resulting finally in their most radically nihilist extension: Thrasymachus' ontological suggestion that "justice is nothing other than the interest or advantage (συμφέρον [I: 338c2]) of the stronger" (I: 338c1–2), and thus all ruling powers are not only *justified* in acting in their own interest, but *should*, if they are to maintain the strength that *ipso facto* defines their justice.[41] That inappropriately ontological, and thus inevitably tautological view that the abstract concept of justice "is" what justice justly finds itself justified in doing—a "perversion" or turning away from justice very much still alive and kicking (justice in the face) today—will find its own, less clearly despotic illustration in Socrates' substitution of an ideally predetermined state for the pitfalls befalling all such necessarily inadequate versions of justice as a mode for exchanging identifiable equivalencies of value upon earth. The dystopian vision of justice that each of these identificatory conceptions of justice entails leads logically to Glaucon's recognition that justice could never be properly identified as such, let alone defined, once perceived as administered by any particular body at all. With perfect relevance to Schiller's theory of aesthetics, not as gateway to a utopian state, but as "material" "form" shaped of the labor of *sublating* opposing drives in this world, Glaucon elegantly sums up the problem inherent in any attempt to define the resolution of opposing claims, or justice, through its external identification—a non-allegorical, but no less figurative transposition of an abstract concept into its ideal agent, identifiable as such—and, with that problem, the difficulty of identifying the idea of justice with any particular embodiment of it, as follows:

> [Since] in the perfectly unjust man we must assume the most perfect injustice ... we must allow him, while doing the most unjust acts, to have acquired the greatest reputation for justice. ... Having set up the unjust man as this sort of character, let us in turn place the just man beside him in this argument. ... We must take away from the just man the outward appearance of justice, for if he is reputed just he will have the honours and gifts this sort of reputation bestows upon him The just man must be and not seem good, unclothed of all but his virtue. Let him be the best of men and let him be thought the worst; then he will have been put to the proof; and we shall see whether he will be affected by the fear of infamy and its consequences. And let him continue thus to the hour of death; being just and seeming to be unjust. When both have reached the uttermost extreme, the one of justice and the other of injustice, let judgment be given which of them is the happier of the two. (II: 361a6–361d4)[42]

The phenomenal appearance of justice, embodied in an individual honored or punished for "acts" whose ability to "seem" just or unjust may be divorced from their actual content, thus irrefutably logically removed from the picture by Glaucon, Socrates proceeds to paint another, "bigger picture," one whose

---

[41] Plato, *Republic* Vol. I, pp. 337–339.
[42] Plato, *Republic* Vol I, pp. 122–124.

willful leap away from the matter at hand, under rhetorical guise of merely offering a better view of it, all future versions of a wished-for state of wish-fulfillment designating itself the object of "utopian thought"—more often than not, uncoincidentally, "futurist" in inflection—will imitate. The generic span of the prescriptive descriptions by which utopian conceptualism, famously critiqued by Marx and Hegel as "fantastic pictures" of "dreamt-up" "duodecimo Jerusalems" and "little Icaria," [43] is compelled to script an *embodiment*, rather than any analysis of its ideational content makes that content not merely a fantasy but a full-scale "ideology" on a par, if not in important ways identical to the "aesthetic ideology" critiqued by de Man, among whose practitioners he reflexively counted Schiller.[44] In de Man's case, that reflex seems to stem from his temporal-theoretical pairing of Kant and Schiller (as he could have similarly have related Wordsworth to the Coleridge of the—post-*Lyrical Ballads*—*Biographica Literaria*) into an historically inevitable odd coupling of comprehensive, structurally rigorous critical thought with its personifying, naturalizing, or otherwise pleasurable aestheticization: on de Man's view, the clearer, the more irreversibly critical and dialectical the thinking, the more aestheticizing, either emotive or otherwise purely self-assertive, but in all instances fundamentally formless the expressions of its reception. (In de Man's version of the history of specifically theoretical reception, it should be noted, by way of Schiller's and other theoretical *Nachfolger*'s defense, that such aestheticization is already positioned several steps ahead of dumb rejection in that its practitioners must be perceptive enough to be admirers in the first place. By contrast, the inability to understand anything of actual significance, to perceive any difference between thinking and, say, plant growth, let alone feel the compulsion to obliterate it, is reserved instead for those who, for several practical reasons, dismiss, because they consistently fail to apprehend, all articulations of thought to begin with.)

Just as the subject of the embodied image of justice he offers is no longer justice but a utopian, because purely ideational state, within whose supremely

---

[43] See Part III, Section 3: "Critical-Utopian Socialism and Communism," *The Manifesto of the Communist Party* (1848), in which Marx and Engel's ever-timely critique of utopian futurist fantasies uncannily recalls the very conception according to which the "best possible state" requires a philosopher-king in Plato, or, in Marx's terms, the special understanding at the disposal of the "ruling class:" "Socialists of this kind ... consider themselves superior to all class antagonisms. ... Hence they habitually appeal to society at large, without distinction of class; nay, *by preference to the ruling class*, for how can people, once they understand their system, fail to see in it the best possible plan of the best possible state of society. ... Such fantastic pictures of future society" (*The Manifesto...* [Marxist Internet Archive: 2010], pp. 32–33 [emphasis added]).

[44] De Man, *The Aesthetic Ideology*, p. 147: "Schiller appears as the ideology of Kant's critical philosophy." De Man's own conflicting accounts of Schiller as both "ideological" "idealist" (147) and "psychological in the empirical sense" (151)—opposing characterizations somehow equally at home within his own unspecified conception of Schiller's "concept ... of an aesthetic state," and still vaguer allusion to the "political institution resulting from such a conception"—are ones his application to Schiller of a non-Hegelian model of mind, by which the history of thinking results not in intellectual progress but reversal, does not address.

anti-"idealist" (in the Schillerian sense), because purely mechanical operation all questions of justice would be out of the question, so Socrates' stated rationale for taking the wholly illogical discursive step of replacing an open inquiry into the nature of justice with the exacting engineering specifications for an ideal state, its ideality demonstrated *post factum* by the allegorical origin story that accompanies it, succeeds in *seeming* logical for no justifiable reason. For Socrates' displacement of his interlocutors' intellectual attention from the potential meanings of an abstract concept onto an explicitly optical illustration of something necessarily entirely different from any concept, claims to base itself on an apparent principle of similarity, that is, of a comparison of like with like differentiated only by magnitude, while executing what turns out to be the illogical origin of our understanding of the "rationale" for the determination of relations of governance—ever modeled on Plato's fully imaginary, "archetypal" state—that would come to be called politics. Socrates' image of the "larger letters" of the state shifts his interlocutors' focus of attention from the insoluble problem of identifying the true nature of justice by way of the identities of individual bodies with which justice can have nothing to do, and changes, with that shift, not only the central subject of the dialogue, but all history of political and aesthetic thought to come. He does this *not* by way of argument, but via a purely empirically based, *ocular rather than logical* analogy:

> The search we are undertaking is no mean task, but as I see it it's one that needs a sharp eye, not a weak one. Since therefore ... we are not good at making an inquiry of this kind, I think we should employ the kind of investigation suitable for people who are not very keen-sighted. If someone had ordered them to read small letters (γράμματα σμικρὰ [368d4]) from a distance, but then someone noticed that the same letters existed written larger and on a larger background (μείζω τε καὶ ἐν μείζονι [368d6–7]). I think it would seem a godsend to read those first and then examine the smaller ones to see if they were the same. (II: 368d1–9)[45]

When Adeimantus bluntly and entirely appropriately asks what relevance the mode of magnification can have to the search for justice, Socrates' answer is, first, to ask rhetorically whether "the state is larger than the individual," and then to conclude from that false analogy that the corresponding *quantity* of "justice in the state would also have to be larger and thus more easily discernible" than it is in the individual (II: 368e4–7)—to which Glaucon, happy to overlook the mortal paradox involved in recognizing justice that he himself first recognized and shift the burden of its appearance in disappearance to the undivided pleasures of the really big screen, responds enthusiastically, to the effect: "wow, I think that's a really good-looking idea!" (καλῶς λέγειν [II: 369a5][46]).

---

[45] Plato, *Republic*, Vol. I, p. 146.
[46] Plato, *Republic*, Vol. I, p. 148.

The state thus enters the history of thinking as big letters written on a big background (μείζω τε καὶ ἐν μείζονι)—of all unlikely figures, a kind of billboard—rather than the "small letters" (γράμματα σμικρά) of the individual agent, the still undefined "just man," now abruptly set aside as a kind of illegible fine print. Framing a traditional 4-part analogy upon an already figurative conception of size alone, Socrates irrationally compares incomparables: if the relation between person and state was indeed simply one of magnification, there would of course be no need for any form of government, let alone political praxis or theory, at all. By using justice as a foil for a state supposedly modeled on the "just" individual, its parts mimicking those of the body, Socrates suggests the justness of a grotesque conception: that of the state as an organic being between whose composite organs no exchange is possible, a bodily machine whose every component part fulfills its "natural" purpose, and, thus, in which *all aesthetic activity*, conducted by those capable of dissimulating or "impersonating" (μιμεῖσθαι [III: 398a2]) any part, *can play no role*, the figuratively magnified "letters" of the state famously spelling out the banishment of poets and forever excluding their *properly* figurative compositions, "poems" (ποιήματα [III: 398a3]), from the perfectly interlocking parts of the completely imaginary, "harmonious" state.[47]

Now Schiller the playwright and "idealist" aesthetic theorist would be the first to agree with the observation of Glaucon, that defining justice on the model of a person cannot be enough, in that no person "is" an idea but rather, in the first instance, a perceptible body, and, as such, is subject to the problem of appearances; that any "outward appearance" (ἀφαιρετέον [II: 361b9]) of "goodness" (ἀγαθόν [II: 361b8]) within any society, because it would reap the potentially corrupting reward of a beneficial reputation (δοκεῖν [II: 361b8, c2]) for justice, cannot be equated with justice.[48] But it is precisely the *ethical* problem of appearances that Plato first raises, and contemporary theorists of "utopian" aesthetics ignore, that made of Schiller, in particular, not an aestheticizing fabulist but avid practitioner of historical-*political* "appearances" (Schein), that is, appearances of the real presence or absence of justice in time. Unlike Goethe, he theorizes aesthetic appearances neither in analogy with the endless permutations of natural metamorphoses, nor as the object and vehicle of an author's or, for that matter, any theorizing empirical scientist's "irony."[49] Artisan of the theater as well as theorist, Schiller understands that, in relation to their meaning, all linguistic, indeed all representational arts are by definition media of *Schein*: the fact that he never failed to distinguish *Schein* from the "material stuff" of the world, without which sharp distinction no aesthetic formation would indeed be possible, made him no more an aesthetic ideologist

---

[47] Plato, *Republic* Vol. I, p. 397.
[48] Plato, *Republic* Vol. I, p. 122.
[49] Goethe, "Versuch als Vermittler von Objekt und Subjekt," in Goethe, *Werke*, Hrsg. Benno von Wiese (Hamburg: Christian Wegner Verlag, 1955), 14 Bde. (XIII: 317).

than an ontologist of phenomenal perception, let alone of any confusion of aesthesis with "Being."

It also endowed his thinking about the formal practice of the aesthetic with a profound sense of historical reality, a deep engagement with the *non*transcendent nature of art within the real limits of historical existence and, therein, of real and consequential political conditions. In that regard, the twentieth-century theorist with whom Schiller most shares a critically *non*utopian understanding of the aesthetic is Adorno, another post-Kantian who took Kant's productive principle of limitation by negation so seriously within his own thinking, made it so fundamental to the very possibility of critical aesthetic theory itself, that, unlike Hegel, he scarcely seemed to notice its pivotal importance to his own.[50] Precisely because his *negative* dialectics of aesthetics are *not* utopianist in orientation, Adorno has not been associated with contemporary theoretical evaluations of Schiller; for the same reason, it is Adorno who best underscores an undervalued aspect of Schiller's thinking: its profound awareness of historicity and of what both theorists understood as "Staatsraison," or the reason of the State. In analyzing the precisely delimited terms on which that understanding is based, something else of enormous cognitive significance opens up: the basis of the acknowledged différand between Adorno and Benjamin that, beginning with their very different understandings of the working premises of the *Institut für Sozialforschung* (University of Frankfurt, 1923–1933) that, in exile, carried the collective moniker, the Frankfurt School, ultimately extended to shape not only all German Departments but the contours of post-Marxist political thinking in the west. Which way the future of theory lies has recently, increasingly appeared to depend on which side of that différand one stands, and a clearer analysis of Schiller's view of the relationship of art to both history and the state may not only relieve him of his worn "idealist" moniker but make the very real stakes of our investments in kinds of philosophy clearer to us today.

For Schiller may have been the first modern theorist to acknowledge in print the actual historical existence of an ideological culture industry—fully

---

[50] Adorno's brief remarks on utopianism in *Aesthetic Theory* focus not only on its material incompatibility with art—"Art is as little capable of concretizing utopia as is theory; not even negatively" ("So wenig wie Theorie vermag Kunst Utopie zu konkretisieren; nicht einmal negative")—but, with real urgency *and* concreteness, on the "total catatrophe" in which any "possible realization" of just such a "paradise" on "earth" would result: "the real possibility of utopia—that the earth, according to the status of productive forces, could here, now, without mediation, be paradise—unites at its highest point with the possibility of total catastrophe" ("dass die Erde, nach dem Stand der Produktivkräfte, jetzt, hier, unmittelbar das Paradies sein könnte—auf einer äussersten Spitze mit der Möglichkeit der totalen Katastrophe sich vereint. Adorno, *Ästhetische Theorie*, Hrsg. Gretel Adorno and Rolf Tiedemann (Frankfurt: Suhrkamp, 1973), pp. 55–56. His, at best, ambivalent acknowledgment of the debt of any critical aesthetic theory, including his own, to Kant, appears in such pointed comments on the opposite view of art as these: "Perhaps our relationship to art today is such that, in Kantian fashion, we approach it as something given; whoever defends it already makes ideologies and art itself into one and the same. There follows upon this, nonetheless, the thought that something in reality beyond the veil ... objectively demands art" [35]).

understanding, nearly two centuries before the cultural sociology of Bourdieu and institutional installation of institutionally critical art by Haake, the anti-"aesthetic" social fact that, within, *rather than contrary to* the rule of *Staatsraison*, "art pays." And while that recognition on Schiller's part, not unlike the one cemented in Adorno's mind by his "*wissenschaftliche Erfahrungen in Amerika*," probably had quite a lot to do with Schiller's practical work as a commercial playwright, as de Man himself acknowledges,[51] de Man just as frankly observes that it may be equally asserted of any of us given to writing for a living.[52] If Schiller understood and accepted the conditions for theatrical "success" dictated by the particular culture industry of which, as we shall see, he was both theoretical critic and practical pillar, no less a theoretical purist than Adorno may also have been empirically forced to acknowledge the thoroughly non-theoretical rule of the empirical when exigent historical circumstances compelled him to be rudely introduced to the American reduction of aesthetic experience to a commodity and power of aesthetic judgment to a

---

[51] Commenting on the pragmatically motivated preference of the playwright for what he calls the "practical" over "theoretical sublime," as a preference for the more stageable representation of "psychological" "terror," caused by "'the desire for self-preservation'" in the face of danger, over "'the drive for knowledge'" heightened and thwarted by experiences of "'the infinite'," de Man observes:

> What is striking in those passages, which are quite convincing and which are psychologically and empirically entirely reasonable—they are also reasonable if you think of them in terms of Schiller's own concerns as a playwright, if you don't ask the philosophical question, "What is the structure of the faculty of the imagination?" but if you ask the practical question, "How am I going to write successful plays?" which was partly and legitimately Schiller's concern—you will provoke a lot more effect on an audience by using terror or using scenes of terror, also using scenes in which Nature is directly threatening, than by using abstractions, such as infinity, which are not easily represented on the stage. ... It doesn't bother him in the least that knowledge would be impossible, as long as he can fill his theater. I don't want to put it in contemptuous terms, but that's practical and that's necessary, whereas the other can wait. (De Man, *Aesthetic Ideology*, p. 141)

[52] In an unusually "practical," "empirically reasonable" observation of his own, rather than belittle, de Man proceeds to defend Schiller's pragmatic concerns as those only the most self-deceiving of us can claim to have transcended, warning the university audience seated before him: "Before you either contest this, or before you not contest but agree with it and hold it against Schiller, or think that it is something we are now far beyond and that we would never in our enlightened days do—you would never make this naive confusion between the practical and the pragmatic on the one hand and the philosophical Kantian enterprise on the other—before you decide that, don't decide too soon that you are beyond Schiller in any sense. I don't think any of us can lay this claim. Whatever writing we do, whatever way we have of talking about art, whatever way we have of teaching, whatever justification we give ourselves for teaching, whatever the standards are and the values by means of which we teach, they are more than ever and profoundly Schillerian. They come from Schiller, and not from Kant. And if you ever try to do something in the other direction and you touch on it you'll see what will happen to you. Better be very sure, wherever you are, that your tenure is very well established .... (De Man, *The Aesthetic Ideology*, p. 142; "Kant and Schiller" was one of the Cornell Messenger Lectures delivered by de Man shortly before his death in 1983).

quantitative "science." His dependence on employment at the so-called Princeton Radio Project whose financial support allowed him to enter the US in 1938[53] (and which, true to the principle of false advertising on which commodification depends, was in fact located in a former brewery in Newark with no relationship to Princeton) brought him face to face with the economic fusion of base and superstructure by which he was *paid* to gather data indicating what the television industry has since come to call "audience-share," so as to determine the popularity of broadcasts that would dictate not only their economic "viability" or lifespan but their future imitation, since they were those for which advertisers would in turn *pay* the most, having *already* correlated the *rate of sale* of their own products with the desire for them created by broadcast *advertising*. Sardonically crediting his experience of "America," embodied and distilled at its very outset by the surreally situated brewery housing the Princeton Radio Project (*"wenn ich dorthin fuhr, durch den Tunnel unter den Hudson, kam ich mir ein wenig wie ein Kafkasche Naturtheater von Oklahoma vor"*), with first "truly" teaching him the "the weight of the empirical" (*"das Gewicht dessen, was Empirie heisst"*[54])—the "blind" external givenness (*"dies da"*[55]) of an unknown, unformed materiality, which, along with the effectively autonomous externality of *Technik*, had already become an important theoretical node of his (posthumously published) *Aesthetic Theory* of the same year—Adorno, supreme critic of culture, nonetheless understood, as did Schiller (and de Man) that, separate from its selective repurposing as *data* for commodification, the empirical is necessary to thought. And like Schiller and de Man, Adorno refuses *either* to seek intellectual refuge from the fact of the empirical in utopian fantasy *or* to forget that, alongside its necessity, as unyielding material resistance, to thinking, the empirical provides ideology with the phenomenal pretext for its aestheticization, and, therein, the required grist for the mill of the culture industry.

---

[53] Adorno's "depressing," ultimately untenable tenure at the Radio Project, ending in his dismissal in 1939 by the Rockefeller Foundation that funded it, despite the special pleading of its director—empirical sociologist, Adorno sympathist, and fellow exile—Paul Lazarsfeld, is extensively recounted and sympathetically analyzed by David E. Morrison, in "Kultur and Culture: The Case of Theodor W. Adorno and Paul F. Lazarsfeld," *Social Research* Vol. 45, No. 2 (Summer 1978): 321–355 (344). Noting Adorno's "alienation" from the empiricist orientation of the Project, Thomas Y. Levin and Michael von der Linn do their best to wrest from his brief period of involvement with an American radio industry that he openly abhorred a somewhat more positive account. See their short preface to their journal publication of the typescript fragments stored in Columbia University's Lazarsfeld papers collection, and forthcoming in the *Nachgelassene Schriften* of the Adorno Archive, which together comprise Adorno's "unsuccessful [attempt] to elaborate," by Adorno's own description, "'a systematically executed sociology and social psychology of radio music'," in Levin and von der Linn, "Elements of a Radio Theory: Adorno and the Princeton Radio Research Project," *Music Quarterly* 76.2 (1994): 316–324 (320–321).

[54] Adorno, "Wissenschaftliche Erfahrungen in Amerika," *Stichworte. Kritische Modelle 2* (Frankfurt: Suhrkamp, 1969), pp. 113–148 (117, 148; epigraph, this essay: p. 123).

[55] Adorno, *Asthetische Theorie*, pp. 38, 47.

Whether or not Schiller's early exposure of culture *as* an industry owed, in the manner de Man describes, to his practical experience as a working playwright, in contrast to Adorno and Horkheimer's inaugural substantivization of a "culture industry" in the *Dialectic of Enlightenment*[56] to signify not the potentially dialectical effect of aesthetic and intellectual-theoretical activity, located by definition within a society's superstructure, upon its base structure—the very potential upon which the conception and practice of "critical theory" by the Frankfurt School was premised[57]—but rather the total absorption of the superstructure by its economic base and inevitable political instrumentalization of "culture" alongside "reason" by totalitarian regimes bent on employing their liberatory capacities against themselves—Schiller instead places his critique of culture as *Lohnkunst* squarely *within* an overarching dialectical argument distinguishing both the unmanipulated or material "reality" of the unaestheticized "work of things themselves" *and* the critical relation to freedom realized in the human work of producing aesthetic form and semblance. As if commenting, in uncannily deManian fashion, on the inherent blindness of any purportedly pure intellectualism, or, for that matter, any supposedly dialectical, whether de Manian or Marxian categorical conflation of the aesthetic with the ideological, Schiller observes:

> Supreme stupidity and supreme understanding have a certain affinity with each other in that both seek only the *real* and are completely insensitive to mere semblance ... in short, stupidity cannot raise itself above the realm of reality and understanding cannot linger in any realm beneath truth. ... Insofar as both the want of reality and the dependence on the real are merely consequences of a lack, so indifference toward reality and interest in semblance is a true enlargement of humanity and decisive step toward culture. ... [I]t affords evidence ... of inner freedom because it allows us to see a power which is capable of setting itself in

---

[56] First published in 1944 under the title, *Philosophische Fragmente* in New York by the Social Studies Association, Adorno and Horkheimer's *Dialektik der Aufklärung* (Frankfurt: Fischer Verlag, 1972 [1st ed. Amsterdam: Querido, 1947]) synthesized reflections composed shortly after Adorno's visa-securing employment by the Princeton Radio Project. Its focus on the medium-induced passivity and manipulation of the commercial radio audience, as prophetic platform of an increasingly technologically dependent culture industry, confirms the influence on this seminal work of what Adorno "learned" while working for a Project whose director had hired him for the purely pragmatic purpose of ensuring his survival. No longer faced with either the prospect of his own or fact of others' mass extermination, but rather a largely student-led "revolution" against the pursuit of both philosophical and cultural inquiry *based in part on his and Horkheimer's own early work*, the postwar Adorno later publicly regretted the polemical message of their now classic Dialektik, its tendentious instrumentalization of all "enlightenment" philosophy, including Kant's inauguration of critical theory itself, as unalloyed tool of totalitarianism.

[57] See esp. Max Horkheimer's great inaugural paper, "Traditionelle Theorie und Kritische," *Zeitschrift für Sozialforschung* (1937), republished in *Kritische Theorie* (Frankfurt a. Main: Fischer Verlag, 1968), Eng. edition: *Critical Theory*, Intro. Stanley Aronowitz (New York: Continuum, 1982 [1st ed. 1972]), pp. 188–243. See also Horkheimer's stringent critique of "refuge taken in utopian fantasy" and defense of "thinking" as neither a "spiritualist" diversion from work nor "moment in the work process" as it is defined by the division of labor, pp. 211–212.

motion of its own accord m independently of external stimulus. ... *The reality of things is their own work*; the semblance of things is the work of human beings, and a mind which feasts on semblance no longer delights on what it receives, but what it *does*.[58]

Rather than idealize "culture" in the inherently ideological manner both de Man and Adorno critique, Schiller recognizes that its semblances can either articulate the otherwise invisible "internal freedom" that is the "power" of human agency, or constitute an industry for the reproduction of ideology, the mere semblances of the semblance of such power. Employing a compound noun of his own coinage to designate the market-based production of such false semblances of "aesthetic semblance"—the remarkably proto-Marxian concept, *Lohnkunst*[59]—Schiller daringly pronounces, 150 years before the Frankfurt School, the material-historical fact that *Kultur*, too, can be tailored to profit, its "salaried" products made to conform to relations of "value" production that are themselves subservient in turn to the singular principle of commodification based in exchange value which determines the products of any commercial industry.[60] In his thoroughly original conception of "Lohnkunst," Schiller simultaneously notes what differentiates it from *Lohnarbeit*. In contrast to the purely quantitative basis by which *Lohnarbeit*, or paid labor, enters an already thoroughly dehumanized market of exchange, Schiller's "Lohnkunst" is definitively *qualified* by him as "kriechende Lohnkunst,"[61] a product which must "grovel" or "crawl" its way into marketability, in that, unlike any practical object, "*art*" made for profit must not only flatter the purchaser but bow to the lie that the spirit that produced it is "free," a purely "internal" "power" heedless of all "external" "material"

---

[58] Schiller, *Briefe*, Letter 26, p. 192 (emphases added in part).

[59] Schiller, *Briefe*, Letter 27, p. 218.

[60] Cf. Adorno's brilliantly cogent summation of the waylaying of the "consciousness" of "intellectual objectivity" by the introduction of "the concept of value" whose subsequent "reification" replaces intellectual objectivity and material objecthood alike: "The concept of value is itself already the expression of a situation in which one's consciousness of intellectual objectivity is weakened. To counter crude relativism one has arbitrarily reified it" ("Der Wertbegriff selbst ist bereit Ausdruck einer Situation, in der das Bewusstsein geistiger Objektivität aufgeweicht wird. Als Gegenschlag gegen den kruden Relativismus hat man ihn willkürlich verdinglicht") ("Thesen zur Kunstsoziologie," pp. 994–103, in Adorno, *Ohne Leitbild. Parva Aesthetica* [Frankfurt: Suhrkamp, 1967], p. 99). In keeping with Schiller's mode of theorizing the aesthetic formally *and* materially, as a sensuous object of "experience," rather than subject of hypostatized rules, he continues: "On the other hand, however, so much does every artistic experience—in truth, even every simple judgment of predicative logic—presuppose the principles of critique, that to abstract therefrom would be as arbitrary and abstract as the hypostasis of values is" [99]). Whether Adorno's emphasis on the necessity of the "experience" of actual material objects to any unreified and "critical," rather than ideological aesthetics would be similarly deemed "pragmatic" by de Man, as opposed to "philosophical" in the mode of Kant, is a question perhaps most revealing of the somewhat paradoxical basis of de Man's own criticism of Schiller, in that the origin of that experience-based critical theory of the aesthetic is Kant.

[61] Schiller, *Briefe*, Letter 27, p. 218.

considerations, indeed one might even say "idealist," rather than self-interested or "pragmatic," to a truly unfathomable degree. For what remains ever-resistant to exhaustive description, indeed unfathomable about the ideological art of superstructural production and reproduction is that it is *necessarily intellectual* in content: ungrounded in any object or objective necessity, it must simulate such a ground by debasing itself, lowering itself to a level of obsequiousness and flatline of amoral, self-aggrandizing deception whose bottom—as nonextant as its summit—it can never quite reach. The trick of *Lohnkunst*, as of every manufactured "tool" ("Werkzeug") and made-to-order servant of a dominant ideology, is that in intellectually exchanging its own actual and inalienable freedom—to negate and critique ideological fictions—for the prospect of profit-by-mystification to whose numbing of the mind it instead substantively contributes, it gives the ideology it "serves" ("dienende"), which is properly nothing, the semblance of something bordering on everything, neither above nor beneath which anyone can go.

To *this* thoroughly capitalized state of aesthetic affairs, Schiller contrasts what he calls "the aesthetic state." Such a state of aesthetic mediation is not a utopian fiction in which negation itself, not to speak of the liberatory effect of thinking, is unthinkable, exactly because, nowhere existent, such freedom "of" thought can never be conceived as necessary—no fantasy of a society that, excluding the referential grounds for its own analysis, "questioning," and contradiction because explicitly posited *in place of* the real, must thus also, as Adorno conclusively observes, exclude *art itself*.[62] Rather, as Schiller profoundly describes such a necessarily "ideal," because spatially nonextant "realm of aesthetic semblance" in which, "every citizen" having "equal rights," the "violent bending" of the "masses" to an ideological "purpose" is upended, and, instead of seeking refuge in either the "lifeless" products of *Lohnkunst* or dream of an immaterial state designed to exclude all difference and opposition, "men make their way through the most complex circumstances" without making that way the only way, because feeling no "need to injure the freedom of others, in order to assert their own":

---

[62] The observation arises as Adorno attempts yet again to dispel the popular misapprehension of his severely mistranslated sentence concerning "poetry" and "Auschwitz," sadly, the single utterance by which Adorno is universally known. Translated in English into two separate sentences seeming to assert that, in Adorno's opinion, any "poetry" written "after Auschwitz" is in fact an act of "barbarism," whereas the single, markedly complex sentence of the original German immediately contradicts that proposition by reflecting that such an assertion must "corrode" (*frisst*) any understanding of the negative constitution of art in the first place, the mistaken truncated reception of the sentence haunted Adorno even as he continued to reflect upon the critical necessity of art, including in the final sentences of the 1967 *Parva Aesthetica,* which take explicit aim at the exclusion of art by the "fulfillment" not of barbarism but of "*utopia*:" "While the situation no longer admits of art—to say as much was the aim of the sentence about the impossibility of poems after Auschwitz—it nonetheless demands it. For the imageless reality is what is become the full reflection of an imageless condition in which art would disappear because utopia has fulfilled itself" (181).

Given wings by [the power of aesthetic taste], even grovelling art-for-profit wrests itself out of the dust, and the fetters of serfdom fall from the lifeless and living alike. ... In the aesthetic state everything—even the [human] tool of [a dehumanizing] servitude—is a free citizen with the same rights as the most noble, and the mindset, which [would] bend the patient masses violently to its purpose, must now ask it for its approval. ... But does such a state of aesthetic seeming exist and where is it to be found? As a need it exists ... wherever not the spiritless imitation of others but our own aesthetic nature directs us, where human beings make their way through the most complex relations with daring simplicity ... without needing to injure the freedom of others in order to assert their own.[63]

Now Schiller cannot of course provide us with the *Stadtsplan* for such an "aesthetic state," since there can be none which would not defeat it, but he has already given us a clear description of the state in which, by contrast, *Lohnkunst* is the only art permitted, because assigned that entirely ideological function by the purely "mechanical" ("mechanischen") state within which it plays a clearly routed, supporting role. The all-inclusive machine of a state in which ideology rules *both* superstructure and rule-generating base, at which Schiller takes direct critical aim, in the single most extensive figurative description in the *Letters*, is one from which the "free movement of the poetic power" ("freien Gang der Dichtungskraft"[64])—central theoretical subject and motivating object of the *Letters*—is excluded *per force*. Far in advance of its future theoretical conception, by Weber, Marcuse, Parsons, and Luhmann, among others (no less than its comic cinematic immortalization by Chaplin), Schiller is the first modern author unflinchingly to depict the autotelic mechanism of the *non*-discursive, purely functional "State" as one whose "members"—*Glieder*—do nothing other than literalize the physical meaning of that term, serving only to rotate the cog assigned them by a machine whose "prescribed" movements control all their own.[65] The resemblance of that vivid description to Socrates' outline of the original "utopian" state is so thoroughly remarkable as to be unmistakable. Yet, whereas Plato surreptitiously introduced one-third of the way through *Republic* Bk. 2 the elaboration of the smoothly running state that will comprise the remainder of the 10-Book dialogue, as merely the facilitating, large print version of the "small letters" of a sufficient answer to the question of "justice" he had sought to that point—only rapidly to abandon and replace that question by its exclusionary opposite, the prescription of a state designed on the purely mechanical model of physical *justesse*—Schiller introduces, in the sixth of twenty-seven Letters, his own unsparing analysis of such a state machine in order to argue for the necessity of its opposite.

Explicitly situated in ancient Greece, the total (and totalitarian) state Schiller describes—"crude and crass mechanism" into which, by dint of pure historical extension, earlier political "organizations" of "independent individuals" had

---

[63] Schiller, *Briefe*, Letter 27, p. 218.
[64] Schiller, *Briefe*, Letter 6, p. 34.
[65] *Ibid.*

sunk—is not posed by him in false analogy with the smaller body (itself standing in for the invisible mind) of the individual, let alone as corporal replacement for the inherently abstract concept of "justice." On the contrary, this unmistakably "Platonic" state is defined by Schiller as a nonhuman "clockwork" out of whose "assembled" "lifeless parts" "the mechanical life" of the "holistic state" is "artificially composed": "ein kunstreiche[s] Uhrwerk ... wo aus der Zusammenstückelung ... lebloser Teile ein mechanisches Leben im Ganzen sich bildet."[66] With stunning insight into the short path from conflict-free "utopian" functionalism to Adorno and Horkheimer's culture industry, with Marcuse's one-dimensional man paving the way between them, Schiller explains the actual experiential *content* composed by prescribed participation in this "pure," *because purely mechanical* form of the state. Along with the concept of instrumental *Lohnkunst* that, he will argue at the conclusion of his final Letter, constitutes the sole version of artistry such a wholly pragmatic state will sustain, the crucial *negative* role played within the constitution of the overarching dialectical thrust of the *Letters* by Schiller's early *critique raisonnée* here, of utopianist parameters that must effectively mimic those of a "solid-state" machine, has attracted none of the theoretical attention that Schiller's purportedly "utopian thinking" *or* "aesthetic ideology" has garnered on both sides of the Atlantic in recent decades. Ironically enough, it is rather *with* this "eternal" utopian archetype (perennially suggested as practical antitype to any society substantively qualified as "unjust") that Schiller's thought has itself been identified, one in which the ideological appropriation and "ownership" of all intellectual capacities make "serving," by conforming to this State—of punitively enforced "harmony"—personally "profitable." For Schiller, this is what the utopian dream of a frictionless "State," or, for that matter, any autotelic formation "eternally" beyond historical relations looks like:

> Eternally chained to a single small fragment of the whole, human beings develop as mere fragments; with only the monotonous sound of the wheel they turn eternally in their ear, they never develop the harmony of their being and instead of giving shape to the humanity in their nature, they turn into merely a mould casting of their occupation, their specialized field of knowledge. But even that meagre fragmentary portion, that still links individual members to the whole, depends not on forms that, through their own activity, they have given themselves (for how could one trust their freedom of action with such a finely tuned and lightless clockwork?), but are rather prescribed to them with scrupulous strictness according to a formula in which their free intelligence is held captive ....
>
> When the common entity makes the administrative office of a man his measure, when in one citizen it prizes nothing but memory, in another the capacity for data-tabulation, in a third only mechanical skill; when, indifferent to character, it insists exclusively on the acquisition of specific empirical knowledge in one individual, while in another it approves all manner of obscuring our ability to understand anything as long as it is accompanied by a spirit of orderly, regulated behaviour; when it insists on driving the development of specialized skills to a

[66] *Ibid.*

level of intensity equal to its abjuring of the subject's extensivity—should one then wonder that the remaining capacities of the spirit are neglected, in order to give succour only to those that reap honour and profit? ...

So jealously does the State insist on its sole ownership of its servants, that it would rather share its man (and who can blame it?) with the Cytherean than the Uranian Venus.[67]

While Schiller must take his "real-life" references for the effects of the perfectly pragmatic realization of the ahistorical or "utopian," because noncontingent, or fully rationalized state, from the history of ancient Greek states whose gradual devolution from the original form of discursive democracy had proceeded past recognition by the time of Socrates, Adorno had another example of such a state fresh in mind. In one of the most stunning rebukes of the theoretical value of utopianism for understanding, let alone of thinking "beyond" historical reality, on record, Adorno recounts a single exchange he had in Paris with Walter Benjamin. Commenting first on the obligation of critical thinking to occupy itself after the war "with the single most important" matter ("mit diesem Allerwichstigsten") before it now and henceforth—clear "recognition of the [internal] mechanisms" ("Kenntnis der Mechanismen") that "burst to the surface in Auschwitz" ("in Auschwitz sich austobten")[68]—he singles out precisely the Platonic model of totally integrated rule by reason of state, *Staatsraison*, in which ideology, rather than the self-disguising content of the aesthetic and intellectual superstructure of the state, is fully transparent across the every aspect of its operation, from the distribution and specialization of functions it prescribes, all the way down to its self-declared "reason" for being, or base. Adorno opens this observation with the rare, directly pragmatic pronouncement, that "political instruction should finally center itself on [the imperative that] Auschwitz not repeat itself" ("Aller politischer Unterricht endlich sollte zentriert sein darin, dass Auschwitz nicht sich wiederhole"), before continuing importantly to note:

> That will be possible only when, without fear of clashing with whatever prevailing powers, it occupies itself openly with what is most important. To do this, it must transform itself into a sociology that deals with the societal play of forces behind the surface of political forms. To give but one model [of these], it is imperative that such a respectable concept as *Staatsraison* be submitted to critique: in that it puts the right of the state above that of its members, it already puts into place the potential for a hellscape.[69]

---

[67] Schiller, *Briefe*, Letter 6, pp. 34–36. In the *Symposium*, Cythera famously designates the Venus of heterosexual, conceived as purely procreative, hence "practical" love, and Urania, the Venus of homosexual, conceived as nonprocreating, hence "intellectual" love.

[68] Adorno, *Stichworte. Kritische Modelle 2* (Frankfurt: Suhrkamp, 1969), pp. 100–101.

[69] Adorno, *Stichworte*, p. 101.

Immediately after this *critically* practical theoretical observation, Adorno recounts verbatim the state of self-induced empirical delusion (alternatively known, before and since, as empirical skepticism, or, in its "positive," post-Freudian or Lacanian version, the power of wishful thinking)—the imminently rationalist "spell" complementary to, but, as it turned out, far more "dangerous" than that of "magical" "Utopian" "immanence" already decried by Adorno in Benjamin's messianic theory of the image—under which his friend in exile, despite every material realization of the all-pervasive "idealism" of the totalitarian state, still labored:

> Walter Benjamin once asked me in Paris, during the period of emigration there, when I sporadically returned to Germany, whether there were still enough torturers to carry out the orders of the Nazis. There were.[70]

Schiller, who described extensively and understood perfectly that the real *practical* consequence of utopian ideology is nothing less than the *pure* reason of the clockwork state, would understand not only that "there were"—more than "enough" not only to make the proverbial (death) trains run on time, but to celebrate the total "politicization of the aesthetic" that Benjamin himself had advocated.[71] If he posited the internally emancipatory "power" of art against "Lohnkunst" and the "act" of making culture against the culture industry, he also knew that those capitalizations of the aesthetic were no less profoundly political, part of Staatsraison itself. His heuristic "aesthetic state," defined only by the dialectic that informs it, represents no "ideal" state—of "total loss of contact with reality"—resulting, as de Man correctly observes, from the ultimately murderous consequences of any ideology of "realism."[72] For, whatever its particular content, that state names the refusal of the total loss of contact with reality on which any administration of an all-comprehensive political "model" of *Staatsraison* is predicated. The conception of such a model, singled out as most urgently in need of contemporary critique by Adorno, itself originates *not ideally but pragmatically*—much as Plato's did and, despite their affection for aesthetic displays, all totalitarian regimes do. For in its original "platonic" conception, *Staatsraison* is proffered as the practicable solution to the otherwise irresoluble problem posed by the idea of justice: the purely figural substitution of a predetermined operating machine for an idea whose relation to phenomenal appearances remains resistant to determination.

No such purely pragmatic entity, Schiller's stubbornly *conceptual* "aesthetic state" is also no pure idea. Like Socrates' method for disproving his interlocutors' worldly formulae for embodying justice, *before* supplanting these with a false appeal to "view" the idea itself "writ large" on the (entirely imaginary)

---

[70] Ibid.
[71] Walter Benjamin, "Das Kunstwerk im Zeitalter seiner technischen Reproduzierbarkeit," in *Illuminationen* (Frankfurt: Suhrkamp, 1977), pp. 136–169 (169).
[72] De Man, *The Aesthetic Ideology*, pp. 142; seen. 36, this essay.

model of an autocratic state, Schiller arrives at his conception of a (nongovernmental) "aesthetic state" by gradual, dialectical discursive means. But rather than foreclosing that dialectical process soon after it begins, Schiller first raises the prospect of such a productive state of imagination in the closing sentences of the *Letters*. The opposite of the externally determined "mechanical" state whose fatal operation he has already described in detail, Schiller's "state" names no ruling design but the unscripted, "double" "experience" of "feel[ing] oneself as matter" while "*simultaneously*" "conscious of one's freedom" not only to act, but to conceive the very "idea" *of* freedom (commended by Jameson) of which human beings alone are capable and the real—destructive and constructive—content of human history is written.[73] Such a state of "experience" cannot be marketed *as* "art" by a culture industry for which all art is *Lohnart*. Unavailable to reification and consumption, it is instead an experience that human beings must first "make" ("wo er diese doppelte Erfahrung *zugleich* machte ..."). Just as Adorno and Marcuse conceive the "autonomy of the work of art" not as a solipsistic retreat into a pointless "aestheticism" represented as such by the very culture industry that cannot sell it, but as a dialectical *political* necessity, Schiller recognized the death of internal life, and with it, freedom, mandated by the equation of art with ideology. It was the refusal of that equation which, definitive of art for Adorno, remained the negative principle shaping the Frankfurt critic's lifelong advancement of aesthetic *theory* and concomitant critique of the culture industry.

The same can be said, if in a different vocabulary and under reversed historical circumstances, for Schiller's understanding of the material component of art in its relation to history. Much as Adorno tried to communicate the significance of the aesthetic, as *form* made of and for the sake of historical dialectical experience, to Benjamin, he just as surely understood that the same conflations of "'the epistemological'" with the "'material'" that made Benjamin's theory of history more closely resemble "magic" than either history or theory, made his friend's "Utopian" conceptions of a similarly unmediated "Golden Age" more immediately visible to him than the terribly concrete and material fact: "Es gab sie."[74] No more ideological than the young Marx in doing so, Schiller calls our "double experience" of "consciousness of freedom" *and* material being "the meaning of human beings, in the fullest sense of the word," which is to say, of freedom within this world not from death but the deathly "harmony" of all necessarily "monotonous" mechanisms for ensuring that their

---

[73] Schiller, *Briefe*, Letter 14, p. 94: "wo [der Mensch] diese doppelte Erfahrung *zugleich* machte, wo er sich zugleich seiner Freiheit bewusst würde und ... sich zugleich Materie fühlte." Jameson, *Marxism and Form*, p. 116.

[74] For these and other central terms in the critical analysis of Benjamin by Adorno, see in particular the key theoretical letters of 1935–1938, in which Adorno attempts to explain the bases of the obfuscating combination of "magic and positivism" he perceives in Benjamin's Baudelaire and Arcades projects, in Theodor Adorno, "Letters to Walter Benjamin," *New Left Review*, 1/81, Sep.–Oct. 1973; *Theodor W. Adorno, Walter Benjamin, Briefwechsel*, Hrsg. Henri Lonitz (Frankfurt: Suhrkamp, 1995).

own intrinsic exclusion of freedom, as of justice, will not even be perceived, let alone missed: from a "clockwork" designed to function irrespective of time, utopian until it falls to earth.

REFERENCES

Adorno, T. W. *Ästhetische Theorie*. Hrsg. Gretel Adorno u. Rolf Tiedemann. Frankfurt: Suhrkamp, 1973a.
Adorno, T. W.. "Letters to Walter Benjamin." *New Left Review*, 1/81, Sep.–Oct. 1973b.
Adorno, T. W.. "Wissenschaftliche Erfahrungen in Amerika," *Stichworte. Kritische Modelle 2*. Frankfurt: Suhrkamp, 1969: 113–148.
Adorno, T. W.. "Thesen zur Kunstsoziologie." In *Ohne Leitbild. Parva* Aesthetica. Frankfurt: Suhrkamp, 1967: 994-103.
Adorno, T. W., and Walter Benjamin. *Briefwechsel*. Hrsg. Henri Lonitz. Frankfurt: Suhrkamp, 1995.
Adorno, T. W., and Max Horkheimer, *Dialektik der Aufklärung*. Frankfurt: Fischer Verlag, 1972. 1st ed. 1947; Orig. pub. under title *Philosophische Fragmente*, New York: Social Studies Association, 1944.
Benjamin, Walter. "Das Kunstwerk im Zeitalter seiner technischen Reproduzierbarkeit." In *Illuminationen*. Frankfurt: Suhrkamp, 1977: 136–169.
Brodsky, Claudia. *In the Place of Language. Literature and the Architecture of the Referent*. New York: Fordham University Press, 2009.
Brodsky, Claudia. *The Linguistic Condition. Kant's Critique of Judgment and the Poetics of Action*. London and New York: Bloomsbury, 2021.
Deleuze, Gilles and Félix Guattari. *Anti-Oedipe: le capitalisme et la schizophrénie*. Paris: 1972.
De Man, Paul. *The Aesthetic Ideology*. Ed. and Intro. Andrezj Warminski. Minneapolis: University of Minnesota Press, 1996
Düsing, Wolfgang. "Ästhetische Form als Darstellung der Subjektivität. Zur Rezeption Kantischer Begriffs in Schillers Ästhetik" In *Schillers Briefe über die ästhetische Erziehung*. Hrsg. Jürgen Bolten. Frankfurt: Suhrkamp, 1984, 185–228.
von Goethe, Johann Wolfgang. "Versuch als Vermittler von Objekt und Subjekt." In *Werke*, XIV Bde. Hrsg. Benno von Wiese. Hamburg: Christian Wegner Verlag, 1955.
Horkheimer, Max. *Kritische Theorie*. Frankfurt a. Main: Fischer Verlag, 1968.
Horkheimer, Max. "Traditional and Critical Theory." In *Critical Theory*, Tr. Matthew J. O'Connell, Intro. Stanley Aronowitz. New York: Continuum, 1982: 188–243. Orig. pub. *Zeitschrift für Sozialforschung* 1937.
Horn, Peter. "Die 'Tochter der Freiheit' und die 'Tendenz' zur Autonomie der Kunst in Schillers 'Über die Ästhetische Erziehung des Menschen' und Schopenhauers 'Die Welt als Wille und Vorstellung'." In *Schiller heute*, Hrsg. Hans-Jörg Knobloch u. Helmet Koopman. Tübingen: Stauffenberg Verlag, 1996, 59–73.
Jameson, Frederic. *Marxism and Form*. Princeton: Princeton University Press, 1971.
Kant, Immanuel. *Werkausgabe*. XII Bde. Hrsg. Wilhelm Weischedel. Frankfurt: Suhrkamp, 1977.
Lévi-Strauss, Claude. *La pensée sauvage*. Paris : Plon, 1962.
Levin, Thomas Y. and Michael von der Linn. "Elements of a Radio Theory: Adorno and the Princeton Radio Research Project." *Music Quarterly* 76.2 (1994): 316–324

Marcuse, Herbert. *The Aesthetic Dimension. Toward a Critique of Marxist Aesthetics.* Boston: Beacon Press, 1978.
Marcuse, Herbert. *Eros and Civilization. A Philosophical Inquiry into Freud.* Boston: Beacon Press, 1966.
Marcuse, Herbert. *Die Permanenz der Kunst. wider eine bestimmte Marxistische Ästhetik.* München: Hanser, 1977.
Marx, Karl and Friedrich Engels. *The Manifesto of the Communist Party.* Marxist Internet Archive, 2010.
Morrison, David E. "Kultur and Culture: The Case of Theodor W. Adorno and Paul F. Lazarsfeld." *Social Research* Vol. 45, No. 2 (Summer 1978): 321–355.
Muller-Seidel, Walter. *Friedrich Schiller und die Politik. "Nicht das Grosse, nur das Menschliche geschehe."* München: C. H. Beck Verlag, 2009.
Niethersole, Reingard. "...die Triebe zu leben, zu schaffen, zu spielen": Schillers Spieltriebkonzeption aus gegenwärtiger Sicht." In *Schiller heute*, Hrsg. Hans-Jörg Knobloch u. Helmet Koopman. Tübingen: Stauffenberg Verlag, 1996, 167–88.
Plato. *Republic.* II Vol. Cambridge, Mass.: Loeb Classical Library, 1978.
Rancière, Jacques. "Aesthetic Revolution and Its Outcomes," *New Left Review* 14, March/April (2002): 133–51.
Rancière, Jacques. *La chair des* mots. Politique et écriture. Paris, 1998a.
Rancière, Jacques. *The Flesh of Words. The Politics of Writing*, tr. Charlotte Mandell (Stanford University Press, 1998b).
Rancière, Jacques. *Le partage du sensible. Esthétique et Politique.* Paris: La Fabrique Editions, 2000.
Rancière, Jacques. *The Politics of Aesthetics.* Trans. Gabriel Rockhill. London: Continuum, 2004.
Rousseau, Jean-Jacques. *Discours sur l'origine et les fondements de l'inégalité parmi les hommes.* Ed. Jacques Roger. Paris: Flammarion, 1971. Orig. pub. 1755.
Schiller, Friedrich. *Briefe über die ästhetische Erziehung des Menschen.* Intro. Elizabeth Wilkinson and L. A. Willoughby. Oxford: Clarendon, 1967.

Author Index[1]

A

Abel, Jakob Friedrich, 28, 30, 31, 66, 73–77, 75n3, 77n11, 79–81, 79n14, 83, 92, 106, 113, 139, 141, 150, 206, 281, 297, 299–301, 303–307, 309, 310, 319, 409, 417, 482, 528, 595, 595n8, 595n9, 596

Adorno, Theodor W., 168, 588, 589, 629, 630n12, 631, 642–647, 642n50, 644n53, 645n56, 646n60, 647n62, 649–652, 652n74

B

Baumgarten, Alexander Gottlieb, 46, 61, 172, 174, 190, 307, 321, 322, 361, 462

Biesta, G.J.J., 243

Burke, Edmund, 23, 63, 153, 156, 172, 174, 190, 201–203, 218, 223, 236, 278, 321, 362, 397n18, 531, 612, 630n12

Byron, Lord, 546

C

Cicero, 78, 306, 328, 417, 594n4, 600, 637n39

Coetzee, J.M., 244

Coleridge, Samuel Taylor, 9, 546, 639

D

Dalberg, Wolfgang Heribert von, 10, 12, 14, 16, 130, 320

Dewey, John, viii, ix, 243

Dubos, Jean Baptiste, 134, 149, 150, 164

E

Eichendorff, Joseph Freiherr von, 543

F

Fichte, Johann Gottlieb, 32, 34, 150, 239, 247, 251, 253–255, 257n18, 259, 332–336, 379, 384n20, 386, 411, 437, 460, 471, 497–509, 568, 580, 612, 613

Fouqué, Friedrich de la Motte, 543

[1] Note: Page numbers followed by 'n' refer to notes.

© The Author(s), under exclusive license to Springer Nature Switzerland AG 2023
A. Falduto, T. Mehigan (eds.), *The Palgrave Handbook on the Philosophy of Friedrich Schiller*, https://doi.org/10.1007/978-3-031-16798-0

G

Gadamer, Hans-Georg, 244, 551
Garve, Christian, 21, 32, 35, 68n7, 77, 82, 82n24, 92, 102, 108, 111, 117, 141, 201, 304, 306, 384, 384n20, 409n1, 484, 485, 501, 528
Gellert, Christian Fürchtegott, 100, 270, 271
Goethe, Johann Wolfgang, vii, 5, 8, 12, 15, 17, 18, 25, 28, 31, 32, 34–42, 45, 48–50, 58, 67, 103, 121, 199, 211n2, 250, 259, 271, 309, 320, 323, 385, 411–413, 415, 459–461, 460n4, 479, 501, 517–519, 530, 574–580, 582, 583, 586, 586n14, 595n6, 608, 608n2, 627n4, 641
Gottsched, Johann Christoph, 135, 264

H

Hardenberg, Friedrich von, *see* Novalis (Georg Philipp Freiherr von Hardenberg)
Hegel, Georg Wilhelm Friedrich, ix, x, 31, 75n4, 77, 211, 229, 240, 243, 281, 285, 310, 327, 383, 414, 507, 533, 535, 544, 544n1, 546, 550, 571, 575, 581, 583, 588, 589, 591–604, 609, 610, 618–622, 619n12, 627n4, 627n5, 633, 639, 642
Heine, Heinrich, 48, 550
Herder, Johann Gottfried, 12, 17, 21, 32, 36, 49, 80, 277, 298, 305, 311, 312, 320, 322, 372, 373, 379, 384, 384n20, 429, 479, 483, 529, 554, 594, 594n5, 595n6
Hoffmann, E.T.A., 543
Hölderlin, Friedrich, ix, 8, 31, 36, 75n4, 77, 217, 220, 230, 530, 533, 535, 542, 542n1, 544–548, 545n2, 581, 591, 635, 635n32
Humboldt, Wilhelm von, 5, 27, 31, 32, 34, 37, 44, 46, 48, 49, 234, 243, 247n2, 258, 258n21, 362, 378n11, 381n16, 385n21, 390n3, 414, 434, 573–589
Hume, David, 59, 64, 77, 150, 157, 219, 297, 304, 327, 480

I

Iffland, August Wilhelm, 11, 12

J

Jacobi, Friedrich Heinrich, 499, 501, 564, 565
Jung, Carl, 244

K

Kant, Immanuel, v, 13, 30, 55, 75, 96, 143, 148, 164, 171, 189, 201, 218, 231, 249, 263, 273, 294, 319, 342, 354, 371, 390n3, 406, 429, 442, 459–475, 477–493, 498, 511–523, 528, 530–532, 541, 559, 568–571, 575, 610, 626
Keats, John, 546
Kleist, Heinrich von, 305, 544, 546, 550–554
Klopstock, Friedrich Gottlieb, 6, 24, 92, 542
Körner, Christian Gottfried, 14–18, 20, 21, 23, 25–29, 31, 32, 37, 38, 41, 47, 49, 113, 137, 139, 144, 147–149, 171–175, 177, 178, 185n20, 189, 201, 202, 231, 232, 320–322, 374, 375n7, 410, 413, 426, 428, 431, 478, 480, 482, 489, 530–532, 563

L

Leibniz, Gottfried Wilhelm, 61, 75n6, 98, 141, 142, 192, 327, 480, 562
Lessing, Gotthold Ephraim, 11, 13, 29, 33, 58, 92, 132–135, 154–157, 166, 167, 207, 209, 211, 264, 270, 271, 309, 312, 322, 372, 379, 412, 413, 424, 466, 531, 601, 602

M

Marx, Karl, x, 392n7, 546, 602, 607–622, 628, 633, 635, 639, 639n43, 652
Mendelssohn, Moses, 6, 29, 55, 57, 58, 61, 63–65, 77, 81, 92, 94, 112, 141, 149, 150, 153, 156, 157, 164, 172, 190, 191, 202, 211, 250, 254, 256, 263, 278, 302, 321, 424, 528, 531
Moritz, Karl Philipp, 11, 61, 121, 126, 296, 322, 528

N

Nietzsche, Friedrich, ix, 211, 243, 294, 304, 305, 368, 420, 428
Novalis (Georg Philipp Freiherr von Hardenberg), 18, 39, 530, 543, 546

P

Platner, Ernst, 150, 297–300, 405, 528
Plato, 6, 92, 100, 119, 121, 151, 233, 237, 248, 280, 328, 355, 392n8, 423, 428, 434, 546, 547, 630n12, 636n38, 637, 637n39, 639n43, 640, 641, 648, 651

R

Reinhold, Karl Leonhard, vi, 21, 28, 191, 238, 320, 332, 373–375, 374n3, 374n4, 378, 379, 379n12, 384–386, 384n20, 477–493, 499, 504, 530, 544, 575
Rousseau, Jean-Jacques, 60, 62, 67, 68, 77, 111, 130, 131, 151, 237, 305, 324, 328, 354, 367, 395, 423, 429, 484, 534, 552, 554, 592, 592n2, 601, 630n13

S

Schelling, Friedrich Wilhelm Joseph, ix, 31, 37, 77, 419, 460, 471, 504, 535, 544, 544n1, 546, 550, 571, 580, 581, 634
Schlegel, August Wilhelm, 32, 36–39, 431, 575, 578
Schlegel, Friedrich, 35, 37–40, 530, 535, 544, 546, 575–583, 576n4, 576n5
Shelley, Percy Bysshe, 546
Stäudlin, Gotthold Friedrich, 26
Sulzer, Johann Georg, 60, 77, 80, 81, 81n23, 135, 150, 151, 153, 164, 191, 202, 205, 211, 250, 254, 263, 271, 296, 297, 300, 321, 322, 327, 328, 407, 528

T

Tieck, Ludwig, 9, 36, 542

V

Voltaire, 100, 103, 111

W

Wieland, Christoph Martin, 8, 17, 18, 155, 191, 258, 263, 270, 303, 320, 426, 431, 478, 479, 485
Winckelmann, Johann Joachim, 209, 234, 466, 547
Wolff, Christian, 74n1, 76, 78–80, 98, 265, 295, 327, 365
Wordsworth, William, 546, 639

Subject Index[1]

A

Aesthetics, vi, 13, 58, 74, 96, 130, 150, 168, 171, 189, 202, 217, 232, 248, 263, 274, 307, 320, 341, 353, 383, 390, 410, 424, 442, 462, 477, 501, 509, 530, 542, 575n1, 608, 625

Animality/animal nature, 7, 62, 92, 97, 98, 114, 116, 118, 122, 197, 308, 309, 343, 354, 396, 484

Anthropology, vi, ix, 5, 76, 78, 80, 85, 85n28, 85n29, 113, 127, 135, 149, 204, 207, 212, 237, 241, 261–263, 266, 267, 269–271, 293–312, 322, 341, 355–357, 373, 379, 405, 407, 483, 528–529, 531, 535, 546

Appearance, vi, ix, 29, 31, 34, 37, 59, 60, 64–66, 69, 94, 121, 122, 177–184, 184n16, 190, 193, 194, 196–198, 203, 208, 222, 249, 250, 252, 280, 294, 308, 310, 311, 331, 344, 360, 367, 373, 381, 393n10, 396–398, 411, 420, 462–467, 511–513, 517–519, 521–523, 533, 534, 537, 538, 545, 564, 569, 570, 588, 591, 617n10, 630n13, 638, 640, 641, 651

Appearances (phenomena), 193, 203, 211, 250, 396, 414, 427, 436, 492, 523, 562, 567, 575, 579, 626

Art, viii, ix, 10, 13, 14, 16, 23, 25, 29, 30, 33–35, 39, 56, 58, 64, 67, 68, 79, 96, 109, 111, 117, 118, 131, 132, 134, 136, 149–154, 163–168, 172, 173, 183–185, 192, 202, 204, 208, 209, 211, 221, 222, 224, 229, 232–237, 239, 241–243, 250, 250n6, 257, 259, 264, 265, 267, 268, 271, 276, 280, 282–285, 307, 321, 323–331, 335, 336, 353, 356–360, 363, 382, 383, 389, 391n6, 392, 392n8, 393, 395, 398, 398n20, 399, 402, 406, 412, 417, 419, 420, 424, 428–431, 437, 442, 444–447, 450, 451, 481, 483, 486, 487, 501, 507, 509, 528–530, 532, 534–538, 542, 543, 545–550, 552, 556, 567, 569, 574, 577, 578, 581–583, 586, 613, 617, 626, 626n2, 628n8, 629, 629n10, 630n12, 633–635, 633n26, 634n30, 641–643, 642n50, 643n52, 646–648, 647n62, 651, 652

---

[1] Note: Page numbers followed by 'n' refer to notes.

© The Author(s), under exclusive license to Springer Nature Switzerland AG 2023
A. Falduto, T. Mehigan (eds.), *The Palgrave Handbook on the Philosophy of Friedrich Schiller*, https://doi.org/10.1007/978-3-031-16798-0

660 SUBJECT INDEX

Autonomy, 17, 35, 40, 42, 43, 45, 48, 62, 65–68, 96, 97, 151, 154, 168, 172, 174, 175n8, 177, 178, 181–185, 190, 192, 197, 198, 209, 235, 239, 264, 281, 306, 309, 310, 319, 326–332, 343, 345, 346, 348, 348n5, 349, 398, 400, 410, 414, 416–418, 429–432, 505, 514, 532, 534, 538, 554, 569, 570, 626, 652

B

Beauty, viii, 29, 30, 34, 56, 59–69, 67n6, 97, 117, 118, 131, 142, 143, 190–197, 202, 212, 219, 233, 234, 237, 239–243, 248, 250, 252, 253, 255–257, 259, 268, 274–277, 279–285, 307, 308, 310, 319–338, 342, 343, 345, 346, 349, 353, 358–360, 364, 383, 390, 390n3, 390n4, 391, 394, 395, 397–402, 397n18, 397n19, 420, 428–432, 444, 450–452, 454, 459–475, 478, 484, 487, 493, 499, 505–507, 517, 527, 530–532, 534, 537, 538, 542, 543, 545, 547, 549, 549n4, 550, 552, 553, 569, 570, 582, 585, 588, 589, 600, 608, 626, 630n12, 631, 634n30
Bildung, 234, 243, 426, 542, 548, 548n3, 554
Body, 57, 69, 81–83, 94, 106, 114–116, 118–125, 131, 181n13, 192, 197, 251, 252, 294, 295, 297, 300, 302, 342, 343, 355, 390n4, 405–407, 411, 449, 463, 466, 507, 528, 585, 599, 600, 603, 636, 641, 649

C

Causality, 297, 310, 349, 381
Character, vii, 9, 19, 20, 34, 36, 56, 60, 64, 84, 94, 98, 101, 104, 111, 121, 123, 126, 132, 133, 152, 157, 165, 166, 177, 181n13, 183n14, 195, 196, 211, 236, 258, 262, 268, 275, 279, 284, 285, 305, 308, 312, 325, 326, 329, 337, 342–344, 355–367, 392n8, 399, 407–411, 413, 414, 417, 418, 420, 438, 442, 444, 447, 448, 450, 451, 454, 463, 465, 466, 478, 487, 520, 522, 533, 534, 536, 594, 595n6, 615–617, 615n8, 617n10, 621, 622, 627n4, 634n30, 649
Conscience, 101, 119, 255, 337, 406, 408, 416, 472n11, 473–475, 490, 493
Consciousness, 109, 111, 155, 164, 167, 205, 207, 208, 224, 226, 228, 310, 417, 493, 504, 505, 537, 553, 563, 568–571, 580, 583, 620, 631n14, 633, 646n60, 652
Critique, vi, 103, 144, 148, 172, 173, 175n8, 185n20, 186, 237, 247n2, 255, 270, 271, 277, 300, 303, 305, 307, 345, 365, 392n7, 401, 408, 411, 415, 425, 437, 438, 468, 478, 536, 537, 547, 582, 607n1, 608, 609n3, 610, 618–622, 636n38, 639n43, 645–647, 645n57, 646n60, 650–652

D

Desire, 29, 34, 62, 64, 66, 69, 93, 94, 97, 110, 111, 115, 119, 142, 190, 197, 205, 221, 242, 249n4, 332, 345, 345n3, 346, 348, 349, 397, 407, 408, 430, 437, 446, 467, 477, 484–486, 512, 514, 516, 519, 523, 530, 532, 541, 570, 587, 643n51, 644
Dialectic, 139, 151, 240, 243, 407, 408, 412, 433, 498, 504–509, 598, 633, 642, 651
Dignity, ix, 101, 130, 191, 193, 197, 198, 210, 224, 241, 268, 270, 276, 281, 327, 336, 345, 360, 418, 461–463, 465–468, 465n6, 470, 471, 499, 546, 551, 586, 588, 608
Drive, vii, 8, 63, 93, 131, 175n8, 238, 248, 275, 306, 333, 346, 354, 396, 407, 433, 442, 477, 489–493, 497, 513, 531, 545, 601, 611, 631n14
Dualism, 149, 193, 198, 233, 238, 251, 253, 262, 275, 295, 332, 406, 432, 438, 528, 529, 533, 534, 542, 555, 613, 621n14

SUJECT INDEX 661

E

Education, vi, vii, 13, 21, 33, 34, 49, 58, 59, 66, 73–85, 112, 126, 130, 131, 133, 154, 212, 234, 238, 240–244, 247, 253–256, 274–277, 279, 281–283, 301, 308, 319, 323, 324, 332, 336, 346–350, 355–364, 372, 376, 385, 389–402, 407, 426, 439, 442–454, 509, 534, 539, 542, 543, 548, 567, 595n6, 608

Empiricism, 55, 57, 59, 65, 141, 263, 294, 300, 301, 306, 333, 435, 585

Ethics, 57, 59, 60, 73, 78–81, 83, 85, 102, 155, 156, 164, 172, 172n1, 192, 197, 198, 205, 206, 209, 231, 232, 242, 262–265, 306, 307, 341–346, 349, 379, 410–412, 417, 419, 433, 436, 454, 461, 513, 515, 515n7, 519, 522, 523, 544–547, 551, 559–561, 563–565, 568, 571, 626n2

F

Faculty, 29, 62, 63, 65, 105, 113, 124, 152–154, 164, 166, 174, 176, 177, 178n11, 194, 219–222, 224, 225, 242, 249–251, 270, 284, 295, 297, 298, 301, 304, 305, 307, 308, 329–338, 347, 349, 354, 355, 357, 358, 361, 364, 374n5, 375n7, 395, 412, 437, 477, 485–493, 499, 507, 545, 565, 571, 588, 610–612, 615, 633n27, 643n51

Feeling, 9, 15, 31, 34, 36, 56, 59–63, 68, 69, 94, 95, 102, 107, 111, 112, 119, 120, 122, 124–126, 131, 132, 134, 149, 151–153, 156, 164–166, 168, 194–196, 203, 208, 210, 227, 229, 230, 236, 249, 251, 255, 256, 263–265, 267, 269, 270, 276–278, 308, 325, 326, 329, 330, 334, 345–347, 358, 361, 391, 395, 396, 406, 408, 411, 418, 434, 444, 448, 452, 461, 464, 465, 469, 471–475, 472n11, 485–488, 498, 503, 504, 507, 511, 514, 517, 521–523, 531, 534, 541, 543, 549, 552, 567, 570, 583, 588, 593, 600, 616, 636, 647

Freedom, 4, 9–15, 18, 22–24, 26, 28–30, 36, 42, 43, 45–47, 81, 93, 101–105, 107, 110, 112, 127, 154, 155, 164, 166, 167, 172, 173, 175n8, 177–181, 185n20, 190–199, 202, 204, 205, 207, 208, 210, 212, 218, 235, 236, 239, 241, 242, 248, 251, 252, 254, 266, 267, 275, 277–281, 284, 296, 298, 306, 308, 310, 311, 319–338, 341, 342, 344–350, 353–360, 362–367, 377, 383, 385, 389–402, 407, 409–413, 415–417, 420, 432, 433, 462, 466, 469, 470, 472, 474, 477, 480, 482, 483, 485, 487–493, 498, 499, 501, 503–508, 514, 532–534, 537–540, 543, 552, 568, 569, 578, 584, 585, 587–589, 593, 594, 594n4, 596, 597, 600, 603, 608, 610–619, 619n13, 621, 629n10, 630, 630n13, 632, 632n22, 633, 645, 647–649, 652, 653

G

Genius, vii, 168, 255, 257, 265, 266, 269, 270, 277, 280, 298, 398, 573–589, 595n6

God, 6, 25, 45, 57, 62, 85, 99, 118, 127, 141–143, 198, 263, 265, 304, 310, 311, 321, 392n8, 407, 426–428, 431–434, 470, 471, 484, 528, 549, 562, 564, 566, 598, 636

Grace, ix, 29, 85, 123, 140, 168, 191–198, 219, 232, 258, 263, 265, 342–344, 392n8, 411, 442, 445, 446, 448–452, 454, 461–471, 468n8, 469n10, 473, 475, 511, 512, 514, 516–523, 517n9, 534, 551, 553, 586

H

Happiness, 7, 9–12, 14–18, 35, 42, 49, 57, 65–67, 81, 93–97, 99–107, 111, 112, 114–117, 120, 125, 140, 142, 164, 185, 198, 211, 249, 256, 266, 267, 270, 324, 325, 361, 365, 380, 382, 382n17, 410, 447, 460, 484–487, 513, 514, 519n10, 562

Harmony, 9, 36, 59, 64, 68, 69, 93, 99, 112, 114, 118–120, 122, 124–126, 142, 195, 196, 202, 221, 239, 249, 253, 258, 258n21, 269, 276, 285, 309, 329, 332, 341, 343–346, 348–350, 359, 361, 364, 375n8, 378, 378n10, 383, 392, 392n8, 396, 397, 399n22, 407, 424, 425, 427, 431, 443, 463, 465, 471, 482, 483, 491, 493, 503, 505, 506, 516–521, 517n9, 523, 535, 537, 538, 543, 552, 570, 577–580, 582, 584–588, 616, 649, 652

History, v, 5, 57, 73, 92, 135, 148, 172n4, 263, 278, 320, 350, 353, 371–386, 410, 423, 477, 482–485, 562, 592

Humanity, 9, 16, 24, 36, 57, 68, 95, 97, 98, 116, 125, 129, 133, 134, 151, 196, 198, 236, 237, 239, 240, 242, 250, 255, 266, 267, 269, 271, 308, 310, 327, 329, 331, 337, 343, 346, 347, 354, 380n14, 383, 391, 392, 394n14, 396, 398, 399, 401, 409, 425–427, 432, 443, 444, 464–467, 465n6, 469, 481, 484, 506, 516n8, 528, 529, 531, 536–538, 542, 546, 552, 567, 569, 570, 574, 582, 584, 616, 635n32, 645, 649

I

Idea, 151, 165, 173n6, 192, 203, 218, 237, 248, 264, 280, 297, 319, 343, 354, 372, 406, 441, 462, 478, 498, 513, 530, 547, 562, 573–589, 593, 609

Idealism, vii, x, 83, 190, 235, 263, 276, 386, 410, 414, 432, 438, 498, 508, 527–540, 543, 544, 589, 607, 626, 634, 636, 636n38, 651

Intelligible, 194, 209, 219, 220, 250, 309, 329, 331, 492, 559

Intuition, 178, 194, 226, 227, 238, 251, 269, 307, 329, 330, 435, 436, 485, 498, 504, 529, 532, 533, 538, 546, 562, 571

J

Judgement, 66, 83, 151, 152, 155, 210, 211, 218–221, 232, 234, 238, 242, 284, 298, 326, 331, 332, 334, 349, 361, 378, 398, 401, 416, 486, 488, 531, 532, 537, 542, 545, 546, 550, 551

M

Metaphysics, 57, 58, 74, 75n5, 75n6, 76, 78, 80, 84, 141, 144, 240, 303, 407, 435, 437–439, 467, 484, 522, 544, 560, 564, 567

Morality/morals, vi, 6, 56, 59–61, 74, 92, 130, 140, 151, 164, 171, 192, 204, 218, 231, 247, 251–253, 262, 275, 305, 319, 341–350, 353, 380, 391, 405, 433, 460, 479, 482–489, 511–523, 528, 541, 567, 593, 608, 628n6

N

Nature, v, 9, 56, 66–68, 97, 113–125, 142, 149, 164, 171, 190, 203, 218, 232, 251, 262, 275, 294, 319, 341, 354, 373, 389–402, 406, 425, 442, 461, 482, 498, 512, 527, 542, 562, 573, 584–588, 591, 608

Noumenon, 250

O

Organism, 114–116, 121, 123, 295, 312

P

Phenomena, *see* Appearances (phenomena)

Political philosophy, 435, 611

Politics, 22, 32, 35, 39, 40, 43, 79, 96, 132, 134, 136, 182, 192, 307, 328, 390, 414, 436, 536, 538, 569, 628n8, 636, 640

A priori, 65, 175, 307, 348n5, 401, 498, 532, 563, 568, 612, 632, 633n27

SUJECT INDEX 663

R

Rationalism, 7, 95, 263, 307, 308, 407, 435

Rationality, 56, 59, 140, 183, 254, 311, 329, 342, 359, 361, 406, 411, 463, 505, 551

Reason, v, 9, 56, 75n5, 93, 140, 148, 165, 177, 190, 203, 262, 275, 294, 319, 341, 354, 391n5, 406, 429, 443, 461, 478, 498, 512, 527, 541, 579, 610, 629n10

Religion, 13, 14, 18, 39, 48, 49, 57, 58, 80, 81, 84, 85, 85n28, 104, 122, 127, 129, 131–133, 140, 141, 309, 323, 324, 365, 482, 528, 529, 549–551, 567, 578n7, 591, 608, 620, 621, 621n14

Right, ix, 16, 40, 43, 45–47, 68, 84, 112, 118, 132, 155, 165, 183, 219, 251, 256, 275, 276, 308, 310, 334, 337, 349, 361, 362, 366–368, 399, 406, 407, 416, 431, 450, 460, 466, 472, 474, 484, 492, 500, 514, 518, 531, 533, 547, 549, 551, 586, 600, 610–612, 614–617, 617n10, 621, 622, 648, 650

Romanticism, 56, 271, 527, 541, 544, 546, 550, 552, 575, 579

S

State, 60, 97, 129, 142, 150, 174, 248–250, 282, 294, 342, 356–364, 393, 406, 462, 482, 506, 514, 529, 567, 582, 592, 610–613

Subject, 10, 24, 29, 46, 62, 93, 105, 107, 108, 115, 122, 124, 149, 156, 164, 165, 176–178, 178n11, 190, 193–196, 198, 204, 210, 221, 227–229, 249, 250n6, 265, 278, 279, 281, 301, 309, 324–326, 329, 330, 332, 334, 343–345, 349, 364, 366, 396, 408, 409, 411, 413, 415, 428, 429, 435, 443, 446, 462, 464, 471, 482, 485, 488, 502, 507, 512, 520, 521, 532, 533, 547, 553, 555, 563, 569, 571, 588, 589, 608, 610, 614, 617n10, 618, 619n11, 622, 630, 630n12, 633n26, 646n60, 650

Subjectivity, 61, 226, 228, 310, 327, 335, 410, 418, 419, 452, 507, 535, 539, 559, 570, 571, 589, 608, 616, 630n12, 631n14, 633n26

Sublime, viii, 7, 8, 29, 30, 44, 94, 96, 99–102, 113, 121, 122, 142, 148, 149, 152–157, 164, 165, 175n9, 181n13, 191, 197, 198, 202–204, 206–212, 218–226, 228, 229, 273–285, 306, 309, 322, 325, 326, 397, 397n18, 412, 414, 417, 418, 418n5, 420, 423, 426, 481, 484–487, 530–532, 547, 550, 566, 587, 588, 630n12, 634n31

T

Taste, 11, 15, 19, 30, 47, 104, 107, 108, 118, 151, 152, 157, 172, 175, 176, 181, 190, 194, 224, 231, 232, 234, 235, 237, 248, 255, 263, 264, 325, 330, 331, 346, 350, 364, 401, 401n29, 477, 478, 480, 483–489, 532, 574, 648

Teleology, 103, 375–377, 380, 529, 533

Theology, 5, 31, 55, 57, 74, 131, 295, 298, 301, 302, 375n7

Transcendental, 190, 193, 234, 237, 238, 240, 243, 248, 279, 298, 307, 326, 332, 336, 354, 363, 400, 410, 452, 472, 498, 499, 504, 508, 522, 535, 537, 555, 634n31

V

Virtue, 7, 9, 13, 15, 22, 23, 26, 35, 56, 57, 62, 64, 65, 85, 92–105, 111–114, 116–119, 126, 127, 132, 140, 142, 149, 155, 192, 195, 197, 198, 211, 219, 227, 232, 233, 264, 324, 337, 341, 342, 344, 350, 354, 365, 366, 375, 393, 401, 409, 430, 433, 461, 467–470, 472, 473n12, 478, 481, 514, 514n5, 514n6, 517, 522, 547, 553, 563, 592, 596, 601, 602, 604n23, 638

Printed in the United States
by Baker & Taylor Publisher Services